HOP ON POP

The Politics

and Pleasures

of Popular

Culture

HOP ON POP

Edited by

Henry Jenkins,

Tara McPherson,

& Jane Shattuc

Duke University Press   Durham & London   2002

© 2002 Duke University Press
All rights reserved
Printed in the United States of
America on acid-free paper ♾
Designed by Amy Ruth Buchanan
Typeset in Minion by G&S
Typesetters, Inc.
Library of Congress Cataloging-
in-Publication Data appear on the
last printed page of this book.

CONTENTS

ACKNOWLEDGMENTS

From the Editors of Hop on Pop:

We would like to express our appreciation to all those who contributed their hard work in the preparation of this book. Early on, Briony Keith facilitated the initial phase of identifying contributors and corresponding with them about their submissions. Shari Goldin did heroic work in battling computer viruses and getting the manuscript into final form for submission. R. J. Bain and Susan Stapleton worked with us to ensure that the proofreading process went smoothly. We also wanted to thank Ken Wissoker, who has believed in this project from the very start, and Deborah Wong, who came to our rescue and turned everything around in our darkest hours.

From Henry Jenkins:

This book centers around the ways that our writing and scholarship are informed by the experiences of our everyday life. So it is fitting to take a moment to thank those people who, on the one hand, keep me grounded in reality and, on the other hand, make my life much more than everyday. Thanks to Cynthia Jenkins, who shapes everything I write; Henry Jenkins IV, who has become almost as good an editor as his mother and a better writer than his father; H. G. and Lucile Jenkins, who continue to inspire me to greatness; and Jim and Ann Benson, who are the most supportive in-laws anyone could ask for. This book reflects a decade of conversations with friends and colleagues too numerous to name (if you think your name belongs here, please insert it on your copy and assume that I meant it to be there all along). This is perhaps a fitting place to acknowledge the contributions Alex Chisholm has made to my intellectual and professional life over the past three years. His energy, his pragmatism, his creativity, and his courage make all things possible. And finally, thanks to Tara and Jane, who have been in there for what has been the longest, bumpiest ride of my academic career, and to the contributors, whose patience surpasses all human understanding.

From Tara McPherson:

This book has been a long time coming, so it almost seems impossible to thank all the colleagues, friends, and family who have provided modes of sustenance throughout its long production. So, here I offer both a "blanket" thank you as well as a couple of more precise ones. The first round of thanks are due to Henry, Jane, and this volume's contributors; I offer each of them my gratitude for riding out this process. Next, because *Hop on Pop* tracks the circuits of exchange between the popular and the political, examining how culture becomes meaningful in daily life, I want to thank several folks outside the confines of the academy. My own engagements with the popular are continually enriched via my association with a circle of friends endearingly known as "The Fun Club." Most of these pals earn their respective livings in what we in academe often disparagingly call the "culture industries," working as film and TV writers, editors, directors, and producers. These friendships have taught me just how impoverished many of our cultural theories of production and consumption really are, for I've watched various Fun Club members tussle with the politics of production on a daily basis. Their struggles to bring together the popular and the political illustrate both the possibilities and the limits of the industry, and I applaud their commitment to bringing new images of gender, sexuality, and race to life in Hollywood. My understanding of the popular is also enlivened by daily conversations with my chief coconspirator, Rob Knaack, whose insights into everyday life and everyday ethics continue to impress me. Finally, I anticipate many years of navigating new dimensions of popular culture with my son, Dexter, as I experience new worlds of fun through his eyes.

From Jane Shattuc:

We launched this project out of the sense of pleasure and community we found in thinking about popular culture. Because of the accessibility of popular culture the book has created an unexpected community for me. My nephew Will Shattuc suggested the title of the book at age four as he gleefully jumped up and down on my brother while screaming "hop on pop!," one of many subversive acts brought on by our shared love of popular culture. My coeditors, Henry and Tara, introduced me to a range of pleasures and politics while accepting our differences. Their intellectual openness and curiosity define much of the book's anarchistic originality. I want to thank the contributors, who were patient yet still so intellectually and politically challenging. I am grateful to David Pearlman, whose thoughtful analysis of popular culture and support of this project undercut any assumption I have about the sciences. Finally, I want to acknowledge Ann Mithona Shattuc, my daughter, who came into my life in the process of this book. She already knows the pleasure of a belly laugh and the politics of being different. Much like Tara and Henry with their respective sons Dexter and Henry, I look forward to the joy of re-experiencing popular culture through the bemused eyes of my child.

HOP ON POP

THE CULTURE THAT STICKS TO YOUR SKIN: A MANIFESTO FOR A NEW CULTURAL STUDIES

Henry Jenkins, Tara McPherson,
and Jane Shattuc

In the 1985 *Mirrorshades* anthology, cyberpunk writer Bruce Sterling issued a call for a new form of science fiction, one less invested in the monumentalism of "the great steam-snorting wonders of the past," and more invested in the technologies of everyday experience ("the personal computer, the Sony Walkman, the portable telephone, the soft contact lens"). Like the other cyberpunk writers, Sterling responded to these emerging technologies with a mixture of exhilaration and dread, unable to shake his impression of "tech [that] sticks to the skin, responds to the touch . . . pervasive, utterly intimate. Not outside us, but next to us."[1]

Sterling's description of the cyberpunks seems oddly appropriate for *Hop on Pop*, which brings together a group of writers representing an emergent perspective in cultural studies. Like the cyberpunks, we are interested in the everyday, the intimate, the immediate; we reject the monumentalism of canon formation and the distant authority of traditional academic writing. We engage with popular culture as the culture that "sticks to the skin," that becomes so much a part of us that it becomes increasingly difficult to examine it from a distance. Like the cyberpunks, we confront that popular culture with a profound ambivalence, our pleasures tempered by a volatile mixture of fears, disappointments, and disgust. Just as the cyberpunks intervened at the point where science fiction was beginning to achieve unquestioned cultural respectability, we are the first generation

of cultural scholars to be able to take for granted that popular culture can be studied on its own terms, who can operate inside an academic discipline of cultural studies.

We confront that phase of institutionalization as a moment of freedom, but also one of danger. The hard fights of the past have won us space to reexamine our own relationship to the popular, to rethink our own ties to the general public, and to experiment with new vocabularies for expressing our critical insights. We have found our own voices and we see this book as a chance to show the world what we can do. It is possible to do work on popular culture now that would have been unthinkable little more than a decade ago, work that doesn't have to bow and scrape to establish the worthiness of the objects of study. The unstable position of the academy in the postindustrial economy, on the other hand, causes uncertainty, as many of the individual contributors to this collection struggle to find jobs. The establishment of a stable base within the academy, if such a base can be called stable when so many can't find employment, threatens to isolate cultural studies from the larger public sphere, to cut it off from its long tradition of engagement with the open universities and the popular press.

This anthology represents an attempt both to play with our newfound freedom and to secure ground for a new approach. For that reason, we are writing this introductory manifesto first of all for ourselves and for other writers in this emergent tradition to try to articulate what we are doing and to explore both the continuities and breaks we represent with the earlier history of cultural studies. We also write this introduction for those who will judge us on the basis of this work. As we struggle with mentors or with tenure committees, we must explain what it is we are doing and why it looks and feels different from what has come before. And as we think about the future of our respective discipline(s) we must ensure its continued popular outreach, committing it to the core principle that knowledge about popular culture must recirculate within the popular.

Manifestos are often written in the heat of battle, with a certain anger toward the past, as part of the process of clearing the ground to make way for new constructions. In practice, they often leave only scorched earth in their path, intensifying the intergenerational battles within the academy, rather than bringing about any clear understanding of how what is to come relates to what has come before. We see this manifesto as doing a somewhat different job, explaining what we borrow from our mentors and what we are offering back in return. What this anthology signals is not anything so dramatic as a paradigm shift. This isn't timidity on our part, simply a recognition that there is no need to burn old bridges when what we really need to do is forge new ones. The essays in this volume show (and, we hope, repay) strong debts to previous work in cultural studies. We have inherited a foundation of core insights and a rich vocabulary of methodological approaches. Many of the founders of cultural studies are still with us and are continuing to grow, continuing to watch changes in their intellectual fields and changes in the popular, and continuing to make fresh contributions to our understanding of politics and pleasure. We have also watched the battles over the creation of cultural studies and we have sought new tactics for responding to long-standing criticisms and new reformulations of old binarisms. If change in the academy has often been likened to an oedipal conflict in which the sons and daughters kill their parents in order to make room for their own accomplishments, we are hoping for something closer to a family reunion, where squabbles may surface but where a strong sense of community and tradition is reaffirmed over potato salad and barbecue. The title of this collection, after all, is *Hop on Pop*, not "stomp on pop." If we do our jobs right here, most of the founders

of cultural studies will still be speaking to us after this book comes out, and that is more than can be said for their relations to the generation that came before them.

Despite the title, we don't necessarily see this essay as a traditional-style manifesto for a future theoretical project. For one thing, we think there have been too many manifestos promising things in the abstract that have never or could never be realized in the concrete. The developments we are describing are already taking place and have been taking place for quite some time. The support for this manifesto's claims can be found by reading the essays in this collection. Many of our contributors do not devote their time to proclamations about what cultural studies should be. They are more interested in defining cultural studies by example through their work and in the end, the work in this book speaks for itself. Many of our contributors would be unlikely to sign onto a single ideological or theoretical project. They have been working independently, doing scholarship within varied traditions, disagreeing among themselves as often as agreeing. Many of them would not even recognize each other, since they come from many academic disciplines and from several different national traditions.

Yet we would assert a "family resemblance," a series of traits, some methodological, others stylistic, that define our work. In this introduction, we sketch the contours of a new direction for cultural studies. Of course, the field has already been moving pretty decisively in that direction the whole time we've been editing and putting together this anthology and we are already starting to see the more mature works in this tradition. Not all of the work we reference or include in this anthology clearly embodies all of the traits we will identify. Some are written in a very personal style and others adopt a more distanced voice. Some are more heavily theoretical than others. Some are historical, others take ethnographic approaches, and still others stay pretty close to textual analysis. Cultural studies is not reducible to a single methodology you can outline, download into your laptop, and take out with you into the cultural arena.

To borrow a concept from Raymond Williams, we speak for an emergent approach to cultural studies. We are not yet dominant and our appearance does not reduce earlier work to residual status. We aren't going to try to turn young Turks into old farts simply with a slip of our pens. However, we are a force of change, a challenge to old ways of thinking and writing. Others can stake out the past and present of cultural studies; we claim a role in its future.

The changes this book commemorates are significant enough that it no longer makes sense to treat our work as a footnote to the Birmingham tradition, yet our ties to the past are firm enough that we don't want to be slid into a new chapter altogether. The temptation is always to understand change in generational terms, and to some degree, the most significant steps toward this new direction have been taken by younger scholars whose intellectual interests reflect different life experiences and cultural backgrounds than those of some of the founders of cultural studies. Yet these changes are being embraced by cultural scholars of all ages, many of whom have been working their entire lifetimes to build bridges beyond the ivory tower to various popular constituencies and are still trying to complicate their understanding of the place of popular culture in their own lives. You will find established names in this collection, alongside scholars whose reputations are still being built. We hope you will see the continuities across these various theoretical, historical, and critical projects.

The goal of rewriting cultural studies extends to the title of this collection, which seems to trigger immediate emotional sparks of passionate pleasure or equally intense discomfort. Some have felt that the title was infantilizing; others that it

represented too crude a reference to oedipal struggles, incest, or opportunism, depending on what meanings get ascribed to "hop" and "pop." Some worried that it would not carry sufficient dignity when they wrote it on their vitae. This anxiety is very real, one challenge of transforming academic language during a phase of disciplinary strength and institutional instability.

The multiplicity of the title's potential connotations, and the intense yet often ambivalent responses to it, make concrete our theoretical and methodological goals. The title reflects our own playful, appropriative engagement with the popular, especially those forms of culture that become a part of our everyday life. Our title pays homage to the formative role that Dr. Seuss's books and popular culture in general played for the postwar generations. More than any previous group, we grew up in an environment steeped in the anarchistic pleasures of popular culture. Our childhoods were fun and we have maintained some of those simple childish and childlike pleasures as we have entered adulthood. We still enjoy the dadaist playfulness of the alliteration of "hop on pop." There is also the irreverent pleasure in using such a name for a serious academic anthology. We wanted the title to challenge the boundary between academic and popular discourses, between work and play, between politics and pleasure, much as the various essays in this collection do. We wanted a title that reflected the diversity of cultural forms and traditions referenced in this book, while at the same time evoking a specific, concrete, and memorable image.

The language of academic titles emerges from a tradition of high culture; we wanted to challenge the ideological hold of that tradition on how we do our work and how we address our audience. Our title thus fuses the playful (which precedes the colon) and the academic (which follows it). One way you can tell we are at a point of transition is that the two still remain separated by that most

scholarly of punctuation marks: remove our co-
lons and we probably wouldn't be considered academics at all.

At one time, we considered calling this collection *The BIG Duke Book of Fun,* yet somehow
that seemed just a little too silly—even for the
most playful of our contributors. Perhaps that's
the spirit with which to take the current title—as
a cheeky attempt to teach old dogmas new tricks
without feeling that we have compromised the seriousness of our own goals or of our political and
intellectual commitments. We are hoping for a
cultural studies that can assume the immediacy
and vibrancy of its objects of study, that can draw
productively on models from vernacular theory
and fan criticism, and that can claim new freedoms in the ways it engages with the political. In
the end, we know that writing and reading cultural
theory is serious work. We also hope it might be
fun.

How will you recognize this emergent cultural
studies? We think that there are a series of traits
or characteristics that, collectively, help to set
it off from earlier work on popular culture. Some
of these traits build upon much older traditions
in the field; some of them reclaim cultural studies' relationship to popular traditions of criticism
and debate; some reflect new directions or new locations from which cultural theory might emerge.
Most reflect the powerful influence of feminism,
queer theory, and other traditions derived from
identity politics on the ways that we conceptualize ourselves and our culture. You might think
of these traits as distinguishing features—sometimes birthmarks reflecting our parentage, sometimes scars from our painful brushes with academic authorities, and sometimes tattoos with
which we adorn ourselves to set us apart from
what has come before. When we spot some of
these distinguishing features across a crowded
conference room, we recognize the writer who
bears them as one of our own. We wink. And

we wait for a safe time and place to conduct the
conversation.

Defining Characteristics

IMMEDIACY

A long tradition of writers, especially in the American tradition, have acknowledged that the "immediate experience" of popular culture demands
our passionate engagement and active participation. Gilbert Seldes and Robert Warshow, for example, saw the immediacy and liveliness of the
popular as its defining trait, what set it off from
the bourgeois cultural refinement of the nineteenth century that they felt had stifled a more
vital American vernacular tradition.[2] Seldes saw
popular culture as liberatory in the ways that it invited intense feelings that he felt were repressed
in the sanctioned space of high culture. Perhaps
too broad a term, immediacy shorthands several
interrelated concepts, such as intensification (the
exaggeration of everyday emotions to provoke
strong feelings or a release from normal perception), identification (strong attachments to fictional characters or celebrities), and intimacy (the
embedding of popular culture into the fabric of
our daily lives, into the ways we think about ourselves and the world around us). If "immediacy" is
what, according to Pierre Bourdieu, distinguishes
the popular from the bourgeois aesthetic, then we
should be suspicious of attempts to write about
popular culture from a distance. Writing about
popular culture requires new epistemologies and
new modes of expression that preserve rather than
ignore this "immediacy."

The ease with which academic critics have embraced the ideal of a rational, political, emotional,
or "objective" distance reflects their own intellectual histories. Some of the founding figures of
this critical tradition were exiles critiquing a culture not their own. Some were working-class intellectuals who saw high culture and high theories

as avenues of escape from their origins. Others struggled to establish a respected intellectual discipline based on the study of the popular. The price of admission into the academy was that we shed our fannish allegiances and enthusiasms at the door, policing our writing for signs of the journalistic and abstracting from our own experiences.

The challenge for our emergent perspective is to write about our own multiple (and often contradictory) involvements, participations, engagements, and identifications with popular culture—without denying, rationalizing, and distorting them. The best cultural critics speak as "insiders" as well as "outsiders." Writers like Ellen Seiter and Marsha Kinder discuss the place of children's media and consumer goods within their own families.[3] Cathy Griggers describes her own fantasies surrounding *Thelma and Louise,* actively rewriting the film as a fan might.[4] Tricia Rose speaks of melding what she learned about rap growing up in the Bronx and what she learned as a graduate student at Brown.[5] They write about the places where popular culture touches their own lives as fans, consumers, thrifters, and parents, provoking a range of emotional responses. In some cases, this relationship may be passionate without being fannish, as represented by recent attempts by writers to explore their conflicted feelings about regional identities or to examine the conservative aspects of popular culture. We can draw on our personal experiences and subjective understandings to critique the popular as well as to embrace it. Even fans are far from uncritical in their relations to cultural producers. However, skeptics have often reduced subjective modes of writing to the "academics as fans" question. We need to start there if we are to understand the perceived opposition between "immediacy" and institutionalized modes of academic writing.

The scholar and the fan, as Joli Jenson notes, remain too closely related to allow for a clean separation: "The Manilow fan knows intimately every

recording (and every version) of Barry's songs; the Joyce scholar knows intimately every volume (and every version) of Joyce's oeuvre." Yet we constantly police the boundary between the two, not simply in terms of the objects of their interest, but also the forms of their attachment: "The obsession of a fan is deemed emotional (low class, uneducated) and therefore dangerous, while the obsession of the aficionado is rational (high class, educated) and therefore benign, even worthy."[6] As academics, we are told that our affective relations to popular texts must be cast aside so we may more fully understand how "they work on us." Romanticizing the fan as engaged in "semiotic guerrilla warfare" simply reverses the polarities without really bridging the gap.

As Lawrence Grossberg has argued, "The collapse of critical distance and the crisis of authority is not epistemological but a concrete historical dilemma called into existence by the fact that, as critical intellectuals, we are inextricably linked to the dominant forms of popular culture; we are fans writing about the terrain, if not the objects, of our own fandom. . . . My existence as a fan, my experiences . . . are the raw material, the starting point of critical research."[7] We must embrace our immediate engagement with popular culture as the source of our knowledge and as the motivating force behind our projects.

Writers like David Morley and Michael Schudson are critical of recent efforts to blur the boundary between academic and fan, insisting that our access to educational capital, our ability to shift between multiple cultural codes and move up and down the cultural hierarchy, makes academics fundamentally different from popular audiences.[8] This warning encourages us to reflect on the differences, as well as the continuities, between our own participation within popular culture and that of other consumers. Yet they make too much of those differences. Contemporary popular culture is consumed as avidly by those of the professional and educated classes as by those of the working classes. The line that separates an academic writing about comic fandom and a corporate lawyer collecting comics may be less real than imagined. Insisting on those differences may be another way of denying that we, as academics, are implicated within the popular culture we critique.

Moreover, this argument devalues the centrality of popular culture to our cultural identities. Claiming to be a "fan," for Morley, seems to mean little more than expressing an arbitrary preference. For many of us, being a fan represents a collective cultural and political identity that links us to other cultural communities. Our cultural preferences and allegiances, no less than our racial, sexual, and political identities, are difficult to shed when we write.

In literary studies, the "intimate critique" has been recognized as an important mode of analysis.[9] In "Me and My Shadow," Jane Tompkins called for feminists to escape from the "straitjacket" of "rational" academic language and to draw on powerful feminist traditions of autobiographical and subjective writing. In this important essay, Tompkins adopts a double voice, speaking both in the abstract discourse of theoretical debate and in the more personal voice of someone who "wants to write about their feelings." The academic "disdain for popular psychology" and passionate language, Tompkins argues, reflects historically gendered splits between public and private, splits that assign women the task of dealing with emotions and men the tasks of dealing with ideas.[10] Norms of academic writing, Tompkins argues, have often denied women their most effective critical tools, forcing them to perform on grounds already defined in masculine terms. A powerful example of subjective criticism, Annette Kuhn's *Family Secrets* discusses her own relations to family, nation, and popular culture. Kuhn's rumination on memory and family life is at times shockingly honest and open about her troubled relations with her mother, while offering sophisti-

cated critical insight into family photographs, British melodramas, and news coverage of Queen Elizabeth's coronation.[11]

Literary criticism is, of course, not the only traditional discipline to rethink the value of "insider" perspectives. In philosophy, feminists have challenged the "rationality" of distanced and abstract discussion, insisting on the value of the "situated knowledge" that emerges when social agents write from the "standpoint" of their own experiences.[12] In anthropology and sociology, powerful critiques have been launched against the "imperial gaze" of traditional ethnography. Instead, anthropologists are adopting new models that value "local knowledge" and acknowledge the complex social relations between researcher and researched subject.[13]

By adopting these new approaches, philosophers and anthropologists struggle with two challenges: on the one hand, there is a common assumption that only those who live within a culture can meaningfully write about it; on the other, there is the pervasive assumption that only trained academics can meaningfully theorize their cultural practices. Writing from an insider perspective about one's culture solves neither problem, since our social identities are forged along multiple vectors. We will always be insiders in some senses and outsiders in others. We can participate in cultural communities in many different ways and as participants we may understand involvement on multiple levels. The challenge is to be honest about how we know what we know about popular culture, while at the same time avoiding having our arguments completely swallowed up into narcissistic solipsism.

Some of the earliest works in the Birmingham tradition, such as Richard Hoggart's *The Uses of Literacy,* emerged from the writers' own experiences of class mobility and cultural hierarchy.[14] Stuart Hall's essays have powerful autobiographical passages.[15] Yet many cultural scholars write a deadening BBC standard prose, which seems to speak from no place in particular. Angela Mc-

Robbie challenged the way that early theoretical and scholarly discourse about subcultures wasn't owning up to scholars' own involvement in the subcultures they were studying. In general, academic cultural studies has displaced more personal voices from its core project.[16] As cultural critics become dissertation advisers and tenure review judges, they often insist on traditional standards of rigor and decorum, which are enforced rigidly due to our "colonial cringe" over our chosen objects of study. As a result, we often find ourselves struggling with the same "straitjacket" Jane Tompkins tried to shed. Even in its most abstracted forms, theory can never allow us to fully escape our own subjectivity, the play of our emotions, the tug of our lived experiences. When we deny those vital forces, we are most likely to get the wrong answers or even to ask the wrong questions.

Writing about popular culture from an "up close and personal" perspective has brought new issues to the foreground, such as the place of mass culture within personal and popular memory, the sentimental value attached to melodramatic representations, the complex political valiances of erotic fantasy, or the roles that "camp" or "gossip" play in shaping the queer community's responses to mainstream media. We can not ask or address these questions from the outside looking in; they require the knowledge of our guts, our hearts, and our longings. Only then can we fully account for the complex tugs and pulls of the popular, the way it fits into our lives, the way it "sticks to our skins," and thus explain its contradictory relationships to politics and pleasure. Only then can we produce writing that has the passion and intensity to make our ideas accessible to a broader public. John Hartley, whom we consider a fellow traveler in our emergent cultural studies, has still expressed reservations about this more immediate engagement with the popular, claiming that it "defers too much to informal, experiential knowledge and belittles too much the practice of formal

knowledge production with its attempts to be scrupulous, testable, and open." Hartley urges us instead to reclaim and revalue the "art" of scholarly writing, to take responsibility for our craft and our skills in using certain technologies for analysis and communication. He writes, "It ought to be possible to do justice to and to learn from popular readerships without de-skilling intellectual culture."[17] We certainly agree. What we are calling for is not a rejection of the academy but rather a new relationship between academic and popular modes of engagement that takes the best of both worlds, recognizes and values alternative forms of knowledge production, and seeks to better map the continuities and differences between them. What we are proposing might better be described as the "reskilling" of intellectual culture or perhaps we simply hope not to be deskilled of what we know as members of a popular audience before we are thought to be adequately prepared to enter academic life.

MULTIVALENCE

The major challenge to "academic distance" has come from groups, such as women, queers, blacks, and other minorities, whose relationship to popular culture could never simply be labeled in "insider" or "outsider" terms. These writers express a core ambivalence about popular culture through writing that speaks from multiple vantage points at once. Corey K. Creekmur and Alexander Doty write, "Many gay and lesbian popular culture producers and consumers have wondered how they might have access to mainstream culture without denying or losing their oppositional identities, how they might participate without necessarily assimilating and how they might take pleasure in, and make affirmative meanings out of, experiences and artifacts that they have been told do not offer queer pleasures and meanings."[18] Such projects cannot be meaningfully described within a vocabulary of "distance" but require an active, even playful appropriation of cultural materials.

At the same time, these modes of inquiry cannot be simply labeled as "proximate" or "insider" perspectives, since these groups have historically been refused access to cultural production and often have been excluded from representation. Frequently, popular culture has been directed against them, framing their identities in stereotypical and harmful terms.

Their engagement with popular culture cannot be dispassionate, disinterested, or distanced. The stakes are simply too high. Their writing acknowledges the pleasures they have derived from engaging with popular culture as well as their rage and frustration about its silences, exclusions, and assaults on their lives. These writers express contradictory responses to the materials of everyday culture and their own dual status as avid consumers and angry critics.

Laura Kipnis's "(Male) Desire and (Female) Disgust: Reading *Hustler*" is a textbook example of such analysis, honestly exploring the writer's contradictory response to contemporary pornography. Far from a "fan" of Larry Flynt, Kipnis explains, "A large part of what impels me to write this essay is my own disgust in reading *Hustler*. In fact, I have wanted to write this essay for several years, but every time I trudge out and buy the latest issue, open it and begin to try to bring analytical powers to bear upon it, I'm just so disgusted that I give up, never quite sure whether this almost automatic response is one of feminist disgust or bourgeois disgust."[19] In struggling to understand (and contain) her own outrage over *Hustler*'s images, Kipnis creates a more complex analysis of its ideological content. She sees "disgust" as a powerful weapon directed against traditional standards of taste and the class politics that holds them in place. She combines a feminist critique of the magazine that holds it accountable for its misogyny and racism with a class analysis that recognizes that *Hustler* provides a powerful "counter hegemonic" voice for some groups excluded from the cultural mainstream. In confronting her own

ambivalence about *Hustler,* she complicates the either/or judgments so often directed against popular culture, refusing to simply celebrate its transgressive qualities without acknowledging its reactionary politics, refusing to condemn it according to the terms of antiporn feminism without conceding the dangers of policing culture.

Writing about the culture that touches our own lives complicates standard clichés. Writing from high places flattens the phenomenon being examined, treating it in one-dimensional terms; writing closer to the ground gives us a stronger feel for the contours of our culture. As we have adopted these new vantage points, the result has not been an uncritical embrace, nor has it been repulsion, horror, or "disgust" over the ideological complicity of popular texts. Rather, writers increasingly recognize the ways we live with and adjust to contradictions. Texts sometimes do and sometimes don't control their meanings. Viewers sometimes do and sometimes don't resist the dominant ideology. People working within the culture industries often compromise but do not always abandon their progressive impulses.

Compared to the old dogmas they are replacing, these new and more qualified claims may seem too hesitant and wishy-washy, yet their power comes precisely in displacing either/or claims with a more multivalent account of how popular culture works. We can neither engage in meaningful conversation with other segments of our society nor can we act with political responsibility until we have a realistic understanding of the culture around us. Complicating previous accounts of popular culture is not an empty academic exercise. In a world where the power to evaluate and rank forms of culture carries tremendous ideological weight, challenging the dominant framing of popular culture has political consequences. Simple univocal accounts of popular culture can be comforting; they can stir us into radical fury; they also are wrong-headed. Insofar as they motivate our political activities, they generate simplistic, feel-good solutions unlikely to have desired long-term effects. The result is a world where reforming the video-game industry substitutes for confronting the economic and social roots of violence in children's lives.

In *Barbie's Queer Accessories,* Erica Rand offers a political economy of Mattel's Barbie franchise, exploring how its production and marketing decisions shape the meanings attached to the popular fashion doll. Yet Rand also explores the meanings that arise when the doll is integrated into children's lives, especially adult memories of their "queer" and unconventional uses of the toy. She is interested in both the "possibilities" and "limitations" of "cultural subversion"; she is interested in both the power of media producers to constrain meanings and the ability of cultural consumers to escape from those constraints.[20] The same consumer may sometimes embrace and sometimes reject, sometimes work within and sometimes think around the ideological construction of femininity, whiteness, and straightness Mattel markets along with Barbie. Even in her account of Mattel, she sees the corporation as something more than a group mind; its decisions are often themselves ideologically contradictory; people at various levels resist or transform corporate ideology through the microdecisions behind cultural production.

For Rand, it is precisely those variable choices, and their complex political implications, that determine how and why popular culture matters. As she explains, "Political battles are fought over and through the manipulation of cultural symbols. People use them to signal political identities, to effect political coalitions, to disrupt and challenge beliefs and connections that have come to seem natural. . . . The world will not change if Brandon and Dylan become lovers and join ACT UP 90210 but it matters that we already know they won't, no matter how often they look soulfully into each other's eyes during the first few seasons."[21] Rand's vantage point acknowledges the uneven forces in these cultural struggles, even as she also recognizes

the pleasures (and political effectiveness) of fantasies that take us beyond what textual ideologies might allow. She avoids both the fatalism of some Frankfurt School-informed writing and the naive optimism of some work on audience resistance. Popular culture promises us no easy victories.

The complexity of Rand's account reflects her theoretical and methodological eclecticism, her willingness to fuse modes of cultural analysis (such as political economy and audience research), which historically have been opposed to each other; part of the complexity comes from a persistent internal criticism that circles around and around the same objects, finding new vantage points and new frames of reference. Such work refuses stasis, moving back and forth across high and low (as when Kipnis compares the self-portraiture of transvestite porn with the playfulness of Cindy Sherman, or when Lynn Spigel invites us to consider the relative value placed on women's crafts and male pop art appropriations of Barbie, or when Wayne Koestenbaum discusses the connoisseurs of opera as if they were another fan subculture).[22] Such work refuses to close off ideological struggles, teaching us new modes of critical thinking rather than offering conclusive judgments. Popular culture matters, for these writers, precisely because its meanings, effects, consequences, and ideologies can't be nailed down. As consumers and as critics, we struggle with this proliferation of meanings as we make sense of our own social lives and cultural identities.

ACCESSIBILITY

Following each year's MLA convention, newspapers in the host city often run articles gently lampooning titles of papers given during the conference. One way to read these jibes is simply as anti-intellectualism on the part of the press, as mean-spirited attacks on academics and their snooty jargon. Certainly, academics have long been misunderstood and misrepresented by the press, and surely we are not the only field that has developed a specialized vocabulary. Yet what else might we learn from these yearly newspaper articles? Might they also lead us to question whether or not the discursive practices of academic cultural theory have limited its viability and use outside of the university? In an era when the university is increasingly under attack as an out-of-touch and archaic institution, being able to explain what we do (and why we do it) to a larger audience is less a luxury than an imperative. Thus, our emergent approach to cultural studies favors the concrete over the abstract and seeks to translate critical insights about popular culture back into popular practice. We are also interested in modes of scholarship that can move beyond the confines of the academy, modes that the popular press might recognize as parallel to their own.

Accessibility does not mean eliminating complexity or abandoning difficult ideas. It does mean taking responsibility for knowing what your reader will need to know in order to understand your writing. Accessible prose is self-contained, providing the context and explanations that the reader requires to make sense of what she's encountering. This may mean defining buzzwords or footnoting background. It also means clarity, but clarity is not the same as triviality. The demands of teaching also encourage attention to accessibility, helping us to rethink some of our professional practices. Students come to our classes with a broad range of experiences and self-expression that does not always match the privileged languages of theory. The new cultural theory recognizes the value of engaging our students in productive dialogues that begin by also valuing their languages.

This move to explain ourselves in accessible terms is not a pandering to market forces (no matter how often our deans and administrators invoke the "bottom line"). Rather, it represents a serious engagement with the notion of the organic

intellectual, a figure important both in the work of Antonio Gramsci and in the formation of British cultural studies, where the organic intellectual was tied to labor politics.[23] Through these traditions, organic intellectuals have come to be defined as those able to articulate the knowledge, interests, or experiences of their own class or social group within wider social and political fields. This version of the organic intellectual within cultural studies has come under attack for encouraging intellectuals to speak on behalf of others, but despite the challenges such a role presents the academic, it is useful to retain the notion as it applies to work that moves beyond the confines of the academy.[24] The organic intellectual not only speaks for her own social group; she also translates the work of the academy for larger publics. Our signaling of the organic intellectual as a key element of the new cultural studies suggests another link between previous forms of cultural studies and our own emergent approach. We herald the emergence of new forms of organic intellectuals tied to new publics and newly organized communities in both "real" and "virtual" spaces.

Today the figure of the organic intellectual often resurfaces as the public intellectual, particularly in discussions of a group of contemporary African American cultural critics, an aggregate that includes bell hooks, Michael Eric Dyson, Gerald Early, Henry Louis Gates Jr., Patricia Williams, Cornel West, Todd Boyd, and Tricia Rose. These critics move beyond the academic in both their writing styles and publication venues, addressing and engaging a wider audience, reaching different publics. They strive, in the words of Tricia Rose, to merge "multiple ways of knowing, of understanding, of interpreting culture and practice, . . . to use theoretical ideas in enabling and creative ways and . . . to occupy as many subject positions as possible."[25] In his *Am I Black Enough for You?*, Todd Boyd compares his critical method and style to both rap's sampling and jazz's improvisation, citing the idioms of the black vernacular as at least as central to his work as the insights of Marxism or postmodernism. His work also highlights the degree to which scholars learn from communities and individuals outside the traditional academy.[26]

Others have also stressed the value of the vernacular to cultural studies. For instance, in his *Street Smarts and Critical Theory*, Thomas McLaughlin claims that to privilege theory as an academic enterprise overlooks the fact that "individuals who do not come of the tradition of philosophical critique are capable of raising questions about dominant cultural assumptions."[27] His work underscores the capacity of a wide range of individuals (fans, cultural practitioners, activists, visionaries) to ask questions about contemporary culture and suggests that we have as much to learn as critics from their questions as these individuals have to learn from our theories. This idea is put into practice in a zine like *Thriftscore;* edited by a nonacademic, this publication produces knowledges that shape academic theory, including an essay in this anthology.[28]

The vernacular is not the only style of this emergent cultural studies. Rather, we embrace multiple styles of scholarship and of teaching. These might include the pro-sex manifestos of Susie Bright published in trade press volumes like her *Sexual Reality* or in magazines ranging from *Elle* to *On Our Backs*. Or they might take the form of the personal, yet still theoretical, writing and poetry of Eve Sedgwick. Umberto Eco's translation of structuralism into the novel *The Name of the Rose* also fits the bill. Certainly we embrace the theoretically informed graphic art of Scott McCloud's *Understanding Comics* and Art Spiegelman's *Maus,* works that suggest new forms cultural criticism might take. While we don't reject what is often termed "high theory," our approach requires the scholar to think carefully about how such work facilitates cultural or political intervention; we understand that these interventions occur on many fronts, both in and out of the classroom.

This support of varied, more user-friendly styles of writing is a political issue that affects our own thinking, teaching, and influence outside the university. The emergent cultural studies challenges what theory can look like. It brings theory to new spaces.

Theory, for instance, might look like journalism, and journalism can look like theory. In fact, the relation between journalism and cultural studies has a long history, shaped differently under different national traditions. To cite one example, John Frow and Meaghan Morris describe the history of Australian cultural studies as being comprised to a great degree of "the partly academic but primarily constituency-oriented work of journalist-critics." They urge us to consider "the actual practices developed by real intellectuals in Australia" and understand that the popular media can be open to "exchanging ideas, rhetoric and research images."[29] They sketch quite a list of scholars they would include in this tradition, and pay particular attention to the careers of adult educator and radio critic John Flaus and of feminist critic Sylvia Lawson. British cultural studies has also benefited from the close relationship between scholarship and journalism and from the development of the Open University. Richard Dyer's career is marked by frequent publication in nonacademic venues, and, as a critic, he moves easily between the ivory tower and less hallowed venues. Indeed, the wide draw of a rack magazine like *Marxism Today* in Britain or of *Ms.* in the United States suggests that the division between the academic and the journalistic has never been firmly drawn (nor need it be.) This insight is shared by a generation of younger cultural critics.[30] Faced with a dwindling market for "traditional" academic jobs in the United States, many of these theorists have turned to other publication sites. Hank Sartin, John Corbett, Rick Wojcik, and others blur the lines between academic and "popular" writing and do much of their work outside of the academy. Other university-based critics like Cindy

Fuchs, Judith Halberstam, Elayne Rapping, Susan Douglas, bell hooks, and Todd Boyd write regularly for non-academic magazines and papers. While their "popular" writing may be stylistically different from their more academic work, the former is no less important or theoretically savvy than the latter. Following the events of September 11 the practice of staging teach-ins has also reemerged in many universities and locales, allowing interaction between community activists, students, and professors.

Borrowing a term from computer lingo, Sandy Stone has written about the importance of the cultural scholar's ability to "code-switch," meaning that it is important that we learn to speak to diverse audiences about our work and why it is important. Her own scholarship and performances reach a wide range of constituencies, including social scientists, media scholars, computer programmers, visual artists, web surfers, and technocrats. Code-switching also gives the scholar an opportunity to interact with communities and enterprises outside of the academy. Cultural scholars consult and work for computer companies and TV shows, speak on talk radio, influence national and local policy decisions, work with web designers, write zines, liner notes, and museum catalogs, and play in bands. These activities are not "more real" or more political than traditional academic scholarship and should not replace it, but they do broaden the cultural spheres from which cultural studies can challenge the dominant ideology.

Finally, a greater focus on accessible language can also affect how cultural studies impacts the academy. One of the great strengths of cultural studies has always been its independence from any one discipline, which has allowed cultural studies to bring together scholars from many fields. A commitment to a more accessible style of scholarship is also a commitment to a cultural studies that can remain interdisciplinary, encourage new forms of pedagogy, and perhaps reach our more resistant colleagues in the natural and applied sciences. If we are not content simply to preach to the converted, cultural studies must take seriously attempts to broaden its reach and appeal.

PARTICULARITY

Details matter. In a far-reaching study, Carlo Ginzburg traces how the theoretical traditions of the humanities and social sciences emerged from a need to explore and interpret fine details of our cultural environment with the same precision with which earlier humans could trace patterns in the natural environment. Ginzburg links hunter-gatherers' attempts to develop a primitive "science of the concrete" from their study of "tracks on the ground, broken branches, excrement, tufts of hair, entangled feathers, stagnating odors" with the science of "clues," represented by Giovanni Morelli's contributions to art history, Sigmund Freud's contributions to psychology, and Arthur Conan Doyle's contributions to criminology.[31] In each case, knowledge emerged from our study of concrete details and method centered around the ways we scrutinized and formed deductions from particulars. Our initial assumptions and global theories are tested against the materiality or particularity of found objects.

Ginzburg's essay helps us to better understand how different methodological traditions relate to details. Some traditions in cultural studies start with broad theoretical generalizations, seeking concrete details only as examples that will neatly confirm their more abstract analysis. In their worst cases, the only proper nouns will be the names of theorists. In the emergent cultural studies, particular examples motivate theoretical and historical inquiry, posing questions or challenges to the critic's initial perceptions and forcing a search for more appropriate models. In these cases, the concrete details of popular culture resist easy assimilation into prefabricated theories.

The dominant form of writing within this tradition is the case study, which makes modest theoretical claims but details a particular example of popular culture at work. Scott Bukatman, for example, takes as his starting point the odd observation that William Gibson wrote *Neuromancer* on a manual typewriter, unpacking this anecdote throughout an essay that circles around the history of the typewriter and its impact on American culture.[32] Ellen Seiter analyzes the physical layout of Toys 'R' Us and contrasts it with the space of more elite toy shops, using this analysis of retail space to explore how class differences shape patterns of cultural consumption.[33] Of course, the case study hardly originates with this emergent tradition. Rather, the closely detailed analysis of particular moments in the production, circulation, and reception of popular culture was a cornerstone of the early Birmingham School writers, who made deft use of particular examples to help untangle the more obscure and abstract formulations of European theory.

In promoting the case study as an analytic tool we should be attentive to its larger history. We might well seek models in foundational work in the disciplines from which cultural studies has emerged, in the "thick description" in anthropology or the New Historicists' elaborate use of the anecdote.[34] Exemplars might include Clifford Geertz's account of the Balinese cockfight or Robert Darnton's exposition of the "great cat massacre," works that bridge the divide between archival research and textual analysis, between ethnographic investigation and cultural critique.[35] These rich, multivalent essays are sparked by the discovery of a telling or surprising detail—Darnton's confusion over why a particular group of French printshop workers found the idea of burning cats funny or Geertz's stumbling upon a cockfight. Their need for a fuller understanding drives them to ask fresh questions that might not have come readily from preexisting theoretical positions. As Darnton writes, "Anthropologists have found that the best points of entry in an attempt to penetrate an alien culture can be those where it seems to be most opaque. When you realize that

you aren't getting something—a joke, a proverb, a ceremony—that is particularly meaningful to the natives, you can see where to grasp a foreign system of meaning in order to unravel it."[36]

Those of us who write about our own cultures have discovered similar points of entry, looking for places where theories chafe against the skin of our own bodies and don't fit the shape of our own experience. Trying to bridge that gap between theory and experience can lead us to more nuanced theories of how popular culture works. This impulse has shaped the best contemporary work on popular culture, work which might adopt a range of models (close textual analysis, ethnography, historical research), either singularly or in combination, and which forces a dialogue between abstract generalization and particular details.

In the case of popular culture, this attention to the particular takes on special importance. If popular culture is always already the site of commodification and alienation, of ideological manipulation, or of cultural resistance, the particulars matter little. Yet the best contemporary essays explode with details, offering exceptions, qualifications, and complications for such master theories. Understanding the particularity of popular culture alters our glib assumptions that it is formulaic, that it always repeats the same messages, that it always tells the same stories and serves the same interests. Looking at concrete moments of cultural production, circulation, and reception helps us to understand the range of possibilities within popular genres and the complex struggles that surround any cultural text.

This attention to details reflects not only the academic's search for "clues," but the fan's celebration of the particular object of his or her fascination. The shift in television studies might be understood in terms of the move from totalizing claims about television as a cultural system toward attention to local shifts within specific series. Marc Dolan's account of the "peaks and valleys of serial creativity" in *Twin Peaks,* for example, explains shifts in network programming that emphasize serialization and a more acute sense of program history, tracing how David Lynch's series recognizes or fails to achieve its artistic potential, episode by episode, season by season.[37] Dolan's essay merges a fan's attention to individual episodes with an academic's understanding of larger social and cultural contexts. Lynn Spigel's *Make Room for TV* examines the representation of early television across different genres of programming, advertisements, advice literature, and popular magazine stories.[38] Spigel's book suggests not one but many different ways that these discourses helped consumers negotiate the anxieties and utopian fantasies surrounding the introduction of this new media technology into the home.

As writers like Virginia Nightingale and James Kincaid have argued, the challenge is to find meaningful ways to assess these details, since not every example is equally representative, not every case study offers us the whole truth, and not every interpretation is equally compelling or illuminating.[39] The historian and ethnographer engage in a process of accessing voices and foregrounding exemplars. The preponderance of details in the new cultural studies suggests a direct record of "what actually happened" or how audiences "really think" about a particular program. We must remember that the details don't speak for themselves; it matters how they are framed and deciphered. Claims about concrete examples still represent interpretations and speculations. When all is said and done, ethnography and history represent alternative modes of theorizing.

We need to recognize and acknowledge the contingent nature of our analysis, to avoid making totalizing generalizations until we have developed a sufficiently rich set of case studies to illuminate larger social and cultural processes. We need to engage in constant critique, questioning the adequacy of our evidence. Such work demands that we be explicit about the interpretive frameworks and procedures we use and the standards by which we select one example over another. The best writing in contemporary cultural studies mixes and matches different modes of cultural analysis, merging history, theory and criticism, or combining ethnographic observation with larger historiographic frameworks, trying to place the details into the most meaningful context.

CONTEXTUALISM
This approach to cultural studies embraces contextualism. We view popular texts not as discrete entities that stand alone but instead exist in relation to a broad range of other discourses, placing media production and consumption within a vast social and cultural configuration of competing voices and positions. Rather than canonize a text for its intrinsic or inherent value, we try to understand and articulate more fully the frameworks within which individual texts are produced, circulated, and consumed. As such, the emerging cultural studies deals with representative rather than monumental texts and is interested in texts in context rather than in texts as isolated phenomena. Studying texts in context also suggests that their meanings are subject to change.

This concern with contextualism reflects the impact and importance of the lessons of work like Richard Dyer's *Stars* and Tony Bennett and Janet Woollacott's *Bond and Beyond,* projects that challenged the primacy of the text in the study of fictional and popular forms.[40] English and literature departments have traditionally focused on the close examination of specific texts, a practice that served both to isolate the object of study from the social networks in which it was embedded and to enable the canonization of particular texts as monuments of high culture. In response to the prevalence of textual studies, some critics turned to the study of the audience, zeroing in on practices of consumption. Dyer, Bennett, Woollacott, and others called for a different understanding of the text: they focused on situating an individual work or figure within a constantly mobile set of intertextual relations; that is, they strove to understand a single artifact in relation to other social events. Dyer's groundbreaking work on the study of stars insisted that "stars are, like all significations, also and always social facts" (1). He urges us to broaden our study of texts beyond formal analysis, for "you need to know what kind of thing a text is in society in order to know what kind of questions you can legitimately pose of it" (2). He also understood that his demystification and analysis of a star like Marilyn Monroe always existed alongside his knowledge that, when "I see her, I catch my breath" (184).

In their study of the "James Bond phenomenon," Bennett and Woollacott situate their reading of this popular hero within a broad network of social and textual relationships. While they carefully examine the formal and narrative devices of the Bond novels and films, they utilize these analyses to illustrate how the figure of Bond has served as a nodal point to condense and articulate a wide range of cultural and political positions. Furthermore, this process of condensation was and is a mobile one; Bond's meaning is not fixed in time and space but is subject to change and variation. Their view of "texts as sites around which a constantly varying and always many faceted range of cultural and ideological transactions are conducted" (8) influences the role of contextualism for the new cultural studies.

A similar understanding of context has been important in other academic disciplines, including the field of labor (and social) history. Rather than simply unearthing or discovering the facts of history, many of these historians strive to situate these "facts" within a larger social and ideological frame, indicating the influence of both E. P. Thompson and Herbert Gutman on the field. In *Counter Cultures,* feminist historian Susan Porter Benson details the history of the department store, examining this cultural institution from many different contexts. Her multiperspectival reading al-

lows her to understand the early-twentieth-century department store not as a monolith of industrial capitalism but as a site of struggle between the competing interests of saleswomen, managers, owners, and customers.[41] These historians understand that traditional historical accounts, in their pursuit of the general and universal, often omit the experiences of the poor, the working class, women, and minorities. Contextualizing historical detail within broader social and ideological frameworks can illuminate the experiences of the underrepresented.

The important work of historian David Roediger draws from both the traditions of labor history and of cultural studies as he investigates the social and historical construction of whiteness. In both *The Wages of Whiteness* and *Towards the Abolition of Whiteness,* Roediger examines the varying ways whiteness has functioned in American history as a kind of "extra" wage for certain members of the working class, often serving to solidify white identity in opposition to blackness.[42] He notes, for instance, that the Irish in America were not unquestioningly seen as "white"; rather, they strategically came to identify themselves as white to gain access to white privilege. But whiteness doesn't always undermine cross-racial alliance. By paying close attention to context, Roediger is also able to investigate those moments when allegiance to whiteness was superseded by class or gender interests, and he recognizes that exploring these moments can offer powerful clues for contemporary struggles for racial justice. Here, Roediger's use of context powerfully links past events to contemporary politics; the reading of the past in the service of the present is also a hallmark of cultural studies, distinguishing it from many traditional disciplines. Contextualism also means situating our readings in terms of their impact on contemporary life.

Cultural studies does not confine its use of context to the study of the past. Contextualism is also a vital aspect of contemporary investigations of popular culture, and this can often lead to what might seem like odd or eclectic juxtapositions of texts and practices. Still, it is understood that knowledge (about texts, events, or practices) is always situated. For instance, in her essay "On the Cutting Edge," Anne Balsamo seeks to understand the meaning of cosmetic surgery in contemporary society. Her examination of a wide range of medical texts, advertisements, and imaging technologies leads Balsamo to conclude that, in many ways, "cosmetic surgery illustrates a technological colonization of women's bodies."[43] But Balsamo also moves to situate cosmetic surgery within broader cultural practices of body modification (from ear piercing to tattooing), noting that we must refrain from the too-easy privileging of the "natural body." Much as in Kipnis's work, Balsamo's contextual reading complicates her analysis, preventing her from dismissing cosmetic surgery as inherently bad, but it does not erase her ambivalence about the complex ways cosmetic surgery gets packaged and realized in our culture. Thus, the emergent cultural studies explores the importance of context without relinquishing the right to judge a work's value or impact. To see context as situational does not mean that we see all situations as of equal relevance or that we embrace an uncritical pluralism.

This understanding of context—the realization that the meaning of texts or practices exists only in relation to complex social and cultural forces—supersedes an attachment to one rigid, global theory. We are not interested in narrowly defining the methods by which an emerging cultural studies should proceed. Cary Nelson has described cultural studies "as a ghostly discipline with shifting borders and unstable contents," arguing that "it needs to continue being so."[44] To be contextual is to understand that cultural studies is relational. Thus, while a cultural scholar may utilize the techniques of semiotics or close textual reading (or psychoanalysis or ethnography or oral

history), none of these tools itself defines what cultural studies is or should be.

SITUATIONALISM

If the emergent cultural studies is contextual, it is also situational, for we know that texts and practices have temporal and spatial properties. We also see the products of the new cultural studies, its own texts and practices, as existing in particular places at particular times for particular audiences. Put differently, we write for specific and concrete situations, with a purpose in space and time. In recent years, this work has included the attempt by academics to engage in public debates emerging in the popular press, debates about the digital revolution, about political correctness, about NEH or PBS funding, about globalization, and about warfare and terrorism. What we say today about these issues (and how we say it) is not the same as it will be in the future when different political and cultural situations may demand a different strategy. This concern with the situational is already manifested in a number of key debates in cultural studies, debates that focus on space, place, and time, on the global and the local, and on the public and the private.

The local was a key terrain for the struggles of the New Left as it moved into the 1970s, as two popular bumper sticker slogans from that period attest: "The Personal is Political" and "Think Globally, Act Locally." Likewise, the familiar union labor call to "support your local" combined labor politics with a concern for specific geographies, while one-time Speaker of the House "Tip" O'Neill's refrain, "All politics are local," also recognized the need for a grounded political practice. While these slogans may imply for some a retreat into the rigid boundaries of identity politics or other parochialisms, the new cultural studies understands them as holding the terms "local" and "global" (or "private" and "public") in a productive tension. We believe that local politics matter, that the practices of situated, everyday life have a ripple effect on the culture at large, and that the abstraction of a strictly global politics may disempower rather than empower marginalized social groups. We also recognize that the local and the everyday are not the same everywhere and that global processes do have an impact on how we can study, understand, or experience the local. We want to keep larger questions of power or inequality in focus, and we read these impacts as they are situated in both the local and the global.

One intellectual legacy of the feminist mantra "the personal is political" can be found in the feminist contributions to the field of geography, an academic discipline concerned with how experiences are placed or situated. Over the past twenty years, urban geographers such as Edward Soja and David Harvey have increasingly detailed the political ramifications of space, insisting that spatial constructions are as central to our understandings of everyday life as are temporal ones. They encourage us to think through the ways in which the spaces we inhabit shape our views of the world and of our selves, precisely situating us.[45] As such, space is a political rather than a natural category. For instance, a map does not neutrally represent a geographic area; it selectively foregrounds some areas at the expense of others. While these insights help to remind us of the spatial realities of daily experience, the work of Soja and Harvey has been taken to task by feminist geographers for displaying a tendency to privilege a view from above. For instance, Doreen Massey points out that Soja's work on Los Angeles tends toward the "overview," a stance that is driven by a need for "mastery" and "detachment," along with the "authority of the viewer which it helps to construct."[46] Soja and Harvey remain attached (though to differing degrees) to a modernist project that privileges a universal (i.e., white, male) perspective. Their understanding of space is still trapped within this global point of view, a perspective that allows Soja to

portray the overall demographic make-up of Los Angeles without ever reaching a street-level vantage point that might tell a different story.

Massey explains that this tendency to think only of the geographic big picture tends both "to rob places . . . of their individual specificity" and "to assign virtually all causality to a somehow unlocatable level of the global" (117). She encourages a turn to the local and to place, insisting that such a vantage point can also lead us to an understanding of wider terrains. She notes that specific places exist at the juncture of intersecting social relations, "tying any particular locality into wider relations and processes in which other places are implicated too." Thus, "theory is not restricted to the sphere of the big, grand phenomena alone . . . the understanding of any locality must precisely draw on the links beyond its boundaries" (120). To be situated demands that one understand how the local impacts the global and vice versa. Massey and other feminist theorists of space put their theory into practice in their investigations of regional communities, domestic architecture, and various work places, outlining how local spatial practices affect our experiences of gender, race, and class. For instance, in *Gendered Spaces*, Daphne Spain explores the degree to which the very architectural design of the plantation home reinforced the Old South's social patterns of gender and racial inequity.[47]

French theorists like Michel de Certeau and Henri Lefebvre have also expressed an interest in the local and the situated, offering a view from the streets, from the urban pedestrian.[48] Still, work such as de Certeau's often feels oddly unspecific, as if the realities of a particular city matter less than the generalized experience of walking. Any city might do, though surely walking in Los Angeles is quite different from walking in New York, let alone Tokyo or Lima. Our approach to cultural studies respects the specificity and integrity of the situation and also recognizes that walking (or driving) in a city as a woman or a minority is not the same as walking as a white man. Meaghan Morris teases out these specific spatial complexities in her essay "Things to Do with Shopping Centres" in which she rejects a semiotic reading designed to show "how shopping centres are all the same everywhere."[49] Instead, she is concerned with the ways in which "particular centres strive to become 'special,' for better or worse, in the everyday lives of women in local communities" (298), and urges us to write the histories of how women inhabit particular places. Her approach moves between many types of reading, including the concerns of managers, urban planners, and local shoppers, allowing her to trace the tensions inherent in one place. This turn to the particular exemplifies the concerns of the new cultural studies, as does Morris's insight that "in researching the history of . . . a particular place, however, one is obliged to consider how it works in concrete social circumstances that inflect in turn, its workings—and one is obliged to learn from that place, make discoveries, change the drift of one's analysis, rather than use it as a site of theoretical self-justification" (306–7).

This call to examine the particular, the local, and the situated has recently had an impact in cultural studies' engagement with mass media as well. Scholars like Anna McCarthy and Victoria Johnson have begun to investigate how our experiences of particular places are influenced by broadcast media that are not confined to a local sphere.[50] In her work on television viewing in 1950s Chicago pubs, McCarthy details how TV brought together specific working-class publics, highlighting television's role outside the domestic sphere. Johnson's work explores how TV mediates between the local and the national, especially in its constructions of the American "heartland." For instance, her examination of *The Lawrence Welk Show* illustrates how national mass media serves to locate "family values" in particular geographic areas like the Midwest. McCarthy's and Johnson's

research pays particular attention to the local, but it is also interested in understanding how places are connected to one another at specific times. Readings such as these, as well as work that investigates the impact and reworkings of U.S. media in other countries, suggest that global forces, while powerful, are never absolute. They are also worked through at the level of the local in diverse and unpredictable ways.

This concern with the specificity of place is not, of course, new to cultural studies. At its best, the tradition of cultural studies inaugurated at the Birmingham Centre was preeminently focused on the specificities and particularities of British life. While this tradition is an important legacy for cultural studies as a whole, Cary Nelson notes that much of their work was "concerned with defining a distinctly British heritage" and that thus much "British subcultural theory . . . is not well suited" to describing the structures of leisure peculiar to American life.[51] An attention to the situational demands that one's approach and methodology be flexible; as such, a simple and strict allegiance to all that emanates from Birmingham limits what cultural studies might achieve. Indeed, what cultural studies means in Birmingham today is not what it meant to Richard Hoggart or Raymond Williams.

Larry Grossberg has written that "there is . . . often a certain fetishization of the local. Cultural analysts are constantly harangued to bring their analysis 'down' to the level of the specific. . . . Yet such celebrations of the local are often untheorized, based on . . . a model of inductive empiricism."[52] But an engagement with the local or situational does not necessarily entail an abandonment of theory; rather, the new cultural studies understands that to explore how the particularities of the local intersect with other networks of power and experience is one way to theorize specific temporal and spatial situations. For instance, in his exploration of the politics of popular music in East Los Angeles, George Lipsitz traces both the global influences that shape this music and the precise and particular ways in which such music reflects life in a specific locale.[53] The music of Chicano rock bands enters into a network of global capitalism while also representing a real and concrete place and the many diverse histories that shape that place. In this approach, an appreciation of the particular is not a "fetishization of the local" but instead offers a way to move beyond the false polarization of the empirical and the theoretical, the global and the local, and the public and the private. A focus on the situational also allows one to ask crucial questions about how notions of identity, belonging, and experience are related to notions of place, space, and time. At its best, theory is not antithetical to details.

On Politics and Pleasures:
Notes Toward a Conclusion

If, as discussed earlier, the title of this volume is open to multiple interpretations, our subtitle, "The Politics and Pleasures of Popular Culture," also charts a volatile terrain. The relationship between "politics" and "pleasure" has been a hotly debated issue in cultural studies. The fear that cultural studies has been de-politicized by a privileging of the pleasures of popular culture is now a commonplace critique of the Americanization of cultural studies, a position voiced in such works as Jim McGuigan's *Cultural Populism* and in Michael Budd and colleagues' "The Affirmative Character of U.S. Cultural Studies."[54] For instance, this latter essay takes American cultural studies to task for failing to consider the relations of culture to "larger economic processes" (176) and for "confusing active reception with political activity" (169).

Such work served to highlight the need for cultural studies to think carefully about a rhetoric of "subversion" and "resistance" that had emerged within the field, but it simultaneously reinforced the tendency to reduce all of cultural studies to a simple binary of production versus consumption. In such a formulation, the site of production becomes the realm of politics, while the site of consumption only speaks of pleasure. As the essays in this volume attest, the relations between pleasure (or pain) and politics is always more complicated. While many of the essays do explore how popular culture can be pleasurable, they also recognize that these pleasures exist in a complex relation to larger socio-economic forces, that one person's pleasure can cause another person pain. Todd Gitlin maintains that "it is pure sloppiness to conclude that culture or pleasure is politics," but this formulation fails to understand that the political is at least partially constituted through culture and the popular.[55]

Arguments such as Gitlin's are limited on at least two counts. First, they tend to view the political as only occurring on the large or global scale. Such a position often raises the rhetorical question, "What can studying the local or the popular do about the war in Bosnia (or the Gulf of Afghanistan)?" This catchall critique cannot recognize that the study of the popular *does* have much to tell us about the politics of warfare. For instance, by understanding how the 1991 Gulf War got played out on the home front in, say, media coverage of the Super Bowl, one can begin to understand the ideological ties between popular conceptions of masculinity, domesticity, and the nation. This understanding is political. Likewise, understanding local notions of family and domesticity have everything to tell us about the U.S. media coverage of the Serbian campaign of rape waged against women during the war in Bosnia. Certainly, any understanding of the American "war on terrorism" post–September 11 must also examine the mass mediations of "ground zero," bringing local and global together.

Gitlin's position also reduces the terrain of the political (not to mention the economic) to a very narrow field, a conception of the political tied to Old Left formulations and perhaps out of tune with the contemporary social landscape and the often mobile social groups that inhabit it. In an insightful essay entitled "Post-Marxism and Cultural Studies," Angela McRobbie has argued that "it is increasingly in culture that politics is constructed as a discourse; it is here that popular assent in a democratic society is sought."[56] Rather than refuse to see connections between the daily experience of popular culture (or the identities it helps produce) and the realm of the political, McRobbie argues that in an increasingly post-industrial society we need to rethink how we understand the connections between the political, the cultural, the ideological, and the economic. While the critics of the "affirmative character" of cultural studies lament the loss of, in the words of Budd et al., "direct thinking about and behavior in politics" (178), the emergent cultural studies understands, in McRobbie's terms, that current social conditions and "the pluralities of emergent identities need not mean the loss of political capacity. Instead, they point the way to new forms of struggle" and new forms of the political (723).

McRobbie's reconceptualization of politics borrows heavily from the project of radical democracy as articulated by Ernesto Laclau, Chantal Mouffe, and others.[57] This project calls for new tactics and advocates a politics of alliance that is more flexible and contingent than the grand claims of more traditional Marxist theory. Such a position accepts that culture and power are not only related, but related in contingent and historically specific ways that preclude a grand and total theory of politics. But advocating a flexible political strategy does not mean that a radical democracy is characterized by passivity, reaction, or endless pluralism. Instead, according to McRobbie, "what we have to expect is not the growing simplification of the class structure as predicted by Marx, . . . but rather the development of a multiplicity of partial and fragmented identities, each with its own role to play in the pursuit of radical democracy" (724). This fragmentation sets the stage for "the possibility of forming chains of connection and articulation across different interest groups" (724), a process that also allows us to envision and move toward other possible (and hopefully pleasurable) futures.

Such a vision of the political recognizes that any viable politics must begin in the spaces people already inhabit, and here the study of popular culture offers fertile ground for understanding the contemporary shape of people's hopes and antagonisms. This does not mean one fetishizes where one is from or retreats to a separatist identity politics, but that politics must begin from somewhere even while we are busy creating and recreating, in the words of Stuart Hall, "imaginary, knowable places." We understand the benefits to be had from a tactical use of identity politics but also know the limits of a fixed politics of identity when one wishes to form productive alliances. Thus, a political position does not derive from fixed origins but from shared, contingent, and temporary places. Popular culture is one area around which such places take shape and are organized.

We recognize that to call for a flexible politics of alliance is a tricky business, for it makes the outlining and privileging of one specific political practice impossible. It also leads to a certain level of abstraction as the foregoing no doubt makes clear. Yet our very commitment to flexibility and specificity makes it hard to be specific when defining the political. Radical democracy is often abstract until the level of praxis. We share an affinity with the political and organizational strategies of alliances like ACT UP, the riot grrls, the WTO protests, and Greenpeace, but also recognize that politics can take other forms, including theoretical excursions less clearly linked to political activism. In fact, we embrace Stuart Hall's insight that theory is an important "detour on the way to something more important" and believe that our intellectual work is political.[58] Politics takes many forms and many valences, ranging from volunteering at a local school to organizing trade unions to intellectual labor. The inherent value of these forms (or the relations between them) is never fixed. Rather than offer one rigid definition of the relation of the political to the popular, we want to consider briefly one example of political alliance that speaks to the power of the popular.

Bad Subjects: Political Education for Everyday Life began in 1992 as a print newsletter written largely by a group of Berkeley graduate students. Its first issue had a run of about 250 copies, the second about 400, and the editors encouraged a policy of "xerox and distribute" among readers. The newsletter, now an online webzine (http://eserver.org/bs), is published by the Bad Subjects Collective and reaches an audience in the thousands. An extensive Web site chronicles back issues, introduces visitors to the newsletter and the collective, invites them to join an Internet discussion group, and solicits writers and workers for the collective. What began as a local effort to link the political and the everyday and to examine the relationship of intellectuals to these links (while also creating a productive space for underemployed young scholars) has evolved into an alliance with a global reach.

While the Bad Subjects often espouse a more manifesto-like style than we've advocated in these pages, their interests parallel many of the concerns we have highlighted throughout this introduction. Their first introductory essay proclaims that "we at BAD SUBJECTS believe that the personal is political; we also believe that the left needs to rethink seriously its understanding of the connections between the personal and the political."[59] The collective also strives to address a public beyond the walls of the academy and takes seriously questions about just what responsibilities the academic has to a wider community. Generally, they do not position themselves as having all the answers, but they realize that taking on certain questions is imperative. "It will take us a lot of time and practice to figure out just what it would mean to conceive of ourselves as public intellectuals. This is where Bad Subjects is relevant. The purpose behind Bad Subjects . . . is to provide a public forum, however limited, in which leftists and progressives

can experiment with imagining and building some kind of new public culture."[60] Though these introductory essays tend to be fairly general, most essays in *Bad Subjects* directly engage with everyday life, addressing topics as varied as addiction, immigration, the Christian Right, cyberspace communities, and *The X-Files*. Through these essays, the collective both explores the contradictions and complexities of popular culture and sketches a vision of other possible worlds, of "other fictions worth believing in."

The futures they outline do not perfectly coincide with the futures we might advocate. Indeed, it is clear that even the members of their collective sometimes disagree, and we are often more comfortable with their specific investigations of culture than with their more abstract theoretical proclamations. Still, they do offer a model of what alliance across difference might look like and of what an engagement with the politics and pleasures of popular culture might produce. We find the urgency and energy of their work inspiring and see it as a viable model of the emergent cultural studies. This spirit is continued and developed in the essays that constitute *Hop on Pop*.

Of course, as editors, our own views of what constitutes the political (or even the popular) often conflict. The process of producing this volume has taught each of us much about our own beliefs and about working as a collective (if a small one.) Despite our disagreements over exact titles or essays or over the relative role of the fan, of theory, or of economics in cultural studies, we each remain firmly committed to the notion that the popular is political and sometimes pleasurable.

Notes

1 Bruce Sterling, "Introduction," in *Mirrorshades: The Cyberpunk Anthology*, ed. Bruce Sterling (New York: Ace, 1988). The cyberpunks were a movement within science fiction associated with such writers as Sterling, William Gibson, Rudy Rucker, Pat Cadigan, Lewis Shiner, and Neil Stephenson who showed increased

awareness of the role of media and global capitalism in shaping contemporary social life. The cyberpunks set their stories in vividly described near-future societies struggling with the repercussions of our contemporary economic and cultural environment. Cyberpunk has often been described as a form of postmodern fiction, but the case can be made that it is strongly influenced by cultural studies' focus on subcultural resistance and appropriation. For a range of critical responses to cyberpunk (although tilted toward the postmodern reading), see Larry McCaffrey, ed., *Storming the Reality Studio: A Casebook of Cyberpunk and Postmodern Fiction* (Durham: Duke University Press, 1992).

2   Gilbert Seldes, *The Seven Lively Arts* (New York: A. S. Barnes, 1924); Robert Warshow, *The Immediate Experience: Movies, Comics, Theater, and Other Aspects of Popular Culture* (Garden City, NY: Doubleday, 1964).

3   Ellen Seiter, *Sold Separately: Children and Parents in Consumer Culture* (New Brunswick, NJ: Rutgers University Press, 1995); Marsha Kinder, *Playing with Power in Movies, Television, and Video Games: From Muppet Babies to Teenage Mutant Ninja Turtles* (Berkeley: University of California Press, 1991).

4   Cathy Griggers, "*Thelma and Louise* and the Cultural Generation of the New Butch-Femme," in *Film Theory Goes to the Movies*, ed. Jim Collins, Hilary Radner, and Ava Preacher Collins (New York: AFI/Routledge, 1993), 129–41.

5   Tricia Rose, *Black Noise: Rap Music and Black Culture in Contemporary America* (Middletown, CT: Wesleyan University Press, 1994).

6   Joli Jenson, "Fandom as Pathology: The Consequences of Characterization" in *The Adoring Audience: Fan Culture and Popular Media*, ed. Lisa A. Lewis (London: Routledge, 1992), 19–28, 21.

7   Lawrence Grossberg, "'It's a Sin': Politics, Postmodernity and the Popular," in *Dancing in Spite of Myself: Essays on Popular Culture*, ed. Lawrence Grossberg (Durham: Duke University Press, 1997), 250–51.

8   David Morley, *Television, Audiences, and Cultural Studies* (London: Routledge, 1992); Michael Schudson, "The New Validation of Popular Culture: Sense and Sentimentality in Academia," *Critical Studies in Mass Communication* 4(1) (1987): 51–68.

9   See, for example, Diane P. Freedman, Olivia Frey, and Frances Murphy Zauhar, eds., *The Intimate Critique: Autobiographical Literary Criticism* (Durham: Duke University Press, 1993); Marianna Torgovnick, ed., *Elo-*

quent Obsessions: Writing Cultural Criticism (Durham: Duke University Press, 1994); Beverley Skeggs, ed., *Feminist Cultural Theory: Process and Production* (Manchester: Manchester University Press, 1995).

10   Jane Tompkins, "Me and My Shadow" in *The Intimate Critique*, ed. Freedman, Frey, and Zauhar, 30, 24, 39.

11   Annette Kuhn, *Family Secrets: Acts of Memory and Imagination* (New York: Verso, 1995).

12   See, for example, Linda Alcoff and Elizabeth Potter, eds., *Feminist Epistemologies* (New York: Routledge, 1993).

13   See, for example, Renato Rosaldo, *Culture and Truth: The Remaking of Social Analysis* (Boston: Beacon, 1993); James Clifford, *The Predicament of Culture: Twentieth-Century Ethnography, Literature, and Art* (Cambridge, MA: Harvard University Press, 1988).

14   Richard Hoggart, *The Uses of Literacy* (London: Penguin, 1958).

15   Stuart Hall and David Morley, eds., *Stuart Hall: Critical Dialogues in Cultural Studies* (New York: Routledge, 1996).

16   Angela McRobbie, "Settling Accounts with Subcultures: A Feminist Critique," in *On Record: Rock, Pop, and the Printed Word*, ed. Simon Firth and Andrew Goodwin (London: Routledge, 1990), 66–80.

17   John Hartley, *Popular Reality: Journalism, Modernity, Popular Culture* (London: Edward Arnold, 1998), 66.

18   Corey K. Creekmur and Alexander Doty, eds., *Out in Culture: Gay, Lesbian, and Queer Essays on Popular Culture* (Durham: Duke University Press, 1995), 1–2.

19   Laura Kipnis, "(Male) Desire and (Female) Disgust: Reading *Hustler*," in *Cultural Studies*, ed. Lawrence Grossberg, Cary Nelson, and Paula Treichler (New York: Routledge, 1992), 378.

20   Erica Rand, *Barbie's Queer Accessories* (Durham: Duke University Press, 1995), 5.

21   Ibid.

22   Laura Kipnis, *Bound and Gagged: Pornography and the Politics of Fantasy in America* (New York: Grove, 1996); Lynn Spigel, "Barbies without Ken: Femininity, Feminism, and the Art-Culture System," in *Welcome to the Dreamhouse: Popular Media and Postwar Suburbs* (Durham: Duke University Press, 2001); Wayne Koestenbaum, *The Queen's Throat: Opera, Homosexuality, and the Mystery of Desire* (New York: Vintage, 1994).

23   See Antonio Gramsci, *Selections from the Prison Notebooks*, ed. and trans. Quintin Hoare and Geoffrey Nowell-Smith (London: Lawrence and Wishart, 1975); and Stuart Hall, "Cultural Studies and Its Theoretical Lega-

cies," in *Cultural Studies,* ed. Grossberg, Nelson, and Treichler, 277–86. Gramsci contrasts the organic intellectual to the traditional intellectual, a figure he aligns with the status quo. The organic intellectual emerges from a subaltern class, representing their concerns within the public sphere.

24 Considerations of the figure of the organic intellectual can be found in Meaghan Morris, "Banality in Cultural Studies," in *Logics of Television,* ed. Patricia Mellencamp (Bloomington: Indiana University Press, 1990), 14–43; and Tony Bennett, "Putting Policy into Cultural Studies," in *Cultural Studies,* ed. Grossberg, Nelson, and Treichler, 23–33. Hall also expresses some reservations about the organic intellectual in "Cultural Studies."

25 Rose, *Black Noise,* 185.

26 Todd Boyd, *Am I Black Enough for You?: Popular Culture from the 'Hood and Beyond* (Bloomington: Indiana University Press, 1997).

27 Thomas McLaughlin, *Street Smarts and Critical Theory: Listening to the Vernacular* (Madison: University of Wisconsin Press, 1997), 5.

28 *Thriftscore* was published by Al Hoff, who can be contacted at P.O. Box 90282, Pittsburgh, PA 15224.

29 John Frow and Meaghan Morris, "Australian Cultural Studies," in *What Is Cultural Studies? A Reader,* ed. John Storey (London: Arnold, 1996), 362.

30 Of course, before the past few generations of academic specialization, many critics bridged scholarly and journalistic writing, as past issues of nonacademic journals such as *Dissent, Saturday Review,* and *Partisan Review* amply illustrate.

31 Carlo Ginzburg, *Clues, Myths, and the Historical Method* (Baltimore: Johns Hopkins University Press, 1992), 000.

32 Scott Bukatman, "Gibson's Typewriter," in *Flame Wars,* ed. Mark Dery (Durham: Duke University Press, 1994).

33 Seiter, *Sold Separately.*

34 See, for example, Lynn Hunt, ed., *The New Cultural History* (Berkeley: University of California Press, 1989); H. Aram Veeser, *The New Historicism* (New York: Routledge, 1989).

35 Clifford Geertz, *The Interpretation of Cultures* (New York: Basic, 1973); Robert Darnton, *The Great Cat Massacre and Other Episodes in French Cultural History* (New York: Random House, 1985).

36 Darnton, *The Great Cat Massacre,* 78.

37 Mark Dolan, "The Peaks and Valleys of Serial Creativity: What Happened to *Twin Peaks,*" in *Full of Secrets:*

Critical Approaches to "Twin Peaks," ed. David Lavery (Detroit: Wayne State University Press, 1994), 30–50.

38 Lynn Spigel, *Make Room for TV: Television and the Family Ideal in Post-War America* (Chicago: University of Chicago Press, 1992).

39 Virginia Nightingale, "What's 'Ethnographic' about Ethnographic Audience Research?" in *Australian Cultural Studies: A Reader,* ed. John Frow and Meaghan Morris (Urbana: University of Illinois Press, 1993); James Kincaid, *Child-Loving: The Erotic Child and Victorian Culture* (New York: Routledge, 1992).

40 See Richard Dyer, *Stars* (London: BFI, 1979), and Tony Bennett and Janet Woollacott, *Bond and Beyond: The Political Career of a Popular Hero* (New York: Methuen, 1987).

41 Susan Porter Benson, *Counter Cultures: Saleswomen, Managers, and Customers in American Department Stores, 1890–1940* (Urbana: University of Illinois Press, 1986).

42 David Roediger, *The Wages of Whiteness* (New York: Verso, 1991), and *Towards the Abolition of Whiteness* (New York: Verso, 1994).

43 Anne Balsamo, "On the Cutting Edge: Cosmetic Surgery and the Technological Production of the Gendered Body," *Camera Obscura* 28 (1992): 226.

44 Cary Nelson, "Always Already Cultural Studies: Academic Conferences and a Manifesto," in *What Is Culture Studies?,* ed. Storey, 276.

45 Edward Soja, *Postmodern Geographies* (London: Verso, 1989), and David Harvey, *The Condition of Postmodernity* (Oxford: Basil Blackwell, 1989).

46 Doreen Massey, *Space, Place, and Gender* (Minneapolis: University of Minnesota Press, 1994), 324.

47 Daphne Spain, *Gendered Spaces* (Chapel Hill: University of North Carolina Press, 1992).

48 Michel de Certeau, *The Practices of Everyday Life* (Berkeley: University of California Press, 1984), and Henri Lefebvre, *Everyday Life in the Modern World,* trans. S. Rabinovitch (New Brunswick, NJ: Transaction Books, 1984).

49 Meaghan Morris, "Things to Do with Shopping Centres," in *The Cultural Studies Reader,* ed. Simon During (New York: Routledge, 1993), 297.

50 Anna McCarthy, "'The Front Row Is Reserved for Scotch Drinkers': Early Television's Tavern Audience," *Cinema Journal* 34(4) (summer 1995): 31–49, and Victoria Johnson, "Citizen Welk: Bubbles, Blue Hair, and Middle America," in *The Revolution Wasn't Televised:*

Sixties Television and Social Conflict, ed. Michael Curtin and Lynn Spigel (New York: Routledge, 1997).

51 Nelson, "Always Already Cultural Studies," 273.

52 Larry Grossberg, "The Space of Culture, the Power of Space," in *The Post-Colonial Question,* ed. Iain Chambers and Lidia Curti (New York: Routledge, 1996), 176.

53 George Lipsitz, *Time Passages: Collective Memory and American Popular Culture* (Minneapolis: University of Minnesota Press, 1990). Lipsitz continues his explorations of the local and the global in his *Dangerous Crossroads: Popular Music, Postmodernism, and the Poetics of Place* (New York: Verso, 1997).

54 James McGuigan, *Cultural Populism* (London: Routledge, 1992); Michael Budd et al., "The Affirmative Character of U.S. Cultural Studies," *Critical Studies in Mass Communication 7* (1990): 169–84.

55 Todd Gitlin, "Who Communicates with Whom, in What Voice, and Why, about the Study of Mass Communication," *Critical Studies in Mass Communication 7* (1990): 191–92.

56 Angela McRobbie, "Post-Marxism and Cultural Studies," in *Cultural Studies,* ed. Grossberg, Nelson, and Treichler, 726.

57 See, for instance, Ernesto Laclau and Chantal Mouffe, *Hegemony and Socialist Strategy: Towards a Radical Democratic Politics* (London: Verso, 1994).

58 Hall, "Cultural Studies." Though "detour" may for some have a negative connotation, Hall's essay makes it clear that his use is more affirmative. Here, the detour can take us to new places, thereby sometimes discovering a value in abandoning the linear.

59 Annalee Newitz and Joe Sartelle, "Bad Subjects: People Building the New Hegemony," in *Bad Subjects: Political Education for Everyday Life* (1992).

60 Sartelle, "Public Intellectuals," *Bad Subjects* 1 (1992).

DEFINING POPULAR CULTURE

Henry Jenkins, Tara McPherson, and Jane Shattuc

When Miles Davis improvised "My Funny Valentine" at Lincoln Center in 1964, jazz stood as an unquestionable art form. Jazz has not always had such respect. In the 1920s the reception of form stood somewhere between "moral opposition and primitivist celebration."[1] Theodor Adorno condemned much of jazz in the 1940s as a form of "pseudo-individualization," or a false attempt at originality. He argued that such fakery was produced by the pressure to standardize within popular or mass culture.[2] In the years since Adorno's critique, jazz did not become somehow "better." Rather the definitions of high culture and popular culture changed to accommodate new tastes. Jazz, and even the "low" form of the blues with all its sexual innuendo, became associated with refined tastes. Should not the capriciousness of cultural tastes cause us to wonder whether today's rap— another "low" popular culture form—might be deified as high culture in the future? The 1990s as the *high* period of rap? What then defines this line between popular and high culture?

Defining popular culture is complicated. It is seemingly the simplest and most pervasive culture and therefore often maligned. Yet for ourselves and many others, popular culture is pleasurable. We are connected to its pleasures and politics in our everyday existence through a diversity of experiences. The range of subjects of this book attests to this ubiquity: television wrestling, children's books, soap operas, home videos, baseball card collecting, and shopping, to name a few. Even our pleasure in playing on multiple levels with Dr. Seuss's title for our book can be understood as a popular culture activity—we based our choice on a favorite children's book and its playful humor and remade it for our own use.

However, the concept "popular culture" belies a simple definition. It has been the subject of debates for three hundred years and has changed, for example, with Romanticism, industrialization, Marxism, American conglomerate culture, and identity politics. Different times have produced different definitions. And we can understand the term only within the complex historical context of its use. Yet one common thread can be traced in the debates: the concept has been used as an instrument by the educated and middle classes to maintain their ideological authority by defining "good" and "bad" culture.

With such a range of meanings, what is "popular culture"? Not only does it evade one simple all-embracing definition, it cannot be easily classified in a list. It undercuts a simple black-and-white history of good and bad culture. An honest history of popular culture is fraught with contradictions concerning economics, class power, theory and criticism, and critical enjoyment. Any attempt to summarize the history of the use of the term (including this essay's) will be schematic at best and often fall into a linear conception that smoothes over the contradictions and nuances. Nevertheless, this essay counters the familiar academic characterization of popular culture—the denigration of popular culture as a form of candy, pollution, or control. Instead it serves as an introduction for those outside cultural studies as a counter-history of how popular culture has stood as a potentially powerful and progressive political force in the battle to define "culture."

Such a positive picture of popular culture has always existed in definitions that consider the experience of makers, consumers, and participants. For centuries, many people have experienced popular culture as a form of liberation from the top-down strictures of high culture—a subversion of dominant notions of taste. This history leads to

the inevitable focus on the hundred and fifty years when mass production led to the vast proliferation of popular culture, and the resulting critical analysis of it comes to the fore.

To begin, the cultural theorist Raymond Williams sees "culture" as one of "the two or three most complicated words in the English language," a word with a range of meanings.[3] It comes from the root Latin word *colere,* meaning "to inhabit, cultivate, protect, honour with worship."[4] By the sixteenth century its previous use—"tending to natural growth"—was extended to human activity, such as the growth of the mind and understanding. Its modern class-conscious usages take hold in the eighteenth century with culture connoting either the development of the intellectual, spiritual, or aesthetic sensibility, a particular way of life, or an intellectual or artistic activity. The term's use as a descriptor of the intellect and/or of artistry took on even greater class distinctions and associations with refinement through class and educational changes in the nineteenth century. Although the term today can often describe the activities of a generalized people (as in "Asian American culture"), it has also remained an ideological tool. Here, "culture" signifies the cultivated or more elite realm of the educated classes as opposed to the debased world of the lower classes, the realm of the popular.

"Popular" was originally a legal term derived from the Latin word *popularis:* "belonging to the people." It began with a political connotation referring to a country's citizenry or to a political system carried on by the whole. Yet according to Williams, this definition always also carried a sense of "low" or "base" and was used by those who wanted to influence the populous. This pejorative meaning remains along side the newer, modern meaning of "well-liked" or "widely liked"—an important shift away from the top-down perspective on popular culture. Here the term refers to the people's own views. But the term remains ambiguous: which "people" are we talking about? All people? Only the underclasses? The marginal classes and groups? Can the middle class be understood as part of "the people"? These two words—"popular" and "culture"—have not historically been easy allies.

Ultimately, popular culture is a self-conscious term created by the intelligentsia and now adopted by the general public to mark off class divisions in the generic types of culture and their intended audience. Yet the divisions have structured a cultural battlefield where the educated standards of the upper class have often been imposed as universal on the other classes. According to Tony Bennett, "the most one can do is point to the range of meanings, a range of different constructions of the relations between popular culture, 'the popular,' and 'the people' which have different consequences for the way in which popular culture is conceived and constituted as a site for cultural intervention."[5]

One has only to consider Shakespeare's *Romeo and Juliet* to begin to understand the problem of defining popular culture. Shakespeare is taught today as high culture in high schools and colleges, yet when the work premiered at the end of the sixteenth century in London, it played to the educated and the lower classes as both wordplay and spectacle. Lawrence Levine claims that Shakespeare became increasingly a class bludgeon in America in the twentieth century. Shakespeare has become the possession of the educated portions of society who disseminate his plays for the enlightenment of the average folk, who in turn are to swallow him not for their entertainment but their education as a respite from (not as a normal part of) their usual cultural diet.[6]

For all of Shakespeare's elite connotations, *Romeo and Juliet* has been adapted in many forms, from the Royal Shakespeare Company's "authoritative" renditions to Franco Zeffirelli's "critically acclaimed" version of 1968 to Baz Luhrmann's 1996 "questionable" adaptation where multiracial gangs in designer label colors fight to the sounds of Prince, the Butthole Surfers, and Radiohead. This postmodern rendering has been converted into a CD-ROM game and has spawned a series of Web pages designed by teenagers comparing the film to other films and the play. What constitutes high and popular culture in these remakings? Not only does this reveal the difficulty of arriving at an all-encompassing definition of popular culture that does not take historical context, audience, and cultural form into consideration; it also reveals how standards are arbitrary—a reflection of social standing and historical circumstance.

Romanticism and the Rise of the People's Culture

Popular culture as a concept was initially defined in anthropological terms. In his *Popular Culture in Early Modern Europe,* Peter Burke argues that the term "popular culture" first appeared in the late eighteenth century as intellectuals became interested in folk or peasant culture as an object of cultural inquiry.[7] Folk songs appeared as a category across Europe—*volkslieder* (Germany), *canti populari* (Italy), and *narodnye pesni* (Russia)—as the middle class began to celebrate these simpler forms. In this period, popular culture encompassed activities as diverse as ballads, religions, carnivals, pantomime, and the making of figurines. Burke credits the German philosopher J. G. Herder with the creation of the term "popular culture."[8] In his famed 1778 essay on poetry, Herder suggested that poetry had lost its moral power in modern times. As opposed to Rabelais's vision of popular culture as anarchistic and pleasurable, Herder looked to peasant culture as a more moral way of life, one that he described as an "Organic Community" of "savages" (*Wilde*) or the lower peasant classes. He thus proclaimed a division between popular and elite culture. This use of culture not only established its anthropological basis as a way of life, but also influenced its modern application to national and traditional cultures. Often implicit in these uses was a romantic nostalgia for a simpler life closer to the organic traditions of thinking about nature.

Although socio-scientific in his logic, Herder established an evaluative hierarchy that is still present in cultural studies debates today. He argued that popular culture, or the oral culture of peasant folk songs, is a morally more effective way to communicate because of its direct and content-oriented approach to meaning. He opposed the utilitarianism of the peasantry to the poetry of the educated middle class culture, which he claimed was formal and therefore frivolous. Jakob Grimm, the writer of fairy tales, followed Herder's lead when he argued that oral folk culture such as ballads, poems, and songs gained its strength from the lack of a single author. Because their authorship was communal, these popular ballads belonged to the people as a whole rather than to an individual.[9] This nostalgia for a peasant-based popular culture can be understood as part of the growing Romantic backlash against a number of converging influences. According to Burke, these influences included the cold formalism of Classicism, the distant rationalism of the Enlightenment, and the inhumanity of industrialization. He argues that intellectuals and artists championed a cultural primitivism where the ancient, the exotic, and the popular were conflated.[10] For example, Jean-Jacques Rousseau espoused the naive and simple experience, Boswell dwelled on the pastoral life, and the Brothers Grimm prized what Burke describes as "the instincts of the people over the arguments of intellectuals."[11] Much of this passion was also fueled by a growing nationalism where peasant culture was conceived of as part of the organic traditions of a country. A century later, Hitler tapped into this same sensibility when he triumphed the *volkishe Kultur* as the basis of German nationalism.

Intellectuals also rushed to preserve this hand-hewn culture of the people as it disappeared in the face of mass-produced culture at the turn of the nineteenth century. Such nostalgia can be linked to a growing upper-class fear of the emerging economic and political power of an industrial class: what once was handmade was increasingly manufactured and bought with the rise of commercial capitalism. Clear cultural divisions between the folk and the educated middle class broke down as industrial capitalism redefined cultural class divisions.

Industrialization and the Rise of Commercial Culture

As industrialization gained momentum, so did the upper classes' fear of the masses. Raymond Williams argues that the association of popular culture with vulgar culture began with the backlash against the new literate classes. As industry grew, the middle class advanced to prosperity and literacy.[12] A second shift in England came in the wake of the Education Act of 1870 as a new mass reading public developed. This growing democratic emancipation provoked an anxiety in intellectuals such as John Stuart Mill and Matthew Arnold, both of whom feared the power invested in this new culture. In *On Liberty,* Mill offered a liberal defense of democracy, but one based on the necessity of "elites" and "minorities." The concept of culture as a "refined" experience is often associated with Arnold. In *Culture and Anarchy* (1869), he wrote about culture as a process of learning the "right" literature and knowledge. He suggested that English literature should be the secular religion in reaction to growing political unrest and class changes in contemporary England. He demanded that England teach "the best that has been thought or known in the world current everywhere" to stem the growth of the power of what he called "the masses."[13]

Although the popular culture of cheap novels, tabloids, and melodrama was not made by but for the lower classes, the intelligentsia in general branded the new forms as a decline in standards in order to control their political use. For example, the novel—a middle-class form—was considered "a new vulgar phenomenon." Consider Flaubert's withering description of Madame Bovary's declassé propensity for dime novels. The new tool of social control became "good taste." The nostalgia for a preliterate, more humble popular culture had waned under the brunt of more moneyed and ideologically aware working and middle classes.

There is no better example to illuminate this class division over mass-produced culture in the 1800s than the response to serial fiction and, in particular, the work of Charles Dickens. Due to the technological revolution that allowed printing of sections of novels in cheap newspapers to reach the "masses," the literary establishment reacted in anger at Dickens's popularity. Jennifer Hayward quotes a literary quarterly of 1845:

> The form of publication of Mr. Dickens' work [serialization] must be attended with bad consequences. . . . [Reading novels] throws us into a state of unreal excitement, a trance, a dream, which we should be allowed to dream out, and then be sent back to the atmosphere of reality again. . . . But now our dreams are mingled with our daily business. . . . The new number of Dickens, or Lever, Warren . . . absorb[s] the energies which, after the daily task, might be usefully implied in the search after wholesome knowledge.[14]

Not only does this quotation echo the same language later used to describe the popular "folly" of the movies and television, but Hayward notes how often nineteenth-century reviews repeated the high culture connection between the commercial "manufacturing" of fiction and an "absence of artistic merit."[15]

Marxism and the Working Class

Conversely, Marxism reinvented popular culture as an idealized working-class culture. Marx himself outlined a cultural theory in his *Critique of Political Economy* (1858) without ever fully developing it.[16] He offered the broad portrait of an economic base and a superstructure that produces culture and its ideology. But there is no explicit mention of a popular or even a people's culture. In one of Marx's few references to high art (Raphael) in *The German Ideology*, he argues that art, like all culture produced under capitalism, results from a division of labor and the alienation of individuals from their labor.[17] Implicit in Marx's writing was the idea that the only truly "popular" culture was one produced outside the alienation of capitalism. This moment would come only after the working class revolted and took the reins of production. Given that within the Marxist framework "the people" translates exclusively into the working class, it has fallen to Marx's interpreters to outline what constitutes popular working-class culture. As Tony Bennett points out, the Marxist construction of "the popular" has gone in two directions. He describes one type as a form of "rear-view mirrorism." Here critics rediscover "the people" in their historically superseded forms and offer these as a guide for action in the present.[18] E. P. Thompson's *The Making of the English Working Class* and Richard Hoggart's *The Uses of Literacy* exemplify this reconstruction of a popular working-class culture. The former celebrates the rising class consciousness of the British lower classes in past centuries while the latter bemoans the loss of working-class communities in northern England with the coming of the American-style "milk bar" in the 1960s.[19] By returning to their working-class roots, these writers write evocatively of how the English working class had developed its own culture in the shadow of industrial capitalist ideology and Americanization.

An important literary version of this love-hate relation with popular culture by the English Left surfaces in George Orwell's writings of the 1940s. Concerned with the moral health of the nation, he found a disquieting brutality and pursuit of power in comic and crime novels. Yet Orwell dedicated much of his writing to constructing an approach to fiction that was egalitarian and sociological. For example, he argued that Virginia Woolf might have been a better writer than Harriet Beecher Stowe. But why should that matter? *Uncle Tom's Cabin* had a wider appeal and therefore had a more profound significance. His *Coming Up for Air* was created out of an intense frustration with the chasm between the intellectual and the person on the street. Much of his criticism was pointed at the pretenses of the middle class while finding a certain honesty and straightforwardness in working-class culture.

A second way into Marxism and working-class culture is what Bennett describes as "'ideal futurism' in which the only version of 'the people' that matters is one that has yet to be constructed: the ideally unified people of a projected socialist future" (9). In this view, present-day popular culture is tainted by the domination of the capitalist production of culture and its enslaving ideology. There is then no truly popular culture of the people. True Marxist popular culture is configured as an ideal in the future when the workers remake capitalism on their own terms after the revolution. Official or state popular culture often replicates this ideal futurism. Soviet socialist realism of the 1930s exemplified the dangers of a top-down tradition where utopian posters and films of healthy and happy workers in harmony with industry and the land belied the cold repression of Stalinism.

The Frankfurt School:
Popular Culture as Mass Culture

The Frankfurt School is usually cited as the Marxist group that described popular culture as a mechanism of modern capitalism's repressive ideology. As German Jewish Marxists in exile in America, Max Horkheimer and Theodor Adorno equated their experience of Nazi propaganda in the 1930s with their experience as European intellectuals of American consumer ideology. They coined the Marxist concept of "mass culture," arguing that mass media in a capitalist democracy manipulates the masses by lulling them into the pleasures of conformity, consumption, and consumer ideology. They broke from Marx's belief in a worker's revolution and culture. The modern capitalist state had gained nearly complete authoritarian control through scientific rationality and capitalist industrialism. Like fascist propaganda, the power of the capitalist media undercuts critical reason, destroying resistance. Horkheimer wrote, "In democratic countries, the final decision no longer rests with the educated but with the amusement industry. Popularity consists of the unrestricted accommodation of the people to what the amusement industry thinks they like."[20] Adorno critiqued a diversity of popular pursuits as ideologically and intellectually corrupting: jazz, the jitterbug, and American TV of the 1950s. According to Ian Craib, "it seems as though the possibility for radical change had been smashed between the twin cudgels of concentration camps and television for the masses."[21]

By the 1940s, Adorno and Horkheimer replaced mass culture with the "culture industry"— a term they considered more critical because of the incompatibility between "culture" and "industry." Adorno's critique of popular music exemplifies this concept. People desire this music because the mass media hammer it into their heads. This mass-produced form is defined by standardization; originality and complexity are slowly squeezed out and a false individualism or novelty is substituted. Adorno argued that "the beginning of the chorus is replaceable by the beginning of innumerable other choruses . . . every detail is substitutable; it serves its function only as a cog in a machine."[22]

Though the Frankfurt School critique does underscore the power of capital, insisting as it does on the role of production, it could not account for the ideas and opinions of the users of popular culture. Adorno saw these people as unrefined observers dulled by exhausting manual labor or by the tedium of nonstimulating work. Ultimately, Adorno's model pictured mass culture as both homogeneous and homogenizing, for he operated from a perspective that made it difficult for him to foresee the diversification that the culture industry would undergo in the late twentieth century.

The culture industry critique of popular culture underlines much of the fear of the "Americanization" of culture. This critique evolved into cultural imperialism theory in the latter half of the twentieth century. In this view international media corporations (such as Disney, Time Warner, Viacom, and Microsoft) spread American consumerist ideology to second and third world countries as a much more insidious form of domination than physical conquest. No essay better evokes this view than David Kunzle's "Introduction to the English Edition" of Ariel Dorfman and Armand Mattelart's *How to Read Donald Duck,* where he heralds the writers' ability to "reveal the scowl of capitalist ideology behind the laughing mask, the iron fist beneath the Mouse's glove. The value of their work lies in the light it throws ... on the way in which capitalist and imperialist values are supported by its culture."[23] The seeming simplicity and innocence of popular culture serve as powerful vehicles for capitalist inculcation. Additionally, the Frankfurt School had a profound influence on American criticism of popular culture spanning from the research of Paul Laserfeld on the effects of television to Fredric Wertham's study of American comics and children, entitled in classic Frankfurt School logic, *The Seduction of the Innocent.*[24]

Although Adorno and Horkheimer's analysis of popular culture as mass culture is the position generally associated with the Frankfurt School, Walter Benjamin, an associate of the school, offered a different view, one that pointed toward the liberatory appeal of popular culture. According to

Benjamin, within capitalism lurks its own seed of destruction—mass production. As opposed to lulling the masses into capitalist consumption, Benjamin argued that reproducibility democratizes a culture. Mass production destroys the social control produced by the aura and authority of original art. Such authority is descended from the ritual function art played for religions throughout the centuries. Icons served as direct connections to God, and individuals marked this power through awe and prayer. It took mass reproduction to break art's ritualized authority.

In particular, the ubiquity of the cinema and photography destroy the uniqueness of art. Mass reproduction brings culture in an accessible form to the people, allowing them to become more analytical. They remake objects for their own political needs—the opposite of the enthrallment by mass culture espoused by Adorno and Horkheimer. "With the screen, the critical and receptive attitude of the public coincide."[25]

Neo-Frankfurt School critics such as Miriam Hansen and Bernard Gendron have also complicated the Adorno/Horkheimer critique of popular culture through their respective studies of the contradictions in the popular reception of Mickey Mouse and doo-wop music.[26] The differences between Benjamin and Adorno mirror the tension in the twentieth century between the consumptionist (what the people do with popular culture) and productionist (what the producer constructed) frames of Marxist interpretation. Much present-day work negotiates this great divide.

American Criticism and the
Aestheticization of Popular Culture

From the 1920s through 1950s, a number of American critics—Gilbert Seldes, Robert Warshow, Dwight Macdonald, and Parker Tyler among them—began to take popular culture seriously in a culture dominated by conservative critics such as

Clement Greenberg (who viewed popular culture as "kitsch"). Long before the auteur theory of film in France in the 1950s, these critics valued film and other popular works based on the objects themselves and on the audience's interaction with them. In 1924 Gilbert Seldes wrote *The Seven Lively Arts* in which he broke from the elite traditions of American criticism, arguing that art included both high and popular cultures. He maintained that much of popular culture, or what he called the "lively arts" of the mass media, was a good deal more entertaining and worthwhile than the so-called serious arts: "My theme was to be that entertainment of a high order existed in places not usually associated with Art, that the place where an object was seen or heard had no bearing on its merits, that some of Jerome Kern's songs in the *Princess* shows were lovelier than any number of operatic airs and a comic strip printed on news-pulp which would tatter and rumple in a day might be as worthy of a second look as a considerable number of canvases at most of our museums."[27]

Seldes expressed an intense emotional pleasure in the complexity of "movies." As opposed to a criticism that saw popular culture as a form of degradation of the high arts leading to a lowering of American tastes, Seldes grouped the high and popular arts together as the "public arts," refusing to keep them in separate categories. He believed that they were two dimensions of the same phenomenon. For example, he lauded the comic strip *Krazy Kat* as "the most amusing and fantastic and satisfactory work of art produced in America today. With those who hold that a comic strip cannot be a work of art I shall not traffic."[28] Yet Seldes's writing also revealed the age-old fear of the emotional power of popular culture. He felt people developed an emotional relationship to popular culture and particularly to film that is akin to passionate love because of "the way a story does all the work for the spectator and gives him the highly satisfactory sense of divine power."[29]

This power had the potential for addiction or what he called "the mood of consent."

Continuing this interest in the popular appeal of everyday culture, Robert Warshow developed a sociological theory of "the immediate experience" of popular culture in American life. His focus was genre films—popular commercial films—that critics had traditionally ignored. He argued that there was no simple division between popular movies and art. All culture depends on the conventions endemic to popular forms. But the frequency of repeated conventions in genre films creates their power. "It is only in an ultimate sense that the type appeals to its audience's experience of reality; much more immediately, it appeals to previous experience of the type itself: it creates its own field of reference."[30] Therefore, the complexity of popular culture lies in the audience's knowledge of previous similar forms and the intricate variations that are carried out.

As a result, Warshow advocated that critics needed to take seriously the knowledge and tastes of the frequent filmgoer. In fact, he broke with the concept of intellectual distance that had defined film criticism to this point. The fan could be a critic and a good critic could only be steeped in film. He was such a person: "I have gone to the movies constantly, and at times almost compulsively, for most of my life. I should be embarrassed to attempt an estimate of how many movies I have seen and how many I have consumed."[31]

Like Warshow, Parker Tyler combined intellectualism with a passion for popular culture. He continued the American interest in the mythic potential of popular culture as opposed to the European emphasis on ideological analysis as the central critical tool. However, he carved out his own critical approach combining psychoanalytic and mythic analysis of popular film and genres. In books such as *The Hollywood Hallucination* and *Magic and Myth of the Movies,* Tyler offered what he called "Magic Lantern Metamorphoses" that transformed popular texts to bring to the surface the "unconscious" content. Tyler saw popular cinema as possessing dreamlike qualities that were experienced all the more acutely because "the movie-theatre rite corresponds directly to the profoundly primitive responses of the audience; the auditorium is dark, the spectator relaxed, the movie in front of him requires less sheer mental attention than a novel or stage play." [32]

Tyler also expanded the scope of serious popular culture criticism in America. He often found profundity in the most banal text and punctured highbrow and middlebrow fare. While he did not have a concept of ideology, he offered a critical mode that we might now call "reading against the grain," uncovering the repressive and repressed elements in popular culture. His late work on sexuality in the cinema expanded the definition of popular culture to encompass gay issues—an early model for the emergence of queer cultural criticism.

Dwight Macdonald, perhaps the most left of these critics, adopted a much more ambivalent attitude toward popular culture. While he was one of the first critics to point out how the Frankfurt School's critique of mass culture insulted the basic intelligence of the average person, he still branded popular culture as an inferior form. He admitted that popular/mass culture was a "dynamic, revolutionary force breaking down the old class barriers, tradition, taste and dissolving cultural distinctions." But, following the Frankfurt School's critique, he argued that mass culture produced "homogenized" culture. "Mass culture is very, very democratic: it absolutely refuses to discriminate against, or between anything or anybody. All is grist to its mill, and all comes out finely ground indeed." Although Macdonald critiqued Adorno's infantilization of the average person, he repeated Adorno's view of the unidimensional nature of popular culture and damned the user's experience as nothing more than "appreciating dust." [33]

For all his disdain for the leveling effects of popular culture, Macdonald saw "Midcult"—the offspring of the marriage of high and popular cultures—as the greatest threat to culture: "This intermediate form—let us call it Midcult—has the essential qualities of masscult—the formula, the built-in reaction, the lack of any standard except popularity—but it decently covers them with a cultural figleaf. In masscult the trick is plain—to please the crowd by any means. But Midcult has it both ways: it pretends to respect the standards of High Culture while in fact it waters them down and vulgarizes them." [34] Here, popular culture remains the loyal "enemy outside the walls" of high culture, but one that has a clear and perhaps more honest purpose: reduction of educated tastes. Midcult is even more insidious because of its lack of clear class boundaries.

Other American critics and institutions have succeeded in legitimizing the study of popular culture. Andrew Sarris created an auteur theory for Hollywood films that applied European notions of expressive individualism to an industrial form to evaluate their worth and legitimize them to an educated population. John G. Cawelti widely expanded the understanding of the Western and other popular genres of film and literature. Reacting against the academic obtuseness of the auteur theory, Pauline Kael wrote in the *New Yorker* eloquent and powerful defenses of certain films and directors such as Martin Scorsese and Robert Altman based on her own take on the auteur theory. She even legitimized the aesthetic importance of violence in commercial film in a magazine whose appeal was based on intellectual distance and not physical transgressiveness. The Association for Popular Culture represents an advocacy group offering an eclectic mix of "popular culture for popular culture's sake" and detailed studies. And finally, the American Film Institute breaks down the wall between the critical and educational establishment and the Hollywood film industry as an institution devoted to the promotion of popular film that ultimately functions as a showpiece for the industry.

British Cultural Studies:
Popular Culture as Everyday Culture

In 1958 British critic Raymond Williams declared "culture is ordinary," a moment that represents the symbolic beginning of what has become "cultural studies."[35] This marked a British Marxist move away from the reductive concept of mass culture as simply a vehicle of false consciousness, while also breaking with the view that high culture was the central liberatory form for all classes. In place of these two critical positions, cultural studies emphasized "culture" with a small "c"—the realm where people exercised their human agency, creativity, and will for freedom within capitalist culture. As a result, cultural studies increasingly focused on everyday life and on how modern society creates and circulates its meanings and values. This critical school "attempts to reclaim culture for the working class, 'common people,' or 'masses' as against antidemocratic and too often academic definitions that identify culture exclusively with elitist ideals of education, leisure and esthetic consumption."[36] Williams saw lived experience as having more social credence than the judgments of critics from afar. As a working-class Welshman at Cambridge University, he argued that his native awareness of the class hierarchy imposed by education and taste was shared by his fellow working-class Britons. This "critical populism" has tempered its interest in the political resistance of the underclasses with much more of a Marxist awareness of how capitalism creates consumption and class divisions than have American cultural studies.

Williams rejected the classic Marxist base-superstructure model of popular culture as a form of vulgar determinism, preferring a more complex model of interaction. No longer could academics study culture as if the economy totally governs

consciousness and average people had no awareness of dominant ideology. British cultural studies sought models that acknowledged the volition of everyday people. They were aware of cultural and economic power and even able to resist the dominant power. This tension between socioeconomic class analysis and a populist notion of resistance has characterized cultural studies' history.

Cultural studies has often focused more on the moment of reception—the individual's experience of everyday culture—rather than the cultural object as the primary source of meaning. With ethnography as a prime tool, critics have attempted to understand the consumption and uses of popular culture by everyday people "in their own terms."[37] Although British cultural studies still perceives itself as a Marxist discipline it is based on the theories of the Italian Marxist Antonio Gramsci. Gramsci saw that dominance was a much more complex process than the traditional view of capitalism and the dominant classes' coercion of the individual, involving a constant battle and the continual necessity of winning consent to the prevailing order.[38]

Gramsci argued that the central ideology was in fact common sense, or "the philosophy of the non-philosophical."[39] This conservative glue makes the social system function. But unlike ideology, its workings are contradictory and multiple, creating a space for the average person to be intellectual and critical. This common sense is tested every time the power (or the hegemony) of the ruling class is questioned. Cultural studies has translated this theory into the study of voices of resistance and opposition. Such forms reveal the contradictions in capitalism that the individual experiences daily where aspects of their social identity—class, gender, race, or sexual preference—knock roughly against the dominant values.

Elaborating on Gramsci's more open-ended notion of hegemony, Williams constructed a model of "cultural materialism" wherein he posed a theory of dominant, residual, and emergent formations. All human cultural practices fall into these categories. The dominant practices—the prevailing forces of power and control—never control the people entirely. There are always residual cultures from the past (such as religion and rural cultures) and emergent cultures (such as the working class and the women's movement) that resist the hegemonic culture. Williams focused on the resistive cultures (which he further subdivided into alternative and oppositional categories) as the site of cultural democracy. He sought to understand the ways in which certain cultural forms were not swallowed up by the dominant ethos and served as an antidote to the class strictures enforced by the cultural base.

The Centre for Contemporary Cultural Studies in Birmingham, England, served as the next locus of British cultural studies and as the site for many studies of resistive cultures. Its analytical framework was fashioned around the founding work of E. P. Thompson (*The Making of the English Working Class*), Richard Hoggart (*The Uses of Literacy*), and Williams (*The Long Revolution* and *Culture and Society*)—all intellectuals who integrated their ideas within a popular and interactive understanding of politics. The Birmingham center moved away from the elitist traditions of the academic disciplines of literature and art and the deterministic concept of "ideology" toward a more interdisciplinary and anthropological definition of culture, and popular culture in particular. Members also took their ideas to a popular audience with a more journalistic approach, publishing their work in magazines such as *Marxism Today* and newspapers such as the *Guardian*.

The work of Stuart Hall, the center's director in the 1970s, exemplified this wide-ranging populist political approach. Chairing the Department of Sociology at the Open University (an adult education program), he mixed French structuralism's awareness of the structural determinants of semiotics and ideology with a culturalist sensibility that highlighted human agency and resistance. Under his direction, the center produced a body of research concentrating on voices of resistance within British working-class culture, including studies of traditional trade unionists, skinhead punks, teenage girls, and Rastafarians. Nevertheless, Stuart Hall argued that "the term 'popular,' and even more, the collective subject to which it must refer—the 'people'—is highly problematic." He cites Prime Minister Margaret Thatcher—"We have to limit the power of the trade unions because that is what the people want"—as a case in point of the difficulty in arriving at a definition of the people and their culture. "That suggests to me that, just as there is no fixed content to the category of 'popular culture,' so there is no fixed subject to attach to it—'the people.'"[40]

In his own and his collaborative work (*The Popular Arts, The Hard Road to Renewal,* and *Policing the Crisis*), Hall attempted to understand the contradictions inherent in the English working class and especially their support of Margaret Thatcher's government, a government that espoused the end of the social support system for that very class. He insisted that there must be an understanding of the "articulation" of the distinctly different, often contradictory, elements that make up culture to avoid either a simplistic economic explanation or a naive populism. Thatcher's success stood as his central case, for she used the language of populism ("the little man") layering it with a competitive individualism and the pleasures of unbridled consumerism to produce a popular "authoritarian populism." Birmingham's work in the 1970s and 1980s provided in-depth studies of the context and history of cultural resistance in relation to the structuring dominance of the economic and class system. The Marxist frame of the economic class system remained central within these nuanced studies.

Using ethnographic studies, these cultural writers sought out how people used fashion, lifestyle, and music as a way of resisting the "we are all one" ideology of the bourgeoisie. This trend spans from the center's collective study (*Resistance through Ritual* [1976]) to Paul Willis's studies of hippie and motorcycle culture (*Profane Culture* [1978]) and shop-floor teenage activities (*Learning to Labour* [1977]) to Dick Hebdige's work on style, particularly punk—as youth resistance (*Subculture: The Meaning of Style* [1979]). Each study highlighted how the smallest element of personal expression could serve as a form of subversion of the class system. Still, throughout this work, there is a continual awareness that these moments of creativity, subversion, and freedom exist as individualized examples of revolt that ultimately do not challenge the social dominance of English capitalism.

Under Pierre Bourdieu's influence, the Birmingham center in the 1980s fostered a series of studies focusing on subcultures. Originating from a view of the 1960s counterculture as a form of political resistance, academics looked at the British working class and the experiences of its youth culture. They focused on how subcultures resisted the class domination represented most immediately by the middle class's penchant for slavish consumerism, respectability, Puritanism, and political obedience. Central to this project was the idea of undercutting the concept of a universal culture—an ethos that the dominant culture seeks to maintain.

A second major influence on British cultural studies in general was the feminist movement and theory. Armed with Kate Millett's manifesto, a rewriting of politics to encompass personal or everyday experience, feminism in the 1960s and 1970s scrutinized popular culture for the ways that it reproduced the patriarchal power structure and falsified the representation of women, finding its worst-case scenario in pornography. Often all of popular film was indicted for its connection to commercialism and mass tastes. Molly Haskell wrote that "the [Hollywood] industry held a warped mirror up to life" producing images that victimized or demonized women. Such male control found its powerful visual equivalent in Laura Mulvey's "gaze"—a psychoanalytic theory of how the pleasure of a Hollywood film emanates from positioning the audience to identify with the controlling look of the male protagonist as he looks at the woman as an object.[41]

During this same period women were busy reclaiming a women's cinema of positive images of strong and independent females. While Haskell mourned Hollywood's disfigurement of female images, she championed the roles of Katharine Hepburn, Bette Davis, and Barbara Stanwyck. Feminists were retrieving the careers of little-known directors such as Stephanie Rothman, Ida Lupino, and Dorothy Arzner.

By the late 1970s, feminist theory of popular culture began to question the repercussions of theorizing women as victims. It moved from an emphasis on production (the text and its making) to an interest in consumption (what the viewer/reader does with the work)—a shift that was central to the rise of cultural studies. Linda Williams wrote in her study of pornography, *Hard Core,* "As long as we emphasize women's roles as the absolute victim of male sadism, we only perpetuate the supposedly essential nature of women's powerlessness."[42] Not only was there a shift in feminism's focus with the rise of the anticensorship movement, there was a growing interest in seeing women as discerning readers and active viewers of popular culture. Central to this shift is Janice Radway's 1987 study of romance novel readers as critical thinkers conscious of the ingredients of the romance formula. "The significance of the act of reading itself might, under some conditions, contradict, undercut, or qualify the significance of a producing particular kind of story."[43] Another important figure in feminism and cultural studies is Angela McRobbie, whose ideological study of teenage girls' response to the magazine *Jackie* challenge the male bias of the subculture studies of the Birmingham School.[44] These girls were not "dupes" nor were they discerning readers. McRobbie later critiqued the ideological determinism of her study and even encouraged her students to work for the mainstream girl magazines because of "the space these magazines offer for contestation and change."[45] This feminist tension between the productionist and consumptionist analyses of popular culture remains a guiding thread in British cultural studies.

Cultural Studies in the 1990s:
The Polysemic Play of Popular Culture

As British cultural studies disseminated its project internationally, its ideas were challenged and changed as it encountered other national and cultural differences. British-trained intellectuals such as John Fiske, Tony Bennett, John Hartley, and Larry Grossberg brought these ideas of cultural studies to other English-speaking countries. Cultural studies affected the critical traditions of Australia, Canada, New Zealand, the Caribbean Islands, and the United States, as well as different disciplines such as women's studies, history, gay and lesbian studies, literature, and anthropology. As the work traveled outside England, some scholars began to question the universality of the British model.

The work of John Fiske in America and Australia represents one of these noteworthy shifts in cultural studies. Combining the theories of feminism, Bourdieu, Hall, Gramsci, Michel Foucault, and Michel de Certeau, he began an extensive study of what might be called the "micropolitics" of consumer practices. His work developed from what he sees as the native intelligence of the people to resist subordination. Following the lead of the subculture studies of the Birmingham School, he believes that popular culture has become the central terrain for resisting repression. The people no longer have access to the self-made or folk culture of the peasant that Herder studied in the

nineteenth century. Rather, the subordinated people of advanced postindustrial society create their own popular culture by remaking the dominant culture of the mass media. "There can be no popular dominant culture, for popular culture is formed always in reaction to, and never as part of, the forces of domination."[46] Fiske sees the forces of domination in clear hegemonic terms—"white patriarchal bourgeois capitalism"—yet, following de Certeau, his focus is on the remaking or "poaching" process by which human beings reveal their talents for resistance.

Borrowing from feminism and the concept of empowerment in his study of teenage girls and Madonna, Fiske looked at the punning strategies of her songs (e.g., "boy toy"), and theorized what the pop star's ambiguous style meant to girls, as well as the girls' responses. He found that the girls created a variety of meanings and this revealed the open-endedness of commercial television as a space where one can resist the force of hegemonic meanings. Critics have argued that he has naively gutted popular culture of its repressive elements in his attempt to affirm a nebulous and idealist category of "the people," creating a model of resistance that forgets the complex interaction of dominant and resistant forms. Fiske's analysis exists in diametric opposition to the Frankfurt School's top-down determinism in which there was little or no room for volition under capitalist ideology. Fiske has substituted the politically conscious and savvy resister of dominant ideology as the typical user of popular culture.

Fiske's and other recent cultural studies research calls upon the work of two French sociologists, Pierre Bourdieu and Michel de Certeau. Bourdieu offered yet another key model of the different experiences of popular culture based on cultural class differences. In *Distinction* he contrasts two aesthetic modes, the "Popular Aesthetic" and the "Bourgeois Aesthetic," to clarify how taste is a reflection of class and particularly of cultural class (e.g., education). The popular aesthetic makes no clear distinction between art and everyday experience. It depends on the willing suspension of disbelief in order to "participate" or "identify" with the fiction. It also celebrates the intensification of emotion and the collapse of the individual into the collective experience. The bourgeois aesthetic is the experience of our dominant cultural institutions (the museum, the gallery, the university classroom, the library). It is defined through its "detachment, disinterestedness, indifference," its refusal to be taken in by popular art, its anxiety about mass culture's lack of emotional control and expressive restraint, and its celebration of high culture's formal experimentation. When the bourgeois aesthetic takes up works of popular culture, it does so by creating "a distance, a gap" between the artwork and its perceiver, placing the popular text in the realm of connoisseurship. Such divisions in experience offer a model of class analysis of the critical reception of popular culture within the aforementioned high culture and low culture traditions.[47]

Michel de Certeau offers a systematic analysis of how everyday people "poach" the established culture to remake it for their own use. The "trickster" of folk culture becomes the modern rule breaker who conducts tactical raids on the established rules that attempt to constrain his activities. De Certeau's central example remains the everyday practices of consumerism where consumers create "clever tricks of the 'weak' within the order established by the 'strong,' an art of putting over on the adversary on his own turf, hunters' tricks, maneuverable, polymorph mobilities, jubilant, poetic and warlike discoveries."[48] For de Certeau, consumers are no longer the mindless pawns of capitalism that the Frankfurt School envisioned. Rather, they are guerrillas making tactical strikes on the occupying army of consumer capitalism through their choices, schemes, and re-creations. Readers/viewers constantly struggle to find their meanings in a popular culture that does not measure up to their needs or social expe-

riences. Through this notion of the active consumer, de Certeau's theory forces us to question to what degree the media producers are able to control the creation and meaning of popular culture. Ultimately, the viewer is also a producer.

A further elaboration of this debate between the production and consumption of popular culture has manifested itself around postmodernism. The term encompasses an academic theory, a condition, an epoch, a form of politics, and/or an aesthetic. As an academic sensibility, it often describes a new social order where "popular culture and the mass media shape and govern all other forms of social relationships."[49] No longer is popular culture simply a reflection of the world around it. Rather, it serves as an active, if not the primary, shaper of social reality. We are caught up in a culture of consumption created by the cultural conglomerates of late capitalism in which reality is determined in the digital haze of television, VCRs, films, computers, cable, and advertising. The critics of such a culture (Jean Baudrillard, Fredric Jameson, and David Harvey, to name a few) bemoan the growing dominance of style over content in our society as we exchange the pleasures of such visual spectacles as MTV, Disneyland, and the Internet for an in-depth critical understanding of consumption and ideological control.

For Jameson this postmodern condition also leads to a problematic collapse of the distinction between art and popular culture; a place where Warhol's artwork playfully dances between commercialism and critical art or the commercial photography and videos by Herb Ritts are treated as thoughtful artworks. We have begun to prefer the simulation of the real over the empirical real, the synthetic and the virtual over reality. The orienting boundaries of time and space are collapsing due to these simulations, the mixing of aesthetic and historical signs, and the ease of global communication and travel. These forces have disoriented us to the point that we have abandoned the desire to make clear moral and political judgments.[50] Ultimately, for the likes of Harvey or Jameson, the postmodern condition is leading to a gutting of political opposition as modern consumers lose their ability to resist and so surrender to the pleasures of late capitalism. This position on postmodernism rewrites the Frankfurt School's culture industry argument, draping it in late-twentieth-century clothing.

Opposing this negative perspective on the postmodern, scholars such as Jim Collins and Barbara Flax argue for the liberatory value of postmodernism because it promotes a multiculturalism that refuses a strict adherence to grand metanarratives or to the canonical power of the theories of modernism, Marxism, Freudianism, Christianity, and capitalism.[51] The fears of Baudrillard and Jameson are often perceived as deriving from their own loss of cultural control as white male intellectuals of European origin. Many feminists, multiculturalists, and global theorists now recognize the possibilities inherent in a postmodern world where identity can be understood as existing at the intersection of many registers. Rather than lament the loss of a totalizing view of the world, they prefer a more nuanced and localized model. For these celebrants of postmodernism, gone is the all-consuming anxiety about the complicity of popular culture in social control. Popular culture provides a plane for the popular remaking of corporate culture and for the fragmenting of power. The totalizing model of capitalist control has been replaced by one of rearticulations and rewritings through popularly created alliances and coalitions.

New Cultural Studies:
The Politics and Pleasures of Popular Culture

Our anthology enters this debate over the politics and pleasures of the late twentieth and early twenty-first centuries, arguing that popular culture is neither simply progressive nor regressive.

Rather, pop culture's politics continue to be formed not only by the historical context and the individual readers who experience it, but also by the ongoing class battle over who determines culture. The discipline of cultural studies has divided over the postmodern emphasis on forms of resistance. This political split has polarized around such dichotomies as British versus American cultural studies, critical versus affirmative analyses, modernism versus postmodernism, and ideological versus multipositional studies. We attempt to move beyond these divides, tracing an emergent position in cultural studies that reflects the contributions of a generation of academics who see that the politics and pleasures of the popular are contingent upon its historical context in late capitalism, as well as upon its forms and users. Central to these debates are the conflicting views about the role of ideology and class in defining the experience of culture. The critics within this newer perspective still question the dominance of a socioeconomic model as the primary mechanism for understanding how people make sense of their identity. Such class determinants stand alongside gender, race, and nation as shapers of social identity for people today. In 1991 Angela McRobbie argued for a middle ground between the extremes of economic reductionism and insouciant hedonism.[52]

There is a growing sense that popular culture cannot be defined as simply progressive or repressive in its social role. A "pure" politics does not exist in popular culture.[53] But we cannot dismiss popular culture for its lack of a purely oppositional or progressive impulse. Manthia Diawara argues that the popular remains the central vehicle for African American expressions of emancipation and a prime source of their victimization. Alex Doty writes about the centrality of popular culture for queer studies: "Part of my queerly realistic view of popular culture then is that queers have always been a major force in creating and reading cultural texts even though pop culture has been a vehicle to reinforce sexism, racism, homophobia, heterocentricism, and other prejudicial agendas."[54] In her work on transnationalism, Ella Shohat maintains that "popular culture is fully imbricated in transnational globalized technoculture," but she still finds it a "negotiable site, an evolving scene of interaction and struggle."[55]

Perhaps such ambivalence about popular culture's role may not provide the definition of popular culture that this discussion has sought to provide. Ultimately, what often defines it is this "indeterminability."[56] Popular culture only "means" something in relation to other readings and readers. We need to know how a particular object of popular culture is presented and experienced before we can begin to define its politics. In the end, these historical and specific contexts of reception, the social positions of readers, and the specificity of form determine the politics and pleasures of popular culture and that shape the work of this volume.

Notes

1 See Nick Evan's essay "'Racial Cross-Dressing' in the Jazz Age: Cultural Therapy and Its Discontents in Cabaret Nightlife," in this volume.
2 Max Horkheimer and Theodor Adorno, *Dialectic of Enlightenment* (New York: Seabury, 1972), 136–37.
3 Raymond Williams, *Keywords* (Oxford: Oxford University Press, 1976), 76.
4 Ibid., 77.
5 Tony Bennett, "The Politics of the 'Popular' and Popular Culture," in *Popular Culture and Social Relations,* ed. T. Bennett and C. Mercer (Buckingham: Open University Press, 1986), 8.
6 Lawrence Levine, *Highbrow/Lowbrow: The Emergence of Cultural Hierarchy in America* (Cambridge, MA: Harvard University Press, 1988), 31.
7 Peter Burke, *Popular Culture in Early Modern Europe* (Hauts: Wildwood House, 1978), 3–4.
8 Ibid., 4.
9 Ibid.
10 Ibid., 10.
11 Ibid., 10–11.
12 Raymond Williams, *Culture and Society* (New York: Harper and Row, 1958), 305–6.
13 Jim McGuigan, *Cultural Populism* (London: Routledge, 1992), 21.
14 As quoted in Jennifer Hayward, *Consuming Pleasures: Active Audiences and Serial Fictions from Dickens to Soap Opera* (Lexington: University Press of Kentucky, 1997), 26.
15 Ibid., 25.
16 Williams, *Keywords*, 265.
17 Karl Marx, *The German Ideology* (New York: International Publishers), 428–32.
18 Bennett, "The Politics of the 'Popular' and Popular Culture," 9.
19 See E. P. Thompson, *The Making of the English Working Class* (London: Gollancz, 1963); and Richard Hoggart, *The Uses of Literacy: Aspects of Working Class Life* (New York: Oxford University Press, 1970).
20 Max Horkheimer, "On Popular Music," *Studies in Philosophy and Social Science* 9(1) (1941): 303.
21 Ian Craib, *Modern Social Theory* (London: Harvester Wheatsheaf), 184.
22 Theodor Adorno, *The Culture Industry* (London: Routledge, 1991), 303.
23 Kunzle, "Introduction to the English Edition," in Ariel Dorfman and Armand Mattelart, *How to Read Donald Duck* (Paris: International General, 1984), 11.
24 See Fredric Wertham, *The Seduction of the Innocent* (New York: Rinehart, 1954).
25 Walter Benjamin, *Illuminations* (New York: Schocken, 1978), 234.
26 See Bernard Gendron, "Theodor Adorno Meets the Cadillacs," in *Studies in Entertainment*, ed. T. Modleski (Bloomington: Indiana University Press, 1986); Miram Hansen, "Of Mice and Ducks: Benjamin and Adorno on Disney," *South Atlantic Quarterly* 92 (Jan. 1993): 27–61.
27 Gilbert Seldes, *The Seven Lively Arts* (New York: Pantheon, 1924), 3.
28 Ibid., 231.
29 Gilbert Seldes, *The Public Arts* (New York: Sagamore, 1957), 7.
30 Robert Warshow, *The Immediate Experience; Movies, Comics, Theater, and Other Aspects of Popular Culture* (Garden City, NY: Doubleday, 1964), 129.

31 Ibid., 27.

32 Parker Tyler, *Magic and Myth in the Movies* (New York: Garland, 1985), 30.

33 Dwight MacDonald, "A Theory of Mass Culture," in *Mass Culture: The Popular Arts in America,* ed. B. Rosenberg and D. W. Manning (Glencoe, IL: Free Press, 1957), 62.

34 Ibid., 38.

35 Raymond Williams, *Resources of Hope: Culture, Democracy, and Socialism* (New York: Schocken, 1989), 3.

36 Patrick Brantlinger, *Crusoe's Footprint: Cultural Studies in Britain and America* (New York: Routledge, 1990), 38.

37 See Renaldo Rosaldo, *Culture and Truth: The Remaking of Social Analysis* (Boston: Beacon, 1993).

38 See Antonio Gramsci, *Prison Notebooks* (London: Lawrence and Wishart, 1971), 419.

39 Ibid.

40 Stuart Hall, "Notes on Deconstructing 'the People,'" in *People's History and Socialist Theory,* ed. R. Samuel (London: Routledge and Kegan Paul, 1981), 238–39.

41 See Kate Millett, *Sexual Politics* (Garden City, NY: Doubleday, 1970); Laura Mulvey, *Visual and Other Pleasures* (Bloomington: Indiana University Press, 1989); Molly Haskell, *From Reverence to Rape: The Treatment of Women in the Movies* (Baltimore: Penguin, 1974).

42 Linda Williams, *Hard Core: Power, Pleasure, and the "Frenzy of the Visible"* (Berkeley: University of California Press, 1989), 22.

43 Janice Radway, *Reading the Romance: Women, Patriarchy, and Popular Literature* (Chapel Hill: University of North Carolina Press, 1984), 102.

44 See Angela McRobbie, "Settling Accounts with Subcultures," in *Culture, Ideology, and Social Process,* ed. T. Bennett, G. Martin, C. Mercer, and J. Woolcott (London: Batsford, 1980).

45 Angela McRobbie, *Feminism and Youth Culture* (London: Macmillan, 1991), 186.

46 John Fiske, "Popular Television and Commercial Culture: Beyond Political Economy," in *Television Studies,* ed. G. Burns and R. Thompson (New York: Praeger, 1989), 43.

47 Pierre Bourdieu, *Distinction: A Social Critique of the Judgment of Taste* (Cambridge, MA: Harvard University Press, 1984), 41.

48 Michel de Certeau, *The Practice of Everyday Life* (Berkeley: University of California Press, 1984), 39–40.

49 Dominic Strinati, *An Introduction to Theories of Popular Culture* (London: Routledge, 1995), 224.

50 See Fredric Jameson, "Postmodernism, or, The Cultural Logic of Late Capitalism," *New Left Review* 146 (1984): 53–92.

51 See Jim Collins, "Postmodernism and Television," in *Channels of Discourse, Reassembled,* ed. R. Allen (Chapel Hill: University of North Carolina Press, 1992), 327–49; Barbara Flax, *Psychoanalysis and Philosophy, Psychoanalysis and Feminism* (Berkeley: University of California Press, 1990).

52 Angela McRobbie, "Post-Marxism and Cultural Studies: A Post Script," in *Cultural Studies,* ed. Lawrence Grossberg, Cary Nelson, and Paula Treichler (New York: Routledge, 1992), 719–30.

53 "Symposium on Popular Culture and Political Correctness," *Social Text* 36 (fall 1993): 27.

54 Ibid., 7–8.

55 Ibid., 27.

56 Ibid., 28.

HOP ON POP

II. SELF

THE TOPICS STRUCTURING THIS AN-thology are not intended to provide an exhaustive or definitive list of the core research interests or buzzwords that define the emergent paradigm in cultural studies. Rather, they are intended to provide nexus points to help us identify the common ground between the specific essays. Many of these essays could have fit under multiple topics, suggesting the multiple relationships which exist between these key terms. Our goal is not to put these essays into cubbyholes but rather to flag issues we think cut across them and thus encourage readers to engage with contemporary debates defining academic research on popular culture. These topics suggest subtle shifts in the ways cultural scholars theorize pleasure, popular culture, and everyday life, especially when read in relation to the critical and theoretical vocabulary of earlier phases of cultural studies.

"Self," for example, is chosen over "subjectivity" to suggest new understandings of the relationship between individuals and larger cultural forces. The term "subjectivity" has become too closely associated with the old "subject-position" model which has increasingly fallen into disfavor because of its implication that individuals are passively woven into ideology through a process of indoctrination. The use of "subjectivity" thus evokes all-too-familiar debates between those who want to emphasize the controlling or regulating force of mass culture and its role in the manufacture of consent, on the one hand, and those who want to emphasize the resistant use of popular culture on the other.

The concept of self found in these essays is one of personal identity as emerging from an ongoing process of negotiation. Such a model maintains some conception of personal autonomy while acknowledging that our self-perceptions are powerfully shaped by social processes, economic realities, and cultural discourses. Our use of "self" does not signal a return to the Kantian subject, but rather a more complex understanding of how individuals and their particular experiences relate to generalized patterns of social and cultural behavior. The self is seen as provisional, under construction, shaped by competing forces, defined through our interactions with popular culture. We agree with earlier generations of critics that one can never fully step outside these social and cultural processes, that there is no "authentic" self. However, we also need to understand that we have differential experiences of those social and cultural processes, that our personal histories shape how we are likely to respond to them, and that we can only understand and analyze how culture defines the self from a situated perspective. Often, ideological criticism adopted a theoretically impossible—and thus alienating—vantage point, pulling back far enough to see ideology at work and thus feigning an exemption from its own claims about how social subjects are constructed. The new discourse on the self, on the other hand, often starts with autobiographical impulses and then explores broader social and cultural contexts that shape those personal experiences.

Discourse analysis has become an important tool for developing a more historically and culturally specific understanding of how the negotiated self operates. Researchers have looked at self-help guides, pop psychology and sociology books, childrearing and etiquette manuals, mass-magazine fiction and nonfiction, and other such sources to better understand the social construction of the self and to specifically understand the ways our assumptions about childhood, sexuality, race, class, and gender took shape at specific historical junctures. Feminism, queer studies, African American studies, and other identity politics movements have played a major role in promoting this new emphasis upon the self and on the value of lived experience in understanding larger cultural processes. Each essay in this section asks core questions about "who we are" and how we come to understand our selves through our relations with popular culture.

Revisiting the old slogan "the personal is political," Elayne Rapping draws upon models of autobiographical criticism to suggest how soap operas fit within family relations and how they relate to a longstanding tradition of utopian thought in American feminism. She understands soap operas as positioning their characters within a complex web of community relations and thus encouraging viewers to understand the self in more collective terms. She describes how discussions about soap characters and their situations became useful in sharing her feminist values with her son and daughter and how they remain one of the ties that continue to bind her family together as her children have become adults.

John Bloom, by contrast, focuses on the more conservative influence of popular culture on white men's conception of themselves and their childhood pasts. He explores the relationship between baseball card collecting and a nostalgia for presexual identities, a means of returning to a simpler past free from the anxieties and failures of adult life. Rebuilding a collection of baseball cards that the collector had as a young boy helps him to take inventory of the relationship between popular memory and the autobiographical past. Heather Hendershot is also interested in the conservative dimensions of popular culture, exploring the religious right's attempts to create an alternative teen culture consistent with its "pro-life" and abstinence campaigns. Hendershot explores the ways that Christian popular culture seeks to regulate, constrain, and channel young bodies into gender-appropriate and church-sanctioned forms of sexuality and sociality.

Peter Chvany uses the fictional alien race, the Klingons, as represented on *Star Trek* and as appropriated by fan culture, to test various contemporary frameworks for understanding "ethnicity." An underlying focus here centers around the ways that the performance of an "imaginary" ethnicity relates to the social and cultural construction of "whiteness." Like Bloom, he helps us to understand the feelings of marginalization felt by members of dominant groups within an era of multiculturalism, while recognizing the potentially reactionary impact of these cultural impulses to redefine the self as cultural other.

Jane Shattuc explores another aspect of the self—our professional identities as academics and how we understand our role as experts in relation to the popular culture we seek to critique. Specifically, Shattuc draws upon her own experience as an expert about talk shows who now appears on talk shows to work through a range of different models that deal with the intersection between academic expertise and the general public. She is interested in the challenge that talk shows pose to traditional academic authority (and especially the concept of objective distance) given their embrace of personal experience as a source of knowledge.

Alex Doty's essay begins with an attempt to map his shifting understanding of his own sexuality in relation to repeated viewings of the childhood classic *The Wizard of Oz*. Part of what makes this MGM musical so effective as a tool for understanding the self is that the story centers around Dorothy's attempts to explore her own emerging sexuality. In Doty's account, Dorothy's struggle to decide whether she is a "good witch" or a "bad witch" forces her to experiment with differing constructions of lesbian identity and desire. Doty argues that queer readings of the film are no less valid than straight interpretations given the total absence of traditional trappings of heterosexual desire one would anticipate from a Hollywood musical.

Elayne Rapping

For only in art has bourgeois society tolerated its own ideals and taken them seriously as a general demand. What counts as utopia, phantasy, and rebellion in the world of fact is allowed in art. There affirmative culture has displayed the forgotten truths over which "realism" triumphs in daily life.

—HERBERT MARCUSE, *NEGATIONS*

A work of art opens a void where . . . the world is made aware of its guilt.

—MICHEL FOUCAULT, *MADNESS AND CIVILIZATION*

It's Sunday night and my daughter, Alison, is calling: "I hate that they have to kill off Eve," she moans, "although I don't blame her for wanting out of her contract—the show is definitely going downhill. And at least they're using her death to make a point about experimental drugs. ACT-UP should be happy about that, if any of them are watching. Probably not. Even the rec.arts.tv.soaps. cbs crowd on the Internet seem to hate her, which I really don't get. She's the only interesting woman left on the show. What do you think?"

We are having our usual weekly check-in call about *Guiding Light*, the soap opera of choice among Pittsburgh women in the 1960s and 1970s, when she was growing up, and the one to which we have both remained loyal for almost three decades, through good times and bad. Neither of us lives in Pittsburgh now, but when we watch and discuss our soap opera, we still share a common community and a set of friends and neighbors about whom we care deeply, even as we laugh at their often ridiculously implausible lives.

But what's this about AIDS, you are no doubt wondering. Dr. Eve Guthrie, after all, as you may know if you are a fan yourself, has died of a rare disease with no links whatever to any activity connected with sex or drugs or even blood transfusions. She has, it seems, picked up this virus while working as selflessly as Mother Teresa (and with as little political sophistication), as a doctor in a war-torn fictional nation. Nothing political or kinky about that.

Nonetheless, as Alison and I both understand, having followed and discussed the murky, contradictory, often subtextual, politics of daytime soaps for so long, there is something progressive, in the most utopian sense of that word, about the conclusion of Eve's story line. In a frenzy of what some would call "denial" about her fatal illness, Eve has made contact by way of the Internet with a colleague doing research on this disease and has been secretly medicating herself with an untested drug. Her fiancé, Ed, himself a physician of the more conservative and typical variety, is adamantly opposed. But lo and behold, the cyber-researcher Eve has hooked up with an old med school pal of Ed's, a woman no less, for whom he has the utmost respect. And this brilliant woman convinces him, in a series of inspiring speeches of the kind Alison and I love to savor, of Eve's courage, her intuitive scientific acumen, and her right to choose her own treatment. Eve even improves for a while on the treatment, but it is too little too late, and she finally succumbs, as the contract of the actress who plays the role demands (and as we who follow the cyber-chat gossip have long known she would), amidst sobbing friends, flashback clips of better days, and a eulogy in which it is predicted that her final act of medical courage will lead to an early cure for the disease. In soapville, this is credible.

The path that led my daughter and me to the soaps is worth tracing briefly, for it was as contradictory and unlikely as many soap story lines. In the 1960s, when Alison was very young, I was a full-time graduate student increasingly caught up in New Left and feminist politics. In those days, hard as it is to remember this now, we of the democratic Left believed that revolution was around the corner; that a post-scarcity world of equality, beauty, pleasure, and material plenty for all was on the horizon.[1] In my socialist-feminist consciousness-raising/study group, we devoured new feminist tracts that corrected for the masculinist biases and blind spots of traditional Left theory. And in our women's caucuses, we developed strategies that challenged traditional Marxist ideology and process, with their artificial splits between public and private, work and play, labor and sexual repression. In our feminist revisions, women would not only be integrated into the public sphere of work and power; the public sphere itself would be transformed, as values such as compassion, nurturance, mutual support, and respect, long marginalized as relevant only to private, family life, were incorporated into public life.

Those were heady days. Also exhausting ones. I would drag myself home each afternoon, after classes and before the evening round of meetings, to find my grandmotherly baby-sitter faithfully watching *Guiding Light* while my two infants napped. And since she would not budge until her "story" was over, and I was too tired to budge myself, we would watch together as she filled me in on what I had missed. The habit stuck. In fact, *Guiding Light* became a daily delight to which I looked forward as a respite from my increasingly hectic life. More than that, although at first I chalked it up to exhausted delirium, the soap seemed, at odd moments, to offer a vision of social and emotional happiness that echoed the social visions my friends and I were constructing in our position papers and organizing projects. "What does a woman want?" asked Sigmund Freud, of penis envy fame (Juliet Mitchell had not yet rehabilitated him for feminism), and I couldn't help but think that, in all the male-run world, only the *Guiding Light* writers seemed to have a clue.

These were very different times in the academic and critical communities. Women's studies, as an academic program, was just being developed, a result of the growing movement of university-based women's liberation unions. But efforts to bring the study of mass media and popular culture into universities, at least in this country, were not yet spoken of. These were the days, in any event, when feminist media analysis was almost exclusively of the "negative"-and-"positive"-image variety. And the gender images that feminists were analyzing in popular culture were rarely considered positive.

Nonetheless, say what they might about "mass culture" and its evils, the Frankfurt School theorists I was then studying could not dissuade me from my instinctive sense that much of what I was trying to teach my kids about what life was supposed to be like in the brave new world I envisioned could most easily be explained with soap examples. In the rest of their world—their school rooms, their friends' homes, the cartoons and sitcoms they watched—women's lives were marginalized and demeaned. But in Springfield, the fictional midwestern town in which *Guiding Light* is set, and in Pine Valley, the somewhat smaller fictional community in which *All My Children*, our other, occasionally watched, show was set, I glimpsed, entangled amid the absurdities and contradictions of the form, a feminized world in which women and their traditional concerns were central, in which women played key roles in every arena, in which, when women "spoke truth to power," even back in the 1960s, power stood up and paid attention.

The idea that bourgeois culture incorporates utopian visions and values, moments during which we are liberated from the constraints of realism and can glimpse, in the distance, a vision of that better world in which our often unarticulated heart's desires are fulfilled, is not of course new. Media scholars have been aware of this at least since Jameson's seminal essay on "Reification and Utopia." Nor is it news that popular culture, often taken so much less seriously than high art forms, has been the most powerful site of imaginative utopian protest. For as Jameson has written elsewhere, it is in times like ours, when "our own particular environment—the total system of capitalism and the consumer society—feels so massively in place and its reification so overwhelming and impenetrable that the serious artist is no longer free to tinker with it," that popular forms that are less "serious," less "massively in place," assume "the vocation of giving us alternate versions of a world that has elsewhere seemed to resist even *imagined* change.[2]

While Jameson does not specifically mention soap opera, feminist media theorists have written extensively and insightfully about the utopian element in daytime soaps. Feminists have discovered in soaps a representation of "a world in which the divine functions"; a world which "exhorts the [real] world to live up to [women's] impassioned expectations of it," as Louise Spence nicely puts it.[3] And John Fiske, taking a somewhat different perspective, has described soap opera as a genre in which "feminine culture constantly struggles to establish and extend itself within and against a dominant patriarchy . . . to whittle away at patriarchy's power to subject women and . . . establish a masculine-free zone from which a direct challenge may be mounted."[4] Other feminist theorists have pointed to any number of specific soap conventions and teased out their utopian implications. It is often noted, for example, that through the incorporation of multiple subjectivities and points of view and the use of multiple, open-ended narrative lines, readers are potentially empowered to question dominant patriarchal assumptions about family and gender norms and to resist hegemonic readings.[5]

But most of this work has focused on the way soaps represent and negotiate the traditionally feminine sphere of private life: the home, family and gender relationships, marriage and maternity. My own pleasure in soaps, and my sense of their usefulness as a tool for raising feminist daughters and sons, came from something much less often mentioned: their implicitly utopian social and political vision. Raymond Williams has written that "community is the keyword of the entire utopian enterprise." And it was their sense of community,

a feminized community closer to my feminist visions of the future than to classic literary utopias, that drew me to soaps.

"The personal is political," we used to say back in the late 1960s. And what we meant by that (and it is a sign of the times that this statement is so often misunderstood, even by feminists, today) was that it was *political* institutions that were responsible for personal suffering, and *political* institutions, the public spaces from which women had so long been excluded, that would need to be changed in order for women to be free and happy. Barbara Ehrenreich and Deirdre English, themselves socialist-feminist activists, eloquently articulated the vision and the demands of that utopian worldview. "There are no answers left but the most radical ones," they wrote in the 1970s:

> We cannot assimilate into a masculinist society without doing violence to our own nature, which is of course *human* nature. But neither can we retreat into domestic isolation, clinging to an archaic feminine ideal. Nor can we deny that the dilemma is a social one. . . . The Woman Question in the end is not a question of *women*. It is not we who are the problem and it is not our needs which are the mystery. From our perspective (denied by centuries of masculinist "science" and analysis) the Woman Question becomes the question of how shall we all—women and children and men—organize our lives together.[6]

The answer to this question seemed vitally important to me as I was raising my children. And despite the derision of most people I knew ("Do you actually watch this stuff," I was asked repeatedly when I first "came out" in print, back in 1973, in a column about soaps and women viewers in a New Left newspaper), the political imaginary of soap opera, in which courtrooms, hospitals, and offices seemed miraculously to bend themselves to women's desires, suggested some answers.

For those not intimately familiar with the always implausible, often incredible, world of soap opera convention, a bit of background on *Guiding*

Light's Springfield community may be in order. The series, which has been on the air since the beginning of television, and before that, as a radio series, focuses primarily on the lives of eight complexly intertwined families who have lived in Springfield forever; they eternally intermarry, engage in personal, business, and political battles with each other, and they see each other, when they aren't feuding, through the constant barrage of mental and physical illnesses, natural disasters, onslaughts by master criminals of the financial as well as physical variety, and via the more mundane events like adultery, unwanted pregnancies, financial setbacks, and addictions that afflict them all, usually in multiple doses and in intensely dramatic ways. They are the Bauers, the Marlers, the Reardons, the Coopers, the Lewises, the Thorpes, the Spauldings, and the Chamberlains.

The show is distinctive in its special emphasis on class differences within a context of community harmony. This explains, in large part, its special appeal in Pittsburgh, where, until recently, the steel industry and organized labor colored the culture of the city. Where many of the newer shows elide issues of class, *GL*'s Reardon and Cooper families are distinctively and proudly of working-class backgrounds. They are proprietors, respectively, of a boardinghouse and a diner, both located on "5th Street" where street life, it is hinted, is a bit rough-and-tumble and folks look out for each other. This sense of working-class community life, while perhaps foreign to audiences in other parts of the country, did indeed ring true in Pittsburgh, where ethnic communities, populated with large networks of extended families, remained for generations in the areas in which the steel mills had provided them work, at least until the demise of the steel industry in the 1980s.[7]

Despite this working-class presence, it is, not surprisingly in a commercial TV text, the Bauers and Marlers, middle-class professionals all, who provide the backbone and set the constant, stabilizing moral tone of the community. Dr. Ed Bauer, grieving fiancé of Dr. Eve Guthrie, is, in fact, the chief of staff at the hospital where so many characters work and spend time healing from physical and mental trauma. And Ross Marler, his best friend, is the all-purpose, ever humane and democratic attorney for the "good" characters and causes. Then there are the Lewises, the Thorpes, and the Chamberlains and Spauldings, who represent big money and high finance. But here too class difference is marked with moral distinction. The Chamberlains and Spauldings are "old money." But where the Chamberlains have class, breeding, and humane policies based on a kind of noblesse oblige, the Spauldings are ruthless, competitive, and cutthroat, among themselves and against all others. The Lewises, by contrast, are Texas oil upstarts of the "good old boy" variety, fairly new to Springfield and closer in style and sympathy to the down home 5th Street crowd. And the Thorpes, represented by the rakishly evil Roger Thorpe, represent an upstart business class, driven by envy of and ire at the respect and love that the nicer and/or more established and self-confident families effortlessly attract.

At any given time there are any number of other characters who arrive in town and remain as semi-permanent or permament residents, usually by marrying into and/or working with one of the clans, until, most often, they wear out their welcome in some way and disappear. Within the permanent families, as regular viewers soon discover and adjust to, characters often change personalities and natures with Jekyll-and-Hyde alacrity. The love of a good 5th Street woman, for example, will temporarily transform a Spaulding into a humane, class-conscious saint. And by the same token, good characters will often stray from the homegrown morals of their Reardon, Cooper, or Bauer roots when lured, romantically or materially, by members of more ruthless families.

Another distinctive feature of the soap genre is its dominant setting. Soaps take place almost entirely indoors, so that interior spaces—kitchens, bedrooms, living rooms, offices, restaurants, hospitals, shops and boutiques, health clubs—are key elements in setting the tone and establishing the theme of story lines. On *GL*, besides the main characters' homes, the Reardon boardinghouse, the Cooper diner, the Lewis and Spaulding corporate offices, the usually Cooper-staffed police station, the country club (where the wealthy characters socialize and where major social events, to which all are invited, are held), and the hospital are the major settings.

In fact, it was the eternal presence of hospital scenes in which healing and nurture were always needed and always provided that inspired my first impulse to share my "escape" with Alison. With a typical four year old's insistence on brute realism, she was refusing to consider the possibility that she might be a doctor rather than a nurse "when she grew up," since, as she scornfully explained to me, "Everyone knows there are no women doctors." I could think of only one counter-example that might bear weight with her: *Guiding Light*. Here, even back in the sixties, women were as commonly cast as physicians and surgeons as men. And why not? On soaps all settings, all institutions, all workplaces are, on one level, merely extensions of the wholly feminized and personalized universe that is soapville.

But this example served me well for reasons beyond the obvious one of offering a "positive" alternative to the *Good Housekeeping* image of Mom as homemaker. It also allowed me to suggest to her that if she did indeed become a doctor, she might be able to act a lot more as she wished the doctors she had often encountered with terror would act. She could, best of all, get to run the hospitals as they did on soaps, and not in the truly terrifying and insensitive ways that hospitals—especially emergency rooms, where we spent more time than I care to remember—then were run. She liked that, for she could see that doctors on soaps, male and female alike, actually behaved like good Mommies at home, caring for and comforting the sick and frightened, and keeping the hospitals warm and friendly.

At Springfield General, for example, doctors and nurses were generally personal friends of their patients, and so every illness was treated with personal attention and concern. Parents and other loved ones, for example, seemed to be allowed to stay with patients at all times and to elicit the most confidential medical information, always provided with kindness and sensitivity, about a patient's condition. This was hardly the case in our own experience. Alison, who suffered chronic ear infections as a child, was plagued by nightmare memories of being wheeled off by silent, white-clad figures to hospital examining rooms where I was not allowed to follow. This did not happen on *Guiding Light*. Moreover, as I pointed out to her, bad, mean doctors, such as the ones we had too often encountered, did not last long on soaps. They and their bad ideas about ignoring patients' feelings and living only for power and money soon came to a bad end, as would be the policy in a right-thinking world.

As time went on, and Alison and her slightly younger brother Jon grew older, soaps continued to play a role in our life together, in our mother-child talks about life and love and politics. For one thing, on the simple level of "positive" images and examples, I found that issues of sexuality and gender were handled much more progressively on soaps than in other popular culture.[8] And since these topics are always difficult for adolescents to talk about, soaps opened up a convenient discursive space for discussing sex and relationships without getting too personal. It was a growing interest in gender relations that first sparked Jon's interest. A girl on whom he had a crush was herself a *Guiding Light* fan and always went home at 3 P.M. to watch with *her* mother. He wanted to find out what was up. As it turned out, we were then following a story line about a girl named Beth, the daughter of Lillian Raines, one of the hospital nurses who has remained a standard character throughout the years, whose stepfather was sexually abusing her. Upon learning of this, her boyfriend Philip, a Spaulding but one clearly uncomfortable with his heritage and heading for class defection, reacted as most boys would have: he ran out in a rage to find the brute and beat him up. But he soon returned, shame-faced, to apologize for being so insensitive. He should have seen that Beth's feelings, not his, were important, he realized, and stayed and comforted her. This was a far cry from what Jon was used to in the (to me) often terrifying boy's culture that he tried to emulate in those sexually insecure years. He said little at the time. Indeed, he often pretended he was not "there" at all. But Alison made sure he got the point. And he still remembers Beth and Philip and mentions them on occasion.[9]

The immediate drama of this story line was intensely personal. But it is a feature of soap opera's strategies for presenting such issues that they never remain merely personal. Rather, they become political and social in the most utopian sense of those words, offering a vision of institutional procedures such as board meetings, trials, hearings, even social gatherings in which serious debate occurs, in which, more often than not, a progressive community consensus occurs. This is what happened on the Beth/Philip story line. The issue of secrecy and shame, important since both Beth and Lillian had been long abused and beaten by the "respectable" husband/stepfather, was endlessly explored, in conversations at a variety of settings, during the course of events related to a variety of other story lines. And in this long, drawn-out process, various community members were forced to accept that such atrocities might indeed be perpetrated in even the "best" homes and families, and that the women were in no way at fault. (Quite often in such story lines, although not in this particular case, characters are actually sent to support groups in which, in a most didactic way, information about the issue is provided to the soap community and the viewer community at once, and generally progressive attitudes and even policy suggestions are advocated.)

And then came the trial in which, in a more public, ritualistic, fashion, the entire community came to terms with and adjudicated the matter, freeing the women from fear and shame and meting out punishment, in this case banishment, to the man. In the course of the trial, which went on for weeks, key characters were heard discussing the shocking events at work, at the hairdressers, over breakfast, and so forth, often arguing with each other, realistically enough, about who was to be believed. And as the pillars of the community, the doctors and grandmothers and police, came to believe and side with the women, so did viewers for whom these characters were equally credible and important. This was back in the late 1970s, it should be noted, long before issues of sexual abuse and violence against women were openly discussed or given the media play they receive today. But on this daytime soap opera they were indeed being discussed and dramatically represented in ways that seemed to me almost daringly oppositional.

How is it possible, in a form in many ways so hokey and even reactionary, for such progressive ideas to appear regularly? Well, for one thing, soaps are presented from a female perspective that is, by its very nature, alterior. The private sphere, as has so often been noted, is privileged and valorized on soaps, and the things women do in that sphere are seen as central to the maintenance and proper functioning of human life. But what is less often noted is the effect that this valorizing of private, feminine experience has on the representation of the public sphere. Soaps portray a world in which reality, as we know it, is turned on its head so that the private sphere becomes all-important. But there is more to it than that. For in so privileging private values, soaps also construct a highly unrealistic but nonetheless prominent and important public sphere in which all institutions are forced to conform to private, feminine values.

The feminist idea that "the personal is political" was a critique of what had, since the rise of the industrial world order, been a sharp delineation between the male-driven public sphere, in which work, business, and public affairs were handled, and the female-driven domestic sphere, the haven in a heartless world, in which took place the work of caring for and maintaining family relations, the socializing of children, and the negotiation of emotional and spiritual matters. In this scheme, issues of morality, and emotional and spiritual health, were designated "female" concerns relevant primarily, if not exclusively, to the home and family life. The male world, by contrast, was understood to be ruled by the competitive, individualist values of the marketplace in which ruthlessness and greed and self-interest were largely accepted as inevitable, if not necessarily desirable. This divide structured a wildly schizophrenic and ideologically contradictory system which maintained that men could escape the maddening crowd of the city via a return to the nurturing hearth and home. This realm was seen to promote values such as caring, emotional openness, mutual support, and concern for the welfare of the group, in this case, of course, the nuclear, or at best, extended family or immediate neighborhood community where one lived one's private life.[10]

In most popular TV and movie genres, the split between these realms and their values is assumed and maintained, and one or the other of the spheres is foregrounded as the central arena of action and thematic concern. Westerns, film noir, and crime dramas, for example, take as given a male world in which violence, greed, and cold-blooded individualism are forever encroaching upon the public spaces of commerce and politics, and the solitary, male hero is seen as single-handedly confronting the worst of this social evil with more or less, always temporary, success. By contrast, sitcoms and theatrical family melodramas are set almost exclusively, and certainly primarily, in the domestic sphere of the family home in which marriages are negotiated, children are socialized, communal and family values figure, and women work feverishly to keep the encroaching evils of urban life, commerce, crime, and corruption from tainting the domestic realm.[11] In sitcoms, this is easily done, since the larger world is rarely visible at all. In melodramas, the job is more difficult, indeed, often impossible. But in all these forms, the gendered bifurcation between the female and male spheres, the values and roles they encompass, and the clear gender roles appropriate to each, are clear.

Soaps are a bit different. While adopting the stylistic conventions of the melodrama, and certainly privileging the concerns and values associated with the feminine, domestic realm soaps claim for their territory, and for their women characters, more than the geographic and social boundaries of home and family. They map out a public realm of political, economic, and legal events and institutions in which women, and the concerns of the feminine, operate as prominently and importantly as in the domestic. By so blurring and eliding the distinctions between the proper concerns of the two spheres, they draw their male characters more fully into the life of the family and the emotions than do other genres. In this way, they create a world in which women are free to take their concerns for such values as compassion, cooperation, and the valorization of spiritual and emotional perspectives into the marketplace, the workplace, and the arenas in which law, justice, public health, and the business of maintaining democratic institutions are negotiated. And, by extension, men themselves, now forced to operate in so feminized and humanized a public sphere, have no choice but to bring home the values by which they now run their public lives to their personal lives. As lawyers, doctors, and policemen, they are, in their good phases at least, caring, humane, and emotionally involved in their colleagues' and clients' lives. And at home they are similarly involved with their children, their wives, their extended family of friends, relatives, and neighbors.

In discussing feminist utopias, Fran Bartkowski notes that, unlike most traditional male utopias, they incorporate "tacit rather than reified models of the state." What is "tacit" in feminist utopias, she suggests, and what distinguishes them from their male-defined counterparts, is a "discourse on the family" that sees the family as the "place where the inhabitants of the projected utopian state [are] formed."[12] It is just such a discourse on the family, as the foundational root of social and political ideology, I would argue, that informs the vision of community and public life on soap operas. If, as I have argued, home is where the heart is, home is located everywhere on soaps. The gathering spots of soap geography, the restaurants, the health clubs, the diners and malls, even the hospital nurses' stations and corporate office buildings—all serve as "homelike" environments. This is a world of public space that is family-driven in every arena. Its laws and policies reek, implicitly, of the values of "interconnectedness . . . nurturance, responsibility, and mutual respect," which Carol Gilligan has defined as informing the feminist moral universe that girls are socialized to maintain: on soaps the binary split between private and public is virtually dissolved.[13] Thus, it is standard on soaps for police officers, district attorneys, and lawyers, who tend to be equally divided between genders, to view their work in fighting crime, for example, as an extension of their roles as parents, keeping the city safe for their children, or, as in the case of sexual predators, for their wives and sisters and mothers. So thoroughly blurred are the sphere distinctions that there is *never* a contradiction between the two roles, never any possibility that one's role as a family member might clash with one's duty to defend a client or uphold the law. In fact, it is not uncommon on soaps for characters in these kinds of positions of authority willfully to ignore the law when their own sense of what is best for the safety of their loved ones is involved. And they are always, inevitably, proven to have been right, even heroic, in their judgment. On soaps, one's instincts about what is right for the family, no matter what the

law might say, are always validated, since the laws themselves are assumed, implicitly, to be in the service of such values.

"Utopia," Angelika Bammer notes, in establishing a theoretical framework for her analysis of feminist utopias of the 1970s, "identifies society as the site of lack." Unlike ideology, she explains, which "represents things as they are from the perspective of those in power . . . utopia is the opposing view of how things could and should be different."[14] Soap operas illustrate this strategy in an interesting way. They construct a world in which women, who do not, in any meaningful sense, participate in public policy formulation in reality, are allowed to have their say about how things should be run. In soaps, women are free to "play house," as it were, with the world; to set up a public sphere informed by the very values they are, in reality, enjoined to maintain and pass on (but only within the home and family of course).[15] Simone de Beauvoir once said that women were most grievously disempowered in not being allowed to "take responsibility for the world." On soaps, they are allowed to do just that. This is what is most empowering about the genre, because it is most at odds with the "common sense" to which women and children are otherwise exposed.

This is, to be sure, a somewhat unorthodox view of soaps. It is usually assumed that romance and the rituals of mating and marriage are what draw and hold women viewers. But while this is certainly a factor, I have always thought it was misleading to focus so heavily on these elements of soaps and to ignore what, to me, has always seemed so much more compelling: the sense of community. Men in soap operas, the good ones in their good phases anyway, are indeed wonderfully nurturing and caring. They become totally obsessed with the needs of the women in their lives and seem to devote every waking moment of work and leisure time to them. It is very common, for example, to see a lawyer, doctor, or cop stare soulfully into the eyes of a woman character in deep trouble and say, "I'm going to drop all my other cases and devote myself entirely to your case, because I care about you so much." And somehow, it's possible to accomplish this without total destruction of the man's career or business.

In a story line on *GL*, for example, Alan-Michael Spaulding, one of the Young Turks prone to switching from evil tycoon to humanistic, selfless community activist under the influence of a good woman, disappeared for weeks at a time from his post as CEO of Spaulding Enterprises when his fiancee Lucy Cooper, of the 5th Street Coopers, was being held by a psychopath who had already committed date rape upon her. And even before her abduction, when Lucy was *merely* suffering the posttraumatic stress of the rape, Alan-Michael seemed to leave his office continuously at the merest hint that Lucy, his office assistant, was feeling down, in order to take her out for a special treat, or to whisk her to his palatial penthouse where she could be pampered and coddled, and allowed to weep, talk about her ordeal as the need arose, or simply sleep. Every woman who has ever complained that her male partner had no time for her because of work, or had no understanding of what she was going through after a traumatic experience, could only drool in envy.

Such are the common characteristics and behaviors of good men. And even the worst of them, if they become regulars, are periodically good on soaps. But, as wonderful as they are , like their real-life counterparts, these men come and go. The sorrows and joys they bring are always fleeting. The marriage vows and family structures to which they commit themselves are always already disintegrating, even as their Friday afternoon wedding vows are being said. Thus, crisis and trauma are always imperiling the sexual and family lives of even the most fortunately partnered women. At the very moment when things seem, at last, to be blissfully perfect in a marriage, every viewer knows that catastrophe looms. In fact, if any marriage goes untroubled for too long, it is a sure sign that the characters will soon be written out, shipped off to another town or country to return, perhaps years later, in different bodies and with new clouds of chaos and tragedy ominously looming.

To avoid such annihilation, it is customary on soaps for even the best of longstanding characters to periodically undergo serious character lapses, if not outright transformations, in which they abandon or lose their wives and families in order to free them up for new storylines. Ed Bauer, for example, among the very best of the "good" men on soaps (as Alison and I, who rarely agree on men in real life, agree) has, in his long career on the series, himself gone through many such periodic marital lapses. At one point, for example, Ed had a brief affair with Lillian Raines, his head nurse. Lillian, having recovered from her ordeal as a battered wife, had just been diagnosed with breast cancer and undergone a mastectomy. Ed, as is common with good men on soaps, was her only confidante. Eventually, he became emotionally involved with her and, in part as a way of reassuring her of her sexual attractiveness despite her surgery, made love to her.

The affair was brief, and Lillian ultimately worked through her trauma with the help of an exemplary support group. But Ed's unbelievably long, blissful marriage to Maureen Bauer (a favorite on the Internet not only because of her lovable character, but also because she was noticeably overweight and still portrayed as sexually desirable) was destroyed. This story line not only served to present the issue of breast cancer progressively, it also saved Ed from storyline oblivion and opened a space for his relationship with Dr. Eve Guthrie. Eve died before Ed could have one of his periodic character lapses and let her down too. But he is destined, as we fans well know, to do it again, at least a few more times, before his character becomes too old for that sort of thing.

Marital and romantic upheaval and disaster, then, rather than family stability, are the norm in the lives of the most prominent and regular members of soap communities. But through all this family turmoil and crisis, the community itself remains stable. This is what really holds the women and children together during all the thick and thin. Every soap character, no matter how battered, how evil, how hopelessly fallen they may seem, can always rely on the emotional and material safety net of the soap community of extended family, social, and political relationships. No sooner has crisis struck than the character suddenly has more friends and attention than ever before. Harley Cooper, another of the Cooper diner/police dynasty, had been something of a hellraiser as a teenager. Abandoned and virtually orphaned by her negligent mother, she became, and remained, a central focus of Springfield concern and activity and enjoyed front-burner status in the story line department for quite a while. As a young adult, however, she was transformed, by love, into a "good" girl, and the beloved of a "good," centrally positioned, man. As nanny to Josh Lewis's two children, after their mother's tragic death, she became Josh's emotional rescuer and ultimately his fiancee.

But no sooner had she achieved the Cinderella happy ending longed for by all soap women, than her fate, luckily for the character and the actress, took a turn for the worse. Josh, upon hearing that his (supposedly) dead wife was spotted in Italy, took off to search for her, leaving Harley jilted and traumatized. The entire community then predictably came to her rescue. Suddenly new career and social opportunities came from all quarters and once more her life was filled with adventure. She eventually became a police officer and something of a local heroine. When, at last, she found true love again, she was given better luck in the romance department, if not the series. She married her new love and so blissful were their prospects that no story line at all emerged for either. Instead they were shipped off to another town and have never been heard of since. So much for happily

ever after on soaps. It happens, but usually off camera, and is not a good career move. Soap actors, who do not know in advance what their story lines hold, watch for telltale signs in their scripts that they are about to be written out of a show. And one sign that provokes anxiety is, indeed, a wedding.

If weddings are often bad news for characters, they are among the most anticipated of delights for viewers because of their lush, festive air of community celebration and ritual. Indeed, soaps, in their portrayal of such events, uncannily call up delightful visions of the kind of post-scarcity plenty and beauty that we on the democratic feminist Left believed in and planned for, back before recessions and Reaganomics gave our youthful optimism a jolt. Soap characters live in splendor and have an endless supply of always up-to-date furniture, clothing and, apparently, hairdressers. They have access to glamorous travel destinations and accommodations on the understandably rare occasions when they need to get away. Should they choose to eat privately, or decide, at the spur of the moment, to call some friends and share an evening of joy, or sorrow, or nervous waiting for the tense outcome of some storyline, they have at their disposal gourmet cooking from places like the Pampered Palate that deliver a world of earthly delights at a moment's notice. Nor are the poorer characters excluded from such treats. Sharing is endemic in soapville, and in fact the first hint that a "bad" character is about to be converted may well be that a wealthy character invites her or him, out of compassion or an instinct that they are savable, to share in some celebration or luxury.

Soaps, then, are in many ways similar to the socialist-feminist utopias of the 1970s. Marge Piercy's Mattapoisett, the utopian community of *Woman on the Edge of Time* in fact offers a similar vision of community, abundance, and pleasure. Here technology, fueled by collective decision-making, is used to produce the very best food and clothing for all, shared in communal dining and recreation areas or, as on soaps, alone if one so chooses. Among the most delicious features, for example, of what a socialist-feminist imagination would do with technology in the service of pleasure and beauty is Piercy's idea of disposable garments called "flimsies," which can be whipped up instantly, cheaply, and to one's personal taste and measurement, for special occasions where formal attire or costumes are required. After wearing, the flimsies are easily disposed of and recycled.[16]

A number of soap conventions resemble this kind of fantasized world of pleasure and beauty. Every soap periodically presents, for example, elaborate celebrations—masked balls, weddings, and so forth—for which everyone, rich and poor, seems magically to acquire the most elaborate, gorgeous evening wear immediately upon hearing of the occasion, even if it is scheduled for the next evening, as it often is. Here too, the costumes seem magically to disappear, never to be worn again, come the stroke of midnight. On soaps, in fact, the entire community seems to coordinate their attire in ways that allow a whole event to take on a particularly collective, communal flavor. Such things do not normally appear in traditional male utopias, but Piercy's feminist world answers real women's dreams, as any proper, technologically advanced, post-scarcity utopia should.

Indeed, the entire utopian world that Piercy spells out in such economic and political detail is filled with feminist-informed, radically democratic details that can be glimpsed, in a far less explicit, less rationalized format, on soaps. The idea of consensus and full community debate, made possible because each community in Mattapoisett was small enough to afford actual town meetings for all decisionmaking, is very much like what happens, in a more drawn out way, in Pine Valley and Springfield politics. The large permanent cast of town residents that make up the communities of these towns afford exactly the kind of structure in which entire populations can debate, differ, and come to consensus. Indeed, the endlessly dragged out story lines, in which every character must weigh every facet of every issue, are in many ways like the endless "consensus-based" meetings that feminists and the more countercultural Left employed in the 1960s. Like soap story lines, these meetings could become irritating, dragging out over many nights and into the wee hours of the morning. All voices, it was insisted, had to be fully, often repetitively, heard. Each interpersonal conflict and disagreement, whether politically or personality-based, had to be aired and "processed," until, at last, everyone not only agreed but "felt okay" about every decision.

So it is on soaps. In fact, the inclusion of complex interpersonal factors not usually allowed in legal and political procedures is one of the most politically interesting aspects of the form. In creating characters who live and interact with each other, sometimes over decades, and who are thrust into so wide a variety of story lines and conflicts and crises over time, soaps allow viewers to see characters as contradictory, complex, and changeable. A good mother can be a terrible friend, an adulteress, or worse. A terrible tyrant in one sphere can be a doting godfather in another. A personally selfish, conniving woman can be a leading figure in a political or legal battle for a progressive cause. Alexandra Spaulding, for example, the matriarch of the Spaulding clan, dotes on the younger members of her dynasty and acts as a good and loyal friend to Lillian Raines and to newcomers to the community at times, even as she ruthlessly schemes to rob and cheat her business and political opponents. Because of this complexity of character and relationship, when consensus actually comes, it is a consensus far more rich in impact and significance than in forms in which a single narrative line, involving a small group of less complicated, contradictory characters, is traced. Thus, the complexity and open-endedness of soap structures serve more than a merely personal, psychological function. They also contribute to the form's implicitly utopian vision of a feminized, radically democratic political process, in which difference and subtlety are recognized and honored within a community structure.

To give one example, on an *All My Children* story line developed over months of endless intrigue and complication in the early 1980s, a woman named Natalie Cortlandt accused her ex-lover Ross, who was actually her husband Palmer's son, of acquaintance rape. As the community discussed the case, taking sides, reviewing in detail her past sins, and recalling bits of their own histories and those of other characters, an ongoing "community meeting" of sorts actually took place around this publicly charged issue. *All My Children,* it should be noted, is set in a town even smaller and more bucolic than Springfield. Pine Valley is a suburb of Llanview, Pennsylvania (setting of *One Life to Live,* which follows it on ABC and which is in turn located somewhere outside Philadelphia). Pine Valley is thus almost village-like in social composition and in many ways far less socially realistic than *GL's* Springfield. On *AMC,* the concept of class is elided in favor of a more fairy tale-like community structure made up of "rich" people, *really* rich people, and temporarily "poor" people. But here too there are long-standing characters who play police officers and lawyers and doctors and their roles in the life of community are central. Here too there are key families who own and control most institutions and who intermarry and tangle with each other incestuously and eternally. There are just fewer of them. The Martins, whose male head is, again, the hospital chief of staff, are the middle-class professional equivalent of the Bauers. And the Chandlers, Cortlandts, and (matriarchal) Wallingfords are the property-holding, economic controllers of the town doings. And then there is Erica Kane, the glamorous, ever crisis-ridden, ever married or in love, ever engaged in some major, glamorous business enterprise, diva of the show, whose campy, over-the-top character gives the show its

peculiarly self-reflexive stamp of irony and self-consciousness.

Nonetheless, even in the more rarefied and more self-consciously campy atmosphere of Pine Valley, social issues and serious, feminized, public rituals and institutional proceedings take place. AIDS, homelessness, and gay and interracial relationships have all been touched upon progressively on this soap. So have more typically feminist-inspired issues such as date rape, domestic abuse, and even, briefly, back in the late 1970s, lesbianism.[17] Indeed, it may well be the very smallness, quaintness, and *un*believability of this particular soap community that has made it possible for *AMC* to lead the way in raising so many charged issues long before other shows dared. Indeed, primetime still hasn't caught up in most cases. And the Natalie/Ross/Palmer Cortlandt adultery/date rape story line was among the earliest and most daring examples.

As the trial itself played out, things, quite realistically in this case, looked bad for Natalie. She had arrived in town as a "bad girl" character, out for what she could get, and had not been rehabilitated sufficiently by the time of this storyline to store up much good feeling. Thus, her recent adultery with the accused made it difficult to imagine a jury believing her. But then, as could only happen on soaps (certainly not, for example, in the O. J. Simpson case), the defendant himself, having witnessed a gang rape that suddenly put his own act in a new perspective, actually confessed, entered counseling, and volunteered, upon release from prison, to work in a rape crisis center. In this way viewers were taken through the experience in real time, in all its subtlety and nuance, and allowed to digest the emotional and political strands gradually, as one would indeed do in an ideal political setting in which all parties had adequate counsel and access to all the time and resources needed to locate and sift evidence, find and bring in witnesses, and deliberate. Soap operas, in this way, open a discursive space within which the characters and the audience form a kind of community. The experience is especially intense since the characters involved are so familiar to viewers and are "visited" virtually every day, for years on end. Court TV, in its best moments, can only approximate the complexity and thoroughness of this kind of coverage of emotionally-intense, politically-contested issues of justice and equity.

The often bizarrely unconventional family and living arrangements that arise from the extended families and community relationships on soaps provide a similarly rich and complex representation of political structure and process. Again, Piercy's Mattapoisett is brought to mind in these utopian projections of a community that honors and accommodates the needs of all members for emotional and material support and security in a feminist-informed manner. Piercy's utopia articulates a private, family realm in which various choices of sexual and child-care arrangements are allowed to suit the varied and often changing tastes and inclinations of citizens. Children in Piercy's world have three biological parents and do not necessarily live with any. They may choose households that suit them, just as those who remain childless may find ways to relate to the children of the community that does not involve custodial care or biological connection.

Similar things happen on soaps. A typical custody decision on *Guiding Light*, for example, ruled that two single mothers, one the birth mother, and one the adoptive mother, should share custody in a way that gave the child two homes and mothers, linked by a common community of support. The fathers, as soap-fate would have it, were temporarily absent at the time. The birth father, Roger Thorpe's then-awful son, had skipped town, and the adoptive father, Billy Lewis, was in prison. The situation was even further complicated, and socially intriguing, because the birth mother, Bridget Reardon, was the working-class manager of the boardinghouse, while the adoptive mother, Vanessa Chamberlain, was the CEO of Lewis Oil.

Thus, the extended family created by the decision crossed class boundaries. This story line was particularly interesting to Alison and me because, at the time, she was herself, as a young single woman recently out of a long-term relationship and deeply immersed in a career, worrying through the issue, so common to her generation, of how and when she might be in a position to have a child. Springfield certainly looked like a utopian heaven to the two of us at that time, for no "solution" to this common social and material dilemma offered in the real world even approached the beauty of the Springfield model.

But parenting isn't the only problem for which soap communities provide utopian solutions. It is also very common on soaps for people to move in and out of relationships and households. And the end of a relationship does not involve the kind of trauma and agony that today sends so many desperate souls searching far and wide, even in cyberspace, for "support groups." On soaps, support groups come to you. They find you sitting alone somewhere, or being beaten by a boyfriend, and they invite you to live with them or with some other character in need of just the service you can provide. Characters who are originally derelicts or exconvicts or worse often wander into town and are immediately recognized for some wonderful character trait or talent and given a home and work.

Roger Thorpe's awful, woman- and baby-abandoning son, for example, returned to town after several years and was promptly left a large inheritance by Henry Chamberlain, who was killed off when the beloved actor who had played him for decades suddenly died. Henry "just knew" that the young man was, deep down, a good person and wanted to provide him with the wherewithal to take responsibility for his young son and become a "productive member of the community." He did just those things and in short order. And, as of this writing, he is a model of nurturing, caring fatherhood, as well as an exemplary member of the

Springfield community, engaged vigorously and virtuously in several story lines in which community issues are at stake.

The Reardon boardinghouse is always full to brimming with such characters. They arrive in town, crash at the Reardons, and promptly give up their wicked ways and criminal schemes to become whatever thing the show seems to be needing at the moment. A black character, David Grant, for example, arrived in town as an ex-convict with a bad attitude. After several years at the boardinghouse, he reformed. But it took a while to find him a career. He flirted with law, police work, restaurant managing and finally settled on becoming a civil rights activist, a job for which he was required to leave town and the show. But each of his previous interests were temporarily central to some major story line, as, in each case, he worked with some other "good" character to solve a crime, try a case, or support and care for a troubled, crisis-ridden female character. In this way, he was integrated into the family and community life of the major characters and, while for the most part unattached and unfamilied, was included in the (largely white) social and family rituals and gatherings.[18]

In the same way, children who have been abused, who are left orphaned and homeless, or who have simply run away from their families because they reject their values, are always instantly incorporated into other, suitable homes, whether a nuclear family, a large home in which a sprawling extended family of relatives and friends live, or a commune-like boardinghouse, like the Reardons'. People thus do not ever really live alone on soaps. Nor are they forced to conform to a single social or sexual norm or lifestyle or family unit in order to have a "family" and community of support. It is no surprise that viewers especially love the holiday celebrations that take place, in real time, on every soap. For so many, especially older women living alone, it is the only family or community celebration they may be invited to.

The way in which these utopian structures and processes are presented on soaps is, to be sure, more fantastic than realistic. Issues of money and power are far less plausibly laid out than in Piercy's Mattapoisett. Modes and forces of production and consumption, if you will, are so distorted as to be laughable. And rituals of order and law and social management are, while not nearly so bizarre, nonetheless far from plausible by any standard of realism. Contradiction and elision are inevitable in all commercial texts, especially those that are most utopian. But the ways in which soaps negotiate and mask their particular contradictions are somewhat unusual in their explicitness and detail.

Most theorists who have discussed utopia in popular or feminist works have described the engines of state as implicit. Richard Dyer, in his well-known analysis of Hollywood musicals, describes the ways in which popular commercial texts attempt, not always successfully, to work through and resolve the contradictions inherent in their efforts to suggest a utopian world within a system of representation very much tied to and dependent upon the existing order. For him, the solution involves a substitution of emotion for detailed political mapping. "Entertainment does not . . . present models of utopian worlds, as in the classic utopias of Sir Thomas More, William Morris et al.," he says. "Rather the utopianism is contained in the feelings it embodies." Nonetheless, I am suggesting that there is indeed something much closer to an actual social model in the soap representation of community than Dyer finds in Hollywood musicals, although the soap model is textured with the same contradictions and "gap[s] between what is and what could be" that Dyer rightly attributes to all such commercial forms.[19]

To see how this is done, it is useful to compare Piercy's Mattapoisett with the soap imaginary. Mattapoisett is a socialist-feminist utopia that does indeed include detailed, discursive blueprints for ownership and decision-making processes, which is plausible, if one assumes the existence of a state government committed to investing in technological development for human rather than military or commercial ends. The political and economic foundations of soap institutions, while also fairly elaborately laid out, are far more contradictory and implausible. The most important difference is in the portrayal of ownership and property issues. Where Mattapoisett's public hearings and trials, elections and economic negotiations, family and child-care polices, all grow organically out of the radically democratic and collectivized ownership and decision-making structures established as foundational, soap operas simply impose a retrograde, almost medieval, and insanely implausible structure of ownership and power relations upon their idyllic communities. In every soap, there are two or three corporate lords who own virtually everything in the town and so provide all the employment and control all the media and other institutions. Nepotism and monopoly are thus givens in these realms.

Nonetheless, while these powerhouses are often the most "evil" of villains, at least in their dominant mode, things always work out in the interest of democracy because justice and virtue always magically triumph, and the corporate, patriarchal tyrant, at the proper moment, invariably undergoes one of those always temporary conversions to "goodness." The Ross Chandler conversion is typical. But such things happen regularly to even the most powerful male figures. Adam Chandler, of *AMC,* for example, has a twin brother who is as pure and simple and good as Adam is usually evil. Nonetheless, when Stewart, the twin, married a woman dying of AIDS and adopted her son, Adam eventually came around and supported the couple in ways that made it possible for him to remain within the feminized utopian community, at least for the moment.

Thus, "good" always emerges out of the "goodness" of human nature, a human nature that—and this would horrify Karl Marx and Marge Piercy—has no relation whatever to the social conditions in which it thrives. Race and gender and class never play a role in one's fate here, at least not for long. A "good" person, white or black, male or female, well born or orphaned, simply prospers, through the goodness of her soul and those of the equally "good" power brokers and owners who provide material security and mete out perfect justice. If soaps are informed by a feminist set of values, then, it is a set of values based, at root, on the most hopelessly essentialist assumptions, if not about gender difference, certainly about human nature.

It is by presenting so patently absurd a view of money and power that soaps manage to elide what I think of as the "Procter and Gamble problem": the problem of how to present a world in which gender justice really reigns without challenging the corporate structure that sponsors these fantasies and uses them to sell heart-breakingly inadequate substitutes for the pleasure and fulfillment that the characters on the shows and in the commercials seem to enjoy. Things happen on soaps in the same "magical" way, to use Raymond Williams's term, that they happen in commercials. In commercials happiness, justice, freedom, and so on are seen, quite magically, to arise out of the consumption of commodities that, in fact, do not have the slightest ability to provide them.[20] Similarly, on soap operas, justice and freedom and goodness and bliss arise quite magically out of a system that, if realistically portrayed, would inevitably thwart, by its foundational principles, the very happiness it is shown to promote. The Ross Chandler date rape trial is a perfect example. A legal system in which, somehow, characters are compelled to act on principle, even if their very lives, fortunes, or reputations are at stake, is a system very different from the one in which O. J. Simpson and William Kennedy Smith were tried.[21] For in the real world, money, class position, and the gender biases that inform all institutions are driving forces not only in legal proceedings, but also in the molding of a defendant's own character and his decision-making processes. Soaps are a bit like extended versions of commercials, then, in the way in which the "magical" thinking of sponsors is drawn out, as in the famous Taster's Choice coffee romantic "miniseries" commercial, into long, equally implausible story lines. The relation between commercials and dramas, after all, is integral.[22] AMC's Dr. Cliff Warner, of "I'm not a doctor, but I play one on television" fame, shamelessly sells aspirin to an audience of viewers who wish to believe that the medical and pharmaceutical industries actually operate by the humane and ethical principles that drive the doctors and hospitals on the soaps.

The feminist-informed public world of soaps is one that bears absolutely no relationship to economic and political reality. Nonetheless, as I have been arguing, there is a fairly elaborate set of laws and rituals and policies, unmoored as they are from economic and political reality, that govern the social world of soaps. The trials do indeed follow actual legal practice, to a point. The board meetings and nurses' stations and police procedures, for all their clumsy gaffes and goofs in the interest of plot, do operate according to a relative coherent logic and system. If it is difficult to recognize these images of public life as "political," it may be because the melodramatic conventions of soaps render their political vision so unrealistic as to seem muddle-headed and naive, as women's ideas about how to run society *are* so often labeled. But it is in fact the very use of melodramatic conventions that allows soap operas so easily to incorporate and transform traditional male political, legal and economic matters into an essentially feminine, and implicitly feminist, worldview. Again, the Chandler trial serves as a perfect example. It did follow understandable, recognizable, procedures of testimony from witnesses and principals, arguments from defense and prosecution, and sentencing hearings and decisions. The way in which characters were allowed to testify, however, was often unbelievably absurd. Characters, for example, were allowed to simply rise up and demand to be heard, because of the "urgency" of the testimony they were suddenly moved to share or the events they were suddenly driven by con-

science to reveal. No real court of law would allow such irregularities. Similarly, hearsay, personal opinion about motives and character, and so on were included with no objections, if they were crucial to the feminist-informed understanding of what the issues in the case were. Ross's confession, for example, would have demanded any number of hearings and rulings to be permitted, once he had pleaded innocent. In soaps, however, doing the right thing, from a feminine, humane point of view, is all that is needed for testimony to be considered relevant or even crucial.

I have mentioned Carol Gilligan's moral vision as an implicit aspect of the soap imaginary. But even more telling in this regard is an essay by Kathleen Jones in which she applies feminist moral assumptions to traditional male theories of public sphere politics and suggests how they might lead to a radically transformed version of justice and political authority. "The standard analysis of authority in modern Western political theory begins with its definition as a set of rules governing political action, issued by those who are entitled to speak," she writes. But these rules "generally have excluded females and values associated with the feminine." Moreover, she argues, the "dominant discourse on authority," in placing "strict limits on the publicly expressible, and limit[ing] critical reflection about the norms and values that structure 'private' life and which affect the melodies of public speech," further ensure that female values will be marginalized within a private realm. Thus "compassion and related emotions" are rendered "irrelevant to law and other policy matters."[23] As Tom Hanks's character put it in the film *A League of Their Own*, "There's no crying in baseball." Or in court or in the military or in Mahogany Row.

This is hardly the case on soaps. There is indeed crying and wailing and gnashing of teeth, as well as other public expressions of emotion and personal concern, in all the public arenas in which right and wrong, justice and human well-being are determined. And they are heeded and considered legitimate. Compassion, especially, is always relevant. Because of this, soaps' hearings and procedures arbitrate public matters in ways that implicitly, if implausibly, echo the political ideals of feminists. The 1960s model of consciousness-raising meetings and public speak-outs, in which women "spoke bitterness" and linked private emotional suffering to public institutions and policies, offers a useful comparison. In both there is an effort to correct for the failings of the masculinist public sphere by recognizing the subjective and emotional realities of women's experience. Again, the Chandler date rape trial comes to mind. But so do many other situations. The Reardon/Chamberlain custody hearing, for example, was interrupted by Bridget Reardon herself who, for love of the child, suddenly offered, without benefit of counsel, the compromise suggestion of shared mothering that the judge, a woman herself, simply accepted as ideal, based on a shared notion of what was best for the child. The key here was the wrenching sincerity of the emotions of the two obviously deeply loving women. The extent of their tears and wails was enough to convince the judge that they would do right by the child in this wholly unprecedented ruling. Nor was there ever any mention of social issues or of the financial arrangements between the two very differently propertied and positioned women. In real life, by contrast, as economically strapped, unconventionally "lifestyled" women who have been through the process know too well, such material and "moral" concerns actually dominate custody hearings.

Thus, that soaps are excessively melodramatic and emotional, and therefore highly *un*realistic, is, from a feminist viewpoint, affirmative. For in feminist theory, as feminist social theorists in so many disciplines have continued to demonstrate, it is the exclusion of the values of the private, domestic sphere from issues of justice and equality that must be addressed and corrected.[24] But because

they so aggressively inject such values into their portrayal of every sphere of life and so flagrantly reject the conventions of aesthetic realism that are valorized in our culture, soaps risk the laughter and derision of those who maintain the artistic and literary canons.

The (gender- and class-based) shame that fans feel in watching soaps is therefore understandable. But it is based on a faulty psychological assumption that fans too often internalize: that pleasure in soaps amounts to taking them at face value. This is hardly the case. In fact, laughter and ridicule are very much a part of the viewing experience of fans. Viewers understand and laugh about most of the contradictions and "gaps" of the form, as any casual scanning of the cyberspace bulletin boards covering soaps will reveal. This indeed is among the more sophisticated pleasures of viewing. Fans happily suspend disbelief for the pleasure of escaping into a fairy tale realm in which dreams and desires and fantasies, despite what we know is plausible, seem magically to be fulfilled.

This aspect of viewership and fandom became an important element in the soap watching sessions I shared with my children. As they grew older and more experienced and sophisticated about politics and narrative, the issue of "realism" periodically came up in contexts that engendered increasingly complex and sophisticated discussions about the vexed relationship between social reality and what is filtered through the lens of popular commercial texts. On soaps the distinction between what is possible and what is desired and deserved is elided if not dissolved. But in life this is hardly the case. Teasing out and dissecting these contradictions was among the most fruitful and exhilarating aspects of our soap habit. It still is.

And, as my own examples of my talks with Alison illustrate, such sophistication about media and politics is not bought at the expense of pleasure. On the contrary, the pleasure becomes richer, more empowering even, as it is inflected with increasingly complex, contextualized strands of knowledge and insight. "Against the grain" reading practices, as is well known by now, are a common ingredient in the pleasures of fandom. As my opening example of a conversation between Alison and me indicates, there is a quite complicated set of assumptions that inflect our by now habitual shorthand discourse about soap opera. We readily jump from one plane to another in our discussions, now savoring a utopian moment, now laughing uproariously at the idiotic apparati that enable such fantasies, now expressing contempt at the ways in which soaps deflect from and distort painful social realities.

Nor is our conversation as one-dimensional in its focus on representation and textuality as it was in the early days, when affirmative images were all we were after. Today, we are likely to jumble together in any given conversation, in ways which make perfect sense to us, facts and tidbits from soap narratives, current headlines, personal issues, and behind-the-scenes information about the industry itself. The reality of AIDS and AIDS research funding; the fantasy world of medical research on TV; the star system and its economics as driving forces in the development of story lines—all these are taken for granted as we continue to watch and derive pleasure from the events and characters on *Guiding Light*. This is, after all, the way in which fans everywhere, as the literature on readerships and interpretive communities teaches, read and discuss popular texts.

Michel Foucault, in writing about the relationship between art and madness, credits art with "interrupting" the long-standing, tyrannical reign of bourgeois reason and creating a space for the return of the repressed. The work of art "opens a void," he writes, "where the world is made aware of its guilt." [25] It is in the nature of oppositional works to invoke this kind of social guilt. But soaps go a bit further than that. They offer a glimpse of a social order in which the guilty may be redeemed. And when we laugh at the absurdity of this vision, we are, at the very least, acknowl-

edging the distance between our dreams and our realities in a way that those whose tastes run only to more fashionably cynical forms may be able to avoid.

Notes

Because of the delay in the publication of this book, some of the examples in this essay are not current.

1 For a vivid example of the amazingly optimistic utopianism of the New Left, see Michael Lerner, *The New Socialist Revolution* (New York: Dell, 1970).

2 Fredric Jameson, "World-Reduction in Le Guin: The Emergence of Utopian Narrative," *Science-Fiction Studies* 2 (1975): 233.

3 Louise Spence, "They Killed Off Marlena, But She's on Another Show Now," in *To Be Continued . . . : Soap Operas around the World*, ed. Robert Allen (New York: Routledge, 1995), 193.

4 John Fiske, *Television Culture* (New York: Methuen, 1987), 197.

5 See especially Tania Modleski, *Loving with a Vengeance: Mass-Produced Fantasies for Women* (New York: Methuen, 1982), and Martha Nochimson, *No End to Her: Soap Opera and the Female Subject* (Berkeley: California University Press, 1992).

6 Barbara Ehrenreich and Deirdre English, *For Her Own Good: 150 Years of the Experts' Advice to Women* (New York: Anchor, 1978), 323.

7 That *Guiding Light* is now in serious ratings decline, causing panicky speculation on the Internet that it will shortly be canceled, is surely related to its rather old-fashioned social geography, in which a sense of old-fashioned working-class culture, based on clearly delineated working-class communities, as was until recently still recognizable in cities like Pittsburgh, is still valorized. Alison's and my nostalgic loyalty to the series is infused, to a degree, with nostalgia for the political climate of that city in those years in which we lived, and I was politically active, there.

8 The importance of feminism's growing influence on women's-oriented popular culture cannot be overlooked as a politically encouraging factor here, one that is not often enough recognized in these depressing political times. For it is encouraging that soap operas, and a bit later other equally disreputable "women's genres," were far ahead of more highly regarded cultural and informational forms in treating gender issues progres-

sively, in accord with feminist thought. At least one reason is surely that the producers of these forms were
aware of, and, for economic reasons, responded to, the
growing influence of feminism on the women viewers
and consumers they targeted.

9   The actor who plays Philip during these years, as I write
this, just returned to the role, along with the actor who
played Rick Bauer, Ed's son (now himself a doctor) and
Philip's best friend. Alison and I are, of course, thrilled
about this, and are eager to share the news with Jon.

10 The seminal, classic texts in which the political nuances
of the public/private split, as articulated by second-
wave socialist feminists, can be found in *Women, Class,
and the Feminist Imagination,* ed. Karen Hansen and
Ilene Philipson (Philadelphia: Temple University Press,
1990).

11 See Thomas Schatz, *Hollywood Genres: Formulas, Filmmaking, and the Studio System* (Philadelphia: Temple
University Press, 1991); Christine Gledhill, ed., *Home
Is Where the Heart Is: Studies in Melodrama and the
Women's Film* (London: BFI, 1987); and Fiske, *Television
Culture.* Francis Ford Coppola's *Godfather* series is a
useful example of how these contradictions may be
used self-consciously to critique the very social structure that enforces them.

12 Frances Bartkowski, *Feminist Utopias* (Lincoln: University of Nebraska Press, 1989), 15.

13 Carol Gilligan, *In Another Voice: Psychological Theory
and Women's Development* (Cambridge, MA: Harvard
University Press, 1982), 57.

14 Angelika Bammer, *Partial Visions: Feminism and Utopianism in the 1970s* (New York: Routledge, 1991), 44.

15 This is a feature of daytime soaps, it should be added,
which strongly differentiate them from their nighttime
counterparts. Ien Ang, in her discussion of *Dallas,* for
example, in *Watching Dallas: Soap Opera and the Melodramatic Imagination* (New York: Methuen, 1985), 71,
points out that it is family that serves as a haven from
the heartless outside world of business and politics,
which is seen as "a hotbed of activity threatening to the
family." This is radically different from the daytime
strategy, in which the line between the spheres blurs.

16 It is worth noting here that it was this very feature that
often served most useful in my talks with my children
about the sticky issues raised by consumerism, in a
world in which social status and peace of mind often
seem, and not only to children, to have so much to do
with the crazy-making need to accumulate more and

more of the right toys and clothing than others do, or at
least to keep up. In trying to tease out the negative and
positive aspects of this culture—pleasure, beauty, and
fun are very real features of commercial culture for
children and adults—soaps pointed to a different kind
of money and production system. It was clear, from
Pine Valley's example, that if one could indeed live in
a world of plenty, in which individual and collective
choices about clothing and other pleasure-providing
items could be easily accommodated, without the anx-
iety-provoking pressures of competition, conformity,
scarcity, and the need to accumulate and hoard, even
Barbie might lighten up and fatten up a bit. The Barbie
issue is also a gender and sexism issue. In Piercy's utopia
this problem is tackled and resolved, again through the
device of offering infinite choice and variety in every
sphere of life. In soaps, this is hardly the case and this
problematic must also be addressed when discussing
their fictional worlds with children.

17 The lesbian story line involved a regular character who
had—as have all women soap characters have had—
bad experiences with men. She became attracted to her
daughter's therapist, an "out and proud" lesbian, and
began a relationship with her. As usual, the community
was fraught with tension and heated debate. Finally, the
decent characters, including the woman's mother, came
to consensus: if the young woman was happy, the relationship was acceptable. The story line abruptly ended
soon after, however. And even as it played out, no physical contact of any kind between the two women was
shown.

18 The problem of race on soaps is vexed. Black characters
do figure increasingly prominently on soaps, and at
times an interracial relationship will be portrayed, generally as a controversial issue for the community (as
Clarence Thomas would like us to believe), with no attention whatsoever to race as a factor in their lives. Of
course, they must be given a black love interest or remain celibate—except when the writers are willing to
tackle "the race issue." Thus the matter of race is always
awkwardly and inadequately handled.

19 Richard Dyer, "Entertainment and Utopia," in *Movies
and Methods,* vol. 2, ed. Bill Nichols (Berkeley: University of California Press, 1985), 229.

20 Raymond Williams, "Advertising: The Magic System,"
in *Problems in Materialism and Culture* (London: Verso,
1980).

21 I am not suggesting that the Simpson verdict was in-

correct. I do not actually think it was, because the issues of racism and corruption in the Los Angeles police department were, in my view, determining factors that compromised the evidence against Simpson enough to produce reasonable doubt, certainly in the minds of a large black jury. I am only commenting here on the behavior of Simpson himself, as a man already known to be violently misogynist, whether or not he committed the particular crime of which he was accused.

22 The tricky relationships among the various elements of soap textuality and viewership are cleverly developed in my Paper Tiger Television segment, "Elayne Rapping Reads Soap Operas." The producer, Dee Dee Halleck, intercut my analysis of the form with ironically juxtaposed story clips, Procter and Gamble commercial clips, and interviews with the residents of Staten Island (where the Proctor and Gamble plant is located) about the health problems they have experienced because of the toxic pollution problems caused by making Ivory soap "99 and 44/100 percent pure."

23 Kathleen Jones, "On Authority: Or, Why Women Are Not Entitled to Speak," in *Feminism and Foucault: Reflections on Resistance,* ed. Irene Diamond and Lee Quinby (Boston: Northeastern University Press, 1988), 119, 130–31.

24 Feminist legal theorists have written extensively and with particular relevance on this point. See especially Martha Fineman and Nancy Thomadsen, eds., *At the Boundaries of Law: Feminism and Legal Theory* (New York: Routledge, 1991) and Martha Fineman and Martha McCluskey, eds., *Feminism, Media and the Law* (Oxford: Oxford University Press, 1997).

25 Michel Foucault, *Madness and Civilization* (New York: Random House, 1965), 278.

Cardboard Patriarchy: Adult Baseball Card Collecting and the Nostalgia for a Presexual Past

John Bloom

Only four sparks [remain] in my memory—four images that root me to this epoch:
1) The sound of Don Pardo's booming voice.
2) The sight of Richard Castellano's sister naked.
3) The fear that Albert Dorish might beat me up.
4) My three shopping bags full of baseball cards.
—BRENDAN BOYD AND FRED HARRIS, *THE GREAT AMERICAN BASEBALL CARD FLIPPING, TRADING, AND BUBBLE GUM BOOK*

Consciously, it may just be a love of the sport. . . . Unconsciously, I'm sure for me, it's vicarious. I was never good enough to play. . . . It's also an unconscious search for order in life. You're always aiming to complete a set, and that's a sense of security.
—ADULT MALE BASEBALL CARD COLLECTOR INTERVIEWED IN THE *DETROIT FREE PRESS,* AT A DETROIT BASEBALL CARD SHOW, 1974.

It sounds to me like they're jealous. . . . Sure we've ruined their hobby, but isn't that what America is all about?
—BASEBALL CARD SPECULATOR ALAN "MR. MINT" ROSEN IN THE *WALL STREET JOURNAL* IN 1990, ON HOW HE AND OTHER BASEBALL CARD PROFITEERS HAVE AFFECTED THE HOBBY.

During the 1970s and 1980s, the hobby of baseball card collecting underwent a radical transformation. For the better part of a century, sports card collecting had been something most North Americans had associated with children, but by the late 1970s, adults, primarily men, had taken an active, if not dominant role in the collecting hobby. As sports card collecting underwent this change, popular news sources began to pay increasing attention to it. Newspapers, magazines, and television news focused mostly upon the extravagant prices for which collectors were allegedly selling their cards at baseball card auctions and shows. Yet, as the epigraphs above illustrate, the hobby also resonated with its practitioners in other more culturally complex and gender-specific ways. As collectors pieced together sets, bought and sold cards, and engaged in a collectors' market characterized by hoarding and inflation, they rendered a popular culture artifact a nostalgic icon of a stable and "innocent" past rooted in male preadolescence and middle-class whiteness.

Over the past twenty-five years, a subculture made up primarily of white, middle-class adult males has emerged around the hobby of baseball card collecting. Many involved in this hobby have understood baseball cards as an authentic link to the past as well as to other men, emblematic of a nostalgia for a presexual boyhood firmly rooted in the white, middle-class home of the 1950s. This particular symbolic understanding of baseball cards is important because it raises questions that help to interpret adult baseball card collecting, and baseball nostalgia more generally, as politically significant cultural expressions, particularly with regard to issues surrounding gender and race. Why would men be interested in representations of their preadolescent years, especially ones that they remembered as exclusively male and relatively homogeneous? To what aspects of contemporary life in the United States is an activity like baseball card collecting a response?

An activity like baseball card collecting is an important one to examine because it provides a concrete site where cultural discourses circulate and where meaning is created and constituted. Central to what I observed within the hobby of baseball card collecting is what I have termed a nostalgia for presexual identity. In the case of card collectors, I see this nostalgia as a particularly conservative expression, but also a contradictory one that draws from alienating circumstances in the present. As Marshall Berman has noted, the progressive ideologies of modern societies often leave individuals feeling alienated and disconnected from one another by continually destroying social formations of the past and recreating them anew. He notes how nostalgia addresses this sense of disconnection, providing a ghost-like memory that questions the validity of modern ideas of "progress."[1] Yet the past imagined through nostalgia can also secure dominant ideologies, such as those surrounding gender and race. In the specific case of baseball card collecting, nostalgia serves as a basis for homosocial bonds that appear universal, but in fact are quite contradictory. Differences between men based upon ethnicity, race, geography, generation, and class are covered over. In addition, even though appeals to values of patriarchal authority and family autonomy are central to nostalgic images that circulate within the hobby, the material basis for the realization of these ideals has been undermined during much of the twentieth century.[2]

When I write that collectors within their subcultural practices nostalgically recall a presexual past, I refer to a nostalgia for a time in their life course that one would most often call preadolescence. However, I deliberately understand their nostalgia as presexual because of the way in which baseball cards seem most often to evoke memories of this period of life. Collectors repeatedly told of how baseball cards became "uncool" when they were expected to begin taking interest in dating, or, in other words, when they were first expected to activate heterosexual identities. Thus, sports memorabilia collectors, and discourses that they engaged with through their hobby, not only tended to associate baseball cards with male, homosocial relationships that characterize white, middle-class boyhood, they understood such relationships as located at a moment within middle-class childhood before socially sanctioned expressions of sexual desire could be publicly addressed.

During the late 1980s and the early part of 1990, I spent a great deal of time attending baseball card shows in the metropolitan area of a major city in the upper midwestern United States. I draw my answers to the preceding questions largely in response to that which I observed firsthand in a particular place at a particular historical moment. My conclusions, therefore, are not meant to provide readers with a definitive meaning of adult baseball card collecting. Instead, I am more interested in opening up questions about the desires that men express through their hobbies, pastimes, and subcultures, particularly those organized around sports spectatorship.

As the brutally honest statement by Alan "Mr. Mint" Rosen suggests, there is a tragic irony involved in the search for authentic community and identity within objects firmly rooted in commercial culture. However, the baseball card collecting hobby that I observed was not only the product of slick marketing and commercial manipulation, but also a popular subculture, one that must be understood as meaningful within the contexts of its practitioners' daily lives and complex personal and social histories. At the same time, it is different from other subcultures that have been studied and interpreted by cultural scholars because of its largely conservative and nostalgic orientation.[3] The practice of "set collecting" provided perhaps the most intimate context in which I observed collectors expressing themselves within the hobby.

Set Collecting and the Baseball Card Subculture

By the time I began interviewing collectors, attending shows, and spending time in baseball card shops in the late 1980s, baseball card collecting had become a large and extremely complex hobby in the United States and Canada.[4] Perhaps the most important changes that helped to promote baseball card collecting in general during the 1980s, however, took place within the baseball card manufacturing industry itself. In 1975, the Fleer Corporation of Philadelphia, manufacturers of candy and gum products, filed a federal antitrust suit against the Topps Corporation of Brooklyn, New York, a company that had enjoyed a virtual monopoly over the production and sale of sports trading cards since 1956. Fleer alleged that the exclusive contracts Topps signed with players, major league baseball, and the Major League Baseball Players Association constituted a restraint of trade. In the late summer of 1980, Judge Clarence Newcomer ruled in favor of Fleer. The ruling opened the door for Fleer, and a third company, Donruss of Memphis, Tennessee (then a wholly owned subsidiary of General Mills), to produce complete baseball card sets for the 1981 season. Fleer only received damages of $3 million (they had asked for $17.8 million), but their new set was very successful. Although the U.S. Circuit Court of Appeals overturned Newcomer's decision only a year later, Topps only maintained exclusive rights to market cards with a confection. Fleer and Donruss maintained the licensing agreements they had worked out with major league baseball and the players' union, and simply sold their cards without gum.[5] Yet I discovered that most collectors practiced their hobby in a manner that was very similar to the way the man from Detroit, quoted at the outset of this chapter, described his collecting practices in 1974. Their primary collecting activities surrounded the collection of "sets."

Most collectors used the term "set" to refer to all of the cards produced by a company during a particular year. Collectors also sometimes created their own sets, defining a particular category and attempting to complete it. The collection of sets comprised the most common collecting practice within my interview sample. Nineteen out of the thirty males whom I interviewed, for example, reported that they either had drawn satisfaction from collecting full company sets in the past, or were continuing to do so in the present. Of the remaining eleven, five collected more self-defined sets, such as so called odd-ball cards, rookie cards, and teams.[6]

The collection of sets is noteworthy for two major reasons. First, it illustrates an active way in which a popular culture audience involved themselves with a form of commercial entertainment. At the very least, the act of collecting a set of either new or old cards required some level of organization, active effort, knowledge, and at times dogged tenacity. Second, and more important, hobbyists who pieced together sets provided me with insights into baseball card collecting as a particularly *male* sports fan subculture. The pleasures and fantasies that made sets meaningful to the collectors I interviewed have an important relationship to gender. The processes involved in recapturing a set of baseball cards were sometimes evocative of the rituals and play that the men interviewed remembered as surrounding baseball cards when they were boys, particularly practices of bartering and hoarding baseball cards. As adults, the act of collecting sets brought them back into the kind of all-male relationships they recalled from their preadolescent years. Collectors often told me that baseball cards reminded them of their childhood friendships with other boys, recalling how the hobby was part of a larger boys' culture that included sports, watching television together, and riding bicycles around the neighborhood. The adult hobby reminded some of a "fraternity," providing an arena for male "bonding." In addition, the set collectors I observed attempted to create a coherent order with their cards, one that linked them to this idealized past without any contradictions, gaps, or digressions. To repeat the epigraph from the Detroit collector, "You're always aiming to complete a set, and that's a sense of security." By striving for such seamless connections, however, adult collectors fragmented their cards from many of the playful games and interactions that had made these objects meaningful to them as children in the 1950s, 1960s, and 1970s. Collecting an ordered set often meant that collectors could not look at or handle their cards very much, for such handling might ruin the condition of cards and

upset the coherence of a set. Once more, even though acquisition was important to childhood collecting practices, men also recalled that they had also often incorporated baseball cards into forms of play with other boys.

The fragmentation of collected objects from the contexts in which they had originally been meaningful, and the subsequent reification of them as constituents of a collected set, is not something unique to baseball card collectors.[7] Yet baseball card collecting is also a fan subculture, and the importance of set collecting within it tells us a great deal about the men I observed and their gendered orientation toward sports spectatorship. Henry Jenkins, in his work on female-based media fan cultures, borrows from the literary criticism of Michel de Certeau, who coined the term "textual poachers" for readers who appropriate aspects of literary texts they read for their own purposes. Like readers of literary texts who "poach," Jenkins sees fans as cultural nomads operating "from a position of marginality and social weakness" in relation to the cultural forms they enjoy. They have very little creative control over the production of commercial culture around them, but they can negotiate their way through it, actively "poaching" certain aspects of their media experiences and reassembling them in ways that are meaningful to their social experiences.[8]

Jenkins draws two conclusions about fans as poachers and nomads. First, they are social—their practices gain meaning from and are reinforced through interactions with others. Second, they blur the boundaries between cultural producers and cultural readers—they create and circulate their own artistic formulations from the representations produced for them on television or within other forms of media culture. These are both characteristic of the baseball card collectors I observed.

Collectors published their own newsletters and magazines, promoted their own shows, and created their own displays for cards. In fact, some even created and circulated their own baseball card sets. "Broders," cards illegally produced by a legendary renegade sports fan whom interviewees identified as "George Broder," were very widely distributed at shows. Such cards featured color photos of athletes printed on one side of a blank card, and were published without the licensing agreements necessary for the sale of such products. They illustrate fans' attempts to take control of media images by evading copyright laws meant to protect the interests of cultural producers over those of cultural consumers.[9]

Yet the sports fan culture I observed was different from the media fan cultures described by Jenkins in important, largely gendered ways. Jenkins argues that the female character of the fan groups he studied was important because their members felt especially marginalized by the processes of media production that, particularly in the case of science fiction, favored male audiences. Because of this, such fan cultures are especially nomadic as they lack any close "proximity to writers and editors" who produce the texts from which they poach.[10]

By contrast, baseball card and memorabilia collectors have a great many allies in the popular media. They have entire sections of the newspaper devoted to the interests of their fan cultures, and writers within them, often current or former collectors themselves, who frequently recollect bittersweet memories of flipping cards and opening their first packs. This creates a remarkable bond among some quite diverse groups of men along commonalities of gender identity. At the same time, it does not create the same sense of marginality from mass media production felt by many other fan cultures. Those I interviewed could often identify major newspaper writers like Thomas Boswell or George Will who felt just the way they did about baseball.

This is not to say that collectors, like other fan cultures, were not trying to "make sense of their own social experiences." But the texts they chose for this purpose, and the ways in which they put those texts back together, did not often represent an attempt to create many new alternatives. Rather, it reflected an effort to find and reestablish a stable sense of order from the cultural symbols of their past.

"Building" Sets

There were two basic ways of collecting sets that I observed. First, some collectors would work at obtaining sets of older cards. Men were often originally prompted to do so after they or (contrary to popular collecting folklore) their mothers *found* their old collection from their childhood. Such collections were usually incomplete sets, so collectors often sought to "fill them in," or buy the cards that were missing from their childhood collection. In addition, as a set might have anywhere from 300 to over 700 cards in it, completing a set could be extremely time-consuming. Depending on the year of the cards they were seeking, collectors could spend hundreds, or even thousands of dollars on these cards. The price of a card depended on a number of factors: its scarcity, its desirability (was the player a star or was he a "common"?), and its condition. Collectors often used nationally published price guides to help them compare costs, and often adopted the standards of those guides. As price guides placed cards in "mint" condition in the highest-priced category, most collectors sought the most pristine cards they could afford so that their collections would have "value." They usually avoided cards with bent corners, creases, writing on them, or off-center printing. Once they finished filling in a set, collectors often attempted to move on to another, trying to fill in the gap of missing cards between their childhoods and the present.[11]

The second kind of set that collectors would buy were those of new cards. At any baseball card show or shop, collectors could purchase an already sorted full set of new cards produced by any of the five companies making baseball cards in 1990. These were called "factory sets," and often collectors would routinely buy all of those produced by each company every baseball season. With the proliferation of card sets by the early 1990s, however, many collectors found this to be a difficult task to manage financially, and in fact could not afford to keep up with all of the cards being produced. In order to do this, or even to afford older cards for sets they might have been trying to fill in, collectors often bought cases of new cards at wholesale prices. They would then open up the packs of cards in the cases and sort them into sets themselves. By doing so, they could get four or even five sets from a case, saving money on the cost per set. They could also potentially get a large number of duplicate cards that featured a valued contemporary star like Cecil Fielder or Kirby Puckett. Collectors used such cards and sets to barter for other cards, either new or old, that they thought they needed.

Collectors often felt very proud of their sets and were somewhat protective of them. Despite the fact that they might be able to sell off their sets for hundreds, perhaps even thousands of dollars, many collectors whom I interviewed were like Tim, a junior marketing executive in his late twenties, who said he would not ever sell his set, even though it included some very valuable cards. "Like I say, it's just a hobby for me. It's just the collecting; I like to—my goal is just to keep building my collection until I get a real nice collection. I feel if I ever have kids of my own and they want to start, then—I can give them some of mine, or we could do it together, or whatever."

Tim's orientation toward his set was not atypical. Many collectors not only valued their sets, but they saw them as extensions of themselves. Even dealers who no longer collected sets would speak of "crossing the bridge" from collecting cards for pleasure to dealing cards for money, and thus severing an important emotional tie to cards, the moment they decided to sell their sets. For Tim, who

still owned many of the cards he had collected as a boy, his sets not only connected him to the past, but also to the future: his potential children. In other words, his baseball card sets, which have remained stable, constant entities over time, were a part of how he both remembered the past and imagined the future. This sense of stability over time illustrates a great deal about how Tim and other collectors imagine the past through their hobby. Like other nostalgic practices, baseball card collecting tends to represent something timeless and stable for its enthusiasts. It connotes a memory that is uncomplicated and straightforward. Baseball cards were part of his childhood, and, as he hoped, might be part of his own child's as well.

Sets became important to collectors in this manner largely through the process of collecting them. This process was at least as important and meaningful to many collectors as the cards themselves. Barry, a thirty-one-year-old UPS delivery driver, characterized his collecting as "almost like an addiction." Like Tim, his hobby was centered around the collection of sets.

> I'm more of a set collector. I try to get the whole set. And yeah, that always makes you feel good when you complete a set. That's what you strive for. And it's really hard to do, especially in a lot of the older sets because of the financial, the prices of the cards are so high now. Those are the goals I do set, to complete the set. I know other people, that's what makes the hobby real good too.

Barry referred to his collecting practices as involving the "building" of sets, a common way of discussing the hobby. It conveyed the idea that a set was something one created by work, craftsmanship, and patience. Bob, a pharmacist in his early forties who was a prominent member of the local sports card collecting club, also used this language to describe his hobby. He told me during one of our interviews, "I'm a set builder." The process of "building" a set was so central to his own collecting that he began to lose interest in baseball cards once he had succeeded. "I'm a goal-oriented person. I like to set goals and if you keep reaching them it takes the challenge away. And that's the way it was with the cards. Maybe I didn't set my goals high enough, like a million dollars or something."

The "goal-oriented" perspective that Bob discussed was a very important aspect of the individualistic and competitive orientation of set collecting. Ironically, although many said they had become involved in collecting because of the "camaraderie" and fellowship they felt with other sports fans, set collecting was largely a solitary activity. Many worked out elaborate forms of trading, selling, and bartering cards to buy the ones they needed. They studied price guides, searched through card shops, attended shows, read publications, and even frequented garage sales and flea markets. They described their purchase of cards as a personal quest.

The whole process of collecting sets in this manner was something collectors often reported as one aspect of their collecting practices as children. In fact, a sort of obsession with set collecting among kids was parodied by *Sports Illustrated* as far back as its first issue in 1954. The magazine included a feature on baseball cards containing two columns and a color centerfold illustrating the cards themselves. The two columns bracketed the cards. The first, by Martin Kane, detailed the marketing and contract wars taking place between the different baseball card producers that year, Topps and Bowman. The second article was by Jerome Weidman, a father of two baseball card collecting boys. Both articles discussed collecting in a humorous manner, portraying it as a typically incomprehensible youth fad. In their humor, however, they conveyed an uneasiness with the desires and emotions that baseball cards evoked in children.

Weidman's essay began as a discussion of his bewilderment over the way baseball cards, objects he would normally have identified as useless advertisements for a product like bubble gum, had become consumer objects that his children desired. He wrote of how his children discarded the bubble gum from baseball card packs, but treasured the baseball cards; and he expressed dismay over the ways gum companies would manipulate their young audiences.

> To make certain that boys will continue to purchase bubble gum as steadily as alcoholics purchase gin, no bubble gum manufacturer publishes pictures of all the members of a given team. This is because our young baseball-card collectors trade their duplicates with other collectors. Thus, much too soon for the bubble gum manufacturers, every boy would own a complete set of 448 cards and be eliminated as a customer.[12]

Weidman's article culminated with a story of how he was with his family on a summer-long vacation in England when his sons realized that they did not have a card for Brooklyn catcher Roy Campanella. Weidman wrote of how he had to have a friend ship a case of baseball cards to England in the middle of their trip. He stretched the case out for the entire summer, giving his sons only one pack to open each day. The boys found six Roy Campanellas, but ended up telling their father on the plane ride home that they were missing one other card. Weidman ended the article recalling that his son said to him, "[It] was awful funny, Dad, but the one card they couldn't seem to get was a Solly Hemus, and what did I think of that? . . . It required quite a bit of self-control on Dad's part not to tell them."[13]

Weidman's column is not only about baseball cards, but also about his inability to direct his own children's desires as he became less important to them than their baseball cards. Even a trip to England could not compete with these cardboard objects. His story was clearly told with tongue in cheek, but his complaints about his children's insatiable appetite for a form of commercial entertainment parallel the concerns about television and the 1950s nuclear family that Lynn Spigel has profiled.[14] He portrays his boys as thoughtless, passive, programmed, and shamelessly manipulated.

This kind of obsessive set collecting was certainly promoted by baseball card companies, but childhood collecting was not necessarily as mindless and alienating as Weidman presented it. Collectors often discussed trading with friends, bargaining over cards in the schoolyard or in their bedrooms, and trying to amass the best collections they could. Yet, those interviewed also remembered the collecting of their childhoods as far more diverse than their adult hobby which was so heavily oriented toward sets. When they recalled childhood collecting, they discussed a variety of games they would play with cards such as "flipping," drawing on cards, or placing cards in the spokes of bicycles to make noise. As adults, they had abandoned such games because they were incompatible with set collecting. The adult hobby of the 1980s that I observed, however, highlighted the most competitive and manipulative aspects of childhood baseball card collecting.

In fact, some of the most successful adult collectors were those who had least playful collecting experiences as children. Thomas, an executive for a local candy distributor, remembered collecting his cards very privately, particularly after his family became the first to move to an isolated suburb when interstate highway construction leveled his inner-city neighborhood. His meticulous habits allowed him to preserve his cards in excellent condition, something he was very proud to show me during our interview.

> From day one, I always, for some reason I was a neat freak. It was like I wanted my own cards. You know my old, well these are my old football cards from the 1960s [showing them to me] and I mean you can see they're beautiful. The corners and . . . now unfortunately, I don't have my baseball. I sold those about nine years ago. And, like everybody else

did, but these are just, they're like new. I mean, it's unbelievable.

Thomas was rewarded for the way he collected when he was a boy, establishing a small sports card side business from the profits he gained by selling off his baseball card sets. However, he also noted how his childhood collecting habits meant he did not enjoy the kind of playful relations with other youths that so many associated with their collecting. Most notably, he did not engage in trading, and only would buy cards new, because he wanted them in the same condition as the moment he bought them.

Likewise, Larry, a full-time dealer in his early thirties who had directed his fledgling career as a journalist toward writing about baseball cards, recalled that he never engaged in fabled childhood games like baseball card "flipping" when he was a boy. Instead, he remembered his collecting to be very much a mirror of his adult collecting.

> I never did—like card flipping. I never heard of that until, I was an adult. . . . Not so much in school, but with friends from school we did a lot of trading. I mean we were fanatics. Well, I mean like any kids I guess. Into baseball and into baseball cards. I'd say back in '68, '69, '70 I had at least two real good friends who were constantly trying to make baseball card deals to add to our collections. You know, one kid had a card that you needed and you tried to get it from him.

Larry's recollections illustrate how set collecting, from a very early age, was linked to a competitive economic relationship with cards, one that mirrored the adult world of capital acquisition. Although Larry created friendships through the competitive trading and negotiating for cards that he described, these friends were at the same time potential stooges.

Doug, a baseball card shop owner in his early forties, collected sets meticulously when he was a child. Like Larry, he built his collection by trading

with friends. More than competition, his memories emphasize the prominence of order that kept
him from sharing his most treasured cards.

> I always traded with my friends. I had a rule that I
> would never trade if I only had one card. That was
> part of my collection, and that got stuck away. I
> would just pull out all the extra cards that I had . . .
> [other kids] thought that was my collection. But
> that would be just trading. I had as many probably,
> duplicates as a lot of other kids would have in their
> collections. . . . My mother bought an Ethan Allen
> dresser drawers, a ten-drawer dresser, and I put my
> collection in there. . . . I organized it by teams. Any
> time a player got traded, I'd put him from one
> box—pull him out of there—put him with the
> other ones.

John, a dealer and salesman in his late twenties,
had similar memories of his private collection.
Like Doug, he never traded any cards from his
core collection. "I never traded anything other
than duplicates." Unlike many other kids, he was
very concerned with keeping his cards orderly and
in good condition. He conveyed this in a story he
told about trading with his school friends.

> We did a lot of trading after school. We couldn't
> wait to get home. Didn't bring a lot of cards to
> school. There was this one kid. He had a paper
> route. I think he probably ripped off half of them, in
> the stores. But he was on a paper route and he had
> money coming in so he could spend his money the
> way he wanted to because he was the main paper
> boy in town. Well, he would bring them to school
> and show them and have them in his pocket the rest
> of the day, and go out and play kickball, or what-
> ever, out in the yard and come back in. It would be
> all bent up and then want to trade them. And I'd say
> no. No dice.

In addition to his discriminating trading practices, John would use his baseball cards to play an
elaborate baseball board game. He often played
against his brother or his friends, but they did not

always have the time to participate. As a result, he
would play games against himself, using his cards
to construct teams and leagues that would play entire seasons and championships. While all of these
different collecting habits and games seem to foreground an individualistic adult hobby centered
around set collecting, John also recalled a sense of
excitement and camaraderie that he shared with
his boyhood friends over collecting cards.

> After school you couldn't wait just to get home and
> go through the cards. Or run uptown and buy some.
> I can remember when, the worst feeling in the world
> is when the small, there was like two stores in that
> town. A very small town. And when they ran out of
> cards, it was like for the next week or so, what are
> you going to do? But as soon as they got the cards in
> we were lined up outside.

John's recollections demonstrate how many
collectors remembered their cards as not only
something they collected, but also as being a part
of a world they shared with their friends during
their preadolescent years. While they may have
competed with one another over them, they also
remembered seeking each other's friendship and
using cards as an expression of common interests.
Most adult collectors, in fact, did not recall collecting sets meticulously when they were kids.
Many traded, invented games with cards, drew
on them, and used them quite informally. Wes, a
second-grade teacher and baseball card show promoter in his mid-thirties, recalled only collecting
the biggest stars when he was a boy. He also remembered playfully using his cards in noncompetitive ways. "We would get together and trade.
That would be about the only extent of games.
And it was always to take the real unknown players, put them in your spokes with a clothes pin,
and just make the sound as your bike tires were
going around."

A number of other collectors also remembered
placing baseball cards in bicycle spokes for noise,
an act that showed no regard for the condition of

one's card. It was also a form of play that was not organized around rule-bound competition, as was trading. Others recalled sorting their cards into "all-star" teams and using statistics on the back to play one team against another.

Differences between childhood collecting practices and adult ones often were most apparent when collectors would discuss how they "ruined" their cards when they were young because of their disregard for "condition." Tim had one such memory.

> We didn't take real good care of them. I don't remember writing on cards too much. But I remember cutting them out one time. Just cutting the body outline so you didn't have any of the edges. We could have had a whole set, like the mid-'60s that my uncle gave us. We were just so stupid. What do six- or seven-year-olds know, you know?

Tim's reflection upon his own childhood play with cards as being "stupid" illustrates an important aspect of the adult hobby and its focus on set "building." Although, for many, childhood collecting often involved putting together sets or an attention to condition, it also was more oriented toward playful, even noncompetitive activities. When a child drew a mustache on a player's face or placed a card in a bicycle spoke, he or she was using a card in an expressive and inventive way with others.

In fact, the fetish over condition created a number of ironies within the adult hobby. For example, when Topps issued sets in series during the 1950s, 1960s, and early 1970s, they also issued checklists for customers to mark off which cards they had in their collections. Most children used these, which ruined their status as "mint" cards in the adult hobby. The most valuable checklists during the 1980s were those that had never been used.

In fact, the kind of drawing on cards that Tim described illustrates how cards were being *used*, how they were a part of the way children would follow baseball as members of baseball fan subcul-

tures. Even gambling games like flipping, the piecing together of all-star teams, or trading, all of which were competitive, also involved children involved in play with one another. The adult hobby, with its focus on completing sets of cards in "mint" condition was a negation of such play. Rather, it placed the focus of collecting upon the individualistic acquisition and organization of cards.

This is not to say that the childhood play with baseball cards that collectors often remembered was more "authentic" than the adult hobby that collectors created. The most important difference between the two, however, is the fact that the adult collecting community that I observed was largely structured through common relations to baseball cards. The friends that collectors made through the hobby were made at baseball card shows, baseball card shops, or through common affiliations with collecting organizations. Many of those whom I interviewed told me that they only saw their baseball card collecting friends at shows or shops, and that few were their neighbors, fellow workers, or family members. When adults recollected their collecting habits as children, however, they recalled how they bought and sold baseball cards with friends whom they already had, children who lived near one another and had relationships that existed in school, on sports teams, or between families that were outside of their hobby.

On one hand, this meant that most adult collectors could draw a stark line between their private collections and most of their public lives. On the other hand, it also meant that the public spaces in which collectors met one another and intermingled were extremely important. Collectors reported that the processes of going to shows, trading for cards, and interacting with others in large part made their collections meaningful, particularly in ways that spoke to their gendered identities. In order to understand the gender dynamics involved in this, it is important to examine the significance of the childhood collecting practices that collectors remembered.

Card Collecting, Sports Fandom, and Male Gender Identity

Modifying and updating the theories of sociologist Janet Lever, Michael Messner has written of the centrality of competition and achievement to sports as a form of boys' play.[15] Messner sees sports as socializing boys for their roles as men in a patriarchal culture, speaking to their already present ideas about gender roles and relations when they first begin to participate in team sports as seven-to-nine-year-olds. Messner argues that gendered identities must be worked out by individuals as they go through the process of individuation, or the setting up of psychological boundaries between themselves and others around them. Within a patriarchal culture, boys most often work out this process by constructing boundaries along gendered lines, particularly separating themselves from their mothers. Messner notes that this is not only an individual, psychological process, but also a social one. Social relations with others provide the context for the creation of such individual boundaries. Messner concludes that "the rule-bound structure of sport" created an important context in which boys were able to construct masculine identities. This was not only true for men who participated in sports, but also for those who experienced them through mediated channels (such as television or baseball cards) as sports spectators.[16]

Such renderings of sports and gender "socialization" suggest a relatively clear-cut distinction between the play of boys and girls, and how such play relates to their maturation into men and women. This may stem from the fact that Messner, by and large, draws his conclusions about children's sports from official, adult-monitored forms of play like Little League.[17] But it also portrays child audiences as somewhat passively molded by the media forms and play activities adults create for them. When I asked collectors about the memories they had of their hobby, they gave me a complex set of answers that suggested that they have engaged in active forms of sport fandom as children and as adults. This engagement may have prepared them for heterosexual masculinity, but it also did so in ways that often involved conflicts between all-male homosocial relations and the social norms of adolescent dating between males and females. Most of those whom I interviewed recalled the carryover of preadolescent sports fan cultures into the teen worlds of heterosexual dating and pairing as being taboo, or "uncool," boyish, and something they either felt compelled to hide or abandon.

During interviews, collectors discussed their childhood hobby as a boy's activity, mentioning primarily male friends with whom they played. This would seem to support Messner's understanding of sports as a significant arena for male individuation. Yet some informants did, in fact, mention girls with whom they remembered collecting cards. John, for example, recalled that his sister was as big a collector as he was, and perhaps a bigger sports fan. He says that she lost interest in sports during her teenage years largely because of external pressures and constraints.

> She was in a situation in high school where she came along at a bad time. Because she always wanted to do girls' sports. . . . She would have loved to do all that but there wasn't anything. And I really think that if she would have grown up in an era where that was there she would still have interest. You know, it's like, all of a sudden it's like, you're beyond that playing with boys stage.

The "playing with boys stage" that John mentioned would suggest that in his preadolescent years, there was more fluidity and less of a rigid structure to gendered relationships. It was only after puberty that sports and playing with boys became inappropriate for John's sister, and thus when gender distinctions became a "line in the sand" one was not allowed to cross over. It is during their teens that most collectors recalled abandoning their baseball cards, or hiding their collecting hobby from public scrutiny to avoid ridicule. Collectors often reported that collecting was something for kids, and that it was not considered "cool" for teenagers. Tim recalled giving up collecting for these reasons. "You go through a growing up phase and you get to the junior high age. You tend to do other things and give up— it's more of a—obviously I don't feel that way now, but—at the time it was more of a childhood thing of now you're moving on to another stage, or something."

Kevin, the clerical worker in his early forties, never gave up collecting baseball cards as a teen. As soon as he became a teenager, however, his hobby became more isolated and less connected to a network of close friends.

It became individual in junior, in high school—'63, yeah. That's about the time your interest turns to girls and cars . . . dates and that thing. You don't have the cash flow, and you don't want to admit that, so that it becomes more of a closet—well I just didn't spend money on girls and cars. What little money I had I put into baseball cards.

Bob explicitly recalled being teased in high school for his interest in cards.

Bob: I can remember I used to read a lot of baseball books, and I got a little grief from that when I was in ninth grade.

Q: How come?

Bob: Well, it was kind of strange. I played baseball all through high school, and out of high school, I played on the team, on the high school team, and that. And the guy that gave me the most grief was the center fielder. I don't know why that was; it was kind of weird.

Q: Sort of like big kids don't . . .

Bob: Yeah, big kids don't collect. That's not the thing to do. That's something little kids do maybe.

John recalled quitting his hobby when he got "into that peer pressure type of thing when people think it's kind of childish to collect cards." Like Bob, he remembered being ridiculed for collecting by his roommates in college who he said would "give me shit" for spending money on cards. Those who did not face this kind of teasing often linked the end of their childhood collecting to the commencement of heterosexual relations with women. Calvin, a dentist in his fifties, had a somewhat typical memory of why he gave up collecting. "I collected until I was fifteen, sixteen and then I quit for a number of years. . . . Just other interests I guess, and I just kind of lost interest and got interested in maybe girls and cars and school and other friends and things like that. . . . Definitely a kids' thing."

Many adults who returned to the hobby well after their teens also reported feeling pressure to hide it from others. Like Kevin, Doug talked of keeping his collecting "in the closet," meaning he did not let many people know about it. Wes admitted that when he began collecting as an adult "it wasn't something I bragged to my friends" about. For most of these men, collecting was something they associated with an earlier stage in life. Yet, even though they reported that stage to have been defined by all male relationships, they also discussed how returning to it was considered less than manly. For those whom I interviewed, baseball card collecting involved informal levels of play that were not directly monitored or controlled by parents or adults, and that allowed levels of intimacy between boys not generally accepted when they became teenagers. This complicates understandings of sports that only see them as preparing boys to be heterosexual masculine teenagers.

In his ethnographic study of high school life in a small south Texas town, Douglas Foley noted how for many youths the competition for success in romance led to the breakup of single-sex relationships, as both males and females sought social prominence through dating. He observed competition for partners to have been more destructive to female friendships than to male ones, but noted that even the boys he interviewed defined their same-sex peer friends as those who "hung out" together, while opposite sex partners were ones with whom one could feel comfortable sharing one's hopes and intimate feelings. Those most likely to maintain more intimate same sex relationships were those with the least social prominence: the "nerds," the "nobodies," the "homeboys/girls." Because they lacked money, good looks, or family connections, they did not have success in climbing the social status ladder in romance. Yet they also had the least at stake in such relationships, and were therefore freer not to be "cool."[18]

Foley's observations parallel those of baseball card collectors who reported that their continued participation in the hobby into their teenage years led them to become stigmatized as immature, strange, or even deviant. Perhaps this is because baseball cards, particularly since the 1930's, have been strongly associated with preadolescent male homosocial relationships. Foley argues that in preadolescence, males are freer to engage in emotionally intimate relationships that, after the commencement of dating, are seen, at the very least, as immature. In fact, the often-repeated statement by collectors that they brought their collections "into the closet" when they became adults even suggests connotations between adult collecting and homosexuality. If Foley is right that those least successful in teenage heterosexual competition are most likely to maintain preadolescent same-sex relationships, then the continued engagement of teenagers and grown men in the baseball card collecting hobby might be seen as a kind of refusal to accept uncritically their gendered socialization.

This complicates how one might understand the homosocial relationships cultivated through baseball card collecting, and even through some forms of sports spectatorship more generally. However, the sports memorabilia hobby is not necessarily a cultural practice that celebrates the elevation of alternative gender identities and relations either. In fact, baseball card shows were a prime example of "male bonding," or the adult homosocial relationships that cultural critics such as Eve Sedgwick note discursively affirm both heterosexuality and male dominance. The only women who attended the many baseball card shows that I observed served primarily traditional roles as supporters of their husbands, sons, or fathers. The adult hobby was, perhaps, even more male-dominated than the childhood collecting that informants often remembered. In terms of gender relations, then, this raises an important question. To what extent did the revival of this preadolescent popular culture form represent a desire by men to shore up gender boundaries by nostalgically recalling preadolescent gender socialization through sports, and to what extent did it represent a desire for more meaningful and intimate human relations? One way to address this is by examining the kind of relations that collectors drew from the processes of set collecting. Many set collectors enjoyed shows for more than the opportunity they provided to buy cards. Shows also allowed men to encounter other men, talk sports, and revel in what one collector called "the commonality of baseball junkies." Tim, for example, said that despite the greed that some dealers exhibited, he looked forward to meeting people whenever he attended a show. [At shows] "usually you can just start talking baseball with [other people]. You know, it's kind of a fraternity type thing. You could walk to pretty much any table there and most of the guys are, you could just start talking baseball. You have a common bond with them."

Tim's comparison of baseball card shows to fraternities is important for it demonstrates the importance of gender to the "common bond" that he shared with other collectors at shows. Not only did he discuss the commonality at baseball card shows in male terms, but he articulated how sports and baseball cards provided for him a context in which he could understand an almost universal bond with other men. Other collectors shared this sentiment, discussing the sense of "camaraderie" they experienced at shows.

If collecting sets allowed men to get involved in all-male social worlds, it often simultaneously created boundaries between themselves and women. In fact, collecting sometimes caused strain between husbands and wives whom I interviewed, actually figuring in the separation and divorce of two informants. Dave, a show promoter claimed that he was divorced from his wife in part because he was more devoted to his cards than he was to her. Calvin told me at the end of our interview that, after he had recently separated from his wife, she refused to let him have access to his large and valuable rookie card collection until it had been appraised and the divorce settlement had been finalized. In other cases, the strain between husband and wife may not have been as extreme, but it was present. Sometimes set collecting created a drain upon family resources, both money and time, that caused tension. Kevin cited this as a factor that eventually drove him from set collecting into dealing. "I was getting a little pressure from [my son's] mom. 'Now you bought the cards, how are you going to pay for it.' So I tried to sell the old doubles."

Doug stated that his wife was not particularly enthusiastic about his collecting and dealing of baseball cards. Like Dave, Doug presented his cards as competing for his time, energy, and affection with his spouse.

Q: Is this your first marriage?

Doug: My only one, other than my baseball cards. It seems like I'm married to the store.

Q: How does your wife feel about your collecting?

Doug: She's tolerated it I guess. She used to help me a while back but she doesn't anymore.

Even those who said their wives had no problem with their hobby also reported how they managed their collecting practices to avoid conflict. Tim explained how he did this by negotiating the finances of his hobby and controlling his desires for cards.

She [my wife] doesn't have any problem with [collecting]. Usually what I try to do, I try to put aside a certain amount of money on a regular basis so that I can just take that money and go to the show. Rather than take a pay check and spend a bunch of it. So I try to budget it that way. She wouldn't be too happy with it if I came home with $500 or $1000 worth of cards, I don't think.

I also encountered evidence that men sometimes used outright deceit to manage the strain their hobby placed on household budgets. One afternoon, I was observing collectors in a baseball card shop called "All-American Baseball Cards." A man entered wearing a suit and tie, looking as if he was just coming from work. He and the shop owner began discussing a display of cards that featured Detroit Tiger slugger Cecil Fielder. The cards were marked at $25 each. The man ended up buying them. As he wrote out his check, he said that his wife was going to think he had gone "nuts." The owner told the man to make the check out to "All-American" instead of "All-American Baseball Cards." He said, "Your wife will think it's All-American Cleaners or All-American Grocers."

Collecting sets not only took up family income, but also household space. Bob, for example, lived in a small three-bedroom ranch house with a walk-in living room and kitchenette with his wife Janet, three children under the age of ten, and a dog. His already crowded living room contained a bookshelf for his collection and a card table where he sorted and priced cards for shows. Janet also collected what are known as "nonsports" cards, or trading cards that have cartoons, comics, celebrities, political figures, war battles, and other "non-sports" related topics printed on them. Her collection was confined to a smaller space on the bookshelf. Terry, a computer company employee in his early fifties, turned the basement of his house into a mini-memorabilia archive. He mounted souvenirs and posters on walls and shelves, had floor-to-ceiling metal cabinets to store his cards (which included every baseball card set ever produced dating back to the late 1940s), and a personal computer for keeping inventory and updating pricing.

The barriers between men and women over their levels of interest in cards was as much a part of the gender dynamics of collecting sets as was the closeness between men that so many reported feeling within the hobby. Like any other popular culture activity, however, baseball card collecting contained its own contradictions that made the "bonds" between men within the hobby more ones of cardboard than those of cement. Most notably, the speculative market and influence of money on baseball card collecting were a significant source of stress between collectors.

Contradictions within Set Collecting

While collecting sets may have allowed men to come into contact with fellow sports fans at shows, it also brought them into conflict with one another over issues of economic exchange. In fact, the monetary value of cards themselves, particularly as cards became increasingly valuable during the 1980s, created stress for many collectors. Wes, in fact, told of how the value of his cards brought his set collecting into conflict with his wife at home.

> It came out a few weeks ago after San Francisco won the Super Bowl, about a Joe Montana card being worth $150 to $200, and my wife asked me, she said, "Do you have that card?" And I said, "Well, I've got everything since '73." And she said, "Why don't you sell it?" And I wouldn't have a full set then. And she can't understand, if you can get $150, you spent $7.00 for the set, why would anyone want to hold it? I said, "Well, if I sell it I won't have a full set. I'm not in it for the money."

For Wes, his commitment to his set was more important than the money he would gain by selling it, while for his wife, the set's potential monetary value perhaps meant an opportunity to gain family income. Wes's story, however, not only il-

lustrates gendered conflict over the importance of sports, but also the strain that financial speculation placed on set collectors in the hobby. High prices for cards made it harder and harder for Wes to justify his desire to keep his sets. For many, the emphasis on trading and making money at shows made the hobby less "fun," and made collecting too much of a "business." For Wes, this tension had driven him in and out of collecting periodically for years. Rather than celebrating the fraternal bonds it evoked for him, he claimed that he had always been turned off by his fellow collectors.

> I didn't enjoy the people at all. I've never associated with people. A couple of my first experiences were with—I'd seen a kid going up with a 1963 Pete Rose rookie, which at the time was worth about $50, and going up to a dealer and the dealer saying, "Oh, yeah, that's an old card. That's not worth anything. I'll give you a half a dollar for it." . . . But the kid knew enough about it. And I think that's where I got . . . I don't appreciate the dealers at all. But it was the only place to go where you could buy your sets. . . . I've gone in and out of loving it and hating it.

Doug, like many other collectors, interpreted his involvement in the hobby in terms of a jeremiad, and felt the hobby had gone through a declension. He said that at one time there had been a sense of community among local hobbyists, but that it had fallen away. "It's more of a business than a hobby. I guess it was always a business, too, but it was more—I guess there was a lot more camaraderie. You could talk to people about different things they were collecting. Now it's kind of like sell, sell, sell."

Collectors often blamed money for disengaging the act of collecting from a genuine interest in sports. If collecting was really only about financial speculation, then anybody could do it. Shane, a factory worker in his late thirties and who collected with his son, saw this as a problem. "[Money] kind of takes away from the way the cards tie into the game itself. . . . I think it used to be a lot more fun when you were looking for particular stars."

Ironically, a number of adult collectors felt that this sort of detraction was worst among contemporary children who copied adult practices of financial speculation. Instead of being interested in cards because of a genuine interest in sports, or in a player or a team, youths were only interested in players who were worth a lot of money, according to informants. Collectors who remembered their own childhood collecting practices as playful often expressed disappointment that contemporary children did not recreate their memories. Instead, they often saw children involved in the hobby during the 1980s and 1990s as crass young business tycoons, carefully placing cards away and hoarding them in plastic binders. Doug discussed how he felt the collecting habits of children had changed over time.

> The kids . . . a lot of them aren't really collecting sets, which is really kind of the back-bone of the hobby. So that's changed. Now they just want hot cards. They want a card if they think it's hot. It seems like that's all they're interested in. I think that, to me, has to do with media hype. So they're not really looking at it for fun.

Ironically, although Dave chides youngsters for not being interested in set collecting, it was adult set collecting that initiated the universal standards for cards that reified their value. Contemporary children who decontextualized their cards, who feverishly searched for those that were "hot" and valuable, were only mirroring what they saw the adults around them doing. Monetary value, an emphasis on condition, and a detachment from play with cards all stemmed from set collecting, which placed a premium on order over creativity, play, or even aesthetic pleasure. In addition, the children that adult collectors disparaged were not altogether different in their collecting habits from what adults remember of their own collecting practices. As adult recollections illustrate, childhood collecting has never been an "innocent," authentic activity uncorrupted by commodity culture. The contemptuous attitude that so many whom I interviewed had for children in the hobby illustrates how nostalgia can stem from a sense of dissatisfaction with the present. Yet it also shows how nostalgic expressions of this dissatisfaction can iron out the complications and contradictions that characterized the past.

In fact, one of the more striking things I discovered while talking to set collectors was how few actually ever looked at or enjoyed their cards after they bought them. Most stored them away and rarely ever looked at them again. Steve, for example, told me,

> I very rarely look. The only time I look through them anymore is if somebody stops by, a sports fan, and we look at them. Or occasionally something or somebody comes up, you know, "Oh, yeah, I remember." And you go back and look at it. But I really don't have them, they're just sitting there collecting dust.

Collectors were more likely to have their cards stored away in a closet, on a shelf, or even in a safety deposit box, than out in the open where they could look at or admire them. As cards were not used in any tangible way, even collectors who complained about greed could only articulate the value of their cards in terms of exchange. However, particularly as inflation and speculation overtook the hobby during the 1980s, the emptiness of such exchange value became apparent even to many whom I interviewed. Wes, for example, told me that he was perplexed by the value of cards.

> I've been telling a lot of people that I think that it's going to . . . it's got to come [down]. It's cardboard. There's no value in cardboard. Topps can print up ten million sets, sell five million to the public, and put the other five million in a warehouse. . . . I've heard they even have the plates from the 1952 sets. They could print up as many Mickey Mantle cards as they wanted. Gold and silver, there's limited

quantities. That's got value to it, but cardboard has no value to me.

Those I interviewed often felt conflicted about the relationship of money to their cards. As compared to other fan cultures, the largely male population of card collectors had a fair degree of economic power so that a relatively large number of collectors were able to turn their fan subculture into a permanent source of income. The monetary value of cards helped to make the hobby seem more legitimate as an adult pursuit, and less of a childish activity. While Wes may have seen the adult hobby as being overwhelmed by a superficial obsession with price and exchange, he also admitted that it made the hobby more acceptable as an adult pursuit.

> *Wes:* I've never looked at [the hobby] in terms of value. But it's, I think, now it's a legitimate collecting, a legitimate hobby business. I think adults now accept it. And it's not anything that we have to hide and say, "Oh, I don't collect baseball cards."
> *Q:* Do you think they accept it because of the money involved?
> *Wes:* Definitely, because of the money.

This speaks directly to the sense of ridicule many reported feeling as they collected sets after their preadolescent years. It made collecting a "rational" activity. In fact, Wes also discussed how the commercial trade of baseball cards that drew from set collecting taught children beneficial values they could use in adult life. While he expressed a common concern over the influence of greed upon kids who collected within the adult hobby, he also felt that set collecting offered benefits.

> It will show them a responsibility for collecting, and taking care of, and not just buying—my own kids will buy stuff and throw it in a drawer and it will be lost. And I see some of these kids who buy cards and save them. They protect them. And they're really

concerned about it if it gets a bent corner. They're concerned about who they get, their organizational skills that they're learning. . . . I've got one kid in this class who can tell me batting averages and where the person fit in the minor league. . . . For a second grader to be reading that much, the reading skills, I think are [very good]. So in that sense I do think it's good for kids. I think they are getting some values out of it.

Janice Radway notes a parallel dynamic at work among the romance readers she surveyed and interviewed in her ethnographic study of female romance readers. They justified their reading, on one hand, by claiming a consumer-oriented right to self-gratification, while simultaneously maintaining that romance reading was edifying, productive, and consistent with values of thrift and hard work.[19] Like romance readers, Wes affirmed the values of work in the way he praised the benefits of collecting for kids. He also discussed how collecting taught thrift, organization, and the value of education. This rhetoric effectively equates cards with the benefits of deferred gratification as opposed to the instant and fleeting sensual pleasures of consumer culture.

Like romance readers, however, adult collectors founded their hobby upon the pleasures and desires that emanated from the consumption of a media artifact. The discussion of the wholesome benefits of baseball card collecting obscured attention away from the desires, fantasies, and pleasures that motivated collecting for adults. Ironically, such childhood play often is about evading the very forms of adult control over children's cultures that Wes talked of baseball cards providing. From what collectors told me and from what I observed, their fond memories of baseball fandom had less to do with memories of learning to read, and more to do with forms of childhood play they associated with baseball cards that served as a foundation for relationships with other boys.

Conclusion: Nostalgia for a Pre-sexual Male Past,
Whiteness, and the Shoring up of a Symbolic Order

In his book on subcultural style associated with
the burgeoning punk rock of the late 1970s, Dick
Hebdige coins the term "symbolic order." Distinguishing his term from the Lacanian understanding of the same term, Hebdige uses the phrase to
mean a general arrangement and understanding
of cultural symbols in a society in a way that gives
that society and the universe surrounding it an
appearance of unity and coherence. A symbolic
order is a key component of a cultural hegemony
that dominant sectors of a society feel they must
continually defend and shore up as its own contradictions are continually at risk of being exposed. For Hebdige, working-class English music subcultures reappropriated objects from daily
life to reformulate or undermine their semiotic
contents and ultimately disrupt a bourgeois symbolic order. In his analysis of punk culture, for example, Hebdige argues that style constantly disrupts meaning, expressing a kind of generalized
"refusal" to make sense to the dominant culture
by "those condemned to subordinate positions
and second class lives." [20]

On its surface, adult baseball card collecting
might seem too mainstream and conservative, its
constituency too comfortable, to ever be considered a subculture. One would not, for instance,
quickly associate most of the white, heterosexual, middle-class men whom I interviewed with
people "condemned to subordinate positions and
second-class lives." Yet, even in spite of their positions of relative privilege, collectors often expressed a sense of social marginalization to me
during interviews, either explicitly through verbal
statements, or implicitly through their collecting
practices. Unlike the subcultures Hebdige describes, however, this one was bent upon salvaging
a symbolic order rather than disrupting it.

The baseball card collectors whom I interviewed did often face social conditions that were
alienating and unsettling. Many, for example,
worked at jobs that were dull, unfulfilling, and
even dehumanizing. Others faced the economic
uncertainties of deindustrialization, which caused
them to endure unemployment, underemploy-
ment, and job insecurity. Some were Vietnam War
veterans who still found themselves struggling to
readjust to postwar life in ways that were quite
lonely.

The particular brand of nostalgia for a presexual past that many associated with baseball card
collecting, however, was an especially conservative
response to such conditions. By seeking authenticity in the all-male, preadolescent worlds of the
1950s-style white, middle-class family, collectors
suggested that their social alienation and instability lay in threats to their positions as white males.
Film critic Viveca Gretton has noted how the nostalgia created by Hollywood baseball films of the
1980s tended to create a mythic formulation of
American life that placed the authority of white
men at its eternal, innocent core. The nostalgia of
baseball card collectors and that of Hollywood
baseball films are linked by more than historical
coincidence. They are tied by the common expression of a desire to reestablish a sense of cohesion
to a symbolic order that places patriarchy and
whiteness at its core.

In interviews, collectors usually were much
more likely to discuss their collecting hobby in
terms that explicitly related to their gendered
identities than they were to discuss it in terms of
race. However, tensions over race and class helped
to fuel nostalgic discourses that they circulated
within their hobby in ways that were perhaps
more subtle, but no less important than gender
tensions. From my observations, very few collectors in the baseball card collecting hobby were minorities, and only one of the collectors in my interview sample was not white. This man was an
African American who at one time was the president of the local sports collectors' club. His leadership, however, generated deep and bitter resent-

ment, which he saw as largely the result of racial bias. The controversy eventually led him to resign and left him feeling somewhat bitter toward many of his fellow hobbyists.[21] This was only one incident, but I see it as symptomatic. By associating baseball with a stable and coherent past, collectors articulated cultural ideals that establish whiteness as a "norm" central to the symbolic order that they were protecting. One can best see this by moving beyond immediate interviews with collectors, and by placing their hobby within the context of the resurrection of baseball nostalgia within popular culture in the 1980s.

Hollywood baseball films of the 1980s such as *The Natural, Eight Men Out,* and perhaps most prominently *Field of Dreams* very self-consciously celebrated baseball as an icon of the American past; a constant, mythic, national tradition that has survived unchanged against the alienating transformations of modern U.S. history. Major publishers released books by celebrated authors such as W. P. Kinsella and Roger Angell, media personalities like George Will, and the late baseball commissioner and Yale University president A. Bartlett Giamatti, all of which glorified the game of baseball as a symbol of transcendent meaning.[22] Many teams in the major leagues cast aside their flamboyant softball-style uniforms of the previous decade for ones that resembled flannel outfits worn during the 1950s, even though teams like the Minnesota Twins and San Francisco Giants created entirely new team logos in the process. By the end of the decade, the Baltimore Orioles had abandoned their old ballpark for a new one that was built to *seem* old, and the Cleveland Indians and Texas Rangers had drawn up plans to do the same.

From its emergence as an adult hobby in the 1970s, baseball card collecting was associated with nostalgic images of baseball as well. In addition, very often this nostalgia evoked particular images of the 1950s suburban nuclear family. Authors Brendan Boyd and Fred Harris, in their popular 1973 book on baseball card collecting, fondly re-

membered baseball cards as a defining aspect of their boyhoods in the American suburbs of the 1950s.[23] Similarly, *Boston Globe* baseball writer Luke Salisbury, in his 1989 book, *The Answer Is Baseball,* spends several pages explaining that the attraction of men to baseball cards has to do with their memory of these objects within the specific contexts of suburban life during the 1950s. Salisbury writes that "almost every American male" collected cards, and he further universalizes the particular experiences of white, middle-class boys by defining his entire age group as the "big suburban generation, sons of World War II vets who did well as the American economy expanded."[24]

As much as the images that surrounded the baseball card collecting hobby were dominated by the experiences of men who grew up in post-World War II suburbs, discourse surrounding baseball during the 1980s also had a great deal to do with cities. Baseball nostalgia during the 1980s often conveyed messages about urban decline. "Photo realist" paintings that I observed collectors selling at shows depicted dream-like images of sunny days in old-fashioned urban ballparks filled with happy, most often white, spectators. Municipalities like Baltimore and Cleveland that constructed old-fashioned looking ballparks each hoped that by doing so, affluent whites would be attracted back into cities that had been devastated by the economic decline caused by deindustrialization. Such nostalgic representations might be seen as offering a critical perspective toward what Marshall Berman identifies as the major thrust of post-World War II modernity toward "killing the street" with urban renewal and freeway construction. But it is also what Berman would identify as a kind of radical anti-modernism built upon a pastoral ideal. As he states, such visions recall an image of "the city before the blacks got there."[25]

Nowhere is this ideal better illustrated than in W. P. Kinsella's 1982 novel *Shoeless Joe,* the book upon which the film *Field of Dreams* was based. Early in the book, the story's protagonist, Ray Kinsella, is driven by the spirit of Shoeless Joe Jackson to build a baseball diamond in a cornfield that he farms in Iowa. Eventually, he decides to leave behind his wife, daughter, and financially troubled farm to pursue a baseball odyssey. His first stop is in Chicago, where he attends a White Sox game at the old Comiskey Park on the city's South Side.

> It is unwise for a white person to walk through South Chicago, but I do anyway. The Projects are chill, sand-colored apartments, twelve to fifteen stories high, looking like giant bricks stabbed into the ground. I am totally out of place. I glow like a piece of phosphorous on a pitch-black night. Pedestrians' heads turn after me. I feel the stolid stares of drivers as large cars zipper past. A beer can rolls ominously down the gutter, its source of locomotion invisible. The skeletal remains of automobiles litter the parking lots behind apartments.[26]

Here, Kinsella's concern is not for those who have to live in the frightening and impersonal projects he describes, but with his own sense of not being in control and of being out of place. In addition, this portrayal of Chicago contains a subtext surrounding urban decline. One senses when reading this passage that Comiskey was, at one time, a ballpark someone like Kinsella could walk to, a place where it would have not been "unwise" for a "white person" to have walked.

In fact, the neighborhood surrounding that ballpark did transform dramatically after World War II. Highway construction and urban renewal eliminated housing and replaced it with the infamous housing projects that Kinsella describes. At the same time African Americans migrated to the South Side of Chicago between 1950 and 1970 in huge numbers. Accompanied by subsequent white flight out of the city to suburbs, the black population of Chicago increased from 14 percent in 1950 to 33 percent in 1970. Because of housing discrimination, however, these new residents faced extreme overcrowding once in the city. In 1960, African Americans were 23 percent of Chicago's population, but occupied only 4 percent of its housing.[27]

It is not necessarily inappropriate for Kinsella to have painted a depressing picture, therefore, of the South Side of Chicago. In fact, it is one that speaks to the historical conditions created by suburbanization, discrimination, red-lining, freeway construction, deindustrialization, and urban renewal. What is significant, however, is the way that Kinsella posits nonwhites as the symbol and cause of instability. As George Lipsitz argues, this association of urban social problems with the culture of minorities and the poor became a central component of neoconservative discourses that have demonized African Americans, Latinos, and immigrants since the late 1970s. Establishing whiteness as a norm not only obscures the experiences of those who are not white, it serves to defend whiteness as a racial category of privilege in and of itself. Lipsitz writes that racial identities are largely constructed through differing life chances afforded to groups based upon their ethnicity.[28] Suburban life during the 1950s and 1960s was central to both racial identities and the differing life options that they connoted, for it rested upon both the exclusion of nonwhites, and upon the homogenization of ethnic groups that, within urban contexts, had seen themselves as separate and different from one another. In terms of reestablishing cohesion and a symbolic stability, nostalgic expressions of urban decline and white "innocence" through baseball imply that the sources of instability in the present have to do with deviations from whiteness as a "norm," rather than from historical factors that created "whiteness" as a norm in the first place.

It is also appropriate that Ray Kinsella in both *Field of Dreams* and *Shoeless Joe* should feel the need to leave his wife and daughter so that he could fulfill a sense of order to his life. Throughout the story, he faces foreclosure of his farm in Iowa, a familiar type of economic problem throughout the 1980s that even some whom I interviewed had faced in their lives. Yet Ray only establishes a resolution to his life's problems by recapturing a sense of pastoral bonding with other men (including the spirit of his own father). This text ultimately represents the complexities and contradictions of universalized male identities as the cause, rather than a symptom, of social instability.

I write this chapter during the mid-1990s, a decade that so far seems to be marked by annual springtime confrontations between "angry white men" and federal law enforcement agencies. Although I conducted my primary research on baseball card collecting over five years ago, the embittered sentiments expressed by right-wing white males today have a strange air of familiarity to me. What I recognize is a common nostalgia for a white, patriarchal symbolic order. Yet the ways in which the sports memorabilia hobby enacted this nostalgia also are quite complex. By imagining boyhood as presexual, and idealizing the homosocial relationships that existed during this period of their lives, many collectors inherently blamed women for the instabilities they experienced as adults. Yet they also recalled moments of male intimacy that were undermined by their own collecting practices, and that in some contexts even called into question their own masculinity. Set collecting may have involved the orderly gathering of pieces that were part of a coherent whole, but the inflation, hoarding, and financial speculation that it spawned also undermined associations collectors had between baseball cards and boyhood innocence. Through their nostalgia and their hobby, baseball card enthusiasts may have worked to sustain a symbolic order that surrounds patriarchal social relationships in the United States, but they did not entirely resolve the contradictions that such a symbolic order conceals.

Notes

1 Marshall Berman, *All That Is Solid Melts into Air* (New York: Simon and Schuster, 1982).

2 Eve Kosofsky Sedgwick, *Between Men: English Literature and Male Homosocial Desire* (New York: Columbia University Press, 1985); Joel Kovel, "Rationalization of the Family," *Telos* 37(1987): 5–21.

3 John Fiske, *Reading the Popular* (Boston: Unwin Hyman, 1989); Dick Hebdige, *Subculture: The Meaning of Style* (London: Methuen, 1979); George Lipsitz, *Class and Culture in Cold War America: A Rainbow at Midnight* (South Hadley, MA: Bergin and Garvey, 1982); George Lipsitz, *Time Passages: Collective Memory and American Popular Culture* (Minneapolis: University of Minnesota Press, 1990).

4 Between 1975 and 1980, ever larger numbers of adult men had begun to gravitate toward the baseball card collecting hobby. *Baseball Card Boom* magazine asserts that "serious" collectors increased from 4,000 to 250,000 during this time, making it the fourth largest hobby in the nation. The number of annual shows increased as well from 20 to 600. Over the next ten years, the hobby continued to grow, involving three to four million people by 1989 (Mark Larson, "1980," *Baseball Land Boom* [February 1990]: 22–23). By the late 1970's, publishers were printing price guides for baseball card collectors, similar to those that antique dealers or vintage car collectors use to assess the "value" of their objects.

5 Ted Taylor, "Court Gives Topps 'Double Play' Decision," *Sports Collectors Digest* 20 (Sept. 1981): 6–10; Ted Taylor, "Fleer: Double Bubble Busts the Trust," *Baseball Card Boom*, 26 (February, 1990).

6 Other researchers have also noted the centrality of set collecting to the adult baseball card hobby. These scholars, conducting their work within the fields of folklore and sociology, have noted the ways such behavior among baseball card enthusiasts matches more general patterns of collecting behavior. See Russell W. Belk et al., "Collectors and Collecting," *Advances in Consumer Research* 15 (1988): 543–53; and Brenda Danet, and Tamar Katriel, "No Two Alike: Play and Aesthetics in Collecting," *Play and Culture* 3 (1989): 227–53.

7 Susan Stewart, *On Longing: Narratives of the Miniature, the Souvenir, the Collection* (Baltimore: Johns Hopkins University Press, 1984); Danet and Katriel, "No Two Alike."

8 Henry Jenkins, *Textual Poachers: Television Fans and Participatory Culture* (New York: Routledge, 1992), 26–27.

9 Jane M. Gaines, *Contested Culture: The Image, the Voice, and the Law* (Chapel Hill: University of North Carolina Press, 1991); Jenkins, *Textual Poachers*, 25.

10 Jenkins, *Textual Poachers*, 48.

11 Of course, a large minority of collectors I interviewed resisted or evaded these trends as well. Some actively searched for cards with writing on them, for example, while others simply did not care about the conditions of the cards they bought, so preferred ones in "poor" condition because they made "filling in" a set more affordable.

12 Jerome Wiedman, "Anybody Got a Solly Hemus?" *Sports Illustrated* (Aug. 16, 1954): 45.

13 Ibid.

14 Lynn Spigel, "Television in the Family Circle: The Popular Reception of a New Medium," in *The Logics of Television: Essays in Cultural Criticism*, ed. Patricia Mellencamp. (Bloomington: Indiana University Press, 1990), 73–97.

15 Michael Messner, "Masculinities and Athletic Careers: Bonding and Status Differences," in *Sport, Men, and the Gender Order: Critical Feminist Perspectives*, eds. Michael Messner and Donald Sabo. (Champaign, IL: Human Kinetics, 1990), 100–103; Nancy Chodorow, *The Reproduction of Motherhood* (Berkeley: University of California Press, 1978).

16 Messner, "Masculinities," 97–108.

17 Michael Messner, *Power at Play: Sports and the Problem of Masculinity* (Boston: Beacon Press, 1992), 24–41.

18 Douglas Foley, *Learning Capitalist Culture: Deep in the Heart of Tejas* (Philadelphia: University of Pennsylvania Press, 1990), 78–79.

19 Janice Radway, *Reading the Romance: Women, Patriarchy, and Popular Literature* (Chapel Hill: University of North Carolina Press, 1984), 188.

20 Dick Hebdige, *Subculture: The Meaning of Style* (London: Methuen, 1979), 127–33.

21 John Bloom, *A House of Cards: Baseball Card Collecting and Popular Culture* (Minneapolis: University of Minnesota Press, 1997).

22 W. P. Kinsella, *Shoeless Joe* (New York: Ballantine, 1982); Roger Angell, *Late Innings: A Baseball Companion* (New York: Ballantine, 1984); George Will, *Men at Work: The Craft of Baseball* (New York: Macmillan, 1990); A. Bartlett Giamatti, *Take Time for Paradise: Americans and Their Games* (New York: Summit Books, 1990).

23 Brendan Boyd and Frederick Harris, *The Great American Baseball Card Flipping, Trading, and Bubble Gum Book* (New York: Warner, 1973), 20.

24 Luke Salisbury, *The Answer Is Baseball: A Book of Questions that Illuminate the Great Game* (New York: Times Books, 1989), 189.

25 Berman, *All That Is Solid Melts into Air*, 324.

26 Kinsella, *Shoeless Joe*, 38.

27 Joe William Trotter, Jr., *The Great Migration in Historical Perspective*. (Bloomington: Indiana University Press, 1991).

28 George Lipsitz, "The Possessive Investment in Whiteness: Racialized Social Democracy and the 'White' Problem in American Studies," *American Quarterly* 47(3) (1995): 369–87.

VIRGINS FOR JESUS:
THE GENDER POLITICS OF
THERAPEUTIC CHRISTIAN
FUNDAMENTALIST MEDIA

Heather Hendershot

Girls don't eat much when guys are around. I guess they assume we're going to think bad of them, or maybe they're too concerned about their appearance . . . many times a girl will look great, but she'll still say she's fat. . . . When I go out to dinner with a girl, I want to enjoy the meal *with* her instead of just watching her pick at her food.

—*BREAKAWAY* BOYS INTERVIEWED FOR AN ARTICLE
IN *BRIO* MAGAZINE

I'd like to order a pizza with pepperoni and olives on my half and a dead frog, some bugs, pocket lint, and ear wax on my little brother's half.

—GIRL ORDERING A PIZZA IN A *BRIO* CARTOON

Focus on the Family is a right-wing Christian organization that produces "pro-family" products, including a wide-range of youth media.[1] Focus puts out two monthly teen magazines, *Breakaway* for boys and *Brio* for girls. These magazines are the only nationally distributed fundamentalist youth magazines.[2] They are sold in some Christian bookstores, but the vast majority of their distribution comes through subscription; there are around 160,000 *Brio* subscribers and 100,000 *Breakaway* subscribers. Parents offer the magazines to their twelve-to-sixteen-year-old children as substitutes for secular magazines such as *Seventeen* and *Boy's Life*. Readers may have started off with other Focus on the Family publications such as *Clubhouse Jr.* for four-to-eight-year-olds and *Clubhouse* for eight-to-twelve-year-olds. As one often finds in secular culture, the magazines for younger children are not targeted to a single sex,

but as soon as readers become teenagers the magazines are marked by insistent gender bifurcation. For girls, the transition from the non-gender-coded *Nickelodeon Magazine* to the highly feminized *YM* is comparable to the move from *Clubhouse* to *Brio*.

Secular cynics who might assume that *Brio* and *Breakaway* are simply phony imitations of "real" youth magazines would be surprised if they read the magazines, for they are actually hi-tech, sophisticated productions in their own right, not just desecularized and watered-down versions of nonreligious youth magazines. While the magazines may seem theologically bizarre to nonconverts, there is something strangely familiar about them too. As someone who avidly read *Seventeen, Teen,* and *Tiger Beat,* and has not looked at such magazines in twenty years, I find reading *Brio* somewhat uncanny. *Brio* and *Seventeen* offer similar advice about make-up and dieting, and share a peppy, slang-laden youth style. Like *Cosmo Girl, Teen,* or *YM, Brio* does not take a radical approach to gender politics. Indeed, both *Brio* and *Breakaway* conceive of femininity and masculinity in essentialist terms.

When I first started reading these magazines, attempting to penetrate their conservative gendered address, I found that the shiny pages of *Breakaway* resisted my highlighter pen. The ink sat on the surface and took a few minutes to dry. If I turned the page too quickly, the ink smeared across the opposite page. Conversely, highlighter ink easily permeated *Brio*'s pages, drying almost instantly. While *Brio* paper is matte, the pages of *Breakaway* are glossy and impermeable. *Brio*'s pages are pastel, and the graphics are easy to read. *Breakaway*'s colors are primary, and its zig-zagged, overlapping, cool graphics are often difficult to decipher. Initially, my smeared highlighter ink simply seemed like a nuisance, but I have since come to see how the unpenetrating ink functions as a metaphor for my relationship to *Breakaway*. These pages were not designed for my eyes at all, as I am reminded whenever I speak to Focus on the Family phone workers ("Are *both* subscriptions for *you?*"). Adults are not supposed to read either publication, and females are certainly not supposed to read *Breakaway*. Conversely, my pen can penetrate the surface of *Brio,* a magazine that I "get" at some level because it's much like the stuff I grew up on. I come to this magazine as both insider and outsider. Outsider as cultural critic, adult, and agnostic. Insider as a former girl recognizing how advice columns make one feel connected to other girls, recognizing how make-up and fashion tips make you feel hip, and recognizing that certain conceptions of "proper" femininity traverse both Christian and non-Christian culture. With *Breakaway,* conversely, I am all outsider. There is no point of connection.

There is a second symbolic dimension to the highlighter pen mishap. On this dimension the differences between *Brio*'s and *Breakaway*'s design symbolize how they, and other fundamentalist youth cultural products such as chastity videos, advice books, and music, function as therapeutic sites that strive to cure teens of sexual desire and other teen "problems." Boys are unemotional surfaces, their interior states difficult to penetrate, while girls are emotionally deep, their feelings constantly exposed, debated, permeated. Boys are cool, funky, and athletic, and use lots of street slang (sans profanity); zig-zagging primary-colored graphics suit them. Girls are sweet, and nice, their feelings never far from the surface. They may exhibit a little pluck, but no grit. User-friendly pastel graphics seem appropriate for this type of girl. Although the construction of teenage girls as emotional and weak and boys as hard and strong is hardly unique to fundamentalist media, it dominates such media to an even greater extent than it dominates popular culture in general, and this dominance serves political and spiritual purposes particular to fundamentalism.

Through their construction of sexual abstinence, food consumption, eating disorders, and weight-lifting, therapeutic fundamentalist youth media define bodily control differently for girls and boys. On the surface, fundamentalism's gender-specific definitions of bodily control seem to construct boys and girls similarly—as equally sexually abstinent, for example—but fundamentalism's discourses of bodily control may actually be more oppressive for girls than boys. The following pages examine how and why *Brio, Breakaway,* and other fundamentalist cultural products such as advice books and chastity videos construct and "cure" male and female bodies differently. The focus is on the therapeutic advice that adults offer teens through these products, and, to a certain extent, how teens respond. Examining the adult-produced artifacts of fundamentalist youth culture cannot reveal all that youth do with those artifacts, but it does elucidate how fundamentalist adults want teens to conceptualize their bodies and how this conceptualization converges with and diverges from secular conceptions of male and female bodies. Secular therapeutic discourse "provides a ready-made and familiar narrative trajectory: the eruption of a problem leads to confession and diagnosis and then to a solution or cure."[3] Fundamentalist therapeutic discourse also entails problem eruption, confession, and cure, but, because of the nature of sin, cures are always extremely precarious. Since sin can never permanently go away, teens are never really cured of carnality. Rather, one might say that fundamentalist therapeutic media help teen desires go into remission.

Chastity through the Roof

Fundamentalist teen advice books repeatedly state that feelings of sexual attraction are a gift from God. Yet God's gift is dangerous; left uncontrolled, it will lead to premarital sexual activity. To prevent such activity, fundamentalists have undertaken a number of nationwide abstinence campaigns, and these campaigns are promoted in *Brio* and *Breakaway*. When you open the magazines, chastity pledge cards tumble out rather than subscription cards. In July 1994, the "True Love Waits" campaign culminated with 25,000 teens planting 200,000 chastity pledge cards in the mall area between the Capitol and the Washington Monument. These cards read: "Believing that true love waits, I make a commitment to God, myself, my family, my friends, my future mate, and my future children to be sexually abstinent from this date until the day I enter a biblical marriage relationship." In 1996, thousands of teens filled out "True Love Waits" cards and assembled at the Atlanta Georgia Dome for a weekend-long chastity extravaganza, featuring various speakers and the hottest Christian bands. These cards had the same words on them as the 1994 cards but were designed slightly differently, with a hole in them so that they could be stacked on a pole soaring up to the ceiling of the Dome. Further cementing the already bizarrely phallic connotations of the event, the gathering's ejaculatory motto was, "My card's through the roof!" (see figs. 1 and 2).

Assuming that God makes "opposites" attract, fundamentalist abstinence campaigns address boys and girls as utterly dichotomous: boys are strong and stoic, girls emotional and nurturing. Yet their faith and their commitment to abstinence unite these opposites. That boys and girls can send their cards through the roof and gyrate to Christian rock to celebrate their shared dedication to chastity may seem strange. Yet chastity celebrations, like Christian youth music festivals, are the ultimate co-ed road trip. Boys and girls who usually aren't allowed to stay out late, go to wild parties, or even touch each other platonically (there is a three inch separation rule at one fundamentalist junior high in California), pile into buses with their adult youth group leaders and spend three or four days in a hotel or camping out. The mutual commitment to chastity, expressed via these events, thus bridges both the metaphorical and literal distance between fundamentalist boys and girls. Chastity—and all the celebratory rallies,

concerts, and parties it entails—is, ironically, the only risk-free activity that teen boys and girls can safely engage in together.

The conundrum is, how do you construct a therapeutic discourse that explains and promotes chastity to teens who have been taught to think of boys and girls as sexually opposite? How can essentialist constructions of gender be maintained if the "inherent" desires of boys and girls can be restructured? In other words, how can boys still be masculine while resisting their active sexual urges, and how can girls still be feminine while resisting the urge to passively submit? These questions represent the fault lines of fundamentalist notions of sexual control. To "cure" teens of sexual desire, fundamentalist adults must sanction the very gender-specific behavioral traits (masculine aggression, feminine passivity) that supposedly compel unchaste behavior.

For example, at the 1994 Washington True Love Waits conference, girls and boys were taught about chastity in separate seminars. Girls were told a sentimental fairy tale about true, eternal love and the achievement of the feminine dream of romance through the preservation of virginity. Boys, conversely, were directed to loudly chant "We are real men! We are real men!" They were told that abstinence was not emasculating, that "Adam was a real man," and that the Garden of Eden housed "Adam and Eve" not "Adam and Steve."[4] The problem of how one could be a "real man" and a virgin was solved by asserting homophobic machismo. Ironically, to control the male body, to save it from its own heterosexual aggression, that body must be constructed as aggressively heterosexual and masculine.

Thus, "natural" heterosexual gender roles are maintained in spite of a constant attempt to control and reconstruct "natural urges." Curiously, the fundamentalist anti-evolution stance represents the key to defusing this apparent paradox. When teens ask why God gives them sexual urges if he doesn't want them to act upon them, videos

Please mail card with punch-out to:
True Love Waits
958 Milstead Avenue
Conyers, GA 30207

My Card's
Thru the Roof!

ATLANTA
GEORGIA
DOME
FEBRUARY
11TH, 1996

T•R•U•E
10
Ve
W•A•I•T•S

5621-39

Believing that *true love waits*, I make a commitment to God, myself, my family, my friends, my future mate, and my future children to be sexually abstinent from this day until the day I enter a biblical marriage relationship.

Signed: _____

Date: _____

❑ I am making this commitment for the first time.
❑ I made this commitment previously; this is a restatement of that commitment.

Mail the top card to Atlanta; keep the bottom card as a reminder of your commitment.

Believing that *true love waits*, I make a commitment to God, myself, my family, my friends, my future mate, and my future children to be sexually abstinent from this day until the day I enter a biblical marriage relationship.

Signed: _____

Date: _____

❑ I am making this commitment for the first time.
❑ I made this commitment previously; this is a restatement of that commitment.

(top) Chastity pledge card with a hole. Cards are stacked on a pole that go "Thru the Roof." Carmel V. France.

(bottom) The fine print reads "Half is for the pole, half is for the teen to keep." Carmel V. France.

and advice manuals often answer that, in biblical times, people married at the onset of puberty, so premarital sex was not an issue. Our bodies have not changed or "evolved" since then, so we still feel "the urge to merge," as one adult fundamentalist puts it, at an age when it is no longer appropriate to marry. Advice books and videos teach teens that history, not God, has made sexual abstinence so difficult to maintain.

Susie Shellenberger and Greg Johnson, the editors of *Brio* and *Breakaway*, have written numerous teen advice books on how to maintain one's faith and virginity.[5] Their co-authored *258 Great Dates While You Wait* tells teens how to avoid sticky situations in which their hormones might carry them away. Like other adult chastity promoters, these two assume that teenagers cannot control their desires. Heavy petting, or even French kissing, will almost inevitably lead down the slippery slope to sexual intercourse. Shellenberger's rationale is "'the law of diminishing returns.' . . . [E]ach time you go a step further, you find that it takes *more* to fulfill your appetite. So you continually let down your barriers to become more and more fulfilled. The result? Two people have had sexual intercourse without planning on it."[6]

By constructing a teen body utterly lacking self-control, a body that can only be controlled/ cured by a spiritual commitment to chastity, fundamentalist chastity discourse may inadvertently encourage boys to be sexually violent and girls to see submission to sexual violence as natural. Boys and girls repeatedly told that, at a certain point, they are no longer in control, may as a result feel less in control. That is, it may actually be more difficult to stop sexual activity if one conceives of one's body as a runaway train. Crudely put, when all bodily control is lost, boys give in to their urge to rape and girls give in to their urge to submit to rape. Significantly, fundamentalists do not speak in such crass terms. In fact, it sometimes seems that rape per se does not exist for fundamentalists.

Instead, boys "lose control" or "force themselves" on girls. This is a scenario in one episode of *Family First*, a fundamentalist sit-com aired on the Trinity Broadcasting Network. A girl ignores her brother's warnings that the boy she is dating has a "bad reputation." The boy eventually forces himself on her, but she simply hits him and escapes. The word "rape" is avoided and the girl is taught a valuable lesson about being led by the spirit, not the flesh. The unstated implication is that she was "asking for it." A teenager who wrote into *Breakaway* was less fortunate than the sit-com girl. She explains that she and her boyfriend were sexually "wrestling," and she kept telling him to stop, but at a certain point she felt that she had "let him go so far" that it wouldn't be fair or possible to stop him. She says she should have pushed him off her and run away, but instead she had sex. Again, what sounds like rape is here defined as the victim's fault because she has been so thoroughly instructed in biologically compulsory fornication.[7]

One way *Brio* and *Breakaway* hope to stymie fornication is by rendering sex taboo by tacitly equating sex with incest. The magazines and spin-off advice books urge sexually aroused teens to consider who their act of sin will affect and to actually picture the faces of all their relatives, as well as Jesus. Boys and girls are encouraged to "date" their parents and to imagine real dates as siblings. One Christian music celebrity actually says, "The best date I've ever had was with my mom!" A cartoon in Shellenberger's advice book *Guys and a Whole Lot More* shows a car parked at Lover's Lane and explicitly places the male sexual aggressor in the paternal subject position. In the caption, the girl tells the boy, "Here's a quarter. Call my dad. Tell him what you want to do. If it's all right with him, it's okay with me."[8] The teen superego is thus maintained by perversely transforming the sexual situation into a primal scene.

Fundamentalist media encourage teens to be chaste by explaining the advantages of abstinence and constructing it as empowering. One video I've seen, however, illustrates the pressures wrought upon both boys and girls by a commitment to chastity. *Edge TV* is a series of videos produced for church youth groups. Each fifty-minute show is designed to be viewed during a youth group meeting and followed by discussion. The videos slickly incorporate funky graphics and MTV-style camera angles in order to look like "real" TV. The first segment in the "Sexual Choices" episode features a dozen kids, many of whom have made sexual "mistakes" in the past. While some feel empowered by their current commitment to chastity, memories of their sexually active history torture many of them. This video shows emotional, introspective teenage boys, which is unusual in fundamentalist media. A large football player type earnestly explains that lust is dehumanizing. He is shot in a soft, Vaseline-on-the-lens, feminine-coded style. Another boy suffers desperately from the urge to masturbate. A third teen is horrified by his homosexual past. This boy remarks that if only he'd talked to someone about his homosexual feelings before he gave in to them he could have properly dealt with his problem, and he wouldn't have engaged in the sexual acts that lead to his HIV-positive status.

The underlying messages of this confessional video are that sex outside of marriage is inherently lustful and unpleasant and that youth desperately need to talk about their sexual feelings. Although fundamentalists virulently oppose ritualize Catholic confession, the organizing principle of much therapeutic fundamentalist youth media is that translating sexuality into language is liberatory, and that if only youth could express their sexual feelings to youth pastors or other mature elders, they would be able to control those feelings. Because of the intransigence of sin, the cure from sexuality is unstable, but it is nonetheless within the teenager's grasp. The fundamentalist directive to speak one's sex is evocative of the forced "infinite task of telling" sexuality that Michel Foucault speaks of in the first volume of *The History of Sexuality,* " You will seek to transform your desire, your every desire, into discourse." [9] There are of course crucial differences between the Catholic confession that Foucault describes and fundamentalist witnessing, which eschews the rituals of the church and the mediation of the priest in favor of a direct, personal relationship with God, but both types of rituals require the translation of the interior self into language, and both serve therapeutic purposes.

The typical witnessing narrative details how one has been born again. It is a public display of the self that is simultaneously spiritually valuable to the evangelizer and of value to listeners as potential converts. The typical chastity narrative, which one might read as a witnessing subgenre, also tells of being saved, now from sexual sin, yet it serves a more overtly therapeutic purpose than the born-again witnessing narrative. Both kinds of narratives are evangelistic, but the chastity narrative is more about the process of healing the self than about healing listeners. Fundamentalist teen sex talk functions as a prophylactic against the commission of sexual acts. The *Edge TV* masturbator, for example, ends his tale by unconvincingly explaining that he feels better now that he has found a support network of tormented fellow masturbators to whom he can confess his sinful feelings rather than acting upon them.

Prophylactic Christian media hope to ease the pressures of the chaste Christian lifestyle by offering pleasurable alternatives to sinful secular culture.[10] There's a whole array of chastity products such as jewelry (True Love Waits rings), clothing ("Don't Even Ask! I'm Waiting"), music ("I Don't Want It" by D.C. Talk), videos (*Edge TV*), and books (*258 Great Dates*). In principle, these products are designed to help kids not think about having sex, but one could not ask for a better example of what Foucault called the "repressive hypothesis." Just when sex is ostensibly repressed, it is actually ubiquitous. Fundamentalists strive to eliminate sex outside the boundaries of marriage, yet it is precisely outside those boundaries that dis-courses of sexuality propagate with reckless aban-don. Focus on the Family dispenses advice to im-prove the sex lives of married couples, but the amount of sex talk directed to those *not* allowed to copulate by far outweighs the amount of sex talk directed to those sanctioned to indulge. Pro-chastity teen media make ignoring sex impossible.

Teen Negotiation of the Chastity Directive

To avoid making the kinds of sexual mistakes dis-cussed in the *Edge TV* video, Shellenberger and Johnson in their dating advice book suggest weird food-centered and highly infantilizing group dates. "Kid's day" requires crayoning in coloring books and playing Candy Land. Airport dates in-volve putting on strange costumes, pretending to meet each other getting off planes, and competing to properly guess how many men will go into the restroom immediately after deplaning. Food dates include eating entire meals by taste-testing at a large grocery store, organizing fruit juice tastings (as opposed to wine tastings), making a giant pop-sicle in a trash can at the local ice plant, and eat-ing all of the leftovers in the fridge. In sum, these adults suggest that one avoids sex by engaging in activities more appropriate for a prepubescent person, and by displacing sexual desire onto desire for food. But do teens accept this solution hook, line, and sinker?

No doubt, many fundamentalist teens reject infantilizing food dates and resist the chastity campaign in various ways. Letters published in *Brio* indicate a constant negotiation of the idea of chastity. The editors receive a thousand letters each month, most of them asking questions about boys and sex.[11] *Brio* letters often focus on looking for loopholes in the chastity mandate. A girl from Ohio writes, "This is kind of an embarrassing question, but if the guy doesn't have a name or face, is it okay to fantasize about your wedding night and what sex will be like after you're mar-ried?" The answer is no, because you should "strive to fill your mind with things that won't leave you frustrated or wanting what you can't have,"[12] but it's hard to believe that teens who have signed chastity pledge cards don't have sexual fantasies made safe through a prefatory marriage fantasy. Although Shellenberger consistently tells girls that even tongue-kissing is off-limits, they continue to ask "how much fooling around is acceptable by God?"[13] One girl, who signs herself "Feeling Guilty," thinks she has found a potential loophole in her chastity pact with God: "I have pledged to remain sexually pure until marriage. But what if Jesus comes back before I get married? I want to know how it feels to have sex. Is this a horrible thing to want?"[14] Since many fundamentalists believe the Rapture could happen at any time, this girl voices a legitimate concern inspired by a fundamentalist, literal reading of the Bible.[15]

Occasionally, *Brio* girls write in to flaunt the fact that they engage in sexual activity without feel-ing guilty. One particularly outspoken girl writes:

> You're probably going to tell me that petting will lead to intercourse . . . [but me and] this guy . . . have done some things that you would probably consider wrong, but I don't think it is, and I don't feel a bit guilty about it. I don't think it will lead to us having sex, because I'm not ready until I'm married. He doesn't pressure me at all and says he respects me for not wanting to have sex. So my question is, what if—because of my own values and beliefs—I don't think it's wrong? And don't tell me to get out of the relationship because I don't want to and I won't.[16]

There's no telling how many of such letters *Brio* receives, since it behooves their own agenda to print more letters from guilty girls than unrepen-tant ones, but it is clear from the letters that *Brio's* adult editors choose to print that readers do not merely internalize the chastity directive without substantial questioning, negotiation, and varying degrees of resistance. On the other hand, it is also clear that such letters also aid *Brio* in constructing the chastity directive. From the editors' perspective, the letters prove that teen sexuality really is out of control; the existence of the "fallen" girl enables the therapeutic salvation narrative to exist.

Breakaway does not represent fallen boys, and does not print letters from Christian boys asking how far is too far to go sexually. Because their desires are uncontrollable once unleashed, the boys given a voice in *Breakaway* avoid any contact, or even being alone with a female: "I prefer group dating because there's a lot less temptation. Because I'm a Christian, I want to stay away from *risky* situations . . . it's better to go out in groups. It's *safer* and it's more fun" (emphasis added).[17] Group dates save boys from their own lustfulness and also shield them from the occasional female temptress. When a boy writes that his girl friend wants to have sex, *Breakaway* advises: "You ought to end this relationship pronto, ASAP, yesterday and real quick. I promise you that your girlfriend is much more likely to bring you down than you are to bring her up. You may think you're strong enough to stay with her without caving in. But be warned: Samson thought the same thing, and before it was all over he was blind, beaten, betrayed and bald (see Judges 16)."[18] This boy, like the girl who feared Jesus would come before she did, is puzzled because his desires don't seem to mesh with biblical directives. He cannot find any place in the Bible that condemns premarital sex. The Bible forbids adultery, lust, and fornication with prostitutes, and it proclaims marriage to be a holy sacrament, but it never explicitly forbids premarital sex.[19] The Bible serves as a rulebook for fundamentalist teens, but the rulebook can backfire when teens study it and recognize the contradictory dimensions of the readings that their church puts forth as unquestionable, or when they notice the differences between isolated scripture and the same scripture in its context. Through the Bible, teens may end up negotiating the very rules that adults say the Bible teaches unequivocally.[20] On the other hand, teens who don't know the Bible

well enough will find themselves trumped by well-versed adults. At one Christian school some boys questioned the rule that their hair had to be short. Their teacher pointed to I Corinthians 11:14, "If a man has long hair, it is a disgrace to him." One student thought he had a winning counterargument: "'But didn't Jesus have long hair?' The teacher was indignant and cautioned the students that the pictures they see of Jesus are just representations painted by sinful men. The Bible teaches that long hair is a sin and also teaches that Jesus never sinned; Jesus, therefore, could not have had long hair. Case closed."[21] The boys lost because they countered with a commonsensical assertion about Jesus' hair rather than a biblically based argument for long hair. ("What about Samson and Delilah?" might have been more productive.)

Negotiating rules is highly problematic for teens wishing to follow commandment number five: honor thy father and mother. In fact, some teens may not negotiate the chastity directive or other rules at all. Why would they want to tamper with their relationships with God and their community? To nonbelievers, the faith of born-agains is almost unfathomable, and one cannot help but wonder what teens get out of it. The peace and joy that can come through a personal relationship with God constitutes the primary earthly reward for being born again. In addition, belief in a rule book (the Bible) offers believers a sense of stability and order, and a place in a community of like-minded folks. Given the tortuous isolation and feelings of helplessness and despair that many teenagers encounter, it's not difficult to see why an ordered belief system and a community of fellow believers might be appealing to some teens. The fundamentalist belief system, which to outsiders may seem to be all rules and prohibition ("don't have sex"), offers structure, stability, and community to youth. This community is a locus for a variety of activities, ranging from picnics and bake sales to hospital picketing and school board electioneering. It is the community's public-sphere activities that cause concern among non-fundamentalists, particularly among those who support reproductive freedom.

Female Retention and Male Expulsion

The adult compilers of the *Teen Study Bible* tell readers unequivocally that "God is pro-life."[22] Psalm 139 is one key text used to support the fundamentalist anti-choice stance. The New International Version of the psalm reads, in part, "You created my inmost being; you knit me together in my mother's womb. . . . My frame was not hidden from you when I was made in the secret place. When I was woven together in the depths of the earth, your eyes saw my unformed body. All the days ordained for me were written in your book before one of them came to be." While the Bible never explicitly condemns abortion, fundamentalist anti-choice advocates use Psalm 139 to prove the personhood of unborn life.[23] Fundamentalists use this passage to show how thoroughly God knows you and your body and, furthermore, to show that your body is not only his creation but also *his*. Another biblical passage supporting this idea is spoken by Paul in 1 Corinthians 6:19–20: "Do you not know that your body is a temple of the Holy Spirit, who is in you, whom you have received from God? You are not your own; you were bought at a price. Therefore honor God with your body."[24] Crucially, this means that you cannot "choose" whether or not to have sex or to terminate a pregnancy in your body, because it is *not your body*. Your body is simply on loan from God. I will turn to a discussion of eating disorders shortly, but suffice it to say here that fundamentalist therapeutic discourses on eating disorders use the same "you are not your own" biblical scripture to explain why eating disorders are ungodly.

As an adult the properly containing (and contained) *Brio* body should retain, not abort, any fetuses that may grow inside her, and she should work to insure that others live by the same belief system. Unlike *Breakaway* boys, whom the magazine conveys as belchers who wear dirty socks and rarely shower, *Brio* girls express great concern about bodily containment: How do I tell a friend she has bad breath? How can I manage my sweaty hair after gym class? The same kinds of anxieties can be found in the letters section of secular magazines, and both kinds of magazines function as public therapy spaces where problems erupt, are confessed and diagnosed, and a solution or cure is offered. A crucial difference between secular and fundamentalist girl's magazines, however, is that whereas both tend to promote certain ideas about "proper" (odor-free, non-sweaty) femininity, the secular magazines promote a gendered body that is only implicitly politicized, while the body promoted in *Brio* is an explicitly politicized, pro-life body. The message sent to teen girls is that God created "your" body, loves "your" body, and lent it to you, and His will is to fill your rental flesh with progeny. Although the young female body is urged to be chaste, once married God has designed her body to be penetrated and filled.

The male teen, conversely, embodies the principle of expulsion and impenetrable hardness. Fundamentalist media endeavor to construct the controlled, chaste teen male body mainly by encouraging rigorous bodily activities *besides* sex. Boys maintain self-control through sports and body building; such vigorous, structured activity is necessary to cure or at least stymie their lust. Inherently more reckless, boys must exert much more self-control than girls. But unlike girls, they are allowed to express their recklessness through their overflowing bodies. Boys are encouraged to ejaculate spit, vomit, and sweat, but not semen. *Breakaway* humor often centers around the very bodily humors disavowed in *Brio*. Once the reader mail column centered on "spew stories," where teen boys wrote about their most embarrassing vomiting experiences.

Breakaway boys' earthly bodies are (ideally) metaphorically clean (chaste), yet they are literally filthy. One *Breakaway* cartoon shows a boy eating junk food and explaining, "Actually, Mom, potato chips are very good for you! The loud crunching scares away germs!"[25] Since boys are assumed to be quite insalubrious, scaring away germs is certainly in order. Interestingly, the dirty, spewing *Breakaway* boy never seems to fart or use the toilet. That is, this boy is only grotesque in carefully circumscribed ways. He transgresses boundaries only from the waist up. The *Breakaway* boy exists somewhere between the "classical body—a refined, orifice-less, laminated surface" that *Brio* constructs, a body whose higher stratum is emphasized while the lower stratum is disavowed, and the vulgar "lower-class" coded body that Laura Kipnis has described as the *Hustler* hardcore porn body: "a gaseous, fluid-emitting, *embarrassing* body, one continually defying the strictures of bourgeois manners and mores and instead governed by its lower intestinal tract—a body threatening to erupt at any moment. *Hustler*'s favorite joke is someone accidentally defecating in church" (emphasis in original).[26] The *Breakaway* body threatens to erupt at any moment, but only through the nose or mouth, and certainly not in church! This body violates what Kipnis, following anthropologist Mary Douglas, calls "'pollution' taboos and rituals—these being a society's set of beliefs, rituals, and practices having to do with dirt, order, and hygiene," but it only does so within circumscribed limits.[27] Both unhygienic *and* unscatalogical, the *Breakaway* body can have its cake and eat it too, as long as the cake exits through an upper-body cavity.

Obsession with the body is considered "vain" in the world of *Brio*, but *Breakaway* encourages boys to build up buff physiques in order to enhance their masculine self-esteem. *Breakaway* de-emphasizes the fact that muscles may increase a boy's sex appeal, and, while *Brio* advises girls not to unfairly arouse boys with "suggestive"

clothing, *Breakaway* never warns boys to hide their sweaty muscles from their horny peers. Yet Christian sports, and body building in particular, are as erotic/masturbatory as secular sports and body building. A *Breakaway* feature on weightlifting describes a sexually charged male body that would be unthinkable in a fundamentalist co-ed environment:

> THE PUMP. It must be experienced firsthand because no sensation compares. Your shoulders throb, your chest aches, your skin tingles. Blood pulses through your veins like a pack of angry earthworms. Sweat streams down the rippled bands of sheer steel you once called your belly. When you stand on your toes, your calves threaten to pop out at the knees. You flex your biceps, and two bowling balls appear. You look at yourself in the mirror and grunt, "Hello, Hulk!"[28]

Although the magazine urges safety and moderation in work-outs, it also applauds (somewhat parodically) the bulging masculine body. Likewise, a study guide on steroids does not find body building problematic or "vain." While advantages of a drug-free work out include "your steady loves your new appearance" and "you look fantastic! Members of the opposite sex are keeping an eye on you," steroids are condemned as a "shortcut" that will make you "overly aggressive" and "cocky."[29] In other words, out of control. By advocating body building, therapeutic fundamentalist media again solve the problem of how virgin boys can be "real men." Weight-lifting represents not a "feminine" obsession with one's looks but rather a business contract with God whereby if you don't cheat with steroids you will gain self-esteem through your muscles. Only through cheating will you become cocky and aggressive—excessively masculine and therefore no longer self-controlled. Paradoxically, lifting should be a diversion from sexuality, yet onanistic weightlifting produces a more sexually alluring—even a cocky and aggressive—body.

To some extent, autoerotic weightlifting is

hoped to function as a substitute for autoerotic genital activity.[30] Although it would be best if boys could avoid erections altogether, according to most fundamentalist experts erections in and of themselves are not sinful, as long as they are not accompanied by mental images of other bodies. This was the source of the *Edge TV* masturbator's agony. He could not masturbate without fantasizing about girls. If masturbation does occur, it must not be accompanied by lustful thoughts. Caught between a rock and a hard place, as it were, the teen boy is basically denied guilt-free penile tumescence. The weightlifter can at least increase the bulk of the rest of his body.

Girls apparently have less to feel guilty about, since they are generally assumed to be less horny than boys. A cartoon in Shellenberger's *Guys and a Whole Lot More* illustrates a "humorous" reaction to the female's puberty-induced anxieties: a girl asks her pharmacist, "Do you have an antidote to hormone poisoning?"[31] Girls are assumed to be sexually curious (hormonally poisoned), but girls' books, magazines, and videos ignore masturbation, since masturbation is basically seen as a boy's problem. Needless to say, weightlifting is not an option for Christian girls wanting to rechannel their sexual energy into the quest for the ideal body.

Fundamentalism and Eating Disorders

Advice from *258 Great Dates While You Wait* includes giant popsicle dates and group dates at fast food restaurants. These dates function, in theory, by displacing desire for sex onto desire for food. For this chastity tactic to work, however, one must not have a fraught relationship with food.[32] The efficacy of fundamentalist media is weakened by its tendency to ignore the ways that girls and boys may view food differently. Transferring desire from sex to food may be easier for the gluttonous *Breakaway* boy than for the comparatively abstemious *Brio* girl.

Appropriating liberal feminist discourse,

Christian books and cassettes on eating disorders argue that secular notions of the "ideal female body" have a negative effect on girls' self-esteem, but fundamentalist media nonetheless tend to replicate secular culture's construction of gendered food consumption. Although *258 Great Dates* emphasizes that all teens live off of junk food, the book also indicates that girls will gravitate to salads on dates and that boys can never be overglutted. One group date involves driving to various fast food restaurants and eating a little bit at a time until you're full: "Still hungry? Though the girls may not be, the guys are!"[33] A *Breakaway* cartoon illustrates the insatiable boy's appetite. As a happy cat enters the kitchen through a hinged cat-door, an equally happy boy, licking his chops, exits the refrigerator via a hinged boy-door.[34]

Another cartoon in *Breakaway* shows a girl speaking to a boy whose mouth is obscenely crammed full of junk food: shakes, pizza slices, hot-dogs, and fried chicken legs (fig. 3). It is unclear from the image whether he is consuming or expelling his lode. The cartoon was part of a contest where boys saw the image without the artist's caption and competed to come up with the best tag line. The artist's caption, printed with the contest winners', interpreted the image as referencing consumption rather than expulsion: "How much weight does coach want you to put on for football?" Several contest winners interpreted the cartoon as representing expulsion: "Biff attempts the world's first atomic burp"; "After hearing what goes into processed food, Hank coughed up every single burger, hot dog and slice of pizza he had ever eaten." One winning caption reads the image as representing both consumption and expulsion: "Suddenly, Warren was forced to admit he had an eating disorder." The humor of this caption, accompanied by the cartoon, would be impossible were it not for the assumption that boys consume excessively, but such consumption is not pathological. If boys really binged and purged, it would be un-Christian to laugh at Warren. This cartoon is symptomatic of how *Breakaway* approaches

Christian boys may consume excessively, but such consumption is not considered pathological. Carmel V. France. Image from *Breakaway* magazine, February 1996.

boys and food. While food articles in *Brio* focus on baking cookies for others or making low-fat milkshakes, in *Breakaway* one finds articles with titles like "More Thanksgiving Maggot, Anyone?"[35] In sum, *Brio* and *Breakaway* assume boys and girls to have different appetites not only sexually but also gastronomically. This represents both a magnification of secular culture's construction of sexuality (where chastity is not encouraged but men and women still tend to be seen as sexually opposite) and a mirroring of secular culture's construction of gendered food consumption.

Fundamentalists often explain eating disorders as problems that are induced by the secular world that can be cured by religion. Because of society's pressure on women to have a certain kind of body, girls lack self-esteem; an improved relationship with Jesus is the key to solving this problem. By studying the Bible, girls with eating disorders will come to see that their bodies are "temples of the Holy Spirit." Thus, the cure for eating disorders is religious, but the causes are not. Fundamentalist therapeutic discourse never portrays girls' eating disorders as stemming from family pressures, an authoritarian home-life, or the tremendous pressures that being a "good Christian" can entail.

Focus on the Family offers therapeutic media

addressing virtually every difficulty of daily life, so it's not surprising that they've produced a cassette on eating disorders. On this tape, former bulimic Jackie Barrille offers some insight into fundamentalist perceptions of eating disorders and the female body. Although fundamentalist media tend to construct girls as emotive, Barrille explains how eating disorders are a means of self-expression resulting from years of *internalized* feelings. In addition, she argues that eating disorders are primarily a matter of taking control of one's life. Barrille says, "In eating huge amounts of food I felt a release, a freedom I had never felt in my life."[36] She explains, however, that by surrendering control to the Holy Spirit, you won't need to binge and purge to seek control over your body. (Interestingly, the same theological concepts can be used for both dieting and for controlling compulsive dieting. A testimonial printed on a fundamentalist weight loss manual reads, "Thanks to First Place, I'm controlling my weight with a power greater than my own.") Barrille does not address how devout fundamentalists who already have a personal relationship with Jesus nonetheless become eating disordered. Might resistance to giving all control to God be a contributing factor to developing eating disorders in the first place? Or might the imperative to surrender oneself spiritually actually contribute to a woman's desire to have total control over her earthly body?

Eating disorders are a way to assert control when faced with difficult and disempowering personal/familial situations. The surrendering of control to parents that is mandated by disciplinary child rearing, the typical fundamentalist parenting style, may thus play a pivotal role in the development of teen anorexia and bulimia. Disciplinary child rearing demands the child submit his/her will and body to parents. As the autobiographical narratives of Christian anorexics explain, authoritarian parents tend to force their eating disordered children to eat, and discipline them harshly when they fail to properly consume. Cherry Boone O'Neill, daughter of Christian singer Pat Boone, recounts how her authoritarian parents made her feel bodily shame when they forced her to wear children's clothing at age twelve, even though she had the sexually mature body of a sixteen-year-old. At eighteen, when she resisted their directive not to vomit, they said she was acting like a child and spanked her. The drive to make her submit to parental control backfired when her resistance was bound up in the development of eating disorders. Anorexia and bulimia became a means of resisting parental control while maintaining the masochism that underpinned the child-parent relationship. That is, O'Neill asserted herself, but only at the expense of herself.

O'Neill begins her autobiography, *Starving for Attention,* by explaining how fasting helped her maintain her anorexic regime:

> Fasting on Thanksgiving Day had really saved me . . . when I was asked why I had not loaded up my plate like everyone else I just answered with spiritual overtones, "I'm fasting today," and that was that! . . . My mother called from the kitchen . . . "Daddy wants to have Communion together before we say the blessing, okay?" . . . My mind was computing feverishly: crackers are about twelve calories and I'll probably eat about one twelfth, so that's one calorie, and . . . how many calories does a six-ounce glass of grape juice have? . . . Too many. I'll just pretend to drink the grape juice . . . maybe I can pretend to eat the cracker, too.[37]

Religion is uncannily woven throughout this family melodrama, as "fasting" sanctifies self-starvation, and Christ's blood and body become an impediment to weight loss. While mother works in the kitchen and daddy presides over the religious ceremony—a familiar division of domestic labor—the resistant daughter destroys herself through the very act of resistance. O'Neill's sad tale stands in stark contrast to the narratives of fundamentalist youth magazines, which, *Brio*'s tormented advice column letters notwithstanding, strive to be relentlessly peppy. Boone had a

personal relationship with Jesus, yet because of her faith her eating disorders continued long after she married and left home. Fundamentalist doctrine demanded that she submit to her husband in the same way she had submitted to her father, and she continued to resist patriarchal submission. Boone explains that only by leaving fundamentalism could she finally cure herself.

I do not mean to valorize fundamentalist anorexics' resistance as a feminist tactic, or to hold up Boone as emblematic of all fundamentalists with eating disorders, but rather to complicate what eating disorders might mean for women of strong faith. Across disciplines (medicine, psychology, feminist sociology), researchers tend to assume that eating disorders are areligious. Yet a number of researchers have argued, erroneously, that anorexia can be traced back to the fasting practices of medieval nuns and other religious women. They assume that eating disorders have always existed, but now they have been drained of their (Catholic) religious impetus and are a result of twentieth-century consumer culture's images of slender female bodies. Historian Joan Jacobs Brumberg has quite rightly argued that tracing eating disorders back to the tradition of medieval fasting women is highly problematic:

> To describe premodern women . . . as anorexic is to flatten differences in female experience across time and discredit the special quality of eucharistic fervor and penitential asceticism as it was lived and perceived. To insist that medieval holy women had anorexia nervosa is, ultimately, a reductionist argument because it converts a complex human behavior into a simple biomedical mechanism. (It certainly does not respect important differences in the route to anorexia.) To conflate the two is to ignore the cultural context and the distinction between sainthood and patienthood.[38]

Calling medieval saints anorexic erases the complexity of their faithful practices.[39] But Brumberg's argument against reading modern anorexia in light of the history of fasting seems to assume that the modern faster lacks spirituality, or, as she further argues, "From the vantage point of the historian, anorexia nervosa appears to be a *secular* addiction to a new kind of perfectionism, one that *links personal salvation to the achievement of an external body configuration rather than an internal spiritual state*" (emphasis added).[40]

For fundamentalists, however, the most mundane acts of daily life can have holy justification. If anorexia is indeed an "addiction" to a particular kind of perfectionism, it need not be a purely secular addiction. There is no transhistorical link between Catholic medieval fasters and contemporary eating disordered evangelical Protestants. But this does not mean that twentieth-century eating disorders must be, by their very nature, "secular addictions." For some fundamentalists eating disorders may have a holy justification. The fundamentalist may see ridding herself of the flesh as an act of purification. For example, Barrille recounts how when one fundamentalist anorexic came close to dying her soul left her body and felt weightless as it headed toward the proverbial white light, but Jesus told her that it was not yet her time, and she returned to her body. In contrast to her freed spirit, her anorexic body seemed unbearably heavy. For her, the desire to lose her body was intricately bound up in the desire to be more spiritual: less body meant more spirit.

Of course, loss of flesh not only means less body, but also a transcendence of sexuality through the reduction or elimination of breasts, of menstruation, and of the wider hips that puberty brings to teens. For both secular and religious women, eating disorders are intricately bound up in feelings about sexuality. By not eating, a girl erases many of the bodily changes wrought by puberty, and for the fundamentalist girl under tremendous pressure to remain bodily and spiritually pure, the desire to erase sexuality may be particularly strong. The desire to drive out sin, to find "an antidote for hormone poisoning,"

may well be a motivation for teen anorexics who have vowed to remain sexually pure. After all, the strictures of eating disorders bear a strange resemblance to those of chastity: maintain bodily control, subdue carnal drives, attempt to displace desire for food/sex onto other activities. Teens who reject the therapeutic advice of chastity manuals and videos may find in eating disorders their own "cure" for their sexuality. I do not mean to suggest that chaste fundamentalists are naturally more inclined to eating disorders than sexually active nonreligious girls. My point, rather, is that fundamentalist adults produce therapeutic media to help their youth escape from tremendous peer pressure to drink, smoke, or engage in sexual activity, but they replace those pressures with another set of potentially overwhelming pressures. Eating disorders are a means of coping with the different ways that religion, families, and popular culture simultaneously strive to discipline girls' bodies.

Walking the Straight and Narrow

Fundamentalist youth media are designed to straighten teens on their already narrow paths, directing them away from sexuality, liberalism, and pro-choice sentiments. Fundamentalist culture offers community and a sense of belonging, and fundamentalist media bolster the potency of that community. The chaste Christian youth of today are, if they stay on track, the youth pastors, Christian pop stars, women's health clinic barricaders, creationism pushers, and school prayer advocates of tomorrow. When you put it this way, these youth seem like "The Enemy." Yet fundamentalist youth are not the most formidable of foes. They are alienated and confused, just like everyone else enduring the torments of puberty. For some, fundamentalist beliefs no doubt exacerbate such torments, while others find their faith helps assuage their suffering.

Parents recognize that during the rebellious

teen years their children may drift from their faith. Adults consider teens the most fragile links in the fundamentalist chain, and this is why so much media is directed to them. If teens submit to the "liberal" values of MTV, as their elders fear, will they come back to the Lord as adult prayer warriors, parents, activists, and voters? And, most important, will they ever enter the Kingdom of Heaven? Salvation is the primary concern of fundamentalist parents, a fact that is all too easily forgotten by secular critics who fear fundamentalist politics but make no attempt to understand the tenets of their faith. If you don't believe in heaven and hell, it is difficult to understand why magazines such as *Brio* and *Breakaway*, or "Pet Your Dog, Not Your Date" t-shirts, which may seem downright silly, are no laughing matter for Christian parents. Fundamentalist media help keep children within the fold, which is absolutely crucial for parents who don't want their children to burn in hell for all eternity.

We must not conceptualize teen religious choices in the same way that fundamentalist adults conceptualize teen sexuality. That is, we should not see teenagers as passive victims of religion, just as their parents see them as victims of their own sexually maturing bodies. Fundamentalist teens are capable of making informed decisions, choosing to follow in their parents' religious footsteps or to leave the church. Sociologist of religion Nancy Tatom Ammerman observes that "although few people who grow up as sectarians drop out of religion entirely, at least 40 percent switch to other denominations by adulthood."[41] In her year-long participant observation study of a fundamentalist church, Ammerman found that many youth "drop out of church when they are old enough to say 'no' to their parents . . . Rather than leaving religion entirely, many 'convert' to other denominations and become among the most committed leaders of the same liberal churches they grew up disparaging."[42]

We need to consistently question our own motivations in studying these youth.[43] For secular critics, it can be tempting to see teenagers as the weak links in fundamentalism, as potential converts to a more enlightened secular humanist (or Marxist, queer, feminist) way of looking at the world. Like fundamentalists, academics believe that words and images have the power to transform. We also allow our lives to be consumed by sequential goals, entering (and sometimes attempting to revise) a highly structured life system that pre-existed us: coursework, dissertation, exploitative part-time teaching, miscellaneous essay publishing and conference-going, book contract, book, job (maybe), committee work, three-year review, more books (maybe), tenure (maybe), retirement courtesy of TIAA-CREF. The ways that these stages can consume our every waking moment are not as far removed from the born-again modus operandi as we might like to believe, and our lives are certainly not devoid of dogma. Academics and fundamentalists are deeply invested in salvation narratives, narratives that we/they hope will seduce others into the fold. Belief sustains us all.

Notes

1   On the history of Focus on the Family's media production, see Eithne Johnson, "The Emergence of Christian Video and the Cultivation of Videovangelism," in *Media, Culture, and the Religious Right*, eds. Linda Kintz and Julia Lesage (Minneapolis: University of Minnesota Press, 1998), 191–210.

2   I use the word "fundamentalist" to refer to conservative, (mostly) nondenominational, evangelical Protestants who identify themselves as having been "re-born" and who take the Bible as the literal word of God. "Fundamentalist" is the mainstream's generic term for right-wing born-again Christians, and I use it with this commonly understood meaning in mind. Some conservative born-agains embrace the fundamentalist label, while others see it as a pejorative word that secular culture uses to deride them. Some non-born-agains mistakenly use the word "fundamentalist" to refer to all

evangelicals, or think that all born-agains are politically conservative. To be evangelical is to believe that disseminating the Word and converting others is crucial to one's faith. All fundamentalists are evangelical, but not all evangelicals are fundamentalists by any means. On the variety of evangelical cultures, see Randall Balmer's *Mine Eyes Have Seen the Glory: A Journey into the Evangelical Subculture in America* (New York: Oxford University Press, 1993). There is also a three-part PBS video series narrated by Balmer and based on the book. For a helpful historical overview, see also Nancy T. Ammerman, "North American Protestant Fundamentalism," in *Media, Culture, and the Religious Right,* ed. Kintz and Lesage, 55–113.

3 Mimi White, *Tele-Advising: Therapeutic Discourse in American Television* (Chapel Hill: University of North Carolina Press, 1992), 177.

4 L. A. Kauffman, "220,000 Jesus Fans Can't Be Wrong: Praise the Lord, and Mammon," *Nation* (September 26, 1994): 306–10.

5 Johnson left the *Breakaway* editorial staff in 1995 but continues to write Focus on the Family books.

6 "Dear Susie," *Brio* (April 1995): 5.

7 Some fundamentalist media seem to blame girls for "tempting" boys to rape them, but when girls write to *Brio* saying that they or their friends have been raped, *Brio* takes them seriously and advises counseling. *The Teen Study Bible,* distributed by Focus on the Family, says that girls are not at fault for being raped, and refers readers to a passage from Deuteronomy that confirms this (22:25–27). However, the biblical passage directly preceding this one says that girls who are raped in the city should be stoned to death along with their rapists, since they did not cry out so that someone could rescue them. Only girls raped in the country, where no one is around, are not at fault. In other words, there are situations when girls could prevent rape but don't. *The Teen Study Bible: New International Version* (Grand Rapids, MI: Zondervan, 1993).

8 Susie Shellenberger, *Guys and a Whole Lot More: Advice for Teen Girls on Almost Everything* (Grand Rapids, MI: Fleming H. Revell, 1994), 160. Shellenberger's advice book is comprised of *Brio* letters and her answers to them.

9 Michel Foucault, *The History of Sexuality, Vol. 1: An Introduction* (New York: Vintage, 1980), 21.

10 See my essay "Shake, Rattle and Roll: Production and Consumption of Christian Youth Culture," *Afterimage* (February/March 1995): 19–22.

11 Susie Shellenberger, "What Is Sexual Purity?" *Brio* (October 1995): 26.

12 Shellenberger, *Guys and a Whole Lot More,* 154.

13 "Dear Susie," *Brio* (April 1995): 5.

14 "Dear Susie," *Brio* (March 1995): 6. Shellenberger responds, "No one knows the time or date of Christ's return. He may come back before you receive your next issue of *Brio,* and if He does, sex won't be the ONLY thing you'll miss out on. What about college life, grad school or giving birth? Heaven is going to be so TERRIFIC that none of the things of seeming importance *now* will matter when we're standing right next to Jesus Christ."

15 Premillennialists believe that the Rapture is when the saved are delivered from the earth, before the Tribulation (when the Antichrist rules the earth for seven years), and the Second Coming of Christ. Postmillennialists hold that believers will not be raptured before the Tribulation. Postmillennialist thought is not extinct, but premillennialism tends to dominate born-again theology.

16 Shellenberger, *Guys and a Whole Lot More,* 155.

17 "Guys Gab about Going Out," *Breakaway* (February 1996): 28.

18 "Yo Duffy!" *Breakaway* (February 1996): 16.

19 While sex outside of marriage is nothing new, as a concept "premarital sex" is a modern invention. When fundamentalists apply the Bible to twentieth-century modes of thought and action, they sometimes find it only addresses their modern problem or issue tangentially. One advice book notes, for example, that "other than condemning gluttony, the Bible does not mention anything about eating disorders. But it does offer great encouragement to those who struggle with poor self-esteem, loneliness, and the frustrating problems of adolescence." Joey O'Connor, "Eating Disorders: Starving for Attention," in *Hot Buttons II,* ed. Annette Parrish (Ventura, CA: Regal Books, 1987), 101.

20 Fundamentalist adults believe that the Bible teaches certain unequivocal lessons, but this does not mean that they do not understand the Bible to be a complicated, nuanced text. Born-agains realize that the Bible's messages are not always simple and easily available to readers. That's why they often participate in Bible study groups. A good illustration of how fundamentalists

study and use the Bible can be seen in James Ault's video *Born-Again* (dist. James Ault Productions Box 493, Northampton, MA 01061).

21 This incident is recounted in Nancy Tatom Ammerman, *Bible Believers: Fundamentalists in the Modern World* (1987; New Brunswick, NJ: Rutgers University Press, 1993), 181.

22 *Teen Study Bible,* 816.

23 There are places in the Bible where inducing miscarriage or killing pregnant women is advocated to smite one's enemies. Some former fundamentalists use these passages to refute the fundamentalist anti-choice platform. See Poppy Dixon, *The NC-17 Bible,* at the Postfundamentalist Web Site: http://www.postfun .com/pfp/NC-17Bible.html. On the development of the fundamentalist anti-abortion platform, see Susan Harding, "If I Should Die Before I Wake: Jerry Falwell's Pro-Life Gospel," in *Uncertain Terms: Negotiating Gender in American Culture,* ed. Faye Ginsburg and Anna Lowenhaupt Tsing (Boston: Beacon Press, 1990), 76–97.

24 Cited in Parrish, *Hot Buttons II,* 102. Paul is actually condemning fornication with prostitutes, but fundamentalists decontextualize the passage to make it pro-life. Parrish uses the passage to discourage eating disorders.

25 *Breakaway* back cover (June 1995).

26 Laura Kipnis, "(Male) Desire and (Female) Disgust: Reading *Hustler,*" in *Cultural Studies,* ed. Lawrence Grossberg, Cary Nelson, and Paula Treichler (New York: Routledge, 1992), 375, 376.

27 Ibid., 379.

28 Manny Koehler, "Don't Gag at the Bench Press," *Breakaway* (March 1995): 8.

29 Edward N. McNulty, *Hazardous to Your Health: AIDS, Steroids and Eating Disorders* (Loveland, CO: Group, 1994), 27.

30 There is a historical precedent for this use of sports to curb lustful activity in boys, the muscular Christianity movement of the turn of the last century. With roots in the English public schools, the idea behind muscular Christianity was that "Christian virtues, morality, manliness, and patriotism can be engendered through physical activity, recreation, and sports" (James A. Mathisen, "I'm Majoring in Sport Ministry: Religion and Sport in Christian Colleges," *Christianity Today* (May/ June 1998): 24–28). Muscular Christianity came to the United States in the 1860s, where it flowered in private high schools before being recognized by the YMCA as a way to evangelize to lower-class urban youth. Evangelist Dwight L. Moody should probably receive the greatest credit, however, for popularizing muscular Christianity in the 1880s. The movement died out by the 1920s. For a contemporary example of the use of sports to evangelize, see Sharon Mazer, "The Power Team: Muscular Christianity and the Spectacle of Conversion," *Drama Review* 38(4) (winter 1994): 162–88. The article title is somewhat misleading, as Mazer does not trace her analysis of contemporary sports ministry back to the muscular Christianity movement.

31 Shellenberger, *Guys and a Whole Lot More,* 156.

32 Like *258 Great Dates While You Wait, The Teen Study Bible* assumes that readers have untroubled relationships to food, asserting that "*physical hunger can easily be satisfied by eating some food.* However, the sex drive isn't like hunger, and intercourse isn't a ham sandwich. Sex isn't just physical—it's spiritual too" (emphasis added). Unnumbered page between 308 and 309.

33 Susie Shellenberger and Greg Johnson, *258 Great Dates While You Wait* (Nashville, TN: Broadman and Holman, 1995), 83.

34 *Breakaway* back cover (June 1995).

35 Andy Fletcher, "More Thanksgiving Maggot, Anyone?" *Breakaway* (November 1995): 22–23. This humorous article marvels at "repulsive" non-American food traditions (fried scorpions, monkey brains), an insect dinner hosted by the New York Entomological Society, and a menu from a Paris restaurant, when the city had been under siege for three months and restaurant patrons were treated to kabobs of dog's liver with herbed butter and cats garnished with rats.

36 Focus on the Family, Eating Disorders (Jackie Barrille), rec. 1982.

37 Cherry Boone O'Neill, *Starving for Attention: A Young Woman's Struggle and Triumph over Anorexia Nervosa* (Minneapolis: CompCare, 1991).

38 Joan Jacobs Brumberg, *Fasting Girls: The Emergence of Anorexia Nervosa as a Modern Disease* (Cambridge, MA: Harvard University Press, 1988), 46.

39 Medieval religious fasters engaged in a number of practices that definitively distance them from modern sufferers from eating disorders:

> Angela of Fogligno, for example, who drank pus from sores and ate scabs and lice from the bodies of the sick, spoke of the pus as being "as sweet as the eucharist." Other women saints were reported to miraculously multiply food. . . . The bodies of women were

also a source of food: mystical women exuded oil from their fingertips, lactated even though they were virgins, and cured disease with the touch of their saliva. (Brumberg, *Fasting Girls*, 45)

40 Ibid., 7.
41 Ammerman, *Bible Believers*, 184. Ammerman acknowledges that the General Social Survey—the source of her data—defines "sectarian" in a way that is "less-than-ideal." In the survey, "groups are categorized as 'sects' based on their small membership and deviance from the American norm, but this category may include everything from Jehovah's Witnesses to the Unification Church" (30).
42 Ibid., 186.
43 My own motivations and objectives in studying Christian youth culture have shifted since I wrote this essay in 1996. See *Shaking the World for Jesus: Media and Conservative Evangelicals* (Chicago: University of Chicago Press, forthcoming).

"Do We Look Like Ferengi Capitalists to You?" *Star Trek*'s Klingons as Emergent Virtual American Ethnics

Peter A. Chvany

The Imperial Klingon Forces, a nonprofit *Star Trek* fan club that advertised itself on the Internet recently, can be reached in care of a residential address at an apartment in Grand Forks, North Dakota.[1]

The prospect of Klingon warriors overrunning the United States from a secret base near Grand Forks probably fails to strike terror into the heart. I am aware of no recent calls for Klingon self-determination, repatriation, or insurgency. *Star Trek* fans, even those as much attracted to the shows' violent warrior races and explosive interstellar conflicts as to its messages of humanist tolerance, are not widely noted for their actual violence. And as a friend to whom I outlined this article reminded me, one obvious problem with treating Klingons as an American "ethnic" group is that they are fictional. Anyone who calls him- or herself a Klingon—and many do—does so in limited contexts, at *Star Trek* conventions or within the discursive subspace of an Internet/ Usenet newsgroup. The "real" ethnic identity of such individuals always proves to be something else. Like National Guardsmen, rather than the Michigan Militia, Klingons are warriors late at night, on weekends, or in moments stolen at the terminal on the job. They can distinguish a fantasy identity (and politics) from their real lives, even if to other *Trek* fans the militaristic rhetoric of some sectors of Klingon fandom comes across as "quasi-ss style."[2]

Yet at the 1994 annual symposium sponsored

by Education for Public Inquiry and International Citizenship (EPIIC), an undergraduate research program at Tufts University, Benedict Anderson noted that several competing factions in the bloody Bosnian ethnic crisis were buying arms with money raised through Internet solicitations. These appeals successfully targeted American and Canadian "ethnics" who identified with one or another Bosnian group attempting to "cleanse" the others, or to resist such cleansing. In North American terms, Anderson implied, the amounts raised were trivial: a few million dollars here and there. But those North American dollars, contributed by interest groups whose connections to the contested homeland were primarily emotional and nostalgic, and who were not at risk when the ordnance they funded did its work, had considerably more buying power on the European market, in "the homeland," than they had back "home" in North America. Anderson's study, *Imagined Communities,* had argued that the New World nation-states of the nineteenth century—and by extension, modern ideologies of nation and nationalism—were narrative byproducts, indeed fictions, of modern print capitalism. Now he extended his argument into the perilous techno-politico-cultural territory of the late twentieth century, where ideas of "the nation," "homeland," "kinship," "true faith," and "blood ties" are as effective and deadly as ever, maybe more so, despite—or because of?—the notorious uncertainties of "postmodern" identity categories. The Internet, that new frontier whose transformative potential had begun to seem a matter of market hype, figured in Anderson's discussion as a very real site of emergent political struggle, a multimedia late-capitalist textual space through which resurgent nationalisms create and disseminate their community self-conceptions, effectively defying both the liberal ideology of harmonious pluralism and the supposed impossibility, in the postmodern era, of taking simply defined ethnic identities seriously any more.

I call Klingons—who likewise throng the Internet—"American ethnics" with this serious set of stakes in mind. I court what Renan called the "grave mistake" of confusing ethnicity with nation, and of attributing to a mere "ethnographic" group the sovereignty of "really existing peoples," in order to investigate the productive lessons of deliberate ethnic misreading.[3] If Klingons are not an ethnic group, as seems obvious, then what are ethnicity's criteria? If it is a self-elected denomination, as we assume when we respect the polite custom of calling each ethnic group what *it* asks us to call it, then would we take *Star Trek* fans in leather armor, latex ridged-forehead masks, and long scraggly wigs seriously if they began to wear their regalia in public, or on the job, and demanded recognition? Would we politely serve them our best imitation *qagh?*[4] Is ethnic nationalism primarily a modern phenomenon that arises as a result of, or in reaction to, the growth of modern capitalist nation-states, as Anderson and many others argue? Or should we follow Anthony Smith's tactic of cross-culturally investigating the historical underpinnings of ethnic differentiation, in a belief that while *nationalism* is "a wholly modern phenomenon," it "incorporates several features of pre-modern *ethnie* and owes much to the general model of ethnicity which has survived in many areas until the dawn of the 'modern era'"?[5] Are ethnic groups best understood as having recognizable, distinct, unique cultures with their own cultural contents, or should ethnicity be regarded as one of the cultural discourses that polices the borders of "otherness," borders defined by the differences between one group and another, not the unique identity of either group alone?

I argue that ethnicity is a socially structured performance of contradictory ideological fictions.

I propose that we look at Klingons as "ethnics" precisely because their group identity *is* fictional and has a traceable history of recent origin, yet is nonetheless the object of debate, ongoing revision, and (re)construction. The shifting, seemingly accidental character of Klingon "identity" sheds light on contemporary popular and theoretical debates about ethnicity as a category of social difference. Like a mathematical "limiting case" that reveals the behavior of a function under nonroutine conditions, Klingons test commonsense assumptions about the nature of ethnicity. They exist outside ethnicity as people ordinarily experience it, since they exist outside reality entirely. Yet emergent Klingons are not *purely* fictional: they appear in living bodies at *Star Trek* conventions, hold Internet discussions, have a language and culture, and participate in the same political and cultural processes as other ethnic groups do— perhaps doubly so, since they participate both "in character" and "out of character." As emergent, marginal, and virtual ethnics (in the sense both of the "virtual" space of the Internet and of the physical sciences—"virtual" photons form the image in a mirror), Klingons allow us insight into the processes by which ethnic fictions acquire their peculiar form of reality in the daily lives of real people. I will discuss how and why the fictionality of those ethnic fictions, the staginess of their performances, gives way to belief in their reality, to conviction, to "identity." Klingon ethnicity is a new American ethnicity; the more interesting question is: where does it fit in the existing, complex scheme of American identities? Who are these emergent American ethnics? Are they truly new at all, or an old group in new clothing?

Ethnic Notions: Klingons on Screen

Literary critic Werner Sollors provides one of several recent reminders that ethnicity, around the world but perhaps especially in the United States, is an "ambiguous and elusive" term. Its slipperiness relates both to its use as a "safety valve" deflecting Americans (and people elsewhere) from discussing better-defined but more troublesome issues (race, power relations, class, gender, sexuality) and to the real contradictions of U.S. and world cultural diversity.[6]

Sollors attempts to make sense of U.S. ethnic confusions by reframing ethnicity in terms of conflicting languages of "consent and descent" that have been employed by groups from around the globe who "consented to become . . . Americans" but wished to preserve distinct descent-based heritages.[7] This approach leads him into difficulty in discussing groups who did *not* so consent (Native Americans, African slaves, conquered Mexicans), and occasionally betrays an urge to simplify ethnic contradictions rather than accounting fully for their complexity. But it has the value of highlighting experiential and cultural similarities across group faultlines and of foregrounding the relational quality of ethnic construction, the fact that one must first compare ethnicities to contrast them.

In America, the idea of ethnicity can refer to the "national" origins of people who immigrated primarily from Europe after the mid-nineteenth century: Irish Americans, Italian Americans, Polish Americans, and so on. Tellingly, earlier Germans, "Dutch," and Scots are generally considered part of the dominant "Anglo" "majority," even if they arrived relatively recently.[8] Ethnicity can also refer to religious groups, such as Jewish Americans, who may be identified (or self-identify) more with their traditions than with their nation of origin.

The idea of "ethnicity" is less commonly ascribed when the difference from the supposed norm is a matter of "race," as with Americans of African or indigenous descent. On the other hand, the Modern Language Association-affiliated Society for the Study of the Multi-Ethnic Literature of the United States (MELUS) tends to generalize the term to such "racial" groups. The case of Asian Americans is still less clear. The long-standing, starkly dualistic, "black or white" quality of "race" relations in the United States leads even many contemporary "multiculturalist" scholars to forget that American society never was only a matter of black and white. Asians have clearly faced devastating oppression, but some historians and critics find that oppression's character difficult to judge while the difference between "race" and "ethnicity" remains murky.[9] Chicanos and other people of Hispanic descent often suffer similar theoretical neglect. Like the category "Asian," the category "Hispanic" obscures some sharp internal differences—cultural, linguistic, or historical—by concentrating on one or two similarities such as language, or by ignorantly conflating disparate groups.[10] Yet "ethnicity" and "race" *can* function synonymously: Sollors reminds us that "before the rise of the word 'ethnicity,' the word 'race' was widely used. . . . The National Socialist genocide in the name of 'race' is what gave the word a bad name and supported the substitution."[11]

Once "ethnics" come to the attention of "mainstream" Americans, concerns about their status often focus on issues of language, which is regarded by many as a primary site of acculturation or resistance—witness the debate in the mid-1990s over "Ebonics" in Oakland, California. Finally, despite the position taken by critics like Sollors who see "race" as a special category of "ethnicity" rather than the other way around, the obvious bodily differences of physical appearance so dear to racist thinking often play a key role in ethnic differentiation even when race is otherwise believed not to be a factor.

Klingons, insofar as they exist, qualify as "ethnic" on all of these counts. Their appearance, especially since the first of the *Star Trek* films in 1979, marks them as non-"white," indeed nonhuman: their bony forehead ridges betoken both a beloved *Trek* tactic of inexpensive alien-making and a routine *Trek* conflation of cultural differences with visible, physical ones.[12] But even in the less high-budgeted original show, Klingons bore signs of racialized body typing. They were universally goateed and mustachioed, at a time when facial hair was most obviously associated with the Beats, and the Beats with jazz and black culture. They sported dark makeup: the color of a Klingon soldier glimpsed briefly in the early episode "Errand of Mercy" varies obviously from "blackface" to "whiteneck," and many other Klingon faces are smudgy, as if the bootblack were melting in the studio lights. And they were played, in two of three starring appearances in the first series, by actors of "ethnic" heritage known for playing "ethnic" roles: John Colicos as Kor in "Errand of Mercy," Michael Ansara as Kang in "Day of the Dove." The exception was William Campbell as Koloth in "The Trouble with Tribbles." Not coincidentally, this was the episode in which Klingons were least threatening, most humorous, and yet most strongly marked by a bodily difference that "told." The episode's Klingon spy who "passes" as a (somewhat swarthy) human aide-de-camp is discovered because tribbles, creatures that coo for all humans and some Vulcans, squawk when brought near him, as they do around all Klingons. Internet *Star Trek* fans claim that when Colicos "was called to play the part of Kor . . . the Cold War was going on, and the general thought was that of the Russians versus US. He suggested to the makeup artist to make him a futuristic Mongol."[13]

In more recent years, with the casting of African American actor Michael Dorn as the continuing Klingon character Worf, the racialized representation of the Klingons took a turn toward the domestic black Other rather than the swarthy foreigner. Klingons had become allies, rather than enemies, of the show's "United Federation of Planets," and the orphaned Worf had been raised on earth by (Russian Jewish) foster parents. The show's resulting "playing in the dark" did not lead to simplistic "black" stereotypes: Klingons also acquired a warrior code reminiscent of samurai *bushido* and ritual swords that might be variants on Middle Eastern scimitars.[14] Like Mr. Spock before him, or his contemporary crewmate Data—the android who wished to become human—Worf offered screenwriters an opportunity to investigate "human nature" by contrasting human crew members with nonhuman others, who usually proved "human" at heart. Such contrasts were all the more dramatically powerful the more nuanced the nonhuman Other in question.[15] But stereotypical ideas about blackness nevertheless affected the ethnic construction of Klingon nature in important ways. Although several guest Klingons were played by white actors (for example, entertainer John Tesh in "The Icarus Factor," or Worf's mate, played by Suzie Plakson), black actors were considered for Worf "mainly to simplify the application of the dark Klingon makeup."[16] The original series' Klingon darkness had thus passed into the realm of natural fact; or, to restate Hollywood's curious racist logic, the best actor for a once-"Mongolian" part is a black man. Dorn's commanding presence also seemed responsible for encouraging the show's production staff to imagine Klingons as sexually potent, emotionally demonstrative, physically threatening (but fully in control of their physicality), and in touch with a genuine, uncomplicated "masculine" identity and spirituality, even when they were female—attributes that had not been routinely combined in earlier representations of Klingons but that *are* routine components of the white imagination of African Americans, especially black men. A *TV Guide* article on guest Klingon James Worthy, the black basketball star, commented at length on his "stealthy moves, leonine grace, and . . . reputation as a gentle soul," traits all paradoxically appropriate to his transformation into the "surly, ferocious Klingon named Koral."[17] The paradox betrays a standard white racist longing for a perceived black authenticity, an erotic admiration of black bodies, and a complex fear of and attraction to cathartic black violence.[18]

But because even the white dominant cultural imagination is contradictory and multivalent, because Klingon ethnic construction had a prior history not limited to "the black image in the white mind,"[19] and because the extended histories and personnel changes of series television and serial film production lend themselves to the creation of formal and narrative counterdiscourses, there have been other notable (if problematic) aspects of Klingon "ethnicity." The sixth *Star Trek* feature

film, *The Undiscovered Country,* extended the old clichéd analogy between the Klingon Empire and the Soviet Union by imagining the Empire beset by energy crises and pollution, and open to both perestroika and détente with the Federation. In the same film, audiences were treated to Klingons with a wide range of skin tones, including Christopher Plummer's Orientalized General Chang, David Warner's relatively light-skinned Chancellor Gorkon, Dorn as Worf's grandfather, and background characters who ranged from off-white to dark black. Whether this increase in Klingon diversity indicated a renewed awareness in Hollywood of *Soviet* or *American* multiethnic complexity is less telling than the differentiation itself. Its offhanded pluralism played against its bizarre assumption that a Klingon named "Chang" might look vaguely "Asiatic" and enjoy tormenting our heroes by quoting Shakespeare while launching torpedoes at them. Was the audience expected to laugh at the stereotyping or with it, or accept it unconsciously, or all of the above? Meanwhile, casual dialogue in one 1988 *Next Generation* television episode hinted that some Klingons—or screenwriters—considered their difference from humans a matter of religion, asking Worf to join their insurrection against Federation "infidels" and Klingons who had too willingly acculturated to human norms. The Klingon rebels represented this mistake as a relinquishment of "birthright" in the biblical language of Jacob and Esau, but countered it with language reminiscent of the American popular conception of Islamic jihads ("Heart of Glory").[20] Later dramatizations of Klingon ritual and religion examined quasi-Buddhist (or Sufi? Hindu? Catholic?) meditation practices and starvation-induced visionary experiences. The Klingon culture-hero Emperor Kahless was resurrected in clone form like a postmodern Arthur ("Rightful Heir"), an allusion further strengthened late in 1995 when Worf and Kor (now an old ridge-headed man rather than a young blackfaced future-Mongol) went in search of Kahless's thousand-years-lost sword on an episode of *Deep Space Nine*. Thus throughout *Star Trek*'s history, Klingons have been markedly different from the Federation/human norm, despite the complex web of specific differences they have signified. But even in being different their culture has paralleled real human cultures at every turn.

Ethnic Notions:
Klingons in the Virtual Real World

Perhaps the most interesting factor in the representation of Klingon "ethnicity," however, is the Klingon language. Developed to add verisimilitude to the opening sequence of the first feature film (so that Klingons fleeing a menacing interstellar cloud entity could be translated in subtitles, like other non-English-speakers), Klingon became unexpectedly realistic when Paramount hired an academic linguist, Marc Okrand, to create something suitable. Okrand took the task seriously, attracting the attention not only of *Trek* fans but of other linguists. Thus at present, Klingon represents one of the most visible *Trek* subcultures. The Klingon Language Institute, for example, is licensed by Paramount; publishes a quarterly journal, *HolQeD* ("Language Science"), which is registered with the Library of Congress and abstracted in the Modern Language Association International Bibliography; boasts an international membership; sponsors a language course through the mails; and is translating the Bible and *Hamlet* into Klingon. But the Klingon Language Institute is only the tip of a Klingon chuchHuD. Because Okrand's *Klingon Dictionary* is available in the extensive *Star Trek* sections of most chain bookstores, Usenet newsgroups devoted to fan culture, Klingon or otherwise, now feature a small but noticeable number of bilingual or wholly Klingon postings.

The Klingon Dictionary cheekily suggests that to study a language, even a created one, *is* to study a recognizable and distinct "culture," promising that one can "learn to speak Klingon like a native"

even as the indicia (dis)claim that "this book is a work of fiction."[21] The text contains many in-jokes, like the fact that the word for the pesky "tribble" is pronounced "yick." But the introduction also employs sophisticated mock-sociological discussions of ethnic differentiation for comic effect, for example noting that "the word for *forehead* . . . is different in almost every dialect," presumably because Klingons' forehead ridges vary greatly.[22] Such moments, though intentionally amusing, repackage certain real-world ideologies of ethnicity in apparent seriousness. For example, the differences among the many Klingon dialects are said to have imperial stakes, since upon succession "the new emperor's dialect becomes the official dialect. . . . Klingons who do not speak [it] are considered either stupid or subversive."[23] In effect, political discrimination on the basis of a simultaneously linguistic and bodily difference—if the dialect and the forehead *do* go together—is so fundamental to "human nature" that Okrand imagines it applies universally to aliens as well.[24]

Science fiction fans who dislike *Star Trek* often point to such assumptions as evidence of the franchise's failure of imagination: *Trek*'s aliens never really think in nonhuman ways. *Trek* fans, on the other hand, proceed in their Internet postings to create an imagined Klingon community largely in accordance with such assumptions. Bison, a fan who wrote recently on the newsgroup alt.shared-reality.startrek.klingon (a space for collaborative fan fiction writing), referred to another fan's created character as a "halfbreed."[25] On the one hand, this remark alluded to fan debates about the smooth-foreheaded Klingons of the original series: they can be regarded as Klingon-human "fusion" hybrids bred by the Empire for use as intermediaries in dealings with the Federation, or overlooked as reflecting real-world budgetary constraints and thus without relevance to the series' internal chronology.[26] But Bison also echoed terrestrial attitudes about "mulattos" and other people of "mixed" descent, who are often believed to be unsure of their identity and to experience automatic rejection by both "parent" groups. The other fan's Klingon-Vulcan hybrid character "would never be accepted" by real Klingons, Bison opined. "Besides," he or she went on, "Klingons and Vulcans cannot procreate but Klingons and Romulans can."[27] This last remark illustrates the powerful certainty fans can bring to bear on topics that, properly speaking, no one can really have a definitive answer to. Since Vulcans and Romulans are pointedly defined in *Star Trek* as closely genetically related, one might expect Klingon interbreeding with either race to amount to the same thing.[28] But Bison believes otherwise and renders a definitive judgment that other fans must somehow respond to. Such certainty illustrates how contemporary real-world ideologies about ethnicity can powerfully constrain the fan imagination of topics which are supposedly marked by science fiction's limitless possibilities. Likewise, an FAQ for the international Klingon Assault Group (a "frequently-asked-questions" document many newsgroups post periodically to help acquaint new users with key terms and procedures) echoes the language of much contemporary "ethnic" writing when it remarks that "the first step" in joining the organization "is to determine whether you have the KLINGON SPIRIT in your heart and soul." Such language represents Klingon identity in terms of an authentic, interior feeling even as it goes on to explain that "your ship's Genetics Engineer [i.e., a sponsoring fan] can assist you in creating or purchasing facial appliances for the ridges"—which is as clear and conscious a statement of the material nuts-and-bolts mechanics of Klingon ethnic "construction" as any academic theorist could labor to uncover.[29] The coexistence of what cultural critics call "essentialist" and "constructionist" perspectives in such statements—the tension between Klingonness as "being" and as "becoming"—should not be a surprise by itself. Critic Diana Fuss, among others, has commented on how even radically anti-essentialist theories such as "deconstruction" often depend on displaced,

repressed, or unexamined essentialisms.[30] But key questions remain. Is it only because Klingon identity is so *obviously* "constructed" that fans think about it in "constructionist" terms? How important is the idea of a Klingon "heart and soul" to these fans? Would they define "real" ethnicities as *only* matters of heart and soul, and not of historical construction and "shared-reality"?

Often, the implicit answer seems to be yes. On the other hand, many fans regard their meaning-making and role-playing activities with a mixture of playfulness and skepticism that allows them to challenge the ideological content not only of "canonical" *Star Trek* product, but of other fans' discourses and, self-reflexively, of their own. To be interested in Klingons might signal a kind of resistance to cultural authority all by itself, since the series' Klingons are uneasy allies at best, and frequently "the enemy"; where Klingon fan culture is concerned, everyone chooses to be an outsider to some degree. Ael t'Arrilaiu, pseudonymous author of an FAQ for the alt.shared-reality .startrek.klingon group, defines her character with coy anti-essentialist self-consciousness as "Half Rihannsu [Romulan], Mostly Jewish, touch of Klingon Blood." She cautions those who would create interesting characters for others to interact with to "Get real? Er, as real as Trek can be."[31] Ael describes herself as a Romulan double agent who admires Klingons and works secretly to promote their Empire. At the same time, she cautions neophyte writers not to react "personally" to other fans who write in character, advising that "if someone offends you" the best course is to "try and make peace."[32] This is not the most obviously "Klingon" of sentiments, but it is repeated by Trekkan in the FAQ for the Klingon Assault Group. Although KAG members enjoy "go[ing] to fan conventions and intimidat[ing] other species," they also "help charities with food and blood drives" and stress "communication, cooperation and participation" rather than the no-holds-barred Klingon aggressiveness depicted on television.[33] A recent fan discussion on the alt.startrek.klingon newsgroup that raised the question of whether "Klingons were basically Russians in space, and Romulans were essentially Chinese" ended by having compared Klingons to Arabs, Vikings, Japanese, Soviets, feudal Europeans, and African Americans; Romulans to ancient Romans (or Greeks) and Japanese; Vulcans to Chinese, Arabs, Romans, and Greeks; Cardassians to Nazi Germans or Israelis (depending on whether the Bajorans they once oppressed are read as Jews or Palestinians); Ferengi to Arabs and Jews.[34] The obvious point—which at least one fan made—is that in all this, the heroic Federation stands in for the American view of itself. But if this is true then why do many Americans (and some fans outside the United States) want to be Klingons? If there is an "ethnic identity" under construction here, it is being negotiated in a number of different ways. Fans' interests and desires neither vary so much that they can be called purely "individual," nor fall into such neat categories that they can be pigeonholed as "racist," "ethnocentric," or even strictly "American."

On the other hand, while there are dedicated *Star Trek* watchers of all races and ethnicities, the active "fan" community *is* predominantly made up of "white" folks. The list of non-U.S. countries that post to Klingon newsgroups tends to confirm this: Northern European or European-colonized locations like the United Kingdom, Canada, Finland, Germany, the Netherlands, Sweden, and Australia predominate. As critic Daniel Bernardi has noted, between the 1960s and the 1990s *Star Trek* has moved from "a liberal humanist project that is inconsistent and contradictory" to an equally inconsistent but noticeably less liberal "backlash trajectory . . . drawing heavily on the discourse of whiteness and the politics of neoconservatism."[35] How much fan whiteness matters—and what whiteness itself is, ethnically speaking—are thus key concerns. How should we regard an emergent ethnicity that emerges from a social space so strongly bounded by prior ethnic and political realities?

Like Ferengi Capitalists?
Klingon Ethnicity and Whiteness

In "DissemiNation," postcolonial theorist Homi K. Bhabha discusses a split, in the production of nationhood through narrative, between "the continuist, accumulative temporality of the pedagogical, and the repetitious, recursive strategy of the performative."[36] We might restate Bhabha's remarks as a comment on the fact that while nations and ethnic groups typically conceive of their existence as a linear progression through historical time, individuals acquire and experience their own ethnicity in the day-to-day performance of ethnic ritual and life. Bhabha's point may help explain why Klingon identity is so powerfully clear to *Star Trek* fans. Fans often write as if that identity were well-understood and stable, though their own activities challenge and transform it. They often see it as invested with profound and clear significance despite its fictionality, its complexity, and its lack of historical depth. Klingons, as an imagined community, are not particularly numerous and have "traditions" only some thirty years old. Yet this is nearly the age the United States had reached as a nation by the date of the Louisiana Purchase; roughly the age of the contemporary concept of Chicano/a ethnic identity (as distinguished from older, less politically-charged ideas of "Mexicans" or "Mexican Americans"); and roughly my own biographical age. This is time enough for repetitious, recursive performances of even a wholly "fictitious" identity to take on an experiential "reality." Many people watch television programs as often as their forebears attended church; given reruns, perhaps more so. Television creates a shared media culture; ethnicity is a cultural process: thus there is a potentially "ethnicity-generating" character to watching television. The question becomes: how does TV-mediated ethnicity relate to the construction and performance of better-known ethnic identities?

In some ways, the relationship is quite direct. French sociologist Pierre Bourdieu has analyzed the processes by which individuals gain a *sens pratique,* a preconscious "feel for the game" of cultural norms. People take corresponding "dispositions" within a cultural "field"—sets of behaviors that feel natural and inevitable, because they are learned in the course of intensely personal life-histories, but which often prove to be strikingly alike for individuals in similar race, class, or gender positions within the larger society. These dispositions can extend to the way people perform and transform the norms of a culture not in actual existence. For example, actor Michael Dorn has attributed his success in gaining the part of Worf to his prior fannish familiarity with the codes of Klingon conduct. On auditioning, Dorn notes, "I did not wear makeup . . . but I took on the psychological guise of a Klingon. I walked into Paramount in character. No jokes. No laughing with the other actors. I sat by myself waiting for my interview. When my turn came, I walked in, didn't smile, did the reading, thanked them, and walked right out."[37] In Bourdieu's terms, Dorn had the right disposition for the part, a combination of inner feelings and outer mannerisms. But he had acquired that disposition without the benefit of growing up Klingon or belonging to a real community. His knowledge came solely from TV and film.

Curiously, however, Dorn emphasized Klingon traits that were not predominant in John Colicos's inaugural urbane-barbarian turn as Kor, William Campbell's cheery Koloth, or Christopher Lloyd's wisecracking Kruge of *Star Trek III: The Search for Spock.*[38] The prior Klingon interpretations closest to Dorn's were Michael Ansara's Kang—a commander under highly unusual stresses—and Mark Lenard's stoic starship captain of the brief opening moments of *Star Trek: The Motion Picture.* But Dorn substantially revised even these portrayals. Like Bison, he had a fannish certainty about Klingon identity and ran with it, bodying forth a complex character in part because he threw aside the wider range of Klingon personae that had been available. His interpretation

might make sense *only* for Worf, the orphan, "the only Klingon in Starfleet": an alien military officer who tries to fit in among humans who believe his race to be overly emotional and violent, who practices strict self-control—much like a black actor trying to fit into a predominantly white entertainment industry that holds similar beliefs about African Americans. But Dorn's performance has become the template for later actors and fans.[39] Such paradigm shifts occasionally overtake even real-world ethnic dispositions: consider the sudden hatlessness of American men after John F. Kennedy's hatless inaugural. And thus such dispositions amount to considerably more than "walking the walk and talking the talk." They remind us that walking and talking are complex, socially-conditioned, learned activities, however obvious and natural they later come to seem. Belief and behavior systems that are originally "ideological" categories, like class membership or ethnicity, naturalize themselves through socially learned individual performance. "Culture turn[s] into nature," and what feels most personal can also be a clear mark of one's group identity. The opposition between individual and group itself is revealed as frequently false.[40]

Similarly, Okrand's *Klingon Dictionary* provides a guide to the pronunciation of Klingon consonants. The text's claim that "the Klingon government . . . has accepted English as the lingua franca" shows why I call Klingons "American" ethnics: the American insistence that the world speak our language is here universalized.[41] But Okrand also frequently warns that "gh" or "H," "q" or "Q" are "not like anything in English" and can only be approximated by sounds from German or Yiddish, or Mexican Spanish or Aztec. And no matter how hard they try, the text claims, "very few non-Klingons speak Klingon without an accent."[42]

These statements are reminiscent of Bourdieu's discussions of class-marked speech habits and the power of social distinctions to shape individual behavior.[43] Linguists like Okrand have shown that the range of sounds produceable by the human speech apparatus is greater than the range of sounds used in any single language or dialect. But the study of multilingual persons shows that past a certain developmental age, most people have difficulty hearing, and learning to properly produce, sounds not recognized as significant in either their "native tongue" or their regional or class dialect. This limitation can be partially overcome by long, hard practice, as actors learn. But that fact in turn suggests that one's own speaking voice, ordinarily counted among the most personal and immutable bodily facts, is likewise the result of early learning and practice, during which the codes of the social environment become internalized and alternative possibilities are excluded.[44] To return to Bhabha's point: behavioral markers of class, nation, or ethnicity, whatever their real or imaginary history, are also a matter of repetition, recursively reproducing that history as lived experience. Internet Klingon fans frequently query each other about the availability of videotapes illustrating combat techniques for the Klingon *batlh'etlh,* the "honor sword." Practicing the *batlh'etlh*—tapes *are* available—may be practicing a martial arts fiction. But it is through precisely such bodily performances that ordinary "ethnic" habits are acquired and become indistinguishable from one's own most genuine persona.

While such a line of argument suggests that Klingon ethnicity is a real quality worth talking about, listing behaviors that characterize Klingons as "ethnics" ignores a cardinal insight of recent anthropological and theoretical studies of ethnicity: that ethnicity is often determined not by the racial, religious, linguistic, or cultural content of each ethnic group but by *relations* among groups, and by the *value* placed upon perceived ethnic differences. As Thomas Hylland Eriksen puts it: "only in so far as cultural differences are perceived as being important, and are made socially relevant, do social relationships have an ethnic element. . . . Ethnicity refers both to aspects of gain and loss in interaction, and to aspects of meaning in the creation of identity. In this way it has a political, organisational aspect as well as a symbolic one."[45] Given this perspective, the ethnic character of Klingon culture becomes less obvious. The crucial issue is not that Klingon ethnicity is "fictional," since every ethnicity is fictional in much the same way, but that we must reinsert Klingon ethnicity in the web of relationships of its social surroundings.

Star Trek is largely a product of the dominant culture. Thus its fans tend to affiliate themselves with the dominant-culture understanding of which groups qualify as "ethnic" and what "being ethnic" means. This tendency powerfully influences fannish activity whatever a fan's individual position with respect to U.S. society. Thus Klingons are neither understood as an ethnic group by the majority culture nor, as participants in that culture, do Klingons understand *themselves* as ethnics. The nonidentification of Klingons as a group is more a matter of *Star Trek* fans' own self-conception than of the invisibility and hostility often visited upon other, better-defined marginalized groups. If there is any widely identified social subgroup Klingons belong to it is "Trekkers."[46] This group *is* often stigmatized in the popular imagination for overindulging in escapist pop-culture pursuits. But Trekkers themselves remain mainstream. Witness the parade of *Trek*-related popular magazine covers, the eight films, the five television series, and the culture industry of both "canonical" (i.e., Paramount-sponsored) and gray-market fan paraphernalia. Trekkers are not a "colonized" people *as* Trekkers. They are not systematically "dichotomized" by the mutual processes of insider/outsider differentiation noted by sociologists of ethnicity. The differences from the mainstream that remain are "undercommunicated" in everyday interactions: no one much cares if you dress like a Klingon in the privacy of your own home, or even at a convention, though other hotel guests are apt to stare.[47] Once you take off the costume, no one can tell you from a mere mortal.[48] The resulting lack of a sense of major stakes in interactions between fans and non-fans makes Trekkers, or Klingons, only an "emergent" ethnicity; ethnicity is not quite ethnic when its boundaries are so vague and the stakes so low.

Furthermore, ethnic borders are difficult to cross despite the internal "dispositional" changes which can and do take place within any given ethnicity—recall how Michael Dorn's dispositional changes to Klingon behavior only made Klingons seem more like who Dorn himself was, a black man among a mostly white crew. The prior ethnic context from which Klingon fans emerge is again crucial. So who are the Trekkers, ethnically speaking? Do they have an ethnic identity of their own, or not? Though there are certainly African American, Asian American, and Chicano *Trek* fans, as well as non-men, non-straights, non-Americans, differently abled people, and so on, the science fiction audience is noticeably whiter on average, speaking strictly of skin color, than the population at large. Having investigated the nature of ethnicity, its status as something fictional that nonetheless has powerful social effects, we are in a position to understand that fan whiteness is not merely a coincidental or easily changeable aspect of *Trek* culture. Whiteness as a *cultural* space, not merely a pigmentation, marks many of the assumptions and activities of the fan community.

Henry Jenkins, an academic and fan who has studied "media fandom" in an openly "ethnographic" manner, but also as an insider, understands media fans not as passive consumers of mass culture but as "textual poachers" who employ complex reading and revising strategies to transform their experiences into acts of cultural production and pop reconstruction.[49] Fans, according to Jenkins, "raid mass culture, claiming its materials for their own use, reworking them as the basis for their own cultural creations and social interactions. . . . Unimpressed by institutional authority and expertise, the fans assert their own right to form interpretations, to offer evaluations, and to construct cultural canons. . . . they often are highly educated, articulate people who come from the middle classes."[50]

As a long-time *Star Trek* fan, I can't help but agree with Jenkins's assertions. But what group can afford to raid mass culture with such confidence, or to be "unimpressed by institutional authority," which is for many other groups an overwhelming consideration? Klingon fan activity represents a triple "investment"—a psychological commitment to representations of Klingon bodies and culture, the "dressing-up" activity of Klingon identity-construction (perhaps similar to the intense labor of "drag" performance), and the investment of time and money serious fan pursuits require. Thus, acting Klingon requires prior access to capital, whether the "cultural" or the ordinary economic kind.[51] Middle-class white Americans, *or* those committed to pursuing that group's dreams of economic autonomy and a de-ethnicized, "assimilated" cultural life, remain more likely on average to possess such advantages. Klingon fandom is not just something engaged in mostly by white fans: it is a choice of interests much more available to those already in possession of, or seeking, "white" middle-class social identity.

In this light, claiming Klingon identity is a less unproblematically positive gesture of anti-mainstream activity. While fans' textual poaching should indeed be read as politically progressive in its refusal to bow to Paramount's corporate control of the *Star Trek* canon, there is nonetheless something politically suspicious about mostly white fans mimicking the performance of a black actor who played an alien who was under considerable pressure to assimilate back into a human (i.e., white) cultural norm. Acting Klingon expresses an acknowledgment of the empty compromises of identifying with the dominant culture. But at the same time it provides relatively advantaged members of society a claim to marginalization without relinquishing their relatively greater access to power. Writing on the political significance of drag in gay male culture, Carol-Anne Tyler has investigated a similarly problematic double bind. Male appropriation of behaviors and styles that the dominant culture codes as "feminine" can both signal a positive identification with women by marginalized gay men and reflect continuing male privilege to appropriate from the disempowered. Such double binds do not tell us that all men (or whites, or straights) are "in power" so much as they caution us against believing that any group is as disempowered as it is sometimes comforting to believe. What counts is the complex and shifting structure of each relationship between people or groups, rather than an absolute hierarchy.

Klingon fans, whose rhetoric of spiritualism and masculinity recalls the "men's movement," are indeed reminiscent of the genuinely self-questioning but still privileged white men's movement participants discussed in Fred Pfeil's recent study *White Guys*. They tell us as much about middle-class self-doubt and political disengagement as about the creation of a culture that could function as a genuine alternative to dominant culture, as many fans believe it already does. Pfeil finds that both the emotional attractions of the men's movement and its political limitations correspond to those of a broad range of alternative cultural movements. A common characteristic of all these groups is "the extent to which political identities are conceived . . . first and foremost as *cultural* identities." [52] Such groups show a "tendency to leap over history for myth, the polity for the tribe." Pfeil believes this tendency reveals an underlying "inability to understand social relations and social change in terms of historically and structurally constituted relations of power." [53] Such movements, that is, respond to a growing awareness of contradictions in late capitalist society which make it desirable to work out new relationships among social groups and even to transform soci-

ety at large. But they persistently misrecognize the solutions to these crises as needing to arise primarily, even exclusively, from the creation of new "cultures" or the recovery of fanciful precapitalist "identities," which may have been genuine in the past but can now only be put into play as marketing niches. As a result, "alternative" cultures end up creating commodities that big business sells back to them at a substantial markup. Similarly, if you've ever priced a good "working phaser" at a *Star Trek* convention, the feeling that your love of imaginative play has been turned into a weapon against your pocketbook (probably by another fan who shares your passions) is a familiar one. It does not necessarily prevent you from cooperating in your own impoverishment by buying one; the urge to acquire the material trappings of one's cultural difference, however little different one really is in one's daily behavior, has itself been successfully promoted by contemporary mainstream society. [54]

In applying such critiques to Klingon fan culture I do not accuse *Star Trek* fans of falling prey to "false consciousness"—at least not more so than anyone else. Few who know me well would miss the irony in my posing as a disinterested critic of *Trek* fan culture rather than a very deeply "invested" fan. But irony is certainly also at work in Trekkan's FAQ for the Klingon Assault Group, which proudly declares that the organization charges no membership dues—after all, "do we look like Ferengi Capitalists to you?"—but notes that members must "create or purchase their own Uniforms," and that ship quartermasters "often can sell Uniforms to ship members at a substantial discount." [55] A kind of pyramid scheme haunts such remarks. But *no one* in contemporary society is entirely free of such profit motives; no one can be secure while failing to think in terms of personal benefit, even the academic critic who writes his fannish experience into his professional work. But clearly, one need not look like a Ferengi to act like a capitalist. Nor will donning Klingon garb and professing warrior virtues, by itself, replace one's white or middle-class social role with something significantly different. Failing to understand how one's activities take place within the constraints of contemporary market forces and ethnic realities, even when the activities seem most freely and "individually" chosen, or most in accordance with some deeply felt "heritage," means relinquishing paramount opportunities for transforming the situation. One lesson of fandom may be that groups with primarily culturalist aims are more likely to make people *feel* better than to make the world better: not a pointless gain, but arguably not a lasting one either.

So whither Klingon—or white—"ethnicity"? Isn't it at least significant that *Star Trek* fans, white or otherwise, are rethinking the terms of whiteness itself? Surely it is. But in what direction is the dominant culture around those fans moving, and does fan activity resist that culture's pressures and refuse its enticements, or merely find friendlier accommodations with them? Another science fiction text of the early 1990s is considerably less confident than the *Star Trek* franchise and its fans about the wisdom of searching for ever-more-fragmented cultural "identities." In his novel *Nimbus,* published in 1993, science fiction author Alexander Jablokov uses the biblical story of the Gileadites and Ephraimites, who could distinguish each other because they pronounced the word "shibboleth" differently, to outline the manipulation of ethnic identity in a postindustrial future where "artificial ethnic groups" could be created by prosthetic mental modification, high-tech brain surgery. "Tie their [ethnic] identity to simple speech accents," one character tells another, "and let all the other artificial ethnic groups identify them that way, and have an emotional reaction. . . . We can fiddle with Rumanian pronunciation and create five different groups within the city of Kishinyov in a matter of weeks."[56] In Jablokov's universe, such ethnic conflicts *have* indeed been promoted, during a series of wars at the

turn of the twenty-first century. The breakdown of society into smaller and smaller groups, which Pfeil identifies as a hallmark of the culturalist response to high-tech postmodernism, has accelerated, in Jablokov's universe, to the point where a group called the Messengers manifests its difference from mainstream humanity not only by communicating in a privately developed language, but by outfitting their foreheads with surgically-implanted skull ridges to mimic a supposed descent from Neanderthals. They might almost be Klingons—or Klingon fans taking the next step in making their fannish identity real. But at the same time, in Jablokov's vision of the future, the obscure imperatives of profit wreak their usual havoc on what's left of human freedoms. The number of ethnic conflicts around the world, and the intensity of ethnic conflict, has increased. But money is still being merrily made by those who have the power to cheerlead and profit from such disasters. Cultural fragmentation benefits those in power far more than it does those who see such fragmentation as a form of resistance.

In short, Jablokov's future looks a great deal like the times in which he wrote about it. As Benedict Anderson has noted, the era of high-tech ethnic conflict, and high-stakes profitmaking from it, is *now*. Without committing the science-fictional sin of believing that Jablokov's grimly clever predictions will inevitably materialize, we should notice that what he imagines as necessary for the construction of artificial ethnicities is a set of technological refinements on processes *already* at work: cybernetic devices to program the human brain to believe in concepts it can already program *itself* for, bodily modifications already implicit in gender-change operations, facelifts, and the burgeoning "cultures" of body art and body piercing. The time when Klingon fans might willingly elect to undergo such modifications in order to improve their performance of a lifestyle that promises relief from postmodern stresses, that promises to make them not-white without subjecting them to the discrimination faced by people "of color," may not be far off. Surely such moves would meet with the usual anti-Trekkie derision. But whether this would be anything other than so many pots calling kettles "black" as they practiced their own ethnic self-delusions is, given the fact that we are only fantasizing here, impossible to determine.

Notes

1 The title of my essay is quoted from Trekkan's KAG FAQ (Klingon Assault Group Frequently Asked Questions) postings (Online posting, Newsgroup alt.startrek .klingon, posted 2 January 1996, accessed 4 January 1996 and "Re: KAG FAQ," Online posting, Newsgroup alt.startrek.klingon, posted 3 January 1996, accessed 4 January 1996). Author has not responded to request for permission to cite. Internet newsgroup postings for which I have secured express authorial permission to cite are annotated in the notes accordingly. I have attempted to contact all Internet authors and have given those who responded an opportunity to comment on this article. Thanks for assistance in preparing this essay are due Henry Jenkins, who validated the study of Star Trek fan culture and pointed the way; Dr. Lawrence M. Schoen of the Klingon Language Institute, and Elliott McEldowney for alerting me to its existence; Shannon Jackson and J. Martin Favor, for suggesting the use of performance theory in the study of ethnicity; and Susan Gorman, Dan Shaw, Kim Hébert, Greg Howard, Min Song, Kathleen Gillespie, Juliet Cooke, Jed Shumsky, and my parents and siblings, who have been listening to my theories about Klingons for years, when not offering their own.

2 SkullBuddy, "Re: What Is KAG . . . ?" (Online posting, Newsgroup alt.startrek.klingon., posted 2 January 1996, accessed 4 January 1996). Author has not responded to request for permission to cite.

3 Ernest Renan, "What Is a Nation?," trans. Martin Thom, in Nation and Narration, ed. Homi K. Bhabha (New York: Routledge, 1990), 8.

4 According to The Klingon Dictionary, qagh is a "serpent worm (as food)," a delicacy portrayed on Star Trek: The Next Generation as best eaten live (Marc Okrand, The Klingon Dictionary: English/Klingon, Klingon/English, rev. ed. [New York: Pocket Books, 1992], 183). Star Trek's fascination with the Klingons' diet as a classic sign of their racial/cultural difference owes a clear debt to eth-

nology; it may likewise signify a race-and-class-marked transgression of social "distinctions" (in Pierre Bourdieu's sense) that mark Klingons as (often gleefully) déclassé and unassimilated.

5 Anthony D. Smith, The Ethnic Origins of Nations (Cambridge: Blackwell, 1986), 18.

6 Werner Sollors, Beyond Ethnicity: Consent and Descent in American Culture (New York: Oxford University Press, 1986), 5.

7 Ibid., 6, 7.

8 Of course even this definition of "the majority" may reflect a dominant-culture perspective. German Americans, we should recall, sometimes faced severe ethnic discrimination during the world wars. "Scots" were identical to "Anglo-Saxons" for Thomas Dixon, the Scottish American author of The Clansman (1905)— but Dixon was a virulent negrophobe whose word should perhaps not be taken as gospel. Historian Leonard Pitt notes that the upper-class Mexican Vallejo brothers, captured by troops of the 1846 "Bear Flag Rebellion" initiated by U.S. adventurers in California, regarded a black prison guard as both an "Anglo" and a "blackguard" in the colloquial sense, for daring to "use the word 'greaser' in addressing two men of the 'purest blood of Europe!'" (Leonard Pitt, The Decline of the Californios: A Social History of the Spanish-Speaking Californians, 1846–1890 [Berkeley: University of California Press, 1966], 27). Mexican social codes, though not race-blind, drew different distinctions from those of the United States: the Vallejos also moved in social circles with Pío Pico, a Californian territorial governor whose grandmother was a "mulatta" and who himself was dark-skinned (Robert L. Carlton, "Blacks in San Diego County: A Social Profile, 1850–1880," Journal of San Diego History 21[4] [19xx]: 11). The question of whose codes applied to Pico and the Vallejos, and when, is thus not simple. Similarly, contemporary Chicano/a critics have highlighted the ludicrousness of representing Mexicans as "foreigners" to the vast U.S. territory wrested from Mexico. Thus it is unasked questions of who constitutes "the majority" and who "the outsiders" that often constitute the crux of ethnic conflict.

9 Theodore Allen has opened a useful way out of such disabling impasses by suggesting a focus on oppression first and the forms it takes second. He goes on to make a provisional distinction between "racial" and "national" oppression according to whether oppressors suppress or cultivate differences within an oppressed

group. See *The Invention of the White Race* (New York: Verso, 1994).

10 For a brief discussion of contemporary conflicts over the naming of communities of Spanish descent in the United States, see Ramón Gutiérrez and Genaro Padilla, "Introduction," in *Recovering the U.S. Hispanic Literary Heritage*, eds. Ramón Gutiérrez and Genaro Padilla (Houston: Arte Público, 1993), especially 17–18.

11 Sollors, *Beyond Ethnicity*, 38.

12 Many of *Trek*'s alien races since the 1980s are distinguished by similar facial "appliances," which create a more thorough visual estrangement than the pointed ears of the Vulcan Mr. Spock or the antennae and blue makeup of the original show's Andorians. Bajorans, featured prominently on *Deep Space Nine*, have only a set of ridges across the bridge of the nose, whereas "Morn," a regular at the same show's interstellar casino, sports an elaborate head appliance which conceals all but the actor's eyes. Meanwhile, on *Voyager*, the visible sign of Commander Chakotay's Native American heritage is a large tattoo across his left temple. The major races discussed in the remainder of this article are summarized as follows:

Race	Physical Features	"Cultural" Features
Klingons	forehead ridges	warlike
Vulcans	pointy ears	logical, stoic
Romulans	pointy ears	emotional, stoic
Ferengi	big ears, bumpy heads	greedy capitalists
Cardassians	gray skin, neck tendons	military state
Bajorans	nose ridges	mystics

13 Todd Hansen, "Re: Klingons = Russians?," Online posting, Newsgroup alt.startrek.klingon, posted 5 December 1995, accessed 4 January 1996. Author has given permission to cite.

14 See Toni Morrison, *Playing in the Dark: Whiteness and the Literary Imagination* (Cambridge, MA: Harvard University Press, 1992).

15 Science fictional play with differences that turn out to be estranged similarities is a hallmark of the genre and by no means limited to *Star Trek*. But each incarnation of *Star Trek* has exerted tremendous narrative pressure on its nonhumans to humanize, perhaps revealing a specifically American preoccupation with normalizing and regulating social difference and assimilating pluralities (though other ideological pressures are certainly at

play as well). Thus the assimilationist "melting pot" paradigm usually takes precedence over the pluralist "salad bowl," despite *Trek*'s widely lauded (and lately deplored, by some vocal Internet critics of *Voyager*'s white female captain and black Vulcan security officer) multiculturalism. The wider field of science fiction is relatively less preoccupied with this theme. Narratives abound in which alienness is preferable to "humanity," or in which human nature undergoes radical change, or in which alien and human remain irreducibly different (though not necessarily antagonistically so).

16 Larry Nemecek, *The "Star Trek: The Next Generation" Companion*, rev. ed. (New York: Pocket Books, 1995), 20.

17 Deborah Starr Seibel, "Klingon for a Day," *TV Guide*, (Oct. 16, 1993): 30.

18 By contrast, the visibly "black" men of recent *Star Trek* productions have been more obviously conceived in an overcautious, polite attempt *not* to play any "race cards." La Forge of *The Next Generation* evinced callow asexuality and even helpless victimizability (as in "The Mind's Eye" and the film *Generations*). *Deep Space Nine*'s Sisko, the station's commander and the show's nominal star, until the last few seasons of the series' run faded into the ensemble. His increasing prominence since the 1995–96 season went hand in hand not only with his character's promotion to captain but with a change of appearance toward the character the actor (Avery Brooks) portrayed on *Spenser for Hire*: the mysterious black sidekick Hawk, who played out white private eye Spenser's aggressive impulses. My black male students have commented on the contradictions of white liberal politics apparent in such facts, noting ruefully that while two "brothers" were stars on *The Next Generation*, one pulled double minority duty as a blind man, one was concealed behind an alien mask.

19 See George Fredrickson's classic study *The Black Image in the White Mind: The Debate on Afro-American Character and Destiny, 1817–1914* (Hanover, NH: Wesleyan University Press, 1971).

20 A later two-part episode explicitly *titled* "Birthright" renewed the implicit connection between Worf and Data, nonhumans whose emotional struggles best revealed the American understanding of "human nature." Interestingly, both characters' problems seemed to lie in the masculine subjectivity of men who lack father figures, and thus male traditions and role models, in a Hollywood renarration of the "men's movement." For comparison, when Dr. Crusher attended the funeral of her

grandmother she wandered into a gothic romance in which a ghostly and lascivious alien life form attempted to seduce her, as it had several centuries' worth of her maternal line ("Sub Rosa"); *Star Trek*'s vision of a "women's" tradition?

21 Okrand, *The Klingon Dictionary*, 1, 4.

22 Ibid.

23 Ibid.

24 The role of physical appearance in motivating ethnic and racial oppression remains debated; for some strong refutations of its importance, see Allen's *Invention of the White Race,* or George Fredrickson, *White Supremacy* (New York: Oxford University Press, 1981). Both studies cite the different racial histories of the United States and the Caribbean as evidence disproving claims that the races "naturally" find each other distasteful.

25 Bison, "SB EPSILON: PERSONEL [*sic*] BIO: Barok Vorkithic," Online posting, Newsgroup alt.shared-reality .startrek.klingon, posted 12 November 1995, accessed 13 November 1995. Author has not responded to request for permission to cite.

26 The *Deep Space Nine* episode "Trials and Tribbleations" (1996) raised this issue only so that Worf could brusquely dismiss it as something Klingons do not discuss with outsiders.

27 Bison, "Barok Vorkithic."

28 The original-series episode "Balance of Terror" established this relationship to highlight the pitfalls of racism: a crewman who believed that the Vulcan Mr. Spock might be a traitor, when the *Enterprise* crew discovered that Romulans looked like Vulcans, was later saved from death by Spock during a battle with a Romulan vessel.

29 Trekkan, KAG FAQ.

30 See Diana Fuss, *Essentially Speaking* (New York: Routledge, 1989).

31 Ael t'Arrilaiu [Heidi Wessman], "A.SR.S.K FAQ ver 1.0," Online posting, Newsgroup alt.shared-reality .startrek.klingon, posted 2 December 1995, accessed 7 December 1995.) Author has given permission to cite.

32 Ael t'Arrilaiu [Heidi Wessman], "UPDATED A.SR.S.K FAQ (ver. 2.0)," Online posting, Newsgroup alt.shared-reality.startrek.klingon, posted 2 December 1995, accessed 6 December 1995.) Author has given permission to cite.

33 Trekkan, KAG FAQ.

34 See note 12 for a description of the various alien races. Dan Joyce, "Klingons = Russians?," Online posting,

Newsgroup alt.startrek.klingon, posted 5 December 1995, accessed 4 January 1996. Author has given permission to cite.

35 Daniel Leonard Bernardi, "The Wrath of Whiteness: The Meaning of Race in the Generation of Star Trek." Ph.D. dissertation, University of California, Los Angeles, 1995, 28, 29. This dissertation was published under the title *"Star Trek" and History : Race-Ing toward a White Future* (New Brunswick, NJ: Rutgers University Press, 1998).

36 Homi K. Bhabha, "DissemiNation: Time, Narrative, and the Margins of the Modern Nation," in *Nation and Narration,* ed. Homi K. Bhabha (New York: Routledge, 1990), 297.

37 Nemecek, *The "Star Trek: The Next Generation" Companion,* 20. At a convention I attended in Denver in late 1988, Dorn reported that he was excited when his agent told him that Paramount wanted to cast a Klingon: his agent did not know what Paramount was talking about, but Dorn put him at ease because he felt he knew exactly what to give them.

38 Campbell's appearance as a Klingon commander is especially interesting since he had, a season earlier, appeared as the bratty infant alien superbeing Trelane ("The Squire of Gothos"), who manifested himself as a kind of twenty-third-century Liberace—not the image one now has of a Klingon warrior, but nevertheless somewhat present in Koloth's easy banter.

39 Leah R. Vande Berg, "Liminality: Worf as Metonymic Signifier of Racial, Cultural, and National Differences," in *Enterprise Zones: Critical Positions on Star Trek,* ed. Taylor Harrison, Sarah Projansky, Kent A. Ono, and Elyce Rae Helford, (Boulder, CO: Westview Press, 1996), 51–68.

40 Pierre Bourdieu, *Distinction: A Social Critique of the Judgement of Taste,* trans. Richard Nice (Cambridge, MA: Harvard University Press, 1984), 190.

41 Okrand, *The Klingon Dictionary,* 10. As critic Leah R. Vande Berg has noted, "cultural imperialism—and not multiculturalism—is the dominant discursive position affirmed" in the *Trek* universe (Vande Berg, "Liminality," 65).

42 Okrand, *The Klingon Dictionary,* 14, 13.

43 See Bourdieu, *Distinction,* 190–93, for one discussion of the various ways class tastes become "embodied."

44 In other words, while it is true that all people from Boston are individuals, and that not all have "Boston accents," it is also true that many Bostonians have very

strong Boston accents, not because of their ethnicity or their genes but because the Bostonian speech environment (which crosses race, class, and gender lines) is so influential.

45 Thomas Hylland Eriksen, *Ethnicity and Nationalism: Anthropological Perspectives* (London: Pluto, 1993), 12.

46 Fans generally prefer "Trekkers" to "Trekkies" since it does not sound like a diminutive or like "groupies" (for further discussion of this point see John Tulloch and Henry Jenkins, *Science Fiction Audiences: Watching "Doctor Who" and "Star Trek"* [New York: Routledge, 1995], 11); given the logic of English grammar it also positively suggests someone engaged in an activity— worker, builder, swimmer, Trekker—rather than a passive recipient of mass culture. Fan resistance to the "Trekkie" label is obviously reminiscent of conflicts between "insider" and "outsider" labels for other marginal groups. As a fan somewhat suspicious of fans' keen sensitivity to outsider criticism, cavalierly dismissive as it often is, I often refer to myself as a Trekkie, perhaps like progressive gay and lesbian activists who have appropriated the term "queer" as a positive marker, but perhaps also like African Americans who use the word "nigger."

47 Eriksen, *Ethnicity and Nationalism*, 27, 21.

48 The case of the *Whitewater* juror who wore her Starfleet uniform to court remains unique, as far as I know, and has excited considerable debate in fan circles. Many *Trek* fans side with the mainstream and believe that her bringing fiction into reality in such a way was distasteful. This fact suggests that we will not be seeing Klingons outside fan space anytime soon.

49 Henry Jenkins, *Textual Poachers: Television Fans and Participatory Culture.* (New York: Routledge, 1992), 1.

50 Ibid., 18.

51 Here I am extending some remarks Bourdieu makes on the dual investment involved in the way individuals acquire cultural competence: "It is in no way suggested that the corresponding behavior is guided by rational calculation. . . . Culture is the site, par excellence, of misrecognition, because, in generating strategies adapted to the objective chances of profit of which it is the product, the sense of investment secures profits which do not need to be pursued as profits" (*Distinction*, 85–86).

It would, of course, be unwise to push the analogy of Klingon performance with "drag" too far without knowing whether fans in their warrior dress are ever physically attacked in the way transvestite and transgendered people often are. Given the "look" of Klingon costuming, the more appropriate parallel would clearly be with leather/biker cultures: the performance is of a "masculine" rather than a "feminine" role. On the other hand, my (outsider's) impression of the leather image is that it usually lacks a "camp" dimension that *Trek* costuming can probably not help provoking in a non-Trekker audience, while camp *is* associated with transvestism to some degree.

52 Fred Pfeil, *White Guys: Studies in Postmodern Domination and Difference* (New York: Verso, 1995), 210.

53 Ibid., 225.

54 This is a good example, in a *Star Trek* context, of what the Italian Marxist thinker Antonio Gramsci called "hegemony": the process by which dominant culture entices willing obedience rather than compelling it from the unwilling.

55 Trekkan, KAG FAQ.

56 Alexander Jablokov, *Nimbus* (New York: Avon, 1993), 160.

The Empress's New Clothing? Public Intellectualism and Popular Culture

Jane Shattuc

Dr. Gilda Carle, "relationship expert," reigned as one of talk television's more popular authorities. She has appeared on more than a hundred programs since the mid-1990s. I first noticed her on a *Sally Jessy Raphäel Show* on February 23, 1994, devoted to the topic of "married women who have affairs with married men." Dr. Carle arrived halfway through the discussion dressed in a bright red tailored suit. Her first act was to hug a crying woman whose husband had just confessed an infidelity. After hugging and stroking the sobbing wife, Carle asked the viewing public: "What about the other party? What about the spouse? What if the other party finds out? All we have been hearing about is: me, me, me." The studio audience erupted in applause. Empowered by their response, she continued: "One of the things we have to do is to take that 'm' in me and turn it around to 'w' in we." The audience greeted this homily with wild applause. Dr. Carle's performance was a popular success.

I tuned into Dr. Carle over a year later on a *Richard Bey* program "Dump Your Jailhouse Boyfriend" (November 2, 1995). By this time, she had shed the physical trappings of professionalism: she entered dressed in a new outfit—spandex Mylar mini-suit—accompanied by Chippendale-style stripper "cops," who draped themselves across her shoulders. She was now introduced as the new "MTV therapist." She lectured angry gang women that they should not date criminals because of female "low self-esteem." What once was

a series of calculated therapeutic homilies constructed for the fragmented logic of television had become overacted muggings at the camera. The women guests and studio audience had become extraneous—mise-en-scène for the expert's performance.

Was I to be pleased that a professional woman was cast as a central authority? Should I have cheered the ways her outrageous performance debunked the "objectivity" of expertise? Yet I cringed at how educated knowledge (mine included) had been reduced to simply an extravagant act by a manipulative woman using underclass women to promote her career. But then I asked: How did her "act" really differ from my own performances of academic expertise?

Dr. Carle's role as a performing "professional" was not anomalous or new. She is a direct descendant of Dr. Joyce Brothers, one in a long line of "genteel women" from Dorothy Dix to Miss Manners to Dr. Ruth who have dispensed advice. They are part of the endless stream of experts—the credentialed society—on which American television depends. There is an array of experts on television from the political pundits on PBS's *News Hour* to the style professionals on the *Today* show to the journalists who give the context to MTV's "rockumentaries." These are middle-class people whose occupations are based on advanced or abstract knowledge. Their role is to use their theoretical understanding to make logic and/or moral sense out of TV's social narratives.

I want to isolate the experts—primarily those on issue-oriented talk shows of the 1980s and 1990s—who performed willingly on the popular medium of TV out of some hope at effecting change outside the confines of universities, government bureaucracies and corporations. Such psychologists, journalists, and writers often share with many academics in cultural studies an eagerness to intervene and change society.

For all their reputation for raucous populism,

talk shows were dominated by experts from the 1980s to the mid-1990s. Usually the experts emanated from mental health fields—psychologists, psychiatrists, psychotherapists, social workers, and relationship counselors—all distinguished by their academic credentials, their PhDs, MDs and MAs. In the next group there were self-help book writers (e.g., Ruth Jacobvitz, author of *150 Most Asked Questions about Menopause*). Next in frequency came various bureaucrats who manage social welfare and health agencies (e.g., Dr. Eric Hollander of the Mount Sinai School of Medicine). Other categories were elected officials (e.g., Senator Orrin Hatch, Utah), religious leaders (e.g., Rabbi Marvin Hier of the Simon Wiesenthal Center), lawyers (e.g., Alan Dershowitz), and journalists (e.g., local investigative journalists). We also saw an increasing number of academics—particularly those out of cultural studies who were called on to interpret culture (e.g., Michael Dyson, E. Ann Kaplan, Marjorie Garber, Naomi Wolf). They willingly digested their educated social knowledge into uncomplicated explanations, formula, and advice for a primarily feminine viewership.

The sociology of the popular expert needs to be teased out not only for its meaning but also to question its political role. How does the popular expert differ from the professional and the intellectual? Is it an oxymoron—"popular expert"—in that expertise depends on a top-down authority within the hierarchy of knowledge? If cultural studies perceives the viewer as an active maker of meaning, might the academic become unnecessary when this person is a capable reader a priori? And if a place for the popular mobilization of learned or academic knowledge exists, how might we understand its relationship to a cultural studies universe?

Traditionally, the work of intellectuals has been to question and explain the assumptions that dominate society, functioning either as part of the bourgeois public sphere, the counter-public sphere, or even the revolutionary vanguard. The bourgeois experts perpetuate class-based values and tastes for a class who could not afford or find the time to live the lifestyle. In Marxist societies intellectuals were also distrusted according to Alvin Gouldner. Their own class-based consciousness was at odds with workers' needs.[1] Yet it would also be naive to suggest that culture can or will dispense with expertise and theory. But we need to question both the Marxist-Leninist and the bourgeois traditions of the intelligentsia as the only vanguard of political change.[2] Such a sensibility goes against a basic premise of cultural studies: the validation of everyday active minds.

What better medium is there to examine expertise than talk shows, which continually pit experts against a public empowered to challenge and test their core claims and arguments. This relationship is not one of slavish respect for authority as some have suggested, nor is it one of complete skepticism. As a degraded daytime form of television, the talk show is an unusual arena, one where women of different colors and classes appear as experts and debate with nonexpert women. Much of the tension in talk shows in the 1980s and early 1990s surrounded the conflict between the educated knowledge of professionals and the lived experience of everyday women. Even though this debate was limited due to production by corporate interests, the programs offer a chance to examine what form of expertise if any succeeds in a popular medium and whether we can call this role political.

Cultural studies remains self-conscious about the relationship of popular culture, power, and expertise. Its goals remain critiquing power and authority, while proving the critical capacity of everyday people and ultimately effecting social change. Theorist Michel Foucault argues that the voice of educated knowledge works as a system of containment. Experts often dispense their knowledge as objective truth, masking the class-based interests of their education and experience. Foucault sees the "productive power" of modern professionals as working "to manage and manipulate people by instilling in them a specific sort of interpretation of whom they are and what they want."[3] Pierre Bourdieu suggests that the power accrued through education or social "distinction" is a form of domination. The ability of the well-educated bourgeoisie to impose its cultural standards on others through distinctions made between "correct" and "incorrect" behavior, "good taste" and "vulgar taste" and "artisan" and "artist" perpetuates the myth of "naturally given" standards or what Bourdieu argues is "a new mystery of immaculate conception."[4]

Following Foucault's lead, Janice Peck suggests that talk show experts function as the "application of social scientific knowledge for the purposes of bureaucratic control." The power relations between these experts and the "ordinary" guests are grossly inequitable. Typically, the advice addressed to women is based on relational issues and their so-called "failure to communicate." Here, experts as "trained communicators" tell guests that they need professional help to communicate "normally,"—i.e., the "help" of the expert. Such circular reasoning ensures the centrality of bureaucratic control and discourse.[5]

Herein lies Bourdieu's paradox for cultural studies academics: intellectuals who theorize and speak about popular culture from within the hallowed halls of the academy.[6] This championing of nonelite culture by elite academics is what Jim McGuigan describes as a "Bourdieuan, infinitely regressing project if ever there was one."[7] Ultimately, cultural studies experts are ensuring their prerogative to define popular or everyday culture through their claim to superior knowledge and education. Yet in *The Last Intellectual,* published in the mid-1980s, Russell Jacoby called for the return to the public intellectual—that dying breed of socially responsible thinkers who speaks to the

broad public. In his eyes, public intellectuals are needed to give direction to popular-based change that is becoming increasingly controlled by corporate and governmental desires.[8]

Toward Defining the Roles of Professional, Expert, and Intellectual

> *professional:* one engaged in a calling requiring specialized knowledge and often long and intensive academic preparation
>
> *expert:* one who has acquired skill or knowledge in or knowledge of a specific subject
>
> *intellectual:* one chiefly guided by the intellect rather than by emotion or experience

Such dictionary definitions (in this case, *Webster's New Collegiate Dictionary*) belie the complex political role these educated positions play in society. Sociology has grown increasingly sensitive about the role that academics and other professionals play in reinforcing the class system. There has been an ongoing debate in the "sociology of professions" distinctions between professional, expert, and intellectual since the nineteenth century. This field has clustered around two major paradigmatic distinctions in the professional classes. Structural functionalism derived from the works of Emil Durkheim and Talcott Parsons argues for the social foundations of the knowledges of the professions including science and medicine, stressing their role in preserving the rational-legal social order.[9] Ultimately, this school of thought sees work and occupations as ethically neutral, while it describes the professions as ethically positive, embodiments of a society's central values.[10]

Within the functionalist paradigm, experts represent the technical side of professionalism, while intellectuals represent what Stephen Brint sees as "the moral aspirations of professionalism as a force in public life."[11] Intellectuals are people who associated with the world of thought and, at least on occasion, address the broadly educated public. They are the "guardians of standards often ignored in the marketplace and the houses of power." [12] In this vein Lionel Trilling (whom Russell Jacoby describes as a model public intellectual) casts intellectuals as the "adversary culture," or critics of established authority, a position echoed by recent Frankfurt School theorists who have called for an oppositional public sphere to weigh against the instrumental reasoning of most experts.

The Marxist professional project offers a diverging perspective. Its proponents agree with Max Weber that professionals are defined by their possession of specialist knowledge. However, professionals construct social closure by building up "a monopoly of their knowledge and establish[ing] a monopoly on the services derived from it." This view of expertise envisions it as a powerful tool to exert control over the other classes. [13] Therefore, social stratification results not only from economic accumulation, but also from credentialism—the main form of collective social mobility and power for the middle class. For example, in his study of the medical field, Robert Dingwall argues that a medical student's knowledge is based not only on acquiring specialized knowledge through education (e.g., medicine), but also through socialization into the style of the field. A central example of this learned style would be the concept of rational detachment or intellectual distance from their work, which is a characteristic that divides the professional from the layperson. Such learned behavior gives the patient and/or the public the sense of a "special" service and therefore, reinforces the idea that the practitioners are "special" people deserving greater status. [14] Here, the professional project echoes Michel Foucault's suspicion of the professional classes' ability to naturalize power distinctions. Sociologist Magali Larson echoes this position when she calls for the questioning of the "expert's collective appropriation of knowledge." [15]

Nevertheless, Keith Macdonald chronicles how the United States has had historically a distinctly more ambivalent relationship to expertise than these European-derived models might suggest. The United States was founded on democratic and anti-elitist principles and in reaction to religious and aristocratic privilege in England. As opposed to Great Britain, America was slow to construct professional associations that legitimize the authority of the professions. In *Anti-Intellectualism in American Life* Richard Hofstadter writes that Jacksonian America's

> deep distrust of expertise, its dislike for centralization, its desire to uproot the entrenched classes, and its doctrine that important functions are simple enough to be performed by anyone, amounted to a repudiation of a system of government by gentlemen which the nation had inherited from the eighteenth century but also the special value of the educated classes in civil life. [16]

The United States has come to define expertise based on the standards of pragmatic capitalism, judging experts based on their practical achievement or experience. Higher education in America has a greater applied orientation than its European equivalents. Educated knowledge alone no longer remains a standard for status; one must "prove" one's knowledge through application. At its worst, this sensibility refuses to recognize the importance of a class of intellectuals who are separated from the dominant norms and therefore able to critique such instrumental reasoning. This ethos has also bequeathed to the country a legacy of quackery where the educated expert has been replaced by those who have mastered the style but not the knowledge of a profession. [17] Expertise has become a democratic theater that anyone can enter. Yet at its best, this American ethos and its disdain for abstract knowledge have come closer than other democratic nations to challenging the hegemony of the bourgeois public sphere. The question remains: what has replaced the professional and the intellectual of the bourgeois public sphere as a figure of popular expertise in America?

Popular Experts on American Talk Shows

> popular expert: one with the ability to make learned knowledge concrete through not only simplifying abstract ideas but making them less "removed" through example and emotion-based experiences.

Talk shows represented a change in the nature of proof we demand of claims made about social truth in the 1980s. In this forum, the distant evidence of expert knowledge was no longer valid. Yet talk show audiences also rejected the synthetic spectacles of television; they were preoccupied with validating the authenticity of lived experience as a basis for social truth. Talk television sought tangible evidence of social truth through personal testimonials, emotional displays, and bodily signs. The pleasure of watching often involved ferreting out "real" from "acted" emotion both in guests and host. The genre still represents a distrust of both learned knowledge of expertise and the simulated truths of media fictions.

Expertise on talk shows of the 1980s and early 1990s involved the ability to make learned knowledge concrete; this process involved not only simplifying abstract ideas but making them less "removed" by drawing on concrete examples and emotional experiences. Gilda Carle might be easily dismissed as a simple quack if it were not for her emotional "skills." Her style reflected a long line of itinerant medicine-show "doctors" beginning in nineteenth-century America who were more often vaudeville actors than trained physicians. Her "Ph.D." is not in psychology, but rather in organizational studies from New York University. She had not written a book; her expertise was based on her professional experiences working at her consulting firm specializing in "applied" communications where she had advised IBM and the New York City government among others.

Carle had created a distinctive performance style that played well in the context of talk television. She gained media access from a video infomercial that she sent the talk show producers. After she was invited onto *Geraldo,* her career snowballed. Like almost all talk show experts, she received no money—only exposure for herself and her consulting firm from appearances. She maintained that she does the work because she simply "cares." Carle argued that she did not do "therapy" on the talk shows; rather she gave "therapeutic tips."[18] Her tips mentioned psychological categories ("dysfunction," "self-esteem," and "ego"), but not the underlying theoretical logic of psychology. Her logic emerged through personal narrative—the "I," "you," and "me," and ultimately the "we" of the American commonsense ideology. Carle's style communicated her pleasure in performing and the audience responded positively to her willingness to engage them.

The power of the expert-as-showwoman was clearly visible when Dr. Pat Allen appeared on an *Oprah Winfrey Show* (as it was then titled) devoted to how to get married (March 14, 1994). Winfrey introduced Allen and her book, *Getting to "I Do"*: "If you follow her advice, you will snag a man within a year!" Allen's first words: "Everyone is both masculine and feminine." She continued, "There is no such thing as a woman that is too masculine." A few minutes later, Allen proclaimed that "the problem is we don't need to marry any more. Men can go to a gourmet cooking class and we can go to a sperm bank." The audience members laughed and applauded wildly. They enjoyed her gutsy proclamation of female independence and her own showwomanship. The use of the all-inclusive "we" of shared experience, the mixing of abstractions with everyday knowledge, and the willingness to entertain powerfully reinforce her American commonsense ideology.

Consider how Naomi Wolf (the second expert) failed initially when she challenged Allen's essentializing feminine behavior as passive. She easily outreasoned Allen, whose analysis of female/

male relationships became increasing incoherent. Wolf preferred a more traditional argumentative approach. She related primarily to Allen and not the audience. In other words, she debated. She did not use an expansive approach. Not only did she respond without references to everyday experience, she initially revealed no pleasure in her own performance; she was annoyed at Allen's circular reasoning. However, Wolf rose finally to the occasion in exasperation and acclaimed emotionally, "I know a lot of wonderful marriages . . . a lot of my friends. The reason that they are wonderful is that they are equal." The audience exploded in applause with appreciation for the intensity of her feeling and the depth of her experience. Nevertheless, she continued to be interrupted by Allen, commercial breaks, Oprah's interjections, and audience questions. An articulated counterstatement could not be made left to only jab at Allen's homespun nonsense.

Conventionally, critics lambast such television discussions as the sites of corporately produced irrationality, spectacle, and emotional extremes.[19] They would have argued that Wolf's resorting to emotion and personal testimony trivializes her ideas about feminism. Admittedly, with their populist and commercial bent, these talk shows were not a platform for scholarly or even well-reasoned treatises. An essential attraction of talk shows as popular culture is their ability to deflate the bourgeois hold on knowledge. Pat Allen implicitly understood the power of iconoclasm, ordinary speech, and performance. Her style echoes Michel de Certeau's point in *The Practice of Everyday Life:* "The critical return of the ordinary, as Wittgenstein understands it, must destroy all varieties of rhetorical brilliance associated with powers that hierarchize and with nonsense that enjoys authority."[20]

Some cultural studies academics have celebrated talk shows because of the shows' open hostility to expertise and educated knowledge. Carpignano and fellow writers embrace an angry show like *Morton Downey Jr.,* which "rejects the arrogance of a discourse that defines itself on the basis of its difference from common sense."[21] For an example, they cite a *Downey* show on the student massacre at Tiananmen Square that allowed an expert from the conservative Heritage Foundation to be shouted down by an anarchist squatter group. Carpignano et al. argued that Downey provided "a forum for the disenfranchised, especially young white men (working and lower middle class) who were not represented in current knowledge-based commodity culture."[22]

Yet the commonsense ideology of popular expertise often forecloses the possibility of political change. "Common sense" is a vague term that veils a complex process by which talk shows individualized what should be understood as social issues. In her study of the popular discourse of race on *The Oprah Winfrey Show,* Janice Peck analyzes how audience members privileged individual experience as the "primary source of truth." Through their self-help logic these programs encouraged taking responsibility for one's *own* feelings and behavior. They base such a belief on a core assumption that the participants are "powerless to change anything beyond our own lives."[23] Through the discourses of Protestantism, liberalism, and the therapeutic, the programs reproduced the dominant ideology of "self-contained individualism"—a foundational cause of the existing social order in America.

Peck looks at a thirteen-part *Oprah Winfrey Show* series called "Racism 1992." Here, racism is understood by the talk show participants because of individual opinions, experience, and rights. Ending racism is reduced to healing oneself of one's prejudice as opposed to collective political change. For Peck, even identity politics with its structural awareness of power fails to offer an avenue for political change; its emphasis on different identities does not imply the necessity of a political struggle.[24]

Despite the repressive nature of commonsense ideology, talk shows still depend on a notion of feminine unity: women share their different personal struggles as part of a shared account of common feminine experience. The vast majority of experts for talk shows have been women. And their expertise is often motivated by personal experience. Their popular success depends on whether they are willing to evoke that background and reject the intellectual distance that traditional expertise demands. Such openness involves a willingness to become the equal of audience members who, as lower-income women, rely more on personal experience than on abstract knowledge for their reasoning.

Talk show audiences' efforts to test expertise against lived experience offers a critique of the traditional standards of proof or research methodology. Classical notions of evidence would exclude the personal as too subjective and not representative. *The Oprah Winfrey Show* has reversed this tradition of objective distance by celebrating the authority of spontaneous emotion and raw evidence. The tension between expertise and experience surfaces during an episode on Prozac (April 14, 1994). Using a direct satellite broadcast from the Pacific Northwest, the program presents the Prozac-taking citizens of Wenatchee, Washington, and their psychologist. From the start of the program, Oprah frames the issue of the psychologist's abundant prescriptions of Prozac for his patients as potentially either representative or anomalous of national trends: "You know our society is always looking for the fastest, the easiest, the quickest fix, but is this right?" The slow process of individual audience members getting up and testifying to their similar experiences suggests that the audience represents a microcosm of a larger community—society-at-large.

Traditionally, the mark of bourgeois propriety has been the clear distinction between the public and private spheres. Almost every issue-oriented talk show starts out with a bit of a risk: Will the guests be seen as anomalous and alone, and therefore, potential "sideshow freaks?" Or will audience members in a fit of spontaneous emotion be led to reveal their shared experiences? Lurking below the surface is the supposition that rational people do not reveal their private lives on national TV unless they deem it socially important. This episode also depends on this tension for excitement.

Even with an audience populated with Prozac takers, the question remains the same. Will these women overcome societal anxieties about the drug and testify? The spontaneous breakthroughs increase as audience members both in Wenatchee and the studio eagerly jump to the mike and passionately profess their relation to Prozac. As one woman stated: "My secret is out." This rising tide of testimony not only leads to a truth based on sheer numbers, but also to a truth based on experience. The audience members are represented as real people whose experiences cannot be reduced to the expert's numbers and sociological language. The close-up and the zoom provides an optical tool for scrutinizing and evaluating the veracity of these performances.

This particular program adopted a classical talk show relay. The guests on the stage begin the emotional displays about the subject—their use of Prozac. Then an invited Prozac user in the audience angrily challenges the assertion that Prozac creates a false personality. This intensity builds through continual testimonials about the normalcy of the experience until one gets the sense that if the audience is representative according to the show's logic, American women are born anew, well-adjusted, highly emotional, and on Prozac.

The emphasis of identity politics on a hierarchy of oppression contributed to *The Oprah Winfrey Show*'s division between audience members and experts. Audience members on talk shows often attempt to close off discussion, asserting that by nature of their oppression—race, gender, or class standing—they are a priori morally right. This "one-up oppressionship" allowed a series of Prozac-taking audience members to disallow experts as having only "academic knowledge" of the pain of depression. When Dr. Peter Breggin (author of *Toxic Psychiatry*) states: "Oprah, people want to believe—we want to believe that it is a biochemical imbalance," the audience of Prozac-takers asserts angrily, "It is!" So powerful was this belief in the power of personal experience (particularly physical and emotional suffering) that the audience claims to know more about chemistry than a psychiatrist who was a leading authority in psychopharmacology. A guest Prozac taker challenges Breggin about a potential contradiction in his personal habits: he has expressed an interest in drinking the liquor in the limousine on the way to the talk show. For her, this incident reveals his own parallel dependency on a chemical. He has failed to "live" his theory and thus has lost his authority.

Finally, the topic of Prozac represents an important test of the authenticity of these displays because of the concern with whether people are "themselves" on Prozac. A central pleasure of talk shows is the ability to judge to what degree the guest is expressing authentic emotions or "'just an act.'" Oprah poses the question: "Does a drug like this hide or enhance who we really are?" and the program becomes an exercise in discerning whether it is the person or Prozac speaking. The Prozac-taking audience members argue that they are in fact themselves, only now "enabled" or "chemically balanced." Yet the two experts argue against the drug's use because it was not "'natural.'"

Even though these talk shows raise the potential for a popular knowledge base, they are commercial institutions that maintain the productive power about which Foucault warns. In this case it still falls to an expert to close the debate. As the credits rolled, Peter Kramer (author of *Listening to Prozac*) argued that the success of therapy and medication is "unarguable," but only for serious situations deemed necessary by the doctor. Here, bourgeois expertise still dominates. Often, expertise bows too willingly to the dictates of commercial TV logic—providing "can-do" individualism

closure to complex social narrative. The audience may be posed as the judges listening and weighing evidence based on common sense and personal experience, but the expert most often gets the final word in the debate.

These talk shows do not follow the classical tradition of the bourgeois public sphere, where J. B. Thompson maintains that "the authority of the state could be criticized by an informed and reasoning public or 'publicness.'"[25] Rather the talk show relies on the tangible proof offered by emotional testimonials and bodily signs (laughter, facial expressions, and tears), all forms of argument and evidence available to the nonexperts. And the acceptance of this proof on these talk shows tests the power of the educated bourgeoisie to define politics and debate. Popular expertise is founded on the ability to extrapolate theory from experience. We may wince at the silliness of the homily of turning the "m" in "me" into the "w" of "we," but that ability to move from personal to collective experience is the power behind the popular expert on television.

In this postmodern age of simulations, talk shows beginning in the 1980s demanded a belief in the authenticity of lived experience as a social truth. Perhaps such direct appeal to raw emotion is what makes the educated middle class so uncomfortable with the so-called oprahification of America. As one *Oprah Winfrey Show* audience member stated on April 14, 1994: "Don't tell me how to feel. I am my experience."

The Organic Intellectual

organic intellectual: a new class of intellectuals who have emerged out of the community they want to represent and enunciate that experience to enact political change.

Talk shows are also arenas for a rare and disappearing political breed: organic intellectuals who are tied to the community they study and publicly represent. They differ from other popular experts such as Gilda Carle who depend on a stylized evocation of experience without the social context. Organic intellectuals draw their power directly from the specifics of their experience. The term, "organic intellectual" itself is derived from Antonio Gramsci:

> Every social group, coming into existence on the original terrain of essential function in the world of economic production, creates together with itself, organically, one or more strata of intellectuals which give it homogeneity and an awareness of its own function not only in the economic but also in the social and political fields.[26]

In this description, intellectuals are no longer only the elites who exist outside or above society. Rather, a new class of intellectuals has emerged from the community they represent. Gramsci rejects simple binaries between bourgeois intellectuals and working-class nonintellectuals. The working-class individual (or the so-called average audience member of a talk show) always has an intellectual or abstract component to her discussion.

Gramsci called for the nomination of working-class thought as a form of intellectualism at its "most primitive and unqualified level."[27] Organic intellectuals understand the sphere of production and day-to-day experience. Their role is to enunciate that experience to enact political change. They are teachers, industrial workers, and organizers who have developed self-consciousness about their culture. These people are "mediators as they are mediated by their constituency."[28] Gramsci writes:

> The mode of new intellectuals can no longer consist of eloquence, which is an exterior and momentary mover of feelings and passions. Rather it participates actively in practical life as constructor, organizer and "permanent persuader" and not just a simple orator.[29]

But how does the potential subversion of bourgeois expertise hold up when there are women or black intellectuals on talk shows? We need to consider how the dominant ideology in America is not only anti-intellectual, but how it does not accord the rights of expertise to women and most particularly to African Americans. Although the American intelligentsia is by and large economically advantaged as a middle class, they are culturally a political minority and women and black intellectuals are even smaller minorities.

Cornel West outlines a model for the organic intellectual in the black community. He argues that intellectuals should not isolate themselves from their community. The black intellectual must stay firmly grounded in African American traditions—gospel and orality, the rhythms of jazz and blues, and the nuances of black popular culture. To build insurgency, the black intellectual works to build high-quality institutions of black critical learning. West struggles to reconcile alternative practices derived from African American culture with European models of intellectualism. In the end, black intellectuals must continually engage in a "self-inventory" to survey their general cultural role, their relationship to historical, and social forces, and their contributions to the community at large. No longer can bourgeois intellectuals un-self-consciously represent the needs of cultural communities with whom they have no direct connection.[30]

How does the model of this black organic intellectual work in practice on a commercial talk show? It would be difficult to describe *The Oprah Winfrey Show*—an internationally syndicated talk show—as an African American (or, for that matter, a feminist) institution even though the host is black, the production company (Harpo Productions) is owned by a race-conscious black woman and its staff is dominated by women of color. As Peck points out, the program neutralizes its racial elements through the leveling effect of individualist ideology. Yet, the show routinely features black experts who often face political resistance.

All talk shows, including *The Oprah Winfrey Show*, have to operate within the dominant Western discourses on race if they want to enjoy commercial success with a broader audience. Because the genre in the 1980s and early 1990s was based on a series of representative social or interpersonal conflicts, the program relied on racial stereotypes. When it came to racial issues, a particular episode's central problem was how to stage these issues as a conflict, with clear and recognizable oppositions leading to a quick solution. Such commercial pressures do not allow for a complex representation of social or historical context. This is why 1980s talk shows were not platforms for the subtleties of racial issues or the complexities of any public-sphere debate. Instead, talk shows dwelled on the universals of personal experience as their core knowledge base. Here, we see the leveling of distinctions as every member of the audience was asked to identify with the program's core narrative. However, the talk show's desires as a capitalist institution must be separated from the discourses and political aims of the intellectual/expert and the audience members.

How did these intellectuals negotiate the limitations of a race discourse on talk shows that continually asserts that "we all are one"? How might have they escaped the naturalization of unstated racial stereotypes (e.g., black perpetrator and white victim) to reach more complex explanations of social and cultural experience? The program, "How Did Black Men Become so Feared" (March 22, 1994) features four black intellectual men: two academics (Michael Dyson, an American civilization professor from Brown University, and Walter Allen, a sociologist from UCLA) and two reporters/memoir writers (Brent Staples of the *New York Times* and Nathan McCall of the *Washington Post*).

Interestingly, when talk shows attempted a traditional public sphere discussion, it does *not* take the form of a debate with the public; rather it was more often a dialogue among the experts themselves. Openly political topics are too volatile for talk shows to throw open debate to an unselected audience; the risk of alienating a potential con-

sumer and thus lowering profits is too great. The episode of *The Oprah Winfrey Show* on fear of black men was no exception. The first ten minutes of the program was consumed in an elaborate retelling of the history of the African American male. Oprah Winfrey and the two academics narrate, quoting historical data, slave narratives, slave advertisements, and the memoirs of renowned black writers, and ending with McCall reading from his memoirs recounting his experiences as a young man on the street. They move through slavery, northern migration, the rise of segregation and northern ghettos to the advent of crack to provide a highly schematic (and problematic) context for their discussion. This introduction's complex use of media and didacticism is a rarity.

The black experts dominate the program and audience discussion nearly disappears. Only three audience members speak. The famed democratic participation of the talk show recedes. On one level this change results from the need to establish the complex context for a less informed audience. But on another level, talk shows can't seem to reconcile the urge to teach politics with their tradition of audience discussion. It is only when such programs populate the audience with preselected "informed citizens" as in the affirmative action program on *Donahue* (March 21, 1994) that the audience comes alive.

Nevertheless, a different notion of democratic participation takes place on this *Oprah Winfrey Show*: the experts become representative of broader communities because their knowledge is based in lived experience. Three out of the four intellectuals describe how they grew up in the ghetto or how they (or a brother) were arrested for illicit behavior. The reporters read from their memoirs full of streetwise experience and dialect. Dyson repeats this style, slipping back and forth between the King's English and black English while peppering his discussion with references to the Christian faith, black writers (Richard Wright), and popular culture (Snoop Doggy Dogg).

Similarly, on the affirmative action episode of

Donahue, Jamie Washington speaks as both an expert (college administrator) and a black who has experienced a world without affirmative action. Yet each of these experts pulls back from their community to reestablish their claims to top-down authority. This is the talk show version of the organic intellectual—urbane middle-class spokespeople who can mix social criticism with personal experience. They do not quite fulfill Gramsci's claim for the self-conscious intellectual who speaks from within the community for which they advocate. Muhammad Ali and Huey Newton would be better representatives of that aspiration.

Nevertheless, *The Oprah Winfrey Show*'s organic intellectuals refuse the simple discourse of self-help or rugged individualism that predominates on talk shows. Following commercial logic, the programs emphasize a "can-do" (or can consume) solution or a spiritual transcendence of complex social issues. The show is the most notorious for this logic; its affirmation of individual will and spirituality is represented by Oprah's battle with weight loss and her references to a higher power. Brent Staples paints a rose-colored affirmation of black life: "The black experience in America has so much vitality and love in it." Oprah continually returns to the individual helping another as the source of change. However, the academics refuse such simple explanations. Dyson describes slavery as "deeply ingrained tradition in the mores and folkways of American culture." Allen asserts that several myths are operating in the discussion: "equal opportunities," "individualism," and "how one makes it in society." But Oprah maintains the talk show's emphasis on individualism: "Isn't the bottom line, you do have to turn to yourself?"

Ultimately, it falls to Nathan McCall—a reporter and writer—to translate between the structural determinism of the academics and the individualist ideology of the host. Instead, he offers a simple parable-like narrative:

I think that there is another element too. You have to be able to look around in your environment and get reinforcement for some of the notions and some of the ideas. . . . It is hard to talk to the brother on the block and say that you can be President of the United States one day. And he goes to the encyclopedia and sees all the presidents thus far have been white males. He's hard to convince him of that.

From the start of the program, when he reads from his memoirs, McCall has been positioned as a street poet who has a tighter relationship to his community than the academics can claim. He has done time for criminal activity. He refuses the formal embourgeoisment of the intellectuals with their European horn-rimmed glasses and tailored suits in that he is in casual attire with African overtones. Yet he balks at simple homilies or answers: "We are dealing largely with perceptions here. When I was coming up, once I became convinced that there was no way out and that I was rejected and despised by this society, I wouldn't even try, man. I wouldn't even try. . . ." Although all the men represent variations on the black organic intellectual, McCall reveals the most about his personal experience, his emotions, and his pain—the hallmark of credibility for talk show audiences. His appeal evolves out of his direct tie to his community—, the very definition of an organic intellectual.

These intellectuals' self-consciousness about their authority is the central marker that reveals their organic connection to their community. Within the first third of the program, the problem of the "exceptional Negro" is posed. Dyson begins:

I have personally been impacted when we talk of slavery. I have a brother also who is serving life in prison. . . . I then get a Ph.D. from Princeton University. People say you made it . . . you got out of it, why should we be any more sensitive to your brother? . . . My answer is not only by the grace of God, but I was identified at any early age as a gifted child and that presented me with a set of opportunities for me to escape in ways that other black men weren't able to make it.

Each man attempts to maintain this balance—repeatedly stating that they are from the community, but are still not representative. In my survey of 260 hours of the four top-rated shows of the early 1990s, I have rarely seen experts as willing to question the limits of their authority (even popular forms of authority) and personal experience. Programs depend on expert authority to organize the discussion and direct the emotion. Yet these men reveal pride in their authority while articulating a discomfort and a responsibility that middle-class black intellectuals carry. Dyson states: "When we get these Ph.D.s, we have got to be responsible for these young black brothers. We must be very careful that our analyses are not harming the very people that we got the Ph.D.s for in the first place." The organic black intellectual, with this high degree of self-consciousness, is a much more complex figure than can be contained within any simple celebration of anti-bourgeois talk shows.

Yet for all this questioning, the program asserts closure through a return to belief and individual agency. In the last ten minutes of the program, Oprah interviews Joe Marshall, a radio talk show host (*Street Soldiers*) from San Francisco. Positioned in the audience, Marshall represents a more traditional talk show expert; he is anti-intellectual and given to quick inspirational answers. "I think it is important for us to drop these labels. Lower class, middle class. These are our people! . . . I think these labels just divide; we don't need any more divide and conquer." Oprah responds nodding in agreement: "Unless everyone comes together to try lift everyone up we are going to fall together." And when Marshall at the close of the program issues "a challenge to all men" to create the extended family or "to be fathers to as many young men and young women," Oprah closes his pronouncement with, "You can be the light." In

the end, the talk show controls the organic intellectual's political impact—not only imposing closure, but also limiting the audience's participation. Such commercial imperatives undercut the motivation of the organic intellectual—, which is the political empowerment of the people.

Popular Culture without Experts

> *vernacular theorists*: individuals who *do not* come out of the tradition of philosophical critique but who are capable of raising questions about the dominant cultural assumptions.

After half a decade of dominance by four programs that showed at least a general commitment to addressing political topics, talk shows by the mid-1990s seemingly lost their tie to the public sphere—that independent sphere where citizens can form public opinion freely. Scores of new talk shows debuted: *The Jerry Springer Show* (1991), *Maury Povich* (1991), *Montel Williams* (1991), *Jenny Jones* (1991), *Ricki Lake* (1993), *Gordon Elliott* (1994), *Carnie* (1995), *Tempestt* (1995), to name but a few.[31] Topics ranged from issues of social injustice to interpersonal conflicts that emphasized the visceral nature of confrontation and sexual titillation. The expert disappeared as the number of guests proliferated, resulting in a rapid succession of five-minute sound bytes (conflict, crisis, and resolution).

Everything also got younger—the guests, the studio audience, the host and the demographics. The hosts—among them, Danny Bonaduce (*The Partridge Family*) Gabrielle Carteris (*Beverly Hills 90210*), Tempestt Bledsoe (*The Cosby Show*), Carnie Wilson (*Wilson Phillips*)—came out of the entertainment industry instead of news. Suddenly they were nominated as "experts" based on claims of their "averageness" as products of middlebrow commercial culture. The studio audience moved from the role of citizens making commonsense judgments to spectators hungering for confrontation. Talk shows came to seem more like a tele-vised coliseum where the screaming battles of an underclass were conducted as a voyeuristic spec-tacle rather than a venue for social change. "Go Ricki!!" had become the rallying cry for not only the death of the public sphere, but the private sphere—nothing was taboo. Much of this change resulted from the jettisoning of the experts and the powerful control represented by their bourgeois ideology.

These new "youthful" programs became the latest stage in the generic evolution of talk shows as the historical circumstances of production and reception changed in the 1990s. Deregulation threw off the shackles of early talk show's pater-nalism. Rising backlash against identity politics and its middle-class do-gooder ideology became fodder for commercial exploitation as witnessed by the phenomenal success of the hold-no-bars *Jerry Springer Show.*

Not surprisingly, the bourgeois institutions of both the right and left reacted in horror at the loss of civility. Liberal-to-left periodicals (*Ms.*, the *New Yorker,* and the *Nation*) decried the pro-grams' lack of social consciousness. William Ben-nett, the neoconservative former secretary of edu-cation, launched a campaign against the new talk shows in October 1995, labeling them a form of "perversion" while oddly praising the older, more liberal programs *The Oprah Winfrey Show* and *Phil Donahue* (once considered purveyors of ab-normality) as upholding family values.

Richard Bey stopped airing in Boston in De-cember 1995. In January 1996 *Gabrielle* and *Rich-ard Perez* were cancelled. That month Phil Dona-hue quit. Geraldo Rivera also announced he would like to be a network anchorperson and changed the title of *Geraldo* to *The Geraldo Rivera Show,* which then featured more hard news. With pro-grams entitled "Advice to Oprah Letter Writers" (December 1, 1995) and "Tipping and Gift Anxi-ety" (November 29, 1995), Oprah Winfrey had

gone on a "spiritual quest of moral uplift"—re-turning to the values associated with the genteel bourgeois tradition of feminine advice as she pa-raded the best and the brightest of American bourgeois culture across her stage while an obse-quious audience oohs and ahhhs. Consider how the selections of her much touted book club (*Song of Solomon, The Book of Ruth,* and *Songs in Ordi-nary Time*) promoted the norms of the educated middle class as a standard.[32]

Over the years talk shows have always had a difficult time balancing their populist underpin-nings with their need for profit. By 1995, the genre had forgone its innovative experiment in partici-pation, settling for the safer and economically more stable forum of bourgeois reformism or the visceral spectacle of confrontation. However, the problem lies in part in how cultural studies has chosen to define the expert and/or the intellec-tual. Gramsci nominated the working-class indi-vidual as the public intellectual—not the Michael Dysons of the academy or even the Nathan Mc-Calls, a former street hustler, and now an edu-cated newspaper reporter. Rather, Gramsci saw working-class knowledge as a form of intellectual-ism at its "most primitive and unqualified level."[33] A problem of understanding expertise in a popu-lar medium is that critics have accepted the talk show industry's categories: the educated profes-sional as expert and the guest and/or audience member as the passive objects of critical inquiry. What distinguishes the expert at his/her most ba-sic evocation Gramsci defines simply as those in-dividuals who have developed a self-conscious-ness of the community out of which they originate and they understand the day-to-day experience of production. How does this differ from the present-day talk show participants who criticize each other's social behavior?

Following Houston Baker's championing of vernacular theory, Thomas McLaughlin, in *Street Smarts and Critical Theory,* argues that we must rewrite what constitutes "theory" or abstract thinking—the hallmark of bourgeois expertise. Vernacular theory is "theory that would never think of itself as 'theory,' that it is mostly unaware of the existence of the discipline." He claims that:

individuals who *do not* come of the tradition of philosophical critique are capable of raising questions about the dominant cultural assumptions. They do so in ordinary language, and they often suffer from the blindness that unself-conscious language creates.[34]

Although this vernacular theory is often inflected by dominant ideology, McLaughlin maintains that it still manages to "ask fundamental questions about culture." Vernacular theory is a form of "situated" knowledge that asks questions about the socially constructed nature of local problems similar in kind to those challenges that academic theory poses on a paradigmatic or global level. The result may be progressive or it may be reactionary. In either case, these vernacular thinkers are no longer treated as passive objects of critical inquiry, empty receptacles waiting to be filled with bourgeois knowledge or problems to be corrected.

Then how does the vernacular theorist function within the talk show model? She has traditionally been stereotyped in the written press as the self-absorbed, fannish, or irrational audience member, worshipping at the altar of televised celebrityhood. However, rarely have the actual ideas and values of the audience been examined by either the established press or academic researchers. When presented with a political issue, audience members reveal their self-consciousness of the relation of the personal to the political. For example, consider the following interaction on an episode of *Geraldo* with two Arkansas state troopers who had accused President Bill Clinton of extramarital relations while governor entitled "Passion and Cover-ups: Clinton's Accusers," which aired on

March 3, 1994. Geraldo starts with classic tabloid sensationalism:

These two men made the most scathing allegation against their boss saying he was a philanderer, a wild and crazy uncontrollable sort of guy who put sex ahead of duty and fidelity. . . . Their former boss is of course the forty-second president William Jefferson Clinton.

After Geraldo quizzes the troopers about Clinton's affairs, the muckraking host asks the accusers about their own questionable reputations for adultery, insurance fraud, wife beating, and drunk driving. Then the program turns the questioning over to the audience:

Audience Member #1: How can you sit there and pass judgment on the president when they both sit there like they're proud? And they both also . . . you cheated on your wife as well.

Audience Member #2: If Hillary doesn't care, why should we? (Resounding applause.) And as far as Clinton's sex life, who gives a damn?! And our Constitution, where is it written that we should have a puritan for a president? . . . What is critical is what the man is doing for the country.

Audience Member #3: What does sex have to do with running this country? This happened before we elected him. Why didn't you [speak up] then? Who cares now?

Audience Member #4: Can't we judge Bill Clinton's ethics, morals, performance by his actions on the job, by his presidency, and leave his love life out of it?

The *Geraldo* audience (usually considered a highly emotional one) takes on the guest accusers and an expert and attempts to cross-examine them based on their commonsense understanding of the difference between the public and the private, what fair play means, and a live-and-let-live attitude toward social difference. This particular program had slowly shifted from its sensational opening to a rather controlled examination of political issues by the audience members. Not all programs offer such a progressive example of the audience as vernacular theorists. However, by nominating everyday thinkers as theorists and noneducated knowledge as intellectually sophisticated, and translating intellectual theory to create a self-consciousness of the relation of their personal experience to politics, critics can begin to push for social class change. Recognizing the cultural authority of vernacular theory will not only help enter other forms of theoretical thinking into circulation but also provide a new basis for the critique of traditional academic ideas as the only meaningful form of theory. Ultimately, vernacular theory breaks with the hegemony of educated knowledge.

The Cultural Studies and Expertise

I am a talk show expert. More than that, I am a *popular* expert in that I wrote a book on a popular subject in vernacular language. I am now an expert about talk shows, on talk shows. And my publisher hired publicists to actively promote my book and get me onto the publicity circuit occupied by the bourgeois experts I seek to debunk. Given this essay, this situation must seem contradictory. However, I have never suggested that the bourgeois expert or ideology will disappear. Her role remains to designate everyday experience and knowledge as a form of abstract political thought. In closing, I offer two very different examples of my experience on talk radio to get at the possibilities and limits of expertise and cultural studies.

No popular venue fits McLaughlin's dictum for vernacular education better than AM talk radio. It is known as the town hall of America's airwaves, where nonelites "ask fundamental questions about culture," as McLaughlin demands. In fact, I wrote the body of this essay to think through

my position before I made my "appearances" on radio talk shows—a truly humbling experience.

Early in my short tour of talk radio I was interviewed on the telephone by an AM morning drivetime program out of St. Louis. Between weather reports about the February snowstorm that had hit the city, I was questioned by a pleasant host who had not read the book and asked me to encapsulate it in three minutes. Knowing the conventions of "talk," I gave a cultural studies answer in vernacular language in one minute: that the guests and viewers were not idiots. We needed to rethink what constitutes political discussion to include personal or everyday experience as political. He thought that it was a provocative argument and essentially agreed with it. He liked the populist liberalism implicit in it. He invited his listeners to call in. Although we talked for ten minutes (wedged between ads for tire chains and cold remedies), no one called. In many ways I would call this a "good interview"—no elitism, sexism, and racism as well as no ad hominem attacks. However, it replicated the bourgeois tradition of educated knowledge or "author interview" where my ideas were not challenged by a larger public.

I also carried my populist logic onto *The David Brudnoy Show* in Boston. As a rather angry and educated libertarian, the host claimed that talk show viewers (and/or guests) were not only "idiots," "crybabies," and "passive" (odd accusations given the parallel between TV viewers and radio listeners), but also "black" and "lazy." He abhorred the use of experience as a marker of truth on TV talk shows and the lack of empirical proof for the claims of guests. I replied that not all classes had access to research or educated knowledge. He said that the guests should go to school and get educated. As I stressed the lack of equal access to education in America, his callers chimed in to agree with the host about the decline of America and relative lack of intelligence of TV talk show viewers. Between Brudnoy's grandstanding as the host and the continual call-ins, I became a secondary figure. Brudnoy so enjoyed the chance to air his disgust with the lack of education in the lower class, he extended the segment from a half hour to two hours.

As much as I wanted to write this off as a "bad interview" (my work became a platform for the host's racism), Brudnoy's listeners were not passive or empty receptacles waiting to be filled with bourgeois knowledge or problems to be corrected. They were primarily active, angry, and reactionary men (and women); they attacked the talk shows and their audiences, taking aim at the women and people of color who predominantly populated TV talk shows. Here, my voice was at best equal to the listeners and often overpowered by the dominant voice of a conservative talk show host and the sheer number of angry listeners. Yet given my position as expert, I was allowed a consistent forum for framing a counterposition in a medium that often dismisses counterpositions via the cut-off button. As much as I worry about providing a platform for reactionary voices, this interview at least allowed political difference to be expressed and pitted diverse kinds of knowledges against each other on something approaching an equal level. Here, I acted as a public intellectual who served to bring to the fore an opposing position to the dominant rhetoric. But am I that ideal—the organic intellectual representing my community? Not really. I am a woman who watched talk shows. I do not represent the average viewer—a lower-income woman with little more than a high school education. At best, I aspire to being a public intellectual.

Ultimately, the goal of a public intellectual is to keep inquiry open, promote questioning, and challenge orthodoxy—even the orthodoxy of the left from which I come. And yes, I have also learned from the popular experts of talk shows. I mix theory with my social and personal experience and speak in the language of everyday cul-

ture. But above all, I am an "act"—one with the privilege to speak with authority. My academic distance from emotion and experience only serves to wedge a greater barrier between academics and those we want to reach. I have learned to take pleasure in a performance from watching hundreds of hours of talk show experts—audience members who have questioned, confounded, and criticized—creating the pleasure of talk shows for me.

Notes

1 Alvin Gouldner, *Fragmentation: The Origins of Marxism and the Sociology of Intellectuals* (New York: Oxford University Press, 1985), 14–15.

2 See Vladimir Ilich Lenin, "What Is to Be Done," in *The Essential Lenin,* vol. 1. (London: Lawrence and Wishart, 1947).

3 Charles Guignon, paper presented as part of the Humanities Seminars at the University of Vermont, Burlington, October 27, 1994, 3.

4 Pierre Bourdieu, *Distinction: A Social Critique of the Judgement of Taste* (Cambridge, MA: Harvard University Press, 1984), 68.

5 Janice Peck, "TV Talk Shows as Therapeutic Discourse: The Ideological Labor of the Televised Talking Cure," *Communication Theory* 5(1) (February 1995): 65.

6 See Pierre Bourdieu, "The Uses of the 'People,'" in *Other Words* (Cambridge: Polity Press, 1990), 155.

7 Jim McGuigan, *Cultural Populism* (London: Routledge, 1992), 12.

8 Russell Jacoby, *The Last Intellectual* (New York: Basic Books, 1987), 3–10.

9 Robert Dingwall, "Introduction," in *The Sociology of the Professions: Lawyers, Doctors and Others,* ed. R. Dingwall and P. Lewis (London: Macmillan, 1983), 3.

10 Keith M. Macdonald, *The Sociology of the Professions* (London: Sage, 1995), xi.

11 Stephen Brint, *The Changing Role of Professionals in Politics and Public Life* (Princeton: Princeton University Press, 1994), 150.

12 Ibid., 151.

13 Macdonald, *The Sociology of the Professions,* xii.

14 Robert Dingwall, *The Social Organization of Health Visiting* (Beckenham, UK: Croom Helm, 1979).

15 Macdonald, *The Sociology of the Professions*, 26.

16 Richard Hofstadter, *Anti-Intellectualism in American Life* (New York: Vintage, 1962), 155–56.

17 Macdonald, *The Sociology of the Professions*, 79–85.

18 Warren Berger, "Childhood Trauma Healed While-U-Wait," *New York Times* (January 8, 1995): 33.

19 See Janet Maslin, "In Dirty Laundryland," *New York Times* (October 10, 1993): 7; and John J. O'Connor, "Defining What's Civilized and What's Not," *New York Times* (April 25, 1989): C18.

20 Michel de Certeau, *The Practice of Everyday Life* (Berkeley: University of California Press, 1984), 13.

21 P. Carpignano et al., "Chatter in the Age of Electronic Reproduction: Talk Television and the 'Public Mind,'" *Social Text* 25/26 (19xx): 33–55.

22 Ibid., 53.

23 Janice Peck, "Talk about Racism: Framing a Popular Discourse of Race on *Oprah Winfrey*," *Cultural Critique* (spring 1994): 94.

24 Ibid., 118.

25 J. B. Thompson, *Ideology and Modern Culture: Critical Social Theory* (Cambridge: Polity Press, 1990), 112.

26 Antonio Gramsci, *Selections from the Prison Notebooks*, trans. and ed. Quintin Hoare and Geoffery Nowell Smith (New York: International Publishers, 1971), 5.

27 Ibid., 9.

28 Maria Koundoura, "Multinationalism: Redrawing the Map of the Intellectual Labor in the Age of Post-coloniality," Ph.D. dissertation, Stanford University, 1993, 26.

29 Gramsci, *Selections from the Prison Notebooks*, 10.

30 Cornel West, *Keeping Faith: Philosophy and Race in America* (New York: Routledge, 1993), 67.

31 Other talk shows debuting in 1995 were *Danny!, Gabrielle, Charles Perez, Marilu, Shirley,* and *Mark.* Other shows that were launched in the early 1990s included *Bertice Berry, Vicki!, Les Brown, Jane Whitney, Leeza, Dennis Prager,* and *Rolonda.*

32 There is even a suggestion that talk shows are going to return the *Mike Douglas*-style of the sixties as the light entertainment of celebrity talk of the 1960s as represented by the success of the *Rosie O'Donnell Show*.

33 Gramsci, *Selections from the Prison Notebooks*, 9.

34 Thomas McLaughlin, *Street Smarts and Critical Theory: Listening to the Vernacular* (Madison: University of Wisconsin Press, 1996), 5.

"My Beautiful Wickedness": The Wizard of Oz as Lesbian Fantasy

Alexander Doty

Like many of you reading this, I have a long and tangled history with *The Wizard of Oz*.[1] For the past thirty-five years or so, *Gentlemen Prefer Blondes, I Love Lucy,* and *Oz* have been the popular culture touchstones for understanding my changing relationship to gender and sexuality. It all started in the 1960s with the annual televising of *Oz*. Watching as a kid, I loved Dorothy, loved Toto, was scared of, but fascinated by, the Wicked Witch, felt guilty for thinking good witch Glinda was nerve-gratingly fey and shrill, and thought the Tin Man was attractive, and the Scarecrow a cringy showoff. But I was really embarrassed by the Cowardly Lion. The supporting cast in Kansas was boring, with the exception of the sharp-featured spinster Almira (which I always heard as "Elvira") Gulch. Only the cyclone could equal this grimly determined bicyclist and dog-snatcher for sheer threatening power.

Looking back, it all makes sense. I was a boy who had a girlfriend who I liked to kiss and to play Barbies with, while also looking for chances to make physical contact with her older brother through horseplay in the pool. I was in love with and wanted to be Dorothy, thinking that the stark Kansas farmland she was trying to escape from was nothing compared to the West Texas desert our house was built upon. The Tin Man might stand in for my girlfriend's older brother (and subsequent crushes on older boys): an emotionally and physically stolid male who needed to find a heart so he could romantically express himself to me. During my first phase with the film, I saw Dorothy's three male companions (on the farm and in Oz) as being like friends or brothers. Well, maybe my heterosexual upbringing had me working to construct some sort of love interest between Dorothy and the showoff Scarecrow. But Dorothy and the Tin Man? Never. Hands off girl, he's mine! Without my being aware of it, these latter responses to *Oz* were signs that I was moving into what would become my initial place within straight patriarchy: as straight woman rival and wannabe.

Then there was that Cowardly Lion, who was teaching me self-hatred. From between the ages of five and fifteen, I was actually far less disturbed by the Wicked Witch than I was by the Cowardly Lion. When he sang about how miserable he was to be a "sissy," I cringed. Because I was a sissy, too. At least that's what certain boys at school and in the neighborhood called me when I'd play jump rope or jacks with the girls—or even when I'd go over to talk with them during recess or after school. At this stage, "sissy" seemed to be a gender thing. It meant being like a girl, liking what they liked. However, in my case, this included boys. But I also liked a girl. While watching the film each year, my gender and sexuality turmoil reached its peak when Dorothy and the Cowardly Lion emerged from their Emerald City beauty treatments with nearly-identical perms and hair bows. And then this ultra-sissified lion dared to sing "If I Were the King of the Forest"! I would sit in front of the television set paralyzed: my desire for and identification with Dorothy battling my loathing for and identification with the Cowardly Lion.

Between my late teens and my early thirties I found my desire for Dorothy cooling as I became a "Friend of Dorothy." Early on in this process of identifying as gay, I was still embarrassed by the Lion. I hadn't come out to anyone, and he seemed to be too out: flamboyant, effeminate, and self-oppressive. Not a very good role model, I thought, even though in the privacy of my room, cocktail in hand, I would dramatically lip-synch and act out "Over the Rainbow" with Dorothy. Dorothy

newly endeared herself to me by her concern about the big sissy she was saddled with. She became my first image of the friendly, caring straight girl/woman. Later someone told me these girls/women were called "fag hags"—a term I thought was mean. I was also told all about Judy Garland. The story of her career and personal struggles intensified my identification with Dorothy as a heroic figure.

Some time in my twenties, I became aware of butches and of camp, both of which fed into my developing "gay" appreciation of *The Wizard of Oz.* Camp finally let me make my peace with the Cowardly Lion. He was still over-the-top, but no longer a total embarrassment. Oh, I'd get a little nostalgic twinge of humiliation now and then (I still do), but by and large I found him fabulously outrageous. King of the Forest? He was more like a drag queen who just didn't give a fuck. Because of this, he seemed to have a bravery the narrative insisted he lacked. Camp's appreciation of the excessive also led me to reevaluate Glinda. She wasn't just *like* a drag queen, she was one! Artifice surrounded her like that pink (but of course) gossamer gown she wore. Who better to guide Dorothy along the road to straight womanhood, I thought. I saw this as a great ironic joke on all those straights who claimed the film as theirs.

And who better to try and prevent Glinda's plans for Dorothy than some horrible, predatory butch dyke? At this point, the only lesbians I could (or would?) recognize as lesbians were butches. To be honest, sight recognition was about as deep as my interaction with butches went, as the gay society I was keeping from the mid-1970s through the early 1980s did not encourage gay and lesbian mingling. You would have thought that Stonewall, with its frontline drag queen and butch dyke fighters, had never happened. So I enjoyed the Wicked Witch of the West as a camp figure: she was just another scary, tough butch dressed in black whom I could laugh at.

The more extensive political and social coalitions formed between gays and lesbians beginning around the mid-1980s, in large part in response to the AIDS pandemic, gave me opportunities to get to know lesbians beyond the tentative looks and "hellos" we'd exchange at bars and on the street. Needless to say, what I learned from them gave new meaning to many popular culture texts. Besides recognizing butches, I might also be on the lookout for femmes—and butchy femmes and femmy butches. And just like gay leathermen, I learned that not all butches are tough and scary. And not all femmes dressed or behaved as they did in order to "pass" in straight culture. Add to knowledge like this my encounters with academic gender and sexuality theory and criticism during the same period, and you have someone who was beginning to see many of his favorite pop culture "classics" in a very different light. Not that all of the ways in which I understood these texts previously were wiped out. Aspects of certain readings and pleasures I let go, but other parts remained to complement or supplement my later interpretations. It now seems to me that heterocentricity and sexism limited and perverted much of my earlier straight, bisexual, and gay readings of Oz. Actually, returning to Oz again and again in recent years has helped me to do battle with some of the remaining limitations and perversions of my straight upbringing. So I'm in love with The Wizard of Oz all over again, and, as with any (re)new(ed) love, I feel compelled to publicly count the ways that I now love Oz.

I'm feeling especially compelled to do this because of the continuing and pervasive influence of heterocentrism and/or homophobia and/or sexism upon both queer and straight understandings of popular culture. To refer to the case at hand: here is a film about an adolescent girl who has an elaborate fantasy dream in which there is not a whisper of heterosexual romance—even displaced onto other figures.[2] Uh, could this girl possibly not be interested in heterosexuality? Well, according to far too many people I've encountered,

including a fair share of gays, lesbians, and straight women, this is not really possible. This cannot be a film about a teenaged girl who is having a rite of passage dream in which she fantasizes about the possibility of a choice outside of heterosexuality. Tell me, then, where *is* the heterosexuality in this fantasy?

In terms of heterosexual readings of The Wizard of Oz, the fantasy, my friends, is not all up there on the screen. Caught within the spell of heterocentrism (and, for some gay and straight men, sexism), viewers of all sexual identities persist in seeing heterosexuality where it ain't. I say it's wishful reading into the text. Or, if not that, it's a subtext. In any case, a heterosexual reading of The Wizard of Oz is appropriative, and clearly subordinate to lesbian readings. OK, maybe I'm overstating the case a bit with some of these remarks, as I certainly don't want to suggest that queer readings should just replace straight ones in some hierarchy of interpretation. But I'm constantly being pissed off at the persistence and pervasiveness of heterocentric cultural fantasies that, at best, allow most lesbian, gay, bisexual, and queer understandings of popular culture to exist as appropriative of and subsidiary to taking things straight.

What I find particularly disheartening is that this heterocentrism (and, sometimes, homophobia) often plays itself out in academic and nonacademic arenas as some sort of contest between straight female or feminist approaches and queer approaches to understanding popular culture. While the following cases in point involve straight women, as they come from my recent experiences surrounding the material in this essay, in another context I could just as easily have illustrated the pop culture territoriality of many gays, lesbians, and other queers. First example, I was discussing stardom with a graduate student, when she asked me to name some gay cult stars beside Judy Garland. As I began to rattle off a list, she stopped me at one name. "Wait!" she said, "Don't take Bette Davis away from us, too!" Before this, I hadn't thought of gay culture—or gay cultural studies— as taking anything away from anyone. Nor had I wanted to believe that anyone apart from white, straight patriarchal types would think that stars and texts were commodities to be owned by one group of cultural readers or another. Was I ever naive: I guess most people out there really are lifting up their leg or squatting to mark their popular culture territory. Regarding the subject of this chapter, there was one student at a college in Louisiana who let me know through her friends that she would not be attending my lecture because she didn't want to have *The Wizard of Oz* "ruined" for her by all my dyke talk about the film. Something similar happened in class during a discussion of *Thelma and Louise*.

One final example: after reading a draft of this essay, a feminist academic (speaking for herself as well as for a group of editors) was concerned that I "[did] not acknowledge that this is an appropriative reading—[a] move from a women-centered film to a lesbian film." Well, 1) a lesbian film is also "women-centered," just not *straight* woman-centered, and 2) my move from reading *Oz* as straight woman-centered to understanding it as a lesbian narrative was an act of revelation, not appropriation. I don't see the process of queer interpretation as an act of "taking" texts from anyone. Just because straight interpretations have been allowed to flourish publicly doesn't mean they are the most "true" or "real" ones. *The Wizard of Oz* is a straight narrative for those who wish it so. As I (half-) jokingly said earlier, if anything, I would now see straight understandings of *Oz* as "appropriative."

Related to the issue of "appropriation," the editor(s) also "would like [me] to discuss more directly the process of reading an externally 'straight' text as 'queer.'" Oh, yes, and while I'm at it, since my "reading will probably outrage many in the straight community," could I "address that anger"? Well, I think I'll address this kind of straight anger by suggesting that any offended

straights address the heterocentrism (and, yes, sometimes the homophobia) that is at the heart of much of the incomprehension, defensiveness, or shock they register in the face of gay, lesbian, and queer readings of popular culture. Oh, and they might also mull over the following, from Terry Castle's *The Apparitional Lesbian:* "When it comes to lesbians . . . many people have trouble seeing what's in front of them. The lesbian remains a kind of 'ghost effect' in the cinema world of modern life: elusive, vaporous, difficult to spot— even when she is there, in plain view, mortal and magnificent at the center of the screen. . . . What we never expect is precisely this: to find her in the midst of things, as familiar and crucial as an old friend, as solid and sexy as the proverbial right-hand man, as intelligent and human and funny and real as Garbo."[3]

ONE OF THE JOYS of working with popular culture as an academic fan is that you never know when or where you'll find material for your current project. It can jump out at you from a scholarly piece you are reading "just to keep up with things," it can pop up during an evening of television watching or magazine scanning, or it can wait for you on a shelf in a store. During a vacation in Provincetown, a largely lesbian and gay resort at the tip of the Cape Cod peninsula, I found myself browsing in a Last Flight Out store. I was looking at a display of t-shirts celebrating famous women aviators, when I was struck by a shirt at the center of the display. On the shirt was a drawing of old-fashioned flight goggles, and within one lens were the ruby slippers from *The Wizard of Oz.* The inscription on the shirt read: "Dorothy had the shoes, but she didn't have the vision. Take the controls. Women fly." In the essay that follows I want to argue that Dorothy really did "have the vision," if you consider that everyone and everything in Oz is a construction of her fantasies. But I understand the frustration with Dorothy expressed by the t-shirt's inscription. Because, at least on the face of it, it seems Dorothy's vision of flying—with all its classic pop-Freudian dream symbol references to expressing sexual desire—is focused on a pair of pretty ruby slippers rather than on the film's more obvious fetishized object of flight, the Wicked Witch's broomstick.[4] I guess for the t-shirt designer, Dorothy unwisely chooses the spectacularized, objectified feminine fetish over its active, phallicized counterpart. But those shoes have their own power, too, even if it is less clearly defined for most of Dorothy's fantasy than is the power of the Wicked Witch's broomstick. And I think the power represented by both the slippers and the broomstick is dyke power.

I know that I'm not the only person who understands the Oz sequences of *The Wizard of Oz* as the fantasy of a teenaged girl on the road to dykedom. But from everything about the film in print or on television, you'd think (as I did once) that *Oz* can only be either a classic heterosexual rite of passage narrative or a gay campfest.[5] Of course, as I've mentioned, within certain gay readings, the Wicked Witch of the West is often understood to be "the mean dyke," but Dorothy is never, ever anything other than straight: Dorothy/Judy Garland is a "fag hag"-in-the-making, skipping down the road with her rather queer male friends.[6] But even children understand that the energy-center of *Oz* has something to do with Dorothy and Miss Gulch/the Wicked Witch—while everyone else, even Toto, is caught up in their passions and desires. Almost every year the telecast of *The Wizard of Oz* inspired my siblings and me to stage an impromptu version of the film using the sidewalk around the block as the Yellow Brick Road. At each of these performances there were only two essential props: one sister's sparkling red plastic high heels and a suitably messy old broom. My sisters and I would then argue about who would play the two star parts—leaving the loser and our two turned-out-to-be-straight brothers to play Glinda and whatever male roles they fancied.

I have already admitted that at the time, and well into my adult years, I understood some of my pleasures in the film as women-centered but not necessarily as queerly lesbian-centered. Like many gay men, the enjoyment I derived from the woman-woman intensities I found in *The Wizard of Oz* had more to do with what I took to be the spectacle of straight women's antagonism, or with "translating" these women's exciting expressiveness to suit my gay needs. I just didn't consider that the women in the film might be desiring outside of straight or gay contexts. I suppose the inability of most people to consider that Dorothy might be (or be becoming) lesbian can be attributed to that general cultural heterocentrism (to which sexism is sometimes added), affecting straight and queer alike, that considers all fictional narratives and characters heterosexual unless denotatively "proven" homosexual. This attitude puts the burden of proof on nonheterocentric fans and/or academic commentators, who find that they must develop their skills in exhaustive close reading if they are going to make any serious impression at all. Without the weight of close readings, it is all-too-easy for non-heterocentric and queer comments of any sort to be dismissed outright or to be patronizingly embraced as "fun" or "provocative." Thank goodness that decades of popular culture fandom has prepared me to do these "close readings"—otherwise known as watching a film (television show, etc.) over and over, examining and raving about every little detail of the text to anyone who will listen, and then using all these details to get someone else to "see the light" about the film (television show, etc.).

In the context of a heterocentrist (homophobic, sexist) culture, close reading often becomes a social and political strategy: perhaps through overwhelming details and examples we can make what is invisible to so many, visible and what is denied, possible. Yes, this is usually a reactive position: I often wish I could just go on and on about my queer popular culture enthusiasms without self-consciously presenting the material with a resistant or hostile listener or reader in mind. But I rarely have this luxury. The straightforward pleasures most fans, academics, and academic fans get in talking or writing about the cultural objects of their affection are almost always heavily mixed for me. Certainly anybody can find themselves in the position of defending their popular culture readings and enthusiasms, but I am often made to feel as if I am also defending my identity or my existence. Or as if I am being chastised for being too visibly gay or queer, and for "recruiting" straight texts as part of some nefarious or misguided plan for a queer takeover of (supposedly) heterosexual popular culture. Or, at the very least, as if I'm about to be caught trying to pull a fast one by "reading an externally 'straight' text as 'queer.'" For some reason, queer and nonheterocentrist interpretations of things are never "just another way to see things" for most people, but something akin to delusional experiences, no matter how many examples you provide.

Having said all this, I will soon proceed with another of my grand delusions and justify my queer love for *The Wizard of Oz* in glorious detail, including juicy bits of behind-the-scenes production factoids and gossip (a.k.a. "archival and fieldwork") without which no academic fan piece is complete. I'll probably have to work even more overtime than usual on this close reading because the tendency toward heterocentrism becomes even more pronounced when people consider characters like Dorothy (and actual persons) who are under eighteen: any signs of homosexual desire and/or lesbian, gay, or queer identity in children and adolescents usually remain unacknowledged or dismissed as evidence of psychosexual "confusion."[7] In the case of *The Wizard of Oz* we also have to remember that for millions of people this film is a sacred text of their childhood, and, therefore, one that is not to be sullied by discussions of sexuality—particularly queer sexuality. Is it any wonder that the idea of twelve-year-old Dorothy Gale (played by sixteen-year-old Gar-

land) as a developing dyke hasn't exactly been at the center of public or academic readings of *The Wizard of Oz*? But the more I look at the film, the more I am convinced that a lesbian angle is essential to interpreting Dorothy's dream-fantasy. Considering this approach seems particularly vital in the face of the plethora of "compulsorily heterosexual" or gay public, journalistic, and academic readings of Dorothy and the film that I mentioned earlier.[8]

For example, in one of the first attempts to use psychoanalytic theory to explain *Oz*, Harvey Greenberg makes a sharp case for the importance of Dorothy's closeness to her Aunt Em on their matriarchally run farm. Rather than celebrate this intense bond, however, Greenberg sees it as a "pathological dependency upon Em-Mother" that Dorothy needs to get over in order to grow up, which in this context means to move on to a heterosexual relationship with someone like Hunk, the farmhand who becomes the Scarecrow in Dorothy's Oz fantasy.[9] What Greenberg doesn't seem to recall is that during his (psycho)analysis of Dorothy's fantasy he also admits that the men in Kansas and Oz are "presented as weak and damaged in some fashion, while the women are far more capable."[10] So, following Adrienne Rich's line of thought in "Compulsory Heterosexuality and Lesbian Existence," why *should* Dorothy want to break her connection with Aunt-Mom-women and realign herself with Uncle-Dad-men?[11]

Salman Rushdie's reading of the film is more self-consciously feminist—at least on two pages. He "rehabilitates" the Wicked Witch by suggesting she "represent[s] the more positive of the two images of powerful womanhood on offer" in Oz—the other being that of Glinda, the Good Witch of the North—because in her rage at her sister's death the Wicked Witch shows "a commendable sense of solidarity."[12] Rushdie also understands that *Oz* doesn't have a traditional male hero and that "the power center of the film is a triangle at whose points are Glinda, Dorothy and the

Witch."[13] And at the center of this triangle lies the magic of the ruby slippers. The power of the wizard "turns out to be an illusion," Rushdie continues, so the film reveals that "the power of men . . . is illusory; the power of women is real."[14] But all this talk about reclaiming "wicked" witches, the absence of a male hero, and the powerful triangular relationship between women in Oz only flirts with the sapphic. Finally, the feminist elements in Rushdie's take on *The Wizard of Oz* remain within the rhetoric of straight sisterhood.[15]

A more consistently straight feminist reading of the film is Bonnie Friedman's "Relinquishing Oz." What is fascinating to me about this analysis is the number of times it suggests contiguous, and even common, ground between straight feminist and lesbian approaches. While she employs a mother-daughter paradigm to discuss the film, as Greenberg does, Friedman's reading more directly addresses the issue of woman-woman erotics. "The story is a mother-romance," Friedman says near the end of her piece.[16] And while she makes a compelling case for the film as a straight mother-romance—Dorothy returns home to become companion to and replacement for Em-as-mother—Friedman suggests the possibility of queering her own reading when she remarks that in the witch's castle Dorothy is "like a girl who leaves home for erotic love and can't come back."[17] So for all her attempts to connect Aunt Em and the Wicked Witch as harsh straight mother figures, Friedman can't help but see the two women as offering very different options for Dorothy. While the tenor of the article as a whole asks us to read this "erotic love" as heterosexual, it just doesn't make sense within the film context for Friedman's statement, which invites us to see the contrast as that between an "erotic love" related to Dorothy's encounters with the witch and a "home" that is connected to fulfilling a heterosexual wife-mother role.

Friedman's article provides a useful starting place for developing a more pointedly lesbian reading of Oz. Indeed, Friedman begins her article by wondering if she "shouldn't have hated that witch so much," as a child because she really represents non-normative female desire and power.[18] Rushdie is also high on the Wicked Witch of the West. Describing her as "lean and mean" in her "slimline black" outfit, Rushdie is on the verge of calling the Wicked Witch "butch," particularly in contrast with Glinda, whom he finds "a trilling pain in the neck" in her "frilly pink."[19] A quick look at *The Wizard of Oz*'s production history reveals that the Wicked Witch's butchness was to a great extent consciously developed—if not, perhaps, called "butch" by the film's collaborators (but you never know). In early versions of the script by Noel Langley, the Witch has been married and has a son, Bulbo. This mother-son relationship is developed to suggest the classic overly-protective-mother-and-gay-son stereotype: "There, my darling boy, mother'll kiss it better! Bulbo musn't cry now; he's going to be King of the Emerald City, and Kings never cry!"[20] Reinforcing this gay rather than lesbian context for the Wicked Witch was the initial casting of Gale Sondergaard in the role. It was producer Mervyn LeRoy's idea to have Oz's Wicked Witch look like the Evil Stepmother in Walt Disney's *Snow White and the Seven Dwarfs* (1937).[21] The result was the Wicked Witch as glamorous diva, with Sondergaard made up "wearing green eye shadow and a witch's hat made out of black sequins."[22]

But as the script changed—particulary with the work of the gay man–straight (I think) woman team of Florence Ryerson and Edgar Alan Woolf—so did the image of the Wicked Witch. It was sometime during the period of making the witch less glamorous that Sondergaard, concerned with maintaining her image, dropped out of the project. Enter Margaret Hamilton and a plainer look for the Wicked Witch. One production still shows Hamilton with her own unaltered features, sans obvious makeup, and with a de-sequined black hat over a near-shoulder-length flip hairdo.[23] But no one was satisfied with this middle-of-the-road approach. It was probably during gay director George Cukor's stint as production consultant on *Oz* that the Wicked Witch got her final look: a sharp nose and jawline, green face and body make-up, a scraggly broom, claw-like fingernails, and a tailored black gown and cape.[24] This is the witch as creature, as alien, as monster, and as what straight, and sometimes gay, culture has often equated with these—butch dyke.[25]

This big bad butch witch, who is loud, aggressive, violent, and wears an obvious "uniform," had been developed by the time of the final script to function on one level as a contrast to good witch Glinda. However Glinda presents complications for lesbian readings of *The Wizard of Oz* that have something to do with Rushdie's complaint that she is a "trilling pain in the neck [in] frilly pink." For Glinda seems to be one of those images of femmes in popular culture that are coded to be able to pass as heterosexually feminine in the eyes of certain beholders.[26] But look at Glinda again: there's more than a touch of camp excess here that finally seems expressive of lesbian femmeness rather than of the straight feminine. And let's not forget that while Glinda may look like a fairy godmother, she *is* a witch, and is therefore connected to the Wicked Witch and to centuries-long Western cultural associations between witchcraft and lesbianism.[27] So what we have set before us in *The Wizard of Oz* is the division of lesbianism into the good femme-inine and the bad butch, or the model potentially "invisible" femme and the threateningly obvious butch.

Into this sexual terrain comes Dorothy, a sixteen-year-old girl just off the farm.[28] Or, rather, it is Dorothy who constructs this sexual fantasy-land after being hit on the head by a flying window frame during a cyclone. The distinction between Oz as a "real" place and Oz as a fantasy is one that the film seems to do its best to blur, however. While almost every commentator and fan has crit-icized the film's final framing device, which, unlike the L. Frank Baum novel, makes Dorothy's adventures in Oz a "dream," *Oz*'s movement from sepia cinematography in the short opening Kansas sequences to brilliant Technicolor during the more lengthy Oz sequences, and back to sepia again in the brief Kansas coda, serves to make the Oz material more vivid and vital. In a very important sense, then, the Oz narrative seems as "real" to the film audience as it is to its adolescent hero. Put another way, the effect of the Oz sequences in *The Wizard of Oz* is true to the perceptions of most teenagers. As one teenaged girl quoted in an essay on *Oz* says: "Fantasy *is* real, necessary, and . . . home is not always the best place to be."[29]

Home down on the farm in Kansas during the latter years of the Great Depression would certainly "not always be the best place to be" for many garden variety heterosexual adolescents, let alone for lesbian, gay, and otherwise queer teens. Among many other sources, Greta Schiller and Robert Rosenberg's documentary film *Before Stonewall* and Allan Berube's *Coming Out under Fire* reveal how the particularly repressive atmosphere of rural and small-town America before World War II worked to force most queer women and men either into an imitation of straight life, into closeted homosexual furtiveness, or out into urban centers.[30] The first and third of these responses are important to understanding Dorothy's farm and fantasy lives in *The Wizard of Oz*. Dorothy, told by her Aunt Em to "find yourself a place where you won't get into any trouble," translates this into "someplace where there isn't any trouble," thereby placing the blame on normative rural culture, not upon herself. Deciding there is such a place, but that "it's not a place you can get to by a boat or a train," Dorothy launches into "Over the Rainbow." While the Land of Oz is most generally this "over the rainbow" place, we discover late in Dorothy's Oz fantasy that at the heart of Oz lies it fabulous capital, Emerald City, through which Dorothy and her friends are conveyed to their beauty makeovers in a carriage pulled by the hue-changing "Horse of a Different Color."[31]

Before letting Dorothy and her gay companions reach what initially appears to be an urban paradise for queers, however, we need to go back to the start of her fantasy, as it is here that the film establishes the terms for its simultaneous expression and disavowal of lesbianism.[32] Two things are central to this expression and disavowal, witches and ruby slippers. To repeat a bit from an earlier section: the distinction Dorothy's fantasy makes between the witches of the East and West and the Witch of the North turn out to be those between two types of witches—wicked butch and good femme—not the one between fairy godmother and evil witches that the fantasy appears to be presenting with its visual and aural iconography.

The film most strikingly reveals its use of witch = lesbian cultural coding, as well as its butch = bad lesbian associations, during the portion of Dorothy's fantasy that takes place inside the cyclone. At one point, Dorothy's Kansas nemesis, the spinster (as with witch, read "lesbian") Almira Gulch comes riding by—or, more accurately, is imagined by Dorothy to be riding by—on her bicycle. The original dyke on a bike, Gulch almost immediately transmogrifies into a shrieking witch flying on her broomstick: spinster = witch = evil butch. Less apparent is how the cyclone episode also sets up the femme-inine woman as the positive model. As the published script puts it: "An OLD LADY in a rocking chair sails past. She is knitting busily and rocking, seemingly unaware that she is no longer on her front porch. The old lady waves as she floats out of sight."[33] So where Gulch's spinster harshness is made the clear model for the Wicked Witch of the West's butch badness (reinforced by the same actress playing both parts), the relationship between Aunt Em and Glinda as images of femme-inine goodness is more obliquely established through the old lady (who looks very much like Aunt Em) floating in front of Dorothy's bewildered eyes, much as Glinda will soon float down toward an equally as-

tonished Dorothy in Munchkinland. This less obvious, more heavily translated, connection between Aunt Em and Glinda falls squarely within the film's sexuality politics, which, at least on the surface of things, opposes butch and femme, demonizing the former for being loud and obvious (the shrieking laugh, the grotesque green makeup, the black uniform), while humanizing the latter with a name (Glinda) and the ability to pass as a non-witch. Recall along these lines that Dorothy doesn't initially allow herself to recognize Glinda as a witch. "I've never heard of a beautiful witch before!" she effuses to a smiling Glinda, who replies, "Only bad witches are ugly." But what can we expect of Dorothy's fantasy when the most readily available cultural images are of "ugly," bad butch spinster-witches? Even after she learns there are "beautiful" witches, however, the term "witch" is used almost exclusively in Dorothy's fantasy to pejoratively label the "ugly" butch variety. What's happening here in terms of Dorothy expressing her dyke desires through her Oz fantasy is complicated. Faced with her own nascent lesbianism, as well as the cultural taboos surrounding the open, positive acknowledgment of these desires, Dorothy's fantasy most clearly represents lesbianism in the conventional form of the evil, yet powerful, butch dyke witch. As she sings to the Munchkins by way of explaining her cyclone adventures: "Just then the witch / To satisfy an itch / Went flying on her broomstick thumbing for a hitch." It appears the "itch" the Wicked Witch wants to satisfy is somehow connected to hitching a ride from Dorothy, who has warily watched said witch from her *bedroom* window.[34] And all of this happens deep within the swirling vortex of a cyclone, which becomes in this context a rather outrageously heavy-handed symbolic representation of the classic dangerous butch stereotype: they possess and desire female genitalia (the vortex) while identifying with heterosexual ("phallic") masculinity (how the cyclone *externally* takes the shape of a funnel). Put it all together and you have a destructive force that sweeps through the conservative heartland of

America, separating a young girl from her family. While presented as threatening and predatory, however, the sexualized ("To satisfy an itch") image of the butch dyke in the cyclone is the only one Dorothy constructs here that will carry over into Oz. Even before we hear the suggestive lines in Dorothy's song, however, the fantasy image of the Wicked Witch has been (homo)sexualized by its pointed visual connection, through that special effects dissolve, to a dyke Dorothy is already acquainted with: the spinster Almira Gulch.[35] There are also moments in the Kansas sequences that suggest everyone knows about Gulch, including a lot of bizarre talk about Dorothy "biting" Miss Gulch, Dorothy's calling Gulch a "wicked old witch," and Aunt Em's "for twenty-three years I've been dying to tell you [Gulch] what I thought of you . . . and now . . . well—being a Christian woman—I can't say it!"

As you might expect, the image of spinster-turned-butch witch is one that Dorothy feels culturally compelled to distance herself from—at least in the "public" spaces (that is, on the manifest level) of her fantasy. So Dorothy also constructs the type of woman she can more safely admire, be in awe of, and perhaps desire: a glamorous witch whom she, and most of the audience, can take to be the epitome of straight femininity. Dorothy's Glinda is both witch and not conventionally witchlike, both lesbian femme and "straight acting and appearing" (to borrow a phrase from certain gay personal ads). Perhaps the ability to pass is the reason Glinda seems a less powerful and compelling figure than the Wicked Witch of the West in this particular lesbian fantasy. But this was not always the case. One Noel Langley draft script suggested the erotic power of Glinda's femmeness as it has her plant a "magic kiss" on Dorothy that protects her from the wiles of the Wicked Witch.[36] However, while the kiss survives in the film, it has lost its magic power.

Given the tangled and conflicted impulses toward lesbianism expressed in Dorothy's fantasy, it comes as no surprise that she both suggests and denies her connection to witches on first meeting Glinda. When a puzzled Glinda asks the tomboyish yet gingham-dressed Dorothy if she "is a good witch—or a bad witch" (a femme or a butch) Dorothy denies being any kind of witch, because, as culture has told her, all witches are old and ugly. It is here Dorothy's fantasy reveals that Glinda is also a witch, thereby establishing a model through which she can begin to explore and come to terms with her own lesbian desires under cover of femme-ininity. But while Glinda provides her with a safe, because straight-appearing, outlet for lesbian expressiveness, Dorothy invests the Wicked Witches of the East and West with the most power and fascination in her fantasy. When she first meets the Witch of the West in Oz, Dorothy tries to convince her that the death of her sister, the tyrannical ruler of the Munchkins, was "an accident."[37] While there are no "accidents" in fantasies, it is clear that Dorothy has the farmhouse, and all it represents culturally, really kill the butch Wicked Witch of the East. She doesn't mean to kill (or want to kill) the witch—something that is reinforced in the later "accidental" death of the Wicked Witch of the West by water. So even while she has the Munchkins and Glinda praise her as a "national heroine" by singing "Ding dong, the witch is dead," Dorothy distances herself from the killing of the butch witch by picturing herself as being trapped within that Kansas farmhouse (and its normative ideology) at the time of the death. But it would appear that the cultural pressure on Dorothy is such that she still feels she must contrive to set herself up in opposition to butch witches. Therefore, the Wicked Witch of the West remains unconvinced by Dorothy's protestations of innocence: "Well, my little pretty, I can cause accidents, too!"

However, Dorothy establishes her connection to witches and with witchcraft—including the butch variety—by dreaming up what has become, along with *Citizen Kane*'s Rosebud, the most fabulous fetish item in film history: the ruby slippers.[38] There is probably no need to rehearse at any length what the sequined blood-red slippers "stand for": teenaged Dorothy's physical entrance into adulthood, as well as her subsequent sexual explorations. It is their particular place within Dorothy's fantasy narrative that give them their dyke associations. As Salman Rushdie puts it, "Glinda and the Wicked Witch clash most fiercely over the ruby slippers"—and, as Dorothy dreams it, over her body once it wears the coveted slippers.[39] "Surrender Dorothy" indeed! Given the "bad butch—good femme" dynamics of the Oz fantasy, however, these slippers come to indicate Dorothy's sexualized genitalia even while disavowing any "obvious" lesbian desire: the butch Wicked Witch can't even touch the femme-inine shoes while they are on Dorothy's feet without getting a shock. However, when they are first placed upon her feet, the shots of the ruby slippers are clearly presented within the narrative as a spectacular display for the Wicked Witch's benefit. While Glinda says to the Wicked Witch, "There they are, and there they'll stay," we are offered a close up of the slippers being modeled by Dorothy against the backdrop of Glinda's pink gossamer gown: the femme displaying herself for the butch? Or, perhaps, the tomboy-in-gingham trying femmeness on for size in front of a potential mentor and a dangerous, yet exciting, butch spectator.

The initial appearance and functions of the ruby slippers in Dorothy's fantasy also work to connect all the major female figures in Oz under the sign of witchcraft. What is particularly fascinating about the ruby slippers in this respect is how they manage to mix together the femme and the butch, suggesting that while there are butch and femme styles and attitudes, they need not work in tension with each other, nor are they necessarily the only ways to be expressive as a dyke. Dorothy herself is the perfect person to wear these slippers, as, perhaps until her Emerald City beauty treatment, she seems to combine butch and femme qualities as a young girl on the (yellow brick) road to discovering what type of "witch" she is. Ultimately, the uses of the ruby slippers in

Dorothy's fantasy suggest that dyke magic resides neither with butchness or femmeness exclusively, but within all sorts of lesbianism.

The tyrannical Wicked Witch of the East wears her powerful, supposedly incongruous, femmy ruby slippers. But femme Glinda can use her magic to whisk the glitzy shoes off the dead butch witch's feet and onto Dorothy's (despite a noticeable size difference). Oddly enough, however, the formidable butch Wicked Witch of the West seems powerless to remove these slippers, although otherwise her magic seems far more potent than Glinda's. To confuse the butch-femme power issue even more, Salman Rushdie points out that Glinda's knowledge about the shoes in these early scenes is "enigmatic, even contradictory," as she initially says she is ignorant about the shoes' power, even while warning Dorothy to "never let those ruby slippers off your feet for a moment, or you will be at the mercy of the Wicked Witch of the West."[40] Good advice, because, as we all know, they never respect you after they have gotten hold of your ruby slippers! Glinda's advice about the shoes is just what you'd expect Dorothy to have the "straight acting and appearing" femme tell her at this stage of her fantasy. At this point, it is impossible for Dorothy's Glinda to admit to full and clear knowledge of the magic power contained in a pair of femme slippers owned by some butch witch—and desired by her even butcher sister. Glinda is only allowed to impart this formerly unspeakable knowledge as/at the climax of Dorothy's dyke rite of passage, which includes a progression through the vaginal-shaped hallways of Castle Oz, which are colored "Wicked Witch green," as is everything else in the Emerald City. So even while Dorothy's fantasy narrative contrives to separate the Wicked Witch from the Emerald City—as it does with the Wicked Witch and Glinda—imagery like the ruby slippers and greenness in this same fantasy reveals that the agents of so-called butch evil and femme(-inine) good are really related after all. However, within the terms of the manifest fantasy narrative, it is only after Dorothy once again "accidentally" dispatches the "threat" of butchness with that famous badly aimed bucket of water, as well as suffers the failure of patriarchy to help her (after she brings the Wizard of Oz the burnt remnants of the butch witch's "phallic" broom), that she lets femme Glinda come forward to declare that she does know something about the special powers of the butch's femme ruby slippers after all.

Actually, what Glinda says is that Dorothy has always had the "power" within her to activate the ruby slippers, but that she had to "learn it for [her]self." And what does Dorothy learn that allows her to use the power of the fetishized ruby slippers?: "It's that if I ever go looking for my heart's desire again, I won't look any further than my own backyard." Dorothy's lesson returns us, in part, to Greenberg's point about the crucial role Aunt Em plays in her life. If we divest his reading of its pathologizing and heterocentrism, Greenberg makes a compelling case for Aunt Em as orphaned Dorothy's "heart's desire."[41] In many ways Aunt Em is the object of Dorothy's fantasy, for it is her desire to return to Aunt Em in particular, rather than to her life in Kansas in general, which is emphasized time and again in the script. Commenting on early scripts in a lengthy memo to Noel Langley (dated April 30, 1938), Oz production assistant Arthur Freed advises the scenarist to concentrate more on what he feels is the film's emotional center, insisting that "it is our problem to set up the story of Dorothy, who finds herself with a heart full of love, eager to give it, but through circumstances and personalities, can apparently find none in return. . . . She finds escape in her dream of Oz. There she is motivated by her generosity to help everyone first before her little orphan heart cries out for what she wants most of all (the love of Aunt Em). . . . We must remember at all times that Dorothy is only motivated by one object in Oz; that is how to get back home to her Aunt Em, and every situation should be related to this."[42]

Considering all this, it's no wonder that the last face Dorothy sees in Oz is Glinda's (the good witch-mother), and that the first face Dorothy sees at the end of her fantasy of dyke discovery is that of Aunt Em, her mother substitute. But while there is a strong mother-daughter aspect to the lesbian erotics represented in Dorothy's fantasy in "a land that [she] heard of once in a lullaby," it has its limits as *the* explanation of this fantasy's dyke dimensions. Recall that it is Aunt Em who tells Dorothy to find a place where she won't "get into trouble." So a temporary separation from Aunt Em seems as important to Dorothy's development at this point as maintaining the bond with her. Also recall that it is Glinda (Oz's Aunt Em figure) who puts it into Dorothy's head that her goal should be to go back home. But consider this: if Dorothy was so hot to immediately go home to Aunt Em, why does her fantasy repress the fact that she can use the power of the ruby slippers to transport herself back to Aunt Em from the start? Clearly Dorothy wants to be constantly reminded of the importance of her bond with Aunt Em, but she also wants to experience the thrills her fantasy will concoct for her with the Wicked Witch of the West.

Far from being a case of lesbianism as simply a regressive "return to mother," then, Dorothy's fantasy represents the complicated process by which she returns home to renew maternal bonds, but only after she has matured through dealing with the dangers and pleasures of becoming lesbian, which involve both the blatant butchness represented by the Wicked Witch of the West and the femme allure of Glinda and the ruby slippers. Clearly, Dorothy's fantasy is as much structured around a series of exciting flights from and encounters with the shoe-coveting Wicked Witch as it is developed around the return to Aunt Em. As it turns out, these are really two sides of the same narrative coin.

The sequence that most strikingly illustrates all this is the one in which Dorothy is imprisoned in the Wicked Witch's castle with her dog, Toto. When the witch threatens to drown Toto, Dorothy is ready to exchange the ruby slippers to save his life. It is here her fantasy finally contrives a compelling excuse for her to surrender the ruby slippers (with their accumulated fetishistic charge) to the butch witch even though "the Good Witch of the North told [her] not to." But Dorothy still shrinks from any direct physical contact. For after offering to give up her ruby slippers, Dorothy has the shoes give the Wicked Witch a shock as she reaches out to grasp them. "I'm sorry. I didn't do it," Dorothy says at this point, thereby adding one more item to the long list of painful "accidents" her fantasy has developed to deal with her ambivalence about butchness (or "obvious" lesbianism). By having her death be the only way for the Wicked Witch to possess the ruby slippers, Dorothy's fantasy also stages a moment that echoes one tragic way many teenagers deal with the pressures and confusions of becoming queer.

After the Wicked Witch leaves to consider how to kill Dorothy, as "these things must be done delicately," a weeping Dorothy approaches a giant crystal ball in which the image of her aunt appears. But just as Dorothy says "I'm trying to get home to you Auntie Em!," her aunt's face begins to fade and is replaced by that of the Wicked Witch who mockingly imitates Dorothy's words: "Auntie Em, Auntie Em! Come back! I'll give you Auntie Em, my pretty!" In a way, the witch *does* "give her" Auntie Em, because the crystal reveals that in some way the witch and Auntie Em are related in Dorothy's mind. At one point in the film's history, this sequence was much longer. Scripts indicate that this longer version contains many elements that reinforce the fantasy connections between the Wicked Witch and Aunt Em, as well as more clearly establish the relationship between the witch and the fulfillment of Dorothy's desire to find a place "where the dreams that you dare to dream really do come true."

In this extended version, after the witch's mocking imitation of Dorothy's cries to Aunt Em, the sequence continues with the witch forcing Dorothy to perform Kansas-like domestic chores. As she scrubs and mops, Dorothy finds herself

singing "Over the Rainbow" again, even as the witch is concocting a "Spell for Rainbows" in her cauldron: "All the brilliant colors found in the prism are reflected upward into [the witch's] face from the bubbling mass." From the liquid in the cauldron, the witch constructs "The Rainbow Bridge," which the script describes as "a beautiful sight," yet it is to be the means of Dorothy's death. It is the power of the ruby slippers, which "seem to come to life with an irridescent glow," that Dorothy has save her by allowing her literally to go "over the rainbow" made by the witch and off to continue her journey of sexual awareness.

Straight, heterocentric, and homophobic readings (not always the same things) might understand what is happening in the long or short version of this sequence as either the expression of a fear of lesbianism destroying heterosexual-homosocial women's bonds, or as the expression of "how intimately bound together is the Good Mother and the Bad" in the mind of a heterosexual teenage girl.[43] Within the reading I am proposing, however, this sequence becomes the central paradigm for the film's incoherent attitudes about lesbianism. For one thing, the attraction-repulsion aspects of Dorothy's fantasy regarding butch witches are fully on display here, particularly in the longer version of the sequence. The butch witch is both the potential source of fulfilled desires as well as the potential source of physical danger. Besides this, the merging and confusion of Aunt Em and the Wicked Witch in the crystal ball suggests that the developing lesbianism Dorothy's fantasy struggles to express requires that she face up to, and work through, her culturally fostered fears, embodied by the figure of the butch dyke, so she can return to her Aunt Em as a more sexually mature young woman—or, to be more precise, a more sexually mature young lesbian. Will Dorothy become a butch, a femme, or remain "in-between" after she wakes up from her fantasy? I think the film leaves this open to some degree, though her strong identification with the ruby slippers and her glamorizing beauty treatment near the end of the film make me think Dorothy enjoys being a femme.

On the other hand, the question of what kind of witch/dyke Dorothy will become might seem unresolved when you consider that her return to Kansas to look "for her heart's desire . . . in [her] own backyard" will actually involve two yards: Aunt Em's and Almira Gulch's. For if her fantasy has revealed that part of Dorothy's lesbian desires have to do with her relationship with her Aunt Em, this same fantasy has also revealed that other aspects of these desires have something to do with Miss Gulch. It is easy to forget that what initiates both the Kansas and Oz narratives is Dorothy's antagonistic relationship with Gulch, or Gulch-as-Wicked Witch. This has all begun, it seems, because Dorothy's relaxed vigilance has allowed Toto to sneak into Miss Gulch's yard more than once to chase her cat. Pleading that "Toto didn't mean to" do what he did and that "he didn't know he was doing anything wrong," Dorothy sets up the first of many "accident" scenarios involving herself (or in this case her canine sidekick) and butches. Just as when she allows the Wicked Witch to take (or try to take) the ruby slippers in order to save Toto, Dorothy's dealings with Miss Gulch over Toto make it appear that Dorothy can only allow herself to satisfy her curiosity about butch dykes (whether spinster or witch) in indirect, and contentious, ways. So time and again in Kansas and in Oz, Dorothy becomes involved in "accidents" that she allows to happen, whether it's letting Toto get into Gulch's garden, "killing" the Wicked Witch's sister, or having the slippers shock the witch. Bonnie Friedman points out that when one of the farmhands suggests that Dorothy avoid trouble with Miss Gulch by finding an alternate route home, Dorothy replies, "You just don't understand," and lets the subject drop.[44] Is it too much to imagine that Dorothy is forced to stage these encounters as antagonistic because of internalized homophobic cultural interdictions warning little girls to stay away from eccentric spinsters and other "witches"?

So while Oz initially appears to be the place where "the dreams that you dare to dream really do come true," my understanding of the much-maligned "no place like home" finale is that Dorothy comes to understand by the end of her fantasy that her daring dyke dreams will really only "come true" when she returns to those two yards in Kansas and works out her feelings toward both Aunt Em and Miss Gulch. Dorothy's last two speeches already indicate how things are sorting themselves out for her, for while she exclaims "And . . . oh, Auntie Em! There's no place like home!" to conclude the film, her penultimate lines reveal what Rushdie sees as signs of "revolt" after Aunt Em gently tries to dismiss Dorothy's attempt to explain about Oz:[45]

> *Aunt Em:* Oh, we dream lots of silly things when we . . .
>
> *Dorothy:* No, Aunt Em, this was a real truly live place. And I remember that some of it wasn't very nice—but most of it was beautiful!

For a moment before she turns back to praise the virtues of home and Aunt Em, Dorothy rallies to validate her experiences in Oz. Although she doesn't consciously realize it, Dorothy's words here pay tribute to that other key figure in her journey to dykedom, the Wicked Witch of the West (Oz's Almira Gulch), who, with her final breath, half-surprised and half-impressed, exclaims, "Who would have thought that a good little girl like you could destroy my beautiful wickedness!" Dorothy's words, like the witch's, reveal that, to the end, *The Wizard of Oz* remains ambivalent and incoherent about its relationship to lesbianism. It is something that has been, at once, a "not very nice" and a "beautiful" part of Dorothy's fantasy about Oz.

Actually, it was partly through the witch's declaration of her "beautiful wickedness" that I was led to my queer appreciation of the film's lesbian narrative. I'm with Derek Jarman who said that from childhood he "often thought" about the Wicked Witch of the West, and "after [his] initial fright, grew to love her."[46] The Manchester, England, group Homocult ("Perverters of Culture") has presented this gay and lesbian rewriting of the Wicked Witch more boldly by using a publicity still picturing Dorothy in the farmyard, one finger pointing upward, under which they have written "GOOD WAS WRONG, EVIL OUR FRIEND ALL ALONG."[47] My growing affection for the Wicked Witch became one of the keys to understanding that a great deal of my enjoyment of *The Wizard of Oz* is dyke-based. Actually, I've noticed that many of the pleasures I take in popular culture representations of strong women, in women icons, and in women-centered narratives have taken a decidedly dyke turn. My cross-gender identificatory investments in reading certain women characters, stars, and narratives as being femininely straight, are now often supplemented or supplanted by the queer-bonding investments and pleasures I have in understanding these women and texts as lesbian. Sometimes I find I'm combining a lesbian angle on popular culture with other approaches, or I discover that certain pleasures and investments I have in lesbian popular culture personalities, texts, and images become the catalyst for questioning conventional gender and sexuality categories. Should I call these pleasures and investments "queer," "bisexual," or "unconventionally gay"?

For example, *Oz*'s Wicked Witch encouraged me to reevaluate my enthusiasms for her animated sisters, the Evil Queen (*Snow White and the Seven Dwarfs*), Cruella de Vil (*101 Dalmatians*), and Ursula (*The Little Mermaid*). All of these characters now seem to be wonderful combinations of straight diva, drag queen, and formidable dyke.[48] Another example: I have come to realize that I am one of those "femme" gays who find certain butch and androgynous dykes and dyke icons (real and fictional, actual and image) very hot: k.d. lang, Katharine Hepburn as "Sylvester" Scarlett, model Jenny Shimuzu, Annie Lennox, Vanessa Redgrave as Vita Sackville-West, Grace Jones, the Patricia

Charbonneau character in *Desert Hearts,* Margarethe Cammermeyer, Glenn Close as Cammermeyer, and a host of butches I've spotted on the streets, at meetings, and in bars. So—to return to Oz—while I haven't fully abandoned all of my previous pleasures and investments in popular culture, the sissy lion, the "hunky" Tin Man, (straight) Judy Garland-as-gay icon, and the kitschy decor in Munchkinland now stand alongside, and sometimes mingle with, the butch witches, "spinster" Almira Gulch, femme Glinda, and "baby dyke" Dorothy in my understanding and enjoyment of *The Wizard of Oz*.

Not surprisingly, it was Dorothy, or, more accurately, a female impersonator performing Judy Garland singing "Over the Rainbow" for a largely lesbian audience, who became another impetus for my re-viewing *Oz*. Before this drag show I would have been among those who would have categorized *Oz*, Garland, and "Over the Rainbow" as "gay things." Perhaps the overwhelmingly gay public claims on Garland, the song, and the film have kept lesbian appreciations in the shade. Or maybe publicly expressing enthusiasms like these has been considered as not being distinctly "dyke" enough in your popular culture fandom within lesbian culture at large. Whatever the case, that night in a Bethlehem, Pennsylvania, club left no doubt in my mind that Judy, "Over the Rainbow," and *Oz* could be "lesbian things," too.[49] Jimmy James-as-Judy was about to leave the stage without singing "Over the Rainbow" when lesbian audience members chanted for him to sing it. Relenting, s/he sat down and proceeded to sing the song to a butch woman who had rushed up to the stage to kiss "Judy" and tell her that she loved her. By the end of the number it was clear the gay drag performer-as-diva and the crowd had found a common ground in *Oz*'s most famous song, turning it from the "Gay National Anthem" into something like a "Queer National Anthem." One big reason I've written all this lesbian stuff about *The Wizard of Oz*, I guess, is to recapture some of the feelings of queer connectedness that I experienced sitting in Diamondz while a drag queen and his dyke fans came together for a while as "Friends of Dorothy."

Notes

I would like to thank Ben Gove for our challenging discussions, and Phyllis Santamaria and Peter Gove for the use of their place in Ealing.

1   *The Wizard of Oz* (dir. Victor Fleming, MGM, 1939).

2   Documented in John Fricke, Jay Scarfone, and William Stillman's *The Wizard of Oz: The Fiftieth Anniversary Pictorial History* (New York: Warner Books, 1989) is producer Arthur Freed's demands that scripts develop a tighter narrative built around Dorothy and Aunt Em as well as Dorothy and the Wicked Witch. One important result was the gradual elimination of all the heterosexual elements in earlier script drafts, which included a princess and prince pair (Sylvia and Florizel, who in Kansas were *Mrs.* Gulch's niece Sylvia and her boyfriend Kenny), a farmyard romance between Lizzie Smithers and Hickory (who became Oz's Tin Man), an attempt by the Wicked Witch (Mrs. Gulch) to force Princess Sylvia to marry her son Bulbo, and even a flirtation between Dorothy and Hunk (who became the Scarecrow). Traces of the latter pairing might be said to remain in the finished film with Dorothy's pronouncement that she'll "miss [the Scarecrow] most of all" when she leaves Oz. How refreshing to have heterosexuality be the repressed thing whose trace returns in a narrative!

3   Terry Castle, *The Apparitional Lesbian: Female Homosexuality and Modern Culture* (New York: Columbia University Press, 1993), 2–3.

4   Among the many examples of texts that allude to or use the idea of flying as (dream-fantasy) coding for women's non-normative, "excessive" sexual desires, whether straight or queer, are Kate Millet's *Flying*, Erica Jong's *Fear of Flying*, and Dorothy Arzner's *Christopher Strong*. So witches don't ride those broomsticks just to get from one place to another!

5   Among the lengthier critical pieces on the film are Salman Rushdie, *The Wizard of Oz* (London: BFI Publishing, 1992); Fricke, Scarfone, and Stillman, *The Wizard of Oz*; Aljean Harmetz, *The Making of The Wizard of Oz* (New York: Delta/Dell, 1989); Danny Peary, *Cult*

Movies (New York: Dell, 1981), 390–93; Janet Juhnke, "A Kansan's View," in *The Classic American Novel and the Movies*, ed. Gerald Peary and Roger Shatzkin (New York: Frederick Ungar, 1977), 165–75; Harvey Greenberg, "*The Wizard of Oz*: Little Girl Lost—and Found," in *The Movies on Your Mind* (New York: Saturday Review Press/E. P. Dutton, 1979), 13–32; Michael Bracewell, "The Never-Ending Story," *Times Magazine* (London) (January 29, 1994): 18–19; Bonnie Friedman, "Relinquishing Oz: Every Girl's Anti-Adventure Story," *Michigan Quarterly Review* 35(1) (winter 1996): 9–28; and Richard Smith, "Daring to Dream," *Gay Times* 211 (April 1996): 60–61. Of course there are hundreds (thousands?) of shorter reviews of and commentaries on the film, beginning from the announcement of its production in 1938.

6   The introduction to the anthology *Out in Culture: Gay, Lesbian, and Queer Essays on Popular Culture*, which I coedited with Corey K. Creekmur (Durham: Duke University Press, 1995), includes a brief discussion of certain gay camp readings of the film. In "Fasten Your Seat Belts: The Ten Gayest Straight Movies—Ever," *Genre* 28 (May 1995): 71, Steve Greenberg quotes college instructor Daniel Mangin: "Gays seem to identify with this [film] early in their lives. Some gays say they've always identified with Dorothy's pals because their body language and manner of speaking seem so gay."

   To this and other remarks by gay journalists and scholars can be added understandings of the film that center around its production history, particularly around the contributions of gay men like production adviser George Cukor and coscenarist Edgar Allan Woolf, who MGM story editor Sam Marx remembered as "a wild, red-headed homosexual" who contributed "whatever levity and foolishness there was in *The Wizard of Oz*" (Harmetz, *The Making of The Wizard of Oz*, 46).

7   For a more detailed analysis of the representation of homosexuality and adolescence in film and popular culture see Ben Gove, "Framing Gay Youth," *Screen* 37(2) (summer 1996).

8   The phrase "compulsorily heterosexual" is, of course, adapted from Adrienne Rich's landmark essay "Compulsory Heterosexuality and Lesbian Existence," which has been reprinted many times since its initial appearance in *Signs: Journal of Women in Culture and Society* 5(4) (1980): 631–60. Most recently, this essay has appeared, with an afterword from 1986, in *The Lesbian*

and Gay Studies Reader, ed. Henry Abelove, Michele Aina Barale, and David M. Halperin (New York: Routledge, 1993), 227–54.

While placed within heterosexualizing contexts, two pieces on *The Wizard of Oz* contain comments that, taken together, might be read as alluding to certain lesbian understandings of Dorothy. The first is by Salman Rushdie to the effect that "the scrubbed, ever-so-slightly lumpy *unsexiness* of Garland's playing is what makes the movie work" (*The Wizard of Oz*, 27). At the other extreme, a review in *Times Magazine* (London) states, "One doubts this film would have resonated so much or aged so well if any actress other than Judy Garland had played Dorothy. . . . That a corseted, nubile 17-year-old was asked to play a 12-year-old adds a muted but persistent undertone of sexuality to an already disturbing film" (June 8, 1994): 41. Not surprisingly, when taken together these remarks echo conventional notions of lesbianism as a state of being either nonsexual or oversexed.

9 Greenberg, *"The Wizard of Oz,"* 25, 30.

10 Ibid., 22. Greenberg's understanding of the men in the film as lacking in some way is echoed by many commentators. For example, Bonnie Friedman finds that "the men of Oz are all missing one key organ. . . . One suspects that, in Dorothy's mind, the men on Aunt Em's farm all lack an organ, too" ("Relinquishing Oz," 25–26). It would seem to be a very short step from comments like these to understanding Dorothy as a dyke-in-the-making. But, where lesbians are concerned, it seems that this one small step is, indeed, a giant leap for most people to make.

11 Rich, "Compulsory Heterosexuality."

12 Rushdie, *The Wizard of Oz*, 43.

13 Ibid., 42.

14 Ibid.

15 In a short story appended to his critical study of *Oz*, entitled "The Auction of the Ruby Slippers" (58–65), Rushdie places the slippers in a heterosexual context as the male narrator recalls making love to his cousin Gail, who liked to yell "Home boy! Home baby, you've come home" the moment he penetrated her (61). After they split up, the narrator wants to buy the ruby slippers for Gail, in the hope that she will remember their sexual activities and come back "home" to him. While heterosexualized, the ruby slippers are still to a great extent associated with women's sexual desires in this story. The story does suggest that lesbianism and gayness are also associated with the slippers as it describes how one female "memorabilia junkie" and her (non-sex-identified) lover are electrocuted when they place their lips to the glass box in which the slippers are being displayed at an auction, thereby setting off an alarm system that "pumps a hundred thousand volts of electricity into the silicon-implanted lips of the glass kisser" (shades of the Wicked Witch of the West). "We wonder . . . at the mysteries of love," the narrator goes on to comment, "whilst reaching once again for our perfumed handkerchiefs" (58–59).

16 Friedman, "Relinquishing Oz," 27.

17 Ibid., 10.

18 Ibid., 9.

19 Rushdie, *The Wizard of Oz*, 42.

20 Harmetz, *Making of The Wizard of Oz*, 43–44.

21 Fricke, Scarfone, and Stillman, *The Wizard of Oz*, 24.

22 Harmetz, *Making of The Wizard of Oz*, 122.

23 Fricke, Scarfone, and Stillman, *The Wizard of Oz*, 62.

24 Ibid., 72–76.

25 For an excellent discussion of cultural associations between lesbianism and the monstrous, see Rhona J. Berenstein, "'I'm Not the Sort of Person Men Marry': Monsters, Queers, and Hitchcock's *Rebecca*," *CineAction!* 29 (August 1992): 82–96.

26 Both Danae Clark's "Commodity Lesbianism," *Camera Obscura 25/26* (January/May 1991): 181–201; and Christine Holmlund's "When Is a Lesbian Not a Lesbian? The Lesbian Continuum and the Mainstream Femme Film," *Camera Obscura 25/26* (January/May 1991): 145–78, discuss the complexities and complications of popular culture coding that seeks to simultaneously represent the straight feminine and the lesbian femme. I use the term "femme-ininity" in this essay to express this coding and decoding dilemma. When I use the term "femme," I am indicating specifically lesbian contexts and readings.

27 Among the many books and articles that discuss the connections between lesbianism and witchcraft are Vern L. Bullough, "Heresy, Witchcraft, and Sexuality," in *Sexual Practices and the Medieval Church*, eds. Vern L. Bullough and James Brundage (Buffalo, NY: Prometheus Books, 1982), 206–17; Judy Grahn, *Another Mother Tongue* (Boston: Beacon Press, 1990), 80–82, 93–98, 218, 242–43; Arthur Evans, *Witchcraft and the Gay Counterculture* (Boston: Fag Rag Books, 1978); and Anne Llewellyn Barstow, *Witchcraze: A New History of the European Witch Hunts* (London: Pandora, 1995), 72,

139–41, 216–17. I'll let two popular culture examples stand in for the many, many others that use the lesbian = witch paradigm. Mrs. Worthington's Daughters, an English theater company, presented "Any Marks or Deviations," by Charles Hughes-D'Aeth, on a national tour between May and June 1997. The play was advertised as "a chillingly witty ghost story harking back to a time when the love of two women could only mean the dealings of witchcraft." In *The Haunting* (1966, dir. Robert Wise), a doctor calls the two central female characters (one an out lesbian, one a closet case) "witches."

28 For most of her fantasy, Dorothy is positioned—or, rather, positions herself—in between the butch and the femme figures. This butch, femme, and femmy butch (or butchy femme) triad is repeated in a number of popular culture texts, such as the Nancy Drew mystery series, which features butch dark-haired cousin George, femme-inine blonde cousin Bess, and in-between red-head Nancy. The major women characters in the film *All about Eve* (1950, dir. Joseph L. Mankewicz, dir.) also fall into these roles: blonde Karen (femme); ambitious, short-haired Eve (butch), and femmy butch/butchy femme Margo. Not surprisingly, the "star" of these kinds of texts always seems to be the character positioned between butch and femme. In *The Wizard of Oz* it seems to me as though Dorothy is moving toward becoming a femme, if her Emerald City beauty makeover is any indication.

29 Juhnke, "A Kansan's View," 175. In an August 28, 1939, review in the *Minneapolis Star-Journal* by nine-year-old Mary Diane Seibel, she says that "everybody but Dorothy and Toto thought it was a dream. I don't know what to think" (quoted in Fricke, Scarfone, Stillman, *The Wizard of Oz*, 186).

30 *Before Stonewall* (1984, dir. Greta Schiller and Robert Rosenberg), Allan Berubé, *Coming Out under Fire: The History of Gay Men and Women in World War II* (New York: Plume, 1990).

31 Rushdie's description of Emerald City is worth repeating as it suggests something of the queerness of the place: "Members of the citizenry are dressed like Grand Hotel bellhops and glitzy nuns, and they say, or rather sing, things, like 'Jolly good fun!'" (*The Wizard of Oz*, 51). It is also worth remembering that Emerald City is where Dorothy and her male companions receive their beauty makeovers, which leaves the Cowardly Lion looking like Dorothy with a curly coiffeur and a bow in

his hair. And while we're pointing out the signs that mark Emerald City as queer, let's not forget "green" as in "green carnation," a favorite gay-coded accessory of urban dandies from the end of the nineteenth century into the early decades of the twentieth. For more on the green carnation in gay culture, see Neil Bartlett, *Who Was That Man? A Present for Mr. Oscar Wilde* (London: Serpent's Tail, 1988), 39–59.

32 While certainly prominent in Dorothy's fantasy, the Scarecrow, the Tin Man, and the Cowardly Lion function as figures Dorothy has "go along for the ride" with her. She seems to have translated the three ostensibly straight farmhands who work for her aunt and uncle into gay companions mostly to help make her fantasy more queer-friendly. The support of these gay men (as well as femme Glinda) allow Dorothy to persist on the path to lesbianism even in the face of the "interruptions" she has the Wicked Witch devise for her. Considering what appear to be Dorothy's problems with more "obvious" signs and forms of lesbianism, it makes sense she would have gay men and femme-inine women represent benevolent queerness in her fantasy.

33 Noel Lagley, Florence Ryerson, and Edgar Allan Woolf, *The Wizard of Oz* (Monterey Park, CA: O.S.P. Publishing, 1994), 12. All further quoted references to dialogue and action in this essay are taken from this version of the script, which is a transcription of the final release version of the film. This script also contains appendices of material cut from the final released version of the film.

34 There is actually some confusion about just which Wicked Witch is the one who flies past Dorothy's window. Dorothy and the Munchkins' duet here suggests it is the Wicked Witch of the East as "the house began to pitch/The kitchen took a slitch/It landed on the Wicked Witch in the middle of a ditch." However, the Witch who flies past Dorothy in the cyclone is played by Margaret Hamilton, who is the Wicked Witch of the West in the rest of the film. Perhaps the two witches are meant to be twin sisters, or the confusion of the two is meant to suggest that Dorothy still conventionally sees all witches (particularly of the butch variety) as being alike. In any case, the points made later in this section about sexualizing the butch witch as well as those addressing the transformation of spinster Gulch into butch Wicked Witch remain valid no matter which Wicked Witch is looking to "satisfy [her] itch" with Dorothy.

35 The associative connection between Miss Gulch's last name and "West"—as in Western locales like "Dead Man's Gulch"—adds one more point to the case for Gulch turning into the Wicked Witch of the West here, and not into the one from the East.

36 Harmetz, *Making of The Wizard of Oz*, 40.

37 Rushdie offers "the heretical thought" that "maybe the Witch of the East *wasn't so bad as all that*—she certainly kept the streets clean, the houses painted and in good repair . . . she [also] seems to have ruled without the aid of soldiers, policemen or other regiments of repression. Why, then, is she so hated?" (*The Wizard of Oz*, 42). So from all that we can gather from Dorothy's fantasy, this particular butch witch may not have been such a monster after all. Perhaps Dorothy understands this at some level, for while she has Glinda and the Munchkins rehearse conventional cultural ideas about "ugly" butch witches by having them tell her how horrible the Witch of the East has been, Dorothy also protests to them that she killed the witch only "by accident."

38 Besides being a fetish item within Dorothy's fantasy narrative, the ruby slippers have become a more general cultural fetish. Outside of the Salman Rushdie short story, "The Auction of the Ruby Slippers," mentioned in note 15, there are many fiction and nonfiction references, stories, and articles about *Oz*'s ruby slippers. Various pairs of the slippers created for the production have been auctioned over the years, and they have always set records for the most money ever paid for a piece of movie memorabilia. Two popular postcards reproduce the shots in the film of the ruby slippers on Dorothy's feet with 1) Glinda's star-tipped wand next to them, and 2) the Wicked Witch's green hands receiving a shock as she tries to take them off.

There is even a book about the slippers, *The Ruby Slippers of Oz* (Los Angeles: Tale Weaver Publishing, 1989), which centers around the attempts of writer Rhys Thomas to discover just how many pairs of slippers existed and exactly how they related to the making of *The Wizard of Oz*. For the record, Thomas found that "four pairs of ruby slippers are known to have survived the fifty years since the making of *The Wizard of Oz* at MGM in Culver City" (219). Thomas labels these four pairs "Dorothy's Shoes" (won in a contest in 1940 by Roberta Jeffries Bauman and auctioned in June 1988 for $165,000), "The People's Shoes" (now on display at the Smithsonian Institution's National Museum of American History, these are probably the pair purchased by an anonymous buyer at the MGM auction in 1970 for $15,000), "The Traveling Shoes" (owned by collector Michael Shaw), and "The Witch's Shoes" (formerly owned by MGM employee Kent Warner, purchased at an auction in August 1988 for $165,000 by Philip Samuels, they are now on display at his art gallery in St. Louis) (218–24).

A more queer-specific cultural appearance of this fetish can be found in its recent translation into glittering rhinestone-studded pin versions of the red AIDS-remembrance ribbons. Shocking Grey, a gay and lesbian mail order outfit, has advertised these pins ("the new gay and lesbian icon") in their catalog with an accompanying photo of an interracial lesbian couple, one of whom wears the ruby pin.

39 Rushdie, *The Wizard of Oz*, 43. One suggestion scriptwriters Florence Ryerson and Edgar Allan Woolf had for revising Noel Langley's script was to have Dorothy actually take the slippers ("Dorothy has always wanted red slippers") from a temporarily stunned, but not dead, Wicked Witch of the East (Harmetz, *Making of The Wizard of Oz*, 48). This would have made Dorothy much more active in expressing and attaining her desires than she is in the final film, where her fantasy consistently places her in the position of being "done to," or "accidentally" doing things to others. This position might be indicative of Dorothy's fears and hesitancies about more directly expressing her "forbidden" dyke desires even in her own fantasy.

40 Rushdie, *The Wizard of Oz*, 43.

41 Greenberg, *"The Wizard of Oz,"* 15–25. Friedman's "Relinquishing Oz" more directly discusses Em as Dorothy's "heart's desire," but largely within a heterosexualized "home vs. the world" analysis of Dorothy's choices in life (21).

42 Fricke, Scarfone, and Stillman, *The Wizard of Oz*, 30. While Freed continued to insist that *Oz* scriptwriters carefully maintain one important emotional center of the film around the relationship between Dorothy and Aunt Em, he also realized that, at the same time, "the Wicked Witch must be made more of an antagonist" for Dorothy (30).

43 Greenberg, *"The Wizard of Oz,"* 25.

44 Friedman, "Relinquishing Oz," 12.

45 Rushdie, *The Wizard of Oz*, 57.

46 Derek Jarman, *"The Wizard of Oz," Observer Magazine* (London) (April 1, 1981). Jarman also cites the film overall as a major influence on his own films.

47 Homocult, *Queer with Class: The First Book of Homo-cult* (Manchester, UK: MS.ED [The Talking Lesbian] PROMOTIONS, 1992).

48 Films cited: *Snow White and the Seven Dwarfs* (1937, dir. Walt Disney); *101 Dalmatians* (1960, dir. Wolfgang Reitherman, Hamilton Luske, Clyde Geronimi); *The Little Mermaid* (1989, dir. John Musker, Ron Clements).

49 Some lesbian enthusiasms for Judy Garland might have their source in the rumors of her affairs with women, which have been variously labeled "lesbian" and "bisexual." As for "Over the Rainbow," recent evidence that suggests this once almost exclusively gay cultural reference is now understood as also relating to lesbian (and also more generally queer) culture, include the rainbow symbol (which is widely used and marketed in various forms—flags, pins, bumper stickers, etc.), and a four-part television documentary titled *Over the Rainbow* (1994, Testing the Limits/Channel Four UK), which traces lesbian, gay, and queer cultures and politics from the 1950s to the present.

III. MAKER

HOP ON POP

IN THE 1970S, ROLAND BARTHES DE-clared "the death of the author," opening up a phase of cultural analysis in which references to individual cultural creation were viewed as increasingly problematic. Earlier models of the "author" often denied the intense collaboration that occurs between artists and their culture. During this period, cultural studies has sought more dialogic understandings of cultural production, drawing on the model of heteroglossia offered by Mikhail Bakhtin. We can write only through borrowed terms. All acts of writing, Bakhtin argues, bear the traces of the previous contexts in which our words and images have circulated. The writer struggles to inflect the meaning of these precirculated materials, to shape the ways they are understood by viewers. Such a dialogic model of authorship runs directly counter to strong traditions in intellectual property law that stress the value of the work as arising from the original creation of an autonomous individual.

The term "Maker" is intended to suggest this new understanding of cultural production, one that emphasizes the activity of generating cultural materials, rather than the authority of the author. "Maker" allows us to place new attention on the process by which cultural works emerged without succumbing to an ideology of autonomous invention. Makers are understood not as superior beings who generate culture through their own creative energies, but rather as craftspeople who have acquired the skills of their trade and draw on broader cultural resources as the raw material for cultural production. "Maker" is shaken free from its association with a deity.

At the same time, a shift from authors to makers allows us new ways of addressing the anxieties about the absence of traditional marks of individual expression within mass production, anxieties that have characterized many traditions of critical theory. Makers may be individual or collective, depending on the mode of production, and value originates from the relationship of the work to the larger cultural context. The danger of abolishing the concept of authorship altogether was that (1) the absence of a theory of authorship made it difficult to acknowledge both the social and cultural basis of creativity and the distinctive or interesting qualities of individual works, and (2) this anti-authorial stance denied affirmation to those traditionally denied the status of authors as they gained greater access to the means of cultural production. The new concept of "Maker" allows us to understand that works have origins, that they are made from earlier works, and that the aesthetic and ideological goals of their makers are relevant to our understanding of their production and circulation. It also allows us to question the social and ideological functions that the concept of "author" plays in constructing cultural hierarchies or maintaining property rights, issues posed by Michel Foucault.

The essays in this section question the social and cultural construction of "authors" while at the same time examine both individual and collective influences on the creation of popular culture. Many of these essays might have fallen as readily into the "Self" section because they often explore the ways that the social construction of authorship depends upon self-disclosure and how the study of cultural production often makes visible the process of performing the self.

Gerry Bloustein's project involves giving teenage girls the technology necessary to become video makers and then encouraging them to engage in a process of self-representation. By examining what the girls choose to record or not record, to preserve or to tape over, Bloustein is able to document the process of rehearsing the social self that is a central part of adolescent life.

In many ways, the most traditional essay in this section, Henry Jenkins's "A Person's a Person, No Matter How Small" contextualizes the postwar children's books of Dr. Seuss in relation to his earlier political activities as a political cartoonist for *PM* and as a propagandist during World War II.

However, this essay sees Seuss not as an exceptional individual but rather as an exemplary figure who embodies larger social and political shifts and becomes a nexus linking together postwar impulses toward popular democracy and permissive-era conceptions of the child.

Alan Wexelblatt also focuses on the process of authorship, in this case the process of self-revelation and self-promotion that shapes community response to a popular television program. Focusing on *Babylon 5* producer J. Michael Straczinski's active involvement in the Internet fan community surrounding the series, Wexelblatt explores how our traditional conception of authorial authority runs against the much-touted democratic potential of digital media. Specifically, he is interested in the conflict between the focus of many fans on Straczinski's revelations and explanations for the program material ("It ain't so until JMS tells us it's so") and fan traditions that encourage popular creativity and multiple interpretations, a blurring of the lines between readers and authors.

Finally, Stephen Duncombe examines the process of popular authorship, focusing on the autobiographical impulses that shape the grassroots production and circulation of zines. Zines, Duncombe tells us, foreground the value of everyday experience, questioning what counts as important and interesting, and expanding the role of authorship to incorporate a broader segment of the population. He draws on comparisons with the earlier tradition of the pamphleteer to suggest how zines are shaped by our shifting understanding of the relationship between the personal and the political.

"Ceci N'est Pas une Jeune Fille": Videocams, Representation, and "Othering" in the Worlds of Teenage Girls

Gerry Bloustien

With good reason postmodernism has relentlessly instructed us that reality is artifice yet, so it seems to me, not enough surprise has been expressed as to how we nevertheless get on with living, pretending—thanks to the mimetic faculty—that we live facts not fictions.
—MICHAEL TAUSSIG, *MIMESIS AND ALTERITY*, XV

Introduction: The Seriousness of Play

Above my desk sits an old postcard print of Magritte's famous depiction of a pipe.[1] It has inspired me for as long as I can remember with its clever drawing together of the concepts of representation and artifice, reminding the spectator of how easily the two become blurred. Michael Taussig's words, quoted above, also point to this dynamic tension between reality and fiction in late modernity. Taussig, in turn, drew *his* insights from the work of Walter Benjamin, a writer fascinated by the work of the dada movement and surrealist artists such as Magritte. Recorded image and artifice, photography and painted image, truth and falsity—how fascinatingly they twist and intertwine!

Hence I begin, aptly enough with a photograph. It was taken by Kate, one of the young women in my project, nearly three years ago at the beginning of my fieldwork.[2] It is a photograph of her, taken by a third party under Kate's direction. Kate and her friend are wearing cosmetic masks and are gazing intently in a mirror at their own reflections, at their own transformation. The photograph immediately highlighted two impor-

Kate and her friend both watch and participate in their own transformation.

tant issues for me: first, I was aware that these two adolescents were simultaneously participating in and observing their own transformation into something different, something "*Other*," while we, the spectators, voyeuristically looked on. Second, the teenage girls seemed acutely aware of the power of the camera; I stress again the photograph was taken by them, or under their direction, not by me. It seemed that they were demonstrating through their *play*, their awareness that learning to be female and "*performing*" femininity is "hard work."[3]

Kate comes from a home where one would perhaps assume that such *performing* or *learning* was easier than for most. Her parents are highly-educated, articulate people, both university lecturers, who sought to give Kate a sense of her own personhood. She is bright, adventurous, attends a single-sex high school founded on feminist principles. The choice of school was her own, in contrast to many other students there whom she told me had their schooling chosen for them by their parents. Even her surname, different from her parents, was deliberately selected for her at birth and taken from a pioneering female ancestor—a symbolic gesture to give Kate a sense of her own identity and opportunities in life.[4] Yet even for Kate, there are particular gender regimes that are

entrenched and inscribed into the institutions of her life—ways in which she has learned to see herself as a developing woman and not simply a developing adult. If she seemed to be gazing at the mirror quizzically and reflexively in this photograph, she was nonetheless adapting and playing with her image in an attempt to suit or contest the perceived hegemonic demands of her world. Because her world is constituted by not one but many intermeshing and often contradictory "domains," or in Bourdieu's terminology "fields," as are most people's worlds, her attempts are carried out through endless strategies and readjustments.[5]

Through my own early experience as a young woman immigrating to Australia, I too had employed many strategies and readjustments. One of my strongest memories of my initial integration into Australian society was that I was suddenly made aware of my physical difference. I was not tall, blonde, and blue-eyed, but rather dark-skinned, shorter than average, and with a body shape that was far more "at home" in Central Europe. I was continually asked where I had come from by my colleagues at my job, by stall holders in the market, by my new neighbors in the street—the implication being that it had to have been from somewhere else! They were pleasant enquiries, not *meant* to be racist, but it was a sudden lesson in seeing myself as different, as "Other," in a way that I had not before. I had not, and still do not think of myself as "different" but I was being immediately identified as such in my new country.

Twenty years later, I found I relived this sense of Otherness, identifying as I do with my teenage daughter's difficulties with self-image. Having brought up both of my two children on a steady diet of what I believed were feminist principles and assertiveness, I noticed with concern their different levels of self-esteem as they reached adolescence. From being a confident and very assertive child, my daughter had become insecure and obsessed with her body image, and (as she saw it) her inadequate intellectual abilities as she grew older. It seemed to me that she and many of her female friends struggled with a difficult balancing act. The discourse that evolved around school and in their social circles suggested a very particular, narrow way that she and her peers felt they could acceptably identify as both female and successful. She did not feel she fit the desired mold. This metaphor is particularly apt as the importance of physicality, body shape, and image seemed to be salient. In her school that immediately seemed to mark her as different and negatively distinctive even though her institution boasted a range of children from diverse ethnic backgrounds. Second, success at school for my daughter and her friends seemed to depend heavily on relationships both in terms of same-sex friendships and boyfriend/girlfriend alliances, far more than on any kind of academic progress, even though the school regarded its university entrance rates as laudatory. Without being seen and acknowledged to be popular and at ease with one's body, it seemed, one could not afford to be seen as successful intellectually. While this seemed to be so for both sexes, it was a far more acute experience for girls. I soon realized that my daughter's experience was not an isolated one.

Having taught over the years in three high schools, one co-educational and two single-sex, I found the same story repeated and amplified. While boys also seemed to face difficulties of socialization, the difficulties of gender relations had particularly long-term implications for young women.[6] The problem is not so much why certain "myths" about femininity or even adolescence persist and exist side by side but, as Sherry Ortner and Harriet Whitehead point out, "precisely one of understanding why certain 'realities' emerge in cultural thought in distorted forms, forms which in turn feed back and shape those realities."[7]

Some time on, as an academic, I find I am still pondering the same questions. This chapter is drawn from my wider ethnographic research in which I was exploring the everyday lived experiences of ten teenage girls through their own eyes.[8] My key participants were directly involved in telling their own stories on video, selecting, framing, filming, and editing the footage themselves. I am using the term "key" to distinguish between the ten young women upon whom my main analytic lens is focused and the other participants—their teenage friends and acquaintances (sixty-five young people in all), their families, relatives, and significant adults such as teachers, youth workers, social workers, and police—the other people who made up and influenced their worlds. The main participants were deliberately drawn from diverse ethnic and socioeconomic backgrounds, but the process was self-selection. I simply offered a number of girls from diverse backgrounds the opportunity to participate in what I called "the video project." Ten of these girls accepted the challenge and all have stayed with the project until the present day.[9] It is important to stress that the ten girls did not constitute a friendship group. The majority of them had never met. The last two to join the project (a few months after the others) were part of the social network of two of the original eight but were not close friends. These ten individuals were offered the opportunity to document on videotape any aspects of their lives that they considered important. I assured them that they would have complete control over the selection, filming, style, and editing and that if they wished we would screen their edited videos publicly at a student film festival. The girls were given no funding nor specific direction on ways of using the camera beyond the fundamentals. The point was emphasized that they were free to videotape what they liked and how they liked, although I would be willing to show them specific video techniques if they requested. No one did. The camera, lent from the university free of charge to them along with videotapes, was a compact Hi8 "superior" domestic camera—deliberately chosen for its low-light capacity, its near-broadcast video quality but also its small size so that it would be as unintrusive as possible in the girls' lives.[10] The girls reserved the camera through me whenever they chose, taking it in turns to videotape their worlds. In my visits to their homes or to other places where they chose to videotape, to deliver the camera, retrieving it, or just meeting to view and talk about their footage, I gradually was able to establish close relationships with the teenagers, their friends, and their larger social networks.

The process thus examined the way each girl chose to interpret, negotiate, and challenge her perceptions; explored her developing sense of self; as well as her relationships with the various social institutions in which she was engaged. The individuals' videos and the filmic processes clearly demonstrated the ways in which the girls understood their social and cultural constraints, through the perceptual frames and boundaries they placed upon themselves in the task. Not everything in their world was for public viewing. Not everything was selected for recording in the first place. The selection, the filming, and the editing processes highlighted the way the girls struggled to represent themselves in ways that cohered with their already established social and cultural frameworks. On the surface such attempts at representation, such as Kate's, seemed like "just play" but under closer scrutiny we can see specific strategies—"the human seriousness of play"—providing insights into the way gendered subjectivity is performed. Femininity itself, as an integral part of a wider identity, is simultaneously constituted and interrogated through enactment.[11]

Such "play" is closely tied to identity and notions of self, ways of dealing with uncertainty. Our contemporary sense of play is intermeshed with notions of the unreal, the invalid, and the false, and so often it is conceived of as "light," "trivial," "free" activity in contrast to notions of "heavy," "obligatory," "necessary" "work."[12] In fact, before industrialization, while there was a distinction between sacred and profane work, work itself was

not separated from leisure and had in all its senses, elements of "play." [13] Here, then, I am arguing for a concept of embodied play as strategy, one that equates with pleasure but not with triviality. Rather, play involves uncertainty, something that can be powerful and disturbing, which makes it a very powerful medium indeed.[14] It has "the potential to meddle with, to disturb. . . . Subversive, it can rock the foundations of a given phenomenal reality by making their presumptions uncertain and unpredictable." [15] Play requires license, a freedom to be able to state or imply that "this is play," "this is not real." [16]

In my own research I use the concept of play to describe a particular process of representation; strategies that incorporate, reflect on, and depict the individual everyday experiences and perspectives of growing up female in Adelaide, South Australia, in the mid-1990s. I am fascinated with the creative power of representation and play, and particularly concerned with the place that self-conscious representation, reflexivity, or posing played in the search for and portrayal of (self) identity for these young women; how that representation becomes "fact" for them. The form of such searching can be deceptively light, a playing with roles and images, but in true late-twentieth-century postmodernist style—especially as young people live it—it can be an earnest endeavor, a "putting on" of several different hats, a "striking of poses," a matter of serious "work, even desperate work in their play." [17] The introduction of the camera into my fieldwork offered this "symbolic" space to play, to experiment—as I shall detail below—but simultaneously it highlighted the usual difficulties and constraints the girls experienced in their search for different strategies to "strike poses."

"Informants" as "Directors"?

The ten young women who were directly involved with telling their stories on video came from different areas of Adelaide, from a variety of socio-economic backgrounds, and from different familial situations and expectations. They could not be said to represent the diversity of female adolescence and yet I argue that each individual applied the same kind of strategies. Comparable processes were utilized through which each person re-presented herself both on and off the camera and constituted her sense of realities.[18] Each individual struggled to constitute a vitally important sense of uniqueness and difference while simultaneously grounding her perceptions within her already established social and cultural milieu.[19] Conformity continually jostled with distinction, involvement with distanciation.

The key participants were Sara, Fran, Kate, Hilary, Janine, Grace, Mary, Pat, Diane, and Claire (not their real names), ranging in age from thirteen to sixteen years at the beginning of the fieldwork period. Of these ten, six were from Anglo-Celtic backgrounds. Janine identified as Nunga, South Australian Aboriginal; Mary was from Papua New Guinea; Fran had an Indian background; and Sara was born in Nepal. Only Kate came from what traditionally would be described as a highly educated middle-class home. The others came from homes where the education levels and class positions were not nearly so clear cut. The definition of what constituted a "family" for these girls revealed a complexity that is belied by the relative simplicity of government census forms: four of the homes consisted of single-parent families, although there were frequently several adults living in the same household. Two of the girls were living with one biological parent and a stepparent, and some lived with additional siblings, who came and went at different times, from blended families. Two of the rest were living with both biological parents. At the beginning of the fieldwork one girl was living independently but later another teenager moved out of home and into a house with several other friends. Even over the period of the fieldwork, which spanned three

years, several household situations changed—exacerbated by unemployment or changes in relationships, reflecting the fluidity of relatedness in many of the girls' lives.

It is important to emphasize that, in all cases, the participants' friendship groups, acquaintances, and household members constituted other networks that directly and indirectly informed the study, adding a further depth and richness. For example, Mary's friendship network was extremely wide as she spent a great deal of her day in the city itself. Her cohorts were often young people who spent most of their time on the streets, their activities involving alcohol and drug abuse, theft, and property damage. Several had been in the juvenile detention center before I met them or were arrested during the time of my fieldwork. Mary herself was arrested for robbery with violence during this time. Another participant spent a great deal of her spare time involved with Cirkidz, a Youth Arts organization originally formed to teach circus skills to disadvantaged young people in Adelaide. Her social life completely centered around the young people she knew through the circus school. Thus, through her, and her video, I met and developed friendships with another group of diverse young men and women.

The centrality of these familial and social contexts to the way the participants viewed and negotiated their sense of personal gendered identity within their wider cultural milieu needs to be stressed. This very specific ethnographic methodology both allowed access to this "core context" and, through the videos, demonstrated its significance as the research developed. The girls' completed videos were thus a foreground to a much wider complex background, two interconnected parts of one whole. Just as out of the chaos of everyday existence emerges a particular framing perspective from any ethnography or similar research, so these young people placed specific conceptual frames around their own understandings of their lives in their self-conscious reflexivity, and in their attempts to make their videos. This perspective allowed differences and a plurality of attitude and behavior to emerge. The resultant insights, highlighting the particular and the local, emphasize the inappropriateness of talking about "teenage girl culture" as though it were uniform and global. It is the concealed, the differences within, that should demand our attention.

"Other" Ways of Seeing: The Power of Mimesis

I initially conceived this unusual use of the video camera as an aspect of a wider ethnography, as a methodological tool. It would be an innovative solution to the extreme difficulty of "entering" or at least having comfortable and regular access to groups that almost by definition would be closed to me as an adult researcher.[20] The alacrity with which the participants took on the task undoubtedly points to the camera's pivotal place and general acceptance in Western culture. Photographs and film have become significant cultural symbols, epitomizing a particular way in which real life experiences are framed, interpreted, and represented. As a recording instrument, the camera is always utilized with an audience in mind. As such, it is the means through which a particular cultural space or context can be created that is different from the real-life experiences it focuses upon. It can also be used for personal reflexivity— a way of seeing ourselves as we think others see us—or to reinvent ourselves the way we would like to be seen. One way to think about such reflexivity is as representation through the creative power of fantasy and play.

This form of play has taken a very particular form since the advent of the camera, the phonograph, and now the complexities of even more elaborate technologies of mechanical reproduction. Michael Taussig, drawing on Walter Benjamin's insights, developed further the concept of mimesis, the embodied ways of becoming "Other"; the innately human way of attempting to gain mastery over that which we do not understand.[21] He describes the way colonized or dominated groups appropriate for themselves the representations of the dominant culture of their societies, and in accepting for themselves the stereotypes laid upon them, they become "Other." With the introduction of highly technologized means of representing self and Other, the fusion between the two has become greater. Mimesis, or embodied mimicry becomes a way of becoming Other, "wherein the replication, the copy, acquires the power from the represented" and "the capacity of the imagination (can be) lifted through representational media . . . into other worlds."[22] Thus the dominated themselves can take on the means of subordination, often re-affirming the process of domination through their attempts to understand, to resist, to self-empower. As a way to appropriate the power of the dominant, it has been sometimes seen by many as a (perhaps misplaced) strategy of "resistance."

In Paul Willis's early work for example, he observed how his "lads learnt to labour." They took on for themselves the particularly narrowly defined, but for them highly valued, notions of masculinity, that would ultimately constrain them, keeping them away from exploring educational advantages and entrapping them in a life of manual labor. John Fiske, Lisa Lewis, and Angela McRobbie's studies have all explored similar aspects of this phenomenon, especially the way young women have created their cultural identities through forms of popular culture and cultural commodities.[23] Such research has tended to assert in various ways that "the everyday culture of the oppressed takes the signs of that which oppresses them and uses them for its own purposes."[24]

The girls in my study would take upon themselves different expressions of femininity, refracted through their identifications with particular aspects of ethnicity and class, sometimes in ways that reinforced traditional stereotypes. Sometimes their exaggerated expressions of femininity seemed to suggest a form of "mimetic ex-cess"—a way of exploring possibilities and simul-taneously rejecting them through play.[25] However, through an analysis of the girls' use of video, I do not see these strategies as resulting from any clear intentionality, from any clearly perceived goals, or even any sense of "resistance." In fact, their behavior renders many of the usual polariza-tions, such as notions of agency or structure or of submission or resistance, as quite impoverished. Rather, their strategies of play reveal an ambiva-lent and contradictory agency, an attempt to "cre-ate a fit" between the structural constraints of their internalized, embodied values and belief sys-tems and the particular demands and expectations of the current social relational world within which they are engaged, the spaces of objective rela-tions.[26] The issue remains, as Bourdieu is fond of explaining, not so much about changing the rules, or of calculatedly implementing strategies, but rather having "a sense of the game."[27] The way my teenage participants perceived, reflected on, and represented their worlds in their everyday activi-ties demonstrated a particular but often tacit re-sponse to the various constraints that surrounded them, including their own sense of place within their familial and social contexts. Their play, their image-making, their use of fantasy highlighted a simultaneous testing, stretching, and affirming of the symbolic and structural boundaries that sur-rounded them.

Taussig asks rhetorically, "Is it conceivable that a person could break boundaries like this, slipping into Otherness, trying it on for size?"[28] The an-swer lies in part in our limited conception of iden-tity. Although we have rejected for the most part the concept of identity as a "unified essence," we haven't yet fully understood the notion of iden-tity as a process of "who one is to become."[29] Ul-timately, identities are narratives—stories we tell about ourselves—and they are fictional, "the nec-essary fiction of action, the necessary fictions of politics."[30] For such a moment of awareness, a

moment of trying to understand who we are, leads not just to a knowing of the self but also to an "in-terrogation" of the self. It becomes "the discursive space from which The Real Me emerges initially as an assertion of the authenticity of the person and then lingers on to reverberate—The real me?—as a questioning of identity."[31] In more prosaic terms Hilary, one of my teenage participants, addressed just this issue in front of the camera stating, "I look at my video and think, 'My goodness! Is that really me?'"

But identity cannot be looked at in isolation. I would argue that the way each girl used the cam-era to interrogate and construct her sense of self revealed a questioning of the concept of a unified self and a great deal about how she saw herself through several different possible engendered subject positions.[32] It pinpointed the sense of un-certainty that the girls experienced as they strug-gled to manage this elusive sense of self. The point that there is no one single subject position offered to these young women growing up but many, that they were aware of these multiple conflicting dis-cursive sites, can be illustrated by a close look at the way these girls constituted themselves, "exper-imenting" with a variety of images and poses.

What Are Little Girls Made Of?

All the girls were seemingly aware that the cam-era was an exciting way of simultaneously explor-ing and constructing themselves, discovering and constituting "the real me." Hilary, for example, wanted to show how "other girls acted and be-haved" and that "not everyone is the same. We are all individuals." She was aware of the power of me-dia representation and was annoyed that, as she perceived it, teenagers were so often depicted in a negative light, especially in the tabloid press.[33] In this way she and some of the others saw the po-tential of the camera as a "political tool," a vehicle for presenting alternative points of view to a wider audience.[34] This did not mean, however, that the

"That is me?"

girls always approached their films with any obvious generic formula in mind. The only times when this issue did become particularly apparent was when they began to include peers in their videos. Then there tended to be an attempt to stage formal interviews and to generalize for the audience about teenage behavior, asking each other questions such as "What do you think about drug use?" "Do you think boys should tell their girlfriends what they should wear?"

From the range of stylistic approaches that they explored at different times, one could see aspects of music video, parodies of "David Attenborough-style" documentaries, or mock current affairs formats—investigating this strange human species "the Teenage Girl." There were also serious attempts to document the fun, movement, and excitement of their social engagements by using handheld camera techniques with the camera in the middle of the activity rather than as an outsider or voyeur. However, one should be wary of assuming this always meant an engagement with media aesthetics as such. Some of this form was a function of pragmatics. I did not provide the girls with lights, external microphones, or tripods in order to deliberately free up their experimentation with the camera. The result was certainly an experimentation with technique rather than genre—sometimes in ways that made me feel very con-

cerned for the safety of the expensive equipment! While this use of the camera in terms of style, genre, and aesthetics is an interesting topic in its own right, there is no space here to detail its occurrence nor its significance.[35]

What is important to highlight here, however, is what I term the "deflection" of the gaze, a realignment of the way self and self-as-other are related in representation. Each girl's activities raised issues about the concept of the "male gaze."[36] While feminism, queer theory, and postmodernism have from their various theoretical perspectives opened up the analytical gaps concerning representations and constructions of masculinities and femininities, there has been a tendency of late to still view experimentation with style and image in terms of opposing dichotomies. Either such "playing" is perceived pessimistically as meaningless, all image and no substance, "young women's street-wise sophistication . . . mistaken for an assault on patriarchal structures" or the "striking of poses" are seen as meaningful parody, targeting, challenging patriarchal cultural conventions.[37] To assume either position alone obfuscates the complexity of identity formation and "the rhetorics of self-making."[38] Rather, I infer from observing the young women in my study that they oscillated continually between these two extremes, like the movement of Newton's cradle.[39] While each seemed to be making arbitrary decisions about what and how she filmed and seemed to be freely exploring boundaries of identity, striking out and creating powerful impacts, underneath her choice were implicit strategies.

In each circumstance, the participant was directly in control of what was videotaped, how it was framed, and how it was filmed. Simultaneously, she was making various choices about the appearance of control and the subject of the gaze. Most of the girls saw the project and the camera as a way of learning about themselves for themselves. As one girl stated at the end of fifteen months, "I noticed from making and watching the video that

I've changed in the way I act towards people. . . . Normally I wouldn't think much about how I talk and think and that, but when I watch, I can see my actual self." Other participants articulated similar feelings toward the project. Kate, age fifteen at the end of the fieldwork, stated, "Relating it back to now we wouldn't hardly do that stuff now. It's fun to see the trends we had and the words we used and the fashions. It's good to see the changes I've gone through. It's odd to think about all the different personalities inside of me." As Fran, sixteen years old at the end of film production time, affirmed, the camera was a means to not simply learn but also construct the desired image: "Since I started making this film . . . I'm seeing myself through other people's eyes, how other people see me. It's been good though because if you see something you don't like, you can change it. It's different to a mirror 'cause it talks to you."

Talking Mirrors and Private Spaces

The appeal of a "talking mirror" and of contemplating "all the different personalities inside" pointed to an awareness of the elusiveness of an "authentic self," and a need to manage and control the uncertainty.[40] One way in which the girls created boundaries of certitude was to mark off what was private and could be considered as constituting "the real me."

> That's why some people keep diaries. A diary can be more important than a best friend. Sometimes, you can't tell a friend what you are thinking because you may not know whether you really believe it. How can you tell someone something when you don't know whether you know it yourself yet? (Belinda, age sixteen, in conversation with the author)

All of the girls began their use of the camera with an exploration of "private spaces," symbolically demarcated areas for aspects of reflection and reflexivity. Private spaces were usually situated within the home. Returning to my notion of freedom to play, we need to understand that areas designated as private also mean areas that one feels one can symbolically bracket off and nominate as "this is (for) play."[41] The domestic domain with family members and their own bedroom space featured prominently in all of the individuals' films—even when they shared a bedroom with others. For most of the girls this was probably a significant place to start because their relatively young ages meant that so much of their social activity was still taking place within the home. Young women, far more than adolescent boys, still tend to be confined within and by the domestic sphere. Whatever symbolic rites of passage exist for Western adolescents, female initiation into adult status is still a process that is constrained by where and when a girl can go into the public arena in safety or without fear of public condemnation. The home and spaces within the home then become areas where not only can the girl often experience more physical freedom but she can also experiment with behaviors and fantasy, trying on different selves for size, playing within different discourses of what it means to be female in her own community. The type of fantasy that can occur here in a designated private space is different from the kind of experimentation that can take place in other contexts. Here the girls played with different notions of what could conceivably be "real"—this was "serious play." In these spaces, the girls knew and understood their own cultural boundaries, arenas that constituted identity understood as "common sense," "natural," and therefore nonnegotiable. A close look at aspects of Diane's story illustrates this point.

Diane's Story

Diane began her video with a close reflexive look at her bedroom, which she called "My own private space where I can do literally what I want to." She talked in voice-over as she filmed how her room reflected her interests and "obsessions" (her

"This is my own private space."

term). She began by zooming in on the name plate on her door and on to some old photos on her dressing table of herself at three and six, "at my mum's second marriage." She focused on the posters of Peter Andre, Michael Jackson, and other male pop stars whose photos decorated her whole wall space, and then panned the room to show her video and CD collection of their music clips. Her room was quite small, painted and decorated in pink and white. It had numerous soft, fluffy toy animals and pretty china ornaments but she did not comment on these aspects with either the camera or her accompanying verbal observations—they seemed a "natural" part of her world, something she took for granted. Instead, she used the camera to establish herself as "a really big fan" of her favorite musicians. She set up her tape recorder to play their songs as background music as she filmed, turning down the volume at a strategic point so that she could then articulate her feelings of fandom.

During her filming, and alone in her room, Diane addressed the camera directly, as though it were a trusted visitor welcomed into her space. Several times after an important evening, a special party, or event, Diane would chat in her bedroom, directly in front of the camera, recording her feelings, excitements, and anxieties on the video. The self she portrayed and projected on these occa-

sions was primarily someone who, in her own words, "enjoyed partying totally" but was concerned about difficulties of friendships, the pressures from peers and parents concerning appropriate social behavior and the difficulties of negotiating relationships with the opposite sex without incurring the reputation of a "slut." Her monologue was punctuated every now and again with qualifications in case the camera should think she was too forward, obsessed with boys or even too self-absorbed. "Have I bored you yet?" she would ask of her imagined audience.[42]

This very space of the domestic that allows more flexibility of behavior can also constrain, as the discourse of femininity is often cemented in the home. If the domestic sphere is an area where domestic obligation and responsibilities such as household chores and babysitting are enacted mainly by women, if the home is a place where very specific confining discourses of femininity are articulated and enacted, then the growing female adolescent is in a double bind: out of the home she is constrained by fear of personal safety; in the home she is constrained by another paradigm of acceptable femininity—domestic obligation and what it means to be a woman and a nurturing female. Her search for a gender-neutral space—if such a place exists—is particularly difficult.

Let's have another look at Diane, using her experience as an example. As she was very protected—she was not allowed to travel by public transport by herself or even with some of her friends—Diane spent a great deal of her spare time at home. She loved teenage soap operas like *Neighbors, Home and Away, Heartbreak High, Beverly Hills 90210,* and *Melrose Place,* which she usually watched alone in her room on her own TV. Her stepfather and older brother "benevolently" tolerated her "obsessions" but simultaneously verbally derided her media tastes. The gender roles in her family were very strictly defined and a very specific form of gendered identity was a constant topic of discussion. Even though finances were difficult, as her father was unemployed, the mother's role as housekeeper was considered paramount. Diane herself was described to me by her parents as outgoing, sensible, domesticated, and hard-working, but perhaps too conscientious as far as school work was concerned; she was lauded and portrayed as academic, "an A student," in contrast to the way in which her brother and most of her friends were portrayed. Yet it was not considered particularly desirable for Diane to go on to tertiary studies. Instead, Diane modeled herself along very traditional feminine lines—taking over the domestic routine when her mother was ill, "being Mum for a while," looking after her brother. Sharply delineated gender roles were constantly rammed home in family conversations. I was told of her brother's boss who continually derided the boys by calling them "hopeless girls." There were anxious family conversations around the kitchen table about teachers or students who were rumored to be homosexual. Diane would frequently be teased by her brother and her father about Peter André, a pop star of whom she was a fan, who they said looked like a "poof." She herself was described by her parents through numerous little anecdotes—usually while she was in the room and part of the conversation—as extremely attractive, and I was told how she got "special treatment" in shops from boys. On one occasion I was told how her mother had gone out to see Diane when she was working part-time at a florist to bring her some dinner at the shopping center. "I asked for a steak sandwich for Diane at the shop and there was a young boy there," she told me. "He said 'I know Diane. I know her brother.'" Her mother put on a mock coy voice imitating the boy. 'I'll bring it to her when it's ready.' Then he asked, 'Does Diane take mayonnaise on her steak sandwich?' I was having a sandwich too but he didn't ask me if I wanted mayonnaise on my sandwich."

The world outside the house was drawn for me in family discussions as morally lax, dangerous, and violent. Diane's acquaintances were described as risk takers and potentially antisocial because they drank and took drugs. The girls were "backstabbers" and their behavior was described as promiscuous. Her mother frequently talked about Helen, the daughter of her old friend who had "stolen" Diane's former boyfriend; she had dropped out of school; she had been before the courts on a dangerous assault charge; they suspected she was pregnant as she had been talking about getting engaged to her current boyfriend. Boyfriends were always represented as difficult conquests that had to be held onto like property or possessions. Boyfriends were also the means of cultural status in Diane's world. She complained to me wistfully one day, "It's not fair. Helen seems to get as many boyfriends as she wants."

What Diane did have, however, was freedom circumscribed by her family situation, to engage in "safe" teenage fantasies involving pop and film stars, but not complete freedom. Her room was crowded with the traditional trappings of a stereotypical girlhood. Her whole room was pink. She had many soft toys, small pretty ornaments as well as her many posters of male pop stars. The fact that her room was only decorated with male stars was also significant. To constitute oneself firmly within female and feminine culture, as it was defined in her immediate world, there could be no hint or suggestion that one identified with female stars or models in case this was interpreted by family or outsiders as a sexual orientation. In Diane's home environment this would be unthinkable and certainly unsayable.

I want to stress again that the camera itself often attained the status of privileged visitor as though whatever was recorded was secret and between the teenager and her video—even though the girls knew that I would see the film and that I would want to talk about the footage with them later. I was from another world in that I was an academic and a filmmaker. But perhaps because I offered an opportunity for self-expression and became a regular and familiar figure to the girls, their social groups, and their families over the two

Dancing to Peter André.

years of fieldwork, I was also allowed to become a friend, and even a confidante at times.[43] My relationship with the girls, but especially their use of the camera, thus became a means for them to test out ideas and experiment with images of self. Actions and thoughts performed on tape, but not in front of a visible audience, created a space for experimentation, a hiatus, as it were. Such play also indicated a moment of blurring, perhaps, of what we usually conceive of as discreet and bounded spheres, of those worlds designated private and those deemed to be public. A fascinating moment illustrates this when Grace suddenly told me that she wanted to dance—she had been filming and talking about her bedroom in my presence— and asked me to leave the room. Once alone, she played her favorite tapes and danced by herself in front of the video camera for about ten minutes. Then I was allowed back into the room and she continued her more mundane filming. It seemed as though here was an instance of music enabling the "saying" of what was perhaps usually unsayable.

"A Room with a View": Music and Mimesis

The centrality of the home in the girls' videos and the various ways in which it was depicted thus indicated both the "investment" and the ambiva-

lence that the participants felt toward this "private" aspect and locus of their lives.[44] One of the most effective links between the different worlds of private and public and the subject positions that the girls negotiated was music. Music served as a cultural thread moving between the worlds that we would popularly designate as private and public.[45] Although the participants sometimes filmed their rooms without verbal commentary, music was frequently played in the background to provide a particular ambience. In these cases the music was chosen quite deliberately to match a particular mood that the individual was trying to create or to tie in with a specific pop or rock star poster. At other times if the participant was in front of the camera talking about herself she often had some appropriate music playing softly—and sometimes not so softly—in the background. In those situations, the music was often selected to underscore an aspect of her sense of group identity. So, for example, Grace deliberately selected music from the Violent Femmes, "a kind of '90s folk punk," she explained to me. Mary, the girl from Papua New Guinea, played reggae music while she was videotaping in her house, taking the imaginary "visitor" on a tour of the rooms.[46] It appeared as though the girls were making the music another symbolic aspect of their sense of self, along with the posters and other cultural icons in their rooms and their houses.

Even when the music was not being played, the importance of its wider meaning as essential commodity was present in the record sleeves, CD covers, posters, and t-shirts that frequently decorated the wall spaces. It was not simply the obvious significance of fan-group membership that the music implied, but the wider meaning that such an icon emitted. For Diane, as I suggested earlier, her musical preferences also implied her (acceptable) sexual orientation within her world. In the bedrooms of Janine and her Aboriginal friends were posters of Bob Marley and sometimes Aboriginal musicians. Mary also had photos of Bob Marley and many posters of other Jamaican performers as well as African American basketball stars. For these girls, obviously the color of the stars and personalities on their wall posters was significant. What their choice implied was not simply their own fandom of these cultural groups but that such membership cohered with their immediate familial and community values and expectations. Their choices suggested an awareness of the constraints in their performed subjectivity and of their investments in these chosen positions.[47] This was another aspect of fantasy, the serious play where "different hats are tried on for size" in the relatively risk-free area of space that is designated "private."

"This is my lost forest."

Fantasies of Fairies and Friends

Another aspect of fantasy that was "serious play"—and where the "unspeakable" is spoken—were the other visual images on bedroom walls. Apart from the posters of pop (and, in one case, sporting) stars on the bedroom walls, another prevalent feature of quite a few of the rooms of the girls were the stylized and often surreal pictures and posters of fairies and magical figures. These images were quite sophisticated rather than child-like simple representations, an aspect of New Age spirituality and "otherworldliness."[48] The female fairy figures were all young adults with long flowing blonde hair and waif-like figures in a complex web of idealized images of forests and lush greenery. The owners of these posters all had colorful candles in their rooms, incense, and often tiny adhesive florescent stars on their ceilings. These particular girls did not know each other before we started filming. The magical element in their posters for these individuals seemed to be part of a much larger representation of fantasy in their bedroom space—a secret, mysterious world that often sat uneasily with the newly acquired demands and responsibilities of imminent adulthood, another aspect of the management of uncertain subjectivities.[49]

The bedroom of one fifteen-year-old participant, Hilary, at first sight was neat, tidy, and ordered. In her video her desk and school books were prominently positioned, for Hilary saw herself as a conscientious student and several times filmed herself studying. Yet her video also revealed a whole "fantasy-inspired" world under her floor boards. About six months before I met her, she had discovered that at the bottom of her built-in wardrobe in her new house were loose floorboards. When she lifted these she had found a tiny rough cellar which she then decorated with cushions, rugs, candles, and wall hangings, thus creating a personal hide-out. She called it "the lost forest." She went there to be alone or with close friends, although she did not hesitate to show this on video. Her subterranean space, in contrast to her bedroom, was exciting, a warm, dark, claustrophobic space lit only by candles, battery torches, and filled with cushions and blankets. It evoked a hidden world of mystery and a return to the secrets of childhood in a way that her ordinary room did not; the latter seemed to represent responsibility and a developing but regretful sense of maturity. The adult world was more public, open to the light and to scrutiny.

Once the girls turned their lenses on their more public selves, the character of their films changed remarkably. Here the boundaries that marked the area as "metaplay"—areas that could be considered safe for fantasy had to be re-signposted. It was a move into more public spheres.

Fantasy vs. Parodic Play: A Move into the Public

Confidence having been established, the girls started to film their activities outside of the home, the aspects of their worlds popularly designated as public. Now there was less direct personal verbal revelation to the camera—but a greater recording of the experience of fun and sense of unity of the group. In this way identity became even more relational—"who I am" became not only "where I came from" but also "who I am with." Here the experimentation and "trying on of hats" became far more an act of parodic play (the unreal) than an act of fantasy (serious play, the possibly real). Frequently in such situations, the camera was invited in as an additional member of the group. It "joined in" their activities and was often beckoned to as though it were a new friend who needed encouragement to feel at home. Because here the "game" has changed, the boundaries are shifting and less secure, the form of experimentation becomes more hegemonic. A particularly appropriate example can be drawn from Sara's film.

Sara's Story

For all the young women in my study, the city was perceived as a place of potential excitement, freedom, and yet also danger. In the daytime, the girls felt they could appropriate the public space by window shopping or "fantasy" shopping, if they were in a group. Only two, Mary and Grace, dared to venture into the city at night; only certain areas were considered safe and even then certainly not when one was alone. Some of the girls were not allowed to loiter even in the daytime. Enclosed shopping malls in the suburbs are seen by parents

as being less dangerous public spaces for their daughters but the representative guardians of law and order in the malls, security guards, were employed to make sure no such pleasant dawdling took place. You either bought or you moved on. However, if one was brave enough and prepared to take the risks, the city could be used for aspects of play.

Sara, along with several friends, took the camera for a day and the girls videotaped themselves trying on hats at a fancy hat shop—until they were thrown out of the shop by the management. This inspired them to obtain special permission from a major department store in the city to film themselves inside the teenage section trying on clothes. The resulting episode revealed some very interesting aspects of the girls' play and experimenting with image and the effect of the camera in a group and in a more public place. I was invited to attend also—so I came with another video camera to film the filming—in true anthropological style!

When we got to the change rooms, which were sectioned off for our exclusive use, Sara, Fran, and Cathy ran off and brought in some garments. They were in such a hurry to dress up that they hardly gave Cindy and Grace time to set up the cameras. It seemed as though they were not dressing up for the cameras but rather for themselves.[50] There actually hadn't been any discussion about who was dressing up first but it was significant who did *not* dress up initially. First, there was Grace who was unsure of her "social standing" and acceptance in the group; her recent experimentation with drugs and attachment to a wider, risk-taking group had caused some distance from these friends. And then there was Cindy who was physically the largest of the group. The clothes that the girls were trying on at this stage were designed for slight, skinny figures with flat chests.

The changing rooms consisted of a long room divided into about eight curtained cubicles on each side. There was a long mirror down one end, which the girls used to view themselves and later as a focal point to walk toward when they were playing at "modeling" the clothes. At first it all seemed very chaotic to me because the girls did not wait for anyone to focus a camera. They dived into the changing rooms and then reemerged wearing the dresses, looking at themselves critically in the mirror, and asking of the others, usually quite seriously, "What do you think?" The cameras were strategically held by the camera people in the changing room space but outside the individual cubicles so that each appearance of a "model" was captured on camera as well as their verbal comments when they were hidden behind the cubicle curtains.

Sara offered to film the others' gleeful selection of several other items of clothing—this time, more evening wear was chosen. Armed with the camera, she recorded their discussions and their trying on of accessories like belts, hats, and beaded jewelry, and then their return to the changing room armed with their eclectic choices. This section was filmed subjectively and evocatively, Sara following the others around the shop floor as though the camera were another member of the group. Fran in particular consciously "performed" to the camera. She smiled, beckoned, and gestured to the camera along the way, held up clothes or put them against her for the viewer's approval. Coincidentally, as the girls explored the shop floor, the pop song being played over the public address system and screened on the large television monitors was Madonna's *Vogue,* exhorting the listener to "Strike a pose!" At one point, Sara filmed these large video screens because "they're an important part of shopping now, aren't they?"

When they returned to the fitting room, an interesting change in their selection of clothes and behavior emerged. First, they came in loudly and confidently with armfuls of clothing and with great glee. They tried on clothes that were very extreme in their eyes, judging from their laughter and scathing comments. A contrast now appeared

"You need a smoke."

in their play with the clothes themselves—trying them on, swirling in front of the mirrors, and making derogatory comments about the garments. They screamed with laughter as they came out of the changing rooms even when such a reaction was unwarranted in my eyes. Now "serious play" had turned into parody.

What was important was the image that these clothes seemed to suggest, so that when Sara appeared in tight shorts and matching top, the others screamed, "What you need is a smoke." Sara obligingly pretended to smoke, assuming a sophisticated stance and then, spare hand hooked into the top of her shorts, swaggering in an exaggerated model's walk along the length of the fitting room. Similarly, when Fran tried on a slinky black dress, Cindy who was behind the video camera at that time, called out, "Act like a model. You have to waggle your butt."

At the end of the session when they all sat in an exhausted heap on the floor of the changing room, I asked them how "real" the exercise had been. They replied that it wasn't. "Oh," I pondered, "well, why did you want to come here and film this?"

"Because this is what we would like to do but can never do," they answered. They did it because it wasn't real? This comment cries out for close analytical scrutiny.

The Blurring of Spaces

In what sense could they mean that this wasn't a real experience? What was happening here? As Taussig has observed, "Once the mimetic has sprung into being, a terrifically ambiguous power is established; the power to represent the world—yet the same power to falsify, mask, and pose—is born; the two powers are inseparable."[51] "Can never do" because such public experimenting involves money and adult authority. Without the camera and the formal request to the store, the girls would not have been so free to try on the clothes and not buy. Unlike the situation in the hat shop, the young women were treated with respect in this store and not thrown out.

It also suggests far more than respect. What seemed to be occurring here was a publicly articulated play with (what was for these girls) an alternative expression of femininity. As a group this collection of girls prided themselves on being "alternative." To be "cool" for them meant to be anti-traditional in terms of femininity: It meant to be unsophisticated (although still greatly interested in and aware of the opposite sex). It meant to talk freely and openly about sex and sexual encounters. It also meant being scathing about what they perceived as the usual female preoccupations with fashion and weight. Their usual choices of clothing were shapeless, oversized t-shirts, baggy pants, or shorts. They scorned the expensive labeled clothes that were so important to other girls in my research group.

But here was suddenly a different scenario. For this "trying on" of image and style was very much concerned with embodiment, with actually seeing and representing themselves, through the long changing-room mirrors, through each other's eyes and comments, and through the lens of the camera. Suddenly there was an intensification of scrutiny. While the girls were trying on the clothes, in spite of their eclectic selection, they seemed to reject anything that closely fit their bodies. They did

not give this as the reason for rejecting those particular garments; they would just say they hated the clothes and would disappear quickly into the changing rooms again. This reaction was even true for Sara and Grace, who were both slight enough to look exactly as the designer had intended them to look.

Yet that rejection was turned into parody at the exhortation of the girls' friends: "Act like a model!" It was an invitation to turn what might usually take place in total privacy, as "serious play" into public, carnivalesque play, an excess of mimesis.[52] With the camera in a semi-official capacity the young women felt they had license to experiment and play with the clothes and accessories in a public arena, to do what can usually only be done in the private spaces of bedrooms or similarly sanctioned areas. However, because this took place in a public space, and because they were not alone and were with other members of their group, the seriousness of the experimentation was transposed into parody, marked out much more clearly as "exaggerated play."

Now You See It, Now You Don't!

As the time progressed, I became inevitably aware of which aspects of their lives the participants regarded as worth filming and exploring for themselves, which would be re-presented or constructed for an outside audience, and which aspects would be closed off to outsiders. In other words, the interpretative and perceptual frames that the girls themselves imposed on aspects of their lives came into focus; what would be regarded as fantasy and serious play and what would be explored through an ironic stance or even parody. Although at first sight much of their everyday lives seemed to have become naturalized, it also became apparent that in fact all areas were actually open to contestation and were the subject of discussion and debate. However, the self-awareness that the girls revealed of their constraints meant that these debates were often rhetorical; some areas of their lives and their subjectivities were clearly marked off as nonnegotiable. These distinctions were clear from the topics that the girls would talk about with me off camera, or even videotape for themselves, and yet decided not to include in their final footage.

For example, all of the girls talked about illicit drug use—either their own use or, even if they did not "indulge," the difficulties they faced when with friends drug taking was so common. They were all quite candid, specific, and detailed in their discussions with me—off camera—as they talked about their various social activities and mused about friendships, parties, or other events. One afternoon Grace spent several hours chatting about her own and her friends' experimentation with illegal drugs. She told me where and how they obtained the substances, the cost, which ones she had tried, and which ones she was too afraid to try. She told me about the large cross-section of friends she had and how they would often meet up in the city. They shared drug use as their main activity in common. ("I can't imagine a world without drugs. It'd be so boring"). It was mainly a combination of alcohol and amphetamines. She told me that her group regularly took "dope, acid trips (LSD), and Rohypnol." I met many of these friends during my fieldwork, several of whom confirmed this information in their casual conversations with each other. At first, she talked openly about such experimentation, casually as we chatted, but the next time she videotaped, she continued the discussion, deliberately recording some of our dialogue on tape. This time, though, she was very careful not to "name names" of her friends who had actually taken some of the harder drugs and announced that she certainly would not select those sections for public viewing. However, she made no attempt to wipe the material completely off the tape by recording over it. It was to be a record for herself.[53]

Similarly, Mary talked about experiments with some drugs, including "magic mushrooms," fungi with hallucinogenic properties that grew wild in the hills. On another occasion, she gave me a detailed account of shoplifting and car theft and subsequent chases through the city. Most of Mary's friends were boys and some were known offenders, frequently appearing before the courts or spending time in the detention center for juvenile offenders. On one occasion one of her friends was also present as she told me of some recent incidents. The two young people interrupted each other in their eagerness to make sure all the details were graphically and accurately narrated.

In this aspect of her life Mary was "one of the boys." She took risks and enjoyed being part of the gang. It was her way of gaining status and being "a person" in the group. However, these details of petty crime or "offending" did not appear in Mary's footage, for two reasons. First, Mary was aware that she was not totally accepted as a member of the street group. Her most important status with the boys was the fact that she had a house, that she lived independently away from family and authority figures. Her house was continually used—and abused—as a base by the boys—with or without her permission. Eventually her telephone and electricity were cut off because she could not afford the huge bills that her "visitors" incurred; her neighbors complained to the youth workers about the noise and graffiti and other damage done to the property. In spite of her attempts to be one of the gang, Mary was assigned the role of "mother" to the boys who came and regularly "trashed" her house and took advantage of her generosity. Desperately, she tried to excuse their behavior to me or to the social workers who helped her fix up the damage. Most of the boys just needed someone to understand them, she said. They were not bad—many had been abused. She was probably right but she was torn between trying to help them and trying to join in their activities because neither strategy managed to gain her full acceptance.

In front of the camera, Mary was anxious to portray another aspect of her life—a more respectable, socially responsible self for others to see and understand. She wanted to portray areas of her everyday experience that were particularly significant and socially acceptable. She videotaped—(and I was recruited to be camera person on this occasion)—her fortnightly routine of going to the local shopping complex, and then to the bank to wait in line for her dole check. (I thought the bank would refuse entry because of security, but on the contrary the tellers grinned and posed for the camera!) Then she led the imaginary camera audience back through the mall, chatting to acquaintances as she went, to window shop at her favorite sports clothing store. The clothes there were way beyond her means but she directed the camera to show her judiciously scrutinizing the items of clothing, feeling the quality, checking the prices, and chatting to the staff as though she were a regular purchaser. She certainly was a regular visitor to the sports store but she was not able to afford the prices of these expensive clothes. At no stage did Mary attempt to talk to the camera. She behaved as though the camera were invisible and had just captured her usual activities on film.

On a separate occasion, though clearly not intended for a wider audience, she gave a detailed verbal account on video—totally unsolicited—of the physical abuse she had undergone as a child when she first was brought into the country by her adoptive parents. This account was later verified to me by her social worker. Before she began to speak she dressed herself in her best clothes and created on the kitchen bench a display of photographs of herself as a small child with her biological parents. This aspect of her life seemed to be recorded for herself—a way of "othering" or distancing events, of enabling her to gain a new perspective on them. These were not to be shown to others, she said. As a companion and a friend in her actual world, which was obviously more

Mary in the sports shop.

than that portrayed on video, I was permitted to be privy to the more intimate aspects of her life. On the parts of the video that were to be selected for public viewing, however, the representation of her life and identity was more carefully and, in some ways, "creatively" drawn.

Clearly Mary's public performance was drawn with far more certitude and confidence than her more "private" self(s). The slippage appears between the shifting subjectivities, the possible and the enacted selves that becomes the problem, the aspect of everyday life and representation that has to be "managed." Identity is as much about exclusion as inclusion—who we are requires a delicate and continual drawing up of shifting boundaries.

Pat and Worlds of Techno

Pat was very involved with techno rave culture and so filmed quite a number of dances. Her material detailed the crowds, the ritualized performances of the DJs and the MCs and, through a strobe facility on the camera, she managed to express the mood of the dances and the effect of the lights and the music impressionistically. The strobe effectively meant that the dancers were shown moving slowly and rhythmically like automatons while the music and the background chat of the dancers continued at their normal pace. Again there was no direct gaze to the camera during these scenes—the operator was effectively invisible as she recorded the event. However, when she filmed some scenes at a techno community radio station where she helped out occasionally or when she filmed the preparations behind the scenes for a number of raves, the people she was filming then did respond by laughing, chatting, and showing a self-conscious awareness of the camera lens. Overtly and publicly she seemed to be very much a part of the "scene," describing herself as a raver and distinguishing between the "real thing" and the many "try hards," those who attempt to be authentic but fail.

Yet off camera, I heard a different story. Pat spoke angrily about the sexism involved in the rave scene—the crude and often ugly violence of the lyrics; the tacit importance of girls dressing in particular clothes, the tight tops and bunched up hair of the "little-girl look"; the control of power and skill that resided in the DJs (an almost entirely male constituency), so that the selection of music and the control of the milieu remained in male hands.[54] When one considers the importance of dance to girls and the fact that often the dances are one of the few public forums for leisure activities, where girls feel that they can be involved safely and legitimately, this has serious consequences.[55]

Conclusion: A Lesson in Threshold Breaking

As the young people in my study hurtle toward adulthood at often breakneck speed, I employ here another metaphor to illustrate their efforts to hold on to certainties. Threshold breaking is a strategy used to control a car under situations of potential danger. It involves learning how to develop a feel for the situation, adjusting one's foot on the brake, applying just enough pressure to avoid a skid. Taussig's comment reminded me of this: "As in so many moments of the mimetic, what we find is not only matching and duplication but also slippage which, once slipped into, skids wildly. . . .

This slippage is its 'secret' so . . . that 'secret' equals slippage."[56]

Taussig refers here to unmanageability—the attempt to control the uncertainties of one identity by appropriating another, one more certain, more powerful, with more status. Frequently, that can involve accepting the identity imposed upon one by others. So Janine and her friends speak with great delight, on her "raw" footage, with winks and nods to the camera, of underage drinking, "experiencing alcohol," at the railway station at night, or stealing money from the War Veterans' Fountain, whenever the necessary bus fare is short after a night on the town. Yet these depictions do not appear on her final footage, neatly edited for final public consumption. Here we only see a Janine who shows us the fun of practicing in her rock band with her friends or being with her extended family at home. But the constructed identity can slip. What has been drawn so "naturally, to look so real" can elude and reveal the mask again. Instead of the beautiful face, we can be left, to refer back again to Kate and her friend, with the cosmetic mask gazing back, reflected in the mirror.

In discussing this slippage, I want to extend the metaphor of "the talking mirror" by revisiting the way the girls used the camera. The girls could see that the possibilities of alternative femininities in their world were theoretically open. Their language was replete with references to images from advertising, film, television, magazines, and music video suggesting the opportunities and possibilities for change, transformation, and control—but at the same time the girls also knew that such "freedom" was a romantic fantasy. This awareness, even implicit, of the symbolic boundaries that constrain and mold their lives—like the strings hanging from the frame of Newton's cradle—produces the gap between the desire and the possibility. There is the struggle and often the failure to control the uncertainty, to grasp hold of the elusive "real self." And so when does the slippage emerge? I argue that we can see it in the blurring of fantasy, serious play, and the parodic, at the boundary of mimesis and mimetic excess. We can see it at the moment when play seems to assume control and become parody. In my research, these were the moments when the implicit, usually invisible gatekeeping processes that the girls imposed upon themselves became more visible.

At first glance it may appear that I had achieved what I had set out (naively) to effect—to give the young women in my research a "voice" that was distinct from mine. Sara comfortably affirmed my view when she told me recently that she decided to participate in the project because she believed in "kids' rights." "Kids have a lot to offer but to be heard they have to have a chance to speak."

Yet I realized during the course of my fieldwork that the issue of selection and portrayal, and the ethics of "voice" itself, was complex. The selection and framing of material that the girls chose for exploration went through several "gate-keeping processes." While each girl was concerned with the construction of her identity and not the reflection of it, her very acts of selection and choice, her playing with image and representation, did not mean that she was always consciously deciding what should or should not be explored even on a primary level. There were subconscious considerations about what would be acceptable for parents or caretakers to see; there were no doubt attempts to please the researcher; there were struggles to construct an image, a representation of "the real me" that would sit acceptably and appropriately with how the teenager already viewed herself. Thus some subjects were barely opened up for scrutiny through the camera although they were regularly a topic for discussion among friends and family. Those aspects taken for granted, for example about sexuality, that were talked about openly with friends while in my company, were skirted around on video, or talked about solely in terms of the dangers of reputation. Other subjects were addressed on camera, such as Sara's experi-

ence of racism, Fran's of violence, Mary's of abuse and neglect—but these are pushed aside through the editing process; they were not for public consumption. Once topics were "chosen" for exploration, the participants thus made decisions about what was purely for their own consumption and about what would be allowed for others' eyes.[57]

What became very clear from the way the girls explored their experiences and perceptions of their worlds were the uncertainties.[58] To return to the issues I heralded earlier in this chapter, the girls' use of the camera also strongly unsettles many of our assumptions about the "gaze." From my research I would infer that the gaze is not monolithic, not necessarily patriarchal, can not be held, and does not reflect one representation but many—and that these many are contradictory and shifting. Far from being able to enjoy and use aspects of popular culture, including music and dance, to assert alternative gendered subjectivities, or even as vehicles of "resistance," it seemed that their involvement was far more complex. Aware of the contradictions, the incompatibilities in their shifting subjectivities, the girls were setting up their own symbolic boundaries—putting their feet on the metaphorical brake pedal to the threshold in order to maintain control, but avoid a skid. One way in which the girls imposed a sense of sameness was to designate "safe" areas, private areas in their lives for experimentation and fantasy.

In the more public areas of their lives they could sometimes use a different kind of play and parody—posing through a mimetic excess—to challenge the untamable through humor, as an "access to understanding the unbearable truths of make-believe as a foundation of an all-too-seriously serious reality, manipulated but also manipulatable."[59] This attempt to bridge the gap between serious play—that which could conceivably be real—and parodic play or mimetic excess—that which is not real—from this very process of a "feel for the game" allows the slippage to emerge.[60] Humor and mimesis, as Taussig reminds us, allows an access—an access though not necessarily to empowerment but certainly to a closer, sometimes terrifying, understanding of what is at stake when we try to grasp reality.

Notes

The material in this chapter is drawn from my forthcoming book, *Girl Making* (New York: Berghahn Books).

1 This 1929 close-up representational painting of a tobacco pipe is entitled *La trahison des images* ("The treachery of images") (*Ceci n'est pas une pipe;* "This is not a pipe").

2 The names used here are pseudonyms. In their documentaries the girls themselves use their own given names but, as I explain below in the main text, this is because what my participants chose to reveal in their videos was selective, what they had decided was appropriate or important to be revealed.

3 The photograph immediately brought to my mind the now famous photograph of the film star, Joan Crawford by Eva Arnold featured on the cover of Richard Dyer's book *Stars, Heavenly Bodies: Film Stars and Society* (London: St. Martin's, 1986). There were three images of Crawford in that photograph; the woman as star before the mirror reflected in a large mirror; the reflection in a smaller mirror that magnified her features and therefore revealed the makeup; and the real woman behind the image. The last image was posed behind her shoulder. Thus the complex images were revealing the various layers of constituted "reality" that we construct and are constituted by our representations. Furthermore, she, like the two adolescents, demonstrated an awareness of the power of the camera. In Arnold's original collection of photographs was the accompanying information that Crawford wanted the photographer to capture the hard work entailed in being a star.

4 It was also a practical decision; as her parents are in a de facto relationship they believed that it should not be a matter of course that their daughter received either or both of their surnames. Kate now appreciates the fortuitous choice as a matter of aesthetics—her given name "did not go well" with either of their surnames, she felt.

5 Bourdieu actually contrasts and distinguishes between the two concepts. In fact, he argues that what has been described by a rather impoverished notion of "society"

is actually an amalgam of relatively autonomous but overlapping spheres of "play" or "fields." Each field is constituted by its own values and principles and possesses two main properties: first, there is a pattern of objective forces, which is like the structure of a game, "a relational configuration endowed with a specific gravity which imposes on all objects and agents that enter into it" (Pierre Bourdieu and Lois Wacquant, *An Invitation to Reflexive Sociology* [Chicago: University of Chicago Press 1992], 17). Simultaneously, a field is constituted as a site of conflict—a relational arena where participants struggle to establish control over specific forms of symbolic capital that function within it. See Pierre Bourdieu, *Outline of a Theory of Practice* (Cambridge: Cambridge University Press, 1977) and *The Logic of Practice* (Cambridge: Polity Press, 1990) for further, specific examples.

6 An article in an Australian publication offered supporting popular fuel for my argument. Margaret Le Roy explores "Why Women Will Always Hate Their Bodies," (*Age* [Oct. 16, 1993]). It is through the body that gender is primarily constructed by others; how one looks, how one perceives that one is observed by others, define one's femininity and masculinity. But even from early childhood the "common sense" way in which boys are discussed is through their behavior, what they do. For little girls the discussion primarily focuses on how they look. I am aware, of course, that little boys are conventionally expected to portray toughness in their stance and dress and little girls are meant to demonstrate more conventional feminine traits through their gestures and behavior as well as their appearance. However, I contend that from very young ages most girls develop a sense of being "naturally" the object of other people's gaze, of being rather than doing, whereas boys develop a sense of "naturally" being the subject—all this despite the advances of feminism and the growing awareness in individual families. If we understand this inevitability as "normality" then, like R. W. Connell, I want to ask, "Where did this 'normality' come from? How is it produced? And isn't there a little too much of it?" Connell, *Gender and Power* (Cambridge: Polity Press, 1987), 2.

It is through the body that girls accept, challenge and experiment with their future roles and statuses as women. It can be seen in the adoption of a physical stance, the development of a particular style, the particular "look" one struggles to acquire. This can also be seen in the forms of ritual that incorporate image, body movement, and dance. In its extreme form, this notion can be employed to understand the phenomenon of anorexia and similar eating disorders that can be read as the ultimate attempt to gain control of one's life through the self-destructive control of one's body. See also Dorothy Smith, "Femininity as Discourse," in *Becoming Feminine: The Politics of Popular Culture*, eds. Leslie G. Roman and Linda K. Christian-Smith (London: Palmer Press, 1988); Beverley Skeggs, *Becoming Respectable: Ethnographies of Young White Working Class Women* (London: Sage, 1996); and Chris Schilling, *The Body and Social Theory* (London: Sage, 1993).

7   Sherry Ortner and Harriet Whitehead, eds., *Sexual Meanings: The Cultural Construction of Gender and Sexuality* (Cambridge: Cambridge University Press, 1986).

8   What a complex notion "everyday lives" has come to be! See Norbert Elias, *The Society of Individuals* (London: Basil Blackwell, 1991), Michel de Certeau, *The Practice of Everyday Life* (Berkeley: University of California Press, 1984) and Kirsten Dortner, "Ethnographic Enigmas: 'The Everyday' in Recent Media Studies," *Cultural Studies* 8(2) (1994): 341–57. Here I use the term to describe the way individuals perceive and engage in their worlds. It is a perception of the world rather than just a sphere of existence. Dortner summarizes it thus: "Everyday life is a means to create some certainty in a world of ambivalence" (352).

9   The post-production editing has of course been completed now and the video won two awards at a student festival (best editing and best documentary) and has been screened internationally.

10 For this reason, I rarely offered external microphones and never video lighting.

11 Claude Lévi-Strauss, *The Savage Mind* (London: Weidenfeld and Nicholson, 1972); Ewing Goffman, *Strategic Interaction* (Oxford: Blackwell, 1970); Victor Turner, *From Ritual to Theatre: The Human Seriousness of Play* (New York: Performing Arts Journal Publications, 1982); and David Handelman, *Models and Mirrors: Towards an Anthropology of Public Events* (Cambridge: Cambridge University Press, 1990).

12 To thoroughly explore this concept it would be advantageous to examine the etymologies of "play," "work," "leisure," and "scholar." For a concise and extremely accessible overview, see Turner, *From Ritual to Theatre*, 33–35.

13 Handelman, *Models and Mirrors*.

14 Leisure has come to mean the freedom from institutional obligations and also the freedom to transcend structural constraints, "to play with ideas, words, with fantasies, with words, . . . and with social relationships" (Turner, *From Ritual to Theatre*, 37). In Western cultural traditions, play has become trivialized because we believe in certainty and yet simultaneously a great deal on which we based our ideas of "certainty," has been eroded. Late modernity has awakened greater possibilities for play because these former boundaries are now perceived as less solid and fixed. Late capitalism has seen great changes in understandings about work and its relationship to identity for example, as unemployment has increased in most industrialized countries. See Handelman, *Models and Mirrors,* for fuller explanation of the paradoxical implications of play.

15 Handelman points out the close affinity between play and terror, which is also an underlying theme of Taussig's concept of mimesis, explicated below in the main text. Eugene Fink argues that, "play can contain within itself not only the clear Apollonian moment of free self-determination but also the dark Dionysian moment of panic self-abandon" (as quoted in Handelman, *Models and Mirrors,* 767).

16 "The profundity of the play medium lies with its uncertain changeability and in its capacities for commentary" (Handelman, *Models and Mirrors,* 70).

17 Paul Willis, *Common Culture: Symbolic Work at Play in the Everyday Cultures of the Young* (Milton Keynes: Open University Press, 1990), 2.

18 For example, there were many ethnic groups that were not represented in my small yet diverse group of participants. However, I was looking at process and discovered that the same processes, the same "strategies" were utilized by all the young women in my research. I am utilizing the concept of strategy in a very particular way, not to indicate any clear intentionality or "resistance" to hegemonic forces but rather to indicate attempts to work within perceived structural constraints.

19 See Bourdieu's concepts of habitus and fields in his *Outline of a Theory of Practice; The Logic of Practice;* and *An Invitation to Reflexive Sociology.*

20 As an adult I did not expect to be admitted into the close friendship and social groups of the young people of my study simply on my own merits or by dint of my being an academic researcher (cf. A. H. Ward, "Gender Relations and Young People," *Cultural Studies* 1[2] [1987]: 211–18, for some earlier observations concerning the difficulty of research in this area). Adolescence seems to demand space and distance from adults

and adult authority. I also needed a means of being a participant-observer in spaces where normally I would not have access and yet, simultaneously, I needed to devise an ethical methodology that would not be exploitative. Somehow I had to develop a way of "ethnography by proxy" that would be both academically acceptable and considered worthwhile by the young women in my research. See S. Wallman et al., "'Ethnography by Proxy': Strategies for Research in the Inner City," *Ethnos* 45 (1980): 1–2.

To understand and analyze differences within what we previously understood to be "bounded cultures" requires a new way of conceiving the task, new methodologies and new ways of expressing the insights to be discovered there. G. Marcus and M. Fischer note that "these experiments are asking, centrally, what is a life for their subjects, and how do they conceive it to be experienced in various social contexts. This requires different sorts of framing categories and different modes of textual organization than conventional functionalist ethnographies, which relied primarily upon the observation and exegesis of the collectively produced symbols of their subjects, to intuit the quality of their everyday experiences." *Anthropology as Cultural Critique* (Chicago: University of Chicago Press, 1986), 46.

21 Michael Taussig, *Mimesis and Alterity* (New York: Routledge, 1993), and *Shamanism, Colonialism, and the Wild Man* (Chicago: University of Chicago Press, 1987).

22 Taussig, *Mimesis and Alterity*, 16.

23 John Fiske, "Cultural Studies and the Culture of Everyday Life" (1992); Lisa A. Lewis, *Gender Politics and MTV: Voicing the Difference* (Philadelphia: Temple University Press, 1990); Angela McRobbie, *Postmodernism and Popular Culture* (London: Routledge, 1994).

24 While these authors have more recently—and quite rightly—questioned the romantic notion of "pleasure equals resistance," there is still in their arguments the implicit tendency to see an intentional, politically motivated expression of frustration, anger, and rebellion behind young people's behavior. These works reveal their underlying links to the classics of subcultural theory and the belief that values attached to "youth subcultures . . . contain the possibilities for social change" (Taussig, *Mimesis and Alterity*, 25).

25 Ibid.

26 Bourdieu and Wacquant, *An Invitation to Reflexive Sociology*, 97.

27 Bourdieu, *An Outline of the Theory of Practice*; Bourdieu and Wacquant, *An Invitation to Reflexive Sociology*.

28 Taussig, *Mimesis and Alterity*, 33.

29 Dennis Hall, "New Age Music: A Voice of Liminality in Postmodern Popular Music," *Popular Music and Society* 18 (2) (1994): 65.

30 Ibid., 66.

31 Homi Bhabha, "Interrogating Identity," in *The Real Me: Post Modernism and the Question of Identity*, ed. L. Appignanesi (London: ICA Publications, 1987).

32 Henrietta Moore, *A Passion for Difference* (Cambridge: Polity Press, 1994).

33 The daily newspapers regularly feature articles on teenage violence, crime, and vandalism. In such articles youth becomes synonymous with a threat to the ordered control of society. See, for example, "Designer Theft: The New Fashion," *Advertiser Saturday* (August 6, 1994): "A thriving black market in stolen fashion clothing is being run throughout Adelaide schools by 'highly organized' teenage groups"; "Anger as Students Trash Park," *Advertiser Saturday* (November 5, 1994): "A wild pre-dawn rampage by hundreds of school students in Elder Park has left a clean up bill of thousands of dollars."

34 The completed footage was to be shown at a statewide youth film festival in December 1996. The films at this festival are screened at a city cinema and open to the public during a long weekend. If available funding (from Community Arts project grants) is available to pay for music copyright then the film can be screened further afield such as community television and other Youth Arts festivals at a later date.

35 See Gerry Bloustein, "Media, Models and Music in the Worlds of Teenage Girls," in *Wired Up: Young People and the Electronic Media*, ed. Sue Howard (London: Falmer Press, 1998).

36 Laura Mulvey, "Visual Pleasure and the Narrative Cinema," *Screen* 16 (3) (1975), and "Afterthoughts on Visual Pleasure and the Narrative Cinema," *Framework* (1981): 15–17.

37 Myra MacDonald, *Representing Women: Myths of Femininity in the Popular Media* (London: Arnold Press, 1995), 34–35.

38 Deborah Battaglia, *The Rhetoric of Self-Making* (Berkeley: University of California Press, 1995).

39 This physical model, which frequently appears as an executive toy, demonstrates the preservation of energy. A series of steel balls are connected on separate strings to an overarching stand. When one of the balls at either end is pulled and then released to strike its partner, the impact is transmitted down the line to the last ball and

then back again. The movement oscillates back and forth, eventually returning again to the still center. While this may seem like a particularly deterministic model, recall that I am arguing for a concept of strategy that is not conscious, "not the purposive and pre-planned pursuit of calculated goals" (Bourdieu and Wacquant, *Invitation to Reflexive Sociology,* 25) but rather "a feel for the game."

40 Goffman, *Strategic Interaction.*

41 See also Shirley Ardener, *Women and Space: Ground Rules and Social Maps* (Oxford: Berg, 1993), for more detailed discussion of the influence of gender on understandings of space and symbolic boundaries.

42 I asked Diane whom she felt she was addressing in these segments of her video and she replied, "whoever would eventually be watching it."

43 I find it very difficult to calculate the exact amount of time I could say I was "in the field" because of the nature of my methodology. I spent at least fifteen months forming relationships with each of these teenagers within their social networks through and around their use of the camera. As is the experience of many ethnographers and in spite of the age and education differential, I found firm friendships were forming, and I was even invited to social functions and family events. In the case of Mary when she was arrested, I was asked to provide a character reference for her before the magistrate. This does not mean that power relationships were not also being negotiated continually. As the final stages of post-production were still ongoing at the time of this writing, I was in many ways still in the field. Just as "play" is both being simultaneously within and without, insider and outsider, involvement and distanciation, I feel as though my field-work experience parallels this phenomenon, as in fact I would argue is the case of all worthwhile ethnographic experience.

44 Wendy Holloway, "Gender Difference and the Production of Subjectivity," in *Changing the Subject,* ed. Julian Henriques (London: Methuen, 1984).

45 See Sarah Thornton's observations drawn from research into British teenagers and club cultures, in her *Club Cultures, Music, Media, and Subcultural Capital* (Cambridge, Eng.: Polity Press, 1995), esp. 19–20.

46 Although of course reggae music does not originate in Papua New Guinea, the connection of music that referenced African American and therefore nonwhite identities was sufficient to suggest a cultural connection for Mary—as it was with the indigenous Australian teenagers in my research.

47 Wendy Holloway ("Gender Difference") argues that particular subject positions are taken up over other possible conflicting ones at specific times according to the amount of "investment" that that person perceives is placed therein. "Investment" here is conceived as both emotional commitment and vested interest. It is an especially useful term because of its obvious connotations of economics and power relations. I would argue further that investment stems from the familial and community framework within which the individual develops her sense of self and thus her possible range of subjectivities. These are, of course, embedded in and parallel to Bourdieu's arguments concerning "symbolic capital."

48 Of course, fairies have long been associated with young girls and childhood but these adolescent girls did not see themselves as children; rather as "marginal beings; those left out from the patterning of society" (Mary Douglas, *Purity and Danger* [London: Routledge, 1969], 95)—or, in Allison James's terms, "nobodies,"—too old to be classified as children and too young to be considered adults (*Childhood Identities* [Edinburgh: Edinburgh University Press, 1993]). They were young women hovering on the brink of adulthood, as it were, but not quite there. The iconography, symbolism, and discourses drawn from the New Age movement allows the bridging between childhood and adulthood in just the ways I have been suggesting—ways that would permit the girls to express and explore this liminal stage of their lives. New Age embodies "a self conscious experience of the indeterminate, the *decentred* and the transitional . . . [it] . . . is a sensibility that deliberately eludes the chains of definition . . . [and] seeks to focus attention on *process rather than products*" (Dennis Hall, "New Age Music: An Analysis of an Ecstasy," *Popular Music and Society* 18 [summer 1994]: 13; emphasis added).

49 Roy Willis notes the acceptance of "the experiences of ego division, which are so radically contrary to the Cartesian cultural tradition of a unitary self" ("New Shamanism," *Anthropology Today* 10[6] [1994]: 18). New Age music also reflects the desire to "confuse boundaries . . . and exhibits the spirit of playfulness, the taste for irony and the penchant for quotation or textual looting associated with postmodernism" (Hall, "New Age Music," 170). Other writers have noted the links of the New Age movement with concepts of "wholeness, spirituality, relationships, self healing, universal brotherhood and sister hood, creativity and oneness of the

universe" (Hall, "New Age Music," 23). Consider these qualities together with the multitude of references to idealized childhood in popular music (Robert Neustadter, "The Obvious Child: the Symbolic Use of Childhood in Contemporary Popular Music," *Popular Music and Society* 18[1] [1994]: 51–68). I would argue that it is important to see the images of fairies and other remnants of childhood in the girls' rooms as not simply nostalgia but as "rooted in particular forms of ideology that have tended to elevate process over being, the inexplicable over the rational. . . . The innocent child becomes a vision of psychic and social wholeness in a world where the self has become problematic" (ibid., 65).

50 As Western culture has become dominated by the visual image, it has also increasingly become one where new technologies have blurred the boundaries of what is popularly understood to be "real" and what is understood to be constructed. Central to this concept is the notion of self-identity—the constitution of the "real me." While not necessarily a function of any kind of implicit conspiracy, the successes of new technologies of mass communication do mean that the question of authenticity has become increasingly blurred, problematic, and even possibly irrelevant for "incredulity towards metanarrative is linked to the successes of systematic technologies of mass reproduction" (Handelman, *Models and Mirrors*, 266). Jean Baudrillard has long argued that we have incorporated the gaze into ourselves so that we internalize an "audience" in all that we do and say: "It is no longer a question of a false representation of reality (ideology) but of concealing the fact that the real is no longer real, and thus of saving the reality principle" (*Simulations*, trans. P. Foss, P. Patton, and P. P. Beitchman [New York: Semiotext(e), 1983], 25).

51 Taussig, *Mimesis and Alterity*, 43.

52 Cf. P. Willis, *Common Culture*, Smith, "Femininity as Discourse," and also L. Goodman, "Comic Subversion: Comedy as Strategy in Feminist Theatre," in *Imagining Women: Cultural Representations and Gender*, ed. F. Bonner (Cambridge, Eng.: Polity Press, 1992) for interesting observations relating to the role of comedy as subversion, "opening up the debate around the subject of the representation of women's bodies" (284).

53 Grace was also quite adamant that when I brought any copy of her video for her to look at and discuss I was to carefully hand it directly to her and not to her mother. She had obviously more concerns than other girls but all the girls treated their "raw" or "wild" footage (untreated material) as private and confidential.

54 One particular CD I was given to listen to was *The Best of Rotterdam Records*, vol. 2.

55 Angela McRobbie, *Postmodernism and Popular Culture*, and S. Lees, *Sugar and Spice: Sexuality and Adolescent Girls* (London: Penguin, 1993).

56 Taussig, *Mimesis and Alterity*, 115–16.

57 Such selection points to what was also unspoken and unsayable, as well as what was unreflected upon.

58 In her "framing" address to the camera, Hilary stated, "I have learned through making this film that the only certain thing about life are the changes."

59 Taussig, *Mimesis and Alterity*, 255.

60 Bourdieu, *Outline of a Theory of Practice*, and *In Other Words: Essays towards a Reflective Sociology*, trans. Matthew Adamson (Stanford: Stanford University Press, 1990).

"No Matter How Small": The Democratic Imagination of Dr. Seuss

Henry Jenkins

Children's Reading and Children's Thinking are the rock bottom base upon which the future of this country will rise. Or not rise. In these days of tension and confusion, writers are beginning to realize that Books for Children have a greater potential for good, or evil, than any other form of literature on earth. They realize that the new generations *must* grow up to be more intelligent than *ours*.

—DR. SEUSS, "BRAT BOOKS ON THE MARCH"

We do not want our children to let protest against domination pile up inside until it has reached proportions beyond all reason. Nor do we want them to be so dependent that they grow willing to follow no matter what kind of ruler. . . . We want our children to resist unfairness and injustice, even in the laws of their land. We want them to cherish and stand up for their own rights and the rights of their fellow men. We want them to reject the rule of all Hitlers.

—DOROTHY W. BARUCH, *PARENTS CAN BE PEOPLE*

When Horton the elephant, in Dr. Seuss's *Horton Hears a Who* (1954), listens to the "very faint yelp" of a microscopic civilization living on a dust speck and tries to rally his neighbors to protect the endangered Who village, he gets caught between two different democratic communities.[1] On the one hand, there is the conformist world of his own friends and neighbors, "the Wickersham Brothers and dozens / Of Wickersham Uncles and Wickersham Cousins / And Wickersham In-laws," who use chains and cages to crush individualistic tendencies: "For almost two days you've run wild and insisted / On chatting with persons who've never existed. / Such carryings-on in our peaceable jun-gle! / We've had quite enough of your bellowing bungle!" On the other hand, there is the civic-minded community of Whoville, "a town that is friendly and clean." Faced by a crisis that threatens their survival, the Whos rally together to insure that their voices are heard: "This is your town's darkest hour! / The time for all *Whos* who have blood that is red / To come to the aid of their country!"

Horton's situation encapsulates the dilemmas that many liberals faced in postwar America—torn between the conflicting values of community and individualism, frightened by mob rule and, yet, dedicated to democracy. *Horton* expresses a nostalgia for the Whoville-like America of the war years, when political differences were forgotten in the name of a common cause and fear over the rigid Wickersham-like conformity of the 1950s. On the eve of the Second World War, many liberals and radicals had joined forces to confront the threat of fascism overseas and to defend the New Deal at home. Under the banner of the "Popular Front," they had sought to contain their differences and broaden their base of support, employing "democracy" as a code word for social transformation (including the resolution of economic inequalities) and "fascism" as a general term for oppression and concentrated power (including the entrenched authority of union-busting corporations). Such rhetorical ploys linked many on the Left to a common vision of what the war was about and what the ideal postwar society would look like. While internal tensions (especially centering around Stalinism) shook the stability of this alliance, the war years allowed many leftists to rally behind broadly perceived national interests. As the war ended, however, the rise of anticommunist hysteria led many liberal "fellow-travelers" to repudiate their earlier ideological partnerships; others expressed their concern over the collapse of individual liberties and the pressure toward uniformity in American culture. Having worked together across a broad political spectrum to win the war, the Left now found its voice excluded from the process of building the postwar era.

Seuss's outrage over the community's pillorying of the nonconformist Horton (a liberal out of sync with his community) contrasts sharply with his disgusted response to Jo-Jo the "very small, *very* small shirker" (who places personal interests ahead of the larger cause). The heroic Horton challenges his community to show greater concern for the weak and the powerless. The contemptible Jo-Jo endangers his community by withholding his small voice from their noise-making efforts. Only when Jo-Jo contributes his voice, "the Smallest of All," do the Wickershams and the other animals hear the Whos and commit themselves to their preservation. *Horton* is not only a plea for the rights of the "small," but also an acknowledgment that even the "small" have an obligation to contribute to the general welfare. Yet, what the story never really addresses—beyond a commonsensical assurance that we all know the right answers—is who gets to define what constitutes the general welfare, the right-thinking Horton or the fascistic Wickershams. Here, as so often in his stories, Seuss trusts the child to find his or her way to what is "fair" and "just."

Seuss's focus on the "small," of course, represents an appeal to children who feel overwhelmed by the adult world and need to find their own voices, but its politics run deeper, speaking on behalf of a broad range of minorities struggling to be heard in the cold war era. Reading *Horton Hears a Who* as a fable about the decline of the Popular Front may seem farfetched. One of the ways that children's literature constitutes, in Jacqueline Rose's terms, an "impossible" fiction is our tendency to treat childhood as a space "innocent" of adult political concerns, protected from the tensions and crises of modern life.[2] In practice, children's literature has been central to adult debates and our understanding of its meanings must be grounded in social, political, and intellectual history.[3]

Seuss often used political terms to describe the writing of his "brat books," seeing his stories as fostering a more democratic culture.[4] Seuss dedicated *Horton* to Mitsugi Nakamura, a Kyoto educator, who he had met during a fact-finding mission to Japan, researching the American occupation's impact on educational and child-rearing practices.[5] Seuss's *To Think That I Saw It on Mulberry Street* (1937) and *The 500 Hats of Bartholomew Cubbins* (1938) had been adopted in both Japan and Korea as part of the official post-war reeducation curriculum. Seuss knew *Horton* would be used to train not only American children, but children in emerging democratic cultures around the world, about the relationship between the individual and the community.[6]

Despite his own involvement in such "reschooling" efforts, Seuss despised the "indoctrination" practices he associated with the German and Japanese educational systems during the war. Overt attempts to moralize through children's literature violated children's trust in adults. The child, for Seuss, was born in a edenic state, outside of adult corruption, yet already possessing, as a birthright, the virtues of a democratic citizen— a sense of fairness and justice, a hunger to belong and participate within the community. The challenge was to protect children from adult's corrupting and antidemocratic influences, especially from the crushing impact of authoritarian institutions. Seuss insisted children were naturally resistant to "propaganda": "You can't pour didacticism down little throats. Oh, you might *cram* a little bit down. But it won't stay down. The little throats know how to spit it right out again."[7]

The children's writer served democracy not by becoming its propagandist (a role Seuss had played during the war, but which he found ill-suited to peacetime) but by teaching children to respect and trust their own internal responses to an unjust world. Often, Seuss "subverted" adult authorities, appealing to children behind their parents' backs, as the closing passage of *The Cat in the Hat* does, when it invites children to claim a secret (and unpoliced) space for their imaginative play. Seuss saw himself as continuing the "nonsense" tradition of Jonathan Swift, Lewis Carroll, Hilaire Belloc, and Edward Lear, employing whimsy to communicate controversial ideas to a resistant audience.[8] The power of such fantasy lay in its indirectness. As he explained, "when we have a moral, we try to tell it sideways."[9]

This "sideways" pedagogy reflected some of the core assumptions behind "permissiveness," then the preferred mode of parenting among middle-class mothers and fathers.[10] Permissive child-rearing saw the explicit display of parental authority as thwarting their offsprings' independence and free will. Instead, Benjamin Spock and his allies hoped to motivate learning and domestic responsibility "sideways," transforming household chores into play and redirecting negative impulses to more constructive ends. Horton's insistence that "a person's a person, no matter how small" perfectly summarizes the permissive paradigm. The ideals of democracy were to be embedded into the micro-practices of everyday life. At the heart of permissiveness was a discourse about power—about the power relations between children and adults—and how that power might best be exercised within a democratic society. Permissiveness, as its name suggests, was defined more through what it permitted—the behavior of children it both tolerated and accommodated—rather than what it prohibited. Contrary to conservative critics, permissiveness did not represent total anarchic "license." Instead, it balanced individualism against community standards. Permissive thinkers struggled with the distinction between "license" and "freedom," seeing the need to "set limits" while calling for implicit, rather than explicit, controls. Spock proposed a model of parental "leadership," rather than patriarchal authority, seeing the parent as soliciting voluntary cooperation, instead of imposing sanctions, and children as socially directed and eager to fit within the domestic "community."[11]

Permissive writers looked with horror at the way that adult problems—the Depression, the Second World War—had introduced desperation and brutality into the lives of America's children; they looked upon the children who would be born into the postwar world as holding a fresh chance for social transformation. Born free of prejudice, repression, and authoritarianism, one writer argued, the "Baby Boom" child "comes into the world with a clean slate, needing only to be guided aright to grow into an adult with the highest ideals to which man has attained."[12] Childhood was imagined as a utopian space through which America might reinvent itself.

Children's fiction, in this context, became a vehicle for teaching both children and adults this new mode of democratic thinking. As child-rearing expert Mauree Applegate explained: "If the democratic process is to improve or even continue, the skills of living together must be taught children with their pablum."[13]

As McCarthyism foreclosed the prospect of meaningful political change within the public sphere, many leftists turned toward the family as a site where the culture could be shifted from below. In doing so, they retained the "Popular Front" habit of framing their social critiques in the language of "democracy" and "Americanism," terms we find it difficult today to disentangle from the nationalistic rhetoric of the cold war. A close reading of these books, however, reveals that their core impulses are progressive (struggling to transform and "democratize" American society) rather than conservative (preserving American institutions from outside challenge).[14]

Dr. Seuss was, in many ways, the poet laureate of this "permissive" culture, with many parents clutching a copy of Dr. Spock in one hand and Dr. Seuss in the other. Seuss wrote five of the ten best-selling children's books of this century.[15] By 1954, when he wrote *Horton*, Seuss was already gaining national recognition as a distinctive voice in children's literature. However, he had spent most of his professional life writing for adults, translating what he had learned from an apprenticeship cartooning for popular humor magazines into the tools for persuasion—first, working in advertising, then, doing editorial cartoons for the Popular Front newspaper *PM*, and, finally, scripting propaganda and training films for Frank Capra's Signal Corps unit. The postwar period saw a gradual narrowing of his attention toward children's writing. This essay focuses on Seuss's transition from war-time propaganda to postwar children's fables, a transition which parallels the emergence of this postwar discourse of "democratic" parenting. Here, I want to focus on works like *Horton,* the Bartholomew Cubbins books, *Yertle the Turtle,* and *The 5000 Fingers of Dr. T,* which reflect the writer's attempt to map the power relations between children and adults. These books shaped Seuss's understanding of his social mission and prepared the way for his later commercial successes, such as *The Cat in the Hat* (1957) and *Green Eggs and Ham* (1960).

The "Family Values" of Radical Democracy

Stephen Greenblatt has spoken of history writing as "speaking with the dead." [16] My desires are more immediate and personal. I want to discover what the grown-ups were talking about behind my back, over my head, in the other room most likely, while I was curled up on the floor reading *Green Eggs and Ham.* As a child of the postwar era, I want to map the political and social forces that shaped my own upbringing.

In the past, changing academic and political paradigms have often created unbreachable generational divides, cutting off the young from the voices of their parents' generation. The politics of the antiwar movement, for example, resulted in a painful rift within the Left, separating the young radicals from an older liberal establishment that had gone through the political upheavals of the 1930s and 1940s. The student Left responded to

real blindnesses and silences in the Old Left, especially having to do with issues of race, gender, sexuality, and nationalism. In the process, however, "liberalism" (and by extension, the kinds of political alliances which tied it to more radical forms of political culture) gained such a negative charge that we have often been unwilling to reexamine its core assumptions and find anything valuable there.

The task of reexamining the legacy of the Popular Front gains new urgency as questions about the nature and function of "democracy" have resurfaced, issues hotly debated within the Left. The emergence of cyberspace has raised new prospects for participatory democracy (certainly on the local and possibly on the national scale) [17] at the same moment that the global collapse of socialism and communism has forced the Left to rethink some of its core ideological commitments. [18] Calls for "radical democracy"—that is, for a coalition of grassroots movements working together for mutual empowerment and enfranchisement—force us to reconsider the cultural factors shaping American citizenship.

Like the Popular Front, the movement for "radical democracy" embraces Western political traditions as the conceptual basis for radical critiques of American society, seeking a new alliance of left-of-center groups behind the goal of combating economic and social inequalities and questioning entrenched power. Radical democracy, Chantal Mouffe argues, recognizes that "modern democratic ideals of liberty and equality . . . have provided the political language with which many struggles against subordination have been articulated and won and with which many others can still be fought." [19] Like the Popular Front, radical democracy is situational and contingent, recognizing the need for constant struggle toward social transformation and constant negotiation and conversation between social groups, who are sometimes aligned and sometimes opposed in their struggles for recognition and empowerment.

For the Popular Front, such affiliations and alliances emerged around issues of class, linking intellectuals with labor union activists, immigrants, the unemployed, the migrant worker, and other proletarian groups, constituting what Michael Denning calls the "laboring" of American culture. More recent efforts toward radical democracy emerge from contemporary identity politics, with its focus on racial, cultural, gender, and sexuality-based groups. Like the Popular Front, radical democracy holds the West accountable for its failures to live up to its own core principles and beliefs: "Such an interpretation emphasizes the numerous social relations where subordination exists and must be challenged if the principles of equality and liberty are to apply."[20]

Grounded in the belief that the "personal is political," many advocates of radical democracy insist that its goals cannot be achieved exclusively in the public sphere through electoral action, but require a reconceptualization of private life and its role in shaping political culture. The power of grassroots movements, Richard Flacks argues, rests "on their capacity to disrupt the routine institutional processes of society, to renegotiate the rules and terms by which people live, and to reorganize the cognitive structures that shape meanings and identities."[21] Otherwise, David Trend contends, the danger is that political culture becomes increasingly "distanced" from everyday life and popular participation in elections declines. What is needed, these critics argue, is the "democratization" of the family, the school, the work place, and the community, as the loci by which we come to understand what it means to participate within democracy: "The means of political representation needs to be spread further into the basic fabric of daily life."[22] Here, as well, the politics of radical democracy closely parallel that of the Popular Front, which sought to link cultural production and domestic experience to broader movements of social transformation.

One way to politicize everyday life would be to reclaim the concept of "family values" from the Right, to reconceptualize the family not as a conservative bastion of traditional authority and social constraint but rather as a localized space of political experimentation and social transformation. Read in this way, the family—the domestic sphere—could become a place where the young learn how to exercise power and where adults learn to rethink core values of jurisprudence. Such a project requires the Left to examine its own practices as parents, as family members, as domestic partners. Without a politics of the family, the Left lacks the means (literally and figuratively) to reproduce itself. Such a project does not turn its back on feminist and queer criticisms of the traditional family, but rather reconceptualizes what it means to participate within a family and what might be the most valuable relationship between personal and public life.[23] Lauren Berlant has been critical of what she describes as the "downsizing" of citizenship under the Reagan-Bush administrations, creating what she calls an "intimate public sphere" where political concerns can only be expressed within volunteerist and individualist terms.[24] What I am calling for, on the other hand, is a reversal of this process, repoliticizing domestic life as the entry point into civic involvement, reforging the links between the public and the private spheres.

In the interest of pursuing such a project, I want to reexamine the history of our current conception of the family, recognizing the utopian strivings of previous generations which similarly sought to locate social transformation within the domestic sphere. One of the most powerful rhetorical devices the Right mobilizes in its campaign for "family values" is our collective popular memory of the postwar period as an age of parental authority and schoolroom discipline, as a period when "father knew best." Conservative representations of the 1940s and 1950s exclude the counter-discourses of progressive school reform and permissive child-rearing, which proposed alternative models of the power relations between adults and children. Reclaiming those earlier voices will help us to question the power of the Right to "naturalize" its peculiar conception of the family.

Dr. Seuss seems an odd and yet oddly apt place to start such an undertaking.

I turn to Seuss not as a hero or an exemplar for the future, but rather, as someone who struggled in his life and his work with the problem of how one might foster a more democratic American culture. Seuss, in many ways, never escaped the blindnesses that crippled the utopian dreams of his generation. He found it difficult, in the wake of the Second World War, to separate his conception of democracy from American nationalism. Strong undercurrents of misogyny run through his stories, and his depictions of exotic places with strange customs often mask orientalist fantasies. Yet, precisely for those reasons, he sheds light on what our fathers and mothers hoped to accomplish and how they fared. What I propose we draw from this earlier progressive movement is not so much its specific solutions as the questions it posed and the goals it set for itself.

Seuss as Propagandist

In 1947, the New Republic published one of the last-known editorial cartoons by Dr. Seuss—who, the magazine reported, "came out of retirement, looked at the current American scene, and temporarily retired again."[25] In the cartoon, Uncle Sam peers down in horror at a community reduced through its mutual suspicions to chaos. Babies name their mothers as communists. A little bird denounces a run-down horse pulling a wagon. Another man suspects a passing bird of leftist sympathies. Fingers point in all directions and wild accusations are flying. The cartoon draws heavily upon images found in Seuss's first children's book, To Think That I Saw It on Mulberry Street (1938). This time, however, adults, not children, had "eyesight much too keen" and needed

Dr. Seuss, brilliant prewar political cartoonist, came out of retirement, looked at the current American scene, and temporarily retired again.

Seuss draws on images from To Think That I Saw It on Mulberry Street to critique anticommunist hysteria in this 1947 New Republic cartoon.

to "stop turning minnows into whales." The cartoon suggests Seuss's growing pessimism about adult politics as he returned to civilian life. This image of a community, unable to trust any of its members, represented the antithesis of the national unity Seuss had hoped to build through his involvement with the Popular Front. Reviewing his earlier political work will help us to understand the ideological contexts out of which emerged the themes and situations found in Seuss's childrens books.

In 1940, Seuss, who was previously known as a light-hearted "nonsense" writer, took up his pen as an editorial cartoonist for the newly created tabloid PM, an important organ of the Popular Front movement. PM's publisher was Ralph Ingersoll, who had quit his lucrative job as publisher of Time to create what he claimed would be a new kind of newspaper.[26] *PM* operated without advertising, in order to be free of obligations to special interests, and it provided regular sections devoted to labor, civil rights, and women's issues.[27] Ingersoll's political philosophy was stated directly and succinctly in *PM*'s 1940 prospectus: "We are against people who push other people around, in this country or abroad. We propose to crusade for those who seek constructively to improve the way men live together."[28] In their account of political activism in Hollywood, Larry Ceplair and Steven Englund identify four dominant strands in Popular Front ideology: (a) opposition to the rise of fascism in Europe and Asia; (b) support for "defenders of democracy and the victims of fascist aggression" around the world; (c) resistance to the rise of "domestic fascism" and isolationism; and (d) criticism of big business's role in busting unions and opposing New Deal social reforms.[29] *PM*'s editorial policy embraced all four strands, despite other internal differences amongst its contributors. Max Lerner would write years later, "the common ground we had was Adolf Hitler and Franklin Roosevelt, one the serpent to be slain, the other the hero to slay him."[30]

Many of Seuss's earliest cartoons lampooned isolationists and fascists, as Seuss took aim at the "American first-isms of Charles Lindbergh and Senators Wheeler and Nye—and the rotten rot that the Fascist priest, Father Coughlin, was spewing out on radio."[31] Increasingly, however, as U.S. involvement in the war neared, Seuss focused on the larger forces dividing American society. In one cartoon, Seuss depicts the American nation as an enormous boat; everyone is rowing together except for one man who fires his slingshot at another crew member: "I don't like the color of that guy's tie" (Feb. 25, 1942). His campaign against defeatism and divisiveness led him to embrace other aspects of the *PM* ideology, including opposition to the anticommunist Dies Committee, the segregationist politics of the South, anti-Semitism, union busting, and corporate greed. Like Inger-

"And on this platform, folks, those most perplexing people...the Lads with the Siamese Beard! Unrelated by blood, they are joined in a manner that mystifies the mightiest minds in the land!"

The Great U.S. Side Show.

soll, he was "against people who push other people around." If, as Seuss would later claim, he rejected many of *PM*'s political and economic policies, he nevertheless was willing to use his pen to promote them, and he drew on Ingersoll's political formulations throughout his later work.[32]

When America entered the war, Seuss enlisted, becoming part of the film unit Frank Capra established in the Signal Corps to explain to the American people "why we fight." Like Seuss, many of the key participants in the Capra unit had close associations with children's literature. Eric Knight, the British-born "local color" novelist, best known for *Lassie Come Home,* helped to determine the overall shape of the *Why We Fight* series. W. Munro Leaf, who had written the children's story *The Story of Ferdinand,* and Phil Eastman, who would author *Are You My Mother?* and other books for Seuss's Beginner Books series, both collaborated with him on the *Private Snafu* animated shorts. These children's writers provided the simple, straightforward prose needed for Capra's films.[33]

Seuss, like many of other Popular Front participants, had hoped that this spirit of "democratization" would keep alive their efforts to transform American society, that the men who wore the uniform would return home changed by what they had experienced through working side by side with those from many other nations or Americans of different races and ethnic backgrounds. A disillusioned Seuss warned in a December 7, 1944, memo:

> Much of what we have gained is, at the moment of victory, threatened. . . . Racial tensions within our Army threatens to grow. . . . .Many soldiers who have seen Europe are eager to turn their backs upon it. . . . Disillusionment, cynicism, distrust, bitterness, are already souring the milk of human kindness; maggots are already eating the fruits of victory.[34]

Increasingly, Seuss saw children, rather than adults, as a more promising audience for those lessons. In many ways, Seuss felt, *PM* and the Capra unit had confronted impossible challenges, trying to instill democratic thought in adults whose prejudices had already been determined by their education and upbringing. Political education might more productively start at childhood.

The Utah Lectures: Seuss and the Post-war Era

In July 1947, Seuss gave a series of lectures and writing workshops at the University of Utah.[35] His previously unpublished notes for those lectures give us insights into his thoughts about children's literature as he entered the postwar era. Seuss took as the theme of his main lecture the need to "wipe out Mrs. Mulvaney-ism"—the rejection of banal and sugar-coated children's books, in favor

of works possessing the "vigor" of popular culture, striving for a middle ground between the high and the low, between "Mt. Namby-Pamby" and "Bunkum Hill."[36] In displacing "Mrs. Mulvaney-ism," Seuss urged would-be children's writers to examine the popularity of comics and other forms of mass culture:

> Over *here*, we put our readers to sleep. Over *there*, they wake 'em up with action. . . . Over *here*, we bore them with grandpa's dull reminiscences of the past. Over *there*, they offer them glimpses of the future.

Seuss was searching for a hybrid form that combined popular entertainment and social uplift. Stressing the centrality of entertainment values in motivating young readers, he warned his students against being "torch-bearers" more interested in message than story: "The Japanese indoctrinated their kids with Shinto legends. Dictators, Hitler, Mussolini, indoctrinated kid's minds politically. (A job the U.S. Army is trying to undo now.)"[37] At the same time, he distrusted comics as having no core social or moral values and no educational content.[38] The ideal children's book, it seemed, would make reading "fun" and meaningful.

Throughout his wartime work, Seuss had shown a particular concern for children and their education. He expressed repeated outrage at people who mislead or manipulate the "small." In one of his *PM* cartoons, an America First mom reads to her children the story of Adolf the Wolf: "And the wolf chewed up the children and spit out their bones—but those were *foreign children* and it really didn't matter" (Oct. 1, 1942). Another cartoon, seemingly looking forward to *How the Grinch Stole Christmas*, depicts Hitler and Mussolini unconvincingly disguising themselves as Santa Clauses, arriving with empty bags and with "Benito Claus" declaring, "This year I'm afraid my kiddies suspect who I really am!" (1942).

What horrified Seuss about fascism was what he saw as its exploitation of children's minds and bodies, its transformation of education into in-

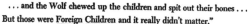

Adolf the Wolf.

doctrination. Seuss's script for the military propaganda film, *Your Job in Germany* warns that the most "dangerous" Germans the Americans would encounter in occupied territory were those who had been children when the Nazi Party rose to power: "They were brought up on straight propaganda, products of the worst educational crime in the entire history of the world." [39] In another such film, *Know Your Enemy—Japan* (upon which Seuss, among many, collaborated) a memorable montage sequence juxtaposes Japanese children at school and at play, with their adult counterparts at war; underneath the images play the sounds of factories grinding out steel and iron.

As he prepared for peacetime, Seuss seemed divided between his recognition of the power of the media to shape core values and his horror over the exploitation of children's minds for political ends. *Design for Death,* another Seuss-scripted film, closes with a call for a more "democratic"

postwar culture, focusing especially on "the problem of educating our kids—*all* our kids—to be smarter than we've been." The postwar world, and the children born into it, would offer "another chance" for peace, social equality, and democratic participation. This formulation is, of course, bound up with American nationalism, seeing "indoctrination" as the fostering of false or foreign ideologies, while seeing "education" as the fostering of the "commonsensical" ideals of American capitalism and democracy. However, Seuss's embrace of "democracy" still contained criticisms of the existing order, recognizing America's failures to fulfill its own ideals.

Old attitudes would need to be transformed through the images and stories parents brought into the playroom. In his Utah lectures, for example, Seuss introduced the issue of race, stressing the "unhappy life" minorities experience in America "which preaches equality but doesn't always practice it." He challenged would-be writers to avoid the racist stereotypes so common in children's literature and to foster a greater commitment to equality and justice. Yet, education needed to be appropriate for the American context, needed to respect children's intelligence and autonomy, needed to be understated rather than overt and preachy.

Seuss saw permissive child-rearing doctrines as reconciling these conflicting demands. He recommended that his students master child psychology, which he said shaped his approach to children's fiction. In many ways, Seuss drew on child psychology to "naturalize" his assumptions about the democratic character of American culture and to justify the political values he wanted to foster in the young. His stories, Seuss told his audience, "rise out of a child's psychology, rise out of a child's basic needs. If you go contrary to those needs, you're headed for trouble. If you write with these needs in mind, you'll have a chance of having children accept you." [40] *Horton,* he said, responded to a child's need to belong, to be accepted by others, to have a secure place within society. The story's success required that Horton's friends finally recognize the wisdom of his actions. Seuss urged potential writers to take seriously children's frustrations over adult privilege and authority, "Children are thwarted people. Their idea of tragedy is when some one says you *can't* do that." Seuss felt that the best children's stories acknowledged and worked through children's anger toward parental rules and that, in doing so, they respected children's innate sense of justice. More generally, Seuss argued, his whimsical stories fulfilled children's needs for spontaneity and change, "They want *fun*. They want *play*. They want *nonsense*."

While Seuss does not cite specific child-rearing authorities, his list of children's needs closely parallels the list of "emotional foods" Dorothy Baruch felt children needed. Baruch was one of the most important wartime authorities on children and a key architect of the permissive approach, merging psychological insights from Freudianism with a core commitment to progressive social reform. Like Seuss, she stressed children's needs for affection, belonging, achievement, recognition, and understanding. Like Seuss, she placed particular importance on the ways children's aesthetic and erotic interests motivated their exploration of the world.[41] Children become subservient to others and come to distrust their own impulses and pleasures, when they are falsely labeled as "dirty" by grownups, Baruch argued. Seuss and Baruch both sought to protect children's imagination and sensuality from adult belittlement.[42]

Rather than "indoctrinate" children, Seuss and other permissive writers sought to protect them from adult's thwarting control, giving them a sense of their own power and potential. Baruch told parents: "There is a propulsion in every human being to fulfill himself in the deepest, richest and soundest way that he can. If only he is not beaten back too unmercifully. If only he is not too defeated. If only he is not hurt so much and made so angry that his real potentialities cannot get through."[43] Freeing children from excessive adult constraint enabled that internal "propulsion" to govern their actions, while frustrating children would warp their development and fuel more anti-social attitudes.

Democracy Begins at Home

Many parents, educators, and child-rearing experts shared Seuss's goal of a more democratic children's culture. Dramatic increases in the birthrate during the immediate postwar period meant that more and more Americans were spending time changing diapers and reading picture books with their kids. The men left behind the wartime camaraderie and adventure, the women the autonomy that had come from working outside the home. Permissiveness made their new domestic duties politically meaningful, a patriotic responsibility, a way to strike a blow for freedom, and thus helped to reconcile them to domestic containment. Focusing on the child give them a way to imagine a world where current social inequalities could be transformed and the threat of war eradicated, through the actions of a citizenry born free of prejudice and selfishness. The fight against "domestic fascism" translated into the demands to raise children who would not be bullies; the struggle against corporate crackdowns on unions was rewritten as a message against hoarding all the toys or the importance of treating the corner grocer as a friend deserving respect.[44] No less than modern-day advocates of "radical democracy," these postwar writers sought "to renegotiate the rules and terms by which people live and to reorganize the cognitive structures that shape meanings and identities."[45]

Dorothy Baruch wrote a series of books during and after the war designed to foster more "democratic" child-rearing efforts, warning parents: "To our children, democracy must not be something you-speak-of-but-do-not-live-by. It must assume reality. It must become a word associated and made real by many small but real experiences."[46]

Initially, Baruch and others were responding to the war's potential disruptions of American family life, the absence of the father, the growing aggressiveness of children's play, the increased government restrictions on civil liberties, and the hostility toward citizens of German and Japanese ancestry.[47] Wartime children, she felt, needed a sense of security, of unconditional acceptance and self-respect; children needed a space to express their frustration over adult rules and restrictions, without censor or penalty; children needed to test their own growing autonomy, through meaningful participation in family decisions.

As the war drew to a close, child-rearing experts reconsidered how the postwar family could help to foster a new era of equality, respect, and internationalism. As Henry Herbert Goddard's *Our Children in the Atomic Age* (1948) explained:

> Eventually we must have men who were born and bred since 1945: men who will be unhampered by the old disproved traditions. That means we must start with the children and give them better care, better bringing-up and better schooling.[48]

With the threat of nuclear war hanging over their heads, they sought to eradicate the divisiveness, the racism, the bullying tendencies, the narrow-minded nationalism that had led to the last war. Some, like Baruch, turned their attention to the psychological conditions behind racism or aggression.[49]

Parents magazine urged mothers and fathers to model their domestic life on the Bill of Rights, making family decisions collectively and including even the youngest of children as active participants in this process: "The voice of the child in his own affairs will not be denied in the democratic home."[50]

Educators, including the Detroit public schools, developed guidelines and recommendations intended to make democratic thinking part of the relationship between students and teachers.[51] The result was a renewed emphasis upon the "civics in action" represented by school councils and class officer elections. Progressive critics condemned the public schools as too regimented, too interested in controlling their students, rather than allowing them to learn at their individual pace and in their own style.[52]

Prewar methods were rejected as having been "authoritarian," "dictatorial," "brainwashing," and "mind control," all metaphors carrying tremendous resonance in the cold war era. Every aspect of family life was now being weighed according to its potential effect on the child's democratic thinking. In *Shall Children, Too, Be Free?* (1949), Howard Lane urged parents to repudiate "the old Germanic-type family and school in which the master was clearly recognized and passively obeyed." He noted, ironically, that "we Americans particularly admired the obedience, respectfulness, discipline of the children of Germany and Japan!"[53] *Our Children in the Atomic Age* (1948) warned that "strict discipline is the kind called for in armies, where men are trained to kill," not for American homes, where children are being prepared for citizenship.[54]

Democratic participation required careful attention to children's psychological development, balancing their need for autonomy with their need to respect community norms. Children who cannot conform to larger social expectations become increasing frustrated. On the other hand, the child was not to be so bound by social convention that "he can not take his part in helping to change society—to weed out its ills and put it into better shape."[55] Permissive writers saw children as progressive forces bringing about a more peaceful world and a more just society. *Your Child Meets the World Outside* (1941), for example, acknowledged that its goal is not simply to help "fit children to an existing world," but to give them "the tools with which to understand it" and "an ability to change it, to shape it toward their own ends."[56] Parents, educators, child psychologists sought to "free" children from the inhibitions, the prejudices, the rigid thought patterns that had blocked their own generation from realizing social transformation.

Here, one sees most dramatically their break with earlier child-rearing experts. Prewar authorities, like the behaviorist John Watson, instructed parents on how to "shape" children's development, seeing their minds as essentially raw materials to be sculpted by adult intervention. Returning to a Rousseauian ideal, permissive writers, on the other hand, placed their "trust" in the natural goodness of children, while distrusting the corrupting influence of adult culture. However, permissive writers could never make the problem of adult power and authority over children's lives disappear altogether; they acknowledged that children needed adults and that adults determined the environment in which children were to be raised. Permissive writers constructed a new representation of childhood as a struggle between authoritarian adults and freedom-fighting children—casting their weight behind the young and urging parents to re-invent their own social and political identities, in accordance with the needs of the future.

Kings, Turtles, and Piano Teachers

Seuss's children's books, from the beginning, display a commitment to the small and the weak (often in the form of the child) against the tyrannies of the strong and the powerful (often in the form of adults). In the opening passages of *The 500 Hats of Bartholomew Cubbins* (1938), Seuss draws a sharp contrast between the realm of the King, rendered powerful by his "mighty view" as he peers down upon his subjects and the realm inhabited by his subjects, and as they look up at the castle: "It was a mighty view, but it made Bartholomew Cubbins feel mighty small." Given the choice between the two perspectives, Seuss consistently chooses the lower vantage point.

Casting a peasant as a protagonist reflects Seuss's knowledge of the folk tale traditions out of which modern children's fiction emerged. However, Seuss takes particular pleasure in ridiculing the pretensions of King Derwin, the pomposity of his court, the arbitrariness of his rules, and the brattishness of his son—all foils for the disruptions caused by Cubbins's uncontrollable proliferation of hats. When the king orders Cubbins to remove his hat, another appears, and then another, "*Flupp Flupp Flupp.*" The king's efforts to control and discipline the child are absurdly misdirected, since the boy has no say over the hats' magical reproduction. As Bartholomew reasons to himself, "The King can do nothing dreadful to punish me, because I really haven't done anything wrong." Seuss seems to be getting at the absurdity of adult demands which run counter to children's natures, parental expectations that transform innocent behavior into misconduct. Seuss also points toward the limits of adult knowledge: "But neither Bartholomew Cubbins, nor King Derwin himself, nor anyone else in the Kingdom of Didd could ever explain how the strange thing had happened." This magical disruption opens a space for the child to have an impact on the adult order, to turn the kingdom upside down and, then, set it right again.

The 500 Hats sets the model for several of Seuss's subsequent stories, such as *The King's Stilts* (1939) and *Bartholomew and the Oobleck* (1949). In these stories, Seuss provides rationales for children to challenge adults' often fickle and irrational behavior. In *The King's Stilts*, Lord Droon is a heartless puritan, outraged that his king ends his hard work days by "having a bit of fun" with stilts: "Laughing spoils the shape of the face. The lines at the corner of the mouth should go down."[57] Droon steals and hides the stilts, reducing the king to an apathetic stupor. Only the page boy, Eric, can outsmart Droon and restore the monarch's missing stilts, allowing him to save the kingdom from an approaching flood.

Here, Seuss introduces two models of adult authority—the repressive Lord Droon, who uses his power to constrain the boy, and the good-natured King Birtram, whose own playful instincts make him an ideal companion for the boy. The king and

Mein Early Kampf   by Adolf Hitler

April 20, 1889

I give the hotfoot to the stork that brings me.

In a series of cartoons published in *PM,* Seuss depicted Adolf Hitler as a spoiled brat.

his page boy bond through play. In the end, the ruler bestows upon Eric a pair of stilts, his reward for unmasking Droon's treachery: "From then on, every day at five, they always raced on stilts together. And when they played they really PLAYED. And when they worked they really WORKED."

As Robert L. Griswold has documented, permissive writers reconceptualized fatherhood, shifting attention from his traditional functions as breadwinner and disciplinarian toward new roles as active playmates.[58] Experts argued that coming home from work and playing with the children rejuvenated world-weary fathers, while exposing growing boys to the masculine realm. Play was understood as an escape from social control and regulation, as a space of the free imagination. At the same time, one can't help but note how this cultural re-valuing of play paved the way for the leisure- and consumption-oriented culture demanded by the postwar economy. In Seuss's modern-day fairy tale, the boy must pave the way for the postwar consumer lifestyle by overpowering Lord Droon's preoccupation with a culture of production.

In *Bartholomew and the Oobleck,* a megalo-

maniac monarch, King Didd, brings destruction down upon his kingdom when he seeks not only to master his subjects, but also to rule over the weather.[59] Bored with snow, rain, fog, and sunshine, the ill-tempered King demands that his court magicians make "something *new* to come down" from the sky. The result is a sticky green substance called "Oobleck," which falls in blobs and gums up the whole city. The commonsensical Bartholomew Cubbins warns the adults about the dangers of the Oobleck, but the adults are so sure of their grasp of the situation that they do nothing until it is too late. In the end, Bartholomew disciplines the king, forcing him to apologize for his error:

> You may be a mighty king. But you're sitting in oobleck up to your chin. And so is everyone else in your land. And if you won't even say you're sorry, *you're no sort of a king at all!*

Permissive writers urged parents to admit their mistakes when they are wrong. In the democratic family, parental rule was neither absolute nor infallible, and children were to learn to take responsibility for their mistakes, observing how their parents have dealt with their own mishaps and misjudgments. As Dorothy Baruch counseled, "When our children begin to protest that which they see as oppression in our dealings with them, we need to stop and think. We need to take stock."[60] When King Didd "takes stock," he finds a way not only to make his own rule more reasonable, but also to heal the harms caused by his past actions.

Adults' dictatorial behavior, Baruch argued, was often rooted in their own childhood, when they had felt belittled by more authoritarian parents: "We, who were once small and helpless, may still need ascendancy to make us feel adequate to cope with life's demands."[61] For these reasons, she warned, adults who boss and bully children were passing these traits onto the next generation. Seuss's stories often depicted tyrants as infantil-

"You Can't Build a Substantial V Out of Turtles."

ized, as spoiled brats pitching tantrums, as never having mastered childish impulses. In one *PM* cartoon, a baby Adolph Hitler ("Adolphkins") rejects, from his crib, in infancy, the milk from Holstein cows as "non-Aryan." In one Seuss poem, "The Ruckus" wants to "make a noise that the whole world will hear," but discovers that he has nothing to say.[62] Yertle the Turtle wants to be "ruler of all that I see," stacking up his subjects so that he can see more and more. In the end, his rule is challenged by the bottom-most turtle, Mack:

> I don't like to complain,
> But down here below, we are feeling great pain.
> I know, up on top you are seeing great sights,
> but down at the bottom we, too, should have rights.[63]

When Mack rises up, he sends Yertle tumbling face down into the mud: "all the turtles are free / As turtles and, maybe, all creatures should be."

In Seuss's world, children, the small, those at the bottom are depicted as clear-headed, rational, capable of achieving a just balance between personal desire and the collective good, expressing their dissatisfactions over unreasonable demands and giving free expression to their natural impulses. Seuss often depicted the adult order as profoundly irrational. In "The Zak," a "North-Going-Zak" and a "South-Going-Zak" meet on the "prairie of Prax" and each refuses to give way to the other, insisting that the path belongs to him alone. Both proclaim, "You will never pass by if I have to stand here on this spot till I die!"[64] Seuss's conclusion suggests the inevitable consequence of such meaningless land disputes: "They *did* both stand there, till they both were quite dead." *The Sneetches* (1961) rendered the whole logic of racism absurd, as the Sneetches developed technologies allowing them to alter and manipulate caste markers, until nobody can be sure who is elite and who is subordinate. Much like the permissive advice literature, Seuss's stories assume that children possess an "instinctive" sense of "fairness." Children, more so than their parents, respect the rights of "all creatures"—sneetches, turtles, or people—to dignity, freedom, and equality. Seuss was continuing Ingersoll's fight against "people who push other people around," whether they were dictators conquering other nations, corporations crushing unions, or parents bossing their children.

CASE STUDY: *THE 5000 FINGERS OF DOCTOR T* Seuss's live-action feature film *The 5000 Fingers of Doctor T* represents the fullest elaboration of Seuss's conception of children as "thwarted people," struggling to find their own voice in a world dominated by dictatorial adult authorities. When we read through Seuss's notes and original drafts for the script, we see strong evidence that he was consciously mapping permissive child-rearing doctrines over images associated with the Second World War.

The 5000 Fingers deals with the plight of an average American boy, Bartholomew Collins (Tommy Rettig), who finds learning to play the piano a fate worse than death. His instructor, Dr. Terwilliker (Hans Conried), is an old-school authoritarian, who insists that "practice makes perfect" and who demands constant drill and repetition. The bulk of the film consists of Bartholomew's dream, in which he and the other boys rise up and overthrow the dictatorial Terwilliker and his plans to dominate the world through his music. As Seuss explained in a memo to the film's producer, Stanley Kramer: "The kid, psychologically, is in a box. The dream mechanism takes these elements that are thwarting him and blows them up to gigantic proportions."[65]

If this description foregrounds issues of child psychology, concerns central to the finished film, the early drafts of the script make frequent references to the struggle against fascism.[66] In Bart's waking reality, Dr. T is "not especially frightening," a "tight-lipped and methodical looking old gentleman . . . no more vicious and harmful than Victor Moore." Once we enter Bart's dream, however, Seuss increasingly characterizes Dr. T as the reincarnation of der Führer. Seuss describes his kingdom as "plastered with posters, showing Dr. Terwilliker in a Hitler-like dictator's pose." His soldiers wear medals that "resemble an iron cross, only it is engraved with a likeness of Dr. Terwilliker in the center." The mother has a "devotion to the man . . . bordering on the fanatical," a "gauleiter-like allegiance" that blinds her to her son's agonies. When he is challenged, Dr. T "flies into a Hitlerian rage." He sees the "piano racket" as a scheme for global domination, and his study is decorated with an enormous world map captioned "The Terwilliker Empire of Tomorrow." He has built a massive piano, designed for the enslaved fingers of 500 little boys, upon which he will perform his musical compositions.[67]

Many traces of this Hitler analogy find their way into the final film. The sets are hyperbolic versions of monumental Bauhaus architecture, and the grand procession borrows freely from Leni Riefenstahl's *Triumph of the Will,* with his blue-helmeted henchmen goosestepping and holding aloft giant versions of his "Happy Fingers" logo. Terwilliker's elaborate conductor's uniform, one reviewer noted, was "a combination of a circus band drum major, Carmen Miranda, and Her-

It's a Cinch, Adolf . . . Once You Learn to Play It

The band leader imagery in *The 5000 Fingers of Dr. T* is prefigured in this *PM* cartoon which depicts Hitler as a one-man-band.

mann Goering."[68] Most of the henchmen bear Germanic names. Hans Conried's long thin body and his floppy black hair closely resemble Seuss's *PM* caricatures of Hitler (minus the mustache). The fact that Conried had provided some of the narration for *Design for Death,* performing the voices of the fascist leaders, could only have strengthened the association for contemporary viewers. Even the film's musical score bore strong Germanic associations; its composer, Eugene Hollander, had studied under Richard Strauss, done music for Max Reinhardt in Berlin before the war, and was the musical director for *The Blue Angel.*[69]

Some of the film's more disturbing images drew on popular memories of the Nazi concentration camps. Arriving by yellow school buses, rather than railway cars, the unfortunate boys are herded through gates, where their comic books, balls, slingshots, and pet frogs are confiscated.

"Presenting a symphony of artists assembled from the twelve great capitals of the world!"

Anti-Comintern Blast.

Then, they are marched off to their "lock-me-tights" in the dungeon. There, Dr. T dreams up fiendish (and Dantesque) tortures for all those who refuse to play his beloved keyboard. The captive musicians have sullen eyes and sunken cheeks and are lean and gaunt in their prison uniforms.

In constructing the more sympathetic plumber, Zlabadowski, Seuss drew upon other associations with the war. In the first draft of the script, Zlabadowski is described in terms that strongly link him to Eastern Europe. "Shaking his head sadly in deep Slavic gloom," Zlabadowski is "a big shaggy edition of Molotov, a kindly Molotov with the cosmic unhappiness of Albert Einstein." As the script progresses, Zlabadowski abandons all of his Slavic associations, except for his rather distinctive name, becoming a more all-American type, a reluctant patriot who must first shed his isolationist impulses before he can be enlisted as Bart's ally in the struggle to stop Terwilliker. In one of his notes about the script, Seuss summarizes the character: "Z's conflict: Desire to help people. Desire to keep out of trouble. An old soldier trying to be a pacifist. He's tired of war. It's futile."[70] In the early drafts, Zlabadowski knows

Terwilliker's evil plans, but he doesn't want to get involved if it means losing his overtime pay for installing the sinks.

In the finished film, many of these adult concerns have vanished. Zlabadowski represents the ideal permissive parent. Initially, he is a bit distracted by his work and eager to make a buck, a bit eager to dismiss Bart's warnings as wild-eyed fantasies. Ultimately, he becomes a warm-hearted playmate (engaging the boy in a pretend fishing trip) and a wise counselor (helping him concoct from the contents of the boy's pockets a sound-stopping device). Angered by Zlabadowski's initial indifference, Bart challenges his adult privileges and sings a song that might have been the anthem for permissive child-rearing:

> Just because we're kids, because we're sorta small, because we're closer to the ground, and you are bigger pound by pound, you have no right, you have no right to push and shove us little kids around.

Proclaiming children's rights, Bart denounces adult assumptions that deeper voices, facial hair, or wallets justify unreasonable exercises of power over children. Zlabadowski regains his idealism:

"I don't like anybody who pushes anybody around." The two cut their fingers with Bart's pocketknife and take a blood oath that binds them together—father and son—in the struggle against Terwillikerism.

In the film's opening scene, Bart offhandedly remarks upon the death of his father, presumably during the war, and Zlabadowski and Terwilliker are cast as good and bad surrogate fathers, respectively. In his nightmare, his piano-crazed mother is hypnotized into accepting Terwilliker's hand in marriage, a deal to be consummated immediately following the great concert. Not unlike Lord Droon in *The King's Stilts,* Terwilliker represents the prewar patriarch who demands obedience and silence from his children. In his fantasy, Bart hopes that the more permissive Zlabadowski will fall in love with his mother and become his father, an arrangement consummated by their blood oath. Zlabadowski understands the needs of boys; he represents the manly virtues of fishing and baseball against Dr. Terwilliker's effeminate high culture, defending America against Terwilliker's Germany.

In the end, the task of finding the right father—and overcoming the bad patriarch—falls squarely on Bart's shoulders. He alone will face down Terwilliker, using his "very atomic" sound-catching device to disrupt the concert and liberate the children. The closing moments, where rebellious children hurl their music sheets in the air, shouting in defiance, stomping on and punching the piano keys, represents one of the most vivid images of resistance in all of American cinema. By this point, Bart's struggle against Terwilliker has absorbed tremendous ideological weight, a struggle of the freedom-fighting all-American boy (with his red-and-white-striped shirt and his blue pants) against an old-school tyrant—the struggle of those who are "closer to the ground" against those who "shout" and "beat little kids about," the struggle of permissive parenting against more authoritarian alternatives.

Conclusion

In the final analysis, Seuss's children's books were as political as any of his war-related work. They helped American parents to imagine how domestic life could be restructured along more democratic principles. They participated in a larger movement to help children overcome the prejudices and the divisiveness that had "poisoned" America's wartime effort. Seuss offered fantasies where powerful rulers are infantile and foolish and destined to end face down in the mud. His stories depicted worlds where children gain control over basic social institutions and remake them according to their own innovative ideas, where children challenge kings and force them to apologize to their subjects, or where kids lead a schoolhouse revolt against unreasonable teachers.

Conservative critics, such as Spiro Agnew and Norman Vincent Peale, blamed Spock and "permissiveness" for the counterculture, suggesting that the anti-war movement reflected the antics of "spoiled" children who needed to be "spanked." To accept such an explanation would be to ignore the real political disagreements that fueled the student revolts of the 1960s. At the same time, one can't help but wonder if the questioning of domestic power, which permissive child-rearing represented, helped to foster a mode of thinking which saw "the personal as political." One can't help but ask whether a mode of child-rearing which empowered children to challenge adult institutions had an impact on how the postwar generation thought about themselves and about their place in the world.[71]

Renewed interest in the project of "radical democracy" forces us to think about how an empowered citizenship might be fostered on the most local levels—not only by changing politics within our communities or our work places, but also by rethinking the politics of the family. We must recognize that this project has a history, even if we do not want, in any simple fashion, to embrace permissiveness. There is much about per-missiveness we might well want to reject. Feminist critics note that permissive approaches often dis-empowered women even as they sought to em-power children, that permissiveness was linked to the domestic containment of women and that writers like Spock helped to "naturalize" domi-nant conceptions of gender roles and normative sexual identities. Permissiveness often mystified the power relations between children and adults, making authority seem to disappear when its mechanisms had only been masked. Permissive-ness placed impossible expectations on parents, which are still being felt as we confront an eco-nomic reality that makes postwar models impos-sible to maintain. Permissiveness romanticizes the child as a Rousseauian ideal. No, permissiveness won't do at all!

Yet, there is something else we can learn from permissive writers like Dr. Spock and Dr. Seuss—the process of rethinking the family, of re-imagin-ing the power relations within the home, and of seeing childhood as vitally linked to the political transformation of American culture. The utopian futures envisioned by permissive writers were never fully achieved. Social institutions and atti-tudes proved too deep-rooted to be transformed by simply changing the ways parents raised their young. But, perhaps, we would do better to evalu-ate permissiveness according to its goals rather than its results. On the Left, we are often slow to acknowledge partial victories, resulting in a pro-found and disempowering climate of pessimism and cynicism. What we need at the present mo-ment are new utopian fantasies, new visions of the future, that will motivate struggles for social trans-formation. Compared to the "real think" of tradi-tional leftism, such utopianism may seem like "fairy tales." However, rediscovering the demo-cratic imagination of Dr. Seuss should remind us that "fairy tales" can become powerful tools for political transformation.

Notes

1 Dr. Seuss, *Horton Hears a Who!* (New York: Random House, 1954). The pages are unnumbered; but, hey, it's a really short book, so you'll just have to read it all!

2 Jacqueline Rose, *The Case of Peter Pan, or the Impossi-bility of Children's Fiction* (London: Macmillan, 1984).

3 For conflicting views on the political content of chil-dren's literature, see Alison Lurie, *Not in Front of the Grown-ups: Subversive Children's Literature* (London: Bloomsbury, 1990), and Jason Epstein, "'Good Bunnies Always Obey': Books For American Children" in *Only Connect: Readings on Children's Literature,* ed. Sheila Egoff, G. T. Stubbs, and L. F. Ashley (Toronto: Oxford University Press, 1980), 74–94. In practice, the political discourse in children's literature has been as varied as that of adult fiction, with competing voices advancing different positions on the core issues the genre circles around, especially on the power relations between chil-dren and adults and on the place of children's play within the larger social sphere.

4 Dr. Seuss is the pen name of Theodor Geisel. It is con-ventional for writers to distinguish between Seuss as a writer and Geisel as a person. However, I believe that this distinction sustains a break between his children's books and his adult political activities which exagger-ates the difference between the two. In any case, most of his adult work either bore the "Dr. Seuss" pen name (his humor-magazine material, his advertising work, his *PM* cartoons) or was unsigned (his military work). Some of his children's books, i.e., those he did not illus-trate, were published under a range of pseudonyms in-cluding Rosetta Stone and Theo LeSeig. I have decided in this essay to refer to Geisel by his pen name in every context.

5 He was impressed by his discovery that Japanese chil-dren, educated according to American principles, were embracing Western cultural values. Asked to draw pic-tures of their future, thousands of Japanese school chil-dren depicted themselves in helping professions, heal-ing the sick, educating the ignorant, and rebuilding their society; Seuss felt children of the previous genera-tion would have seen their futures as warriors. Young girls imagined business careers for themselves that would have been closed to their mothers. For back-ground on Seuss's investigation of Japanese education, see Judith and Neil Morgan, *Dr. Seuss and Mr. Geisel: A Biography* (New York: Random House, 1995).

6   Like many of his generation, Seuss's hopes for bestowing democracy on the world ran against his fear that the world was not ready to receive it. In confronting postwar Japan, Seuss saw both the prospect of legitimate friendship across cultural differences and the dangers of a culture that only a few years before he had viewed as hopelessly militaristic and imperialistic. His participation in the reeducation of Japan cannot simply be reduced to cultural imperialism, without regard to his idealistic goals or to the historical context. Yet, at the same time, it never can be separated from the imperialistic mechanisms by which those goals were achieved.

7   Lecture Notes, University of Utah Workshops, July 1947, Seuss Papers, Geisel Library, University of California-San Diego, Box 19, File 6. Subsequent references will refer to Seuss Papers.

8   In my longer work-in-progress, an intellectual biography of Dr. Seuss, I argue that nonsense writing was far from meaningless; rather, it was the expression of a peculiarly modernist sensibility, an acknowledgment of aspects of contemporary social experience that either destabilized traditional structures of meaning or seemed senseless, mechanical, or nonhuman. Its common themes reflect crisis points in the hegemony of the nineteenth-century middle classes, where the old was giving way to the new and where narrow consensus confronted expanding diversity. Given Seuss's rather stylized and fanciful representations, which constitute a vernacular version of surrealism or dadaism, his fit within the aesthetics of the Popular Front might seem problematic. The Popular Front has most often been associated with an aesthetic of realism or naturalism. However, Michael Denning, in *The Cultural Front: The Laboring of American Culture in the Twentieth Century* (New York: Verso, 1996), notes strong elements of modernism running through the cultural politics of the Popular Front, and has stressed the non-naturalistic elements in many of the central artistic accomplishments of this movement. Seuss's children's books, I would argue, represented an odd negotiation between naturalism, which was the dominant aesthetic of children's literature of the period, and the New Humorists' fascination with the fantastic and the nonsensical.

9   Robert Cahn, "The Wonderful World of Dr. Seuss," undated and unidentified magazine clipping, Seuss Scrapbook, Seuss Papers.

10 What I am calling "permissiveness" was far from a coherent or univocal discourse. Permissive impulses entered American life from many different directions, from the work of Yale's Gessell Institute, from the anthropological research of Margaret Mead, from the best-selling "baby books" of pediatrician Dr. Benjamin Spock, and from the commercial discourse of advertising and popular magazines. Permissive thought dominates child-rearing advice in the postwar period, though not without challenge and controversy. The emergence of permissiveness reflected many shifts in postwar America's conception of childhood—a changing understanding of child sexuality and the place of sensuality and pleasure in development and learning; a fascination with the "primitivism" of the child and its "natural" and "pure" knowledge of its own basic biological needs; a restructuring of the family unit which served to justify the domestic containment of women by granting children greater authority at the expense of their mothers; new sociological and psychological understanding of the stages of children's "normal" maturation and of the centrality of play in their growing sense of themselves and the world; changing ideals about what parents valued in their children, stressing autonomy and creativity over obedience; a shift within the economic climate of the country, away from a culture of production and toward a culture of consumption. The multiplicity of permissive discourses, as well as the variety of their manifestation within popular culture, is the focus of my current research interests.

11 For a useful discussion of the political theories underlying Spock's work, see William Grabner, "The Unstable World of Benjamin Spock: Social Engineering in a Democratic Culture, 1917–1950," *Journal of American History*, 167 (3) (spring 1980): 612–29. Grabner's understanding of this postwar period closely parallels my own focus here: "Through control over the child-rearing process, Spock sought to create a society that was more cooperative, more consensus-oriented, more group-conscious, and a society that was more knowable, more consistent, and more comforting."

12 Henry Herbert Goddard, *Our Children in the Atomic Age* (Mellott, IN: Hopkins, 1948), ix.

13 Mauree Applegate, *Everybody's Business—Our Children* (Evanston, IL: Row, Peterson, 1952), 59.

14 Most accounts of the American Popular Front, such as Michael Denning's epic study, *The Cultural Front*, focus on the movement's public sphere politics, on *Waiting for Lefty*, WPA projects, and political rallies. The relationship of the American Popular Front to domestic

sphere issues in general and permissiveness in general remains underexplored, in part because our standard narrative focuses on the collapse of the movement in the wake of the Hitler-Stalin Pact. Denning, however, makes the case for its influence on American culture extending well beyond the end of World War II. The cliché of the "red-diaper baby" suggests that adults' political commitments had some influence on child-rearing practice, however.

15   *Green Eggs and Ham* (1960), *One Fish, Two Fish, Red Fish, Blue Fish* (1960), *Hop on Pop* (1963), *Dr. Seuss's ABC* (1963), and *The Cat in the Hat* (1957) represent the top five best-selling children's books between 1895 and 1975. *The Cat in the Hat Comes Back* (1958) came in eighth place, preceded only by *Charlotte's Web* (sixth) and *The Wonderful Wizard of Oz* (seventh). See Ruth K. MacDonald, *Dr. Seuss* (Boston: Twayne, 1988), 11.

16   Stephen Greenblatt, *Shakespearean Negotiations: The Circulation of Social Energy in Renaissance England* (New Historicism: Studies in Cultural Poetics no. 84, vol. 4) (Berkeley: University of California Press, 1989). "I began with the desire to speak with the dead."

17   See, for example, Lawrence K. Grossman, *The Electronic Republic: Reshaping Democracy in the Information Age* (New York: Viking, 1995).

18   For an essential overview of these debates, see David Trend, ed., *Radical Democracy: Identity, Citizenship and the State* (New York: Routledge, 1996).

19   Chantal Mouffe, "Radical Democracy or Liberal Democracy?" in *Radical Democracy,* ed. Trend, 25.

20   Ibid., 24.

21   Richard Flacks, "Reviving Democratic Activism: Thoughts About Strategy in a Dark Time," in *Radical Democracy,* ed. Trend, 110.

22   David Trend, "Democracy's Crisis of Meaning," in *Radical Democracy,* ed. Trend, 14.

23   Of course, one important first step would be to redefine the family to include a broader range of social arrangements based on mutual trust and social alliance, including same-sex partnerships.

24   Lauren Berlant, *The Queen of America Goes to Washington City: Essays on Sex and Citizenship* (Durham: Duke University Press, 1997).

25   Dr. Seuss, the *New Republic* (July 28, 1947): 7.

26   Roy Hoopes, *Ralph Ingersoll: A Biography* (New York: Atheneum, 1985).

27   Among his regular contributors were some of the leading literary and political voices of the period, including Margaret Bourke-White, Leo Huberman, Max Lerner, Tom Meany, I. F. Stone, Hodding Carter, Erskine Caldwell, and Albert Deutsch. Dr. Benjamin Spock offered a regular column of advice for new parents, writings that would provide the basis for his best-selling *Baby and Child Care.* Stone's role in the publication is discussed in detail in Andrew Patner, *I. F. Stone: A Portrait* (New York: Pantheon, 1988), and in Robert C. Cottrell, *Izzy: A Biography of I. F. Stone* (New Brunswick, NJ: Rutgers University Press, 1992).

28   Ralph Ingersoll, as quoted in Patner, *I. F. Stone,* 73.

29   Larry Ceplair and Steven Englund, *The Inquisition in Hollywood: Politics in the Film Community, 1930–1960* (Garden City, NY: Anchor, 1980).

30   Max Lerner, "Preface," in *Ralph Ingersoll,* by Hoopes, viii.

31   Edward Connery Lathem, interview with Dr. Seuss, undated transcript, Seuss Papers, Box 8, File 14, 141. The complete transcript of this interview is held in the Baker Library Collection at Dartmouth. All *PM* cartoons cited are included in Seuss Papers, Box 18, Files 11–19. Where information about their dates is provided, I have included it parenthetically in the text. In other cases, the clippings are currently undated.

32   "When I joined up I told them I didn't care for a lot of their economic policies and a lot of their political policies." Lathem transcript, Seuss Papers, Box 18, File 14, 128. Many participants in Popular Front organizations distanced themselves from their political commitments in the wake of the rise of McCarthyism. Seuss, as a children's writer, had added concern in preserving the "innocence" of his audience from adult political concerns, and indeed, most of the publicity and writing about Seuss has tended to ignore his earlier adult writings and political activities. We will probably never know how deeply committed Seuss was to *PM's* politics, though his continued participation in progressive contexts throughout the 1940s and early 1950s suggests that he was minimally a "fellow traveler." At the same time, we must not duplicate a McCarthyist logic of "guilt by association" in our attempts to claim Seuss for the Left. Michael Denning, in *The Cultural Front,* cautions us against placing too much stress on party membership or seeing the Popular Front as a cohesive political strategy or organization. Rather, Denning argues, the Popular Front represented a "structure of feeling," a way of understanding contemporary social experience, which shaped the political and cultural activities of many

artists and intellectuals who would not have viewed themselves as radicals. Seuss's participation within a succession of groups which writers like Denning associate with the Popular Front (*PM,* the Capra unit, UPA, Stanley Kramer's production group, etc.) suggests that his thinking bore some "affiliation" with its cultural politics, even if we can not place a label on his actual political beliefs. This rereading of the Popular Front as a "historical bloc," rather than as an organized political movement, may help to explain why many of Seuss's associates, who read this manuscript, felt uncomfortable with the term "Popular Front" or its application to one or another of the contexts discussed here. Participants in such groups might or might not have seen themselves as contributing to the Popular Front, a political term in circulation during the period but only retrospectively ascribed to this "historical bloc" as a whole. For a contemporary account of his involvement with *PM,* see "Malice in Wonderland," *Newsweek* (February 9, 1942): 58–59. Largely forgotten today, Seuss's cartoons enjoyed broad circulation. They were republished in national news magazines, distributed by Nelson Rockefeller's Inter-American Affairs operation at the State Department, as well as employed by the Treasury Department in its Defense Bond campaign.

33 After the war, Seuss worried that their address to the enlisted men had been too childish and simple-minded: "Being remote from the soldier, we tend to talk down to the soldier when we should be talking *with* the soldier. His world is mud and we tend to talk to him from our world of clean sheets. The information we give him is the information he wants—and is greedy for—but we often irritate him by the way we present it." T. S. Geisel, Memo to Chief, Army Inform. Branch, IED, Feb. 5, 1945, Seuss Papers, Box 230, File 34.

34 T. S. Geisel, Memo to Chief, Special and Information Services, December 7, 1944, Seuss Papers, Box 230, File 29.

35 Other participants in the lecture series included Vladimir Nabokov, Oscar Williams, and Wallace Stegner.

36 Dr. Seuss, Lecture Notes, "Mrs. Mulvaney and the Billion Dollar Bunny," University of Utah Workshop, July 1947, Seuss Papers, Box 19, File 7.

37 Lecture Notes, University of Utah Workshop, July 1947, Seuss Papers, Box 19, File 6.

38 Seuss's focus on comic books in this lecture reflects the emergence of reformist campaigns leveled against the relationship between children and popular culture,

most notably Dr. Frederic Wertham's campaign against the comics. Seuss clearly shared some, though not all, of Wertham's concerns. At the same time, he had himself been a cartoonist and popular humorist and had briefly published a comic strip for the Hearst newspapers. Seuss saw the opportunity for children's writers to engage with those themes and materials that made the comics so popular with children, while, in the process, reshaping children's tastes in a more palatable direction.

39 T. S. Geisel, Final Continuity Script, *Your Job in Germany,* Seuss Papers, Box 9, File 6.

40 Lecture Notes, University of Utah Workshop, July 1947, Seuss Papers, Box 19, File 6.

41 For a fuller explication of the permissive conception of children's sensuality and sexuality, see Henry Jenkins, "The Sensuous Child," in *The Children's Culture Reader,* ed. Henry Jenkins (New York: New York University Press, 1998). This collection also reprints some of the primary source materials cited in this essay.

42 See, for example, Dorothy W. Baruch, *New Ways in Discipline: You and Your Child Today* (New York: McGraw-Hill, 1949).

43 Ibid, 14.

44 See, for example, Elizabeth A. Boettiger, *Your Child Meets the World Outside: A Guide to Children's Attitudes in Democratic Living* (New York: Appleton-Century, 1941).

45 Flacks, "Reviving Democratic Activism."

46 Dorothy W. Baruch, *You, Your Children and War* (New York: Appleton-Century, 1942), 90.

47 See also Munro Leaf, *A Wartime Handbook for Young Americans* (Philadelphia: Stokes, 1942), and Angelo Patri, *Your Child in Wartime* (Garden City, NY: Doubleday, Doran, 1943). For additional background on American child-rearing during this period, see William M. Tuttle Jr., *"Daddy's Gone to War": The Second World War in the Lives of America's Children* (New York: Oxford University Press, 1993).

48 Goddard, *Our Children in the Atomic Age,* iii.

49 Dorothy W. Baruch, *The Glass House of Prejudice* (New York: William Morrow, 1946).

50 Evelyn Emig Mellon, "Democracy Begins at Home," in *The Child Care Guide and Family Advisor,* ed. Phyllis B. Katz (New York: Parents' Institute, 1960), 515–20.

51 See, for example, Detroit Public Schools, *Democratic Citizenship and Development of Children* (Detroit: Wayne State University Press, 1949).

52 Mary Elizabeth Byrne Ferm, *Freedom in Education* (New York: Lear, 1949), 13.

53 Howard A. Lane, *Shall Children, Too, Be Free?* (New York: Anti-Defamation League of the B'nai B'rith, 1949), 11.

54 Goddard, *Our Children in the Atomic Age*, 135.

55 Baruch, *New Ways in Discipline*, 72.

56 Boettiger, *Your Child Meets the World Outside*, 9.

57 Dr. Seuss, *The King's Stilts* (New York: Random House, 1939).

58 Robert L. Griswold, *Fatherhood in America: A History* (New York: Basic, 1993).

59 Dr. Seuss, *Bartholomew and the Oobleck* (New York: Random House, 1949).

60 Baruch, *New Ways in Discipline*, 115.

61 Ibid., 123.

62 Dr. Seuss, "The Ruckus," *Redbook* (July 1954): 84.

63 Dr. Seuss, *Yertle the Turtle and Other Stories* (New York: Random House, 1950).

64 Dr. Seuss, "The Zaks," *Redbook* (March 1954): 84.

65 T. S. Geisel, "Some Notes by the Professor," undated, Seuss Papers, Box 7, File 13.

66 Unless specifically cited, all subsequent references will be to T. S. Geisel, First Draft Script, *5000 Fingers of Dr. T*, Seuss Papers, Box 7, Folder 13.

67 Conried's campy performance often transcends any rigid parallels between Dr. T and der Führer, making his monomaniacal musician the comic centerpiece of the film. He rolls his villainous lines with relish, offering Zlabadowski a toast with his "best vintage" of Pickle Juice, before ordering the hapless plumber to be disintegrated slowly —"atom by atom—at dawn!" Across several musical numbers, T seems more like a child at play, enjoying "glorious weather for zipping and zooming," demanding that his men "dress me up" in more and more extravagant duds, including such effeminate clothing as "pink brocaded bodices," "Peek-a-boo blouses," and "chiffon Mother Hubbards." Dr. T fits alongside Yertle the Turtle and young "Adolphkins" within the long tradition of infantile and impulse-driven tyrants that run through Seuss's work.

68 Dick Williams, "Roaming the Sound Stages," *Los Angeles Mirror* (March 7, 1952), *5000 Fingers of Dr. T* clipping file, Margaret Herrick Library, Academy of Motion Picture Arts and Sciences, Los Angeles.

69 Mildred Norton, "Just What Music Has Always Needed," *L.A. Daily News* (August 10, 1952), *5000 Fingers of Dr. T* clipping file, Margaret Herrick Library, Academy of Motion Picture Arts and Sciences, Los Angeles.

70 T. S. Geisel, Loose Notes, *5000 Fingers of Dr. T*, script files, Seuss Papers, Box 7, File 13.

71 Ironically, when the student protesters accused their parents of being "fascists," they chose the one word most likely to sting them. Permissiveness's widespread adoption reflected postwar anxieties parents felt about their own exercise of power and an attempt to police the American family of its remaining vestiges of authoritarianism.

An Auteur in the Age of the Internet: JMS, *Babylon 5*, and the Net

Alan Wexelblat

For starters, I have problem with the auteur term. . . . I do consider myself the author of the B5 story, the creator of its characters and universe. Insofar as we enter other areas, my position is that of navigator . . . I point to a spot on the horizon, and say "That's where we're all going."

—J. MICHAEL STRACZYNSKI, *BABYLON 5*
CREATOR/WRITER/PRODUCER

JMS is King. As to whether he belongs here [in rec.arts.sf.tv.babylon5], everybody gets one vote, and JMS gets one more vote than the rest of us put together. Be polite to the King, even though you think he's not as honest as he says.

—ALEX ROOTHAM, *BABYLON 5* FAN, USENET POSTING

I'm fairly disinterested in the auteur. I don't think they're best qualified to comprehend the breadth of their work in many ways: I prefer the perspective of the recon balloon to that of the front line.

—WILLIAM HUBER, *BABYLON 5* FAN, USENET POSTING

What we know of an author changes our relationship to that author's texts. What if we not only knew about an author but could talk to him during his process of creating a work? What if he not only listened, but participated—talking about the work, about himself, and about his readers—and it all happened at the speed of the Internet? How would the power of the author shape the reader community and vice versa? New-media theorists such as Howard Rheingold have argued that the Internet democratizes discussion.[1] I would like to present a different point of view, one that illustrates the constrictive power that an active author can have on a reader community. Specifically, I

analyze the relationship between an auteur and a fan community in the process of an ongoing dialog of mutual- and self-construction. In this case, the auteur is J. Michael Straczynski—JMS, as his fans call him and as he signs himself—the creator of the science fiction television series *Babylon 5;* the fan community is comprised of viewers of the show who use the Internet to gather information about the show and/or communicate with similarly enabled fans.

I look particularly at the means by which the author is constructed through interactions in these new media. This construction happens through three major processes. The first is conventional: the author is constructed by fans through the text created by the writer, where the primary interaction medium between author and fan is the text. The second is that the author is constructed by himself, through self-revelation in the manner of a speech-maker. This is a new process that is greatly facilitated by the new media. Finally, the writer and the fans jointly construct an author by means of dialog in the new media. I believe that the dialog participants work from partially shared models of what the author should be and relate their interpretations to this model, which they co-construct.

This last process is the most interesting because it is one which has not been so pervasively available to authors before the widespread use of the Internet. The Internet allows near-real-time interaction between discussion participants and thereby speeds up a process that is critical to fans' reading of a complex, episodically unfolding text such as *Babylon 5,* a text subject to a large number of constructions and interpretations. In the past this process was carried out in fanzines and other print or broadcast media, which have not generally been so fast or so widespread as the Internet. In other media, various intermediaries usually intercede. Interviews, press releases, information kits, and so on all place human and physical barriers between the author and the fans. Even when authors spoke directly to their fans, such as the Beatles' releasing Christmas records to their fan club members, there was little interaction and few means of direct feedback from readers to author. The new media provide interaction and feedback opportunities that could change the entire character of the relationship.

To analyze the JMS-fan relationship I discuss new-media resources available to fans and examine fan activities within the media. I then discuss JMS's responses to fan activities and his self-characterizations. I close by discussing three separate incidents in which the new media played a significant part in the construction of the author.

Background

Babylon 5 is a science fiction television serial set nearly three hundred years in the future. Humans have established colonies in the solar system and, via technology purchased from visiting aliens, have begun to expand to other stars. Earth operates under a united government, and humans rapidly become one of the five major empire-building races, among dozens of other space-faring sentients. Ten years before the events depicted in the television series, a misunderstanding caused the Minbari—one of the most advanced races—to go to war with the humans. On the verge of wiping out earth, the Minbari suddenly halted their advance, surrendering for unexplained reasons. To prevent the kind of misunderstanding that started the Earth-Minbar war, the major races agree to the construction of a massive space station in neutral space which will serve as a United Nations-like place for meeting, trade, and negotiation. This station, called Babylon 5 (because the first four never became operational) serves as the home of the major characters in the series and the focal point of much of the action.

As a dramatic series, *Babylon 5* resembles *Twin Peaks* in some ways and *Star Trek* in others. One of the key ways in which *Babylon 5* is like *Twin*

Peaks and some contemporary series such as *Murder One* and *The X-Files* is that all follow a continuing story. As JMS notes, "[Babylon 5] is, as stated, a novel for television, with a definite beginning, middle and end."[2] The arc is the name given to the overall plot outline which JMS wrote describing the major events and actions, the main characters, and associated stories of *Babylon 5*. The arc features centrally in discussions among the fan community. For example, all episodes are labeled as either "arc" or "not arc." Arc episodes are expected to advance the overall plot and to contain major or important information. Not-arc episodes may tell interesting stories and develop characters but they do not answer central questions of the series or resolve key mysteries.

The arc is plotted for five years and each year has a theme; although there has been discussion of spin-offs or related stories, JMS has been adamant from the beginning that *Babylon 5* would be a show with a definite end, resulting from the completion of a planned story, following the development of the important themes. These themes are often mythic, in the sense described by Joseph Campbell: they deal with basic concepts such as good and evil, fall and redemption, and the relationship between a public hero and a private person.[3]

Viewers are promised (by experience and by JMS's public statements) that all the major questions raised in any given year of the arc will be answered in the next year's arc episodes. Thus, ongoing fulfillment and revelation is combined with continuing mystery. A similar thing was done within *Twin Peaks*, which initially turned on the central mystery of who killed Laura Palmer, but eventually revealed that to be only one detail of a larger series of unanswered questions.

Author(ship)

The centrality of the authorial myth to fan interpretation is not surprising. Media fandom emerged from literary science fiction fandom where issues of authorship are more clear-cut than in network television and where readers often have direct interactions with the writers of their favorite books and short stories. Many important science fiction authors came from fandom, while many writers in the genre regularly attend fan conventions.[4]

JMS is himself an avowed member of science fiction fandom, acknowledging important influences from such series as *The Prisoner,* and of being an ongoing watcher of *The X-Files* television series. *Babylon 5* also lists the well-known science fiction writer Harlan Ellison as a creative consultant, and D. C. Fontana (associated with science fiction in general and *Star Trek* in particular) wrote some of the early episodes.

As evidenced by public postings, JMS is acutely aware of the place that *Babylon 5* might have in the history of science fiction fandom. He understands the need to cultivate an active fandom in order to help a show which does not do well in the standard (Nielsen) ratings. Fans of several such shows—including *Star Trek, Beauty and the Beast,* and *Quantum Leap*—have played important parts in keeping these shows on the air when networks or studios threatened to cancel them:

> In the final analysis, I think we've made a little history with this show, . . . had an effect on how SF Television will be done henceforth, and brought a "screw 'em, let's go for broke" philosophy back to the genre, which (personal opinion) had grown, in TV, a bit on the stuffy side. Bar fights, main characters who lie, bad guys who do good things and good guys who do bad things, bathrooms, fasten/zip and lessons in Centauri anatomy, we've broken some of the taboos, and I think that's a positive thing.[5]

Note the construction of *Babylon 5* as a special, groundbreaking entity that is better than other texts with which it might be compared. Fandom, particularly science fiction fandom, has always posited itself as apart from, and superior to, the other viewers of other television series. Participants in the new media are generally from the upper classes of society because of the financial requirements for net access; they are also overwhelmingly from the literate classes because written text remains the primary means of communication in the new media. Both these selection mechanisms lead to a fandom which is trained to value high-culture artifacts and to separate itself from "mundanes," as non-fans are often derogatorily labeled. As Foucault notes, auteur discourse concerns taste: "Discourse that possesses an author's name is not to be immediately consumed and forgotten; neither is it accorded the momentary attention given to ordinary, fleeting words. Rather, its status and its manner of reception are regulated by the culture in which it circulates."[6] Fans need a powerful, or at least well-known, author in order to maintain a superior feeling; JMS needs a fan base heavily invested in a superior view of the show in order to justify his sense of his show being exceptional in the television medium and his own sense of being an exceptional television author. This move to superiority and separation from "low" or popular culture is a familiar one. For example, Bourdieu argues that creating an author is one of the ways that bourgeois (cultured, refined) taste makes a space for itself in the realm of the popular.[7] High culture is authored; pop culture is not.

Authorship, and the construction of the author, also serve several useful pragmatic purposes for readers/viewers. First of all, they allow readers to group artworks together in meaningful and coherent ways; for example, fans of *Star Trek* often speak of the episodes written by D. C. Fontana as a whole. Authorship also plays a large part in demarking the value of artworks. Something written by a well-known writer commands a higher price than something by an unknown. Additionally, fans are often collectors and will seek out obscure material by a named author, thereby raising the value of a previously ignored item. Finally, authorship provides a simple and readily accessible causative explanation. Fans seek explanations in their model of the author for actions taken by characters in the series.

Each of these purposes encourages fan construction of an author. In an episodic series such as *Babylon 5,* some means must be found for rationally associating actions, plot elements, and characters across episodes (grouping artworks). In a fan culture, it is common to see tie-ins appear that are associated with the main text. For example, *Babylon 5* has spawned artifacts such as associated novels, that are given weight and value by virtue of their having been approved by JMS (demarking value). His name appears prominently on the cover of the novels even though he does not write them, and buyers read on the book jacket that these novels describe episodes of the plot which were not made into television shows.

JMS denies himself the auteur label. However, I argue that JMS deliberately constructs himself as an auteur, in much the same way as David Lynch did in *Twin Peaks,* and as Chris Carter did in *The X-Files* and *Millennium.*[8] JMS fits this construction even more than the usual television series producer because he is also the series' main writer. Not only did he originate the concept for the series and write the arc, but he also wrote most of the individual show scripts. In the third season of *Babylon 5* he wrote the script for every episode, a feat never before achieved in American television. Thus he is strongly associated with both the overall trajectory of the show and with the individual episodes. Recovering authorial intent is the most prevalent activity in the *Babylon 5* online fan community. It is also precisely the mode in which most of the interactions with the writer occur: fans ask questions to clarify or validate their interpretations of what they see in the episodes and JMS responds, or not, as he sees fit.

The Net Parts

Two media are the most significant for understanding this author-construction process: Usenet newsgroups and the World Wide Web. Rec.arts.sf .tv.babylon5, the major discussion newsgroup during the period researched (January 1995–January 1996) is distributed worldwide. Many of the fan quotes used in this paper come from postings to this newsgroup, now archived at Google (news .google.com). The newsgroup, like much of Usenet, is anarchic. The group has opinion leaders, members who are particularly respected and members who are particularly reviled, but among the fans there is no single authority or source of direction. There is no central organization filtering and ordering postings to the group as a whole.

The World Wide Web (or simply the Web) adds a new media dimension to fan activity. In some ways, the Web acts like a journal of record. Newsgroups are transient and postings are composed quickly; Web sites exist for much longer and are often designed by professional graphic artists. Newsgroup postings have no specific sponsorship and sometimes lack even the authorship of a nameable writer; Web sites often have corporate or other official status. Two Web sites in active use during the first airing of the series particularly highlight the competing models of reader interaction with the show.

THE LURKERS VERSUS BABCOM

Note: this episode is more momentous than most. Think twice before proceeding to the spoilers; it's worth seeing unawares at least once. (Warning posted in the Lurker guide)

"The Lurker's Guide to *Babylon 5*" is a fan Web site. It is one of the first, having been established early in the show's history. Babcom was an official *Babylon 5* site, established and maintained by Warner Brothers, the show's producing parent. The site had only been on the Web for a few months at the time this research began. The two sites could not be more different if they tried. The Lurker site is organized along lines similar to the way a viewer experiences the shows; that is, by episode. Babcom only added an episode guide as an afterthought.

The Lurker site is meticulous in its attention to

detail, both in terms of its own accuracy and in terms of what its creators expect viewers to want; for example, each of the episodes in the Lurker's Guide has hints as to what details a sharp-eyed viewer might watch for in order to gain clues, an important part of the construction process. On the other hand, Babcom contained numerous errors which would be caught by even a casual viewer of the show; for example, the character Delenn was referred to as "he" in the official biography despite being decidedly female.

Babcom also clearly had little respect for fan conventions. Babcom plot descriptions contained significant spoilers; any fan scanning this list found it impossible to watch the episodes with a fresh mind. By contrast, the Lurker site provided summaries which carefully do not reveal plot surprises. Potentially revelatory information was placed farther down the page where it would not be seen inadvertently.

Babcom promoted a personality-based television model of fan viewing. The site featured the actors and characters of the show, greeting visitors to the site with a contextless picture of a character. The character descriptions were short and static—reflecting the status of each character as revealed to a point in the airing of the show's episodes. Readers could jump from a character's description to an equally short description of the actor playing that character, possibly including credits for work other than *Babylon 5*. By contrast, the Lurker site avoided featuring the characters. Although it provided much more complete cast lists than Babcom, character descriptions were avoided. The avoidance of featured characters acknowledged that in the *Babylon 5* series (unlike many other television series) characters change. Not only do their personalities change, their appearances change and their centrality to the story changes. To describe the characters absent their context in the unfolding narrative would be to do a disservice to fellow fans who might thereby be misled.

Perhaps the starkest contrast between the two sites was how they treated the author. In the of-ficial site, JMS was listed as simply one of three "creators" of the show. His official titles were given as "executive producer/creator," and his status as the writer of episodes was not acknowledged. The arc was not mentioned on the official site, and JMS's biography was visibly shorter than that of the other executive producer, Douglas Netter. JMS's words appeared nowhere on the site, nor were there any clues or hints that there might be such a thing as authorial intention which readers might strive to recover.

The Lurker site, by contrast, was a testament to the strength, depth, and variety of that form of reading. The Arc featured prominently, Arc episodes were specially identified as such, and the developed Arc up to the point of a given episode could be read with the information about each episode. Complete, detailed plot synopses were also available. JMS was significantly foregrounded at the Lurker site, which contained an extensive searchable index of "all of the JMS posting archives" as well as the episode guides and synopses. This kind of resource allowed fans to cross-check and cross-correlate information, both key activities in recovering authorial intention.

The "Backplot" section gave facts about the *Babylon 5* universe which were revealed in that episode, or inferred from casual references, sets or props. Details were meticulously searched by fans for story significance. "Questions" referred to unanswered questions raised in a given episode around plot elements, and were expected to be resolved in future episodes, or even in other material. JMS encouraged these explorations and questions within the confines of the plot. He rejected, however, the idea that any plot inconsistencies come from a failing on his own part.

> What you have picked up on are not flaws, but story points in the making . . . areas that will be explored down the road. These questions WILL be answered. . . . I've always taken pride in the fact that my stories are generally airtight. I hate loose ends and unanswered questions and inconsistencies. So

feel free to poke and prod. It'll either be something I've deliberately built into the show, or something that I should attend to.[9]

The most interesting section for critical analysis is the JMS portion. For each episode, the fans gathered and sorted those remarks by the author which seemed to pertain to the episode or that were posted in response to discussion about a given episode. This foregrounding of the auteur's words is key to the particular construction going on in this interchange. As the fan site of record, the promotion in the Lurker archives of JMS's words to an equal level of importance as direct textual evidence must be seen as a specific move to assert the auteur's authority.

> After speaking to the program director at [a TV station in San Antonio], I found out he was interested in airing *B-5* next season (this season they have a full lineup). The program director (at the moment I can't remember his name) said he was awaiting a call back from Warner about *B-5* etc. So I sent JMS a message telling him that his gentleman was awaiting a call back and could he have someone at Warner who is knowledgeable about *B-5* call him. JMS said no problem.[10]

FANS' ACTIVITIES AND JMS'S RESPONSES
Advertising for the show by Warner Brothers was lacking. The show was distributed by an independent production company, and there was no assurance that any station in a given market would carry the series. Additionally, the series suffered from initial low ratings, leading some stations to cancel it in favor of other, possibly better-rated, shows. In response to this situation, fans mobilized to lobby stations and convince them that an audience for the show existed. This sort of activity is not new; indeed, the original *Star Trek* series was preserved for a while by a similar sort of fan campaign. However, *Babylon 5*'s fan community has had to deal with the completely decentralized decision-making authority of hundreds of

different local stations in its attempts to save the show.

The new media excel in quickly mobilizing a large, dispersed population. Messages on newsgroups propagate across the nation in hours or a few days. Fans outside the direct broadcast area of a particular station can contribute to write-in or call-in campaigns and can react quickly to changes in station policy; speed and numbers are critical to this kind of campaign. JMS's presence on the Net allowed fans to get his direct involvement in a way not possible with previous shows. Additionally, the Web's ability to act as a journal of reference is invaluable in collecting information for mobilizing fan action. For example, a fan collected information about writing to a variety of local stations and writing to Warner Brothers, as well as relevant notes from JMS, in a page called "KEEP B5 ALIVE: Write your local station now!" JMS's close contact with the fan community made him the natural spokesman for this sort of effort, given Warner Brothers' silence on the issue, leading to JMS coming to be seen as a saving presence. In the minds of fans, not only did he personify the show, but he also began to personify the power that the show may wield in the commercial arena.

Fan Fiction

> DO NOT POST STORY IDEAS to the *Babylon 5* newsgroup. Since the show's creator/Executive Producer (J. Michael Straczynski, "JMS") is here and reading this group right along with us, he would have to withdraw for legal reasons if story ideas were posted. We don't want that! (The full FAQ explains/defines "story ideas.") DISCLAIMERS DO NOT WORK. Releasing the idea into the public domain does not work. Please respect the group's charter and do not post story ideas here at all. A mailing list exists elsewhere for creative ideas.[11]

As with any series, it is impossible for the official *Babylon 5* text to satisfy all the desires for fans to see certain stories told. Therefore, some fans are moved to write their own stories. The new media play a unique role in the process of fan fiction creation and dissemination. There was an absolute and well-respected ban on posting fan fiction to the rec.arts.sf.tv.babylon5 newsgroup. Fan fiction could easily be construed as promoting story ideas, something which the newsgroup charter prohibits; this prohibition has been the subject of repeated controversy in the group. Fan fiction mostly finds its home on the Web, where the basic paradigm is that anyone can be a publisher. Probably the most comprehensive fan fiction site is the *Babylon 5* creative site. Even here, in what should be the bastion of countercanon fan activity, JMS's presence and authority are felt. For instance, JMS is quoted not quite encouraging fan fiction:

> Obviously, I can't say anything officially here saying "Go write fanfic to your heart's content." Because PTEN would (correctly) stick my head on a pike in the middle of downtown Hollywood. However, let me be ABSOLUTELY clear in this: I have NEVER said, "Don't write it." All that I have EVER said is, "Don't put it in a place where I can see it or stumble over it." [12]

This quotation is interesting because it seems to promote two models at one time. On the one hand, there is the model of JMS as the creator of the *Babylon 5* universe, inviting others in to play with his creation, to share in the authorship as it were. On the other hand, there is the assertion that PTEN would lose something by the act of fan fiction being created. What is that loss? Since no fan can create television broadcasts, fan fiction cannot compete economically with the original text. Instead, the model of loss that seems to lie unspoken behind this assumption is that fan fiction would represent a challenge to authorial control over the text, and this is not permissible for an auteur. If JMS were to encourage fan fiction actively, it would be tantamount to suggesting that not only are alternative interpretations of the main text possible, but that the direction and tone of the

text could be determined by someone else, or that sources other than the officially sanctioned one could produce desirable material. Thus, the potentially dangerous (permissive) first model has to be counterposed with the second (restrictive) model.

Newsgroup Activities

Many of the fan activities are based around ongoing discussions, particularly on the rec.arts.sf.tv .babylon5 newsgroup. We will next take a look at themes which take up most of the discussion threads in the newsgroup.

LOOKING FOR CLUES

> Let me dive in for a second on the general issue of "what means what." One of the things I learned doing other shows, like being on *Murder, She Wrote* for two years, was that you *must* play fair with the audience. The clues cannot be so small, or so diminished, that they will zip by too easily. There has to be at least a reasonable chance that people will glom onto things.
>
> So the odds are that a single word, or a look, or something going on in deep background is probably *not* significant. Anything in foreground, which is given some weight, *may* be significant. [13]

One of the favorite activities of fans of any complex or ambiguous text is the search for clues, and *Babylon 5* fans are no exception. Contributors to the newsgroup take apart the smallest details of the episodes, searching for the clues that they know are in the text. They know the clues are there because the auteur has told them so.

Fans use these clues to build complex models of character, character motivations, plot twists, and so on, in an attempt to anticipate what might be coming next. Jenkins noted that a *Twin Peaks* fan used an analogy between that series and Charles Dickens's novel *The Mystery of Edwin Drood* to anticipate the identity of a mysterious character. Similarly, *Babylon 5* fans build models of the show in terms of what they know—such as J. R. R. Tolkien's *The Lord of the Rings* and Shakespeare's *Macbeth*—and use these models predictively. For example, *The Lord of the Rings* uses a particular thematic structure, in which characters take certain parts in the drama and, as a result, express particular motivations. Using this as a model, fans hypothesized that analogous characters in *Babylon 5* would take certain future actions or were motivated by certain beliefs.

JMS's reaction to the proliferation of models among fans is bifurcated, as are so many of his other responses. On the one hand, he rewards fans who pick up on clues he deliberately places: "Congrats; you're the first person I've seen to get the Macbeth parallel." [14] On the other, he actively discourages the use of these models for predictive purposes:

> Though I may sometimes nod to one or another landmark of SF, I'm not doing The Prisoner, Lord of the Rings, Childhood's End, MacBeth, the Iliad, The Mountains of Madness, or any of the thirty other works that I'm supposed to be doing, all mutually contradictory. I'm telling this story, my story, and though it's nice to be compared to such other works, it does become bothersome after a while when everybody tries to pin down which work I'm supposed to be "doing" when they NEVER do this to novelists, because this is TV. C'mon, people, I've written published novels, and short stories, and plays, and radio dramas, and I *do* have a brain in my head to maybe make up something on my own, y'know. [15]

Surely it is obvious to JMS, as a published novelist, that this sort of activity in fact happens in all kinds of print media. Even leaving aside cases where a writer is accused of outright plagiarism, a major activity of criticism is the search for inspirational models. Novels seen to be too derivative are looked down upon; this is particularly true in science fiction/fantasy fandom where the predominance of media-derived product and multi-

volume series have led to a growing complaint of lack of originality. Even within supposedly "original" works, comparisons are constantly made between new material and predecessors. For example, it is a rare book that deals with robots and is not compared to the works of Isaac Asimov. JMS is not the first to suffer these slings and arrows, no matter what he protests. A writer who was less married to the auteur model might be more willing to accept the predictive power of analogy models, seeing them less as losses of control than as ways in which fans can participate in the co-creation of the text.

JMS also seems to be concerned lest his master work be seen as more common or less original than he sees it. This leads us back to Foucault and his description of how the attachment of an author's name to a work gives it value. JMS might have responded, for example, by pointing out that no work of art is completely original; for example, Shakespeare's plots were often drawn from the common oral stories of his time and from the commedia dell'arte. However, JMS holds a model of ownership, one in which the story is a possession that remains solely his, by virtue of the (undisputed) long hours and hard effort he has put into creating the *Babylon 5* scripts and show. As the creator of this unique work, he elevates himself to auteur status. Clearly he is not only pointing toward the horizon; he is claiming to have made the horizon exist. It is the job of the readers to see only that authorized story and to focus their efforts on recovering authorial meaning.

RECOVERING AUTHORIAL MEANING

> IMO [In my opinion] nothing which we see on the TV screen in B5 is "self-evident." That is IMO part of the "rules" of this series. It ain't so until JMS tells us it's so. (David Shao, *Babylon 5* fan [unarchived rec.arts.sf.tv.babylon5 posting])

The project of recovering authorial intention or meaning takes the entire text and, rather than attempting to form predictive models about the future course of the plot, seeks to assign meaning to what has been viewed. In particular, of course, the meaning to be assigned is the one purportedly encoded in the text by the auteur. This linear model of encode-transmit-decode is not widely accepted these days by critical theorists, but it closely matches the model under which JMS and most of the fans seemed to be operating.

This poses a direct challenge to theorists such as Howard Rheingold and Douglas Schuler who posit the Internet as a democratic leveler of differences.[16] In this utopian discourse, the oft-quoted fact that "on the Internet no one knows you're a dog" should cause a peer-based interpretive community to form in which the author (though not dead) would be merely one voice among many and where his ideas would wield no more weight than any other. That clearly is not what is happening here. Even discounting the special voice of the author, the egalitarian model among fans does not hold. Within the fan community there are opinion leaders such as prolific message-posters and the writers of the episode summaries. These opinion leaders shape discussion by the topics they choose and by how they engage those topics. Standards of right and wrong are enforced in the interpretive community.

Simplistic formulations of the effects of new media on author-reader relations cannot account for the complexity of the phenomenon we see here. My own theory is that there is no reward structure in the fan community for oppositional critical analysis, whereas the rewards for friendly analysis are direct and obvious. For those who "guess correctly" there is the vindication of being proven right in later episodes; there is a demonstration of one's superiority to one's fellow fans. In some cases, there is direct reward in the form of a positive comment from JMS himself, such as the one acknowledging the fan who caught the *Macbeth* parallel. This direct reward can also have the effect of promoting fans to authorlike status: they

are recognized for a special act that creates value within the community.

DISCUSSING ALTERNATIVE
INTERPRETATIONS WITHIN THE CANON

Babylon 5 contains enough ambiguities that even those who subscribe to authorial intent models can find and debate different interpretations. The show must do this, or risk losing all mystery. Here, fans forward different theories in any space that authorial intention leaves them. They agree on the general framework, but introduce different sets of clues into evidence to support their varied, often contradictory, hypotheses about events not seen directly or fully on screen. For example, in the episode "Divided Loyalties," one of the characters is shot at. The shooter is not seen on screen; we only see the gloved hands holding the pistol. Immediately, a mystery is suggested: who is the shooter? Resolution of this mystery appears to come in the episode: a character is identified as a traitor and removed. But the episode does not state definitively that this character is the one who did the shooting, and this character arguably lacks certain skills shown onscreen being used by the assassin. As a result, a number of conflicting theories emerged in the newsgroup. Each theory acknowledged that there was one, right, answer, but each cited different supporting evidence for its conclusions. Some even went so far as to hypothesize that characters' onscreen dialog was mistaken in some way, thus allowing more room for theorizing.

> I don't think Talia was Control, either. The statement by Talia indicated that the sleeper was codenamed Control, but it seems that there's the possibility that the spies made a mistake and either picked up disinformation or conflated two different plans. Control may well be someone else.[17]

These theories are often related back to the author. JMS's previous surprises and plot twists which were not anticipated or understood by fans are cited as evidence for the more outlandish theories—if the author was so clever before, simple explanations must be wrong in this case.

Throughout these interactions, JMS has acted to define the program's ideology by his (often Delphic) answers to fan questions, by labeling interpretations as right or wrong and by offering explanations of key events both in the *Babylon 5* universe and in our universe where the show is created.[18] He has given a consistent bifurcated response, simultaneously attempting to maintain strict interpretive control, while encouraging the growth and development of the fan community which is essential to the show's survival.

How JMS Views Himself

> When I'm up on stage, I'm in ***PERFORMANCE MODE*** thinking up the next line, setting up the next segment, whatever . . . and combined with the fact that despite what I cobble together in my JMS "persona" I'm actually very shy. . . . I don't hear the applause. I'm so riddled with anxiety that I don't hear it.[19]

More than any other author in television history, JMS has been willing (perhaps eager) to share details of himself, his private life, his beliefs, and his thoughts with fans. As the quotation above suggests, he is aware that he presents a construct, a selective excerpt of things chosen from all that he might say about himself. Still, at other moments, his view of his own self-presentation is differently assessed:

> Regarding how I present myself here [in the newsgroup] . . . I don't think about it one way or another. I honestly don't much care how I'm perceived. Who and what I am, if I'm annoying or a saint or just another Joe, is utterly and completely irrelevant to the work. Fifty years from now, when I'm long gone to dust, no one's going to remember me for being a swell guy, or a rotten guy. All that matters, all that re-

mains, is the work . . . if I did a good job, the work will live on. If not . . . nothing matters.[20]

Here JMS again seems to be wanting to have it both ways. On the one hand, he claims that the revelatory details are not important, that what matters is the text itself. But that begs the question of why personal information is brought into the discussion in the first place. Presumably, JMS brings in just that personal information which supports his desired self-construction.

JMS AND CHARACTERS

JMS repeatedly indicated the special status of characters bearing the initials "J.S.," such as both the station commanders (John Sinclair and James Sheridan). In general, when considering works of fiction, the degree to which the writer can be identified with any particular character or characters is always uncertain. It is common for fans to select one particular character in a text and identify him with the author. For example, the science fiction author Robert Heinlein was often identified with the words and actions of Lazarus Long, one of his recurring characters; however, Heinlein created hundreds of characters in his career and the identification with any one particular character to the exclusion of all others is arbitrary at best. JMS has vocally resisted identification with any particular character: "Often I slice off parts of my own character (what there is of it) and invest it into all of my characters. There's a lot of me in Ivanova, Delenn, G'Kar, and the others."[21] This construction allows fans to read the words and actions of any character in the text in the light of JMS's self-revelation.

At the same time as he puts himself into his characters, JMS repeatedly claims to avoid promoting his particular views on issues. This has been his defense several times in discussions on the net about the portrayal of religion in the show. The show repeatedly addressed religious issues, and religious figures featured prominently in many episodes. JMS, however, consistently characterizes himself as an atheist.[22] JMS's claim has always been that his views as an atheist are not per se represented by any of the characters.

In other cases, JMS very clearly promotes his particular views. For example, the issue of having a gay character or gay relationship has been raised a number of times by fans. JMS has resisted the notion of having a specifically gay character:

> Let me put this as simply as I can . . . in the year 2258, nobody *cares* about your sexual orientation. It doesn't come up. No one makes an issue out of it. There are no discussions, no proclamations, no inquiries, no "how will they react?" It's like being left-handed or right-handed; no one really cares one way or another.[23]

Here JMS has taken a major social and political issue in modern American society and projected his own particular view of it into the series. No character speaks the lines quoted above, or anything directly reflecting this view, but it is reflected in the characters' dialog and actions, in what they do not say as much as in what they do say. In many ways this pronouncement resembles those made by people around the *Star Trek* series, which has also come under fire from sections of the fan community for its failure to represent a gay relationship as a significant part of their view of the future. Sex, sexuality, and interpersonal relationships of a heterosexual nature are regularly featured in the series, but homosexuality and queer representations are marginalized or excluded.

Again, we see the duality wherein JMS claims not to be promoting himself or his personal views in any character, and yet it takes no great stretch of imagination to see that he is doing precisely what he claims to be avoiding. His point of view seems to be that silence on queer relationships is the same as support, and so characters on the show never utter the word "gay," yet they are claimed to be indifferent to others' sexuality. JMS's choice of

when to deny his own points of view and when to promote them acts not only to shape the story told by the text, but also acts to shape the view of the storyteller constructed by the fans who search for the author.

JMS THE STORYTELLER

My use of the term "storyteller" here is not accidental. On many occasions, JMS has spoken of his activities in terms of story-telling and in particular of his attempts to work within the framework of a traditional storyteller:

> We try to emphasize the voice of the storyteller as much as possible, that we are creating . . . well, I don't want to say creating new mythologies, because I don't think they are really created, they stretch back to the foundations of civilization, and show up repeatedly in works of literature . . . but reinterpreting and reinventing and clarifying the structure of myth for a new generation.[24]

It is not surprising to see that someone who considers himself to be operating in a traditional story-telling mode would turn to using traditional story-telling mythic structures, in particular those described by Joseph Campbell, whom JMS has noted as an influence:

> I knew that the best series set up places where the stories come to you, in a police station or a hospital or a law office, and decided in an SF environment a space station would work well for that . . . added the backdrop of myth and archetype, constructed a Hero's Journey, and took it from there.[25]

Here JMS specifically references the Hero's Journey, an archetypal form of story described by Campbell as being present in virtually all story-telling cultures around the world. However, despite clearly being a student of Campbell's writings, he does not seem to subscribe to Campbell's belief that these archetypal forms belong to no one and that their particular instantiations are less important than the presence of the prototypical elements, which resonate with our experiences and expectations.

JMS is quite aware of *Babylon 5*'s possible place in the tradition of science fiction television. In discussing archetypes and myth he shows his awareness of the larger structures that society, history and language bring to bear on the text he produces. However, the implications of that awareness seem to be different for him than they might be for other critics. JMS draws meanings from the texts that circulate around him; he reworks their images and themes to add new meaning to his series. This is the essence of the process that Campbell describes. JMS, though, seems to deny that others could legitimately take images and themes from his series and constitute from them meanings different than the ones he imposes.

Fans are extremely active in detecting elements, structures, and parallels between *Babylon 5* and other works both inside and outside the science fiction genre. However, JMS is often quick to dismiss these parallels:

> Is *Babylon 5* supposed to be a parallel world to Tolkien's *Lord of the Rings?*
>
> There is no 1–1 corrolation [*sic*]. No. Why should I want to do that, instead of telling my own story? [Tolkien] and I used the same tools in our writing; archetypes and mythic structure, and the hero's journey, so some tools are reflected, as in sagas going back to the Illiad [*sic*] and the Odyssey and Sir Gawain.... and Camelot and endless other mythic stories.... I constantly get mail from people saying, "Oh, you're doing WW II, or you're doing ancient Babylon, or you're doing Kennedy, or Camelot," and they're all sure they're correct, and they all find evidence ... but they can't be all correct, and they're not.[26]

And yet, in some sense, these meaning-seeking fans are all correct. The stories belong to no one. The mythic elements and issues drawn from the cultural fabric are amenable to many interpretations, each of which has meaning relevant to the reader creating that interpretation. Each reader brings to the text his or her own backgrounds and associations and each sees within it a different story.

The models fans and JMS use to frame their discussion undergo constant evolution. Often that evolution is in response to a direct challenge of some form. In the following sections, I will discuss three incidents, each of which challenged some significant aspect of the author/fan models and each of which led to major changes in the discourse.

STORY IDEAS

> Just today I received a legal piece of paper from a pinhead in Georgia who thinks I swiped his idea for a ZONE, and that's probably going to involve lengthy legal stuff to prove that I didn't do it.[27]

In any society that attempts to establish precise ownership of intellectual property, creative artists must exercise great care in limiting their exposure to material related to what they are creating. Yet one cannot be a creative artist without training and knowledge of the field in which one creates. The paradox of appropriation plays itself out in many forms. In an environment where a writer is in frequent contact with the thoughts, ideas and suppositions of fans, there is a constant danger of contamination, in a legal sense. Usually the ideas that circulate on the net are nebulous and, given the wide variety of possibilities in a complex universe such as *Babylon 5*, there is little overlap between fan speculations and the aired material. But it can happen. On August 15, 1994, JMS posted this message:

> Kwicker: What if Joe wrote a story in which a "memory-challenged" person DISCOVERED records of who or what he was?
>
> I was in the process of developing that as a b-story in an upcoming episode. Because of that comment, I now have to scuttle the story. I understand that this proceeds from enthusiasm on everyone's part, but let me repeat this as forcefully as

I can: NO STORY IDEAS. No matter what anyone says, what disclaimers are put up, if I see a story idea that is something we're doing or contemplating doing . . . I have to scuttle it to protect the series. This has just torpedoed what would've been a very compelling little b-story.[28]

The reaction to this incident was an almost universal condemnation of the fan in question. The absolute control of the auteur had been called into direct question and the fans closed ranks in response to what was perceived as a threat to the show. In response to the threat, a group of fans on Usenet stepped in. Previously, JMS had been receiving Usenet news messages directly; now the Rangers (as the fan group called itself, after the Rangers in *Babylon 5*) interceded and removed messages that could be construed as story ideas.

A solution was found and the story was produced in the third season, under the title "Passing through Gethsemane." In essence, the sinner recanted his sin, as JMS reported:

This was the story that someone else (don't want to use names, no sense in blaming anyone) had accidentally suggested while I was working on it early in season two. So I had to scuttle the script for nearly a year. Finally, very chagrined over what happened, the individual gave me a notarized form explaining the situation. At that point, I was able to reactivate the story. So no, it's not any kind of "it's okay to do this" notion about story ideas; as it is, the story was tied up for about a year, and might never have seen the light of day had not the other person made great efforts to set the situation straight.[29]

It is ironic that the group set up to deal with the story ideas "problem" and prevent possible resulting charges of plagiarism is called Rangers; that title is itself appropriated from the works of Tolkien, as the Rangers in *Babylon 5* serve much the same function as the Rangers in *The Lord of the Rings* who, in turn, can be related to American park rangers and to lawmen such as the Texas Rangers.

RACISM CHARGES

At one time our Xenobiologist was Indian, named Chakri Mendak. It was only after careful deliberation that I decided to change the character to an African-American, which was done for several reasons, not the least of which being that it would let me bring in some Indian characters in other roles that could be quite interesting. And yes, overall I want to draw from a number of different ethnic groups and heritages, because they each add something new to the mix. And the context throws into relief the fact that those OTHER guys are all aliens, but we—whatever the ethnic background—are all equally human, and I think that will do a lot to ease or even eliminate racism.[30]

A recurring theme in several of the net discussions has been charges of racism or tokenism, made against JMS and against *Babylon 5* in general. It has taken several forms, from the very mild: "Well, (gulp) has anyone else noticed that the only major black character on B5 is a junkie" (Harry Knowles, unarchived usenet posting), to the very aggressive: "Racism is in the heart of this show and if not why did they replace the asia[an] woman that was commander before Ivanova. We are to be impressed with the guess [*sic*] stars that are minority and yet there is only one minority on the show" (Blacnight9 [AOL screen name, real name unknown]).

Accusations of racism are always hard to deal with, particularly for white men in positions of power. It is easy to read JMS's quotation at the beginning of this section as promoting tokenism; the notion that having one Indian character somehow prevents other Indian characters from appearing is hard to rationalize. On the other hand, JMS clearly constitutes himself via his public commentary as being against tokenism and in favor of color-blind casting. This "party line" is echoed by fans like this one, defending JMS and *B5* against

Knowles's comment: "Franklin was a junkie before a black actor was chosen for the part. B5 casting is totally color-blind. This is because jms is, and everyone is in 2260" (Jay Denebeim, unarchived usenet posting).

Of course, Denebeim has no way of knowing that this is the case; rather, he is stating his belief in the author-function he has constructed. In this model, JMS embodies what is good about the series, a common phenomenon in fandom, as Tulloch and Jenkins note:

> The tendency is to ascribe the series' virtues to those agents with whom the fans have the most direct personal contact (the producers, the writers, the actors) and to ascribe its faults to forces more removed from the fan's world and less easily conceptualized in personal terms (the studio, the network, the ratings system).[31]

So Denebeim naturally assumes that what is true of his model must also be true of the person behind the model. Interestingly, though perhaps not unexpectedly, JMS views his "color-blind" casting in personal terms. In his response to Blacnight9, he makes this confession:

> I didn't come into the world with a silver spoon. We were poor. I'm not talking poor lower case letters, I'm talking POOR. We lived in houses without roofs, without heat in the winter, always on the run from creditors. You know where poor folks live, Blacnight? In the poor part of town, which was usually the ethnic part of town. Most of my life I lived in areas that were mainly black, or hispanic, or puerto rican. I lived in Newark just before the riots, as a kid, the only white kid on the whole BLOCK. I've got class photos from schools as a kid, and you look for row after row, and in the lines of brown and black faces, you find one—ONE—white face. Mine. It ain't a case of "well, sure, some of my friends were black," ALL of them were. Or Puerto Rican. Or Hispanic.[32]

By introducing his own lower-class and multi-ethnic upbringing, JMS is seeking to bring to bear

a set of associations which would make him impervious to the charges of racism leveled against *Babylon 5*. However, the logic does not hold. Even if we grant JMS's premise that his childhood makes him "not a racist"—whatever that might mean—we still must make the further leap of granting him absolute power over the show in order to completely constitute the show itself as nonracist. JMS has repeatedly asserted that he has some degree of casting control over the series. To the extent that the characters seem to be racial or ethnic tokens, JMS must bear a larger share of the responsibility, whatever his personal background or upbringing. Any reader could observe the cast composition, deconstruct its meanings vis-à-vis racial makeup and the standard American stereotype of the drug user, and arrive at the interpretation Knowles writes about. JMS's choice of a black actor for that role has racial meanings and overtones regardless of his personal views on the matter or his upbringing.

JMS Leaves rec.arts.sf.tv.babylon5

> Rastb5 has been virtually taken hostage by a very few people who have no interest in this forum except to tear down this show in general, and me in particular. To that effect, they lie, manufacture facts, speculate based on premises that have no basis whatsoever in reality, engage in smear campaigns, insult and abuse users of this area, drop innuendo when they have nothing else to grab onto . . . they leap into threads that should by all rights be reasonably safe from flame and turn them into referendums on whether or not jms is a liar, in the kind of logic that stems from "are you still beating your wife?" premises.[33]

On November 27, 1995, JMS announced he was leaving the usenet newsgroup rec.arts.sf.tv.babylon5. Perhaps the most important element of this incident is that it happened at all. JMS's decision and the manner in which it was done changed the character of the newsgroup discussion in many ways. The public way in which it was broadcast affected every fan in the group: specific miscreants were named as the targets of JMS's wrath but the implication was that the group as a whole was either hostile or passively complicit. In fact, most group members simply ignored abusive postings and went on with their own discussions; one of the important features of Usenet newsgroups is that they can support an almost unlimited number of parallel conversations, and readers can choose which conversations they want to read and to which postings they want to reply.

The timing of JMS's departure also raised more than a few hackles: he left Usenet at almost precisely the same time as he was invited to host a *Babylon 5* area on AOL. Usenet is an open, free forum in which anyone can participate; AOL is a closed pay service that restricts its content to members only. This led to unsubstantiated charges that JMS was profiting from the AOL venture and had withdrawn from Usenet in order to line his own pockets at the expense of the fan discussion.

Finally, JMS's departure changed the newsgroup he had left. For several weeks, well over one hundred postings per day responded to JMS's resignation. Even after the torrent of messages on the topic had died down, rec.arts.sf.tv.babylon5 was different. Some members left the group, echoing JMS's sentiments. Some complained bitterly but stayed. However, no one could miss the fact that the auteur was no longer present. His answers to fan questions disappeared, as did his reports on himself and his writing. Fans often remarked on this absence, both positively and negatively, and fans new to the group were quickly apprised of what had happened. Eventually, a moderated newsgroup was formed, the justification for which grew almost entirely out of this incident.

On one level, what happened can be framed as a fracas about technology and thin skins. One could be surprised that someone who had been on the networks for so long would be unfamiliar with the extremely common Usenet habit of "flaming." Vitriolic personal attacks are nothing new to this medium, and they can be directed against anyone who attains notice. Simply put, one would have expected JMS to have a thicker skin. In general, our society has forced thicker skins upon public figures of all sorts. Celebrities learn that with notice come detractors, and they learn to ignore the clearly outlandish ones; this is why no one bothers to sue the *Weekly World News*. However, new media present three difficulties for this conventional model of celebrity.

First, there is the issue of celebrity itself. JMS still publicly maintains his "innocence" in the face of the cult of personality he has helped create. He denies the auteur label and may indeed believe that fans do not see him this way, despite all the evidence to the contrary. While fan icons—such as Gene Roddenberry—have previously attained this status, none have done so in such a direct personal spotlight as the new media cast on JMS.

Second, the new media encouraged unprecedented closeness and intimacy. JMS has felt free to discuss his religious beliefs, his childhood, his writing technique, his relationships with cast and production company members, and many other details of his life that would likely have remained unexplored without the new media. This degree of intimacy and self-revelation place Usenet vituperation in a different category: much closer to home than slander in a supermarket tabloid. In a way, personal attacks became truly personal because the man against whom they were directed chose to put so much of himself online.

Third, there is the sense that the attacks on the auteur poison the fan community as a whole. For better or worse, fans develop and maintain relationships through the new media. They begin by reading each others' postings to the newsgroup and often move to private email exchanges and to face-to-face meetings at fan conventions. As JMS put it, the flames had . . .

> ruined this forum for not only me but a great deal of other people who've emailed me to say that they don't post here any more, because they've gotten

tired of being attacked, tired of reading the endless tirades and smears and assaults on me and other users. . . . I have become, in many ways, the football used to pull others on either side of the line into an ugly and destructive game. And the only way to stop it is to remove the football.[34]

JMS's interpretation of the situation was incredibly paternalistic. JMS seemed to see fans as needing his protection in their discussions, just as they needed his help to keep *Babylon 5* on the air in their local community.

JMS's departure spawned a host of messages by fans who indicated that they were "leaving" the community. One wrote: "With your [JMS's] departure, the worth of bearing their pettiness has evaporated, and I am content to leave it to the slavering visigoths that have made camp here." Clearly this fan subscribed to a model of community where the word of the auteur was the only currency of interest, and he was far from alone. The fans named in JMS's message as responsible for his departure received significant vilification from the majority of those publicly posting to the newsgroup. Messages suggesting that the named miscreants be "hanged" vied with messages suggesting they be banned from the newsgroup. Each posting they made generated a dozen or so followups, including many urging the fan community to ignore or shun the offenders. Of course, such a coordinated campaign is impossible, and the resulting debate only added in notoriety.

Condemnation was not universal:

> I would like to voice my unqualified support for Fuller et al. You would think someone in JMS's line of work would have thicker skin. B5 is ONLY a TV show!!!!! If JMS gets upset because some people think it sucks then he has serious problems that have nothing to do with this group. . . . Criticism is part of the real world. Most of you are posting from the US so you don't cherish concepts like free speech, but I for one think Fuller et al. have the right to say anything they please.[. . . Now that the King

is dead perhaps this group might get an injection of democracy.[35]

This posting raises key questions about how disagreements between authors and fans can take place in the auteur-centered space that the newsgroup had become. Not the least of the telling points above is the jab at fans in the United States for lack of respect for the speech of others who disagree with them. In effect, the fans in the newsgroup adopted a model of censorship that simply denied space for unpopular viewpoints to be heard.

Another sector of the fan community responded with sympathy for JMS, but condemnation for fans who abandoned the group. Huber expressed it this way:

> I'm mildly insulted (very mildly) by the "JMS is gone? Then I'm out of here!" posts. Are the rest of us chopped liver? Are you just looking for a Q&A session? I hope that many of the folks who've posted here will continue to do so; I enjoy reading much of what is written, and hope that some of you like some of my posts as well. I prefer seminars and panel sessions to Q&A sessions.[36]

This posting expresses the most cogent critical response to this incident. Here we find an explicit critique of the operative models used to support the auteur and a plea for more egalitarian forms of reading, wherein fans working together would create meaning without necessarily referencing an absolute authority for dispute resolution and wisdom dispensation. The analogy of a seminar, presumably modeled on the free intellectual exchange of seminars in university graduate programs, seems closer to the egalitarian models discussed by Schuler and Rheingold than the models expressed by the vast majority of the fans.[37]

A logical question to ask is why this situation ever developed. Given that the Rangers already filtered the group for story ideas, couldn't they simply eliminate undesired postings? Human beings can perform filter functions that software can only poorly emulate. Ron Jarrell, one of the leaders of the Rangers, addressed this point directly:

> We can eliminate anything out of the group. However Joe's not really interested in that, because even if we DID pull them out of what's HE'S seeing, they're still there. We'd also start having to delete messages that refer to them, and messages that refer to those, etc., etc.[38]

Thus the fans, notably the opinion leaders in the newsgroup community, support the rationale of authorial personal responsibility outlined above. In a sense what seemed to happen was a form of reification, in which the abstract fan community came to identify with the concrete person of the writer, and vice versa. In a sense he is "one of us"—a fan of his own creation, and yet he is somehow special.

On December 7, 1995, the Lurker site announced that JMS would "rejoin" the newsgroup, via some (unspecified) mechanism similar to that initially rejected by Jarrell. It appears that he received a filtered version of the group, consisting solely of the questions and posts directed specifically to him, presumably from approved posters only. It is hard not to draw a comparison to a medieval king and his food tasters, sampling each dish to be sure poison would not pass the lips of the sovereign.

Closing Comments

In this chapter, I have tried to analyze the relationship built through the new media between JMS and the fans of *Babylon 5* who make their meeting place on the Internet. Their models of author-reader interaction are relatively simple, despite the intelligence and sophistication of the fan community. Repeatedly, JMS's actions and reactions worked—overtly or covertly—toward reinforcing an auteur model of one meaning for all fans. This relationship and the underlying models provide a strong challenge to strictly egalitarian and more optimistic formulations of new media and their effect on discourse and authority structures. Instead of the predicted one-voice-among-many, JMS and the fans have built a traditional hierarchical structure, with the auteur at the top, favored fans (such as the Rangers) below that, and the vast mob of serfs below that.

I feel a sense of surprise and disappointment at some of these findings; I would have hoped my fellow fans would have more concretely established their challenge to authorial power. However, I also acknowledge that this is the community that these *Babylon 5* fans have constructed for themselves, and readers should not take my comments as being prescriptive; rather, I have simply tried to describe what I have seen in the theoretical terms I have available to me.

That the fans have built this kind of operating structure presents a warning to those who see new media as a technological quick-fix for the purportedly stultifying effects of television. Old models of authorial power operate just as well within the literate computer-accessing population as they do anywhere else, especially given a strong authorial presence whose words and actions reinforce that kind of model at every turn.

Notes

1 Howard Rheingold, *The Virtual Community* (Reading, MA: Addison-Wesley, 1993).

2 J. Michael Straczynski, posting titled "Overview of the 5-Year Plan," 1993.

3 Joseph Campbell, *The Hero with a Thousand Faces* (Princeton: Princeton University Press, 1949).

4 John Tulloch and Henry Jenkins, "Infinite Diversity in Infinite Combinations," in *Genre and Authorship in Science Fiction Audiences: Watching "Doctor Who" and "Star Trek"* (New York: Routledge, 1995).

5 J. Michael Straczynski, posting to Genie computer network, August 19, 1994.

6 Michel Foucault, "What Is an Author?," in *Language, Counter-Memory, Practice: Selected Essays and Interviews,* trans. Donald Bouchard and Sherry Simon (Ithaca, N.Y.: Cornell University Press, 1977).

7   Pierre Bordieu, *Dinstinction: A Social Critique of Judgment* (Cambridge, MA: Harvard University Press, 1984).

8   Of course, the notion of the "auteur" has been elaborated upon in contemporary film theory, owing much to the work of Andrew Sarris, who argued for the stylistic analysis of a film to be organized around the figure of the author-director. Ironically, Roland Barthes was at the same time dismissing the concept of the author. The tension between these two perspectives on the auteur/author, drawn from film and literary studies respectively, is in some ways played out in the discussions between JMS and his critics on the Internet. See Roland Barthes, "The Death of the Author" in *Image, Music, Text,* trans. Stephen Heath (London: Fontana/Collins, 1977), and Andrew Sarris, "Notes on the Auteur Theory in 1962," *Film Culture* 27 (1962–1963): 1–8. For additional reading on theories of authorship, see John Caughie, ed., *Theories of Authorship: A Reader* (London: BFI, 1981).

9   J. Michael Straczynski, posting to Genie computer network, September 1992.

10   Desiree Nehr, unarchived posting to rec.arts.sf.tv.babylon5.

11   Joseph Cochran, automated mailing sent to new posters to the rec.arts.sf.tv.babylon5 newsgroup.

12   J. Michael Straczynski, cited in the "JMS on Story Ideas" section of the *Babylon 5* Creative site.

13   J. Michael Straczynski, posting to usenet titled "Key Questions to Be Answered," June 1994.

14   J. Michael Straczynski, posting to usenet titled "Spoiler of Geometry of Shadows," 1994.

15   J. Michael Straczynski, posting to usenet titled "Enough of This 'B5 Is This and That,'" May 1995.

16   Douglas Schuler, *New Community Networks* (Reading, MA: Addison-Wesley, 1996).

17   Leo Maddox, usenet posting titled "Re: Wait! Talia Isn't Control!," December 19, 1995.

18   JMS has been known to answer fans' elaborate interpretive questions with pronouncements like "good question" or "interesting hypothesis." On one level, this avoids having to give answers that might spoil upcoming plot points. On another level, it reinforces the model of JMS as the sole font of wisdom. Fans cannot be seen to outguess him.

19   J. Michael Straczynski, posting to Genie computer network, September 20, 1993.

20   J. Michael Straczynski, posting to Genie computer network, date unknown.

21   J. Michael Straczynski, Compuserve conference dialog, December 2, 1995.

22   J. Michael Straczynski, posting titled "Straczynski Seems to Be an Ann [*sic*]," November 1993.

23   J. Michael Straczynski, "Will There Be a Gay Character?" Entry in the Lurker JMS Answers file.

24   J. Michael Straczynski, posting to AOL titled "Why I Watch," December 9, 1995.

25   J. Michael Straczynski, CompuServe conference dialog, December 2, 1995.

26   J. Michael Straczynski, in response to a question from Anne and Scott Cald, *Babylon 5* fans, CompuServe conference dialog, December 2, 1995.

27   J. Michael Straczynski, posting to Genie computer network, January 1992.

28   J. Michael Straczynski, posting to Genie computer network, August 15, 1994.

29   J. Michael Straczynski, posting to CIS, November 1995.

30   J. Michael Straczynski, posting to Genie computer network, April 1992.

31   Tulloch and Jenkins, *Genre and Authorship in Science Fiction Audiences.*

32   J. Michael Straczynski, posting to AOL titled "Blacnight9," December 12, 1995.

33   J. Michael Straczynski, posting to usenet titled "jms resigns rastb5," November 27, 1995.

34   Ibid.

35   Colin E. Manning, posting to usenet titled "Support for Fuller, et al.," December 6, 1995. This post was from Ireland.

36   William Huber, usenet posting titled "Aftermath: Should We All Go?" (Attn: JMS).

37   Schuler, *New Community Networks;* Rheingold, *Virtual Community.*

38   Ron Jarrell, posting to usenet titled "Re: jms resigns rastb5," December 2, 1995.

"I'm a Loser Baby":
Zines and the Creation
of Underground Identity

Stephen Duncombe

It takes a special breed of person—someone who doesn't even have a life to begin with—to shun the pleasures of the big city and lock themselves away to toil over something like this. Let's face it folks, all fanzines are put out by total fucking geeks, and *Stuff and Nonsense* is no exception.

—ANDREW JOHNSTON, "I'M A NERD," IN *STUFF AND NONSENSE*

Freaks, geeks, nerds, and losers, that's who zines are made by. "If you had to stereotype a zine editor," says Cari Goldberg Janice of *Factsheet Five,* "it would be someone who was usually a social misfit, who doesn't 'fit in' in many respects, who might be a loner who does better in a written forum than face to face."[1] Don Fitch, a long-time science fiction fan, sketches a similar portrait of the typical SF fan and zine writer as "something of a nerd, rather above average in intelligence and below it in social skills . . . alienated from his peers and finding in s-f and Fandom a means of escaping some of the unpleasantness and stress of The Real World."[2]

That zines are a haven for misfits is not too surprising. For people who like to write and want to communicate, but find it difficult to do so face-to-face, zines are a perfect solution: The entry price is facility with the written word, and the compensation is anonymous communication. "How else could I get up the courage to talk to people at [punk] shows?" asks Mitzi Waltz of *Incoherent*. "'Wanta buy a zine?' isn't much as opening lines go, but it's the best this congenitally shy gal can do."[3]

So what are zines? Zines are noncommercial, nonprofessional, small-circulation magazines that their creators produce, publish, and distribute themselves. Most often laid out on plain paper and reproduced on common photocopy machines, zines are sold, given away, or as is common custom: swapped for other zines. They're distributed primarily through the mail, advertised along the grapevine of other zines, and in the pages of review zines like *Factsheet Five*. Filled with highly personalized editorial "rants," comix, stories and poems, material appropriated from the mass press, and hand-drawn pictures and cut-and-paste collages, the breadth of the zine world is vast. Topics range from the sublime (for example, the travelogue entries and philosophical reflections of a wandering outcast in *Cometbus*), to the ridiculous (*8-Track Mind,* a zine devoted to eight-track tape enthusiasts), making a detour through the unfathomable (pictures of bowling pins in different settings in *Eleventh Pin*). The print runs of these zines are as small and intimate as their character: averaging about 250, but the phenomenon, while hidden, is much larger. Anywhere from 10,000 to 50,000 different zine titles are circulating in the United States today. They are produced by individuals—primarily young people, raised with the "privileges" of the white middle class—who feel at odds with mainstream society, and feel that their interests, voice, and creativity are unrepresented in the commercial media. In brief, zines are the most recent entry in a long line of media for the misbegotten, a tradition stretching back to Thomas Paine and other radical pamphleteers, up through the underground press of the 1960s, and on toward the Internet.[4] Zines are also the voice of an underground culture that for the past two decades has been staking out its ground in the shadows of the mass media.

I began my study of zines in earnest near the end of the twelve-year conservative drive of the Reagan-Bush era. Against this juggernaut, the radical political opposition—in which I was an active participant—acted out a tragedy seemingly

Front cover of *Absolutely Zippo* #27.

self, zines were the crack in the seemingly impenetrable wall of the system; a culture spawning the next wave of meaningful resistance.

As I spent more time with zines and zine writers, immersed in this underground world—reading thousands upon thousands of zines, interviewing scores of zine writers, and publishing zines myself—I realized there was a minor flaw in my theory/fantasy of underground culture as vanguard of world revolution. Witnessing this incredible explosion of radical cultural dissent, I couldn't help but notice that as all this radicalism was happening underground, the world above was moving in the opposite direction: politics were becoming more conservative and power more concentrated. More disturbing was that zines and underground culture didn't seem to be any sort of threat to this aboveground world. Quite the opposite: "alternative" culture was being celebrated in the mainstream media and used to create new styles and profits for the commercial culture industry.

But these are the contradictions of creating an alternative culture within a consumer capitalist society, and something I deal with at length in another study. These limitations don't mean that underground culture doesn't matter, just that by itself—to paraphrase W. H. Auden—it makes nothing happen. What it does do, however, is create a space in which individuals can experiment with alternatives to the status quo: new ways of configuring community and solidarity, counter definitions of work and consumption, and—what I want to explore in the pages that follow—reimagining the most basic of political building blocks: *identity*. Not satisfied with a culture produced for them and identities given to them, zinesters take the first of all political steps: imagining and creating these things themselves.

unchanged for decades. In zines I saw the seeds of a different possibility: a novel form of communication and creation that burst with an angry idealism and a fierce devotion to democratic expression. A medium that spoke for a marginal, yet vibrant culture, that along with others, might invest the tired script of progressive politics with meaning and excitement for a new generation. Perhaps most importantly, zines were a success story. Throughout the 1980s, while the Left was left behind, crumbling and attracting few new converts, zines and underground culture grew by leaps and bounds, resonating deeply with disaffected young people. As an ex-punk rocker, weary politico, and scholar of culture and politics, I was intrigued by its success. Perhaps, I thought to myself,

Zine writers may be shy, awkward, and lacking social skills, but there is more to the loser label than this. Zine writers are self-conscious losers; they wear their loserdom like a badge of honor.

Front cover of *Function* #8.

Mike Appelstein proudly displays rejection letters from jobs he has applied to as a writer in *Writer's Block,* and in *Scatologica,* Jokie Wilson reprints his letter of rejection from art school. A writer named Doug begins his zine with his ex-girlfriend's accusation: "You've got no money, no friends, you live in a slum, you never do anything interesting and you're too damn fat to have sex. Your life is pathetic." The name of Doug's zine? *Pathetic Life.*[5]

For those unsure as to exactly what a loser is or does, John Foster outlines "Three Days in the Life of a Loser" in *Ched.* A snippet: "*9:00 PM–10:30 PM:* Go to local bar. Hang out with drummer for local underground band sensation. Get dissed: bad musical taste, bogus attitude. Protest charge of bogus attitude. Attempt to present a facade of cool. Talk about records so obscure that nobody present has heard of them. Fail to present facade of cool. Convince drummer for local underground pop sensation to leave at the same time so as to avoid appearance of total friendlessness."[6]

The loser, as John unabashedly admits, is himself. It is also assumed to be whomever is on the receiving end of the zine. "You're a geek, c'mon admit it," accuses Aaron Lee in *Blue Persuasion,* "There's no need to be defensive. . . . You don't have to act tough around me, or point the finger at someone else, or make apologies and hem and haw. . . . You're a geek. Just like me. So now that the horrible truth is out, we can stop pretending. And get to know each other. Hi, how are you?"[7]

Being a loser is so firmly imbedded as an identity in the zine world that Jery Vile of *Fun* parodies it in a regular column in the old *Factsheet Five,* "Why Publish?"

> I publish because I was fat and wimpy in high school. Everyone beat me up. Even girls. I had a horrible complexion and my mother made me wear sissy clothes. . . .
>
> I was in good shape after 'Nam. Of course there was no parade for me when I got back. They called me babykiller. My dad had a parade after WWII. He was fond of telling me the reason was because he was a winner, they don't have parades for losers. I floated from town to town, trying to adjust and keep from killing innocent babies.
>
> I couldn't hold a job. I was desperate, suicidal. I turned to crime. . . . A book of matches changed my life. "How About a Career in Publishing?" Thank God for the Acme Institute. It's a good job. I get to work with my hands without getting my fingers dirty. I have a nice car, a beautiful wife, and a set of power tools that every neighbor would kill his mother to use. It is almost like being a God.[8]

Jery's humor only works because it takes for granted the knowing audience of *Factsheet Five;* an audience of people who see themselves and other zine writers as losers—and aren't ashamed. "For losers who strive to lose," the zine *Losers* proudly emblazons across its cover.[9] In the zine world, being a loser isn't something to quietly accept and then slink away. It is something to yell from the rooftops and explain to the world.

Marginalized people with little power over their status in the world still retain a powerful weapon: the interpretations they give to the circumstances and conditions that surround them, and the ideals and character traits they possess.[10] Such is the case with zine writers. While there isn't much they can do about being losers in a society that rewards interests they don't share and strengths they don't have, they can redefine the value of being a loser, and make a deficit into a benefit. Labeled losers by mainstream society, zinesters write to one another, glorifying their loserdom, and in the process making this negative label a positive one. By extolling losers as role models zinesters create a new identity, a *Cool Loser* (as the title to one zine attests), and claim it proudly as their own.[11] In *Hex* for example, Jane draws a comic of karmic revenge on a boy who thought she was a "dork" in grade school. "I'm still a dork," she writes in the last frame, but now she's "also a punk."[12] The glorification of the loser is the revenge of the nerds.

American society, always unequal, has gotten more so in the past two decades. In terms of wealth, three-quarters of income gains during the 1980s and 100 percent of increases in wealth went to the top 20 percent of families in the United States, while the wages for most Americans remained stagnant or dropped.[13] The ability of the elite to maintain order in the face of this redistribution of the nation's wealth, and without—for the most part—the use of overt force, has to do with the fact that America, while not much of a democracy, *is* a fairly well-functioning meritocracy.

In a meritocracy people have to compete for their place in society, and those with merit move to the top while those who lack it drop to the bottom. It is a fixed class system, but not necessarily with fixed classes. While the elite tends to be re-

placed by their children, the possibility exists for a bright young nobody to die a bright old somebody. This Horatio Alger, rags-to-riches story is a powerful stabilizing influence. Anybody can be a winner, "A Dollar and a Dream" as the New York Lotto slogan goes. But this is no cause for congratulation, because where there are winners there are also losers—and lots of them. The winners are celebrated with power, wealth and media representation. The losers—the majority of Americans—are invisible.[14]

But they are visible in zines. The prominence of the loser in the pages of the zine is certainly the handiwork of socially awkward individuals—losers in a *personal* sense. But loser ethics also stem from and appeal to those considered losers in a *societal* sense. That is: people who are losers not because they are awkward and shy, but simply because they are denied or reject the wealth, power, and prestige of those few who are the winners in society. "Above average in intelligence and below it in social skills" is how Don Fitch describes science fiction fans. Overlapping this, however, is the membership description of another subculture which has had a major influence on zines. "Punk," explains Legs McNeil, a high school drop-out and cofounder of the first punk zine in 1975, "was what your teachers would call you. . . . We'd been told all our lives we'd never amount to anything."[15]

Most people in America will "never amount to anything" as the concept is defined in our society. They won't be the "best and the brightest" because what they excel at doesn't fit the elite criteria of merit, because the traditional ladders of education and social services are being dismantled, because they consciously reject the paucity of a life spent in competition, or because they are just regular people, nothing special. But by celebrating the fact that "we'd never amount to anything," the zine world does amount to something. It becomes a place where losers who have found their way into the underground can have a voice, a home, and others to talk to. As individuals, zinesters may

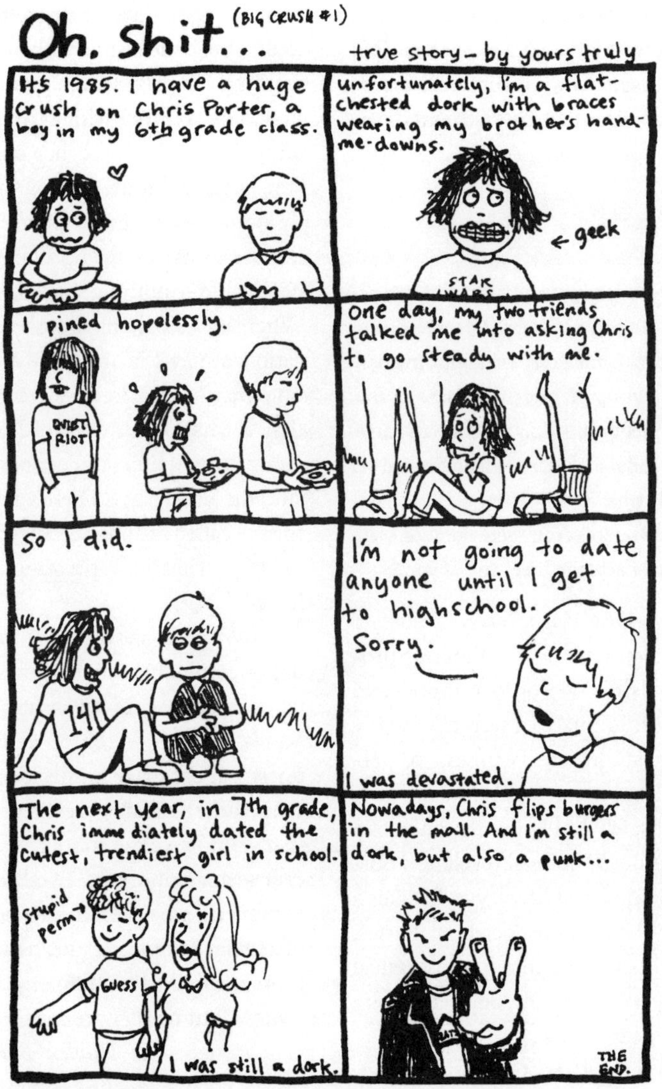

Revenge of the nerds in *Hex* #1.

be losers in the game of American meritocracy, but together they give the word a new meaning, changing it from insult to accolade, and transforming personal failure into an indictment of the alienating aspects of our society.

Everyperson

> I just lost the one person in the world that I can actually say I loved, and this is where I've decided to vent my frustrations. I must tell you about my personal life in order to purge myself of some of this depression and loneliness. I don't usually tell anyone about my personal life, keeping it all bottled up inside because it is what it is—personal. But I have decided I can trust you folks out there because, well, I will probably never actually meet any of you.[16]

So begins *The Elana Rosa Veiga Torres Newsletter for This World and Beyond* in which the heartbroken Josh Abelon tells his tale of love found and lost, sharing his most intimate of secrets with the most anonymous of strangers. "Perzines," or personal zines, like Josh's above, read like the intimate diaries usually kept safely hidden in the back of a drawer or under a pillow. Personal revelation outweighs rhetoric, and polished literary style takes a back seat to honesty. Unlike most personal diaries, however, these intimate thoughts, philosophical musings, or merely events of the day retold, are written for an outside audience.

What makes perzine writers unique, however, is not the fact that they share the intimacies of their lives—that's what famous authors of published memoirs do—but the fact that zinesters lack the connections and credentials to be published, yet do it anyway. They don't wait for anyone's approval: no editors imposing standards of content and style, no publishers imposing fiscal or advertising related constraints. In other words, perzines are created by people who have not been "authorized" to do this kind of writing: losers.

Jen Payne, for example, shares *The Latest News*

about her quiet life in a shoreline town in Connecticut. One issue begins with her reminiscing about working at a coffee shop and the regulars who visited there, another with a trip to New Hampshire, and still another with her love for photography (the latter including photos straight out of a family album: Jen at the prom, her and her husband, a picture of her cat). The zine itself is a scrapbook of Jen's life—nothing special, nothing outrageous. Whereas the rule of thumb regarding the publication of news in the mainstream media is "dog bites man"—that is, what is considered "newsworthy" is what is out of the ordinary—what Jen and many other writers of perzines honor is the opposite: the everyday. "There's much to celebrate in this so-called mundane, everyday life," one of Jen's readers writes in appreciation, and "*TLN* shows it well."[17]

BudZine is another celebration of the everyday—complaints about Christmas fill one issue, taxes another—of an everyperson: John "Bud" Banks. As the editor of a trade magazine that doesn't allow space for his ideas, Bud understands that "there probably aren't too many publications that would give me space to carry on about whatever seems important." And so he creates his own forum, thereby refusing to accept that the lives of regular people are not news. "It's not that my thoughts and ideas have any *special* worth," Bud writes, "but neither are they worth*less*."[18]

Through *The Duplex Planet*, David Greenberger chronicles the thoughts and ideas of forgotten and "worthless" people: the elderly. Hired as activities director of the Duplex nursing home in Massachusetts with little qualifications and less of an idea of what such a director was supposed to do, David started asking the residents questions. Amazed by the life, humor and just plain oddness encapsulated in the responses he received, he bundled their musings together as a newsletter for the home, then later made it into a zine.

"It's one of the greatest shoe states in the country. Especially ladies shoes," William "Fergie" Fer-

Front cover of *Budzine* #19.

gusen, tells David and his readers about Massachusetts in one issue. "They have ladies shoes that go right up to your knee—and I mean up to your knee. And they didn't used to have much on. And when they'd lace those babies up you could see from here to Winston Churchill, and you know what a tall sonofabitch he was! And they'd fall down and say it was their equilibrium—ha! Equilibrium my ass! Those decks were as slippery as a cake of ice and we went to the South Pole."[19]

The hilarity of such offbeat ruminations accounts for the popularity of *The Duplex Planet*, and there's an initial temptation to dismiss David's zine as a carnival freakshow which allows his young audience a laugh at the kooky old folks. But the ultimate effect of *The Duplex Planet* on

the reader is the opposite. Through his ruminations Fergie and the other residents of the Duplex Nursing Home come alive as genuine people, and their ideas develop a logic, albeit an insane one. Reading their words it's impossible to ignore the fact that they—whether they're off their rockers or not—have something to say, and want to be heard.

"I am a tard. So what?" shouts out punk rocker Aaron Rat in his zine *Tard Nation*, angrily questioning assumptions about who gets to be heard and who has the right to publish and share their ideas. "I was born with Down's Syndrome," he explains, "You might think it's funny but it's not. I have it better than most people with Down's. I can still write and talk and do most things that normal people can do." And like "normal" people who do perzines, Aaron insists that what he has to say is important, even if he feels—probably correctly—that most people think it isn't. "So fuck you if you don't like it! I'm doing this zine for tards everywhere. I can still be proud of what I do."[20]

In stark contrast to the funny, exciting, glamorous, dangerous, or tragic lives of the personalities who populate the sitcoms and dramas of television and the pages of magazines and newspapers, perzines chronicle the lives and events of normal (or normally abnormal) people—by the standards of the mass media, dull people. Vicki Rosenzweig, for instance, begins her inaugural issue of *Quipo* with a tale of spilling soup on her lap at a local Chinese restaurant, continues with a description of swans near her New York City home, and finishes with her thoughts on deli counters. By the standards of car chase narratives, this is boring stuff.

But the narratives told in these zines are of and by real individuals, and the events chronicled and personalities revealed are far more textured than their scripted and handled counterparts in the mass media. Jen, after recalling her days in the coffee shop, gives her views on the national debt.[21] In his "The Play's the Thing" issue on his acting experience, Bud slips in a critique of how the

"Fergie" on the front cover of *Duplex Planet* #112.

vision tonight or leaf through *Time* or *Newsweek*. How many "regular" people do you see or hear? Of these, how many have their views expressed in a form different from a statistical average or in a space larger than a sound bite, or play a role other than victim or freak on a talk show? As a meritocracy, the voices heard in America are of the best and brightest: experts, business leaders, politicians, and celebrities. Perzines are the voice of a democracy: testimony to the unrepresented everyday, the unheard from everyperson.

By expressing the experiences and thoughts of individuals, perzines are illustrations of *difference*. Not the difference offered in abundance through mass culture—style, sound bite, and lifestyle—but a distinction far more profound. As Vicki suggests, real difference is not to be found on the fifty-plus channels on cable TV, but through searching for its expression in out-of-the-way places and creating that expression oneself.

The "difference" zine writers frequently express is the one deviation rarely tolerated or represented in the mass media: rejection of the "good life" as it is defined in consumerist terms. Dennis Brezina records his simple life, living close to nature in *America's at our Doorstep*.[24] Terry Ward—a former manager of the town dump—sends out his almost biweekly *Notes from the Dump*, sharing personal memories and opining on national politics from the perspective of a man who has "dropped out" of society.[25] Ernest Mann—another older man who has left society behind—puts out *Little Free Press*, telling of his exploits trapping squirrels in a warehouse and traveling to Mexico to purchase affordable false teeth.[26] And in *Cometbus*, punk rocker Aaron shares his hobo life traveling the fringes of America.[27]

Alienation can sell in America. The culture industry knows its market, and if enough people feel estranged from the norms and practices of society, it will make room for, and profit from, a *Rebel Without a Cause* that speaks to this malaise. But there is a profound difference between the

mainstream news frames and interprets events.[22] And Vicki uses her commonplace observation of delis—"The typical grill is the same: many variations on the hamburger, a BLT, hot dogs"—to launch into cultural analysis: "The deli counter is like many other aspects of modern American culture: it gives the appearance of great variety, but mostly offers the same thing in a number of disguises. . . . As with food, real variety is available, but you have to look for it, or make it yourself—it doesn't come prepackaged."[23]

These personal zines are testimony that regular people *think:* about themselves, about their experience, about politics, and about their role as creators and consumers of culture. If this doesn't seem radical—and it shouldn't—watch the tele-

rebel represented by the mass culture industry and the rebel who speaks through zines. The rebel of mainstream media is on the outside, howling at the world for its injustice, but invariably wanting to get in, to be accepted, but on his (for invariably it is a him) terms. While there is plenty of howling at injustice done in zines, the strategy of the zine rebel is one of removal: communicating feelings of alienation by alienating herself from society. And the zine that records this struggle is not used as a medium to broadcast discontent to the dominant society, but as a way to share personal stories of living on the outside quietly with other disaffected individuals.

As such, Dennis's rural, contemplative life, unfolding day by day in *America's at Our Doorstep,* is as "mundane" and "everyday" as Jen Payne's. Dennis relates seeing a deer, the books he read, finding a mouse nest in the oven. And even though Aaron—as he takes readers with him bumming across the country, visiting decrepit towns, sleeping on buses, and reporting his impressions of local punk scenes—fits the American ideal of the misunderstood rebel loner, he is more interested in exploring and communicating the forgotten little features of life outside the public gaze than fighting for a place in its light. "I had an hour to kill before the bus arrived, so I looked around downtown Janesville [Wisconsin], where I'd been assured by the locals that there was 'nothing at all,'" Aaron writes. "As usual, 'nothing at all' turned out to be pretty cool. I passed a beautiful river, old crackly neon signs, a farmer's market, an old 'Chop Suey' district, and a shopping cart guy with a tiny general store junk stand and a sign that said 'Everything You Need Can Be Bought Here.' Yeah, nothing at all." [28]

It is these sort of things—the experiences, ideas—that are "nothing at all" to the dominant society, whether it is because they are too regular, or too far outside what is regular, that zines represent and communicate. Perzines are a way that individuals, who in the eyes of the political and media elite are themselves "nothing at all," can assert, if not as Karl Marx's angry revolutionary would have it: "I am nothing and I should be everything," then at least, less egotistically: I am nothing and I should be *something.* [29]

The Political Is Personal

Emphasis on the personal is not limited to perzines; it is a central ethic of *all* zines. In the first serious survey of science fiction and fantasy fanzines, psychologist Frederic Wertham (of *Seduction of the Innocent* infamy) highlighted their "intensely personal" quality as a defining characteristic. [30] What Wertham argued back in 1973 is equally true today; zine writers insert the personal into almost any topic: punk rock, science fiction, religion, sexuality, sports, UFOs, even the exploration of pharmaceutical drugs.

In an issue of *Pills-a-go-go,* Jim Hogshire, eager to dispense knowledge on Dextromethorphan Hydrobromide (the "DM" in commercially available cough syrups), experiments on himself, guzzling eight ounces of the medicine and recording its effect:

> At four o'clock in the morning I woke up suddenly and remembered that I had to go to Kinko's and that I had to shave off about a week's worth of stubble from my face. These ideas were very clear to me. They may seem normal, but the fact was that *I had a reptilian brain.* My whole way of thinking and perceiving had changed. . . .
>
> The world became a binary place of dark and light, on and off, safety and danger. I felt a need, determined it was hunger, and ate almonds until I didn't feel the need anymore. Same thing with water. It was like playing a game.

Jim makes it to a Kinko's copy shop where a friend tells him that his pupils are of different sizes. He wanders out alone again, later recalling that

> I found being a reptile kind of pleasant. I was content to sit there and monitor my surroundings. I was

alert but not anxious. Every now and then I would do a "reality check" to make sure that I wasn't masturbating or strangling someone, because of my vague awareness that more was expected of me than just being a reptile.

The life of a reptile may seem boring to us, but I was never bored when I was a reptile. If something started to hurt me, I took steps to get away from it; if it felt better over there that's where I stayed. Now, twenty-four hours later, I'm beginning to get my neocortex back (I think). Soon, I hope to be human again.[31]

Obviously written to be funny, Jim's piece nevertheless follows a convention of zine writing: viewing a topic through a highly subjective lens, then sharing those personal insights, experiences and feelings with others, making it clear that the teller is as important as what is being told.

Zines are not the first "underground" media to personalize the news. This was a cardinal feature of the eighteenth-century pamphlet: little booklets of only a few pages, unbound and without covers, selling for a shilling or two. While Thomas Paine's *Common Sense* is certainly the most well known and influential of these pamphlets—between 100,000–250,000 copies were printed—he was not alone. Bernard Bailyn, in his collection *Pamphlets of the American Revolution, 1750–1776*, estimates the full bibliography of those that have survived from this pre-Revolutionary period at over four hundred.[32]

Zine writers of a historical mind like Gene Mahoney liken zines to pamphlets, calling *Common Sense* the "zine heard 'round the world."[33] And there is some validity to this hereditary claim, as the pamphlet, in the words of George Orwell, is primarily, "a one-man show. [Where] one has complete freedom of expression, including, if one chooses, the freedom to be scurrilous, abusive, and seditious; or, on the other hand, to be more detailed, serious and 'highbrow' than is ever possible in a newspaper or in most kinds of periodicals."[34] And before the reader thinks that such a comparison between the high and mighty pamphlet and the lowly zine sullies the reputation of the former, they should be aware that many pamphlets *were* scurrilous, abusive, and seditious, and not above, as Bailyn writes, "depicting George Washington as the corrupter of a washerwoman's daughter, [or] John Hancock as both impotent and the stud of an illegitimate brood."[35] The political analysis put forth in pamphlets frequently degenerated into crude conspiracy theories, and many pamphlets were far from "highbrow." Some were quite terribly written, filled with illogical arguments, poor sentence structure, and painfully bad poetry. After all, they were for the most part— like zines—the work of literary amateurs.

As Orwell points out, these early pamphlets were the words and ideas of individuals, and again like zines, the intimate literary style they employed underscored this point. A popular pamphleteer like John Dickinson, for example, wrote a pamphlet as a letter "to his friend," using the pronoun "I" frequently when making his points.[36] The aim of the pamphlet, however, was not to tender the purely personal musings of its author. Its function lay in offering a medium with which to think through, articulate, argue, and persuade others on *political* issues of the day. While the language of pamphlets may have been personal, the content and purpose was explicitly political.[37]

Zines, too, are often explicitly political, and it is rare to come across one which doesn't express an opinion of some sort on a political issue. But the type of political analysis in zines is markedly different than that found in eighteenth-century pamphlets. Pamphleteers used a personal voice, but the politics discussed were, for the most part, abstracted from themselves, of interest to the public. American pamphleteers, while personally slandering their opponents, would delineate what the stamp tax, English rule, or the quartering of the British army would mean for American *society*. Although uttered with a personal voice, theirs was a public discourse.

For zines, politics—like all other topics—is

primarily a personal discourse. Part of this reflects how politics have been popularly defined since the late 1960s. One of the prominent ideas to come out of tumult that was the New Left was the idea that the "personal is political," a notion best and most frequently articulated by the feminist movement. Simply stated the idea went something like this: Politics not only existed on the level defined in the *Oxford English Dictionary:* in terms of policy, states, and governments, but also on the plane of personal interaction: on the street and in the bedroom.[38] With this new definition, what could be considered within the realm of "the political" was significantly expanded.

But zines put a slight twist on the idea that the personal is political: they broach political issues from the state to the bedroom, but they refract all these issues through the eyes and experience of the individual creating the zine. Not satisfied merely to open up the personal realm to political analysis, *they personalize politics,* forcing open even what the *OED* defines as politics with a personalized analysis. In *Dishwasher,* Dishwashin' Pete surveys class politics through his own stories of dishwashing throughout the country.[39] Patrick Splat explores the issue of discrimination against homosexuals through stories about "coming out" both to the mainstream and underground world in his zine *Loring Punk*.[40] And Adam Bregman exposes the sham of democracy in an age of money politics by writing about his own campaign for mayor of Los Angeles—financed by selling lemonade outside City Hall—in the pages of his zine *Shithappy*. In his zine, Adam backs up his assertion that "democracy is a farce" and that "the worse crimes that politicians commit are legal" not with abstract logic, but with personal, detailed and engaging description of the ins and outs of his campaign. "I always knew that the government was completely corrupt," he concludes, "but after running for mayor I've learned how and why it is corrupt."[41] (Needless to say, Adam lost his bid for mayor, though he did get 643 votes.)

None of the zines mentioned above print reams of statistics on class inequality, prejudice against gays and lesbians, or election funding. Instead, they tell stories. It's not that zines don't present any information which has not been experienced personally. They do: *Loring Punk,* for example, reprints some news clippings on acts of bigotry in the Minneapolis area. But often that information will be presented in such a way as to keep it from being just another floating statistic in a sea of information, making some sort of personal connection between the zinester and "the facts."

One way that zine writers do this is through interviews. This format has strong traditions in music fanzines, and it's in the punkzine *Fenceclimber* that Josh MacPhee uses an interview to introduce the subject of class conflict. After beginning with personal testimonial about how he never had any contact with labor unions until the Emergency Medical Technicians were locked out at a hospital down the street, Josh, through a give-and-take discussion with the union's leader, lays out the context of the union's struggle: what the term "lock out" means, what the EMTs are asking for, new management strategies in the health care industry, and so on. This is straight political analysis of a labor/management struggle, but because it is introduced as a discussion between two people, *Fenceclimber* puts a human face on what are often presented as abstract social forces and political actors.[42]

Another way that zines personalize their politics is to position political issues within a stream of other, more intimate matters. Adam of *Shithappy* segues out of his run for Mayor into the story of a painful breakup with his girlfriend; Patrick of *Loring Punk* moves from tales of coming out to a list of the guys and girls he finds sexy. This placing of the borrowed "fact" and the "personal" plea side by side also finds its way into the pages of another feminist zine, *Finster,* where editors KJ, Erin, Rebecca, and Mary add their hand-scrawled commentary to each reprinted fact on young women and body weight.[43]

For some politically minded zine writers the

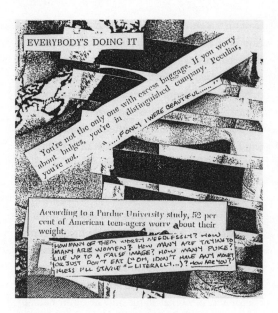

Personal Commentary in *Finster* #3.

personalization of politics is understood as a way to cast off the "preaching" model of persuasion they feel is too common in political discourse. "i hate preachers," writes Jason Page in *Cheap Douchebag*, "what I am trying to do is inform and educate people, so they can form their own opinion."[44] By putting the personal first, political persuasion is cast in terms of emulation rather than conversion. The message isn't "you should do this." Instead, it's "look what I've done." "Change ourselves so others can change," writes the editor of *Forever and a Day*, giving an example: "If you throw away your television and tell me your reasons then perhaps I will do the same and tell someone my reasons and they will discard theirs."[45] In this way, making politics personal is a way of giving away authority, saying to your reader that this—unlike the claims that politicians and professional journalists make—isn't "the truth," it's just what I think.

But at the same time, stressing the personal is a way of taking authority. It's a way for zinesters to assert that they have the right to think and write about the stuff that they are passionate about—whether it be cough syrup or class politics. The same stuff may have been written about a thousand times by skilled journalists and well-educated experts, but as Joshua, the editor of *Notes from the Light House*, writes, "everyone has their own way of telling a story. It's the individual's perspective that makes the same ole story somewhat unique in its own way."[46] Personalization is the mark of individuals who don't have a voice that matters in public discussions about culture and politics saying: Yes I do matter, I have a voice, this is what I believe, *this idea is mine.*

The personalization of politics is a way that zinesters confront the distance between themselves and a mainstream political world in which they effectively have no say. When pamphleteers wrote in the eighteenth century, some were arguing for a hands-on democracy; a political system in which individual citizens could participate directly, and one which seemed within their power to create. Even those who argued against such a participatory democracy, like James Madison, did so because they feared it was a real possibility. It no longer is. The republican ideal of a personal attachment to politics remains part of our ideological heritage, but in practice it is repudiated. Politics for most people has become something "out there," something to leave to the professionals: the politicians, pollsters, and media pundits. As a 1995 poll reveals, 89 percent of Americans feel that the people running the country are somewhat or definitely "not like them."[47] The "public" only appears every four years, when a fraction of it is sighted in a voting booth. The personalization of politics within zines is an attempt for people to redraw connections between everyday "losers" like themselves and the politics that affect them, to collapse the distance between the personal self and the political world.

This same impulse, however, can widen the gap as well. Zinesters are primarily young people seasoned on post-Vietnam, post-Watergate, post-actor-as-president mainstream politics. As such, they have little faith in the "reality" of politics as it is presented to the public. Confronted with a world of stage managed falseness, the only thing they are sure is real is themselves. When Elayne Wechsler, editor of *Inside Joke,* writes that "in the end, the only Reality in which any of us can believe involves our own personal experiences," then the move toward the personal circles in on itself, closing out the world of people and politics. Zines like *Interesting!,* Richard J. Sagall's "compilation of things I find interesting" or Paul Goldstein's *Goldstein: A Newsletter about Me, Paul,* are examples of this solipsistic turn.[48] "Everything is bullshit," begins a rant in *Forever and a Day.* It concludes with the editor's advice: "Close your eyes and build your own meaning. You will be right."[49]

The Politics of Authenticity

Why Publish? To cut through TV horseshit reality to something better—something more personal.
—Edgar "Bolt" Upright, editor of *Tales of the Sinister Harvey*

Ours is a society where things aren't always what they seem. Politicians speak of the people then do the bidding of big business. Corporations befoul the planet then claim to be environmentally friendly. Service workers smile when they don't mean it, successful artists create what will sell. The ends of profit turn nearly everything into merely a means for getting there. It is a world of spin, promotion, public relations, and pseudo-events: *TV horseshit reality.*

To cut through all this zinesters look to "the only Reality in which any of us can believe," that is: themselves. But to connect to this self, everything that stands in the way must be jettisoned. "Man was born free," Jean-Jaques Rousseau began his 1762 treatise *The Social Contract,* "and everywhere he is in chains." Following the Rousseauean creed, zinesters believe that authenticity can be found only in a person unshackled by the contrivances of society. An authentic individual, therefore, is one who cuts through the conventions of manners, norms, and communication and connects to his or her "real" self.[50] This search to live without artifice, without hypocrisy, defines—more than anything else—the politics of underground culture.

Zines are bursts of raw emotion. Their cut and paste look is a graphic explosion unbeholden to rules of design. The "rant" editorial which opens each zine is the spontaneous disgorge of whatever the editor has on their mind. "I think I should say what I want here," Christina begins her *Girl Fiend,* "and not what others expect me to say or what I hope will be of interest. this is my zine, right?"[51] *Right.* "With fanzines you're doing it because you're passionate about it," explains Al Quint of *The Suburban Voice,* "And even if the writing isn't at a professional level, sometimes the excitement, the enthusiasm can compensate for it."[52]

I would argue the point stronger than Al. The excitement and enthusiasm of zines don't compensate for lack of professionalism, they are the replacement for it. Professionalism—with its attendant training, formulaic styles, and relationship to the market—get in the way of what Freedom, the young co-editor of *Orangutan Balls,* told me was the most important aspect of zines: the freedom to just "express."[53] After describing Tom Paine's *Common Sense* as a zine, Gene Mahoney goes on to write, "Even if you're not out to change the world . . . self publishing allows you to be yourself and express your real thoughts. Your real feelings."[54] Saying whatever's on your mind, unbeholden to corporate sponsors, puritan censors, or professional standards of argument and design; being yourself and expressing your real thoughts and real feelings is what zinesters consider authentic.[55]

This celebration of the pure freedom to express helps explain the fact that traditional practices of publishing are sometimes absent from zines.

Pure expression:
Chaos Collage in *Egg*.

A zine from Atlanta, fittingly called *Decontrol*, commands the reader to "make up your own number" instead of listing an issue number on their zine, and many zines, including some of the biggest like the old *Factsheet Five* and *Maximumrocknroll*, use page numbers only intermittently, if at all.[56] But within the zine world itself, traditions begin to form. And because zines are meant to be read, certain protocol—like decipherability—must be followed. Or not. Having been criticized in a *Factsheet Five* review for putting together a sloppy zine, the publishers of *Sick Teen* respond that

> A punkzine laid out neat and tidy is like a punk show with reserved seating. Complaining about not being able to read them is like asking the band to stop playing so you can hear what lyrics the vocalist is singing. . . . That is not what punk is about. Not tidy layouts, not slow and carefully enunciated lyrics. . . . A phrase like "a good and tidy punkzine" is self-contradictory. It can be good, it can be tidy, but not both. As you must have noted, *Sick Teen* is considered the ideal among most punkzine editors.[57]

Also reveling in disorder is the editor of *Frederick's Lament*, who, in addition to sending out his artfully crafted, but nonlinear zine, sent me a NASA photo of Saturn, an official memo form filled out with a nonsensical rant, and a card explaining the germination process of lawn grass.[58] This was not the first nor will it be the last time I've received nonsensical text, images, and mass culture ephemera in the mail as part of a zine. Stretching this ideal of pure expression to its extreme is *Punk and Destroy* "about the punk scene in Portland, Ore." Hand lettered, smudged, and badly reproduced, it is literally unreadable.[59] What matters is unfettered, authentic expression, not necessarily making sense.

This command to stop making sense has an honorable lineage in the cultural underground.

> Ah
> Eh he
> He! hi! hi! Oh
> Hu! Hu! Hu!

Profession of faith by the author, reads the preface to a book by Dadaist Theophile Dondey, who once explained to a sympathetic friend that his writings were nonsensical because, "Like you, I despise society . . . and especially its excrescence, the social order."[60] Early in the twentieth century Dadaists responded to the "sense" and "order" that was World War I by creating nonsense. Similarly the refusal of some zines to make sense or have any order can be considered a reaction against the order and sense of more recent times, in particular the tendency for expression and identity to be packaged as a nice, neat product. But such nonsense is also the—perhaps illogical—conclusion to the ideal of pure expression. By eschewing standards of language and logic the zine creator refuses to bend their individual expression to any socially sanctified order. That this nonsense communicates nothing (except its own expressiveness) to the reader of the zine matters little, for the fact that no one except the creator can understand it means that they've finally created something absolutely authentic.

An "anarchist," Mike Gunderloy defined in *Factsheet Five,* is "one who believes that we would all be better off without government. Most anarchists know what the true anarchist society would look like. They all disagree about it."[61] Mike's wry humor is on target, for it is exactly this predicament of honoring absolute individual thought and action while at the same time building a political movement which has plagued anarchist theorists and practitioners for centuries. And out of all traditional political philosophies it is anarchism which turns up most often in the pages of zines. *Assault with Intent to Free, Profane Existence* ("making punk a threat again"), *Anarchy,* and *Instead of a Magazine,* are all explicitly "anarchist zines." But more common is the anarchy Ⓐ symbol and anarchist ideology scattered throughout the pages of personal, punk, feminist, queer—just about any—zines.

Anarchism in the zine community has its roots: Anarchy has always played a starring role in punk rock and thus punk zines, and prominent zinesters like *Factsheet Five* founder Mike Gunderloy

have also been active in the anarchist movement. More significant, however, are the homologies between the nascent philosophies of the zine scene and those of anarchism. On the most basic level, anarchism is the philosophy of individual dissent within the context of voluntary communities, and zines are the products of individual dissenters who have set up volunteer networks of communication with one another. But the connections run even deeper: the underground ideal of authenticity is part of the tradition of anarchism as well.

William Godwin, the eighteenth-century father of anarchist theory, was himself deeply concerned with the topic of authenticity and creativity. Writing of culture in a hypothetical anarchist Utopia, Godwin asks "should we have theatrical exhibitions?" He concludes: *No,* as theater, "seems to include an absurd and vicious cooperation. . . . Any formal repetition of other men's ideas seems to be a scheme for imprisoning for so long a time the operations of our own mind. It borders in perhaps this respect on a breach of sincerity, which requires that we should give immediate utterance to every useful and valuable idea that occurs to our thoughts."[62]

Godwin's celebration of immediate individual expression and distrust of cooperation and abstraction is extreme even for anarchists, most of whom value spontaneity and liberty *as well as* solidarity and organization. But nonetheless Godwin's emphasis on sincerity as defined through the spontaneity of individual thought and action occupies a prominent place in the anarchist pantheon of ideals, and in the politics of underground culture. Michael Harrington, a socialist critic of the counter culture of the 1960s, commented on later political variants of this form of "authentic" expression, describing both Bob Dylan and members of SDS as practitioners of "the stutter style. It assumed that any show of logic or rhetorical style was prima facie proof of hypocrisy and dishonesty, the mark of the manipulative. The sincere man was therefore supposed to be confused and half articulate and anguished in his self-revelation."[63]

What worried Harrington, besides a bit of generational rivalry, was that by privileging "the sincere man," logic and rhetoric—the rules of argument and patterns of persuasion necessary to communicate political abstractions to large audiences and thus further social movements—would be sacrificed. What mattered to the sincere man was not whether he was getting his message across to others but whether he was truly expressing what he thought and felt. In other words, what was important was the expressivity of the act, not the effectiveness of the result. What Harrington was criticizing has a long history in cultural and political undergrounds, represented in its most extreme form by anarchist practitioners of "propaganda of the deed" in the late nineteenth and early twentieth centuries.

Propaganda of the deed collapsed political strategy and individual expression into a single act—frequently one of terrorist violence (giving rise to the popular caricature of the bomb throwing anarchist). The results of these acts were usually disastrous, when not ludicrous, but the political impact of destroying property or killing a particularly odious capitalist or statesman was never really the point.[64] The deed was a means for individuals to express their dissent without compromising their individuality or spontaneity. What mattered within this odd strategy was less political efficacy and more the purity of the deed itself, "the immediate, apocalyptic value of an act" as historian James Joll puts it.[65]

Most zine writers do not revel in complete chaos, nor are they given to throwing bombs, but they do share this emphasis on the act over the result. This is not merely a means-over-ends political strategy, for most zine writers (like practitioners of propaganda of the deed) there is no abstract strategy at all, no means or end: just *the authentic act.* Alienated from mainstream political institutions, and wary of any constraint on their individuality, they reject a strategic model of politics and communication entirely in the search for a more "authentic" formula. The only thing that stands this test of authenticity is a highly personal act of expression. That is: *making a zine.* For in producing a zine the individual commits non-violent propaganda of the deed, creating an authentic medium of communication, expressing the thoughts and feelings of an authentic individual.

Manufactured Selves

What is an authentic individual? Zinesters argue for a world without any artifice, where they can express what they *really* feel and who they *really* are, but what is this "self" they are trying to be true to? Rousseau believed in a quasi-mystical "natural man"; a "noble savage" then corrupted by civilization. Authenticity, for him and many other Enlightenment thinkers, meant reconnecting to this pre-historic identity—recapturing its essence before it had been shaped by society. But zinesters aren't doing this. They may not want to adopt values and identities fashioned by the mainstream world, but they are not trying to resurrect some sort of pristine identity which only exists outside the web of social construction. In fact, through their zines, they are engaged in the opposite: manufacturing themselves.

No one is born a punk rocker or science fiction fan. Individuals form these identities for themselves out of the experiences and values of the subcultures which they are a part. They listen to bands and cut their hair, or read science fiction and go to conventions—and put out zines. In this process they define who they are. Through his zine a suburban middle-class kid becomes a gritty punk rocker, while a librarian recreates herself as a starship captain. Zines—like computer mediated communication and other such media—allow people, if only for a short time, to escape the identity they are born into and circumscribed by and become someone else. Zine writers use their zines

Turkey in a space helmet in *STET*.

as a way to assemble the different bits and pieces of their lives and interests into a formula which they believe represents *who they really are.*

For Leah Zeldes Smit, the editor of *STET*, even categories like science fiction fan don't fully describe who she is. So in her zine she tells of Thanksgiving dinner with the same emphasis as her trip to Holland for WorldCon (the world science fiction conference). Understanding that this is a rather odd combination, she concedes that her husband, "complains that there is nothing fannish about recipes. That's true . . . But it's my fanzine and I can do what I want to."[66]

Equally reluctant to be pegged to any identity not of his own choosing is Brian Shapiro, who complains about a review of his zine in *Factsheet Five* that attempted to stick it in a category. "It was never my intention to 'mix' punk and politics in CANCER or to make a connection between politics and music," stresses the author, "Animal rights and music and art etc. . . . are all great interests of *mine*. The reason that I publish CANCER is to provide an outlet in which I can express those interests. . . . If key chains and sperm interested me, I would probably do a publication on those things."[67]

I found this to be true in my own case as well. The second issue of a small zine I published—

Notes from Underground—included a mix of personal essays, political diatribes, comix, poems, pirated news articles, and two letters from friends overseas. When it was reviewed by Seth Friedman in *Factsheet Five* he placed it in their "personal zine" section, but commented that it was "Situationist inspired" (certainly news to me). It was also reviewed by Larry-Bob Roberts in his *Queer Zine Explosion*, who didn't pick up on the Situationism, but did mention among other things that one of the political essays was on the latest Gay and Lesbian March on Washington.[68] So what was *Notes from Underground*? A perzine, queerzine, poetry, comix, travel, political, "Situationist" zine? Well, actually all of the above (I do like the Situationists after all), and none of the above. It was simply *my* zine. And the fact that it is mine is what matters. In an era when every conceivable identity has been cataloged and packaged, yet ordinary people have little say in this process, zines offer a way for their publishers to "package" the complexity of themselves and share it with others.

As zines offer a way of communicating that frees individuals from face-to-face interaction (with all of its accompanying visual and auditory cues of gender, race, age, and so forth), and the writer is only known by what he or she puts down on paper, the notion of who and what one is in a zine is potentially very flexible. It is with this in mind that John Newberry, editor of *The Raven*, argues that one of the great things about writing for a zine is that it, "allows people to become something else, someone else. If they contribute to the zine, they have the opportunity to assume identities of their own choosing, and not be molded into beings they don't want to be."[69]

In the middle of an interview with Kali Amanda Browne, editor of *Watley-Browne Review*, I remembered John's words. I had asked Kali about her "correspondent" Kandi: the svelte woman who was often drawn lingering at bars, telling stories about her nights out, and ranting about the general unworthiness of the opposite sex. "Oh, she's me," she replied, laughing. And the other contributors? I asked. "They're all me . . . different parts of me."[70]

Kali uses her zine to construct her identity—but she does it by dividing up her identity into different characters. Tracing her ethnic roots to Africa, Latin America, Europe, India, and China, she understands the limitations of any identity except a hybrid that she creates. She uses her zine to act upon the motto she includes on the cover of her envelope—"Never make anything simple and efficient when it can be complex and wonderful"—by creating for herself a multi-faceted, virtual identity.[71]

An equally complex cast of characters speak through *Sweet Jesus,* a zine put together by a group of precocious high school students. It begins:

> This zine was supposed to begin in September. Me, Chaz, and Bloody Mary had been planning it all summer. A publication for the masses to combat the honor-roll, squeaky clean school newspaper and lit mag which we never could get into even though we tried an awful hell of a lot. We'd publish all the rejects like us and become saviors to the socially downtrodden. . . .
>
> But life got in the way. Mary started working weekends at Mickey O's so she could buy herself a scooter, my father started making me study since the tuition went up and all, and Chaz fell into some strange black hole and never quite got out and finally ended up hanging himself in his bedroom one Monday night in December with only ten shopping days till Christmas.

In this issue and the three that follow, interviews, recollections, illustrations, and poems from Chaz (found after his death), St. Xeno (who penned the introduction above), Bloody Mary, Nasha, Mia X and others trace the hidden life of their dead friend and in the process reveal their own intertwined life stories. Hoping to be able to interview some of the authors of this haunting zine, I turned to the back of the first issue looking for addresses. There, under a list of the writers,

was the note "and those characters sprung from the amazingly twisted mind of Franetta L. McMillian." Franetta was all of the characters—and none of them . . . and none of them were real.[72]

But in a way they were. Some characters introduced later, like a young black girl who integrated her school, were based directly on Franetta's own experience, while others were based on interviews with real individuals. But talking to me later Franetta pointed out that *all* of them were a part of her: different memories, different experiences, different facets. Like a novelist—which in many ways is what *Sweet Jesus* is in zine form—she creates a densely populated world out of herself. I don't think it was any accident that Kali and Franetta—the two people I discovered "passing" as others in their zines—are women of color. As both women and minorities they are acutely aware of the constraints of identity as defined by others.[73]

For zine writers, the authentic self is not some primal, fixed identity that precedes them, it is something flexible and mutable that they existentially fashion: out of their experiences, out of subcultural values which they take as their own, and in the case of editors of zines like the *Optimistic Pezzimist,* even out of a fascination for decidedly "unauthentic" items like Pez candy dispensers. What makes their identity authentic is that they are the ones defining it. The "modern ideal of authenticity," writes philosopher Charles Taylor, resides in the belief that "being true to myself is being true to my own originality, and that is something that only I can articulate and discover. In articulating it, I am defining it."[74] The underground call for authenticity doesn't demand that you be who society says you are. Since the mainstream world is "TV horseshit reality," it's better if you're not. Instead you are who you create yourself to be.

In a way, zinesters are doing the same thing that a big-money politician does when he projects himself as a man of the people. Both are manufacturing themselves. The identity creation that takes place in the pages of zines is a reflection of a larger world where reality and representation seem to occupy separate spheres—the society of spin which zinesters profess to abhor. Yet to the underground there is a difference. Politicians are in search of votes and money; zinesters are looking for their authentic selves. Politicians attempt to fit into pre-scribed roles—carefully thought out and tested in front of focus groups—as an instrumental means to become part of the dominant system. Zine writers are using the same freedom of self-creation, not to enter into the mainstream, but to escape it. Predictably, they rarely do.

I'm Against It

> I don't like Burger King
> I don't like anything
> And I'm against it.
> —"I'm Against It," the Ramones

"I think the Reagan Years, paradoxically, were good to zines," Mike Gunderloy argues. "[They] encouraged people to think about being self-sufficient and to look for alternatives. . . . A lot of people discovered they had a voice."[75] Mike is right: Being shut out of the mass media and feel-ing alienated from a conservative society is what led a lot of zinesters to develop their voice. But the voice those in the underground discovered may not be so "self-sufficient."

Fantasies of an authentic individual unsullied by society's conventions aside, people don't con-struct their identity in a vacuum; they create who and what they are in conversation with others.[76] This is what zinesters are doing by writing to each other, sharing their everyday lives, assembling their identity, figuring out their politics. But there is yet another interlocutor that precedes the un-derground culture of zines: the aboveground world of straight society. Notions of identity, poli-tics, and authenticity, so important to the zine world, are arrived at in discussion with, or rather in argument against, mainstream society and cul-ture. As staunch contrarians, zinesters construct who they are and what they do in opposition to

the rest of society: Their identity, forged, in inter-action with the dominant society, is a *negative identity.*

This negative identity is in many ways a legacy of punk rock. Punk rock itself was created, to a great degree, in opposition: *against* the commer-cial music of the mid 1970s, *against* the peace and love vibes of the hippie scene that by that time seemed like a sham. Punk was rebellion. In re-sponse to *Maximumrocknroll*'s effort to channel some of the punk energy into "constructive" po-litical engagement, reader Matt writes in: "I re-spect *MRR* for what it is, but as long as I can re-member, punk rock is a totally different thing. It's not positive, it's not intelligent, and it's cer-tainly not political. Punk rock is hate, chaos, nihil-ism, destruction. Punk rock is being fifteen years old and getting a hair cut your parents hate."[77] Pure rebellion, pure negation. Summed up in "I'm Against It," an early punk song by the Ramones, and in the names of later bands like Born Against. Epitomized by the nihilistic titles of zines like *The I Hate People Gazette* and *Oh Cool Scene Zine: I Hate Everybody, I Hate Poetry (but that's all I can write).*[78]

This ideal of the negative is bolstered by how anarchism came to be defined within the punk movement. Dave Insurgent, lead singer for Reagan Youth, a punk band interviewed in *Maximum-rocknroll*, asserts: "[Anarchy] just comes down to showing no authority over other people. . . . Just no authority. . . . Live your life the way you want to live it." The bassist, Al Pike, elaborates: "We don't preach political anarchy, just self anarchy . . . no one telling you what to do."[79]

A nice ideal, one that complements Godwin's principle of unfettered expression—and raises just as many problems. For "liv[ing] your life the way you want to live it," meaning: "no one telling you what to do," easily becomes doing what some-one is telling you *not* to do. Consider the claim above that "punk rock is . . . getting a hair cut your parents hate." This is the paradox of negative identity: who you are is contingent upon who you

Comic in
Scrambled Eggs #1.

are rebelling against. Nate Wilson, illustrating who he is in a comic, tellingly defines "My Own Me" through the distaste others have for him. Without their opposition, he writes, "I would know I was just like them."[80]

Setting yourself apart from "them" is integral to underground identity. If you identify "them" as the forces of "Just Say No" Puritanism, you celebrate substance abuse, as *Sauce* and *Exercise with Alcohol* do.[81] And argue, even if half in jest, that "Drunk driving is a birthright, not a privilege, no matter what some pansy-assed teacher or cop tells you," as *Tussin' Up* counsels.[82] If "they" are the legalized peddlers of alcohol and tobacco, then you define yourself as a teatotalling Straight Edge punk and reject these things.

For a self-consciously rebellious subculture, such identity formation makes a certain sense, but it also contains a serious contradiction. A negative identity only has meaning if you remain tied to

what you are negating. Reveling in the fact that you are a loser only makes sense if there is a society that rewards winners you despise. Thus, the authentic self that zinesters labor to assemble is often reliant upon the inauthentic culture from which they are trying to flee. Josh Norek of *Howhywuz, Howhyam,* for example, concludes his introductory rant with an explanation that his zine "stem[s] from a perpetual sickness of the sterile and homogeneous lifestyle found in greater suburbia."[83] This begs the questions: What would happen if Josh moved out of the sterile landscape he hates? Would he lose the inauthentic world that is so necessary for constructing his opposing authentic one? Would he lose his identity? Would he stop putting out a zine?

Emancipatory narratives are always linked to repressive ones. This is their weakness as well as their strength, for it allows radicals to have a purchase on what they oppose.[84] However, if it stays in this stage, rebellion is not really a rebellion at all, merely a dependent relationship, what Richard Sennett calls a *bond of rejection*.[85] Far from being autonomous, zinesters' negation binds them to the mainstream culture they loathe.

But before condemning zines as little more than vessels of negation, it is important to remember a few things. Zines offer a space for people to try out new personalities, ideas, and politics. While it's true that these things often take the shape of a negation of the world above ground, this isn't the only world that zinesters have to compare themselves to. Zines are a medium of communication, written to be shared with others underground. Through this sharing, the argument with the outside world can begin to be replaced by a conversation among comrades. The network of zines, imbedded within a larger underground culture, creates a forum through which individuals can construct their identity, formulate their ideals of an authentic life, and build a community of support, without having to identify themselves— either positively or negatively—with mainstream society. While mainstream society certainly proceeds an alternative community in terms of reflexive identity construction, this doesn't mean it has the last word. "What's the matter?" ask the editors of *Losers*, "The jockos and beauty queens don't take you seriously? Don't kill yourself. We'll love you and feed you."[86] Zines foster a community of losers within a society that celebrates winners.

The alternative ways of seeing and acting upon the world that arise out of such communities and cultures are pregnant with possibility—and fraught with contradiction. We can learn from both.

Notes

This chapter, with minor variations, also appears as a chapter in my book *Notes from Underground: Zines and the Politics of Alternative Culture* (London: Verso, 1997).

1 Quoted in J. C. Hertz, "Zine Stream: An Undercurrent Magazine Culture Explodes," *New York Perspectives* (May 6–12, 1993): 10.

2 Don Fitch, personal communication, April 22, 1994. "A gallery of grotesques," is how Damon Knight once described the Futurians, an early and famed science fiction club of which he was a member (*The Futurians* [New York: John Day, 1977], 149). In describing parties he used to throw for zine publishers at his house in upstate New York, Mike Gunderloy highlighted their odd dynamic: people would come, talk to one another for a bit, then invariably retreat alone to corners, walls, nooks, and crannies and start reading each other's zines. Mike Gunderloy, personal interview, December 6, 1992, New York City.

3 Mitzi Waltz, "Why Publish?" *Factsheet Five*, no. 23, 1987.

4 Zines have made their way onto the Internet, and since the early 1990s their numbers have been steadily growing. The theme of the summer 1995 issue of *Factsheet Five* was electronic zines, with six pages of e-zine reviews, articles on how to put zines online and an essay arguing for a "new definition for zines," one that includes e-mail zines and Web pages. This crossover shouldn't be any real surprise, for zines and computers have never been strangers. Zinesters regularly use computers to create their zines, and interest in computer-mediated communication in the zine world stretches back to *Factsheet Five* no. 1, where computer BBSs were listed among the handful of zines. Parallel to the rise of zines—though on a far larger scale—has been the development and maturation of the Internet. I doubt, however, that the virtual zine will ever completely supplant its paper predecessor. After all, the telegraph, telephone, radio, and television never did away with the underground presses. There is something about the materiality of a paper zine—you can feel it, stick it in your pocket, read it in the park, give it away at a show— that I myself would be reluctant to give up. I suspect many others feel the same way.

5 Mike Appelstein, *Writer's Block*, no. 8, late 1991/early 1992; Jokie X. Wilson, *The Olecatronical Scatologica Chronicle*, July 1991; Pathetic Doug, *Pathetic Life*, no. 11, April 1995.

6 John Foster, "Three Days in the Life of a Loser," *Ched*, no. 2, October 28, 1993.

7 Aaron Lee, "Your Reflection," *Blue Persuasion*, no. 4, 1994, 58–59.

8 Jery Vile, *Why Publish?* ed. Mike Gunderloy (*Factsheet Five Collection*, New York State Library).

9   *Losers*, no. 2, no date.

10 Writing in 1887, Nietzsche attempted to trace the genealogy of Western morality. Its genesis, he argued, was in Judaism, and its character stemmed from the fact that Jews were slaves. Held in bondage, the Jews inverted their wretched state by creating a moral order in which powerlessness, introspection, and other traits of servitude are virtues. By doing this they remade themselves as the virtuous (and symbolically victorious), and cast their powerful enemies as wicked (and morally vanquished). This morality became the basis for Christian ethics, as early Christians, themselves oppressed, gathered around the figure of Christ, the crucified and powerless son of God the all-powerful.

Nietzsche despised these *slave ethics*, as he called them, for being "reactive," that is, not created tabula rasa but in reaction against dominant ethics. While his ideal of a pure ethics, like that of an authentic primordial self, is flawed, his insight into how a deficit can be turned on its head and made an advantage is brilliant. (For as much as he loathed slave morality he acknowledged that it was the foundation of all that was beautiful and intelligent in the West.) Friedrich Nietzsche, *The Genealogy of Morals* (1887; New York: Doubleday Anchor, 1956).

11 Wendy and Monica, *Cool Loser*, no. 2, no date.

12 Jane, *Hex*, no. 1, 1993, 49

13 Editorial, *New York Times*, April 18, 1995, A24. The data come from a study done by Edward N. Wolff for the Twentieth Century Fund.

14 For an interesting discussion of the problems of the American meritocracy, see Christopher Lasch, *The Revolt of the Elites, and the Betrayal of Democracy* (New York: Norton, 1995).

15 Quoted in Jon Savage, *England's Dreaming* (New York: St. Martin's, 1992), 131. McNeil cofounded *Punk*.

16 Josh Abelon, *The Elana Rosa Veiga Torres Newsletter for This World and Beyond*, vol. 1, no. 1, July 7, 1991. Josh also puts out the music zine *Cramped*.

17 Letter from David Demming in Jen Payne, *The Latest News*, vol. 4, no. 2, summer 1992, 4.

18 John Banks, *BudZine*, no. 1, May 1993.

19 David B. Greenberger, *The Duplex Planet*, no. 112, 1991.

20 Aaron Rat, *Tard Nation*, no. 3, 1995(?).

21 Jen Payne, "Jen on . . . the National Debt," *The Latest News*, vol. 4, no. 2, fall 1992, 6.

22 John "Bud" Banks, "News Casting," *Budzine*, no. 9, March 1994, 5.

23 Vicki Rosenzweig, *Quipo*, no. 1, 1993.

24 Dennis W. Brezina, *America's at Our Doorstep*, vol. 4, no. 4, September/October 1991.

25 Terry Ward, *Notes from the Dump*.

26 Ernest Mann, *Little Free Press*.

27 Aaron Cometbus, *Cometbus*, no. 31, early 1990s.

28 Ibid., 72.

29 Karl Marx, "Contribution to the Critique of Hegel's *Philosophy of Right*: Introduction," in *The Marx-Engels Reader*, 2d ed., ed. Robert C. Tucker (New York: Norton, 1978), 63.

30 Frederick Wertham, *The World of Fanzines* (Carbondale: Southern Illinois University Press, 1973), 35. *Seduction of the Innocent* was Wertham's salvo in the 1950s war against comic books.

31 Jim Hogshire, *Pills-a-go-go*, spring 1993.

32 Bernard Bailyn, ed. *Pamphlets of the American Revolution, 1750–1776, vol. 1: 1750–1765* (Cambridge, MA: Harvard University, 1965).

33 Gene Mahoney, publisher of *Good Clean Fun*, in "Why Publish?" *Factsheet Five*, no. 29, 1989.

34 George Orwell and Reginald Reynolds, eds., *British Pamphleteers VI*, p. 15; cited in Bailyn, *Pamphlets*, 3–4.

35 Bailyn, *Pamphlets*, 15–16.

36 John Dickinson, "The Late Regulations Respecting the British Colonies" (1765, Philadelphia); reprinted in Bailyn, *Pamphlets*, 688.

37 Also unlike zines, however, the purpose of the pamphlet was not to present the musings of an "everyperson" unrepresented in the media of the day. John Dickinson might sign a later pamphlet "from a Farmer in Pennsylvania," but this member of the Philadelphia elite was a far cry from a simple yeoman.

38 *politics*: the science and art of government; the science dealing with the form, organization and administration of a state or part of one, and with the regulation of its relations with other states. *political*: of, belonging, or pertaining to the state or body of citizens, its government and policy, esp. in civil or secular affairs. *Oxford English Dictionary*, 2d ed. (Oxford: Clarendon Press, 1987).

39 Dishwashin' Pete, *Dishwasher*.

40 Patrick Splat, *Loring Punk*, no. 1, 1993.

41 Adam Bregman, *Shithappy*, no. 3, 1993(?), 9.

42 Josh MacPhee, *Fenceclimber*, no. 2, early 1990s.

43 KJ, Erin, Rebecca, and Mary, *Finster*, no. 3, 1992.

44 Jason Page, *Cheap Douchebag*, no. 11, 1990s.

45 Editor, *Forever and a Day*, no. 7, 1993.

46 Joshua, "How to Use a Zine," *Notes from the Light House*, no. 7, 2.

47 Poll conducted of 1,045 registered voters by *U.S. News and World Report* reported in Michael Barone, "The New America," July 10, 1995, 22.

48 Paul Goldstein, *Goldstein: A Newsletter about Me, Paul,* 1992; Richard J. Sagall, *Interesting!* premiere issue, 1994.

49 Anon., *Forever & a Day* no. 7, 1993.

50 This authentic self marches through history: reappearing in the nineteenth century as the young Marx's "species-being," at the root of existentialism in the first half of the twentieth century, and in Norman Mailer's "White Negro" beat of the 1950s; the idea of living an authentic life weaves through the SDS's Port Huron Statement in 1962, and colors the New Left that follows.

51 Christina, *Girl Fiend,* no. 3, August 1992, 1.

52 Al Quint quoted in J. C. Hertz, "Zine Stream," 10.

53 Freedom, personal interview, June 13, 1992.

54 Gene Mahoney, "Why Publish?" *Factsheet Five,* no. 30, 1989, 95.

55 At a discussion I attended, David Mandl, a disc jockey at a New York-area noncommercial, "alternative" radio station, was asked to describe his station's politics. He began speaking about how WFMU broadcasts lectures by Noam Chomsky and other notable dissidents, but then quickly changed direction, locating the politics of the station somewhere else. Lauding his friend and fellow DJ, Vanilla Bean, Mandl explained that sometimes "he'll go off on some political tirade, but a lot of the times he won't . . . but he's just done stuff that's so incredibly exciting and impassioned, so wonderful, that it's blatantly political in an implicit way." For Mandl, as for many in the underground, the politics reside less in the content of what is said and more in the form of expression that the saying takes. David Mandl, talk at the Libertarian Book Club, April 17, 1995, New York City.

56 Crash Rats, *Decontrol.*

57 "Letters," *Factsheet Five,* no. 20, 1986. Incidentally, the cover of this issue of *FS5* shows an illustration of a woman in ancient Egyptian dress dumping mainstream magazines in the garbage.

58 *Frederick's Lament,* 1991.

59 David Alvord, *Punk and Destroy,* no. 1, late 1980s-early 1990s.

60 Cited in Cesar Grana and Marigay Grana, eds., *On Bohemia: The Code of the Self Exiled* (New Brunswick, NJ: Transaction Publishers, 1990), 7.

61 Mike Gunderloy, *Factsheet Five,* no. 5, 1985.

62 William Godwin, *An Inquiry Concerning Political Jus-* tice, vol. 2 (London, 1793), 846–47, cited in James Joll, *The Anarchists* (Cambridge, MA: Harvard University Press, 1980), 19. Setting the stage for Godwin's passion for original and experiential thought is Gerard Winstanley: "Men must speak their own experienced words, and must not speak thoughts" (cited in Christopher Hill, *The World Turned Upside Down: Radical Ideas During the English Revolution* [London: Penguin, 1975], 369).

63 Michael Harrington, "We Few, We Happy Few, We Happy Bohemians: A Memoir of the Culture before the Counterculture," in *On Bohemia,* ed. Grana and Grana, 781.

64 A politically disastrous example: Alexander Berkman's botched assassination attempt on Henry Clay Frick gained Frick and the Carnegie Steel Company public sympathy while they were violently suppressing a strike; and a ludicrous one: the 1886 case of Charles Gallo, who threw a bottle of acid from one of the galleries of the Paris stock exchange, then fired three random revolver shots, hitting no one. At his trial—where he insisted on addressing the judge as Citizen President—he shouted, "Long live revolution! Long live anarchism! Death to the bourgeois judiciary! Long live dynamite! Bunch of idiots!" Gallo's case is from Jean Maitron, *Histoire du mouvement anarchiste en France (1880–1914)* (Paris, 1951), cited in Joll, *The Anarchists.*

65 Joll, *The Anarchists,* 111.

66 Leah Zeldes Smith, *STET,* November 1990, 25.

67 Brian Shapiro, "Letters," *Factsheet Five,* no. 22, 1987, 66.

68 *Factsheet Five,* no. 50, December 1993, 46; *Queer Zine Explosion* (with *Holy Titclamps*), no. 13, 1994.

69 John Newberry, *Why Publish?* ed. Mike Gunderloy (Albany: Pretzel Press, 1989), 25.

70 Kali Amanda Browne, personal interview, June 22, 1992.

71 This letter, by BVI, appeared in *Factsheet Five:*

> What I want to do is form groups of five people who will correspond with each other and who will not refer to their sex/gender, race, economic status, or sexual orientation for a period of six months. At the end of that time, the group will vote to decide whether or not to reveal their identities in terms of the above categories. The purpose is to try to learn just how profoundly we identify with those categories and to try to determine other levels at which humans can communicate. Interested parties should use gender-ambiguous names or aliases, and inquiries may be sent to . . .

"Letters," *Factsheet Five*, no. 32, 1989, 106.

72 Franetta L. McMillian, *Sweet Jesus*, no. 1, early 1990s.

73 The ability of zines to project a virtual identity can lead to misunderstandings. There have been well-documented incidents of deception—often with hurtful results—on another medium of virtual identity: computer bulletin board systems (BBS). But these misunderstandings can have their positive sides as well. Franetta tells the story of talking to a white supremacist skinhead by phone while doing research for a character she was creating for *Sweet Jesus* no. 3. Unable to categorize her by looks, he spoke with her as a person. They got along so well that at the end of the conversation the racist skinhead asked Franetta if she would like to come out West and be part of the survivalist community that he was forming. When she told him she was African American, he was silent for a moment, then admitted that he had never really talked at length to anyone black before, and again made his invitation (Franetta declined).

For accounts and analysis of virtual identity in computer-mediated communications, see Lindsy Van Gelder, "The Strange Case of the Electronic Lover," in *Computerization and Controversy*, ed. Charles Dunlop and Rob Kling (New York: Academic Press), 365–75; David Myers, "'Anonymity Is Part of the Magic': Individual Manipulation of Computer-Mediated Communication Contexts," *Qualitative Sociology* 10(3) (fall 1987): 251–66.

74 Charles Taylor, *The Ethics of Authenticity* (Cambridge, MA: Harvard University Press, 1991), 29.

75 Quoted in Jim Hogshire, "You Can Be the Publisher," *Nuvo*, December 26, 1990-January 2, 1991, 9. Jim Hogshire is the publisher of the zine *Pills-a-go-go*.

76 "The self is something which has a development," social psychologist George Herbert Mead argued at the turn of the century, theorizing that "[the self] is not initially there, at birth, but arises in the process of social experience and activity, that is, develops in the given individual as a result of his relations to that process as a whole and to other individuals within that process." George Herbert Mead, *Mind, Self, and Society* (Chicago: University of Chicago Press, 1934), 135.

77 Matt, "Letters," *Maximumrocknroll*, no. 85, June 1990.

78 Born Against is the name of a punk band whose lead singer puts out the zines *I*, *Yeast Roll*, and *Dear Jesus*; Kevin Person Jr., *The I Hate People Gazette*, no. 5, early 1990s; Anon., *Oh Cool Scene Zine*.

79 Interview with Al Pike and Dave Insurgent of Reagan Youth, *Maximumrocknroll*, no. 4, Jan.-Feb. 1983.

80 Nate Wilson, *Scrambled Eggs*, no. 1, 1993.

81 Zak Sally and Mike Haeg, *Sauce*, 1993; Bruce Clifton, *Exercise with Alcohol*, 1994.

82 Cited in Jim Hogshire, "You Can Be the Publisher," *Nuvo*, December 26, 1990-January 2, 1991, 8.

83 Josh Norek, *Howhywuz, Howhyam*, 1992, 1.

84 Terry Eagleton, seminar, October 17–19, 1991, New York Marxist School, New York City.

85 Richard Sennett, *Authority* (New York: Norton, 1980), 15–49.

86 The Raven, *Losers*, no. 2, no date.

HOP ON POP

THIS SECTION REFLECTS A SIGNIFICANT shift of interest in recent years, from the study of narrative structures or characterization as the primary vehicles for ideological analysis, toward a new focus on issues of performance. The study of performance introduces issues of the body and affect, inviting attention to what Roland Barthes called the "grain of the voice," the emotional immediacy created by performance which is not reducible to characterization. The study of performance also enables us to talk about forms of popular culture (vaudeville acts, freak shows, street performances, magic shows), which are not narrative-based but which depend on the staging of personalities and the direct interactions between performers and audiences. There is, of course, a danger of romanticizing the authenticity of performance as a source of individual expression which can not be contained within ideological and narrative structures, as occurs when early feminist critics spoke of Katharine Hepburn's strength and intelligence transcending the domestic containment suggested by the resolutions of her film vehicles. As research on performance has matured, it has led us to think less about the distinctive or idiosyncratic aspects of stars and more on the social and cultural construction of star identity and on the various cultural codes which shape performance styles.

The study of performance invites a consideration of culturally specific ways of inhabiting bodies which performers often push to an extreme to achieve emotional effects. Critics have argued that comic female performance exaggerates or parodies the codes of conventional femininity, claiming the right to make a spectacle of oneself rather than being turned into a spectacle for male consumption. Others have explored how the performance of racial stereotypes can call into question essentialist constructions of blackness or whiteness, while others suggest that the ability to transcend such stereotypes is unequally distributed between groups within a culture. Other writers,

such as Judith Butler or Eve Sedgwick, have drawn on theories of performance to examine the construction of self in everyday life, suggesting that our every social interaction represents an (un)conscious mobilization of bodily signs to achieve a desired effect.

The essays in this section explore the aesthetics and politics of performance, ranging from karaoke to professional wrestling, from opera to camp. Robert Drew describes the process of karaoke performance from the inside out, stressing the strategies by which amateur performers preserve "face" given the impossibility of matching professional quality performances. Drew explores the aesthetics and sociology of amateur music production, stressing how participatory forms of music can cement social ties within groups and how they contrast with the celebrity and commodification associated with the music industry. Sharon Mazer uses her research into the training of professional wrestlers to open larger questions about the performance of ethnography, which she understands to be the translation of experience into texts. She asks critical questions about the ethics and politics of studying performance, especially given the difficulty of separating the performed body from the self.

Diane Brooks and Pamela Robertson examine the racial politics surrounding performance. Brooks looks at how the black opera diva Leontyne Price negotiated the shifting racial politics of the civil rights era, caught between the demand to be a representative of her race and the desire to avoid being trapped into black roles. Price is understood in relation to the complex cultural construction of black ladyhood, a social role that has been criticized for adopting a class-conscious politics of "racial uplift and cultural respectability" and praised for embodying black female authority. Robertson, on the other hand, reconsiders her own previous analysis of Mae West, questioning whether work about the transgressiveness of female comic performance can be meaningful if it ignores the ways that white women are privileged over women of color. She questions whether camp offers the same opportunities for the ironical presentation of racial identities that it poses for the self-parody of sexual and gender identities, and suggests the ways that white stages of camp femininity often occur against a backdrop of black authenticity. Ed O'Neill's work on Tallulah Bankhead continues this reassessment of the cultural politics of camp performance. Through examining the various anecdotes which we choose to tell about this colorful performer, O'Neill seeks to explain the properties that made her into a "camp icon." He is especially interested in the epistemological instability of such anecdotes and the ways that the impossibility of determining their truthfulness results in our fetishistic relationship to star performers.

"Anyone Can Do It": Forging a Participatory Culture in Karaoke Bars

Robert Drew

Maybe you've noticed it on your way home from work, the hotel lounge marquee missing a few letters: "K RAOKE HAP Y HOUR 5–9 PM." You've contemplated stopping in now and then, just as seriously as you've now and then contemplated suicide. Or maybe, silently screening CDs at the listening bar of your local music superstore, you've leafed through one of those free entertainment guides dropped in bundles at the entrance. Among the cover bands, copy bands, and live deejays, there it was again: "KARAOKE HAPPY HOUR 5–9 PM."

Most Americans' closest encounters with karaoke don't get much closer than this. Yet since the peculiar, high-tech hybrid of recorded music and live song performance was introduced stateside in the late 1980s, it has captured the interest of a growing minority. While sales of home karaoke equipment have risen steadily, what's more impressive is that, despite manufacturers' efforts to maximize profits by privatizing it, karaoke continues to thrive in public. It's impossible to know just how many karaoke bars there are, but one Internet-based directory, offering an incomplete survey of only fourteen states, lists over seven hundred establishments that have karaoke at least once a week.[1] Karaoke's growth in the United States signals a widespread yearning to have an active voice in the public performance of music.

Even so, like many amateur musical practices in Western societies, karaoke remains a largely hidden culture.[2] The mainstream press granted it a flash of attention when it first appeared, discovering and discarding it as summarily as any fad.

Tampa's hottest karaoke bar, Good Time Charlie's. Most Americans don't get much closer to karaoke than the marquee of their local restaurant-lounge.

Since then, it has provided comedic fodder for late-night talk show hosts, political speechwriters, and filmmakers. When karaoke appears in movies, Ben Fong-Torres observes, "It's got to be at some big, sloppy party, there've got to be drunks, and whoever's doing the singing has got to be doing it poorly."[3] Such portrayals tune out all the wonderful singers who perform in karaoke bars; they betray a common belief that the only people with the ability, even the right, to sing publicly are professionals.

It's hard for Americans to imagine how, in Japan and much of East Asia, karaoke can be conspicuous, omnipresent, even routine. It is found in nearly every bar, as well as in arcades and bowling alleys, taxicabs and buses, public halls and hospitals. One Japanese observer cites a local study suggesting that over 50 percent of Japanese citizens perform karaoke in a given year.[4] But then, in many Asian societies, karaoke has smoothly harmonized with local culture: voice training has long been a part of every child's education, and singing a requisite activity at ceremonies and social gatherings. Westerners may have laughed at televised images of Imelda Marcos crooning at diplomatic dinners, but to Filipinos and other East Asians, there was nothing laughable about it.[5]

A century and a half ago, singing was as much a part of daily life in the West as it is in the East. Choral societies and church choirs covered the United States and Europe; the piano was a fixture, and the sing-along a sustaining ritual, of middle-class homes.[6] But in the late nineteenth century, cultural entrepreneurs urged policies to safeguard what they saw as legitimate culture, and part of that effort was the strengthening of boundaries between performers and audiences.[7] This professionalization of music and the arts coincided with a new set of cultural assumptions: musicians and artists came to be viewed as quintessential outsiders, set off from society by extraordinary talent. It was taken upon faith, in John Blacking's words, that "being a passive audience is the price that some must pay for membership in a superior society whose superiority is maintained by the exceptional ability of a chosen few."[8]

Even today, despite the much-touted blurring of lines between high and popular culture, the notion of cultural production as both the prerogative and the proof of exceptional individuals remains with us. As Joshua Gamson shows, one of the constants in media texts tracking film and pop stars has been the attribution of fame to some "indefinable internal quality."[9] And yet, more populist discourses of celebrity have also surfaced: exposing the machinery behind stardom, disclosing an urge to tear down the stars, and, occasionally, expressing the Warholian conviction that anyone can be a star.

This schizoid perspective on cultural performance—anyone can do it or, maybe, almost no one can—infuses the rhetoric around karaoke in the United States. Many karaoke performers and emcees will insist that anyone can do it; nonperformers will counter that they most certainly cannot do it. The truth is somewhere in between: karaoke may not demand intensive vocal training, but it imposes its own work and demands its own skills. Notwithstanding its advocates' assertions that it allows everyone to feel like a star, karaoke performers bear less in common with celebrities than with the legions of uncelebrated amateur musicians.[10] They often face unfavorable performance conditions, impassive audiences, unclear role expectations. Most of all, they face the challenge of forging a participatory culture in contexts where people are accustomed to consuming their culture passively. In karaoke, we find people devising ways to break the silence of a non-singing culture; perhaps we even get an idea how we can do so ourselves.

What follows is the result of a pilgrimage through dozens of karaoke bars, most of them located in and around the three cities I've called home over the past five years: Philadelphia, Albany, and Tampa. I found a few bars in each town through newspaper ads, and far more in "snowball" fashion through performer and emcee contacts. I started out logging performers' actions onstage and interrogating them afterward. Yet it quickly became clear that much of the action was offstage, and that my notebook and tape recorder were as often as not obstacles to inquiry. So I began to forestall documentation for experience, to immerse myself in karaoke's world, to seek understanding through relationships with nonperformers as well as performers. Sometimes I invited friends or relatives along, giving as much attention to their responses as those of my new acquaintances. And I performed myself on many occasions, taking my cue from the ethnomusicological injunction to participate in the music one studies, as well as from the current interpenetration of ethnography and autobiography.[11]

In writing this chapter, I've attempted to envision the participants—including myself and even my reader—as characters in a story rather than subjects of a study. It is assumed that narrative can itself be a legitimate mode of inquiry, that, as Richard Rorty suggests, "Theory [is] always a second-best, never more than a reminder for a particular purpose, the purpose of telling a story better."[12]

Anyone Can Do It

When karaoke's promoters claim that "anyone can do it," they are not just selling their wares. They are echoing a sentiment shared by partisans of so many revolutions in popular music, from rockabilly to punk, from rhythm and blues to rap. It is a sentiment eloquently expressed by ethnomusicologist John Blacking: "There is so much music in the world that it is reasonable to suppose that music, like language and possibly religion, is a species-specific trait in man." Or, by the famous injunction that appeared in an early punk fanzine, under illustrations of finger positions on the neck of a guitar: "Here's one chord, here's two more, now form your own band."[13]

Everything about karaoke seems calculated to convince prospective performers that it is a no-risk proposition. Emcees solicit applause before,

Non-performer Tony Cowdry prefers to watch from a safe distance. The most common reason given for not performing is "I can't sing."

after, and often during every performance. Audiences are encouraged to be, and typically are, almost ridiculously supportive. There is a place here for everyone, you are told. Ability doesn't matter. Anyone can do it.

And yet, down in the pit, you find that anyone cannot do it, and that ability matters very much indeed.

"I CAN'T SING"

Donna is a thirty-nine-year-old, single mom living outside Albany. She's a music lover, the sort whose daily round is organized by pop songs. At her data processing job, she says, the only thing that sustains her is her Walkman. Flipping through the three thousand titles in the Tally-Ho Pub's karaoke song book, she knows more songs than I know, and I know a lot. Donna isn't shy: when I do Marshall Crenshaw's "Someday, Someway," she joins me onstage and dances magnificently. And despite her thick New York patois, she isn't afraid of her voice. She recalls that when she worked in telemarketing, men would ask her on dates just from hearing her on the phone.

Donna has all the makings of a karaoke performer. All, that is, except one: she can't sing. Or so she claims.

"Everybody can sing," I say.

"Not me," she insists. "If I get up there and sing, I'll drive this crowd right outta here."

She's jotting down titles from the song book for her friends to perform, enjoying the second-hand pleasure of a playlist arranger. I look over her list: TLC's "Waterfalls," Janet Jackson's "Escapade," Salt 'n' Pepa's "Let's Talk about Sex."

"How's this one go?" I ask her, knowing full well how it goes.

Let's talk about sex, baby, let's talk about you and me, she sings, no worse than dozens of performers I've seen.

"That's singing," I say. "That's called singing." She laughs. "I don't think so!"

"Do you like to sing?" I ask her. "Do you ever sing?"

Her response is one I've heard from so many people who are intrigued by karaoke but categorically refuse to try it. "Sure I sing," she says, "when I'm alone."

BEING "UNMUSICAL"

Few would deny that music's meaning and value—
that music itself—originates in society. Music,
like language, is both seed and fruit of human
contact. Why, then, do so many of our most active, creative musical moments—those moments
when we break out in song—take place in soli-
tude? We sing in the shower or in the car. At the
traffic light, we catch the person in the next car
staring at us, and we clam up. Despite every reas-
surance from karaoke emcees (or ethnomusicol-
ogists, or do-it-yourself punkers) that music is a
universal human capacity, we run and hide to exercise this capacity. We all *do* sing, yet we remain
convinced that we *can't* sing: a logical contradiction that remains, for many of us, an experiential
given.

Every attempt to extend music-making runs
up against the widespread belief that "musicality"
is an innate gift that some people have and others don't.[14] Musicians refer to a singer's voice as
her "instrument," as if it were something as solid
and self-evident as a horn or a woodwind. And
indeed, for many people, "I can't sing" becomes
an unproblematic description of a physical handicap. Such self-appraisals often can be traced to
early childhood experiences: a grade-school music
teacher's offhand insult, a failed bid for the glee
club. The prescription such people internalize is
not to sing, *not* to make music—thus rounding
out a cycle that assures their "unmusicality."

As fate would have it, now and then, these souls
who are convinced they can't sing end up in a spot
where they just might prove themselves wrong.
Maybe they're dragged there by friends; maybe
they're out for a drink and have no idea what
they're getting into; or maybe they're just curious.
They watch intently, fascinated and repelled. They
laugh, then frown, then recoil. "No, no," they cry,
if someone suggests they try it. They'd just as soon
go sky diving, or volunteer for a root canal. You
can see it in their eyes: they fear karaoke.

The only ones who may fear it more are those
who are convinced they *can* sing.

VOICES BREAKING

Tommy Starr—a consummate stage name. A former amateur boxer, his white t-shirt and jeans
stretch tightly over his trim, muscular frame. With
his light brown skin and short, curly black hair,
he resembles the handsome pop singer Jon Se-
cada—except for his fractured nose, which, like
Brando's, only makes him more striking. I met
Tommy last Monday at Spanky's in West Philly—
a cramped, dingy place with poor sound that
draws only a handful of singers. He sat with three
other people, his girlfriend and another couple, all
of whom seemed content just to watch him perform. Tommy stood out effortlessly, caressing ballads by George Benson and James Ingram with
his luscious tenor. Men in the audience cheered;
women screamed.

I complimented him after his smooth take
on Ingram's "Just Once," and we got to talking.
He moved quickly from his career (manager at a
rental center) to his former avocation (boxing)
to his new passion: singing. He always sensed he
could sing but never did so publicly until he discovered karaoke. I told him about Saturday night
at Chollett's, my favorite place in town, where the
crowds are huge, the song selection seemingly infinite, and the sound of professional quality. As he
left, he pointed at me and said, "See ya' Saturday,"
and I wasn't sure if I was being addressed as a fellow performer or as a fan.

Such late-night, barroom promises usually
amount to nothing, but Tommy is there at Chollett's the following Saturday. His entourage is
streamlined tonight: just his girlfriend, Hillary, a
tall, pretty blonde who acts as Tommy's sounding
board and moral supporter. She peruses the song
book with him, now and then suggesting, "That
one would be good for you." Tommy's easy manner can't hide the fact that he really cares about

this. He sweats over the song book for a good half hour before settling on Marvin Gaye's "Sexual Healing." During our long wait to perform, he endows me with pointers on vocal technique: sing from the chest, let your breath out slowly, don't hold the mike too close.

Finally, our turns come up. I do U2's "Mysterious Ways," and mangle it until it's almost unrecognizable and I'm almost voiceless. Bombing always leaves me a bit deflated, but I'm so used to it by now—so acutely aware of my limits—that it hardly matters. Besides (I tell myself), I'm getting something else out of this: I have a book contract. Tommy's up right after me. The emcee introduces him as "a new face here," and people turn to check him out. Sometimes, when you get onstage and hear your song's opening chords, you can tell that you're doomed before you even open your mouth. From the look on his face, Tommy can tell very soon after he opens his—and so can everyone else.

Bay-aay-aay-bee-eee. Gaye's melody extends to heights where most of us mortals, Tommy included, become prone to nosebleeds. So he breaks off, and asks the emcee to restart the song in a lower key. The emcee pushes some buttons and tries again, but it's no use. As each high note approaches, Tommy's face strains, and his voice breaks like a pubescent boy's. I anticipate the breaks, and feel myself inwardly cringing: *Whenever* (gasp) *bloo-ooo tee-eeerdrops are fallin'* . . . *I just get on the telephone and* (gasp) *caa-all yoo-ooo up, bay-bee.*

Most of the crowd has turned back to their conversations or just turned away. It seems like only two of us are left watching: me, standing in back, and Hillary, standing a few feet in front of me, her arms folded. I can't see her face. Tommy struggles through the song and descends to quiet applause. I offer the obligatory pleasantries—you did fine, that was a tough song, etc.—but they sound hollow even to me. There doesn't seem

to be much more to talk about, and pretty soon, Tommy and Hillary leave.

VOICE AND FACE

In karaoke, the conviction that you have failed by purely formal standards of vocal competence can bring on all the symptoms of a personal, even moral, lapse. Singing ability can come to anchor a performer's *face,* the image pressed upon her by her own and others' efforts within the moment. Erving Goffman notes that "a person . . . cathects his [*sic*] face; his 'feelings' become attached to it." [15] Vocal competence can come to mandate a performer's temporary sense of self; those who sing well tend to feel well, and to evince well-being. Henry Kingsbury's observations regarding conservatory students' investment in their competencies could as easily describe many karaokists: "The association . . . between their musicality and their self-image was not unlike the link between a teenager's self-confidence and sense of sexual attractiveness." [16]

Audience members also have an investment in the success of performances. The performer's image of herself as a skilled vocalist and audience members' images of themselves as supportive listeners are mutually dependent. Because loss of face tends to be contagious, maintenance of face is a collective effort. Sometimes this machinery hums along magnificently, regardless of the performers' empirical competencies. There are bars where nary a performer can hit the broad side of a note. Passers through may sit in back, snickering, wincing, or scratching their heads. Yet a cluster of regulars stands in front, admiring and applauding and sustaining one another.

Other times, this face-saving pact between performer and audience dissolves. A performer may lose face even as others strain to help her preserve it. Another may maintain copious face even when others feel she should rightfully have forfeited it. And now and then, a performer may move along mindlessly even as the disparity between what others think of her and what she thinks they think of her widens into a perilous chasm, as in this story recounted by an emcee:

> The girl was absolutely horrible. I mean, she screamed, and it was horrible. Well, a woman who was there told the girl as a joke that she was a talent agent, and that she liked her singing. And she said, "Would you sing this song for me? It's my favorite song and I want you to do it." And we were even running low on time and the girl insisted, "This talent agent wants to hear me sing this song! Let me sing!" And people had said, "Don't let that girl back up there." Well, when she got up there, people took napkins and stuffed them in their ears, and walked around with these napkins sticking out of their ears. This girl was completely oblivious to it. She was so into what she was doing and where that other woman was, she completely ignored that anyone was ridiculing her.

Such an incident offers glaring proof that in karaoke, devastating aesthetic failures also can be

Emcee Billy Ray. A first-class technician, he admits he wouldn't know the key of your chosen song if he fell over it.

devastating personal failures. It is at these moments, when an individual has become a laughingstock and yet remains "completely oblivious," that hidden feelings have the potential to break out into the open and genuinely hurt someone.

NO ONE CAN DO IT

In karaoke bars, then, your sense of self can come to hinge quite precariously upon your singing success. And yet it's hard to think of any place where you'd less want anything to hinge upon your success. Don't be fooled by emcees' cheerful avowals that karaoke is easy; in the words of one of the more capable performers I've encountered, "It's the rawest form of performing you can do."

The power of public performers can be gauged by their ability to dictate the framework of their performances. Famous singers (and famous people who feel an inclination to sing) can have their background music tailored to their competencies and their characters. The right recorded backdrop can flatter even the narrowest voice, as is proven, for instance, by Ringo Starr's many hits. As Steve Jones writes, "The ability to record sound is power over sound." [17]

Now, imagine that you are a first-time karaoke performer, and consider the scope of your power. Though you have thousands of songs to choose from, bear in mind that these songs have been recorded in a studio in Pineville, North Carolina, or Long Beach, California, or some other place that's hundreds of miles away. Also remember that the musicians who recorded the songs don't know a thing about you and couldn't care less if you are a bass or a soprano. These musicians have recorded each song in a particular key, and you have no way of knowing in advance the key of the song you are pondering. The song book doesn't tell you; the emcee usually can't tell you; and even if someone could tell you, if you are like most performers (myself included), it wouldn't mean much to you anyway.

Maybe you've got your eye on a certain tune

you've always loved. Be warned, though, that in karaoke your competencies bear no necessary relation to your tastes. Or maybe you've found a tune that sounds good when you sing along with it on the radio. In that case, remember that the key of the karaoke version bears no necessary relation to that of the original recording, and that there is a world of difference between singing along with a song and singing the song oneself.

You might invent little tricks in an effort to control your fate. You might, like one performer I've met, convince the emcee to let you screen your songs privately with the aid of his headphones before performing them publicly (though this is highly discouraged, since it holds up the show). Or you might, like another performer, exploit the chances taken by your fellow volunteers, holding your fingers over your ears and singing their songs to yourself until you come upon one that you think you can do (though you'll have to wait until the following week to do it, since there is an unofficial rule against doing a song that's already been done that evening).

If you are lucky, whatever song you cast your lot on will land squarely within your vocal range. For me, this occurs about one time in five. Many performers do better, and some do worse. I can recall only one regular performer I've met who never did a song out of her range. She had worked up a large collection of karaoke discs, which she would screen at home and get emcees to play for her at bars. (Feel free to follow her lead; the discs are available for about $30 each at most music stores.)

If the song you choose is not in your range, you have two choices. You can either sing it in the key it's in, and leave the impression that you have no voice; or sing it in your preferred key, and leave the impression that you have no ear. After shredding my vocal cords on far too many high notes, I have come to prefer the second alternative. Be advised that this decision requires a degree of confidence. It requires you to stay stubbornly off key even as

In choosing their songs, performers rummage through thousands of choices. Each song poses its own challenges and possibilities.

many others present sing insistently on key—trying to bring you into line, assuming you're not aware of your error.

Leaving the stage before finishing your song is not an option. On those rare occasions when performers do so, they affirm their failure all too decisively and sacrifice the token applause that greets even the most miserable performances. You may become so hoarse that you find yourself nearly incapable of uttering another lyric. You may reach the point where, watching the members of your audience hightailing it to the bar or to the bathroom, rather than resenting them, you find yourself envying them. Still, you're expected to go the distance.

After many trials and almost as many errors, you may build up a little collection of songs within your compass. To have a repertoire of tunes you know you can do lends you a tactical advantage. You can open with them to establish your competence or fall back upon them when you've thrown it in doubt. In the minds of your fellow patrons, these songs become identified with you no less than with their original artists: "Once you get a hit," one performer observes, "it's like a hit on the radio."

And yet, like hits on the radio, you'll find that your repertoire items have a limited shelf life. "You get bored with the same old stuff," says another performer. "You figure that people are tired of hearing you do the same songs all the time." When you are operating in a social world as small as the typical karaoke bar, with a catalogue of expressions as large as the typical karaoke song book, it becomes difficult to remain in your niche. Yet every time you hazard a new number, you're back to square one.

Throughout this ordeal, you are liable to feel vaguely troubled about how good you are and how good you ought to be—particularly in comparison to the singers whose voices you displace. The anxiety of influence looms large in karaoke. The very absence of the familiar star's voice seems to summon you to fill it in. You find yourself instinctively reproducing the most convoluted cadenzas and subtle sighs of the original recordings without any prompting from the lyric monitor. You may prepare for your performances by studying the originals; you may even (like one performer I met) listen to tapes of your performances side-by-side with the originals to evaluate yourself. As among the amateur rock musicians observed by H. Stith Bennett, it may seem to you that your "ability to copy music [is] the exhibition of [your] technical accomplishment."[18]

As Bennett and others will inform you, however, the task you have set for yourself is "humanly impossible."[19] In an age of tape splicing and digital recording—when popular songs are no longer documents of real-time performances but assemblages of the best moments of many performances—not even the stars themselves can replicate the sounds of their recordings in live performance.[20] And you are attempting to do so with inferior equipment and minimal preparation.

It would seem, then, that karaoke is impossible. Not only can't "anyone" do it; no one can.

DO IT ANYWAY

I've done my best to provide every reason not to try karaoke: the pervasive assumption that singing

skill is uncommon; the damage that a failed performance can inflict upon one's sense of self; the many obstacles to virtuosity. Still, for the remainder of this essay, I'll make the case for trying it anyway.

Up until this point, I have abided by a particular vocabulary to describe singing. I have distinguished performers' voices based on accuracy, flexibility, and purity; I have characterized them as on- or off-key, broad or narrow in range, clear or distorted. These are the terms of traditional voice training, terms that most people understand and accept.

Alternatively, we might begin by regarding song as an extension of speech. The distinction between speaking and singing, while universally recognized, is hard to define empirically; singing is, as one music educator notes, "primarily elongation of the vowels and extension of the pitch inflections commonly heard in the speaking voice."[21] Yet while we've come to see that any language engenders innumerable ways of speaking, and that even apparently incorrect utterances can be appropriate within certain communities and contexts, we are not always willing to grant the same variability to song.[22] Our understanding of singing as a form of competence can blind us to its flexibility as a means of expression.

Simon Frith writes: "In songs, words are the signs of a voice. A song is always a performance and song words are always spoken out—vehicles for the voice. . . . Song words, in short, work as *speech*, as structures of sound that are direct signs of emotion and marks of character."[23] If a song is chiefly the vehicle for a voice, then singing voices should be potentially as diverse as speaking voices. Against the conventional vocal standards of range and intonation, we might come to value a singing voice for the cogency and force with which it communicates.

This is how many of the popular singers whom karaoke performers emulate beg to be regarded. Most popular songs seem inferior when judged on traditional musicological grounds, and popular singers rarely measure up to the standards of classical vocal training.[24] In the estimation of an operatic critic like Robert Rushmore, Elvis Presley had only "a passing baritone range with a pleasing quality in the middle compass"; Bruce Springsteen's songs "rely totally on the tonic, dominant and subdominant chords and scarcely range an octave."[25]

What popular singers, especially rock singers, *do* have over opera *prime donne* is access to the everyday "signs of emotion and marks of character" extolled by Frith; those shouts, moans, wails, and squeals that, while stifled by classical training, are vital components in the expressive repertoire of the human voice. Frith continues: "Because so much of rock music depends on the social effects of the voice, the questions about how rock's effects are produced are vocal, not musicological. What makes a voice haunting? sexy? chilling?"[26] From this angle, the lack of formal training among popular singers and their listeners does not handicap them but simply forces them to fall back on more quotidian faculties.[27] "Ignorance of *how* their music makes sense certainly puts no limit on a rock audience's appreciation: all that needs to be taken for granted is the common experience of desire, hope, fear."[28]

Experienced karaoke performers sense that each of the myriad voices they select amongst bears its own marks of character, and poses its own challenges and opportunities. As a result, song choices often are based on a subtle feeling of affinity—of a kindred voice and sensibility—with the original vocalist. A performer who sounds all wrong emulating the crystal-clear tones of Karen Carpenter or Maureen McGovern may be right at home belting out Janis Joplin. Another may struggle with Elton John's and Billy Joel's vocal gymnastics, only to find his niche in Lou Reed's flat murmur. For my part, I've found that some of my best karaoke covers are of puppy-dog crooners like the Everly Brothers, the Beach Boys, and the Fleetwoods (thus forcing me to come to terms with my own mawkishness).

Pop songs and stars, then, are conduits as well as exemplars of public culture; they do not merely impose their voices on listeners but make their voices available. The presence of singers as diverse as Bob Dylan, Tina Turner, and Joe Cocker on karaoke lists sanctions every Dylanesque whiner, Turneresque screecher, and Cockeresque grunter to take the stage. Through karaoke, pop stars become direct facilitators of musical participation; those vocal deviants whom the mass audience has granted a pulpit, in some sense, return the favor.

THREE MORE WAYS TO DO IT

The plenitude of popular music sets a mood for karaoke and, at its best, infuses it with a rare spirit of tolerance and playfulness. Contrary to the fears of many neophytes, there is no one right way to do karaoke. Experienced performers routinely move and involve audiences even while transgressing dominant vocal standards. As I will show in the following sections, they do so by communicating in ways their audiences can relate to: by conjuring a feeling of hangdog humility, or irreverent foolishness, or careless spontaneity. I begin with a personal story.

"I Don't Know These Words!": The Self-Deprecator The Reform synagogue that my family attended when I grew up was a center for social interaction and cultural continuity. Thankfully, it was not a rigorous inculcator of language and doctrine. In seven years of attending Hebrew school, my brothers and I learned little of the alphabet and less of the language. For our bar mitzvahs, Rabbi Agin would tape record our *haftorahs,* the excerpts of the Hebrew bible we had to recite. We would take our tapes home and listen to them and repeat them, and the rabbi would drill us every week. Though we didn't understand the words we were singing, they mattered deeply to us. This was an exercise in mnemonics. It was like "Simon," that board game we played where you had to push

the buttons in the sequence they lit up in. Also like Simon, there were winners and losers.

My youngest brother, Ken, was bar mitzvahed in September, which meant that his haftorah was one of the longest of the year. It filled four pages in his study book and almost a full side of his tape. Ken wasn't much of a student in Hebrew school or any other school, but he somehow took to the task. He'd sit up on his bunk bed with his tape recorder, listening and repeating and rewinding and listening again, taking in the strange speech bit by bit.

The day of his bar mitzvah arrived, and Ken put in a masterful showing. Even Uncle Max, the Orthodox cantor, praised the little *mensch* for his command of scripture. My parents were hopeful that this success might spill over to Ken's school performance, perhaps even spark his interest in temple services. Instead, Ken returned to his cassette player, not with Torah tapes, but with tapes of rap music given to him by his best friend, Melvin "Beh-beh" Watson. Instead of Rabbi Agin, his new tape tutors were the Sugarhill Gang, Grandmaster Flash, Run-D.M.C. Again, Ken sat up on his bunk, listening and repeating and rewinding.

Before long, Ken could rattle off any rap on demand, reciting chapter and verse. They'd flow osmotically in and out of his everyday speech. (Dad, driving us to school: "This new clutch is tricky." Ken: "IT'S TRICKY-TO-ROCK-A-RHYME-TO-ROCK-A-RHYME-THAT'S-RIGHT-ON-TIME-IT'S TRICKAAAY!!!") Sometimes he'd just sit with a glazed look, unraveling rhymes under his breath like some autistic homeboy. My brother Larry and I marveled at this miniature, melanin-deficient Melle Mel—as did kids of all persuasions, at least in our little town.

Then Ken went away to college, and the first white rap group, the Beastie Boys, came out. And Ken said, "That shoulda been me." And Ken went to graduate school, and the dopest white rap group, 3rd Bass, got famous. And even though Ken thought 3rd Bass was fresh, he still said, "That shoulda been me." And Ken started his career as a social worker, and the phoniest white rapper, Vanilla Ice, hit it big. And even though he knew Vanilla Ice was a sucker, Ken still said, "That shoulda been me." And nowadays, every white boy from the suburbs reckons himself a "gangsta."

So when I bring Ken to Mickey's in Albany for one of his first karaoke outings and, leafing through the song book, he comes upon the Sugarhill Gang's "Rapper's Delight"—the first U.S. rap hit, and the first rap Ken ever learned—there is no doubt what choice he'll make. There's something to prove here. This is *old school,* from *back in the day.* And although he's not sure what toll the years have taken on his verbal magic, he is willing to find out. Besides, there's a teleprompter here to fall back on. Waiting his turn, Ken quietly rehearses, mouthing the words to himself a little less assuredly than he did fifteen years ago.

Ken's name is called. He gets up in front of the mostly white rockers at Mickey's and starts rapping. His opening is mesmerizing: he whizzes through the hip-hip-hops and bang-bang-boogies like an exquisite machine. He summons the crowd in those open, inviting terms of early rap: *I am the Wonder Mike and I'd like to say hello, to the black and the white, the red and the brown, the purple and yellow!* The rockers in the audience call back, gettin' funky.

Then, about two minutes in, something awful happens. Ken launches into the third verse: *I'm the C-A-S-AN-the-O-V-A.* But different words appear on the screen: *I'm Imp the Dimp, the ladies' pimp.* "Rapper's Delight," which may be the only rap ever written that's as long as Ken's haftorah, has been edited for karaoke. The version on the teleprompter has jumped over several verses and landed at a point that's hard to situate. His template ruptured, poor Kenny looks as though he's been dropped in the middle of the South Bronx circa 1980—a clueless, thirteen-year-old wannabe.

Ken silently scans the screen for a familiar lyric to get his bearings. But silence screams in karaoke; people who hadn't been watching turn to see what's wrong; those who had been watching look away in pain. So he tries to fake it, but the words roll by too fast: *That shock the house . . . you do the freak, spank . . .* . Reduced from a million-dollar man to a five-dollar boy in a matter of seconds, Ken announces desperately: "I don't know these words!"

"Just read 'em!" comes a voice from the crowd.

Ken lowers his 6'2" frame and squints into the teleprompter. "I can't!" he sputters.

The folks at Mickey's are not ones to ignore a cry for help. They're the kind who would offer a hand if you got your car stuck in the Albany snow, even if it meant getting their feet wet. Or who'd lend a voice if you were stuck in the middle of a song, even if they could only mitigate your discomfort by sharing it. So the rockers join in, tripping through the rap and collectively producing some semblance of a narrative: *We're a treacherous trio, we're the serious joint.* And Ken, lifted by their effort, recovers his rhythm and takes the lead: *She said she's heard stories and she's heard fables, that I'm vicious on the mike and the turntable.* And when the hook line comes around, the line of "Rapper's Delight" that most everyone knows, we all shout out: *Ho-tel, mo-tel, Ho-li-day Inn!*

Ken never quite regains the mastery of his opening lines. (Though he comes pretty close with the verse that starts, *Have you ever gone over to a friend's house to eat and the food just ain't no good*—the verse he once used to diss Beh-beh's mother's cooking.) His memory has compressed the script very differently from the karaoke software producers. Nonetheless, he gets through the performance, he engages the audience, and he's rewarded with healthy applause and some slaps on the back. What's more, the folks at Mickey's thereafter address him by name, they kid him about his troubles onstage—they like him.

Aside from the natural appeal of watching a sibling squirm, what intrigued me about Ken's performance was the metamorphosis of the vaunting persona who took the stage into the vulnerable one who eventually won the audience's approval.

It seemed that his very loss of composure ("I don't know these words!") was the act that precipitated his recovery. Such "one-down" moves—excuses, apologies, disclaimers—are common face-saving strategies in everyday interaction but tend to be suppressed in onstage performance. In karaoke, though, the crowd's sense of inclusion, as well as its understanding of the severity of the task, foster a readiness to accept performers' hedges.

And so performers preface their songs with coy disavowals: "I don't know if I can sing this," or "Don't expect me to be good." Or they signal their frustration with their execution by frowning, shaking their heads, and critiquing themselves: "Can't do it, can't do it." Although such gestures and comments digress from performers' song scripts, they often seem no less scripted than the songs themselves. They are gambits in the sort of corrective process triggered by face-threatening events of all kinds.[29]

The audience, too, plays a role in this process. I found that whenever I complained about my performances, no matter how atrocious they were, others would dispute my self-assessment. Audience members' acceptance of a performer's apologies seems to absolve them no less than the apologies absolve the performer. As one emcee stated, "If somebody says, 'That was terrible,' you sort of have this obligation to say, 'Oh, no, it was good,' even though you know it stunk." Along with obligations, though, such moments present the crowd with opportunities to put karaoke's "anyone can do it" creed into action.

These little dramas of supplication and expiation need have little to do with anyone's true feelings. Crowd members may pardon a performance even when they "know it stunk," and performers may beg the crowd's pardon even when they're inwardly self-assured. Hence, one performer gleefully recounted how he went to a strange bar and performed all the songs he'd rehearsed and honed at his regular bar. As he took the stage, he'd adopted the demeanor of a novice, inspecting the equipment confusedly and asking, "What's this thing? How does this work?" His fumblings thus composed a performance in themselves, a fabricated show of humility of which he was secretly quite proud.

"This Could Get Ugly": The Clown If Laurel and Hardy were reincarnated as a couple of Northeast Philly goombahs, they might look something like Ed and Dave. Ed's the big one, sporting a sweatsuit circa 1970, a greased-back scalp, and a slightly demented smile. Scrawny Dave wears a t-shirt, jeans, stringy hair, and an expression that is not all there. Ed spits into the mike to test it out. "So I'm in line at the bank," he says. "I got my tongue up this—." He breaks off just before the sordid payoff of his Andrew Dice Clay joke, and his friends in the audience chuckle.

"He's up here doing the Diceman," announces the emcee. "This could get ugly." As if to stifle Ed, the emcee quickly spins the disc they've requested, "You've Lost That Lovin' Feelin'." It doesn't take long to discern why whoever they're singing to has lost that lovin' feelin'.

As the song begins, Dave suddenly emerges from his trance and takes the lead, such as it is. He's the one who howls the tune like a stray mutt, miles off-key, laughing and waving his arms ridiculously. He's the one who, midway through the song, starts whacking his partner over the head with his mike. He's the one who unceremoniously drops the mike on the floor and walks offstage as the last chorus ends—followed closely by Ed, who announces broadly, "I ain't never singin' with him again!"

And he's the one who gets the biggest hand of the night.

The fool and the clown: deft negotiators of pratfalls, donners of lampshades, depositors of foodstuffs in oversized trousers. Orrin Klapp first noted the paradox that, though fools themselves are ridiculed, the role they perform is often prized: "The fool upsets decorum by antics and eases routine by comic relief. He also acts as a cathartic symbol for aggressions in the form of wit."[30] More than a mere scapegoat or steam valve, however,

the fool can be an innovator, a source of insight and power. Barbara Babcock views clowning as a form of native theorizing, an epistemological critique: "The clown's performance . . . disrupts and interrupts customary frames and expected logic and syntax, and creates an open space of questioning."[31]

In karaoke, clowning serves as a critique of the classical voice and as yet another way for participants to convince themselves that "anyone can do it." Whereas other performers fret over minor slips off-key, the clown sings wildly, incessantly, shamelessly off-key. Where others maintain a solemn bearing, the clown objectifies himself with contorted postures and expressions. Like the small-time Liverpool rock musicians who "adopt an aesthetic of musical incompetence," or the amateur punkers of Austin, Texas, who "display their musical ineptitude like a badge of honor," karaoke clowns overturn and relativize prevailing standards of song performance in pursuit of a more open, direct mode of musical practice.[32] As one emcee states: "If you get up there and act like, 'I'm being a clown and I want you to know it,' then they will treat you like, 'Hey, this guy's funny! He was wonderful that way!'"

While some performers are clownish from the outset, others seem to have clownishness thrust upon them: "I have seen people get up to do songs, they start out serious but it's just not working, and they immediately go into, 'I'm doing it as a joke.'" Clowning here works as a face-saving stopgap when performers are failing. When a pair of young men try "Little Red Corvette" and find themselves unable to keep up with the words, one of them resorts to a coarse, Durante-esque dialect that is out of joint with Prince's sexy number. This draws some laughter from the crowd and some dissipative ribbing from the emcee: "I bet you'll wake up in the morning feeling really good about doing that!"

Clowning has its limits: its suitability depends on the song, and it can yield diminishing returns if pursued too relentlessly. Yet in karaoke, it is not

You don't have to be able to sing to do karaoke. Ken and Yvette happily warble their way through "Sympathy for the Devil."

unusual for the folly to mount until it dominates the event. At such times, it is the serious performer who can come to feel out of place. Consider the comments of one smooth-voiced karaoke regular: "It's the funniest thing. The singers that people seem to enjoy the most are the ones that are drunk out of their minds, acting stupid, and don't sing a note right. It's so funny, people would rather see that sometimes than the good ones—which is just as well, because that's what makes it fun." Though she struggles to be tolerant, the performer can't hide her bewilderment that some audiences would prefer travesties of songs over faithful renderings. She is, understandably, torn between her respect for karaoke's pluralist ideal and her resentment at karaoke's demotion of her own painstakingly-nurtured voice.

"It Just Popped Into My Head": The Improviser
A well-dressed woman is doing "Midnight Train to Georgia," backed by three male friends. The division of labor recalls the hit version by Gladys Knight and the Pips, and the performers try to reproduce the call-and-response of their template. But the boys' Pips impersonation is so convincing that Gladys can't help laughing, and as she breaks up, unable to continue, her Pips go right on sing-

ing. Their backing vocals are thrust absurdly to the foreground—*Leavin' on a midnight train! . . . Goin' back to find! . . . I know you will!*—and the longer they continue, the more thoroughly they disable their lead singer.

It sometimes seems as though these little routines ("you be Gladys Knight, we'll be the Pips") are put together just so they can fall apart. The laughter, raised eyebrows, and fumbling for words give the impression that these are no longer performers, but real human beings appearing before us. Suddenly, their problems seem twice as arduous, their solutions twice as ingenious. Among karaoke performers, as among amateur musicians, spontaneity has an almost magical effect:

I'll sing a song and a phrase will pop into my head, and I'll change the words right then and there on the spot. I was singing a song last week, "Jessie's Girl." There's a phrase in the song, "I'm looking in the mirror all the time, wondering what she don't see in me." The next phrase says something, I don't even know what it says because I changed the words, it just popped into my head. I said, "Could it be that he has thirteen inches and I just have a little peewee?"[33]

Onstage and off, performers take pains to assure us that such emendations "popped into their heads." So strong is the appeal of miscarried schemes and makeshift recoveries that some performers are tempted to contrive them. A college student doing "Jailhouse Rock" appears to be thrown off by the song's breakneck tempo and abruptly shifts to a weird hybridization of Presley's lyrics and scat-style nonsense syllables—*Obada oobada eebada let's rock!*—animating the whole with bowlegged, jitterbug-style movements. Later, he describes his performance as an ad hoc response to a mnemonic impasse: "My friend chose the song, and the reason I improvised the way I did was because I didn't quite know all the words. . . . My high school band teacher was into the weird kind of phrases I was using. So I was like, might as well pull it out of the hat right now.

'Cause I had nowhere to turn, I didn't know the words!"

Yet the following week, he does the same song, the same scat singing, the same jitterbug dancing. His performance is improvised to the degree that it could hardly be identical to his previous one, but this is clearly a planned and polished form of improvisation. Even so, it is as good for the audience, as good for me, and evidently as good for the performer as it was the week before.

AN AMATEUR AESTHETIC

Karaoke performers, no less than other amateur performers, routinely put themselves on the line in ways professionals rarely have to. Despite their paucity of formal training, they take the stage under conditions so unstructured and unpredictable as to frighten off many trained singers. They risk failure in the most intimate, diffuse performance contexts, where failure can feel very personal. Though emcees claim that karaoke allows anyone to be a star, performers are all too clearly themselves once they descend from the stage and must themselves suffer the consequences of their performances.

Performers willingly shoulder this burden in support of the radical notion that culture is ordinary—that creativity is not marginal to daily life, something to be supplied by a few chosen artists.[34] A quarter of a century ago, John Blacking asked: "Why bother to improve musical technique if the aim of performance is to share a social experience?"[35] Many musicologists undoubtedly still consider the question an affront to their discipline, but to karaoke performers it is mere common sense. If judged by their musical expertise, karaoke performers' achievements are often modest; but if judged by their readiness to make music in a society where amateur music-making remains strange, their achievements are substantial.

Those who have observed karaoke from afar and thought about joining the fray can take comfort in the enormous flexibility of karaoke's aesthetic. Most participants come to karaoke with little preparation and few expectations, fostering a tolerance for deviations from dominant vocal standards. Karaoke often accommodates as wide a range of voices as speech itself and is defined as much by quotidian social skills as by formal musical skills: technical virtuosity often seems less important than the ability to feel others out, humble oneself, laugh at oneself, think on one's feet. In this sense, karaoke recalls the many grass-roots musical crusades that value the vernacular over the esoteric, social utility over individual expertise.

All of which suggests that if you can cast aside your conditioned fear of your own voice; if you can remain alive to the hazards without letting them hold you back; if you can imagine a place where breaking into song is as natural as saying "hello"; then perhaps you, too, can do it—in a karaoke bar or anywhere else.

Notes

1 Casey Allen, "Karaoke Establishment Listings," *Where to Sing,* http://www.wheretosing.com, February 2, 1997.

2 Ruth Finnegan, *The Hidden Musicians: Music-Making in an English Town* (New York: Cambridge University Press, 1989).

3 Ben Fong-Torres, "Pass the Popcorn . . . and the Microphone," *Karaoke and DJ USA* 25 (1996): 28.

4 Hiroshi Ogawa, "The Socialization Process in Karaoke Singing in Japan," in *Karaoke around the World: Singing Culture in the Era of Digital Technology,* ed. Toru Mitsui and Shuhei Hosokawa (London: Routledge, 1998).

5 Deborah Wong, "'I Want the Microphone': Mass Mediation and Agency in Asian-American Popular Music," *Drama Review* 75 (1994): 158.

6 Conrad L. Donakowski, *A Muse for the Masses: Ritual and Music in an Age of Democratic Revolution* (Chicago: University of Chicago Press, 1977), 188–215.

7 Paul Dimaggio, "Cultural Entrepreneurship in Nineteenth-Century Boston, II: The Classification and Framing of American Art," *Media, Culture, and Society* 4 (1982): 312; Lawrence Levine, *Highbrow/Lowbrow: The Emergence of Cultural Hierarchy in America* (Cambridge, MA: Harvard University Press, 1988), 139–40.

8 John Blacking, *How Musical Is Man?* (Seattle: University of Washington Press, 1973), 34.

9 Joshua Gamson, *Claims to Fame: Celebrity in Contemporary America* (Berkeley: University of California Press, 1994), 32.

10 H. Stith Bennett, *On Becoming a Rock Musician* (Amherst: University of Massachusetts Press, 1980); Sara Cohen, *Rock Culture in Liverpool: Popular Music in the Making* (New York: Oxford University Press, 1991); Ruth Finnegan, *The Hidden Musicians: Music-Making in an English Town* (New York: Cambridge University Press, 1989); Barry Shank, *Dissonant Identities: The Rock'n'Roll Scene in Austin, Texas* (Hanover, NH: Wesleyan University Press, 1994).

11 John Blacking, "Fieldwork in African Music," *Review of Ethnology* 23 (1973): 181; Laurel Richardson, "Writing: A Method of Inquiry," in *Handbook of Qualitative Research*, eds. Norman K. Denzin and Yvonna S. Lincoln (Thousand Oaks, CA: Sage, 1994), 520–23.

12 Richard Rorty, *Essays on Heidegger and Others* (New York: Cambridge University Press, 1991), 80.

13 Blacking, *How Musical Is Man?*, 7; Dick Hebdige, *Subculture: The Meaning of Style* (London: Routledge, 1979), 112.

14 Henry Kingsbury, *Music, Talent, and Performance: A Conservatory Cultural System* (Philadelphia: Temple University Press, 1988), 59–83.

15 Erving Goffman, "On Face-Work," in *Interaction Ritual* (New York: Pantheon, 1967), 6.

16 Kingsbury, *Music, Talent, and Performance,* 5.

17 Jones, *Rock Formation,* 38–47.

18 Bennett, *On Becoming a Rock Musician,* 154.

19 Ibid.

20 Jones, *Rock Formation,* 38–47.

21 Van Christy, *Foundations in Singing* (Dubuque, IA: William C. Brown, 1973), 3.

22 Dell Hymes, *Foundations in Sociolinguistics* (Philadelphia: University of Pennsylvania Press, 1974), 4–5.

23 Simon Frith, *Sound Effects: Youth, Leisure, and the Politics of Rock 'n' Roll* (New York: Pantheon, 1981), 35.

24 Susan McClary and Robert Walser, "Start Making Sense: Musicology Wrestles with Rock," in *On Record: Rock, Pop, and the Written Word,* ed. Simon Frith and Andrew Goodwin (New York: Pantheon, 1990), 277–92.

25 Robert Rushmore, *The Singing Voice* (New York: Dembner Books, 1984), 156.

26 Frith, *Sound Effects,* 14–15.

27 Bennett, *On Becoming a Rock Musician,* 3; Finnegan, *The Hidden Musicians,* 133–42.

28 Frith, *Sound Effects,* 15.

29 Goffman, "On Face-Work," 19–23.

30 Orrin Klapp, "The Fool as a Social Type," *American Journal of Sociology* 55 (1950): 161.

31 Barbara Babcock, "Arrange Me into Disorder: Fragments and Reflections on Ritual Clowning," in *Rite, Drama, Festival, Spectacle: Rehearsals Toward a Theory of Cultural Performance,* ed. John J. MacAloon (Philadelphia: Institute for the Study of Human Issues, 1984), 107.

32 Cohen, *Rock Culture in Liverpool,* 173; and Shank, *Dissonant Identities,* 113.

33 Cohen, *Rock Culture in Liverpool,* 101–2.

34 Raymond Williams, "Culture Is Ordinary," in *Resources of Hope: Culture, Democracy, Socialism,* ed. Robin Gable (London: Verso, 1988), 3–18; Paul Willis, *Common Culture: Symbolic Work at Play in the Everyday Cultures of the Young* (Boulder, CO: Westview Press, 1990).

35 Blacking, *How Musical Is Man?*, 35.

Watching Wrestling/
Writing Performance

Sharon Mazer

Hey Professor, lemme tell you a story.
—DAVE (THE "WILDMAN") TO JIM FREEDMAN,
IN *DRAWING HEAT*

"Why don't you take pictures of us naked? Huh? Huh? You want pictures? Take pictures of us naked!" Vito, a large wrestler with a shaved head who sometimes jobs as "Von Kraut" for the World Wrestling Federation (WWF), is shouting, hounding me as I circle the ring at Gleason's Gym with my camera.[1] The other wrestlers watch and listen, but otherwise leave us alone. Taken aback, I reply: "Why would I want to do that? I'm an academic." It's a lame response, I realize immediately. But nothing more effective springs to mind. Instead, I remember the incident on ABC-TV's *20/20* when reporter John Stossel had his ears boxed by wrestler Dave Schultz after insisting that the monster wrestler admit that professional wrestling is not "real."[2] Instead of coming up with a pithy response, I realize once more that I don't belong in a steamy gym watching as a bunch of men practice hitting each other, or pretending to hit each other. I belong in the library, at a computer, at a coffee bar with a friend discussing Foucault. . . . I remember that Vito is a big man who could inflict considerable injury if he stops shouting at me and decides to act. I remember that he is a man and I am a woman, and that there are sexual tensions created by the mere fact of my presence in the gym that could explode at me if I am not careful.

But Vito doesn't do more than repeat his challenge, which I continue to parry without much success. The exchange goes on for what seems like an hour until he at last stalks off to the locker room. When he reemerges and joins the other men hanging around the ring, Johnny—as in "the

Johnny Rodz School of Professional Wrestling"—jokes that we should do a series of photos in which I'm wrestling the men to the mat, and then he casually offers me a ride back into Manhattan, an escape I gratefully accept. Upon my rather cautious return to the gym the following Saturday, Vito ignores me for an hour or so and then approaches me. I try to contain my anxiety, but instead of attacking me once more, he earnestly asks me about his chances of breaking into the film business as an actor, and we resume our customary, if wary, dialogue.

What happened? What was I—a member of the cultural elite—doing on the receiving end of a wrestler's tirade? For that matter, what was I—short, round, and female, not inclined to athletics of any sort—doing sitting on a metal chair ringside watching a group of men working out on yet another hot and humid Saturday afternoon?

It's been almost ten years since I first found my way to the Johnny Rodz School of Professional Wrestling. I've spent months at a stretch watching wrestlers train, taking notes and photographs first for an article published in the *Drama Review* in 1990, and subsequently as part of ongoing research for a series of conference papers and now a book which focuses on the inculcation of masculine, patriotic values both in training and in performance.[3] Because Johnny accepts me, the younger wrestlers have, for the most part, tolerated my presence, ignoring or welcoming me according to their individual, moment-to-moment inclinations. The confrontation with Vito was an exception, a vivid reminder that no matter how much time I spend ringside at Gleason's, I don't really belong.

Watching wrestling requires, among other things, a certain tact. To win the wrestlers' acceptance—not just permission to sit ringside, but to hear the stories, to be allowed to take photographs, and ultimately to be "let in on the game"—has obliged me to accept a kind of dynamic invisibility.[4] I have been silent for long hours and then, suddenly, asked to perform more actively as a kind of model spectator: "Ask Sharon. She knows," Johnny will goad a youngster.[5] "Sure!" I chirp. Or on stopping two wrestlers who appear about to shoot the practice, he will reiterate that it's not enough to do the moves and remind them that "before you hit the guy you have to ask the audience 'what should I do?'" When he turns to me, I contribute as cued: "Kill him."[6]

The wrestlers, following Johnny's example, have created their own ways of incorporating me into their domain, of converting my watching—my intrusion into their private practice—into something less disturbing. Often a wrestler first begins to engage me in dialogue by "inviting" me to wrestle with him. The offer to teach me the moves is half jest, half test. What is at stake is not so much whether or not I'm going to get into the ring. I won't. But more how I will respond. Will I attempt to lecture them on what is theirs, patronize them? Will I be offended at the implication that I might come to their level, become touchable? I laugh because it's silly to expect me to last more than a fleeting second in the ring. The wrestler generally laughs with me and on subsequent afternoons will find other ways of acknowledging me at least once or twice. Often the last wrestler to jest/test me will tease a newcomer by introducing me as his "teacher" who has taught him everything he knows about the game. Inevitably, within about a month of encountering me for the first time, a wrestler will sidle up to me at ringside and interrogate me, as Vito once did: "So, you're writing a book, huh? You have a husband? What does he think of you hanging out at the gym with a bunch of wrestlers?"

My role as observer has thus evolved via a series of interactions directed by Johnny and negotiated with the wrestlers on a day-to-day basis. Over the years I have come to realize just how problematic our transactions are. In that I am permitted to show up at the gym week after week, allowed to watch while refusing to enter the ring myself, I occupy the position of voyeur. That is, I am privileged to observe a group of men engaged in secret, essentially intimate exchanges. The exchange between them, and with me, is implicitly charged with sexual energy. Watching wrestlers in their private training sessions is not exactly the same activity as being a spectator at a striptease or a Times Square peepshow, but what I do, literally, is spend hours in close proximity to men in various stages of undress as they toss and hold each other, sharing secrets and experiences that ordinarily would exclude me completely.[7]

Moreover, my status relative to that of the wrestlers is marked by two contradictory and intersecting identities: that of a scholar and that of a woman. The first problematic is located in assumptions of class difference, the second in assumptions about gender difference.[8] As a scholar doing research, even before my articles are written, I am potentially a threat to the culture of the ring, to the way in which these men construct their relations to each other, and to their ambitions in the highly competitive industry that is professional wrestling, already problematized as the least legitimate of sports. I represent what they perceive as a dominant culture that effectively excludes and marginalizes them as lower class men. "We've had people like you here before, come in here, think they can tell us what we're about," Larry—who was, at the time, working toward a doctorate in sports sociology—said to me early on. Because my status outside the gym has been perceived as higher than theirs, they have consistently monitored my words and manner for signs of arrogance or condescension. Their decision that I am "alright" is largely founded in the second of my primary cultural identities, in my femaleness.

Indeed, the way in which the wrestlers monitor my behavior appears to be attached to, and reflective of, my status as a woman in an arena defined and dominated by men. While as a scholar, I might represent an otherwise remote intellectual elite, as a woman I am, superficially at least, familiar, proximate to their everyday experiences and expectations. My acceptance in the gym has, as a result, been contingent upon my own performance within conventional assumptions of femininity. To remain silent and effectively invisible while present, to speak only when spoken to and even then only according to the cues given, has signalled to these men my willingness to perform according to their (generally unspoken) rules. Because I have been what they term "respectful"— or perhaps more properly, because I have not been disrespectful—I have been told by Johnny that I "don't have to get [my] face pushed to the mat to be let in on the game." Or haven't I?

Getting your face pushed to the mat is the rite of passage any newcomer to wrestling faces in the early weeks. Typically he unintentionally provokes the wrath of a more experienced wrestler who then verbally and physically abuses him as the others stand back and watch. If the newcomer sticks it out and returns subsequently, he has passed a crucial test, is deemed worthy of a higher degree of respect than before, and is assimilated into the group. It is possible that Johnny's statement is not so much a compliment as an acknowledgement that my physicality makes me an obviously unsuitable candidate for rigorous athletic training. It may indeed be my short round femaleness that softens the threat implied by my watching.[9] But it is obvious, too, that Vito's verbal assault served as an equivalent initiation, a test of my willingness to stand my ground, to stick it out, and to return the next week for more if necessary.

So, given that I was conscious of, and playing by, the rules, that I was being a good girl, why was Vito shouting at me? The short answer is that I spoke out of turn. Or rather, I spoke properly in response to a prompt from Johnny, but failed to take into account the volatility of the particular wrestler. In brief, Johnny had stopped Vito, who was about to pummel his partner, and asked him what he thought the spectators' response would be to his failure to invite their participation. This is a standard exchange in Johnny's pedagogic reper-

toire, a lesson in engaging the audience in the action with which I am quite familiar. He turned to me, as he has on many occasions, and I chimed in with the expected spectator response: "Bor . . . ring." At which point, the shouting began.

While it is true that I had acted according to the role assigned to me by Johnny, my shift from silent observer to jeering spectator, however playful, at that moment transformed Vito's private lesson into a public humiliation, his workout with the men into a display in front of a woman. His demand that I take pictures of them naked was, at this level, a direct response to his coming to awareness of being watched. His sense of having been exposed was to be matched by my own, his loss of face redeemed by mine. In his assault I was to be denied the safety of the sidelines. My invisibility was revoked. Given that I had spoken, the last word was to be his.

But of course the last word is literally mine. After leaving the gym I find a quiet café and record the events of the day into my notebook. And more than a year later I write the first draft of this essay. I have been doing fieldwork, gathering material for my book. These wrestlers are not chance acquaintances or friends, but figures in a narrative I am constructing. I am not writing a fan letter, or an article for one of the many fanzines, or an entry into the rec.sport.pro-wrestling discussion. I am composing treatises in which my experiences in the gym are processed and re-presented, commodified for scholarly consumption. I am acting as a performance studies scholar, a cultural anthropologist, an ethnographer. This is not a surprise to anyone reading this, I am sure. But it has been to me. The work of my work is something I tend to forget for long stretches of time as I navigate the boundary between my world and Gleason's Gym. I am Margaret Mead, I am Clifford Geertz, I am Richard Schechner.[10] Sharon Mazer wears khakis!

Well, I'm not exactly ready to pose for a Gap ad. What I am attempting to make perfectly clear is how utterly naïve I have been, how slow my coming to consciousness has been. My naiveté has

Rubio pins Frankie and looks to me for approval. Photograph by Sharon Mazer.

Rubio lifts Frankie in a hold typical of Mexican wrestling, which is more visibly "choreographed" than is Anglo wrestling. Photograph by Sharon Mazer.

been justified to some degree by my proximity to the objects of my research. Gleason's Gym is not in Bali. It's in Brooklyn. I am not watching a cock-fight, at least—and here I am mindful of Clifford Geertz's self-conscious punning, as well as that common to the WWF—not of the poultry per-suasion.[11] I journey thirty minutes by subway—not hours by plane, canoe, horsecart—from my home. My computer, the library, a terrific coffee bar, and a good friend are mere minutes away. Yet the distance traveled is no less far, the borders I've crossed no less emphatic for being in the neigh-borhood. When I return from watching wrestling, what I write is not wrestling as such, but perfor-mance. When I re-constitute myself from watcher to writer, I also re-position the wrestlers from subjects in their tales of training and wrestling to characters in my own story of life as a scholar. As James Clifford acknowledges in his essay, "On Ethnographic Allegory": "Whatever else ethnog-raphy does, it translates experience into text. There are various ways of effecting this transla-tion, ways that have significant ethical and politi-cal consequences."[12] Consequences, in my case, which are moved and marked by the dialectics of class and gender.

What, then, is the terrain navigated between watching wrestling and writing performance? And how is the map of these activities both animated and complicated by the fact that the objects of my study are men in a male-defined space? In asking these two questions, others arise, and from these still more emerge—far more, in fact, than I can properly answer at this point in my work. Instead of pretending to naiveté, I find myself genuinely naïve, only just beginning to comprehend the ac-tual complexities and potential consequences of my undertaking.

In the wrestlers' workout the exchange is ex-plicitly between men. That is, a number of men practice their moves while being watched and ad-vised by other men. The lone woman wrestler, a professional body builder who calls herself Sky Magic, is accepted, treated, and respected as one of

Sky Magic kicks Rubio to the mat. Photograph by Sharon Mazer.

the guys. She has had her face pushed to the mat and returned for more. It is, perhaps, ironic that of all the wrestlers who regularly work out at Glea-son's, Sky profits the most. She makes a living of sorts from "phone wrestling," in which she talks wrestling, literally, to men who call her on a 900 number, and from "apartment house wrestling," where for $300 an hour she wrestles a man in his apartment. No sex—at least in the superficial sense. In fact, she claims that "as a feminist" she would never cross the line into phone sex, escort services, or prostitution. Still, it is an enterprise for which her gender qualifies her over the other wrestlers, one which in very specific ways belies Johnny's oft-stated doctrine of neutrality: every-one is treated the same way regardless of gender, dependent upon their physical performance, their willingness to take the hits and do the work.

Sky had been training at Gleason's for only a month or so when I returned there after more than a year's absence. She immediately approached me and, offering a firm handshake, confided her pleasure in seeing another woman present during workouts. Her immediate assumption of a bond between us as women, while it highlights the problem of gender in the gym, was touching in the moment. Treated by the other wrestlers as one of the guys, and accepting me on the same terms as the others, she nonetheless also explicitly engaged me as "one of the girls."[13] Her ambivalence—apparently treated as "one of the guys" and at the same welcoming the bracing presence of another "girl"—in some ways reflects my own. It is certainly possible that, having passed my own approximation of the wrestler's initiation by withstanding Vito's assault, I then, like Sky, might be considered an insider on the wrestlers' terms, one of the guys.

At the same time, just as the men's insistence on gender neutrality in their workouts with Sky implicitly carries with it unspoken anxieties of difference, so too my position in the ring as a woman who has been accepted on the wrestlers' terms is more paradoxical in ways that remain largely unacknowledged and uninterrogated. When I sit on the sidelines—unlike Sky, a watcher rather than an active participant—my position is far more difficult to explain. I am a woman watching men perform physically with each other. I do my best to reassure by acting in ways that mark me as "feminine," but the fact of my watching, in experience as well as theoretically, seems to position me in ways that are remarkably like that of a man watching women dance for his pleasure. Put another way, if I am truly "one of the guys" then I must according to the protocol of the gym do as well as watch. If I do not, and therefore am not, then what am I? And if I am an academic, as well as a not-fully assimilated woman, observing their moves and translating them into my own language for my own purposes, then I am certainly not neutral insofar as (in theory) to watch is a

masculine, subject position, while to do while being watched is a feminine, object position. As long as I remain silent and effectively invisible at the sidelines, it is possible to overlook the contradiction between what I am—female—and what I do—watch. If I call attention to myself at the wrong moment, these contradictions become potentially disruptive.

To return to my original question: Why was Vito shouting? My speaking was cued by Johnny as the voice of the spectator who authorizes the wrestlers in performance. A relatively large proportion of training time in the gym is spent learning and practicing ways of making openings for spectator participation; this triangulation with the spectators as it constructs and manipulates response forms a central part of my own work. An invitation to play with the wrestlers on this level, then, might be considered a gift from Johnny, both as an opportunity to share more directly in the experience and as a piece of material for my research. At the same time, however, my speaking made my watching and the wrestlers' being watched visible, thus violating rules for which Vito and the others probably have no language, at least not the theoretical discourse of the scholar. My speaking claimed for me the masculine place in the dialectic, leaving Vito the feminine. His challenge—"Why don't you take pictures of us naked?"—didn't simply cast me in the role of voyeur, more a spectator at a striptease than a researcher doing fieldwork. It sexualized the encounter. If my speaking threatened his manhood, then his response was to reclaim that manhood by reminding me that I was the "girl" in the room and, as such, in a position of relative vulnerability in fundamental, sexual terms.

How, then, am I to consider the implications of this exchange as sexualized and potentially dangerous? How do I detach from my visceral response to this experience, an experience that is still vivid to me now? Can I, simply, deny my (feminine) vulnerability and reclaim a position of (masculine) objectivity by stepping back into my role as a performance studies scholar? Do I, simply, proceed with my project, translate my experiences at Gleason's into narratives which can then be interpreted, reconstituted and represented as authoritative analysis? If I do so, can the shift from my apparent submission to the dominant male culture of the gym—my performance as a "good girl"—to my subjugation of them into my own narrative, therefore, be seen as deception? Is what I enact inevitably a mis-representation of my "self" in the first instance and of the wrestlers' selves in the second? That is, do I violate an unspoken contract with the wrestlers when I translate their workouts into the language of performance, when I use theoretical discourses drawn from performance studies and anthropology to describe the initiation protocols by which new wrestlers are assimilated into the group, when I discuss the parallels between watching wrestlers train and watching actors, and most of all when I theorize about the gender dynamics of the ring, in particular what I consider to be the homoeroticism implicit in the codified yet expressive physical engagement between men? Is it a betrayal—or rather, what kind of betrayal is it—this retroactive transgression of masculine space and identity? And is it another, perhaps inevitable, betrayal when what I write ceases to be about them and becomes—as does the story that opens this essay—about me? How can I possibly tell the truth about watching and writing in this essay, infected as it is by the necessary tension between experience and representation, if indeed that is what I am to do?

Perhaps the first step is to leave my own questions, which begin to turn against the possibility of answers, to one side and explore the questions that are implied by Vito's original question: Why don't I take pictures of them naked? My answer at the time—"Why would I want to do that? I'm an academic"—is not only lame. It's superficial and disingenuous. Sure I'm at Gleason's as part of my ongoing scholarly explorations of popular performance, in particular the representation of mas-

culine identity in certain types of physical display. But I might just have easily continued to write about didacticism, the representation and transmission of cultural values and identities in Middle English drama. There's no obvious justification for my decision to spend my Saturdays in the gym watching men in tight-fitting lycra going through multiple series of physical moves when the logic of my academic conditioning would rather place me with a book in the library or a playbill in a theatre. Clearly I must take some pleasure in watching these men, their bodies in action as they work on the moves, toss and cover each other. Must I now admit that I am to some degree engaged, animated, titillated by the act of watching, by the fact that I am an audience of one, a short round woman peeping at muscular men as they engage in otherwise exclusively masculine activities? That I am gleeful in my privilege as the only woman watcher, and that I relish and derive a certain amount of status from the telling of my stories to my friends over coffee later? That it is a real hoot to turn my adventures into scholarly writing and to be rewarded with a book contract for making public the private dealings of these men? That I derive pleasure, power, and profit from this "work" in a way that would not be available to me were I still writing about the English Middle Ages? [14]

The issue is one of ethics, of truth-telling as well as of truth-asking, centered on the idea and act of translation, situated as it is at the border between experience and explanation. Somewhere between the watching and the writing discrepancies inevitably arise. The re-presentation of, and theorizing about, a series of experiences by someone who acts both as insider and outsider is rendered less true and, as such, potentially unrecognizable to its original participants. In *Between Theatre and Anthropology*, Richard Schechner asks:

> How can a "good" performance be distinguished from a "bad" one? Are there two sets of criteria, one

for inside the culture and one for outside? Or are there four sets: inside the culture by the professionals who also make performances; inside by ordinary audiences; outside the culture by visiting professionals; outside by ordinary audiences? Who has the "right" to make evaluations: only people in a culture, only professionals who practice the art in question, only professional critics? Is there a difference between criticism and interpretation? (Has Clifford Geertz studied, interpreted, criticized, or reviewed the Balinese cockfight?) [15]

In the wrestler's gym I am not simply an outsider, identified as scholar and woman. I am also a wrestling spectator who has frequently attended matches at Madison Square Garden and who has watched hours of wrestling on television. As such, I might be classed by insiders as a "hard-core fan" if not a "mark." A hard-core fan is one who considers himself (almost exclusively *him*self) in on the game. That is, he not only follows wrestling avidly by attending matches, watching television, subscribing to newsletters such as the *Pro-Wrestling Torch,* and engaging in fierce debates on the Internet, but also prides himself on knowing that the finish is fixed with scenarios mapped in advance. A mark is one who may be avid but who hasn't quite attained full knowledge of the game. Obviously the boundaries between the two types are subjective, and wrestling is not so much a case of inside/outside as of degrees of inside-ness. In this regard, I was once asked by Larry, the wrestler-academic, if I considered myself a fan. After some thought, I answered: "Probably not, not after so many years here." His answer was one of identification rather than distancing: "Me neither."

But if I am neither wrestler nor fan—in Schechner's terms, neither a professional nor an ordinary audience member from within the culture of the ring—perhaps, as a theatre director who has invested more than twenty years of training and practice in creating performances for audiences, I can be considered a "visiting profes-

sional." I am simultaneously inside and outside the game, knowledgeable and naïve, powerful and vulnerable, an experienced wrestling spectator and professional producer of theatrical spectacles who is learning another performance language just as I might were I to study Kathakali or, for that matter, ballet. My experience of watching and writing can be represented as familiar or strange depending on which identity I claim, which I chose to ignore.

Far from neutral or, despite my protestations to the contrary, naïve, my interactions with the wrestlers as both watcher and writer are "laced with power," a phrase Renato Rosaldo uses in *Culture and Truth: The Remaking of Social Analysis* as he considers the ethnographer's role in relation to the cultures s/he studies. Rosaldo asks: "What are the complexities of the speaker's social identity? What life experiences have shaped it? Does the person speak from a position of relative dominance or relative subordination?" [16]

In the hierarchy of the gym, no matter how articulate and self-possessed I may be as a scholar/writer, as a watcher I must perform according to role assigned to me by the dominant culture of the gym or risk verbal, even physical, abuse. In the academy, with the wrestlers present only as material from my research, I become dominant. My scholar/writer's authority frames and contains, objectifies and abstracts, and above all extracts and constructs a narrative that supersedes that of the wrestlers, no matter how articulate and self-possessed they are, no matter how proximate their world may be to mine. Vito may shout at me for talking out of turn, might even chase me from the gym. His size and ferocity are indeed intimidating. But my voice is, in the end, heard more widely in the talks I give at conferences and in the documents I produce for publication. His shouting was heard by eight or so wrestlers and forgotten in the weeks that followed. What remain of his words are, literally, in my hands.

What is it that I write when I re-write wrestling into performance? At the first level, I endeavor to

(clockwise from top left)

Larry teaches Tommy a lesson in "respect." Photograph by Sharon Mazer.

Tommy attempts to escape Larry's grasp by squirming through the ropes. Photograph by Sharon Mazer.

Larry's dominance of Tommy is apparently effortless. He converses with Chris while keeping Tommy under control. Photograph by Sharon Mazer.

describe precisely what the wrestlers do: how they train and what they say to each other and to me about their training, about their ambitions, and about their identities as wrestlers and as men. That is, I describe the culture of the gym and the activity of a group of men there. The narrative I produce is not solely description, of course, and certainly not pure. Beyond the exigencies incumbent upon the transcription of the wrestlers' actions and words into prose, my narrative is inflected by the language both of the scholar and of the theatre director, the accumulated vocabulary of years of theatre training, education and experience. I watch them practice what they call "the game"—the moves, the rules of engagement. They talk about the "babyface" and the "heel," about how to perform a "face turn" or a "heel turn," about "exchanges," about what is "cheap heat" versus what is not and how to generate it.[17] I translate their language into mine, as I've done in many of the notes in this chapter. Then I write about Aristotelian definitions of character and structures of conflict, the positioning of protagonist and antagonist, the escalation of action through conflict and reversal, the climactic moment of recognition and final reversal, and the denouement. I write about patterns of action as they resemble the interactions between scenario, lazzi, and improvisation in commedia dell'arte and *wayang kulit*. I write about a theatrical didacticism, about a presentational dynamics and spectator engagement that resembles Middle English drama, about arenas and audiences which are uncannily like those described by Brecht when he declares:

Make no bones about it, we have our eye on those huge concrete pans, filled with 15,000 men and women of every variety of class and physiognomy, the fairest and shrewdest audience in the world. There you will find 15,000 persons paying high prices, and working things out on the basis of a sensible weighing of supply and demand. . . . When people in sporting establishments buy their tickets they know exactly what is going to take place; and

that is exactly what does take place once they are in their seats.[18]

Our cultures are discrete but analogous. The wrestlers talk strategies for getting a shot at the big leagues, the World Wrestling Federation (WWF) and World Championship Wrestling (WCW). I submit essays to the *Drama Review* and work at a book for the University Press of Mississippi, hoping to accumulate a viable vita and with it a high-level teaching job. The wrestlers gossip. They name-drop. They compare themselves to, and often are critical and even contemptuous, of pro wrestling's stars: Hulk Hogan, Randy Savage, Lex Lugar, Ric Flair, Shawn Michaels, the Undertaker, Bam Bam Bigelow. I pick up what they drop as evidence from my research. I drop their names and use their words to authenticate my own, then go on to drop the names of star scholars: Roland Barthes, Mikhail Bakhtin, Angela Carter, Michel Foucault, Judith Butler.[19] The wrestlers hang out in Johnny's office, with its poster-and-news-clipping-papered walls, listening to Johnny tell stories of wrestling with Hulk Hogan and barhopping with Andre the Giant. I hang out with them, then write about oral tradition, the transmittal of performance knowledge from one generation to the next as it finds parallels in a multitude of practices and cultures. They take their cues from Johnny Rodz and other wrestler/teachers. I take mine from Richard Schechner and other scholar/teachers, just as I used to hang on and now transmit the words of my acting teachers:

Performance knowledge belongs to oral traditions. How such traditions are passed on in various cultures and in different genres is of great importance. Some surprising parallels exist, for example, between the way professional sports in America and traditional performances in Asia are coached and taught. Sports are fine examples of non-verbal performance—dramatic and kinesthetic yet not "dance" or "theatre" in the classical, modern, or postmodern sense. The coaches of sports teachers are usually former players. They personally give their "secrets" to younger players. Older players, even when they can't play anymore, are respected for their records; participants and fans alike delight in anecdotes about the old great ones. Some of these ancestors are enshrined in "halls of fame," and some are kept on as coaches or in the front office.[20]

The wrestlers greet each other by swiping two fingers gently in a modified high-five. They practice holds and lifts; they toss and cover each other. I write about the cultural implications of masculine display, about the homoerotics implicit in the play of domination and submission between men. They learn the ropes and talk about "getting your face pushed to the mat before you can be let in on the game." I write about initiation and rites of passage, tests of manhood and the presentation/articulation of masculinity in/as performance. They quote other wrestlers and promoters, the stars of the game. I quote the wrestlers, attempting to capture their ways of speaking about who they are and what they do. But their words are not left unattended. What they say is framed by my words and those of others. I cite authorities, anthropologists, pop philosophers, social historians and feminists, name-dropping in my own way as much as the wrestlers do in theirs. I cite Umberto Eco:

> Contest disciplines and neutralizes the aggressive charge, individual and collective. It reduces excess action, but it is really a mechanism to neutralize action. . . . The athlete is a monster, he is the Man Who Laughs.[21]

I cite Clifford Geertz:

> In the cockfight, man and beast, good and evil, ego and id, the creative power of aroused masculinity and the destructive power of loosened animality fuse in a bloody drama of hatred, cruelty, violence, and death.[22]

I cite Victor Turner: "Initiations humble people before permanently elevating them."[23] I cite Robert Bly:

It's becoming clear to us that manhood doesn't happen by itself; it doesn't happen just because we eat Wheaties. The active intervention of the older men means that older men welcome the younger man in to the ancient, mythologized, instinctive male world.[24]

I cite John Preston's history of the Mineshaft, one of the most (in)famous gay sex clubs of the pre-AIDS era:

> The most important aspect of these public displays has to do with the masculinists' observations of the need for ritual. Without doubt, sadomasochistic behavior has many roots. . . . But the public display of gay male sadomasochistic sex acts is primarily an exhibition of the gay man going through the rite of passage. It is the way many gay men accomplish their gender needs of leaving adolescence and entering male adulthood.[25]

I cite Andrea Dworkin:

> The principle that "the personal is political" belongs to patriarchal law itself, originating there in a virtual synthesis of intimacy and state policy, the private and the public, the penis and the rule of men. The regulation of men in intercourse is a prime example. It is not enough to have power as a birthright; power must be kept—over living human beings born to rebellion, arguably a human trait, certainly a human potential. The regulation of men in sex creates a seamless state of being internal and external; experienced in the world as real and imposed on the body, experienced in the body as real and imposed on the world; in the body and in the world called "nature." The restraint on men, operating inside and outside, is efficient, smart about power.[26]

The disparate voices—wrestlers, scholars, cultural critics—are wrapped in and with my own. I don't simply describe or transcribe. I create a narrative, re-presenting the wrestlers, their words and actions from within the frame of scholarly discourse, according to my own scenarios and in my own language. The practice and performance of wrestling is more than "the game"—it's a "mechanism to neutralize action" (Eco), represents the "creative power of aroused masculinity" (Geertz), acts as a kind of initiation (Turner) by which men come into a man's world (Bly), and as such carries with it homoerotic implications which are at once celebratory (Preston) and assertive of patriarchal values (Dworkin). I string together references to a wide range of philosophers, cultural critics and theorists. At times I catch myself turning to their words when my own fail. Sometimes the point is not only to contextualize my readings of wrestler culture, but more to reify and legitimize my excursion into low culture itself. Once in a while, if I am to tell the truth, I collate their words with my own simply to prove that I do more than hang out in the gym and the arena, am more than someone who stays home Saturday mornings on purpose to catch the "All-Stars." I am a real scholar. You can tell because I've read Umberto Eco.

In "Hermes' Dilemma: The Masking of Subversion in Ethnographic Description," Vincent Crapanzano considers the ways in which three ethnographers, including Clifford Geertz, interpret cultures. Crapanzano begins by citing Walter Benjamin on translation: "All translation is only a somewhat provisional way of coming to terms with the foreignness of languages"[27] and adds: "Like translation, ethnography is also a somewhat provisional way of coming to terms with the foreignness of languages—of cultures and societies. The ethnographer does not, however, translate texts the way a translator does. He must first produce them."[28]

In his essay, Crapanzano re-reads Geertz's presentation of himself as "strain[ing] to read over the shoulder" the cultural texts of the "native"[29] and recognizes the imbalance of authority implicit in Geertz's representation:

> The image is striking: sharing and not sharing a text. It represents a sort of asymmetrical we-relationship with the anthropologist behind and above the native, hidden but at the top of the hierarchy of understanding. . . . There is never an I-you relationship, a dialogue, two people next to each other reading the same text and discussing it face-to-face, but only an I-they relationship. And . . . even the I disappears—replaced by an invisible voice of authority who declares what the you-transformed-to-a-they experience.[30]

In these terms, my dialogue with, my experience of the wrestlers, whatever its imbalances and however I acknowledge its problematics, is never fully reproducible in writing.

The problem Crapanzano articulates, and what I seek to recognize without necessarily apologizing for in this essay, is explicitly connected to ideas of colonization and orientalism as developed over the past few decades. My work is inescapably situated in relation to that of the anthropologist who travels to a distant land, plants him (or her) self at the boundary of, and attempts to integrate him (or her) self into, an alien culture for a period of time, observes the natives of that alien culture in everyday and/or ritual activities, and then returns to "civilization" where he (or she) re-presents that alien culture to other, similarly positioned "scientists." It is, as it were, an act of cultural voyeurism, my own and that of the readers for whom I act as a guide.

In writing about wrestling as performance what I seek to make visible, I realize, is the nature not of wrestling but of performance. The questions I seek to answer are not those of the wrestling fan—is it "fake"—but those of the performance studies scholar—how is it constructed to look "real," what pleasures might accrue as a result of the "fake," and what values are reified in the process. I don't care if Hulk Hogan, who is uniformly derided in wrestling circles as an incompetent and massively egotistical wrestler, switches from the wwf to the wcw. I am fascinated by his phenomenal success, which I attach to the heat he generates, to the way in which he works a crowd, especially when he stays in the arena posing for photographs long after the match is over, and to the particular way in which he presents an ideal of the American man. That punches generally don't land on the opponent's face and that matches are fixed by the promoter are not interesting notions in and of themselves. How wrestlers learn to take punches and lose matches is. I am engaged in considering the cultural assumptions by which a promoter maps scenarios, the signs by which we recognize the face and the heel, and how the turn from one to the other is constructed over time. I am absorbed in the problem of understanding and explaining the ways in which wrestlers negotiate with the demand that they give ground as well as take it, especially in the context of a performance that is explicitly about masculine prowess and power. I am fascinated by the audience's apparent sophistication, by the ways in which spectators simultaneously accept both the real and the fake in what is at base a low-culture performance genre.

If I am to tell the truth about what happens when I watch wrestling and write performance, then I must admit that the experience of the wrestlers and fans is, in the end, largely irrelevant to my enterprise. I am writing towards a theory of performance, concerned with the ways in which that experience is articulated and displayed, and in its convergences with my experience of theatre and the theatrical. I am, perhaps, more like Clifford Geertz at this moment than I generally care to admit. Richard Schechner asks:

> Granted that the Balinese "use" the cockfight the way Geertz says they do (and not all those who have lived in Bali and experienced cockfighting there agree with Geertz), do they "interpret" the cockfight the way he does? That is, even if the cockfight is like *Lear,* do the Balinese believe it is like *Lear?* And if they do not, how much attention should we pay to the Balinese interpretation and how much to Geertz's? . . . Geertz has not written his interpretation at the request of the baffled Balinese driven to understand their cockfights. The Balinese are perfectly happy with things as they were ante Geertz. Also, he is writing in what is, to them, a foreign lan-

guage. His interpretation is addressed to people who cherish *Lear,* not the topeng pajegan play, *Jelantic Goes to Blambangan.*[31]

I don't deny the wrestlers and fans their separate, other experience of wrestling. But it is not mine.

When I began work on this essay it seemed most odd to consider the transaction between writer and wrestler in the same light as that between Clifford Geertz and his Balinese protagonists. After all, the map of my own daily life—until my move to New Zealand in 1994—and theirs have been convergent: Larry is now an assistant professor in sports sociology at Washington State University, after earning a doctorate at the University of Connecticut; he also did his undergraduate degree at Wesleyan, after which he taught high school social studies for several years before working on Wall Street. When Chris meets me at one of my favorite Upper West Side coffee bars to talk about wrestling, our conversation often digresses into a discussion of his girlfriend's experiences teaching at a local elementary school as well as into stories of the army and growing up in the neighborhood. Sky sets up a girl-wrestler video with a couple of budding filmmakers from SoHo and then disappears for several months, ostensibly on tour in a musical about girl wrestlers that is said by its German producers to be modeled after the Cirque du Soleil. And when not debating which bicycle to buy at the bike shop where my husband works, Johnny works for the *New York Times* and hangs out at jazz clubs in Greenwich Village.

More importantly, I have to ask, in the economy of the gym what is my authority worth? How relevant is any of this musing to those who would seem to have most at stake? To Johnny who once worried that I might reveal secrets of the game in a way that would embarrass or injure him? To Larry who wrote a dissertation about boxing from his wrestler's perspective? To Vito whose anger at being watched flared so easily and provoked this writing? A couple of years ago I offered Johnny and the others the issue of the *Drama Review* containing my first article on wrestling. I was, need-less to say, more than a little anxious. After all, not only was I discussing the game in public—a clear violation of the game's primary ethical code—but the bulk of my theoretical writing featured words like "homosocial" and "homoerotic," words that could conceivably deeply offend the men in that masculinist, fiercely heterosexist culture. It could trigger, I imagined, a response far more dangerous than mere shouting. Johnny examined the article with enthusiasm, exclaiming when he saw his name in print. Then he handed it to José, one of his students, for photocopying. That's the last I heard or saw of it. Johnny is not a stupid man; indeed, he is both smart and shrewd. And Larry is certainly capable of translating my theoretical ex-positions back into the language of the street. These men are not "natives." Or if they are, they may be seen in the light of Schechner's reading of Geertz's Balinese informants. They were, and are, simply not all that interested in what I have to say.[32]

Having problematized Geertz's reading of the Balinese cockfight as the cultural equivalent to *King Lear,* Schechner asks: "Ought Geertz, there-fore, abandon his project?"[33] I ask, if my transver-sal from watching to writing is, in essence, a be-trayal of the wrestlers' subjectivity and the codes of the game, if my writing performance ultimately misrepresents what it is the wrestlers believe they do, if what I write is, in the end, relevant only to the intellectual elite, then ought I, now, abandon *my* project? Schechner asks, "Is [Geertz's] work leading to a better understanding among peoples, or is it a further imposition of alien categories on Third World cultures?"[34] I ask, now, what does my work do? What is the point of my watching wrestling and writing performance? Schechner never gets around to answering his questions about Geertz's work. Perhaps he cannot. Perhaps the questions can only be answered with new, in-creasingly complex questions. Perhaps the ques-tions are the point.

Ideally, what I write does not simply impose an

irrelevant if sophisticated theoretical discourse on a highly popular performance genre. Nor does it elevate the form inappropriately and inauthenti-cally to the high culture status of, say, opera. Ide-ally, situated as it is at the intersection between high and low culture, what I write about wrestling leads to a better understanding of the representa-tion and transmission of cultural values in per-formance. In particular, what I write, ideally, makes visible the theatrical processes by which ideas of nationalism and masculinity are both represented and affirmed in performance, that is to say, as vis-ceral experiences between performers and spec-tators rather than as texts per se. To recognize the effective collapse of the assumed borders—geographical as well as experiential—between my life and those of the wrestlers I study is to ac-knowledge a genuine kind of "sameness" without necessarily "saming" them. To problematize the journey from experience to representation is not to obviate the results of my work. Ideally, by open-ing my own (inter)actions to examination my the-ories of masculinity as performed in popular cul-ture are amplified without being nullified. In interrogating my position in the exchange, my writing potentially acquires the force of truth-telling in a way that "objectivity" and "authority" as a rule seek to mask. Ironically, in revealing my-self as short, round and female, I may attain the musculature—at least in abstraction—that is otherwise denied to me.

A final anecdote: several weeks after my run-in with Vito I found myself sitting ringside with the men watching several female body builders struggle to learn enough moves to make the "girl-wrestler" video convincing. In the ring with the women, one of the wrestlers—Chris—was working very hard to show them how to make their holds and throws as authentic-looking as possible given their lack of training. Perched on the turnbuckles were two skinny film-student types who periodically framed the women with their hands in true movie-director-cliché-style and urged: "Show her your

(top to bottom)

Chris gives Sarah a lesson in being pinned as Deb observes and the men at Gleason's watch. Photograph by Sharon Mazer.

Deb "dominates" Sarah. The men watch. Photograph by Sharon Mazer.

The "girl wrestlers" square off. The men watch. Photograph by Sharon Mazer.

contempt, Deb!" and "Strut your stuff, Sky!" Also watching the women, opposite us at ringside, were most of the other men in the gym, the boxers, clearly titillated by the display. As I sat there next to Larry, Vito, Rubio, Frankie, Mohammed, and the others, I sensed that something had shifted, if only for a moment. Each prompting from the "directors," each rejoinder from the boxers on the other side of the ring, brought a smile from the wrestlers, a smile that was shared with me. Afterward, Larry and Chris explicitly included me in their conversation with the women, asking me to affirm their judgment that Deb in particular, if properly coached, could be quite successful as a wrestler. For a moment, and without getting my face pushed to the mat, I felt that I was indeed in on the game. And after the day's session was over, I accepted Johnny's offer of a ride back to the city, found a coffee bar, pulled out my notebook, and began to write.

Notes

1 To "job" in wrestlers' parlance is to be hired on a per-match basis to lose to the circuit's stars. Some wrestlers, such as Barry Horowitz in the WWF, have spent years and built entire careers as jobbers. It is interesting to note that, having built a considerable following of his own, Barry Horowitz at the time of this writing wrestles as a star. Located at the edge of the Brooklyn side of the East River, Gleason's Gym is best-known for producing world-class boxers.

2 A "monster" is what other wrestlers call a very big wrestler.

3 "The Doggie Doggie World of Professional Wrestling," in *The Drama Review* 34(4) (winter 1990). See also "In Search of the 'Morality' in Professional Wrestling's All-American Play," presented at the meeting of the Association for Theatre in Higher Education/American Theatre and Drama Society (Chicago, 1990), and "From Beefcake to Cheesecake: The Appearance of Women in Professional Wrestling," presented at the meeting of the Association for Theatre in Higher Education/Women and Theatre Program (Seattle, 1991). A version of this chapter was first presented at the annual meeting of the Association for Theatre in Higher Education/Perfor-

mance Studies (San Francisco, 1995) and appears in *"Real" Wrestling: Professional Sport/Theatrical Spectacle* (Jackson: University Press of Mississippi, 1998). For an alternative personal account of an academic's journey into the world of professional wrestling, see Jim Freedman, *Drawing Heat* (Windsor, Ont.: Black Moss Press, 1988). For an academic reading of wrestling from a distance, see Gerald W. Morton and George M. O'Brien, *Wrestling to Rasslin: Ancient Sport to American Spectacle* (Bowling Green, Ohio: Bowling Green State University Popular Press, 1985).

4 Definitions of "the game" are rather ambiguous, implying both the sport and the con. Superficially, to be "in on the game" means to understand the moves and the way they are combined in performance. But the rules by which the performance is constructed, in particular how the wrestlers win and lose, are what really constitute "the game."

5 A "youngster" is someone new to the game, generally but not always young.

6 To "shoot" a match is to cross over the line from the rules of exchange into a "real" fight.

7 I am indebted to my colleague Peter Falkenberg (University of Canterbury) for his observation that my watching wrestlers can be considered an illicit activity, as such more like watching a peepshow than watching a play on Broadway. I must also acknowledge Robert Vorlicky (New York University) who, several years ago, persisted in questioning me about the sexual implications of my watching wrestling.

8 Elizabeth Grosz calls sexuality a "slippery and ambiguous term." Her recognition, in the context of philosophical history, that sexual difference is "a mobile, indeed volatile, concept, able to insinuate itself into regions where it should have no place, to make itself, if not invisible, then at least unrecognizable in its influences and effects" is no less apt in the wrestlers' gym (*Volatile Bodies: Toward a Corporeal Feminism* [Bloomington: Indiana University Press, 1994], viii-ix).

9 Again I must thank Peter Falkenberg for this observation.

10 Here I must add my appreciation to Richard Schechner who edited and published my first essay on wrestling for the *Drama Review*.

11 "To anyone who has been in Bali any length of time, the deep psychological identification of Balinese men with their cocks is unmistakable. The double entendre here is deliberate. It works in exactly the same way in Balinese as it does in English, even to producing the same

tired jokes, strained puns, and uninventive obscenities" (Clifford Geertz, *The Interpretation of Cultures* [New York: Basic Books, 1973], 417). Or, as the Red Rooster, a star in the wwf for several years, used to crow: "Poultry in motion!"

12   James Clifford, "On Ethnographic Allegory," in *Writing Culture: The Poetics and Politics of Ethnography,* ed. James Clifford and George E. Marcus (Berkeley: University of California Press, 1986), 15.

13   Women wrestlers are commonly referred to as "girl wrestlers," with no insult intended.

14   Particular thanks are due to Bob Vorlicky and Peter Falkenberg for pushing me to explore my position in this exchange seriously, to Bob for forcing me to admit to the sexual tensions inherent in my watching, and to Peter for calling what I do while watching "peeping" and while writing "gossiping."

15   Richard Schechner, *Between Theatre and Anthropology* (Philadelphia: University of Pennsylvania Press, 1985), 25.

16   Renato Rosaldo, *Culture and Truth: The Remaking of Social Analysis* (Boston: Beacon Press, 1989), 169.

17   The "babyface," often referred to simply as the "face," wrestles as the good guy; the "heel" as the bad guy. Matches rarely pit face against face, or heel against heel, but scenarios often anticipate or feature what is known as a "face turn" or "heel turn" in which a face or heel converts himself, or is transformed by events, into the opposite type. Such turns, if well set up and staged, generate tremendous "heat" and are at the heart of the wrestling event. "Exchanges" are the reversals between winning and losing within matches. "Heat" is the energy provoked in the audience. An example of "cheap heat" often used by the wrestlers is the waving of a flag—American to signal face status, Russian or Canadian to signal heel status. Once at a match in Brooklyn I saw a girl wrestler named Linda Dallas grab the microphone and shout "Brooklyn sucks" as she was introduced. Cheap or not, it was certainly effective.

18   *Brecht on Theatre: The Development of an Aesthetic,* ed. and trans. John Willett (New York: Hill and Wang, 1964), 6.

19   It must be noted that Barthes and Carter have written brilliant essays on wrestling in their own right, see Barthes, "The World of Wrestling," in *Mythologies,* trans. Annette Lavers (1957; New York: Hill and Wang, 1972), and Carter, "Giants' Playtime," *New Society* 29 (January 1976): 227–28.

20   Schechner, *Between Theatre and Anthropology,* 23.

21   Umberto Eco, *Travels in Hyperreality,* trans. William Weaver (1967; Orlando, FL: Harcourt, Brace, Jovanovich, 1986), 161.

22   Geertz, *The Interpretation of Cultures,* 420–21.

23   Victor Turner, *From Ritual to Theatre: The Human Seriousness of Play* (New York: paj Publications, 1982), 25.

24   Robert Bly, *Iron John: A Book about Men* (Reading, MA: Addison-Wesley, 1990), 15.

25   John Preston, "The Theatre of Sexual Initiation," in *Gender in Performance: The Presentation of Difference in the Performing Arts,* ed. Laurence Senelick (Hanover, NH: University Press of New England, 1992), 332.

26   Andrea Dworkin, *Intercourse* (New York: Free Press, 1987), 158–59.

27   Walter Benjamin, *Illuminations,* ed. Hannah Arendt, trans. Harry Zohn (New York: Schocken, 1969), 75.

28   Vincent Crapanzano, "Hermes' Dilemma: The Masking of Subversion in Ethnographic Description," in *Writing Culture: The Poetics and Politics of Ethnography,* ed. Clifford and Marcus, 51.

29   Ibid., 74 (citing Geertz, *The Interpretation of Cultures,* 452).

30   Ibid.

31   Schechner, *Between Theatre and Anthropology,* 309–10.

32   It has been suggested to me by Rosemary Du Plessis (University of Canterbury) that, given professional wrestling's self-conscious occupation of the boundary between the fake and the real, wrestlers might be less concerned with the relative authenticity of my representation of their culture. They are not, after all, an indigenous peoples struggling to establish an authentic identity against that imposed from outside by the colonizer. I am not certain this explains the wrestlers' indifference to my writing so much as it points to the problematic implicit in considering my work with wrestlers in the same light as Geertz's with the Balinese.

33   Schechner, *Between Theatre and Anthropology,* 310.

34   Ibid.

Mae West's Maids: Race, "Authenticity," and the Discourse of Camp

Pamela Robertson Wojcik

In recent years, subcultural studies have merged increasingly with academic identity politics. But while much work has been done on queer and camp representation and also on racial stereotypes, subcultural studies have unwittingly advanced artificial barriers between audiences and between subcultures. We tend to talk about only one audience, one subculture, one difference at a time, and only in relation to the in-that-instance Other, dominant culture. Most analyses of camp do not, therefore, remark upon the relation between camp's sexual politics and race discourse. Moe Meyer, for instance, discusses the controversy over African American drag queen Joan Jett Blak's 1991 bid for mayor of Chicago as Queer Nation candidate exclusively in terms of gay debates about the effectiveness of camp; Meyer never mentions Blak's race as potentially affecting the debate nor examines Queer Nation's political stakes in running an African American drag queen.[1]

Alternately, in discussions of *Paris Is Burning*—a film that foregrounds the links between queerness, camp, and racial discourse—critics tend to treat the African American and Hispanic use of camp to gain access to fantasies of whiteness as a special case. Such critiques never fully acknowledge the degree to which the film's invocation of "realness" testifies to inextricable links between race and sex and never consider whether or how race discourse operates in camp generally. An important exception is bell hooks's essay "Is Paris Burning?" hooks views the film as

> a graphic documentary of the way in which colonized black people (in this case black gay brothers, some of whom were drag queens) worship at the throne of whiteness, even when such worship demands that we live in perpetual self-hate, steal, lie, go hungry, and even die in pursuit.[2]

However, hooks claims that rather than interrogating whiteness, the entertainment value of the film obscures its "more serious critical narrative," a narrative of the pain and sadness behind the camp spectacles. For hooks, the white filmmaker and white audience both evade the race politics of *Paris Is Burning* in their focus on and pleasure in the film's camp effect. But, by mapping the relationship between the film's race politics and its camp effect onto a narrative vs. spectacle paradigm, hooks similarly masks the link between race and camp in the film. She suggests that the film is *really* about race and *not* camp. She therefore maintains the barrier between race discourse and camp discourse by viewing camp spectacle as being in the service of white pleasure and at a remove from "the more serious narrative" about blackness.

Most discussions of camp, whether about gay men, lesbians, or heterosexuals, assume the adjective "white." Because whiteness, as Richard Dyer says, "secures its dominance by seeming not to be anything in particular," representations of normative whiteness foreground race and ethnicity as categories of difference.[3] Queer and camp Western representations, though nonnormative in terms of sex and gender, are still consistently defined through categories of racial difference and especially blackness.

This racial specificity becomes clear in the frequent analogies made between camp and blackness. Dennis Altman, for instance, says, "Camp is to gay what soul is to black."[4] Describing post-Stonewall attitudes toward camp, Andrew Ross refers to camp falling into disrepute "as a kind of blackface," and George Melly dubs camp "the Stepin Fetchit of the leather bars, the Auntie Tom of the denim discos."[5] We could ask why Uncle Tom and blackface haven't been recuperated as camp clearly has (by queer identity politics and in academic discourse). If this question seems problematic, and it should, it points out how thin these analogies are, and it also points to the fact that the flexibility of sex and gender roles promised by theories of camp performativity does not yet extend to race. In part these analogies suggest, as David Bergman says, the fact that camp raises the issues of any minority culture—issues having to do with appropriation, representation, and difference.[6] But the consistency with which the category "black" is posed as the counterpart to camp not only signals the degree to which camp is assumed to be white but also mirrors the way tropes of blackness often operate in white camp as an authenticating discourse.

This essay focuses on Mae West and how she enlists racial difference in the service of queer performativity. Elsewhere, I have argued that West created a form of feminist camp through her dual appropriations of the live entertainment traditions of female impersonation and female burlesque. My interest in that earlier essay was in locating the role women have played as producers and consumers of camp, "to de-essentialize the link between gay men and camp, which reifies both camp and gay male taste; and to underline camp's potential for asserting the overlapping interests of gay men and women, lesbian and straight."[7] Like other theorists of camp, I ignored the racial specificity of West's queer and feminist performativity. Emphasizing how West forged a feminist camp character from gay male and heterosexual female traditions, I dodged the question of how West's simultaneous appropriation of African American music and her characters' interactions with African American performers complicated or delimited the flexible and porous model of queer identity I saw in West's films. Yet, neither aberrant nor exceptional, West's use of blackness as an authenticating discourse runs through most white camp and needs to be taken into account to fully understand camp.

This chapter, then, attempts to correct or complement my previous analysis of West. Hopefully, however, this essay can do more than fill a gap in my analysis and will instead provide a point of entry into a discussion of the seemingly contradictory reliance in camp and queer discourse on tropes of racial authenticity; I hope this essay will enable us to rethink how camp codes of sex and gender intersect with racial codes. Using West as a point of departure, then, this essay examines the racial dimension of camp, considering (1) how tropes of blackness are used in camp performance; (2) the degree to which the camp spectator is textually constructed as white; and (3) how a consideration of an African American spectatorial position modifies our understanding of camp practice.

Little Eva

In his piece on West, John Kobal mentions that West's earliest theatrical experiences were as Little Eva in *Uncle Tom's Cabin* and as a "coon shouter." Kobal mistakenly identifies "coon shouter" as an old vaudeville term for African American singers who perform for white audiences not in blackface or whiteface, but "as themselves." In fact, the term "coon shouter" or "coon singer" was used to describe white, often Jewish, performers like Fanny Brice, Sophie Tucker, Eddie Cantor, and Al Jolson, who sang, not only in Negro dialect, but also in blackface.[8] Eliding the links between "coon shouting" and blackface, as well as the links to Jewish entertainment traditions, and aligning it instead with African American performers, Kobal describes the "Mae West character" as "the first white woman with a black soul." And he wistfully posits the unfounded assertion that West has "a touch of colour in her blood."[9] Thus, in Kobal's narrative, West is identified simultaneously with the white child Harriet Beecher Stowe says is representative of her race, with black singers, and with blackness itself. If we take into account the more accurate definition of "coon shouting," Kobal's narrative also links West with blackface. If camp is, as Melly says, an "Auntie Tom," it may be appropriate to think of West as camp's Little Eva, Tom's dearest friend; but, more importantly, I want to use Kobal's odd narrative to suggest that the Mae West character is not just a white woman with a black soul, but manages to be representative of her race and of camp style because she identifies so closely with blackness and especially black music.

Kobal's account differs from most accounts of West's early career, which tend to focus on her role as Little Lord Fauntleroy and suggest that she dropped her imitation of black styles when she adopted the style of female impersonation and white female burlesque. However, as much as West aligned herself with gay male culture both by borrowing aspects of gay style and by writing antihomophobic plays about gay life, she also aligned herself with African American culture. In addition to her potential cross-sex, cross-gender identification as a female female impersonator, West also participates in complicated cross-racial identifications with blackness which are key to her transgressive image.

As Kobal suggests, West appropriated black musical styles and she also adopted the shimmy after seeing it in a Harlem nightspot. In addition, she wrote a novel, *The Constant Sinner*, about an interracial love affair. According to Clarence Muse, West gave him money for an antilynching campaign. West frequently featured African American performers in her films, including Louis Armstrong, Hazel Scott, and Duke Ellington, whose band she forced Paramount to sign for *Belle of the Nineties*. And West garnered extremely positive receptions in the African American press. One article in *The Chicago Defender*, for instance, applauds her for being more attentive to the African American journalists than Hazel Scott, who is accused of being "high hat" with them.[10]

But, although West affiliated herself with black performers, and, to a degree, race issues, the roles of African Americans in her films are still quite limited. The musical performers in her films do not figure in the plot and are typical of African American specialty acts in Hollywood films. The African Americans who do figure prominently in her films play maids and include Gertrude Howard, Louise Beavers, Hattie McDaniel, and Libby Taylor, who played the role both on and off screen for West. Their representations are stereotypical. As Donald Bogle describes them: "The domestics were always overweight, middle-aged, and made up as jolly aunt jemimas . . . they had the usual names: Pearl, Beulah, and Jasmine. Their naive blackness generally was used as a contrast to Mae West's sophisticated whiteness."[11] West employs racist language with her maids, calling them Eightball and Shadow, for instance, or accusing them of being slow and lazy, but the maids are also pictured as confidantes and trusted good friends, in a manner similar to movies like Jean Harlow's *Bombshell*, *Imitation of Life*, Shirley Temple movies, and others in the 1930s, a decade Bogle tags "the Age of the Negro Servant."

Bogle claims that because West's barely concealed status as a prostitute places her at the bottom of the social scale, she enjoys a livelier camaraderie with her black maids than with white women. Bogle is correct that West's friendly interactions with her maids can be read as a class affiliation but the camaraderie West enjoys with her black maids differs not only from her interactions with upper class white women (who are often failed rivals) but also from her interactions with other subordinate women, with whom she also shares her low social status.

In her films, West's interactions with other female characters are mediated by both class and race. As James Snead suggests, "insofar as all of West films are about consolidating women's power in spite of a limited social context," she achieves a greater rapport with lower class women of all races than with upper-class women.[12] West's character frequently functions as counselor to subordinate women, like the fallen white Sally in *She Done Him Wrong* whom she counsels on men ("Men's all alike . . . it's their game. I happen to be smart enough to play it their way") and whose shame she ameliorates with the worldly wisdom that "when women go wrong, men go right after 'em." Similarly, in *Belle of the Nineties,* when her African American maid, Libby (Taylor), asks, "What kind of husband do you think I should get," West advises her, "Why don't you take a single man, and leave the husbands alone?" In *Klondike Annie,* West helps her Chinese maid, Fah Wong, played by Soo Yong, escape to her lover, and even speaks Chinese with her. In West's interactions with Fah Wong, however, there is none of the joking and play West enjoys with her black maids. This is true also of her interactions with her French maid in *The Heat's On* and Native American servants in *Goin' to Town.* In contrast to these relationships, West's connection with her African American maids signals not only a class affiliation but also West's identification with, and privileging of, tropes of blackness.

One scene in *I'm No Angel* shows West bantering and singing "I Found a New Way to Go to Town" with four maids. The five women discuss West's character Tira's whirlwind romance with Kirk Lawrence, the gifts he's given her, Tira's sexual attractiveness to men, and the kind of men the maids like. The maids serve, as Bogle says, as "foils," straight (wo)men and yes (wo)men, "paying homage to the supreme power of their white mistress." The scene thematizes the class affiliation Bogle describes. From her position as a cooch dancer in the circus who imitates the Harlem shimmy, as West herself did, Tira, "the girl who discovered you don't have to have feet to be a dancer," has risen to become a lion tamer in a high-hat circus. In her new penthouse apartment, she first mistakenly assumes that the doorbell signals a house detective, then must be reminded by her maid Beulah to call Kirk's gift of diamonds a "necklace" rather than "beads."

Still, barking orders to the four maids as she talks with them (famously, "Beulah, peel me a grape"), West is clearly the boss and center of attention. The maids frame her and set off her whiteness as well as the whiteness of the room. West's glowing whiteness is carefully constructed here and throughout her career. In a TV documentary about West, Herbert Kenwith claims that white women in West's stage shows were required to have dark hair, to wear darker make-up and clothes than West, and even to put a grey gel on their teeth, so that West's whiteness would make her stand out as the star and center of attention.[13]

West's conversation with her black maids, however, masks racial difference by focusing on gender. West talks about men, sex, and clothing, and treats Libby Taylor's comment that she likes "dark men" not as a given, but much like her own quip that she likes two kind of men, "domestic and foreign." Snead describes a similar moment later in the film:

> So when West looks over her shoulder and says, referring to Cary Grant, "My man's got rhythm," and the giggling black maids say "Yes'm, I knows what you mean," West commits a certain breech of racial taboos in order to share both the terminology and presumably the content of sexual secrets of white and black male "rhythm."[14]

West thus simultaneously foregrounds her racial difference from the maids and her gendered identification with them. Stuart Hall describes this double move of "othering" and identification as typical of racist discourse—a complex play of repulsion and attraction combining racial insult with racial envy, one marked by the "surreptitious return of desire."[15] In his analysis of the racial politics of blackface, Eric Lott describes this "complex dialectic" as "a pattern at times amounting to no more than two faces of our particular mode of racism, at others gesturing toward a specific kind of political or sexual danger; and all of it comprising a peculiarly American structure of racial feeling."[16] *I'm No Angel*, like other camp uses of blackness, constructs a porous and mobile queer identity through this double move of othering and identification.

Queen B

West's homosocial bonding with her maids might be readable as homosexual, if we consider Linda Nochlin's point that in painting "the conjunction of black and white, or dark and light female bodies, whether naked or in the guise of mistress or maidservant traditionally signified lesbianism."[17] This potential homosexuality is raised obliquely when one of the maids (whose face we never see and who isn't identified in the credits) says, "Well, men don't mean a *thing* to me." The homosexual connotations feed off the contrast between the women, but also depends on the way the scene portrays the maids as West's back-up singers. McDaniel and Taylor not only sing along to "I Found a New Way to Go to Town" with West, but also dance across the room following West's lead.

In his analysis of the mythology of the back-up singer, John Corbett claims that, while the role of the back-up singer has historically been filled by male and female performers of all races and ethnicities, the unspoken adjectives that precede the mythologized stereotype of the "back-up singer" are always "black" and "female" and that the unspoken adjectives preceding "lead singer" in stereotypical configurations of "lead" and "back-up" are "white male."[18] Kaja Silverman argues that West's voice is coded masculine, an assertion in line with those who see West's persona as masculine.[19] West's presumed masculinity is, however, mediated by her imitation of female impersonators and is a self-conscious feminine masquerade that plays masculine and feminine codes against each other. And, similarly, her whiteness is mediated through and constituted by her imitation of black female musical styles.

Ramona Curry, in line with Kobal, notes that as a stage performer, West adopted a style of singing characteristic of "dirty blues," similar to that of Ma Rainey and Bessie Smith, and maintained this style in a somewhat modified, censored, form in her films. West's performance of "dirty blues," according to Curry, associates West in the public mind with "the unbound sexual behavior that the dominant U.S. society frequently attributes to lower class African Americans."[20] Once established, West's association with working-class black female sexuality carries over, regardless of what she sings.

In appropriating a black female blues style, West takes on the persona of what Hazel Carby refers to as the "mythologized" blues singer, and embraces "an oral and musical woman's culture that explicitly addresses the contradictions of feminism, sexuality, and power." Carby describes women's blues of the 1920s and 1930s as "a discourse that articulates a cultural and political struggle over sexual relations":

> a struggle that is directed against the objectification of female sexuality within a patriarchal order but which also tries to reclaim women's bodies as the sexual and sensuous subjects of women's song.[21]

West's performance of blues inflected songs across her films not only aligns her with black female working-class sexuality, but also enables her to address her position as a sexual subject and object in much the same way as the direct sexuality of female burlesque.

Not coincidentally, as Carby points out, the figure of the black female blues singer whose style West appropriates was historically transplanted into the figure of the black maid, as many female blues singers, including Hattie McDaniel and Ethel Waters, moved from making race records into film careers and maid roles. Rather than a white male lead, West, coded as simultaneously a female impersonator and a black woman, backed-up and fawned over by the maids, plays the Queen-B or Bulldagger, a figure SDiane Bogus claims is common in and peculiar to African American lesbian fiction and culture, a "female blues singer who bonds with other women." The Queen-B was "a central figure in the community at large" whose sway over her followers relates both to her singing and her unorthodox sexuality.[22]

Crucially, the Queen B requires an adoring audience. And in West's films, her sexuality is typically performed *for an audience* whose attention, approval and admiration she explicitly seeks when she says, "Here goes my big moment" and "How'm I doin'?" In *I'm No Angel,* West's encounter with Cary Grant requires the presence of her maids who (1) stand in for the film audience, (2) underscore West's sexuality as a form of masquerade, and (3) offer an alternative site for West's desire as she diverts our attention, and Grant's, to the maids, whom she proclaims to be "great gals." I am not suggesting that the Mae West character be read as a closet lesbian. Rather, West's lively homosociality with her maids, in conjunction with her affinity for African American music and her association with female impersonation, marks her sexuality as particularly fluid and deeply transgressive, not merely ironic. As Snead claims, "If some white actresses derive their aura of purity and chasteness by their opposition to the dark and earthly maids who surround them, then West's image benefits by her kinship with, rather than her difference from, the same kinds of figures."[23] West masks racial difference through a seemingly race-neutral gendered discourse and simultaneously reinscribes that difference through the maids' support for her camp performance and authentication of her racial impersonation.

West's sexual and racial identifications are fluid (she is white and black, male and female, gay and straight). However, the maids necessarily remain static markers (black and female) of her transcendence (they set off her whiteness and potential masculinity, authenticate her blackness, foreground her sexuality). West uses camp to theatricalize sex and gender roles to reveil their constructedness, yet she depends on her maids' stable identities to do so, underlining Hortense Spillers's suggestion that there are at least two female genders, one white and one black.[24] The racial difference ultimately remains in place. Although West is *like* a black woman, she is not one. Her transracial mobility merely reaffirms her whiteness. This whiteness, constituted through its appropriation of and difference from blackness, is neither a color nor the absence of color, both impervious to racial markers and able to absorb them.

The Real West

At the same time, West's identification with blackness sometimes goes against the grain of camp, suggesting the possibility that West might have an "authentic" self beneath or behind the discourses of camp and masquerade. As trusted good friends, the maids are pictured as knowing the real West better than anybody else. West, in effect, lets her hair down with them, and tells them her true feelings. In *I'm No Angel,* West's Tira never tells Cary Grant that she loves him. Instead, he finds out from Gertrude Howard's Beulah, who testifies in a breach of promise suit that Tira said "she never knew she could love a man like she loves him." West also uses the "authenticity" of African American music to portray her true feelings.

When West performs African American styles of music, she updates the burlesque tradition of minstrelsy. Performing blackness, but without blackface, West, in John Szwed's terms, "marks the detachment of culture from race and the almost full absorption of a black tradition into white culture."[25] Almost. What's crucial is that the black tradition still be marked as "other." While commodifying African American community life and culture, minstrelization requires that the commodity still signifies blackness to the consumer. In West's films, this is signified and authenticated by the presence of African American performers.

As is common in the musical, West's numbers are often keyed to her characters' moods and situations. In *Belle of the Nineties,* for instance, she plays a woman, Ruby Carter, who moves from St. Louis to New Orleans to forget an old lover. She sings "Memphis Blues" and "My Old Flame" with the Duke Ellington band. More striking, and unusual for West, is her rendition of "Troubled Waters" in the same film. This number is the only time in her films West sings a song without a diegetic audience. Prior to the number, Ruby explains to her maid Jasmine (Libby Taylor) why she has an unfair reputation as a bad woman: "You know, people get reputations from people talking about people when they don't even know the people." Giving Jasmine the rest of the night off to attend a prayer meeting, Ruby provides her money for the collection and tells her to pray for her. Then, after Jasmine leaves, Ruby is drawn to the balcony to listen to the revivalists at the prayer meeting sing "Pray Chill-en and You'll Be Saved."

Karl Struss films the revival meeting in an expressionistic style reminiscent of Vidor's *Hallelujah* (1929). After a verse of "Pray Chill-en," the scene cuts back to West who sings a verse of "Troubled Waters." The lyrics of "Troubled Waters" repeat the sentiments West has previously expressed to her maid:

> They say that I'm one of those devil's daughters.
> They look at me with scorn. I'll never hear that horn.
> I'll be underneath the water judgement morn-ing.
> Oh Lord, am I to blame? Must I bow my head in shame?
> If people go 'round scandalizing my name?

Rather than simply present West singing "Troubled Waters" as reflecting her state of mind, this scene uses intercutting and dissolves to link her song with the revival meeting. Jon Tuska describes the scene:

> The beat of the spiritual is merged with hers in a fused counterpoint. By means of complex process shots, double exposures, and superimposed images, Karl Struss pictorially integrates for McCarey the sequences of Ruby's song with the Negro chant. As it becomes increasingly wild, there are sudden close-ups on faces, feverish dancing, the torchlit scene backlighted from reflections from the river. Struss brings off a split-screen effect with the revellers, one half their dancing, one half the reflection of their dancing. Ruby's image is superimposed over this. Her song rises and blends with the jazz spiritual, only to drown it out on the soundtrack, hitting a single pitch as the camera pans a succession of grotesque faces.[26]

At the very end, one male revivalist in closeup drowns out the two songs with his chant of "My soul's on fire, my soul's on fire." While the song is private and reflects Ruby's interiority, it depends on the external presence of the black revivalists. Her song functions as a call and response with the revivalists' song. This marks West as authentic in a double sense. First, the revival meeting provides a back-up for West, who is visually and sonically inserted into the meeting. Her song's fusion with the "jazz spiritual" lends it the presumed authenticity and spirituality of African American religion and music, despite the fact that the song "Troubled Waters," though explicitly coded as an African American spiritual, was written for West by the Hollywood songwriting team of Johnston and Coslow. Second, the intercutting suggests that the out of control revivalists ("souls on fire") are reacting to her scene. It sets up a contrast between her individual controlled whiteness and the familiar stereotype of the frenzied emotions and spirituality of the African Americans; it thus sets West's character off as an individual, a white angel, authentic in the sense of belonging to oneself.

Imagining the Audience

West's affiliation with African American culture underscores her identification with the marginal and her status as a transgressive woman within mainstream representations of sexuality. It also authenticates her identity—an identity that is particularly porous, fluid, and mobile, but nonetheless whole. Within camp representation (and, of course, in other arenas as well), her use of blackness for authentication is quite typical. As critics' frequent analogies between blackness and camp indicate, tropes of authenticity and "realness" operate both within camp discourse and within academic identity politics. Representations of queer white subjectivity are constituted, in large part, by their constant coupling with, and contrast to, images and sounds of blackness.

Lott views the double move of othering and identification in blackface minstrelsy as a "peculiarly American structure of racial feeling" but the use of blackness as an authenticating discourse has become part of a transnational camp aesthetic. To cite a few brief examples, Madonna, clearly, foregrounds her affinity with African American culture as much as with gay male culture. Consider her video for "Like a Prayer," where images of black religion authenticate her passion, or "Vogue" where she sings "It doesn't matter if you're black or white, a boy or a girl," all the while obscuring vogueing's racial and homosexual specificity. In a different vein, Joan Crawford's status as a grotesque is reaffirmed by her performance in blackface in *Torch Song*. Similarly, as Patricia Juliana Smith argues, Dusty Springfield's camp masquerade transforms her into simultaneously a black woman and a femme gay man; and Ronald Firbank's novels, according to William Lane Clark, tie their camp effect to representations of transracial desire and the employment of black jazz tropes in much the same manner as Fassbinder does in *The Bitter Tears of Petra Von Kant, Ali: Fear Eats the*

Soul, and other films.[27] Elsewhere, I have described how the Australian film *The Adventures of Priscilla, Queen of the Desert* privileges its scenes with Aboriginal people—in stark contrast to its scenes with the Filipino bride or butch white woman—a transnational example of camp's reliance on black imagery and stereotypes.[28]

Often, in these examples, by no means meant to be exhaustive, an appreciative black diegetic audience is inscribed as both spectator and back-up for the white performers. I've described how this audience supports West and stands in for the film audience in its appreciation of West's camp masquerade in *I'm No Angel*. Similarly, in *The Adventures of Priscilla, Queen of the Desert,* Aboriginal people not only perform African American blues for (and, in the case of one man, lipsynch with) the white men, but also form the most enthusiastically appreciative audience for the white drag act. They thus authenticate the group's act and their gayness which, in turn, lends the Aboriginal people an aura of "coolness" denied to various groups of white rednecks elsewhere in the film. The African American gospel singers in Madonna's "Like a Prayer" video perform a similar function, backing up and seeming to respond to Madonna's performed identification with blackness.

Although these black diegetic audiences stand in for the film audience, blackness's authenticating discourse seems to be addressed primarily to a white film audience. Rather than provide points of identification for the audience, these supportive audiences primarily produce a spectacle of spectatorship that situates the white performer within a black context; such images authenticate the white performer's performance as not only imitative of black culture but also appreciated by a black audience. But what difference would it make to our conception of camp to imagine the external audience for these various texts as black instead of white?

To begin to address this question, my discussion will take a short detour through *Without You I'm Nothing*, the 1990 film version of Sandra Bernhard's 1988 one-woman off-Broadway stage show. The film operates on the premise that Bernhard has gotten away from her "roots" and that she has returned with her show to Los Angeles to perform in a mostly black nightclub. Rather than an authenticating back-up and appreciative audience for Bernhard's camp appropriations of blackness, the mostly black audience is represented as singularly bored by Bernhard's performance. By placing the show in a black nightclub, the film, for Jean Walton, shifts the "emphasis from issues of gender and sexuality to issues of race." [29] But camp is always already about race, and the film *Without You I'm Nothing* uses the black audience's unenthusiastic reaction to create feelings of spectatoral discomfort.

In various segments, Bernhard performs a minstrelization of blackness without blackface. In her first number, for instance, she imitates and appropriates the music of Nina Simone. Wearing an African costume, she sings "Four Women," the first line of which is "my skin is black." She also parodies Diana Ross, Dionne Warwick, and Prince as well as various unspecified images of blackness (a "pretty" lesbian nightclub singer who sings "Me and Mrs. Jones," a "funked up" version of white Patti Smith). Seeing these appropriations in the context of the black nightclub, the film viewer feels embarrassed and uncomfortable and cannot respond with camp pleasure.

The film also includes scenes of a character, whom the credits name as Roxanne, played by African American model Cynthia Bailey. Roxanne "enigmatically haunts the margins of the film until she enters the space of the performance as the last and only member of the audience at the end." [30] As Lauren Berlant and Elizabeth Freeman point out, she "personifies authenticity." [31] Roxanne serves as a potential object of desire and double for Bernhard throughout the film. In

Berlant and Freeman's account, she "perpetuates the historic burden black women in cinema have borne to represent embodiment, desire, and the dignity of suffering on behalf of white women." [32] At the end, Bernhard looks to Roxanne for approval after performing a striptease to "Little Red Corvette," and Roxanne rejects her, writing "Fuck Sandra Bernhard" in lipstick on her tablecloth before exiting into blinding white light.

Bernhard's show is also about being Jewish and female and includes monologues that fantasize about a WASP existence—as an attractive preppy named Babe on Christmas Eve and a Mary Tyler Moore-ish existence as an executive secretary who marries her boss. These monologues, like the show's use of 1970s pop music, depend on the viewer's recognition of and identification with their fantasies. But the "me too" of identification is blocked by the viewer's recognition that the members of the nightclub audience do not share this "me too" response.

The film creates a distance between our imagination of Bernhard's "successful" stage show and her "failure" here by "othering" the L.A. audience as racially different from both the New York audience and the film audience. It enacts the split between white camp pleasure and a "more serious narrative" about race which bell hooks descibes. The film viewer's experience is distracted and divided. The film viewer senses the difference between Bernhard's "summer of success" playing to a presumably mostly white hip New York audience (filled with white stars like Liza Minnelli) and her failure to engage this diegetic black audience. While recognizing how Bernhard's camp performance might have worked for a white audience, the viewer also guiltily recognizes how it can't work for a black audience.

Ironically, but not surprisingly, the film's deconstruction of whiteness could be seen as authenticating the "real" Bernhard for black and white audiences, showing the comedian to be self-

reflective about the racial dynamic of her character "Sandra's" appropriations of blackness. Z. Isiling Nataf writes:

> The film speaks to black audiences about an ending
> of the fraud of white supremacist myths and de-
> grading black stereotypes. It speaks to white audi-
> ences, the new generation of whom have grown up
> in a miscegenated and multicultural world, through
> the media if not in their own neighbourhoods, and
> a hope for resolving the 'racial gap which they don't
> feel responsible for.' And it does so by crossing over,
> by loving instead of fearing blackness, by having
> black heroes, by refusing racism, and ultimately by
> embracing African-American culture which is all
> Americans' culture.[33]

Given the unidirectional crossover she describes and its similarity to minstrelsy and other
appropriations of blackness in American culture
(including the hero worship of African American
sports stars), Nataf's view seems utopian at best.
To me, the film's deconstruction of whiteness still
seems to be geared toward a white audience. The
film creates the shock of displeasure by forcing a
critical recognition of blackness's frequent use in
camp as an authenticating discourse. But this
shock is still mediated through the authenticating
black presence of the on-screen audience and the
figure of Roxanne.

On the surface, *Without You I'm Nothing*'s en-
coding of a critical African American response to
the white star's appropriation of blackness may
seem more subversive than *I'm No Angel*, which
depicts the African American response to West's
similar appropriations as affirmative and supportive. But *Without You I'm Nothing* still locates camp
pleasure strictly in the white star's persona, reen-
acting hooks's split between white camp pleasure
and a "more serious" race narrative. *I'm No Angel*,
however, suggests the possibility of an alternate
mode of camp pleasure available to an African
American audience.

Reading the maids' performances as camp re-

quires shifting the viewer's emphasis from the
film's presumed center (West) to the film's presumed margins (McDaniel, Beavers, Taylor, and
the unnamed African American actress). Arthur
Knight's work on African American constructions
of stardom between 1925 and 1945 is helpful here.[34]
Drawing on the writings of James Baldwin, Richard Wright, bell hooks, and Ralph Ellison, as well
as contemporary responses to Hollywood in the
African American press, Knight suggests that black
"audiences' relationships with stars overlapped
with but were also voluntarily and necessarily
more multi-valent than white audiences' relationship with stars." Knight describes how African
Americans might have defined stardom "from
within a different set of values (and constraints)."
Asking "what were Black movie-goers' relationships with Hollywood stars (and their films),"
Knight describes the polar options I have identified in terms of the diegetic black audiences
in *I'm No Angel* and *Without You I'm Nothing*: (1)
black identification with and desire for white stars
and (2) critical distraction or interrogative resistance. But he also points to African American
communities' attempts to create African American stars despite the constraints of Hollywood,
where black players were largely isolated in white
worlds or segregated in wholly black worlds. In
addition to creating independent "race" films
and "race" stars (like Lorenzo Tucker, "the Black
Valentino"), African American publicity and live
touring elevated even minor black performers to
the status of stars for African American audiences.
These mechanisms could effectively transpose
center and margin, foreground and background,
lead and back-up.

Hattie McDaniel's performance, in particular,
seem available to be foregrounded and doubly encoded (as double entendre) for black audiences.
Billed early in her career as the "colored Sophie
Tucker" and the "female Bert Williams," McDaniel
began her career as a band vocalist and became the
first African American woman to sing on Ameri-

Louise Beavers and Mae
West in a scene from *She
Done Him Wrong*. Cour-
tesy of the Museum of
Modern Art.

can radio. She appeared on *Amos 'n' Andy* and *The
Eddie Cantor Show,* and starred in *Beulah* on radio
and TV. As Bogle notes, in films, her comments
and reactions "often can be read as a cover-up for
deep hostility. Indeed, she seemed to time her lines
to give her black audience that impression." [35]
When West responds to Libby Taylor's comment
that she likes "dark men" by saying she "ought to
have a big time in Africa," McDaniel's facial expression—eyes widening and rolling in a kind of
mock horror as she laughs—could be seen both as
a stereotypical eye-popping response to the white
woman's outrageousness (á la Stepin Fetchit) and
as McDaniel's own campy theatricalization of that
stereotype. McDaniel makes a spectacle of herself,
drawing our attention to her response and to the
stereotype she embodies, offering critical commentary on West's joke and on "the historic burden" she and the other actresses playing maids
have borne as authenticating back-up for white female stars.

Thus, at the same time that West's maids support her camp performance and direct attention
to her as star, they could also be seen as camping it
up—overplaying their delight in the white star to
point to the constructedness and unauthenticity
of their supportive role. Where West uses race as
support and back-up for her sex and gender masquerade, the maids play off West's performance
and campily highlight the element of masquerade
in their own presumably "authentic" personae.
Instead of an appreciative audience, they might
be seen as a critical chorus, momentarily foregrounded to comment on the white star's actions.

The double nature of African American performances in white Hollywood films have been
noted before, but are generally described in relation to practices of "signifying" rather than
camp. By viewing them as camp, however, we can
broaden our conception of camp to acknowledge
the degree to which camp is always already about
race as well as sex and gender and, conversely, to
acknowledge that signifying is a sexed and gendered practice as well. We can also consider how
camp can be used as a strategy from within both
African American and gay communities to create
a distance from oppressive stereotypes. By viewing
the maids' performances as camp, we can perhaps

escape the polarity of imagining the black audience's response as either affirmative or critical of the white star and instead consider the possibility of a two sided camp response, involving both identification and irony, recognition and mis-recognition, affirmation and critique. Perhaps, too, by recognizing the maids' performances as masquerade, we can begin to rethink the relationship between camp and race discourse as an exchange between two modes of masquerade rather than simply a white appropriation of black authenticity.

Conclusion

Authenticity seems antithetical to camp which is so doggedly committed to artifice. "Realness," as *Paris Is Burning* demonstrates, is precisely a subversive category meant to dissolve difference and any notion of authenticity. We need, though, to reconsider how "realness" operates in camp and in queer academic discourse as a racial fantasy for both white and non-white queers and the degree to which camp and queer performativity reinscribes racial difference. We need further to acknowledge the degree to which we use essentializing tropes of authenticity to position a *more authentic,* because less fixed, queer identity. Acknowledging the links between camp's sexual politics and race discourse may enable us to consider non-queer forms of racial masquerade—such as the over-the-top sensationalist stereotyping of blaxploitation, or the Auntie Tom performances of Mae West's maids—as forms of camp; to rethink what it means for camp to be a "Stepin Fetchit" or "Auntie Tom" and whether Stepin Fetchit and Auntie Tom were camp all along. It should also remind us to bring pressure to bear on our camp icons, and on our own camp readings and practices, to ensure that we do not naively assume that camp has a consistently progressive politics. Camp may be, after all, a kind of blackface.

Notes

Portions of this chapter appear in *Guilty Pleasures: Feminist Camp from Mae West to Madonna* (Durham, NC: Duke University Press, 1996). Thanks to Corey Creekmur, respondents at the Society for Cinema Studies and the Humanities Research Center, and especially Arthur Knight, for comments and suggestions.

1 Moe Meyer, "Reclaiming the Discourse of Camp," in *The Politics and Poetics of Camp*, ed. Moe Meyer (New York: Routledge, 1994), 5–7.

2 bell hooks, "Is Paris Burning?" in *Black Looks: Race and Representation* (Boston: South End Press, 1992), 149.

3 Richard Dyer, "White," in *The Matter of Images: Essays On Representation* (New York: Routledge, 1993), 141.

4 Quoted in Richard Dyer, "It's Being So Camp as Keeps Us Going" (1976), reprinted in Dyer, *Only Entertainment* (New York: Routledge, 1992), 146.

5 Andrew Ross, "Uses of Camp," in *No Respect: Intellectuals and Popular Culture* (New York: Routledge, 1989), 143; and George Melly, preface to Philip Core, *Camp: The Lie That Tells the Truth* (New York: Delilah, 1984), 5.

6 David Bergman, "Introduction," in *Camp Grounds: Style and Homosexuality,* ed. David Bergman (Amherst: University of Massachusetts Press, 1993), 10.

7 Pamela Robertson, "'The Kinda Comedy That Imitates Me': Mae West's Identification with the Feminist Camp," *Cinema Journal* 32(2) (winter 1993): 57.

8 June Sochen, "Fanny Brice and Sophie Tucker: Blending the Particular with the Universal," in *From Hester Street to Hollywood: The Jewish American Stage and Screen,* ed. Sarah Blacker Cohen (Bloomington: Indiana University Press, 1983), 45. The links between Jewish and African American cultures are too complex to delve into here. It is, however, worth considering the contrast Susan Sontag sets out between homosexual camp and Jewish "moral seriousness" in her "Notes on 'Camp'" and how the mutual appropriation of African American culture in camp and in Jewish entertainment traditions might complicate that model, especially since the references to blackness found in most other theorists of camp are absent from Sontag's model. See Susan Sontag, "Notes on 'Camp'" (1964), reprinted in Sontag *Against Interpretation* (New York: Farrar, Straus and Giroux, 1966), 275–92.

9 John Kobal, "Mae West," in *People Will Talk* (New York: Knopf, 1986), 154.

10 Lawrence F. LaMae, "Writers Fear Hazel Scott Has Become 'Hollywood,' One Writes," *Chicago Defender,* July 31, 1943.

11 Donald Bogle, *Toms, Coons, Mulattoes, Mammies, and Bucks: An Interpretive History of Blacks in American Films* (1973; New York: Bantam, 1974), 60.

12 James Snead, "Angel, Venus, Jezebel: Race and the Female Star in Three Thirties Films," in *White Screen/Black Images: Hollywood from the Dark Side,* ed. Colin MaCabe and Cornel West (New York: Routledge, 1994), 68.

13 *Mae West and the Men Who Knew Her* (dir. Gene Feldman, 1993).

14 Snead, "Angel, Venus, Jezebel," 69.

15 Stuart Hall, "New Ethnicities," in *Black Film/British Cinema,* ed. Kobene Mercer et. al. (London: Institute of Contemporary Arts, 1988), 28–29.

16 Eric Lott, "'The Seeming Counterfeit': Racial Politics and Early Blackface Minstrelsy," *American Quarterly* 43(2) (June 1991): 227. See also Eric Lott, "Love and Theft: The Racial Unconscious of Blackface Minstrelsy," *Representations* 39 (summer 1992): 23–50.

17 Linda Nochlin, "The Imaginary Orient," in *The Politics of Vision: Essays in Nineteenth-Century Art and Society* (New York: Harper and Row, 1989), 49.

18 John Corbett, "Siren Song to Banshee Wail: On the Status of the Background Vocalist," in *Extended Play: Sounding Off from John Cage to Dr. Funkenstein* (Durham, NC: Duke University Press, 1994), 56–67.

19 Kaja Silverman, *The Acoustic Mirror: The Female Voice in Psychoanalysis and Cinema* (Bloomington: Indiana University Press, 1988), 61.

20 Ramona Curry, "*Goin' to Town* and Beyond: Mae West, Film Censorship and the Comedy of *Un*Marriage," in *Classical Hollywood Comedy,* ed. Kristine Brunovska Karnick and Henry Jenkins (New York: Routledge, 1995), 220.

21 Hazel Carby, "It Jus Be's Dat Way Sometime: The Sexual Politics of Women's Blues," in *Gender and Discourse: The Power of Talk,* ed. Alexandra Dundas Todd and Sue Fisher (New York: Ablex, 1988), 231.

22 SDiane Bogus, "The Queen 'B' Figure in Black Literature," in *Lesbian Texts and Contexts: Radical Revisions,* ed. Karla Jay and Joanne Glasgow (New York: New York University Press, 1990), 275–90.

23 Snead, "Angel, Venus, Jezebel," 69.

24 Hortense J. Spillers, "Mama's Baby, Papa's Maybe: An American Grammar Book," *diacritics* 17(2) (summer 1987): 65–81.

25 John F. Szwed, "Race and the Embodiment of Culture," *Ethnicity* 2 (1975): 27.

26 Jon Tuska, *The Films of Mae West* (Secaucus, NJ: Citadel Press, 1973), 93.

27 Patricia Juliana Smith, "'You Don't Have to Say You Love Me': The Camp Masquerades of Dusty Springfield," and William Lane Clark, "Degenerate Personality: Deviant Sexuality and Race in Ronald Firbank's Novels," in *Camp Grounds,* ed. Bergman, 185–205 and 134–55, respectively.

28 Pamela Robertson, "The Adventures of Priscilla in Oz." *Media Information Australia* 78 (November 1995): 33–38.

29 Jean Walton, "Sandra Bernhard: Lesbian Postmodern or Modern Postlesbian?" in *The Lesbian Postmodern,* ed. Laura Doan (New York: Columbia University Press, 1994), 248.

30 Z. Isiling Nataf, "Black Lesbian Spectatorship and Pleasure in Popular Cinema," in *A Queer Romance: Lesbians, Gay Men, and Popular Culture,* ed. Paul Burston and Colin Richardson (New York: Routledge, 1995), 76.

31 Lauren Berlant and Elizabeth Freeman, "Queer Nationality," *boundary 2* 19 (1) (1992): 150.

32 Ibid., 173–74.

33 Nataf, "Black Lesbian Spectatorship," 77.

34 Arthur Knight, "Star Dances: African American Constructions of Stardom, 1925–1945," paper presented at the meeting of The Society for Cinema Studies (Dallas, 1996).

35 Bogle, *Toms, Coons, Mulattoes, Mammies, and Bucks,* 120.

"They Dig Her Message": Opera, Television, and the Black Diva

Dianne Brooks

Some black women like myself, born in the late 1950s, are culturally schizoid. As children of progressives, our youth was marked by transition, boundary crossing, and integration. My mother, educated in the black middle-class style and a true progressive thinker supplemented my cultural education with Youth Symphony Concerts, ballet lessons, and opera.[1] Here the notion was both of uplift (the now hackneyed notion that black people could and should do anything whites or anyone else did) and of true artistic and intellectual curiosity. Television further enhanced this cultural conflict by providing us with the possibility of becoming both addicted and exposed to absurdly populist fare like *The Beverly Hillbillies* and sublimely artistic attempts at mass elevation like *Omnibus* or the *Children's Film Festival*. And OPERA! It was everywhere for me, blaring through the house on weekend afternoons, emanating from our black-and-white television set, and taking place in downtown Boston, where I, little ten-year-old me, actually met the great Leontyne Price.

Of course, I didn't fully appreciate Leontyne Price when I went backstage. I didn't appreciate her status as symbol, icon, and nexus of a cultural hurricane. Price was, after all, the first African American singer to make it to the Met in her prime, and to break ground on the NBC-TV Opera. But more significantly, I did not really understand her vocal greatness although I knew it and felt it. Despite my mother's best efforts I had rejected the sublime as embodied by opera during my childhood and adolescence. It took the visual to bring me back around, when, several years ago,

I saw Francesco Rosi's film version of Bizet's *Carmen*. I had wound up majoring in foreign languages so there were no further barriers to librettos and I had matured enough to recognize the similarities with my other cherished forms of melodrama. Soon after, I bootlegged my mother's Leontyne Price aria collection and have become increasingly obsessed.

I still struggle to understand my and my mother's relationship to this particular form of iconic, hero worship. First there is the sheer excess that is everywhere—the music and voices that cause chills, the largeness of the visual spectacle, and the tawdriness of the stories. This is the easy part to understand. Then there is the black lady, representing the possibility of beauty and dignity in a world which maligns and disrespects her and assumes her to be coarse, ugly and tasteless. Then there is the more transcendent opportunity to see oneself across culture, beyond one's culturally limited role. In opera, black ladies are glamorous, beautiful, desired, princesses, nuns, maids, aristocrats, actresses as well as French, Italian, Germanic, Ethiopian, Japanese. Yet in the early 1950s when Leontyne Price first appeared on the operatic scene, black women were mainly culturally visible as passive servants or tragic mulattoes.[2]

Nevertheless, opera represents an antiquated intercultural dream. In this dream, we are able to experience the whole wide world beyond the boundaries imposed because of race, gender and class. Such limits don't allow you to imagine traveling to foreign countries or to experience alternative perspectives. They choke your identity and inhibit you. However in the dream opera world a black woman can even be "difficult"; not just sassy, but defiant. For example, I saw Kathleen Battle and Thomas Hampson several months ago in a televised concert performance together telecast on *Live from Lincoln Center*. Battle has always fascinated me and especially recently: she is the "bad" girl black diva. I love her because she has the audacity to be haughty. She is the anti-stereotype.

Black women aren't supposed to be haughty: we're supposed to be grateful for opportunities, as well as strong and sensible and big and buxom. But Battle is a svelte and sexy brat, punished for her bad behavior by being fired by the Met. Despite her troubles, she represents the dream that many of us black women have: to be elevated and cherished, rather than abused and denigrated. Many of us, even those of us who are strong feminists, crave the opportunity to be valued for our femininity far away from our experience. We are so desperate for this kind of visual recognition that when matinee-idol-like Hampson, at the closing of one of their duets, sweeps her up into his arms and carries her off stage, I cheer out of my own desire to be recognized.

My aim in the following discussion is to consider one way in which the black female operatic persona, constructed via television, opened an alternative narrative space for black women. In this space, black women were allowed to be something other than poor, pathological members of the underclass, even allowed to represent people who were not necessarily black. I will investigate this apparent representative transgression by looking at the television career of the first black diva to sing lead roles with the Metropolitan Opera, Leontyne Price. Beginning in the 1950s, black Americans recognized that television was probably the best way to get the larger culture used to the ideas of integration and the world beyond their back doors. At this time, the United States also realized the need to expand its cultural markets both domestically (from just whites to whites and blacks) and internationally. It needed to project an image of tolerance and inclusion. Television, opera, and Leontyne Price were employed as the vehicles of this integrationist task.

Ms. Price's television career demonstrates how this culture insists on constructing oppositions between opera and television, art and entertainment, black and white. Such oppositions do not entirely succeed in the case of Leontyne Price. She challenged conventional notions of representation, who could stand for whom, and became a commercially and socially viable sign. Price's image was always complex, a plethora of shifting representations. But she did not give over her black identity; she was neither absorbed by white, operatic culture, nor was she limited to black roles in black productions.

Historically, Marian Anderson broke important ground with her appearance on the steps of the Lincoln Memorial. Anderson had been scheduled to appear at Constitution Hall but had been denied access at the last minute by the Daughters of the American Revolution, owners of the hall.[3] They refused to allow a "colored" person to appear there. Eleanor Roosevelt stepped in, resigning from the DAR and securing for Anderson her place at the Lincoln Memorial, where she stood and sang before an enormous, integrated audience, a symbol of black achievement in the face of American racism.

The film of the performance remains a striking visual moment as a lone black woman sings out in front of a national monument. Yet Anderson's performance, although similar to Price's public role, differs in artistic significance. Although, that moment stirs much race pride in African Americans, it forced Anderson to be understood socially as "a proud black woman, dignified in the face of indignity." This remains an important political message but it limited Anderson's artistic and social role. At that time it remained impossible for an African American person to be read as other than race victim, a reading which necessarily limited the artistic and representational roles available to that person. So, in the case of Anderson, the image that we most remember is, the only preserved and oft-used one: the Lincoln Memorial moment. Such an iconic moment obscures the fact that although she debuted too late for starring roles at the Metropolitan Opera, she was the first black woman to receive an operatic performance contract with the most prestigious opera company in the United

States. We may also not realize that Marian Anderson had a rich operatic, concert career. Regardless of race, this further knowledge can free us to
imagine ourselves as other than what we are told
we can be despite the very real limitations that
stand before us. We need the reality of the consequences of oppression as well as the opportunity
to imagine something beyond it.

Television came along early on with endless
promise eventually invading and penetrating our
homes. In an age of increasing image bombard-
ment, the nature of the diva changed. Just as politicians had to pay attention to television after the
1960 election, divas now had to emerge on or
somehow be anointed by television. Stardom became increasingly attached to the visual image.
Despite the Lincoln Memorial moment, Marian
Anderson could not be the first black opera "star"
because she was known by way of radio. She was
loved and admired, but she was also already fifty-
eight by the time she stepped on stage for her first
full-length operatic performance with the Met. By
1955, the year of Anderson's Met opera debut, Leontyne Price had already eclipsed her signification by
way of the medium that has changed the nature of
all stardom. Price debuted that year nationwide in
the NBC Opera Theatre production of Tosca, at the
age of twenty-eight.

They Dig Her Message:
Leontyne Price's Televisual Construction

A 1961 *New York Daily News* photo shows Leontyne Price being presented with an award by black
church members and runs the caption: "They Dig
Her Message."[4] This caption highlights one of the
many roles Leontyne Price played according to the
media. Price wasn't simply an opera star, she was a
star with a "message," a translator who can "get
down" with the folks and show them the way to
the mysterious yet sublime world of high culture.
This caption reveals certain misconceptions about
the black churchgoer of the time: that they only

understood the vernacular, that the black population is culturally homogenous, that they needed a
translator and that they are not opera fans. But by
the late 1980s one can no longer assume that Price
was a "translator" or that she was an out of touch
anomaly. A 1982 *New York Times* article strained to
read Price's accomplishments in a more contemporary context, noting that Price always had a
black business manager who "refused roles she
thought inappropriate for a black woman," and
"consciously avoided a public romantic attachment with a white man."[5] The *Times* article again
assumed a black cultural homogeneity and unity
of values but one that no longer saw integration as
important. Thus Price's early symbolism worked
to erase her presence; there is little sense of the real
Price anywhere in the thirty-five years of coverage.
Ultimately the mainstream media scrambled to
reconstitute her as a black heroine only at her
retirement.

Since so much of Leontyne Price's professional
life was public, it's become difficult to separate coincidence from construction. Significantly, 1952,
the year in which the United States Supreme
Court changed history by declaring in *Brown v.
Board of Education of Topeka* that separate but
equal was no longer the law of the land, was also
the year Price debuted in her first full-length
opera, Virgil Thomson's *Four Saints in Three Acts*.
This opera was first presented at the Hartford
Athenaeum in 1934 and has always been recognized as a consciously modernist and progressive
achievement. Thomson's contact with black culture through Josephine Baker in Paris and the Carl
Van Vechten scene in Harlem led him to the decision to "have my opera sung by Negroes."[6] Using
blacks to play Spanish saints destabilized the representation. Such iconoclasm was supported by
the already modernist libretto contributed by
Gertrude Stein. Leontyne Price appeared on the
scene around this beginning of the end of legally
sanctioned segregation. Both of the events were
symbolic: Price signaled the possibility of integra-

tion by way of "non-traditional casting." *Brown v. Board of Education* did not end segregation, but signaled the end.

Once she began to be recognized as a vocal phenomenon, the various presses searched for a narrative into which Ms. Price could be fit. They constructed the tale of Price, born in Laurel, Mississippi, in 1925, the only daughter of a teacher and laundress who ultimately attends and graduates from the Juilliard School of Music. Leontyne Price easily fit the role of the "black lady." She was talented and ambitious, attractive and extremely well-educated, and from a family that seemed to have transferred the values of hard work to their daughter. The accounts do not offer many insights into the black part of her life. They assume that she had very simply assimilated. This Horatio Alger narrative was instantly seized upon by government media to aid in its attempts to promote an anti-racist world image. In the 1950s the U.S. State Department was actively employed in the business of countering criticisms by Communists that America's racist social policies were anti-egalitarian, anti-democratic and ultimately supported the corrupt, exploitative capitalist elite. Once the Cold War began and the USSR began increasingly to support anti-imperialist struggles in Asia, Africa, and Latin America, the department organized tours with African American performers to these areas. Not surprisingly, Anthony Carlisle, writing about "Negroes in the News" for the U.S. State Department, seized upon Price's narrative of happy southern race relations. Carlisle foregrounds the benevolent Mrs. Chisolm who recognized the talent of her laundress's daughter and who then sponsored her by providing use of her piano, music and records and later by "assisting her financially, providing clothes and defraying travel expenses ... also making it possible for Miss Price to sing before a jury of musicians at ... Juilliard where she was granted a scholarship."[7] This account provided the beginning of the good black diva image.

Price's next debut was on the Broadway stage as

Bess in Gershwin's *Porgy and Bess* which revealed a more commercial image of a black diva. She took this role instead of going off to Paris to study voice. In *Porgy and Bess* unlike *Four Saints and Three Acts,* Price performs the more limited and more commercially viable role of poor black woman. This opera was also intentionally written for blacks but without any modernist attempts to destabilize notions of representation. Here Gershwin celebrated black life using a musical mixture of popular jazz and opera. So, by very early in Leontyne Price's career, she had already traveled across a spectrum of roles for black artists but her social influence was still limited to the stage.

Leontyne Price and Television

Leontyne Price's image was narratively and symbolically overloaded from the beginning. She stepped in to take up Marian Anderson's place as the black operatic voice. But more importantly, she appeared just in time to be taken up by the new visual, television—a medium of the home. Because she was now "seen," producers and audiences could not separate her vocal artistry from what she represented, despite their constant insistence on color blindness. Although a highly accomplished vocal artist independent of television, Price was immediately taken up and constructed via press and television as a sort of affirmative action opera star. Leontyne Price became the first great black diva, one of the means by which opera and television would become integrated. She was at first cherished as a boundary crossing hero, a symbol of possibility at a time when integration seemed to be a utopian objective. But as the integration project began to fail, and as opera receded to remotest reaches of PBS, Price's blackness, the black lady version, became relatively valueless.

Leontyne Price's television resume is extensive. She appeared in four separate productions of the NBC Opera Theatre (1955–1962); was the subject of a WCBS-TV biography called *This Is Leontyne*

African American opera diva Leontyne Price.

Price (1965); performed two segments in a *Bell Telephone Hour* (1965); appeared in the *Bell Telephone Hour*'s coverage of the opening of the new Metropolitan Opera House at Lincoln Center (1966); appeared as part of yet another *Bell Telephone Hour* special entitled "The First Ladies of Opera" (1967); won two Emmys (one for a 1979 White House concert, the second for a 1980 *Live From Lincoln Center* telecast) and finally closed out her televised full-length opera career with *La Forza Del Destino* and *Aida* (what became her signature role) both in the 1984–1985 season. She was also the subject of a public television biography in 1984.

I would like to discuss five of these numerous television appearances which occurred in three socially distinct decades. I am most interested in charting Price's shifting signification as a sort of trajectory of the black lady. Wahneema Lubiano discusses the "black lady" as a culturally recognizable narrative that walks a fine line between hero-

ism and cultural betrayal.[8] The black lady narrative can be traced back to uplift messages found in, for example, the Black Clubwomen's movement. This movement, similar to that begun earlier by white women, organized large numbers of mainly middle-class black women into reformers. Prominent black women activists like Mary McCleod Bethune and Ida Wells-Barnett were members of the National Association of Colored Women which by the turn of the century represented 50,000 members.[9] These reformers believed in values of hard work, education, and morality, similar to the white women reformers who preceded them. Black women's colleges like Spelman in Atlanta trained women to be teachers in their communities and taught them to be morally above reproach.

Fictional versions of these black ladies appeared in novels by black women writers like Francis Ellen Watkins Harper and Pauline Hopkins. Writing in the late nineteenth century, these women constructed heroines who were well-educated, career-oriented, moral and chaste. Since black women, at that time, were presumed to be ignorant and licentious, writers and other black women urged actions that would counter these stereotypes. Visual representations of these black ladies are found in early black independent films, such as Oscar Micheaux's *Symbol of the Unconquered.* In that film the main character, Sylvia Landry, is a chaste and honest teacher, raised by hard-working folk; she survives various adventures and hardships in her attempts to raise money for the school in which she teaches. But these black ladies were both revered and resented. Black ladies were suspect because of their uncritical support of a class hierarchy that presumed poorer blacks to be ignorant and immoral. On the other hand, black clubwomen / black ladies always understood that their fates were bound with that of the masses of less well off black people. The motto of the NACW, "Lifting as We Climb," was explained by president, Mary Church Terrell, as necessitating that members, "come into the closest possible touch with the masses of our women, through whom the womanhood of our people is always judged." [10] By the 1950s, however, the black community was beginning to disperse, and middle-class blacks moved away from exclusively black communities leaving the poor behind. Leontyne Price appeared at a time when black middle-class achievement and assimilation were still the dominant goal. This notion, however, essentially failed to address how class is as potent a factor in oppression as race. Eventually, the chaste black lady represented assimilation and moral uplift. She no longer served the broadest notion of a unified community. That community ceased to exist in the common geographical and social location it had under de jure segregation.

The "black lady" was always subject to criticism by black men. They distrusted and resented these women who the men perceived as having greater opportunities and accomplishments. The traditional role of black women has been primarily understood to be as supporters of black men. Often their achievements were viewed as a threat to the dominant model of male identity in the larger culture, even when, for example, black women offered fairly traditional views of marriage. According to a prominent clubwoman of the early 1900s, "the true woman takes her place by the side of the man, as his companion, his helpmate, his equal, but she never forgets that she is a woman, not a man." [11] A popular notion at that time was that black women would be unfit to do their work in the home if they studied certain subjects like Latin, Greek, and the higher mathematics. From the all-male American Negro Academy, formed in 1897 to bring together leading intellectuals like W. E. B. Du Bois, to civil rights organizations and black nationalist groups of the 1960s, black women's public achievement and activity have been a great source of contention. In the late 1960s, with the ascension of black power movements, women were relegated to support positions within the prominent organizations. [12] By that time, the black lady as a prominent symbol of uplift was likely to be ridiculed as a participant in the oppression of the urban black poor. Although she had been recognizable as a role model through the 1950s and into the early 1960s, she soon disappeared as an authentic black representative. She had become merely a symbol of assimilation into the white world and denial of opportunity to black men. Not surprisingly, by the 1980s Clarence Thomas could impose this narrative on Anita Hill, as Wahneema Lubiano suggests. As a result, he garnered almost unflinching support from many in the black community, despite his own obvious desires for whiteness. [13]

We can follow this downward trajectory of the black lady via the television visibility of Leontyne Price. The early Price of the 1950s is the ground breaker, the Jackie Robinson of opera, televisually constructed to demonstrate television's beneficence and its self-proclaimed color blindness. By the mid-1960s American television realized that it needed to appear more than simply colorblind. The policy of pretending blacks were just like whites and would not be noticed did not work. Civil rights had put the issue of race discrimination into the forefront in such a way as to call attention to blackness. Leontyne Price was a ready symbol, now fully embraced by television as a cultural representative/translator of the 1960s. But non-violent, integration did not give way to peaceful assimilation either. Once black power came into the forefront, and opera was finally relegated to public TV land, Leontyne Price's version of the black lady really had no place. [14] By the 1980s Ms. Price had lost her status as black icon. She was pressed into service at a time when progress was thought to be assimilation and discarded when identity politics began to limit, rather than expand, the available narratives for black women. Although she is still admired and respected within the small world of opera, Leontyne Price's status as ground-breaking hero has not remained intact in the American cultural scene.

Leontyne Price, like many "black ladies" of her era, was identified by her iconography. Despite the early promise, Price could not move far beyond the narrative of black lady representative of the race. And once that narrative was discredited she was no longer televisually useful. Although praised with laudatory comparisons like "the Stradivarius of singers," Ms. Price was also criticized for her lack of gesture, her stiffness on stage. Black ladies were often taught to be stiff and reserved which translated into in control of emotions and passions. Gentility and reservation won out over in-your-face emotion and anger. We learned to play a role for public consumption that became oppressive in itself. The early Price of NBC's *Tosca* was a much more supple and open actor than the later symbolic Price, weighed down by the social significance of being the only black woman to open the new Metropolitan Opera House in 1966. The later Price of the 1985 farewell *Aida* is the stiffest of them all: she seems totally worn out; she did not act, she just said goodbye.

Constructing Ms. Price: Tosca and the Audience

One reason that I insist on linking Leontyne Price, an operatic star, to television is because of her place in the medium's history. Although this fact is not widely known, Price's 1955 appearance in *Tosca* on the *NBC Opera Theatre* was her first in a grand operatic performance. More importantly it was the first time any black woman performed a grand operatic role before a wide audience and the first such performance of a black woman on television.[15] The *NBC Opera Theatre* and the *NBC Opera Company,* a combined full-fledged touring company, was the brainchild of Samuel Chotzinoff, the NBC executive who, among other things, brought Arturo Toscanini to NBC, and Peter Herman Adler, the conductor of the New York Opera Company. Both Chotzinoff and Adler believed that the *NBC Opera Theatre* would be a way of acculturating the masses through television and increasing the audience for opera. Thus all productions were sung in English and used a combination of telegenic singers and actors. *NBC Opera Theatre* productions began in 1948 and lasted until the mid-1960s.

The *NBC Opera Theatre* began during the ear-liest period in the broadcast history of television when producers fought battles about what kind of programming should air and about who should produce it. But the program died at just about the time when consolidation of television production practices was complete. Over the course of the decade, television production moved from New York to Hollywood. Live "theater-like" programming gave way to filmed series. Perhaps most significantly, television programming control shifted from advertiser/sponsors to networks. Television critics and writers saw these changes as a retreat by the industry from earlier commitment to aesthetic experimentation, program balance, and free expression. According to some contemporary critics, however, marketing considerations were always the primary motivator: there had never been any serious commitment to the values of culture, taste or aesthetics.[16]

Pat Weaver was the master of putting the rhetoric of culture and taste in the service of network consolidation campaigns.[17] Weaver outlined his strategy for attracting the light viewer to television in a 1953 staff memorandum, which states that "we must get the show that gets the most talk in the coming season, that wins the Peabody award, that enables me to keep carrying the fight to the intellectuals who misunderstand our mass-media development, and that can be profitably sold without affecting any of our present business."[18]

So, although artists worked in television hoping to keep television independent of the low-brow aesthetics of the Hollywood film industry, the market dictated that television would not serve the public by elevating their tastes. Rather, by the 1960s, the appearance of the black lady opera star was affected by TV's transformation.

The black lady survived as a sort of hybrid between high and low culture. Her mission was elevation but she did not forget her roots. Network television tried to produce both high and low culture, but ultimately abandoned the high art aesthetics. Leontyne Price's first few operatic appearances happened on the network produced *NBC Opera*

Theatre during the period of network experimentation with high culture. By the 1960s *Bell Telephone Hour* programs were no longer produced by the network and were obviously intruded upon by low-brow influences. Her final broadcast—a non-network, public television production with corporate underwriting—was the purest in its high art aesthetic and the least accessible.

At the time of Leontyne Price's television debut, black artists had been singing and performing grand opera, but they were relegated to all-black companies in the United States.[19] Marian Anderson appeared at this time in a supporting role with the Metropolitan Opera, the first black woman to ever sing there. Black performers, such as Sammy Davis Jr. and Ella Fitzgerald made guest appearances in television variety programs but none were allowed a controlling role. In fact the viewing public had not seen a black woman performing as the tragic Italian heroine opposite white men. Although the early network claimed that it simply hired the best person for the role, casting a black woman as a white woman on live television would have called attention to the text, infusing it with numerous possible and potentially "uncomfortable" meanings.

By 1955, the year of the *Tosca* broadcast, NBC had already been actively practicing a policy it called "integration without identification." NBC's public relations director, Sidney Eiges, explained that "people who work for us whether in office work or on programs as entertainers are all employed on the basis of ability without regard to race or color."[20] The wording of this policy seems to indicate that the objective was to simply assimilate blacks into NBC without paying any special attention—just sort of inserting them into places in between whites, as if no one would or should notice. Copies of the RCA employee newsletter, *The Baton,* contains several articles under the subheading "News of Significant Developments in Home Entertainment and Electronics" which mentions new black employees and performers. This policy was successful enough that it garnered

an Urban League award in 1953. So, in this context, it seems Price was just simply to play Floria Tosca and no one was supposed to identify her as black.

But NBC did want people to identify with her for a number of reasons. At the time, the network base was New York City, which had a large black population who were not shy about criticizing their lack of visibility in programming. The emerging civil rights movement was creeping onto network television. NBC executives like Pat Weaver saw the network as a necessary participant in the molding of a domestic ideology that would inform and enlighten viewers and "liberate them from their primitive tribal belief patterns."[21] The politics of the time necessitated a presentation of America as a tolerant, inclusive democratic society. NBC's public relations director, Sidney Eiges, promoted and defended their integrationist policies at the time of Price's television debut. Much of his correspondence explained the new visual narrative constructed around Price as that of the well-mannered, highly cultured artist of superior talent, who happens to be black and achieving the dream of uplift and upward mobility. A memo from George Norford to Eiges, dated 6/7/55, several months after Price's NBC debut, reveals further evidence of NBC's more conscious attention to race than simple race-blind hiring. Norford's memo expressed concern that NBC was losing the "integration race." Norford attaches a copy of Alvin "Chick" Webb's column in the *Amsterdam News* which cautioned NBC that "they are being outdistanced considerably by their rival, CBS, along the integration-of-Negro performer's front."[22] Norford came up with a number of suggestions to "extend this daring and imagination" [in programming] to encompass Negro performers in its top programs in the coming season. Number three on the list was "an NBC Opera with a Negro star or co-star (which would help put to rest the feeling that 'Tosca' was a one-shot 'accident.'")[23]

Leontyne Price then helped to introduce a new version of the black lady to a wider audience via television opera since neither black nor white audiences had seen her in this particular context. Television audiences may have caught a glimpse of the black lady elsewhere in variety show performances, for example, but they had never seen her play a white woman. Price's interracial casting really pushed beyond the boundaries of any and all narratives available to black women at the time. So, in spite of their stated policy that we do not "identify," NBC seemed to expect that black and white audiences would recognize and accept an integrated American landscape where blacks can stand in for whites. Leontyne Price continued to carry out NBC's integrationist pledge while she boosted her own career visibility by performing in three more *NBC Opera Theatre* Productions: *Don Giovanni, Dialogue of the Carmelites,* and *The Magic Flute.*

The destabilizing presence of Ms. Price in the 1955 televised *Tosca* elicited numerous responses which do not adequately address the specialness of the event. In a letter to NBC president Sylvester "Pat" Weaver, Mrs. Rapp, an opera fan, seemed to recognize that the black lady was out of place. She wrote:

> I had looked forward to hearing your presentation of *Tosca* this afternoon but was shocked and dismayed by your casting of a negress vis-a-vis white men in such necessarily romantic scenes. Since there is no dramatic excuse for this casting, as there would be in *Aida,* for example, I find this deliberate inter-racial propaganda extremely offensive and believe it to be both premature and mis-guided. Let us not mis-use our arts for propaganda in the communist manner. When inter-racial romances become part of the folkways of America will be time enough for such casting as ruined my enjoyment of today's TV performance. I have no objection to Miss Price personally. She has an excellent voice and I have previously enjoyed her work many times.[24]

Although we know that Mrs. Rapp knew Ms. Price's work and race, we know she had never seen Ms. Price play a white character since the only available film and television roles for black women at that time were as overweight maids like Beulah or as variety entertainers. Mrs. Rapp may not have minded reveling in the golden tones of Leontyne Price's black lady voice, but the visual spectacle of her acting as other than black was too disruptive to be pleasurable. Mrs. Rapp could no longer identify and could no longer recognize herself in the heroine and the romantic excess which drove the opera.

On the other hand, letters of praise, such as the following from Henry Lee Moon, Public Relations Director of the NAACP, suggested that some people recognized and identified with the black lady. This position provided a useful and oft-repeated defense of her visual existence:

> We have received many calls from members and friends of our Association this week expressing their enjoyment of the program and their appreciation of this significant step by NBC in setting aside the ancient taboo against Negro performers in opera. . . . I have no doubt but that the vast majority of the American people, irrespective of race, color or region, shares the enthusiasm of those who spoke to me. However, I do recognize that there is an articulate, organized minority which opposes every advance made toward securing the equality of opportunity for all Americans, regardless of race, creed or color. . . . I am sure that many televiewers join us in the hope that NBC will not now rest on its present laurels but will continue to employ talent on the basis of individual merit.[25]

This response assumed a tolerance level that was inconsistent with the times, but Moon was, like Eiges, a PR man who was trying to put the best possible spin on a truly disruptive event. Eiges suggested to Mrs. Rapp that since the "majority" of American people did not care, why shouldn't casting be colorblind. The strategy was to stem the fear of the "other" by making the "other" the same. And since the normative television image was and still is that of the upwardly mobile middle-class, the theory was that visually representing the black versions of this little by little would be acceptable.

The NBC responses to irate white viewers summon up an image of an integrated, tolerant nation where the pools of highly qualified blacks compete evenly with whites, especially in the arts:

> In carrying out our policy [of bringing to the American public the very best in music], our artistic directors have only one yardstick in choosing performers—and that yardstick is ability. We would be shirking our duty to the music-loving public if we let other considerations enter into this choice. In the opinion of our opera directors, Leontyne Price was the most artistically fitted to sing the role of Tosca.[26]

At the same time that television was evoking a fantasy of a racially diverse America, it attempted to elevate itself via high culture. The network promoted the ideas that art knows no compromise and that art transcends the literal and banal concerns of politics, law and sociology. Apparently, a Mrs. Caldwell raised a concern specifically about interracial relationships to which Eiges responded,[27] "We realize that the subject of Negro-white relationships tends to be controversial. And, as you point out, there are laws governing such relationships in Mississippi and elsewhere. But our sole concern in our operatic productions is music, and not sociology. Furthermore, we feel that questions of race, color and creed can have no place in the world of the arts, nor in any aspect of our NBC operation."[28]

But this fantasy of a colorblind America has never been represented anywhere. There was no real visual context for this evocation; NBC then (as it does today) did the affirmative action dance, adjusting its textual readings and responses depending upon which direction the criticism was coming from. When blacks criticized NBC's lack of visual integration, Eiges could turn to Price's performance in *Tosca* as an example of NBC's good race relations. He offered a slightly different reading from that given to whites, as in the response to Lorraine Tucker of the Bronx Council of the National Council of Negro Women.[29] The National Council of Negro Women had conducted their own "survey of conditions relating to the employment of Negroes in the media of Radio and Television" and from the results had concluded that there was an "absence of shows headed by outstanding Negro personalities."[30] In response, Eiges referred again to the "integration without identification" policy, to the upcoming *Tosca* broadcast and enclosed a list of black performers who had appeared on NBC in the previous three months.[31]

Eiges used the Price performance again in response to a similar complaint from a Mr. John Randolph who expressed his regret over his participation in "blackout," whereby black audiences turned off their television sets protesting against NBC's lack of inclusion of black performers. Eiges stated that:

> We think NBC's record of the use of persons on the basis of their abilities without regard to race, creed or color is an outstanding one.... It is perhaps best exemplified by the recent appearance of Leontyne Price during the NBC *TV Opera Theatre* performance of "Tosca" on January 23. NBC has a policy of integration without identification under which the number of Negroes appearing on our programs and joining our work force is constantly increasing.[32]

As with most cases of racial ground-breaking at the time, audiences were supposed to notice but expected to either applaud the progressiveness of the medium or get used to the changing world. Leontyne Price is the black lady plus in this context; she is a well-educated credit to her race, but even this very first appearance signals her attempt to step beyond those narrow definitions. Leontyne Price is the black lady who dares to study Latin, Greek, and the higher mathematics; the black lady who is both expected to uplift and held responsible for failure.

Leontyne Price as Text

In my own specific, post-1960s context I have always understood the importance of the black lady.

My mother, my aunts, some of my teachers were all "ladies" in this sense: both devoted to the families and communities from which they came and interested in culture beyond the boundaries of race. These women were our teachers and provided us with positive models of limitless potential. And although the black lady suffers under the degrading label of bourgeois assimilationist, she continues to exist from Jessye Norman to Angela Davis.[33] Yes, even with her sophisticated nationalist, class, and gender critique, Davis's education, manner, and comportment betray the black lady underneath.

There are several reasons why a form as steeped in high art tradition as opera resonates with some black women. Black women, from Elizabeth Taylor Greenfield in the 1700s to Kathleen Battle, have been singing concert operas; it is part of black American history. There have also been consistent black audiences for opera across generations and centuries, who formed their own independent fan groups and opera companies. And opera remains one of the few mediums that engages in non-traditional casting, and thus one where black women can indulge in the old world fantasies of glamour and excess, which are usually denied to us.

When I finally saw the NBC opera broadcasts at an archive in Wisconsin, I had a deeper understanding of what Leontyne Price's significance was to my mother and other black ladies of her generation. I had grown up with her recordings as a sort of background to my life and had seen her perform in an opera house, but the visual immediacy of television put her in a place I had never seen any black women in before, a place that is different even from the contemporary *Live at the Met* broadcasts, which do regularly feature reigning black divas. The *NBC Opera Theatre's Tosca*, however, was made in 1955 for television rather than for the operatic stage. Most full-length operas shown on television now are *Live at the Met* broadcasts which place seven or more cameras at strategic points in the opera house, filming per-

formances that are organized for the stage. In the case of the *NBC Opera Theatre*, the performances were written and staged for television, blocked and shot on sets in television studios. The visual was almost more important than the musical: this was opera for television, not televised opera. The setting was thus more intimate, the spaces were closer and most shots were medium shots and close-ups. In *Live at the Met* broadcasts, the seven cameras fight to capture the breadth and the hugeness of the Metropolitan Opera House, zipping from close-ups to wider and longer shots of the great sets and masses of singers. When I watch the Leontyne Price of that first *Tosca* I am struck by the joy and exuberance of her acting; she touches and embraces her Cavradossi with no apparent hesitation. She moves gracefully, smiling lovingly and glaring haltingly when demanded by the story. I am stunned at how beautiful she looks, costumed as a Floria Tosca, the Italian actress in flowing gowns, flatteringly lit (always an issue for darker skinned performers); it's almost like watching the Rodgers and Hammerstein's *Cinderella* but with better music. When Price is directed for the small screen, by an experienced television director, there is virtually none of the rigidity of her later more distanced, literally outsized, performances. I find myself so able to identify that I am practically absorbed by the text. Finally, someone who more closely resembles me, at least in skin tone, gets to wear tiaras and die for love. Finally, a black woman gets to represent a more conventional object of desire.

When I read this televisual opera as a text, I am able to see the possibilities beyond the traditional black lady. Leontyne Price was not yet the great icon, even I recognize this. So, while we notice that she is a black woman in the role, she is singing the familiar arias and following the familiar plot trajectory for Floria Tosca, and she is Floria Tosca. And to that extent, she reminds us of the possibility of having an identity that is something more than one wholly based on race.

But, as I pointed out earlier, after the performance and beyond the text itself, Price was already overloaded with symbolism and significance, a fact which only escalated as her career continued. I would suggest that it is this very significance which invaded her other operatic texts, closing off the hopeful possibilities of that first milestone performance. By 1966, in the middle phase of her television career, one of her primary televisual roles was as an example of U.S. civil rights progress. Ten years after her debut, blacks were much more visible on television and society was grappling with images of peaceful black protesters being set upon by police dogs. Martin Luther King Jr. had become a television icon of sorts and promoted integration as an ultimate goal. Leontyne Price was still the only black opera star around and her performances became as weighted as they are weighty. For example, an appearance in a *Bell Telephone Hour* aired in March of 1966, hosted by Charles Boyer and opening and closing with quotations from Keats, placed Price's performances between a can-can re-creation and Benny Goodman playing in front of a Matisse painting.[34] Amidst this mishmash of cultural symbols, Price was virtually unrecognizable as the liberating, beautiful and exuberant black lady from *Tosca* eleven years before. She was the "great" Leontyne Price, but there was no freedom in her role. She was just the black lady, dignified symbol of uplift. In her first segment, singing "Ritorna Vincitor" from *Aida,* she appears to have been sandwiched between two large tablets meant to suggest Egypt. Her second and third appearances underscore this confused displacement—in one segment she sings "Summertime" from Gershwin's *Porgy and Bess* in a gown and in the other she joins in a closing medley with, among others, the New Christy Minstrels. In fact, this program demonstrates an almost naked use of Price as racial signifier: she was Aida, the Ethiopian princess, and the downtrodden Bess.

Two television programs in the 1960s further illustrate this fully formed and narrowed black lady narrative. First, Price appeared in a 1966 "documentary" produced for the *Bell Telephone Hour* entitled, "The New Met: Countdown to Curtain." This program used relatively fast-paced editing and camera movement to construct a suspenseful narrative with Leontyne Price as one of the main, heroic protagonists. Price shares the spotlight with then Met director Rudolf Bing and Franco Zeffirelli on the occasion of the opening of the new Metropolitan Opera House at Lincoln Center, the dramatic denouement of this mini-spectacle. But the choices of what to stage, who should stage it and who should "open the house" were carefully considered and are loaded with significance. The greatest living American operatic composer at that time, Samuel Barber, was commissioned to write a new opera, *Antony and Cleopatra.* This premiere was staged and directed by Franco Zeffirelli, celebrated opera, theatre, and film director, who had been trained by the great master of visual spectacle, Luchino Visconti. Finally, the finest American and African American soprano is given the lead, the ultimate liberal gesture at the height of the civil rights movement.

Here Price was "heaped with responsibility," as even the voice-over narrator remarked that she must open the great house, work with the notoriously chaotic Zeffirelli, and master an entirely new modernist opera that she will perform while connected directly to her hometown audience.[35] Here Price was the symbol of black achievement. Again, she was "the black lady plus," but she could not extend her representative boundaries. She was type-cast. The camera rushed between scenes of departure and arrival of the "stars," set construction, rehearsals, and even a brief scene of Marc Chagall describing the great painting that had been commissioned for the glass foyer.

One particular segment, however, visually and metaphorically demonstrates Price's lack of mobility. At one point during a dress rehearsal, Price is trapped in a huge mechanical pyramid that is supposed to enclose her and move her offstage. The pyramid gets stuck and does not move for over an hour. Price is heard, trapped inside, saying, "I'll never get out of here with my life."[36] In many ways Price never got free. This broadcast never showed the up-close performance. It only narrates the events with a relatively happy ending even though the pyramid never quite worked. Price only represented the black lady as symbol of progress.

In 1967, when Price is featured as one of four "First Ladies of Opera," yet another *Bell Telephone Hour* program, she is about as different from the Price of the earlier *Tosca* as she will ever be.[37] On this program, Birgit Nilsson, Leontyne Price, Joan Sutherland, and Renata Tebaldi are each given a segment to perform and discuss their own status as one of the "four outstanding operatic sopranos of the world."[38] Here Price is "diva" placed in a visually spare, contemporary setting offset by curtains and gauze where she sings "Pace, Pace Mio Dio" from *La Forza del Destino*. The camera is utterly static. She remains placed outside of the dramatic operatic context, giving first a mini-concert performance followed by an interview. She is the graciously mannered black lady, but she was not allowed to act or to visually represent other than herself. In her interview she referred to her Congressional Medal of Honor and said, "It's marvelous to be back." So worn out had she been by ten years of symbolic demands, she had been forced to take several months off after she lost her voice during a performance.

Price maintained her dignity as the "black lady" in the 1960s performances in spite of the indignity of her surroundings. In these broadcasts, however, she has stiffened as if somehow shielding herself. In contrast to her former loose gesturing and movement which played directly to the camera, she had evolved into a figure, a symbol, in various set pieces. She was no longer singing/acting directly to anyone; she represented civil rights progress. And the pleasure derived from the pos-

sibility of transcendence seemed to be lost. In most of these examples, her performances are so isolated and out of operatic context that our ability to infuse her actions with meaning is severely limited. Only in the documentary about the Met opening is this picture slightly complicated. There Price was the cool and dignified "black lady" amidst the overpowering chaos of Zeffirelli's "vision," an opera that was not entirely well-received. But Price gave a slightly more relaxed performance during some scenes in which she is shown greeting her family in her dressing room. Here we get only the slightest suggestion of what the pre-television Price might have looked like.

From the early to mid-1960s, Leontyne Price was narrativized as the ultimate example of the black woman achiever and as a symbol of progress in American race relations. Early in the 1960s she was shown with the black church members who dug her message. She had become a boundary crosser, a translator and most importantly a symbol. Roy Wilkins, the director of the NAACP, in an editorial for the *New York Post* in 1965 noted that Leontyne Price's achievement truthfully showed that a combination of luck, patronage and hard work can help an individual. He recognized her "symbolic stature of possibility" while acknowledging that "many if not most" will fall short of her success.[39] Wilkins heralded the black lady but his status as black leader was about to be put into question. The NAACP and other mainstream black integrationist groups would recede when the voices of angrier, younger blacks proposed alternative models of public black identity.

By the late 1960s, Price's star had inevitably begun to crack under the overloaded weight of this symbolism. In 1967, Price went ahead and honored a contract to sing at the Atlanta Music club, despite protests by Coretta Scott King because the club had no black members. Here two black ladies faced off, with King's widow bound to have popular support. But Coretta King, too, suffered from the discrediting of the black lady. Her leadership was not widely accepted after her husband's death. This clash was only the beginning of Leontyne Price's fall from public grace and visibility. Price's relationship with the Metropolitan Opera began to be on-again/off-again, mainly, according to Price, due to a lack of new roles.[40] She had become locked into the role of Aida, the Ethiopian princess, and by the late 1960s, she was also of diminishing symbolic significance. In an era of upheaval when an integrationist policy had taken a back seat to more nationalist expressions of blackness, there was no place for a black opera star, at least not on television. Television reconstructed the black narrative so that cultured black ladies (i.e., Diahann Carroll's *Julia*) gave way to symbols of black power and seemingly more authentic versions of black culture. As the most visible public black culture was governed by identity politics, the upwardly mobile black middleclass became the comic figures lampooned in programs like *The Jeffersons*.

Thus, by the early 1980s, when Price retired from full-length operatic performances, her symbolic significance had all but disappeared. There was a need to "reconstruct" her for audiences who no longer recognized her narrative. This reconstructed television phase had actually begun in 1979 at the twilight of Jimmy Carter's presidency. Price won her first Emmy award for a White House concert. Carter introduced Price with, "Opera is not just a luxury for a few but a thing of beauty to be enjoyed by everyone." This seems to be a curious statement to make when introducing a star of Price's stature. And opera really isn't for everyone, nor is it trying to be. The televisual reconstruction continues with a second Emmy award-winning concert in 1980 for a *Live from Lincoln Center* broadcast. The new narrative painted Price as aging diva, someone from a forgotten past with practically no reference to her earliest television achievements.

This reconstruction is exemplified in, for example, a *New York Times* article that attempted to reconfigure Price as recognizably black to a post-nationalist audience. Popular culture and mass media were no longer interested in high-culture symbols. The only available black narrative must encompass an "authentic," urban and primarily youth culture. So, although Price was inauthentic musically, proof of her blackness could be found in, for example, her lack of public romantic attachments to white men and her refusal of the whitest operatic roles. This picture was the opposite of the possibility Price offered viewers in the 1950s when she could play non-black roles. But, in her own words, Price placed herself above this merely reductive symbolism by, for example, saying that she always thought of herself as too healthy for frail consumptive roles like Mimi in *La Bohème*, Violetta in *La Traviata*, and Desdemona in *Otello*. And, as stated earlier, part of Price's falling out with the Met was based on limited type-casting as Aida.

Price's farewell *Aida*, televised in a 1985 broadcast, was the closing chapter in this narrative of integration, identification, and diva construction via television. Aida had become her role as much because it was a Verdi opera and Price was a Verdi soprano as because Aida was an Ethiopian princess caught in a tragic love affair with an Egyptian soldier. Price had debuted on television close to the camera, in a role which suggested a future of interesting representational possibilities. And Price performed those roles but not, for the most part, in front of the television camera. Price appeared in only two *Live at the Met* broadcasts, both in her retirement season: *La Forza del Destino* and *Aida*. So, although *Aida* is one of the great and popular operas, not surprisingly her last televised performance conveyed a mixture of meanings. Rather than a joyous, festive performance, this text was heartbreaking. Here she was no longer playing to the camera. She was no longer young and pliant but heavier, older, and wooden. Not only had she aged as every star does, the burdensomeness of her role was apparent. Only during the signature aria of this opera, "O Patria Mia," does the rigid exterior of the now extremely reserved black lady briefly crack. Price made her farewell at this point in the middle of the opera. Here the camera held her tight in a long close-up. She put her head down after finishing, holding back tears. Ten full minutes of applause followed which held up her performance. At this point as well as during her curtain calls I am reminded of the earlier Price, the one about to be buried under signs and symbols—the Price of the television *Tosca*. Throughout the performance she held back, seemingly not wanting to upstage, weary, and restrained.

In an adulatory article in *Opera News* (Met Opera Guild publication), Reynolds Price (no relation) called Leontyne Price the "finest soprano of our time" and more. He pointed out that by the early 1960s she had become a "national emblem of excellence . . . the actual scope of her accomplishment . . . almost never acknowledged frankly in her own country."[41] Indeed, it is stunning to contemplate the extent to which Leontyne Price was, for a time, everywhere and is now almost nonexistent, except to diehard opera fans. At the same time, this is not an unusual fate for a television "star," only as long-lived as whatever trend they represent. Leontyne Price both benefited from and suffered as a result of her relationship with television. She first appeared, fortuitously, during a brief moment which attempted to blend high art and pop culture, black with white. Perhaps, she would have remained completely unknown without the television boost. But, to some extent, she was confined to one narrative with which television ultimately dispensed. Still, Leontyne Price has survived with dignity as the black lady always does. At the close of the farewell *Aida* performance she knelt, clearly emotional, and mouthed "I love you" to an audience that even after ten curtain calls refused to let her go.

Notes

1 My mother grew up in segregated Washington, D.C., and although from a working-class family, attended the best black high school at the time. Many of her teachers had earned Ph.D.s but were unable to find work in universities. Thus my mother got intensive training in high-level subjects like Latin and Greek.

2 The different versions of *Imitation of Life* (1934, dir. John Stahl; 1959, dir. Douglas Sirk) serve as useful examples of the visually limited roles available to black women. Half of the story centers on the conflict between a passive darker-skinned black servant and her white-looking daughter who lives a life of misery and deception trying to pass. Although these films are among the very few that address any aspect of race relations, they do not offer black women the opportunity to imagine themselves as other than either servants or tragically doomed figures. Films produced by blacks did imagine blacks in other roles but were not widely seen by whites. Black-cast musicals such as *Stormy Weather*, produced by big studios, relied on stereotypes and depicted a small, circumscribed community.

3 It is important to note that Marian Anderson was not the first black "opera" star. Many other black operatic concert performers preceded her, including Sissereta Jones (1890s), Marie Selika (1900s), and Elizabeth Taylor Greenfield (late 1700s), to name a few. For more complete discussion of black opera stars, see Rosalyn M. Story, *And So I Sing: African-American Divas of Opera and Concert* (New York: Amistad, 1990.)

4 *New York Daily News*, February 20, 1961.

5 Susan Heller Anderson, "Leontyne Price—Still the Diva," *New York Times*, February 7, 1982.

6 Story, *And So I Sing*, quoting Virgil Thomson in *Virgil Thomson* (New York: Knopf, 1966).

7 Anthony Carlisle, "Negroes in the News," Reference Branch, IBS, U.S. Department of State, New York, June 30, 1953.

8 Wahneema Lubiano, "Black Ladies, Welfare Queens, and State Minstrels: Ideological War by Narrative Means" in *Racing Justice, Engendering Power*, ed. T. Morrison (New York: Pantheon, 1982), 323–63.

9 Paula Giddings, *When and Where I Enter: The Impact of Black Women on Race and Sex in America* (New York: Bantam, 1984).

10 Ibid., 98.

11 Josephine Turpin Washington, quoted in Giddings, *When and Where I Enter*, 109.

12 Elaine Brown offers numerous examples of the problems encountered by women in the Black Panther Party and black nationalist organizations in *A Taste of Power: A Black Woman's Story* (New York: Anchor, 1992).

13 Ibid.

14 Another black lady pressed into service in the late 1960s was Diahann Carroll's *Julia,* a single, working nurse, who is raising her child and living in a fairly integrated world. The program was criticized for its soft approach to race issues and its middle-class message.

15 No black singer had yet appeared on the Metropolitan Opera stage at the time of Price's Tosca. Both Robert McFerrin and Marian Anderson had signed contracts with the Met in 1955, but note that Anderson's subsequent debut was in a relatively minor role.

16 William Boddy, *Fifties Television: The Industry and Its Critics* (Urbana: University of Illinois Press, 1990).

17 Ibid., 108.

18 Ibid., 104.

19 See, for example, John Lovell Jr., "The Operatic Stage" in *The Crisis* (Feb. 1948): 42–62.

20 Letter from Sidney Eiges to Lorraine Tucker, January 14, 1955 (Wisconsin Historical Society—NBC Papers, Box 169, Folder 1).

21 Boddy, *Fifties Television,* 105.

22 Interdepartmental Correspondence from George Norford to Sidney Eiges, June 7, 1955 (Wisconsin Historical Society—NBC Papers, Box 169, Folder 1).

23 Ibid.

24 Letter from Mrs. William Jordan Rapp to Sylvester Weaver (Wisconsin Historical Society—NBC Papers, Box 169, Folder 1).

25 Letter from Henry Lee Moon to Sidney Eiges (Wisconsin Historical Society—NBC papers, Box 169, Folder 1).

26 Letter from Sydney Eiges to Mrs. William Jordan Rapp, (Wisconsin Historical Society—NBC papers, Box 169, Folder 1.)

27 The actual complaint letter from Mrs. Caldwell is absent from the file that contained the letter cited here. There were other letters of protest in the file, but it certainly seems as if much of the correspondence regarding Price's performance is absent.

28 Letter from Sidney Eiges to Mrs. John T. Caldwell (Wisconsin Historical Society—NBC Papers, Box 171c, File 28).

29 Letter from Sidney Eiges to Lorraine Tucker, January 14, 1955 (Wisconsin Historical Society—NBC Papers, Box 169, Folder 1.)

30 Ibid.

31 This list was not located anywhere in the file.

32 Letter from Sidney Eiges to Mr. John Randolph, March 3, 1955 (Wisconsin Historical Society—NBC Papers, Box 171c, File 28).

33 Ibid. Again, Lubiano very skillfully demonstrates Clarence Thomas's successful use of this trope in his attack on Anita Hill.

34 "Masterpieces and Music," *The Bell Telephone Hour,* 1966.

35 "The New Met: Countdown to Curtain," *The Bell Telephone Hour,* March 23, 1966.

36 Ibid.

37 "First Ladies of Opera," *The Bell Telephone Hour,* January 1, 1967.

38 Ibid.

39 Roy Wilkins, *New York Post* editorial (from Metropolitan Opera Press Clippings File).

40 Anderson, "Leontyne Price—Still the Diva."

41 Reynolds Price, "Bouquet for Leontyne," *Opera News,* April 1, 1995.

How to become a Camp Icon in Five Easy Lessons: Fetishism—and Tallulah Bankhead's Phallus

Edward O'Neill

This essay is dedicated to the memory of Richard Iosti.

First, you're another sloe-eyed vamp,
Then someone's mother—
then you're camp.

—STEPHEN SONDHEIM, "I'M STILL HERE"

The Truth about Tallulah

I would not speak ill of the dead—not for all the world. Yet in speaking of the dead, or of those who are absent, and in not knowing whether what one says is true or not, one certainly runs a risk of being taken as speaking ill, and the dead, like those absent, can't speak for themselves. I will be speaking of Tallulah Bankhead (who died in 1968, when I was six years old), and I cannot vouch for the veracity of much of what I will say. Happily, it is the very *lack* of veracity which is the point: the way Bankhead excites interest in part because of the very *difficulty* in knowing her. The story I have to tell about Bankhead consists in the way she becomes for gay men such as myself a figure for certain epistemological dilemmas which also affect us *as gay men*.

Since we habitually ground our stories in their truth-value, and since I have no assurances of knowing the truth about Tallulah, I would like instead to ground the significance of at least one of the stories I will tell about Tallulah not in its truth but rather in who has told it before, in the chain of tellers and listeners whom some other cultures inscribe at the beginnings of their stories in order to ground the speaker's authority.[1] (In our academic

culture this tradition is preserved in the footnote.) In fact, I *had* to be told the story many times because each time I forgot its punch line.

The first anecdote I will recount was recounted to me years ago in New York City by my friend Leonard Dietz, a talented actor, ardent cinephile, and gay man. The last time I saw Leonard was 1990 in San Francisco. His AIDS had worsened, and he was en route from New York City to his native Australia to escape the burdensome private health care costs of the United States. By the time Richard Iosti, a graduate student in art history at UCLA, told me the story again a few years later, I had already forgotten the punchline, although I enjoyed the story as much because of Richard's throaty-voiced recounting of it as because of the story itself. And finally, my friend Phillip Mendelsohn told me the story again, as well as telling me where I could find a written account.

What's become of Leonard now I do not know, for I have lost touch with him. Richard Iosti died of AIDS around Christmas of 1992. Phillip Mendelsohn is alive and well and HIV-negative and living in Los Angeles to this day. Since my topic is not just Tallulah Bankhead but also camp and gay men's investment in figures like Bankhead, what I will say of the dead and absent Tallulah will have as much to do with my investment in Leonard and Richard and even Phillip as with my investment in Tallulah. If camp is often framed as a morbidly nostalgic attachment to things of the past, my own campy attachment to Tallulah is intensified by the fact that this attachment came by and through people some of whom are now far away or dead—and not for just any reason but because of AIDS.

Epistemological Trouble

There *is* a documentary source for this anecdote about Tallulah which I had to be told so many times: Truman Capote's last, unfinished "novel" *Answered Prayers*.[2] Although the three extant chapters which make up Capote's book scandalized and alienated the many one-time friends he portrayed therein in thinly-veiled portraits when the chapters were published in *Esquire* during his lifetime, this hardly lets us know the extent to which these portraits are accurate, since it may have been their very *inaccuracy* which offended so—whence in part my reluctance about speaking ill, even of the dead.[3] Capote died without finishing the novel, and whether Capote's death was tragic or squalid, it effectively prevents us from finding out from him how much of *Answered Prayers* is truth and how much fiction. As Capote's editor, Joseph M. Fox, writes in his "Note" to the text: "There is only one person who knows the truth, and he is dead. God bless him."[4]

Although Capote often contended that what he'd written was "true," the novel itself contains a commentary on its own status as "docufiction," a commentary which does not make it easy to determine what Capote might have meant by saying the novel was "true." Capote himself described the process of writing the novel as affected by a personal crisis which changed his feeling about "the difference between what is true and what is *really* true."[5] The crisis seems to be mirrored within the novel by the odd form of literary criticism practiced by Capote's surrogate, the down-and-out writer and sometime-hustler P. B. Jones. In one passage, Jones marks out the distance between unconvincing truth and believable illusion by reference to the infamous gender reversals of *Remembrances of Things Past* (Albertine for Albert, etc.), a novel that Capote meant to imitate with *Answered Prayers*:

> Because something is true doesn't mean that it's convincing, either in life or in art. Think of Proust. Would *Remembrance* have the ring it does if he had made it historically literal, if he hadn't transposed sexes, altered events and identities? If he had been *absolutely factual*, it would have been *less believable*, but . . . it might have been better. . . . That's the question: is truth an illusion, or is illusion truth, or are

they essentially the same. Myself, I don't care what anybody says about me as long as it *isn't* true.[6]

The Jones character later amplifies this view, not in terms of what he said but in terms of what he *neglected* to say, by reference to the gender reversals of female impersonation. Had he been able, he *would* have said as truth is nonexistent, it can never be anything but illusion—but illusion, the by-product of revealing artifice, can reach the summits nearer the unobtainable peak of Perfect Truth. For example, consider female impersonators. The impersonator is in fact a man (truth), until he re-creates himself as a woman (illusion)—and of the two, the illusion is truer.[7] What seems to be a mere reversal—truth is illusion, illusion truth—is actually a three-step process: 1) the truth of gender—"the impersonator is *in fact* a man"—is covered up 2) by an illusion of gender—"he *re-creates* himself as a woman." If 3) seems merely to reverse the two—"the illusion is truer"—what should be emphasized is that this third step retrospectively rewrites the values of the terms "truth" and "illusion," and this step can only take place because "truth" was in the first place "*nonexistent*" or transcendent—i.e., "the unobtainable peak of Perfect Truth." The third step is not a reversal or collapse of an opposition, but rather reveals a lack at the origin, an aboriginal emptiness, an emptiness which allows for a play of unstable reversals.

Enter Tallulah: her Perfect Truth the aboriginal emptiness in question. Capote could easily have imbibed his doubts about the categories of truth and fiction from Bankhead herself, whom I will be taking as a figure for certain epistemological and ontological instabilities which I will argue are inseparable from Bankhead's very campiness. But I must make clear at the outset: I have no interest in giving the "truth about Tallulah," in tearing away the veil, in denuding Bankhead. As we will see, she would have been the first to denude herself. What interests me is not the truth about Tallulah—if, indeed, one could find such a thing—but rather the way the play of the veils that surround her is it-self a part and parcel of Bankhead's fetishistic fas-cination, her star power and her camp appeal. If Bankhead was fond of saying that her first name was a Native American word for "trouble," what I would like to underline is the way "Tallulah Bank-head" signifies a sort of *epistemological* trouble. I would like to draw out the ways in which Bankhead becomes available for a camp reading because of this epistemological trouble, the implicit assump-tion being that this trouble has significance for gays and lesbians because we bear the burden of being similarly troublesome to a homophobic so-ciety, whether in terms of the problematic visibil-ity of our identities (as Sedgwick and Edelman, among others, have argued), or because of the way we reveal gender to be a masquerade or perfor-mance (as Butler has suggested).[8]

Three Ways of Looking at an Anecdote; or, Literal Homosexuality, D-d-darling

Capote's anecdote about Bankhead is of interest not merely because it's funny but because it poses male homosexuality precisely in terms of an epis-temological enigma, and because this anecdote al-lows us to read an affinity between an insufficiently legible male homosexuality and a fetishistic in-vestment in Bankhead. That is: in this anecdote, consider how the doubtful status of the Bankhead anecdote (i.e., is it true?) coincides with the doubt-ful status of homosexuality (i.e., is he gay?) and so male homosexual curiosity *about Bankhead* sud-denly finds itself reflected back in the form of cu-riosity *about male homosexuality*.

The anecdote runs as follows. Dorothy Parker, Montgomery Clift, and Tallulah Bankhead attend a dinner party—smashed out of their minds. Miss Parker runs her hands over Mr. Clift's face in a fashion which for Tallulah calls to mind Helen Keller reading Braille. Parker murmurs, "He's so beautiful. . . . Sensitive. So finely made. The most beautiful young man I've ever seen," finally culmi-nating her tribute to an unobtainable peak of Per-fect Male Beauty (to paraphrase Capote) with this capper: "What a pity he's a cocksucker." Capote indicates that Ms. Parker took some heed of the possible offense to modesty embodied in her re-mark and so gave two rejoinders or defenses. First, Capote writes, "sweetly, wide-eyed with little girl naïveté, [Ms Parker] said: 'Oh. Oh dear. Have I said something *wrong?*'" And then, second, ap-pealing to Bankhead: "I mean, he is a cocksucker, isn't he Tallulah?" To which Miss Bankhead re-plied, "Well, d-d-darling, I r-r-really wouldn't know. He's never sucked *my* cock."[9]

My interest in this anecdote is primarily episte-mological. What's important about the anecdote for me is the way it marks a site where the difficulty in getting the truth about Tallulah Bankhead and about male homosexuality come together. What's interesting about Bankhead's riposte is that it un-derlines the way certain obscurities about Bank-head, such as her gender, take up the burden of an epistemological obscurity around male homosex-uality. Indeed, one reason this anecdote is so inter-esting is because it already helpfully produces for us within its narrative certain epistemological posi-tions we might be tempted to take vis-à-vis male ho-mosexuality and vis-à-vis the anecdote itself. These positions which are not limited to the historical in-dividuals in the anecdote (Clift, Parker, and Bank-head) but which have also been held by various writers about Bankhead and about homosexuality. Namely, we might like to ascertain the truthfulness *of* this anecdote in much the same way as Parker *within* the anecdote would like to ascertain the truthfulness of her ascription of homosexuality to Clift. The possible impropriety in saying risqué things about Bankhead or about Clift's sexuality, signaled in the anecdote by Parker's "Have I said something *wrong?*," would be ameliorated on the one hand by the truth of the anecdote and on the other hand by the truth of Parker's claim about Clift: I mean, it *did* happen, didn't it? "I mean, he *is* a cocksucker, isn't he?" If we are to speak of the dead in this way, we could at least know if what we're saying is true—or even "*really* true."

In this story, Miss Parker holds an epistemological position we can identify roughly as *empirical,* one based on a certain *literal* conception of language. She seems certain that it is possible to know whether a given man is or isn't a cocksucker. Whatever breach of etiquette or propriety may be involved in such an assertion would at least be lessened by the appeal to a *literal homosexuality,* a concrete thing which can be known and given an equally concrete (even colorful) name. Here Miss Parker's position is much like that of cultural readers like Robin Wood and Richard Dyer and, in a different way, Vito Russo, who take as their interpretive task identifying a concrete and namable but hidden homosexuality, bringing it to light, protecting it from misnaming.[10] Such critics would aim for a certain representational transparency, whether of images to things or of language to the world; they would like to see pictures that matched up with reality and words that matched up with both; they would like to *see* homosexuality and to *say* what it is, to call, in other words, a spade a spade, or, using Parker's word, a cocksucker a cocksucker.

This position has in no way been entirely superseded by recent discussions of the epistemology of homosexuality. Rather, a certain *literalism* seems to inhere in gay and lesbian critical projects as a kind of necessary starting point always to be surpassed or as a stumbling block never to be overcome, depending on one's point of view. When D. A. Miller evinces the status of male homosexuality as a *connotation* rather than a *denotation* in Alfred Hitchcock's *Rope* and in Hollywood cinema of a certain era more generally, Miller does not throw into question the primacy and stability of male homosexuality as an object which can be denoted, named and known. Indeed, he takes considerable pleasure in imagining a spectacle which *Rope* refuses its spectators, a literal spectacle almost as colorful as Parker's, what Miller calls "men kissing, sucking, fucking one another," as if

this "idea and image," *had it been* represented, *would* have given some "*direct* evidence" of the "homosexuality of the protagonists . . . *visually displayed* (with a kiss) or *verbally disclosed* (*by a declaration*)."[11] Male homosexuality in this framework is something you can *see* ("visually displayed") and say ("verbally disclosed . . . by a declaration"). Miller, much like Parker, takes a certain glee in unveiling this brute fact, in showing what often remains hidden, in tossing aside propriety and stating the unstated but by no means unstatable, even if this spectacle remains in an unrealized conditional.

Indeed, whether homosexuality *is* or *is not* there (whether in Montgomery Clift or in *Rope*) is hardly of much import compared to the fact that one has already decided that *this* is the question to be answered. Gay approaches to cinema in particular and cultural studies in general would to a certain extent be encompassed by this question, one which, like Ms. Parker, tries to excuse the social opprobrium attached to making homosexuality visible ("Have I said something wrong?") by appealing to the potential referential accuracy involved ("I mean he *is* . . . isn't he?"). If "vulgar" psychoanalysis and "vulgar" Marxism consist in reducing every sign to a phallus in the former case and every ideological superstructure to a mere mask for a material base in the latter, then the kind of *vulgar gay interpretation* with which I am taking issue in this essay consists in trying to grant to homosexuality an ontological solidity and epistemological availability—homosexuality as something you can *see* and *say*, call, however rudely, by its correct name—which would enable homosexuality to be a concrete entity hidden and repressed underneath the textual surface. Discussions of camp enter into this vulgar interpretation as soon as they must base camp on a gay "sensibility" which they imagine to be more solid and easy to recognize than camp itself. This move of trying to ground camp in something ostensibly more recognizable is hardly a surprising critical move. Few

critics agree on a definition of camp, let alone—
and this is a separate issue—a set of objects or
works which possess this flighty characteristic of
campiness.[12]

A different position would question the project
of trying to ascertain the truth of the anecdote,
and likewise, of trying to denote, to name, and to
represent such a literal homosexuality. Here we
can follow the path of Eve Kosofsky Sedgwick,
whose trajectory I take to be anticipated in certain
ways within the anecdote by Bankhead. This position would pay heed to the very doubtfulness of
homosexuality. Indeed, Sedgwick has invited us
not to consider male homosexuality as a question
whose truth is to be decided, and instead to consider the ways in which the very epistemological
perplexities, the dubiety or doubtfulness of a
ghostly male homosexuality, what Sedgwick calls
the "epistemology of the closet," are very much a
part of how homophobia functions.[13] The very
difficulty in ascertaining the truth about male homosexuality is not, on this view, something separate from the construction of that sexuality. This
difficulty is not merely a doubt to be traversed in
order to reveal the real thing-in-itself. On this
view of homosexuality, camp (as an aesthetics of
or at least appealing to homosexuals) would no
longer be grounded in either specific characteristics of camp objects, nor would camp be grounded
in a gay subject or "sensibility," a certain way of
perceiving the world. Rather, *camp would on this
view be structured similarly to and marked by the
very same epistemological difficulties which help to
(and which fail to) define male homosexuality.* That
is: something's being or not being camp is no less
tricky than someone's being or not being queer.

We can read Bankhead's position in this anecdote along such lines, finding therein a form of
empiricism far more radical than Miss Parker's.
What Bankhead in this anecdote, like Sedgwick in
her work, underlines is the very epistemological
trickiness of male homosexuality. More precisely,
much like Sedgwick's reading of Henry James's

"The Beast in the Jungle," Bankhead's witticism
underlines the way women may be placed in a position of needing to know a man's sexuality in a
way which the men themselves, under the burden
of homophobia, cannot or must not, thus of needing to know what cannot (if the man is gay) be
gleaned through what might loosely be called
"firsthand" experience: "He's never sucked *my*
cock." On this reading, Dorothy Parker takes the
role of James's May Bartram, longing for a sexually
and emotionally unavailable and possibly gay
man, and Tallulah, like Sedgwick reading James's
story, or like Poe's Inspector Dupin in Lacan's famous reading, takes in the trickiness of the whole
intersubjective situation and picks up the trick by
trumping the other players.[14]

While it might seem like this shift from the
possibility of getting a *correct* answer to the necessary impossibility of getting *any* answer *at all* is
dramatic and final, this third position still unwittingly shares certain assumptions with the first
two, and therefore requires modification. Namely,
Bankhead's epistemological position in the anecdote is not as clear as I have made it seem above.
On the reading implied above, Bankhead would
seem to be saying that it is *in principle* impossible
for *any* woman to know whether *any* man is "a
cocksucker" or not, since no woman would have
direct or (euphemistically) "firsthand" access to
the proof of the kind that Miller imagines might
have been possible in viewing some alternate-
universe version of *Rope*.[15] But close attention to
Bankhead's words show that she eschews such
generality—*in principle, any* woman, *any* man—
instead hewing to an even more radically empirical or particularist stance. More precisely, Bankhead does not say that she *can't* know if Clift is a
cocksucker or not, but only that she *happens not to
know*.

That is, although the humor of the anecdote
would seem to devolve on Bankhead's advancing
the hypothesis of the quite empirical *impossibility*
of her ever knowing if a man were "a cocksucker"

or not, nothing in the anecdote precisely states what both the above readings must assume: namely, that Tallulah Bankhead does *not* have a phallus. *And yet* nothing in the anecdote *states* that Bankhead does *not* have a cock. What Bankhead says is *not* that she does *not* have a cock, but only that Clift has never *in fact* sucked it.[16] That is, Bankhead's lack of knowledge (about whether or not Clift is a cocksucker) is purely *contingent* rather than *necessary*. It's not at all that Bankhead *can't* know whether or not Clift (or Capote, or anyone for that matter) is or isn't a cocksucker; it's not that it would be *impossible* for her to know this; it's rather that she simply *happens* not to know.[17] The purported and presumably comical "impossibility" of Bankhead having a cock is in fact not empirical at all. Capote reproduces (or imagines?) an intonation which he inscribes in his text via italics in a way which emphasizes this phallic possibility: "He's never sucked *my* cock." When I laugh at this story, I cannot help but feel that as a Bankhead fan I have been caught not just in my admiration for Bankhead's brilliant riposte but in my secret belief in *Tallulah Bankhead's phallus*.[18]

Saving Fetishism from Its Fans

If this, my preferred reading of this anecdote, has a fetishistic cast, it is no accident. I began by posing this anecdote in terms of its epistemology or doubtfulness: its *status* as a doubtful anecdote in gay camp lore and its *content* as the doubtfulness of homosexuality. But the anecdote also reproduces within itself a fetishistic construction of Bankhead. This occurrence seems to me significant in part because the image of Bankhead's phallus crops up in this doubtful, apocryphal text precisely to answer the riddle of male homosexuality. Rethinking the concept of fetishism in this context could shed some light on the epistemology of camp. And camp might in turn then reflect some light back onto the epistemology of fetishism. Here at the outset I'm understanding "fetishism" rather

literally in terms of the way the anecdote (or my reading of it) constructs Bankhead as a phallic woman, but what I'd like to do in what follows is to reinterpret fetishism in less vulgar terms. Such terms that allow us to think about camp in ways that avoid the vulgar gay interpretation discussed above and that hew instead to the epistemological instabilities which Sedgwick, Edelman and others have underlined with respect to male homosexuality. Indeed, in what follows I will use Bankhead's status as a camp icon to rethink fetishism, and fetishism in turn to rethink camp. In this framework, Bankhead plays the role which in Freud's conception of fetishism is played by the maternal phallus, the one she sports in my reading of this anecdote. Capote names as "the unobtainable peak of Perfect Truth": lost to an archaic past, she exists only through an almost-infinite series of proxies.

Indeed, everything that this anecdote articulates about male homosexuality, not only its impropriety but also its doubtfulness, also applies to Bankhead herself as a site of camp meaning. She remains as a shared point of significance for certain gay men. Bankhead's legend or myth, so often marked by such ribald frankness, also shrouds her in doubt and makes her an object of a phantasmatic belief sustained by exactly such narratives passed (often) from gay man to gay man. Indeed the article by D. A. Miller mentioned above is richly suggestive exactly because it cannot be shoehorned into the kind of vulgar literalism of the kind I imputed to Parker. Miller's reading of *Rope* rather depends upon a highly phantasmatic elaboration of an image of male homosexuality: not just "the idea and image of men kissing, sucking, fucking one another," but moreover Miller's phantasmatic articulation during his reading of the film of an "x-ray vision, from behind the gorgeously tailored suit . . . [an x-ray vision that sees] through the cleft of the buttocks all the way to the perforation of the anus itself . . . [and its] cavital darkness."[19] Moments such as this in

Miller's text suggest a highly productive form of phantasmatic elaboration which is neither more nor less phantasmatic than my own image of Tallulah Bankhead's phallus.

My frankly fetishistic reading of this anecdote, then, would represent one particular strategy for untangling the complex routes of association which link fetishism, male homosexuality, cinema, stars and camp. If fetishism has gotten a bum rap in film studies, it is not just because of fetishism's detractors, but rather because of its fans. Indeed, the concept of fetishism has achieved a spectacular degree of currency exactly because its fans *are* its detractors. The feminist use of psychoanalysis as a critical tool construed fetishism as a defensive strategy operated by Hollywood cinema to construct a masculine viewing position and to defend that masculine construction against the threat of castration embodied by even the most circumspect images of women.[20] This concept of fetishism also relies on an implicit Marxist condemnation of commodity-fetishism as a kind of delusional seeing which imagines an impossible form of value shining forth from the material and economic reality of the commodity. Indeed, in this context stars, especially female stars, would mark a perfect conjoining of psychoanalytic fetishism and commodity-fetishism. The woman's image functions as a visible fetishistic defense against castration while at the same time reifying the star-as-commodity by putting a human face on what is essentially a mass-market product. The star personifies the commodity by commodifying the person and vice versa. The life and body of the star, and above all the female star, would seem to be the extracinematic point around which cinematic fetishism condenses, the point where the fetishism within the classical Hollywood text overflows into paratexts, like publicity, fan magazines and gossip, and so takes on a shadowy life on the borders of public texts and private desires.

But both psychoanalytic and the Marxist readings of fetishism end up reinstating a naive form of empiricism within the desiring and consuming subject by constructing fetishism as a *delusive modality of seeing*, as a question of blindly *not* seeing what's there (the absence of the phallus, the commodity as the product of labor having an exchange-value) or of seeing something that's *not* there (the imaginary maternal phallus, a value unrelated to either labor or exchange). Freud's fetishist has refused to see what's right before his eyes (the fact that his mother lacks a phallus) and instead displaces the value represented by this imaginary organ from a primordial past onto all the more visible, accessible and mobile fetishes with which we are all familiar.[21] Likewise, Marx points out that the consumer's behavior in relation to the commodity goes beyond 1) the *positive* qualities and uses of the commodity, its use-value, and even beyond the commodity as 2) what it's *not*, as a sign for the labor and commodities for which the commodity can be exchanged, which exchanges determine the commodity's exchange-value. And Marx explicitly states that the fetish-character of the commodity cannot be described according to optical metaphors. Rather, the fetishistic aspect of the commodity adds a third dimension to the commodity, which Marx calls "spiritual" or "transcendental."[22]

This kind of reading of fetishism is quite plausibly based on Freud's and Marx's texts, *and yet* another reading is possible, one which is equally plausible but is less frequently advanced in the study of film and popular culture. Such a reading is implied when Jean Laplanche and J.-B. Pontalis emphasize the fact that the "reality" of castration is not a simple act of perception, since what is "perceived" is exactly an *absence*, which can be the object of a cognition, but never a perception.[23] That is: one never *sees* "nothing," since "nothing" is precisely the lack of something to see. On this reading, fetishism would *not* be a delusive avoidance of the reality of the presence or absence of a phallus, nor of the positive qualities of the commodity or the negation of those qualities. Rather, fetishism would mark a *modality of value which protects belief and pleasure from the certainties and unanimities of a shared public code,* whether the code of gender (the presence or absence of the phallus), or a code of exchange values.[24] *Fetishism allows desire to circulate within the social field without yielding assent.*

The very fact that Freud conceives of fetishism not as a denial to an assertion but rather as a *disavowal* or refusal of belief suggests that Freud's concept of fetishism involves some *third* dimension beyond either a literal perception or a signifying presence or absence. On such a reading, the words "*and yet*" in Octave Mannoni's famous formula for fetishism—"I know very well . . . and yet all the same"[25]—would separate a public code organized by presence and absence, truth and falsity—"I know very well . . . e.g., that my mother doesn't have a phallus"—from a private investment which refuses the certainty of public agreement of presence and absence, truth and falsity—"but all the same I *believe* she does!" The question of the truth about Montgomery Clift's homosexuality—was he or wasn't he?—or the truth about Tallulah Bankhead—did she say this or didn't she?—is suspended by this third option: not the *necessary impossibility* of truly knowing, but a *contingent belief,* a belief which provides a way out of an epistemological impasse by *refusing* the options of truth and falsehood. I *know* the anecdote Capote tells may or may not be true, I *know* Montgomery Clift may or may not have been gay, I *know* Tallulah Bankhead cannot have had a phallus, *and yet* all the same I *believe everything.*

If fetishism has been construed along psychoanalytic and Marxist lines in terms which are primarily *negative* or *privative*—in terms of a *loss* of vision, a *loss* of the phallus—analyses of stars have tended by contrast to emphasize the *positive* function of the star as a point of identification for specific viewers in the context of specific social antagonisms. The analysis of stardom thus offers the potentiality for rethinking fetishism in less nega-

tive terms. In Richard Dyer's work on stars, for example, stars are understood not simply as masks covering social conflict but rather as rallying points which actually allow for the articulation of specific identities which find themselves caught up in the same kinds of antagonisms and conflicts as those which surface in star discourse. Here Dyer's writing on the star image of Judy Garland has particular relevance for gay and lesbian approaches to cinema. He shows how the conflicts condensed in Garland's onscreen and offscreen star image have spoken to the conflicts that structure gay and lesbian experiences.

The anecdote I have given above about Bankhead, as well as the constructions of Bankhead's persona which I will articulate below, will provide a way of rethinking fetishism. It allows a framing of the issue not as false, delusional belief but rather as an epistemological arrangement which permits the flow of phantasmatic belief by protecting that belief against reality testing. By giving that belief a minimally public discursive form (in this case, gossipy speculations organized around a central figure whose very unknowability spurs on unverifiable suppositions) untenable and even "impossible" stories and hypotheses take on an autonomy by virtue of their circulation rather than their truth.[26] Indeed, consider the fact that both Dyer's lengthy studies of individual stars and subsequent influential star studies like Miriam Hansen's have focused on figures who are either gay icons, as with Dyer's writing on Marilyn Monroe and Judy Garland, or who are handsome male stars who are rumored to have been bisexual or gay, like Dyer's study of Paul Robeson or Hansen's writing on Valentino. Such happenstance suggests that gay men and camp may have been more definitive for star studies as a whole than has yet been recognized.[27] An analysis of Bankhead's camp appeal in terms of fetishism might thus shed light not only on the *content* of the construction of Bankhead through rumor, hearsay and gossip, but also on those very devalued *modalities.* Such anecdotes are subject to doubt *as evidence.* Yet such questioning does not at all preclude them from functioning as evidence *of the way doubt and belief function*—indeed, quite the contrary.[28]

Examining Tallulah Bankhead's campy appeal to gay men can serve as an inductive starting point in answering the question: What becomes a camp icon most? Indeed, Bankhead's career can be taken as a vast how-to lesson in achieving the status of camp iconicity: How to Become a Camp Icon in Five Easy Lessons. Such an analysis of Bankhead's persona would thus hope to save fetishism—even from its biggest fans. It would displace a negative image of fetishism as failed vision and hallucinatory excess with an understanding of the positive role of fetishism. Now it would be understood as forms of belief significant to a minority but articulated outside or against the power of a dominant majority to impel its own authority under the name of "truth."

Easy to fetishize: Tallulah Bankhead in the film *The Cheat* (Paramount Pictures, 1931). Courtesy of the American Museum of the Moving Image; photographer unknown.

"Tallulah" Means (Gender) Trouble

The construction of Bankhead's star persona through anecdotes seems consistently tinged by a literally fetishistic fascination with Bankhead's body, specifically her genitalia. Perhaps the most famous anecdote about Bankhead concerns the filming of Hitchcock's *Lifeboat:* when climbing daily into the gigantic pool in which *Lifeboat* was shot, Bankhead's habit of not wearing underwear apparently caused a commotion among the film's crew members, who clambered to steady the ladder that Bankhead climbed so that those crew members might see—well, we can only imagine what. A visiting journalist from a proper women's magazine, having observed the commotion and noted its cause, approached the studio, whose publicity department insisted that in the interest of publicizing the film, Bankhead's lack of underwear must *not* be publicized, and so either Bankhead must cover up, or the set would have to be closed, thus effectively putting the entire produc-

tion under wraps, and so depriving it of publicity. An underling was forced to confront Hitchcock with the issue, but Hitchcock claimed indecision about whose responsibility the problem was: Was it a matter for wardrobe? Or hairdressing?[29] The anecdote constructs a Bankhead who is flagrantly visible while also, no doubt for reasons of modesty, saying nothing about what it was (or wasn't) that the stagehands were fascinated to see (or not see). Hitchcock's eminently fetishistic witticism turns the stagehands' interest in the sight of Bankhead's genitals into a question of covering up what's there or not there, of hiding what was to be seen or not seen (wardrobe), or of shifting one's attention to the outlying areas (hairdressing).

If this anecdote would seem to suggest a certain fascination with Bankhead's gender, or at least her genitals (which isn't entirely the same thing), this fascination must stem in part from Bankhead's very undecideability in terms of gender. While also a famously beautiful and captivating woman, Bankhead's myth is peppered with anecdotes which underline not her feminine beauty but rather her masculinity—mostly arising from the depth of her speaking voice (about which, more later). Winston Churchill is said to have asked Bankhead if she was ever mistaken for a man on the telephone. Bankhead's reply was, "No. Are you?" And an actor who once worked with her was identified by a critic as "a kind of masculine Tallulah Bankhead," which caused Bankhead to respond, "Don't be redundant, darling."[30]

If Tallulah Bankhead has a particular appeal for gay men, at least *part* of this appeal consists not only in a doubt about her gender but also in a doubt about her sexuality.[31] *How to Become a Camp Icon, no. 1:* Allow yourself to be *imagined* to be gay. Those rumored to have numbered among her female lovers include such unlikely suspects as Sister Aimee Semple McPherson, Patsy Kelly, Hattie McDaniel, as well as her lifelong friend Estelle Winwood.[32] And rumors about Bankhead's lesbian experiences were fomented by Bankhead herself, who was purportedly quoted as saying, "My family warned me about men, but they never mentioned women!"[33]

But part of Bankhead's camp appeal, as well as the suspicions about her sexuality, may also arise out of a sort of "guilt by association": the way queers have become accustomed to reading innuendo into fact under the pressure of a homophobic imperative of gay invisibility. Bankhead's career seems to have been marked by an insistent, almost fatalistic pattern of connections with gay writers, other camp icons like herself, and at least rumored-to-be-gay performers. The fact that one cannot know precisely the truth of Bankhead's sexuality, rather than forming an obstacle to a reliable knowledge, as it would be for critics and historians, functions to enable an investment

in Bankhead as she can be constructed via social networks which are as intricate as they are obscure. Of course, it would be hard to imagine any modern theatrical career entirely devoid of such associations. Yet with Bankhead these collisions seem to acquire a certain density which becomes persuasive.

How to Become a Camp Icon, no. 2: Associate with gay writers and artists. Bankhead was associated early on professionally with Somerset Maugham and socially with Noël Coward, whose *Private Lives* Bankhead performed first in 1946, later touring in the piece extensively. In 1947 she appeared in a New York production of gay polymath Jean Cocteau's *The Two-Headed Eagle*. During her radio appearances Bankhead also frequently recited poems by another camp icon whose writing and life combined like Bankhead's equal measures of irony, savage wit, and bathetic sentimentality—namely Dorothy Parker.[34] When Bankhead appeared in *The Skin of Our Teeth*, her understudy was Lizbeth Scott, who went on to sue *Confidential* in 1955 for printing stories about her reputed lesbianism. And in 1937–38 Bankhead was to appear with Clifton Webb in a show with music by Cole Porter, only to be replaced by none other than Lupe Velez, whose grotesque write-up in *Hollywood Babylon* subsequently made her available for campification.

A Tallulah Well Lost

Beyond the appeal Bankhead would have to potential gay and lesbian fans as *possibly* "one of us," much of what seems to be appealing about Bankhead stems from her very *inaccessibility*. Like the maternal phallus lost to a primeval past of childhood, the very lack of access to Tallulah impels a desire to fill out this epistemological void. This absence seems to spur on a fetishistic project of accumulation, the desire to collect scraps, stories and anecdotes. One wants to restore a wholeness and plenitude lost to time, partly for a love of such scraps and partly with the aim of constructing a whole and entire Tallulah from them. Probably the ultimate such project, not entirely distinguishable from a thoroughly respectable academic drive toward completeness, can be found in Jeffrey L. Carrier's remarkable *Tallulah Bankhead: A Bio-Bibliography*. Therein Carrier gives a short (forty-seven-page) biography, a year-by-year and even sometimes month-by-month chronology, a list of all stage, film, radio and television appearances, as well as a discography and a list of awards, honors, and tributes, not to mention a list of roles for which Bankhead was considered, screen tests she shot, and even fictional references to her.

But what such a massive drive toward documentation tends to obscure, even while it reveals it, is the way Tallulah is treasured *as lost and inaccessible*. Since it is a mere proxy or substitute for an imagined maternal phallus, no fetish can ever live up to the glory of what it replaces. The fetish is always a pale copy. Likewise, Bankhead as an object of investment mobilizes exactly this kind of comparison between the "real thing" and all the substitute proxies to which we have greater access. A director who worked with Bankhead commented that "no one has ever captured Tallulah on paper and no one ever will"[35]—a strange comment for someone in the process of trying to do just that.[36]

Bankhead is lost to us. In part because the roles she played on stage were so frequently played by other actresses on the screen. We can only imagine (for better or worse) Bankhead on stage in Dumas's *La dame aux cameilles* in 1930, since Garbo played Dumas's heroine on the screen. Bankhead appeared in the play of *Let Us Be Gay* in 1930; the film role went to Norma Shearer. In 1941, Bankhead appeared in Clifford Odets's *Clash by Night;* Barbara Stanwyck played the role onscreen in 1952. Bankhead was considered for *Humoresque,* for *Mr. Skeffington,* and for *Gone with the Wind* (but then who wasn't?); the parts went to Crawford, Bette Davis, and Vivien Leigh, respectively.[37]

Bankhead opted to perform in Noel Coward's *Private Lives* rather than playing Lady Macbeth in Welles's stage and subsequent film version of the Scottish play; Jeanette Nolan took the role instead. And, perhaps most sadly, she screen-tested for the role of Amanda Wingfield in Tennessee Williams's *The Glass Menagerie.* Irving Rapper directed the test, which was shot by the great cinematographer Karl Freund, who, it is said, cried while Bankhead performed. But when Bankhead showed up drunk on the set (on the day she was to feed lines from off-camera), Jack Warner, shell-shocked from working with the often-drunk Errol Flynn, refused to hire her; Gertrude Lawrence, who preceded Bankhead in Coward's *Private Lives,* played the role on the screen.[38]

But to mention Bankhead's *not* getting a part in *Mr. Skeffington* is to touch on what is arguably *the* defining feature of Bankhead's status: as a double for and as doubled by Bette Davis, a better-known and even-more-travestied camp icon. Part of Bankhead's inaccessibility derives from Davis's greater accessibility. Among the roles that Bankhead played or was to play which were eventually filmed by Davis were Julie in *Jezebel,* the heroine in *Dark Victory,* and, most famously, Regina in Lillian Hellman's *Little Foxes.*[39] This uncanny replacement of Bankhead by Davis was so well-known that it became the subject of a much-publicized but perhaps fictional feud between the women, Bankhead's occultation in the public eye by Davis becoming dramatized as a rivalry between the actresses. In Bankhead's 1951 radio show, *The Big Show,* the writers capitalized on the whiff of a catfight, striking lines for Bankhead like, "Just wait 'til I get my hands on her. I'll pull every hair out of her . . . mustache."[40] Since Davis's on-screen persona included a series of memorable catfights (with Miriam Hopkins in *The Old Maid* and *Old Acquaintance,* with Mary Astor in *The Great Lie*), including those rumored to have transpired offscreen, Bankhead's ongoing catfight with

Davis practically takes on the status of a meta-catfight.

Further, Bankhead is also reputed to have served as the model for a number of dramatic and cinematic figures who became more well-known than Bankhead. It is not hard to imagine Tallulah as a model for Tennessee Williams's Blanche Dubois in *A Streetcar Named Desire* or Flora Goforth in Williams's *The Milk Train Doesn't Stop Here Anymore,* roles which Bankhead eventually played on stage, *Streetcar* in 1956 and *Milk Train* in 1964. (The latter screen role in Joseph Losey's film of the play went to Elizabeth Taylor.) Geraldine Page also claimed that the character of Princess in Williams's *Sweet Bird of Youth* was modeled on both Rita Hayworth and Bankhead. Zoë Akins purportedly modeled the heroine of her story "Morning Glory" after Bankhead,[41] and Hitchcock told writer Ben Hecht to model Alicia Huberman's manner of speech in *Notorious* on Bankhead's.[42] Even Davis's role of Margo Channing in *All about Eve* has been said to have been modeled on Bankhead: Bankhead called the film *All about Me.*[43]

Remembrances of Things Past

The entire narrative construction of Bankhead as past, as lost, as an ever-receding and never-reachable origin and original, helps to construct Bankhead as an object of *nostalgia.* If camp has been understood as involving an investment in the devalued aesthetic products of outmoded eras, the downside of this construction of camp has been that it continues the psychological and psychoanalytic construction of the male homosexual as fixated on an earlier developmental era. Such focus grounds camp in a definite form of subjectivity, rather than *understanding camp as an effect of historical processes.* By grounding a nostalgic camp in a regressive subjectivity, one loses the opportunity to understand the ways in which "sub-jectivity" itself arises at specific junctures as a historical effect. In his insightful (but "utterly humorless") discussion of camp, Andrew Ross underlines such a historical perspective.[44] Camp, which revalues earlier and devalued modalities of cultural production, is likely to come into effect when a medium whose cultural power is on the wane (film, for example, during the 1950's) comments on its own decline: "The camp effect . . . is created not simply by a change in the mode of cultural production, . . . but rather when the products . . . of a much earlier mode of production, which has lost its power to produce and dominate cultural meanings, become available, in the present, for redefinition according to contemporary codes of taste."[45]

Ross's key example is Robert Aldrich's *Whatever Happened to Baby Jane?,* a film that activated memories of Davis's earlier on-screen and rumored offscreen fights with various costars to such an extent that the same rumors surfaced about its production: in *Baby Jane,* Bette Davis and Joan Crawford portray degraded has-beens locked in a perpetual struggle, Crawford's movies now running in the afternoon on television. Whatever "nostalgia" is involved in such texts can no longer be understood as a personal or collective psychological experience but rather as a certain potential within technological and cultural changes, a potential which, like electrical potential, arises from differences. E. H. Gombrich has pointed out in the field of decorative design that new technologies and materials seem to begin by modeling themselves on earlier ones. Stone columns imitating trees, Formica imitating wood grain, linoleum imitating brick, the computer screen imitating a desktop, and, most recently, compact disks including *faux* surface noise which recalls the era of the record (Madonna's *Erotica* being only one example).[46] Ross's insight about camp can be understood as the obverse. Namely, as a temporal reversal wherein the *earlier* technology or medium in the process of being superseded attempts to reproduce within itself the newer technology or medium in order to acknowledge and comment on its own impending irrelevance. Such a situation is "nostalgic" but in a sense which is no longer psychological but rather historical.

If a camp effect attaches itself to Bette Davis or Joan Crawford after *Baby Jane,* then it is because these icons come to serve as indices of historical processes of cultural and technological change. Certainly her appearance in the *Baby Jane*-clone *Die! Die, My Darling* brings Bankhead into the orbit of such a discussion. Here Dyer's writing on stars, and on Judy Garland in particular, is helpful insofar as certain of the meanings Dyer finds in various star personae have a specifically *temporal* or *historical* dimension such that the star in question becomes a signifier of a temporal moment or a historical process. If, as Dyer suggests, specific star images crystallize not only an ideal but also an idealized and idealizing historical and biographical moment—the young Shirley Temple, the maternal Kate Smith—so other star images, like Bankhead's, seem always to contain within themselves a minimal temporality, a retention of the past in the present.[47] Dyer underlines in Garland's image (among other things) androgyny and the "comeback" syndrome as part of Garland's appeal. Dyer clearly marks Garland's androgyny as implying a developmental *phase,* thus suggesting that Garland's image serves to mark a temporal moment, and likewise Garland's "comeback" syndrome, her successive failures and successes, imply that her image encompasses a sort of historical periodicity.

Stephen Sondheim's song "I'm Still Here," quoted in the epigraph to this chapter, frames this kind of temporal moment, as well as these historical transitions across cultural regimes, in terms of the minimal personal triumph of the show-biz "survivor." "First you're another sloe-eyed vamp, / Then someone's mother, / Then you're camp." These lines function well to suggest the way the camp effect involves condensing significations which are not only opposed but which also have specific temporal and historical markings. Not only does "vamp" suggest an anterior historical period, but "vamp" and "mother" each suggests a different *age;* at the same time these two lines also recall ontological oppositions between a generalized kind of copy ("*another* sloe-eyed vamp") and a particular and original origin ("*someone's* mother"). When these opposing temporal, historical and ontological significations become condensed into a single point, "then," as Sondheim tersely puts it, "you're camp," where the "then" can be read as marking *both* temporal succession and logical entailment.[48]

Likewise, Bankhead's fitful fame and her tendency to rise only to be eclipsed make her entire career path also a cyclical one, such that her fame is practically synonymous with a prior obscurity, and her obscurity marks a by-gone fame. Dyer's analysis of the same pattern in Garland's career suggests *How to Become a Camp Icon, no. 3:* Have many highly visible public failures such that all one's successes are "comebacks" (also known as the "Judy Garland Rule"). And the historical condensations of camp suggest a corollary to the "Judy Garland Rule," namely, *How to Be a Camp Icon, no. 4:* Since it's very difficult to become the object of a cult of nostalgia in the present, try to accelerate the passage of time by identifying yourself with waning cultural institutions. The effect is familiar from Garland's identification with vaudeville, both through musical numbers in her films and through her vocal borrowing from Al Jolson, and from Bette Midler's later cultivation of a camp following through her early and assiduous association of herself with music of the 1940s and with vaudeville through her adoption of the jokes and persona of Sophie Tucker. Bankhead's career shows a similar pattern: during the era of Hollywood cinema's dominance, her screen roles were woefully few and all-too-marginal, and she was identified instead with theater, as well as with radio.[49] In 1950, as television was effectively replacing radio as the broadcast entertainment medium of choice, Bankhead was chosen to be the hostess of what was agreed to be radio's last hurrah, a program called *The Big Show*. Bankhead's career path thus made her an index of media (theater, radio) whose cultural authority was waning in the face of new media and technologies (first film and then television).

But if Bankhead comes to signify a certain collapsed temporality or the waning of specific cultural institutions, it is important to underline that she is not therefore a figure for a past which actually existed. Just as Freud emphasizes that the fetish is not a sign for a maternal phallus which actually existed, so we think not merely of what Tallulah *was* and *did* but of what she *might have been* (e.g., more famous, more filmed) and what she *never was to have done* (e.g., be fellated by Montgomery Clift). Narratives construct Bankhead's "lostness" not merely in terms of an inaccessible past but rather in terms of *alternative modalities* of being: not an *indicative* "is" or "was" but a *subjunctive* of what "might have been" or a *negative future anterior* of what "never was to have been."[50]

Bankhead's most acute fans are most susceptible to this sense of regret. Carrier's writing is particularly rich in constructions of Bankhead which need to be articulated in the conditional or subjunctive: "*Had* Tallulah been cast as Amanda Wingfield, it *might have* halted her tailspin into the depths of camp and caricature, but probably not for long."[51] Here I would say rather: it is the "had [she] been" and "might have" which are precisely what *make* Bankhead camp and caricature. Or:

> That she *was never* universally recognized as a major talent is probably her own fault. As many critics have noted, the *potential* for greatness was there, but, *regretfully*, the discipline wasn't. By living exactly as she wanted—with reckless abandon—she allowed her antics to upstage her art.[52]

These constructions of Bankhead implement linguistic and narrative potentialities which have a powerful political valence for disenfranchised groups, as well as a certain melodramatic appeal.[53] Just as fetishism splits off an alternative modality of belief which need not answer to the presence or absence of the phallus, so these alternative modalities open up an imaginative, counterfactual space (like Miller's imagined version of *Rope*) against which reality can then be measured and found wanting. Such unrealized potentialities implicitly criticize reality by providing an Archimedean external point from which it might be leveraged *elsewhere*.

From Copies to Copying

If Bankhead is constructed as lost in an Edenic past overshadowed by mere copies, this relation between original and copy is also susceptible to reversals in which Bankhead herself becomes a mere devalued copy, derivative not fundamental. After all, Bankhead was notably belated in many of her stage portrayals: she followed Jeanne Eagels's in Somerset Maugham's *Rain*, Gertrude Lawrence in Coward's *Private Lives*,[54] Jessica Tandy and Vivien Leigh in *A Streetcar Named Desire*, and she played the leads in *Humoresque*, *Dark Victory*, and *All about Eve* on the radio *after* Joan Crawford and Bette Davis had played them onscreen.

If Bankhead was often a secondary repetition of a prior original, she was in a sense always playing herself, always playing the role of the (in)famous person who she herself was. When she appeared on Broadway in Thornton Wilder's *The Skin of Our Teeth*, Bankhead adlibbed lines to the audience that expressed Tallulah Bankhead's feelings, rather than those of her character Lily Sabina: "I don't understand a word of this play, not a word." As Carrier observes, "Tallulah Bankhead's greatest portrayal was Tallulah Bankhead."[55] With film cameos in *Stage Door Canteen* and *Main Street to Broadway*, Bankhead had the opportunity to appear on screen, but only by playing her most famous creation: herself. Indeed, the tragic narrative of a fallen and degraded Tallulah can only be brought forth by presenting Bankhead as exactly a degraded copy *of herself.* Carrier again exemplifies this type of narrative construction by describing Bankhead's 1956 appearance as Blanche Dubois in Williams's *Streetcar:*

> She became a parody of herself, and the caricature that she presented on radio and television was a tragic distortion of a rare and original talent, a talent that fell victim to the whims and caprices of the formidable Tallulah Bankhead.[56]

In the media, in her role as radio hostess, in 1950 on her "lecture tour," in 1953 during her performances in Las Vegas, and later as TV guest, Bankhead was asked to play herself—endlessly, and the performance took its toll. Bankhead was fond of saying: "If I have to go out on a stage once more and say, 'Hello, Dahlings,' I shall go stark raving mad."[57] Such constructions make Bankhead not only into a faded copy of herself, but also into a part of what was once a whole. An anecdote which I have often heard recounted about Bankhead finds a drunken Tallulah, having stumbled and fallen, only to be recognized by the gentlemen picking her up: "Aren't you Tallulah Bankhead?" "I'm what's *left* of her."[58]

Perhaps Bankhead's campiest performance took the form of her playing the luridly seductive "Black Widow" during the 1967 season of the camp-lite television series *Batman.* The program marked one of those moments to which Andrew Ross has drawn attention: the crossover of camp from a minority audience to a mass market. If Bankhead was both lost original and failed copy (even of herself), this construction of Bankhead's star status in terms of copying, helps us to understand the way camp functions as a two-way site of struggle. In the kind of mass-marketification of camp to which Ross draws attention and which

has, if anything, intensified since he wrote about it, the margin and the mainstream enter into a dialogue. When the excluded margin has acquired a certain caché of cultural capital because of its very marginality, this marginality can in turn be sold back to the mainstream which has effected this very marginalization to recapture that elusive caché. The net effect is that the very difference between the margin and the mainstream is both *capitalized* upon (literally, in the economic sense) and yet in the process the difference is capitalized is also *effaced.*

Such circulation from margin to mainstream and the corresponding effacement of difference between the two are not without certain effects which become evident in the way the iconography of gay male subcultural styles functions. It sells merchandise, thus effacing the specificity of those very styles. From the macho gay style popularized after Stonewall in the 1970s to single earrings to black denim to double earrings to tattoos (or, more recently, nipple-piercing), the same effect takes place: a devalued style, often associated with a phantasmatically transgressive, working-class masculinity. It acquires a new, sexualized valence and meaning through its appropriation in gay culture, only to be then reappropriated by the mainstream through fashion and advertising, ads for underwear and cologne having spearheaded this strategy. When the subcultures from which these styles emerge are the objects of phobias, like homophobia and racism (as in the case of R&B, jazz, and, most recently, rap and hip hop), the difference between the margin and the mainstream is not diminished. Rather the anxiety over the difference increases as the signifiers of that difference circulate freely back and forth and thus cease to function as differential signifiers, as marks of difference.

This circulation of signifiers which fail to mark differences is not something secondary and derivative which is added on to camp afterwards and from the outside. Rather, what is at stake in the camp effect as it is legible in Bankhead's persona is precisely such a process of copying, of reversals of original and copy, of earlier. Later, such that the ontological priority and security of such differences are effaced, and these apparent oppositions are replaced by a process of mimetic copying and doubling which are dramatized and narrativized in Bankhead's bitchy witticisms and purported catfights with Bette Davis. Indeed, two witty Los Angeles performance artists have constructed a nightclub act called the Dueling Bankheads in which, among other things, these two men dress in drag as two rather tipsy Bankheads and sing the song "Dueling Banjos" as if it were a chain of insults, using for words the title of Bankhead's film *Die, Die, My Darling* in lieu of lyrics.[59] By not only copying Bankhead but by doing it *twice*, and by aiming Bankhead's famous bitchiness at *herself*, the artists cleverly condense the aggressivity Bankhead has come to connote with her status as doubled by others and by herself, and the music itself aligns this aggressivity with the phobic construction of male homosexuality in the movie *Deliverance*, for which "Dueling Banjos" served as a theme.

The constructions of Bankhead alternately as a lost original and a failed copy thus opens the way for a third construction of Bankhead: namely "Tallulah Bankhead" as a proper name which marks a *process* of copying or imitation, the "Tallulah Bankhead effect," a process which is neither a subject nor an object. After all, whether Bankhead is imitated or an imitation, original or copy, subject or object, is somewhat irrelevant from the perspective of the process of copying involved. Tallulah Bankhead *as a camp icon* is thus less a sign which refers to or denotes an actual person and more a signifier, "Tallulah Bankhead," which indexes this process of copying. "Tallulah Bankhead" is one name for the camp effect, which is to say that "Tallulah" indeed means "trouble."

What's Left *of Her: Mourning and Laughing*

The paradox of a camp figure like Bankhead is that she serves as a unique sign for a process of copying which involves the opposite of uniqueness. To be a camp icon requires this unique mark or trait— Bankhead's and Davis's voices, the resonant, pleading sob and catch in Judy Garland's voice or Maria Callas's. *How to Become a Camp Icon, no. 5:* To be imitated you must be original, striking, different (also known as the "Derrida Rule"). To imagine a confrontation between Bankhead and Davis is to imagine two of the most distinctive voices of the American theater and cinema. One can hardly overlook the fact that many of the traits of camp icons are ensconced in the voice as the most traditional metaphysical image of the subject's self-presence, and in particular the voices of *women*, women having also been constructed as the very image of a private emotionality.[60] Although the gay male attachment to this sign of feminine interiority emphasizes the expressiveness, transparency and theatricality of such voices, this attachment also subverts the very interiority that is being cited.[61] What is imitable about Bankhead's voice is not just its gruff, subversively "masculine" texture, but above all its special pattern of *emphasis*: "He's never sucked *my* cock." Indeed, on a record she made in 1957 called *Co-Star*, Bankhead demonstrates for the listener the art of acting through exactly such shifts in emphasis: "*What* are you doing? What *are* you doing? What are *you* doing? What are you *doing?*"[62]

Further, such an attachment to the voice is one of the marks that moves camp even as a fetishistic attachment to signifiers, to voices, away from a conception of fetishism in terms of castration and visibility and toward an understanding which emphasizes the partiality of fetishism, its success in *making desire portable, mobile*. If fetishism and castration are generally understood in terms of seeing and not-seeing, the gay camp fixation on the voice and the transmission of camp anecdotes by ear certainly moves away from such a visual and objectifying understanding. Bankhead's extensive radio appearances and her recordings no doubt helped prepare the way for the separation of her voice from her body, for the transmission through gay male culture of that voice: the record I mentioned above has in turn been sampled and cited in the work of performance artist/drag queen John Epperson/Lypsinka.[63] The voice, although seemingly intimately tied to the body, is also subject, via impersonation, to the same kind of drifting by which the fetish as a substitute allows the phallus to be displaced and made mobile. Bankhead's career was very much bound up with this drifting of signs into ever new contexts. Much of the end of her life was taken up first with mobility: touring in summer stock and then with appearing as a guest on shows like *The Andy Williams Show, What's My Line?, The Red Skelton Show, The Tonight Show, The Mike Douglas Show,* and *The Merv Griffin Show.*[64]

This separation of the voice from the body and of words from a context is also legible in another aspect of Bankhead's camp status, namely in the way so many anecdotes about Bankhead terminate in a quip, an epigram, a bon mot. The fetishism of gay male camp depends in part upon this fragmentation, this separation of the part from a whole which opens up the anecdote to endless performances and citations. Such fetishism, far from preserving the wholeness and integrity of a phallicized body, dismembers that body, taking a supplementary prosthesis in place of a lost totality. Anecdotes *about* Bankhead—"Are you Tallulah Bankhead?" "I'm what's *left* of her"—thus actually *perform* Bankhead's status as leftover by *being* that very remainder. Here Bankhead belongs alongside Dorothy Parker and Oscar Wilde, figures whose reputations depend in part upon those witticisms, ripostes, and epithets which are often transmitted orally: the mini-narratives leading to a bon mot that help to make up the patchwork quilt of gay culture. We have sewn our culture not from whole cloth but particolored and patchwork like the harlequin's costume. We campers are queens of shreds and patches, handing on our secret legacies in oral culture, from mouth to ear. If we can be a spectacle to others, or if we are insistently forbidden from even being visible to others, the ear takes up what the eye lets go, and gay culture reverberates with these stories like so many echoing whispers, like the voices of the dead.

Speaking of her autobiography, Bankhead mentions a caveat that impelled the writing of the work, a caveat of silence, of respect, of modesty. "I tried to be completely honest. . . . Of course, one has to protect people who are dead *and can't answer back.*"[65] In thinking of Tallulah, I situate myself in relation not only to her and her lost voice, but to those voices who have spoken in her voice, who have quoted her and imitated her: the voices of the living and the dead. If camp has been seen as a nostalgic fixation on the past, as a defense against time and loss, stars as fetishes displacing a nonexistent value in order to preserve it, I would prefer a third alternative: not holding on to the past, nor giving up on it as absent and lost, but rather preserving the past *as irretrievable.* Appealing to Julia Kristeva's discussion of women's relation to the phallus, Tania Modleski has insisted that men, because they have the phallus, can avoid the experience women have, namely of *mourning* the phallus.[66] But what I have tried to suggest of Tallulah Bankhead's status as a camp icon for gay men is that her appeal consists precisely in the way Bankhead as a fetish, as a proxy phallus, is treasured in the very *inaccessibility* which permits the articulation of phantasies about her. I would also like to suggest briefly in closing that this relationship to an absent figure performs a work of mourning, a work which takes on a new meaning after the advent of AIDS. Could our relationship to an irretrievably absent Tallulah not point ways for us to think through our relationship to others who are absent?[67]

If we understand camp in terms of the way our

voices can quote the dead and absent, then we might believe that camp delusively tries to revivify the dead, to make them live again. But I would argue that there is nothing delusive about camp, for in endlessly conferring upon Tallulah the power of speech, in making her speak again and again, do we not *italicize* that voice and mourn the impossibility of hearing it? Can we, after all, be assured that in adoring Tallulah what we want is her full presence, her life? For could it not also be that such nostalgia has no wish to revive what is lost but rather cherishes it *as lost,* without thereby celebrating loss? The title of Capote's novel in which he remembers Tallulah, *Answered Prayers,* derives, he says, from a quotation whose origins are uncertain: "More tears are shed over answered prayers than over those left unanswered."[68] What I am saying about Bankhead is that our memories of her should be thought of as prayers which are *unanswered* and *unanswerable.*

But it is not *only* Tallulah's words nor her inflections, not, in sum her *speaking* voice, which transfixes me in her wake. In *Stage Door Canteen* her perhaps two minutes of screentime begins with Tallulah, surrounded by sailors, laughing. It seems significant that Tallulah should be introduced through her laughter. The fact that she and all the men around her are laughing makes it seem that perhaps she has just tossed off one of her famous witticisms, saltier than any sailor's, and that she laughs in appreciation of herself, and of the sailors' appreciation of her. Bankhead herself was sensitive to this aspect of her appeal when she ascribed this very appeal in part to her "hoarse laugh."[69] I would like to think of Tallulah as "she who, unbelieving, still plays with castration. . . . She takes aim and amuses herself with it as she would with a new concept or structure of belief, but even as she plays she is gleefully anticipating her laughter, her mockery of man," just as I would like to think that Jacques Derrida, in writing this passage, was thinking not of Nietzsche's "woman" but of Tallulah.[70]

When I think of Tallulah's voice, I imagine such an eruption of laughter—perhaps staging the way time and history laughed at her, or the equanimity with which she might have laughed at them, or perhaps implying the aggressively bitchy power to ridicule which she had and which I quote, covet, and, as a victim of homophobia, need. Nor am I alone in remembering this laughter. At Bankhead's 1968 memorial service, a telegram arrived from Alfred Hitchcock. "My warmest and most vivid memory of Tallulah is *laughter.* To be with her was a time of fun and enjoyment. When the laughter *subsided,* there always *remained* my good friend, a strong and courageous woman."[71]

I like to think that in the laughter of the gay men I have known and loved and who shared stories of Tallulah with me there is a fun and enjoyment which is also a token of friendship, strength, and courage. And that when other memories subside, this sound, this echo, will remain in our accursed hearts—those chambers of eternal mourning.[72] When we think of, recount, and imitate Tallulah, is it the voice and the long-lost full presence that we long for, or is it not what "always remained" when the laughter subsided?

Probably Tallulah would laugh at such speculations. Incredulous, no doubt she'd upbraid me. "*What* are you doing? What *are* you doing? What are *you* doing? What are you *doing?*"

And then, she'd laugh, and I would too, for no one would enjoy her laughter more than I.

Notes

1 Jean-François Lyotard and Jean-Loup Thébaud, *Just Gaming,* trans. Wlad Godzich, in *Theory and History of Literature,* vol. 20 (Minneapolis: University of Minnesota Press, 1985), 32–33.

2 Truman Capote, *Answered Prayers: An Unfinished Novel* (New York: Random House, 1987).

3 The existence of other chapters is itself one of the things about Capote's novel which is in doubt, a doubt that intensifies the doubts within the book as it stands.

4 Capote, *Answered Prayers,* xxii.

5 Ibid., xvii, emphasis in original.

6 Ibid., 48, emphasis added.

7 Ibid., 49, emphasis in original.

8 See, for instance, Eve Kosofsky Sedgwick, *Epistemology of the Closet* (Berkeley: University of California Press, 1990); Lee Edelman, *Homographesis: Essays in Gay Literary and Cultural Theory* (New York: Routledge, 1994); and Judith Butler, *Gender Trouble: Feminism and the Subversion of Identity* (New York: Routledge, 1990).

9 Marc Siegel tells me that his research into Tab Hunter reveals that Bankhead repeated the joke with reference to Hunter. Whether this shows that she originated the line or appropriated it from Capote—or Parker, for that matter—is not clear.

10 See, for instance, Richard Dyer, ed., *Gays and Film* (New York: Zoetrope, 1984), *The Matter of Images* (London: Routledge, 1993), and *Now You See It: Studies on Lesbian and Gay Film* (New York: Routledge, 1990); Robin Wood, *Hollywood from Vietnam to Reagan* (New York: Columbia University Press, 1986); and Vito Russo, *The Celluloid Closet*, rev. ed. (New York: Harper and Row, 1981). I do not mean to single out for blame these critics in particular; rather I take them as exemplary of a widespread type of critical project whose usefulness is by no means a thing of the past but whose goals and limitations are certainly eligible for discussion and revision. For a further discussion of the differences between such reading practices and my own, see the author's "*Poison*-ous Queers: Violence and Social Order," in "Do You Read Me? Queer Theory and Social Praxis," ed. Eric Freedman, special issue of *Spectator* 15(1) (fall 1994): 8–29.

11 D. A. Miller, "Anal Rope" in *Inside/Out: Lesbian Theories, Gay Theories,* ed. Diana Fuss (New York: Routledge, 1991), 122, 121; emphasis added.

12 See, for instance, Moe Myer's insistence that camp be construed as a gay species of parody in his introduction to *The Politics and Poetics of Camp,* ed. Moe Meyer (New York: Routledge, 1994). In the present case, Bankhead's status as a camp icon is itself demonstrable but unprovable.

13 And here Sedgwick also draws inspiration from Miller, whose reading of *Rope* pays heed exactly to the "dubiety" which he describes as "constitutive" of the production of homosexuality as a connotation (Miller, "Anal Rope," 124).

14 See Jacques Lacan, "Le séminaire sur "la lettre volée," in *Écrits* (Paris: Éditions du Seuil, 1966), or Jacques Lacan, *The Seminar of Jacques Lacan. Book II: The Ego in Freud's Theory and in the Technique of Psychoanalysis, 1954–1955,* ed. Jacques-Alain Miller, trans. Sylvana Tomaselli (New York: Norton, 1991), 175–205. For the connection between the epistemological status of male homosexuality and the intersubjective structure outlined by Lacan, I am indebted to an unpublished paper by David Gardner on queer cinema spectatorship and cruising.

15 This reading (emphasizing the impossibility) of Bankhead's knowing if Clift were gay would take up the motif of the deprivation of sight already within the anecdote—in the form of Parker's feeling Clift's face as blindly trying to feel something she cannot know by seeing.

16 And it is this kind of attention to such anecdotes which, however absurd, characterizes precisely the fan or "fanatic's" attention to the object of his fanaticism.

17 Such "impossibility" could never be empirical but is rather always transcendental; i.e., nothing is empirically impossible, since our empirical knowledge is always "corrigible" or subject to revision or correction.

18 I say "phallus" here rather than "cock" in order to indicate the fetishistic status of this imaginary organ. Such an organ is not imaginary because it is impossible, but rather is imaginary in the present instance because its existence and nonexistence are both equally in doubt.

19 Miller, "Anal Rope," 134.

20 Nor is this conception of fetishism as a defensive relation to castration limited to male heterosexual spectators, since male homosexuals, according to the psychoanalytic theory, are all the more invested in the phallus and can tolerate even less its absence in a love object and so might thus have an even greater need of fetishism in such situations as the cinematographic one. On the canonical psychoanalytic reading of male homosexuality, see Kenneth Lewes's highly admirable *The Psychoanalytic Theory of Male Homosexuality* (New York: Meridian/New American Library, 1988).

21 See Sigmund Freud's oft-cited "Fetishism," in *Sexuality and the Psychology of Love,* ed. Philip Rieff (New York: Collier, 1963).

22 Karl Marx, *Capital,* vol. 1, trans. Eden Paul and Cedar Paul (London: J. M. Dent and Sons, 1930), 43–58, esp. 43–48.

23 Jean Laplanche and J.-B. Pontalis, *The Language of Psychoanalysis,* trans. Donald Nicholson-Smith (New York: Norton, 1973), 120.

24 For a further discussion of fetishism, see the author's "Making Politics Perfectly Queer," forthcoming in *Strategies*.

25 O. Mannoni, "Je sais bien, mais quand même . . ." in *Clefs pour l'imaginaire ou l'autre scène* (Paris: Éditions du Seuil, 1969), 9–33. See Slavoj Žižek's discussions in *The Sublime Object of Ideology* (London: Verso, 1989), also see *For They Know Not What They Do: Enjoyment as a Political Factor* (London: Verso, 1991), notably the discussion of Mannoni at 245–49.

26 In *Epistemology of the Closet* Eve Kosofsky Sedgwick underlines the significance for minorities (such as gays) of gossip as a tentative epistemic modality for thinking about social types: "It is probably people with the experience of oppression or subordination who have most *need* to know it [i.e., the crudeness of recognized typologies of social groups and relations as against their actual diversity and complexity]; and I take the precious, devalued arts of gossip, immemorially associated in European thought with servants, with effeminate and gay men, with all women, to have to do not even so much with the transmission of necessary news as with the refinement of necessary skills for making, testing, and using unrationalized and provisional hypotheses about what *kinds of people* there are to be found in one's world" (23; all emphases in the original). I owe a debt to Marc Siegel for drawing my attention to this passage, which I must have read many times without noticing it—much the same way I encountered Capote's anecdote about Bankhead.

27 See Richard Dyer, *Stars* (London: BFI, 1982), and *Heavenly Bodies: Film Stars and Society* (New York: St. Martin's Press, 1979); Miriam Hansen, *Babel and Babylon: Spectatorship in American Silent Film* (Cambridge, MA: Harvard University Press, 1991).

28 For a discussion of the modality of gossip as devalued yet central to the novel, see Patricia Meyer Spacks, *Gossip* (New York: Knopf, 1985), esp. chapter 1, "Its Problematic," and chapter 2, "Its Reputation."

29 Cited in Donald Spoto, *The Dark Side of Genius* (New York: Ballantine, 1983), 282. Spoto cites Hume Cronyn as his source for the story; it was Cronyn whom I first heard recount this story on an appearance on *The Tonight Show*. Carrier also refers readers to Doug McClelland's *StarSpeak: Hollywood on Everything* (Boston: Faber and Faber, 1987) and John Russell Taylor, *Hitch: The Life and Times of Alfred Hitchcock* (New York: Pantheon, 1978).

30 Harold J. Kennedy, *No Pickle, No Performance: An Irreverent Theatrical Excursion from Tallulah to Travolta* (Garden City, NY: Doubleday, 1978), 71. I had a strange sense of deja vu when reading this book: eventually I realized that when I was a child, or perhaps almost a teenager, one of the two newsstands in my small hometown for some unknown reason had a copy of this book on its single rotating rack of paperback books. I would read it standing up while loitering about trying to get a peek at some "adult" magazines. Somehow Kennedy's backstage stories of a theatrical life exerted a powerful draw for me, whether because of the book itself or because of its connection with other illicit "reading" materials. In any case, I find it oddly uncanny that Tallulah made a sort of appearance at this particular moment in my nascent sexuality and/or reading habits.

31 For a discussion of Bankhead's putative lesbianism, as well as her association with drugs both licit and illicit, see Barry Paris, *Louise Brooks* (New York: Knopf, 1989).

32 See Kenneth Anger, *Hollywood Babylon II* (New York: New American Library, 1984).

33 Quoted in Jeffrey L. Carrier, *Tallulah Bankhead: A Bio-Bibliography*, Bio-Bibliographies in the Performing Arts, no. 21 (New York: Greenwood Press, 1991), xvii.

34 These included: "The Waltz," "Advice to the Little Peyton Girl," "Sentiment," "The Telephone Call," "The Little Hours," and "Here We Are." See Carrier's chronology of Bankhead's radio appearances. Parker's own status as arch-origin of camp as a verbal practice is in part documented in Arthur Dong's documentary, *Coming Out Under Fire*, in which one former soldier describes how he and his friends would read Parker's short stories and imitate her language, including the use of expressions such as "divine" and "darling." Whether these were gay coinages before Parker ever got her hands on them I do not know. What is more certain is the good effect to which Bankhead put them: Bankhead's summer stock revue of sketches at one point included a sketch in which a very middle-aged Bankhead played (of all things) Peter Pan. When Bankhead as Peter asked Wendy her name, Wendy would reply "Wendy Moira Angela Darling. What's yours?" This of course provoked Bankhead's response: "Peter Pan, Darling." See Kennedy, *No Pickle, No Performance*, 68.

35 Ibid., 67.

36 The comment is quoted in Carrier, *Tallulah Bankhead*, 201.

37 Ibid., 250.

38 Ibid., 33. See also Mike Steen, *A Look at Tennessee Williams* (New York: Hawthorne, 1969).

39 Charles Higham recounts in his biography of Davis that Davis modeled her own interpretation on Bankhead's, even against director William Wyler's strenuous objections. See *Bette: The Life of Bette Davis* (New York: Macmillan, 1981); see also Arthur Marx, *Goldwyn: A Biography of the Man Behind the Myth* (New York: Norton, 1976).

40 Carrier, *Tallulah Bankhead*, 35.

41 Anne Edwards, *A Remarkable Story: A Biography of Katharine Hepburn* (New York: William Morrow, 1985).

42 Leonard J. Leff, *Hitchcock and Selznick* (New York: Weidenfeld and Nicolson, 1987); quoted in Carrier, *Tallulah Bankhead*, 203.

43 Bankhead did a 1952 radio version of the 1950 film; a recording was released on Moving Finger Records, number 002; referred to in Carrier, *Tallulah Bankhead*, 176.

44 Andrew Ross, "Strategic Camp: The Art of Gay Rhetoric" in *Camp Grounds: Style and Homosexuality*, ed. David Bergman (Amherst: University of Massachusetts Press, 1993), 102. The remark perhaps demonstrates that humorlessness, like humor, is very much in the eye of the beholder.

45 Ibid., 58.

46 E. H. Gombrich, *The Sense of Order: A Study in the Psychology of Decorative Art* (Ithaca, NY: Cornell University Press, 1979), 174.

47 See especially Dyer's *Heavenly Bodies*.

48 The fact that subsequent camp icons like Eartha Kitt have taken this song as a kind of anthem suggests that Sondheim's insight has not gone unappreciated by those to whom the matter is of some urgency.

49 See Carrier's chapter on Bankhead's radio performances.

50 And the "subjectivity" which corresponds to this narrative modality will no longer correspond with the traditional philosophical subject defined in terms of an immediacy of consciousness and perception manifested in the indicative modality which is so often the unthought basis for the philosopher's construction of the subject.

51 Carrier 33, *Tallulah Bankhead*, emphasis added.

52 Ibid., xvii, emphasis added.

53 On melodrama and the "might have been," see Mary Ann Doane, *The Desire to Desire: The Woman's Film of the 1940s* (Bloomington: Indiana University Press, 1987), 106–8; on minority discourse, see Gilles Deleuze and Félix Guattari, *Kafka: Toward a Minor Literature,* trans. Dana Polan, *Theory and History of Literature,* vol. 30 (Minneapolis: University of Minnesota Press, 1986), 16–27, and *A Thousand Plateaus: Capitalism and Schizophrenia,* trans. Brian Massumi (Minneapolis: University of Minnesota Press, 1987), 104–7.

54 And it must also be remembered that Lawrence returned the favor by beating out Bankhead for the part of Amanda in the film of Tennessee Williams's *The Glass Menagerie.*

55 Carrier, *Tallulah Bankhead.*

56 Ibid., xvii.

57 Ibid., 38.

58 Kennedy recounts a similar story, but describes the events as having happened to Kay Francis (*No Pickle, No Performance,* 71).

59 The Dueling Bankheads can be glimpsed in the documentary *Wigstock: The Movie* (1995).

60 See Jacques Derrida's *Speech and Phenomenon, and Other Essays On Husserl's Theory of Signs,* trans. David B. Allison (Evanston, IL: Northwestern University Press, 1973), and *Of Grammatology,* trans. Gayatri Chakravorty Spivak (Baltimore: Johns Hopkins University Press, 1974).

61 Dyer's essay on Garland in *Stars* is particularly acute on this issue of the expressivity in Garland's voice and performing style, which seems to appeal to a male homosexuality constructed in a constricting closet of secrecy. For a richly suggestive meditation on male homosexuality, the voice, and fandom, see Wayne Koestenbaum, *The Queen's Throat: Opera, Homosexuality, and the Mystery of Desire* (New York: Vintage Books, 1993). Readers of Koestenbaum's book will recognize that the current writer's debt to his is much greater than can be indicated by a single footnote.

62 Roulette, CS109.

63 For an interview with the eloquent Epperson, see *Re/Search* #14, *Incredibly Strange Music, Volume I* (1993): 152–63. His most recent performances featured notable samples of Bankhead.

64 See Bruce Hainley's astute discussion of the career of Paul Lynde in "Special Guest Star: Paul Lynde," *Yale Journal of Criticism* 7(2) (fall 1994): 51–84. This article, along with Koestenbaum's book, got me started on the present project.

65 John Kobal, *People Will Talk* (New York: Knopf, 1985); cited in Carrier, *Tallulah Bankhead,* 36.

66 Tania Modleski, "Time and Desire in the Woman's Film," *Cinema Journal* 23(3) (spring 1984): 19–30.

67 On gays and mourning, see Douglas Crimp's thought-

provoking "Mourning and Militancy" *October* 51 (winter 1989): 3–18.

68   Capote says the quote is from St. Teresa of Avila, but as he never gives a source, I have reworded the phrase, rather than quoting Capote's version of it.

69   Carrier, *Tallulah Bankhead,* 11.

70   Jacques Derrida, *Spurs,* trans. Barbara Harlow (Chicago: University of Chicago Press, 1978), 61.

71   Carrier, *Tallulah Bankhead,* 44, emphasis added.

72   Here I am translating, quoting, and paraphrasing from the first verse of Baudelaire's "Obsession," in part in reference to Paul de Man's discussion in *The Rhetoric of Romanticism* (New York: Columbia University Press, 1984), 259–62. For an acute discussion of mourning in de Man's work, see Jacques Derrida, *Mémoires: For Paul de Man,* Wellek Library Lectures at the University of California — Irvine, trans. Cecile Lindsay, Jonathan Culler, and Eduardo Cadava (New York: Columbia University Press, 1986).

V. TASTE

HOP ON POP

WE INCLUDE TASTE AS A CATEGORY IN this anthology not so that we might celebrate the decorous but, rather, in order that we can investigate the social and cultural processes by which cultural objects or practices come to be deemed tasteful (or tasteless) in the first place. Socially, the term functions as a rubric in which class and culture often intersect, although the cultural construction of taste is rarely revealed or foregrounded. To declare an object tasteful is to imbue it with aesthetic value and cultural capital, securing a place for the object within society's hierarchies and canons. Taste serves as one of the important means by which social distinctions are maintained and class identities are forged. Following on the work of Pierre Bourdieu, the critical analysis of "distinction" has become an important element of cultural studies. Recognizing the significance of this endeavor, we retain the term "taste" for the emergent cultural studies.

When fans of lowly cultural objects (like TV shows) are ridiculed as "needing a life" or when overweight women are perceived as undisciplined and out of control, the moral judgments implicit in cultural constructions of taste are expressed. To include taste as a topic in this volume is to call for an analysis of the ways in which cultural concepts of decorum shape our understandings of class, gender, race, and sexuality. For instance, the widespread cultural perception of soap fans as less in tune with reality than sports fans has everything to do with the relative social value assigned to differently gendered leisure activities. As a social category of judgment, taste places us, or, more accurately, puts us in our respective places, reserving the best spots for those labeled tasteful, proper, or refined. But the borders of the tasteful are not easily maintained and must be carefully managed and produced. This process of containment creates gaps and fissures in which the tasteless can emerge as a challenge to the proper and the decorous. We are interested in how taste is maintained and how it is challenged, and the following essays explore this terrain.

The essays in this section prove the lie inherent in the cultural truism "there's no accounting for taste." While this expression serves to naturalize taste, rendering its cultural work transparent, these essays suggest that there are myriad critical frameworks that allow us to "account" for taste, particularly as it masks the play of power in society. Surveying a wide range of periods, practices, and texts, these essays foreground the varied roles taste plays in shaping our cultural experiences and understandings of values and aesthetics, the high and the low, the esteemed and the trashed.

Louis Kaplan's investigation of the role of humor during the Holocaust brings many issues of taste to the foreground. Generally, humor is not a form of expression deemed appropriate in analyses of this period of history. Kaplan pushes us to consider why the Jewish deployment of jokes during the Holocaust has been repressed in our contemporary accounts of the period, a repression that denies the possibility of a subversive use of laughter as a means of resistance against the Nazi oppressor. Kaplan's work underscores that melancholy is not the only mode of remembrance. Tony Grajeda's essay looks at a very different cultural production, lo-fi music, in order to examine how processes of distinction work within various categories of "alternative" and rock music. Grajeda examines the diverse ways in which cultural standards of taste work in conjunction with our understandings of the technological and the aesthetic to code certain types of music as "corporate" or as "alternative." In turn, these value judgments are closely tied to cultural perceptions of modes of production and to notions of authenticity and gender.

The next trio of essays looks at the role taste played in the regulation of and cultural discourses about three forms of popular entertainment in the early decades of the twentieth century in the United States. While each of these works analyzes the cultural function of censorship in different ways, all three share an interest in the relationship between standards of decorum, "low-brow" practices, and the resistance to mainstream notions of taste. In their exploration of the regulation of early nickelodeons, Roberta Pearson and William Uricchio encourage us to read against the grain of official accounts of history. They stress the importance of rethinking our historical narratives of criminality in order to entertain the possibility that what is officially labeled "criminal" might also represent a challenge to dominant modes of control. Thus, they suggest that the "tasteful" obedience of our historical methodologies often overlooks the discontinuities that Benjamin reminds us categorize the history of the oppressed.

Though he moves away from actual legal records, Nick Evans's account of cabaret nightlife during the Jazz Age also takes up issues of regulation, albeit a regulation via broader cultural discourses. More specifically, Evans investigates the "racial cross-dressing" of white jazz dancers of the period, elaborating the degree to which white participation in jazz culture replayed colonizing strategies, allowing whites to appropriate the "wildness" of African American culture while also distancing themselves from the culturally unacceptable aspects of blackness. He also offers up an alternative model of racial alliance and cross-racial identification in the form of a small group of ethnic white musicians whose struggles delineated other, less colonizing ways of being white. In her essay on burlesque in La Guardia's New York, Anna McCarthy is also interested in the ways in which official and unofficial social discourses effect a form of censorship. To this end, she explores the ways in which the formal aspects of burlesque challenged bourgeois theatrical codes and thus provoked dis-ease on the part of moralist reformers. McCarthy extends her analysis to point out the degree to which our present-day theories of voyeurism and the female body make it difficult to understand the cultural and historical specificity of a form like burlesque. Our theoretical tendency to privilege sight over sound erases the degree to which music and noise were an integral part of the

burlesque experience. McCarthy's project highlights the necessity of testing our theoretical claims against actual cultural practices. Only then can we begin to understand the limits of a reformist mentality when confronted with the gyrating bodies of burlesque.

Eric Schaefer's and Eithne Johnson's chronicling of Boston's Combat Zone extends this critique of the reformist mentality into the urban politics of the second half of the twentieth century. Their study unpacks the rhetorical framework used to position adult entertainment as "both lethal and contagious," a conceit used to justify the regulation of a physical area of Boston by comparisons to "lowly" areas of the body. This research, along with the other essays of this section, serves to remind us that matters of taste and morality often slip and slide between bodies, geographies, and psyches, eroding and reestablishing the borders of the decent and the deviant.

"It Will Get a Terrific Laugh": On the Problematic Pleasures and Politics of Holocaust Humor

Louis Kaplan

Memorializing Laughter

Had I known of the actual horrors of the German concentration camps, I could not have made *The Great Dictator;* I could not have made fun of the homicidal insanity of the Nazis.

—Charles Chaplin, *My Autobiography*

These regretful remarks may sound somewhat strange coming from the most significant comedian of the twentieth century, from the little tramp who made his living out of directing barbed ridicule and tendentious laughter against the big meanies of this world. Charles Chaplin's circumspect comments about *The Great Dictator* (1940) are marked by backtracking. They partake of none of the careless brashness of his silent slapstick days nor even of the committed satire of his anti-Nazi comic campaigns. Instead, this elder statesman seeks to demarcate the borders of comedy and to ban Holocaust humor as taboo. He suggests that the grave horrors of the concentration camps or the insanely homicidal tendencies of the Nazis are no place for comedy. The old clown steps back, takes off the greasepaint, and situates Holocaust humor as something to be avoided. In this account, the figure of the enlightened moralist ("Had I known . . .") has gained the upper hand over the comic anarchist.

Yet beyond all these regrets, the fact of the matter is that the world is fortunate to have these exceptional comic film documents like *The Great Dictator* or Ernst Lubitsch's *To Be or Not to Be;* only these films had the audacity to attest to the power of a life-affirming laughter in the face of a homicidal death machine and to overstep the lines of good taste. Such audacity is, after all, one of comedy's trademarks. This attitude might lead one to invert Chaplin's statement and to insist that the more one knows about the horror of concentration camps and or the homicidal insanity of a political regime, the more one has the responsibility to resist and to use black humor as a weapon against such tyranny. Indeed, it was this line of reasoning that led Chaplin in 1939 to direct an anti-Nazi film against his evil twin with the mustache in the first place. The latter-day naysayer to Holocaust humor ("Had I known . . . ") is challenged by the compelling insistence of the Chaplin who proclaimed that he "had to do it."[1] In this way, the bounded moralist who authorizes the restrictive position that one should not joke about the Nazi's atrocity exhibition is contrasted with the anarchic moralist who feels that one has a duty and an obligation to exercise Holocaust humor at whatever costs in an economy that would recognize no reserves nor reservations. The anarchist is bound to transgress those limits as he/she laughs in the face of death.

Now it should not be surprising to learn that the late Chaplin's reticence and rationale finds resonance in many official accounts of Holocaust memory. The wave of memorializing activities in the public sphere to commemorate the fiftieth anniversary of the Jewish Holocaust—whether in the form of museums, monuments, memoirs, or narrative and documentary films—occurred with the utmost piety and gravity. Such officially sanctioned stagings continue to demarcate the Holocaust as a site of mourning and melancholy that excludes the possibilities and powers of levity. These monuments have "hallowed out" the Holocaust and repressed the comic dimension, however caustic, ironic, or sarcastic. There is the underlying fear that the subversive and anarchic power of laughter—even if registered as laughter directed against the oppressor—would make a mockery of these sanctification efforts. This is the view tacitly expressed in *In Fitting Memory*, the somber volume reviewing the art and politics of Holocaust memorials.[2] Heavy funereal objects like gravestones and tombstones are sanctioned by official Holocaust culture as appropriate and fitting ways to remember the Jewish catastrophe.[3] But the lift of humor and jest is said to just not fit.[4]

To take another notable instance, there is not much room for humor in a manipulatively melodramatic film like Steven Spielberg's *Schindler's List* (1993) which cranks out a conditioned set of overdetermined meanings and fitting responses. Its cathartic effect lies only in the tear-jerking realm of pathos which it extracts from its audience from beginning to end.[5] It should be recalled that those who manage to survive its tragic narrative find themselves transported to the burial ground of Oskar Schindler in Jerusalem. There is no denying that this final documentary framing device is an attempt to ground the fictional narrative in the lived experience of the survivors and thereby achieve both temporal and narrative closure. Here, the audience is made to identify with the survivors in a mourning ritual where there is no acceptable alternative to shedding tears of sorrow.[6]

But there is another commemorative pathway. In 1995, I was given the opportunity to lead a session at a seminar attended by an international group of educators at the same Yad Vashem Memorial Museum in Jerusalem but with a very different agenda. This session sought rather to memorialize a strain of laughter buried deep within the Holocaust. It was devoted to the use of Jewish humor about the Holocaust as a means of resistance against the Nazi oppressor.[7] It was a restaging and discussion of the jokes told by ordinary Jews whether living in urban centers, ghettos, or concentration camps during the Nazi reign of terror. The session was an attempt to give voice to this subjugated and marginalized form of expression that has been repressed far too often in the

Holocaust memory banks of an official culture that has placed a taboo upon such laughter. In juxtaposition to the efforts to conserve, contain, and control the memory of the Holocaust within the discourse of gravity, this counter-discourse seeks to uncover the liberating laughter of Holocaust humor. This humor ranges from the clandestine "whisper jokes" told as a survival mechanism in the ghettos of the Third Reich to the recent transgressive stagings of the Akko Theater Group in Israel exposing the sacred taboo against levity to the blackest of humors.

The transgressive quality of Holocaust humor raises the question of the limits of humor—where what is "funny" exchanges places with what is "sick." But all humor that matters moves its audience out of the comfort zone in order to force a consideration of more questionable areas of human experience. Thus, it becomes clear why Holocaust humor would be an anathema to discourses of closure and containment. The authoritarian reading of the Holocaust as a discourse of gravity and its attempt to repress Jewish humor and render it taboo seeks to take this anarchic weapon of contestation and provocation out of circulation.[8] However, Jewish Holocaust humor is a testament to the politics and the pleasures of popular culture even in the most extreme and perverse of circumstances. Its strategy for surviving in the face of death contrasts with the cult of death at the center of Holocaust monumentality. Jewish Holocaust humor enacts an old Yiddish folk saying: "If your heart aches, laugh it off." Throughout the history of a persecuted people, Jewish humor has transmuted suffering into laughter.[9] In contrast to officially sanctioned mourning rituals and state commemorations, Holocaust humor provides an alternative way to memorialize the horrors of the past, one that stresses the need to work through mourning via laughter.

It is the goal of this essay to recall the problematic pleasures and politics of humor during the Holocaust era via two case studies in the popular media of jokes and film comedy. Unlike the official demand of Holocaust monumentality for a strictly delimited reading, these transgressive modes of pop cultural expression (i.e., jokes, cartoons, and film comedies) are based on the refusal to be circumscribed within the confines of officialdom. They offer more decentralized, heterogeneous, polysemic, and anarchic transmissions of the Holocaust memory. The first case study involves a number of anonymous jokes between 1940 and 1942 that were recorded in the diaries of Immanuel Ringelblum who served as the underground archivist of the Warsaw ghetto. The second case study focuses on Ernst Lubitsch's controversial Hollywood film comedy, *To Be or Not to Be* (1942), which deploys a provocative and tendentious humor to deal with a Final Solution already in progress. There are many differences regarding the functions and audiences of these pop cultural artifacts: jokes circulated among the Jews of the Warsaw ghetto versus a Hollywood film production about life in war-torn Warsaw made by a German-Jewish emigre for a predominantly non-Jewish audience. However, both of them demonstrate how Jewish humor could be used as a political weapon and as a provocative form of entertainment during (and in response to) an extreme state of a culture under threat of extermination. The investigation of these two case studies and their liberating laughter offers an anarchic antidote to the reigning death cult that has forgotten the Holocaust's own problematic sense of humor.

Ringelblum Records the Joke Resistance

There's a joke going around . . .
—Emmanuel Ringelblum, *Notes from the Warsaw Ghetto*

As the chronicler of the Jewish experience in the Warsaw ghetto and as a social historian of great reputation in Poland, Emmanuel Ringelblum (1900–1944) understood that a valuable resource for Jewish cultural expression like jokes warranted a place in his accounting of everyday life in the ghetto from 1940 to 1942.[10] Indeed, the transient and ephemeral nature of the Jewish joke partakes of the same spirit as the chronicle itself—in its documentation of the fleeting instant and the passing moment. This is not to deny that there is a tendency toward fixity when the oral joke moves to the more codified form of written transcription. There are dozens of timely and topical jokes in Ringelblum's *Notes from the Warsaw Ghetto*. Ringelblum composed his *Notes* as a personal diary to accompany his more official editorial labors as the head of underground "Oneg Shabbos" project whose task it was to document the political and social life of the Jews of Warsaw during the Nazi occupation and oppression. When the ghetto was destroyed, Ringelblum buried these handwritten manuscripts in a rubberized milk container in the hope of finding a post-Nazi posterity. They are read today as the astonishing eyewitness record of a period of intense persecution and its resistance.

As a leader of the underground movement, Ringelblum realized implicitly that such jokes served as a liberating means of psychological and spiritual resistance in the Jewish struggle for survival.[11] While Ringelblum made the following comments in June 1942 in connection with the ghetto's fascination with Leo Tolstoy's novel *War and Peace* and its depiction of the Napoleonic disaster in Russia, they might be extended to the function of the Jewish joke in the collective consciousness as well. Here, the social historian plays pop psychologist: "In a word, being unable to take revenge on the enemy in reality, we are seeking it in fantasy, in literature."[12] In other words, the Jewish joke must be viewed as one of those fantastic weapons in the ghetto's literary arsenal that enabled the oppressed to take revenge against their persecutors before organized armed resistance, the Warsaw Ghetto Uprising of April and May 1943.[13]

Given the psychological premise that the Jewish joke expressed the wish fulfillments of the persecuted against their oppressor, it should come as no surprise that a number of jokes collected and narrated by Ringelblum express a death wish aimed at Adolf Hitler directly. For example, one joke depends upon the homonymic word play embedded in the word *Platz* (as the noun plaza and as the imperative verb form of "burst") in both German and Yiddish. "There's a joke about a Jew riding in a streetcar. When he comes to the Hitler Platz, he cries, 'Amen!'"[14] This veiled witticism is a perfect example of an anti-Nazi "whisper joke": while it appears on the surface as if the Jew supports Hitler with his affirmative exclamation when he hears about the plaza named after the dictator, the underground subtext reveals that this "Amen" expresses the concealed wish that Hitler should explode.

Ringelblum did not transcribe this joke in the form that it appears in this English "translation" of the original Yiddish. Fearing that the manuscript would be seized by the Nazi authorities, the director of Warsaw ghetto underground archives would usually refer to Hitler in abbreviated fashion as H. or as Horowitz. In its uncanny way, this latter usage marks an overdetermined nickname for Hitler in this black humorous genre of "horror wit." In the specific case at hand, Ringelblum omits the proper name of the dictator completely. "It is narrated that a Jew rides with the tram and when he comes to the Platz, he answers 'Amen.'"[15]

It is possible to interpret such jokes directed against Hitler in light of the model of the tendentious joke outlined by Sigmund Freud. Freud explains the debasing mechanism at work. "By making our enemy small, inferior, despicable, or comic, we achieve in a roundabout way the joy of overcoming him."[16] A pointed barb in Ringelblum's *Notes* exposes the exact function and purpose of the anti-Nazi joke: "A new society has been formed, called Strength through Malicious Joy."[17]

If the Nazis seek to organize the German people around the propagandistic slogan of "Strength through Joy" ("Kraft durch Freude"), the Jewish joke retaliates with a dose of malicious joy (*Schadenfreude*) that draws its strength from Nazi defeats and failures.

Meanwhile, another joke recounted by Ringelblum fits perfectly into the Freudian model of tendentious deprecation and depreciation. While Hitler starts out at the beginning of this joke as "the big fellow," his stature steadily shrinks in the course of the narrative until he is reduced to pygmy status by the time the Jewish tailor has delivered the final punchline. This joke turns the tables on the Nazi's racist rhetoric that subhumanizes the ghetto Jew. However, this joke also can be read as a parable for life in the ghetto itself and the pressing need to make everything "stretch" to survive the dire and worsening circumstances.

The big fellow ordered three different tailors each to make him a suit and furnished the material. One tailor said. "There's only enough material for a vest." The second tailor said, "There's enough material for a whole suit." The Jewish tailor said he could make three suits out of the stuff: "He may be very big to Them, but to us he's a pygmy!"[18]

Another joke designed to make Hitler seem small and inferior is scatological in nature. Here, the Führer's reduced status is identified with the infant rather than with the pygmy. Countering Nazi anti-Semitic rhetoric that equated the Jews with feces, this Jewish joke retaliates by giving Hitler a taste of his own medicine so that a frightened Führer appears to be unable to control his own bodily functions. In this jocular wish fulfillment, the oppressor who treats the Jews as feces undergoes scatological humiliation himself. The joke plays with the identification of the Nazis as the brown shirts by providing them with a matching uniform on the bottom. The juxtaposition of Hitler and Napoleon and the hidden longing that the Russian campaign will spell disaster for the Nazis as it did for the French becomes quite explicit here. "They say that at the beginning of his Russian campaign Napoleon put on a red shirt, to hide the blood if he should be wounded. H. put on a pair of brown drawers."[19]

At times, however, the tendentious joke that dreams of the defeat of the Nazi enemy reveals the grim reality of the true circumstances with bitter irony. For instance, one Warsaw ghetto anecdote recorded by Ringelblum on May 8, 1942, draws upon the traditional Jewish joke figure of the *Wunderrabbi* (wonder rabbi) to make this point. These traditional jokes mock the charismatic Hassidic rabbi's supposed supernatural powers or his belief in miracles. In its inversion of the natural and the supernatural orders, this joke makes the super-natural event (angel's descent) appear more probable than the natural event (parachutist's descent). Even while the witty rabbi of Ger dreams of a miracle, one senses how fantastic and apparitional the odds.

> They tell this story: Churchill invited the Chassidic Rabbi of Ger to come to see and advise him how to bring about Germany's downfall. The rabbi gave the following reply: "There are two possible ways, one involving natural means, the other supernatural. The natural means would be if a million angels with flaming swords were to descend on Germany and destroy it. The supernatural would be if a million Englishmen parachuted down on Germany and destroyed it."[20]

In contrast to the Warsaw ghetto jokes that deflate the enemy, another category seeks to transmute the marks of subordination and humiliation imposed by the Nazi oppressor into signs of privilege and status. This has always been a strategy for those who are victimized or stigmatized by the dominant discourse. This transmutation process might be seen as directly linked to the Jewish joke's attempt to transform suffering into laughter. A few of these jokes focus specifically upon the armbands with the blue and white Star of David that were compulsory for Jews in the ghetto after January 1940. In these jokes, the badge of shame undergoes a radical reversal that makes it seem as if it were to be worn as a badge of honor. But unlike the rather naive call made by the German Jew Robert Weltsch in his editorial in the *Jüdische Rundschau* during the first Jewish boycott in Germany in April 1933 that encouraged the Jews to honor the yellow badge with pride ("Tragt ihn mit Stolz den gelben Fleck!"), these joke fantasies are laced with a bitter irony in their attempt to counteract the stigmatization process. On February 23, 1940, Ringelblum records: "Nalewski Street looks like Hollywood nowadays—wherever you go you see a star!"[21] The joke inverts the "special treatment" (*Sonderbehandlung*) to which the Jews have been subjected in the ghetto and its negative connotations (e.g., outsider, criminal) into a positive virtue—the singling out that goes with Hollywood fame, celebrity, stardom. In this way, a Jewish joke fantasy transforms the streets of the wretched Warsaw ghetto into Grauman's Chinese Theatre in Hollywood and its honorary walk of stars. It should be noted that this joke has uncanny resonances in relation to Ernst Lubitsch's film comedy released two years later. For in *To Be or Not to Be*, Hollywood stars play the inhabitants of Nalewski Street in an American-style act of comic resistance against the Nazis.

Similarly, Ringelblum relates another joke about the yellow star dated from May 1942 that specifically involves Jews who have been deported to the Warsaw ghetto from Germany and who must wear the brand on their chests. Again, the strategy of ironic resistance seeks to convert the badge of humiliation into a badge of honor. In this rewriting of history, the stigmatization of the Jew (*Jude*) is decoded and thereby revealed to be an acronym which spells out the news of the inevitable victory against the Axis powers.

The German Jews, deported here from Hanover, Berlin, etc., have brought a number of jokes with them. One of them is that they explain the emblem "Jude" that they have to wear on their chest as being the initials of the words: Italiens Und Deutschlands Ende (the end of Italy and Germany).[22]

This radical reversal is similar to the Jewish joke's response to the economic decree stating that Jews were forbidden to use German money that bore the likeness of Hitler. Rather than taking this economic hardship lying down, the Jewish joke offers a playful response and mocking means of resistance to fight evil with evil by means of an ancient folkloric explanation that strikes fear into the heart of the enemy. As Ringelblum exclaims, "Apparently they're afraid Jews might give him the Evil Eye!"[23]

Yet one more flight of fancy involving the ubiquitous armbands takes place in Paradise. Hitler notices that one "Jewish boy" does not have to wear his armband and has received a special exemption from the rule. On an institutional level, this joke would point to the possibility of an ideological conflict between Hitler and the Church. On the level of everyday life, the joke meditates on the question of privilege and its relationship to survival. It provides a case study in the receipt of special privileges, or what each ghetto dweller needs to survive the Nazi reign of terror. In this regard, the Jewish listener—fantasizing a way out of Jewish identity amid Nazi racism and racialism—cannot help but identify with the Jesus character in the following joke "conversion": "Horowitz comes to the Other World. Sees Jesus in Paradise. 'Hey, what's a Jew doing without an arm band?' 'Let him be,' answers Saint Peter. 'He's the boss's son.'"[24]

While the last joke finds a loophole out of a specific decree, there are other jokes that make fun of Nazi propaganda in general. Indeed, it is possible to understand Jewish jokelore in this period as a form of counter-propaganda whose function was to expose Nazi rhetoric as a discourse of lies, deceit, and empty promises. The Jewish joke reveals the Orwellian world view of the Nazi propaganda machine and its brainwashing strategies of inculcation when it comes to matters of mathematical calculation. As Ringelblum recounts: "The populace was just bursting with jokes about the New Year. One of them was that 1942 would be called 1941, because H. had promised his people he would end the war in 1941."[25]

The primacy of the Jewish joke in the service of resistance against the Nazi oppressor also helps to account for the fact that Ringelblum's *Notes* contain only one joke that is completely self-directed in character. In this way, the jokes of the Warsaw ghetto do not conform to Freud's contention in his *Joke* book that the Jewish joke is basically self-critical in nature.[26] This one exception mocks the Jewish Social Self-Aid Organization (for whom Ringelblum himself worked as an administrator). This joke is an ironic displacement of aggressive feelings from the Nazis to Jewish authorities—or what was left of them. However, when one considers the degree of corruption in this organization, one can understand it not so much as self-abuse but rather as the subordinated ghetto dweller's valid criticism against a corrupt Jewish authority.

> Horowitz asked the local Governor General [Hans Frank] what he has been doing to the Jews. The Governor mentioned a number of calamities, but none of them sufficed for Horowitz. Finally, the Governor mentioned ten points. He began: "I have set up a Jewish Social Self-Aid Organization." "That's enough; you need go no further!"[27]

This joke depends upon a surprising contrast when one learns that the Jewish Self-Help Organization has done more harm to the Jews of Warsaw than the Nazis have done. This ironic twist might be contrasted with another joke of the Warsaw ghetto whose punchline goes in the opposite direction in setting up the differences between Nazi and Polish authority. Taking the form of the dream of an oppressed Jew, it again performs the wish fulfillment which unites the joke work and the dream work.

> A Jew alternately laughs and yells in his sleep. His wife wakes him up. He is mad at her. "I was dreaming someone had scribbled on a wall: 'Beat the Jews! Down with ritual slaughter!'" "So what were you so happy about?" "Don't you understand? That means the good old days have come back! The Poles are running things again!"[28]

However, whether the Jewish joke wishes for the return of Polish pogroms as "the good old days" or bemoans the Jewish self-aid as the biggest calamity to befall the ghetto, both of these black humorous tales—as most jokes of the ghetto—involve the transmutation of suffering into laughter. Aptly enough, one notices that the Jewish dreamer in the latter joke is engaged in an alternating current of laughing and screaming. This might be understood as an explanatory mechanism for the very transmutation process in which the Jewish joke is engaged. For it was never a free and easy laughter. Rather it bore the mark of what, as Ringelblum records, served as the title of the special number of an underground newspaper called *Liberty* in early 1940, issued to celebrate the Jewish holiday of Purim which commemorates victory over Haman who sought unsuccessfully to exterminate the Jews of ancient Persia. This issue was called "Laughter through Tears."

Lubitsch Touches Holocaust Humor

A shocking confusion of realism and romance. Frankly, this corner is unable even remotely to comprehend the humor in such a juxtaposition of fancy and fact. Where is the point of contact between an utterly artificial plot and the anguish of a nation which is one of the great tragedies of our time? You might almost think Mr. Lubitsch had the attitude of "anything for a laugh."

—Bosley Crowther, review of To Be or Not to Be

There is a scene in *To Be or Not to Be* (1942) where Ernst Lubitsch stages a "meta-joke" about the deadly stakes of anti-Nazi joke-telling in the Warsaw ghetto. It is a scene that underscores the risks of Ringelblum's operation as well as the distance between the Hollywood stage set and the Warsaw underground. The Polish actor Joseph Tura in the guise of the double agent Professor Alexander Siletsky "reveals" to Nazi Colonel Ehrhardt the name of one Rovansky whom he claims to be the leader of the Polish resistance. However, it is soon ascertained that this same Rovansky has been shot by the Gestapo just yesterday for committing the crime of anti-Nazi joke warfare. He was murdered for "telling some outrageous, supposedly funny stories about der Führer." Here, Lubitsch calls attention to the stakes of political humor in a totalitarian regime and, in this manner, he offers both an unconscious homage to Ringelblum's risky project and a self-reflection on his own outrageous strategy of joke resistance. In "Miming the Führer: *To Be or Not to Be* and the Mechanisms of Outrage," Stephen Tifft deftly reviews how Lubitsch engages in a political act of resistance in this film by adopting "a *strategy* of comic bad taste—of imposing comic pleasure for subversive ends."[29] In contrast to Nazi propaganda aggressively aimed at a unified meaning, Lubitsch's comedy "starts to scatter its aggression and to disseminate germinal political meanings unexpectedly."[30] The ambivalence and subversive quality of the humor of *To Be or Not to Be* led many critics (such as Bosley Crowther) to speak so negatively about it at the time of its release and to view it as "an artistic blunder" and "in the poorest taste."[31] There was the general impression on the part of the opponents of Lubitsch's comedy that the gravity of the Nazi menace could not lend itself to his discourse of travesty.

But in his famous defense of *To Be or Not to Be* against the charges that it constituted a perversion of film genres, Lubitsch insists that this unsettling mixture of levity and gravity—what is being marked in this essay as "Holocaust humor"—can not be accounted for nor contained by traditional film conventions.

> It is true that I have tried to break away from the traditional moving-picture formula. I was tired of the two established, recognized recipes, drama with comedy relief and comedy with dramatic relief. I made up my mind to make a picture with no attempt to relieve anybody from anything at any time; dramatic when the situation demands it, satire or comedy whenever it is called for.[32]

Thus, from Lubitsch's perspective, it is not surprising that a critic like Bosley Crowther would be "unable even remotely to comprehend the humor in such a juxtaposition of fancy and fact." As a master of mix up, Lubitsch challenges the doctrine of comic relief which would use comedy in order to defuse tension or toward cathartic ends. Instead, he suggests that the Holocaustic humor of To Be or Not to Be (which, after all, is the question) does not seek to resolve anything. It seeks only to unsettle and to discomfort its viewers with no relief in sight. It is also important to recall how a specific brand of Jewish humor enters into the mix of To Be or Not to Be at strategic points in the narrative. In other words, the film offers a number of tendentious jokes that one might expect to find in Ringelblum's diaries. For instance, there is the recurrent "whisper joke" that makes its rounds among both the Nazis and the resistance. It is a joke directed against the Führer that takes him for a piece of cheese and offers the veiled suggestion that he stinks. It circulates against the censors in its tripartite transmutation of political leader into product brand. "They named a brandy after Napoleon, they made a herring out of Bismarck, and the Führer is going to end up as a piece of cheese!" Curiously enough, one finds a variant of this joke delicacy (with the title "The Recognized Brand") in a Jewish joke book published in the United States at the same time. In 1941, a rabbi from Chi-

cago by the name of S. Felix Mendelsohn (who collected and published a number of Jewish joke books) devoted a full chapter to jokes of "The Third Reich." Given the contraband nature of the anti-Nazi joke, it is not surprising to find them resurfacing among German-Jewish emigres in New York (or in Hollywood as in Lubitsch's case).[33] The title of Mendelsohn's book calls attention to the liberating power of Jewish humor in its equation of laughter and freedom as inalienable rights—Let Laughter Ring.

> A German walked into a Jewish grocery store on Grenadierstrasse and asked for a Hitler herring. The grocer's wife, not knowing what the customer wanted, shouted to her husband: "This man wants a Hitler herring. Do we have it?"
>
> "Sure thing," replied the grocer. "Give him a Bismarck minus a head."[34]

This pointed barb imagines a decapitated Hitler in the form of a further subtraction from the second term (i.e., the Bismarck herring) rather than as an independently rotten third term (i.e., the stinky cheese) in Lubitsch's version. Nevertheless, both of these witticisms reduce the vegetarian dictator to more manageable and digestible proportions.[35]

Meanwhile, Lubitsch feeds another classic Jewish joke retort to the character Greenberg (played by Felix Bressart) who is the only ostensibly Jewish character in his Polish acting troupe in the film.[36] This casting gesture further compounds the irony of Jack Benny—an American Jew of Polish descent who was born with the name of Benny Kubelsky—in the role of Joseph Tura, the great Polish actor who plays a Nazi impersonator throughout the twists and turns of the plot. In criticizing his fellow actor Mr. Rawitsch for his histrionics, the irrepressible Greenberg remarks: "Mr. Rawitsch, what you are, I wouldn't eat." Rawitsch then proceeds to fill in this punning punchline by naming the taboo for our general delectation. "How dare you call me a ham!" This joke form has a long history in the annals of Jewish humor and it was often used as a classic Jewish defense mechanism against the slanders of anti-Semitism. For instance, Moshe Waldoks and William Novak narrate a joke in their *Big Book of Jewish Humor* attributed to the British Zionist Israel Zangwill where the hamminess of Rawitsch is replaced by the piggishness of a well-dressed matron.

> Israel Zangwill, the British-Jewish writer, once found himself at a fancy dinner party, seated next to a well-dressed matron. Zangwill was tired, and without thinking, he yawned—right in the face of the woman beside him. Taken aback by this rude behavior, she said to him, "Please mind your Jewish manners. I was afraid you were going to swallow me."
>
> "Have no fear, madam," Zangwill replied. "My religion prohibits my doing that."[37]

This parallel case study suggests that the subtext of Greenberg's Jewish joke "reactions" (as he refers to these pointed barbs) needs to be understood in the context of German anti-Semitism and Polish collaboration.

Furthermore, one should not forget how Jewish humor enters into the multiple layers of simulation revolving around the persona of Hitler as portrayed by the Polish actor Bronski. In the opening sequence, the one-liner that breaks the flow of the narrative and the audience's identification with Bronski's Hitler involves a case of overt Jewish self-irony. The irony is compounded when one considers that it comes out of the mouth of an actor who is playing the arch-enemy of the Jewish people. Bronski responds to the cascade of official greetings of "Heil Hitler!" with a rather offhanded "Heil myself!" At the point of Hitler's turning into travesty and with a dose of Jewish self-irony that provides the faux Führer with the knock-out punchline, the producer Dobosh plays the Crowtherlike critic seeking relief in

documentary realism. He interrupts the anarchic mixing of the genres with a call to order and a return to the spirit of the letter ("That's not in the script!").

But this intervention leads only to further complications that further link Lubitsch's film to Holocaust humor. There is a comic refrain in *To Be or Not to Be* that allies itself to the old Yiddish maxim, "If it hurts, laugh it off!" Greenberg literally sticks his nose in and offers his profoundly Jewish judgment on these black humorous scenes that mercilessly mix travesty and tragedy. The initial instance occurs when Maria Tura (played by Carole Lombard) appears for the first time on the set wearing a sexy evening gown. She asks Dobosh what he thinks of it for "the concentration camp" scene in the *Gestapo* drama that they are rehearsing and she even suggests to him that it will offer a "tremendous contrast." But while the straitlaced authority figure Dobosh is rather appalled by such a contrast, it is the comic Greenberg who exclaims intuitively, "That's a terrific laugh!" It is almost as if the difference between the authoritarian and anarchic receptions of Holocaust humor for the next fifty years were already being played out here in the stark contrast between Dobosh's and Greenberg's reactions. Greenberg's response suggests an implicit understanding of the terror and fright behind the laughter circulating through Nazi Germany, Poland, and the United States circa 1942. In this one-liner, Greenberg has captured the terror at the heart of Holocaust humor's problematic pleasures.

In the film's climactic scene, Greenberg plays the part of distraction (or scapegoat) by feigning an assassination attempt against the Führer (Bronski) in order to open an escape route for the rest of the acting troupe. The straight man Dobosh again sets up the scene in a relatively somber manner: "If we can manage it such that Greenberg pops up among all those Nazis." But Greenberg does not think about it this way. Imagining only the terrible contrast that will be triggered by his "popping up" amid the brown shirts, Greenberg interjects his tragi-comic philosophy of life once more. "It will get a terrific laugh!" Dobosh counters with an air of finality. "It won't." In this amazing exchange of dialogue, the two approaches to Holocaust humor are starkly contrasted. On the side of the "pop up" and its terrific pleasures, Greenberg locates the jest that is buried in the lethal gesture. His exclamation openly flouts the directorial gaze of the documentarian Dobosh who sees only the gravity of the situation and its horrible end.

In these ways, Greenberg functions as Lubitsch's stand-in for the typically Jewish world view that jesting resistance—no matter how harrowing the stakes or the punchline—operates as a politically directed gesture against oppression. Greenberg's terrific and terrible laughter manifests the Jewish credo at the level of pop culture that affirms the transmutation of pain into pleasure or of "laughter through tears." All in all, Greenberg's brand of Holocaust humor affirms laughing in the face of death.

Postwar Elaborations

Tura: Bronski, now we belong to history.
Bronski: Well, they might even erect a monument to us.
Tura: They will. I can see myself sitting on a horse for the next hundred years.
—*To Be or Not to Be* (1942)

This study has focused on two case studies that demonstrate how the politics and pleasures of Jewish humor served as a means of laughing and surviving in the face of death at the time of the Holocaust. In the course of the last fifty years, the pop cultural historian can point to any number of examples that have deployed black humor as a means to deal with the horrors of the Holocaust and have built and elaborated upon the precedents of Lubitsch and Ringelblum. In the postwar era, the dialogic exchange between Joseph Tura and

Bronski in *To Be or Not to Be* on their place in the annals of comic Holocaust monumentality has proven to be prophetic. Mel Brooks's *The Producers* (1967) directly takes up the question of bad taste in offering a Broadway production that stages Hitler's reign of terror as a Busby Berkeley musical. Like Lubitsch's earlier example, this transgressive film was accused of frivolity and of making light of Jewish suffering.[38] But Brooks's aggressive and anarchic strategy must be seen as a post-Holocaust installment of the old Yiddish maxim that preaches the need to laugh off suffering. In this light, *The Producers* defuses the pain by reducing the Holocaust to bad theater.[39]

Similarly, a number of joke books appeared in Germany and Austria in the sixties and seventies which explored how humor served as a means of resistance in the Nazi era. These publications put into printed form the underground jokeloric genre of the *Flüsterwitz* or the oral tradition of jokes circulating from mouth to ear and mouth like smuggled or contraband goods.[40] Many of them include specific jokes from Ringelblum's diaries in the same or somewhat altered versions. Such alterations testify further to the difficulties of containing or controlling anti-Nazi jokes and subjecting them to a definitive version.

Finally, there are a couple of recent phenomena that have approached the Holocaust through the empowering and liberating lens of black humor in contradistinction to conventional commemorative practices. The most striking of these investigations in the United States can be found in Art Spiegelman's two-volume autobiographical comic book history, *Maus*.[41] Here, Spiegelman appropriates the propagandistic imagery of Nazi caricature and its representation of the Jew as parasite (e.g., rats and vermin) in order to stage a resistant counterdiscourse through the life story of his survivor father, Vladek Spiegelman.

In narrating Vladek's story of how he survived the Auschwitz concentration camp, Spiegelman tells the troubled history of his own life as a child of survivors. Spiegelman's "mouse-querade"—the transposition of his Jewish family into mouse people and the similar transposition of Nazis and Poles into cats and pigs—provides the narrator with the ironic distance he needs to tell this grueling tale of suffering and woe. At the beginning of the second volume, Art reflects upon the problem of representing the Holocaust. "I feel so inadequate trying to reconstruct a reality that was worse than my darkest dreams and trying to do it as a comic strip." [42] Yet it is exactly the antirealism of the comic strip and its cartoon world that enables Spiegelman's impossible attempt to represent the unrepresentable.

Nevertheless, while presented quite literally in a comic form, Spiegelman's narrative relies heavily on melodrama and pathos which often blunts comedy's transgressive force. Humor is quite often used as relief to his recounting of the atrocities perpetrated against the mouse folk. One instance is the character of Mandelbaum, Vladek's inmate friend, who acts like a traditional Jewish schlemiel character who loses his spoon and his belt, spills the soup, and comports himself in a general state of disarray. "I hold onto my bowl and my shoe falls down. I pick up the shoe and my pants fall down. But what can I do, I only have two hands!" [43] But this comic interlude soon gives way to the documentary account of the horrors at Auschwitz and Mandelbaum's subsequent extermination. In an insightful analysis, Art's psychiatrist Pavel exposes the backlash of guilt felt by this child of survivors on account of his comic book's success. Pavel's remarks sound the return of the repressed symbolic order (in the name and the law of the father) that would chastise the transgressive element of ridicule in *Maus* and help to explain the tempering of the anarchic thrust of the Holocaust humor in the comic book. "Maybe, you believe you exposed your father to ridicule." [44]

In sharp contrast, the recent performance "Arbeit Macht Frei" ("Work Makes Free") by the Acco Theater Group directed by Dudy Ma'ayan

and Asher Tlalim's filmic version of the group "Don't Touch My Holocaust" (1994) makes no such apologies in offering a direct violation of the Israeli taboo against the humorous or blasphemous desecration of the Holocaust. The cultural historian Steve Aschheim has situated the Acco performance as an "act of desacralization" that challenges "what they take to be the self-righteous, sacrosanct, indeed, taboo status of the *Shoah* within Israeli society." [45] The German documentary directed by Andres Veiel bears the title of *Balagan*—which is the Yiddish and Hebrew word for confusion and chaos. *Balagan* is a fitting title for the anarchic aspects of this project, which applies the black humorous techniques of the Artaudian theater of cruelty to a post-Holocaust setting. The hysterical antics of Madi Ma'ayan put the viewer in a problematic space where it is very difficult to determine whether one is bearing witness to farcical parody or horrific tragedy, and where there seems to be no relief in sight. As the title indicates, "Arbeit Macht Frei" takes the position that only a theater of cruelty can work through the horrors of Auschwitz (and its concentration camp slogan) on the path toward liberation. In this way, the project might be understood as another variant of Jewish humor's central aim to transmute suffering into liberating laughter.

One of the most fascinating aspects of the postmodern staging of this non-localized theatrical presentation involves a trip by bus to the Ghetto Fighter's Museum (*Lochamei Haghetto'ot*) in Acco. The roles of actors and audience in the theater are reframed in the space of the museum as tour guides and visitors. Dressed up as an elderly female concentration camp survivor who speaks Hebrew with a thick German accent and who throws in a smattering of Yiddish, German, and English in her cynical and black humorous monologue, Madi Ma'ayan takes up a number of subject positions in offering her account of the Holocaust story. She speaks in a splintering voice that not only destabilizes cultural viewpoints and linguistic codes, but also plays around with and passes through the variegated roles of objective observer, tyrannical authority, impassioned survivor, and insane anarchist. This constant slippage disrupts any totalizing reception by the participant-observer.

All of these examples demonstrate that humor offers an alternative way to memorialize the Holocaust in the postwar era. This transgressive commemorative practice values the power of laughter as liberating and as a means of survival in the face of death.[46] How different is this life-affirming strategy from the sanctioned forms of commemorative practice that transforms the Holocaust into a cult of death. Let us imagine the following open-ended scenario. What would happen if one were to visit the Holocaust Memorial Museum in Washington and, instead of being provided with an identity card of a victim to accompany one along the stations of the museum, the visitor were to be provided with a card with anonymous whisper jokes that were told by ghetto dwellers against their Nazi oppressor? One wonders what would be the consequences of such a different museological, psychological, and pedagogical practice. Instead of the grave identification with the victim engendered by the U.S. Holocaust Memorial Museum,[47] this memorial would foreground the problematic politics and pleasures of jokes and their relations to popular culture—seeking Greenberg's terrific laugh.

Notes

The author wishes to gratefully acknowledge the generous support of the Lucius C. Littauer Foundation and Franz Rosenzweig Research Center at the Hebrew University of Jerusalem for providing funding that allowed him to undertake the research necessary for this particular article in the period between 1992 and 1995.

1 See Theodore Huff, *Charlie Chaplin* (New York: Pyramid, 1964), 212–13, for Chaplin's wartime defense of his compulsion to a laughter without reserves or reservations.

2 Sybil Milton, *In Fitting Memory: The Art and Politics of Holocaust Memorials* (Detroit, MI: Wayne State University Press, 1991).

3 The most thorough and thoughtful exploration of Holocaust monumentality is to be found in James E. Young, *The Texture of Memory: Holocaust Memorials and Meaning* (New Haven, CT.: Yale University Press, 1993).

4 The only exception to this general tendency is the compilation and analysis provided by Steve Lipman in *Laughter in Hell: The Use of Humor During the Holocaust* (Northvale, NJ: Jason Aronson, 1991). Lipman's volume is an important resource for all further study of Holocaust humor.

5 But this only applies to those who know how to read the film in relation to the official narrative and its codes. The case of the black schoolchildren in Oakland laughing at the scene of Goeth's target practice where he picks off the Jews from long range shows that there are even ways to misread a canonical text trying its best to maintain itself in the discourse of Holocaust gravity.

6 For a different reading of the final scene as redemptive of Hollywood melodrama, see Geoffrey Hartman's recent essay "The Cinema Animal." He writes, "This sentimentality is redeemed only by the final sequence: it takes one out of docudrama, and presents the survivors, the Schindler remnant, together with the actors who played them, as they place a ritual pebble on Schindler's tombstone in the Jerusalem graveyard." Hartmann's analysis seems to forget the possibility that melodrama can invade the staged space of this "documentary" footage just as easily. See *The Longest Shadow: In the Aftermath of the Holocaust* (Bloomington: Indiana University Press, 1996), 84.

7 This session was held on January 15, 1995, at one of the biannual seminars on teaching the Holocaust organized by Ephraim Katz and sponsored by Yad Vashem: The Holocaust Martyrs' and Heroes' Remembrance Authority in Jerusalem, Israel. The session was entitled "The Jewish Joke as Weapon of Resistance against the Nazis."

8 This bears a certain resemblance to Henry Jenkins's distinction between "anarchistic comedy" and classical Hollywood cinema: "If a dominant tendency of classical narrative is its push to unify its materials into a coherent story, the tendency of anarchistic comedy is toward heterogeneity, even at the risk of disunity and incoherence." Transposing this logic, the authoritarian approach to the memorializing of the Holocaust would seek narrative homogeneity and seek to avoid

the heterogeneity, disunity, and incoherence set off by the comic detonation of the anarchistic approach. See Henry Jenkins, *What Made Pistachio Nuts? Early Sound Comedy and the Vaudeville Aesthetic* (New York: Columbia University Press, 1992), 22.

9   In "Why Jews Laugh," Nathan Ausubel discusses how this expression illustrates the life philosophy of "laughter through tears." "In Jewish humor comedy and tragedy are joined together like Siamese twins. 'Laughter through tears' is what the Jewish folk philosopher chooses to call it. You laugh in order to give yourself courage not to grieve, and you shed a tear or two because the human comedy is often no mere laughing matter" (Ausubel, *A Treasury of Jewish Humor* [Garden City, NY: Doubleday, 1951], xvi). One should not forget that Ausubel's folkloric editions—the other one being *A Treasury of Jewish Folklore,* published in 1948—typify the attitude of American Jewry about the function of Jewish humor in the immediate wake of the Holocaust.

10   Even the translator and editor of the *Notes* calls attention to the unusual place of jokes in Ringelblum's daily accounts: "Most of the notes are overpoweringly sober. But the common man in the Ghetto had his own way of relieving tension—by making up and telling jokes. The *Notes* tell dozens of these jokes—sardonic, bitter, violent, wishful. Why did Hitler put on brown drawers when he invaded Russia? What did the newborn baby say to its mother? How did the rabbi of Ger answer Churchill when that great statesman came to him for advice? And that man who was buried up to his neck in the sand—what did *he say* when they let him go, laughing that it was 'only a joke.' These jokes have a desperate quality, they are all the stronger for being part of a tradition of wit that Jews share with Negroes and other people who have a long history of oppression behind them. In *Notes from the Warsaw Ghetto* humor is a brilliant counterpoint to the dominant note of repressed anguish." See Jacob Sloan, "Introduction," *Notes from the Warsaw Ghetto: The Journal of Emmanuel Ringelblum,* ed. and trans. Jacob Sloan (1958; New York: Schocken, 1974), xxvi.

11   It should be noted that a number of other major diaristic accounts of the Warsaw ghetto are also sprinkled with jokes. These include *Warsaw Ghetto: A Diary of Mary Berg* (New York: L. B. Fischer, 1945); *The Warsaw Diary of Adam Czerniakow* (Briarcliff Manor, NY: Stein and Day, 1982); Shimon Humberband, *Kiddush Hashem: Jewish Religious and Cultural Life in Poland Dur-*

ing the Holocaust (Hoboken, NJ: Ktav, 1987); and Chaim Kaplan, *Scroll of Agony: The Warsaw Diary of Chiam A. Kaplan,* trans. and ed. Abraham I. Katsch (New York: Collier, 1965).

12   Ringelblum, *Notes,* 300.

13   For an account of how the joke arsenal was replaced by military means in the Jewish resistance, see Ber Mark, *The Warsaw Ghetto Uprising* (New York: Schocken, 1975).

14   Ringelblum, *Notes,* 68.

15   Emmanuel Ringelblum, *Notizen von Warshauer Ghetto* (Warsaw: Verlag Yiddish Buch, 1952), 55.

16   Sigmund Freud, *Jokes and Their Relation to the Unconscious,* trans. James Strachey (New York: Norton, 1960), 103.

17   Ringelblum, *Notes,* 252.

18   Ibid., 153.

19   Ibid., 68.

20   Ibid., 265.

21   Ibid., 22.

22   Ibid., 288.

23   Ibid., 289.

24   Ibid., 40.

25   Ibid., 251.

26   To recite the famous Freudian Jewish folk maxim, "Incidentally, I do not know whether there are many other instances of a people making fun to such a degree of its own character." See *Jokes and Their Relation to the Unconscious,* 112.

27   Ringelblum, *Notes,* 55. This same joke (dated September 26, 1940, in Ringelblum) also appears as "Jewish Joke II" in Chaim Kaplan, *Scroll of Agony,* 205. Here it is dated from October 8, 1940, and reads: "The Führer asks Frank, 'What evils and misfortunes have you brought upon the Jews of Poland?' 'I took away their livelihood; I robbed them of their rights; I established labor camps and we are making them work at hard labor there; I have stolen all their wealth and property.' But the Führer is not satisfied with all their acts. So Frank adds: 'Besides that, I have established *Judenraten* and Jewish Self-Aid Societies.' The Führer is satisfied, and smiles at Frank. 'You hit the target with the *Judenraten,* and Self-Aid will ruin them. They will disappear from the earth!'" A comparison of this more elaborate version of the joke with Ringelblum's reveals substantial differences and it points out the difficulties of acquiring a standardized text in folk cultural production which depends upon performance. Kaplan's punchline

is that much bleaker and blacker than Ringelblum's in its self-ironic and prophetic realization of eventual extermination, which it jokingly relocates from Nazi menace to Jewish self-aid.

28 Ringelblum, *Notes,* 79.

29 Stephen Tifft, "Miming the Führer: *To Be or Not to Be* and the Mechanisms of Outrage," *Yale Journal of Criticism* 5(1) (1991): 6.

30 Ibid., 7.

31 For another discussion of the negative criticisms launched against *To Be or Not to Be* and Lubitsch's defense, see William Paul's "Playing for Keeps," in *Ernst Lubitsch's American Comedy* (New York: Columbia University Press, 1983), 225–56.

32 Ernst Lubitsch, *New York Times Magazine,* March 29, 1942.

33 For another example of anti-Nazi emigre humor, see B. D. Shaw, ed., *Is Hitler Dead? and Best Anti-Nazi Humor* (New York: Alcaeaus House, 1939).

34 S. Felix Mendelsohn, *Let Laughter Ring* (Philadelphia: Jewish Publication Society, 1941), 109.

35 In this context, one should also recall Mendelsohn's chapter "Hitleria," which contains anti-Nazi and anti-Hitler jokes in his post-Holocaust volume published two years after the war, *Here's a Good One: Stories of Jewish Wit and Wisdom* (New York: Bloch, 1947), 75–93.

36 For an elegant and sophisticated analysis of the normally marginalized Greenberg character as the center of Jewish interest in the Lubitsch film, see Joel Rosenberg's essay "Shylock's Revenge: The Doubly Vanished Jew in Ernst Lubitsch's *To Be or Not to Be*" *Prooftexts* 16(3) (September 1996): 209–44.

37 William Novak and Moshe Waldoks, ed., *The Big Book of Jewish Humor* (New York: Harper Perennial Library, 1981), 83. As a black-humorous performer himself, Rabbi Waldoks recently teamed up with fellow child of survivors Lisa Lipkin in order to stage a bit of Holocaust humor entitled "There's No Business Like Shoah Business."

38 In this context, we should also recall Brooks's rather weak remake of the Lubitsch classic *To Be or Not to Be,* released in 1984.

39 For a further elaboration of this view, see Sanford Pinsker, "Mel Brooks and the Cinema of Exhaustion," in *From Hester Street to Hollywood,* ed. Sarah Blacher Cohen (Bloomington: Indiana University Press, 1983), 245–57.

40 This includes such titles as Franz Danimann, *Flüsterwitze und Spottgedichte unterm Hakenkreuz* (Vienna: H. Boehlau, 1983); Alexander Drozdzynski, *Das verspottete Tausendjährige Reich* (Düsseldorf: Droste, 1978); and Max Vandrey, *Der politische Witz im Dritten Reich* (Munich, Goldmann, 1967).

41 Art Spiegelman, *Maus: A Survivor's Tale* (New York: Pantheon, 1986); and Art Spiegelman, *And Here My Troubles Began (From Mauschwitz to the Catskills and Beyond)* (New York: Pantheon, 1991). Both volumes have now been published together as *The Complete Maus* (New York: Pantheon, 1997).

42 Spiegelman, *The Complete Maus,* 176.

43 Ibid., 189.

44 Ibid., 205.

45 Steven E. Aschheim, *Culture and Catastrophe: German and Jewish Confrontations with National Socialism and Other Crises* (New York: New York University Press, 1996), 28.

46 One final example is offered in Roberto Benigni's *Life Is Beautiful* (1997). As Roger Ebert recalls, "At Cannes, it offended some left-wing critics with its use of humor in relation to the Holocaust" (*Chicago Sun Times,* October 30, 1998). Ebert notes that the second half of the plot located in a fairy-tale concentration camp follows the Jewish comic survivalist strategy of "smiles through tears."

47 See Michael Berenbaum, *The World Must Know: The History of the Holocaust as Told in the United States Holocaust Memorial Museum* (Boston: Little, Brown, 1993).

The Sound of Disaffection

Tony Grajeda

You engage the play function on your compact disc player, but something isn't quite right. The player's normally crystal clear sound suddenly produces the sort of noise one would expect from an old portable tape recorder. An unbearable buzzing, the kind that sounds suspiciously like tape hiss, is competing with—even drowning out—the music itself. You can barely make out the vocals, which are unspeakably muffled. The entire thing sounds abysmal. What at first seemed a seriously defective CD gives way to the impression that this sound must be some weird experimental art thing masquerading as pop music, or some pathetic pop band with the audacity to release its crappy demo tapes. Or, perhaps, it could be a little of both, which would then bring the result within proximity of what has come to be known as "lo-fi."

In part defined within and against the notion of high-fidelity, lo-fi gained currency in the mid-1990s to signal the sound associated with a range of mostly "alternative" music: Beat Happening, Guided by Voices, Sebadoh, the Jon Spencer Blues Explosion, Royal Trux, the Grifters, Strapping Fieldhands, Tall Dwarfs, Lisa Germano, Daniel Johnston. These bands are not exactly *Billboard* material. But the label has also served to encompass a wider array of pop activity, bandied about in the company of everyone from Beck, Liz Phair, and the Flaming Lips to Neil Young, Sheryl Crow, and John Mellencamp, as well as 1995 Lollapaloozers, Pavement.

Referring primarily to production values, lo-fi stands as technical shorthand for "home recordings," those small-scale efforts made on (relatively) inexpensive equipment such as four-track tape machines. Unlike state-of-the-art recording techniques, low-fidelity equipment produces an altogether rough and ragged sound quality, often failing to mask hum, static, tape hiss, and other noises endemic to the very process of recording. Not simply a case of technology but also of technique, lo-fi has been used further to describe those musical performances marked by amateurish playing (often on minimal instrumentation), off-key singing, and a certain casualness in delivery. This dual aspect of amateurism (in terms of performance) and primitivism or minimalism (in terms of equipment and recording processes) has set the tone for what constitutes lo-fi, leading discussion in the music press to a binary between art and commerce: to what extent has lo-fi been a question of either aesthetics or economics?

But such questions of cultural production, often crisscrossing debates over format (i.e., analog vs. digital, vinyl vs. CD), remain symptomatic of the ongoing issue over what is meant by "alternative" music.[1] That is to say, what is often at stake in the ethos of (anti-corporate) independent music is precisely what it means to *sound* alternative, to signify sonically an oppositional sensibility, regardless of one's position in relation to the music industry. While the cultural politics of popular music are frequently limited to an analysis of the economic struggle between independent and major labels, much less attention has been given to how that struggle is played out both aesthetically and technologically. What interests me here, then, is how production values become coded as either corporate or alternative, the ways in which those values are determined historically, and the degree to which those production values as formal properties can be read politically.[2]

Since lo-fi is still playing itself out on the cultural field, what follows is necessarily a preliminary sketch. What I hope to establish, however, is a kind of genealogy of lo-fi by tracing a brief history of the vexed relationship between music, or recorded sound in general, and technology.[3] Indeed, the discourse on lo-fi could be read as offering a condensed version of debates on sound going back to the late nineteenth century, to the inception of the mechanical reproduction of sound. This analysis will suggest that the issues raised by the particularities of lo-fi (and mid-1990s pop music more generally) allow us to consider not only a wider band in the history of pop music but also to take in a wider perspective on a range of social and cultural conditions. Therefore, I will explore the contours of lo-fi by setting the context for its emergence, which is nothing if not overdetermined: technologically in the digital era of high fidelity, aesthetically in the musical era of grunge and the general valorization of noise, as well as politically, in the so-called postmodern era of well-nigh total corporate hegemony over culture and the attendant widespread anxiety over the possibilities for adversarial or oppositional culture. Finally, I will briefly suggest how the making of lo-fi and its history coincide with debates on modernism, mass culture, the avant-garde and gender — debates which in many ways have yet to be resolved.

Lo-Fi as a Discursive Formation

According to the magazine *Musician,* "1994 was the year lo-fi arrived."[4] But no sooner did it appear on the cultural graph as something resembling recognizability than the sound was declared already over and done, yet another "stylistic and cultural dead end."[5] Given the propensity for dramatic pronouncements in pop music writing, both assertions could be read as equal parts prediction, bluff, and wish fulfillment. What one could say with some certainty is that, by 1995, lo-fi had arrived—arrived indeed as a discursive formation.

Although the term itself has been tossed around for years in the music press, it was none other than the paper of record, the *New York Times,* that give lo-fi headline status as far back as April 1993. A year later the *Chicago Tribune* chimed in, shortly followed by another *Times*

Sunday feature. Late 1994 found the decidedly alternative publication *Option* defining the field of contenders, with *Musician, Spin,* and the *Alternative Press* soon placing what were said to be lo-fi recordings high up on their year's best lists. Predictably bringing up the rear, *Rolling Stone* managed to label every other band it featured in the first half of 1995 as somehow lo-fi.

Subject matter aside for the moment, such writing has invariably eluded the degree to which lo-fi itself results from a discursively constituted trend. Accordingly, each round of articles never fails to point out the increasing attention lo-fi receives in the media, while simultaneously failing to acknowledge their own role in contributing to the development of that trend. In other words, the fiction of objective reporting—the proverbial window on to reality—is embraced by specialty and mass-circulation publications alike. The media reports claiming merely to reveal a trend also serve to perpetuate it, functioning as an organizing principle for fans, writers, industry apparatchiks, even and especially other musicians. Thus the term itself is not only called upon to describe passively or innocently what has been going on; it also *produces* interest at both the community and commodity levels, reproducing itself in a circulation of discourse. What follows, then, is a quick read of lo-fi as a discursive formation, not to figure out necessarily what lo-fi *is* but to track how it is used and what is being invoked in its name.[6]

In a profile on the otherwise obscure duo Ween, *Times* music critic Jon Pareles sets the stage for "low-fi rockers": the "suburban slackers," who had just released *Pure Guava* on Elektra following several independent label recordings, are found to be utilizing "primitive two-track and four-track recorders." According to Pareles, the group's music "sounds casual and unadorned; instruments tend toward low-fidelity, and voices pop up at various speeds, exaggeratedly low or chirpy."[7] The last of these qualities resulted apparently from a malfunctioning tape recorder, the kind of happy accident over authorial agency that repeatedly crops up (as we will see) in stories on lo-fi.

A greater sense of artistic intentionality underwrites a *Chicago Tribune* feature on Beck, appearing, almost to the day, a year later. Beck's song "Loser," which had made the top fifteen on the *Billboard* pop charts, is said to be "the apotheosis of a rock underground subculture built around crude, four-track home taping instead of polished studio recordings." Along with Daniel Johnston, Pavement, Sebadoh, Guided by Voices, Ween, and Beat Happening—reviewed under the banner "Low-fi is the Latest Trend in the Music Biz"—Beck and "these other cassette-mongers," it is argued, "have been releasing records with a living-room ambiance, celebrations of spontaneity and humor that meld noise, melodies and good old-fashioned goofing around into music that is the antithesis of Bon Jovi."[8]

This "latest trend" is further elaborated in another *New York Times* Sunday feature, "Lo-Fi Rockers Opt for Raw Over Slick." Familiar traits of rock mythology course through the article: lo-fi's do-it-yourself methodology is "rooted in rock-and-roll history," from 1960s garage rock to 1970s punk, while "the combination of available technology and impromptu techniques democratizes pop music, putting creative power into the hands of anyone with a will." (Notice, by the way, how artistic agency has returned to the musician from temperamental technology in the earlier account, a contradiction at work over who or what authors the sound, about which more later.) The political implications of such populist sentiment notwithstanding, the discourse of lo-fi has begun to take on the trappings of rock ideology: "In a world of sterile, digitally recorded Top 40, lo-fi elucidates the raw seams of the artistic process."[9]

Finally, yet another *Times* piece, a mere half year later ("Fleeing Sterile Perfection for Lovable Lo-Fi Sound"), secures the terms of debate. Set against a world of "advanced technology" which "make[s] recordings as pristine and clear as pos-

sible," where production values are felt to be "too slick" and "sterile," lo-fi appears as the perfect response to "a very processed, perfect sound." Where aesthetics, economics, and method meet, lo-fi is posited as the "genuine" article, offering "an intimate sound with a raw edge." And where sound can be read as ideology, the discourse of lo-fi preserves a sense of authenticity: "Instead of trying to eliminate all incidental room sounds, a lo-fi artist embraces incidental noise and incorporates it into the mix to achieve a heightened sense of reality."[10]

The investment here in notions of authenticity persists, of course, in conventional rock discourse, and rather predictably attaches itself to any debate over the function of technology. As Simon Frith has noted, where "the authenticity or truth of music" is at issue, "the implication is that technology is somehow false or falsifying," adding that the "continuing core of rock ideology is that raw sounds are more authentic than cooked sounds."[11] Certainly our experiences of music, whether "live" or recorded, are always and no doubt already technological.[12] What repeatedly takes place at the discursive level, however, is that these same debates get played out at every stage of technological development. Likewise, the case of lo-fi reveals the latest cultural form to embody an enduring contradiction in pop music mythos, one which elicits a certain anxiety over the insoluble interdependence between the technological and the human, an interdependence in place since at least the late nineteenth century. That is to say, the widespread fiction in pop of an opposition between technology and music—as if music somehow *precedes* technology, as if the latter distorts rather than enables the former—blithely ignores the extent to which technology remains a constitutive element to music. In short, and somewhat irrespective of such periodizations as modernity and postmodernity, what is always at stake in the discourse of musical authenticity and audio fidelity is a question of the real or the referent, how it is defined and constituted, how it is "captured" or represented.[13]

The Question of Fidelity

As a technical notation, fidelity refers to the quality or condition of faithfulness to an original, and audio fidelity—the signifying practice that invariably subordinates the assessment of music as such to a description of sound—is simply the degree of accuracy in the reproduction of sound. In the nineteenth-century context of rapid industrialization, expanding mass culture, and cultural precedents such as photography, the mechanical reproduction of sound—inaugurated by Edison's phonograph in 1877—coincides temporally (and spatially) with what Miles Orvell calls the "culture of imitation," that pervasive (and particularly) American dispensation "fascinated with reproductions of all sorts."[14] From the very beginning of sound's technological reproducibility, then, the realm of aural culture presupposes the terms of debate—natural and constructed, authenticity and artifice, original and copy, reality and simulation. These binaries will carry through from the period of modernity and the industrialization of sound to our own so-called postmodernity and the digitalization of sound.[15] An early moment in the history of sound technologies provides a case in point.

In 1915 the Edison Company began marketing a new line of phonographs by staging what became known as Tone-Test Recitals, evenings of "musical entertainment" featuring phonograph recordings and live accompaniment. In order to prove that "the Edison Diamond Disc's re-creation of the music cannot be distinguished from the original," performers—including well-known opera stars of the day (such as soprano Anna Case)—sang along with their phonographic reproductions, thereby challenging audiences to determine the differences between vocal renditions.[16] These highly ritualized performances, thousands of which took place across the country over the next several years, typically culminated in "the so called dark scene, where the artist steals from the stage, while the phonograph is playing."[17] Count-

less reports celebrated the machine's achievement in fidelity: "Just how true and faithful is this Re-creation of the human voice was best illustrated when Miss Christine Miller sang a duet with herself, it being impossible to distinguish between the singer's living voice and its Re-creation by the instrument that bears the stamp of Edison's genius."[18] Initiating an aesthetics of fidelity, the tone tests and their responses also set in motion the cultural coding of reproductive technology to blur incontestably the distinction between original and copy, and the experiential differences of each.

"Just how true and faithful" echoes throughout the history of audio fidelity and sound reproduction, resonating most recently within the discourse of lo-fi, with its "special air of intimacy" and "goal of greater realism." As one musician put it, "I prefer the lo-fi thing over a more slick sound because we get more of a live, organic feel that way—the snaps, the pops, the accidents that always happen make it more human."[19] What is curious about the terminology of naturalism here is that we're still talking about *recorded* music. How sounds become coded as "organic" or "slick," let alone "more human," requires a brief visit to the site of sound (re)production—the recording studio.

Fidelity and Dissimulation in the Studio

By at least the mid-nineteenth century, a particular standard for acoustics had been set by the concert hall. The history of audio fidelity doesn't end, however, at that moment when recorded sound was considered to have successfully approximated this ideal.[20] As Edison's anticipation of the Memorex "test" suggests, sound reproduction not only aimed to re-create the "real," rendering the original indistinguishable from the copy (the two were now inseparable); such reproduction also revealed the referent's susceptibility to being displaced. Consequently, over and beyond achieving fidelity to the real, specific developments in recording techniques eventually superseded it, thereby ushering in a new level of aesthetic criteria to which all else would be measured.[21]

Studio recording in the first half of this century involved the direct registering of sound onto a disc, one that couldn't be edited. In other words, a recorded performance (no matter how many times rehearsed) was still a singular performance by musicians captured in one "take." With the advent of magnetic tape in 1948, however, a recording could be assembled out of different takes, a final version made up from patches of several performances.[22] Along with the development of multitrack recording facilities in the 1960s, tape technology irretrievably transformed the recording process. The recording of a performance in its entirety was now, for the listener, the *appearance* of an uninterrupted performance. The editing process of cutting out mistakes and splicing in preferred extracts allowed producers, as Frith has noted, to "make records of ideal not real events."[23] The studio became the site where music was entirely constructed, manufacturing a sound without any reference whatsoever to a "live" event. Indeed, live performances soon came to be measured against the sound standards of studio recordings.

The entrenchment of this aesthetic of audio fidelity (the idealized state of music) continues to set conditions on and for a listening subject, shaping the ways in which aural pleasure is experienced through a technological apparatus. And the aesthetic cuts both ways. The studio standard raised the stakes on the notion of an immaculate sound, altering the terms of assessment—spontaneity, artificiality, and accuracy. Once an unblemished sound has been judged, say, to be "sterile" (the result perhaps of what is called "recording consciousness" said to afflict some performers), the blemished sound subsequently takes on new meaning, now valued over the "artificial" studio recording.[24] Put another way, once it has been socially and culturally determined what constitutes "perfect" sound (the flawless performance for instance), what returns dialectically as the other of this order is nothing less than imperfection—the

"flawed" performance as a privileged (anti-)aesthetic for what the system supposedly can never tolerate.

Imperfection is a key term in the discourse of lo-fi. It underwrites not only the celebration of amateurism (itself both a critique of rock's professionalist cult of technique and an alibi for poor musicianship) but, moreover, the kind of happy accidents that keep popping up, as already noted, in lo-fi stories.[25] Yet the notion of imperfection has taken on additional cultural significance in our current era of digitalization, one heralded as the latest manifestation of what could be called the "technological sublime."[26] A rather less sanguine treatment of digitalization, however, taking into account the exultation over its efficiency and accuracy—since "precision is fundamental to any digital system"[27]—would consider those qualities and values digital instantiates as something much more akin to the procedures of instrumental rationality.[28]

Digitalization: The Sound Remains the Same

A few short years into the digital 'revolution,' one could be treated to the full-throated singing of its virtues:

> What you hear on the CD is flawless sound reproduction, free from the scratches, ticks, pops, and surface noises that frequently (and naturally) bedevil conventional LPs. . . . You only have to hear a Compact Disc once, through headphones or through speakers, to understand why older analog playback media inevitably will become obsolete. On CD, climaxes gain explosive strength. High notes are reproduced with startling realism. Even the lowest passages sound amazingly clear. The difference between analog and digital sound is as striking as the distinction between mono and stereo.[29]

Even as sales talk, one can detect here the installing of an aesthetics of audio fidelity, the cultural coding of a sound-related technology dominated by notions of perfection, purity, and permanence. Given the heritage of these specific traits, the discourses of digital technology, from advertisers to audiophiles, could be thought to imply less a radical postmodern break with the past its adulators proclaim than a continuation and perhaps intensification of previous social and cultural relations. For in its valorization of perfection, purity and permanence, digitalization appears as the result of a curious intersection between social modernity and a particular musical history. While the former can be encapsulated by Antonio Gramsci's notation of "order, exactitude and precision" necessary to the imperatives of capital (efficiency and technical rationality, the standardization of production and consumption, the commodification and reification of culture),[30] the latter has been supported, according to Michael Chanan, "by the long tradition, going back to Pythagoras, which assimilates music to the laws of mathematical harmony and proportion."[31] This narrative of an aesthetic form, in which it is believed that "all is founded in perfection,[32] has reached eminent articulation through a technological form that demands precision, infallibility, certainty, clarity and so on. This remarkable confluence of aesthetics and technology speaks as much to the persistence of social modernity as to its supposed eclipse by postmodernity.

Similarly, such fictions of audio fidelity ("flawless sound reproduction") suggest the contours of an ideological interpolation, one intent on the production of a listening subject as an effect of both an aesthetically and a scientifically inflected discourse on sound.[33] But this discursive structuring of subjectivity infers not just any subject since, it could be argued, it has been gendered masculine on two accounts: socially, in terms of an economy of "leisure" (audiophiles as a demographic are overwhelmingly male)[34] and theoretically, in terms of a libidinal economy of mastery, control, and the fetishization of technology. (After all, one trusts that those *explosive* "climaxes" spoken of in the previous quote remain strictly musical in nature.)

That condition of "imperfection," then, constitutive to lo-fi (which, as we shall see later, is also laden with gendered characteristics), seems rather out of tune with the overall digital aesthetic of "perfect sound forever." This commonly heard mantra invokes a dual desire for permanence and perfection.[35] The first of these traits speaks to the scourge of early technologies which degraded in time and degraded with use. The guarantee of the compact disc, however, promises not just durability but no appreciable wear. This appeal for a stable, immutable object, one impervious to the passage of time, could be traced back to the late-nineteenth-century crisis of modernity around notions of decay, disintegration, and deterioration, a time when, as Marx put it, "all that is solid melts into air."[36] One response to this crisis of modernity, as Mark Cheetham claims, was a reassertion of Platonic "transcendental purity" (inspiring at least the abstract painting of modernism): "Purity and purification are powerful tools for organizing and controlling otherwise inchoate experience."[37]

This "rhetoric" of purity can also be found as a normative principle in the discourse of audio fidelity. For example, the phenomena of noise as unwanted sound persists as the dire enemy of audiophiles. (Performance standards, of course, have traditionally castigated errors, flaws and inconsistencies.) Digital engineering has installed the purity aesthetic technologically (e.g., with "error correction" circuitry): production values consist of a cleansing process to expunge whatever is thought to contaminate the recording of sound—mistakes are corrected, impurities expelled, accidents prevented, uncertainty predicted. Indeed, if earlier technologies foregrounded their material production (tape hiss, radio static, turntable hum), then digital technology offers a kind of groundlessness of profound absence from the very materiality of its instrumentation. As one commentator noted, "All describe digital technology by its absence: the absence of any interference with simply experiencing the music, the absence of that sense of spatial distance one gets from an LP, the absence of surface noise, of rumbles, pops, and scratches. Digital *is* what it isn't."[38] In that it "*is* what it isn't," concealing nevertheless its means of production, the "ideological effect"[39] of digitalization fulfills the putative desire for eliding any mediation between sound and its reception—the metaphysics of presence.

To be sure, this desire for the infallible, untainted object constitutes an aesthetic with an ancient pedigree, although one that was rehabilitated more recently, for example, inhering in the codification of (late) modernism issued by Clement Greenberg, who famously valorized form as the essence of art. By eliminating whatever was considered to be extraneous to a specific art-form (since each particular art was "unique and irreducible" to itself), Greenberg claimed that "each art would be rendered 'pure,' and in its 'purity' find the guarantee of its standards of quality as well as of its independence."[40] What Hal Foster termed this "will-to-purity" in modernism can be found coursing as well throughout the discourses of audio fidelity.[41] Until, that is, the rather unexpected unfolding of less than perfect sound, represented by such cultural moments as lo-fi (among other developments) and its altogether noisy soundscape, quietly casting doubt on our apparent yearning for at least the appearance of perfect incarnations of pure, untarnished sound.

Noise Annoys

> There's definitely a trend toward dirtier tracks. Tape hiss, guitar-amp noise, low-level garbage. Five years ago, we would have cleaned all that up. But today, the prevailing wisdom is to go lo-fi and let that noise become part of the music.[42]

As a technical term in the field of electronics, noise is that phenomena which disturbs or interrupts a transmission and interferes with a signal, such as static on a phone line or "snow" on a TV screen.[43] We could never apprehend such noise, however, without the very technology that broadcasts it. In other words, the technology itself produces noise, which then requires further developments in technical formats for noise reduction (e.g., the Dolby system). But the technological imperative to eliminate anything perceived as noise also entails a judgment: what is signal, what is noise.[44] The apparatus, after all, must be read, and the reader, no matter how white his or her lab coat, must enter into an act of interpretation. Calling into question the distance between cultural values and scientific evaluation, Jacques Attali reminds us that "noise had always been experienced as destruction, disorder, dirt, pollution, an aggression against the code-structuring messages."[45] This conceptualization of noise as a figure of disorder, a metaphor for subversion and resistance, functions as shorthand for a kind of excess or radical outside to any system. And this accords with a cultural avant-garde (reaching back at least to Italian Futurist Luigi Russolo's "art of noises" in 1913) that privileges what has been deemed unacceptable by social convention. The discourse of lo-fi plays upon both senses of noise—as a cultural signifier of revolt and as a technical term for the "unwanted." We need to bear in mind, however, that the ideology of audio fidelity constitutes itself through a differential relationship to "noise," without which it could never define itself as fidelity.

The noise associated with lo-fi turns upon technological dissonance commonly at odds with the digital drive for pure signal. In production lingo this means "working in the red"—the distortion zone on recording equipment.[46] This intentional distortion in the recording process, disrupting the expectation for "clean" sound, overlaps with the typical lo-fi practice of utilizing limited machinery—machinery technically incapable of noise-free recording. In failing to eliminate its own workings, the equipment's noise, as John Corbett points out, "foregrounds the music object as such."[47] And incorporating sounds dwelling in the medium itself (such as tape hiss) assumes that this noise can be attributed solely to cheap equipment. But what are we to make of noise produced not out of necessity but rather by choice? An article on Guided by Voices, for example, reveals an intentional breach of both technological expectations and audible trust: "About half our last album was recorded on twenty-four-track, then re-mixed to seem like four-track stuff—it sounds like messed-up arena rock!"[48] Recordings that play on this relation between production and consumption hover amidst artistic intentionality, aural perceptions, and the vicissitudes of what the medium itself produces. They confound the treatment of lo-fi as emblematic of romanticism, leading us back once again to the issue of authenticity.[49]

The Feminization of Rock

Most discussion on lo-fi emphasizes *home* recording, whether as an effect of low-rent studio work or as an actual site of production. One hears of Liz Phair's bedroom or Beck's kitchen, basement tapes and garage tapes—spaces that function ideologically to signify intimacy, immediacy, authenticity. In contradistinction to the outside world, with its impersonal high-tech studios and alienated and alienating mass culture, home is regarded in the discourse of lo-fi as a "safe space," one presumably free of most social constraints. Here one's "self" is more clearly or easily itself, allowing the "true" self to emerge; meanwhile, the low-tech presentation is said to offer quite unproblematically direct access to this act of the artist's revelation. This echoes Walter Benjamin's observations on the technology of the cinema over half a century ago: "The equipment-free aspect of reality here has become the height of artifice; the sight of immediate reality has become a 'blue flower' in the land of technology."[50] Rather than mediate the experience between listener and performer, the technology of home recording—at least in the mythology of lo-fi—actually enacts the unconcealing of the artist.

Axiomatic of the discourse of romanticism,

this fantasy of direct communication is either celebrated as a form of personal self-expression or ridiculed as a form of self-indulgence. To move beyond this particular reading of lo-fi, however, requires us to consider the extent to which such a reading is gendered. I want to suggest that not only is the home or bedroom recording characterized as a "feminine" site of production but, moreover, that lo-fi itself has been gendered feminine within the overall masculinist discourse of rock, a characterization that serves to devalue it on those very same grounds.

In August of 1995 the *Village Voice* ran a major feature on the state of pop music. In "The Rock Beyond" critic Simon Reynolds ruminates on the aftermath of corporate "mainstreaming" of alternative music:

> Lo-fi, the mess-thetic of record collector bands like Guided by Voices, was the U.S. underground's first response, and a weak one, since lo-fi is just grunge with even grungier production values. As the ersatz folk culture of fanzine editors and used-vinyl store clerks, lo-fi was always gonna prove a stylistic and cultural dead end (which won't stop Pavement, the genre's R.E.M., from taking the sensibility into the mainstream, four albums from now).

The article goes on to explore what Reynolds calls "post-rock," "a new breed of guitar-based experimentalists struggling to escape lo-fi's retro-eclectic cul-de-sac."[51] Setting aside for the moment Reynolds's inscription of lo-fi as "weak," I want to examine briefly the article's implicit model of culture, one which relies on a surprisingly traditional notion of mass culture.

The first principle of Reynolds's argument holds that the "mainstream" is little more than a lost cause, a corporate wasteland, seemingly free of contradiction; further, whatever has been assimilated or incorporated into the mainstream—or mass culture—is utterly compromised artistically. What manages to evade commercial conformism though is this "new breed of experimentalists" (who sound pretty interesting by Reynolds's account), but why, we might ask, does this account require a dichotomy between the innovators and the mainstream?

In valorizing the experimental risk-takers over the mainstream—which presumes a fairly undifferentiated mass culture—the article posits a decidedly modernist cultural model premised on a stark binary operation, with an avant-garde uniquely outside or, literally, in front of a corrupted or degraded mass culture. This opposition between high culture and "low" or mass culture—what Andreas Huyssen calls the Great Divide that persists across modernity—entails a model of culture that many have argued is irredeemably gendered. In particular, Huyssen's landmark essay, "Mass Culture as Woman: Modernism's Other," examines a range of discourses which, since the industrialization of culture, "consistently and obsessively gender[s] mass culture and the masses as feminine, while high culture, whether traditional or modern, clearly remains the privileged realm of male activities." [52] The cultural work such documents perform, he maintains, is to "ascribe feminine characteristics to mass culture" (49). Indeed, such texts signify not only "the identification of woman with the masses as political threat" (50); what is also at work generally is "the persistent gendering as feminine of that which is devalued" (53).

Apart from reinforcing the modernist assumption of mass culture and its other, celebrating some radical cutting edge thought to be in opposition to the sorry state of everything else, what's curious about the configuration delineated by Reynolds's text is the way in which lo-fi is denigrated: not merely "retro" or "ersatz folk culture," it is the stuff of "record collector bands," "fanzine editors," and, perhaps worst of all, "store clerks." In other words, and again set against vanguardist trendsetters paving the way toward a "post-rock" future, lo-fi appears as a past-oriented culture based in consumption, a hopelessly consumerist culture of collectors, fans, and clerks. [53]

This feminization of lo-fi—as a form of (de-graded) mass culture, as a form of (banal) consumption—is exacerbated by its principal distinction as home recording. [54] To be sure, this activity coincides with the political economy of the rationalized household endemic to a post-industrial society, where work and play, production and consumption are now merely a key stroke and modem away. But the specifics of this "emergent" culture of home recording also consist of a "residual" culture. [55] An archaeology of the arrival of the mechanical reproduction of sound in the late nineteenth century reveals that the first casualties of the phonograph's entry into the domestic sphere were amateur musicians, many of whom were women. [56] So in many ways this activity of home recording could also be read as staging a series of reversals: inverting the conventional treatment of domestic space as a private, "feminine" sphere, the bedroom—our trusted guarantee for reproduction—has become instead (or perhaps once again) a site of cultural production, inverting as well the gendered coding of consumption and mass culture as "merely" feminine. History enters the bedroom, we might say, from which it never left. [57]

This notion of the feminization of rock is further suggested by facets of the lo-fi aesthetic. As mentioned earlier, its sound typically is marked by a seemingly amateurish approach to both recording and performance, effects that shape what loosely can be called song "structures." Several critics have noted, given the standard three-minute pop framework of verse-chorus-verse-etc., the rather fragmentary nature of lo-fi songs that often clock in at less than two. Unlike the punk predilection for compression of standardized compositional forms through speed, many lo-fi songs (especially those of Pavement, Guided by Voices, and early Sebadoh) simply end "prematurely," abbreviated and provisional pop numbers, shards instead of songs that come and go without resolution. Instructive here is a review of Pavement's *Wowee Zowee* from 1995: "Good, complete songs" are in short supply, insists the reviewer, with "the album as a whole feeling scattered and sloppy"; producing merely "song fragments," one of "which sounds like an unfinished rehearsal," the group is faulted for having "turned in a handful of half-baked performances."[58]

The sound of incompleteness, indefinite structure, lack of resolution—such traits have been gathered up by traditional music theory as "feminine endings." Evidently lacking a "strong tonic," these features, as musicologist Susan McClary argues, have been castigated in the discourse of music criticism as passive and "weak."[59] Such "weakness," I would suggest, characterizes lo-fi both formally, as fragmentation, and technologically, as disruption. This latter notation of instability, the breakdown of technology and its concomitant loss of mastery, control and order, throws into question the status of the authoring agent of lo-fi sound. For how else are we to take all those happy accidents but as minor ruptures in our sense of authorship? With the autonomous artist no longer fully in charge—sharing credit for the source of a sound with an apparatus that makes itself heard, with a technology somewhat out of control—such proceedings recast the dismissal of lo-fi, to return to the Reynolds passage, as "weak," a weakness due in part no doubt to a lack of artistic agency and technical virtuosity.

Since the text in question predicts the inevitable mainstreaming of Pavement, let us turn to a Pavement story, in which the group's Steve Malkmus, recalling an early encounter opening for the hard-core band Black Flag, describes a telling moment:

> I was backstage before the show and all those guys, they looked so scary, I was afraid of them. . . . And before they played, Henry Rollins was back there with this pool ball, this white cue ball, just squeezing it to get pumped up for the show. I mean, squeezing a cue ball! . . . It's like smashing your head against a brick wall. That's what I thought punk was, you know. That's when I knew that maybe I'm just not punk enough.[60]

Rollins comes up again, this time in an article on Lou Barlow's group Sebadoh. Barlow is reminded of reports in the music press that Rollins has thrashed Pavement for "slacking," deriding them and other bands believed to be playing "losercore." (Another Barlow project, Sentridoh, released the 1991 single "Losercore.") Acknowledging the significance of Rollins to post-punk culture and the influence of Rollins on his own work, Barlow good-naturedly impersonates the hardcore icon: "I fuckin' hate that Sebadoh losercore shit! They're weak! Why celebrate weakness?! You need to have strength in the world today!"[61]

Of course, the insinuation here is that the musical traits of hardcore as aggressive, angry rock are bound up with the corporeal dimensions of an almost histrionic masculinity. Getting "pumped up" after all is precisely the hardcore virtue of a hard (male) body, "impenetrable, invulnerable, invincible, one it is hoped that is entirely under control.[62] As for "losercore," in the dread of and amusement in someone getting "pumped up" by squeezing a cue ball could be heard a latent quarrel with rock as a masculine form, one dominated by the loud, hard and fast school of rebellion. For, how else is one to articulate dissatisfaction with the way things are? And what if the way things are included this very same masculinist ethos? What, in fact, would that dissatisfaction sound like?

Lo-Fi Suicide [63]

The metanarrative of "high fidelity," running the length of the twentieth century, consists of one long march of sound production incessantly striving to at first more accurately reproduce "real" sound (in the phonograph and early studio era) and then to displace this take on the real with a simulacra of autonomous sound (the digital era of disembodied abstraction, de-materialized purity). Every industry development in sound technologies—from 78 to LP, mono to stereo, AM to FM—moves without fail in the direction of bringing the listener ever nearer to some perceived idea of the "truth" of sound.[64] The technological rationality of digital precision and the CD's promise to eliminate "noise" is only the latest chapter in the drive for perfect sound forever. But a curious counternarrative has appeared, gaps in the trajectory of high fidelity that include such "reversals" as the comeback of vinyl[65] and the latest craze for "vintage" equipment.[66] Enter also the discontinuity of lo-fi and its accompanying debates on aesthetics, reception, and the phenomenology of sound.

We need to keep in mind that lo-fi practices— i.e., not *no* production values but *low* production values—remain thoroughly technological. What inheres in the discourse of lo-fi, however, is another rehearsal of the same old story about the natural and the artificial, *the* story, in other words, of nature and culture. The same story gets mapped onto nearly every shift in technology, played out, for example, in the analog vs. digital debates.[67] While new or emerging technologies render our relationships to previous technologies differently, the arguments remain fairly static: older forms of technology are usually set against newer forms as less alienating, less anti-humanistic, indeed, *almost as if they have become naturalized.*

Most of the groups heretofore mentioned as lo-fi have already moved on (if not to major labels, then certainly to "cleaner" sound productions), implying that, as an aesthetic device, lo-fi is the stuff of home recordings prior to a group's seemingly inevitable professionalization. But such movement isn't always perceivable, so insinuates the previously mentioned example of simulation staged by Guided by Voices, providing as well something of an object lesson in rock's order of things. Still, such reversals remain rare, and usually reinscribed (if our earlier reading of the pop press on lo-fi is any indication) as a more genuine form of authenticity. Nevertheless, the entire history of sound production demonstrates how recorded music is fundamentally a construct, one sufficiently given over to the realm of simulacra.[68]

With the success of alternative largely defined in market terms (major label signings, AAA ["album adult alternative"] radio everywhere, MTV apparently sticking around for awhile), what it means to *sound* alternative has been circumscribed by a certain level in production values. This sound threshold, below which (commercial) radio and TV will not tolerate—and where lo-fi seems destined to reside—offers us another way of reading formalist properties politically, at least those associated herein with the hegemony of digital aesthetics (humanist subjectivity, bourgeois ideology of autonomous art, dematerialization of perception, "transcendental purity," masculinist fetishization of technology). But by resisting industry incorporation and testing the limits of acceptability, lo-fi remains at the margins of social and cultural production, effecting, if nothing else, the verve of the unassimilable.

What I've also tried to suggest, however, is the attempt to circumvent the somewhat deathless opposition of authenticity and artifice underwriting much of the rock mythology. Primarily by instantiating how technology has been a constitutive element to all of pop, certain lo-fi recordings deliberately incorporate rather than mask noises of the medium, thereby calling attention (as in dub and some tendencies in hip hop) to their own construction.[69] Willful obscurity notwithstanding, the Mountain Goats, Daniel Johnston, and the Folk Implosion have produced some of the noisiest recordings around. Or consider the Silver Jews (which once included members of Pavement) and their 1993 EP *The Arizona Record.*

In typical lo-fi fashion, the entire work sounds as if it was recorded on a cheap portable cassette recorder—all muffled and murky and not a little bit difficult to actually hear. One can expect such sounds for lo-fi aesthetics, until one of the songs suddenly drops out, followed by silence and then just as suddenly resumes—as if someone had accidentally erased a segment. Another track just ends in mid-song—as if the recorder had shut off, and the tape had run out and clearly before the song is "resolved." It is an altogether jarring experience, with songs ending abruptly or interrupted by other songs. Moreover one is unsettled that such seemingly avant-gardist tactics have been employed in the recording process of fairly "traditional" pop songs. In this gorgeous mess of a recording, you can never not know what you're experiencing, never not hear the sound of the recording in the very act of revealing its own means of production.

Usually reserved for work produced by the historical avant-garde (in Peter Burger's configuration) such a tactic of "exposing the instrumentation" seems out of place on a pop record.[70] But this collision of formal experimentation and mass cultural production is exactly the strategy of a politicized avant-garde, one which casts doubt on the reified dichotomy between high and low culture, or in this case, between an aesthetics of estrangement and the pleasures of lo-fi pop music. "What is elided in the construction of standard music history," as John Corbett argues, "is precisely the materiality of the apparatus."[71] This very process shores up the bourgeois notion of autonomous art, an art free from social constraints, economics, politics and history.

Music has always been conceptualized as the most idealized of art forms, the one least beholden to the grubby world below. Even pop music, the first to be soiled in the strict hierarchy of musical idioms, is not immune from this faith in some rarefied pure outside. In part this situation attests to the staying power of nineteenth-century romanticism and its belief, as Caryl Flinn reminds us, "that music's immaterial nature lends it a transcendent, mystical quality, a point that then makes it quite difficult for music to speak to concrete realities."[72] But this desire for autonomy that forges an identification between high and mass culture has also been attained and sustained through technology, the "hidden dialectic," in Huyssen's phrase, holding in tension the still vested interest in hierarchical cultural categories.[73] That is to say, the aesthetic of autonomy linking high and low

through the discourse of romanticism is also an effect upheld by historical change through digital technology. As already mentioned, this form of technology paradoxically brings into being its own absence, that seeks to erase any trace of its mediation.

Either by refusing or failing (both produce the same effect) to repress the signifier and foregrounding its own constructedness, lo-fi sustains a strategy of "baring the device." Developed through the historical avant-garde, the concept has long become a function, as Thomas Crow insists, of the culture industry.[74] Yet in terms of cultural theory, to return to the feminization of rock, this gendered inscription of lo-fi as a feminized form of commodified culture would, perhaps dialectically, appear to complicate that treatment of the historical avant-garde itself, one that traditionally has been rendered as a masculinized form of rebellion against bourgeois society.[75] Not only does lo-fi offer, then, a specific instance of interdependence between high and mass culture (which of course has long been under way—in theory if not always in practice)[76] but it also suggests a kind of redistribution of methods and sentiment related to issues of gender and culture. Here we need only recall the question of artistic agency in lo-fi "accidents," events that serve to dispel the shroud of authenticity and intentionality enveloping creative autonomy while transmitting an implicit critique of a gendered will to mastery through technology. Hence, to the extent it has been rendered feminine, lo-fi's appropriation of avant-gardist procedures from within rather than against mass culture reminds us of the permeability of both traditional cultural boundaries and conventional cultural theory. The politics of "popular" music, however attenuated, also involve a politics of gender and sexuality that hit home, so to speak, in daily life.

The lo-fi practice of "making strange" and defamiliarizing our experiences of sound in the digital age seems to be taking up what was, for

Huyssen, "the historical avant-garde's insistence on the cultural transformation of everyday life." [77] And while all this revealing and exposing and unmasking pretty much leaves lo-fi in the same predicament the historical avant-garde found itself in: how to address the politics of representation. The experience of lo-fi appears to entail less a political tract than a gesture of dissonance, the sound of disaffection with a culture evidently impelled toward permanence, purity, perfection.

Notes

This essay has benefited greatly from conversations with Paul Dickinson, Brent Keever, and Joe Milutis, as well as with colleagues at the Society for the Study of Social Problems (New York City) and the International Association for the Study of Popular Music (Denver) conferences in 1996. I am indebted to Charles Weigl and Gary Weissman for music that mysteriously fell through the cracks at my nearby chain stores. I also wish to thank Ghislaine McDayter, Kathy Green, and the editors of this volume, especially Tara McPherson, for their generous critical readings of this essay.

1   Although "alternative" has become one of the more notorious floating signifiers of 1990s rock discourse, provisional distinctions of institutional contexts might still be drawn between college radio and AAA ("album adult alternative") commercial programming, MTV's "120 Minutes" and VH-1, or independent record shops and chain retailers such as Tower, Sam Goody, or Best Buy.

2   The noisy garage aesthetic of 1970s punk provides an obvious example of encoded production values, a direct assault on what was taken to be the creeping professionalization of rock that extended to "subcorporate" distribution, circulation, and reception (crack labels, zines, and clubs). An initial hearing of lo-fi suggests that, in its attempt to reclaim recording processes from high-tech studios, it has inherited from punk this aim of demystifying rock's means of production.

3   My use of the term "technology" should be taken to function not merely as "a set of tools or techniques" but as "a relation of the technical and the cultural, as a material and cognitive form of social process." Teresa de Lauretis, Andreas Huyssen, and Kathleen Woodward, eds., *The Technological Imagination: Theories and Fic-*

tions (Madison, WI: Coda Press, 1980), viii. I should add that I'm less interested in *how* the technologies under discussion actually work than in the ways they are represented.

4   Nathan Brackett, "Lo-Fi Hits Big Time," *Musician* 195 (January/February 1995): 44.

5   Simon Reynolds, "The Rock Beyond: To Go Where No Band Has Gone Before," *Village Voice* (August 29, 1995): 26–32.

6   That is to say, I'm less interested in attempting to define lo-fi as such than I am in parsing out its symbolic function, exploring both the formal traits determined as lo-fi and the range of issues interpellated by the term. To that end we should note how lo-fi will be riven with contradiction through the competing, overlapping and rather incompatible discourses of romanticism, realism, modernism, and postmodernism.

7   Jon Pareles, "Low-Fi Rockers," *New York Times* (April 11, 1993): sec. 9, 6.

8   Greg Kot, "Taking Up the Slack for a Whole Generation," *Chicago Tribune* (April 3, 1994): sec. 13, 7, 21–22.

9   Matt Diehl, "Lo-Fi Rockers Opt for Raw Over Slick," *New York Times* (August 28, 1994): sec. 2, 26. As standard procedure, the article also makes reference to the murky recordings of the Velvet Underground, forerunners, it would seem, to anything perceived as "noncommercial."

10 Rene Chun, "Fleeing Sterile Perfection for Lovable Lo-Fi Sound," *New York Times* (January 10, 1995): B-1, 4.

11 Simon Frith, "Art versus Technology: The Strange Case of Popular Music," *Media, Culture and Society* 8 (1986): 265, 266. This essay, crucial to my own argument, goes on to sketch the degree to which technological developments (recording processes, the microphone, magnetic tape) "have made the rock concept of authenticity possible" (269). Elsewhere, Frith insists that the "most misleading term in cultural theory is, indeed, 'authenticity.' What we should be examining is not how true a piece of music is to something else, but how it sets up the idea of 'truth' in the first place—successful pop music is music which defines its own aesthetic standard." "Towards an Aesthetic of Popular Music," in *Music and Society: The Politics of Composition, Performance and Reception*, ed. Richard Leppert and Susan McClary (Cambridge: Cambridge University Press, 1987), 137.

12 To quote Frith again: "The industrialization of music cannot be understood as something which happens *to* music, since it describes a process in which music itself

is made—a process, that is, which fuses (and confuses) capital, technical and musical arguments." "The Industrialization of Music," in *Music for Pleasure: Essays in the Sociology of Pop* (New York: Routledge, 1988), 12.

13 Against the modernist preoccupation with an artwork's formal traits, privileging as well an artistic practice of suspending the referent, Jacqueline Rose argues that the "transition to postmodernism . . . has been read as a return of the referent, but the referent as a problem, not as a given." *Sexuality in the Field of Vision* (London: Verso, 1986), 229.

14 Miles Orvell, *The Real Thing: Imitation and Authenticity in American Culture, 1880–1940* (Chapel Hill: University of North Carolina Press, 1989), xv.

15 Although turn-of-the-century sound technologies were technically incapable of faithfully replicating non-recorded sound, these forms of mechanical reproduction—what Michael Taussig calls "mimetically capacious machines"—involved both a desire to preserve and a desire to imitate, to offer both a document of what has been and a representation of the "real." This double function of preserving and reproducing will carry through to current forms of machinery, becoming intensified, as I will suggest, through notions of permanence and perfection. Michael Taussig, *Mimesis and Alterity: A Particular History of the Senses* (New York: Routledge, 1993), 198. For an intriguing take on phonography involving the imperative to preserve, see Charles Grivel, "The Phonograph's Horned Mouth," in *Wireless Imagination: Sound, Radio, and the Avant-Garde*, ed. Douglas Kahn and Gregory Whitehead (Cambridge, MA: MIT Press, 1992).

16 Evan Eisenberg, *The Recording Angel: The Experience of Music from Aristotle to Zappa* (New York: Penguin, 1987), 111.

17 For a fascinating cultural history of the tone test campaign, see Emily Thompson, "Machines, Music, and the Quest for Fidelity: Marketing the Edison Phonograph in America, 1877–1925," *Musical Quarterly* (79)1 (spring 1995): 152. The above quote is taken from correspondence between the Edison Company and one of its dealers sponsoring tone tests. See also Neil Baldwin, *Edison: Inventing the Century* (New York: Hyperion, 1995), especially 337–39.

18 This account from the *Boston Herald* is quoted in Walter L. Welch and Leah Brodbeck Stenzel Burt, *From Tinfoil to Stereo: The Acoustic Years of the Recording Industry, 1877–1929* (Gainesville: University Press of Florida, 1994), 147.

19 Scott Taylor of the Grifters quoted in Brad Lips, "We'll Take the Lo Road: On the 4-Track Trail," *Option* 59 (November/December 1994): 78. The lo-fi aesthetic seems to function immanently to this Memphis quartet's riveting blend of churning guitars and junkie blues, one that privileges echo, distortion, and feedback. And I'd swear that's a blown speaker front and center of the mix on "Bummer" from *One Sock Missing* (1993), perhaps yet another recording "accident."

20 The approximation model of recording lasted well into the 1940s and 1950s. As Edward Kealy describes it, record corporations "encouraged their engineers and mixers to develop their craft skills and strive for a recording aesthetic of 'concert hall realism' and 'high fidelity.' This required the construction of large studios and the development of microphone and mixing techniques in order to record whole symphony orchestras and dance bands in a way that simulated the psycho-acoustics of a live performance." Edward R. Kealy, "From Craft to Art: The Case of Sound Mixers and Popular Music," in *On Record: Rock, Pop, and the Written Word*, ed. Simon Frith and Andrew Goodwin (New York: Pantheon, 1990), 210.

21 On how developments in the recording process increasingly impacted on the cultural practices of making music, see Steve Jones, *Rock Formation: Music, Technology, and Mass Communication* (Newbury Park, CA: Sage, 1992), and Michael Chanan, *Repeated Takes: A Short History of Recording and Its Effects on Music* (London: Verso, 1995).

22 See Iain Chambers, "Contamination, Coincidence, and Collusion: Pop Music, Urban Culture, and the Avant-Garde," in *Marxism and the Interpretation of Culture*, ed. Cary Nelson and Lawrence Grossberg (Urbana: University of Illinois Press, 1988).

23 Frith,"The Industrialization of Music," 22.

24 For H. Stith Bennett, "an understanding of the acoustic control that is possible in the recording studio has promoted a unique consciousness of the make up of sounds in general—what I call the recording consciousness." "The Realities of Practice," in *On Record*, 229.

25 Addressing the "fuzzy-needle surface buzz" of early Pavement recordings, band member Steve Malkmus claims that it "was actually a mastering mistake as much as anything else." Such an incident is consistent with one of the great myths of rock—the cosmic accident. The story of "Rocket 88," for instance, itself considered one of the earliest rock records, always includes mention of the damaged amplifier that had fallen off

the band's truck en route to the song's recording, thus producing a distorted sound fundamental to rock's emergence. See Jim Dawson and Steve Propes, *What Was the First Rock'n'Roll Record?* (Boston: Faber and Faber, 1992), 88–91. The collision of art and technology, author and accident, persists through the lo-fi discourse of ego reduction, to which we will return. Pavement quoted in David Sprague, *Option* 45 (July/August 1992): 33.

26 Consider, e.g., two recent titles: Steven Holtzman's *Digital Mantras: The Languages of Abstract and Virtual Worlds* (Cambridge, MA: MIT Press, 1994), and Nicholas Negroponte's "national bestseller," with its vaguely Heideggerian invocation, *Being Digital* (New York: Vintage, 1995).

27 Ken C. Pohlmann, *Principles of Digital Audio* (Indianapolis: Howard W. Sams, 1989), 40.

28 For a particularly pessimistic view of digitalization as "the final culmination of a process of alienation," see Jean Baudrillard, *Simulations*, trans. Paul Foss et al. (New York: Semiotext(e), 1983). For a particularly perceptive critique of Baudrillard's work, see Peter Wollen, "Modern Times: Cinema/Americanism/the Robot," in *Raiding the Icebox: Reflections on Twentieth-Century Culture* (Bloomington: Indiana University Press, 1993), 67. See also Jonathan Crary on the "modernization effect" of the CD within the "ongoing rationalization and industrialization of the cultural" at work since late nineteenth-century modernity, in "Capital Effects," *October* 56 (spring 1991): 122. "The compact disc digitalizes the gramophone," observes Friedrich Kittler, "numbers and figures become (in spite of romanticism) the key to all creatures." "Gramophone, Film, Typewriter," trans. Dorothea Von Mucke, *October* 41 (summer 1987): 118.

29 "The Compact Disc Phenomenon: How It All Began," *Digital Audio's Guide to Compact Discs,* ed. Larry Canale (New York: Bantam, 1986), 1.

30 Antonio Gramsci, "Americanism and Fordism," *Selections from the Prison Notebooks,* ed. and trans. Quintin Hoare and Geoffrey Nowell Smith (New York: International Publishers, 1971), 298. While Gramsci's work (much of it written within Mussolini's prisons) has been extremely influential on contemporary cultural theory (especially for British cultural studies), I am using his remarks here somewhat ironically, at least to the extent that a radical Italian communist could be said to have argued for the appropriation of Fordist principles of capitalist production for socialist means. Less directly political but no less incisive, critical soci-

ologist Georg Simmel had already noted at the turn of the century how "punctuality, calculability, and exactness," along with precision, were key components of the rationalization of European societies, "The Metropolis and Mental Life" (1903), in *On Individuality and Social Forms* (Chicago: University of Chicago, 1971). For a compelling account of the often fraught relations between social and cultural modernity, see Anson Rabinbach, *The Human Motor: Energy, Fatigue, and the Origins of Modernity* (Berkeley: University of California Press, 1992).

31 Michael Chanan, *Musica Practica: The Social Practice of Western Music from Gregorian Chant to Postmodernism* (London: Verso, 1994), 8. See also Richard Leppert, *The Sight of Sound: Music, Representation, and the History of the Body* (Berkeley: University of California Press, 1993) for a skeptical look at that strain in the Western tradition intent on forging an identity between music and mathematics (rational order, pure form, the logic of numbers, etc.).

32 Thomas Levenson, *Measure for Measure: A Musical History of Science* (New York: Touchstone, 1994). For more on "music's mathematical underpinnings," see Sir James Jeans, *Science and Music* (1937; New York: Dover, 1968) and Edward Rothstein, *Emblems of Mind: The Inner Life of Music and Mathematics* (New York: Random House, 1995).

33 The digital era offers not only a discourse of aesthetics but also, as already suggested, a discourse of science. Even a cursory glance at the audiophile magazines reveals a preponderance of theory in the abstract language of audiologists. Such experts debate whether the latest mathematically measurable and scientifically documented technical achievements (a system's specifications) are even audible—i.e., not immediately apparent—but theoretically possible. If the technology itself has far surpassed our ability to discern its claims of difference, then the rhetorical maneuvers of the specialists—intent on having us believe we're actually hearing qualitatively improved sounds—approach something resembling an article of faith.

34 The early vestiges of audio fidelity, from this 1907 account, already presupposes a male listening subject invested in "perfect specimens of the recording art. To this man the class of record is immaterial, his aim being only records which for clearness, volume, and quality of tone are absolutely faultless" (A. Lillingston, *The Living Age* [August 24, 1907]: 488). Or, consider this anonymous tongue-in-cheek piece from 1957: "A new neurosis has

been discovered: audiophilia, or the excessive passion for hi-fi sound and equipment." These "audiophiliacs," it is claimed, "are middle-aged, male and intelligent," exhibiting aggressively emotional attachments to their hi-fi sets: "To many it has a sexual connotation: addicts may be seeking a 'sterile reproduction without biological bother,' and in extreme cases, a record collection becomes a 'symbolic harem'" ("Audiophilia," *Time* [January 14, 1957]: 44). For more recent (but less jocular) evidence of "audiophilia," see Barry Willis, "Toys for Boys?" *Stereophile* 16 (1) (January 1993): 101–11.

35 An early Pavement recording, before the "major" indie releases on Matador, is called, appropriately enough, *Perfect Sound Forever.* This Stockton, California, group, known for assembling a wild pastiche of pop styles and sounds, are sort of the postmodern pranksters of lo-fi, incorporating as well the discourse of audio fidelity self-reflexively. They are also clearly aware of the blatant artifice of pop, evinced by this response to the alleged spontaneity of lo-fi: "The Beatles managed to do it in the most expensive studios, like on *The White Album.* At least they simulated spontaneity, anyway." Diehl, "Lo-Fi Rockers Opt for Raw Over Slick."

36 "Constant revolutionizing of production, uninterrupted disturbance of all social conditions, everlasting uncertainty and agitation distinguish the bourgeois epoch from all earlier ones. All fixed, fast-frozen relations, with their train of ancient and venerable prejudices and opinions, are swept away, all new-formed ones become antiquated before they can ossify. All that is solid melts into air, all that is holy is profaned, and man is at last compelled to face with sober senses, his real conditions of life and his relations with his kind." Karl Marx and Friedrich Engels, "Manifesto of the Communist Party," *The Marx-Engels Reader,* ed. Robert C. Tucker (New York: W.W. Norton, 1978), 476. On the "terror of disorientation and disintegration" as an overriding condition of modernity, see Marshall Berman, *All That Is Solid Melts into Air: The Experience of Modernity* (New York: Simon and Schuster, 1982).

37 Mark Cheetham, *The Rhetoric of Purity: Essentialist Theory and the Advent of Abstract Painting* (Cambridge: Cambridge University Press, 1991), 112. On "the role of the unclean and the impure" in the history of philosophy, see Susan R. Bordo, *The Flight to Objectivity: Essays on Cartesianism and Culture* (Albany: SUNY Press, 1987), and Mary Douglas, *Purity and Danger: An Analysis of the Concepts of Pollution and Taboo* (1966; London: Ark Paperbacks, 1984).

38 Gerald Seligman, "The Compact Disc Experience: Concert Hall Sound at Home," *Village Voice,* "Video Vision/Audio Adventures" supplement (October 22, 1985): 71.

39 Against the "ideological effect" of, in particular, the cinema, in which "the instrumentation itself [is] hidden or repressed," Jean-Louis Baudry posits Althusser's notion of a "knowledge effect": Manifestation of the apparatus and its techniques "produce a knowledge effect, as actualization of the work process, as denunciation of ideology, and as a critique of idealism," Baudry, "Ideological Effects of the Basic Cinematographic Apparatus," in *Narrative, Apparatus, Ideology: A Film Theory Reader,* ed. Philip Rosen (New York: Columbia University Press, 1986), 288. This "knowledge effect" will come up later in my discussion on the production of lo-fi sound.

40 Clement Greenberg, "Modernist Painting" in *The New Art,* ed. Gregory Battcock (New York: E. P. Dutton, 1973), 68.

41 Hal Foster, "Re: Post," in *Art after Modernism: Rethinking Representation,* ed. Brian Wallis (New York: New Museum of Contemporary Art, 1984).

42 David Kahne, senior vice president of artists and repertoire at Columbia Records, quoted in Chun, "Fleeing Sterile Perfection for Lovable Lo-Fi Sound."

43 R. Murray Schafer, *The Tuning of the World* (New York: Knopf, 1977), 182.

44 Ibid., 93.

45 Jacques Attali, *Noise: The Political Economy of Music,* trans. Brian Massumi (Minneapolis: University of Minnesota Press, 1985), 27.

46 On the similar practice of "working in the red" found in hip hop production, see Tricia Rose, *Black Noise: Rap Music and Black Culture in Contemporary America* (Hanover, NH: Wesleyan University Press, 1994), 74–80. A good deal of lo-fi sound was anticipated by Public Enemy's *It Takes a Nation of Millions to Hold Us Back* (1988) in its radical textural dissidence engineered by the Bomb Squad production team of Hank Shocklee, Carl Ryder (Chuck D), and Eric (Vietnam) Sadler. More specifically, the sampling of decrepit vinyl record effects (scratchy needle sounds, brittle pops, raspy static) has become a staple of "black noise," from the etched surfaces of Arrested Development's *3 Years, 5 Months and 2 Days in the Life of . . .* (1992) to the crackling backdrop of Tricky's "Hell Is Around the Corner" from *Maxinquaye* (1995)—all of which was paved long ago by the extraordinary work of reggae musician and producer Lee "Scratch" Perry.

47 John Corbett, "Free, Single, and Disengaged: Listening Pleasure and the Popular Object." *October* 54 (fall 1990): 89.

48 This Dayton, Ohio, group's penchant for British Invasion-era rock (by way of Big Star and R.E.M.) crystallizes the lo-fi aesthetic: placing a premium on melody (harmonies and hooks galore), their sound is scruffed up with a glaring amount of recording noise (static and tape hiss, e.g., are prominent features). Recalling the initial debate on lo-fi as a question of either economics or aesthetics, GbV's production process bridges both: four-track recordings out of necessity (apparently they have been laboring for years, releasing their own basement tapes) intersect with deliberately experimental techniques (vocals run through guitar amps for instance). Moreover, fairly traditional song structures are fractured unexpectedly (the twenty-eight numbers on *Alien Lanes* [1995] in forty-one minutes), suggesting a kind of avant-pop at odds with their reception in the music press as nostalgic bearers of a by-gone era when rock was "innocent." Indeed, as the above quote attests, GbV's "authenticity" is entangled with dissimulation: "We used to do pretend interviews, pretend photo spreads, pretend liner notes, pretend lyric sheets." Robert Pollard of Guided by Voices, quoted in John Chandler, "I Heard You Call My Name," *Puncture* 28 (fall 1993): 61.

49 Although a highly contested field, my use of "romanticism" here functions generically to denote a belief in the potential for access to poetic/artistic subjectivity— that somehow unmediated communication with the artist's (oftentimes tortured) soul.

50 Walter Benjamin, "The Work of Art in the Age of Mechanical Reproduction," in *Illuminations,* trans. Harry Zohn (New York: Schocken, 1969), 233. For a trenchant reading of Benjamin's already much-discussed text, see Miriam Hansen, "Benjamin, Cinema, and Experience: 'The Blue Flower in the Land of Technology,'" *New German Critique* 40 (winter 1987), as well as Susan Buck-Morss, "Aesthetics and Anaesthetics: Walter Benjamin's Artwork Essay Reconsidered," *October* 62 (fall 1992).

51 Reynolds, "The Rock Beyond," 26–27.

52 Andreas Huyssen, "Mass Culture as Woman: Modernism's Other," in *After the Great Divide: Modernism, Mass Culture, Postmodernism* (Bloomington: Indiana University Press, 1986), 47. Page numbers of further citations given in the text.

53 As Patrice Petro argues, "It is remarkable how theoretical discussions of art and mass culture are almost always accompanied by gendered metaphors which link 'masculine' values of production, activity, and attention with art, and 'feminine' values of consumption, passivity, and distraction with mass culture." What's also curious about the cultural model ineluctably inhering to the *Voice* piece is that Reynolds himself has co-authored, with Joy Press, *The Sex Revolts: Gender, Rebellion, and Rock'n'Roll* (Cambridge, MA: Harvard University Press, 1995), the most ambitious attempt yet to apply 1970s French feminism and psychoanalytic concepts to rock. Indeed, the book opens with a critique of the same "negative association of femininity and popular culture" (5) that I've been tracing, even making use of the very same essay by Huyssen. Regardless of the rhetorical maneuver of the *Voice* article to set up a foil to what Reynolds champions, the text nevertheless attests to "the tenacity," as Petro puts it, "of hierarchical gender oppositions both in our culture and our theoretical discussions" (6). Patrice Petro, "Mass Culture and the Feminine: The 'Place' of Television in Film Studies," *Cinema Journal* 25(3) (spring 1986): 5–21.

54 Of course, the home of our cultural imaginary, as both private refuge and as a "woman's place," also has a history. As Griselda Pollock contends, the long-standing dictate (especially in the West) legislating a dichotomy between public and private and its attendant assigning of sexual difference intensified in the nineteenth century, becoming a constitutive feature of modernity: "As both ideal and social structure, the mapping of the separation of the spheres for women and men on to the division of public and private was powerfully operative in the construction of a specifically bourgeois way of life." "Modernity and the Spaces of Femininity," in *Vision and Difference: Femininity, Feminism, and Histories of Art* (London: Routledge, 1988), 68.

55 The temporal concepts of residual and emergent cultures were developed by Raymond Williams, one of the key figures in British cultural studies, to differentiate historically those "experiences, meanings and values" which "cannot be expressed in terms of the dominant culture." "Base and Superstructure in Marxist Cultural Theory," *Problems in Materialism and Culture* (London: Verso, 1980), 40.

56 This displacement of "family" musicians was anticipated by the player piano, but the phonograph accelerated empirically the passing of "the piano girl." See Holly Kruse, "Early Audio Technology and Domestic

Space," *Stanford Humanities Review* 3(2) (1993); Judith Tick, "Passed Away Is the Piano Girl: Changes in American Musical Life, 1870–1900," in *Women Making Music: The Western Art Tradition,* ed. Jane Bowers and Judith Tick (Urbana: University of Illinois Press, 1986); Emily Thompson, "Machines, Music, and the Quest for Fidelity," and Richard Leppert, *The Sight of Sound.*

57 Liz Phair's bedroom recording, prior to her breakthrough Matador release *Exile in Guyville,* is called *Girly Sound.*

58 "What does a defiantly anti-corporate rock band do when it starts getting too much attention? In Pavement's case, they recoil." So begins a *Rolling Stone* review—for our purposes confirming as well a sense of how production values are coded corporate or alternative—which also ends sounding betrayed, if not a tad resentful: "Maybe this album is a radical message to the corporate-rock ogre—or maybe Pavement are simply afraid to succeed." Mark Kemp (review), *Rolling Stone* (April 20, 1995): 70.

59 Susan McClary, *Feminine Endings: Music, Gender, and Sexuality* (Minneapolis: University of Minnesota, 1991), 11. See also Claire Detels, "Soft Boundaries and Relatedness: Paradigm for a Postmodern Feminist Musical Aesthetics," *boundary 2* 19(2) (1992), and John Shepherd, "Music and Male Hegemony," in *Music and Society.*

60 Quoted in Jason Fine, "Catching Up with Pavement: Lo-Fi Leaders of the Stockton Scene," *Option* 59 (November/December 1994): 92.

61 Quoted in *Milk* magazine, issue 6.

62 Reynolds and Press, *The Sex Revolts,* 99. For, if one needs "to have strength in the world today," the "fully armored body image of (especially) working class masculinity," as Fred Pfeil points out, is strictly for show, and a show increasingly put on for a world on the wane. While maintaining "a hierarchical order within masculinity and the domination of women," Pfeil argues— in regards to the pumped-up Bruce Springsteen of the mid-1980s—"that a certain kind of white working class masculinity associated with Fordist regimes of mass production and capital accumulation is being rendered artifactual," *White Guys: Studies in Postmodern Domination and Difference* (London: Verso, 1995), 77, 88. On rock as a masculinized form of rebellion, see Leerom Medovoi, "Mapping the Rebel Image: Postmodernism and the Masculinist Politics of Rock in the U.S.A.," *Cultural Critique* 20 (winter 1991–92).

63 "Lo-Fi Suicide" is a song by the Folk Implosion (Lou Barlow and John Davis) from their *Electric Idiot* EP (1994). Although Barlow's group Sebadoh has abandoned lo-fi on the last couple of recordings for more conventional production values, the Folk Implosion's contributions to the movie soundtrack for *Kids* sustain a noisy lo-fi sensibility.

64 Frith, "The Industrialization of Music," 20–21.

65 On the creation of vinyl collectors as a new subculture, see George Plasketes, "Romancing the Record: The Vinyl De-Evolution and Subcultural Evolution," *Journal of Popular Culture* 26(1) (summer 1992). On the "resistance" to CD format and the significance of vinyl to the fields of alternative, rap, dance music, and club culture, see Richie Unterberger, "The CD Takeover," *Option* 29 (November/December 1989), 13–15, and Parke Puterbaugh, "The Wax Factor," *Rolling Stone* (January 26, 1995): 22. On how "the major labels have gotten wise to the fact that vinyl speaks of authenticity and passion," as a form of "street credibility," see Trip Gabriel, "Not So Fast with the Last Rites; The Vinyl Underground Lives," *New York Times* (July 24, 1994): sec. 2: 30, 35.

66 The "re-claiming" of vintage equipment such as tube amps for recording obtains not only in the more expected sounds of roots and retro stuff (Ben Vaughn's *Mono U.S.A.,* for instance, an eight-track mono recording, seems intended to invoke the sensibilities of 1950s rockabilly and AM radio), but also in the techno and acid house of such outfits as Prototype 909, who utilize "obsolete" analog circuitry for a sound that paradoxically isn't meant to be "too refined, too polished, or too synthetic." Marisa Fox, "Taylor 808," *Option* 61 (March/April 1995): 24. Or consider the "nostalgic futurism" of Stereolab, St. Etienne, and Pram, largely electronic groups who employ such dated technology as the Ondioline, Moog synth, and the theremin, reminding us of the technological sublime of yesteryear's imaginary futures. Simon Reynolds, "Plasticine and Heard," *Artforum* 33(9) (May 1995): 15–16; see also interviews with Candi Strecker, Robert Moog, and Juan Garcia Esquivel in *Incredibly Strange Music,* vol. 2, ed. V. Vale and Andrea Juno (San Francisco: Re/Search Publications, 1994). Finally, it should be noted that 1994 brought the first increase in sales of vinyl albums in thirteen years, coinciding with the "arrival" of lo-fi. John Leland, "Sound and the Fury: The Revenge of Low Tech," *Newsweek* (February 27, 1995): 75.

67 As Andrew Goodwin states, "Playing analogue synthe-

sizes is now a mark of authenticity, where it was once a sign of alienation." "Sample and Hold: Pop Music in the Digital Age of Reproduction," in *On Record,* 269.

68 As for this postmodern aesthetic often attributed to such digital technologies as the sampler, Andrew Goodwin asks, "is it in fact an aspect of economic, historical, and technological developments in pop that need to be understood in the context of the continuing dominance of realism, modernism, . . . and romanticism?" Goodwin, "Sample and Hold." This disjunction between postmodernism and the discourses of *contemporary* music reflects my earlier argument on how digitalization involves an extension of features associated with social modernity rather than a clear transition to postmodernity, suggesting, at least in terms of sound and technology, an utter lack of consensus on what is said to constitute the "postmodern condition."

69 On the ways in which dub "remind the audience they are listening to a recording," see Paul Gilroy, "Steppin' Out of Babylon: Race, Class, and Autonomy," in *The Empire Strikes Back: Race and Racism in '70s Britain* (London: Hutchinson in association with the Centre for Contemporary Cultural Studies, University of Birmingham, 1982), 300.

70 In Burger's initial conceptualization, the historical avante garde is defined against both the bourgeois realm of autonomous art and the elite modernism of purely aesthetic experimentation, one set over and in opposition to everyday life and mass culture. This aestheticist version of modernism came to be conflated with a rather traditional notion of the avant garde, typified by Clement Greenberg's famous 1939 essay "Avant Garde and Kitsch" and codified in Renato Poggioli's 1968 treatise *The Theory of the Avant Garde.* Burger's rendering of dada, surrealism, and the Soviet avant garde, however, attempts to distinguish between a politically charged avant garde, which sought a reintegration of art and life, and the modernist ideology of aestheticism, which insisted on the separation of aesthetics and politics (a separation often believed to counter commodification). Peter Burger, *Theory of the Avant Garde,* trans. Michael Shaw (Minneapolis: University of Minnesota, 1984). See also Andreas Huyssen, *After the Great Divide,* and Victor Burgin, "Modernism in the *Work* of Art," in *The End of Art Theory: Criticism and Postmodernity* (Atlantic Highlands, NJ: Humanities Press International, 1986).

71 Corbett, "Free, Single, and Disengaged," 84.

72 Caryl Flinn, *Strains of Utopia: Gender, Nostalgia, and Hollywood Film Music* (Princeton, NJ: Princeton University Press, 1992), 7.

73 Andreas Huyssen, "The Hidden Dialectic: Avant-garde—Technology—Mass Culture," in *After the Great Divide.*

74 As Crow maintains, "the avant-garde serves as a kind of research and development arm of the culture industry: it searches out areas of social practice not yet completely available to efficient utilization and makes them discrete and visible." Thomas Crow, "Modernism and Mass Culture in the Visual Arts," in *Pollock and After: The Critical Debate,* ed. Francis Frascina (New York: Harper and Row, 1985). Although speaking to "high" culture practices, Crow's argument also applies to the "low" culture of lo-fi, suggesting as well the extent to which such phenomena manage to straddle the Great Divide, and which finally assigns something like lo-fi to a now rudimentary diagnostic of the postmodern. I would like to thank Bernard Gendron for bringing Crow's essay to my attention.

75 See Susan Rubin Suleiman, *Subversive Intent: Gender, Politics, and the Avant-Garde* (Cambridge, MA: Harvard University Press, 1990).

76 Fredric Jameson's approach, for example, "demands that we read high and mass culture as objectively related and dialectically interdependent phenomena, as twin and inseparable forms of aesthetic production under late capitalism." "Reification and Utopia in Mass Culture," *Social Text* 1(1) (winter 1979): 133–34. For a related argument more specific to the British context, see Simon Frith and Howard Horne, *Art into Pop* (London: Methuen, 1987).

77 Huyssen, *After the Great Divide,* 7.

CORRUPTION, CRIMINALITY, AND THE NICKELODEON

Roberta E. Pearson and William Uricchio

We begin with the sad story of the rise and fall of Gaetano D'amato, a young Italian American who went from bootblack to the relatively prominent position of deputy chief of New York City's Bureau of Licenses, the government office that issued common show licenses to the city's nickelodeons. In October 1908, following an extensive investigation of the Bureau, D'amato was arrested, "charged with grafting."[1]

> The facts indicate that in place of allowing these matters to take the regular course, he put himself to considerable trouble in many cases, and interested himself beyond the limits of his usual duties, in order to "expedite" the issuance of licenses, notwithstanding that in so doing, he was acting contrary to rule and prescribed practice.[2]

In one such instance, D'amato issued a license contrary to the Fire Department's expressed disapproval of the proposed nickelodeon premises. Despite such "expediting," often done for his fellow countrymen, the majority of those testifying against D'amato were also Italian. Others among his countrymen supported him, as D'amato's plight called forth contradictory reactions from the "Italian colony of New York, with its several hundred thousand members," which the *New York Times* reported was "split wide open over [his] arrest."

> Little else has been talked of all week among the politicians of the colony. The older men, the ones who have always resented D'amato's rapid rise, shake their heads and declare they had long foretold it. But with the younger element, who accepted D'amato as a sort of leader, they declare it is all a plot.[3]

The story of D'amato concerns us not for its rarity but for its typically negative portrayal of the cinematic institution. Emerging alongside the social upheaval attendant upon rapid urbanization, increasing immigration, labor strife, and so forth, the new film medium quickly found itself caught up in the social debate over national values and identity that raged during the first two decades of the new century.[4] As the cinema struggled to disassociate itself from the workers and immigrants perceived as threatening the status quo and to establish itself as mainstream, respectable entertainment, tales of corruption, immorality, fires, collapsing balconies, and other outrages circulated publicly in the popular press and privately in the official reports of state and civil institutions. Government officials, both corrupt and upright, clergymen, both moralistic and supportive, civic reformers, both repressive and progressive, and theatrical entrepreneurs, wanting simply to crush the competition, all pursued their own agendas, in the process contributing to this negative discourse about cinema.[5]

During the nickelodeon period, anecdotes about D'amato and his ilk formed part of a master narrative constructed in the popular press and private documents, and it is possible to trace in this tale a move from the disequilibrium of anarchy and corruption associated with the marginalized worker and immigrant classes to a rational equilibrium associated with social/cultural elites imposing control on the new medium. The period's archival record (court cases, fire insurance records, journalistic reports, police investigations, city ordinances, and civic reform groups' investigations) resulted directly from the attempt to impose this master narrative and thus both constituted and was constituted by the discourse of rationality. The period's master narrative positioned Gaetano D'amato as a corrupt individual, an exploiter of the underclass, vanquished by the powers of progressive reform.

Today, the archival record established by the

period's elites constitutes the "facts" that comprise what we normally consider to be historical evidence. Given this limitation upon the available data, scholars reassessing the nickelodeon period are in danger of partially reproducing the elites' master narrative, as we speak of "Americanization," of "bourgeoisification," of "industrialization," or of the "social control" of the cinema.[6] In fact, when we began our investigation of cinema exhibition in New York City between 1907 and 1913, master narratives of this kind appeared to provide powerful explanatory paradigms. At first, Mayor George B. McClellan and other city officials relied upon the powers granted them by pre-existing state statutes and city ordinances, but this legislation rapidly proved an inadequate means for dealing with the social upheaval engendered by the growing popularity of the new film medium. Faced with such ineffective control mechanisms, various social elites—McClellan's successor, Mayor William J. Gaynor, civic reformers, fire underwriters, and others—joined together to draft a detailed ordinance regulating moving picture exhibition venues, eventually passed by New York City's Board of Aldermen in 1913. Were one seeking to impose coherence upon these events through the customary historiographic practice of periodization, one could characterize the 1907 to 1909 period as fairly anarchic, with the state's primary response being outright suppression, and the 1910 to 1913 period as one of containment, regulation, and rationalization. One might even detect in the period's discourse a Foucauldian trajectory from morality and personified authority to rationality and systematization, in which highly visible means of control, such as suspending licenses, were replaced by the disciplinary micro-techniques of the regulation of architectural spaces, employees, and the cinema audience. These interpretive frameworks would position Gaetano D'amato as a relic of an outmoded and rapidly transforming system.

Given the origins of archival evidence within the period's master narrative, data that would permit an alternative and perhaps more favorable positioning of D'amato may never be forthcoming, but re-examining the available data from a slightly different perspective, reading it against the grain, as it were, might cast a more favorable light upon D'amato's behavior. The *New York Times* tells us that "the younger element [among the Italians], who accepted D'amato as a sort of leader" declared that "it is all a plot." Might D'amato have been a hero of sorts to some of his people, even after the discovery of his grafting? Might they have appreciated the fact that he "expedited" their license applications? Might they have seen his approval of premises disapproved of by a Fire Department inspector as an appropriate response to a city department reputedly controlled by and run for the benefit of the Irish immigrant population? Might they have perceived the case against their peer as yet another in a series of systematic discriminatory actions directed against Italians? These questions must remain unanswered but posing them suggests that trying to hear the voices of the marginalized social groups whose perspectives were largely excluded from the period's master narrative might lead us both to reposition D'amato and to question many of our assumptions about "corrupt" and "criminal" behavior during the nickelodeon period.

Does questioning these assumptions entail condoning graft, or, worse yet, the truly appalling conditions existing in some New York City nickelodeons before the enactment of the 1913 ordinance? Were we ourselves somehow magically transported back to 1908 New York City, we must admit that a serious concern for life and limb might outweigh the immediate urge to undertake a personal investigation of some of the less salubrious nickelodeons. Between 1907 and 1909, the popular press and official reports indicate that nickelodeon owners obtained licenses illegally, safety inspectors demanded payoffs, projectionists smoked while handling volatile celluloid film, and understandably panicky audiences made conditions even worse. (And conditions seem to have been bad enough, with fire exits leading to bricked-up walls, balconies collapsing, and a general failure to meet even the minimum safety requirements well in evidence.) Consider a few excerpts from the official report to Mayor McClellan that preceded the famous 1908 nickelodeon closings:

> A wooden stairs led up at the left side to the top of the fence at the rear of the yard. Nine steps take one up to a small platform and three higher lead to the top of the fence. On the left is a sheer drop of eighteen or twenty feet into the yard of the adjoining house. There is no stairs leading from the before described stairs to the yard behind that of the yard of the moving picture show.
>
> The exit on the right hand side of the hall was blocked up by a chair behind the door. The courtyard is bounded by a board fence about 6' 6" and by a four or five story brick building. There are no doorways through the fence. To get out of the yard one must scale the fence or else go through an iron door leading into an adjoining building. This was not open when I inspected the premises.
>
> Here one is given his choice of leaping a picket fence, behind which there is a drop of ten feet, or of going up a stoop into the kitchen of the adjoining house.[7]

Do we mean to excuse such flagrant disregard of basic safety standards? Can we even understand it? We could challenge the "accuracy" of the "facts" reported in the press and official documents—was the fire exit really bricked in? Did the balcony really collapse, killing three people? We could "explain" these conditions in terms of the excesses of an early-twentieth-century capitalism, concerned with profit at any price, that gave rise both to robber barons such as Andrew Carnegie and to cockroach capitalist nickelodeon owners with few means and fewer scruples. But, as we did with D'amato, we might once more read the evidence against the grain, attempting to take the perspective of those marginalized social form-

ations largely excluded from the period's archival record and from the construction of the period's master narrative, who nonetheless played a prominent part within it. How might members of such social groups, from whose ranks came many nickelodeon proprietors, employees and audience members, regard the laws which mandated compliance with safety standards or forbid grafting?

The law, as the discursive realm of definition, regulation, and arbitration, might have seemed the quickest route for the motion picture's incorporation into (or exclusion from) the social order. Yet, as we have said above, the social order was itself in flux, undergoing change so rapid that some historians speak of a hegemonic crisis in the decades between 1880 and 1920, perhaps most apparent on a local level, in the cities that were initially the primary site of both cinema production and exhibition. The medium found itself caught between two different modes of social organization, roughly characterizable as the "old" and the "new." On the one hand, there was the charismatic, ad hoc, and personalized authority of the clergy and of the political machine: Tammany Hall in New York City. On the other, there was the rationalized, systematic authority of the managerial classes: civic reform groups, professionals such as fire underwriters and engineers, "progressive" city officials. Tammany saw the new medium as yet another opportunity for personal gain in a field that had already yielded them a rich harvest. As John Collier of the People's Institute, a civic reform group concerned with the film industry, noted, "All the exhortations that can be made and all the laws that can be passed won't break the grip of Tammany as long as Tammany controls the people's amusements."[8] Some Tammany politicos quickly added nickelodeons to their existing theatrical interests while the Tammany aldermen (city councilmen), whom the City Charter granted the ultimate authority for the issuance of licenses, demanded payoffs from nickelodeon proprietors. Many of these proprietors, hailing from the "old country," found nothing surprising about a personalized authority that demanded individual tribute, and the aldermen may indeed have been more responsive to their needs than an impersonal government bureaucracy.[9] Even the organ of a progressive reform organization, the *Civic Journal,* was sympathetic to this perspective, as it answered the question: "What, *in practice,* is an alderman?"

> In the congested districts the alderman is the poor man's lawyer (getting people out of trouble by politics not by law). He is an employment agency (representing his political organization always, whether helping out those on civil service lists or getting the applicant a place with some friendly corporation). He gives stand permits for news dealers, bootblacks, and the like. In some districts he collects toll for these services, and those affected pay the five or ten dollars as if it were a fine imposed by law; it is imposed by custom and tradition.[10]

Some clergymen hailed the new medium's potential for "uplift," but others, like the Tammany politicos, simply extended their previous practices and rhetoric to encompass it. These repressive clergy associated the cinema with all the other "cheap amusements" that wreaked havoc by distracting the "lower orders" from their religious obligations and exposing them to texts of dubious morality. Seeking to counteract the deleterious influence of these cheap amusements, the clergy mounted a rigorous defense of "blue" Sundays, bringing pressure to bear upon civic officials to enforce archaic laws that prohibited various activities on the Sabbath day. Unlike many European countries, but like England, the United States had a strong tradition of Sabbitarianism, and even the entertainment media of a cosmopolitan urban center such as New York City were occasionally subject to Sunday closing laws, despite the fact that for many working people the Christian Sabbath was the single day of leisure. Many New York clerics associated the danger to the Sabbath, and by extension to fundamental American values, with the ever-rising influx of "aliens" from southern

and eastern Europe, ill-disposed to conform to dominant, i.e., white, Anglo-Saxon, Protestant values, yet constituting a large proportion of the city's population and, according to the clergy, of nickelodeon audiences. Banning the Sunday showing of moving pictures, thought certain clergymen, was a tactic for disciplining these unruly elements, who, as Methodist minister John Wesley Hill said, substituted "the red laws of riot, carnival and immorality" for the blue laws of puritanism.[11]

The managerial classes saw the new medium as yet another field for rationalization through the imposition of their professional expertise. This ethos drew upon an emerging social science paradigm predicated upon the gathering of data that would "objectively" reveal patterns of human behavior and thus enable predictions about the ameliorative possibilities of particular regulations. During the first decade of the twentieth century, surveys proliferated on various aspects of the urban condition: demographics, living conditions, the "social evil" (prostitution), and cheap amusements, among others.[12] These surveys rendered individuals as statistical constructs marked only by aggregate variables such as age, gender, ethnicity, and occupation. Here, the reformers' stance closely resembled reform rhetoric about tenement conditions, with researchers investigating conditions such as crowding, sanitation, and potential fire hazards. Evidence such as this enabled these reformers to make both predictions and recommendations, as they called for better air flow or more frequent fire inspections, hoping that such ameliorations would better the lot of an underprivileged and relatively powerless audience whom the reformers saw as dependent upon their intervention. Casting the audiences as victims, they often ignored the immigrants' established folkways, avowedly seeking to abolish such "anachronistic" practices in favor of a modernized bureaucracy.[13]

In the film industry, the more successful producers, whose opinions were represented in such trade journals as the *Film Index* and the *Moving Picture World,* generally allied themselves with the managerial classes and supported the framing of legislation to rationalize and modernize their industry (as well as providing a way to rid the industry of its "lowest" elements), viewing this as a route to respectability and increased profits. At the same time, they resisted those laws, often framed and/or supported by the repressive clergy, that aimed at the outright suppression of cinema exhibition, seeing them as emanating from a groundless moral panic over the new medium. The more marginal nickelodeon proprietors, the cockroach capitalists, shared their more fortunate brethren's suspicion of repressive legislation, while sometimes suffering on the one hand, from Tammany's use of the law for personal gain, and on the other, from their more powerful rivals' use of the law to drive them out of business.

Caught as they were among these conflicting discourses and practices of corruption, morality, and rationality, members of the film industry harbored a certain justifiable suspicion of the law. Articles in the trade press reveal that the successful producers, both the members of the Motion Picture Patents Corporation and their independent rivals, considered negative discourse about the cinema a weapon employed by those hostile to the industry who wished to frame repressive legislation. With a certain (justifiable) paranoia, members of the industry may have deemed everything from official reports about bricked-up exits to the popular press's constant refrain about fire as easily discounted "enemy propaganda." For example, in 1910, the *Nickelodeon*, a trade journal for the moment allied neither with the MPPC nor the independents, complained of the law's attitude toward motion picture exhibition.

> Municipal authorities seem generally prone, without reason, to assume that the proprietors and managers of motion pictures theatres are natural violators of the law, and that special ordinances are requisite to hold them in restraint. This spirit is responsible for much of the peculiar legislation that

has harassed the exhibitor since the first picture theatre opened.[14]

Once more reading the available evidence against the grain, we conclude that the "cockroach capitalists" of the film industry's low end suspected the motivations not only of municipal authorities but of the financially more secure producers, whom they believed were attempting to impose control over the industry through such means as the establishment of the MPPC and an alliance with the managerial classes. Hence, some nickelodeon owners probably appreciated the power of their many enemies—conservative clerics, rival theater and vaudeville owners, the MPPC—to use the law and the press against them. However "true" the reports about health and safety dangers, however necessary regulatory statutes, low-end nickelodeon proprietors may have had ample grounds to discount them as yet another attempt to drive them out of business. From their perspective, discrediting both "disaster reports" and the "laws" designed to prevent them might have been simply the necessary evasion of their opponents' knavish tricks.

Certainly the more prosperous elements of the film industry constantly fulminated against the more marginal nickelodeons as they strove for a "middle-class" respectability. In December 1908, Francis V. S. Oliver, Chief of the Bureau of Licenses, included the views of a Mr. Rubenstein in his report on the Bureau's inspection of moving picture theatres:

> Every man who has the interest of the business at heart is looking forward to the time when every moving picture show in the country will be shown not in a cut-out front store, but in an actual theatre put up for the production of moving pictures as they are put up at the present time for plays.[15]

Rubenstein's statement is an early example of the Trust's anti-storefront rhetoric, oft-repeated during the following years' debate over nickelodeon regulation. In 1910, the *Film Index*, jointly owned by trust members Vitagraph and Pathé, lauded New York City's efforts to curb the "moral" and safety hazards of the storefront shows:

In New York, the authorities are going after the dark houses and the irresponsible machine operators with a vengeance that is wreaking havoc among cheap exhibitors of the East Side. This is as it should be. There is no excuse for a dark house where unmentionable evil may flourish, and there is no excuse for a ten dollar a week foreigner turning the crank of a picture machine on the ground floor of a tenement containing a hundred other excitable foreigners.[16]

Any "foreign" entrepreneur, struggling to make a go of his "dark house," would probably have sensed the anti-immigrant bias here and may have had good grounds to regard regulations concerning theater lighting and the employment of qualified projectionists as yet more unfair impositions originating from his business rivals. Indeed, during the battle over the framing of the 1913 audience, the smaller proprietors repeatedly claimed that some of the more stringent requirements were specifically designed to drive the "small fry" out of the business.

Reports of dark houses, irresponsible machine operators and excitable audiences may have circulated primarily to the detriment of the low-end operators, but the industry as a whole resented the exaggerated and often groundless reports of cinema-related fires, distrusted a popular press that sought to boost circulation through attacking the highly visible film industry and believed some of the more stringent regulations proposed by frightened legislators to be unnecessary. The Iriquois theatre fire of 1903 had forged a popular association between fires and theatres, reinforced by the Boyertown fire of 1908, that led to great public concern about the mandating of safety standards to avoid future disasters. Said the National Board of Fire Underwriters in 1909:

The Iriquois fire in Chicago, December 30, 1903, in which 600 persons lost their lives, was a terrible object lesson in bad construction and equipment, yet this was not sufficient to stop these disasters. The January 13, 1908 fire in an opera house in Boyertown, PA, cost the lives of nearly 200 women and children.[17]

Neither of these famous fires, however, occurred in nickelodeons. And, despite the widespread impression to the contrary, while the Boyertown opera house was exhibiting films on the disastrous day, official reports stated that the motion picture equipment did not cause the fire.

Industry representatives continually sought to counter the conviction that motion picture projectors inevitably led to fires. Gustavus Rogers, representing the New York exhibitors at the hearing that preceded the Christmas Eve, 1908, nickelodeon closings, spoke directly to the issue of fires.

So as far as fires and panics are concerned—and I challenge contradiction of the statement I now make—an examination of the records of the Fire Department of the City of New York will show that there have been more fires in butcher shops and in other places where articles of merchandise are exhibited than in moving picture places.[18]

A year later, the *Nickelodeon* said much the same thing about Chicago.

There were 7, 075 fires in Chicago in 1909. . . . There is no reference whatever to picture theatres or to motion picture films. It will be noted that they are not represented under "explosions"—that favorite expression of the theatre fire reporter; neither are they mentioned under "ignition." The conclusion grows upon us that there were no film fires in Chicago in 1909.[19]

Given the disparity between public impressions and what seem to have been the actual "facts" of the matter, members of the film indus-

try might be excused for taking a fairly cynical attitude toward fire regulation laws, viewing them
not as necessary for the preservation of life but
rather as a necessary public relations ploy.

> So much exaggeration has existed in the treatment
> of picture theatre fire reports that exhibitors have
> come to detest and avoid the very word, even when
> used in a protective way. They are inclined to over-
> look the fact that the danger lies not in the actual li-
> ability to fire, but purely in the minds of the people
> themselves.[20]

A broader public shared the film industry's
cynical attitude toward the law, since the period's
hegemonic crisis entailed a widespread critique of
the legal system as corrupt and inefficient, particularly within the nation's machine-ruled urban
centers. New regulations or changes in existing
ones were frequently viewed as but another means
of extorting graft from the struggling businessman. New rules meant new payments, and, thus,
more often functioned to exclude those who
would not pay than to regulate the behavior of
those who would. City inspectors, policemen,
firemen, and petty city bureaucrats like Gaetano
D'amato found new ways to supplement their incomes through new regulations. The "law," in
practice rather than theory, often came down to a
matter of whom to pay, not what regulations to
follow. A 1913 article written by New York City's
Commissioner of Accounts Raymond Fosdick,
head of the department charged with investigating
illegalities in city agencies, makes it clear that corruption on all levels had become an accepted business practice. Talking about the city's building
trade, he asserted that even the initially honest city
inspector came to participate in the corrupt system. "By and by he comes to expect it [the pay-
off], and learns how, by rigorous application of
minor features of the law, to make the life of the
non-tipping contractor miserable."[21] In paying
city inspectors or bribing Gaetano D'amato or
their aldermen to issue them licenses, nickelodeon

proprietors simply followed the era's standard operating procedures.

Seeing the potential for corruption everywhere, the film industry's trade organs, as well as
progressive reform organizations concerned with
cinema regulation, often denounced legislators,
their proposed legislation, and the entire legal
system. For example, a 1910 editorial in the *Film
Index* suggested that New York state politicians
wished to establish a state censorship board not to
protect the people but to line their own pockets
and continued by extending its critique to the law
generally. "The way not to have a thing properly
done is to give someone authority by law to do
it."[22] The *New York Times* reported on a meeting
in which members of civic reform organizations
denounced the Board of Aldermen for obstructing
the ordinance to regulate motion picture theatres.

> Some of the speakers said that the reason the ordi-
> nance was being held up was because "the motion
> picture show proprietors had 'reached' the Tam-
> many Aldermen." Other speakers said that the Al-
> dermen had been "reached" by the vaudeville the-
> ater propritors who didn't want the rival business of
> motion pictures to improve and develop. All agreed,
> however, that the Aldermen had been subjected to
> some mysterious and malign influences and they
> were characterized generally as "grafters."[23]

But critics went beyond excoriating only the
most obvious excesses of corrupt politicians, as a
ubiquitous lack of respect for the law, its framers
and its agents made suspect every aspect of the legal system, from the drafting of legislation to its
enforcement. This was especially true with regard
to the often vague laws regulating entertainments,
cheap amusements, and the cinema. Highly regarded public figures openly challenged legal decisions and the motivations of those who made
them, while the press represented aspects of the
legal process, especially the deliberations of the
Board of Aldermen, as a cross between a circus and a prize fight. William Sheafe Chase, canon

of the Episcopal Church and one of motion pictures' most vociferous opponents, was once charged with contempt of court for having "viciously and maliciously criticized" a New York judge who made a Sunday closing decision favorable to the film industry.[24] Theodore Bingham, having resigned his position as New York City's police commissioner, asserted that Mayor McClellan had closed the nickelodeons merely to appease his political opponents. "I asked the Mayor why he had taken such a sudden interest in the moving picture question, and he answered: 'I am playing a little game to win the ministers.'"[25] Newspapers delighted in reporting on the more bizarre aspects of legal decision making and the Board of Aldermen proved a ready source of good material, with the aldermen engaging in name-calling and even the occasional fist-fight. In 1907 the *New York World* reported on the aldermen's deliberations on the Doull ordinance, a piece of legislation designed to amend Sunday closing requirements.

> The Aldermanic meeting yesterday was a peppery occasion literally and figuratively. Soon after it began a man in a crowded gallery sifted about a pound of cayenne pepper among the throng of spectators standing below. Sneezing and coughing and the wiping away of tears became the occupation of everybody in the rear of the chamber.

Later in the same meeting, an Alderman Peters who refused to be quiet and take his seat had to be restrained by two sergeants at arms and forcibly put back in his place.[26]

The situation did not improve once the laws were on the books, as those charged with their enforcement seemed unclear as to their intent and even questioned their usefulness. After the 1908 closings that also affected vaudeville and other theatres, entertainment executives asked Police Commissioner Bingham to clarify the Sabbath laws. Said Bingham, "I'd like to know what the law is myself." A little while later, in answer to another question, the commissioner said: "Oh, I don't know the law myself. Why don't you go at once to the Corporation Council's office?"[27] The famous Tammany magistrate "Battery Dan" Flynn dismissed a complaint against a nickelodeon proprietor charged with admitting an under-age (under sixteen) patron, saying, "The law is an outrage. It deprives poor people of going to the theatre, and I believe it was passed in the interest of the big theatres that don't want people to go to the five and ten cent shows." Flynn said that he himself had bought nickelodeon tickets for unescorted children.

Not only were the laws represented as unclear or unjust, they were also represented as unequally enforced. Some interpretations of the statutes held that both nickelodeons and saloons should be closed on Sundays, yet a widespread system of payoffs enabled the latter to continue their operations even on the "Lord's" day. In 1909 the *Moving Picture World* complained of this inequity, reprinting an article from the *Brooklyn Standard Union* that criticized the police for permitting the saloons to sell liquor on Sunday.

> Few people could be convinced, in view of the evidence on all sides, that the police knew the excise law was placed on the statute books to be enforced. . . . And perhaps not until hypocrisy is banished from local police affairs and intelligent and fearless leadership directs police activity will the laws be enforced impartially.[28]

An unlucky but ingenious nickelodeon proprietor, Mr. Cohen, of whom we shall hear again shortly, was arrested numerous times for showing films on Sundays. On the occasion of his fifth arrest, Cohen said that "he was being harshly treated by Captain Reynolds, who allowed other men to do the same things without arrest. 'He says he can't arrest them because they sell soda water,' said Cohen. 'Well, last week I was selling soda and he arrested me.'"[29]

Faced with unjust or unequally enforced legislation, opponents of the law could simply ignore legislation and face the consequences of fines or imprisonment, but the more astute used the legal system against itself in an attempt to get specific laws repealed. Said the *Nickelodeon* about the under-sixteen admission requirement: "The quickest way to kill an obnoxious law is to enforce it so rigidly that the people grow sick of it and see that it is repealed."[30] The test case—arresting a violator in the hopes of a judicial decision invalidating the law—was also a useful tactic. The *Tammany Times* asserted that this was Mayor McClellan's motivation for strictly enforcing Sunday closing laws.

> Mayor McClellan wants neither a blue Sunday nor the pleasure of the people unduly curtailed or restricted.... What the Mayor wants is to obtain from the courts a proper definition of the laws now on the statute books. There is only one way of getting this desired information, and that is through the medium of a test case.... To make a test case arrests are necessary.[31]

As we have seen, several factors, ranging from corruption to unequal enforcement, combined to undermine the legal systems' authority during the nickelodeon period. The nickelodeon entrepreneurs, often drawn from the ranks of lower or immigrant classes, had good reason to share the period's general disdain for the law. Not yet fully acculturated within the idealized ethics of the system, nor economically able to stand by and watch their investments destroyed (and perhaps even inspired by the model of robber-baron entrepreneurial capitalism), nickelodeon proprietors seem to have developed a set of unorthodox, innovative responses to legal constraints. But since the historical records (popular and trade press reports, police, fire and judiciary records, and the published observations of concerned clerics, progressive reformers, and even the fire insurance industry) contained relatively few of these responses and they formed no coherent pattern, we at first invalidated them as historical "evidence" and

tended to relegate them to the status of period "color." Then we realized that such relegation might result in our unwittingly reproducing the period's own preferred discourse and confirming its own biases. In this article we are endeavoring to empower the voices of those who in their own period might not have "fit"—in terms of class, or ethnicity, or cultural background—and who in our period do not "fit" historiographically. Our method is to read the available evidence against the grain of the period's interpretation, reconsidering practices that period elites categorized as corrupt or criminal, in order to see the sometimes curious, sometimes outrageous, and sometimes startlingly dangerous actions of nickelodeon proprietors and their personnel operators as the guerrilla-like activities of those simply struggling to survive.

Nickelodeon owners adopted several survival strategies. Some worked within the legal system, cooperating with those who sought test cases or seeking court injunctions to prevent city officials like McClellan from suspending their licenses. Others evaded the law, violated fire-regulations or Sunday closing statutes and paid off city officials like D'amato. And others responded in a more imaginative fashion, claiming to stay within the letter if not the spirit of the law. The same Mr. Cohen who was frequently arrested for violating the Sunday closing laws continually contrived ingenious defenses. At one of his court appearances, "Captain Reynolds told Magistrate Hylan that Cohen had been charging admission to his show by a subterfuge. Persons were admitted free of charge, but when seated on the inside everyone had to purchase five cent's worth of candy, or incur the displeasure of the management."[32] Cohen had earlier claimed that the profits from Sunday exhibitions went to charity or that he charged his patrons for soda water, not the films.[33] Two nickelodeon owners fined twenty-five dollars for admitting under-age minors attempted to make life difficult for the court clerk by paying in nickels from three large paper bags they carried under their arms. Court clerk Fuller refused to count the money in court and said it must be taken up to a quieter room. . . . On their way up one of the bags broke and the contents scattered in all directions. This was too much, and the two prisoners were taken before the justices again while the question of legal tender was considered.

The pair relented when told to pay their fine in paper money or go to jail.[34]

Proprietors also engaged in less veiled ridicule of the law. When the police department finally enforced Sunday shutdowns in 1907, ironic signs appeared on the closed nickelodeons: "Little Old New York died to-day. We have gone to the funeral. We will be back to-morrow"; "We are on the ice temporarily. Will get off to-morrow"; "We have not gone into the undertaking business. Not yet, but . . ." and, most mordant of all, "We are thinking of moving to Boston."[35] The next year's closing gave rise to unintentional humor as the proprietors of Hammerstein's Victoria (a vaudeville house) strove to keep within the letter of the law by providing a lecture to render a travel film of northern Europe an "educational" show suitable for the Sabbath.

> "A railroad track," said the lecturer, the moving pictures having been taken evidently from the front of a train.
>
> "Some men," continued the educationalist presently when a group of men on skis were shown. The next scene revealed them speeding downhill.
>
> "Men skiing," announced the man.
>
> The pictures again switched to the railroad track.
>
> "Another railroad track."
>
> The track ran across a low trestle.
>
> "The Brooklyn Bridge," bellowed the announcer.
>
> Pictures showing reindeers tramping about in the snow were explained as "animals eating snowballs."[36]

Sometimes the owners of moving picture venues engaged in a more active resistance aimed at the lawmakers themselves. At the "peppery" meeting at which the aldermen debated the Doull Ordinance, a Mr. Moses, owner of an establishment that showed films, first raised the issue of corruption, saying to those who opposed the bill, "What do you mean by voting against an open Sunday? Is it another hand-out for graft?"[37] When this tactic produced no results, Moses resorted to more strongly persuasive means, physically attacking Alderman Cornelius D. Noonan, who had voted against the ordinance.[38]

Isolated incidents of selling candy instead of charging admission, posting humorous signs and hitting public officials do not normally constitute "valid" historical evidence, since their comparative rarity and random occurrence mitigates against their fitting into our historiographical models of consistency, resonance, etc. But we have argued that this lack of "fit" stems from the period's own archiving practices—in which the records that were kept tended to support the period's master narrative—and the present-day unwitting reproduction of that master narrative. We have attempted to use these examples of "random, non-patterned" evidence to suggest a counternarrative by drawing upon the probable perspectives of the period's marginalized social groups with regard to the legal apparatus.

Survival tactics that entailed flouting the regulatory apparatus constructed by law and civil statute occasionally resulted in violations with disastrous consequences such as the collapse of a balcony at a Rivington Street nickelodeon that cost several lives. More often, however, the potential for danger was subject to strong discursive amplification. We do not wish to trivialize attempts to "better" the conditions of film exhibition, but, rather, to offer a new vantage point on seeing "transgressions," that is, the many incidents of "criminal" or "corrupt" behavior associated with the emergent nickelodeons. As noted at the outset of this essay, the limited array of interpretative paradigms currently used to understand the period tend to emphasize the sordid nature of these "violations" and the subsequent triumph of "progress." We have suggested an alternate paradigm that might see these "violations" as perfectly consistent with the period's dominant practices. The laws regarding nickelodeons—from their conception and formation to their deployment and enforcement—were seen as corrupt and sometimes as specifically designed to subvert the film business. In this context, the various tactics deployed by nickelodeon owners seem less "corrupt" or "irrational" as they do motivated and reasonable acts of survival.

In concluding this chapter, a return to the kind of anecdotal evidence with which we began may help to reinforce our point concerning reading period evidence against the grain or within the perspective of the periods' marginalized social formations. In 1908 the *Moving Picture World* ran a story titled "Audience Applauds His Shrieks of Agony," relating the horrifying experience of projectionist John Riker.

> Reaching into the sheet-iron cage that covered a moving-picture machine with which he was giving an exhibition, John Riker seized a bare electric wire instead of the switch. He was held fast while a current of 1000 volts went through his body. He shrieked for help. His cries, coming through the narrow aperture of the booth, sounded to the audience like a phonographic accompaniment to the blood and thunder drama that was being portrayed in the moving pictures. The audience, not suspecting the dangerous plight of the man, applauded. . . . [When he was rescued] Riker's hand still gripped the wire and had to be pried off. His hand was almost roasted by the strength of the current. [When will operators learn? We cannot understand why a bare wire was allowed to be used. Every operator ought to use only properly insulated wires, and if any bare surface shows they should be bound with tape.—ED.] [39]

Why did the journal print this story—to appeal to their readers' rubber-necking propensities, their potential schadenfreude? For that matter, why do we reprint it? We do so because we wish to suggest that such anecdotes might have had a powerful communicative function. The top-end of the film industry joined with groups such as the fire underwriters or New York City's Department of Water, Gas and Electricity in promulgating certain "reasonable" (nonmoral, nonjudgmental) propositions: "Don't touch bare wires"; "Don't smoke around nitrate film"; "Don't hire inexperienced projectionists." But in an environment where authority was so fundamentally subverted, so suspect, where statute, law, or even "common sense" safety standards were undermined and questioned, where every law could be seen as yet another another attack or opportunity for graft, how were "rules" to be communicated? With the discursive structure of laws and regulations invalidated, cautionary tales, narrativized vignettes of operators with horribly maimed arms and others that we have found, were called into service.

Notes

1 "D'amato's Arrest Stirs Italians," *New York Times* (Oct. 4, 1908).

2 The complainants and prices paid for a $25 initial license and/or $12.50 renewal included M. di Christopero, $185; Roger di Pasca, $100; and Joseph Brunelli, $75. Special examination of the accounts and methods of the Bureau of Licenses, Office of the Commissioners of Accounts, Nov. 2, 1908, Accounts, Commissioner of, MGB 44, New York City Municipal Archives.

3 "D'amato's Arrest Stirs Italians," *New York Times* (Oct. 4, 1908).

4 For a detailed discussion of this situation, particularly as it regards the workers and immigrants so often assumed to constitute cinema's audiences, see William Uricchio and Roberta E. Pearson, *Reframing Culture: The Case of the Vitagraph Quality Films* (Princeton: Princeton University Press, 1993), especially chapter 1.

5 William Uricchio and Roberta E. Pearson, "Constructing the Mass Audience: Competing Discourses of

Morality and Rationalization in the Nickelodeon Period," *Iris* 17 (1994): 43–54.

6 For example, see Tom Gunning, *D. W. Griffith and the Origins of American Narrative Film* (Urbana: University of Illinois Press, 1991); Miriam Hansen, *Babel and Babylon: Spectatorship in American Silent Film* (Cambridge, MA: Harvard University Press, 1991); and Uricchio and Pearson, *Reframing Culture.*

7 Francis V. S. Oliver, Chief, Bureau of Licenses to George B. McClellan, Mayor, "Regarding Inspection of Moving Picture Theatres," December, 1908, Folder 4, Bureau of Licenses, MGB 51, New York City Municipal Archives. The inspections were carried out under the city's mandate to protect the safety of its citizens, even though specific statutes regarding nickelodeon construction were not approved in New York City until 1913.

8 "People's Amusements," *New York Daily Tribune* (Dec. 19, 1908).

9 Mario Maffi, among others, argues that the organization of social life particularly in southern Italy was based upon a pattern of social stratification and personified power which was transferred to and quickly adapted by the immigrant community in the United States. See *Gateway to the Promised Land: Ethnic Cultures on New York's Lower East Side* (Atlanta: Rodopi, 1994).

10 "Worrying about the Aldermen," *Civic Journal* 1(7): 3, 8.

11 "Commends the Mayor," *New York Times* (Dec. 28, 1908).

12 For an overview of these surveys, see Alan Havig, "The Commercial Amusement Audience in Early-Twentieth-Century American Cities," *Journal of American Culture* 5 (1982): 1–19. For period surveys see, among many others, Edwin R. A. Seligman, ed., *The Social Evil: With Special Reference to Conditions Existing in the City of New York* (New York: G. P. Putnam's Sons, 1912); Robert Coit Chapin, *The Standard of Living Among Workingmen's Families in New York City* (New York: Russell Sage Foundation, 1909); and Louise Bollard More, *Wage-Earners' Budgets: A Study of Standards and Cost of Living in New York City* (New York: Henry Holt, 1907).

13 One of the problems faced by the managerial classes in their reform program was the entrenched corruption of the system upon which they were forced to rely for social change. After he was pushed out of his office by Mayor McClellan, former Police Commissioner Bingham said that the mayor ordered a hearing about the nickelodeons but the man put in charge was the head of the license bureau. "Not only was it [the License Bureau] found to be doing a land office business in graft, by charging double and sometimes treble the legal cost of common-show licenses, but it was also trafficking in peddler's licenses in the same outrageous way." Theodore Bingham, "Why I Was Removed," *Van Norden's; World Mirror* (Sept. 1909): 595.

14 "Putting the Picture Theatre Right," *Nickelodeon* 4(2) (July 15, 1910): 27.

15 Francis V. S. Oliver, Chief, Bureau of Licenses to George B. McClellan, Mayor, "Regarding Inspection of Moving Picture Theatres," December, 1908, Folder 4, Bureau of Licenses, MGB 51, New York City Municipal Archives.

16 "Answer New York Sun's Editorial," *Views and Film Index* (Dec. 31, 1910): 245.

17 Proceedings of the 43rd Annual Meeting of the National Board of Fire Underwriters, May 13, 1909, 70.

18 Francis V. S. Oliver, Chief, Bureau of Licenses to George B. McClellan, Mayor, "Regarding Inspection of Moving Picture Theatres," December, 1908, Folder 4, Bureau of Licenses, MGB 51, New York City Municipal Archives.

19 "The Causes of Fires," *Nickelodeon* 4(5) (1910): 120. The list of probable causes curiously includes seventeen fires resulting from "rats and mice with matches." Beware of pyromaniac rodents!

20 "Panics," *Nickelodeon* 2(5) (Nov. 1909): 136.

21 Raymond B. Fosdick, "Driven from the City: Another Point of View," *Outlook* (Jan. 18, 1913): 134.

22 "Casual Comment," *Film Index* (Nov. 26, 1910): 2.

23 "Denounce Fight Law Fight," *New York Times* (June 18, 1912): 6.

24 "Rector Chase Found Guilty of Contempt," *Moving Picture World* (Jan. 18, 1908).

25 Theodore Bingham, "Why I Was Removed," *Van Norden's; World Mirror* (Sept. 1909): 596.

26 *New York World* (Dec. 18, 1907): 2.

27 "Diluted Vaudeville To-Day's Show Menu," *New York Times* (Dec. 27, 1908): pt. 2:1.

28 "Trade Notes," *Moving Picture World* (Oct. 1909): 521.

29 *Moving Picture World* (June 1, 1907): 201.

30 "Putting the Picture Theatre Right," *Nickelodeon* 4(2) (July 15, 1910): 27.

31 "The Mayor No Puritan," *Tammany Times* (May 22, 1909): 8.

32 *Moving Picture World* (June 8, 1907): 217.

33 *Moving Picture World* (June 1, 1907): 201.

34 "Nickles to Pay Their Fines," *Nickelodeon* 5(10): 282.

35 *New York World* (Dec. 9, 1907).

36 *New York World* (Dec 28, 1908).

37 "Aldermen Fail to Doctor Blue Laws," *New York American* (Dec. 11, 1907): 1.

38 "One More Silent Sunday Certain; Aldermen Halt," *New York Herald* (Dec. 11, 1907): 1.

39 "Audience Applauds His Shrieks of Agony," *Moving Picture World* (Feb. 22, 1908): 138. Countless of these cautionary tales appeared in the *Moving Picture World*, usually with an admonitory comment at the end (see also Aug. 8, 1907, 359, and Sept. 14, 1907, 438).

"Racial Cross-Dressing" in the Jazz Age: Cultural Therapy and Its Discontents in Cabaret Nightlife

Nicholas M. Evans

In his 1933 autobiography, *Along This Way,* James Weldon Johnson recalls delivering a lecture in 1917 containing a controversial proposition: "that the only things artistic in America that have sprung from America soil, permeated American life, and been universally acknowledged as distinctively American, [are] the creations of the American Negro." Johnson reasserts this idea in the autobiography, identifying ragtime and jazz ("lighter music") as particularly influential cultural creations:

> It is to this music that America in general gives itself over in its leisure hours. . . . At these times, the Negro drags his captors captive. On occasions, I have been amazed and amused watching white people dancing to a Negro band in a Harlem cabaret; attempting to throw off the crusts and layers of inhibitions laid on by sophisticated civilization; striving to yield to the feel and experience of abandon; seeking to recapture a taste of primitive joy in life and living; trying to work their way back into that jungle which was the original Garden of Eden; in a word, doing their best to pass for colored.[1]

The basic terms of Johnson's formulation reproduce a social, cultural, and racial binary popular well into the twentieth century—the idea that "sophisticated civilization," or bourgeois rational culture associated with upper-middle-class "Anglo-Saxons," was divided irrevocably from "primitive joy in life," or intense physical and emotional pleasure associated with African Americans and other social minorities. Johnson clearly satirizes this distinction as untenable; his invocation of "passing," for example, reminds of the manner in which educated, light-skinned African Americans traversed the color line and appropriated "sophisticated civilization" as their own. Johnson himself, like many other black intellectuals, accessed "civilization" even without disguising his background. Yet his more poignant satire lies in reversing the direction of passing: in Harlem cabarets, he posits, "civilized" whites sought to appropriate a supposedly black, primitive state. This ironic reversal of terms is all the more piercing given that it echoes the discourse used by many white Americans in the 1920s to articulate their own experience of jazz dancing. Cabaret goers often openly expressed their desire to recapture primitive physical and emotional intensity because oppressive civilization robbed them of such feeling. Johnson's argument, historically positioned by his autobiography between World War I (1917) and the Depression (1933), identifies the racialized cultural dynamic in white, American, 1920s popular culture with which my essay is primarily concerned.

This cultural dynamic was situated principally in northern urban centers such as New York and Chicago, where dancehalls, ballrooms, nightclubs, and cabarets sprouted before and after World War I. These venues offered food, alcohol, dancing, and other entertainment to their white, well-to-do clientele of wealthy (sub)urban sophisticates, business professionals of the middle and upper-middle class, and upwardly mobile youths.[2] Elements of this popular culture also spread to suburban country clubs and college parties, as represented in the fiction of F. Scott Fitzgerald. Historically, this white fascination with cabarets and jazz coincided with a period of heightened racial tensions in the North. African American migrants were perceived to invade northern cities, inspiring reactionary fear and anxiety among—as well as violent reprisals from—the white bourgeoisie. Paradoxically, then, embracing leisure activities deriving from black culture correlated with

promoting social policies that oppressed black Americans. I suggest that this correlation manifested a quasi-imperial relation between white and black Americans, in that larger African American populations challenged northern Anglo-Saxons' sense of social and cultural dominance. To maintain control, the latter group pursued colonizing strategies, enforcing the socioeconomic inequality of African Americans as well as expropriating and commodifying their culture.[3] Whites' jazz dancing in cabarets, their passing for colored, manifested such cultural expropriation: it represented a complex and paradoxical desire to control threatening "black" energy by confronting it within the confines of white selfhood, thereby defusing racial anxiety imaginatively. If white Americans could master "black" identity in bodily cultural performance, they could supposedly manage a black social presence in the body politic.

However neatly I have just phrased it, this project was fraught with complexities. Bourgeois white discourse about jazz and jazz dancing in the 1920s was far from monological; what Johnson calls "passing for colored" was a controversial cultural phenomenon whose meanings were highly unstable. The only issue on which all 1920s white commentators agreed was that jazz dancing manifested primitive experience. With respect to two other crucial issues—the relation of the primitive to African Americans, and the value assigned to primitive experience—1920s discourse about jazz reveals a diversity of perspectives not evident in Johnson's passage. This discourse divides roughly into two strains, moralist opposition and primitivist celebration. Jazz's moralist opponents equated primitive dancing with blackness, but their evaluative orientation conflicted with the one Johnson emphasizes: for them, emulating the primitive state of African Americans signified a perverse embrace of inferiority. They found jazz degrading mentally, physically, and spiritually, as many subsequent studies of jazz's reception demonstrate.[4] These moralists—whose views dominated the popular press—expressed faith in the absolute difference of the races, privileging the supposed whiteness of "sophisticated civilization" over and against the presumed blackness of the primitive.

In contrast, jazz's celebrants—a diverse, subdivided group—promoted primitive experience to varying degrees. One celebrant camp consisted of "Negrophiles" like bohemian Carl Van Vechten. In George M. Fredrickson's words, these "romantic racialists" valorized African Americans as "exotic primitives" admirable for their "natural spontaneity, emotionalism, and sensuality."[5] These "Negrophiles"—many of whom were associated with artistic modernism—were no doubt the primary targets of Johnson's satire, for they reversed the order of valuation in the primitive–civilized binary. However, the primitivism of many of these figures also often proved to be subtly reactionary by insisting on the separate (and not quite equal) status of African American culture, thereby reinscribing the color line.[6] Another camp of celebrants who also reversed the binary managed, at least initially, to avoid this reinforcement of dominant racial ideologies. These figures consisted mostly of white, ethnic musicians, especially in Chicago, whose embrace of African American jazz problematized the color line. My brief consideration of these musicians concludes the essay. A third group of celebrants that reversed the binary did so in more qualified fashion than "Negrophiles." These figures, represented by jazz bandleader Paul Whiteman and music critic Henry O. Osgood, maintained primary allegiance to civilization but promoted primitive jazz dancing as a temporary, therapeutic escape from civilized life. Their compromised position derived from ambivalence about the relationship between the primitive and African Americans: Osgood and Whiteman shared with moralists the fear that proximity to "blackness" brought degradation. Their project thereby combined conflicted impulses. They sought to expropriate jazz's "primitive" qualities—its spontaneity, emotionalism, and sensuality—but also to distance those qualities from associations with African Americans. My analysis focuses principally on Osgood and Whiteman's projects.

Osgood's *So This Is Jazz* and Whiteman's *Jazz*, both published in 1926, are generally considered the first two full-length books on jazz.[7] Both celebrate jazz's primitive energy; both try—and fail—to hide jazz's black origins. To dissociate themselves from this past, Whiteman and Osgood promote only "refined" jazz, the music that Whiteman performed. They take pains to distinguish "early" jazz—supposedly raucous noise of roadhouses and brothels patronized by African Americans, ethnics, and poor whites—from Whiteman's "symphonic" jazz, consisting of melodic pop music heard by the white bourgeoisie in cabarets, hotel ballrooms, and even concert halls. To Osgood and Whiteman, good jazz has been elevated aesthetically and socially, removed from suspect black conditions—like those in Johnson's Harlem cabaret—to respectable white ones. Yet, since their project also depends upon claiming that jazz's transformation and transportation does not deplete the music's primitive energy, they never fully distance themselves from jazz's "blackness." Their emphasis on refinement and elevation is thus a counteractive effort to obscure persisting, ultimately irrepressible anxiety about jazz's racially "contaminating" effects. Osgood's and Whiteman's works help to demonstrate that many bourgeois white celebrants remained profoundly ambivalent about jazz; they desired its primitive intensity but feared the imagined cultural miscegenation that embracing it manifested. They worried that jazz dancing did mean passing for colored, that it comprised racial cross-dressing.

I borrow the term "racial cross-dressing" from Eric Lott. His essay "White Like Me: Racial Cross-Dressing and the Construction of American Whiteness" extends his work on mid-nineteenth-century minstrelsy in *Love and Theft: Blackface Minstrelsy and the American Working Class*.[8] In "White Like Me," racial cross-dressing refers to cultural praxes derived from blackface performance that involve the conscious or unconscious imitation of "black" behavior, with or without the literal minstrel trappings of grease paint or burnt cork. For Lott, blackface serves a dual ideological function: it allows whites the luxury of playing with stereotypical "black" behavior while leaving intact both the stereotypes and the illusion of absolute racial difference that they perpetuate. That is, through blackface, whites imaginatively clarify their own racial identity by maintaining contradistinct notions of blackness. However, because these stereotypes of blackness exist in the white imagination, they paradoxically reveal blackness as a "constituent element" of white subjectivity, an internalized component of "black" identity immanent in whiteness. As Lott puts it, "The other is of course 'already in us,' a part of one's (white) self."[9] Especially in moments of rapid industrialization, when bourgeois-liberal ideologies of rationalized social order and self-control become paramount, the particular configurations of this Other relate to pleasure and the body. Sander L. Gilman's work on race and sexuality at the turn of the twentieth century confirms this idea: in an implicitly imperial relation, whites attributed to blacks the sexuality they believed lacking in themselves, so that ambivalent identification with black figures gave imagined access to that sexuality.[10] Lott, following the Lacanian work of Slavoj Žižek, elaborates:

> Because one is so ambivalent about and represses one's own pleasure, one imagines the Other to have stolen it or taken it away, and "fantasies about the Other's special, excessive enjoyment" allow that pleasure to return. Whites get satisfaction in supposing the "racial" Other enjoys in ways unavailable to them—through exotic food, strange and noisy music, outlandish bodily exhibitions, or unremitting sexual appetite. And yet at the same time, because the Other personifies their inner divisions, hatred of their own excess of enjoyment necessitates hatred of the Other. Ascribing this excess to the "degraded" blackface Other, and indulging it—by imagining, incorporating, or impersonating the Other—[those] confronting the demand to be "respectable" might at once take their enjoyment and disavow it.[11]

In *Love and Theft* this argument applies to laborers during the industrial revolution of the early nineteenth century, but the formulation is also relevant to social dynamics of the second such revolution at the turn of the twentieth century. Lott's description of whites' experience of internal tension between self-indulgence and self-control, and their expression of that tension in ambivalent feelings toward a racial Other, captures well Osgood and Whiteman's conflicted stance toward jazz and jazz dancing.

Still, applying Lott's argument to Whiteman's work, in particular, requires a few crucial qualifiers. Some bourgeois whites in the 1920s did enact precisely the dynamic that Lott identifies—they temporarily set aside "white," rational self-control in cabarets to enjoy the primitive, "black" pleasure of jazz dancing, all the while unconsciously imagining the two modes of experience as discrete. However, this assumed discreteness became much more tenuous for whites, like Whiteman, who wanted consciously to deny jazz's "blackness"— who, in effect, refused to see jazz dancing's relation to blackface performance. Since these figures were aware of jazz's "blackness" and sought to dissociate its valued primitive qualities from African Americans, they necessarily reconceptualized whiteness to encompass those same qualities. That is, they reconfigured the racial categories—white/ civilized vs. black/primitive—on which Lott's formulation of racial cross dressing, like Johnson's idea of passing for colored, rests. In *Jazz* Whiteman tries to resolve the internal conflict of self-indulgence and self-regulation by deracializing the idea of the primitive, making it generically "human." This vexed effort, as I will elaborate later, hinges on extracting race and ethnicity from contemporary views on the linear-historical development of civilization. Only with this work could jazz's spontaneity, emotionalism, and sensuality become colorless. Ultimately, then, *Jazz* does perpetuate myths of absolute racial difference, a condition for racial cross-dressing upon which Lott insists; however, first, it smuggles features of blackness across the color line and whitewashes them. Whiteman tries—and fails—to remove race from racial cross-dressing. He promotes a type of performative identity that masquerades openly, in whiteface, as primitive cross-dressing. The bleached suit that Whiteman fashions for respectable white Americans to wear at cabarets only covers his persisting fears that the dancing white body is racially mongrel.

Accelerating industrialization comprised the general context for early-twentieth-century racial cross-dressing. Further grounding lies in the specific social and historical conditions of northern cities during the second and third decades. African American migrations to these urban centers inspired local hysteria that related significantly to growing white interest in black music and dance. These cities' Anglo-Saxon elites hated and feared the migrants' growing presence even as they engaged, fascinated, in activities perceived to manifest blackness.

Flipside Phenomena:
Ragtime, Jazz, and "Negro Invasions"

At the turn of the twentieth century, dramatic socioeconomic changes wrought by industrialization coincided with vast immigration from southern and eastern Europe. Americans of northern European descent anxiously perceived the complexion of the national body politic to miscegenate and darken, its health to fail. Anglo-Saxon "nativists," especially those in northern cities, believed that Italians, Poles, and other groups threatened the racial purity of the nation-state. Russian Jews

in particular became anti-immigration targets due to racist fears that they would "semitize"—miscegenate and weaken—Anglo-Saxon America. The dominant social group reacted to this threat (if I may pursue the body-politic metaphor) by trying to close all orifices: the immigration policies and quotas established by Congress in 1924 were the strictest to date. Vast African American migrations comprised a similar, internal "race problem." Racial tensions exploded in riots and demonstrations after the war, especially in 1919, but white reactions to the "problem" of a black social presence began earlier. In 1915 a rejuvenated Ku Klux Klan began to garner popular support among millions of Northern white urbanites. A major goal consisted of instituting segregation—federally legalized by the 1896 *Plessy v. Ferguson* Supreme Court decision—in the public sphere. Segregation would supposedly excise and isolate the racial "disease" from the (white) body politic, amounting even to partial amputation when separate-and-unequal social conditions suffocated those who were forcibly segregated.

Gilbert Osofsky's sociohistorical work, which traces the demographic shifts that accompanied black migrations to Northern cities from 1890 to 1930, identifies segregation's function as ambivalent social amputation.[12] African Americans had registered a cultural presence in the north since at least the early nineteenth century, but the migrations at the turn of the century seemed a threat of unprecedented proportions. As Osofsky reports, the case of Harlem dramatizes well Northern whites' anxiety about a growing black social presence. At the turn of the century, many longtime Harlem residents were of Dutch origin; more recent ones were upwardly mobile Italian and Russian-Jewish immigrants. At this point, Harlem was a "respectable" middle-class and upper-middle-class neighborhood, "a symbol of elegance and distinction." In the first two decades of the century, when African Americans increasingly moved to the area, many panicking white residents sought "to repulse what they referred to as the Negro 'invasion.'" By the early teens, virtually all white-owned real-estate companies in Harlem refused to rent to black tenants. However, as the Dutch-American and other residents began to flee to other parts of the city, reversals in these policies were "forced upon" the landlords, as a 1916 building notice stated. The African American "invasion" effectively defeated white opposition. By 1920 many blacks living in other parts of New York moved to Harlem, and "practically every major Negro institution moved from its downtown quarters to Harlem by the early 1920s." [13]

Paradoxically, in 1912–1916, at the same time that whites perceived and combated the black "invasion," a ragtime dance craze erupted on Broadway. How did this racial cross-dressing cohere with anxiety about the body politic's penetration, hysterically figured as a miscegenizing rape? Why would affluent white Americans embrace (masked) "blackness" culturally in their leisure time, while sociopolitically they supported the violent effort to repel African Americans? Lott's psychosocial analysis of self-regulation and racial projection suggests an explanation that can be further elaborated with reference to Freudian theory. Racial cross-dressing arguably manifested a reaction formation in which certain impulsive feelings—revulsion, fear, hatred of African Americans—were repressed in a coping mechanism that generated opposing impulses—attraction to, desire for, enjoyment of "blackness." [14] Psychoanalyst Otto Fenichel notes that reaction formations do not erase the initial impulses, but "primarily serve the purpose of keeping still existent opposite tendencies in the unconscious." [15] This formulation captures Osgood and Whiteman's radical ambivalence about the "blackness" of white jazz dancing.

Though reactions to ragtime (before and during the war) and jazz (during and after) were similar, urban social policy toward African Americans shifted in the third decade of the century. Osofsky observes that, as white flight from Harlem accelerated in the early 1920s, Harlem became a symbol of material black success. However, at this point, the city's powers turned toward a strategy of quarantining the "disease" that had invaded the body politic. By 1930, when approximately 72 percent of Manhattan's African American population lived in Harlem, landlords and neighborhood-protection organizations had begun to restrict them there. Residents of Washington Heights, Yonkers, and Westchester warded off black "invasions" in the 1920s; the Bedford-Stuyvesant section of Brooklyn became one of the few other areas to house a growing African American population. By the end of the decade, New York's black populations were concentrated in dense pockets: "Most Negroes were 'jammed together' in Harlem—even those who could afford to live elsewhere—with little possibility of escape." [16] At the same time, the material quality of life in Harlem and Bedford-Stuyvesant declined rapidly. Landlords, white and black, exploited a captive residential market, raising rents drastically while allowing buildings to deteriorate. Overcrowding and congestion contributed to poor sanitation and health problems, including comparatively high mortality rates. Furthermore, bootlegging, the narcotics trade, illegal gambling, and prostitution (with most brothels owned by whites) became more prevalent, or at least more visible, in Harlem than in other parts of the city, dubbing the area a vice district. [17] Such was the partial amputation: social policy gave up sections of the city to the "invaders," but then built walls around those areas and induced the development of destructive conditions.

Harlem's vice-district reputation obviously cohered with images of primitive black sensuality, contributing to whites' growing fascination with the neighborhood in the 1920s. In his study of New York nightlife, Lewis A. Erenberg notes that Harlem was perceived as "too far away to be dangerous yet close enough to be exciting." Late at night, wealthy white slummers drove up to Harlem through Central Park, describing their trips in imperialist terms as journeys "out from civilization" and into the "heart of darkness." [18] There they frequented cabarets and nightclubs such as the Cotton Club and Connie's Inn, which catered directly to whites' perceptions of African Americans as self-indulgent pleasure seekers. Geographically, Harlem became marked as the primitive space within sophisticated New York, a conceptual counterpart to the "black" primitive within civilized "white" subjectivity. White slummers who went there accessed the intense selfhood they believed their civilized selves lacked, but then imaginatively regained rational self-control on the journey home. These whites—"Negrophiles" like Carl Van Vechten—most directly tried to pass for colored.

The openly "Negrophilic" pursuit of racial cross-dressing in Harlem represented a variant of whites' reaction formation that can be characterized in at least two ways. Either the geographic containment of the African American "invasion" tempered feelings of fear and anxiety, making whites less conflicted about the racialized dimension of their pursuit of the primitive; or, in contrary fashion, the realization of a *permanent* black presence in the city (however restricted) intensified those same negative feelings, thereby also intensifying the reactionary feelings of attraction. Given the persistence of racial tensions in twentieth-century America, the latter contention seems more likely, as manifested also in the later popularities of big-band swing, rock music, and rap and hip hop.

The confluence between Anglo-Saxons' oppression of African Americans and their simultaneous indulgence in black music and dance conflicts with James Weldon Johnson's optimistic (and possibly ironic) claim that in cabarets "the Negro drags his captors captive." African American social power did register indirectly in white anxiety about black "invasions," but white/black power relations were hardly reversed in racial cross-dressing. On the contrary, thanks to figures like Osgood and Whiteman, jazz dancing could participate in systems of racist domination. This process through which cultural expropriation joined social oppression is fundamentally imperialist. Fascination with the supposedly primitive nature of ragtime and jazz coincided with similar interest in the cultures of other non-Western peoples— and, significantly, with U.S. colonialism at the turn of the century. As "black" dances became popular on Broadway, so did "Latin" dances like the tango as well as (after the war) the Hawaiian hula, "Egyptian dances, South Sea Island dances, and other exotic forms of bodily expression."[19] It is perhaps no accident that this wide-ranging primitivism followed the Spanish-American war and coincided historically with other U.S. interventions in South and Central America, the Pacific, and European colonies involved in World War I. As the U.S. military dominated racial others abroad, and segregation did so domestically, affluent white Americans commodified those others' cultures.[20] Even if isolationism characterized U.S. foreign policy in the teens and 1920s, that orientation involved anxiety about racial others "at home"—an "internal" colonial situation.

Exploring the sociopolitical issues attending turn-of-the-century African American migration further historicizes the psychosocial analysis of racial cross-dressing, but it does not address *how* members of the urban white bourgeoisie attempted ideologically to justify their pursuit of primitive "blackness." In what terms did they articulate their fascination with the practices of ostensibly inferior cultures? One answer lies in another phenomenon related to accelerating industrialization.

The Therapeutic World View: Recovering the "Black" Childhood of the "White" Race

White Americans sought "the feel and experience of abandon" in cabarets, as Johnson puts it, for complex reasons stemming from a crisis in cultural authority at the turn of the century. As T. J. Jackson Lears argues, nineteenth-century bourgeois-liberal ideology proved insufficient to account discursively for shifts in material relations and subjectivity relating to heightened industrialization and the rise of corporate capitalism.[21] The bourgeois-liberal idea that Western, rational, Anglo-Saxon society represented the pinnacle of world civilization, and its corollary that moral progress conjoined with material progress, were challenged by at least two factors. The first threat came from within the ranks of the bourgeoisie. Prescribed bourgeois-liberal subjectivity—the autonomous, willful individual, exemplified by the self-made man—seemingly became untenable in the increasingly interdependent social structures of corporate bureaucracies. This sense contributed to feelings among the bourgeoisie of unstable selfhood, of widespread emotional debilitation, anxiety, and nervousness, manifesting the condition known as neurasthenia.[22] The second, "exterior" threat, which also contributed to this condition, related to anti-immigrant sentiment. A "radical specter" of labor activism and unionism seemed to invite social disorder and disintegration and was often attributed to foreign insurgents from southern and eastern Europe. In this context, elements of republican ideology, which also privileged rational, autonomous subjectivity, reemerged discursively among the bourgeoisie to compete with bourgeois liberalism. Republicanism offered an alternative interpretation of the historical situation: the American middle class and social elite were effete, nervous, "overcivilized" milquetoasts vulnerable to overthrow by the "rabble"—the (ethnic) working classes—because wealth and comfort had severed them from the invigorating intensity of "real" life. By the turn of the century, republicanism helped to inspire leisure activities intended to restore the bourgeoisie's contact with "real" life, to combat their debilitating nervousness, to recover their prized, willful autonomy, and (in some cases) to return them to unquestioned social dominance. These activities registered what Lears calls the therapeutic world view.

The leisure activities on which Lears focuses—the arts and crafts movement, orientalism, cults of medieval religious mysticism and knighthood—related generally to the emergence of purportedly more scientific, neurological forms of psychological therapy. The fundamental programs of all of these therapies were relatively consistent: conflicting with bourgeois liberalism's equation of moral and material progress, they portrayed "modern civilization" as the cause of the bourgeoisie's nervousness. From this perspective, Victorian social conventions were to blame: their demand for absolute, rational self-control unhealthily repressed vital emotions and impulses. To combat this condition, Lears writes, "mind-cure panaceas ... advised the overstrained to put themselves in touch with [inner] psychic energy in order to win back and perhaps even increase lost mental and emotional vigor." These therapies, liberating affluent Americans from "the constraints of the modern superego," were believed to return repressed parts of identity and the feeling of "real" life—to dispel anxiety through restoring psychic wholeness. Such was precisely the case for leisure activities in cabarets, which Lears does not discuss: in Johnson's words, jazz dancers were "attempting to throw off the crusts and layers of inhibitions laid on by sophisticated civilization; striving to yield to the feel and experience of abandon; seeking to recapture a taste of primitive joy in life and living." The so-called revolution of morals and manners that dominates characterizations of the 1920s owes much to the therapeutic worldview.[23]

Republican images of "real" life were nostalgically primitive in romanticist terms—pastoral, preindustrial, premodern—and intersected with racial discourses, as Johnson satirizes in equating the primitive with the "jungle" and "colored" people. Lears provides historical detail to ground the discursive confluence of race and historical nostalgia. At the turn of the century, popular conceptions of human development were linear or scalar. Macrocosmically, development was historical: different "races," conceived of as discrete, biological lineages, occupied different locations on a timeline of progress. In one respect, this model supported belief in northern-European superiority. Supposedly, the Anglo-Saxon race had advanced beyond stages of savagery and barbarity to the highest state of rational civilization, while "contemporary primitives" such as African Americans had not advanced beyond a lower position on the scale—and could never do so, according to racist eugenicists.[24] Yet this system's portrayal of racial development also harbors at least one paradox that destabilizes belief in racial discreteness: the premodern, medieval forebears of Anglo-Saxons were considered, in many ways, to be as undeveloped as—and, hence, as analogous to—"contemporary primitives." In contradictory fashion, then, Western and non-Western peoples became members of the same family, with the latter all but embodying the former's ancestors. Thus, representations of medieval culture oddly converged with those of contemporary non-Western cultures. In an August 25, 1917, *Literary Digest* article that Osgood quotes in his book, jazz and the bodily movement attending it are associated not only with "those jungle 'parties'" of "the Kongo" but also with "the medieval jumping mania." The same article confirms the salience of the therapeutic world view in quoting the views of Professor William Morrison Patterson of Columbia University (on which, as we shall see, Whiteman draws). Patterson, too, implies a relation between presumed savages and a deep-seated part of the white self: "Modern sophistication has inhibited many *native* instincts, and the mere fact that our conventional dignity usually forbids us to sway our bodies and tap our feet when we hear effective music has deprived us of unsuspected pleasures."[25] His implication is carried by the ambiguity of the term *native,* signifying both foreign primitives and an inescapable inheritance.

The instability of genealogical relations between Anglo-Saxons and groups like African Americans also found expression at the microcosmic level of personal development. A corollary of the linear model of civilization was that each indi-

vidual's life progressed through the same stages that his or her race traversed historically. The recapitulation theory—ontogeny recapitulates phylogeny—summarizes this notion. As children and adolescents, twentieth-century Anglo-Saxons were supposedly savage primitives; they attained civilized status only upon achieving self-controlled adulthood. Thus a nostalgic past, primitive races, and contemporary children became mutually associated. In romanticist fashion, children—like medieval life, that "childhood of the race"—were repositories of "spontaneous feeling and intense experience" on which contemporary Anglo-Saxon adults could draw for therapy. By the same token, African Americans and other non-Western groups were perceived as "childlike premodern types."[26] Such romantic racialism stretched from antebellum days well into the twentieth century; "the child Negro" was central to "the restored 1920s plantation myth."[27]

The idea that a contemporary, adult Anglo-Saxon could possess residual primitive traits deriving from childhood or adolescence recalls Lott's notion that "the [racial] other is of course 'already in us,' a part of one's (white) self." Seeking to embrace one's repressed inner child in processes of therapeutic self-reconstitution dovetailed with seeking the primitive in ragtime and jazz dancing. That is, the process of racialized Othering that Lott identifies obtained in the specific historical moment that Lears details. Lott's work also elaborates on the particular notion of accessing racialized adolescence when he discusses constructions of white American manhood. He contends that white men adopt masculinity by borrowing the perceived behavioral inflections of black men and, furthermore, that whites commonly associate "black maleness with the onset of pubescent sexuality."[28] Hence, in some cases, white men who don personae characterized by dynamism, strength, spontaneity, and sexual potency engage with what they imagine, unconsciously, to be their inner, "black," adolescent selves. The sense of restoring contact with this masculinity via ragtime and jazz dancing would therapeutically dispel neurasthenics' "feminized" state, an effect sought by "new" women as well as men in an era that prized headstrong self-assurance.

Imagining that blackness comprised raw, chaotic, premature energy also bolstered the tendency to consume such primitive images while oppressing African Americans sociopolitically. Marianna Torgovnick's analysis of primitivist discourses helps to articulate these threads of imperialistic logic. Notions of primitives as childlike suggested that they "needed guidance in order to emerge into modernity, the cultural equivalent of adulthood," while notions of them as "sexually volatile and, by a further extension, naturally violent" led to belief that they "required severe control." [29] One thinks here not only of discourses that criminalized and pathologized African Americans, legitimating segregation, but also of lynching, that ultimate expression of white hysteria about black men's alleged propensity for sexual violence. Torgovnick follows both sets of notions to their shared, "inevitabl[e]" conclusion: "whites [believed] they were destined, indeed obliged, to control and dominate primitive peoples." [30]

The therapeutic worldview helped ease ideological tensions for members of the white bourgeoisie who adopted forms of "racially primitive" behavior. Yet these tensions were never fully resolved; the embrace of "blackness" was always conflicted and ambivalent. If Anglo-Saxons were to remain civilized as adult representatives of their race, they could not embrace their intense, "black," adolescent self, even temporarily, without reservations. They felt the need to "civilize" their bodies' primitive emotions and sexuality—to discipline, domesticate, control, and master these feelings and impulses. The dominative order is clear: a white superego constrains a black id to maintain a well-balanced ego. This perspective helps to clarify Osgood's and Whiteman's convoluted discourse. Ragtime and jazz, symbolizing African American sociocultural threats "from below" akin to the radical specter of labor unrest,

provoked anxiety about white social control that Osgood and Whiteman sought to allay ideologically. In their texts they expropriate jazz's therapeutic intensity to reconstruct bourgeois white identity, masking and disciplining the music's vitality by transforming it into an aesthetic form appropriate for civilized, adult, Anglo-Saxon consumption. This sanitary racialized therapy supposedly dispels anxiety, restoring belief in white control and dominance by containing African Americans' potentially subversive power. [31] Osgood and Whiteman's approach to managing black music and dancing follows precedents offered by actual performers—musicians, singers, and dancers—who enacted similar ideological work in cultural praxis. This work largely took place in a site marked out for it—cabaret nightlife.

Bourgeois Cabaret Culture, 1911–1929: Disciplining "Blackness" for the Drawing Room

Cabarets, which began appearing on Broadway around 1911, provided a novel space in which bourgeois white Americans could engage in activities associated with the supposedly primitive state of African Americans. Erenberg's study of turn-of-the-century nightlife supports this thesis. Erenberg extensively documents the social history of cabaret performance as well as the cultural discourses about (including perceptions of the significance of) such performance. [32] Although his scholarship lacks a theoretical framework, the material it provides conforms to the dynamics of racial cross-dressing and the therapeutic world view. For example, Erenberg shows that "prosperous urbanites" believed that cabaret culture allowed them "to throw off the weighty hand of civilization," to "revitalize and reorient their lives," and to regain "their true, more vital selves." [33]

Whites' engagement with racialized leisure activities in cabarets came in roughly two forms. The first consisted of consuming the supposedly primitive performances of racially charged vaudeville acts; the second involved both witnessing and participating in ragtime and jazz dancing. Erenberg notes that the format of cabarets blurred distinctions between performers and audience, encouraging slippage between these two forms of engagement. Dispensing with a separate, elevated stage, cabarets featured performers who mingled with the audience. Patrons often became part of the performance, and they effectively constituted "the act" when they took to the dance floor. In other words, cabarets promoted ritualized conditions in which both designated performers and patrons could racially cross-dress.

By the turn of the century, African American performers were relatively prominent in urban vaudeville and musical theater. Many had been appearing in New York nightclubs and saloons, especially in the Bowery and the Tenderloin, since as early as the 1880s. "Although black artists and audiences were still [largely] excluded from the informality of Broadway cabarets," there were a few notable exceptions.[34] In the second decade of the century, probably the best-known African American performer was the classically trained musician, composer, and bandleader James Reese Europe. Europe led various orchestras before World War I that performed at benefits and dances for black organizations as well as "for private social gatherings and entertainments of the eastern [white] social elite." In 1914–1916, his well-known Europe's Society Orchestra played ragtime-styled dance music in premier Broadway cabarets. By 1919, the year of Europe's death, this group's popularity in the U.S. earned its leader the titles of Jazz King and King of Jazz. For those bourgeois Anglo-Saxons who attended cabarets featuring Europe's groups, the racialized aspect of ragtime dancing was relatively unmediated. The music of African American performers seemed "infectiously" dynamic, inspiring dancers to lose self-control and succumb to the pleasurable "disease" of primitive experience.[35]

Despite the prominence of some African American musicians, by far the most common and popular Broadway-cabaret performers at this time were of distinctly ethnic European extraction—Irish, Italian, Polish, and especially Russian-Jewish[36]—who occupied a vaguely intermediary position in racial hierarchies. These figures' relative prominence reveals that many bourgeois whites remained anxious about racial contamination even as they desired racialized therapy. By virtue of these performers' ethnicity, they were perceived as premodern types who could supply the "black" spontaneity, emotionalism, and sensuality that bourgeois whites consumed therapeutically; by virtue of being qualifiedly white, they appealed to elite Anglo-Saxons who wished to avoid exposure to African Americans. This dual role was performed particularly well by vaudeville and cabaret stars such as Al Jolson, Eddie Cantor, and Sophie Tucker, who were of Russian-Jewish origins and sometimes wore blackface. These performers were seen as translators of black culture for white audiences at least partially because some racial discourses figured Jews as "middlemen between whites and blacks."[37] Tucker, for instance, not only wore blackface early in her career; she also sang "coon" and ragtime songs with "mixed Jewish and Negro inflections," leading some listeners (hearing her phonograph recordings) to mistake her "for a southern black girl." Billed as the "Last of the Red Hot Mammas" and, in the early 1920s, as the "Queen of Jazz," Tucker was believed to enable her audiences to "explore the intense emotions associated with [racialized] sensuality" while also holding such intensity "at arm's length."[38] She provided sanitized therapy by transferring "black" vitality while displacing and partially veiling the original African American referent.

If ethnic performers provided one imaginary method of dampening ambivalence about indulging in racialized intensity, more elaborate strategies were needed to mitigate the potentially contaminating effects of "black" dance. In the 1912–1916 dance craze, moralists condemned steps like the turkey trot, grizzly bear, bunny hug, and fox-trot as racially tainting. The prominence of these "animal dances" made it seem "as if Uncle Remus had joined high society." Such dances supposedly illustrated "the influence of lower-class sensuality," "a reversion to the grossest practices of savage man," and whites' "uncontrolled inundation by inferior peoples" such as "swarthy, lower-class Italians and Jews" and "sensual blacks and Latins."[39] Even primitivists who celebrated the therapeutic "pep" or "kick" of ragtime feared that cabaret dancing involved cultural miscegenation. Simply adopting black dance steps was exciting, but it still seemed too dangerous; further sanitizing strategies were believed necessary to protect whites from ("their own") black bodies.

The famous dancing team of Vernon and Irene Castle emerged in the teens to provide such strategies. The Castles emanated white, bourgeois gentility. Irene hailed from a "respectable middle-class" family, while the British Vernon generated an air of European classiness.[40] In their exclusive dancing school, Castle House, this team took it upon themselves to regulate the steps of the new craze. The Castles' dance instructions became influential nationally through distribution in short films; their 1914 book *Modern Dancing;* printed interviews; and exhibitions on tour as well as in their Broadway cabarets, the Sans Souci and Castles in the Air. In revising the animal dances, the tango, and other steps, the Castles claimed that they refined and disciplined overly savage movements while still preserving terpsichorean vitality. In her introduction to *Modern Dancing,* Elisabeth Marbury—aristocrat, reformer, and Castle patron—wrote: "Refinement is the keynote of [the Castles'] method." Their style allies "the spirit of beauty and art" with "the legitimate physical need of healthy exercise and of honest enjoyment." True to the therapeutic world view, Marbury argues that dancing helps "working men and women" to "fling off morbid introspection"—a feature of neurasthenia—and to recover the "joy"

of "the tiny child."[41] Tellingly, achieving such refined therapy involved proscribing overt sexuality. *Modern Dancing* concludes with a list of commandments entitled "Castle House Suggestions for Correct Dancing":

> Do not wriggle the shoulders.
> Do not shake the hips.
> Do not twist the body.
> Do not flounce the elbows.
> Do not pump the arms.
> Do not hop—glide instead.

Dips should "not mean an exposure of silk stocking"; "a man [should] stand far enough from his partner to allow freedom of movement; he should not hug or clutch her."[42] The Castles' emphasis on grace as "another form of discipline" manifested assumptions of aesthetic and racial superiority. In 1914 the team was instrumental in introducing the fox-trot, which "slow[ed] down the faster one-step" and "allowed variation in movement . . . without being too raucous or too expressive." Since the fox-trot and one-step became widely popular and remained so after the war, the Castles' influence (despite Vernon's death in 1917) extended well into the 1920s. When in 1921–1922 the popular black musical revue *Shuffle Along* popularized the Charleston and black bottom among white audiences, dance instructors carefully removed objectionable "hip and pelvic thrusts" and combined the dance with the one-step.[43]

Serving to reinforce the Castles' reputation for civilizing primitive dances was the fact that, from 1913 to 1916, James Reese Europe's Society Orchestra provided the music for many of their performances. Europe's energetic, big-band ragtime symbolized the "black" energy that the Castles ostensibly tamed with elegant bodily grace and self-control. (That Europe's bands were themselves extremely disciplined could be obscured by racially charged perceptions.) In Irene Castle's own words, she and Vernon "toned down . . . nigger dance[s]" like the shimmy of 1918–1919 so "they can be used in the drawing-room." [44] As the racialized dimension of the recapitulation theory demanded, the Castles sought to civilize the adolescent, sexual energy of (internal) "blackness" so that Anglo-Saxon adults could indulge in it temporarily without fearing the loss of "white," rational self-control. This mode of mediating between "black" culture and white bodies differed from that of figures like Sophie Tucker, consisting more of disciplining and masking than of transmitting "blackness."

The cultural functions that Sophie Tucker and the Castles respectively performed reappear symbolically in discursive strategies of Osgood's and Whiteman's works. Racially ambiguous, intermediary figures like Tucker appear in their texts, but the two writers ultimately reject these figures' roles in favor of emulating the Castles' approach to dancing. Osgood, and even more so Whiteman, sought not only to sanitize jazz as commercial therapy but also to legitimate it in terms of fine-art aesthetics. This goal requires that jazz be presented unambiguously as civilized, rationally ordered, "white." Such presentation was challenging in the face of 1920s anti-jazz discourse. Moralists portrayed jazz in exactly opposite terms: as anthropologist Alan P. Merriam summarizes, they not only "regarded [jazz] as a symbol of barbarism, primitivism, savagery, and animalism" but also "associated [it] with crime, feeble-mindedness, and . . . individual physical collapse." [45] Hence Osgood and Whiteman's convoluted discursive strategies. They necessarily invoke images of primitive blackness as the source of jazz's therapeutic energy, but they must also mask those images and assert that civilized whites can master their potentially dangerous energy. Sexuality figures prominently in this process: for Osgood and Whiteman, jazz inspires a battle between the "white," civilized adult and the internal "black" primitive, between the rational mind and the unruly body. As it provides therapy, jazz sexualizes—

"blackens"—its performers and audiences, but, Osgood and Whiteman anxiously insist, bourgeois Anglo-Saxons can control and dominate the desires that jazz awakens.

Happy Feet: "Black" Sexuality and "White" Self-Control in So This Is Jazz

Henry O. Osgood, of New England, Yankee stock, served as music critic for and editor of the *Musical Courier*. In *So This Is Jazz*, he promotes the kind of 1920s "jazz" that most white dancing enthusiasts enjoyed: Tin Pan Alley songs by Irving Berlin, George Gershwin, and Jerome Kern as performed by the white society orchestras of Paul Whiteman, Vincent Lopez, and Isham Jones. I am concerned only with the book's first, brief chapter, in which Osgood distinguishes this supposedly legitimate jazz from other styles. Presumably to assuage moralists, this chapter summarily rejects "early," implicitly African American jazz in favor of Isham Jones's "refined" music.

For Osgood, early jazz is epitomized by comedian-clarinetist Ted Lewis, who, with Paul Whiteman, was among the best-known "jazz" performers. In the chapter's opening, Osgood recounts hearing Lewis's band playing at a New York banquet sponsored by commercial recording manufacturers. The music was "nerve-harrowing, soul-wrenching noise," consisting of animal-noise imitations and apparently wild improvisations. His distaste for the performance takes on racial overtones: "all the players jolt[ed] up and down and writh[ed] about in simulated ecstasy, in the manner of Negroes at a Southern camp-meeting afflicted with religious frenzy. . . . All-brass circus and minstrel bands were as nothing compared to it." Osgood laments that Lewis's fans emulate the performer. He reports and then jokingly dismisses a friend's admission that "when Ted and his old clarinet got shrieking on top of all the other instruments it acted on me just like a couple of drinks. I'd get so excited I couldn't sit still—I just had to get up and dance. I like the modern jazz. It's pretty, but it doesn't give me the kick the other used to. . . . (Jazz, a state of mind!)" [46]

Half a page later, Isham Jones arrives to represent "the modern jazz." A few years after hearing Lewis (circa the early 1920s), Osgood accompanied another friend to the dining room of "a big lake-front [Chicago] hotel" where Jones's orchestra was performing. This jazz, played by "eight gentlemen," was "music, languishing, crooning music, rude neither in sound nor tempo, music that soothed and yet, with insinuating rhythms, ear-tickling melody and ingenious decorations, stirred me within as much as Ted Lewis's racket had agitated the friend just quoted." Osgood is so stirred, so therapeutically invigorated, that he wants to dance:

> My feet began tapping of themselves. Had there been an acquaintance among the women in the room, I should unquestionably have challenged her to dance in spite of the fact that those feet had been strangers to a ballroom floor for at least fifteen years. Luckily for the possible victim, I knew none there except my host, a man every inch of him. I began to expatiate with enthusiasm upon this marvelous new thing in music. . . . Somebody had put music into jazz.

Osgood's approval derives partially from the discipline with which Jones's musicians perform: "there was no careless improvising in what the men played. . . . Each one played a definite part that some clever musician had written for him in preparing the score." This is the "jazz" that Osgood seeks to legitimate, with formal musicological analysis, in the rest of his book and in related essays.[47]

In constructing a version of jazz historiography, Osgood's first chapter follows a linear emplotment structurally consonant with the recapitulation theory: jazz advances from a raucous "black" adolescence—"the grotesque extravagances of Lewis"—to the sedate, disciplined, and yet still energized "white" maturity of Jones's gen-

teel musicians. Since this emplotment requires that mature jazz outgrow its primitive state, Osgood distances Jones's jazz from images of blackness with various rhetorical maskings and displacements. First, he avoids associating jazz with blackness directly: African American culture—the stereotyped "Southern camp meeting"—appears only as background for Lewis's music. Additional displacements protect mature jazz from its raucous past: Osgood distances Jones from Lewis aesthetically, temporally (by "three or four years"), geographically (from New York to Chicago), and situationally (from a crass commercial banquet to a swank hotel dining room).[48] Furthermore, Osgood's discourse recalls and deploys cultural icons analogous to Sophie Tucker and the Castles. The fact that Lewis was of Jewish extraction—and sometimes performed in blackface, which Osgood notes only obliquely by comparing Lewis's group to "minstrel bands"—suggests that he, like Tucker with her "black" singing style, displaces yet still transmits jazz's racialized energy. In contrast, Jones's genteel jazz, like the Castles' disciplined dancing, is seemingly purged of all racial connotations and made safe for bourgeois consumption.

However, Osgood's representation of the effects of Lewis's and Jones's jazz suggest his suppressed anxiety that racial contamination is still occurring. He seems particularly concerned about his friend's response to Lewis. He tries to put a good face on it: since Lewis supposedly tempers jazz's "black" energy by displacing it, Osgood's friend experiences not frenzied "Negro" affliction, but the mild inebriation of "a couple of drinks." Yet even the latter image, possessing illicit connotations during Prohibition, blends into the possible danger of losing rational, "white" self-control: the friend says "I'd get so excited I couldn't sit still—I just had to get up and dance." Osgood half-heartedly dismisses the logical conclusion of his friend's statement—that the "blackness" of the body can overthrow prescribed "adult" status—with the joke that constitutes its own one-line paragraph: "(Jazz, a state of mind!)." He suppresses worry about the dangerous physicality of the "state" he invokes by correctively recontaining it—emphatically, as the exclamation point reveals—under the safer rubric of the rational mind. His use of parentheses seems to indicate that further suppression and containment of the "state" is necessary.

That this defense fails—and that the failure is then whitewashed—is evident in Osgood's own engagement with Jones's music. He says his response to Jones equals that of his friend to Lewis, yet his reaction is superficially more sedate: Osgood suppresses his desire to dance and instead joins in intellectual conversation with his dining companion. The particular figuration of his desire and the channels into which it is directed deserve closer inspection. Osgood's wayward feet "tapping of themselves" expose the sensual "black" primitive that already lies within him. Acting on their own, the animated appendages are initially beyond his control; Osgood himself suggests their independence later in the passage, when he denies ownership of "*those* feet." It is perhaps this unruly bodily rebellion that leads Osgood to compare his experience to the hyperphysical "state" that Ted Lewis inspired in his friend. Indeed, there are sexual connotations in Osgood's response: the mutinous feet may serve to displace another image associated with (male) blackness, the erect penis. In Freudian symbolic systems, feet can replace the penis, and Sander L. Gilman identifies whites' frequent conceptual "reduction of the black to the genitalia" at the turn of the century. Jazz and jazz dancing, imaginatively awakening the internal, adolescent, "black" self, sexualize the dancer. This equation is reinforced by widespread belief that *jazz*, the verb, can designate copulation. Osgood himself, in retracing the origins of *jazz*, finds one genesis in the trade vocabulary of the Barbary Coast—the name of "the once notorious red-light district of San Francisco" as well as a punning reference to northern Africa.[49]

The jazzy feet, then, initially pose a threat, inspiring Osgood's internal, "black" id to supersede his "white" superego. Yet Osgood the bourgeois Anglo-Saxon cannot let this occur, and he carefully details the process through which he sublimates and masters his sexual desire. First he attempts to channel the desire into a polite heterosexual ritual: he seeks union with an absent woman, who indeed is lucky to be spared his terpsichorean/sexual favors given his unpracticed "feet." Osgood then turns to another polite form of sublimation, this time with homoerotic overtones: he professes relief that the only "possible victim" present was his male companion—suggestively denoted "a man every inch of him"—with whom he enthusiastically engages in intellectual verbal intercourse. Osgood's ultimate ability to control his desire, to refrain from sexualized dancing, would seem to prove his superior, civilized status. In contrast with the Ted Lewis fan who dances uncontrollably, Osgood presents himself as master of his body. He thereby also distances himself from the fear that his feet invoke—that the internal racial primitive, which jazz strengthens, can destabilize white rationality. However, this distancing is only partially successful, since Osgood's adoption of all aspects of prescribed bourgeois subjectivity—including heterosexuality—is interrupted by the homoerotic overtones of his final sublimation, overtones indicative of Victorian views about the consequences of uncontrolled sexuality.[50] Thus Osgood's efforts to suppress fears of jazz's "black" sexuality, and hence to legitimate refined jazz, remain unstable. He insists paradoxically that white jazz orchestras and their audiences are purged of "blackness" and yet also that they must, can, and do discipline and dominate jazz's (black) "frenzy." He wants to enable himself and his readers to indulge in jazz's pleasurable, racialized therapy without fracturing belief in absolute racial difference. Osgood attempts imaginatively to maintain the color line despite his own admission—evident in the image of "the Southern camp meeting"—that "blackness" irrepressibly underwrites white jazz dancing. In *Jazz*, Paul Whiteman—who, in 1930, popularized a song fittingly entitled "Happy Feet"—supports and extends Osgood's project.[51]

Let's Get Physical: Whiteman's Jazz and "Human" Rhythmic Liberation

To Osgood, Whiteman—even more than Isham Jones—embodied mature jazz. Whiteman's supposed racial superiority, like that of Jones and Osgood, enabled him to obscure and refine the "black" energy of jazz more thoroughly than could ethnic transmitters like the Jewish Ted Lewis. His name nearly overdetermines the argument: Whiteman sought to transform jazz and jazz dancing into safe therapy—good clean fun—for the white social elite and middle class. As Erenberg incisively observes in his brief commentary on jazz, Whiteman "became a star by doing for jazz what the Castles had done for black dances."[52] *Jazz*, written with the assistance of Mary Margaret McBride, reinforces Osgood's narrative in many respects: it emplots the music's aesthetic maturation in the same way, and it exhibits the same ambivalent, conflicted process of noting yet still tenuously masking jazz's racialized meanings. In this fashion, Whiteman also reaches Osgood's conclusion—that jazz dancing can be unproblematically civilized. Yet *Jazz* also employs another strategy to reach this conclusion: Whiteman admits to the primitive qualities of jazz even as he deracializes the concept of the primitive. This pursuit takes the form of dramatically recasting a musical emblem of racial difference—rhythm—as a racially unmarked component of primitive existence. In this respect, Whiteman's discourse diverges from Osgood's somewhat: he concedes that jazz dancing involves temporarily crossing into a primitive field of experience, though one still purged of imagined racial contamination. *Jazz* implicitly acknowledges that jazz dancing constitutes racial

cross-dressing, but only in the guise of a sanitized, whitewashed primitive cross-dressing that (in therapeutic doses) poses no threat to white, bourgeois subjectivity.

In 1920, as his recordings gained national popularity, Whiteman usurped James Reese Europe's title and proclaimed himself King of Jazz.[53] He toured the country incessantly and managed a national network of orchestras, which promoted the aesthetic preferences evident in *Jazz*. One measure of Whiteman's popularity, and of his wide impact upon the meanings of jazz and jazz dancing, was the manner in which *Jazz* was serialized in 1926 in the *Saturday Evening Post*—arguably the nation's most popular periodical at the time. Three sizable excerpts were printed in consecutive installments on February 27, March 6, and March 13; the first of these featured the article on the front page.[54]

Both in performance and print, one of Whiteman's central aspirations was to render jazz acceptable as serious music according to fine-art criteria. For example, in *Jazz*—and in the March 6 *Post*—Whiteman emphasizes his "experiment in modern music," his orchestra's concert at New York's Aeolian Hall on February 12, 1924.[55] Well-attended by various fine-art composers and pop-culture stars, the concert supposedly documented the history of jazz. It concluded with the premiere of George Gershwin's *Rhapsody in Blue*. After the event, Whiteman continued to pursue high-art pretensions by performing at venues like Carnegie Hall, sometimes labeling his music "symphonic jazz" or "modern American music."

This pursuit of artistic legitimization conflicts with the other main discourse that Whiteman deploys in *Jazz*, that of the power of and need for jazz therapy. These two discourses' competition generates major ideological contradictions extending beyond representations of race. Whiteman's presentation of jazz's musical refinement as comprising artistic progress and improvement not only involves veiling and disciplining the music's originary "blackness" but also intersects more broadly with bourgeois-liberal ideology—specifically its faith in material progress. The latter intersection appears in Whiteman's unabashed proclamations (also in the March 6 *Post*) that "symphonic" jazz performance is a major financial industry that achieves "business-like" stature in Tin Pan Alley's "song factor[ies]." This echo of Coolidge's famous dictum that "the business of America is business" also finds more general expression when White-man touts the industrial productivity of the United States as a whole. For Whiteman, effecting artistic progress by elevating jazz complements and even engenders the accumulation of wealth, enabling the so-called American dream. In direct contrast, Whiteman's claims about jazz's thera-peutic power intersect with republican ideology's *suspicion* of notions of material progress. When Whiteman promotes jazz therapy, he condemns industrialism as alienating and dehumanizing and depicts the music's rhythms as a corrective tonic. The two discourses coexist apparently without in-tended irony, sometimes appearing side by side in the same passage.[56]

Whiteman's overall treatment of jazz thus har-bors unresolved ideological fissures and tensions. My main concern is the discursive process by which he attempts to resolve these tensions, to refine jazz while still preserving its implicitly "black" intensity. Like Osgood, Whiteman para-doxically invokes the referent of African Ameri-can jazz to expropriate primitive rhythm as a ther-apeutic device, only to obscure and discipline the "blackness" in white jazz that this acknowledg-ment exposes. Yet even here, where Whiteman's and Osgood's projects cohere directly, their rhe-torical strategies differ somewhat. Since White-man articulates jazz therapy openly and exten-sively, he qualifiedly concedes the influence of African American culture on his own music. Still, this concession is hardly an open acknowledg-ment of debt, as in James Weldon Johnson's por-trait of white dancing in a Harlem cabaret; rather, it heightens anxiety about the instability of belief in racial difference. Whiteman's relatively direct representations of "blackness" generate a counter-balancing rhetorical strategy that suppresses this anxiety: when images of African Americans ap-pear in *Jazz*, rational, self-controlled, white figures of the Castles' ilk always accompany them to re-strain their unruly energy. If expropriating jazz can destabilize constructed black/primitive and white/civilized subjectivities and thus invoke fears of miscegenation, Whiteman's rhetorical strategy represses this possibility by imaginatively rein-scribing those subjectivities.[57]

One need go no further than *Jazz*'s first para-graph to perceive its anxious, conflicted represen-tation of whiteness's relationship with blackness:

> Jazz came to America three hundred years ago in chains. The psalm-singing Dutch traders, sailing in a man-of-war across the ocean in 1619, described their cargo as "fourteen black African slaves for sale in his Majesty's colonies." But priceless freight des-tined three centuries later to set a whole nation dancing went unnoted and unbilled by the stolid, revenue-hungry Dutchmen.[58]

Whiteman tries to draw an uncrossable color line in *Jazz*'s first sentences, to insist on faith in white rationality's distance from and control over black bodies and their energy. The Dutch traders are willful businessmen; the slaves are powerless, chained, objectified cargo. Whiteman, as the one who finally does "note" and "bill" jazz, presum-ably inherits the Dutch's potent autonomy—a move that unwittingly underscores the relation between his cultural expropriations and the slave trade. However, these contradistinct notions of racial identity are inherently unstable: Whiteman must necessarily cross the color line to expropriate jazz's cultural power, its ability "to set a whole na-tion dancing." To obscure this implied foray into "blackness" and suppress the ideological tensions that it invites, Whiteman dissociates jazz from the Africans grammatically: the "jazz" in the first sen-tence, apparently synonymous with the slaves, paradoxically becomes a separate, disembodied entity—other "priceless freight"—by the third sentence. That is, jazz's original referent is displaced even as the referent itself, in muted form, is present. Black contributions to jazz are erased; the Africans and their descendents are denied autonomous culture and agency. A few pages later, Whiteman caps this reinscription of the color line by, gallingly, crediting *the Dutch* for giving jazz "its start in life." He notes offhandedly that the music, disembodied, just so happened to "bid[e] its time among black laborers." The first pages of *Jazz,* vacillating between admission and obfuscation of a racial debt, reveal anxiety about white "ownership" and use of black cultural praxes.[59]

The same narrative pattern frames Whiteman's portrayal of an early jazz band. (He necessarily discusses only the band's "discovery," studiously ignoring its formation and development—implicitly among or influenced by autonomous ex-slaves—since his racially polarized discourse cannot account for them.) This passage, in chapter 2 of *Jazz,* was among the first paragraphs of the front-page *Saturday Evening Post* installment of February 27. Here, another willful white expropriator—Whiteman's de facto father figure—controls jazz's power: "A showman, Joseph K. Gorham, gets credit for first realizing the possibilities of the underworld waif."[60] Gorham serves as mediating reporter (narrative overseer) of the musicians' intense display of "black" energy:

> Gorham, a newcomer to New Orleans, heard a group of musicians playing on the street to advertise a prize fight. He was halted first by the perspiring, grotesque energy of the four players. They shook, they pranced, they twisted their lean legs and arms, they swayed like mad men to a fantastic measure wrung from a trombone, clarinet, cornet and drum. They tore off their collars, coats and hats to free themselves for a very frenzy of syncopation.

"With the sure instinct of a good showman," Whiteman assures us, "Gorham pushed his way

through the crowd and interviewed the leader." Soon, "Brown's orchestra"—the invocation of color is necessarily explicit—"had been taken over by Mr. Gorham and placed at Lamb's Cafe" in Chicago.[61] Racist minstrel imagery abounds in this passage; the jazzy "frenzy of syncopation," for instance, echoes Osgood's Southern camp-meeting. Moreover, the excessively physical scene—the prize fight, the musicians' sweat—takes on bestial connotations as the prancing, swaying performers take off their clothes. These "bucks" resist the constraints of polite civilization, of domestication—until Gorham reins them in. He masters and contains the musicians' virile sexuality by commodifying its musical expression. By extension, Whiteman and his readers also supposedly begin to learn how to master "black" intensity; the audience imaginatively encounters and manages their own internal primitive through symbolic exposure to Brown's orchestra. Even so, the presence of this black "interlocutor" (as Lott would put it) again complicates Whiteman's project, since the Africanness that he previously dissociated from a disembodied "jazz" returns irrepressibly as the music's undeniable essence. Such is the conflicted, uneven process through which Whiteman alternately invokes and veils jazz's racial origins.

This process of representation takes another ambivalent turn later in the same chapter (and the first *Post* article), when Whiteman effaces Brown's display of "blackness" in retelling his own originary experience with jazz in San Francisco. This episode serves as the epiphany leading Whiteman to his career in jazz. He invokes blackness only indirectly at the beginning of the passage, where he employs the same geographic pun that Osgood mentions: "We first met—jazz and I—at a dance dive on the Barbary Coast." The rest of the account, despite its implicit references to African Americans, displaces blackness by silently refusing to identify the venue's racial character. Finding "the jazziest of the jazz places," Whiteman "ambled at length into the mad house. Men and women were whirling and twirling feverishly there. Sometimes they snapped their fingers and yelled loud[ly]." This scene of intense vitality, reminiscent of Brown's street performance, causes Whiteman to lose self-control:

> My whole body began to sit up and take notice. . . . My blues faded [Whiteman had been depressed] when treated to the Georgia blues that some trombonist was wailing about. My head was dizzy, but my feet seemed to understand that tune. They began to pat wildly. I wanted to whoop. I wanted to dance. I wanted to sing. I did them all.[62]

More like Osgood's friend, the Ted Lewis fan, than Osgood himself, Whiteman experiences jazz therapeutically, discovering his internal primitive self. Despite Whiteman's superficial suppression of African American referents in the account, his invigorated persona is of course characterized by "black" adolescent sexuality: his initial, full-body erection leads to the familiar image of his wildly happy feet as well as other displays of sensual dynamism. The trombonist's "Georgia blues" reinforces the "blackness" of this persona, while Whiteman's "whooping" invokes Native Americans, other purported noble savages. This depiction of Whiteman's first experience with jazz, suggesting more direct contact with originary "blackness" than does Osgood's experience with Isham Jones, is somewhat risky. Whiteman presumably invokes this contact to authenticate his career in jazz, yet this authentication has a cost: he nearly admits to losing self-control and succumbing to the hyperphysical, primitive state that so concerned Osgood. Whiteman's management of the same concern in *Jazz* is not limited to the passage's suppression of black referents. Just after relating this episode, he worries about possessing "stores of vitality" that will debilitate him unless he can turn them "into some channel." His solution is to regulate his vitality by regulating jazz itself: he studies various jazz bands—implicitly white ones in this case, perhaps because they pose less of a racial threat—and masters the music by

devising a formal, "scored, trained" method of jazz orchestration. This disciplined effort, like Osgood's turn from dancing to conversation, supposedly reassures Whiteman's audience that jazz need not destabilize bourgeois subjectivity: mastering jazz through structured work means sublimating the desires jazz enflames. As Whiteman puts it, suggesting both "black" jazz's adolescent hypermasculinity and jazz orchestration's mature rationality: "in the good old phrase, [jazz] 'ma[d]e a man of me.'"[63]

When Whiteman discusses jazz orchestration and professional jazz performance, bourgeois-liberal ideology shapes his narrative. Making jazz progress artistically by scoring it in regimented, trained fashion coincides with Whiteman's personal, moral progress in gaining self-control. These ideological equations are prominent in chapter 9 of *Jazz*, which details the instrumental devices of Whiteman's jazz "orchestra," and in chapter 12, where Whiteman emphasizes his band members' formal academic training and their moral status as "conscientious" married men who "stick to their jobs with greater persistence." These chapters constitute the bulk of the March 13 *Post* article. Such discussions seek to legitimate jazz to music educators and fine-art composers, but they also pose a problem when Whiteman begins to pursue his project of jazz therapy. The problem first arises when Whiteman, like Osgood, dismisses the early jazz that he heard in San Francisco as "raucous," "crude," and "unmusical." Echoing Irene Castle, he asserts in chapter 9 that early jazz's "demoniac energy, fantastic riot of accents and humorous moods have all had to be toned down."[64] Such refinement produces Whiteman's "melodious" jazz, which uses "every kind of legitimate orchestral instrument" and requires fine-art "discipline" to perform.[65] In a passage reprinted in the March 13 *Post*, Whiteman casts his band as an "army" and himself its "commander." The similar image of Isham Jones's regimented gentlemen symbolically concluded Osgood's civilizing project, but Whiteman's work continues past this

point. The conflicting ideological principles underwriting jazz therapy interrupt his full-fledged
investment in bourgeois liberalism. Jazz, he insists, cannot be so refined that it loses its primitive
vitality, which here takes on the more generic label
"life": "I hope that in toning down we shall not, as
some critics have predicted, take the life out of our
music. I do not believe we shall. It seems to me
that we have retained enough of the humor, rhythmic eccentricity, and pleasant informality to leave
us still jazzing."[66] Whiteman tries to avoid destabilizing his efforts to civilize jazz by carefully hiding his therapeutic project under the bland,
racially unmarked rubric of "life"—a term resonating with republican ideology's "real life." This
term obscures the traces of "black" vitality necessary for therapy, and with it Whiteman hopes to
resolve ideological fissures between therapy and
refinement. *Life* signifies something much more
friendly and reassuring than "the perspiring, grotesque energy" of Brown's orchestra or the uncontrolled animation of Whiteman's own whooping,
dancing, singing persona.

Whiteman advances his therapeutic claims
fully in chapter 7, where rhythm—syncopation,
"irregular" accents—surfaces as a focal component of "life." Rhythm, of course, was (and still is)
a stereotypical metonym for African American
identity: black people supposedly "have" rhythm.
Such racist equations can dovetail with linear-historical models of civilization, in which hyperphysical primitive peoples are supposedly dominated
by rhythmic movement—the savage equals the
drum. Also relevant here is the association of
rhythm with sexual intercourse that arises in Osgood's book: his etymology of *jazz* fluctuates between the bawdy vocabulary of the Barbary Coast
and the ritual language used in "jungle 'parties'
when the tom-tom throbbed." Moralist attacks on
jazz's sensuality often had these meanings in
mind. Osgood's book responds to such attacks
by muting jazz rhythm's implicitly sexual connotations: refined jazz has tepidly "insinuating"
rhythms that are mainly of intellectual interest.

Whiteman pursues a different strategy, openly
admitting the sensuality of rhythm while harness-
ing it to sanitized therapy. He concedes "the effect
the rhythms have on the emotions—their intoxicating effect," but he finds such emotional awak-
enings healthily liberating: jazz "stir[s] up the
whole human being." The primitive already lies
within, Whiteman allows, but—true to the therapeutic world view—it represents a simple side of
the civilized ("human") self that must be reclaimed
and explored. Strategically, Whiteman neglects to
mention the racialized network of associations
that surround rhythm—reminders of the color
line—as he proceeds to reclaim it as a necessary
feature of generic "human life." Adopting rhetoric
derived directly from therapy-oriented neurolo-
gists, Whiteman condemns industrialism:

> I believe all the tendencies of modern living—of
> machine civilization—are to make crippled, per-
> verted things of human beings. The machines are
> standardizing everything. . . . At their work, men
> and women are the victims of efficiency, the [Fred-
> erick Winslow] Taylor system [of systematizing la-
> bor tasks], so that humanity itself is being made into
> machines. On their way home, on the streets, in the
> cars, subways, trains, humans are transported in
> masses, like wheat run through a mill.

Such a lifestyle unhealthily suppresses emotions
and impulses: "The Machine Age is as bad as the
Puritan Age, in that it brings repression." It is rational, industrial life, says Whiteman—not *jazz*,
as his critics would have it—that "might conceivably plunge a whole nation into nervous prostration or insanity."[67]

Whiteman's solution, of course, is the therapy
of jazz's rhythmic effects. Jazz intoxicates, yes, but
intoxication is "natural"; Whiteman surveys the
animal kingdom to cite behavior illustrating that
"[all] life needs intoxication now and then." Such
intoxication is generically human:

> Every society of human beings known upon this
> earth has had intoxicants—not only drinks and

drugs of various kinds, but seasons of intoxicating themselves with song and dance. The lowest sub-men in the jungles of Africa have these seasons in common with the ancient Greeks, citizens of the highest civilization in the modern world.

Blackness irrepressibly reemerges here as the ultimate referent for jazz, but it is immediately re-contained and legitimized by the image of Greek bacchanalia. Invoking the unreproachable prece-dent of ancient Greek society, Whiteman attempts to assuage Anglo-Saxon fears about losing Apol-lonian rationality. Indeed, he argues that rhythm's therapeutic effects can actually help reconstitute civilized self-control. Rhythmic intoxication is healthy, he says, not destructive like other intoxi-cants. This position requires a grand theory about human nature: "Maybe this will seem fantastic, but I almost believe that everything wrong— disease of the body, unhappiness of the spirit— may be due to a disturbance of the natural rhythms." In an obvious appeal to Prohibitionists (who often associated jazz with alcohol), White-man assures that "drink and drugs" cannot com-bat internal rhythmic disturbances. In contrast, jazz, a "good" intoxicant, can "get one back into the right rhythms." Earlier I cited a 1917 *Literary Digest* article that quotes William Morrison Pat-terson's authorization of the nostalgic, therapeutic pursuit of the primitive. At this point in *Jazz*, Whiteman recirculates that authorization:

> Professor Patterson of Columbia University says somewhere in his studies of rhythm that the music of contemporary savages taunts us with a lost art. Modern life, he points out, has inhibited many nor-mal instincts, and the mere fact that our conven-tional dignity forbids us to sway our bodies, to tap our feet when we hear rhythmic music, has deprived us of normal outlets for natural impulses.

Jazz restores internal rhythmic order by re-turning the experiential intensity that modern, in-dustrial life suffocates. This therapy's racialized nature, thoroughly obscured, nevertheless peeps through:

> In America, jazz is at once a revolt and a release. Through it, we get back to a simple, to a savage, if you like, joy in being alive. While we are dancing or singing or even listening to jazz, all the artificial re-straints are gone. We are rhythmic, we are emo-tional, we are natural. We're really living—living to a pitch that becomes an intoxication. And it's good living.

The term *savage* displaces "blackness" only barely, given the invocation a mere nine pages ear-lier of "sub-men in the jungles of Africa." Still, Whiteman does his best to distance himself from the word ("savage, if *you* like"), and the preceding, deracialized discourse—life, humans, ancient Greeks—recasts savagery as a less threatening, even desirable premodern condition. With such strategies Whiteman attempts to construct a rhythmic, emotional, natural "we" for white America, a "we" that experiences a "joy in living" quite distinct from the malodorous, bestial, "gro-tesque energy" of Brown's orchestra. He seeks to provide imaginary solutions to racialized anxiety about jazz by arguing that the primitive lies within civilized selfhood without tainting the latter. He idealizes this paradoxical dynamic elsewhere in the book—and in the *Post* of March 6—in the figure of the Prince of Wales, whom he met while touring England. "His Royal Highness" is not only an eminent symbol of European civilization but also "an extraordinarily good dancer, I should say, with a splendid sense of rhythm" and a penchant for playing drums. Whiteman's discourse about jazz therapy helped fashion this rhythmic-yet-civ-ilized persona for bourgeois Americans, a persona also popularized by George and Ira Gershwin's fa-mous 1930 song "I Got Rhythm." This persona has figured immensely in the creation and reception of popular culture far beyond the 1920s and 1930s, from swing to postwar rock music—as in Lott's analysis of Elvis—to contemporary rap and hip hop.[68] According to Whiteman, whites can adopt this persona temporarily in cabarets and ballrooms to revitalize their civilized selves, without cultural miscegenation.

Having said that, it is difficult to measure the direct impact of Whiteman's discourse on white dancers' material experience. There are few if any indications that Whiteman espoused his arguments at concerts, for example, and persuaded his audiences to accept them. Available evidence of this nature relates mainly to Whiteman's disciplined regulation of his bands' performances, which necessarily affected dancers' experience. "At present there are . . . fifty-two Paul Whiteman orchestras located all over the U.S. and in Paris, London, Havana and Mexico," Whiteman wrote in 1924. "All these orchestras receive careful supervision and training, and play according to specific directions which I have personally prepared."[69]

Direct evidence is available on *Jazz's ideological* impact, as seen in an unsigned evaluation of the book in the *New York Times Book Review*. The reviewer summarizes the text and its main arguments sympathetically; for example, he or she agrees with Whiteman's narrative of the linear development of jazz, from its "African background," to its "raw and wild" stage "out in California," to its "uplift" at Whiteman's hand. Because "Mr. Whiteman . . . invented the orchestration of jazz, . . . he achieved being taken seriously. He got his jazz taken seriously." Most importantly, the reviewer accepts Whiteman's sanitization of racialized jazz therapy: "The decriers of jazz proclaim that it makes those who listen to it (and especially those who dance to it) drunk. So it does, answers Whiteman; jazz does make the listener drunk; it makes him alive, awakens all his faculties, stimulates him. But it is a good drunkenness, not a bad drunkenness."[70]

Such ideas found acceptance not only because of Whiteman's popularity, but also because he— and Osgood—were not alone in promoting them. *Jazz* and *So This Is Jazz* participated in a general discursive trend of the mid-1920s, a civilizing mission led by music critics and educators. This mission involved conceding the emergent distinction between early ("black") jazz and refined ("white") jazz as well as privileging the latter's ordered regulation of the former. In August 1924 the music-educator journal *Etude* sponsored a forum in which only five of the thirteen participants "rejected jazz without qualification." The other eight distinguished between jazz styles and promoted "'advanced' or 'refined' jazz."[71] The lead editorial of the *Etude* issue also expressed the latter position, as did a *New York Times* editorial that documented the forum. When the forum continued in the *Etude's* following issue, about half of the contributors concurred with Osgood and Whiteman. Music educators who championed the "better" jazz generally believed that making the music "less vulgar and more refined" would help to control it, to keep it in "its 'proper' place."[72] By the 1930s swing era, it became common to treat sanitized "black" music and dancing as safe therapy for middle-class whites.[73] Whiteman and Osgood popularized a cultural aesthetic of controlling and restraining "blackness" that, directly and indirectly, affected Americans' material experience of music and dance for years to come.

Whiteman's and Osgood's texts show that white fascination with ragtime and jazz dancing resonated with reactionary, racist social practice toward African Americans in at least three ways. At the broadest level, the confluence manifested the paradoxical dynamic of a psychosocial reaction formation of racial feeling. The conflicting impulses of this dynamic were rationalized, at a second and more specific level, by the therapeutic world view: embracing "blackness" in jazz therapy would presumably reconstruct the bourgeoisie's agency, empowering that group to battle social threats posed by African Americans and other minorities. At a third level, the confluence appears in another paradoxical claim that Whiteman makes—that his therapeutic project has different effects on different social classes. Whereas jazz heals the overcivilized bourgeoisie, he suggests that it *disempowers* the discontented masses, dissipating their threatening energy and *robbing* them of their agency.[74] All three dimensions of this project of sociocultural control have proven influential in the United States, yet even in the 1920s the project failed to attain hegemonic status. Among other variant formations of racial feeling, in 1920s Chicago a small group of ethnic white musicians pursued cultural praxes relating to racial cross-dressing but manifesting more constructive social relations. My brief consideration of these figures concludes the essay.

The Exceptional Chicagoans?

Chicago's South Side hosted a dynamic jazz scene in the 1920s, attracting white patrons to integrated "black and tan" cabarets. Circa 1925, a number of young white men from ethnic-immigrant families frequented cabarets to hear African-American performers such as Joe "King" Oliver and Louis Armstrong. This group included Eddie Condon and Jimmy McPartland (both of Irish extraction), Benny Goodman and Mezz Mezzrow (Russian-Jewish), and Bud Freeman (French Catholic). Their black idols influenced them so dramatically that they committed their lives to playing "authentic" black jazz. Condon, McPartland, and Mezzrow remained steadfastly loyal to New Orleans jazz, while Goodman and Freeman became famous big-band performers. Initially, social relations between these figures and African American musicians were significantly different from those between blacks and bourgeois whites, distinguishing the so-called Chicagoans from other 1920s racial cross-dressers.

In visiting the South Side, the Chicagoans did pursue therapy based on primitivist notions of black culture. Their autobiographies display intense, even "Negrophilic," investment in such notions; Mezzrow's *Really the Blues* (1946) does so

most dramatically.[75] However, the therapy they collectively sought was not a temporary respite from the office or parlor, but an altogether different mode of lived experience. As ethnic immigrants or their children, these figures experienced forms of discrimination that rendered them suspicious of assimilatory bourgeois-liberal ideology. Rather than pursue bourgeois (white) American identity, the Chicagoans rebelled: they skipped school, joined street gangs, ventured to the South Side. When they found "therapy" for their alienation in black jazz, they dedicated themselves to the music, making it a shared avocation that (initially) held no promise of financial reward.[76] It is possible that their dedication expressed a particularly intense, variant reaction formation, but the similar aspects of marginalized social experience among African Americans and white ethnic immigrants also suggests a more constructive cross-racial identification.[77] The Chicago phenomenon may have represented what anthropologist Victor Turner calls "a loving union of the structurally damned"—a tentative coalition among those similarly alienated—that "pronounc[es] judgment on normative [social] structure and provid[es] alternative models for structure."[78] The most prominent aspect of prescribed social structure that these musicians critiqued was segregation: Goodman, Condon, and Mezzrow helped to organize some of the earliest interracial jazz bands.

Even if this argument holds for the Chicagoans' early contact with African American musicians, it becomes more untenable in later periods. Jazz historian William Howland Kenney notes that the Chicagoans' "appropriations of black jazz" contained the seed of expropriation, of "racial exploitation."[79] Indeed, as Benny Goodman and Bud Freeman became swing-band stars from the 1930s onward, they arguably updated the roles of Sophie Tucker and Ted Lewis, displacing and decontaminating the supposed intensity of African American culture for white, middle-class audiences. Furthermore, even purists like Condon and Mezzrow (who condemned swing's commercialism) eventually traded on their association with "authentic" New Orleans jazz to establish careers in various Dixieland revivals. If the Chicagoans initially embodied an alternative response to the Northern influx of African Americans, eventually they participated in cultural projects resembling Paul Whiteman's.

I highlight the early Chicagoans because I want to believe that more constructive white identities did and can exist. Processes of racial cross-dressing so impact twentieth-century U.S. whiteness that they seem always to threaten alternative white subjectivities. This essay nevertheless participates in efforts to redefine white selfhood. If, as Lott suggests, white Americans delusionally explain their own psychosocial crises about pleasure and the body with reference to racial hierarchies, then those crises do not resolve but persist and self-perpetuate—as do their contributions to processes of social oppression. Excavating these aspects of formations of whiteness should, at the very least, prompt white Americans to devise other, more constructive methods for confronting fragmentations of selfhood wrought by industrial—and late—capitalism.

Notes

1 James Weldon Johnson, *Along This Way: The Autobiography of James Weldon Johnson* (New York: Viking, 1933), 327, 328.

2 A 1925 study that surveys the social atmospheres of New York dancehalls, restaurants, and cabarets provides specific statistics about the venues' clientele that are probably reliable. The authors assert that "the majority of patrons fall in the age group between seventeen and forty" and estimate that 10 percent of Manhattan's women and 14 percent of its men "attend dance halls [at least] once per week." Average admission charges ($0.75–0.80 per person), costs for refreshments and coat checking ($0.20), and dancing charges ($0.20)—the latter usually for single men—suggest a clientele with a fair amount of expendable income (at least $2.00

per couple or single man per evening). See LeRoy E. Bowman and Maria Ward Lambin, "Evidences of Social Relations as Seen in Types of New York City Dance Halls," *Journal of Social Forces* 3(2) (Jan. 1925): 286–91. For patrons who purchased bootleg liquor commonly supplied by some dancing venues, the cost of attendance per evening probably doubled. In 1922 the going rate for half-pint bottles of gin or whisky was $2.00. See "Izzy, Ebon in Hue, Raids Rum Bazaar," *New York Times* (Mar. 3, 1922).

3 I should clarify immediately that white jazz dancing, as cultural performance, derived at best only partially from African American cultural praxes. What Eric Lott says of blackface minstrelsy applies equally well to 1920s jazz dancing: "What was on display in minstrelsy was less black culture than a structured set of white responses to it which had grown out of northern . . . social rituals and were passed through an inevitable filter of racist presupposition." See Lott, *Love and Theft: Blackface Minstrelsy and the American Working Class* (New York: Oxford University Press, 1993), 101. When I surround the terms *black* and *blackness* with quotation marks, I refer to what many bourgeois Anglo-Saxons *believed* to constitute, or what they associated with, African American culture.

4 See Morroe Berger, "Jazz: Resistance to the Diffusion of a Culture-Pattern," *Journal of Negro History* 32 (1947): 462–68; Neil Leonard, *Jazz and the White Americans: The Acceptance of a New Art Form* (Chicago: University of Chicago Press, 1962), 29–46; Alan P. Merriam, *The Anthropology of Music* (Evanston, IL: Northwestern University Press, 1964), 241–44; MacDonald Smith Moore, *Yankee Blues: Musical Culture and American Identity* (Bloomington: Indiana University Press, 1985), 82–92; and Kathy J. Ogren, *The Jazz Revolution: Twenties America and the Meaning of Jazz* (New York: Oxford University Press, 1989), 139–61.

5 George M. Fredrickson, *The Black Image in the White Mind: The Debate on Afro-American Character and Destiny, 1817–1914* (1971; Hanover, NH: Wesleyan University Press, 1987), 327.

6 Michael North pursues this argument regarding modernist writers in *The Dialect of Modernism: Race, Language, and Twentieth-Century Literature* (New York: Oxford University Press, 1994), 27–28.

7 Henry O. Osgood, *So This Is Jazz* (Boston: Little, Brown, 1926); Paul Whiteman and Mary Margaret McBride, *Jazz* (New York: J. H. Sears, 1926). A third major work

addressing jazz and ragtime is Gilbert Seldes, *The Seven Lively Arts* (New York: Harper, 1924), a study of several forms of American popular culture. Seldes's handling of jazz's racialized meanings largely resembles that of Osgood and Whiteman. See Nicholas M. Evans, *Writing Jazz: Race, Nationalism, and Modern Culture in the 1920s* (New York: Garland Publications, 2000).

8 Eric Lott, *Love and Theft*; Lott, "White Like Me: Racial Cross-Dressing and the Construction of American Whiteness," in *Cultures of United States Imperialism,* ed. Amy Kaplan and Donald E. Pease (Durham: Duke University Press, 1993), 474–95.

9 Lott, "White Like Me," 476, 481.

10 Sander L. Gilman, *Difference and Pathology: Stereotypes of Sexuality, Race, and Madness* (Ithaca: Cornell University Press, 1985), 126.

11 Lott, *Love and Theft,* 148.

12 Gilbert Osofsky, *Harlem: The Making of a Ghetto,* 2d ed. (New York: Harper and Row, 1971).

13 Ibid., 111, 105, 110, 112–13, 120.

14 On reaction formations, see Otto Fenichel, *The Psychoanalytic Theory of Neuroses* (New York: Norton, 1945), 151–53; Sigmund Freud, *Three Contributions to the Theory of Sex,* trans. A. A. Brill (New York: Dutton, 1962), 40, 94.

15 Fenichel, *Psychoanalytic Theory,* 151.

16 Osofsky, *Harlem,* 130, 248 n.15, 130–31.

17 Ibid., 135–49.

18 Lewis A. Erenberg, *Steppin' Out: New York Nightlife and the Transformation of American Culture, 1890–1930* (1981; Chicago: University of Chicago Press, 1984), 255, 256.

19 Ibid., 226.

20 This argument echoes Frances S. Connelly, *The Sleep of Reason: Primitivism in Modern European Art and Aesthetics, 1725–1907* (University Park: Pennsylvania State University Press, 1995), 112–13.

21 T. J. Jackson Lears, *No Place of Grace: Antimodernism and the Transformation of American Culture, 1880–1920* (New York: Pantheon, 1981), 4–58.

22 For more on neurasthenia, see Tom Lutz, *American Nervousness, 1903: An Anecdotal History* (Ithaca: Cornell University Press, 1991).

23 Lears, *No Place of Grace,* 51, 53–54, xviii.

24 Ibid., 142–49.

25 Osgood, *So This Is Jazz,* 11; "The Appeal of the Primitive Jazz," *Literary Digest* (Aug. 25, 1917): 28 (emphasis added).

26 Lears, *No Place of Grace,* 143, 145. The prominent neurologist G. Stanley Hall popularized these ideas about childhood, race, and the recapitulation theory. See Gail Bederman, *Manliness and Civilization: A Cultural History of Gender and Race in the United States, 1880–1917* (Chicago: University of Chicago Press, 1995), 77–110.

27 Michael Rogin, "Blackface, White Noise: The Jewish Jazz Singer Finds His Voice," *Critical Inquiry* 18 (spring 1992): 442. See also Fredrickson, *Black Image,* 97–129, 327–28.

28 Lott, "White Like Me," 480.

29 Marianna Torgovnick, *Gone Primitive: Savage Intellects, Modern Lives* (Chicago: University of Chicago Press, 1990), 99.

30 See Gilman, *Difference and Pathology,* 131–149; Torgovnick, *Gone Primitive,* 99.

31 See Lott, *Love and Theft,* 113.

32 When I speak of social history, I mean that Erenberg's text not only documents performers' repertoires, reputations, and biographies but also extensively describes venues' locations, clienteles, floor plans and shows, financing, and the like. Based on exhaustive research of primary documents in library archives and the public record, the book's reconstruction of cabaret culture comes as close as is possible to offering a "factual" record. I rely heavily on Erenberg in this section of the essay because his secondary work provides access to primary materials that are otherwise unavailable to me.

33 Erenberg, *Steppin' Out,* 242, 259.

34 Ibid., 187; see also 22–23, 72–74.

35 Reid Badger, *A Life in Ragtime: A Biography of James Reese Europe* (New York: Oxford University Press, 1995), 52, 217, 311 n.11, 88.

36 Erenberg, *Steppin' Out,* 187.

37 Moore, *Yankee Blues,* 132.

38 Erenberg, *Steppin' Out,* 196, 194, 250.

39 Marshall Stearns and Jean Stearns, *Jazz Dance: The Story of American Vernacular Dance* (1968; New York: Da Capo, 1994), 96; Erenberg, *Steppin' Out,* 79, 81.

40 Erenberg, *Steppin' Out,* 159.

41 Elisabeth Marbury, introduction to *Modern Dancing,* by Mr. and Mrs. Vernon Castle (New York: Harper, 1914), 20–22.

42 Castle, *Modern Dancing,* 177, 136, 135.

43 Erenberg, *Steppin' Out,* 164, 163, 250–51.

44 Irene Castle, quoted in Erenberg, *Steppin' Out,* 163–64.

45 Merriam, *The Anthropology of Music,* 242.

46 Osgood, *So This Is Jazz,* 5–6.

47 Ibid., 7–8; Osgood, "The Jazz Bugaboo," *American Mercury* (Nov. 1925): 328–30; Osgood, "The Anatomy of Jazz," *American Mercury* (Apr. 1926): 385–95.

48 Osgood, *So This Is Jazz,* 7.

49 Sigmund Freud, *Introductory Lectures on Psychoanalysis,* ed. and trans. James Strachey (New York: Norton, 1966), 155–56; Gilman, *Difference and Pathology,* 126; Osgood, *So This Is Jazz,* 13.

50 Another way to interpret Osgood's homoerotic sublimation finds its effects less disruptive to his project. Following Eve Kosofsky Sedgwick's notion of the homosocial, one might argue that Osgood's conversation with his companion embodies male bonding that reaffirms his "legitimate" masculinity. "Refined" jazz, which can be seen as a feminized version of hypermasculine "early" jazz, serves as the discursive matter through which the two men triangulate their desire for relations with one another. In this sense, Osgood's figuration of his companion as "a man every inch of him" can suggest his need to reclaim prescribed masculinity through identification with an ample source. For more on this dynamic, see Eve Kosofsky Sedgwick, *Between Men: English Literature and Male Homosocial Desire* (New York: Columbia University Press, 1985).

51 Paul Whiteman and His Orchestra, "Happy Feet," in *Swing Time! The Fabulous Big Band Era, 1925–1955* (Columbia C3K 52862). This song made something of a comeback in the late 1990s, as part of the revival of swing music's popularity. See, for example, the compact disc *Happy Feet* by the Austin, Texas, cabaret band 8½ Souvenirs (Continental 8121; RCA Victor 63226).

52 Erenberg, *Steppin' Out,* 252.

53 It should be noted that most jazz critics, beginning as early as the late 1920s, have discounted Whiteman's music (not to mention James Reese Europe's music) as being "jazz" at all. To them, Whiteman's schmaltzy pop music for polite social dancing literally pales beside the authentic 1920s African American musical expressions of figures like Joe "King" Oliver and Louis Armstrong. While I acknowledge the importance of such definitions of authenticity, I also recognize that they derive from retrospective, canon-forming narratives of jazz's musicological development that efface the complexly varied cultural contexts in which "jazz" circulated and registered in the 1920s. Whiteman was synonymous with jazz both for his moralist opponents and his fans, who comprised the population of Fitzgerald's jazz age. See Evans, *Writing Jazz.*

54 Paul Whiteman, "Jazz," *Saturday Evening Post* (Feb. 27, 1926): 3+; (Mar. 6, 1926): 32+; (Mar. 13, 1926): 28+.

55 Whiteman, *Jazz,* 87–111; Whiteman, "Jazz" (Mar. 6, 1926): 33, 180, 185.

56 Whiteman, *Jazz,* 155–58, 163, 7, 145–58; Whiteman, "Jazz" (Mar. 6, 1926): 186, 188.

57 Lott suggests this possibility with respect to minstrelsy. See *Love and Theft,* 57–58.

58 Whiteman, *Jazz,* 3.

59 Ibid., 9. On similar white anxiety about "owning" minstrelsy, see Lott, *Love and Theft,* 55–62.

60 Whiteman, "Jazz" (Feb. 27, 1926): 3; Whiteman, *Jazz,* 17. See also Osgood, *So This Is Jazz,* 12–13.

61 Whiteman, *Jazz,* 17–19. The basic details of this story are true: in 1915, Gorham did bring Brown's band to Chicago from New Orleans. However, in apparent contradiction to my argument, members of the band were in fact not black but "white" (some were Creoles). See Richard Sudhalter, *Lost Chords: White Musicians and Their Contribution to Jazz, 1915–1945* (New York: Oxford University Press, 1999), 3–8. This information need not qualify my interpretation of Whiteman's writing in racially polarized terms. Whiteman never identifies the musicians' racial identities explicitly, and, as my analysis shows, his representation of Brown's orchestra relies heavily on imagery of "blackness." I propose that Whiteman's (perhaps intentional) ambiguity *encourages* a racially polarized interpretation of the passage, as does the Barbary Coast episode discussed next. Even if Whiteman assumed his readers knew that the musicians were "white," his portrayal of them closely resembles Osgood's treatment of Ted Lewis.

62 Whiteman, "Jazz" (Feb. 27, 1926): 4–5; Whiteman, *Jazz,* 32–33.

63 Whiteman, *Jazz,* 34, 40, 35.

64 Ibid., 238, 33, 210; Whiteman, "Jazz" (Mar. 13, 1926): 137.

65 Whiteman, *Jazz,* 94, 192, 211.

66 Ibid., 248, 210; Whiteman, "Jazz" (Mar. 13, 1926): 142, 137.

67 Whiteman, *Jazz,* 12, 145, 153–54, 155, 16.

68 Ibid., 146, 149–50, 153, 155, 79; Whiteman, "Jazz" (Mar. 6, 1926): 32; Lott, "White Like Me," 483–85.

69 Paul Whiteman, "What Is Jazz Doing to American Music?" *Etude* 42 (Aug. 1924): 523.

70 "If Jazz Isn't Music, Why Isn't It?" review of *Jazz,* by Paul Whiteman and Mary Margaret McBride, and *Blues: An Anthology,* ed. W. C. Handy. *New York Times Book Review* (June 13, 1926): 5.

71 "Where Is Jazz Leading America?" *Etude* 42 (Aug. 1924): 517–18, 520; (Sept. 1924): 595–96; Berger, "Jazz," 474–75. See also Leonard, *Jazz and the White Americans*, 82.

72 "Where the Etude Stands on Jazz," *Etude* 42 (Aug. 1924): 515; "A Subject of Serious Study," *New York Times* (Aug. 11, 1924): Berger, "Jazz," 463.

73 For similar arguments, see Berger, "Jazz," 467, 472–73; Stearns and Stearns, *Jazz Dance*, 328–34.

74 This recipe for social control hinges upon reconfiguring jazz therapy as an assimilatory agent. When Whiteman warns that America "might conceivably plunge . . . into nervous prostration or insanity," the specific segment of "America" he refers to is factory workers, including Asian and eastern European immigrants. "Americans—and the term included Slavs, Teutons, Latins, Orientals, welded into one great mass as if by the machines they tended—lived harder, faster than ever before. They could not go on without some new outlet." From this perspective, jazz's therapeutic effects unite all "Americans," including minorities, helping to dispel their shared alienation with a shared culture. However, nervous prostration and insanity were not the only possible results of the laborers' discontent. Whiteman also gestures generally toward social unrest: "the incredible pressure was bound to blow off the lid." Hence, covertly, jazz also defuses dissidence and maintains productivity among workers, *especially* minorities. This suggestion is reinforced later in the book when Whiteman muses that "Music has been used by Southern planters of all time to speed up work among the negroes." See *Jazz*, 16, 295. The portrayal of jazz as a tool for social control coheres with Lears's general conclusions about the therapeutic world view. Lears argues that the bourgeoisie's quests for intense, primal, authentic experience ultimately failed to restore their autonomous subjectivity and performed instead the hegemonic function of easing "their own and others' adjustments to a streamlined culture of consumption" commandeered by corporate capitalism. See *No Place of Grace*, xvi. In other words, jazz and cabarets, as commercial culture, helped to disempower all classes. This perspective, of course, echoes Theodor Adorno's notorious analysis of jazz (for Adorno, jazz is Whiteman's music). Mia Carter observes that "Adorno saw jazz as the ultimate fetishized commodity of the 'soulless modern age'" because it appealed to "base" sensuality. Rather than liberating subjectivity, jazz—even more than other products of the Culture Industry—provides only simulated liberation and leaves the subject further alienated and controlled: "Emotional responses and expressions are 'katharsis for the masses, but katharsis which keeps them all the more firmly in line.'" In this respect, the pop-music conductor "became a dangerous, mesmerizing wizard of capitalism's fascistic impulse, the band or orchestra, his destructive tool: Paul Whiteman became the Fuhrer." See Mia Carter, "I Jam, Therefore I Am: Modern Jazz, Critical Postures and Performances" (unpublished essay).

75 Mezz Mezzrow and Bernard Wolfe, *Really the Blues* (1946; New York: Citadel, 1990).

76 An idea similar to this one appears in Burton W. Peretti, *The Creation of Jazz: Music, Race, and Culture in Urban America* (Urbana: University of Illinois Press, 1992), 98–99.

77 Since some ethnic immigrants were already associated with "blackness" and the primitive, their embrace of African American culture could have manifested repressed resentment about the association. Michael Rogin proposes a similar idea in his work on the blackface performances of Al Jolson. Jolson, seeking to appropriate bourgeois white identity, paradoxically seized blackface as a vehicle for assimilation: blackface "liberates the performer from the fixed, 'racial' identities of African American and Jew. Freeing Jack [Jolson's character in *The Jazz Singer*] from his inner blackness, blackface frees him from his [Jewish] father." See Rogin, "Blackface, White Noise," 440. "Blackness," then, could be embraced as a means to achieve whiteness even as it is loathed for symbolizing both a racial "inferior" and a part of the ethnically Jewish self. See also Evans, *Writing Jazz*.

78 Victor Turner, *From Ritual to Theatre: The Human Seriousness of Play* (New York: Performing Arts Journal, 1982), 51. On the musicians' cross-racial identification, see also William Howland Kenney, *Chicago Jazz: A Cultural History, 1904–1930* (New York: Oxford University Press, 1993), 116.

79 Kenney, *Chicago Jazz*, 111.

The Invisible Burlesque Body of La Guardia's New York

Anna McCarthy

She comes out fully clothed. Slowly to the music, and to encore after encore, she takes off hat, gloves, and other minor accoutrements. Coyly or brazenly, depending upon her style, she slips off dress, skirt, smock, blouse or pajamas. Then the brassiere. A few turns wherein she gyrates, flings, undulates or fingers her breasts, and she begins to operate in the nether regions. Panties come off. Finally, in some burlesque houses, in the split second of the blackout, the G-string . . . comes off. In some theaters the girl then continues, if applause warrants, dancing with breasts and buttocks bare and a hand or strip of cloth held decorously over the Mound [*sic*].

—EYEWITNESS ACCOUNT OF STRIPTEASE ACT, CA. 1935

"Underworld Exhibition"

Beginning in the mid-1920s and continuing through the 1930s, striptease acts like the one described above became a standard ingredient in the entertainment offered by burlesque theaters. Prior to this time, burlesque consisted primarily of risqué comic sketches, solo vocal performances by both men and women, and saucy chorus numbers. The addition of strip acts to this formula was, as observers from the period pointed out, an attempt to rejuvenate burlesque. This was a time when the ribald sensibility that had once been the trademark of burlesque was becoming an increasingly standard element of the legitimate theater, from semi-nude Broadway "revues" to scandalous plays such as Mae West's notorious *Sex*. For burlesque operators facing a loss in revenues, the striptease act injected the necessary amount of extra sexual titillation to turn a profit, despite the fact that it condemned burlesque and its artists to a furtive

and tawdry existence on the margins of urban popular entertainment.[1] Indeed, by the end of the 1930s, the burlesque show was a form of amusement rivaled in its ability to transgress and offend reformist middle-class sensibilities only by the taxi dance hall, where men paid women to dance with them, and the penny arcade, which proffered peep-show pornography for the price of a few coins. One of burlesque's most vigorous reformist opponents proclaimed in 1937 that

> the so-called burlesque of today is not in reality a burlesque—certainly nothing like the sprightly and amusing music hall entertainment of an older generation . . . This type of underworld exhibition should not be tolerated in the City of New York. It may give temporary entertainment to "morons and perverts," . . . but there is no demand for it by the public in general, and its effect upon the weak and upon the young and impressionable is deplorable.[2]

So what exactly was the "underworld exhibition" of the 1930s burlesque show like, and what exactly was the source of its offensiveness? Certainly the show revolved around female nudity, but the fact that nudity was a central part of numerous Broadway revues suggests that it alone was not enough to render burlesque as loathsome as the above description paints it.[3] The explanation seems to have more to do with the class lines that distinguished forms of popular entertainment and which guided reformist beliefs about both the motives of audiences and the "effects" of such entertainments upon them. Thus, on Broadway, middle-class "legitimate" theatergoers might snicker and gasp at daring nude displays and sexual jokes without being characterized as a group seeking sexual arousal in such material. In burlesque shows—which often included lewd satires of high culture (for example, a Minsky show entitled *Desire Under the El* staged during the Broadway run of Eugene O'Neill's controversial *Desire Under the Elms*)—the meaning of nudity and dirty humor was far less flexible, and the motives of the burlesque public were correspondingly characterized in one-dimensional terms. From the perspectives of reformers (and of "slumming" middle-class audience members), the interest of the burlesque-goer could only be prurient. In what seems to be the only in-depth eye-witness documentation of 1930s burlesque, the 1937 doctoral dissertation of a sociologist named David Dressler, we find the burlesque audience described as "a little in-group bound together by a temporarily common interest. Nothing else matters but sex."[4]

It is true that burlesque created a theater experience saturated with a salaciousness that seemed irredeemably "low," integrating sex and scatology into all levels of the performance, from the comedy sketch to the chorus number. Even before the raising of the curtain, the audience was treated to an innuendo-drenched sales pitch from the "candy butcher"—a stock entr'acte figure who sold various products from pornography to sex aids. The show would then open with a barely-costumed chorus doing a suggestive song and dance number, sometimes offering the audience an extra glimpse of flesh (buttocks, for example) as they exited the stage. These chorus numbers would be interspersed with comic routines and sketches, usually extremely vulgar ones. The transcript of a city Bureau of Licenses hearing for New York's Republic Theater in 1935 gives us a sense of what these sketches were like. Here, police witnesses testified to the "indecent" nature of comic dialogue interwoven with nudity with examples such as this:

> Couple walk on conversing about marriage . . . when the female asks her friend, "'what is a baby?'"; comic says "'nine months interest on a small deposit'"; all exit. Chorine [chorus girl] now appears in a Mexican number as Toreador while one show girl stands nude to the hips in red; they engage in a dance routine and six show girls wearing red capes, skirts, and black hats with breasts exposed walk on stage.[5]

Such smutty humor and unabashedly coital female performance styles were not the only aspects of the burlesque show that repelled reformers, however. Other features of 1930s burlesque, notably indecorous audience behavior and the addition of a unique architectural feature, the runway, were also held responsible for burlesque's depravity. Both were insistent violations of bourgeois theatrical codes; the disgust they provoked further illustrates how class politics shaped the anti-burlesque sentiment of the 1930s.[6] With the addition of the runway—a narrow extension of the stage into the audience space—burlesque violated the visual relations of classical theater by perforating the invisible "fourth wall" separating the imaginary world onstage and the "real" world of the audience. Allowing members of the company to move freely between the space of artifice and the space of reality blurred the boundary between performed sex acts and sex acts performed on others. Many strippers took advantage of this confusion, using the runway to work interactive components into their acts; some strippers would talk to or even touch orchestra and audience members.[7]

This sense, or promise, of interactivity points to a second way in which burlesque violated bourgeois theatrical codes and norms: in the range of audience behaviors it allowed and even promoted. Irving Zeidman, the eyewitness author of a popular history of burlesque, described the atmosphere of the burlesque show in this period as

> a frenzy of congregate cooching such as had never been presented on a public stage. The chorus girls on the runway yelling, shimmying directly at and over the men, the music blatant, jangling, and dissonant, the audience alternately hooting or derisively encouraging—it was a demoniacal, orgiastic spectacle.[8]

This frantic spectacle of screaming, gyrating, sexualized female bodies—situated dangerously close to a roaring audience and competing with a discordant orchestra—was, for some observers, a frightening thing. Film director Rouben Mamoulian described a 1920s visit to a burlesque theater with abject horror: "Frankly, it made me sick in the stomach, this kind of titillation. The audiences were ugly. The girls were bored. The whole thing was tawdry, shoddy, unworthy of a human being, woman or man."[9] Mamoulian's revulsion at the audience and the performers is typical of mainstream reactions to the alien environment of working class amusement and recreation. Time and again, moralistic descriptions of the burlesque experience from this period resonate with the language of class difference. An article in *Fortune* magazine offered the following evaluation: "The most repulsive thing about a burlesque show is its audience . . . the backwash of a depressed industrial civilization, their eyes slight and most of their mouths open. It is not a pretty sight."[10]

It is quite likely that the horrifying coupling of sexual spectacle and working-class, masculine enjoyment was itself a titillating, transgressive thrill for the middle-class viewer, whether reformist or slummer. However, in Dressler's study, the non-working-class regulars at burlesque shows seemed more interested in signaling their distance—in moral and class terms—from the patrons around them. As one anonymous burlesque-goer, described by Dressler as an "intellectual," explained:

> In the burlesque show I would indulge in [masturbation] through my clothes. I would even have an ejaculation in the theater. The peculiar thing was that when I did this, I had the utmost contempt for anyone else about me whom I suspected of doing likewise. I always considered myself above the audience, and perhaps I was in that I had a certain amount of insight.[11]

Another of Dressler's informants, also a well-educated man of the middle classes, described his feelings at being in the theater and watching the show as "mingled—some erotic enjoyment and some disgust."[12] These bourgeois expressions of disgust were probably occasioned not simply by the frank display of female sexuality, but by contact with an alien audience culture imbued with an uninhibited air of salaciousness expressed vocally,

and often collectively, in "guffaws, applauds, calls out, whistles."[13]

For reformers, the anarchy of the 1930s burlesque show, so different from the decorous ethos of the bourgeois theatrical tradition, was evidence of its obscenity. Burlesque, according to this argument, made no pretense at entertainment; indeed, "entertainment" served only as a pretext for the inartistic sexual display onstage. The striptease act was crucial to these arguments against burlesque's cultural worth. Dressler described the non-striptease portions of the show as "rest periods," whose only purpose was to "rest the gonads so that they may be revived or refreshed for the next strip act."[14] As he explained, during these rests "a singing woman will probably come forward, the chorus cavorting about as she sings, in an untrained, off-key voice, a song to which no-one listens, the attention being riveted on her body and her movements."[15] This "sick" fascination with showing sex, to the exclusion of any other concerns was, for the reformist mind, the core of burlesque's degeneracy.

The Burlesque Body

Our contemporary understanding of burlesque, and striptease in particular, is perhaps not terribly different from that of the reformers of the 1930s. In their eyes, the libidinal power (and corrupting threat) of burlesque was its visuality—its ability to *show* the female body, miming sex, to a screaming, out-of-control audience. Today, although motives and methods may differ, most attempts to theorize the power relations of strip-tease are, like the psychoanalytic models they tend to draw upon, similarly fixated on visuality. From a Freudian perspective, striptease spectatorship dramatizes Oedipal anxieties about the precise meaning of sexual difference, anxieties in which the sight of female genitals can both deny and confirm the threat of castration for the (male) subject.[16] But this explanation, although it makes sense as an abstract model, denies striptease and its diversely pleasured audience members any historical specificity. After all, it works just as well as an explanation of a medical examination, and it doesn't allow us much room for thinking about striptease as a kind of performance, that is, as a representation empowered with the ability to make something happen *as* it happens. A visit to the burlesque theater must have yielded pleasures beyond a reassuring sense of the stability of sexual difference. Among these might have been the thrill of experiencing sex in public, of sharing a sexual context with other men, of being confused about what one was seeing, hearing, and feeling; these and other (un-Oedipal?) pleasures were surely targets of anti-burlesque censorship in the 1930s just as much as the disrobing act itself. On its own, psychoanalytic theory seems too blunt an instrument for an adequate exploration of such pleasures, and of burlesque's hectic, carnal world.

The rest of this chapter will explore other ways of reconstructing and accounting for the pleasures of public sexual amusement in striptease. My focus is on the sexual forces—homoeroticism, for example—released by invisible aspects of the performance such as music and sound, and the role of censorship in the *production,* as well as suppression, of these forces. I choose to focus on the sense of hearing because it seems so glaringly absent from any psychoanalytic treatments of striptease, even though historical descriptions of burlesque immediately confront us with a riotous and cacophonous aurality.[17] To overlook this aural complexity is to risk ignoring striptease's potential for dissonance, its power to deviate from the narratives of heterosexual masculinity that the visual components of the striptease act seem so readily to embody. We already know what striptease *looks* like; it is time to stop and *listen* as well, asking what social and sexual identifications are set into play, what bodily sensations are experienced and imagined when desire is expressed in sound.

This essay's deliberately perverse interest in the "un-visual" side of striptease stretches a premise that has been central to much recent theoretical and practical work in feminist cultural critique, namely, that bodies and bodily sensations are produced in performance, or through performative acts. Gender identity, in other words, comes into existence only when it is enacted; it is not something inherent, or essential to, the person it describes. This premise, which underpins the work of Judith Butler and others, has provided a valuable basis for exploring how categories of social identity such as gender are experienced as imperfect, mutable, and negotiable. However, much of the fruitful work in this vein rests upon a visually-centered framework of ideas; witness the proliferation of metaphors and concepts like "marking," "passing," "inscription," etc. to describe how identities are "performed" in cultural practice. I want to extend this concept of the performative beyond the visual and into the realm of the *invisible* by focusing on three sonic aspects of striptease that are central to the performative dynamics of pleasure and identification: the voice of the performer, the vocal intervention of the audience, and the sound of the music itself. These sonic and musical structures allowed certain unexpected desires to be embodied and experienced, unseen, alongside the manifestly visible bodies of performers and audience members. They defined a field of sensation, transgressions, and fantasies— an invisible body—that was sexy and sensuous like its visible counterparts. As we shall see, this invisible burlesque body, like the manifest body of the stripper, came into being through the actions and interactions of diverse agents—performers, band-members, audience-members, and even reformists and lawmakers—all of whom had a stake in defining the kinds of pleasure made available by the performance of striptease.

Of course, the invisible burlesque body I'm describing here is not a literal body, or object, but rather a metaphorical, sonic structure that can be felt and not seen within striptease's structure of looking. However, I've chosen to describe the structuring functions of music and sound in striptease as a kind of "body" because the word suggests both representation and sensation: one's body is both a place to experience *from* and a thing one experiences. The mystery of the human body's line between the subjective and the objective is, it seems to me, the source of much erotic affect and performative power. Exploring how this power operates in striptease beyond the range of vision will, I think, illuminate the pleasures of popular entertainment as a polymorphous, incoherent, and sensuously complex realm of experience to which censorship, obsessed as it is with the visual, can never adequately respond.

Censorship And Sensuality

From a visual perspective, striptease eroticizes censorship; a strip act is, after all, a censorious performance. Its goal is to act out the process of making something visible (stripping) but also to censor this process at the very last moment (teasing). External censorship, in the case of the strip act, becomes a process of imposing a point of onset for the performance's own censoring mechanisms, a condition which can make for a certain amount of confusion between the erotic and the juridical. Indeed, the history of burlesque censorship is largely a history of eroticizing the civic regulations that were enacted precisely to *de-eroticize* stripping.[18] This subversion became increasingly difficult throughout the 1930s, however, with the severe censorship campaign set in motion by the La Guardia mayoral administration and civic organizations such as the Society for the Prevention of Vice. By the end of the decade, burlesque was no longer censored in the city of New York, it was simply prohibited entirely. The campaign to stamp out burlesque, initiated by Paul Moss, La Guardia's licensing commissioner and a Broadway producer, precipitated a cataclysmic change in the legal and economic status of striptease performance.[19] However, Moss's abolition of the institution by no

means removed striptease from the map of popular amusements in the city. After a brief revival of burlesque in a sanitized, authorized (and not very popular) form known as "Vaudesque," the institution of the "strip joint" emerged, and strip acts became a new form of cabaret entertainment.[20] During these years of transition, as burlesque operators fought for and lost their licenses, watching a strip act was a highly policed form of pleasure; like the saloon, the movie theater, and the city streets, the burlesque theater was an entertainment environment organized by the watchful eyes of both municipal authority and civic anti-vice organizations.[21]

The performance style of striptease in the final days of theatrical burlesque was greatly shaped by municipal laws governing what could be seen. Even so, the ways in which the performance remained *beyond* regulation can be discerned in the very same regulatory structures. Consider, for example, the following journalist's report on the municipal codes governing striptease in New York:

> Strippers must perform on a darkened stage, all *bumps* must be toward the wings, not frontwise, during *grinds* the hands may stray but they mustn't touch, the *flash* (the apparent moment of complete nudity) must be at one of the wings, may only last for eight bars of music, and may only expose one breast.[22]

This absurd legalistic choreography tells us more than just the extent of striptease's surveillance. It also communicates a great deal about the ways that public sexuality could draw upon invisible forces such as regulation and, in a quite different way, music. It is hard to conceive of a form of censorship more charged with eroticism; the anxious legal code simultaneously prohibits and enables a titillating display, transforming the monitoring function of municipal authority into a ritual structuring of desire. One can imagine that this close imbrication of salaciousness and pro-scription, a pairing that Robert C. Allen identifies as the key to burlesque's anti-bourgeois erotics in the nineteenth and early twentieth century, could only have added to the lascivious and transgressive force of the strip act.[23]

The musical nature of this set of legal codes is a particularly interesting element in the structuring of desire in the strip act. When we stop to consider the eight-bar limit on the revelation of nudity, its inadequacy and ambivalence as an instrument of regulation becomes clear. After all, a bar of music can last almost any amount of time, depending on the overall tempo of the piece. A stripper can show a great deal—too much, even—in the time it takes for an orchestra to play eight bars. Indeed, one is tempted to speculate here on whether the emblematic *ritarde* that stretches out the final verse of many striptease numbers works as a sly circumvention of such limitations (recall, for example, the well-known recording "The Stripper"). Music, in these regulations, is a way of enabling, and not simply suppressing, the display of the female body, a condition which suggests that music played a central and generative role in burlesque's production of desire.

Sounding the Burlesque Body

It is significant, I think, that the most readily accessible representation of the strip act of the 1930s—burlesque's golden age in popular memory—is a musical number: the oft-recorded instrumental standard known as "The Stripper."[24] Written by David Rose in the 1950s for a never-produced television show entitled *Burlesque* and scoring a number two hit for the MGM label in 1962, the recording is an attempt to recapture what *Variety* referred to as the "Goona Goona" of burlesque.[25] As a kind of popular historiography, this number's nostalgic recreation of a striptease act offers us some preliminary contact with the ways that music inscribes an invisible burlesque body. Consider how MGM vice president Jesse Kay tried

to explain the appeal of the record's lush orchestration: "It's because it's well done with a big orchestra, but still has the feel of walking down the runway in a strip joint . . . you listen to those little three and four piece combos in a strip joint and the music is dirty. This isn't. It's naughty—naughty and nice."[26] The language here is significant. Kay suggests that the recording facilitates several different kinds of auditory identification: the feeling of being in the audience and the feeling of appearing in the show itself. Rather than specifically conjuring up an image of a stripper, the number allows for a variety of possible identifications—audience member, stripper, orchestra-member. Paradoxically, then, Kay's description signifies a bawdy, bodily pleasure but manages not to specify which body and whose pleasure it represents.[27]

This understanding of sound as material for the fantastic production of a bodily sensation recalls Roland Barthes's remarks on the grain of the voice, the quality of recording that refers the listener to the body of the performer, and constructs a form of sensual pleasure based in "the image of the body (the figure)."[28] But unlike this Barthesian body, the burlesque body produced in "The Stripper" refuses to be fixed as an image.[29] It uses sound as a medium for multiple embodiments, inviting the listener to shuttle between imagining the feeling of performing and imagining the feeling of watching, collapsing the distinctions between the two in the process. Listening to orchestration of "The Stripper," which usually involves punctuating drum accents and trombone slurs, we hear a salacious abandon that can serve simultaneously as a sonic replacement for the come-ons of an imagined stripper, as an incitement to identify with the imagined excitement of the stripper herself, as a way of encouraging the formation of a visual image of the body, and, at the same time, as an invitation to feel vicariously the bodily sensation of stripping.[30] The burlesque body "The Stripper" constructs is beyond vision, and so are the auditory projections, identities, and pleasures it makes possible.

A similar sense of music's invisible eroticism and the urgency of the perceived need to regulate this force is relayed to us from the heyday of burlesque through an anecdote related by former burlesque impresario Morton Minsky. The anecdote concerns one of the first obscenity trials brought against performers and managers, a trial immortalized in Rowland Barber's novelistic account, *The Night They Raided Minsky's*. According to Minsky, some of the most crucial testimony for the prosecution came from anti-vice activist John Sumner. Sumner, who seems to have spent a great deal of his free time personally policing the performances offered in burlesque theaters, told the court that he had observed women on Minsky's stage moving their bodies in obscene ways. When asked by the judge to demonstrate these movements for the court, Sumner replied that he *could not possibly do so without the music*" (emphasis added).[31] The anecdote raises some interesting questions about what striptease music signified in the context of public performance. What exactly did Sumner want the music to "do" for him in his attempt to mimic the sexual display of a female performer? And what kind of music did he hope for as accompaniment?

The answer to the latter question is not immediately clear, as the music that women stripped to in this period encompassed an eclectic range of musical forms, including current popular tunes of all types, sentimental ballads, ribald parodies of popular songs, and numbers written especially for the performer.[32] Indeed, as theaters were increasingly censored, songs such as "A Pretty Girl Is Like a Melody" became increasingly popular as accompaniment. When a covert signal informed the stripper that undercover detectives had entered the theater, it was easy to expunge the sexual content of the act and conform to the innocuous sentiment associated with the song.[33] What linked these widely divergent types of accompaniment

for striptease, from the sentimental to the comic, was a set of formal codes that served as the signatures of striptease's "goona goona"—a sensibility that Sumner probably hoped music would endow on him, and which would apparently not be present should he simply rotate his hips in silence. David Rose's famous 1962 recording of "The Stripper" can serve as a touchstone for the sound of striptease, as it contains many of the stylistic devices that characterized burlesque music in the 1930s and 1940s—muted trumpet, slurred trombone, and punctuating drum accents. As slide whistles highlighted certain gestures and movements onstage, a drum technique known in burlesque parlance as "catching the bumps" underscored the performer's pelvic thrusts. This latter percussive embellishment was crucial; as stripper Ann Corio remarked: "I don't know what a stripper would do without that drummer. He controls her movements like a drill sergeant—and when the big moments come in her act, he's tattooing that drum like a civil war drummer at Bull Run."[34] In addition to these "bumps," shrieks, and slurs in the brass section would accompany the performer as she "shimmied," "cooched," and went into a grind.[35]

Sumner's request for musical accompaniment in his courtroom reenactment suggest that these stylistic flourishes were crucial to the bodily affect of stripping, an affect which—even when reproduced in the legislative arena—could not clearly be labeled obscene. As Sumner's reluctance to perform in silence indicates, music was an apparently necessary ingredient in the sexuality displayed onstage; it is as if merely taking off one's clothes in front of an audience would not be enough. The orchestral accompaniment thus did not simply *add to* the sexuality of the stripper's bodily display. Rather, this sexuality was somehow *produced by* the invisible forces of sound. Sexuality, in this scenario, is inextricable from its environment; it is something in the air and the ear as much as in the eye and the (shown and hidden) genitals. Even

Dressler had to acknowledge the importance of such intangible environmental factors, in the production of striptease's erotic charge: "The burlesque-goer is titillated not by nudity alone, but by the salaciousness accompanying it."[36] Sumner could not make his body burlesque—that is, he could not mime the transgression he had witnessed—without the invisible cloak of smut that music provided.

Though the raucous musical style of the burlesque orchestra was necessary for stripping's bodily affect, the nature of this affect remains an open question. For even as percussive accents and slide whistle interjections supplied a salacious environment, they also added a defamiliarizing distance to the performer's "bumps" and "grinds," movements which were intended to invoke the act of sexual intercourse. These sound effects must thus have operated not only as ways of fabricating eroticism, but also as ruptures in the process of producing a "realistic" sexual display. Music both provided a titillating sensibility and undercut it, through the humor of the sound effect.[37] Foregrounding artifice called attention to the absurdity of the situation of the strip act; it reinforced the *impossibility* of actual sexual contact. The imaginary body produced in this relation between sound and performance thus exploited both realism and artifice simultaneously, refusing to rest in one or the other mode of representation. Its tease was not simply the tease of showing and hiding the genitals, but the tease of oscillating between suspended belief and distanciation, of revealing the artifice of the act and inviting the spectator to be "taken in" all at once.

It is tempting to read this comic kind of teasing as a means by which a performer could distance herself from the dreariness of taking off her clothes for an anonymous and scary audience. There is a potential (though admittedly problematic) form of empowerment for the performer in striptease's musical emphasis on the absurd. Refusing to get too serious could be a way of feeling

a sense of control over the objectifying sexuality that this audience came to produce and consume. And indeed, it is important to note that strippers, or at least the stars canonized in celebratory histories of burlesque, were highly aware of the comic dimensions of their acts. Sound and music were primary ways of conveying this awareness. One popular strategy was to subvert chaste lyrics by placing heavy-handed emphasis on or pausing before certain words in a song, as in "would you like to lay your head upon my—er—pillow."[38] Another involved cracking jokes during the performance. Zeidman writes of a Mutual wheel stripper named Jeri McCauley who "would converse with the boys while in the throes of her specialty . . . swinging her hips way out of line, stopping suddenly, and screaming 'get me out of this position, boys!'"[39] Famous Minsky strippers like Gypsy Rose Lee and Gladys Clark would talk to the audience throughout their acts. While Gypsy was known for her sartorial asides, Clark was a little more blunt, uttering cutting lines like "Hey you, take your hands out of your pockets, you're a big boy now."[40]

These instances of feminine vocal authority complicate any understanding of the stripper's body as a mute puppet of male desire. But at the same time, they are probably atypical examples of the ironic use of the voice in striptease. In many other instances, the performer's voice was the only way she could acknowledge, and perhaps protest, the conditions of striptease that made her a victim and an object. This latter voicing of resistance emerged from a web of speech acts that included the utterances of the audience. Zeidman describes the 1934 audience at the Star in Brooklyn as "a heckling, sarcastic, filthy mob that barely permitted the performances to proceed . . . as the finale strippers prepared to introduce the other women principals for the final curtain, a ruffian's voice would rasp 'bring the rest of the whores out!'"[41] Although contemporaneous sociologist David Dressler argued that this level of abuse led "the girls [to] become inured to the shouts of the audience, the masturbators, the perverts,"[42] it is also true that in the rougher theaters in Brooklyn and on the Bowery, strippers were often heckled so much they would have to stop stripping and ask for a break, threatening to leave the stage altogether.[43]

In such cases, the stripper's voice was not the vehicle for displacing or deflecting male desire, but rather a way of throwing male anger back at itself. Talking back could thus serve the stripper as a way of repositioning the meaning of her body in relation to masculine sexual authority. A famous cinematic example of this use of the voice to reposition the body appears in Dorothy Arzner's 1940 film *Dance, Girl, Dance*. In an oft-cited scene, Judy—the ballet dancer played by Maureen O'Hara—is hired as the "clean act" for a burlesque show. However, when she actually goes on stage and performs a sensitive, expressive dance she has choreographed herself, the audience responds with jeers, catcalls, and whistles. Judy stops her dance and faces the crowd, verbally confronting and shaming it into silence. As she speaks, close-ups show the leering faces of the audience (comprised of both high class slummers in tuxedos and hardened lechers) become chagrined and sheepish. Won over by Judy's insistence that she is not an object, they finally stand and offer her an ovation of applause.

In this scene, Pam Cook has argued, the film actually redeems the men in the burlesque audience, letting them off the hook by showing them to be swayed by feminist rhetoric and therefore as basically "decent."[44] But for my purposes, the most interesting aspect of this cinematic example of feminine resistance and masculine redemption is not the film's reformist feminist fantasy. Rather, it is the way that the film registers the audience's transformation: though it gives us visual cues via shots of the men's faces, the decisive moment is expressed in sound, through the extended round of applause (presumably meant to encourage a simi-

lar affective transformation for the audience of the movie). The use of applause here is highly significant; in burlesque theaters applause was one of the most crucial and highly complex means of communication between audience and performers. Indeed, it is possible that Arzner is adding some irony to the redemptive moment here, by having the "transformed" male spectators do essentially what they would be doing at a burlesque show anyway.

Burlesque applause served several signifying purposes. It played a structuring role in the performance, as it ostensibly motivated the removal of items of clothing.[45] It was common for performers to present the strip as a series of encores, leaving the stage after shedding a garment and returning when prompted by the sound of clapping. As Dressler noted, applause was the currency in which a stripper's worth was measured: "since salary is often in direct relation to applause, they [strippers] rather like to strip to the point of arousing the audience . . . "[46] And, as Jeffrey Smith has pointed out, in one notable moment in Rouben Mamoulian's 1930 film *Applause*, the audience's clapping could make the stripper aware of her own sexuality. In a crucial scene in the film, a stripper tells her boyfriend, "You'll never know, Tony, what it feels like to be on the other side of those footlights, to hear them clap and clap for you. It does something to a girl. I don't know what." Smith sees this line as part of the film's construction of a space of feminine sexuality that ruptures the patriarchal ideology of the film's manifest content.[47] Whether or not this was actually the case for "real" performers, the film's emphasis on applause as an expression of the desires of both audience and performers underscores its centrality in the erotics attributed to striptease. Indeed, the idea of the encore was so crucial to the structure of striptease that the trade press referred to striptease as "the encore business."[48] The sonic cue of applause prevented the act from being a continuous, realist performance, making it instead a serial play of false climaxes in which a pretense of coaxed exhibitionism was corroborated by both audience and stripper. However, the raucous, shameless roaring and clapping of the burlesque audience involved a kind of "letting go" that was not always easy to achieve; applause apparently signified a lower class sensibility for one of Dressler's sociological informants, a white, middle-class, college-educated young man. In a detailed account of his reasons for frequenting burlesque theaters and masturbating during the show, this informant signaled his "moral" (read class) difference from the rest of the audience, by noting that "I would not applaud any of the numbers . . . I still, for some reason, react the same way." Not participating in what was a ritual part of the performance was, for this audience member, a way of conveying that he "considered [him]self above the audience."[49] It also created a protective barrier between him and the others in the theater. Applause expressed a fantasy of tactility; it substituted for touching oneself, or another audience member, or the performer. Not to applaud was to avoid symbolic contact with the lower class world of burlesque and its denizens.

The pressures and ignominy of contact and participation that this anonymous spectator fought to resist call attention to the ritual character of applause in striptease. Burlesque applause was unlike applause in other theatrical situations. Clapping in vaudeville or legitimate theater communicated the audience's gratification and acknowledged closure; clapping in burlesque was a way of communicating the audience's *need* for gratification, and an attempt to *deny* closure. The "tease" of the act thus derived its structure as much, if not more, from the audience's *sonic* presence than from its powers of vision—the strip was controlled by the *clap* rather than the gaze. The affective specificity of this applause structure in striptease underscores the idea that pleasure was produced as much through the *frustration* of desire as through its satisfaction. Clapping at a

striptease performer, in other words, expressed a fantasy of lack of control rather than of mastery. It did not support the certainty of masculine vision; rather, it called attention to the inadequacy of this vision.

Aside from clapping, other sonic forms of audience participation included wolf whistles, foot stamping, and—of course—constant exhortations to "take it off." In this third scripted vocal intervention, spectatorial engagement again seems to revolve around a complicated game of thwarted mastery. The performer, while exposed to and pinioned by the eyes of her public, nonetheless controlled the process of meting out glimpses of her sexual organs and breasts. The spectator's voice, in begging the stripper to "show it to me" acknowledged his vision's inability to show it by itself. Given this structure of desire and frustration, we can see striptease as a performance form that constantly dramatizes, through the dissonant pleasures of its sounds and sights, the neediness inherent in the search for sexual gratification. Going to a burlesque theater to watch and participate in a striptease act was both a fantasy of sexual risk and failure, in which the spectator humiliated himself by begging to see more, and an illusory fiction of mastery and control, in which the stripper seemed to obey the shouted orders to "take it off" (but only up to a point that she, the management, and the watchdogs of vice determined). This discrepancy between what was seen and what was heard—or uttered—made the performance into a play on the fear of missing something. It invited spectators to share in the fantasy activities of begging, pleading, and capitulating, to identify, in other words, with a sonic body that challenged, rather than supported, the security of masculine vision.

The Gaze in the Theater

Along with the vocalized body of the audience's thwarted pleasure and desire, other invisible sexual dynamics also countered the idealized one-way visual relationship between audience member and stripper. Rather than the singular stare of the audience member toward the performer, the theatrical context of striptease involved a network of looks in which the visual was not always pleasurable. To begin with, audience members were themselves objects of scrutiny from theater management; during periods of close municipal and civic supervision, theaters adopted extensive surveillance techniques to police audience behaviors. The audience at the Bowery Theater was kept in line "by diligent ex-pugs who paraded up and down the aisles, even cutting off any applause they considered too prolonged." [50] And, when the Star in Brooklyn attempted to clean up its act, a few heckling audience members were arrested as a result of management complaints. Other extreme measures were also implemented at the Star: "When applause for the strippers was too prolonged, or uncalled for comments persisted, a huge flashlight was spread over the entire theater to detect the culprits." [51] It is significant that these attempts to monitor the audience centered on the decibel level and duration of its sonic responses to the spectacle. While municipal supervision was primarily concerned with regulating the visual display of the performer, the managerial surveillance of the burlesque theater attempted to regulate the sonic "display" of the audience. Again, sound apparently held the key to the obscenity and eroticism of the sexual spectacle; it is as if the audience's sonic participation in the performance was too clear a demonstration of its pleasure. [52] For even though this pleasure derived from a thwarted peek and not a gratifying look, it signaled a dialogue with the visible performer and, by extension, a too intimate involvement between her and the audience.

The theater searchlight not only regulated sonic intercourse between audience and performer, it also served an additional supervisory purpose, namely, discouraging masturbation and touching in the audience. Dressler made the hyperbolic claim that in certain theaters, "an entire row of poorly riveted seats will vibrate with the masturbatory movement." [53] But self-love was not the only kind of desire policed within the theater. As George Chauncey has shown, burlesque theaters were crucial sites in the social and sexual geography of gay New York. [54] In this geography, known public sites of "legitimate" desire—from the consumer desire of the department store window to the economized desire of the prostitution district—sheltered the emergence of gay male desire. [55] According to Dressler, burlesque theaters were favored pickup sites; hence the following (characteristically homophobic) description of the audience environment: "Here and there a homosexual will make stealthy advances to a likely neighbor. One will touch the genitals of the other. Another will try to 'date up' a young man through the preliminaries of polite conversation. Here is the abnormality of the burlesque business." [56]

It is impossible to know the extent to which the theatrical text of burlesque accommodated this segment of the audience, although it is clear that gayness and gender bending were often referenced explicitly within an evening's performance. Some theaters employed transvestite men in the chorus, and a stereotypical stock character named "the nance" appeared in numerous sketches. In addition, comics would occasionally appear in bra and panties and parody a striptease number. [57] We can discern a nascent homoeroticism in at least one other aspect of the performance; a stock performer male tenor who would croon love songs from the wings as the stripper performed. Known as the "tit serenader," or "bust developer," this unseen male principal "sang offstage of Mother Machree, and a luscious lady undulated on the stage proper." [58] In this odd voice/body figuration, the gyrations of the female performer would add bawdy meanings to the chaste lyrics carried by the disembodied male voice.

In heterosexual terms, the gender dynamic of

tit serenader and stripper at once confirmed and inverted the power relations of striptease. On the one hand, the tit serenader served as a kind of ventriloquist, a masterful man controlling and orchestrating the bodily display of a voiceless female performer. On the other, the female performer's risqué send-up of the "feminine" sentiments expressed in the songs thwarted the singer's control over her expressiveness. However, this dualism confines the pleasures of striptease to a heterosexual model of desire, whereas the presence of gay audience members suggests a less unitary, triangular circulation of erotic identifications. After all, the tit serenader's effeminate sincerity aligned masculine affect with love and sentiment, opening up a homoerotic relationship between singer and audience. As identification and desire circulated between male voice, female body, and male spectator, the structural possibility for a homoerotic relation between spectator and voice emerged, despite the seemingly straightforward heterosexual nature of striptease.[59]

What we find, finally, in striptease, is less a one-way relationship of viewer to viewed, of male subject to female object, and more a network of such relationships, involving a range of participants switching between, and sometimes acting simultaneously in, each role. Although documentation of the genre's history is rare and ephemeral, it is important that future studies embrace these complexities, seeing striptease as not simply a symptom of larger cultural prejudices, but as a cacophonous arena in which those prejudices both did and undid themselves.

Notes

1 "The Last Legs of Burlesque," *Theatre Magazine* (February 1930): 36–37.

2 John Sumner, secretary of the New York Society for the Prevention of Vice, quoted in "5 Tons of Books Seized in Vice War," *New York Times* (May 6, 1937): 26. Prior to the emergence of striptease, reformers did still challenge burlesque's raciness, but primarily on artistic grounds, arguing that there was no merit in the entertainment other than its salaciousness. For example in 1919, William Burgess, director of the Illinois Vigilance Association, described burlesque shows as "displays of fleshly debauch of semi-nudeness, more repulsively lewd than the naked form can ever be and these are employed chiefly as setting, for sensual song, filthy story, dialogue, or action, all of which it is libel to call 'comedy.'" From *Proceedings of the National Conference of Social Work* (1919): 502–6, reprinted in Lamar T. Beman, ed. *Censorship of the Theater and Moving Pictures* (New York: H. W. Wilson, 1931.) A similar reformist description of burlesque from around this period is quoted in Abel Green and Joe Laurie, Jr., *Show Biz: From Vaude to Video* (New York: Henry Holt, 1951), 76.

3 Indeed, in the previous decade, the bulk of Sumner's anti-vice vitriol was aimed at nudity and immorality on the Broadway stage. See John Sumner, "The Sewer on the Stage," *Theatre Magazine* (December 1923): 9, 78; "Effective Action against Salacious Plays and Magazines," *American City* (November 1925): 523–25. See also "Naked Challenge," *The Nation* (September 5, 1923): 229.

4 David Dressler, "Burlesque as a Cultural Phenomenon," Ph.D. dissertation, New York University, 1937, 64. This dissertation follows a "Chicago School" model of qualitative sociological inquiry, based on six months of field work involving site visits, interviews, and questionnaires. Studies in the Chicago School vein tend to present in-depth descriptions of the norms, values, and beliefs associated with working class and lumpenproletarian social institutions (such as taxi dance halls, numbers rackets, etc.) within a larger urban ecology. Dressler's study indicates a similar concern with the social ecology of the city as in, for example, his detailed catalogue of the role of burlesque theaters within the community life of a neighborhood. Unfortunately, Dressler's overarching goal in such cataloguing was to "prove" that burlesque theaters produced vice; hence his somewhat spurious attempts to connect the presence of burlesque theaters with an elevated number of venereal disease cases, or sex offenses, or prostitution arrests in any particular area. These moralistic conclusions raise the question of whether the study is a useful account of burlesque life. However, in conformity with the Chicago School method, Dressler's study includes several unedited transcripts of interviews and statements (from audience members and performers), and displays, overall, a surprising amount of sympathy and

compassion for participants in the world of burlesque. In this article I draw extensively upon Dressler's dissertation as a primary source, i.e., as a place for basic information and eye-witness accounts, and attempt to avoid reproducing the moralizing attitude that colors the social analysis. Interestingly, Dressler's subsequent publication, *Parole Chief* (New York: Viking, 1951), based on his experiences as executive director of the New York State Division of Parole manages to downplay the moralizing and offers an interesting set of well-rendered character sketches and humorous anecdotes. Dressler later went on to hold a professorship in sociology and social welfare at California State College at Long Beach; he published several books on parole and criminology, most of which were fairly liberal-minded.

5 "Exhibit D, City of New York Department of Licenses," Testimony of inspector Frank J. Donavan; reprinted in Morton Minsky and Milt Machlin, *Minsky's Burlesque: A Fast and Funny Look at America's Bawdiest Era* (New York: Arbor House, 1986), 292–99.

6 For a similar argument on the class politics of anti-obscenity movements, see the chapter on *Hustler* magazine in Laura Kipnis, *Ecstasy Unlimited* (Minneapolis: University of Minnesota Press, 1994).

7 After the City of New York banned runways in the mid–1930s, undeterred theater operators simply relocated the orchestra and added stairs leading from the stage to the orchestra section so that the strippers could still interact with the audience. See Dressler, "Burlesque."

8 Irving Zeidman, *The American Burlesque Show* (New York: Hawthorn, 1967), 110.

9 Interview in James Silke, ed. *Rouben Mamoulian: "Style Is the Man"* (Washington, D.C.: American Film Institute, 1971), 7.

10 "The Business of Burlesque, A.D. 1935," *Fortune* (February 1935): 142.

11 "X," quoted in Dressler, "Burlesque," 190.

12 Ibid., 180.

13 Ibid., 159.

14 Ibid., 73. See also Laurence Bell, "Strip-Tease as a National Art," *American Mercury* (September 1937): 60; "The Last Legs of Burlesque," *American Mercury* (September 1937).

15 Dressler, "Burlesque."

16 See, for example, Roland Barthes, "Striptease," in *Mythologies*, trans. Annette Lavers (New York: Hill and Wang, 1972). Drawing from this essay, feminist film critics have theorized striptease through a close reading of Rita Hayworth's gestural strip in the film *Gilda* (1946;

dir. Charles Vidor). See Mary Anne Doane, "*Gilda*: Epistemology as Striptease," in *Femmes Fatales: Feminism, Film Theory, and Psychoanalysis* (New York, Routledge, 1991), and Kaja Silverman, *The Subject of Semiotics* (New York: Oxford University Press, 1983), 230–31. More recently, Eric Schaefer has complicated the straightforward understanding of striptease as the dramatization of patriarchal visual relations in "The Obscene Seen: Spectacle and Transgression in Postwar Burlesque Films," *Cinema Journal* (winter 1997): 41–66. Drawing upon the work of Judith Butler, Schaeffer proposes that the performative aspects of striptease call attention to the performative character of gender identity. Stripping, Schaeffer contends, is a process of de-gendering in which the discarding of costume is the discarding of cultural cues of femininity: "The degradation of the stripper often alluded to by critics does not occur on a personal level but is instead the degradation of a construction, the feminine, which is valued by the dominant society" (57).

17 For a related critique of the omission of sound in psychoanalytic accounts of the striptease in *Gilda*, see Adrienne McLean, "'It's Only That I Do What I Love and I Love What I Do': *Film Noir* and the Musical Woman," *Cinema Journal* (fall 1993): 3–16.

18 In 1933, the first of many codes for burlesque was established to regulate sexual display. As it turned out, burlesque operators were fairly pleased with the restrictions, which prohibited the removal of clothing except "in immobile tableaux and statuesque presentation with distinctly artistic appeal, provided the vital parts are clad in opaque raiments." As Irving Zeidman notes, the codes were "a boon rather than a ban, for in practice it gave official sanction for the first time to the baring of breasts, whereas the verbiage about removing clothes 'in an indecent manner' added nothing to what was already on the statute books." Operators found ways to add "artistic merit" to strip acts and burlesque continued in much the same vein as before. Prohibitions against movement continued to be enforced throughout the next decade across the country; by 1950, ingenious costumes evolved in which a "bib-like covering" would expose a breast for a split second in between steps of the stripper's dance.

19 Under Moss, the new code for burlesque stipulated that "no female shall be permitted on the stage in any scene, sketch, or act with breasts or the lower part of the torso uncovered." It appears that this code was enforced only selectively, and mainly along a class axis, given the con-

current rash of nude Broadway productions. In this period burlesque was targeted by federal legislation as well. FDR's National Reconstruction Act prohibited encores and enforced the wearing of brassieres. As burlesque performers and management continued to violate obscenity codes, raids became more frequent and licenses harder to renew each year. Finally, in 1937, almost all burlesque theaters in New York were refused licenses, the word "burlesque" was banned as a description of any type of entertainment, and the name "Minsky" was prohibited from appearing on any theater marquee.

20 After the failure of "Vaudesque," stripping's re-emergence in the 52nd Street nightclubs was fairly tolerated, although sporadic raids occurred during the war years. This geographical and venue change for striptease moved it into a sphere of regulation separate from the licensing of theater and closer to the demi-monde of adult entertainment. This move also aligned striptease with jazz, a musical form which was also subject to strict regulation via the cabaret laws. These required musicians to carry cards bearing their fingerprints in order to play live. Striptease thus became detached from the working-class world of burlesque and recoded as part of the margins of middle-class amusement, the place in the habitus of the urban bourgeoisie where pleasures border on the illicit. See "Two of the Minsky's Strike Their Flag," *New York Times* (May 6, 1937): 26; Laurence Bell, "Strip Tease as a National Art" (*American Mercury* (September 1937): 62; Allen Chellas, "It's Still Burlesque, *Holiday* (August 1950): 20; Paul Chevigny, *Gigs: Jazz and the Cabaret Laws in New York City* (New York: Routledge, 1994); Minsky and Machlin, *Minsky's Burlesque*, 138–39; Arnold Shaw, *52nd St.: The Street of Jazz* (New York: Da Capo, 1971), 339; and Zeidman, *The American Burlesque Show*, 225–26.

21 For an excellent discussion of the ways that minoritized groups—in this case gay men—have historically managed to construct a social world within these policed environments, see George Chauncey, *Gay New York: Gender, Urban Culture, and the Making of the Gay Male World, 1890–1940* (New York: Basic Books, 1994).

22 Paul Ross, "Lid Is off Strip-Teasing," *PM* (April 1, 1941): 23; cited in H. L. Mencken, *The American Language, Supplement II* (New York: Knopf, 1948), 694.

23 Robert C. Allen, *Horrible Prettiness: Burlesque and American Culture* (Chapel Hill: University of North Carolina Press, 1991). Allen proposes that burlesque operated through performative excess, resisting containment within a single level of analysis. However, the body of the stripper remains a problem even within this nuanced cultural history. For Allen, the complexity of burlesque is unrelated to striptease. Indeed, in the historical narrative he details, the emergence of the strip act in twentieth-century burlesque marks the beginning of the decline of a vibrant and subversive popular amusement. From then on, the dynamic interaction between female performer and her audience, an interaction charged with her "verbal and physical insubordination" in classical burlesque theater, were gradually replaced by a strict separation of "silent feminine sexual display and verbal, male-dominated humor" when stripping came to dominate the show (271–72). However, Allen continues to emphasize the uneasiness of burlesque's relation to dominant culture, and refuses to see striptease purely as an enactment of patriarchy's voyeuristic and fetishistic mastery games. It is, instead, one of the central elements in "the inescapable cultural and political paradox of burlesque" (284). My historical "resurrection" of the invisible embodiments that striptease made possible foregrounds powerful paradoxes and ambiguities in the erotics of burlesque during the late 1930s, the moment in which Allen locates the death of the form's transgressive potential.

24 This period has, from the 1950s onward, become the object of nostalgia: see histories such as Zeidman's *The American Burlesque Show,* and "revivals" such as former 1930s Minsky stripper Ann Corio's Broadway musical *This Was Burlesque.* Corio co-wrote a history of burlesque to accompany this show: Ann Corio and Joseph DiMona, *This Was Burlesque* (New York: Madison Square Press, 1968).

25 *Newsweek* (June 25, 1962): 60.

26 Ibid.

27 A parallel kind of polymorphous pleasure can be found in Dressler's description of a striptease routine from the 1930s: "She closes her eyes, postures ecstatically and passionately, voluptuously taking the part both of herself and her lover. Her face and body are herself, responding lasciviously to her lover, symbolized by her hands, which caress her sexual parts, her buttocks, her breasts, on top of and beneath her clothing as she sways and quivers hypnotically." Dressler, "Burlesque," 78.

28 Roland Barthes, *Image, Music, Text,* trans. Stephen Heath (London: Flamingo, 1977), 189.

29 As John Corbett has pointed out, Barthes's use of the word "image" in his attempt to discern the workings of the grain of the voice reveals a contradictory form of

audio fetishism, one which seeks both to recover the visual in sound, filling in the discrepancy between visible and invisible forms of pleasure, and at the same time asserting the autonomy of sound through the valorization of the recording as material plenitude. See John Corbett, *Extended Play: Sounding Off from John Cage to Dr. Funkenstein* (Durham, NC: Duke University Press, 1994), 42–44.

30 This multiplicity of identifications is a mode of representation not confined to music, although Peggy Phelan argues that it is prominent in performance and is particularly associated with the female body in representation. See Peggy Phelan, *Unmarked: The Politics of Performance* (New York: Routledge, 1993).

31 Minsky and Machlin, *Minsky's Burlesque*: 81–83. The anecdote is retold in Rowland Barber's *The Night They Raided Minsky's: A Fanciful Expedition to the Lost Atlantis of Show Business* (New York: Simon and Schuster, 1960), 331–2.

32 Dressler, "Burlesque as a Cultural Phenomenon," 70; Zeidman, *American Burlesque Show*.

33 Zeidman, *American Burlesque Show*, 77–78, 228.

34 Corio, *This Was Burlesque*, 76.

35 See Mencken, *The American Language*, 693.

36 Dressler, "Burlesque," 74.

37 A comparable double role of sound in performance would be the hollow "clunk" we hear when the Three Stooges hit each other over the head (and it is hardly coincidental that the Stooges's style owed a great deal to the comedy "bits" that comprised burlesque's comic interludes). Although it is beyond the scope of this paper, it is interesting to note that a similar effect of sound governed much of the live accompaniment in the cinema of the first few decades of the twentieth century. Rick Altman explores this condition of film sound in a paper presented at the Society for Cinema Studies Conference, Syracuse, NY, 1994.

38 Dressler, "Burlesque," 78.

39 Zeidman, *American Burlesque Show*, 117.

40 Ibid., 97–98, 164.

41 Ibid, 177.

42 Dressler, "Burlesque."

43 Zeidman, *American Burlesque Show*.

44 Pam Cook, "Approaching the Work of Dorothy Arzner," in *Feminism and Film Theory*, ed. Constance Penley (New York: Routledge, 1988), 48.

45 Morton Minsky notes that in "clean" burlesque shows, stripper Georgia Sothern would coax applause from the audience as a way of delaying the realization that she was very carefully managing to avoid removing her clothing. See Minsky and Machlin, *Minsky's Burlesque*, 182. In Ann Corio's words, "Georgia stripped and Georgia teased, but that was only a minor part of her act. Her music, 'Hold That Tiger,' was wild, the orchestra played at full blast and full tempo, and Georgia came on stage in full flight. . . . You didn't shout from the audience to Georgia to take it off; there was no time, no cause, and the music was too loud, anyway. You just sat there and watched—and wondered how she could do it." Corio, *This Was Burlesque*, 91–92.

46 Dressler, "Burlesque," 155.

47 Jeffrey Smith, "'It Does Something to a Girl, I Don't Know What': The Problem of Female Sexuality in *Applause*." *Cinema Journal* (winter 1991): 47–60.

48 "The Last Legs of Burlesque," 37.

49 Dressler, "Burlesque," 197.

50 Ibid., 188

51 Ibid., 178.

52 Of course, it is also possible that audience members experienced an exhibitionist thrill from the knowledge that they were being watched.

53 Dressler, "Burlesque," 161.

54 George Chauncey, *Gay New York*, 290–95.

55 According to Minsky, Gypsy Rose Lee once attempted to convey the queer desires of the burlesque audience to her sister, June, by proclaiming: "While they sit there jerking off, I'm the one using *them*. Because there's another audience coming to watch my audience watch me" (Minsky and Machlin, *Minsky's Burlesque*, 141).

56 Dressler, "Burlesque," 161, 204.

57 Zeidman, *American Burlesque Show*, 110, 78–9. Zeidman also notes that female principals would also crossdress from time to time; Mutual Burlesque's Gladys Clark would often appear in a suit and tie during a chorus number and spank the chorus girls with a cane before removing her masculine attire. Dressler saw the inclusion of such moments, and other kinds of nonnormative sexual material, in burlesque comedy as an attempt to create "situations which would appeal to the homosexual, the pederast, the sodomist, the fetichist [*sic*], the sadist, the masochist, the necrophiliac." Dressler, "Burlesque," 77.

58 Zeidman, *American Burlesque Show*, 143; Minsky and Machlin, *Minsky's Burlesque*, 146; Corio, *This Was Burlesque*, 75; Mencken, *The American Language*, 693.

59 There is limited material available for speculation on the relation of the occasional women in the audience to the striptease act in general. Sporadic references to

couples attending burlesque together appear in Dressler's sociological study; more telling, perhaps, is the fact that he employed an anonymous female participant observer to attend a performance and offer her "objective" response to what she saw on stage. Her description is a curious mixture of dispassionate scientism and frank same-sex curiosity:

> There may be some identification by women in audience with teaser. As to excitation, much depends on mood. If craving sex relations or stimulation, would say that woman's gyrations have strong effect, partly homo-sexual in aspect, partly identification with woman . . . Coming as an observer, removed, scientific, has tendency to remove any personal feelings . . . Nevertheless, in retrospect, would say that . . . curiosity re: breasts, removal of brassiere, shapes of breasts, etc. lead[s] to thought identification [sic]." (Dressler, "Burlesque," 83–4)

QUARANTINED! A CASE STUDY OF BOSTON'S COMBAT ZONE

Eric Schaefer and Eithne Johnson

In 1974, Boston received nationwide publicity for officially designating an "adult uses" district in a skid row section of downtown. With its descriptive nickname, the Combat Zone figured prominently in national debates about adult entertainment and pornography. Those debates became especially heated in 1976 following on the January release of *Snuff.* That X-rated sexploitation film was marketed to capitalize on rumors of foreign "snuff" films (in which women were allegedly killed during sex acts), prompting the public to speculate that *Snuff* was the real thing.[1] In April 1976, as the snuff issue began to frame debates on pornography, *Time*'s cover story exploited the controversy, suggesting that an unchecked contagion had swept across the nation. Boston's strategy for dealing with adult entertainment and pornography was described in sensational terms: "Boston lures the licentious—or the curious—to an anything-goes 'combat zone,' and other cities are rushing to find out how to emulate the zone, a device to quarantine the porno plague."[2] Seven months later, on November 16, 1976, two white Harvard football players were stabbed—and one subsequently died of his injuries—as they were leaving the Naked i nightclub in the Zone. Given that the Combat Zone was long known for its rough and rowdy atmosphere, why did this case garner so much attention? We suggest that there was much more at stake than a local tragedy. At the national level, the *Snuff* controversy had linked adult entertainment with murder; at the local level, the Combat Zone "crisis" appeared to prove that there was indeed a direct connection. This rhetorical framework, which positioned adult entertainment as both lethal and contagious, demanded a moral response—locally and nationally—that had implications for individual bodies and on the body politic.

Reacting to the "crisis" in the Combat Zone, statements by police, city officials, and opponents of adult entertainment repeatedly corporealized the Zone as the place "down there." As we will argue, this representation of the Zone illustrates Stallybrass and White's contention that "the axis of the body is transcoded through the axis of the city, and whilst the bodily low is 'forgotten,' the city's low becomes a site of obsessive preoccupation, a preoccupation which is itself intimately conceptualized in terms of discourses of the body." [3] By exploring the discursive linkages among the domains of the body, psychic forms, topography, and social formations, Stallybrass and White seek to explain the excessive attention the bourgeoisie has historically directed at the "*city's* 'low'—the slum, the ragpicker, the prostitute, the sewer—the 'dirt' which is 'down there.'" [4] Not surprisingly, in Boston's Combat Zone, specific bodies—prostitutes, pimps, muggers, gays—especially "black" and female bodies became signifiers for "down there"; they became carriers of the "porno plague" threatening Boston.

This mapping of the city's "low" as a spatialized body already coded as pathological emerged from preexisting discourses—a "discursive domain" in Stallybrass and White's terms. First, we will address the discourse of urban planning and how it came to be applied in Boston. Following on Lewis Mumford's organic model for the city, postwar urban planning initiatives called for curing a "sick" Boston by clearing away its "diseased" areas. The Combat Zone emerged from just such a "low" area, which city officials then designated as the only permitted site for adult entertainment. Second, we will examine popular and moralizing accounts of the Combat Zone. We will argue that the Zone was represented as a hybrid space, a threatening and thrilling urban carnival. Third, we will investigate the official vice war mobilized

in reaction to the football players' stabbing case of November 1976. Much as Simon Cottle argues in his analysis of a racially stigmatized neighborhood in England, Boston journalists reported on the Zone within a "trouble frame," drawing on powerful metaphors of illness and warfare, linking them to bodies already coded for race, sex, and class. In 1976, the Zone came to be regarded as symbolically central to Boston's Imaginary. [5] Stallybrass and White provide a useful definition of this process: "The point is that the exclusion necessary to the formation of the social identity at one level is simultaneously a production at the level of the Imaginary, and a production, what is more, of a complex hybrid fantasy emerging out of the very attempt to demarcate boundaries, to unite and purify the social collectivity." [6] To date, local discourses continue to represent the Combat Zone within the "journalistic 'trouble frame' even when no actual trouble has occurred." [7] Summarizing this case study, we will consider how the combat zone controversy helped (re)stigmatize adult entertainment as it verged on legitimacy. [8]

This local conceptualization of adult entertainment as pathological and dangerous interests us for a number of reasons. It provides an opportunity for us to work together since our specialties overlap at the emergence of hard-core sexual representations in the period from the late sixties into the seventies. Our research into the issues surrounding the designation of the Zone, as an adult district, was aided by Helene Johnson (Eithne's mother), who was active in civic affairs at the time. She designed a report in favor of the liberal zoning law that effectively contained adult entertainment. At present, the Zone, and its representation in public discourses, affects our lives directly. Not only did we live near it (across the Boston Common) when this article was researched and written, but one of us works in the area at Emerson College, which relocated to that end of downtown. Indeed, as Emerson refashions itself as "the College on the Common," it has to wrestle with preconceptions of the Zone that understandably worry students, parents, and alumni. In April 1995, a student commentator offered this sensational description in the campus newspaper: "Everyone has heard horror stories about the Combat Zone. The very name is intimidating. . . . The rumors are mild compared to the reality."[9] Despite the fact that the Zone has shrunk from its heyday—from thirty-nine adult businesses in the area in 1977–78 to five in 2002—it clearly remains a highly stigmatized space. The student essay repeated the journalistic "trouble frame" that has become the standard reporting for the area—conflating the few remaining adult businesses with the street trafficking of prostitutes, drug users, and muggers. By looking at the ways the Zone was represented in the seventies, we will offer a cultural and historical context for this "trouble frame."

The Diseased City

When blight sets in . . . the inhabitants or the owners of buildings can no longer pay their share of municipal taxes; the street-cleaning department tends to overlook the more run-down neighborhoods, where the need for public hygiene is often worst, and even the fire inspectors and sanitary inspectors become lax: the repairs needed to keep blighted properties up to standard would do away with what little profits may remain in the investment, and so, by indifference or collusion or bribery, the city officials permit the blight to deepen.
—Lewis Mumford, *The Culture of Cities*

During the postwar years, the American city was increasingly conceived of as a "sick" place. Lewis Mumford's influential book, *The Culture of Cities* (1938), had promulgated an organic model for thinking about urban space: "To maintain its life-shape the organism must constantly renew itself by entering into active relations with the rest of the environment."[10] To fight the "uglification" of American cities drastic measures would be needed. As Mumford had put it, "the failure to act

and re-act means either the temporary suspension of life or its final end."[11] In their 1966 book, *Boston: The Job Ahead,* Martin Meyerson and Edward C. Banfield summed up the general consensus on the urban condition: "The American city—so we are told from every side—is in a state of crisis. Its residential neighborhoods are blighted, its streets congested, its economy moribund, its services deficient, and its government ineffective. The 'urban crisis' will soon, it is said, produce an urban catastrophe."[12] While cities were "withering," drained of people and businesses in a gradual process of "decay," the suburbs appeared to flourish. Titles of articles from specialized and popular magazines of the period reveal the sentiments of many urbanists, journalists, as well as the general public: "Prescription for the Ideal City"; "Does Your City Suffer from Suburbanitis?"; "Flight to the Suburbs"; "Blight on the Land of Sunshine"; and "Rx for Tired Town." "Crisis," "blight," "flight," a lack of "life" called for a response in the form of "prescriptions" and "cures." This organic model inscribed a body on the cityscape. Here we will examine the official transcoding of bodies and space in downtown Boston. In the postwar period, local officials sought to reinvigorate the "sick" corpus by cutting out its symbolic "low"—that is, the slum in the urban core—and replacing it with a new symbolic head in the form of a monumental City Hall Plaza.

Although "blight" affected all northern industrial cities, Boston seemed to have been hit particularly hard. Once known as the "hub of the universe," it had suffered the collapse of the textile industry, a decline in commercial fishing, and its diminution as a banking center, making Boston a prime target for planning initiatives and federal policies that called for the removal of blighted areas—often low-income housing—in favor of large tax-producing developments. "Urban renewal" became the nostrum for sick cities. The 1950 *Plan for Boston* developed by Boston's Planning Board called for redeveloping 20 percent

All but a few of the adult businesses in Combat Zone have closed, yet it remains a highly stigmatized space. Photo by Eric Schaefer.

of the city's land over a twenty-five year period.[13] In 1957, the Boston Redevelopment Authority (BRA) was established as a "semi-autonomous, five-member board, with four members appointed by the mayor and one by the state."[14] The BRA promptly embarked on redevelopment projects in the West End and in the New York Streets areas. In both instances multiracial and multiethnic neighborhoods were bulldozed as a means of clearing "slums." In the West End, thousands of low-income households were replaced by the luxury apartment buildings of Charles River Park; light industrial and commercial buildings went up in the New York Streets section of town. Residents were displaced by the projects quickly and cruelly. Boston's redevelopment during this period—particularly the clearance of the West End—was the subject of national controversy.[15] Local critics attacked Charles River Park as sterile and character-

less and blamed the city administration for giving the developer a sweetheart deal. In contrast, relatively little protest occurred when the city, backed with millions of federal dollars, bulldozed Scollay Square for the new City Hall and Government Center.

At the center of a tangle of narrow streets, Scollay Square had served residents, visitors, and servicemen as a marketplace of cheap diversions since the mid-1850s.[16] A popular haunt for sailors from nearby Charlestown Navy Yard, Scollay Square bustled with activity, especially during World War II. Round-the-clock movie theaters and vaudeville houses stood next to bars, shooting galleries, arcades, bookstores, and joke shops. Hotel dining rooms and coffee shops offered steak and lobster, while Joe & Nemo's purveyed hot dogs and coffee. Photo galleries took snapshots of locals and sold stills of striptease queens; tattoo parlors provided permanent souvenirs from Boston. The Square's most infamous product was adult entertainment. Not only were strippers popular at burlesque palaces such as the Casino and Old Howard, but also Sally Keith—"Queen of the Tassels"—was famous for her nightclub act at the Crawford House. Although women were welcome at these shows and specials were offered to attract them, local lore focused on the cadre of "bald-headed men," Harvard professors, and college students who frequented these places. Indeed, these venues followed in the nineteenth-century trend toward sexually explicit entertainments for men. According to Kathy Peiss, the nineteenth-century music hall "was closely tied to the male subculture of public amusements," and it attracted "a heterogeneous male clientele of laborers, soldiers, sailors, and 'slumming' society gentlemen."[17] Although men and women of "polite society" were known to enjoy the Scollay Square entertainments, public and official discourse increasingly disdained them; for example, the Old Howard came to be seen as "a sink of sin" and "a social cancer."[18]

By the 1960s, Scollay Square had lost its vitality

as an entertainment center. City censors had closed the Old Howard in 1953. However, the Square still provided shelter and shopping for working-class people as well as transients who could shack up for the night in one of its many flophouses. Edward J. Logue, head of the BRA, described the area as "a rundown and notorious skid row."[19] The Old Howard burned to the ground on June 20, 1961, and, by Labor Day, the city began claiming the land by eminent domain. Demolition of the area started in February 1962.[20] In a short time the razing of the "mean-spirited, sour, brutish, and nasty" district was complete, and the new City Hall, state and federal buildings, and private office complexes were underway. The "cancerous" Scollay Square was cut out and paved over in an effort to realize "the New Boston."[21]

According to Larry Ford, the typical development in North American downtowns results in a "dumbbell" pattern with a "zone of assimilation" along a "retail spine" that connects a newer central business district at one end with an older skid-row area—"zone of discard"—at the other end.[22] At one end of Boston's "retail spine," Washington Street, stands the city's modern central business/government district, including the Quincy Market retail complex, City Hall Plaza and, nearby, Bulfinch's State House with its golden dome. Following Stallybrass and White's thesis that "thinking the body is thinking social topography," this cluster of official buildings can be conceptualized as the symbolic "head" of the city. From there, Washington Street winds through the shopping district to the section designated as lower Washington Street, where the Combat Zone emerged. That name, "lower Washington Street," took on value in the city's Imaginary as the place "down there" once adult entertainments began to accumulate in the area in the early sixties. In this way, official and popular discourses created symbolic distance between high and low areas that were geographically close. This discursive purification of the body politic located pathology in the city's "lower" regions,

away from its monumental power base. (As we will argue in the third section, this process of official purification intensified during the Combat Zone "crisis" of 1976.)

Most of the adult businesses that opened on lower Washington Street were new, rather than displaced Scollay Square enterprises.[23] The area was home to the majority of the city's aging movie palaces, and by 1962 the 1,500-seat Pilgrim Theater was showing "adults only" films—primarily nudie-cutie and nudist pictures. At least two newsstands or bookstores were selling adult magazines.[24] At some point in the 1960s, lower Washington Street and several side streets, including LaGrange and Essex, came to be known as the "Combat Zone." This moniker was apparently inspired by the presence of rambunctious youth and servicemen who were notorious for their brawls in and around the area.[25] More adult bookstores were established as the decade advanced. The Combat Zone began to attract more notice, and adult businesses were targeted as evidence for the decline of the area, even though it had already been a skid row. In 1969, Theodore Glynn Jr., the assistant district attorney for Suffolk County, asserted that adult businesses served as a magnet for the abnormal: "The people who sell this stuff are preying upon a very sick element of our society.... It's garbage and trash. They are real purveyors of filth."[26] By 1970, ten "adults only" bookstores were clustered in the area along with nine bars that featured adult entertainment, usually in the form of strip dancing.[27] The New Boston's Combat Zone had replaced Old Boston's Scollay Square as a "zone of discard" or "dangerous movement zone."[28] Moreover, the term "Combat Zone" came to be used for several areas in the city that were considered blighted, until the lower Washington Street area was officially zoned as the city's only permitted adult uses district.[29]

The Combat Zone was bounded by the edges of other geographically distinct areas including the downtown shopping district to the north, the

legitimate theater district to the south, the garment district and a growing Chinatown to the
east, and the Park Square skid row to the west. In
addition to adult businesses, the Combat Zone
and Park Square included other mixed-use buildings, including single-room-occupancy hotels
(SROs) for transients, retired merchant marines,
and working-class men.[30] However, such residents
were largely overlooked in urban renewal plans.
As Larry Ford points out, "From the 1920s
through the 1960s, city plans and policies aimed at
eliminating the blight of single-room-occupancy
hotels."[31] In Boston, proposals to renovate Park
Square had been floated since 1960 and later called
for elimination of the adjacent Zone. In the late
1960s, the BRA put forward a two-phase redevelopment plan dubbed the Park Plaza. Phase I called
for the clearance of several blocks around Park
Square and the construction of new hotels, apartments, office buildings, shops, and entertainment
sites. Phase II entailed demolishing the Combat
Zone to make way for luxury apartments, a parking garage, and other facilities.[32] Both plans met
with opposition as well as a lack of federal funding.[33] In June 1973, the Park Plaza Civic Advisory
Committee (CAC), a local group formed to give
citizens a voice to the BRA on the Park Plaza plan,
concluded "the BRA proposal for Phase II was neither convincing nor practical."[34] Experience from
the destruction of Scollay Square had convinced
many in the neighboring communities that clearing the Combat Zone would only scatter adult
businesses to other parts of the city.[35]

Back Bay Association representative and newspaper columnist Dan Ahern had argued in 1972
that the city had to take over six blighted areas, including the Combat Zone: "Action must be taken
to fence in and civilize these areas [including
lower Washington Street]. . . . Each district should
be geographically restricted. . . . There is a tendency for all of these areas to sprawl and spread
into adjacent neighborhoods."[36] Fear of blight
and contagion—linked to "dirty streets, dirty

The Combat Zone was quarantined off from the rest
of downtown Boston as illustrated in this city planning document, "Boston's Adult Entertainment District," from January 1976. Courtesy of Boston Redevelopment Authority.

movies"—prompted neighborhood groups and
business alliances to advocate a containment strategy for adult businesses, urging the city to clean itself up, in particular for "middle class adults."[37]
As David Sibley notes in Geographies of Exclusion,
"The fear of infection leads to the erection of barricades to resist the spread of diseased, polluted
others. The idea of a disease spreading from a
'deviant' or racialized minority to threaten the
'normal' majority with infection has particular
power."[38] In April 1974, the BRA and the Park
Plaza CAC's Subcommittee on the Entertainment
District released an interim report on the issue.
This Entertainment District Study concluded,
"that a special Adult Entertainment Zone be created in the Lower Washington Street area between
Essex and Kneeland Streets. Containing a majority of the adult entertainment facilities for the entire city in this compact area would facilitate the
policing of such activities and would avoid their
spread to other areas of the city where they create

incompatibilities with neighboring land uses or inhibit needed real estate investments."[39] Zoning could be used to inscribe a "little island" around an "E" district for "adult uses"—to preserve the "health" of the downtown and to prevent the proliferation of such businesses into respectable residential districts.[40]

At Boston Zoning Commission hearings in September 1974, BRA Director Robert T. Kenney stated, "The spread of [adult entertainment] creates a blighting effect. We think it is time to face the issue and try to contain it."[41] Neighborhood groups from Back Bay, Beacon Hill, and Chinatown tended to support the move, while representatives of businesses and institutions that abutted the area, such as the Sack Theater chain and the Tufts New England Medical Center, opposed the new zoning. Without any evidence to back up the claim, George McLaughlin Sr., lawyer for the Sack chain, sinisterly opined that "no one's life is respected [in the Zone] and death is the all too common reward for one who resists assaults."[42] The Medical Center representative expressed concern for employees walking through the district, but acknowledged, "Our main concern is not the morality issues. We understand why people in other parts of the city prefer to keep undesirables out of their areas and in ours."[43] Two months later the Zoning Commission approved the measure as an amendment to the existing zoning code.[44]

The BRA's director of public information claimed, "We believe it is the first time an American city has zoned to allow adult entertainment in one specific part of the city."[45] Boston's experimental therapy for treating the hard-core "epidemic" was considered liberal and risky in comparison to the dispersal strategies practiced by most cities that prohibited the clustering of such businesses; however, city officials were well aware that the Zone served as a profitable attraction.[46] Journalists emphasized that the city's rationale "for this quarantine was pragmatic rather than

moral.[47] Even so, this zoning strategy was guided by moral assumptions about the nature of adult entertainment and its patrons. For instance, the BRA warned that the businesses it was sanctioning in the district were "often associated with a high incidence of illegal activity" without addressing the fact that such activities had already been permitted to flourish in that skid row.[48] To ensure that the Zone remained a space apart, the city allowed moving signs and flashing lights, signage considered as evidence of blight and forbidden elsewhere by the city's restrictive codes. These gaudy adornments gave the area, as one BRA document asserted, "a distinct character appropriate to its use."[49] At the same time, they signified a contaminated space, drawing those that sought it out while warning others who wanted to stay away.

By officially designating the Combat Zone as a unique district and encouraging architecture and signage that signified blight, Boston officials effectively laid the foundation for the area as a site of crisis, arising from congestion, neglect, and an "anything goes" atmosphere. In March 1976, the Park Plaza CAC issued a report charging that the "flamboyant scheme to preserve the Combat Zone" was implemented at the expense of the theater district, "a depressing bombed-out scene," suffering from the city's continued neglect of the whole area.[50] According to evidence offered by Zone establishments, the city neglected regular street lighting, arbitrarily issued safety and fire code violations, and ineffectually policed illegal street activities. Debra Beckerman, spokesperson for Zone businesses, claimed that they had requested "additional police protection between 1 and 4 A.M.," to no avail.[51] The manager of the Naked i nightclub illustrated the way the Zone was treated compared with other areas of the city: "If someone passed out drunk in the Prudential Center [an upscale development], someone would have him removed. Here they're just left to lie."[52] Even garbage pickup was neglected. In the city's Imaginary, the Zone's literal trash merged symbolically with its figurative trash—the polluting presence of adult entertainment. By setting up a quarantine "down there" on lower Washington Street, the city attempted to purify its official body. Yet, the Zone was understood to be a space with a threateningly perverse mix of pleasure and commerce.

Combat Zone as Carnival

Except for the Back Bay, Boston's streets are routinely narrow and twisted. Washington Street where it descends into the Combat Zone is notably so. Cars cruised slowly by. Often they were filled with young men drinking beer from the bottle and yelling out the window at women. Sailors from other countries, women in suggestive clothes, men in stretch fabric suits and miracle fabric raincoats with epaulets and belts, an elderly Oriental man moving through on his way to Chinatown, seeming oblivious of the crudely packaged lust about him. Winos shuffled about down here, too, and kids wearing black warm-up jackets with yellow leather sleeves that said Norfolk County Champs 80–81 in the center of a large yellow football on the left front.
—Robert B. Parker, *Ceremony*

Much like Robert B. Parker's novel, *Ceremony*, popular accounts of the Combat Zone typically featured a cast of characters that included leering college boys, seedy "B" girls and saucy prostitutes, flashy pimps, winos, wayward husbands, co-ed strippers, muggers, shady operators, conventioneers, frightened pedestrians, and hard-bitten cops. While no doubt "real" in certain respects, these characterizations must also be understood as representations—that is, as the "combat zone" of the city's Imaginary. Robert Campbell, the *Boston Globe*'s architecture columnist, pointedly observed: "There's a kind of theater of violence in the Zone—pimps lolling on street corners, knives and boots and green berets for sale in what used to be Army-Navy stores—but it's not the real thing. Perhaps we descendants of the Watch and Ward

[Society] need to believe that sin is seedy and violent, so the Zone merchants play it that way."[53] Regarding the historical distrust of popular sites, Stallybrass and White observe that "the fair had to be split into two opposed parts: in so far as it could be thought of as low, dirty, extraterritorial, it could be demonized (and in time idealized) as the locus of vagabond desires. In so far as it was economically useful, it could be seen as part of what Norbert Elias has called 'the civilizing process.'"[54] Much like the fair and the carnival, the Combat Zone was split in local representations as a hybrid space in which proper commerce was mixed up with "dirty" transactions. Even as the Zone was represented by most (even those who worked there or frequented it) as morally problematic and dirty, it was also seen as economically viable, pumping money into the city by attracting suburbanites and conventioneers. In this "world upside down," the powerful Congressman Wilbur Mills could become an alcoholic buffoon, discredited by his association with stripper-dancer Fanne Foxe, while Foxe could shine for a while as a highly paid, nationally recognized celebrity.[55] In the subsections below, we examine the characters who dominated this urban sideshow as they were represented in popular accounts, especially drawing on newspaper reports from November 1976. What resulted were ambiguous, hybrid characterizations. On the one hand, they served to differentiate legitimate, if morally dubious, capitalist enterprises from what were vilified as parasitic, criminal, and illegitimate trafficking. On the other hand, they perpetuated a logic of contamination in which clear distinctions could collapse—between entrepreneurs and criminals, between patrons and johns (straight and gay), between entertainers and prostitutes.

ENTREPRENEURS/CRIMINALS

Like the carnival, the Combat Zone was represented as a heterogeneous, chaotic "commercial convergence," through which money was ex-

The Combat Zone was characterized as "an urban sideshow" that
was populated with "transients"
who had been kicked out of other
areas and suburbanites and conventioneers who would stop briefly
to patronize the adult businesses.
Courtesy of *The Boston Herald*.

changed for a variety of entertainments and services.[56] Ordinarily, cities encourage business ventures that attract paying customers and increase
tax revenues. However, Boston was ambivalent
about the money generated by adult businesses,
since such goods were illegal elsewhere in the city
due to the zoning mechanism. In effect, the Zone
was a commercial ghetto, a marketplace for adult
entertainments that, because of their ambiguous
constitutional status, were legally available, yet potentially subject to prosecution. Owners and operators were dubiously depicted, even as they behaved like legitimate entrepreneurs—organizing
a trade association, hiring a spokesperson, and
lobbying for city services. Since so many similar
enterprises were concentrated in a small area, they
were motivated to raise the stakes for thrill-seeking consumers—the harder the core, the dirtier
the dance, the greater the opportunity for profits.
Despite doing the "right" things as businesses, this
capitalistic impulse was seen as morally questionable because it catered to what were perceived as
base instincts. This ambivalence about the products was inscribed on the bodies of the sellers
through popular and official accounts. In turn

they cultivated their liminal status in the "low"
Zone, even as they resisted their representation as
criminals.

In newspaper accounts, allegations about "organized crime" in the Zone served to give the stories a well-known "trouble frame." Historically,
many forms of adult entertainment had been illegal, but they had been incrementally granted a
provisional legitimacy, which continued to be
tested in the courts. Blurring the distinction between legal and illegal capitalist activities, local
newspaper accounts continued to insinuate allegations of criminality. Reports frequently referred
to rumored "twice-weekly tribute" payments to
mobsters.[57] That some of the operators and employees of Zone establishments had police records
was used as evidence to condemn them all. According to Marvin Finkelstein's study published in
the *Technical Report of The Commission on Obscenity and Pornography*, vol. v (1970), a sample of
sixty-three bookstore operators and employees
was divided between those who had police records
(excluding obscenity violations which were
viewed as hazards of the trade) and those who
could not be classified as "criminal types."[58]

Finkelstein argued that "there [was] no necessary correlation between individual or collective criminality and 'organized crime'"; furthermore, he noted that no case had been "fully adjudicated" nor were Boston police able to bring forth any incriminating evidence.[59]

According to newspaper stories, police sources supported the idea that "organized crime" was the sinister power behind adult entertainment.[60] Finkelstein observed that police speculated that some Zone operators were connected with the Mafia, in part because some adult materials were distributed and/or produced by an outfit in Providence, Rhode Island, an area with a reputation for harboring mobsters.[61] Yet such statements by the police appeared to be based solely on personal perception, rumor, or evidence that was, at best, circumstantial, such as Providence's role as a distribution center. As reported in Boston newspapers, police called on the perceived threat of "organized crime" and "illegal activities" on downtown streets to justify frequent charges against Zone businesses on all sorts of violations, from obscenity to poor lighting.[62] By depicting Zone operators as criminal and negligent, officials attempted to stigmatize them. Moreover, since the Zone was deprived of city services, street criminals concentrated there—muggers, pickpockets, pushers, and prostitutes—known in the *Herald American* as "'freelance' predators."[63] Thus, adult entertainment was further stigmatized, and the adult district remained a "dangerous movement zone," visibly marked not only by glaring signage and blighted buildings, but also by the transient types routinely chased out of other neighborhoods.

For their part, Zone operators charged that they were harassed when it was good for police publicity.[64] Not surprisingly, some operators attempted to remain anonymous. In those cases, news accounts intimated that "hidden" or "undisclosed" ownership of Zone businesses was an indication of "organized crime" involvement, over-looking the possibility that the fear of public stigma itself may have encouraged some owners to remain invisible.[65] Other owners may have preferred anonymity to ensure privacy for themselves and their gay customers; among the eight adult bookstore owners personally interviewed by Finkelstein, three were "admitted homosexuals."[66] Making the best—or worst—of their liminal status following the 1976 crisis when the Harvard football players were stabbed, sixty Zone operators established an alliance they called "BAD" for Boston Adult District.[67] Surely, no business alliance would choose such an acronym if it feared losing customers during a controversial period. However, this "bad" attitude also fed into the rumors that Zone businesses were associated with "organized crime." Whether or not such allegations were based in real relations of production, they may have served a variety of capitalistic interests: an enterprise with little regulation and "low" social standing may have attracted certain entrepreneurs, including seasoned criminals; stigmatizing rumors of criminal and deviant types in the adult business may have functioned to keep away all but the most adventurous, preserving the bulk of the profits for the select few.[68]

PATRONS/JOHNS/QUEERS

Recalling descriptions of burlesque patrons in Scollay Square, Combat Zone patrons were typically described as a mix of men across class and social lines. Parker's *Ceremony* (1982), one of his popular novels about Boston private eye Spenser, colorfully illustrated the Zone's attractions for men:

> Time stood still in the Combat Zone. You could see a dirty movie or a quarter peep show at most hours of the day or night. You could purchase a skin magazine specialized in almost every peculiarity. You could get a drink. Fellatio. Pizza by the slice, adult novelty items. Everything necessary to sustain the human spirit. The neon lights and oversized flash-

ing bulbs and crudely drawn signs that advertised all of this and much more (*All Live Acts! Nude College Girls!*) were plastered onto old commercial buildings, some of them once elegant in the red brick and brownstone that Boston had been built in. Above the one-story glitz of the Combat Zone the ornamental arched windows and intricate rooflines of the old buildings were as incongruous as a nun at a stag film.[69]

Parker's passage stereotypically inscribes gender and sex into the Zone's cityscape: the proverbially fallen woman is written into the contrast between the "once elegant" ornamentation and the seductive "glitz," beckoning the male visitor. With its mobile gaze and sophisticated appreciation for this urban arcade, Parker's prose not only draws on the traditional address of hardboiled detective fiction but also invokes that much discussed literary figure, the "flaneur." According to Elizabeth Wilson, this particular bourgeois subjectivity inscribes an "essentially male consciousness. Sexual unease and the pursuit of sexuality outside the constraints of the family [is] one of its major preoccupations."[70]

Not surprisingly, press accounts of the Combat Zone wrestled with the issue of sexual contact between male and female bodies. In this way, the Zone was seen to follow in—and was called on to perpetuate—the tradition of a separate sphere for adult male entertainments. Zone patrons were comically hailed as thrill-seeking men, among them suburbanites, conventioneers, professors, and inexperienced college students. Detailing a 1976 tour of the area with two plainclothes detectives, Eleanor Roberts provided this description for the *Herald:* "A DISTINGUISHED GRAY-HAIRED MAN TAMPED DOWN THE TOBACCO IN HIS PIPE, PUFFED ON IT—and never took his eyes off the performer. Hollywood might have cast him as a judge or a stockbroker. There were a couple of florid-faced, bald types and a handsome dark-haired young man with a neatly-clipped mustache who could have been taken for a young

lawyer or businessman."[71] Roberts's rhetoric recalled the cast of characters—particularly the "bald-headed men"—typically associated with the Old Howard in Scollay Square. Due to the Zone's sexually permissive environment, newspaper stories hinted or charged that otherwise respectable, married men might be inclined to take up with prostitutes. Lt. Det. Anthony J. DiNatale provided this characterization for Roberts's provocative article: "Men from truck drivers to college professors frequent [the Zone]. And that includes the husband who comes in town for Christmas shopping with his wife, but spends his time watching erotic dancers or porno films and then goes off with a hooker."[72] Thus, sexual contact was presumed to follow exposure to sexual entertainments as if they were contaminants. Following this logic of contamination, any man might be converted into a john.

If this temporary transformation could be excused for unattached men, particularly college students, it could not be so easily tolerated for others because of the potential negative impact on home and family life. Moreover, in this homosocial environment, men might be presumed to engage in sex acts with men, even men dressed like women, as with gay drag show performers and prostitutes. *Herald* columnist and Back Bay business representative Dan Ahern urged law enforcers to end the "chauvinism" that allowed male prostitution to continue without punishment, especially in residential neighborhoods adjacent to the Zone.[73] Based on her tour, Roberts's article provided the most sinister mix of porn, pimps, and gays. Of the "tacky, tarnished" Carnival—a gay bar—she wrote: "It was a dismal scene. Seedily-dressed men drooping on stools over drinks, trying to pick up other homosexuals." Sounding the alarm for the heterosexual family, Roberts described a "three-year-old [girl] perched on a stool at the bar with her lesbian mother and a friend," who watched as "two homosexuals kissed, embraced and whispered terms of endearment."[74]

Demonizing both gay sex and lesbian mothers, Roberts focused on sexuality—and its presumed potential to contaminate public space—rather than on the sociality of these environments. Accounts like this opened up the gay bar scene to official scrutiny, jeopardizing one of the few public spaces in Boston for gays and lesbians to meet openly. As Elizabeth Wilson observes regarding the experience of gays and lesbians in cities: "Urban life provided the space in which subcultures could flourish and create their own identities, yet the more visible they became, the more vulnerable that made them to surveillance and containment."[75] That Boston's Combat Zone could be perceived as a transgressively queer space was a convenient threat bandied about by adult entertainment opponents. From the mid-seventies to the early eighties, as City Councilor Raymond Flynn launched his successful bid for mayor of Boston, he promoted a concerted effort to drive out all sex businesses. The Zone was vilified as "a notorious gathering place of homosexuals."[76] Taking the contamination theory of sex exposure to its logical extreme, not only might patrons of adult entertainment become johns, but also they could become truly queer, shaking the city by dismantling its foundation in the bourgeois family.

ENTERTAINERS/PROSTITUTES

Eleanor Roberts's tour implied that the Combat Zone was too dangerous for any respectable woman to visit without official male chaperones. Other accounts also implied that any woman entering the Zone might be taken for an entertainer or prostitute, even those who had to pass through the area on their way to shops, offices, or the nearby medical center. In *The Sphinx in the City,* Elizabeth Wilson observes that both flaneurs and city planners have long feared that any woman might be mistaken for a streetwalker, especially in disreputable areas. According to Wilson, this problem for women stems in part from the fact that "there is no identity without visibility, and the

city spectacle encourages self-definition in its most theatrical forms."[77] Comparing the Combat Zone to a carnival, *Globe* reporter Robert Campbell described it thus, "Architecture and schlock, mystery and a little sin, plus a lot of theatrics."[78] In the Zone, entertainers and prostitutes, who also make theatrical self-display their business, were thrown together in a very tight space. Like historical characterizations of popular entertainers, from nineteenth-century ballerinas to twentieth-century burlesque dancers, local accounts of women working in the Zone tended to collapse the boundary between displaying the female body for pay and providing sexual contact for pay.

Like the Zone's spectacular signage, women working in the area were described as deliberately drawing attention to themselves. In *Ceremony,* Parker provided this dramatic description of Zone prostitutes, as seen by Spenser: "They both wore blond wigs. They both had on slit skirt evening gowns with sequins and cleavage. The white girl wore open-toed sling-back high heels. The black girl had on boots."[79] Spenser's investigative gaze was conveniently unobstructed because they were both wearing "transparent plastic raincoats." Not only were flamboyant prostitutes a staple in local press coverage of the Zone, but also the college student/stripper was frequently mentioned.[80] The "totally nude college girl revue" was a big draw at Zone clubs. Area advertising exploited the sensational and stereotypical concept of the seemingly respectable "co-ed" who stripped for fun. To distinguish between stripping and prostitution, news accounts emphasized that the "real" students were usually drawn to the work to pay tuition or earn money for more respectable goals.

Regardless of their status, women working in the Zone were suspected of criminal intent, much like the owners of adult businesses. News stories took special interest in scams and tricks that might befall thrill-seeking male patrons, especially where women's bodies were displayed. A *Herald* story noted a typical ploy involving women: "Money can go fast inside a drinking spot. As the nude dancers weave what is intended to be an exotic spell, the bar girls go into action. They ask for a drink that can cost $6, and a 'gero bomb' (Jeroboam—large bottle of champagne) can go for up to $500 if the man is a 'real sucker,' undercover investigators report."[81] Although prostitution was never legal in the Zone, the "anything goes" atmosphere and sluggish enforcement of existing laws allowed it to occur. In news stories, distinctions between "good" and "bad" prostitutes emerged. Good prostitutes were those who provided their services for a set price and moved on to the next trick without attracting too much attention. Bad ones might use the job as a ruse to steal money without servicing patrons. Debra Beckerman, the spokesperson for Zone businesses who also danced in clubs, described such women as "pseudo prostitutes [and] robber barons."[82] As she explained in news accounts, these "robber barons" were female muggers disguised as prostitutes who duped prospective johns and deprived good prostitutes of opportunities to work. In the Combat Zone, everyone was suspected of having a duplicitous, hybrid nature, and nothing was ever quite what it appeared to be. In the city's Imaginary, the Zone was mapped as a stereotypically sexualized body, impure yet desirable.

Combat Zone as Theater of War

Although the Combat Zone was characterized as a blighted place populated by an unsavory lot, violent crime in the Zone received little attention prior to November 1976. Indeed, one police spokesman claimed early that year that crime in the area "hasn't changed much. It's still a haunt for purse-snatchers and pickpockets, but crimes such as murder and auto theft are much lower than in other parts of Boston."[83] One reason crime was seldom noted may have been dictated, in part, by the profile of typical victims in the downtown area. In October 1976, *Boston Globe* reporter Jerry Taylor provided the following victim

profile drawn from a local survey: twice as many males as females, predominantly teenagers and young adults, from low-income, nontraditional families.[84] Quoting expert opinion that "most robberies and assaults are intraracial," Taylor added that the local survey indicated blacks and whites suffered victimization equally. Thus, poor, especially male, youth were depicted as most in danger of being robbed and/or assaulted and most likely by their peers. Such cases were not considered especially newsworthy. The events of November 16, 1976, challenged this victim profile. Indeed, the journalistic "trouble frame" for representing the Zone could now map it as a theater of war in which power relations (regarding race, sex, and class) were dangerously inverted—predatory prostitutes and transient black men were seen to prey on privileged white men.

Following an annual celebration at the Harvard Club, several Harvard football players went to the Zone's Naked i nightclub. This outing came to a violent end in the early morning hours. Newspaper articles on the case invariably described how, after leaving the club, the athletes attempted to retrieve a wallet allegedly stolen by one of two or three black prostitutes they rebuffed as they prepared to leave the Zone. As typically reported, several black men—accounts ranged widely from six to ten—came to the aid of the prostitute by attacking the players, stabbing Thomas Lincoln and Andrew Puopolo. News accounts hailed the heroic patrolmen who transported the wounded Puopolo to the hospital instead of following regulations and waiting for emergency medical technicians.

The swift response to the stabbing was coincidentally determined by an increased police presence following the release of an internal report on November 8 by outgoing Commissioner Robert DiGrazia. The report charged the Boston Police Department with corruption and laxity—particularly District 1, which included the Combat Zone. Subsequently, the new commissioner vowed to improve the force. As described by Richard Steele and Richard Manning for *Newsweek,* on

When this photo appeared in *The Boston Herald* in November 1976, following the stabbing of two Harvard football players in downtown Boston, it was captioned, "More police in evidence on Washington St. in the heart of the Combat Zone, now reportedly being 'squeezed' by organized crime." Courtesy of *The Boston Herald*.

November 15, "the police reacted to the report with a massive show of force, assigning the 25-man vice-control unit to 'saturation' duty in the area and hauling off prostitutes to jail by the dozens."[85] Thus, an unusually large number of police were on the streets, and the "atmosphere in the zone grew increasingly ugly" (35). The *Globe's* first story on the football players case observed that "the stabbings coincided with the first night that a substantial increase in patrolmen was ordered for the Combat Zone by new police commissioner Joseph Jordan."[86] Their rescue effort and concern for Puopolo's condition diverted attention away from the charges against the police force. The Harvard athlete never regained consciousness and died several weeks later. During those intervening weeks, press and public scrutiny was focused on the Zone and the adult entertainment it contained.

Building on the "trouble frame," press coverage quickly exploited metaphors of illness and warfare. For instance, the first report on Puopolo from the *Boston Evening Globe* was titled "Quick Action by Doctors, Police Saved Puopolo." The story's lead sentence stated, "Because of its proximity to the Combat Zone and South End, Tufts-New England Medical Center gets plenty of opportunity to practice what one of its surgeons calls 'combat medicine,' not unlike the Medevac-style medicine of Vietnam."[87] When the story was reprinted verbatim in the next day's morning edition, it became "Tufts New England Saves an Athlete's Life with Its Combat Medicine." If once the Combat Zone earned its name for the off-duty military men it attracted, now it could clearly be associated with the horrors of the battlefield itself. The war on vice was subsequently waged in and around the Zone to prevent contamination from this area, which was variously identified as a "sewer," a "cesspool," and, by City Councilor Raymond Flynn, as a "terminal cancer zone."[88] On the meaning of military terms to represent illness, Susan Sontag writes, "To describe a phenomenon as a cancer is an incitement to violence."[89] People who called for the elimination of the district ominously hinted that violence and vice presented a kind of unwinnable urban war so long as the Zone was officially sanctioned for adult entertainment. According to critics, this quarantine was now seen as irresponsibly liberal and ineffective in protecting the city from contamination. What was to have been "a little bit of Copenhagen" was becoming a whole lot of trouble.[90]

After the football players were stabbed, the marginal people associated with the Zone suddenly became larger than life in the popular Imaginary; alarmist reports suggested a forcible invasion of the city. Newspaper accounts dramatically rendered the events of November 16 by privileging binary oppositions: white, male, ivy leaguers vs. black, knife-wielding males and predatory prostitutes. These narratives frequently referred to a "group" of black men who, according to a police source, "materialized 'from nowhere'" to aid the prostitute and attack the football players.[91] Sinister descriptions of an organized agency on the part of these men and sensational terms—"fracas" and "melee"—to describe the scene suggested that the attackers employed guerrilla-style tactics, recalling the way the Viet Cong had been characterized.[92] Several days after the stabbings, Donald Gould, an off-duty state trooper, died of a heart attack brought on by fighting in the Zone with a shadowy figure identified only as "Richie."[93] Outrage over the Combat Zone mounted. *Herald* columnist Jim Delay scripted this sensational account of Zone denizens: "There are super-sedulous murderers and thieves. Mostly, though, there are creeps. These creeps are difficult to see clearly in the dark. In the sunlight—even if touched by one pale sunbeam—they would melt into sticky little puddles on the Combat Zone sidewalk."[94] An illusive, even supernatural, ability was also attributed to area prostitutes. None were apprehended nor charged for stealing the football player's wallet. Nevertheless, not a single reporter from the major dailies raised any doubt about the guilt of the prostitutes or the validity of the athletes' accounts of the incident. Not coincidentally, the most strident opposition to the Combat Zone decried the "aggressive hookers" who defied public morals and resisted police efforts at control.[95]

Two days after the Harvard football players were stabbed, the *Herald* ran a front-page story in which then City Councilor Raymond Flynn railed against the Zone. He warned that "Downtown Boston is going to become a smut capital of the nation unless we take some swift, decisive, forceful action" and further asserted that citizens were "fed up with what's going on *down there*."[96] This spatialization of the Zone as "down there" was articulated mostly by the police, city officials, and especially opponents of the Zone. Quotes that located the Zone "down there" appeared regularly in the more conservative Hearst-owned *Herald* and were echoed in subsequent stories both locally and nationally. The liberal, independent *Globe* also discursively located the Zone as a place of violence and vice represented through women's bodies and the traffic in prostitution. *Globe* reporter John Cullen quoted a patrolman stationed in the Zone after the stabbings: "'This place looks like the Berlin Wall,' he said. 'Every 10 feet there is an armed guard and every place you turn *down here,* there's a uniformed cop.'"[97]

That the Zone was "down there" indicated more than a geographical location on lower Washington Street; rather, this sexualized spatialization related to an "imaginary geography."[98] As an inverted world, the Zone was seen to privilege the lower part of the body, particularly the female genitals. What was normally "down" was "up" in the Zone—on signs, stages, and screens. Women who worked in the Zone, especially "common streetwalkers," were marked as threats to the social order when they stepped out of the containment area. According to Sibley, dominant discourse seeks to reject polluting bodies by displacing them: "This 'elsewhere' might be nowhere, as when genocide or the moral transformation of a minority like prostitutes are advocated, or it might be some spatial periphery, like the edge of the world or the edge of the city."[99] In Boston, prostitutes came to represent desires mobilized, and made mobile, by the presence of adult entertainment in the core of the city. To keep them in their place "down there," police had usually herded them back into the Zone rather than booking them all. However, after November 16, 1976, such leniency was publicly criticized. For instance, on November 21, 1976, *Herald* columnist Dave O'Brian summed up the "official tolerance" of the

This *Boston Herald* photograph of lower Washington Street was captioned, "The hookers are definitely more aggressive." Courtesy of *The Boston Herald.*

Zone since 1974: "even as . . . the vice squad insisted that its job was still to enforce the letter of the law *down there*, the police were leaning more toward chasing the hookers out of Park Square, the theater district and Bay Village, and back into the [Combat Zone]. Where they belong." [100] Because this "down there" was the city's "elsewhere" of vice, such women could contaminate the city by crossing out of the Zone.

Indeed, violence *and* vice could both be mapped onto the bodies of those "aggressive" prostitutes and "common streetwalkers." Especially from the *Herald*'s perspective, the city was seen to be invaded by an "army" of hookers and undesirables intent on "savagery." [101] This alarmist view dates from the nineteenth century when Western city planners interpreted the "urban experience as a new version of Hell," represented as the "female Sphinx, the 'strangling one,' who was so called because she strangled all those who could not answer her riddle: female sexuality, womanhood out of control, lost nature, loss of identity." [102] Exploiting the traditional association of female sexual agency with urban danger, *Herald* columnist Dan Ahern wrote: "Hookers do more

than undermine the economy. They rob pedestrians and when people resist they are kicked, gouged and knifed." [103] In sum, from November 16, 1976, on, issues of gender, race, and capital were transcoded into a discursive domain of vice warfare wherein the bodies of the Zone's marginal people appeared to be grotesquely out of proportion, threatening to overpower Boston's respectable citizens. [104] From November 15 to 30, the *Globe* reported that "93 persons [had] been arrested in the Combat Zone, including 43 for prostitution, 13 for liquor violations and seven for common night-walking. Also 66 complaints were drawn up . . . charging a number of persons with disseminating obscene material." [105] Moreover, press stories made it seem that the city's very economy was the spoil of this urban battle. By clamping down on the Zone's legitimate businesses as well as the street traffickers, city officials could appear to be attacking the cause of violence—this quarantined district afforded the police a theater of war in which dangerous Others could always-already be located. In contrast to press coverage of the football players' case, little sympathetic ink was spilled nine months later when Debra Beckerman, now identified as a "dancer-publicist" for Zone businesses, mysteriously disappeared.[106]

Assimilating the Zone

After the football players' case, newspaper stories began predicting the death of the Zone. The 1976 vice war so stigmatized the Combat Zone as a dangerous place—especially for middle-class, white men—that it peaked as an adult attraction a short time later, 1977–1978. Every time a theater, an adult bookstore, or strip joint closed after that, officials and reporters rushed to pronounce the death of the adult district.[107] However, since it was the only area zoned for adult businesses, such entrepreneurs persisted; thus, observers had to concede that the ailing Zone was always "down but not out."[108] This popular framing of the Zone as a perpetually moribund place echoed the anthropomorphized discourse of urban planning, which had mapped a body—subject to health and sickness—onto the cityscape. Instead of eradicating the Zone in the manner of Scollay Square, the city had used a zoning amendment to quarantine the blighted "low" within the official body politic. The 1976 crisis allowed the city to begin to constrict the Zone by two means without having to confront First Amendment issues regarding adult entertainment: first, by discouraging adult businesses through bureaucratic procedures—license hearings, building codes, and safety citations; second, by encouraging developers to assimilate the area along the downtown spine.[109] Assimilation was contingent on the exhaustion of adult entertainment as an economically viable attraction. Because the containment strategy clustered adult businesses in an area badly neglected by the city, property values dropped over time. Only as adult entertainment dispersed to the suburbs and video stores in the 1980s, could the Zone be safely domesticated for new development projects.[110]

In order for "spoiled" space to be assimilated, it has to be purified through the purging of its "low" Others. According to David Sibley, "Often, but not invariably, [moral] panics concern contested spaces, liminal zones which hostile communities are intent on eliminating by appropriating such spaces for themselves and excluding the offending 'other.'"[111] Just such a moral panic was created in Boston as a result of the coverage accorded the Harvard football players' case. As the *Globe*'s Robert Campbell recalled a few years later, "About the same time as the Puopolo murder, an acquaintance of [a BRA] planner was strangled on Mt. Vernon Street [on Beacon Hill]. No paper or TV station mentioned the crime. It didn't have the myth-power of the killing of a Harvard student in a den of iniquity."[112] Not only were the athletes stabbed in an area considered disturbing to the official body politic, but also this case followed the recent revelation that the police department was troubled by lax law enforcement as well as corruption. In this moment, the difference between domains—official culture's "high" and the Zone's "low"—threatened to disappear in the city's representation of itself. By making the Zone and its marginal people symbolically central to the city's Imaginary as contaminants, popular representations perpetrated a moral panic. Periodic crackdowns on prostitutes and transients forced their displacement from the area without having to address the economic needs of such people through any official process. In this way, Boston police served notice that such people would not be tolerated in an area that had once been conceded to them.

Although people lived in the Zone and in the adjacent Park Square—in single-room-occupancy hotels (SROs), in the retired merchant marines' home, or in homeless shelters—these places were never perceived or treated as residential areas. A manager of the Naked i put it this way in 1984, "The Combat Zone really isn't a neighborhood. It's more like the reverse of a neighborhood, where a person can be anonymous if he feels like it. The zone is the orphan of the city for the orphans of the city."[113] Over time, illegal squatters were evicted, the shelters closed, the merchant

The Pilgrim Theater and the
Naked i fall to the wreckers in
January 1996. Photo by Eric
Schaefer.

marine home was demolished, and SROS were converted to other uses.[114] Adjacent to the Zone, Chinatown suffered from the dominant anti-residential perception of the urban core, in part because mixed commercial/residential zoning had already been implemented in that area. Indeed, Chinatown civic groups had opposed the adults uses district. Nevertheless, a growing immigrant population, especially "more women and children," forced that neighborhood to expand in the direction of the stigmatized Zone.[115] In 1980, the Chinese Economic Development Council purchased the Zone's Boylston Building, which housed several adult establishments, including "some kind of men's health club," as reported by Ahern.[116] Replacing those businesses and a gay bathhouse with a Chinese cultural/commercial center was seen as a major step in reclaiming the Zone for other business ventures. Writing about efforts to shrink the Zone in 1981, John Yang commented, "the combatants that appear to be the most effective in this battle against the profiteers of sex are the profiteers of real estate."[117]

New landlords within the Zone evicted adult businesses. Low rents for theaters and storefronts, which had once attracted such entrepreneurs to the area, began to shoot up, forcing others to close.[118] The State successfully assimilated one corner of the Zone with a multimillion dollar Transportation Building. A mall development on the downtown spine, Lafayette Place, failed but is undergoing revival. The adult businesses that anchored the Zone—the Pilgrim Theater and the Naked i—closed after property owners decided to demolish those buildings for a parking lot.[119] Moving into the area, Emerson College purchased and refurbished the Majestic Theater and acquired buildings for office and classroom use. In 1995, the college turned the massive 1916 Little Building, abutting the Zone, into a student dormitory. Suffolk University followed Emerson's lead, converting a building a few blocks away into a dormitory. Thus, in these more lucrative versions of the SRO, college students have replaced the "college revue." Perhaps the most striking change can be found in the construction of the Ritz-Carlton Towers on former parking lots running along Avery Street between Washington and Tremont. The creation of luxury condominiums on what was once the most feared piece of real estate in the city represents the final phase in the purification of the Combat Zone.

The history of Boston's Combat Zone paralleled adult entertainment's emergence into the public sphere in the United States in the 1960s and 1970s: moving from a gaudy high profile expression of sexual liberation, to concern over its negative impact on individuals and families, to its gradual disappearance as it moved into the home via domestic technologies—vcrs, cable, and home computers.[120] The Combat Zone briefly flourished, with official sanction, during a period when adult entertainment appeared to be achieving respectability. During the late 1960s, more and more "sexploitation" films had moved into general release. Films made by Russ Meyer (*Vixen, Goodmorning and Goodbye*) and Radley Metzger (*Camille 2,000, The Lickerish Quartet*) were notable because they appealed not only to men, but also to growing numbers of women and the valuable "couples" market. With the advent of hard-core features and "porno chic," sparked by the release of *Deep Throat* (1972), adult entertainment began to attract a wider audience. Boston's zoning strategy was offered as a fair-minded acknowledgment of the pragmatic coexistence downtown of adult entertainment and legitimate theaters. Opponents resisted this zoning strategy, and, in the wake of the football players' case, sought political power by vilifying "liberals" for making the city, and by implication the family, vulnerable to this "cancer."

Both locally and nationally, the Combat Zone came to represent a failed social "experiment" initiated during a more liberal era; and its blighted appearance signified contamination at the center of a major city. During coverage of the 1976 vice war, the *Herald* quoted Thomas Walsh of Morality in Media of Massachusetts, who reportedly said: "We wouldn't go there [Zone] after 8 P.M. because you're liable to get killed."[121] The *Herald*'s political editor, William J. Lewis, opined: "Life, of course, is cheap in the Zone. Deaths are commonplace."[122] These conservative comments echoed the moral outrage that emerged around *Snuff* in

early 1976. Protests against that film provided a guiding logic for opposing adult entertainment—that exposure can lead to physical violence—for the antipornography discourse that rapidly gained ground. That logic contributed to the virtual evacuation of the Combat Zone by adult businesses. It did not, however, kill the ostensible contaminant itself, since adult entertainment was dispersed across Boston through other means, especially in legitimate video stores.[123]

We suggest that adult entertainment was further stigmatized at the very moment in which what had historically been "low" culture for (presumably) heterosexual men became more public and accessible to women and to gays. The Combat Zone crisis following on the heels of the *Snuff* controversy indicate that 1976 marked a shift in the contemporary elaboration of sex as contaminant and the ways in which certain bodies were positioned in such discourses. This shift has had enormous implications as socially conservative arguments have been officially popularized, while others—"liberal" and "sexual liberationist"—have been marginalized. The Combat Zone crisis illustrates the way adult entertainment has been demonized as a pathological form of culture—particularly on the grounds that it contaminates public space. Urban planning, whether Burnham's "City Beautiful," Le Corbusier's "Radiant City" or any of the myriad schemes carried out in urban spaces around the world, has been unable to turn the city into a utopia. But, as Elizabeth Wilson cautions, "Both the utopia and the architectural treatise proceed from the assumption that human deviance and unreason can be wiped out by the perfect plan."[124] The effort to move Boston closer to utopia, first by quarantining then by shrinking the Combat Zone, was rife with contradictions. The morality and antipornography campaigns that began gaining ground in 1976 sought to eliminate that which was presumed to be deviant in the name of saving women and bourgeois families. However, as we have indicated, deviance was not only identified with a space that was sexually and racially demarcated, but was also located on the very bodies of marginal people—especially female prostitutes—taken to represent the "porno plague." To purify the public space contaminated by adult entertainment, not only did those bodies have to be swept away, but also the legitimate adult businesses had to be so stigmatized that patrons, especially middle-class men, would be repelled. Perhaps most ironic, this purging of adult entertainment in public spaces, in the name of the bourgeois family, helped speed pornography's domestication via cable, VCRs, and the Internet. Boston and other cities were "saved" by taking pornography out of public spaces and putting it into the private space of the home.

Notes

Our thanks to Helene Johnson for sharing original documents from the Park Plaza Civic Advisory Committee and the Back Bay Association. With Dan Ahern, she prepared and designed the *Downtown as an Arts Center* report (1976); they also worked with the BRA to develop the interim report, *Entertainment District Study* (1974).

1 For more on the snuff controversy, see Eithne Johnson and Eric Schaefer, "Soft Core/Hard Gore: *Snuff* as a Crisis in Meaning," *Journal of Film and Video*, 45 (2–3) (summer–fall 1993): 42–59.

2 "The Porno Plague," *Time* (Apr. 5, 1976): 58–63.

3 Peter Stallybrass and Allon White, *The Politics and Poetics of Transgression* (Ithaca, NY: Cornell University Press, 1986), 145.

4 Ibid.

5 Stallybrass and White cite and elaborate on Babcock's formulation: "What is socially peripheral is often symbolically central" (ibid., 20).

6 Ibid, 193.

7 Simon Cottle, "Stigmatizing Handsworth: Notes on Reporting Spoiled Space," *Critical Studies in Mass Communication* 11 (1994): 249.

8 Cottle argues that a neighborhood populated by lower-income, minority residents became a "racialized sign" through media coverage, receiving far greater visibility than warranted (ibid., 239). The area became "news-

worthy because of its prior association as a place of trouble"; therefore, journalists continued to use the "trouble frame" when reporting on that neighborhood (249).

9 Mary Ellen Carter, "The Combat Zone: Our New Next Door Neighbor," *Berkeley Beacon* (Apr. 6, 1995): 4–5.

10 Lewis Mumford, *The Culture of Cities* (1938; New York: Harcourt, Brace, Jovanovich, 1970), 301.

11 Ibid.

12 Martin Meyerson and Edward C. Banfield, *Boston: The Job Ahead* (Cambridge, MA: Harvard University Press, 1966), 1.

13 Lawrence W. Kennedy, *Planning the City Upon a Hill: Boston since 1630* (Amherst: University of Massachusetts Press, 1992), 158–59.

14 Ibid., 161.

15 Sociologist Herbert Gans's study, *The Urban Villagers: Group and Class in the Life of Italian Americans* (1962), became a classic in participant-observation research. The last section of the Charles River Park complex is currently being developed but continues to stir controversy due to issues relating to the displacement of the original area residents.

16 Our understanding of Scollay Square is based on planning documents, newspaper accounts, and, to a large extent, David Kruh's book, *Always Something Doing: A History of Boston's Infamous Scollay Square* (Boston: Faber and Faber, 1990).

17 Kathy Peiss, *Cheap Amusements* (Philadelphia: Temple University Press, 1986), 141–42.

18 Stewart Holbrook, "Boston's Temple of Burlesque," in *The Many Voices of Boston: A Historical Anthology, 1630–1975*, ed. Howard Mumford Jones and Bessie Zaban Jones (Boston: Atlantic Monthly Press/Little, Brown, 1975), 387.

19 Kennedy, *Planning the City Upon a Hill*, 177.

20 Kruh, *Always Something Doing*, 133.

21 Although the phrase "New Boston" was coined early in the century, it was popularized in the postwar period. Lawrence W. Kennedy credits Mayor John F. Collins "for making 'New Boston' a reality as well as a watchword" in the 1960s (*Planning the City Upon a Hill*, 157).

22 Larry Ford, *Cities and Buildings: Skyscrapers, Skid Rows, and Suburbs* (Baltimore: Johns Hopkins University Press, 1994), 86.

23 Boston Redevelopment Authority/Park Plaza Civic Advisory Committee, *Entertainment District Study*, In-

terim Report (Boston: Boston Redevelopment Authority, April 1974), 4.

24 M. Marvin Finkelstein, "The Traffic in Sex-Oriented Materials in Boston," in *Technical Report of the Commission on Obscenity and Pornography*, vol. 4, ed. W. Cody Wilson (Washington, D.C.: U.S. Government Printing Office, 1970), 104–5.

25 We have not been able to pinpoint the exact date when this area became known as the Combat Zone, but sources suggest that it emerged in the early to mid-sixties. Most likely, reporters popularized a name that was already in circulation on the streets. According to landscape architect Shirley Kressel, "servicemen came to the garment district for uniforms," which suggests that the adult spots were established nearby to take advantage of this preexisting pattern of movement in the area (Carter, "Combat Zone," 4).

26 Bob DiIorio, "Smut Sales Are Booming in Boston," *Sunday Herald Traveler* (June 29, 1969): 37.

27 Finkelstein, "Traffic in Sex-Oriented Materials," 105.

28 Ford, *Cities and Buildings*, 89.

29 Dan Ahern, *Boston's Red Districts* (Boston: Back Bay Association, 1972), 5.

30 According to Larry Ford, SROs were a tradition in the United States: "For at least a century, hotel living was considered an acceptable and respectable housing alternative for (male) bachelors, retirees, and others who were not interested in the task of running a home" (*Cities and Buildings*, 69).

31 Ibid., 70–71.

32 Park Plaza Civic Advisory Committee, *Park Plaza* (Boston: Park Plaza Civic Advisory Committee, n.d.), 4.

33 Citizen groups feared that the high-rises permitted in these plans would "Manhattanize" Boston, so they lobbied against them; a scaled-down version was finally completed in the 1980s to attract wealthy residents and visitors (Park Plaza CAC, *Park Plaza*, 6).

34 Ibid., 4.

35 Kennedy, *Planning the City Upon the Hill*, 208; Ahern, *Boston's Red Districts*, 6.

36 Ahern, *Boston's Red Districts*, 3.

37 Ibid., 1.

38 David Sibley, *Geographies of Exclusion* (London: Routledge, 1995), 24–25.

39 BRA/CAC, *Entertainment District Study*, Interim Report, 26–27.

40 Earl Marchand, "Troublesome Combat Zone Here to Stay, City Planners Say," *Boston Herald American* (Dec. 9, 1976): 3.

41 Janice Elliott, "BRA's Proposal to 'Contain' City's Combat Zone Is Blasted, Defended," *Boston Herald American* (Sept. 12, 1974): 4.

42 Ibid.

43 Ibid.

44 Robert Jordan, "Boston Board Approves Zone for Adult Shows," *Boston Globe* (Nov. 15, 1974): 1, 17.

45 Ibid., 1.

46 "Boston Designates 'Combat Zone' as Only Permissible Area for Porno," *Independent Film Journal* (Dec. 11, 1974): 8; "High Court Mulls Legality of Anti-Smut Zoning Maneuvers," *Independent Film Journal* (Oct. 29, 1975): 5. The city made a half-hearted effort to give the area a new identity by renaming it Liberty Tree Park after a historic tree that had once grown on the site. The "park" amounted to a stretch of brick sidewalk and a few spindly saplings. As Ahern and Johnson put it, the "BRA built the expensive brick-lined, brightly lit Liberty Park as a 'catalyst for investment' and they got three more dirty bookstores and a strip club" (*Downtown as an Arts Center* [Boston: BRA, 1976]).

47 Carter, "Combat Zone," 4.

48 "Combat Zone," *Newsweek* (Dec. 2, 1974): 43.

49 BRA, *Boston's Adult Entertainment District* (Boston: BRA, Jan. 1976).

50 Ahern and Johnson, *Downtown as an Arts Center*, n.p.

51 Paul Corsetti and Jim Morse, "Combat Zone Concept Held Failure; Tight Enforcement Plans Revealed," *Boston Herald American* (Nov. 30, 1976), 11.

52 Terry Minsky, "Those Who Live, Work, or Hang Out in Area Feel It Serves a Need," "The Combat Zone: Can It Survive? Second in a Series," *Boston Globe* (Dec. 28, 1984): 14.

53 Robert Campbell. "They're Out to Get the Combat Zone!" *Boston Sunday Globe* (April 16, 1978): B4.

54 Stallybrass and White, *The Politics and Poetics of Transgression*, 31.

55 Carter, "Combat Zone," 5.

56 Stallybrass and White, *The Politics and Poetics of Transgression*, 27.

57 William J. Lewis, "Pleasures in the Zone Not Cheap," *Boston Herald American* (Nov. 27, 1976): 18.

58 Finkelstein found that a fairly high percentage of employees in adult bookstores had juvenile offense records; in comparison, those operators who had police records had been charged with a high percentage of white collar crimes ("Traffic in Sex-Oriented Materials," 62–65).

59 Ibid., 66, 67, 77.

60 Paul Corsetti and Earl Marchand, "Zone Known Far, Wide, 'Secret' Owners Sought," *Boston Herald American* (Nov. 24, 1976): 3.

61 Finkelstein, "Traffic in Sex-Oriented Materials," 76–77.

62 Joan Vennochi, "Cleanup Poses Its Own Questions," "The Combat Zone: Can It Survive? Last in a Series," *Boston Globe* (Dec. 29, 1984): 2.

63 Earl Marchand and Paul Corsetti, "Crime Bosses Squeeze Zone Clubs," *Boston Herald American* (Nov. 26, 1976): 1.

64 According to Finkelstein's study, adult bookstore owners "complained of what they perceived to be police 'harassment.' All but one of them complained of alleged pilferage of the stock and/or name-taking with threats of arrests" ("Traffic in Sex-Oriented Materials," 147). For their part, police complained in news accounts after November 16, 1976, that club and store owners posted "lookouts" and used "closed-circuit television" to spot police (Eleanor Roberts, "What's Behind Doors Along the Combat Zone," *Boston Herald American* [Nov. 28, 1976], 29; Earl Marchand, "Civic Drive on to Purge Combat Zone," *Boston Herald American* [Nov. 18, 1976]: 1, 10). These tactics recalled those used in Scollay Square's Old Howard, where secret buttons at the front of the house could be pushed to signal strippers and comedians to clean up their routines when city censors or police appeared (Kruh, *Always Something Doing,* 78).

65 During the November 1976 crisis, *Herald* reporters Corsetti and Marchand floated a sensational story, charging that a "highly placed state Welfare Department official owns a piece of the Combat Zone's most corrupt bar" ("Welfare Aide Owns Bar in the Combat Zone," *Boston Herald American* [Dec. 2, 1976]: 1, 8). Subsequent news stories failed to connect anyone in that department with the bar (Marchand and Corsetti, "Crime Bosses Squeeze Zone Clubs," 1, 24; "State Police Join Probe of Zone Bar Ownership," *Boston Herald American* [Dec. 3, 1976]:1, 7).

66 Finkelstein, "Traffic in Sex-Oriented Materials," 102.

67 "State Trooper Dies of Heart Attack Following Fight in Combat Zone," *Boston Herald American* (Nov. 20, 1976): 1.

68 In his study of adult bookstores, "Traffic in Sex-Oriented Materials," Finkelstein argued that the "adult bookstore business, although moving in the direction of oligarchic control, retains some characteristics of the free market" (127). Certainly, collusion to restrict trade is nothing unusual in a capitalist economy, whether or not those charged are rumored to be associated with so-called organized crime. Other industries—from waste management to mainstream film making—have been accused of such collusion, as well as rumored to include mob and criminal types. However, such rumors have usually failed to generate as much moral indignation as those that connect criminals with sex businesses. Therefore, cultural critics must continue to question the rumors and their discursive effects. In 1977, *Herald American* columnist Dick Flavin facetiously suggested that Zone operators fight reformers by forming their own union, "Purveyors of Illicit Morals and Pornography (PIMP)" ("Combatting the Combat in the Zone," *Boston Herald American* [Jan. 9, 1977]: 10).

69 Parker, *Ceremony* (New York: Delacorte, 1982), 45.

70 Elizabeth Wilson, *The Sphinx in the City* (Berkeley: University of California Press, 1991), 5.

71 Eleanor Roberts, "What's Behind Doors," 29.

72 Ibid.

73 Dan Ahern, "Mobile Pimps, Hookers Poser for City," *Boston Herald American* (Nov. 24, 1976): 11.

74 Roberts, "What's Behind Doors," 29.

75 Wilson, *The Sphinx in the City,* 120.

76 David Farrell, "Ray Flynn's War on Combat Zone," *Boston Globe* (Dec. 23, 1984): 14.

77 Wilson, *The Sphinx in the City,* 12.

78 Campbell, "They're Out to Get the Combat Zone!," B4.

79 Parker, *Ceremony,* 46.

80 Perhaps recalling the 1976 allegations that a Welfare Department official had investments in the Zone, Parker's novel hinges on the exploitation of minors by an Education Department official-turned-pornographer.

81 Marchand and Corsetti, "Crime Bosses Squeeze Zone Clubs," 1, 24.

82 Corsetti and Marchand, "Charge Made Muggers, Pickpockets Rule Combat Zone," *Boston Herald American* (Dec. 1, 1976): 3.

83 David Gumpert, "X-Rated Businesses in Boston Are Given Home on the Raunch," *Wall Street Journal* (Jan. 6, 1976): 1, 34.

84 Jerry Taylor, "Analysis of Crime in Hub Lists Causes, High-Risk Areas," *Boston Evening Globe* (Oct. 27, 1967): 1, 7.

85 Richard Steele and Richard Manning, "Mortal Combat," *Newsweek* (Dec. 6, 1976): 35.

86 Stephen F. Crimmin, "2 Harvard Athletes Stabbed in Hub," *Boston Evening Globe* (Nov. 16, 1976): 1, 20.

87 Richard Knox, "Quick Action by Doctors, Police Save Puopolo," *Boston Evening Globe* (Nov. 16, 1976): 1, 20.

88 Corsetti and Morse, "Combat," 11; George Ryan, statement in *Boston Herald American* (Nov. 21, 1976); Marchand, "Civic Drive on to Purge Combat Zone," 3. George Ryan, president of Morality in Media in Massachusetts, issued a statement after the stabbings that was treated differently by the *Herald* and the *Globe*. The former used it as the basis for an article without a byline; the latter printed a truncated version under letters to the editor ("Combat Zone a 'Cesspool,'" (letter to the editor), *Boston Sunday Globe* [Nov. 21, 1976], A6).

89 Susan Sontag, *Illness as Metaphor* (New York: Farrar, Straus and Giroux, 1978), 81.

90 Ahern and Johnson, *Downtown as an Arts Center*, 10.

91 Crimmin, "2 Harvard Athletes Stabbed In Combat Zone," *Boston Herald Americana* (Nov. 17, 1976): 1, 18.

92 Alexander Hawes Jr., "Harvard Athlete Is Stable after Combat Zone Melee," *Boston Globe* (Nov. 17, 1976): 1, 7.

93 George Croft, "Trooper Dies After Beating in Combat Zone," *Boston Evening Globe* (Nov. 19, 1976): 1, 7

94 Jim Delay, "What About the Zone? A Few Suggestions," *Boston Herald American* (Nov. 22, 1976): 13.

95 Ahern, "Mobile Pimps," 11; John Cullen, "Prostitutes Invade the Back Bay," *Boston Sunday Globe* (Nov. 21, 1976): 14; Corsetti and Marchand, "Charge," 3.

96 Marchand, "Civic," 1; emphasis added.

97 Cullen, "Prostitutes," 1; emphasis added.

98 Sibley, *Geographies of Exclusion*, 49.

99 Ibid.

100 Dave O'Brian, "'Zone' Experiment Isn't Working Out," *Boston Herald American* (Nov. 21, 1976): A1; emphasis added.

101 Paul Corsetti and Jim Morse, "Hub Official Warns Zone a "Fire Trap,'" *Boston Herald American* (Nov. 23, 1976): 6; Joe Heaney, "Prostitution Rap May Also Hit Men," *Boston Herald American* (Nov. 28, 1976): 27.

102 Wilson, *The Sphinx in the City*, 6–7.

103 Ahern, "Mobile Pimps," 11. Extending the threat posed by the streetwalker to bourgeois propriety, Ahern called for the end of "chauvinist" legislation that failed to charge male as well as female prostitutes (11). This call was not taken very seriously, although it may have served to heighten local homophobia. On the other end of the spectrum, State Representative Barney Frank humorously floated the idea that other areas of the city, especially the financial district, should be given over to prostitutes at night, so that they could freely ply their trade (Marchand, "A Frank Suggestion: Hookers in the Financial District," *Boston Herald American* [Nov. 25, 1976]: 29. Frank's benign perspective on sex-for-pay would be revisited some years later after he became congressman (and openly gay) when it was widely reported that his roommate was operating an escort service from Frank's home.

104 The city was already embroiled in race- and class-based clashes over court-ordered busing to implement desegregation of the public schools.

105 Paul Feeney and Peter Mancusi, "Officials Say Concept of X-Rated Zone Failed, Plan Crackdown on Violations," *Boston Globe* (Nov. 30, 1976): 1, 12.

106 Her allegation that an "unnamed bar . . . was 'immune from harassment'" by the police because an unnamed politician had a hand in it was left dangling in her absence (Jerome Sullivan, "Dancer-Publicist for Combat Zone Reported Missing," *Boston Evening Globe* [Aug. 30, 1977]: 41).

107 Tom Ashbrook, "Going the Way of All Flesh," *Boston Globe* (Aug. 2, 1988): 53–54; Dan Caccavaro, "Zoned Out," *Boston Tab* (Feb. 1, 1994): 10, 11; John F. Cullen, "The Shrinking Combat Zone," *Boston Globe* (Dec. 23, 1987): 1, 24; Jonathan Kaufman, "Real Estate Development Boom Threatens 'Adult Entertainment,'" "The Combat Zone: Can It Survive? First in a Series," *Boston Globe* (Dec. 27, 1987): 33.

108 Richard Kindleberger, "Down but Not Out," *Boston Sunday Globe* (Dec. 17, 1995): A1, 7; Vennochi, "Cleanup," 1, 2; Jane White, "Combat Zone Hangs Tough," *Boston Ledger* (Oct. 12–18, 1979): 3, 5, 8; John E. Yang, "Whither Boston's Combat Zone?" *Boston Sunday Globe* (Feb. 8, 1981): C3.

109 Richard Hudson, "Combat Zone Plan: Shrink It," *Boston Globe* (Aug. 22, 1977): 1, 6.

110 Ian Menzies, "Combat Zone on the Prowl," *Boston Globe* (Aug. 26, 1982): 25.

111 Sibley, *Geographies of Exclusion*, 39.

112 Campbell, "They're Out to Get the Combat Zone!," B4.

113 Minsky, "Those Who Live," 14.

114 Though gentrification elsewhere in the city SROs were converted into pricey condominiums. Many people, especially single male lodgers, were subsequently displaced. In reaction to citizen lobbying, some condo buildings had to include a percentage of low-income units.

115 Anthony Yudis', "The Plan: Chinatown to Grow, Evict Combat Zone," *Boston Sunday Globe* (June 4, 1978): D1, 2.

116 Dan Ahern, "Monumental Peeping," *Boston Herald American* (Nov. 18, 1976): 17.

117 Yang, "Whither Boston's Combat Zone?" C3.

118 Kaufman, "Real Estate Boom."

119 Despite opposition, club owners have announced plans to reopen the Naked i at some other location in the Zone, and an upscale "gentlemen's club," Centerfolds, has recently opened across from the remaining strip club, the Glass Slipper.

120 The moral panic over "smut" on the Internet follows much the same pattern that it did with the Combat Zone: there is the fear that an unsuspecting net surfer might stumble across porn in cyberspace; there is the fear that predators lie in wait for the innocent and the inexperienced; and, finally, there is the fear that the "filth" of adult material will contaminate this new "community" with all its utopian potential. Although we can only point to this similarity here, the topic deserves further research.

121 "Citizen Group Blasts Combat Zone Legality," *Boston Herald American* (Nov. 16, 1976): 6.

122 Lewis, "Pleasures in the Zone Not Cheap," 18.

123 Andrew J. Dabilis, "The Shrinking Combat Zone: Is It Shifting Toward Suburbia?" *Boston Globe* (Dec. 23, 1987): 33. Following on the publicity gained by their reaction to *Snuff* in 1976, antipornography activists have been able to attract a lot of attention and support through public protests at X-rated movies. They have also found support in other venues where their provocative lectures and slideshows are seen arguably to raise awareness about date rape and violence against women. The antipornography movement slowed as home videotapes replaced X-rated theaters. In contrast, protests against video stores renting adult tapes are rare, but when they occur it is usually a contest over community space and the alleged "threat" of adult entertainment. Like moral conservatives, antipornography feminists perceive urban space as dangerous for women. But, as Elizabeth Wilson warns, "we must cease to perceive the city as a dangerous and disorderly zone from which women—and others—must be largely excluded for their own protection" (*The Sphinx and the City*, 9).

124 Wilson, *The Sphinx in the City*, 20.

HOP ON POP

CULTURAL FEELINGS AND ANXIETIES about change surface in popular expressions like "Change is good" and "The more things change, the more they stay the same." Our anthology seeks to explore change as a social process and to offer models for thinking through the critical analysis of change. One of the hallmarks of the past decade in cultural studies is an increasing attempt to negotiate between the twin demands of theory and of history. Certainly, both the historical and the theoretical implicitly embrace change but not consciously enough. During the reign of "high theory" in the academy, the two terms were often seen as antithetical: history dealt in the empirical while theory addressed the abstract. The term "change" is offered as a bridge term, a concept which can mediate between the concerns of history and theory. To focus on change is to refuse to see history and theory as inevitable binaries, two camps which cannot meet. The concept allows the scholar to see both the continuities and discontinuities inherent in social and cultural processes without resorting to a predetermined or narrow model of historiography. To chart change is also to move beyond the notion of history as simply a temporal process, opening up our analyses of social formations to considerations of the spatial and of movement.

Certainly, embracing the term "change" does not mean we are abandoning history. From its origins in the work of Walter Benjamin or Raymond Williams, cultural studies has always been cognizant of the importance of the historical. Rather, the shift to the term "change" permits the cultural studies scholar to avoid several of the pitfalls of historiography as it's been constituted as a modern discipline. To think about change shifts our understanding of the historical away from the grand and evolutionary metanarratives of history, away from a notion of progress as the engine of history. For many, history also signals the distant past, those events which occurred in earlier eras. "Change" is also about the present, creating a space from which to analyze the present as well

as the past, the micro as well as the macro, and to explore the productive relations and tensions between previous moments and our own. Neither do we wish to jettison theory, but we recognize the need to imbue theory with history, avoiding the temptation of mapping nineteenth century models onto contemporary periods or vice versa.

Each of the chapters in this section investigates how change is manifested in cultural texts and contexts. Some of these works look more like "traditional history," tracking the change of social relations as significant historical events unfold. Some pursue the changing nature of cultural forms, particularly generic forms. Still others are interested in how changes have occurred in our intellectual traditions, tracing, as it were, the intersections between popular culture and shifts in theoretical paradigms. What holds these essays together is their recognition of patterns of difference and similarity across time and form.

Matthew Tinkcom, Joy Van Fuqua, and Amy Villarejo query the changing meaning of concepts like use value from the time of Marx to the contemporary period, but their investigation does not remain on purely abstract or theoretical terms. By bringing together the shifting validity of different ways of understanding value with the intricacies and idiosyncrasies of modern thrift shopping, the trio highlights ways in which we might rethink the relationship between production and consumption in specific cultural contexts and also points the way toward interesting reformulations of our intellectual histories. The playful form of their essay also emphasizes newly emergent styles of critical practice. In her essay on women's early writings about shopping, Elana Crane also teases out the changing nature of consumption in a precise historical moment, focusing as she does upon the intersections between the emerging urban sphere, cultural understandings of gender, and the shift toward new forms of production and display. Her essay most closely resembles what we commonly recognize as history, but it too weaves together an analysis of a specific period in history with a consideration of the implications of this moment for our present-day interpretations of the relation of the public to the private. Popular culture becomes a vehicle for discerning the interplay between these realms, particularly as they impact our notions of class and gender.

The chapters by Greg Smith and Angela Ndalianis survey a different type of change, a change seemingly rooted in very recent history. Both turn to an analysis of specific electronic texts in order to map the changing nature of cultural and critical forms, suggesting that new technologies certainly have long histories. Smith navigates the computer game *Myst* as he highlights its hybrid nature. Though heralded as a radically new interactive technology, Smith points out the ways in which *Myst* actually combines the old and the new, referencing the role of the author and the premodern technology of the book at the same time that it subtly reworks these traditions. He also points out that our critical methodologies will need to be as flexible as these new objects of study if we are really to understand them. Ndalianis also explores this blending of old and new in the realm of computer entertainment in her investigation of the rules of genre at the end of the millennium. Here, genres are theorized across cultural forms, tracing the continuities and discontinuities that occur when horror travels from film to CD-rom, recognizing the role that audience familiarity with popular forms plays in this process. This research also reminds us that the on-going horizontal integration of entertainment companies impacts formal and aesthetic issues as well. Both essays are thus concerned with medium specificity in a time of changing modes of production and technological forms.

Tara McPherson's essay is quite literally about change as she explores the different forms popular myths of the U.S. South take in two distinct historical periods. Focusing on the intersections of femininity, place, and race in the novels *Gone with the Wind* and *Scarlett,* she notes the ways in which the different cultural contexts of the 1930s and the 1990s produce two distinct versions of the southern lady for popular consumption. Furthermore, these two versions reflect shifting cultural modes of representing race, modes which are closely tied to U.S. history before and after the civil rights movement. Though the contributions in this section tackle a wide range of texts, practices, and periods, each produces insights into different ways of thinking cultural and social change in the realm of the popular, asking how popular culture shapes and is shaped by the movement across space and time.

On Thrifting

Matthew Tinkcom, Joy Van Fuqua,
and Amy Villarejo

Thrift: from Old Norse, "prosperity"

A long time ago, we stopped buying our lives' commodities in retail stores. We didn't stop shopping, and we didn't undertake shoplifting to any significant degree. We began thrifting. This chapter is the product of years of discussion and argument about the role that thrift-shopping plays in our lives, and what "thrifting" has taught us about elaborating (in both senses) the critique of capital. We write as a collective because we learn and shop as a collective, and this essay is offered in the spirit of an open-ended discussion about thrifting and value. It also offers tips about thrift-shopping and how to equip your life in ways perhaps unimaginable to the nonthrifting among us. This chapter will have been successful if you, reader, have thrifted this book. Thrift on.

DAILY LIFE ENCOMPASSES advertising, television, cinema, popular music, journalism, art, photography, architecture, fashion, and cuisine, as well as cultural studies, literature, teaching, feminism, Marxism, psychoanalysis, and, as Marx says, "carbuncles on our asses," by which we mean to designate, as he did, the closely felt and lived minutiae of the everyday. In thrift, we are speaking of thrift stores (Salvation Army, Value Village, St. Vincent de Paul, etc.). Thrift cuts across each of these domains. We are aware that we are isolating heuristically certain practices of consumption for close attention; it is therefore incumbent upon us to distinguish carefully among the practices we invoke. To begin, then, on the level of consumption, for the sake of distinguishing between the various ways in which we are encouraged as consumers to buy new goods, here we differentiate between retail and thrift shopping and focus our attention in the latter part of this piece on the anatomy of thrift. As an initial distinction, we name all types of shopping that involve the "debut" of the commodity within the store, "first-order shopping." First-order shopping organizes consumer goods in fairly predictable (but changing) ways with which most of us are familiar: department stores, "specialty" shops, megastores (or, a phrase we like from the French, hypermarchés), and so on. Thrift forms a second-order form of shopping, and insists on organizing the merchandise, and therefore the thrift experience itself, in often quite strikingly different ways. Cultural studies' attention to shopping incessantly focuses its gaze on first-order shopping; even when that attention shifts from "consumption" to the "commodity" (consumption socially coded, consumption's minimal predication, the consumer good "first produced in order to be exchanged for profit").[1] While cultural studies work on shopping, consumerism, and commodities is proliferating, infused with its most productive paradigms, it has rarely touched thrift.[2]

"The Immense Collection of Commodities"

In order to investigate the distinction between the commodity's debut and its recirculation (retail shopping and thrift-shopping, respectively) we need to address the *problem* of value.[3] By value, we mean to designate that "contentless and simple" abstraction which structures the production and circulation of commodities and money. By the problem of value, we enjoin with the longer history of critique which wrestles with the fragmented and contradictory effects of value-coding rather than treating value as a unified phenomenon. For example, value embeds hierarchical distinction (a PBS "quality drama" vs. a soap opera), a sense of frugality or a good deal within the exchange matrix (a Taco Bell "extreme value meal"), a sense of necessity or utility (impact air bags in cars), and a sense of emotional investment ("When you care enough to send the very best®"). These dimensions of the abstraction "value" emerge in practices of value-coding, practices which are overlapping, difficult to distinguish, and conceal the relations of production which make possible and structure them. Such hierarchies are lived as crises in the day-to-day confrontation between one's income and one's spending. But they mirror the dynamic movement of capital (its political economy) centrifugally from the home to the neighborhood, city, state, nation, and globe. (For example, commodities made in Hong Kong and purchased in the department store might well find their way through the thrift store into our kitchens, but might then if not purchased in the thrift store be "discarded" by way of international aid into Haiti or Bosnia, the abjected underside of the international division of labor.[4])

Thrift Tip #1: Most prices are not negotiable. Nothing that is not priced will sell. Rule: Do not contest this. Know the scheduled sales: Ladies Day, Seniors Day, Colored Price Tags, etc.

We turn to Marx, whose explanation of these relations has for years challenged us in our reading and our shopping. In his attempt to show how the labor demanded in an object's production abets in the creation of value within human societies, Marx uses the example of a linen coat. Noting that the coat, a commodity itself, comprises both other commodities, such as thread, buttons, and linen, and the human labor demanded for the production of a garment, Marx traces the production of the linen coat, in terms of how capitalist societies produce (a) commodities, (b) money as money, and money as capital, and (c) more abstractly, the sense of value, in all of its complexity. In the *Grundrisse*, Marx focuses on the consumption of the commodity; he was hardly in a position to anticipate that the wealth of capitalist societies would itself lead to the current bizarre matrix of surfeit and scarcity of consumer goods mapped unevenly throughout the globe. Marx understands and reads the coat as it is made, circulated, and worn, but an enormous and mostly neglected activity around the continuing circulation of commodities has recently arisen. We are, of course, talking about thrift stores. At the historical moment at which Marx was writing, he was, in other words, unable to foresee that capitalism would be unable to clean up after itself.[5] It would whip itself into the frenzy of consumer culture we call postwar America, dive into the murky waters of late capitalism (cf. Jameson), and leave in its wake the detritus of material goods and broken promises of its efficiency and essential democracy.

Thrift Tip #2: Acknowledge the dirt in thrifts: stains, tears, outmodedness can teach us about the commodity's trajectory through its production and consumption. Also, remember that a good dry cleaner can remove many stains, but if in extreme doubt, pass it up.

If a Marxist critique can teach us about the world of contemporary capital, what can thrift teach us about contemporary Marxism? While Marxist philosophy would direct us toward questions of value, labor, profit, exploitation, and class difference, thrift ushers us toward those questions and also to the commodity itself—its apparent death and its rebirth within a nexus of crises of value.[6] We find these crises in the soiled racks and shelves of old sweaters, discarded fad appliances ("The Hotdogger," "The Popcorn Pump," "The FryDaddy"), unmatched martini glasses, and aluminum Christmas trees. And the lessons that both habits of radical critique and afternoons of sorting through thrift stores can teach us simultaneously make us realize that seldom is the commodity exhausted of its value. Its potential handiness, its circulation, and, most important, *re*-circulation, and its potential to have any number of meanings (sentiment, nostalgia, camp, loving disdain) attributed to it are hard to seize within the "economic," as traditionally and rigidly understood. The problem of thrift is not simply one of the use/

exchange nexus, but rather how that opposition can be productively undone by the vibrant improbabilities available in thrift. Both an object of inquiry and a critical practice, both a strategy for coping with graduate student salaries and a template for value-coding, thrift challenges our received notions about how to learn from and about late capitalism. Why do one's research in the library when Raymond Williams's *Keywords* appears, priced at 65 cents at the Salvation Army, or for the cinephiles among us, a bag of 1932 *Photoplays* can be had for $1.95? Why run to Dean and Deluca for a new spice grinder when a selection of Braun coffee grinders, the debris of 1980s yuppie culture, awaits the fussy thrift shopper for $4.95? Not only does the thrift store offer this variety of goods, but thrifting has been central to our intellectual work in that it also makes differences among shoppers visible. In the encounter among an astonishing variety of thrifters of different ethnicities, races, classes, genders, regions, and sizes, a theory of thrift necessarily must involve distinguishing among people's differential relations to capital. Typifying the thrift shopper is as difficult as typifying the thrift merchandise: this is late capital in one of its most complicated settings.

Thrift Tip #3: Evaluate your relationship to racism and your anxieties about class privilege. Thrift will reconfigure your notions of privilege, mainly because thrift erases the semiotic determinants of distinction. Your habitus will not remain intact.

To return briefly to Marx, within the realm of exchange-value, we are told that "all commodities are merely definite quantities of *congealed labortime.*" This sense of labor's coalescing within the commodity and defining its movement through production and consumption helps us to understand the making and selling of new commodities. But what does it say about those goods that come to have no perceived use *or* exchange value within contemporary socio-semiotic registers? Exempting for the moment the fascination with old things that sell for large sums, such as high art and an-

tique furniture, the mere fact of thrift stores' existence suggests different forms of work and different social relations than those determined by the initial productive labor of commodities in their debuts. Thrift may force us to shift our analysis of capitalism from productive labor to consumption (often understood as a form of reproductive labor), yet in that shift we must acknowledge the imbrication of production and consumption. Thus, in *Capital,* when Marx generalizes the wealth of all economies as being the "immense collection of commodities" which that society produces, is he anticipating the very problem of capital's tendency to produce, simply, too much for some in some spaces? "Consumerism," as a name given to postwar economies, has defined the analysis of how we live and work. But too often the term consumerism conceals the fact that the proliferation of goods cannot rely upon, and indeed must ignore, the fact that not all goods are ever, and indeed seldom, completely used up. (To rejoin the example of the linen coat, barring the coat's physical disintegration, it continues to exist in the world after it has been purchased in a first-order setting. Yet, in Marx's analysis, that purchase marks the final moment in the circuit of production and consumption.) Thrift stores embrace the commodity at this very moment in which it becomes entangled in a web of labor and seemingly unrecognizable forms of work (both remunerated and unremunerated via charity). For that reason thrift stores appeal not only as a way of clothing and furnishing our lives, but because they can teach us something about the way that certain facets of capitalism make themselves felt in daily life, by turning our critical attention to practices of consumption hitherto unexplored.

The Crisis of Distinction

We are often surprised that more people don't thrift or address thrift, out of need and out of the pleasure to be found in the acquisition. A common reaction by first-time thrifters (we know what we're talking about: we recruit) to the spectacle of an old Safeway store converted into a Salvation Army is that there's too much to take on here. Likewise, the critical literature on "consumption" has not and cannot begin to sort through all the stuff on the racks and shelves of the thrift store: "lifestyle shopping" is *not* thrift-shopping and the subject of consumption is neither thrift nor the thrifter.[7] While one seldom hears the complaint (except maybe from Jean Baudrillard) that a shopping mall is scaring him or her, one recognizes that the average thrift store, while smaller than a department store, seems to instill a dread in those unfamiliar with thrifts. In part, this may be to some because thrifts obey the logic, anathema to retail, that "used" goods don't need to be distinguished—they are used up, exhausted of value, unworthy of further attention, and it is therefore a challenge to encounter the commodity as it languishes in the realm of uselessness. Simultaneously, though, by putting all the commodities into a sort of crisis in the refusal to distinguish relative worth (that is, exchange), the sense of fear in which it seems that the thrift store cannot be managed by generally acknowledged rules of value-coding confronts the thrifter with the work of adjudicating value beyond or outside its more typical designations: the work demanded by finding something worth buying in the thrift, and perhaps the even greater challenge of deciding that it is worth the price being asked. Not to mitigate matters, thrifters are vocal in their assessment of other thrifters' potential purchases: as one woman announced while looking at our giant framed 1950s photo of Old Faithful: "You couldn't PAY me to take that." No hushed murmurings of the department store are heard here.

With respect to the items apparently in-themselves, in its failure to distinguish among commodities in a hierarchical fashion, thrift value operates through a logic that inverts commonsense determinations of a commodity's worth. The monetary value of a thing can only be known by its small asking price. The value of the commodity is thus deferred to other notions of what might make it desirable, that is, the specific social relations in a given moment whereby an agreed-upon price is met.[8]

More often than not, this leads to a weird amassing of stuff by some thrifters (regular thrifters can often be assumed to collect in delightfully different and aberrant ways) and a sense of the unexpected distribution of thrifted oddities and their accompanying affects. Such collecting is not solely the hallmark of a particular social type such as the "hipster" or the slumming record collector; thrift-shopping seems to lend itself to collecting among many kinds of shoppers who appear in thrifts. Within our own personal experiences, we have met some people with remarkable collections: 1960s "barf-ware" (brown-tinged plastic used in bowls and vases), union badges, religious commemoration photos (christenings, weddings, bar mitzvahs), glitter-rock platform shoes, plastic-bonnet hairdriers, and a rather dizzying array of "I Love You This Much" statuettes. In addition, we have had occasion to witness the unsolicited appearance of these thrift tastes within popular venues.[9] Rather than asserting that the shopper will know the value of the object by its customary, "appropriate" (and, to thrifters, exorbitant) price, as in retail shopping, thrift stores often confront the shopper with the cheapness (i.e., the low price) of a sweater or chair. This act forces the thrift-shopper to contemplate its pleasures and uses in another way. While we would hesitate to call this "use" in a simply nostalgic way (for example, the liberal fetish for Guatemalan clothing or Icelandic hand-knit sweaters), it is vexing to consider what other descriptive term we might bring to bear upon the crises of value which thrift so handily demonstrates.

In order to dispel any fast utopianism around the specter of thrifting, it is important to recall that thrift is itself a product of capitalism, and the convergence of Marxist theory and thrift store shopping for our work appears on the side of abundance and commodities, not in their dearth. It is truer than ever that money, and the relation between labor and value which the money form regulates, is central to capital's concealing of its operations, and the relative lack of money among all but the most affluent classes is said to mete out commodities in a supposedly even fashion. But what thrift reveals through the fact of superabundance among the wealthy is the fallacy of the commodity's alleged depletion: retaining its materiality, but not its cachet, the linen coat of Marx's analysis moves quickly to the thrift, entering another sphere of distribution or continued circulation. There is nothing necessarily democratic about thrifts—they do not operate with an ethos of who needs what the most—but at the same time, thrift stores effectively demonstrate that more customary notions whereby class difference is detected in everyday social interaction are not identical with the decisions that thrifters make to come to the thrift store, nor indicative of the choices they make within the store. The problem is not that class dissipates as a category of critique, but that thrift complicates class beyond a notion of "simple" material circumstances. Indeed, while we do not deny that many shoppers in thrifts form part of the expanding pool of the working poor, unemployed, and "downsized," the effects of the work of thrift are unpredictable.

Further, the differences among people who appear in thrifts can disable the sense in which income is any indicator of possession. Working in a cultural studies program, we have had occasion to hear a number of our senior colleagues from our own and other universities bemoan the fact that the working class in the United States is difficult to ascertain. This lament leads to all sorts of arguments about post-Fordism, the global economy, the sense of a disappearance of a working class (by which they mean the disappearance of a working-class *culture,* which apparently cannot be specified

or identified) in the "information age." These are persistent arguments, but if one wants to behold the effects of capital's reorganization of class, visit your local Value Village or Salvation Army. Most of the shoppers are there because they need to be: the age of "late capital" has bypassed them, at least to the extent of their purchasing power in the domain of the upscale (i.e., anything but thrift stores). Spending time in thrifts can teach us how communities devastated by the economic joyride of the 1980s and 1990s remobilize, and this is not simply shopping to make do. The fact is that most commodities are discarded because of the velocity of fashion, and thrifters know this in ways that even the savviest of cultural critics may forget.

One of the challenging problems that we have had to consider in relation to thrift is our position as consumers of thrift and as allegedly socially mobile professionals of the academy. The problem here is that we are said to be promised greater income with our eventual change in status from graduate students to faculty members. Therefore, the logic runs that someday we will no longer need to resort to such seemingly desperate measures as going to thrift stores, drinking non-imported beer and serving substandard imported cheeses at our parties. Someday, the logic continues, we will be Nordstrom (or Bergdorf) shoppers, too. But, there is a fiercely difficult professional ideology at work in this promise, which runs counter to our experience of the academy. Given the fact that the university, as a site of knowledge production, is being rapidly corporatized, and despite so much polite hand-wringing in the publications of professional associations, whose pages regularly feature "get it off your chest sessions" for frustrated graduate students and junior faculty, the fact is that the university is not going to be divested miraculously of its status as training site for upwardly mobile technocrats. Thus, when we thrift, we are not slumming in order to prepare us for the real shopping that lies ahead, but we thrift to learn, and for life.

*The Anatomy of Desire: "You Can't Always
Get What You Want, But . . . Sometimes . . .
You Get What You Need"*

The rest of this chapter is devoted to the more specific analysis of thrift shopping, attempting to answer the ontological question "What is thrift-shopping?" We continue by comparing "second-order" shopping with "first-order shopping." We acknowledge at the outset that our first-order designation is increasingly problematic in the face of retail's strategies of proliferation and differentiation, in the form of outlet malls, "discount" stores, and the like. Nonetheless, it is possible to make some preliminary comparisons between thrift shopping and the bulk of retail practices. For instance, thrift shopping shares with retail shopping the pleasure of goods on display, immense quantities of items, the promise of satisfaction through the commodity. Like the department store as well as the outlet mall, the finer thrift store will cover every dimension of life's pursuits, offering clothing, furniture, appliances, kitchen gadgets, curtains and towels, bedding, office supplies, toys, china and glasses, accessories, children's clothing, coats, shoes, the occasional snack bar, and, in the largest Goodwill store in Seattle, an espresso bar *and* a museum.

Like retail shopping, too, thrift shopping is complicated. It is less often based on the desire for a novel commodity available on the market (such as a George Foreman grill, although those are already in the thrifts). But it does hold the promise if not its fulfillment of a targeted object of necessity or desire (a linen coat for the summer, a replacement fan, a black dress for the holiday party, larger clothes for growing children).

Thrift Tip #4: Avoid arriving at the thrift with a specific commodity on your mind. Recently, one of us overheard two Gen-X women asking a pricer for aluminum Christmas trees; to their horror, the pricer responded, "We just threw ten or twelve of those into the dumpster," gleefully knowing that

dumpster-diving would be beyond the women's boundaries of acceptable "shopping." It was.

As with all shopping, it is an outing (in both senses, perhaps—you will notice that many thrift shoppers are queer), if a necessary one, requiring leisure time. But it can be a collective activity pleasurable in itself, regardless of the aim or even the presence of an aim. And, like retail shopping, thrift shopping can also be tiring, frustrating, confounding, a haphazard experience designed to toy with desire. For the working poor, the temporarily poor, the increasing poor, the homeless, the privileged, and the marginal (measured by class but also by other axes of social definition, such as vectors of sexuality, race, locale, and ethnicity), thrift shopping is nonetheless shopping, although a shopping experience that often reconfigures how decreasing purchase power can result in gainful expenditures.

But of a significantly different sort. Thrift shopping differs from retail shopping in at least several ways, some of which we provide in axiomatic fashion.

A. Thrift shopping *rarely* satisfies the hunt for a particular object, even if that desire motivates the shopping experience. It instead requires fluidity and is structured by chance and surprise. When you buy your life's goods from a thrift, you are as much at the mercy of time, chance, and luck as the next shopper, and showing up with twenty bucks in your pocket offers no assurances that you're more likely to find the $4.95 coat you've been looking for than the person with a five dollar bill and two ones. It is this sense of chance, of the aleatory threats and rewards that thrifting can offer, that makes retail begin to reveal the assurances it offers, at much higher cost: multiple units of the same thing, repeated in a variety of colors and sizes, with no panic that the "good stuff" might disappear before the store opens. There are, of course, important material differences of income that show up in thrifts—where the most affluent shopper may pick up the ten dollar lamp without a second thought, we may agonize over the purchase of so expensive an item.

Thrift Tip #5: With the exception of Goodwill, thrifts don't permit you to return any item. Ever.

Because thrift store merchandise is most often donated, to continue with our coat example, it is rare that one will find the coveted linen overcoat (a) in one's size, (b) with both sleeves and lining intact, (c) without a large grease stain on the front lapel, or (d) of an acceptable cut. More than likely, one will settle on a tan wool overcoat or no overcoat at all . . . until the next trip. Thrift forces the issue, literally and metaphorically, of the stain and the question of style (and therefore of taste).

B. Thrift shopping has an entirely different relation to novelty and quality than does retail shopping. Very few items at thrift stores are new (see axiom D below), and none carries the guarantee that it will function, or fit, or contain all the requisite pieces, etc. This is marked in thrifts by the ubiquitous disavowal, "as is," the retail name for broken, damaged, tainted, or stained (as in our favorite room at IKEA). Like the "save as" command on computers, the "as is" reminds us that the commodity, like the text, has a mutable identity, and that it has a history. The stain thus exceeds the fiction (for it is a fiction, as anyone who has ever returned a new purchase knows) of the guarantee. The stain gestures to the commodity's past, it functions as an ever-present reminder of its recycled nature, and it hints at a realm, which we might call the abject (literally, moving away, not simply from the normative but in the sense of traveling further afield from the paradigms through which the normative is intelligible), that the new commodity attempts to erase. It is a reminder of dirt, of sweat, of piss or shit, of grease and grime. Of labor: unlike the new commodity, which conceals these relations in its fetish-character, the thrift item reminds us of its past by forcing us to consider, "Where did this come from?" That is, the very fact of its circulation in this realm forces the question of its production. The effects of this recognition

are not guaranteed to lead to anything at all, much less revolution, but it does produce a different awareness of commodity-relations and the affect, or "aura," surrounding different items which can be political. Our central example of this effect would be the sudden appearance at one of our local thrifts of what signified as a gay man's wardrobe (Mr. Stein, his name tags indicated). In purchasing Mr. Stein's lavender Barney's dress shirts and flamboyant ties, we were forced to contemplate the likelihood that Mr. Stein died of AIDS, a legacy which we literally wear and remember to the present day. If this represents a transformation of memory, of mourning, it is a form of preservation shared by a community pressed to contemplate the signifying complexities of "these things," the title of an *Out* magazine article which opens with the very problematic we seek to elaborate in this chapter:

> A confession, Mark: When you died, last August, what I wanted most was your clothing. Others in attendance just wanted you back, but what good would that have been, in your condition? No, I coveted the leather jacket and the dozen pairs of pleated chinos (though they'd have needed taking up by several inches), the cashmere scarves, the ottery overcoat I'd seen so often, gleaming in the street light, with you gleaming inside it. I wanted these things not as mementos to hang in the closet and remember you by but on their own merits, as merchandise.[10]

This vexed form of wearing history, both personal and proximate, and emphatically aware of clothing as a commodity, is substantially different in its affective dimensions from the practice of buying something retail which is "environmentally responsible" or shopping at a retail store that promises to contribute a percentage of the profits from a given item to a "good cause," still at some remove and rarely embodied in this way. Significantly, the flip side of this affective recognition is that the luxury items Mr. Stein or Mark "passed on" more than likely were produced under relations of exploitation (a Turkish sweatshop) than in an environmentally sound Newbury Street entrepreneurship. This circumstance forces us, on the underside of our example, to remember that "sexual orientation" rarely guarantees a swerve in the international division of labor.

C. Thrift shopping will not cooperate in one of the central functions of retail: to determine mass taste, and therefore to determine "appropriate" social signification, including the lines of gender division. Not even the minimal requirement that an item be appropriately gendered (by department, say, or specialty store) functions at the thrift, since "cross-shopping" is easy without hovering salespeople, and the items themselves are rarely separated "correctly" along gender lines. A paradigmatic rack of "men's" overcoats, to continue Marx's and our example, will likely look something like this: leathers gathered together, from the 1970s calf-length through the late 1980s bomber jackets (think Shaft to Banana Republic) followed by coats sorted by color (a thrift principle) of various fabrics (wool, cashmere, camel hair, blends) followed by tweeds and, finally, trench coats, lined and unlined. All are of different origins in time and in style, some reaching back to as early as the forties or even earlier (depending on where in the country one thrifts) and some roughly contemporary. Many will retain labels, indicating origin and size (and occasionally something more fanciful, such as the cashmere blazer Matthew recently found for Amy with a label that boasts, "This garment made of 100% pure shit"), but others will have no label at all. The sizes themselves are not uniform and are of mixed gender designation. While the retail store sanctions the acceptability—in terms of quality, style, and gender specificity—of any given garment merely by carrying it (and therefore by advertising it and/or relying on national if targeted ad campaigns), the thrift store carries any item donated to it which is

in "saleable" condition, and that term is obviously broad indeed. The question one most often hears in the aisles of thrift stores, "Is this OK?," means something like, "Is this absolutely weird, anachronistic, or ugly, or might it be cutting edge, anticipatory of coming trends or fabulously hip?"

D. Thrift shopping necessarily links the question of style with the question of value in ways different from retail shopping. Thrift stores are not uniformly 501(C)(3) non-profit establishments, but many of them are (Goodwill, Salvation Army, church-related stores such as St. Vincent de Paul, Junior League, SPCA, etc.). Both types, though, have a relation to "charity" beyond their IRS status: thrift stores exist ideologically to provide goods at low cost to those who cannot "afford" retail goods. Due to this ethos and because their only overhead expenses are connected to the building and staff and not the inventory, thrift stores are able to price goods at levels lower than required by a retail calculus. But what rules does thrift pricing obey, if any, and how does one determine value within the thrift codings?

Thrift Tip #6: Uniformly, as we suggested above, new goods are priced higher than used goods. An acrylic sweater with a tag from K-mart still on it may be $7.95, but a cashmere sweater from Saks Fifth Avenue may sell for as little as $.90. On a practical level, this means that one can purchase a glamorous birthday gift for less than the cost of a Taco Bell Extreme Value Meal.

Even without value-coding the cultural significance of fabric (acrylic vs. cashmere), the thrift pricing scenario is divorced from value-coding based on what equivalent items would sell for if they were new.

Thrift Tip #7: "Old" items perceived to be of "collectable" value are priced higher than "simply" old items. At one thrift store where we shop, a set of 2' tall ceramic Billie Jean King and Bobby Riggs statues have remained unsold for $125 for the past four years.

Thrift pricers rely on antiques and collectibles guides wherein certain items are designated as desirable and therefore of higher value than those not mentioned. Examples in this category include Fiestaware and McCoy, Kirby vacuum cleaners, certain "antique" furniture, Oriental rugs, cinema and popular culture artifacts, old metal fans, anything with identifiable art deco lines, clothing perceived as "vintage" as opposed to "just" old, quilts, and cameras. This method of pricing, however, clearly relies upon the cultural knowledge, the ability to identify and value-code, of the pricers themselves (and their participation or lack thereof in the circulation of these items outside the thrift as well as their perceptions within the thrift of desired commodities, since pricing relies equally on the patterns of consumption of regular thrift shoppers), the comprehensive nature or reliability of the pricing guides, and, most important, the ebb and flow of value within the spheres of antique stores, flea markets, collectors' circles, and the like. Certain items in our area therefore evade this logic: ties from the 1940s and 1950s are rarely marked up, likewise unmarked china and porcelain, and the "just" old which cannot be marked by pricers as valuable. The pricers' attribution of value forces the thrift shopper to reconsider the "worth" of certain items s/he may have passed up; a $4.95 bag of plastic dinnerware (Melmac, now increasingly "hot") may draw the thrifter's attention to "value" which may have escaped her/him otherwise. Clearly, part of the challenge and fun for some thrifters involves "scoring" items perceived as valuable by them, and not by the pricers, for as little money as possible. But equally challenging for the thrifter is the tracking of value as it finds determination within notions of trash, debris, the unworthy. Unlike the auction, the supreme example of the so-called democratic determination of value, thrift shopping cannot presume the equal distribution of cultural capital upon which the ethos of equal competition relies.

Whereas the auction is always assumed to have the force of driving the price of the commodity up, the thrift store displays a countervailing tendency of driving the price of the commodity down. The thrill of the auction depends upon the shared knowledge that a kilim from the 1920s among the cognoscenti is worth upward of $1,200, but the thrift presumes that not a soul, regardless of what she or he knows about the marketplace, can or will pay more than $79.95 for any commodity whatsoever.

But this slippage raises, then, the second half of our question: How does one determine value within thrift value-coding? When is an item "worth" its price, and what arithmetic is required for such a determination? The answer, "it depends," can be demystified as a matter of individual taste and whimsy through an analysis of the dimensions and specificities, the economy, of the phenomenon itself. Since thrift shopping is an exercise in chance and surprise, as we indicated above (*Thrift Tip #4*), it is virtually impossible to say, as one says on the way to the mall, "Today I would like to buy a pair of running shoes for less than $50." This example produces some of the most unwieldy contradictions of thrift shopping, first among them the nexus of knowledge involved in the measurement of value (a risk minimized by the retail "guarantee" of newness and the promise of the return). The thrift, unlike the Foot Locker, may not have a single pair of running shoes in one's size that day, and, if a pair is found, the willingness to accept the hand-scrawled price involves a number of questions.

It is necessary here, as it is in examining retail, to explore the determinations on the "I" of our example. If the "I" is a yuppie running for leisure/exercise, the "I" will likely be overeducated on the characteristics, brand names, and worth more generally of running shoes: if they have been worn by a previous runner, that runner may have had problems with pronation leading to problems for the thrift shopper in stride or in physical stress as a result. The thrifter may not be able to run in the shoes, let alone go thrift shopping in them; members of the underclass know as well as over-educated technocrats what thrifting, and leisure, involve. The thrift shopper may also know that even shoes which have never been worn lose their cushioning as the materials age, and may even know as well that only New Balance running shoes come in very wide sizes. If a pair of appropriately sized New Balance running shoes is available in the thrift that day, priced at $3.95, is it worth the risk that the previous wearer may have molded them in such a way that the shopper will encounter poten-tial physical problems? (Thrift shopping *is* physi-cally demanding.) Any variation in the cultural capital our shopper possesses leads to variations in consuming decisions: running shoes may be in vogue for a particular constituency, and s/he may want only those which "look best." (And, thrifting reveals that even the most "debased" shopper car-ries with her/him questions of socio/cultural aes-thetic evaluation.) And a middle-aged heart attack victim who is beginning an exercise plan may only demand that the shoes hold up on the treadmill, whereas the inveterate thrifter will worry primar-ily about their ability to move through the nasti-ness of snow, oil, and gravel of the parking lot, all of which pertain to our specific locale. Balanc-ing knowledge with the *risk* of any purchase is a hallmark of value-coding in certain dimensions of thrift shopping, where the risk that any given item will be "flawed" is minimized in retail shopping. Thrift calls attention, then, to commonsense as-sumptions about pricing in relation to affective matrices of value-coding (i.e., "it just feels good— I don't know why"), while retail relies on a less flex-ible grid for determining a commodity's worth.

Thrift shopping also, however, poses chal-lenges to the division between function or neces-sity and desire (use and exchange: our vexing bi-nary). Someone shopping for a functional soup pot may snap up a $3.95 Wear-ever crock ("plug in

it when you go to work: it's a full meal when you come home, barring any fire hazards"), while an-other consumer with more upscale pretensions (but not necessarily knowledge or income) may opt for the $7.95 Le Creuset or Calphalon equiva-lent. This type of "brand hunting" might seem only to characterize those more formally educated thrift shoppers whose cultural capital is dispro-portionate to their income (such as graduate stu-dents!) or those who are shopping for the thrill of the bargain rather than the so-called utility of the purchase or, The Enemy, the thrift shopper buy-ing goods for resale at "vintage" or "consignment" shops. But these distinctions quickly break down, both in the store and in the analysis: thrift begs the question, "When is something necessary?" They also break down to the extent that one realizes that *all* shoppers are "label conscious," so that seeking an All-Clad omelette pan is just as haphazard and labor-intensive as pursuing a "utilitarian" Revere-Ware two-quart saucepan lid. More particularly, thrift shopping demystifies the manufacture of necessity by capitalism, and one is not required to have read Marx to know this.

E. Thrift stores, however, harbor some of the same contradictions as retail, but they tend to make at least one of them more visible. Thrifts are filled with bodies that "don't fit" idealized and ostensibly normative contours, yet the donated clothing, especially, reproduces the disdain for those bodies held in contempt by the retail mar-ket. As one woman on an Internet discussion group eloquently lamented,

> To bring in another thread topic, anyone wanna join me in griping about the lack of big-people clothes in most thrift stores? I spend a lot of time in thrift shops (Goodwill, St. Vincent de Paul, ReVisions, etc.) and about all I find for larger sizes are polyester stretch pants (the kind with that funky "crease" "sewn" down the fronts of the legs) and those Omar-the-Tentmaker muumuu dresses (usually in table-cloth-size-flower patterns).

Women of size may be able to cross-shop a few cotton flannel shirts in men's big sizes (in the "XL" section, usually separated for both men and women), but thrift is generally not congenial—either logistically or in terms of the merchandise—for bodies that contest the industry's standard 4–16 range. Thrifts do, on the other hand, expose the fact that "most" shoppers are not in that range at all. Rather than consign them to a dark corner of a large department store or to a specialty "plus-size" shop, thrifts guarantee that the often self-satisfied "normative" shopper will encounter a range of bodies during any given outing: big folks, wheelchair-bound folks, folks on crutches, etc. While that juxtaposition again does not ensure a politics, it certainly does prompt thrift shoppers to contemplate the calculated designs of the fashion industry and its regulation of bodies and "looks."

F. Lastly, thrift shopping produces its own "organic" intellectuals; thrift is a field of knowledge production outside the academy and has tentacles into zine culture, Gen-X culture, Martha Stewart features, Internet discussion groups, and the like. More than a rest stop on the information highway, thrift "sites" reveal modes of pleasure in and coping with the morphing dimensions of late capital. Al Hoff, Girl Reporter, publishes a zine on thrifting, *ThriftSCORE,* recruiting the thrift army with tips on how to: get banned from a thrift, tell alpaca from acrylon, buy paint-by-numbers, make a TV star wear a crocheted beer hat, etc. Reading *ThriftSCORE* (or teaching *ThriftSCORE* to our undergraduates) is an exercise in popular history, in the vagaries and determinations of style, in the constitution of communities across regional and economic borders. Retro denim and tiki parties, swimsuits and star culture: all are occasions for inquiry, historicizing, and contemplation equal to or surpassing academic commentary on popular culture; the way in which second-order shopping becomes socially inscribed has become a field in itself worth seeking out for the ways it can inform pop culture analysis.

A sampling of Hoff's work might entice the reader to seek out other thrifters and their knowledges. For example, here are the first ten items from Al's "75 Things I HATE about Shopping in Thrift Stores":

Everything reported below is TRUE and happened to me (though thankfully not on the same day). [with apologies to John Waters for ripping off his style . . .]

Arrgh! The alarm goes off at 7:45 A.M. I hate to get up, but you gotta be at the thrifts early. [1] I go and grab half a cup of joe. I really need two cups but thrift stores never have bathrooms. [2] OK, let's go!

The First Thrift: It's freezing in here and I left my jacket in the car! [3] The store is set up so everybody has to sidle down this one narrow little aisle to get to the rest of the store. [4] It is also the shoe and dishware aisle, so it's clogged. [5] *"There's a kind of hush all over the world tonight."* [6] There's some guy taking up the whole aisle while he's super slowly moving plates one at a time from one pile to another. [7] Excuse me, excuse me, excuse me—I bug outta there for another aisle.

I eyeball a magnificent fold-up snack tray with pink-and-rhinestone poodles watching '50s TV, but it's too awkward to haul around. [8] I stick it between some bad paintings, and cut myself on a rusty picture frame nail. [9] *"My baby loves love, my baby loves lovin'"* [10] [11]

Thrift Protocols: Before You Go . . .

The premise of this essay is that knowledge is produced in various sectors which licensed academic critique frequently fails to recognize. To that extent, we would fail as Marxist shoppers if we left the reader without bearings in the arena of thrift. Thus, we would close with some final suggestions for practical and theoretical understanding of the anatomy of thrift:

— Pee before you leave home and dress in layers. Thrifts provide only the most rudimentary of services (lighting, over- or underheating, soft 1980s hits and a preponderance of Christian ballads—expect to hear "From a Distance"), but they seldom provide restrooms. Also, wear clothing that allows you to try on other clothing over it: shorts, leggings, tights, etc. Thrifts rarely provide fitting rooms, and, if they do, they are occupied or otherwise undesirable.

— Don't go on an empty stomach. Thrifts rarely have food, and you won't want to lose shopping time to eating. Exception: Akron, Ohio, Village Discount Outlet with Snack Bar, 69 cents for hotdog and small beverage.

— Carry rope or string in your car, or, better, borrow a truck.

— Look in the phone book under used furniture, thrift, consignment. *Do not tear out the page if it is a public phonebook;* this is just good manners (thanks to Al Hoff for this necessary reminder). Make a map. Give yourself time. Things to look up: Goodwill, Salvation Army, St. Vincent de Paul, Value Village, Thrift Town.

— Get a cart. Watch your cart. People will shop your cart.

— Go at the beginning of the month, or when you know there will be new stuff.

— Bend over and examine the space beneath the racks. An occasional cashmere item falls through, since most merchandise is on wire hangers. Check the pockets of things you examine or buy. Get in there. Look inside old books for items such as postcards, photographs, recipes, letters, bookmarks, and the like.

— Surrender preconceived notions of what "your size" is, particularly if you're going to cross-shop. Even if you really like something, make sure that you won't mind throwing it away or giving it away or redonating it later. Sometimes you can have too much stuff.

What is degraded to some only reveals how degradation works, how certain practices, including those of the university, maintain their own legitimacy by continually coding some texts or practices as "valuable" and others less sacrosanct as "trash." To those keepers of the gate, we (the dubious, the queens, the poor, the marginalized, the big, the trashy) say "thrift on."

Notes

1   Martyn J. Lee, *Consumer Culture Reborn: The Cultural Politics of Consumption* (London: Routledge, 1993), xi.

2   See Angela McRobbie's *Zoot Suits and Second-Hand Dresses: An Anthology of Fashion and Music* (Boston: Unwin Hyman, 1988), and Daniel Miller, *A Theory of Shopping* (Ithaca: Cornell University Press, 1998).

3   We will attempt here to define several of the specific Marxist terms that we use in this essay. By invoking value, we refer to Marx's struggle to differentiate *use value* from *exchange value;* according to Marx, use value is the sense of an object's necessity ("I need these shoes to keep my feet warm") whereas exchange value is what the object will bring on the marketplace. In prior historical moments, exchange fluctuated in relation to what an object might be bartered for, and for which precious metals could be said to stand in for, whereas in contemporary capitalist societies, the exchange value *appears* to be determined by the marketplace of goods and money. What such exchanges conceal is the fact that the object is made through industrial means using standardized labor, and exchange can conceal the creation of *profit.* Through his analysis of the movement of money through social relations of production and exchange, Marx argues that what is circulating most powerfully in capitalist societies is not commodities, but money itself as it functions both as the medium of exchange and the medium of profit.

4   *Labor* is central to an analysis of cultural value because it is the human production of commodities, most commonly in industrial settings, that allows for many commodities, and indeed many different kinds of commodities, to become available. Despite glowing reports of the new "information economy" in industrialized nations that is said to have dispelled the function of the working class, the fact remains that "knowledge work"

in the United States, Europe, and Japan retains the conditions of labor under capital, while the production of clothing, cars, and stereos has been dispersed to the venues of the "developing world" where wages are substantially less and regulated with more considerable force than might be allowed elsewhere. The painful irony of a woman making Disney sweatshirts in Haiti, and then having them "donated" back through charitable means after they have circulated through France or California, drives home the perverse logics of globalization.

5   An important companion historical investigation into those institutions contemporary to Marx, such as pawn shops and flea markets, would provide a context for this essay.

6   The history of human societies, according to Marx, is the history of struggle among classes. In contemporary societies, this means that there are primarily two classes, those who own the means of production (whom Marx identified as capitalists and their allies, the *bourgeoisie)* and who enjoy the fruits of profit, and those who have only their labor to sell (the *proletariat)* and who thus are exploited, in the sense that their labor, extracted beyond compensation, is both maximized to its fullest extent and used to expand profit. The reality of this situation is, of course, more complicated, as the exploitation that a migrant worker in the San Fernando Valley experiences is considerably different from that of a unionized French truck driver. Nevertheless, both enter the scene of production with theoretically the same thing, namely their labor power to sell.

7   See Rob Shields, ed., *Lifestyle Shopping: The Subject of Consumption* (London: Routledge, 1992).

8   Much of this discussion expresses our debt to Gayatri Chakravorty Spivak's work on value and its discontinuous and textualized status. See "Scattered Speculations on the Question of Value," in *In Other Worlds: Essays in Cultural Politics* (New York: Methuen, 1987), 154–78. Spivak's reading through Derrida disrupts the use/exchange binary, a reading which makes visible the labor ignored by certain "orthodox" Marxist analyses of the commodity and concealed through the commodity's circulation.

9   Joy's Tale of Unexpected Thrift:

> It was Austin, Texas, 1988. k.d. lang's *Shadowlands* had just been released. I went to Waterloo Records, bought the CD, came home and started to play it. While perusing the CD cover and insert, I saw my shirt. I mean, I saw my #@!*& shirt! What was k.d. doing in the shirt that I had thrifted in Austin and then given to my girlfriend Jan?
>
> I called Jan and said, "Hey, why is k.d. wearing the shirt I gave to you?"
>
> Let me tell you a little about the shirt so you can understand why it was so special. See, I thrifted the shirt in a Salvation Army in Austin, Texas, in about 1986. It was lime green, long-sleeved, cotton with tiny raised felt horseheads all over it. It was a western-style shirt with those "snap" buttons and all. And, it had really, really long lapels and sleeves. It was hand-tailored for an air force serviceman who must have been stationed in Korea—the tag was stitched in the collar with his name on it. I loved the shirt but thought that Jan—a wistful grunge girl before they were so classified—could really do it justice.
>
> Well, Jan explained that she had worn the shirt and that her roommate Danielle had wanted to wear it also. At this time, Jan and Danielle were friends with k.d. lang, and she would party with them when she came to Austin for gigs. k.d. and Danielle were sort of "involved" for a while, and k.d. saw The Shirt. Jan had loaned it to Danielle for a fancy dyke night on the town, and, to make a long story short, k.d. saw The Shirt and had to have it.
>
> And, now she does.

10 Jesse Green, "These Things," *Out* (June 1995): 128–30.
11 "75 Things I HATE about Shopping in Thrift Stores," *ThriftSCORE* (issue 2, summer 1994), 6–7. (*ThriftSCORE* P.O. Box 90282, Pittsburgh, PA 15224; e-mail: al@girlreporter.com).

Shopping Sense: Fanny Fern and Jennie June on Consumer Culture in the Nineteenth Century

Elana Crane

In her critique of *New York Times* columnist Maureen Dowd, Susan Faludi sketches out the two roles between which women journalists have historically been forced to choose: "Since women first broke into press punditry, they've had to play either the primly principled commentator or the wickedly frivolous disher." Contemporary women columnists, though, "have been breaking down these molds by voicing passionate beliefs—particularly on women's rights—with wit and impudence." Faludi now fears, however, that "we seem to have been returned to the days of Jennie June's shopping and gossip columns."[1] Faludi juxtaposes politics (women's rights) with shopping; in her view the two are mutually exclusive, but this was certainly not the case during the second half of the nineteenth century at the time Jennie June and other women were writing. Shopping, as it developed in the 1850s, demanded that participants learn new ways of acting, understand the new language of consumer culture, and adopt or reject new styles of fashion. All of these areas were considered political and at times controversial, as shopping took place in the public sphere and raised important questions about women's economic and political independence. In contrast to Faludi's trivializing of shopping as a topic not worthy of a columnist's attention, many prominent nineteenth-century women journalists devoted a considerable amount of copy to women's interaction with consumer culture. These writers saw themselves as consumer experts, guiding women

around what historian Mary Ryan calls "the invisible tentacles of the urban market."[2]

June and her contemporary, Fanny Fern, offer complicated and detailed reactions to the emergence of consumer culture. These professional journalists run counter to the still prevalent characterization of nineteenth-century women authors as "largely ignorant of the developing economic situation of which they were a part."[3] For more than twenty years, from the 1850s through 1870s, Fern and June devoted a great deal of attention to examining fashion, shopping, and the ways in which women's movements were routed through consumerism.

Fanny Fern, the persona developed by Sara Willis Parton, started writing for several weekly papers in Boston, and her success enabled her to move to New York City in 1854.[4] From 1855 until her death in 1872, Fern wrote a weekly column for the *New York Ledger,* a story paper with national syndication; over the years she also published them in a series of books.[5] As one critic has commented, Fern was "a combination of advice columnist, gadfly, and social reformer."[6] Fern based many of her columns on things she observed in the city or news items she read in the papers, and her columns often responded to modern goings-on with biting sarcasm and a caustic common sense approach. Shopping was not spared from her sharp appraisal; in Fern's work, shopping is a nuisance, an arduous task, or a ridiculous waste of time. In "A Glance at a Chameleon Subject," for example, Fern adopts the persona of a fashion writer to satirize the enterprise. She advises women to "puff your hair and your skirts. Lace your lungs and your handkerchief." Responding to a reader's question, "Tell you the fashions?" Fern replies, "Take a walk down Broadway and see for yourself. If you have a particle of sense, it will cure you of your absorbing interest in that question during your natural life, though your name be written Methuselah."[7]

While Fern used sarcasm to discuss the topic of shopping, Jennie June employed a more straightforward and serious approach to her work as a fashion columnist. The monthly articles June produced informed readers about new styles and directed women through the complicated world of fashion and consumer culture. Though known more today for her part in organizing the late nineteenth-century women's club movement, Jennie June, the pseudonym of Jane Cunningham Croly, was also a prolific fashion writer.[8] In the 1850s, June syndicated a monthly fashion column, "Fashionable Intelligence," and in the 1860s, while editing and writing for the women's fashion magazine *Demorest's Monthly*, June started another monthly fashion column, "New York and Paris Fashions" carried in urban newspapers across the country.[9] Though June's work predated the creation of women's pages in newspapers, it does reflect the more commercial enterprise of the newspaper business that emerged during the second half of the nineteenth century. Financial support for newspapers shifted from political organizations to advertisers; the largest source of revenue for many newspapers came from department stores, and these advertisers urged newspapers to introduce material to attract women readers.[10]

I focus on Fern and June because of the great deal of writing they generated about shopping and their interest in exploring what shopping meant for women. They wrote during the time department stores first emerged, when ready-made clothing was beginning to be produced, and when stores first started the work of transforming shopping into a leisure pursuit for women. Stewart's Marble Palace, which opened in 1846, was one of the first department stores in America. Other department stores emerged in the 1850s and with them selling techniques changed; owners sold items at fixed prices, created a free entry policy to encourage browsing, and made their profits through quick stock turnover. Stores built up near

each other to establish shopping districts, pushing out housing and transforming residential areas into commercial zones. By 1869, the stretch of New York City's Broadway between Tenth Street and Madison Square was known as the "ladies' mile." It consisted of a number of large department stores (including Stewart's as well as Lord and Taylor's), jewelry stores, dressmakers, and ladies saloons. Although other women writers certainly contemplated the new demands of shopping, Fern and June each produced a significant body of writing observing, advising, and often complaining about the role of shopping in women's lives. Their writings serve as a bridge between the domestic-focused work which dominated the first half of the nineteenth century and the direct critiques of consumerism made by theorists such as Charlotte Perkins Gilman at the end of the century.[11]

Fern's and June's work, as it envisions a readership of both men and women, differs from that of many nineteenth-century women fiction and advice writers who address an exclusively female audience and view the marketplace primarily through the lens of the domestic sphere.[12] For example, in Catharine Beecher and Harriet Beecher Stowe's 1869 *American Woman's Home,* the authors offer women guidance on home management; they focus on how women might care for their families and homes more efficiently. Consequently, Beecher and Stowe's chapter on clothing spends very little time on women's fashions, with most of the chapter devoted to how to dress one's daughters: "There is no duty of those persons having control of a family where principle and practice are more at variance than in regulating the dress of young girls, especially at the most important and critical period of life."[13] Their guide imagines an audience of women who do their own sewing and who shop only to purchase the necessary supplies. In contrast, Fern and June both see shopping as occupying a larger part of women's lives and involving more than just purchasing necessary household items; in their work, shopping signals a shift from woman's identity being formed through her role as wife and mother to the more individualistic pleasures afforded by consumer culture. These writers also insist that shopping requires all parties involved to learn new forms of behavior. While their work does offer women advice, it is in the form of how to analyze the retail market, and just as much advice is proffered to businessmen. Examining their work not only revises assumptions about women's roles but expands our understanding of women's writing at mid-century. Instead of discussing women's lives in relation to the domestic sphere, Fern and June emphasize women's public role as consumers. As active consumers, women can lobby to effect better working conditions for store employees, advocate improvement of the ready-made clothing industry, and begin to question their status within patriarchal culture.

The meaning of consumption for women has also engaged theorists of women's experience of modernity. Recent discussions of shopping consider whether the female shopper can serve as a counterpart to the male flâneur, the urban figure introduced by Charles Baudelaire and later discussed in several essays by Walter Benjamin.[14] The flâneur, with his aimless city strolling, browsing, and observing, has served as a figure representative of modernity, but his experiences have largely been thought to have excluded women. Janet Wolff argues that modernity has been defined as what is experienced in the public sphere; she rightly argues that this version of modernity has left women out of the picture. Wolff argues that because women were relegated to the private sphere, their experience of modernity has never been considered. She does not believe women had a visible presence in the public sphere and says that there is no point in trying to search for the figure of the flâneuse because she did not exist. Conceding that department stores created new sites

for women in public, Wolff dismisses shopping as an experience comparable to those of the flâneur: "although consumerism is a central aspect of modernity, and moreover mediated the public-private division, the peculiar characteristics of 'the modern' which I have been considering—the fleeting, anonymous encounter and the purposeless strolling—do not apply to shopping or to women's activities either as public signs of their husband's wealth or as consumers."[15] As Elizabeth Wilson notes, Wolff relies on Thorstein Veblen's analysis of women's role as conspicuous consumers to inform her understanding of women's shopping and views shopping as a fairly passive activity.[16] Wolff believes that no female counterpart to the flâneur exists; women simply could not wander alone throughout the city. Instead, Wolff says that we must look at the private side of modernity. She seems to be saying that we have had too narrow a definition of modernity, but her own understanding of modernity's "private manifestations" is equally as confining in its exclusion of shopping. Shopping, though, did entail more than consuming or publicizing wealth, and if we think about it creating a separate urban space for women, it is possible to see how studying shopping can also contribute to redefining modernity.

Opposing Wolff's dismissal of the female shopper as a counterpart to the flâneur, film theorist Anne Friedberg considers shopping a useful site for examining women's experience of modernity: "It was as a consumer that the flâneuse was born."[17] Friedberg sees shopping as a practice that allowed women to participate in the new mobile models of vision. "To shop: as a verb, it implies choice, empowerment in the relation between looking and having, the act of buying as a willful choice. To shop is to muse in the contemplative mode, an activity that combines diversion, self-gratification, expertise, and physical activity."[18] Friedberg does, however, acknowledge that while shopping could be empowering, "new freedoms of lifestyle and 'choice' were available, but . . .

women were addressed as consumers in ways that played on deeply rooted cultural constructions of gender."[19] Overall, though, Friedberg finds that many of the characteristics associated with the flâneur (the aimless walking, browsing, and musing) can also be applied to the shopper, and Friedberg considers women's access to these experiences positive.

Wolff and Friedberg represent two approaches to an understanding of the role consumption played in women's lives, but neither adequately addresses the complicated and at times contradictory aspects of shopping. During the nineteenth century, shopping was a new experience and appeared to disrupt social norms. Women consumers were considered a threat to urban order; just being visible in the city challenged assumptions about women's position within society. Some commentators argued that shopping was dangerous; they described it as a vice or mania and criticized women for the hours they spent downtown. As one 1881 editorial complained: "The awful prevalence of the vice of shopping among women is one of those signs of the times which lead the thoughtful patriot almost to despair of the future of our country. Few people have any idea of the extent to which our women are addicted to this purse-destroying vice."[20] This writer clearly felt threatened by women shoppers. Historian William Leach argues that too many scholars have followed this lead and treated shopping as a kind of disease infecting female consumers. Missing is any consideration of the positive impact consumer culture may have had on women. His own interest, he explains, lies "largely with those patterns of consumer life that implied a new freedom from self-denial and from repression, a liberation that promised to expand the province of rewarding work and individual expression for women."[21] Leach examines late-nineteenth-century women's diaries and argues that women were fascinated with the opportunities shopping provided for pleasure and escape from the home.

As Gillian Swanson argues, we need to avoid the traps of either pathologizing or celebrating consumption. "Both the fixity of sexual categories and an inherently negative view of consumption need to be superseded so that the involvements of women in the city and the various forms of cultural consumption that form part of modern urban experience can be included as components of civic life."[22] My understanding of the role of consumption is similar to Swanson's. In order to see shopping as part of public life, it is necessary to shed the belief that consumption is at worst an affliction or at the least a triviality; it is equally important not to overstate the liberatory powers shopping might hold for consumers. What fascinates me about Fern and June's work is the intense scrutiny they bring to shopping, avoiding sensational or derisive commentary, which suggested shopping was a vice and that women were unable to control themselves from wanting things. However, they do not imagine shopping as an entirely positive way for women to spend their time. In contrast to the private diaries Leach discusses, the women's public writing on consumer culture is more ambivalent. Instead, their work advises women how they might use their position as consumers to improve labor practices and shape the new manufacturing and retailing industries while recognizing that shopping served as a hollow substitute for the careers and opportunities routinely denied them by the cult of domesticity. Fern, who consistently identified with and showed concern for working-women, emphasized improving labor practices to create a better shopping environment. June's role as a fashion expert led her to focus on the manufacturing industry's production of ready-made clothing and retailers' selling strategies. Both writers describe shopping as creating a separate female urban sphere, and they worry about the channeling of all of women's energies toward shopping. Although they do make specific recommendations for improving consumer culture, Fern and June ultimately see shopping as preventing women from assuming other public roles such as learning a profession or gaining the right to vote. A close examination of these writers' columns suggests both a necessary revision of existing scholarship and a more nuanced approach to women's involvement in consumer culture.

Store Manners

The space of the shopping district demanded new ways of behaving. In her history of women sales clerks in the early twentieth-century department store, Susan Porter Benson has shown that the intersection of male managers, female employees, and female customers often created shifting power alliances. Although managers and customers had a shared class background, women customers were often suspicious of store managers and managers despaired of women customers' demands. Similarly, although class differences separated the women customers from the women sales clerks, their shared gender also allied them against the managers.[23] These different relations among shopping's participants, though, existed even before the period Benson examines. Fern's columns between the 1850s and 1870s examine the relationships between women customers and male and female clerks, male bosses and their employees, and women customers and bosses and attempt to negotiate among the interests of each of these three groups. As Fern understands it, women customers want to be able to shop in peace and receive polite service, store owners want to sell their goods, and employees want not to be at the mercy of time-monopolizing customers and mean employers. Balancing these interests, Fern directs her attention to what middle-class women can do to meliorate working conditions, and the kinds of recommendations Fern made were as concerned with political activism as etiquette. She believes women consumers have power to affect labor issues in the stores; if they will be aware of how they treat clerks and speak out against the employees' exploitation,

store owners will be compelled to improve their management, and in turn, employees will improve their service.

The male sales clerks most stores employed irritate Fern because of their lack of expertise and rudeness. In one column, Fern describes a shopping trip where a series of store clerks she collectively refers to as "Yardstick" offends her and sends her all over the big stores and into little ones in search of the items she needs. First she goes to a dry-goods store and asks the clerk for blue silk. "Yardstick, entirely ignorant of colors, after fifteen minutes of snail-like research, hands me down a silk that is as *green* as himself." At another store, the clerk ignores her request for pointed collars and tries to persuade her to purchase round ones because he declares pointed ones no longer to be the fashion. Undeterred, Fern attempts to purchase some wool:

> Dear me, how tired my feet are! nevertheless, I must have some merino. So I open the door of Mr. Henry Humbug's dry-goods store, which is about half a mile in length, and inquire for the desired article. Young Yardstick directs me to the counter, at the *extreme* end of the store. I commence my travels thitherward through a file of gaping clerks, and arrive there just ten minutes before two, by my repeater; when I am told "they are quite out of merinos; but won't Lyonnese cloth do just as well?" pulling down a pile of the same. I rush out in a high state of frenzy, and, taking refuge in the next-door neighbor's, inquire for some stockings.[24]

However, inexpert service again thwarts her mission, and Fern gives up in defeat. Fern, who knows what she wants, has her choices ridiculed and ignored. Over and over, Fern's columns describe customers as at the mercy of ill-trained and inconsiderate employees.

To make shopping more enjoyable, clerks need to be trained to know their stock and to treat customers more politely. The clerks at Stewart's measure up to her ideal and are a foil to the employees she has previously encountered. She commends owner A. T. Stewart's organization and management of his establishment: "You may stroll through his rooms free to gaze and admire, without being annoyed by an impertinent clerk dogging your footsteps; you can take up a fabric, and examine it, without being bored by a statement of its immense superiority over every article of the kind in the market. . . . . You will encounter no ogling, no impertinent cross-questioning, no tittering whispers, from the quiet, well-bred clerks, who attend to their own business and allow you to attend to yours." [25] In contrast to the usual frustration she experiences elsewhere, Stewart's clerks please her because she is able to shop without interruption. This passage directs women to a store characterized by good service and advises store owners to follow Stewart's model. Fern's dual address foregrounds the connections between women's lives and the business world.

While Fern is usually critical of male clerks for their aggressive and surly behavior, she also recognizes that days spent helping customers who simply want to fill time can explain the men's attitudes. Fern tries to teach women how to behave in stores, not out of deference to the managers, but to the clerks. In "Counter Irritation" Fern reproves "a heartless woman, who had been diverting herself with turning a store full of goods topsy-turvey." [26] Her "Advice to Ladies," sarcastically counsels: "When the spirit moves you to amuse yourself with 'shopping,' be sure to ask the clerk for a thousand-and one articles you have no intention of buying. Never mind about the trouble you make for him; that's part of the trade. Pull the fingers of the gloves you are examining quite out of shape; inquire for some nondescript color, or some scarce number, and, when it is found, 'think you won't take any this morning;' then, keep him an hour hunting for your sunshade, which you, at length, recollect you 'left at home;' and depart without having invested a solitary cent." [27] Fern implies that with so many women wasting clerks'

time, it is no wonder so many clerks are rude. In addition, she suggests that clerks may be irritable from overwork and poor pay. Fern asks her readers to consider, "What if their employers looked upon them merely as tools and machines, not as human beings? What if they ground them down to the lowest possible rate of compensation?" She urges women to feel empathetic toward the clerks. For Fern, though, empathy on the part of women customers only goes so far; she then turns from customers to address employers: "Oh! if employers sometimes thought of this!" [28] Fern moves from complaining about service to calling for better working conditions. [29]

The women workers who were gradually hired for retail positions concern Fern even more, and many of her columns discuss the ways that store managers poorly treat their female clerks. As with her columns about male clerks, Fern envisions a readership comprised of both businessmen and women consumers. "Female Clerks" urges owners to treat clerks as they would their daughters, allowing them to sit down when tired and refraining from criticizing them in front of customers: "I have sometimes heard such brutal things said by employers to a blushing young girl, whose eyes filled with tears at her helplessness to avert it, or to reply to it, that I never could enter the store again, for fear of a repetition of the distressing scene, although, so far as I personally was concerned, I had nothing to complain of." [30] Fern warns managers to treat their employees more fairly or face a dwindling clientele. It also models consumer activism for other women shoppers; she demands that employees be better treated or threatens not to shop at the store.

According to Fern, women consumers also need to understand how they can unwittingly participate in the exploitation of store employees. In "Tyrants of the Shop" Fern describes an incident at a store in which a manager berates a female clerk in front of customers. This passage illustrates Fern's connection of writing with activism; she demands that women speak out against the unfair treatment of female employees. "You wonder if you were to sit down and write about this evil, if it would deter even one employer from such brutality to the shop-girls in his employ; not because of the brutality, perhaps, but because by such a short-sighted policy, he might often drive away from his store, ladies who would otherwise be profitable and steady customers."[31] Her analysis recognizes the interests of the different participants. If employees were better treated, Fern suggests, customers would be more comfortable shopping and might spend more money.

Her concerns extend to the workers who produce these stores' goods. In "Working-girls of New York" Fern tries to educate readers about working women's daily lives. She asks readers to imagine these women's work day: "Now follow them to the large, black-looking building, where several hundred of them are manufacturing hoop-skirts. If you are a woman you have worn plenty; but you little thought what passed in the heads of these girls as their busy fingers glazed the wire, or prepared the spools for covering them, or secured the tapes which held them in their places."[32] Women need to be better educated in economics, so they can see how shopping is part of a much larger system and how women consumers can promote poor working conditions simply by purchasing certain products.[33] Later in the piece, Fern reports on conditions at a dressmaker's where employees are packed into basement rooms with no ventilation. "Oh! if the ladies who wore the gay robes manufactured in that room knew the tragedy of those young lives, would they not be to them like the penance robes of which we read, piercing, burning, torturing?"[34] The article ends by discussing The Working Woman's Protective Union, an organization that secures workers' wages and finds work for seamstresses outside the city. In Fern's mind, "there is no institution of the present day more worthy to be sustained," implying that middle-class women should contribute funds for its support.[35] Fern's work demonstrates

how shoppers might be transformed into activists, and by instructing women in this manner, she anticipates the concerns of turn-of-the-century consumer activists, reformers, and researchers who studied working conditions of women employees.[36] Fern appealed to women to educate themselves and to understand the larger systems connected to shopping.

Ready-Made Expertise

Though Jennie June became interested in labor issues through her work in the women's club movement and eventually wrote a book about working women, she remains silent in her fashion columns about the workers in the shopping industry.[37] Instead, she scrutinizes the goods themselves, seeking to improve the manufacturing and retailing industries, balancing businessmen's interests against those of women consumers. June tries to redirect the actions of clothing makers and sellers and urges women not to blindly accept whatever goods stores offer. June felt shopping could be made into a better experience by improving the quality of "ready-made" clothing. In her mind, ready-made clothing held the promise of simplifying women's lives.[38] Some comment on the ready-made industry appears in nearly all her columns from the late 1860s and early 1870s, when the industry first began producing garments for women. Tailors, who made men's clothes, were the first to mass produce their garments, and the first women's clothes to be manufactured were outer garments such as cloaks and jackets since they did not need to be as fitted as dresses. June lobbies manufacturers to produce high quality retail clothing and stores to carry ready-made wear. "A ladies' furnishing establishment, where outfits could be obtained, tasteful and lady-like in design, careful and good in material, neat in workmanship, and of various grades, is an absolute want in New York City, and would realize a fortune, if properly conducted."[39] She directs her comments to store owners, to improve their lines of ready-made clothes, and to shoppers, alerting them to the problems with stores' merchandise. This dual address illustrates June's awareness of her role as a public commentator. June shows how her expertise is indispensable to the business world: if it wants to succeed, it needs to listen to women.

The promise of ready-made clothes was often far from the reality, and June details the problems with poorly designed and cheaply produced garments. June turns an expert eye on the clothing sold, demonstrating how readers might assess their quality. She explains that the idea of wearing out these clothes seems implausible until one actually puts them on: "How people can buy them and wear them out is a mystery, until you buy them and wear them, and then you find that they have been put together easily, to be replaced quickly. That they have a way of dropping apart and becoming demoralized to an extent which, while it does not really wear out the fabric, wears out human patience, and induces the owner to set out on a quest after something better."[40] This description of ready-made clothing certainly does not inspire consumer confidence in the new trend of purchasing clothes instead of remaking older garments to fit the changing fashions.

In effect, June translates between the needs of consumers and the business of manufacturers and retailers. A column, subtitled "How Not to Do It," criticizes the clothes as being made with ill-chosen fabrics and incongruous trimmings. She urges companies to devote more attention to production: "So far as women's clothing is concerned, I think the art of not making any thing they want, in any way that they want it, has been brought to perfection. There is singular lack of enterprise and knowledge of what is required in every department of ladies' ready made garments, a condition of things probably due to the fact that business in this direction, as in all others, is monopolized and presided over by men who know nothing about it themselves, and depend upon the judgment of ignorant and unscrupulous employees." Although June avoids directly blaming the heads of the

manufacturing companies, she does question their expertise. She continues by presenting an alarming picture of the retail industry: "There are tuns [*sic*] of black silk cloaks that nobody wants; of mixed woolen suits, trimmed all in the same stereotyped way, and looking as if they were turned out like sailors' shirts at twenty-five cents apiece, by contract. Acres of coarse gray cloth sacs, mounted with bone buttons; plenty of embroidered Breton jackets, at $20 to $25 each; and round cloaks made of the heavy, water-proof cloth, which can only be worn with the thermometer in the neighborhood of zero." The piles of unsold clothes underscore her point that businessmen need to consider what women want. June positions herself as an expert in consumer matters by describing in detail the quantities of unsold goods. She concludes by proposing the kind of ready-made garment that should be produced: "But try to get a light tweed cloak, heavier than linen, but not so heavy as the ordinary thick waterproof cloth, and just what is needed for summer traveling wraps, or a pretty jacket for $5, or a neat suit in a good summer washing material for $10 to $15, and you will discover that they are not to be had, and you will take something that you don't want, in all probability at a higher price."[41] This conclusion reveals frustration at an industry deaf to its customers' needs. Her columns rely on precise description to identify the problem and to propose a solution to it. Here, the wrong fabrics and wrong trimming are contrasted with the right fabric and practical design. June often used this negative-positive strategy to illustrate the changes that the industry needs to make. For example, following her discussion of the poor execution of ladies' suits and coats, the column's next section, "A Bright Idea," discusses the success of one company's ready-made morning wrappers (printed cotton dresses for home wear). Although these dresses have nothing unique or outstanding about them, she explains, they are well made and the quality of the product "created quite a furor, the sale averaging sixty per day." June includes this statistic to encourage producers to improve their ready-to-wear lines: "This single fact speaks volumes in favor of a popular ready-made clothing system for women and children, something like that which has been reduced to a science for man. At present, women generally are at the mercy of high-priced stores and dress-makers, their means and earnings, at the same time, averaging not more than half those of men."[42] If stores really want to appeal to women consumers, she suggests, they need to offer a better made, more affordable, and wider variety of ready-made clothing.

June also finds store sales to be frustrating experiences, displaying the worst aspects of manufacturing and retailing; her columns show women how they might scrutinize marketing techniques. One column assesses the vast quantities of leftover stock selling at reduced prices: "The past month has been signalized by the selling off of summer stocks and summer goods, and at such rates as must have filled the hearts of the innumerable Mrs. Toodleses with joy and triumph." For June, though, this is not cause for celebration. Indeed, she describes the sales as a gloomy affair: "Thousands of the dingy-looking suits which make the large furnishing houses dismal, which you wonder how anyone could ever have the conscience to make, or any one else the heart to buy, which are never seen on the street, which are bought by no one knows who, and worn no one knows when, have disappeared, and are leaving vacancies which will only be half filled for months to come, by dreary odds and ends, generally kept out of sight, but are resurrected for a few weeks in July, in order to afford summer visitors to the city a glance at New York fashion."[43] This passage's elaborate clauses uses mock bafflement to disparage retail methods retailers use and to warn tourists about this ploy. June suggests fabrics on sale offer better bargains than leftover clothing.

June pays close attention to the ways in which sales encourage spending. She observes that the economic panic of 1873 enables merchants "to get rid, at a "reduced" price, of quantities of old, shop-worn goods, which otherwise they would never think of being able to sell at all. There is a curious idiosyncrasy in the minds of people at such times, which makes them, even when they have money to spend, willing to do a sort of penance by buying something they do not like, and do not want, for a little less than they would pay for something they do want and would like. In this way merchants get rid of a terrible lot of trash, and women accumulate it."[44] By exposing retailers' marketing techniques, June instructs readers how to analyze consumer culture, reminding them to be critical of products and selling strategies.

The Female Urban Sphere

Fern and June make it clear that women were actively engaged shaping the shopping experience. Their work, as it appeared in newspapers and was addressed to both men and women, informed readers of new ways to approach retail stores and to scrutinize goods. As Mica Niva notes, "Consumption (as a feature of modern capitalism) has offered women new areas of authority and expertise, new sources of income, a new sense of consumer rights; and one of the consequences of these developments has been a heightened awareness of entitlement outside the sphere of consumption."[45] In addition to their discussions of retailing and manufacturing issues, Fern and June use shopping to explore women's lack of economic and political independence. As much as Fern and June offer women specific advice for becoming consumer experts, these journalists also believe shopping diverts women from intellectual or professional pursuits. In the shopping world Fern and June observe, women are infantilized by their lack of economic independence, react to their limitations by engaging in a critical surveillance of one another, and fill their hours with devotion to mere fashion.

As shopping became popular as something

to do apart from the task of purchasing needed items, commentators complained about the hours women spent shopping. June uses these opinions to examine women's limited control over their household incomes. One column uses browsing and windowshopping to bring attention to middle-class women's restricted social position: "There have been quantities of virtuously indignant articles written about shopping; about women who occupied their time in looking at articles which they did not want, and could not afford to buy. But how do we know they did not want them? Might it not have given them a poor sort of consolation to look at articles, simply because they could not afford them? Women are so poor there are some who live in very fine houses who do not know what it is to have a dollar in their pockets which they can spend freely." Here, she illuminates the compensatory pleasure shopping provides; if women cannot always buy, they can certainly look.[46] June criticizes a culture that encourages women to spend, spend, spend, yet does not allow them to control their finances:

It is this which very often makes women seem mean, and like children, pleased with trifles. A very nice looking old lady was made completely happy this morning by having two inches on a remnant of ribbon "thrown in." I thought then if one only could be a beneficent fairy about this time, how delightful it would be to touch with a wand the thin, scant looking pocket-book of some women and have them find unexpected treasures in the shape of bills and crisp new currency, stretch ribbons to unimaginable lengths, duplicate gloves, attach the wished for ornament to the waist, or clasp it round the neck, and witness the joy of discovery.[47]

June turns observers' criticism on its head: women only appear puerile because of their economic dependence on men.[48] Her humor, imagining herself as the good fairy, suggests the ridiculousness of not allowing women any economic independence. Shopping, in June's eyes, often

encourages women to engage in verbal and psychological skirmishes; it creates a culture where women combat one another in order to appear the most fashionable:

For dress being so important to those who have nothing else, every faculty is devoted to it, and it would no more do for a flaw to exist in a toilet which will be certainly examined by every lady acquaintance the wearer may meet, than it would in the armor of a knight of the olden times. In both cases the chances of meeting an opponent, would be the almost certainty of being vanquished, a dreadful possibility of being beaten, and one which at any cost, to somebody else, the American young lady insists upon guarding against.

The great thoroughfares, therefore, from 12 in the morning to 5 o'clock in the afternoon, are thronged with beautifully dressed women, nearly all of them young and most of them unmarried, who seem to have no object in life but to put on elaborate attire and go out and display it.

The spectacle, on a clear bright day, is brilliant in the extreme, but to me it is a sad and sickening sight. There is little more trace of gentleness or womanliness about these daily promenades than among the painted but less bedizened creatures who walk there at night. They are bold in look, loud in speech, obtrusive in manner, and measure every woman they meet by the cost of the material of her dress, or the number of yards and trimming that she wears.[49]

June characterizes the endless showing off from noon to five as a battle, where a woman's opponents are other women and their weapons are their evaluations of each other's outfits. Her description of the women, "who have nothing else" to do but stroll on Broadway, indicts the way middle-class women's lives become absorbed by shopping because other avenues are closed to them.[50]

More forcefully than June, Fern examines the impact of shopping culture upon women's minds and skills; denied other opportunities, they turn mean, maligning one another. Fern describes lady shoppers as frivolous and mindless, and labels women who shop "'for fun'" as "silly."[51] She explains, "When ladies 'go shopping,' in New York, they generally expect to enjoy themselves; though Heaven knows, they must be hard up for resources to fancy this mode of spending their time, when it can be avoided."[52] Fern characterizes herself as someone who doesn't like to shop; three columns about shopping begin by asserting her disdain for it. For example, one column begins with the declaration, "I detest shopping."[53] Shopping is bothersome and time-consuming; it keeps her from doing the things she likes—writing, thinking, going places, being with her family.

Devotion to fashion and shopping does not make women happy: "You should see the gay little bonnets, and oh! you should see the vapid, expression-less, soul-less faces beneath them. You should see the carriages, . . . and the faces, seamed with *ennui* and discontent, which peer through the windows, from beneath folds of lace and satin."[54] In assessing the women of 1868, Fern laments their preoccupation with shopping: "I had hoped that *all* their time would not have been spent in keeping up with the chameleon changes of fashions too ugly, too absurd for toleration. It is because I want them to *be* something, to *do* something higher than a peacock might aim at, that I turn heart-sick away from these infinitesimal fripperies that narrow the soul and purse, and leave nothing in their wake but emptiness."[55] While the pleasures of consumer culture fill a void in women's lives, Fern argues, it is a temporary salve that ultimately prevents women from finding fulfilling vocations.

In Fern's work, shopping does not establish a female community; rather, it seems to bring out the worst in women. As critic Lauren Berlant argues, "The failure to cultivate intellect, talent, or simply self-expression has a sublime range of effects on women: most parodically, the woman becomes a grotesque slave to surfaces and form, ded-

icating herself to policing both her own and other women's adherence to rule while often becoming massively hypocritical."[56] Fern delivers a pronounced satire on the New York woman's obsession with appearances: "The New York woman thinketh it well-bred to criticise *in an audible tone* the dress and appearance of every chance lady near her, in the street, shop, ferryboat, car, or omnibus. If doubtful of the material of which her dress is composed, she draweth near, examineth it microscopically, and pronounceth it—'after all—silk.'"[57]

This mode of relating to one another extends beyond the spaces of shopping. Observing women attending a lecture, Fern charges that they occupy themselves by assessing other women: "the first bonnet within range passes under the inspection of an inexorable, martinet, vis: 'Did *she* make it herself?' or, 'Is it the approved work of a milliner?' 'Does her hair curl naturally?' or 'Does she curl it?' 'Is her collar *real* lace?' or 'Only imitation?' These professional detective queries, so amusing to the general female mind, while away the time edifyingly, especially when there is a variety of heads within in eyes-range for minute inspection."[58] Even female clerks participate in the surveillance of other women; they "are too often taking an inventory of the way you dress your hair; of the cut and trimming, and probable cost of your sacque and dress. No lady who shops much can be unaware of the coroner's inquest, favorable or otherwise, thus held over the dry-goods on her back."[59] Characterizing women's mutual surveillance in such clinical terms (engaging in "professional detective queries" and performing a "coroner's inquest") depicts the female urban sphere as a sinister, threatening environment. "Women," Fern continues, "*always* dissect each other the moment they meet, and never leave so much as a hair-pin unmeasured."[60] Fern's choice of words suggests the consequences of women's closed opportunities. Though women have the skills to be detectives, coroners, analysts, they use that energy to disparage one another.[61]

While the activities associated with shopping are considered appropriate feminine behavior and sanctioned by society, women are discouraged from entering other public arenas, such as politics or professional employment. Fern satirizes the inconsistent codes of proper feminine behavior in an attempt to open more doors for women. For example, Fern juxtaposes the fashion-obsessed audience in the passage above with a defense of female lecturers against claims they are unwomanly.

> If conservatism is shocked to hear a woman speak in public, let conservatism stay away; but let it be consistent, and not forget to frown on its own women, who elbow and push their way in a crowded assembly, and with sharp tongue and hurrying feet "grab" —yes, that's the word—the most eligible seat, or who push into public conveyances already filled to over-flowing, and, with brazen impudence, wonder aloud "if these are *gentlemen*," as they try to look them out of their seats. There are many ways a woman can "unsex" herself, beside lecturing in public.[62]

Her complaints about women's conduct while shopping are part of her larger examination of the hypocritical standards of conduct applied to women. While many people consider it perfectly appropriate for women to spend their days shopping, or to "scramble at a matinee for seats," they feel that for women to cast votes, "would be to forfeit man's love, and soil both your skirts and reputation."[63] Fern uses her observations of women's experience shopping to connect the daily, the seemingly trivial, with the political.

Fern's strongest but also most alarming critique of the designs of consumer culture on women is her piece "A Morning at Stewart's," which demonstrates her acute awareness of the power retailers had in directing the inclinations of women shoppers. She shows that what could feel like constraint could also feel like freedom, and that is precisely what is so insidious about shopping. Though stores attempted to entice women to spend their days shopping, to the exclusion of other activities, they also provided moments of delight and pleasure. In the piece, Fern describes a visit to Stewart's department store: "It is not often that I treat myself to a stroll into Stewart's great shop. Mortal woman cannot behold such perfection too often and live. It is like a view of the vast ocean, so humiliating and depressing by its immensity and sublimity that little atoms of humanity are glad to creep away from it, to some locally-big elevation of their own."[64] Although Fern writes tongue-in-cheek here, evidenced by the passage's exaggeration and mock seriousness, the rest of the section illustrates Fern's appreciation of the great store: "Once in awhile, when I feel strong enough to bear it, . . . I put on a bold face and plunge in with the throng. When I say 'throng' I don't wish to be understood as meaning anything like a mob. It is a very curious circumstance that given how objectionably some 'throngs' may behave elsewhere, even the most disorderly of all throngs, a *woman-throng*—yet at Stewart's so suggestive of order and system is the place, that immediately on entering, they involuntarily 'fall into line,' like proper little Sunday scholars in a procession, and never shuffle or elbow the least bit."[65] Though she admits she does not know why women behave so much better at Stewart's, Fern suggests that it is because of the efficient, machine-like work of the employees and the disembodied, luxurious display of goods: the "statuesque" clerks, the "eel-like manner" of the cash boy darting through the aisles, the "artistic" exhibition of silks "so that, as the light falls on it from the window, it looks like a splendid display of folded tulips and roses."[66] Fern delights in the order Stewart's imposes: "Indeed, I sometimes think that if the great Stewart himself were bodily to order them out, they would neither mutter, nor peep mutinously; but turn about, like a flock of sheep, and obediently leap over the threshold."[67] She praises the store because it is able to control the shoppers' behavior. Paradoxically, this restraint is represented as a kind of freedom; Fern is able to shop because the store is efficiently managed and the crowds of shoppers are controlled. As Gillian Swanson argues, in the nineteenth century, "consumption was used as a means of addressing the public management of individuals."[68] While she describes ways individual women can mediate fashion and resist commercialism, she is not interested in celebrating subversiveness in consumer culture. Her work, alarmingly, applauds efforts to systematize and regulate women's appearance and public behavior. The article's conclusion, though, belies the idea that Fern approves the way stores attempt to control women's behavior. She ends with the speculation, "Perhaps husbands wink at the thing and give the little dears coppers to spend there on purpose—I don't know."[69] While her tone appears humorous, the point she makes is anything but; Fern suggests Stewart and husbands collude to control women's behavior; women fall into line at his store, and, for their husbands, that is well worth whatever money women spend. Though Fern retreats from this analysis with an exasperated "I don't know," she leaves the door open for women to explore the many different directions shopping pulls their lives.

Their work enables Fern and June to assume other public roles through their columns. Indeed, Fern and June highlight the visibility of women's experiences in urban life. Their own experiences as flaneuses gave them an authority for their commentaries, and it was this experience and authority that lent them the expertise to become writers about urban space. As shoppers they became flaneuses, and as flaneuses they became writers about shopping and urban life. Their work confirms the need for more complicated analyses of consumer culture and of the roles female columnists have played in American life.

Notes

1 Susan Faludi, "Does Maureen Dowd Have an Opinion?" *Nation* (May 13, 1996): 10.

2 Mary P. Ryan, *Women in Public: Between Banners and Ballots, 1825–1880* (Baltimore: Johns Hopkins University Press, 1990), 87.

3 Ann Douglas, *The Feminization of American Culture* (1977; New York: Doubleday, 1988), 60.

4 Biographical information about Fern can be found in Joyce Warren, *Fanny Fern: An Independent Woman* (New Brunswick, NJ: Rutgers University Press, 1992). As professional journalists analyzing the emerging service economy, Fern and June insist that shopping demands serious inquiry. Importantly, they do not see consumer culture as moving in one direction, where women can only be duped by its designs on them. They do not view the consumer as a passive figure; rather, their columns suggest ways women can use their roles as consumers both to improve the shopping world and to expand their positions within the world beyond. Combining practical advice with more analytical speculations, Fern and June offer a way to reassess this moment in the history of nineteenth-century literature and enhance our understanding of female responses to the emerging consumer culture. Fern and June imagine shopping as an experience that enables women to move beyond the confines of the home, but one that also may prevent them from assuming other roles in public life. Ironically, shopping did.

5 Though the collections of Fern's columns are out of print, a substantial selection of her journalism can be found in the reprint of Fern's novel *Ruth Hall* (New Brunswick, NJ: Rutgers University Press, 1986).

6 Nancy Walker, *Fanny Fern* (New York: Twayne, 1993), 199–204.

7 Fanny Fern, *Fresh Leaves* (New York: Mason Brothers, 1857), 297.

8 Fern and June did know each other and were both active in forming Sorosis, one of the first women's clubs. It is not clear, though, how familiar with one another's work they were.

9 Though none of June's fashion columns were collected, June did author a number of books, including a history of the women's club movement. Biographical information about Croly can be found in Elizabeth Bancroft Schlesinger, "The Nineteenth-Century Woman's Dilemma and Jennie June," *New York History* 42 (1961):

365 79; Madelon Golden Schilpp and Sharon M. Murphy, *Great Women of the Press* (Carbondale: Southern Illinois University Press, 1983), 85–94; and Karen J. Blair, *The Clubwoman as Feminist: True Womanhood Redefined, 1868–1914* (New York: Holmes and Meier, 1980).

10 Women's pages in newspapers did not become common until the 1880s. See Gerald. J. Baldasty, *The Commercialization of News in the Nineteenth Century* (Madison: University of Wisconsin Press, 1992), 126.

11 For example, in Susan Warner's 1850 novel *The Wide, Wide World* (New York: Feminist Press, 1987), shopping is a site for cultivating a bond between mother and daughter. For a discussion of the way *Godey's Lady's Book* envisioned consumer culture as an extension of the domestic sphere, see Gillian Brown, *Domestic Individualism: Imagining Self in Nineteenth-Century America* (Berkeley: University of California Press, 1990), 178–84. See also Charlotte Perkins Gilman, *Women and Economics* (1898; New York: Harper and Row, 1966).

12 For example, Nina Baym argues that women fiction writers "were thinking about a social reorganization wherein their special concept of home was projected out into the world. . . . If worldly values could dominate the home, perhaps the direction of influence could be reversed so that home values dominated the world." *Woman's Fiction: A Guide to Novels by and about Women in America, 1820–1870* (Ithaca: Cornell University Press, 1978), 48–49. See also Jane Tompkins, *Sensational Designs: The Cultural Work of American Fiction, 1790–1860* (New York: Oxford University Press, 1985).

13 Catharine Beecher and Harriet Beecher Stowe, *The American Woman's Home* (New York: J. B. Ford, 1869), 158.

14 Charles Baudelaire, *The Painter of Modern Life, and Other Essays* (London: Phaidon, 1964); Walter Benjamin, "On Some Motifs in Baudelaire," in *Illuminations* (New York: Schocken, 1968), 155–200, and "Paris, Capital of the Nineteenth Century," in *Reflections* (New York: Schocken, 1978), 146–62.

15 Janet Wolff, *Feminine Sentences: Essays on Women and Culture* (Berkeley: University of California Press, 1990), 46.

16 Elizabeth Wilson, "The Invisible *Flâneur*," in *Postmodern Cities and Spaces*, ed. Sophie Watson and Katherine Gibson (Cambridge: Blackwell, 1995), 66.

17 Anne Friedberg, *Window Shopping: Cinema and the Postmodern* (Berkeley: University of California Press, 1993), 34.

18 Ibid., 2.

19 Ibid., 36.

20 Editorial, *New York Times* (June 13, 1881): 4:5, quoted in Elaine S. Abelson, *When Ladies Go A-Thieving: Middle-Class Shoplifters in the Victorian Department Store* (New York: Oxford University Press, 1989), 30.

21 William Leach, "Transformations in a Culture of Consumption: Women and Department Stores, 1890–1925," *Journal of American History* 71 (1984): 320.

22 Gillian Swanson, "'Drunk with Glitter': Consuming Spaces and Sexual Geographies," in *Postmodern Cities and Spaces*, ed. Watson and Gibson, 93.

23 See Susan Porter Benson, *Counter Cultures: Saleswomen, Managers, and Customers in American Department Stores, 1890–1940* (Urbana: University of Illinois Press 1986).

24 Fanny Fern, *Fern Leaves from Fanny's Portfolio*, second series (1854; Freeport, NY: Books for Libraries Press, 1971), 378.

25 Ibid., 340.

26 Fern, *Fresh Leaves*, 321.

27 Fanny Fern, *Fern Leaves from Fanny's Portfolio* (Auburn: Derby and Miller, 1853), 317.

28 Fern, *Fresh Leaves*, 321–22.

29 Though Fern's recommendations, as they evoke the familial model, are similar to the reforms other women writers advocated, the fact that she directly addresses employers is a departure from the way novelists employed the idea of woman's "influence" to effect change. For a discussion of Fern's views on labor, see Kristie Hamilton, "The Politics of Survival: Sara Parton's *Ruth Hall* and the Literature of Labor," in *Redefining the Political Novel: American Women Writers, 1797–1901*, ed. Sharon M. Harris (Knoxville: University of Tennessee Press, 1995), 86–108.

30 Fanny Fern, *Ginger Snaps* (New York: Carleton, 1870), 66.

31 Fanny Fern, *Folly as It Flies* (New York: G. W. Carleton, 1869), 194.

32 Ibid., 221.

33 In another column, "Where the Money Is Made," Fern argues that women should visit the market and warehouse districts, and she hopes that seeing commerce laid bare will curb their spending. See Warren, *Fanny Fern*, 264.

34 Fern, *Folly*, 226–27.

35 Ibid., 229.

36 For example, Maud Nathan organized the New York consumers league in 1890 to ensure that manufacturers treated their employees fairly. Nathan's group established boycotts of goods not produced under decent labor conditions. See W. Elliot and Mary M. Brownlee, eds. *Women in the American Economy* (New Haven: Yale University Press, 1976), 314–28 and Kathryn Kish Sklar, "Two Political Cultures in the Progressive Era: The National Consumers' League and the American Association for Labor Legislation," in *U.S. History as Women's History: New Feminist Essays,* ed. Linda K. Kerber, Alice Kessler-Harris, and Kathryn Kish Sklar (Chapel Hill: University of North Carolina Press, 1995), 36–62.

37 Jane Cunningham Croly, *Thrown Upon Her Own Resources, or What Girls Can Do* (New York: Thomas Y. Crowell, 1891).

38 Not everyone shared June's opinion. Co-operative housing visionary Melusina Fay Peirce, for example, wrote in 1868 that women had lost some of their power with businessmen taking over clothing production. See Susan Strasser, *Never Done: A History of American Housework* (New York: Pantheon, 1982), 196.

39 Jennie June, "New York and Paris Fashions for January," *Cincinnati Commercial* (Jan. 31, 1867): 2.

40 Jennie June, "New York Fashions for June," *Cincinnati Commercial* (June 1, 1876): 2.

41 Jennie June, "New York and Paris Fashions for August," *Cincinnati Commercial* (Aug. 1, 1868): 4.

42 Ibid.

43 Jennie June, "Fashions for July," *Cincinnati Commercial* (July 1, 1871): 2.

44 Jennie June, "Fashions for December," *Cincinnati Commercial* (Nov. 29, 1873): 4.

45 Mica Niva, "Consumerism and Its Contradictions," *Cultural Studies* 1 (1987): 208.

46 June anticipates a theme Kate Chopin later explores in her short story "A Pair of Silk Stockings," in *Portraits* (Great Britain: Women's Press, 1979), 143–47.

47 Jennie June, "Fashions for December," *Cincinnati Commercial* (Dec. 1, 1875): 2.

48 See also Elaine Abelson's discussion of this issue as it relates to women's shoplifting in *When Ladies Go A-Thieving,* 166–67.

49 Jennie June, "New York and Paris Fashions for November," *Cincinnati Commercial* (Nov. 1, 1869): 2.

50 The women's club June helped to found, Sorosis, was devoted to women's intellectual and professional development. See Blair, *The Clubwoman as Feminist,* 15–31. It is important to note, however, that June clearly was not anti-fashion; her brand of feminism was compatible with fashion, and she encouraged women to develop fashion sense independent of the styles dictated by designers and retailers.

51 Fanny Fern, *Caper Sauce: A Volume of Chit-Chat about Men, Women, and Things* (New York: G. W. Carleton, 1872), 38.

52 Fern, *Folly,* 193.

53 Fern, *Fresh Leaves,* 212.

54 Ibid., 295.

55 Fern, *Ginger Snaps,* 96.

56 Lauren Berlant, "The Female Woman: Fanny Fern and the Form of Sentiment," *American Literary History* 3 (1991): 438. For a discussion of Fern's representation of women's mistreatment of one another in her novel *Ruth Hall,* see Hamilton, "The Politics of Survival."

57 Fern, *Fresh Leaves,* 98.

58 Fern, *Folly,* 209.

59 Fern, *Caper Sauce,* 37.

60 Ibid., 38.

61 Here I am indebted to Amelie Hastie for her reading of Fern's work.

62 Fern, *Folly,* 211.

63 Fern, *Ginger Snaps,* 80.

64 Fern, *Folly,* 216–17.

65 Ibid., 217.

66 Ibid.

67 Ibid., 218.

68 Swanson, "'Drunk with Glitter,'" 81.

69 Fern, *Folly,* 218.

Navigating Myst-y Landscapes: Killer Applications and Hybrid Criticism

Greg M. Smith

Persuading consumers to purchase expensive new technology usually requires a software application demonstrating the medium's distinctive capabilities. If these pieces of software, called "killer applications," can show that the new medium offers new pleasures, consumers can justify purchasing the new equipment, thus opening up previously untapped commercial markets for further development. At the time of its introduction, an innovative software blockbuster such as Brøderbund's CD-ROM *Myst* not only sold CD-ROMs (over two million copies),[1] but it also sold consumers on the need for CD-ROM technology.[2] It helped to create a widely held understanding of the nature of the CD-ROM.

Killer applications are by definition shining examples of the "new." Showing that a groundbreaking product is radically different from its predecessors is necessarily a part of creating a killer application. Popular hyperbole promises that "you've never seen anything like this before," or "you ain't heard nothing yet" (as Al Jolson was widely reported as saying in *The Jazz Singer*, 1927's killer application, which paved the way for widespread conversion to sound film). The lure of new ways of seeing and hearing helps create consumer demand, but this emphasis also hides the continuities between old and new paradigms of media use.

By heralding *Myst* as "one of those works that irrevocably changes the parameters of an artform, multimedia's equivalent of *Don Quixote* or *Sgt. Pepper*," popular discourse at the time of the game's release necessarily emphasized *Myst*'s innovations over the ways it continued and extended earlier multimedia trends.[3] This emphasis on what made *Myst* new made it difficult to see clearly what *Myst* actually did. Rather than create a radically distinctive form of multimedia, *Myst* reworked characteristics of previous CD-ROMS combined with various techniques borrowed from other media. This essay in part traces how *Myst* reconfigured strategies borrowed from earlier media paradigms. Viewing *Myst* in terms of preexisting media helps us to see the blend of old and new that is necessary for a commercially successful killer application. Reconnecting *Myst* to other media helps us see more clearly what was so distinctive about this CD-ROM.

Even if the software was in many ways revolutionary, our way of talking and thinking about the medium were not revolutionized. The terms we used to describe the CD-ROM medium and the expectations we had regarding what a CD-ROM should do were a crucial part of the background against which we made sense of *Myst*. Discussions concerning *Myst* in the popular press and on the Internet were rooted in the utopian rhetoric surrounding virtual reality and hypermedia. Over and over the discussions about *Myst* refered to its "interactivity" and its "virtual reality," and these terms mystified as much as they enlightened the game. What did these words mean specifically in relation to *Myst*? This chapter investigates several common observations about *Myst* that circulated in public discourse at the moment of the game's release in 1994 and amplifies what these terms mean in relation to this particular CD-ROM.

A closer understanding of *Myst* proves useful for understanding our society's definition of multimedia's capabilities. Since such killer applications demonstrate a medium's capabilities early in its history, they can powerfully shape our understanding of what the medium is and what it should do. The *New York Times* acclaimed *Myst* as coming close to "the Holy Grail of multimedia developers: finding a way to immerse the viewer in a narrative but to let them shape it freely."[4] A killer application is important not only as a model for future development (e.g., *Qin: Tomb of the Middle Kingdom, 9, Drowned God, Timelapse*) but also as a particular definition of the goals of a medium itself. The capabilities exploited by a killer application loom large in our conceptions of the pleasures offered by the medium. Better understanding the social network of meanings activated by *Myst* should help us understand our past, present, and future conceptions of multimedia.

Nonlinear Narrative

Computer games found their first economically viable audience by positioning themselves as an outgrowth of arcade video games. A generation of players whose fine motor reflexes were honed using joysticks at arcades further developed those skills in their homes as they played Nintendo or Sega home versions of arcade games. Once the technology was domesticated, computer games found a ready-made audience by providing similar visceral pleasures of quick moves executed against the clock. Beginning with two-dimensional games such as *Donkey Kong* and *Super Mario Bros.*, the computer game then called upon the detailed graphics information that could be provided by CD-ROMs to create simulated three-dimensional games. Based on the same principles of quick action, hand dexterity, and time pressures, CD-ROM games such as *Doom* offered the player the pleasures of racing through a maze of corridors while accumulating a staggering body count before dying.

Doom epitomized an important early paradigm for CD-ROM games. We the player play the part of the hero who has been sent to investigate a crisis. Our mission, we are told, is to find out what went wrong with interdimensional space travel between the moons of Mars. Once transported into the eerie landscape, we are suddenly besieged by a variety of lethal attackers, and we must fight our way through by blasting a swath through these marauders. Although *Doom* has a

story, the story quickly loses narrative significance, leaving us only with the goal of staying alive. *Doom* has only one rule: "if it moves, shoot it." This dominant paradigm of CD-ROM games (as embodied by *Doom*) offers the spectacular pleasures of nonstop violent action, supplying the player with sufficiently de-veloped hand reflexes with graphic pictures and digital sound of their lethal triumphs. Such games provide an interactive version of the culturally devalued pleasures of wrestling, martial arts movies, and the splatter film.

Almost immediately *Myst* announces itself as a very different kind of game from the *Doom* paradigm. When we the *Myst* players arrive on Myst Island, we find an uninhabited virtual world of placid landscapes, strange equipment, and burned books. We learn of Sirrus and Achenar, two brothers, and their father Atrus, a man who creates fantastic worlds or "ages" by writing them into books. These books provide links which allow travelers to venture from one spectacularly realized age to another. However, the library of books has been virtually destroyed by fire, and Atrus leaves messages for us casting suspicion that one of his two sons is responsible for foul play. If we solve the puzzles which protect the few remaining books, we can use the books to travel among five other ages, urged on by Sirrus and Achenar (who are both trapped in books themselves and who accuse the other of evil via distorted Quicktime video). Collecting loose pages in the different ages enables us to unravel the mystery of what happened to Atrus and his two sons.

Some have called *Myst*'s story "compelling" and "engaging," but most note how minimal the plot is.[5] For example, *PC Magazine* says that "if you like a neat plot with defined goals, you'll be disappointed [by *Myst*]."[6] Given the enormous popularity of *Myst*, it is remarkable how little plot there is in *Myst*. We learn what happened before we arrived on Myst Island through some extraordinarily terse expository devices: the opening credit sequence, three brief video clips, and the unburned pages of several handwritten journals. After the initial exposition is over, we do not learn about any more significant plot events until the end of the game when we get the denouement. This is an astoundingly flat narrative structure: a setup of the situation and the resolution, separated by hours or even months of player activity without any payoff provided by new story information.

Experienced CD-ROM game players will recognize this structure from playing "shoot-em-ups" such as *Doom*. The brief exposition and denouement frame and provide a rationale for the primary game activity. Although *Myst* works hard to differentiate itself from the *Doom* paradigm, it calls upon a similar narrative framework for its action.

However, *Myst* structures its action without the urgency characteristic of most CD-ROM games. One of the most commented on features of *Myst* is its almost complete lack of time deadlines. *MacWorld* notes that "there's no time pressure to distract you, no arbitrary punishments put in your way."[7] But time pressures and the threat of arbitrarily punishing characters are two of the primary driving forces in CD-ROM games. Without these local structures pushing the plot forward, *Myst*'s narrative comes to a standstill.

This standstill differs from the plot structure in *Doom* because *Doom* incorporates norms from modern spectacle-oriented Hollywood product, as Angela Ndalianis argues (in this volume). Low-budget popular films such as *Evil Dead II* and big-budget blockbusters such as *Twister* are now structured so that the narrative progress of the film comes to a halt while the film stages an action spectacle (explicit gore, expensive special effects, etc.) intended to elicit a visceral reaction. Rather than the action-packed narrative stasis of the modern action-adventure spectacle or the deadline-driven progression of the classical Hollywood film, *Myst* chooses a time scheme more characteristic of art cinema narration, which is less dependent on deadlines to drive the plot.[8] After a brief taste of *Raiders of the Lost Ark*-style narration, the *Myst* player suddenly finds him/herself in *L'Avventura*. Like a protagonist in an episodic art film, the *Myst* player wanders through an ambiguous world without time pressures exerted by the narrative.

Myst is not so much a nonlinear narrative (as some commentators have described) as much as it is a linear narrative which stops and transforms into a game only to return to the narrative for ending closure.[9] The destabilizing force in this narrative is not simply that *Myst* has four possible endings, nor is it that a player can visit the Channelwood, Stoneship, Mechanical, and Selenitic Ages in any order. The reason it doesn't matter in what order the player visits the different ages is because the narrative has been stilled.

Of course there is some new narrative information offered along the way to the *Myst* player, but that information has more to do with gaining insights into characters than it does depicting new plot occurrences. Visiting Sirrus's and Achenar's rooms in various ages helps us understand their characters. Sirrus's rooms are plushly and lavishly decorated, and Achenar's rooms are filled with weapons, implements of torture, and poisons. After solving the puzzle in each age, we revisit Myst Island where we receive another Quicktime video message from Sirrus and Achenar, allowing us to examine their performances in detail. This information is useful in helping the player to decide which brother is guilty and which is innocent, but this information does not advance what we know about the storyline. *Myst* does not show us plot occurrences (formative events in their past, battles in the present) to help us decide between the two brothers. Instead, *Myst* transmits its narrative information (after the intense early exposition) through the art direction, not through character action.

As the player traverses *Myst*'s lushly detailed environments, his/her primary activity involves solving puzzles. Solving these puzzles provides local payoffs to the *Myst* player, which keeps him/her involved. The narrative framework not only provides a forward impetus to the player's activity but it also provides justification for the puzzles. Commentators have noted that "*Myst*'s challenges aren't shoehorned in to the landscape. The puzzles, for the most part, are logically and integrally linked to place, time, and story. Instead of confronting you with brainteasers that have no more purpose than extending play time, *Myst* demands that you have a hands-on interactive experience manipulating the clocks, valves, machinery, and gadgets found in the game." [10] Unlike many other games, *Myst*'s story justifies the presence of the puzzles we players have to solve. Rather than seeming to be added arbitrarily as an obstacle for the player to overcome, the puzzles' existence makes sense in terms of the narrative: the books that link the various ages need to be protected from people who might use them for evil purposes. In this sense *Myst* plays by one of the rules of the well-made classical narrative form. Obstacles that protagonists have to overcome must not be thrown into the story arbitrarily to delay their progress toward the goals. Instead obstacles in classical narratives (and in *Myst* ages) must be justified in terms of who these particular characters are and what events have happened to them. In *Myst* the story, as brief as it is, underwrites the activity of puzzle solving and the fantastic construction of these worlds.

The game of puzzles and panoramas cannot be separated from the narrative framework, however. The narrative framework provides an overall trajectory for the player by setting up a large question to be answered: which one is guilty, Sirrus or Achenar? The framework energizes the player's search and buoys us with the hope that (eventually) the enigma will be solved. The narrative construction maintains a classical sense that the hermeneutic code will eventually be unambiguously disclosed, and this long-delayed hope propels us through the CD-ROM. Without this narrative setup, the puzzles would provide less pleasure. In fact, after successfully completing the game, the player is told that he/she is free to do exactly what they've been doing: explore the various worlds of *Myst*. But few players do because the overall narrative goal has already been achieved. Without the promise of narrative closure, the spectacular views and intricate puzzles lose much of their appeal.

Myst has much at stake in trying to differentiate itself from the *Doom* conception of CD-ROM games. If this killer application can distance itself from the fast action and abundant violence of the *Doom* paradigm, it can open up new audiences whose reflexes have not been trained by arcade games. Rejecting time deadlines and relying on subtle art direction as a primary means of conveying narrative information help *Myst* position itself in opposition to the "shoot-em-up." Classically justifying its puzzles in terms of the narrative differentiates *Myst* from games whose puzzles are merely arbitrary obstacles added to the landscape. But these strategies which distinguish *Myst* are supported by the same narrative structure used in *Doom*. A narrative standstill makes possible both the gory pleasures of *Doom* and the quieter pleasures of *Myst*.

Intuitive Immersion in Virtual Reality

Real life is what happens between *Myst*.
—*Myst* player Arthur Siegel[11]

A computer designer quoted in *Rolling Stone* called *Myst* "a real breakthrough, imaginative, hypnotic, as close to virtual reality as we've come." [12] Erik Davis in *Village Voice* says that "*Myst* is the first home-computer game I've experienced that produces the almost haunting sense of having passed into some parallel place." [13] This frequently-alluded-to sense that *Myst* immerses players in alternate virtual universes may seem peculiar to students of new media because this cutting-edge software most closely resembles the hoary technology of the slide show (with accompanying music and effects). At first glance a slide show of tourist snapshots seems antithetical to the promises of a virtual reality which can envelop us.

However, the still images do rely upon some qualities media scholars discuss as giving a socially convincing sense of the real. Many have commented on the level of detail in *Myst*'s 2,500 images, stating that the intricacy of these 3D modeled images helps give them their virtual reality. This echoes Christian Metz's argument that the rich detail of the cinematic signifier helps us disavow the absence of the actual object being depicted.[14] *Myst*'s seeming real similarly depends on its level of detail, as *Myst* co-creator Rand Miller says: "A lot can be done with texture. . . . Like finding an interesting texture you can map into the tapestry on the wall, spending a little extra time to actually put the bumps on the tapestry, putting screws in things. These are the things you don't necessarily notice, but if they weren't there, would flag to your subconscious that this is fake."[15] *Myst* takes full advantage of the CD-ROM's capability to present lavishly detailed still images in its attempt to create images which seem "real," or even "hyperreal."[16]

Many have commented on *Myst*'s soundtrack (a combination of New Age-ish music and digital sound effects), suggesting that it also bolsters the sense of virtual reality in a way reminiscent of film sound. Bob Lindstrom in *Compute!* magazine calls attention to *Myst*'s "brilliant digital samples with the realer-than-real impact that we normally associate with motion-picture audio."[17] Mary Ann Doane has argued that sound provides a sense of presence which is crucial to the cinema's sense of seeming-real, that sound reawakens our early childhood awareness of space (which is first defined by the audible, not the visual).[18] Sound for Doane provides a sense of nearness which counterbalances the necessarily distant cinematic signifier,[19] and the crispness of digital sound (in CD-ROMS, DVDS, or present-day Hollywood films) only increases this effect. *Myst* recognizes that "the ear builds a sense of embodiment as much as the eye," as the *Village Voice* puts it, and uses this

CD capacity to lend its visuals a sense of intimate presence.[20]

A crucial aid to *Myst*'s seeming real is its seamless interface that does not call attention to the computer medium but encourages us to concentrate solely on the diegetic world it depicts. Unlike many software applications, *Myst* appears onscreen as a series of images with no computerized instrument panel or pulldown menus in sight (unless your mouse pointer wanders to the top of the screen to reveal a standard Windows-style menu). For most of the time the *Myst* player receives relatively few cues which remind you of the game's "computerness."[21] Lindstrom notes how *Myst* "almost entirely does away with the interface. . . . With no artificial computer layer between you and the game, *Myst* effectively lures you into its own reality and enhances its hands-on illusion of life."[22]

Myst's primary brilliance lies in the way it provides narrative justification for the very things that are most annoying about CD-ROMS. Compared to the utopian promises of the potential of hypermedia and virtual reality, CD-ROMS are quite humble objects. Instead of rising to the potential of tomorrow, CD-ROMS are often mired in the technology of today: slow access time, difficult installation procedures, animated images much fuzzier than the worst television. *Myst* ingeniously makes the medium's limitations part of the story it tells. For example, Quicktime video clips are of extraordinarily poor visual quality and are frequently presented in a small window occupying a fraction of the computer screen. *Myst*'s creative solution is to locate these clips in books and small viewers in the various story ages. *Myst* even alludes to the difficulty most CD-ROM users have experienced when running too many programs in the background while trying to run a CD-ROM application with video clips in the foreground. *Myst* duplicates the erratic, interrupted quality of CD-ROMS under multiprocessing in the disjointed video messages from Sirrus and Achenar.[23]

Since animation in CD-ROMS tends to be considerably less fluid than media savvy audiences are accustomed to, *Myst* avoids relying on animation and justifies this in terms of the story. Either Sirrus's or Achenar's vandalism has assumedly caused the populations of these ages to be wiped out, resulting in a series of uninhabited landscapes that require minimal animation.

Then there is the issue of CD-ROM's slowness. Anyone used to channel surfing on cable would have found waiting on the response time of early CD-ROMs agonizing. According to *MacWorld*, however, "*Myst* is the first CD-ROM game we've seen that doesn't constantly remind us how slow the medium is."[24] This has less to do with *Myst*'s seek time than it does with the structure of the game. The lack of timed deadlines is a major factor here, but more subtly *Myst* emphasizes the necessity of waiting in order to complete the game successfully. You cannot simply get into the tree elevator on Myst Island, press the button, and have the elevator respond. You must wait for the steam boiler to build up pressure before the elevator will respond. Unlike timed games such as *Super Mario Bros.*, *Myst* trains the player to wait (a handy skill in dealing with early CD-ROMs).

Things take time in *Myst*. Like the real world, movement through *Myst*'s (virtual) space involves real time, and much of the player's time is spent traveling through diegetic distance. A puzzle frequently will be located away from the corresponding book-link to another age. This situation requires that the player travel a significant distance from the solved puzzle to the linking book (for instance, after solving the puzzle in the clocktower, the player must "walk" to the other side of the island to go to the next age). *Myst* arranges its objects in such a way that the player must spend a great deal of time shuttling back and forth between locations.[25] In Channelwood, for instance, a player must navigate through a maze of water pipes, turning on multiple valves located across the island to enable the machinery to work properly.

In contrast to the *Doom* player, much of the *Myst* player's time is spent tediously traversing the space. This reminds us that this space is recalcitrant to our desires, just as the real world is. Although we would like to be able to move instantly from one place to another, the real world requires time to walk through, fumble with keys, and unlock doors. Because *Myst* keeps us from moving through its spaces too quickly, it reminds us of the real world which also does not bend so easily to our desires.

And yet we are frequently reminded that the *Myst* worlds do not respond as the real world does. The *Myst* player must use somewhat non-Cartesian tools to explore these virtual worlds. Clicking the mouse on a portion of the screen allows you to "move" left or right, up or down. However, directionality in *Myst* is not as straightforward as this would suggest. A click left in a particular location may shift you either 90 or 180 degrees left; clicking right is similarly unpredictable.[26] In a fairly distinctive location, there are enough overlapping spatial cues to keep your movements from becoming too confusing. In spaces with great redundancy (e.g., the network of very similar treehouses in the Channelwood age), this unpredictability can become quite confusing. Why are the *Myst* player's movements structured this way? In the real world we can control whether we're making a 90- or 180-degree turn. Why not let a click left always execute a 90-degree left turn in *Myst*?

Myst suggests that the new CD-ROM medium does not have quite the same fear of losing the spectator in space that the new medium of film had when it created the classical cinema's stylistic norms. *Myst* seems more concerned about losing the spectator narratively. It is designed so that only one clue is so absolutely crucial that if you miss it you cannot progress at all. The box even includes an actual paper brochure revealing this clue (concerning the tower rotation on Myst Island) just in case you miss it. This suggests that once the player understands the basic narrative trajectory, he/she can tolerate significant ambiguity of spatial cues without becoming disoriented.[27] Narrative trajectory seems more important here than consistency of movement.

Movement commands in *Myst* are structured so that you will go where you *need* to go, instead of being structured to maintain a clear spatial orientation. If you click left and turn 180 degrees, you can assume that there is nothing significant in the space you would have seen had you turned only 90 degrees. *Myst* will let you see what you need to know, editing out spatial perspectives which are not significant to the narrative or to solving the puzzles.[28]

The sense that the *Myst* player moves based on where his/her mind *wants* or *needs* to be (and not on a purely logical, Cartesian system of movement) recalls the argument that hypermedia is supposedly arranged to approximate the human mind more closely. According to this line of thinking, the mind functions not based primarily on formal binary logic but on nonlinear associations, links, intuitions.[29] We can move from one subject to another as long as these subjects are somehow mentally linked, regardless of whether that link makes purely logical sense. *Myst* takes this principle and maps it onto a virtual space, and the player's moves through this space are consistent with this popular model of mental functioning.[30] By allowing us to visit potentially significant spaces and preventing us from seeing insignificant spaces, *Myst* simulates the mental landscape of a player who intuits the significance of the various locations. Instead of duplicating most games' literal conception of a player capable of simulated physical movement in any direction, *Myst* positions the player in a world whose operating principles are both physical proximity and mental connection. The result is a compromise world that samples from both the real and the virtual. *Myst* (like the real world) denies us the freedom of moving at the speed of our intuitions, and yet it shapes our movements to simulate a limited sense of intuition.[31]

Jon Katz in *Rolling Stone* writes, "*Myst*'s strange, mystical world rewards not the quick reflexes of *Super Mario Bros.* but creative reasoning. The more we guess, the more we guess right, and the more we guess right, the more our confidence builds. . . . The thrill is not in the story so much as in discovering that this technology can be mastered by intuition."[32] *Myst* activates the fantasy that many of us have: that we will be able to master our technology without resorting to manuals, that technology will so closely duplicate the workings of the human mind that we can use it based purely on intuition. The non-Cartesian method of movement in *Myst* enables the player to interact with the virtual spaces in ways that feel more naturalistic.

Myst, therefore, gives the impression of immersion in an alternate reality through its simulation of the processes of intuition, its intricately detailed art direction, its atmospheric sound, and its narrative justification of the limitations of the CD-ROM medium. Immersion figures largely in discourses about *Myst*. "It will become your world," announces the *Myst* packaging. A woman allegedly wrote to Brøderbund Software, *Myst*'s publisher, that her children had to sleep in sleeping bags because she was too immersed in the game to do the laundry. The director of marketing at Brøderbund says that they receive online messages saying, "I've lost my job, I've lost my girlfriend. When is *Myst 2* coming out?"[33]

Stories such as these are part of the *Myst* legend, which is initially puzzling because there is little in *Myst* which would seem to elicit traditional visual immersion: few moving images, few images of humans to identify with, a stagnant narrative. Immersion usually occurs when you're swept up in narrative progression, not when you're mired in digression.

The fact that *Myst* is widely acknowledged by its players to provoke immersion in the game/diegesis suggests that an alternative paradigm of immersion (or engagement) is at work in CD-

ROMS.[34] The requirements for this form of immersion seem to include a narrative framework providing forward direction; a cohesive detailed virtual world which makes logical sense on its own terms; and the lack of an intrusive interface which might remind us of "computerness." These three qualities characterize both *Myst* and the game which seems to be its antithesis: *Doom*. *Doom* supplies a narrative framework (as discussed earlier), and its atmospheric details and digital sound create a cohesive and detailed world with little visible interference from a computer interface. Within this paradigm of CD-ROM immersion there is considerable room for variation, and *Myst*'s version of immersion is distinguished by its simulation of mental intuition (rather than slavishly literal-minded understanding of the player as moving through a physical environment). *Myst* and *Doom* share certain fundamental requirements for CD-ROM immersion while offering very different experiences based on the qualities that shape their interactivity.

Interactivity

Although popular discourse seems to have given new technology a monopoly on the word "interactive," reader response theory has made the academy aware that all reading is interactive in some sense. The important question is, what kinds of interactions are promoted and discouraged in a reader's encounters with various kinds of texts? What does "interactivity" mean in different texts?

In *Myst* interactivity clearly refers to the fact that the player can control the order in which he/she visits the various ages instead of the CD-ROM dictating the order. This clearly differentiates the game from the form of interactivity proffered by *Doom*, in which the player must progress through an ordered sequence of numbered levels. But even more importantly, interactivity in *Myst* means that you can choose which portions of the space to attend to and manipulate.

Myst asks the player to conceptualize its virtual spaces in a distinctive manner. We are encouraged to treat almost everything in the space as being potentially significant to the narrative/game. *Myst* teaches us that we should "handle" (click on) every panel, every decoration, and every object in a room because each of these could provide information needed to solve the puzzle. This makes you aware of the possible significance of the smallest items in the space.

With few human figures and little spoken dialogue, *Myst* foregrounds its spaces as being the most important object of our attention. Our early experiences with *Myst* teach us to treat the space in this manner, just as neoformalist film criticism suggests that the initial moments of a film teach us how to watch and listen to this particular film.[35] We are initially placed on Myst Island with no overt instructions on what to do, no clear sense of what the object or goal of the game is. The lack of clear instructions on how to proceed is one of the innovations most frequently noted about this killer application. The discussions of this highly praised aspect of *Myst* need to be tempered with the acknowledgment that for most of the time one plays *Myst*, one knows exactly what the goal is and how to maneuver in the space. However, this initial (though temporary) lack of clear orientation is crucial to teaching us the importance of close attention to the space. The narrative standstill and the intricate detail of the images also encourage us to explore the landscapes carefully, as does the lack of a time deadline. A timed game such as *Super Mario Bros.* or an action-intensive game such as *Doom* do not promote perusing the scene; all the emphasis is on the figure's actions. In *Myst* we haltingly uncover the narrative and the unwritten rules of playing as we click on various objects, and along the way we discover the potential importance of the most negligible objects.

Myst encourages you to interact with all the objects, but it discourages purely random guessing since many clicks don't do anything at all. The game does provide intermittent reinforcement for our clicking behavior, however. Just because one

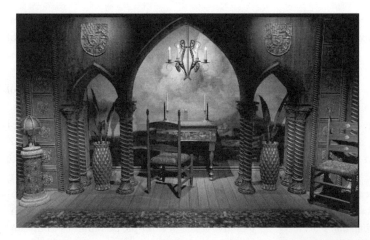

Myst's intricately detailed spaces (such as Sirrus's room in the Stoneship Age) encourage the player to click on or "handle" all these objects to determine if they are significant to the game.

clicked-on object doesn't do anything does not mean that another very similar object will not be the key to the puzzle (for instance, in the Stoneship Age most of the semicircular panels lining a hallway do nothing, except for one which is the gateway to the compass room). *Myst* encourages a continuous curiosity about the minutiae of its detailed spaces, shaping the quality of our interactions with the CD-ROM.

In addition to training us to watch its virtual spaces, *Myst* instructs us that close attention to sounds is just as important. Musical motifs cue you to whether or not a place is significant to the narrative/puzzle (e.g., intriguing music plays in the Myst tower only when a clue is available).[36] In some cases being able to remember and reconstruct a sequence of sounds in *Myst* is crucial to working the puzzle (sound memory is crucial in order to get to the Selenitic Age and to leave it). The crisp, overly near, omnipresent digital sounds we hear on our first visit to Myst Island prepare us to recognize the importance of sound in *Myst* problem solving.

So *Myst* foregrounds portions of the signifier which are generally relegated to the "background" in mainstream visual media.[37] In *Doom*, for example, players must pay much more attention to the lethal demons hurtling toward them than to the patterns on the wall. *Myst* restructures the way the reader/player encounters the CD-ROM

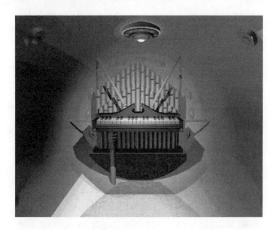

Sound plays an important role in alerting the player to crucial information. To solve this particular puzzle, the player must duplicate a series of tones heard elsewhere on the organ.

text, similar to the way hypertexts has been argued to restructure the hierarchy of traditional written texts. In a hypertext, items which play a secondary role on the conventional page (for instance, the footnote) can become prioritized, forming the basis for a reader's interactions.[38] *Myst* also rearranges the normal hierarchy of dealing with visual media, making typically subordinate elements such as setting and sound effects crucial to navigating the virtual spaces.

This restructuring makes the *Myst* player very aware of the possibilities of this space. The act of constantly clicking on things that *don't* do anything makes you aware of how many things *could* have a function. There is no obvious difference between objects that are significant to the narrative/puzzle and objects that are not, so the player is constantly aware of things that could lead to a solution but do not. In *Myst* you are frequently aware of the road not traveled by the software designers. While playing *Myst*, I experienced a bit of what Julia Kristeva's concept of the chora must be like: a space of generative potential, a space structured by possibility more than by firm actuality.

It is much more difficult to get a sense of this possibility in narratives which unfold at a pace outside the viewer's control (such as film or theater). For example, Hollywood film opens up narrative possibilities (will she be rescued? killed? will she escape?) only to close them down with a clear answer in a few minutes, giving the particular arrangement of plot events in a film a sense of inevitability. After we have seen the outcome, it is sometimes hard to reconstruct the feeling we once had that there could have been other possible outcomes. In *Myst* our narrative questions can remain open for a much longer time (even indefinitely). This makes us intensely aware of all the potential solutions for this particular *Myst* puzzle which unfortunately do not work. Because we stay in this limbo for such a long period of time, this awareness of the narrative roads not taken is heightened. The difference between traveling through diegetic space in *Myst* and in classical film

is comparable to the difference in the attention you give to a new location when making a map of it as you travel versus the attention given to a new place when you already have a map in hand.

Oddly enough, that sense of the potential of *Myst*'s landscapes seemed to disappear once I had solved the puzzle. Once I hit upon the solution I found it difficult to remember the many other solution attempts I tried unsuccessfully. The space transformed from chora to topos in my memory, with the designer's solution seeming somehow obvious. The space changed in my mind from the interactive space of multiple possibilities to the singular space designed by the CD-ROM's authors.

Author

I read about some of those mysteries [of science and nature] and look at the world around me in its complexity, and I am just awed. From my point of view, there is a creator in all that. It is hard to express my awe at the detail and craftsmanship in what I see.
—Rand Miller, cocreator of *Myst*[39]

As the player becomes aware that some objects perform functions when clicked on while other objects do not respond, he/she becomes aware that someone has chosen what is significant and what is not. In other words, this is not a real world in which everything can be handled and manipulated; it is an authored world where someone has chosen to imbue certain objects with significance. *Myst*'s structure consistently reminds us of the presence of this author.

Myst has the narrative conciseness of a well-made classical narrative, with few loose ends or red herrings. There are no spaces which are there merely to be admired. Virtually every space has significance to the narrative/puzzle. Unlike the real world, in which a detective must sort through which clues are important and which are not, every clue provided in *Myst* is needed for the solution, with nothing left over. If you can handle a book of patterns or a faucet or a key, you can be

Myst foregrounds the importance of the author who "wrote" these fantastic worlds and emphasizes the significance of a particularly old-fashioned piece of technology: the book.

certain that it is required to solve the puzzle. An author assures us that, unlike the real world, there is a lock corresponding to every key you find.[40]

The game relies on the same privileging of the ending, on the Barthesian drive to solve the narrative enigma and reveal the hermeneutic code, that characterize classical narratives. But unlike the reader of a novel, you are prevented by the author or the medium itself from skipping to the last chapter. There are limitations imposed by the author on our interactivity. You can visit the four ages in any order you wish, but you can only see the ending after you have completed all the tasks assigned to you by the author.[41] In addition, *Myst*'s authors perform the classic authorial function of withholding information until the ending. All of the rhetoric of the game is phrased to ask us to choose which *one* of the brothers is evil and which is good, never directly raising the possibility that *both* are evil, which is the case.[42] *Myst* does not offer us free access to the narrative information and diegetic spaces promised by utopian notions of hypermedia. Instead our interactions are bound by an authorial presence which withholds narrative information from us in a way resembling classical narrative practice.

The process of playing *Myst* involves becoming familiar with "*Myst* logic," or in other words, trying to reconstruct how the authors think in order

to better understand how these worlds are put together. While I was stuck trying to solve a puzzle, I would envision all kinds of possible solutions to attempt, many of them relying on elaborate and minute connections among the various elements in the space. I pondered the fact that the bedrooms and elevators on Channelwood and the Mechanical Age were in a similar spatial arrangement in relation to each other, and that the bedrooms on these two ages used the same musical motifs. Once the significance of the virtual environments was foregrounded in my mind, I found numerous obscure points of connection. However, I finally realized that some of the patterns I noticed were too obscure for a mass audience to find dependably and use in the solutions. I realized that the creators of *Myst* could not use too simple nor too complex a solution if they were to sell mass numbers of CD-ROMs. So it was helpful to conceptualize an author trying to reach a mass audience, an author more resembling a Hollywood director than an idiosyncratic artist such as a Jean-Luc Godard. *Myst* asks you to mindread the implied author in order to understand better the world he has created.

One might argue that playing *Myst* simply involves learning the intrinsic rules of this diegetic world without reference to an authorial presence, but the *Myst* story itself foregrounds the notion of a creator of worlds. A character in the diegesis

(Atrus) has "written" these worlds into existence from his own imagination. These ages are creations of his mind, according to the story. This emphasis in the story on the creator of these worlds points us not only to Atrus but to the real-life creators of *Myst,* Robyn and Rand Miller. It is not coincidental that the Miller brothers have received an unprecedented level of publicity for CD-ROM designers (they have been interviewed in *People* magazine and have appeared in Gap ads).[43] Each *Myst* disk even includes a thirteen-minute self-promotion video detailing their efforts in *The Making of Myst.*

This authorial presence can be considered as yet another way that *Myst* narratively justifies the properties and limitations of CD-ROMs. By definition we cannot write to a CD-ROM. As much as we "interact" with it, our interactions are bound. We cannot transgress outside where the authors want us to go. And *Myst* itself is a story about what happens when wanderers stray outside the limitations placed on them by creators. Atrus gives Achenar and Sirrus access to the various ages, but their curiosity overwhelms them, causing most of the ages to be destroyed. In the "winning" ending of *Myst,* these transgressors are themselves seemingly destroyed by the creator.[44] *Myst* is a cautionary tale about the potential perils of giving people unbridled access to information, about the dangers of the same curiosity to explore virtual worlds that the game encourages in its players.

Although hypermedia is sometimes thought of as the physical embodiment of poststructuralist freedom, this is clearly not true of the hybrid medium of the CD-ROM. As Mireille Rosello argues, "the relationship between hypertext and authorship may never be radically reconfigured. . . . The dream of collaborative writing and participatory reading often falls short of the theoretically infinite possibilities offered by hypertexts."[45] Barthes and Foucault notwithstanding, the author is not dead. He/she is alive and well and living on Myst Island.

The foregrounding of the author is perhaps the primary means of shifting a text from a low popular culture status to a high culture status as Art. Works authored by corporate entities (such as Campbell's soup can labels) tend not to be given the cultural cachet associated with works by an individual artist, which poses a problem in gaining status for media which are necessarily collaborative because of their complexity (such as filmmaking or CD-ROM developing). Associating the cinema with "auteurs" such as Fellini and Bergman, the art cinema in the 1950s raised the status of the cinematic medium. The art cinema offered film style that was clearly different from the industrially manufactured product of the Hollywood studios. By marketing these works of individual "artists," the art cinema brought the "lost audience" (those who preferred books and theater over Hollywood) into the theater, and therefore gained a new customer base and a new status as "art."

Through extratextual discourse and the structure of the game itself, *Myst* emphasizes the presence of a Creator, a Maker of worlds, an Author.[46] Publicity about the Miller brothers encourages us to read the software as being "written" by their artistic visions rather than "developed" by a faceless corporate entity. Emphasizing authorship is a crucial part of *Myst*'s attempt to distance itself from the dominant conception of CD-ROMs. This strategy complements *Myst*'s rejection of certain lower cultural associations of the *Doom* paradigm. Rejecting explicit physical violence, emphasizing deliberative thought over muscular reaction time, and foregrounding authorship, *Myst* creates a coherent strategy to gain higher cultural status than other CD-ROMs. It also opens up CD-ROMs to a "lost audience" who values the rarefied pleasures of intellectual reflection, not the "lower" pleasures of gore and quick reflexes. *Myst*'s emphasis on the author announces that the CD-ROM game is now capable of "art" and not merely diverting products such as *Doom.* As *Myst* demonstrates, when a killer application changes our conception of a medium, it also frequently changes its class appeal to an audience.

Hybrid Text, Hybrid Criticism

Myst uses new technology to emphasize the status of the author and to commemorate that antiquated technology called the book. By making books the central links between ages, it celebrates the book's capacity to take readers to new worlds. Less overtly, *Myst*'s intricate imagery points out a shortcoming of books: the inability to portray those worlds with detailed signification. The blend of postmodern technology and premodern imagery (books, gears, boilers) helps *Myst* to position itself on the frontier of a new medium.[47]

Myst blends old and new in creating worlds that are undeniably fabricated and yet familiarly worn. Details in its virtual worlds show that the "wood" has been "aged," the surfaces have been "worn," and that nails have been "hammered." This is a world that has been built by hand (authored) as much as it has been manufactured. This calls to mind the industrial practice Stuart Ewen mentions that was used at the beginning of the nineteenth century to make manufactured goods seem handmade. When industrial capitalism began to boom, many factories used mechanical production to stamp a hand-worked look onto the surfaces of the goods they produced, providing a link to the recent artisanal past and making the mass-produced surfaces seem more familiar.[48] *Myst*'s hybrid form allows us to mix our pleasures: the pleasure of handmade craftsmanship and the pleasure of cutting-edge technology; the pleasure of being told a story by a storyteller and the pleasure of exploring a story space on our own.

Mixing the familiar with intriguing new technology works well for new commercial objects of material and symbolic culture. Killer applications are heralded as embodiments of the new, but they tend to blend in established forms with their innovations. This mixture is similar to early narrative cinema, which took plots from well-known novels, plays, and tales (*Uncle Tom's Cabin, Little Red Riding Hood*) to root its narrative and stylistic experimentations in comfortably familiar terri-

tory. Recall that even the novel itself began as a mix of components taken from other familiar forms (Greek classical literature, picaresque tales, romantic and pastoral cycles). A killer application by definition must be new, but not so new that its foreignness makes it commercially unviable.[49] To see clearly what is innovative about a killer application, it is productive to view it as a hybrid, a mix of current entertainment forms. Treating *Myst* as part game, part book, and part movie helps show what makes it truly distinctive as a CD-ROM: its seamless interface; its narrative justification of the drawbacks of the new technology; the way its player movements simulate intuition; its rejection of time deadlines; the way it encourages curiosity about the possibilities of its spaces; and its foregrounding of the author.

A hybrid conception of new media can create criticism which goes beyond the commonplace descriptions in the popular press. To say that *Myst* is "interactive" or "intuitive" or "close to virtual reality" is correct, but what do those general terms mean? Paying attention to the components of CD-ROM narration helps us to see better how these terms, which are inherited from utopian popular discourse, structure the meanings provided by a particular text.

Such a hybrid media form using hybrid content seems to call for a hybrid criticism. A critical approach which samples from established methodologies can provide close attention to individual instances of new media. I began conceptualizing this paper as a straightforward narratological investigation of how we make sense out of *Myst*'s narrative, space, and time, given that we are initially given no overt goals and no instructions on how to proceed. I soon felt that such a programmatic approach missed much more than it explained, and I began this essay with its blend of Julia Kristeva, David Bordwell, Stuart Ewen, and Greg Smith. Close attention to the surfaces of these texts should usefully counterbalance some current scholars' emphasis on the potential of the medium, which too often tends to fall into the trap of accepting the utopian rhetoric of popular marketing concerning the "interactivity" of new technologies. These discourses are important, but they and the technological objects they describe should both be scrutinized through critical eyes. Just as *Myst* switches from movie to game to book, the CD-ROM critic should be able to switch from one analytic tool to another to follow the path blazed by this new and old medium.

Notes

I wish to thank Bob Lisson for acting as therapist and coach during my *Myst* playing experience.

1 *Myst*'s sales figures are even more remarkable because *Myst* is primarily sold as a stand-alone product rather than being bundled into a package with other software (a common marketing practice to boost sales).

2 Mike Snider, "*Myst* Remains a Solid Best Seller," *USA Today* (Feb. 1, 1996): D1.

3 Erik Davis, "Into the *Myst*," *Village Voice* (August 23, 1994): 45–46.

4 James Sterngold, "Multimedia: CD-ROMs Hitch a Ride with a Man on a Spider," *New York Times* (Apr. 2, 1995): B1.

5 Michael Desmond, Steve Fox, Jeff Bertolucci, Eric Bender, Michael S. Lasky, Heidi Wolff, Gregg Keizer, Leslie Crawford, and Laurianne McLaughlin, "Games and Leisure," *PC World* (December 1994): 132–35; Lori Grunin, "Solve, Shoot, and Puzzle Your Way to Holiday Gaming Happiness," *PC Magazine* (Dec. 6, 1994): 508–9.

6 Lance Ulanoff, "*PC Magazine* Picks the Top 100 CD-ROMs," *PC Magazine* (Sept. 13, 1994): 156.

7 Although commentators such as Levy say there are *no* time deadlines in *Myst*, there is one (the battery in the Stoneship age runs out of power after a period of time, shutting off all the lights). However, this time deadline is temporary, since it is relatively easy to recharge the battery and reactivate the lights. Steven Levy, "*Myst*," *Macworld* (January 1995): 102.

8 David Bordwell, *Narration in the Fiction Film* (Madison: University of Wisconsin Press, 1985), 205–33.

9 Michael J. Miller, "After Hours," *PC Magazine* (December 20, 1994): 144.

10 Bob Lindstrom, "Entertainment Choice," *Compute!* (Aug. 1994): 86.

11 Jon Carroll, "Guerillas in the *Myst*," *Wired* (Aug. 23, 1994): 80.

12 Jon Katz, "Rom and Roll," *Rolling Stone* (Apr. 7, 1994): 44.

13 Erik Davis, "Into the *Myst*," *Village Voice* (Aug. 23, 1994): 45.

14 Christian Metz, *The Imaginary Signifier: Psychoanalysis and the Cinema,* trans. Celia Britton, Annwyl Williams, Ben Brewster, and Alfred Guzzetti (Bloomington: Indiana University Press, 1982), 61–74.

15 Rand Miller, quoted in Marilyn Gillen, "Interactive Gamers Try to Follow Enveloping *Myst*," *Billboard* (July 1, 1994): 100.

16 In fact, Lindstrom says that "the lure of seeing all of *Myst*'s stunning locales is a major motivator pulling you through the game" ("Entertainment Choice," 86). This suggests that, although *Myst*'s narrative drive comes to a virtual standstill, the player's curiosity concerning the virtual environment may provide an important forward impetus. If classical narratives are structured around the question "What happens next?" portions of *Myst* may be structured around the question "Where will we visit next?"

17 Ibid., 87.

18 Mary Ann Doane, "The Voice in the Cinema: The Articulation of Body and Space," in *Movies and Methods,* vol. 2, ed. Bill Nichols (Berkeley: University of California Press, 1985).

19 In addition, Doane's argument that sound when not clearly tied to an onscreen sound source conveys a sense of the uncanny provides useful explanation for the common feeling that the landscapes in *Myst* (which frequently uses atmospheric sound without a clearly specified source) are somehow unsettling.

20 Davis, "Into the *Myst*," 45.

21 This is comparable to the way a darkened film theater helps audiences to become immersed in the cinematic diegesis and less aware of the theater.

22 Lindstrom, "Entertainment Choice," 87.

23 This discussion has important parallels to Rudolf Arnheim's argument that the potential of cinema is defined by its limitations. Rudolf Arnheim, *Film as Art* (Berkeley: University of California Press, 1957).

24 George Beekman and Ben Beekman. "*Myst* 1.0," *MacWorld* (March 1994): 76.

25 *Myst*'s emphasis on traveling through space while finding and carrying objects which allow you to solve puzzles reveals the game's origins in *Adventure*. *Adventure* (and its descendant, *Zork*) were early text-based games which sent the player on an interactive quest involving puzzle solving and object manipulation. Various ver-

sions of *King's Quest* took this structure and added increasing amounts of graphics. Such quest-based object manipulation remains central to the conception of computer games.

26 Whether a click executes a 90- or 180-degree turn depends on the player's location in the diegetic space. A click left at a particular location will always execute the same turn, no matter how many times one revisits that location and clicks left. The system is not random, in other words.

27 My experiences trying to teach post-MTV undergraduates about continuity errors seem to bear this out. As long as a character's overall narrative trajectory is clear, many seem able to tolerate jump cuts and 180-degree rule violations without significantly experiencing discontinuity. It is difficult to convey a sense that crossing the 180-degree axis was once considered a radical and jarring stylistic choice in film.

28 The game creates a position roughly comparable to the ideal observer position promised by classical cinema. Classical Hollywood narration promises that the spectator will be given the "best" view of the action. Classical cinematic narration excises "unnecessary" actions (e.g., going to the bathroom) which do not advance the story. See Bordwell, *Narration in the Fiction Film,* 161.

29 John Slatin, "Reading Hypertext: Order and Coherence in a New Medium," in *Hypermedia and Literary Studies,* ed. Paul Delany and George Landow (Cambridge: MIT Press, 1991), 158.

30 In fact, *Myst* itself seems structured to exemplify the commonsense understanding of human memory articulated by Christian Metz. Metz says that "all one retains of a film is its plot and a few images" (*The Imaginary Signifier,* 46). The experience of playing *Myst* resembles Metz's description of what we remember after seeing a film: the narrative and still images.

Playing *Myst,* however, exposes the insufficiency of our own (human) memory. Players cannot remember all the details they need to know to solve the various puzzles, so they must keep a journal of their observations to navigate the various ages successfully. A CD-ROM can keep these details stored, but we must rely on other technology (the paper journal) to aid our own limited memory.

31 *Myst* does have a "zip mode" which allows a player familiar with an age to move faster through the space. I have argued that the necessity of so much tedious traveling time in *Myst* makes us aware of this space's recalcitrance, which reminds us of the real world. Zip mode

only changes this argument slightly. Zip mode allows the player to move through the space more quickly, but it is roughly limited to moving about as far as the "eye" can see. Were it not for zip mode, moving across a known space would be significantly more tedious and frustrating. Thus zip mode allows a *comparative* but not an *unlimited* freedom of mobility, more like leaping across space rather than teleporting to a new space. This allows us to be aware that moving through *Myst*'s spaces requires time (as it does in the real world), while simultaneously providing a means of moving which is optimal given these bounds.

32 Katz, "Rom and Roll," 46.

33 Don Steinberg, "The *Myst* Mystique," *New York Times* (July 17, 1994): A31; Chris McGowan, "CD-ROM Successes: How They Happen," *Billboard* (Feb. 18, 1995): 68, 75.

34 Davis suggests that the belief that CD-ROMs should emulate film, that "immersion is identical with simulating the movement of physical bodies," is a "naive literalism that drives much VR design." Instead he roots *Myst*'s structure in comic books and fairy tale picture books, arguing that "the enchantment provided by these pictures is empowered rather than weakened by stillness and defined borders" (Davis, "Into the *Myst*," 45).

35 Kristin Kristin, *Breaking Through the Glass Armor: Neoformalist Film Analysis* (Princeton, NJ: Princeton University Press, 1988), 38–44, 89–95.

36 This resembles the filmic practice of using music to alert us that crucial actions are imminent.

37 Lighting also provides cues to the *Myst* player. Objects which are not at least partially lit are not significant to the narrative/puzzle. The player eventually learns to click on all lit objects, ignoring all totally dark spaces.

38 Terence Harpold, "Threnody: Psychoanalytic Digressions on the Subject of Hypertexts," in *Hypermedia and Literary Studies,* ed. Delany and Landow, 172.

39 "The *Mystery* in Learning," *Electronic Learning* (May/June 1995): 28.

40 Some spaces in *Myst* almost seem to be dead ends, but even these maintain some narrative justification. Taking the tree elevator on Myst Island upward seems to provide you with nothing more than a bird's-eye view of the island, but once I realized that this elevator *had* to be there for a purpose, I recognized that there had to be a way to make that elevator go down below ground level, which was crucial to finding my way to Channelwood. Working on the assumption that there are no gratuitous machines in *Myst,* the "dead end" trip up the

elevator helped me to rethink my assumptions about how the elevator worked.

Of course not absolutely every space you can click on can be significant to the plot/puzzle. Sirrus's and Achenar's rooms in the various ages primarily exist to house the "pages" we are collecting and to give us clues about the brothers' personalities. Thus there are some objects which exist as "atmosphere" or as character-oriented informative cues. A player can experience considerable frustration if he/she tries to find narrative/puzzle functionality in an object that is decorative. But every object which can be manipulated and which clearly is not solely decorative is crucial to the puzzle solution.

41 Many consider *Myst*'s ending to be an anticlimax after spending so much effort on arriving at the denouement, but the promise of an unambiguous ending (even if it turns out to be disappointing) is crucial to the player's forward progression through the game. Few seem to feel outraged by the disappointing ending, however. As Siegel puts it, "Games can get away with sucker endings if the puzzles are good." The emphasis on the process of exploring the ages and solving the puzzles seems to compensate for the relative lack of payoff in *Myst*'s ending. David Siegel, "Spinning Pizza into Gold: A Structural Analysis of *Myst*," http://www.upandrunning.com/storyweb/film/myst.html.

42 How *Myst* cues you to suspect one brother or another is interesting. Atrus tells us that he suspects Achenar, and I initially trusted him. But Sirrus's performance is so nasal and condescending that he quickly comes under suspicion. I read Achenar's performance as more guileless, but he seems overly emotional to the point of instability. Eventually we figure out that Achenar's rooms are more warlike and ethnic (using native masks as decorations, for example), and Sirrus's spaces are more plushly decorated according to European standards. When I played *Myst*, I decided that Achenar was the evil one, relying on Eurocentric, classist notions, which made me feel more comfortable with Sirrus's plush rooms. Thus I duplicated the game's own emphasis on set decoration over more common sources of information about characters (such as acting performance). The Gap ad (photographed by Richard Avedon) appeared in *Wired* (May 1995): 18–19.

43 Susan Reed and Cathy Free, "CD(ROM) of Brotherly Loves," *People* (Jan. 16, 1995): 185–86.

44 This fact is overlooked by many reviewers who state that no one gets killed in *Myst*, or that the player cannot be "killed." More accurately, no one gets killed until the end of *Myst*, and the player can get trapped in total darkness for all eternity if he/she chooses the wrong ending.

45 Mireille Rosello, "The Screener's Maps: Michel de Certeau's 'Wandersmanner' and Paul Auster's Hypertextual Detective," in *Hyper/Text/Theory*, ed. George P. Landow (Baltimore: Johns Hopkins University Press, 1994), 143–44.

46 The fact that Rand and Robyn Miller are sons of a fundamentalist minister has received much commentary in popular discourse, tying together *Myst*'s story of creation by a father, the creation of CD-ROM worlds by the Millers (Rand plays father Atrus in the game's video clips), and the ultimate act of Creation. Robyn Miller noted that "sometimes late at night, after I had done something really cool, I would look down on my creation and I would say, 'It is good'" (Jon Carroll, "Guerrillas in the *Myst*, *Wired* (August 1994): 73.

47 Many have made the connection between the juxtaposition of old and new objects in *Myst*'s fantastic landscapes and surrealism. For instance, Rothstein says, "Myst . . . in its combination of surreal futurism and old-fashioned imagery . . . seems to reflect the condition of the video game itself, poised at the brink of something new even before it has finished mastering something old" (Edward Rothstein, "A New Art Form May Arise from the *Myst*," *New York Times* [December 4, 1994]: 25). Descriptions of playing *Myst* frequently rely upon this connection: "This is a dream which can alternate from beautiful to eerie and back with no effort, a waking dream. That perhaps describes the experience best—a waking dream" (David Pipes, "*Myst* by Broderbund," *Game Bytes* 18).

48 Stuart Ewen, *All Consuming Images: The Politics of Style in Contemporary Culture*. (New York: Basic Books, 1988), 32–33.

49 The academic criticism of new media early on emphasized hypertext's radical capabilities to restructure narrative. However, it is this hybrid entertainment form (and not a radically destabilizing narrative such as Michael Joyce's *Afternoon*) that developers soon envisioned as the future of the medium. For discussions of *Afternoon*, see Stuart Moulthrop, "Hypertext and 'the Hyperreal,'" in *Hypertext '89: Proceedings, ACM Conference on Hypertext, November 5–8, Pittsburgh, PA* (New York: Association of Computing Machinery, 1989); David J. Bolter, *Writing Space: The Computer, Hypertext, and the History of Writing* (Hillsdale, NJ: Lawrence Erlbaum, 1991).

The Rules of the Game: *Evil Dead II . . .* Meet Thy *Doom*

Angela Ndalianis

The Evil Is Unleashed—Science Fiction and Horror Meet the Shoot-'em-Up

Interdimensional doorways finally make possible space travel between the two moons of Mars: Phobos and Deimos. The Union Aerospace Corporation's research into interdimensional travel is a success. Or is it? In a climactic series of events, things start to go terribly wrong. Some people sent through the gateways disappear. Others return from Mars's moons as zombies. Then the moon Deimos vanishes without a trace. Enter the hero-leader of a specialized team of space marines. He sends his troops ahead of him through the interdimensional gateway; armed with a Space Marine Corporation gun, he follows them through, but once on Phobos his worldview changes. The space marines have vanished. Instead, dark surroundings envelop him, and eerie, atmospheric music accentuates the suspense-filled moments. The marine leader begins to scour the corporate installation in search of any living human being . . . but it's not the living who come to greet him. Seemingly out of nowhere, an array of bizarre creatures charge down dim-lit corridors and through automatic doors: zombified humans, demons, imps, minotaur-like forms, evil spirits. And so it begins. He must explore the installation to find out what happened, then get the hell out of there at any cost! Picking up weapons along the way, he attacks the monsters like a man gone berserk—with fists, chainsaw, gun, rifle, and missile launcher. His body takes a beating, but his victims also pay the price. Hundreds of those demonic bodies audibly erupt, explode, and splatter

before him—and he revels in every gory detail. A sequel to *Aliens: Aliens Meets the Demons of Hell*? Or perhaps *Evil Dead II* in outer space? This is no film space. The horror of this story belongs to the cult computer game released by id Software in 1993: *Doom: Evil Unleashed*.

Doom reveals the complex relationships that currently exist between entertainment structures. The cross-over between popular culture forms such as films and computer games tests the clear separation between diverse media forms, and this overlap has ramifications for genre analysis. Hans Jauss has argued that a genre's development involves both the repetition of previous conventions within a genre, and the introduction of elements that extend and alter those conventions. Each new addition to a genre calls upon "rules of the game," or sets of generic conventions, which are familiar to the audience. These rules can "be varied, extended, corrected, but also transformed, crossed out, or simply reproduced."[1] Genres are viewed as language games that can introduce radical changes within a category, even leading to the "transformation into another genre through the invention of a new 'rule to the game.'"[2] One question that needs to be addressed is what happens when the "rules of the game" extend beyond the one medium? Do genres cross media borders?

A more flexible account of genre's functions in contemporary media would acknowledge the dynamic interchange between various popular culture forms. Genre films and computer games are not closed systems drawing purely on their own genre and media specific conventions. Their "meaning" also crosses into other media. Clearly, audience familiarity with genres from related media is economically advantageous to computer game and film companies. This is especially the case given the horizontal integration currently operating across a variety of entertainment media.[3] Genre and media hybridization is crucial to creating a larger cross-over market. Economic motivations aside, this cross-over suggests that the boundaries of our critical models must expand to consider cross-media hybrids such as the "interactive" computer games *Under a Killing Moon* and *Phantasmagoria*. Not only do both these games depend on mise-en-scènes and cinematography that owe a great deal to filmic modes of production, but their very structures are influenced by film genres. *Under a Killing Moon* combines its game format with detective, noir, and science-fiction conventions, and *Phantasmagoria* is a combination of the psycho-killer and splatter horror films.

While the game *Doom: Evil Unleashed* does not employ film production techniques in the way these other two examples do (including film actors and directors), the game does depend on player familiarity with science fiction and horror conventions, especially those evoked by *Aliens* (James Cameron, 1986) and *Evil Dead II* (Sam Raimi, 1987). As a superhybrid form that ruptures generic and medium-specific boundaries, *Doom* has become the blockbuster success of the gaming industry. *Doom,* and its equally addictive sequel *Doom II: Hell on Earth,* introduced a filmic quality to game spaces and thus helped to broaden the digital market. An analysis of the *Doom* games reveals how film genres have extended and opened their borders; the "old rules" of the generic game spill outward from films into new media products such as computer games.[4] The *Doom* games created new generic rules and new audience responses: not only did the games alter the rules of the genre in their own medium, but their impact also reveals the potential computer games have for influencing the development of film genres.

In *Doom* we play the main protagonist (a marine). The aim of the game is to navigate this character through the three worlds of Phobos, Deimos, and Hell to discover what went wrong with the interdimensional experiments. In the process, we must also destroy all monsters that come within shooting distance. When (and if) we get to the end of the game, we will have defeated the demon hordes, returning to Earth victoriously ... until the sequel *Doom II*. The sequel was made possible because someone left open one of the dimensional doors. The result? Demons of Hell gained access to Earth. So, it begins again. We reprise our role as hero and return to kick some more demon butt as we struggle to save humanity from being transformed into a population of zombies. The full dramatic—and at times horrific—effects of this story would have been impossible to experience without the genre's technically innovative three-dimensional graphics and texture and the atmospheric sound effects; these effects added to the hyperviolent and hyperaction dimensions of the game.

Before *Doom* graced our computer screens, the game effects of id software's *Wolfenstein 3-D* (1991) had transformed the two-dimensional game format known as the "platform game" into a separate genre known as the corridor game, or shoot-'em-up genre. Before *Wolfenstein 3-D,* platform games like *Donkey Kong* had stressed action that took place on a two-dimensional plane that ran parallel to the computer screen. The layout of the games resembled a mazelike ant farm; the player navigated a two-dimensional, cartoonish character through this maze while trying to avoid obstacles placed in his/her path. Corridor games like *Wolfenstein 3-D* were instrumental in transforming this two-dimensional platform space into a more convincing three-dimensional environment. Rather than moving characters across a series of platforms that ran parallel to the screen, the player maneuvered them through a series of corridors; the corridor format stressed movement into the simulated depth of the computer screen space. The title "corridor games" has recently been superseded by the term "shoot-'em-up" (or first-person shooter) because shoot-'em-up action is the main emphasis in much of the game play. The most common example of the corridor games, therefore, is these "shoot-'em-up," body count variations that require the player to move through corridors shooting all enemies that come toward him/her.

However, even a game like *Wolfenstein 3-D* (which was groundbreaking for its time) remains "unrealistic" when compared to *Doom*.[5] *Doom* further extended the conventions of the shoot-'em-up. The differences between *Doom* and *Wolfenstein 3-D* are visible primarily in the ways we experience the environment that the hero, and we, immerse ourselves. In most shoot-'em-ups we adopt the view point of the main protagonist. The player does not see the hero's entire body; often only his hands and the weapon he wields are visible at the bottom of the screen. The game play logic is that our own body—which exists beyond the computer screen—"fills in" the protagonist's body. Despite the movement into a simulated three-dimensional space, in *Wolfenstein 3-D* the cartoonish, two-dimensional articulation of that three-dimensional space persists. We discover a game world based upon blocky, monotonous environments composed of minimal color arrangements and flat surfaces lacking in texture and attention to detail. *Doom*, on the other hand, envelops us in environments filled with realistic details, details that flesh out laboratories, torture rooms, infernal landscapes, and military installations. Such visual details are accompanied by sound effects: background music, the demons' cries of attack, and groans of pain coming from the hero's aching body. The result is an atmosphere of suspense, action, horror, and grueling tension. The movements of the hero further enhance this convincing experience of an alien world. In *Wolfenstein 3-D*, we slide robotically along the corridors and confront our enemy (a continual assault of identical, cartoonlike Nazis) with a limited range of weapons. In *Doom*, not only do we face a whole barrage of demonic forms of different shapes and sizes (complete with matching arsenal of weapons with multiple sound and visual effects), but we also move along corridors and up and down stairs in bobbing, jerky motions that simulate running actions more realistically.

Doom's articulation of more realistic and atmospheric effects in the shoot-'em-up emphasizes Jauss's argument that some new additions to a genre can alter the rules so much that a new genre can emerge. Working with the conventions of many of its shoot-'em-up predecessors, *Doom* introduced enough new rules to allow for a redirection in the aesthetics of the shoot-'em-up genre. The redirection cemented the break between platforms and shoot-'em-ups instigated by *Wolfenstein 3-D* and made possible our more convincing immersion into the game narrative spaces. The game was also pivotal in broadening the conventions and expectations of the shoot-'em-up genre. *Doom* became the form that all shoot-'em-ups would aspire to and was even compared to other "classic" examples of other genres from other media. As one review noted, "To describe *Doom* as a first-person perspective action adventure would be like calling *Blade Runner* 'a film about robots.'"[6]

The *Doom* duo triggered a craze in *Doom*-like shoot-'em-ups. These included games that repeated conventions formulaically such as *Alien vs. Predator* (also an offshoot of Dark Horse comics); *In Extremis* (which borrows heavily from *Aliens*); and *Terminator Rampage* (also influenced by the *Terminator* films). However, innovative new additions such as *Dark Forces, System Shock, Duke Nuke 'em 3D*, and *Quake* have expanded the boundaries of the genre by incorporating new features, adding an even greater realism and more intensive form of game play. Graphics and sound effects have become even more detailed and three-dimensional, and the character movement includes greater mobility: aside from walking, running, and turning, heroes can now also look up and down, jump, swim, and crouch.

Besides influencing the genre within its own medium, *Doom*'s entry onto the shoot-'em-up scene technically and creatively bridged the gap between the genres and styles of two separate media. The enhanced graphics, special effects, digital sound effects, musical track, as well as the level and articulation of violence and "realism," amplified the shoot-'em-up genre's connections with contemporary Hollywood cinema. Discussing *Doom*'s influences, Jay Wilbur, the chief executive officer of id, stated that "[id] wanted to make an *Alien*-like game that captured the fast-paced action, brutality and fear of those movies. Another fine influence was the movie *Evil Dead II*—chainsaws and shotguns are an unbeatable combination!"[7] While the games draw upon various science fiction and horror film conventions, these two specific film sources—*Aliens* and *Evil Dead II*—stand out when playing both *Doom* games.

The Doom *Duo, the Shoot-'em-Up,*
and Action Sensibilities

While emerging from a different tradition, many conventions of action cinema intersect with those of the shoot-'em-up game genre, reflecting the hybrid nature of entertainment media. In *Aliens*, the hero Ripley goes back to an alien-infested planet with a specialized marine squadron to discover the whereabouts of the inhabitants (who have been used as incubators for the alien spawn). The film's hybrid structure collapses the boundaries of several genres—science fiction, horror, and the combat film—into one by incorporating all these genre forms into an overriding action cinema trajectory. For example, a dominant plot concern of the film is a science fiction interest in corrupt corporations that misuse technology and science and endanger humanity. Often, however, this story is frozen for the sheer spectacle displays of bodies, special effects, violence, and blood-pumping action. The film invites us to take part in a series of adrenaline-rushing scenes that focus on chases, explosions, gun blasts, and spectacular special effects as humans hunt aliens and aliens stalk humans.

A comparison of action cinema with the shoot-'em-ups reveals interesting parallels. Shoot-'em-ups (along with beat-'em-ups like *Mortal Kombat*,

Street Fighter, and *Rise of the Robots*) corner the action game market. As with action cinema, both game genres reveal their capacity for generic surfing. Examples of this surfing include the referencing of science fiction (*Rise of the Robots* and *Duke Nuke 'Em 3D*), science fiction-horror (*Doom*, *Doom II*), war/combat (*Wolfenstein 3-D*), science fiction-medieval-horror (*Quake*), and martial arts and fantasy (*Mortal Kombat, Street Fighter, Virtual Fighter*). The articulation of the "'em" becomes the means by which iconography associated with film genres is called upon. The "them" gives form and shape to the visuals, particularly to the environment we move around in, and to the appearance of the antagonists that we destroy. In *Doom* and *Doom II* the visual generic references vacillate between an array of creatures—specters, imps, cacodemons, hell knights (thus calling up horror iconography and character types), as well as a series of cyberdemons, arachnotrons, and corporate military zombiemen (which merge science fiction-horror components with the combat film). In addition, we're thrust into science fiction environments that consist of moon bases, technological gadgets, and teleporters; these are coupled with an atmosphere dominated by dim lighting and eerie sound effects that recall the ghoulish backdrops that dominate in horror films. As with action cinema, generic specificity of an iconographic, narrative, or thematic kind is no longer central to the genre. The only stable, defining characteristics that exist are those prolonged moments of pure, adrenaline-rushing action.

The role required of the game player adds a further action cinema sensibility to the game experience. Action cinema is defined by the physically active roles required of the protagonists. This genre of games is also classified according to the dominant action it requires of its player: to shoot "them" up. The games not only contain the role of sole vigilante against a multitude of no-good futuristic demonic spawn (complete with arsenal of weapons), but also focus on spectacles of action encapsulated in the never-ending gun battles and fist fights that players engage in as they fend off their enemies. The physiques of some of the "human" baddies ("The Heavy Weapon Dude" and "The Shot Gun Guy") also reflect the connection with action cinema. Their chunky, muscular bodies and assortment of machine guns and bullets recall characters who populate action films like *Commando* and *Broken Arrow.* Action cinema, however, focuses its spectacles of action around the bodies of its muscular, half-naked protagonists—the most popular being Bruce Willis, Jean Claude Van Damme, and Arnold Schwarzenegger. But in shoot-'em-up action games like *Doom, Duke Nuke 'em, Quake,* and *Dark Forces,* we are invariably the protagonists. Rather than seeing a display of main protagonist hyperbodies on the computer screen, we have to make do with the knowledge that our own muscular, well-oiled, and sweaty bodies occupy the real space beyond the screen.

The action of the *Doom* games has enough in common with action films to allow for a two-way flow between these media. Universal Studios had been seriously considering producing a film version of *Doom* with Arnold Schwarzenegger—the man who brought the capital A into Action—everyone's favorite for the lead role.[8] Jay Wilbur saw the *Doom* film as likely following the game's lead in providing "mainly, just nonstop seat-of-your-pants sweat-of-your-brow action."[9] Contemporary blockbuster movies' greater emphasis on action and spectacle at the expense of tighter, more literary-oriented narratives is no new phenomenon to the cinema. It is, however, an aesthetic that has become more pronounced because of the exchange with computer and arcade game formats. The chase and action scenes that take place in corridorlike spaces in films like *Die Hard 3* and *Under Siege 2,* for example, reflect a certain "shoot-'em-up" sensibility.

While these overlaps reveal the extent of the convergence of popular culture forms, the games themselves provide a different experience to that provided by action films. In action cinema, no matter how economically pruned down the narrative and no matter how often the story is frozen for the spectacles of action, the action is still placed within a rigidly ordered sequence of narrative events. For example, in the final, climactic scene in *Aliens* (after Ripley and Newt's tension-riddled and action-packed "escape" from the alien mother's den), we find ourselves engrossed in the duel between the alien mother and Ripley. As viewers, we are enticed by the action in its own right: the build up of nail-biting suspense as the alien mother stalks Newt; Ripley's exit to change into her "transformer/terminator" outfit; and the final explosive encounter as alien and human engage in hand-to-hand combat. However, the presentation of these events is unchangeable. And, eventually, this action sequence returns us to a storyline concerned with unraveling events about the Corporation, Ripley and Newt, and the aliens.

In the shoot-'em-ups (overt connections to film aside), game players would profoundly resent the freezing of the visuals, spectacle, and action for the sake of the linear unraveling of the story. The *Doom* storyline outlined earlier may sound like the foundations of a great action-science-fiction-horror film and may soon be one, but when we play this game (and others like it), we desire different experiences than we do as film spectators. In game play reality is the last thing a *Doom* player thinks of when in the throes of shoot-'em-up action for the higher purpose of saving humanity. Intricate science fiction-horror plot details are difficult to glean (and of little interest) once within the game itself. The primary directive is to exterminate (and revel in exterminating) the barrage of aliens as they pour out of corridors, secret passageways, and multidimensional doors and come straight for us. As protagonists, we work according to the principle: "shoot first, and shoot anything that moves—and don't even bother about asking questions later." The game revels in those moments of spectacle so typical of action cinema, but now the action has become the essence of the game experience.

The Aesthetics of Gore:
Doom *Meets* Evil Dead II

Aliens' impact on *Doom* is reflected in the way the action tendencies in the game move beyond the generically specific. The influence of *Evil Dead II*, however, draws *Doom* back to the specifics of horror. In *Aliens* and *Evil Dead II*, different kinds of action spectacle are evoked. The display of bodies and violence is a feature that sprawls across several genres and is present especially in action cinema. However, horror differentiates its brand of body horror and bodily destruction through the self-conscious play and graphic articulation of the visual (and aural) sense of horror. Splatter horror films like *Evil Dead II* amplify the gore factor that runs across many contemporary horror films; the audience responds to spectacles of action that radiate around bodies in revolting states of destruction.[10] This visual assault of splatter horror aims at extracting an emotive response from the audience and targets a gut-level reaction. This reaction vacillates between revulsion and comedy and, like action, is always at the expense of the narrative. The playful intensification of the sound and visual effects of gore and the splatters of blood and flesh in *Doom* and *Doom II* reveal an undeniable debt to the erupting and audibly splattering bodies of the *Evil Dead* films, particularly the over-the-top quality of the second film. The *Evil Dead* films and *Doom* computer games depend on games played with the spectator; these games converge around gore and, through this gore, around issues of genre.

The "buckets of blood" attitude to bodily destruction finds its perfect expression in *Evil Dead II* in a frenzied series of morbidly hysterical scenes. The story begins in a way that recalls the prequel. A couple—Ash and Linda—arrive at a cabin in the woods only to discover that an evil has been unleashed from the Realm of Darkness. Only

minutes into the film, Ash's girlfriend Linda becomes possessed. After Linda's death, a group of travelers join Ash and, one by one, similarly become possessed, leaving Ash behind to play the hero. From the beginning of the film, we are thrust into what can only be described as a roller-coaster ride of gore and splatter. Three examples will suffice. Gore moment number 1: Within the first few minutes of the film, Ash dispenses with his demonically possessed girlfriend by chopping off her head with an axe; later that evening, he sees her decaying, decapitated body performing pirouettes in the woods outside the cabin—with her head rolling along the ground in accompaniment. In a series of events that deal with this struggle between the living (Ash) and the dead (Linda), Linda's body (minus the head) attacks Ash with a buzzing chainsaw. But since Linda's head is lying on a bench in the tool shed, her body has no access to vision, and she accidentally slices her own body in half from the neck down. The result? Every inch of space in the tool shed is flooded with sprays of blood. Gore moment number 2: Ash's hand becomes possessed. The solution? First he stabs it, tacking it onto the floor. Then he saws it off with the chainsaw, complete with more blood-spraying effects as the blood gushes over Ash's face, and he victoriously cries out, "Who's laughing now?" Gore moment number 3: Ash tries to push a demon spawn into the basement by slamming the trapdoor down on its head. He succeeds. In the process, however, one of the demon's eyeballs vacates its socket at a super velocity, making its way full speed across the room and into the mouth (and, presumably, down the throat) of a hysterical, screaming character. While blood may not be involved, the abject events we witness make our own blood curdle and our flesh tingle in a combination of revulsion and humor.

We are invited to participate in a film that takes the violence and gore of horror cinema to their absolute sensory limits. The horror genre is reduced to moments of excess: excess of style and excess gore. Besides the gut reactions that the film's bloody sequences provoke in us, this sensory involvement is also present on a stylistic level—especially through the hyperkinetic camera movements that thrust our vision into the narrative space. This is nowhere more evident than in the high-velocity tracking shot used in the beginning of the film. The camera glides rapidly through the woods and cabin, then collides into Ash, sending him spinning in a clockwise direction at an incredible speed. All along, sound effects amplify the visual disorientation that assaults us.

In calling upon *Evil Dead II* and the tradition of the "gross-out" splatter film, the *Doom* games deploy the destructive sensibilities of the splatter film. Many shoot-'em-ups also have this crucial link to the splatter factor of horror cinema; while the narrative and iconography may alter, the combination of violence, gore, and splatter remains stable.[11] But by the time this spectacle of gore emerges in *Doom* and *Doom II*, it has reached a state of transcendental purity. In a homage to Ash, the *Doom* hero has the option of replacing his hand with a chainsaw appendage while (again, like Ash) also having access to a shotgun. With these two weapons (among many others), the hero exposes the game player to a series of visual and sound extravaganzas that circulate around bodies in states of destruction. Masses of these evil beings erupt and explode as they become the recipients of the hero's punches, chainsaw attacks, and shotgun bursts. Even the visual style of the games recalls *Evil Dead II*: the high-velocity, out-of-control, point-of-view tracking shots of *Evil Dead II* find their parallel in the point-of-view movements of the game hero. *Evil Dead II* and the *Doom* games invite us to interact with an experience that is intent on the aestheticization of gore.

Lights, Camera, Interaction! . . .
Let the Games Begin

Despite overlaps, it's inevitable that the shift of a genre from one medium into another alters the presentation of various conventions and formu-

lae. In the shift of films to games, a main difference is found in the role of the audience/game player. In film the extent of our physical involvement within the film space is limited; a linear narrative exists before we see it and has been preorganized in a precise temporal sequence. Unlike their filmic counterparts, computer games provide us with "narratives" that transform and extend the nature of film spectatorship. In computer games, rather than perceiving the narrative through the protagonists of a predetermined narrative, we often are the protagonists.

In her exploration of the human-computer interface, Brenda Laurel attempts to articulate the precise nature of the interaction between human and computer. She imagines a situation: if, during a theatrical performance, audience members were taken up onto a stage and made to perform, their relationship to the performance would shift from that of spectators to that of "audience-as-active-participant."[12] Computer games display precisely this sense for theatrical and performative possibilities that allow the game player a more active role. The player must interact with and propel the narrative events that are taking place. The programming of the games appears to offer limitless (though often highly controlled) options and choices in the sequence of these narrative events. In *Doom* and *Doom II*, the temporal structure branches off like a web into multiple directions that break up any signs of strict linearity. When replaying a specific game level, for example, we can change the direction and order of our character's movements; we can take different routes; we can fight a different sequence of demons; we can die in a variety of ways, then return to the game reborn again. In other words, the same "story" is retold—or, rather, replayed—in a series of different ways, and the notion of the singular, linear narrative no longer holds sway.

This alteration and loosening up of closed narrative structures can be taken further still through the use of patches or .wad files. While not allowing the player to alter the actual game play itself, the

.wad files can modify the sound effects and the level data that affect the look and texture of the game environment (the walls, lifts, doors, ceilings, sky, landscape, etc.) and can also transform the appearance of the aliens. If we were to categorize the *Doom* games according to film genre categories that place a great deal of emphasis on setting and iconographic details, the .wad files would actually allow the player to take an active part in altering the genre of the game itself. For example, popular .wads include "Porndoom" (which decorates the game architecture with pornographic images of women, thus aligning the game to pornographic genres); "Pacdoom" (which transforms some of the nasty demons into not-so-nasty-looking Pac Men, therefore reliving the game's links with the platform game format); "Simpsons Doom" (which swaps the characters of *Doom* with characters from *The Simpsons*); and "Aliens Doom" (which samples Hudson's voice from the film *Aliens* and transforms the *Doom* demons into the film's aliens). In other words, despite the plot layout as outlined on the *Doom* game cover, in the game itself, due to cheats, .wads, and general game play, the "narrative," character types, setting, iconography, and sound effects do not stay still long enough for us to impose on the games the generic form of categorization more traditionally aligned with film.

The types of interaction required of the spectator and game player therefore differ between the two media. However, it is problematic to assume that computer games provide an active type of involvement and a "truer" form of interaction, while films only offer the audience passive levels of engagement. Brenda Laurel has suggested that the notion of "interactivity" is a troublesome term. One assumption is that "interactivity" is viewed as the "unique cultural discovery of the electronic age."[13] Interaction can, however, also be achieved in other ways—including "sensory immersion" into an illusory space.[14] This idea of interactivity and immersion depends greatly on *feeling* as if you

are participating; in this process of participation, the imagination and "playful instincts" have an important role to play in collapsing the boundaries between illusion and reality. In the human-computer interface experienced in playing computer games, the illusion or representation "invite(s) us to extend our minds, feelings, and senses to envelop" the games *as if* they were real.[15] While not a computer game, *Evil Dead II* extends just such an invitation. Not only are we thrust into the narrative space through our emotional reaction to the gore, but our senses are also plunged into the film every time our point of view merges with the view of the camera as it races through the narrative space.

"Interaction" encompasses a dual function. The first is concerned with an interactivity particular to the computer game medium. This consists of a more active interaction in shaping the game "narrative." The second form of interaction is not restricted by medium limits. Besides reflecting our willingness to immerse ourselves in illusionary spaces as if they were real, interaction also depends upon our more active and critical engagement with these fictive spaces. The *Doom* games and *Evil Dead II* achieve this in the way they dare us to become engrossed in a game about genre.[16] In particular, *Doom II* and *Evil Dead II* ask us to consider the function of the sequel in a genre. Jauss has argued that the relationship between author, the work, and the public is never a passive one. Active participation of the public is central to the production of a genre's meaning.[17] *Evil Dead II* and *Doom II* acknowledge the central role the audience plays in actively shaping and participating in a genre's conventions.

Generic Game Play and the Sequel:
Evil Dead II

In her book *Broken Mirrors, Broken Minds,* Maitland McDonagh makes a comment about Dario Argento that could easily have been written about

Sam Raimi. Argento's films, she argues, often "sublimate their narratives to mise-en-scenes whose escalating complexity is characterized . . . by a series of baroque stylish devices." [18] This function of excess is an important component of the post-1980s horror film and, as McDonagh points out regarding Argento, excess does not just imply "more." Excess involves a process that causes the mind of the spectator to rebel because expectations have been shattered and everything does not seem to make sense "according to the rules." [19] In *Evil Dead II*, Raimi produces precisely such a response from the spectator, forcing us to stand outside the film and interrogate its structure.

Evil Dead II is preoccupied with its status as a sequel. This fact becomes one of the most challenging aspects of the film's interaction with its audience. In the prequel *The Evil Dead*, a group of vacationing teenagers—including Ash and Linda—arrive at a cabin in the woods. In the cabin they discover a book called *The Book of the Dead*, which unleashes an evil spirit from the depths of hell itself. This evil spirit attacks and possesses the characters—including Ash's girlfriend Linda—leaving Ash alone to fend off the forces of darkness. The film ends with Ash emerging from the cabin in broad daylight. We, and he, assume that his struggle has been successful, but in the final shot of the film we are plummeted into a high-speed tracking shot that we associate with a demon's viewpoint as it races through the woods and the cabin and, finally, toward Ash. And so the film ends.

In case the viewer missed the first film, the opening scene of *Evil Dead II* provides the audience with a brief narration that outlines the significance of *The Book of the Dead*. This narration commences: "Legend has it that it was written by the dark ones. *Necronomicon ex Mortus,* roughly translated *Book of the Dead.* The book served as a passageway to the evil world beyond." After this opening sequence, the film's status as a continuation of the first film is further driven home. The

film is literally marked as sequel when a "II" insignia stamps itself visibly and audibly through the "Evil Dead" titles. From its beginning, the film tells us "I am a sequel" and establishes an expectation in the audience of the sequel as repetition of the "original."

After the opening narration and the opening titles, we're introduced to the two main characters, Ash and Linda, as they drive up toward the cabin. This sequence presents us with a minifilm that is quite self-consciously presented as a reduced version of the events that occurred in the first film, *The Evil Dead.* We are introduced to the same lead actor (Bruce Campbell) with the same name (Ash); in a similar drive through similar woods with a similar girlfriend, they come across a similar bridge and arrive at a similar cabin in the woods; then, as the ominous feeling of doom mounts, they profess their love to each other in a similar way (with the narrative dwelling on the locket that Ash gives to Linda). All these cues wreak of copy, formula, and repetition of the "original." On the one hand, we have this familiarity to cling to. On the other, something is not quite right and our expectations for the familiar are undercut. A series of details begin to accumulate and the opening scene not only focuses on points of repetition and familiarity that connect the film to *The Evil Dead,* but also introduces several variations that contradict its status as sequel.

The differences pile up. While Ash is familiar, the girlfriend is not the same. She has the same name—Linda—but is played by a different actress. Additionally, this cannot be the identical event depicted in *The Evil Dead* because none of the other characters are present. In the sequel, only Ash and Linda make the trip to the cabin. An alternative interpretation would be that it's just the beginning of another, different story also starring Bruce Campbell, who appears as a "different guy" who coincidentally happens to be named Ash. But things are still not quite right. If Campbell plays some "other guy," and if the story taking place in the first five minutes is taking place sometime after the events in the first film, then the bridge that Linda and Ash drive by (which was destroyed in *The Evil Dead*) should not be present at the beginning of *Evil Dead II*. Raimi presents us with a puzzle to be solved, and this puzzle dares us to become involved in a game of actively interrogating the film's structure.

The beginning of the film therefore introduces us to false leads that depend on our sense of generic and sequel expectations. There are enough familiar elements to suggest a reworking of *The Evil Dead* as a reduced flashback. However, the opening story also establishes itself as a new story that is intent on denying the fact that Ash was ever in the woods in *The Evil Dead,* that is, until the death and burial of the possessed girlfriend (which occurred halfway through the first film and occurs only minutes into the sequel). At this point, *Evil Dead II* picks up at the precise point that *The Evil Dead* left off: with the high-speed tracking shot through the cabin headed at breakneck speed for Ash. This movement seems to send the camera and our vision spinning in all sorts of acrobatic directions, making us feel as if we truly are on a rollercoaster ride that takes us on a one-way trip back to the prequel. It takes about seven minutes before our desire for repetition appears to be unproblematically fulfilled, and the film suddenly seems to remember it is a sequel. Or does it? Again, issues of generic repetition are complicated because, even in this tracking shot, the beginning of the film again presents itself as a film that both is and is not a sequel, a narrative that is and is not a narrative continuation. In the "sequel" version of the tracking shot, the camera propels forward in an "over-the-top" way that is eager to establish its superiority to the first film. The camera does not stop once it arrives at Ash's location; it follows Ash as he is sent flying and somersaulting through the air.[20]

This poses some riddling questions. Is this a sequel to the first film, or is this a continuation of the events that we see in the opening sequence of the beginning of *Evil Dead II*? Is the opening scene, perhaps, the prequel to the rest of the film? Is this a copy or an original? Are these old rules or new rules?[21] Somehow, the film is all these things, with two "narratives" (one present in the prequel and one in the sequel) coexisting and struggling with each other and with the audience. The contradictions, the plays on repetition, the undercutting of expectations, all have the effect of making us contemplate the production of generic "meaning" and how we extract it. Rather than passively accepting *Evil Dead II* as a sequel, the film invites the audience to ask the question "what is a sequel?" and furthermore "what is a sequel's relationship to genre?" Raimi refuses to give us a continuation or sequel that is about sameness and repetition. Instead, the beginning of the film plays on the idea of a sequel as similar to *and* different from the original.[22] Like genre films, *Evil Dead II* draws on our expectations while simultaneously altering and adjusting those anticipated conventions and patterns. As extensions of both *The Evil Dead* and of the horror genre, *Evil Dead II*'s refusal to repeat formulaically the prequel explores the generic process as a dynamic system. While doing this, the film does not deny us the thrill of the ride that we are taking.

Generic Game Play and the Sequel: Doom II

The kind of interaction involved in our critical immersion in *Evil Dead II* suggests an audience interaction that exists at the level of generic game play. While the notion of game play and interactivity may be more literal in the *Doom* games (in the way the medium itself embraces player interaction), interaction also works on this second level in computer games. This level of interactivity depends on the audience's critical awareness and recognition of the way the games self-reflexively and deliberately manipulate generic conventions. Both *Doom* games exhibit an obvious playfulness in the references they make to *Evil Dead II*. Besides the splatter sensibility already mentioned, the most obvious allusion is the way both games allow the hero to part with his hand and brandish a chainsaw arm in the style of Ash in *Evil Dead II*. Beyond this, as with *Evil Dead II*, the sequel *Doom II* develops a tongue-in-cheek attitude that goes further than *Doom*. Not only does the latter game acknowledge some of its sources, but, like *Evil Dead II*, it also explores the relationship that exists between generic repetition and generic variation in the extension of a genre's vocabulary.

Taking its lead from *Evil Dead II*, *Doom II* plays a clever game with the genre of its own medium. *Doom II* consists of thirty levels (and two secret levels) located on Earth, Mars, and Hell. Having traveled through fourteen levels of gore, destruction, and mayhem, the hero arrives at the richly textured and layered settings of *Doom II's* "Industrial Zone" (level 15). Having undergone some genuinely hair-raising and heart-pumping moments fighting an array of imps and demons (to the accompaniment of atmospheric music tracks, sound effects, and suspense-filled horror lighting), the player enters not one but two secret levels hidden behind a secret doorway on this level. This secret doorway transports us to the corridors of *Wolfenstein 3-D*, id Software's predecessor to *Doom*. The first secret level ("Wolfenstein") takes us back to the first level of *Wolfenstein 3-D*, and the second ("Grosse") to the final level of *Wolfenstein 3-D*. After the hyperrealism of *Doom II*, we find ourselves in the rigidly angular, monotonously decorated and colored corridors of *Wolfenstein 3-D*, where we battle against two-dimensional images of soldiers that all look exactly the same. This shift of game experience is both a treat and a disappointment. It is hysterically funny and quite jolting. The atmospheric game play of *Doom II* is suddenly replaced by a type of game play that had, before the emergence of *Doom*, been quite innovative and exciting. But to quote one reviewer who grappled with the differences in the game play experience between *Doom* and *Wolfenstein 3-D*: "Next to the horrors of *Doom*, *Wolfenstein* is a front seat at a Johnny Mathis concert (or something like that)."[23]

One of the most disorienting experiences while in the *Wolfenstein 3-D* levels occurs when touches of *Doom II* spill into this game predecessor, making the "3-D" addition to the "Wolfenstein" title seem quite hollow when compared to changes that have been introduced into the genre since *Wolfenstein 3-D*. Occasionally we encounter this spill as three-dimensional decor (e.g., in the textured, 3-D trees and skies) that invades the two-dimensional space of the *Wolfenstein 3-D* world. We are also continually reminded of *Doom II's* presence through the superweapons still at our disposal; these contrast to the limited and primitive weapons used in *Wolfenstein 3-D*. The player also experiences the occasional and unexpected minotaur figures that charge forward, catching the player off guard by introducing a blast of suspense and horror that is so much the trademark of *Doom II* (now buried deep in other levels of the game). The most spine-tingling moment that escapes into this secret "Wolfenstein" level from the depths of *Doom II* occurs when the cyberdemon (the most awesome creature in the game) comes seemingly out of nowhere—intent on never allowing us access to the *Doom* levels again. The processes of generic variation emphasized in this exchange between predecessor and successor reflect the crucial impact that innovative graphics and design had on the development of this shoot-'em-up genre during and post-*Doom*.

The play on the *Wolfenstein 3-D* secret levels reveals an awareness of an audience familiar with the generic conventions of these games and with the filmic tradition being referred to. As Brophy states in reference to the contemporary horror film, we are dealing with a genre that "mimics itself mercilessly" and exposes a "violent awareness of itself as a saturated genre."[24] Exactly the same point may be made of the shoot-'em-up genre in the wake of the *Doom* games, which are to the shoot-'em-up what the *Evil Dead* films were to the splatter film. As Brophy argues in response to the horror film, *Doom II* in particular recognizes that the player is aware of its place within the shoot-'em-up genre's historical development. It "knows that you've seen it before. It knows that you know it knows you know." [25] In laying out its film and game predecessors, the makers of *Doom II* are telling us that they have outdone their predecessors. The predecessors, however, are not only *Wolfenstein* and earlier, more primitive shoot-'em-ups; they also include *Doom II*'s prequel *Doom*. This idea of an example saturated with allusions that stress its generic superiority is driven home quite jarringly when we roam back through the door that separates the *Wolfenstein 3-D* levels from level fifteen of *Doom II:* we shift from the angular, simplistic visuals into the labyrinthine, weaving complexities and hyperreal environments of *Doom II*—and its accompanying mayhem, monsters, and ultragore.

In an interview on his film *The Evil Dead,* Sam Raimi discussed the role of allusion in the horror film. Discussing Wes Craven's allusion to *Jaws* (via a poster) in *The Hills Have Eyes* (1977), Raimi stated that in Craven's film the poster was there to make the point that *Jaws* was "pop" horror whereas *The Hills Have Eyes* was "real" horror. [26] The subsequent appearance of a *The Hills Have Eyes* poster in the basement in *The Evil Dead* undercuts its predecessor by suggesting that, by 1983, it was Craven's film that produced "pop" horror and Raimi's that presented "real" horror. It is precisely this sentiment that the makers of *Doom II* are expressing, and often, as with Raimi's films, with a wicked sense of humor. The inclusion of the "Wolfenstein" level asks us to ponder the differences between the "real" game horror of *Doom II* and the "pop" game horror of *Wolfenstein 3-D.*

The "Grosse" level (which is also the exit level out of level 15) introduces a different game—one filled with humor. Having successfully pulverized the cyberdemon, in order to exit level 15 and move on to the "Suburbs" (level 16), we must enter the exit room. In this room we find four identical cartoonlike figures hanging from nooses on a futuristic gallows in the center of the room. To complete this level the player must first shoot these characters down, releasing them from the nooses that keep their two-dimensional, primitive, cardboard-cutout little bodies swaying in midair. These "cute" little additions to the level have some historical significance. These characters are clones of "Commander Keen," another id Software product dating back to 1990; *Commander Keen* even predated *Wolfenstein 3-D* and reigned back in the days when id was still making platform games. Again, the joke involves *Doom II*'s sense of historicity. The game asks its audience to celebrate the advances made in extending the shoot-'em-up genre's rules. [27]

The humor stays with us until the end of the game. When we enter level 30, an onslaught of demons attacks us. Finally, we make our way to the doorway decorated with a ram's head—the doorway that separates us from the exit to the entire game. Once beyond the ram (in my case, thanks to the cheat codes that not only made me invincible and powered me up with every weapon under the *Doom* sun but also allowed me to walk through walls), we find ourselves face to face with John Romero, or, more to the point, his head on a stake. Romero was one of the game's programmers and one of the individuals who made every *Doom II* player's life both a joy and a nightmare for many weeks and months of torturous game play. Having played (and suffered because of having played) the game, we can now destroy one of its makers. Just as post-1970s horror cinema treads a fine line that distinguishes it from comedy, *Doom II* plays off the same sentiment. The game injects a refreshing bout of comedy into the shoot-'em-up and, taking its cue from *Evil Dead II,* is very much a virtuoso performance that displays the ease with which it has perfected and developed the conventions that preexisted it and into which it has injected new life.

In all these scenarios, a game is being played with the spectator, a game that depends on audience familiarity with conventions of the genre—a game that bargains on outdoing and outgrossing examples that preceded it. It is a game that celebrates its genre's rules while also actively altering those rules, inviting the audience to acknowledge that alteration. Those exhilarating moments in which the *Doom II* game player is transported back to a past time when *Wolfenstein 3-D* ruled the shoot-'em-up genre are precisely about such a ploy. In response to the horror film, William Paul has argued that "there are values in gross-out horror . . . (that have) more to do with the immediacy of play than the delayed satisfaction of ultimate purpose."[28] For both film spectator and game player, the experience of *Evil Dead II, Doom,* or *Doom II* is about an immediacy of play that greatly depends on audience recognition of the conventions of horror and shoot-'em-ups—conventions that celebrate, parody, and take to absurd limits the codes drawn upon.

Popular culture forms have evolved into a complex web of interconnections, connections that often refuse the enclosed, self-contained structures imposed by many genre critics. The movements within and beyond generic and medium borders fluctuate in perpetual motion, refusing to be contained in any definitive way. *Aliens, Evil Dead II,* and the *Doom* games reveal the way the boundaries between film genres, computer game genres, and other media are continually shifting as they intersect with diverse media in a multitude of ways. This nexus of popular media will further expand as vertical mergers in the entertainment industries continue. Our methods of analysis need to be revised to consider generic processes in light of cross-media overlaps. John Hartley has discussed the blurring of boundaries currently witnessed in television, describing this cross-fertilization between different types of programming as

categories of "dirt." Within these categories of dirt, it becomes difficult to discern a clear separation between one text and another. It is at this point of intersection, in this "ambiguity of boundaries" rather than in the "clear oppositions and demarcations," that the "power of (generic) dirt lies."[29]

Notes

This chapter was written in 1994 at the peak of *Doom* frenzy.

1 Hans Jauss, *Toward an Aesthetic of Reception* (Minneapolis: University of Minnesota Press, 1982), 88.

2 Ibid., 90.

3 The economic viability entailed in this intersection of entertainment media has not been missed by the Spielberg, Geffen, and Katzenberg "Dreamworks" project. The Dreamworks company focuses on the integration of a variety of popular culture forms—including films and computer games.

4 This cross-over and intermingling of genres is, of course, nothing new. The difference is that in recent years this trend has become more pronounced. Not only have generic borders become more malleable, but this cross-over is now occurring on a grander, blockbuster level that emphasizes spectacle.

5 The same may be said now of the *Doom* games following the release of new breeds of shoot-'em-up realism in games like *Duke Nuke 'Em 3D* and *Quake* in 1996.

6 "*Doom:* Evil Unleashed," *Edge* (March 1994): 30.

7 "Violence is Golden," *PC Gamer* 1(4) (March 1994): 43.

8 "*Doom* the Movie!" *PC Zone* (December 1994): 8. The question of who will be the lead protagonist of *Doom* the film was a topic of great discussion on the Net, and Schwarzenegger was a hot favorite.

9 "Doomed: In Extremis," *PC Gamer* 1(3) (April 1994): 42.

10 Philip Brophy has provided an engaging discussion of contemporary cinema's "rampant body-ness." His analysis of the bodily destruction present in action and horror cinema becomes a means of exploring the complex overlaps between genres and media. See "The Body Horrible: Some Notions, Some Points, Some Examples," *Intervention* 21(2), (1988): 58–67.

11 Michael Arnzen, "Who's Laughing Now? . . . The Postmodern Splatter Film," *Journal of Popular Film and Television* 21(4) (Winter 1994): 179.

12 Laurel states that "people who are participating in the representation aren't audience members anymore. It's not that the audience joins the actors on stage; it's that they *become* actors—and the notion of the "passive" observer disappears." *Computers as Theatre* (Reading, MA: Addison-Wesley, 1991), 17.

13 Ibid., 20.

14 Ibid., 20–21.

15 Ibid., 32.

16 In relation to *The Evil Dead*, Scott McQuire argues that "the movement of this film is structured around a series of dares, the tension spring-boarding the viewer into realms of dismemberment and disembowelment. You wonder how far the film will go. It dares you to watch it and go further and constantly takes your breath away with its obviousness and its unrestrained transgressions, its (technical) sophistication and its (narrative) bluntness." See "Horror: Re-makes and Offspring," *Antithesis* 1(1) (1987): 23. This dare factor and transgression of boundaries goes even further in the sequel.

17 Jauss, *Toward an Aesthetic of Reception*, 19.

18 Maitland McDonagh, *Broken Mirrors, Broken Minds: The Dark Dreams of Dario Argento* (London: Sun Tavern Fields, 1991), 14.

19 Ibid.

20 Similarly, on this issue of variation, the tracking shot may duplicate the ending of the first film, but the two holes present in the cabin door in the first film (the damage caused when Ash was attacked by a demon who thrust his hand through the door) are no longer there.

21 This question of original or copy is further complicated by the fact that the film reveals the impossibility of the existence of such a thing as "the original," especially as far as genre is concerned. While the use and assimilation of conventions may reveal originality and may instigate new directions in a genre, genre films depend greatly on that which has gone before, even if only to contest or reject a previous form. As an example, while *Evil Dead II*'s absurd, darkly hysterical, and over-the-top nature may appear original and new within the context of the horror genre, this morbid humor owes a great deal to the tradition of EC comics, which influenced the deconstructive tendencies of contemporary horror cinema. For more information on the comic book/horror film connections, see Kim Newman, *Nightmare Movies: A Critical History of the Horror Film, 1968–88* (London: Bloomsbury, 1988), 18, 207; Farrah Anwar, "Bloody and Absurd," *Monthly Film Bulletin* 57(683) (December 1990): 347; Philip Brophy, "Horrality—The Textuality of Contemporary Horror Films," *Screen* 27 (January-February 1986): 12.

22 Steve Neale has convincingly argued that in genre, repetition and difference are inseparable and that "they function as a relation." Therefore, rather than revealing the generic process as "repetition *and* difference," it is more appropriate to claim for "repetition *in* difference." See *Genre* (London: British Film Institute, 1980), 50. This point is aptly illustrated in the opening minutes of *Evil Dead II*.

23 "*Doom:* Evil Unleashed," 31.

24 Brophy, "Horrality," 3.

25 Ibid., 5.

26 Phil Edwards and Alan Jones, "The Evil Dead Speak," *Starbust* 57 (1983): 27.

27 id Software is, of course, also presenting us with an homage to the company's own contribution to the development of the shoot-'em-up genre—particularly its crucial role in transforming its own platform game *Commander Keen,* to corridor/shoot-'em-up games like *Wolfenstein 3-D* and the *Doom* games.

28 William Paul, *Laughing Screaming: Modern Hollywood Horror and Comedy* (New York: Columbia University Press,1994), 422–23.

29 John Hartley, *Tele-ology: Studies in Television* (New York: Routledge, 1992), 22–23.

Seeing in Black and White: Gender and Racial Visibility from *Gone with the Wind* to *Scarlett*

Tara McPherson

The winter of 1991 found me roaming around the Mississippi Delta, on paid leave from a northern graduate school beginning my doctoral research on southern femininity. I was born and mostly raised in the South, so this return to the region felt fairly comfortable, and I soon settled into the rhythms and rituals of the area. These rituals included almost daily sojourns to any of a number of small diners that dot the area, in search of home cooking and plate lunches. At one of these establishments, a combination gas station/country store/lunch-counter-type place, I came across a dusty postcard tacked up near the cash register. It was one of those plastic, ridged postcards I've always called "3-D," composed of two interlaced images. This particular card most often depicted a young hoopskirted belle standing before an antebellum mansion on the scale of Tara, much like the opening moments of the film *Gone with the Wind*. However, if you stood in just the right spot as you paid your bill, this vision of southern architecture and femininity was supplanted by the familiar iconic image of a grinning, portly Mammy. The owners wouldn't sell me the postcard, but it stuck with me over the years and came to symbolize for me a very particular mode of racial visibility, one I see as a prominent way of seeing in black and white in the latter half of the twentieth century that dovetails with much of critical scholarship on race in the past two decades.

Critical Blindness and Lenticular Logics

Hazel Carby's work on early African American women novelists, *Reconstructing Womanhood*, underscores that "we need more feminist work that interrogates sexual ideologies for their racial specificity and acknowledges whiteness, not just blackness, as a racialized categorization," highlighting the always racialized dimensions of the white southern lady.[1] Critical writings before and after Carby have insisted that race is not just a "black thing," but this insight has not necessarily permeated wider culture (or even most of the academy). As discussions with both my students and with family and friends make clear, many people (and especially white ones) still understand "race" to be a category applicable largely to minorities. This chapter continues the project to decenter the "race = black" binary that permeates much of late-twentieth-century thought and underscores the inevitable impossibility of understanding whiteness apart from its connections to blackness.[2] Although it may seem all too obvious to say that whiteness exists in relation to blackness, there is real labor involved in training one's eye (particularly the white eye) to discern these relationships and their changing valences in different historical and geographic registers. In *Playing in the Dark,* Toni Morrison uses the analogy of the fishbowl to describe this difficult-to-achieve process of recognition, noting that "it is as if I had been looking at a fishbowl—the glide and flick of the golden scales, . . . the tranquil bubbles traveling to the surface—and then I saw the bowl, the structure that transparently (and invisibly) permits the ordered life it contains to exist in the larger world." She goes on to insist that is a "willful critical blindness" that allows us not to see race.[3] Perhaps one cause of the difficulty in discerning the interrelations of our cultural constructions of race derives in part from the changing trajectory of these images over time and space. Thus one of the aims of my work is to suggest the differing ways in which the figure of the white southern lady and other iconic southerners is cast against, beside, or in front of various figures of blackness, highlighting some of the myriad configurations these relationships have produced. She serves as a powerful nodal point for various cultural understandings of the connections of race, class, and gender in America. To underscore that these relationships change is not to suggest that any connection or any meaning can exist at any time, but rather to insist that what relationships are visible is less a function of empirical fact or critical whimsy than of historical process and shifting economies of the visibility of race. I focus here on blackness and whiteness, even as the South as a whole becomes less black and white, because the black/white axis in southern culture remains so prominent. Indeed, as Zillah Eisenstein has argued, despite racial and ethnic diversity in the United States, "blackness is made the bedrock signifier of race and racial hatred, and African-Americans stand in for the multirace threat. Blackness, repressed in the mind's eye, threads through the process of creating 'others.'" This American obsession with blackness owes much to the particularities of the South's role in national history and culture.[4]

In what follows, I detail some of the ways in which the different economies of visibility that were prevalent in the 1930s and the 1990s structure different representations of the relation of white and black femininity in the novel *Gone with the Wind* and in its sequel, *Scarlett*.[5] To summarize briefly, the earlier novel in many ways foregrounds the interdependence of its images of black and white femininity (though critics have rarely read it this way) if only to insist upon racial difference. *Scarlett*, on the other hand, attempts a dismissal of black femininity, an erasure that denies the historical webs that bound black and white southern women (and their representations) together during the period in which the novel is set. These two modes of representing racial difference, which might be labeled as *overt*

versus *covert*, differ in that the former *brings together* figurations of racial difference in order to fix the categories, while the later *enacts a separation* that nonetheless achieves a similar end.[6] While these two modes are not entirely distinct historically and can coexist in any one era, this covert strategy of representation is more prevalent in the present than it was in the pre–civil rights era. Certainly, overt racism continues to exist today, as a well-documented litany of contemporary hate crimes attests, but even groups like the Ku Klux Klan have adopted more covert styles of representation and discourse to their ends. Moreover, these representational modes are complexly related to politics and to forms of racist practice, structuring particular ways of feeling and acting southern that expand the scope of the lenticular from a mere visual strategy to a way of organizing knowledge about the world. This chapter explores the workings of these twin logics in two twentieth-century triangulations of race, place, and gender, tracing the transit loops between ways of seeing and ways of knowing, although I move away from the term "covert" as a name for this more recent logic, preferring instead to designate this frame of reference a "lenticular" one.

A lenticular image is composed when two separate images are interlaced or combined in a special way. This combined image is then viewed via a unique type of lens, called a lenticular lens, which allows one to see only one of the two views at a time. By slightly rotating the picture, the second image comes into focus, displacing the first. The most familiar type of this image is probably one of those thick, plastic-coated postcards like the one I described above.[7] The ridged coating on each card is actually a lenticular lens, a device that makes viewing both images together nearly impossible. I have a large collection of these cards, but the reason the phrase "lenticular logic" struck me as a particularly apt trope for the racial economy of visibility I denoted "covert" above derives from that country-store postcard, with its southern belle and mammy. As critics we can read these two images (and the connections between them) in a variety of ways, but the structural logic of the card itself makes joining the two images within one view difficult if not impossible, even as it co-joins them at a structural level. Like the fishbowl logic that Morrison identifies as prevalent today, a lenticular logic is capable of representing both black and white, but one approaches the limits of this logic when one attempts to understand how the images are joined or related. Such a positioning naturalizes images and their possible meanings, erasing context and connections. Unlike the image of the fishbowl, the term lenticular also moves us away from a division between form and content, container and contained, toward a more flexible model.

I prefer *lenticular* to *covert* because the first term allows one to move away from an understanding of this logic as an always intentional one, as strictly a sneaky practice of bad faith. Though racial images in the late twentieth century can certainly derive from ill intent (one need only recall the infamous Willie Horton ads of the elder George Bush's presidential campaign), this way of thinking is also often an unconscious or unrecognized one, one of those economies of visibility produced at a specific historic juncture that can derive from multiple intentions ranging from the naive to the liberal to the insidious. The "additive" strategy of race in much contemporary critical theory is one example of a lenticular logic, in which images of race (and class and gender and sexuality; name your favorite) get tacked onto an initial image or narrative, but without a framework that will allow us to understand the images or narratives in relation.[8] Such a framework operates in tales like the one told in Ken Burns's PBS special, *The Civil War*. This five-night, eleven-hour journey through the history of the war does include segments on black soldiers and slaves during the conflict, but the overall force of the series segregates these details about race from the overall narrative drive of the series. Because the program ultimately portrays the Civil War as a story

of the (white) national family's conflict and final reunion, it can never integrate the story of the slaves it images into its tale.[9]

During its first season, the television series *Savannah* deployed another version of a lenticular narrative, one that froze the dual image in its first frame, for Spelling's *Savannah* was almost exclusively a white world. This move served to erase blackness from the South at precisely the historic moment when African Americans were for the first time in the twentieth century returning to the South at a rate faster than they were leaving it. In the words of Michael Eric Dyson, *Savannah*'s pretense "of colorlessness [is] actually an investment in whiteness."[10] Exploring the varied economies of visibility that structure twentieth-century representations of the South illustrates the degree to which the cultural and material meanings of race in America are both definitive and shifting. As such, my work is part of an ongoing project of antiessentialist racial critique that investigates how race, an unstable category, gets fixed, especially in relation to gender, in particular landscapes and temporalities. Put differently, this project explores how race gets made via narrative and image at precise moments in place and time.

In an age when race seems increasingly to be a cultural pressure point and to be ever present, it also retains an opacity, a now-we-see-it, now-we-don't quality that makes adequate explanations of its workings in today's society difficult to produce. This is partially due to the tendency described earlier to see "race" as equivalent to "minority" and to attempt to understand it by adding it on to already existing structures or categories. Thus, it is crucial to explore how race—especially as it is yoked to gender—continues to recede from our field of vision.[11] By exploring, in two wildly popular texts from very different historical periods, how race becomes visible in relation to gender, I am not suggesting that one novel is "better" or "less racist" than the other. I instead want to foreground the notion that racial categories like "white" and "black" not only are interrelated but are related differently at different historical moments. Thus, this is not an argument that *Scarlett* (or *Savannah*) should simply include more African American characters, but rather an exploration of what its strategies of racial representation reveal about how race was made visible at the end of the last millennium. Such an argument also suggests that visibility is not inherently something to be desired, as work on the commodification of minority and lesbian images has made clear.[12]

If I chose here to focus on two novels set in the South, this is largely an acknowledgment of the nation's tendency to locate its racial past on southern terrain. Thus, it is not surprising that two of the most popular and best-selling epics of the twentieth century deploy their racial logics south of the Mason-Dixon line. Elsewhere I have considered the relative "southernness" of each of these two books, but here I want instead to read them as indicative of larger national frameworks for understanding race and its visibility vis-à-vis gender.[13] The two tales are separated by nearly sixty years, a period characterized by the South's move toward industrialization and away from a period often referred to as the "colonial South." If, as Franklin D. Roosevelt maintained in 1938, the South was "the Nation's No. 1 economic problem," the intervening six decades saw substantial changes in the area.[14] During the 1970s, the South became a center of growth and economic expansion, attracting new industry and stimulating urban growth due to a variety of factors.[15] And, of course, the 1950s through the 1960s saw the rise and initial success of a black southern-born civil rights movement. In the 1930s, the South was a fiercely segregated society; by the 1990s, it was (at least nominally) integrated, with Atlanta recently deemed by *Ebony* readers the "best U.S. city" to live and work in as an African American.

The decade preceding 1990 also marked an "improvement" in the nation's popular images of the South. In his *Media-Made Dixie*, Jack Kirby notes that, during the 1960s and 1970s, "neoabolitionist professional and popular history," combined with media representations of a "devilish" South, had "tarnished the sentimentalist image of the plantation and slavery" (166).[16] By the early 1990s, works like *Scarlett* signal a return to this image, particularly to a national fascination with the image of the southern lady.[17] These images may feel familiar from *Gone with the Wind,* but their reprisal deploys very different linkages of race and gender than did that earlier work.

An Old South

The Pulitzer Prize-winning novel *Gone with the Wind,* a bestseller virtually from the moment of its publication in 1936, has sold nearly thirty million copies to date. It has been issued in nearly two hundred editions in forty countries. The book's author, Margaret Mitchell, was born in 1900 and came of age in a South that was experiencing the onset of industrialization, a process that was rife with hardships but also with possibility. In the early twentieth century, southern cities, including Mitchell's own Atlanta, were challenging rural areas as the center of the region, and racial violence and widespread lynching characterized the area. Mitchell's early years coincided with moments of sharp increases in lynching throughout the South and with the Atlanta race riots of 1906. These years were also marked by a black resistance to such violence, including the efforts of Ida B. Wells and the NAACP. From 1882 to around 1930, lynching was woven into the very fabric of southern society, a normalized aspect of subjugating the black minority, and Georgia and Mississippi had the highest rates of lynching. The practice began to decline around the time Mitchell was revising her novel, for, as the South moved toward increasing modernization, lynching was seen as bad for business, both because it was driving away a cheap labor force as African Americans migrated north and because it hindered southern efforts to court northern business by damaging the region's image.[18] I am interested in how *Gone with the Wind* might be situated vis-à-vis this history. Mitchell's novel can be read as a story about the South during this transition to modernity, a tale about the formulation of region and race as material conditions shifted in the 1920s and 1930s, even if the novel's subject matter focuses on an earlier period.

Central to Mitchell's concerns was the role of woman in this move to modernity, an issue Mitchell was fully aware of from early childhood. Her mother, May Belle Mitchell, had been an active participant in southern suffrage campaigns, and Margaret Mitchell once wrote, "My earliest memories are of my mother and the women's suffrage movement." Mitchell displayed mixed feelings about her mother's political activism, and *Gone with the Wind* becomes a platform on which to play out the author's deeply conflicted feelings about women's progress. Of course, women's rights in the South have never been only about gender, for southern suffrage campaigns often staged their populist appeal by offering white women's votes as a counter to the black male vote.[19] And, while at one level *Gone with the Wind* debates whether Scarlett should side with modernist Atlanta or the agrarian past, this struggle is not just about gender; her character's development also hinges upon a very specific and overt relationship to blackness, particularly via the novel's representation of slaves and slavery. Here, I want to focus on the degree to which the novel's construction of Mammy becomes intricately tied to that of Scarlett in at least two ways.[20]

First, the figure of Mammy provides the (dark) background against which the (white) image of Scarlett can take shape. Throughout *Gone with the Wind*, representations of white femininity, particularly as embodied by Scarlett and her mother, are sketched in stark and deliberate contrast to those of black femininity. On the opening page of the novel, Mitchell details Scarlett's "magnolia-white skin—that skin so prized by Southern women"; of course, such white skin was "so prized" precisely

because it was not dark skin. In and of itself, white skin would signify little; it only takes on value in contrast to darker skin, which in the antebellum South signaled low-class status or "mixed blood." Through a running series of contrasts, Scarlett's (white) femininity gets set up as the opposite of Mammy's blackness. The darkness in the text demarcates the white characters, and this darkness serves as a central feature of almost every description of Mammy afforded by the novel.

Mammy enters the story "shining black, pure African" with a "lumbering tread," "huge ... with the shrewd eyes of an elephant" (15). She is consistently described as either old and gnarled, as gigantic, or as animalistic, all images that portray her as unfeminine and as desexualized.[21] She is not, of course, ever called a "lady"; rarely is she even designated "woman," although she sometimes serves as a source of maternal comfort, an image to which I will return. She is often like "an old ape" (701) or a "restless bloodhound" (15); her "mountainous figure" waddles and quakes (701); she wears huge men's shoes and her "shapeless body overflows" into the spaces it inhabits. Mammy is here figured via "metaphysical condensation," which, in the words of Toni Morrison, "allows the writer to transform social and historical differences. Collapsing persons into animals prevents human contact and exchange" (68). This constant barrage of imagery pointedly contrasts Mammy's "figure" to that of the "feminine" ladies who are identified as contained, petite, high class and, it goes without saying, white. Hence, *Gone with the Wind* is a novel that defines femininity, and this definition has everything to do with how Mitchell conceptualizes and focuses on race. Mitchell deploys blackness as a background against which she elaborates the details of white female subjectivity in the South at precisely the moment the region begins to recover (from a white perspective) both economically and politically from the years following the Civil War. Of course, this recovery operates in both senses of the word: as a recouping of the losses of the war for white southerners and as a covering over of the brutalities during and after Reconstruction for the former slaves.

Mammy's role in defining who counts as a lady does not end at the level of descriptive detail. As the narrative unfolds, she will also come to play a key role in the actual production of white femininity. The novel's first sentence asserts that "Scarlett O'Hara was not beautiful," underscoring that it is not beauty but something to do with appearances that defines (white) Southern womanhood. A certain "veneer of femininity" (42) is key, and we soon learn of Scarlett's consummate skill in manipulating this veneer. *Gone with the Wind* underscores that to be a southern lady required the observance of certain strict codes of etiquette and decorum, and many feminist critics of the novel praise the character and the narrative precisely because they subtly push against the established codes of ladylike behavior. Though Scarlett ultimately longs to be a lady in the novel, she does at various moments resist her training in proper femininity. Much as in feminist valorizations of Madonna during the 1990s, these optimistic critics read these moments of Scarlett's (or the text's) performance as a campy subversion of the rigid boundaries of southern femininity. For example, literary historian Anne Goodwyn Jones praises Mitchell's decision to have Scarlett deploy feminine wiles in order to gain entrance into "the male, public, economic and competitive world." Literary critic Ann Egenriether reads Scarlett as "the quintessential American heroine" because "she capitalizes on her womanliness," while Harriet Hawkins goes further, calling Scarlett's masquerades "radically, breathtakingly liberating."[22]

Of course, figurations of femininity as tied to masquerade or performance have occupied a key position within feminist theory during the past twenty years, particularly in feminist film theory via its return to the work of psychoanalyst Joan Riviere. In her 1929 essay, "Womanliness as a Masquerade," Riviere structures an equation between femininity/womanliness and masquerade, a position elaborated on by contemporary feminist film theorists like Mary Anne Doane. However, Riviere, Doane, and the feminists celebrating Scarlett—all of whom place different values on the strategic potentials of feminine masquerade— read femininity only as a performance of *sexual difference,* a move that renders invisible the degree to which femininity also indexes other markers of identity, highlighting the limits of many accounts of masquerade.[23]

For instance, Riviere's essay centers on her analysis of a female patient, a successful career woman who exaggerates her performance of femininity whenever she enters the masculine work world, a performance Riviere reads as a kind of reaction formation against the prohibited assumption of masculinity. Here, as is the case with Scarlett's celebrants, femininity is defined strictly in relation to masculinity, and its performance allows women access to the new spaces. Yet, within the text of her analysis, Riviere points out that her patient is a woman from the "Southern States of America" who repeatedly had dreams and fantasies that "if a negro came to attack her, she planned to defend herself by making him . . . make love to her, ultimately so that she could then deliver him over to justice." That the patient is a southern woman being attacked by a black man is then dropped by Riviere who goes on to read the dream as an expression of the woman's fear of reprisal for having "killed mother and father," a fear that leads her to then perform womanliness with a vengeance.[24]

Although Riviere certainly makes a case for her reading, a more compelling analysis would account for the culturally specific racial dynamics at work in her patient's dreams. Such a reading would make it hard to position the black man, as Riviere does, as primarily an instrument of "the retribution of the father"; much more likely would be an interpretation that reads this execution of an exaggerated femininity as about a performance of racial as well as sexual difference, particularly given the fact that Riviere's patient came of age in a region and era—Margaret Mitchell's South—where ideologies of femininity were deployed to prop up apartheid-like conditions. Essentially, Riviere's reading—and much of the feminist theory that follows from it—posits femininity solely against masculinity and thus cannot discern the racial or regional contours of the masquerade.

Scarlett may indeed manipulate femininity but to what end? Scarlett's "play" with femininity works in the service of capitalism and chain-gang labor as she uses her feminine wiles to maintain her lumber business, while simultaneously allowing Mitchell to appropriate for women larger social spaces within the organization of urban and public spheres. But this appropriation only serves upper-class white women. Then, at the narrative's end, rather than overturning or challenging Southern codes of behavior, the novel ultimately reinforces them as Scarlett embraces tradition and returns home. Furthermore, celebrations of Scarlett's manipulations of femininity and entry into public life also miss what has historically shaped and supported her masquerades; namely, a whole geographic system of social and economic production—the slave system—has enabled this play. As literary theorist Cora Kaplan has explained in relation to *The Thorn Birds*, "The reactionary political and social setting [of the novel] secures . . . a privileged space where the most disruptive female fantasy can be 'safely' indulged." [25] Scarlett's performance as a "strong" yet feminine woman is possible because it is situated within a scenario that romanticizes the Old South.

This symbiotic relationship between Scarlett's strategic femininity and the reactionary social setting that supports it is best illustrated by returning to the figure of Mammy and her role in producing white femininity. Throughout the narrative, Mammy's physical labor and "supporting" role allow Scarlett to perform femininity. For instance, when Scarlett decides to dress up in curtains to work her feminine wiles on Rhett, it is Mammy who sews the dress and, thus, "assists" in

her performance. Likewise, as Scarlett's "maid," Mammy laces her into her corset, pulling and jerking vigorously, and, "as the tiny circumference of whalebone-girdled waist grew smaller, a proud, fond look" comes into Mammy's eyes (55). Paradoxically, Mammy is here figured as a chief co-conspirator in the production of a system of femininity that simultaneously works to deny her own status as a bearer of privileged womanhood. Mitchell consistently represents Mammy as the enforcer of southern etiquette, thus supporting her narrative claim that Mammy has authority over Scarlett and the whole plantation. But Mammy's "power" is only the power to labor in the maintenance of white femininity. Her "power" is the power to police Scarlett (at home and on the streets of Atlanta), thus producing Scarlett as a lady (i.e., as *not* Mammy) and simultaneously maintaining Tara as the space of the family and of white rule.

Of course, this policing of white femininity has everything to do with class as well. For Scarlett is not just *any* white woman; she is also a woman of the planter class, and whiteness, proper femininity, and class position are all closely bound in *Gone with the Wind*. One need only recall the novel's representation of the Slattery family to understand that true femininity is no more within the reach of the average lower-class white woman than it is achievable by Mammy. In fact, nearly each of the tale's "white trash" women functions as a degraded third term that holds the novel's black-white equation in place. Emmie Slattery's description as an "overdressed, common, nasty piece of poor white trash" serves as a nightmare image that works to underscore the effect on the social order of not maintaining clear distinctions between black and white. Emmie's very touch had killed Ellen O'Hara, and her attempts at proper femininity miserably fail her, revealing as they do her "rabbity face, caked with white powder" (376). Scarlett's masquerades are not available for Emmie, and the novel's representations of the lower classes only underwrites its black-white logic.

To privilege Scarlett's uses of femininity or to read her masquerades as being only about sexual difference is to forget that this narrow view of the southern belle erases the historical specificity of the lives of many poor and working-class white women in the South. It denies the suppression of black femininity that helped produce Scarlett's masquerades while also ignoring the historical resistance slave women waged against their own cultural positioning as "unwomanly." [26] And, finally, it overlooks the degree to which the narrative punishes Scarlett for her transgressions, highlighting what happens to independent women in the postbellum (and, by extension, the modern) South.

The novel's final scene firmly reinscribes the interdependency of white and black femininity while simultaneously naturalizing those connections and their class connotations. On the last page, after losing Rhett, Scarlett realizes she must go home to Tara and plantation life, and "it was as if a gentle cool hand were stealing over her heart" (733). The narrative paints an Edenic picture of Tara, a portrait that, of course, includes Mammy:

> [Scarlett] stood for a moment remembering the small things, the avenue of dark cedars leading to Tara, . . . vivid green against white walls. . . . And Mammy would be there. Suddenly she wanted Mammy desperately, as she had wanted her when she was a girl, wanted the broad bosom on which to lay her head, the gnarled black hand on her hair. Mammy, the last link with the old days. (733)

The novel closes by bringing black and white femininity together within a sentimental frame, a frame which cannot allow for any range in its definition of the lady.

Scarlett's (and the text's) desire to return to Tara is a desire for a space undisturbed by racial difference, a space where Mammy becomes part of the landscape of southernness, one of the "small things" allowing white safety and white privilege within the secure space of home. Such a memory cannot include the history that lies behind the im-age of Mammy's "broad bosom," the history of enforced wet nursing. [27] From its early pages, *Gone with the Wind* stages an inevitable return of Scarlett to Tara, to a utopian, safe space of white southern identity that can allow no memory of how white safety has been secured by practices of omission, exclusion, or violence. Such a vision also freezes the origins of white southern identity within the physical and mental geographies of the past, situating the plantation home as an essential landscape of desire and escape. Margaret Mitchell and her heroine, Scarlett, in the words of film critic Thomas Cripps, "remained ever Southern" in a familiar southern landscape that modernity neatly altered to its own ends. [28]

Still, Scarlett's longing for a return to the safety that Mammy symbolizes points toward a contradictory impulse in Mitchell's portrait of the slave. While Mammy repeatedly emerges in the text as dark, animalistic, and dehumanized (one recalls her "lumbering tread," her "elephantine" form), she simultaneously comes to connote the maternal, as the foregoing passage strongly suggests. In these moments, white and black womanhood are no longer cast in strict opposition but joined via the desires of white feminine subjectivity. Hence Scarlett and Mitchell are at once repelled by Mammy's blackness and also powerfully attracted to it, a doubling that points to the complexity and ambiguity of southern racial experiences, particularly as they unfold for white women. [29] For the white woman (as character and as author), blackness becomes a shadowy source of comfort and security, a desirable space of safety. The presence of Mammy underwrites Scarlett's fantasy of a return to the world of childhood and also allows Mitchell to explore her character's capacity for love. If Scarlett has failed at loving Rhett, Melanie, her children, and her mother, Scarlett's devotion to and desire for Mammy enables Mitchell to reveal her character's worthiness and humanity as the novel draws to a close. Thus this black presence sets the stage for Mitchell's playing out of the often contradictory and complex imperatives of power, guilt, and desire.

Here, *Gone with the Wind* exhibits a desire for commonality or connection that we might term a white southern structure of feeling, a latency in the text that is in tension with the novel's overtly racist expressions. Although the dominant culture in Mitchell's South deployed Jim Crow tactics to disavow and guard against this very commonality, the culture's visual logics continually joined black and white, defining each race via and against the other. Beneath the surface of this logic coursed a subterranean desire for connection, a hunger for the other. Cultural critic Raymond Williams notes that "structures of feeling" are "concerned with meanings and values as they are actively lived and felt, . . . characteristic elements of impulse, restraint and tone, specifically affective elements of . . . relationships." He singles out art and literature as having a particular purchase on structures of feeling and further argues that these structures "can be defined as social experiences in solution." We might say that Mitchell's latent longing for connection is an affective mode still "in solution," hovering as it is at "the very edge of semantic availability"; the novel's precipitated meaning is its overt racism.[30] Very few whites in Mitchell's time had moved beyond this affective suspension, although some had. Of course, reading the mammy as a maternal figure of comfort for whites is a tricky game, and Mitchell offers an array of harsh images to distance the figure of Mammy. Mitchell's representations range from monkey-faced to maternal, and Mammy also functions as a shadowy substitute for Scarlett's mother, Ellen. This ambiguity hints at a longing for racial union even while it labors to hold black and white apart, a familiar pattern across southern history and racial representation. For whites, Mammy could be a "great mother" (via the psychic and cultural mechanisms of nostalgic fantasy) and also absolutely *not* the mother (via the dictates of language and the law: she's black and beastly), inhabiting

two seemingly contradictory modes at once. This fantasy of union is too unsettling to be simply presented; rather, it is contextualized via the dehumanizing images of Mammy that permeate the text, framed strictly via white desire. Let me be clear: though the novel does reveal a desire for union, this latency in no way mitigates the novel's racism. It does, however, signal a current that might be accessed differently by a more radical white subjectivity.

Historian Deborah Gray White has written that the mammy image developed from an attempt by pro-slavery propagandists to demonstrate that the plantation South benefited slaves by providing moral instruction. Hence the mammy was figured as capable, content, and nurturing, an example of slavery's good effects, and her large, desexualized form countered claims that white masters might be attracted to slave women. One could read Mitchell's Mammy simply as an extension of this ploy, as a lost-cause justification for "the benevolent institution" of slavery. Certainly, her portrait of the excesses of freed field hands as wild, terrifying, and out of control supports such an interpretation, as does her insistence that "good darkies" like Mammy and Peter "stood loyally by their white owners" after the war (476). But the relationship of Scarlett and Mammy also reveals Mitchell's simultaneous desire to picture a more harmonious version of women's relationships, particularly interracial ones. Of course, this relationship is only figured via white longing, for Mammy's own interiority is denied by the novel. Although Mitchell amply explores Scarlett's performances of white femininity, the text never attributes a similar mimetic capacity to Mammy. Critics such as Hazel Carby have repeatedly noted slave women's own performative strategies, skills that allowed them to "play" the Mammy while simultaneously resisting the white definition of that image. But the Mammy of Mitchell's world is content to serve white power, always working to ensure it. Thus while Mitchell represents black and white femininity coming together in the space of Tara at the novel's close, this (re)union must be read as a white fantasy.[31] Other potential affective possibilities of longing and union are short-circuited, rewired back into the plantation and the landscape, trapping Mammy and Scarlett within Tara's deep verandas.

That Mitchell is ultimately unable to envision black female subjectivity as existing in any relationship to white women beyond a supporting one suggests a limit to her critical imagination while also highlighting the contradictory movements of her text. But Mitchell's failures do not mean that we should simply dismiss this impulse toward union in the novel. Literary critic Minrose Gwin points out that fictional re-creations of southern women's interracial experiences offer "a powerful lens through which we may envision new critical relationships, new illuminations," an insight that suggests that we can explore the contours of Mitchell's vision to understand how she uses black womanhood in her delineation of white southern femininty.[32]

Gone with the Wind is not particularly subtle in its delineation of whiteness in relation to blackness. It is a novel that proceeds in black and white, foregrounding the mutual dependency of the two terms. In an essay on another early-twentieth-century tribute to the Old South, D. W. Griffith's 1915 film *The Birth of a Nation,* film theorist Richard Dyer notes that "*Birth* knows that it is about racial purity or, to use a contemporary phrase, ethnic cleansing." He also argues that the film's representation of race "includes the whites just as much as blacks, something *Birth* itself is clearer on than most current white discourse about race."[33] Both of his observations apply to *Gone with the Wind* (as novel and as film), for it is a text that proceeds via the more overt of the two logics of racial visibility I outlined in the previous section. Mitchell writes, for example, that "[Scarlett] knew what Reconstruction meant. . . . The negroes were on top

and behind them were the Yankee bayonets. She could be killed, she could be raped and, very probably, nothing would be done about it" (456). She thus writes in the service of an ideology of which she is aware and supportive. This is not, moreover, a lenticular logic. Rather, her construction of racial difference is overt and pointed. Mitchell's presentation of the Ku Klux Klan's slaughter of black men and women (in the name of white women's "protection") underwrites and justifies the racial violence of her own era.[34] Since it seems quite evident that *Gone with the Wind* is a novel about race, racial difference, and racial representation, it is at first surprising to learn that until quite recently most critics denied that the novel was about race at all. This reinforces the claim that much current white discourse on race does not understand whiteness as itself a racialized category.

Literary critic Kenneth O'Brien argues that "as extraordinary as it may sound, Mitchell's novel would . . . still make sense if all the . . . black characters disappeared. . . . Race, and politics too, are essentially negligible elements" in the book.[35] O'Brien's sentiments are typical of those of many commentators on the novel, all of whom read it as being about issues of survival, tradition, or womanhood. In fact, only a small and very recent percentage of the mass of critical articles written about *Gone with the Wind* focus their remarks on issues of race.[36] Instead, critics like O'Brien and Anne Goodwyn Jones maintain that the novel is about "the struggle of one individual against the confines of Southern womanhood,"[37] and each traces the various ploys of Scarlett as she attempts to outwit southern tradition and its ideals of femininity. Such interpretations frame *Gone with the Wind* as a struggle between "tradition" and "change" and read Scarlett as sympathetic to and as representative of change or modernity. Hence, both Jones and O'Brien must view Scarlett's (and Rhett's) return to tradition at the novel's end as a "strangely ambiguous and unsatisfying conclu-sion."[38] Rather than being mystified by the novel's ending, I would argue that this final scene (where Scarlett leaves "modern" Atlanta to return to tra-dition at Tara) makes perfect sense if one carefully examines the role and representation of race in the novel. Indeed, rather than being a "negligible ele-ment" of the relationship of gender to region, race is the key to understanding both the narrative tra-jectory of *Gone with the Wind* and its final return to a fairly conservative figuration of southern womanhood.

In arguing that race is not an issue in *Gone with the Wind*, analyses like O'Brien's repeat an ingrained pattern of western thought that sees "race" as only applying to people of color; in such thought, whiteness remains a category somehow unmarked by race.[39] Specifically, it overlooks the degree to which the social construction of white southern womanhood in the antebellum period depended upon a simultaneous definition of black women as unfeminine and unwomanly. In their explorations of racial dynamics, feminists from Sojourner Truth to Angela Davis to Hazel Carby have long recognized that ideologies of black and white female sexuality "only appear to exist in iso-lation while actually depending on a nexus of figu-rations which can be explained only in relation to each other."[40] This relationship is evident in *Gone with the Wind*, for Scarlett's role as the "transgres-sive belle" and her relationship to southern society are both played out on a racialized and highly charged terrain.

Writing on the erasure of the consideration of race from literary criticism, Toni Morrison sug-gests that "what is fascinating . . . is how [literary scholars'] lavish exploration of literature manages *not* to see meaning in the thunderous, theatrical presence of black surrogacy . . . in the literature they do study."[41] Given the highly detailed racial contours of Mitchell's novel, it is particularly fas-cinating that critics could miss its racial content

for so long. Certainly, this oversight has more to say about the shifting economies of racial visibility at the close of the twentieth century than about the racial politics of Margaret Mitchell or of the 1930s. As such, this refusal to see the structures that shape our understanding of race stands as a prime example of the lenticular racial logic that characterizes post-civil rights discourse on race. In the remainder of this chapter, I want to explore how this economy of visibility, one that operates quite differently than the overt economy deployed by Mitchell, can be traced across the rewriting of *Gone with the Wind* in the 1990s.

A New South

Scarlett, Alexandra Ripley's 1991 sequel to *Gone with the Wind*, was, much like its predecessor, an instant bestseller, with many stores' stock sell-ing out as soon as it arrived. Over two million cop-ies were sold in the novel's first year, before the book's paperback issue in 1992. The sequel was also filmed as a television miniseries (in seventeen languages), which, upon its premiere in 1994, gar-nered a worldwide television audience of more than 275 million and was the top TV movie of the year in several countries, including the United States, Germany, Spain, and Japan.[42] Although Ripley was praised by some critics for capturing the essence of Mitchell's style (and roundly hated by most), the two novels deploy strikingly differ-ent economies of visibility in regards to race. Much like the television series *Savannah*, *Scarlett* finally deals with the interrelation of black and white by erasing blackness. In the end, Ripley, who no doubt faced quite a dilemma in deciding how to capture the "essence" of Mitchell's overt de-fense of racism during Reconstruction, displaces the text's considerations of blackness onto an en-tirely new geographic terrain. But before this dis-placement occurs, Ripley first constructs a view of ante- and postbellum southern race relations that retains all the nostalgia of Mitchell's accounts with none of the vituperative defenses of the Klan that might today serve to warn reader's away from Mitchell's rosier portraits.

More specifically, Ripley reproduces an old tale familiar from *Gone with the Wind* and other lost-cause ideologies about the tight bond between former slaves and their masters. Throughout the first half of the novel, casual references to former slaves "still loyal to old pre-War owners" (243) paint a picture of these "servants" as longing for the "early days at Tara" (34). These slaves are incorporated into the white family much as the "good" slaves were in Mitchell's novel, once again erasing their specificity beyond the confines of white society and rehabilitating the plantation household for contemporary tourist consumption. Mammy is once again deployed as the key figure who justifies master/slave (or, more accurately, mistress/slave) relations, and, much as in *Gone with the Wind,* her characterization underscores her love for the white characters. Early in the sequel, Scarlett returns home to Tara, hoping to "rest her wounded heart on Mammy's love" (9), only to find the former slave on her deathbed. In an odd reversal of the care-taking sequences of the first novel, Scarlett nurses Mammy until her death, watching with loving eyes as Mammy dreams of "those . . . happy times" before the war when, as a slave, she cared for Scarlett's mother, Ellen O'Hara (15). Though Mammy is occasionally figured as (at least formerly) "big" and "fleshy," and once referred to as a "creature," the conscious depiction of her as representative of blackness is missing in the sequel, as are characterizations of blackness and blacks as ominous and lethal. And Scarlett is no longer repeatedly delineated via images of pale whiteness. Whiteness is given meaning in other ways.

The novel's primary linkage of black and white femininity is thus less pronounced than that of *Gone with the Wind,* resting as it does on a subtle equation of Mammy and Scarlett's mother, Ellen O'Hara, as both women are drawn as objects of Scarlett's deepest daughterly affection and are, at her insistence, buried side by side. Still, Mammy dies within the first thirty of nearly nine hundred pages, and the novel quickly moves on to define femininity without the dark background of *Gone with the Wind,* thus naturalizing the whiteness of southern femininity. As the novel begins to take up the question of the southern lady most forcefully, blackness fades from view, erasing the historic interrelatedness of constructions of black and white womanhood in the era of the novel's setting. Black and white are thus held apart as Ripley dispatches Scarlett to Ireland in the sequel's second half, conveniently expunging black characters from her text. If *Gone with the Wind* and *The Birth of a Nation* foreground racial representation, the second half of *Scarlett* seemingly enacts a blanching in which whiteness is the *implicit* but *unspoken* telos or goal. Still, the very necessity of this narrative displacement of the racism of the South and the United States during Reconstruction—a displacement compelled by the text's own lenticular logic—simultaneously serves to highlight racism's very intractability. At first glance *Scarlett* may hardly seem to be about race at all, but a closer look reveals a tale deeply concerned with securing the meaning of whiteness in an era of multiculturalism.

Indeed, the specter of the first novel's overt defense of plantation owners' rights reappears in Ireland's seemingly white landscape at the novel's close. Though Scarlett is, at first, sympathetic to the fight for Irish independence and the text initially represents the plight of Ireland as a conquered land as similar to that of the South (658–662), the narrative trajectory of the novel finally figures the Irish revolutionaries as ungrateful and rebellious laborers, unable to appreciate "a good landlord" (860). The characterization of the Irish peasants as "so inhuman, so like . . . yowling . . .

wild beasts" echoes Mitchell's portrayals of "evil negroes," and, thus, the sequel condenses the earlier novel's figuration of blacks and of white trash onto one group. Finally, the moral force of both novels rests with the aristocratic landowner, for all is fair in defense of the plantation. Interestingly, in *The Wages of Whiteness*, historian David Roediger points out that Irish immigrants to the United States were often considered "black," and he tracks the process by which the working-class Irish came to claim whiteness as an appropriate label by distancing themselves from blacks. To the degree that it maps the ascent into aristocratic culture of Irish immigrant Gerald O'Hara, *Gone with the Wind* can be seen to trace a similar "whitening" of the Irish. *Scarlett* reverses this process, again "blackening" the Irish, who come to represent a threat to white southern femininity, as the marauding hoards attack Scarlett, Rhett, and their daughter in the final chapters of the novel. Still, this threat is covertly figured—that is, the racial displacement is not foregrounded, and not the primary interest in femininity that the text displays. Indeed, the novel selectively reclaims aspects of Irishness, as it links Scarlett's vitality and independence to her Celtic roots. When mediated through Scarlett's white southern femininity, the "wilder" aspects of Irishness are tamed and repurposed, severed from their class associations. If *Gone with the Wind* plumbed its heroine's depths via associations with and appropriations from black characters, the sequel's Scarlett finds her humanity and depth via the text's theft of ethnic, and not racial, difference. Thus, rather than mobilizing the earlier novel's latent and suppressed desire for cross-racial alliance, illustrating a new capacity to imagine integration in the post-civil rights era, the sequel flees from a vision of racial union, sketching instead the contours of a blindingly white American subject, dolled up via strategic raids into the emotional textures of ethnicity. Such an inability to imagine racial union is a failure of

many recent southern (and American) texts, illustrating our continued inability as a nation to come to terms with the meaning of race in southern history.

Although race is suppressed in the novel, *Scarlett*'s overt narrative question is an inquiry into the viability of the southern lady for a new era (our own as much as the one of the novel's setting). On its surface, *Scarlett* appears to call the ideal of the southern lady into question, echoing the early ambivalence to this figure displayed in *Gone with the Wind*, but like the earlier text, Ripley's novel finally resolves the dilemma of femininity in favor of the lady. Early in the novel, Scarlett strives to be a lady, recalling the example of her mother, who, the text relates, was "always occupied with the perpetual work required to produce the orderly perfection that was life at Tara under her guidance" (33), for "Ellen O'Hara had quietly ruled the plantation" (39). When an aunt comments that Scarlett had "grown up to be the image of Ellen," the narration assures us that "there was no greater compliment in the world that anyone could pay [Scarlett]" (124). The novel also offers a surrogate for Ellen in the figure of Eleanor Butler, Rhett's mother, who smells of lemon verbena, "the fragrance that had always been part of Ellen O'Hara" (130). Eleanor "was a Southern Lady . . . [and] ladies were trained from birth to be decorative . . . [but] they were also trained to manage the intricate and demanding responsibilities of huge houses . . . while making it seem that the house ran . . . flawlessly" (130). This new southern lady picks up on the earlier Scarlett's "New Woman" spunk, transforming her into a slightly veiled version of the career woman of the 1990s.

Once Scarlett moves to Ireland (where she manages her own estate), she begins to question certain aspects of the ideal woman her mother and Eleanor each appeared to be. Well into the story, Scarlett is enraptured by her new daughter, redeemed from the bad mothering traits evident in the first novel, when she realizes that she loves her daughter, Cat, more than her mother loved her. Her insight propels her to think, "Being a lady like her isn't the only way to be. It isn't even the best way to be" (629). Scarlett then rejects the superficial and hypocritical standards of those people in Atlanta who deemed her un-ladylike, seemingly dispensing with an interest in being a lady at all, but the text itself redeems the finer traits of ladylike behavior for a more modern Scarlett. Indeed, Scarlett's newfound sense of self-worth derives precisely from her position as the head of a new plantation, a landscape she manages with all the efficiency of the classic plantation mistress. Thus, *Scarlett,* much like its predecessor, initially critiques the social restrictions heaped upon the southern lady only to triumph the "time-honored" traits of ideal womanhood: maternal love, quiet strength, serenity. *Scarlett* insists the ideal woman can have it all: she can run the show, have her Cat, and get Rhett, too.

Scarlett's gentle refiguring of the lady as self-reliant might seem a welcome change to her status as "decorative" object, but this is not an entirely new configuration of the southern lady. Throughout the postbellum south, the ideology of the lost cause triumphed the strength of the southern lady, exalting her hard work and courage and firmly securing her place upon a pedestal. For instance, in a speech delivered to the graduates of Franklin Female College in June 1873, the Honorable J. W. Clapp draws upon familiar rhetoric when he urges the young women "to renounce all ostentatious display" and resort to "those lessons of energy and self-reliance" that are the hallmarks of each "cultivated southern woman."[43] His celebration of southern women's management skills and inner strength coincides perfectly with the figure of ideal southern womanhood popular in that period, a figure that both *Gone with the Wind* and *Scarlett* rework and finally triumph. And, as the recent popularity of *Scarlett* and countless television mini-series like *The Blue and the Gray* might sug-gest, it is precisely this figure of southern womanhood who is now enjoying a late-twentieth-century renaissance.

Central to this process of reclaiming the southern lady for our times is a lenticular logic of race that allows for a selective revamping of southern mythologies that conveniently displaces the racial context of the past while cherishing the images a previous racial economy had supported. Thus, both *Gone with the Wind* and *Scarlett* privilege the figure of the southern lady, but they do so through quite different logics. While I do not mean to suggest that an overt (and often racist) racial visibility is at all preferable to the lenticular logic deployed in the post-civil rights era, it is crucial to recognize that these two logics each strive to give whiteness a meaning. If, as Toni Morrison suggests, whiteness is mute, meaningless, and empty, both novels illustrate their authors' (and their respective cultures') attempts to fill the category with meaning, to give it voice.

Gone with the Wind carves out whiteness's definition by foregrounding difference and what whiteness is not. *Scarlett* also struggles to give whiteness contour and content but does so by highlighting Irish ethnicity and that mythic figure of an all-white past, the southern lady. We could simply dismiss the two epic tales as racist, if differently so, but little is gained in such a move. Instead, in exploring the different ways in which whiteness comes to voice in these stories of twentieth-century women, we might hear also the expression of a need to understand whiteness as a category that is not meaningless. *Scarlett*'s travels to Ireland thus become not only a way to avoid representing blackness and slavery but also an attempt, in an era which "celebrates" multiculturalism, to discern the heritage of whiteness, reclaiming select aspects of Irishness in order to give Scarlett both spunk and a history that is not tied to slavery. We can recognize that drive while also underscoring those aspects of race that the novel will not acknowledge.

While exploring the racial logic of each novel does suggest that to reclaim the southern lady is a dangerous move, understanding the impulses behind each logic also points the way toward better understanding the varied meanings whiteness and blackness have had throughout our nation's complex racial history. Neither the original myths of Scarlett nor her sequels can account for the myriad possibilities for femininity which the two tales excise. We might begin new explorations of race and femininity by examining these very omissions, asking what other ways a southern woman might be. What stories might Prissy or Belle Whatling or Emmie Slattery tell us if we were to listen to them? Surely, the social relations of race, class, and gender are more complex than two figures trapped in a postcard would suggest. These complexities may be good or bad, but nothing is gained in not addressing them.

Notes

1   Hazel Carby, *Reconstructing Womanhood: The Emergence of the Afro-American Woman Novelist* (New York: Oxford University Press, 1987), 18.

2   A brief listing of such works would include Toni Morrison, *Playing in the Dark: Whiteness and the Literary Imagination* (New York: Vintage, 1992); bell hooks, *Black Looks: Race and Representation* (Boston: South End Press, 1989); Ruth Frankenberg, *White Women, Race Matters: The Social Construction of Whiteness* (Minneapolis: University of Minnesota Press 1993); Fred Pfeil, *White Guys: Studies in Postmodern Domination and Difference* (New York: Verso, 1995); David Roediger, *The Wages of Whiteness: Race and the Making of the American Working Class* (New York: Verso, 1991) and his *Towards the Abolition of Whiteness* (New York: Verso, 1994); and Vron Ware, *Beyond the Pale: White Women, Racism, and History* (New York: Verso, 1992), as well as numerous anthologies on whiteness. While this turn to whiteness has been likened to the men's movement's tendency to appropriate the hard work of feminism in reactionary ways, much of the work in the books mentioned above springs more from an attempt to understand racial oppression than from a move to

valorize or triumph whiteness. Still, this early writing has spawned an academic subspecialty, work not always sensitive to the relations of whiteness to other registers of racial difference.

3   Morrison, *Playing in the Dark,* 17–18.

4   Zillah Eisenstein, *Hatreds* (New York: Routledge 1996), 79.

5   Margaret Mitchell, *Gone with the Wind* (New York: Macmillan, 1936) and Alexandra Ripley, *Scarlett* (New York: Warner Books, 1991). Further citations of these works appear as parenthetical page numbers in the text.

6   I borrow the phrase "economies of visibility" from Robyn Wiegman's development of the term in *American Anatomies* (Durham, NC: Duke University Press, 1995). What I have labeled overt and covert visual economies correspond to the different economies of visibility Wiegman sees as typical of the regimes of vision predominant in the pre- and post-civil rights eras, economies that she designates (following Foucault) as specular and panoptic. She notes that the "primary characteristic of the modern panoptic regime [in late-twentieth-century life] is its reliance on a visual production which exceeds the limited boundaries of the eye. . . . It is for this reason that the signs of race . . . are today seemingly unleashed in a proliferation of circulating images: integration beckons now the rising primacy of difference as commodity" (41). She links this shift in visual economies to the ascendancy of "cinema, television and video" which "serve up bodies as narrative commodities." While this focus on a proliferation of images of race (which for Wiegman means an abundance of images of blackness) might seem to run counter to my observation that *Scarlett* erases blackness, this simultaneous proliferation and erasure of blackness is characteristic of the covert or panoptic visual economy of race today. Thus, televisual productions of race today, to take just one example, are generally populated by black *or* white casts, but representations of "integration with equality" (to borrow again from Wiegman) are rare.

Ruth Frankenberg similarly discusses the likenesses and differences between what she calls "essentialist racism" and "color-evasive" racism, categories that would also correspond to my "overt" and "covert" designations. Frankenberg also posits a third category, "race cognizance," in which the workings of power vis-à-vis race are made visible. In this way, her work is more optimistic than Wiegman's, who remains critical of "the easy turn in contemporary critical theory toward an emancipatory rhetoric that rings increasingly hollow to many ears" (*American Anatomies*, 42).

7 Many thanks to Anna McCarthy for alerting me to the correct label for all these postcards I have been collecting.

8 Cf. Wiegman, *American Anatomies*, especially pages 189–90.

9 This analysis of Ken Burns's *The Civil War* is developed in my "'Both Kinds of Arms': Remembering the Civil War," *Velvet Light Trap* 35: 3–18. See also my *Reconstructing Dixie: Race, Gender, and Nostalgia in the Imagined South* (Durham, NC: Duke University Press, 2002), chapter 3.

10 Dyson, "Three Black Men Define the Image," *Los Angeles Times* (Oct. 22, 1995): M1.

11 Ruth Frankenberg writes of the inability of whites to perceive race as "lacunae in perception" enabled by racial privilege (*White Women*, 9).

12 I am thinking here of Danae Clark's insightful essay on the explosion of lesbian visibility in the mass media in the past decade. Clark rightly points out that the increased inclusion of lesbian images in visual culture has more to do with corporate financial interests than with an interest in lesbian civil rights. Likewise, one could argue that the O. J. Simpson trial certainly increased racial visibility but that increase in no way signaled an automatic or "positive" advance in our understanding of racial relations in the late twentieth century. Danae Clark, "Commodity Lesbianism," in *The Gay and Lesbian Studies Reader*, ed. Henry Abelove, Michèle Aina Barale, and David Halperin (New York: Cassell, 1994).

13 My *Reconstructing Dixie* explores both the meaning of "southernness" in a variety of twentieth-century texts and the ways in which the South comes to hold a variety of meanings for the nation at large at different historical moments.

14 For a useful "textbook-style" tracing of both the "colonial South" and the pre- and postindustrial South, see John B. Boles, *The South through Time: A History of an American Region* (Englewood Cliffs, NJ: Prentice Hall, 1995), especially chapters 4 and 5.

15 See, for example, Richard M. Bernard and Bradley R. Rice, eds., *Sunbelt Cities: Politics and Growth since World War II* (Austin: University of Texas Press, 1983), 1–30, and John D. Kasarda, "The Implications of Contemporary Distribution Trends for National Urban Policy," *Social Science Quarterly* 61 (December 1980):

373–400. Kasarda lists several factors leading to the South's growth in the period, including its lower cost of living, its improved consumer services, changing racial attitudes, and the spread of air conditioning. I would suggest that the South's weak labor unions and right-to-work policies, its cheap labor force, and a widespread campaign of "image building" by southern cities were equally important, if not more so. This period of growth was not equally distributed among the South's citizens; the New South developed along fairly familiar lines of racial geography.

16 Jack Kirby, *Media-Made Dixie* (Baton Rouge: Louisiana State University Press, 1978).

17 I provide an in-depth examination of this post-1970s return to a "new old South" in my *Reconstructing Dixie*. There I argue that the Reagan-Bush years saw a return to a more sentimental version of the old South than had been possible during the civil rights movement or the *Roots* years. I also detail the marked return of the southern lady as a popular image after 1980, a reprisal I link to a backlash against both feminism and the gains of the civil rights era.

18 I am indebted in this analysis to E. M. Beck and Stewart Tolnay's *Festival of Violence: An Analysis of the Lynching of African-Americans in the American South, 1882–1930* (Urbana, IL: University of Illinois Press, 1995), a statistical history analyzing patterns of lynching across the south from 1882 to 1930. They note the "bloody nineties" as marking the period of the worst violence, but they also single out 1908 and 1915 as particularly brutal years. They underscore the fact that lynching continued throughout the 1940s, 1950s, and 1960s, and that the decline in numbers doesn't reflect lynchings that were attempted but thwarted. While *Festival of Violence* provides important analyses, it does, in its drive to the scientific, downplay the relationship of the economic to the cultural. In underplaying these links, the authors neglect the powerful ideological work popular culture did in the service of this reign of terror. For studies that explore these links with more nuance, see chapter 5 of Grace Hale's *Making Whiteness: The Culture of Segregation in the South* (New York: Pantheon Books, 1998), and Fitzhugh Brundage's *Lynching in the New South: Georgia and Virginia, 1880–1930* (Urbana, IL: University of Illinois Press, 1993).

19 Mitchell's remark on her mother's career as a suffragist along with a brief recounting of May Belle's work is reported in Darden Pyron's *Southern Daughter: The Life*

of Margaret Mitchell (Oxford: Oxford University Press, 1991), 43. Pyron largely neglects the racist populism of the southern suffrage campaign, but this history has been well documented.

20 Leslie Fiedler also notes the link between Scarlett and Mammy in *The Inadvertent Epic* (New York: Simon and Schuster, 1980), though his analysis veers in a decidedly different direction.

21 Several feminist critics have incisively detailed the stakes and the terrain of the mammy image, including bell hooks, Patricia Morton, Hazel Carby, K. Sue Jewell, and, in the context of *Gone with the Wind*, Helen Taylor and Diane Roberts. Hazel Carby and Thomas Cripps also comment on Hattie McDaniel's performance as Mammy in the film version, pointing out the ways in which McDaniel briefly transcends the script's imaging of race, calling its construction of racial stereotypes into question, particularly for the African American viewer. Thus, the film is able to reveal (particularly for its black audiences) the performative nature of black femininity in a way that the novel is not.

22 Anne G. Jones, "*Gone with the Wind* and Others: Popular Fiction, 1920–1950," in *The History of Southern Literature*, ed. Louis D. Rubin Jr. et al. (Baton Rouge: Louisiana State University Press, 1985), 372; Anne Egenriether, "Scarlett O'Hara: A Paradox in Pantalettes" in *Heroines of Popular Culture*, ed. Pat Brown (Bowling Green, Ohio: Bowling Green State University Popular Press, 1987), 125; and Harriet Hawkins, "The Sins of Scarlett," *Textual Practice* 6(3) (winter 1992): 492. See also Amy Levin, "Matters of Canon: Reappraising *Gone with the Wind*," *Proteus* 6(1) (1989): 32–36.

23 A more detailed elaboration of this key debate within feminist theory can be found in my *Reconstructing Dixie*. While southern literary scholarship rarely intersects with the terrain of feminist film theory, the issue (and debates on the value) of feminine masquerade surface in both. The work of Jones, Hawkins, and Egenriether is certainly more celebratory in its assessments of masquerade's subversive potential than are the articles by Doane and Riviere, but each shares an inability to discern the racial contours of the masquerade. Doane's work on masquerade began in two early essays, "Film and the Masquerade: Theorizing the Female Spectator" (1982) and "Masquerade Reconsidered: Further Thoughts on the Female Spectator" (1989); both are available in her *Femme Fatales: Feminism, Film Theory, Pscyhoanalysis* (New York: Routledge, 1991), 17–32,

33–43. Joan Riviere's essay, first published in 1929, is reprinted in *Formations of Fantasy*, ed. Victor Burgin, James Donald, and Cora Kaplan (New York: Methuen, 1986), 35–44. Patrice Petro has recently extended my analysis of Riviere and race in her work on Weimar cinema.

24 Riviere, "Womanliness as Masquerade," 37, 38.

25 Cora Kaplan, "*The Thorn Birds*: Fiction, Fantasy, Femininity" in *Formations of Fantasy*, ed. Burgin, Donald, and Kaplan, 164.

26 For an excellent description of the discursive and material forms of resistance deployed by African American women, see Hazel Carby's *Reconstructing Womanhood*, bell hooks's *Ain't I a Woman? Black Women and Feminism* (Boston: South End Press, 1981), and Angela Davis's *Women, Race, and Class* (New York: Random House, 1983). In *Between Men* (New York: Columbia University Press, 1985), Eve Kosofsky Sedgwick offers a reading of Mammy that supports the interpretation I delineate here. She notes that Mammy is "totally in thrall of the ideal of the 'lady,' but in a relation that excludes herself entirely . . . her personal femaleness loses any meaning whatever that is not in relation to Scarlett's role" (9). This corresponds to what I call a "lack of interiority" in the character.

27 For a discussion of the use of slave women as wet nurses, see bell hooks, *Ain't I a Woman?* and Deborah Gray White, *Ar'n't I a Woman?: Female Slaves in the Plantation South* (New York: Norton, 1985). Additionally, female slave narratives discuss the impact of the historical use of wet nurses by wealthy slave-owning families, and Julie Dash's moving film, *Daughters of the Dust*, also provides illuminating commentary.

28 Thomas Cripps, "Winds of Change: *Gone with the Wind* and Racism as a National Issue," in *Recasting: Gone with the Wind in American Culture*, ed. Darden A. Pyron (Miami: University Presses of Florida, 1984), 140.

29 Nell Irvin Painter provides insightful comments on a "psychological" interrelatedness among black and white southern daughters in her examination of the psycho-social role dynamics of southern families in "Of Lily, Linda Brent, and Freud: A Nonexceptionalist Approach to Race, Class, and Gender in the Slave South," in *Half Sisters of History: Southern Women and the American Past*, ed. Catherine Clinton (Durham: Duke University Press, 1994), 208–10. Eric Lott also notes the affective consequences of racial proximity in his *Love*

and Theft: Blackface Minstrelsy and the Working Class
(New York: Oxford University Press, 1993).

30 Raymond Williams, *Marxism and Literature* (New York:
Oxford University Press, 1977), 132, 133, 134.

31 This is not to suggest that African American women
might not also desire unity. Indeed, it is in the work of
African American novelists like Margaret Walker and
Sherley Anne Williams that the possibilities for such
a unity are most powerfully explored. As feminist theorist Michelle Wallace notes in *Invisibility Blues: From
Pop to Theory* (New York: Verso, 1990), 145, the power
of work like Williams's resides in its definition of
"friendship as the collective struggle that ultimately
transcends the stumbling blocks of race and class."

Other African American women have also reconstructed the image of the mammy. The work of artist
Bettye Saar refigures the mammy and her twentieth-
century counterpart, Aunt Jemima, via tropes of militancy, while Cheryl Dunye's film *Watermelon Woman*
seeks to reinscribe the agency of mammy. This film also
suggests the complex ways in which black women (as
the slaves who "played" the mammy and as the actresses who later portrayed the figure onscreen) performed black femininity as a survival strategy.

32 Minrose Gwin, *Black and White Women of the Old
South: The Peculiar Sisterhood in American Literature*
(Knoxville: University of Tennessee Press, 1985), 17.

33 Richard Dyer, "Into the Light: The Whiteness of the
South in *The Birth of a Nation*," in *Dixie Debates:
Perspectives on Southern Cultures*, eds. R. H. King
and H. Taylor (New York: New York University Press,
1996), 169, 167.

34 Mitchell's novel clearly defends the Klan night rides as
a necessary defense of white women, though her politics outside the novel seem quite contradictory. She
at once claims to love the novels of Dixon while supporting and championing the revisionary history of
W. J. Cash. For a longer contextualization of *Gone with
the Wind* within contemporary Atlanta, see my *Reconstructing Dixie*, chapter 2.

35 Kenneth O'Brien, "Race, Romance, and the Southern
Literary Tradition," in *Recasting*, ed. Darden A. Pyron,
163.

36 During the time that this volume was in preparation,
what I term an emergent strand of southern studies began to take on the racial implications of Mitchell's epic
quite directly, while a few earlier critics also discussed
race as an important element of the novel. Of the work

already mentioned, Hales, Cripps, Fiedler, and Kaplan
consider race to varying degrees, as do Elizabeth Young,
*Disarming the Nation: Women's Writing and the Ameri-
can Civil War* (Chicago: University of Chicago Press,
1999), Linda Williams, *Playing the Race Card* (Princeton: Princeton University Press, 2001), Diane Roberts,
*The Myth of Aunt Jemima: Representations of Race and
Region* (New York: Routledge, 1994), and Helen Taylor,
*Scarlett's Women: Gone with the Wind and Its Female
Fans* (London: Virago Press, 1989). In addition, Eve
Sedgwick, Hazel Carby, Joel Williamson, Toni Morri-
son, and Alice Walker all offer critical commentary in
the context of larger works on other topics.

37 O'Brien, "Race, Romance," 163.

38 Ibid., 165.

39 In her book *White Women, Race Matters,* anthropologist Ruth Frankenberg characterizes such "color-blind-
ness" as "color-evasive," noting that such strategies actually evade an acknowledgment of the privileges of
whiteness by arguing against racial difference.

40 Carby, *Reconstructing Womanhood,* 20.

41 Morrison, *Playing in the Dark,* 13.

42 For an interesting look at the miniseries' statistics and
self-promotion, see the advertisement for the sequel in
the *Hollywood Reporter* (November 29, 1994): 6. In addition, *TV Guide* published many articles on the series.
Another odd bit of *Gone with the Wind* trivia is the huge
success in Japan of a musical based on Scarlett O'Hara
(see the introduction to Pyron's *Recasting*). In a longer
consideration of the novel, I also examine "the place" of
Charleston in *Scarlett*, noting its role as historic setting
and also as a nodal point of 1990s global capital. See my
Reconstructing Dixie, chapter 2.

43 A copy of J. W. Clapp's speech is housed in the archives
at the University of Mississippi, Oxford, Mississippi.
It was first published by the Public Ledger Printing Establishment in Memphis in the spring of 1873. Clapp
also urges the young women to honor the confederate
dead and to retain their influences within the domestic
sphere.

HOP ON POP

HOME IS A POWERFUL WORD: DOROTHY'S refrain at the end of *The Wizard of Oz,* "There's no place like home," legitimizes the solidity of the conservative Midwest over the excitement and adventure of Oz. Karl Reitz self-consciously titled his made-for-TV film *Heimat* (homeland) to reawaken and rethink the German nationalist nostalgia surrounding this word. The film turned into a beloved work for both the Right and Left. And consider how the term "Palestine homeland" incites violent disagreement in the Middle East yet is an oddly unquestioned phrase in U.S. news nomenclature. "Home" remains one of the most emotionally charged and ideologically loaded terms in common use. To say "my home" releases a number of meanings (and potential misunderstanding) associated with family and/or country that are central to the pull of popular culture.

Academics have traditionally distanced themselves from its complex everyday usage by substituting "site," "space," and "origin," thereby evoking a structural or geographical sense of a place, beginning, or source. But such language does not get at the sense of belongingness, allegiance, and sentiment conjured up by "home." Jürgen Habermas offers a sociological understanding of home in Western society when he translates the word into the "private sphere"—the realm where nonpolitical activities such as emotion, pleasure, and domestic tasks take place. As feminists point out, home becomes gendered as the place of feminine activity. They argue that home is opposed to and ultimately devalued as compared to the all-important public sphere, where men engage in work and political discussion and actions.

We have chosen "home" to tackle these thorny ideological and gendered issues and question the lack of academic analysis. Our interest in the word reflects the rise of autobiographical accounts in feminism and cultural studies that look at the present and historical role of one's home in popular culture. The title of a popular anthology on the subject, *Home Is Where the Heart Is,* reveals the

new sensibility where psychological and gender studies take central stage. Home represents more an ideal than a reality in its usage. Such nostalgia for the lost simplicity of this model home often covers a deep-seated resentment at the modern world, family, and/or woman.

The writers in this section provide vivid, often personal portraits of the different ways home is used in popular culture. All essays tie home to nation. Nabeel Zuberi and Maria Koundoura offer intimate accounts of how home is not an easy concept for them given their multiple cultural identities. Both are drawn to popular culture in all its progressive and regressive ideology as a venue for understanding and transcending their places in the world. Zuberi discusses the contradiction of his attraction to Morrissey, formerly of the British rock group the Smiths. The allure is based on the singer's representation of sexual androgyny, working-class rage and alienation—a sensibility shared by the writer who is working class and gay. Zuberi does not feel at home in Britain as a Pakistani and an educated child of the working class nor does he feel a direct connection with Pakistan as a gay new Britain. Yet Morrissey's music does not provide a comfortable home. Zuberi recognizes the white nationalism and neo-fascist appeal of the singer in his nostalgia for a bygone Britain where the [white] worker had status as opposed to the new labor market of Asians and Caribbeans. It is only in reading Morrissey's lyrics as ironic that the writer can find an ambivalent resolution.

Interestingly, Maria Koundoura picks a seemingly much less complex object from popular culture, *I Dream of Jeannie,* to weave a theoretical account of her identification as a Greek girl living in Australia with a product from commercial America. *Jeannie* in its foreignness first allowed the writer as a child to transcend location and her painful outsider status as an immigrant in Australia. Now as an academic in America, she uses her cultural capital to theoretize and write about "displacement," where she sees her own past and still present joy in a program as reflecting the complexity of identity in the late twentieth century: "It still is the means through which I can blink my way home, in the current instance, through this personally theoretically narrative. The show represents my 'as if' self, my ability to transport myself to a better place, a place that is both familiar and foreign: the imagined community of a nation that, in my case, can only be represented in the multiple cultures in which I have lived." Home becomes an imagined return to unreachable previous identity.

Aniko Bodroghkozy continues the examination of the possibilities of forging a popular identity by looking at images of "Canadian-ness." Her home—Canada—often relies on either American popular culture or British high-culture traditions to define itself. By reanalyzing traditional Canadian economic determinism and cultural imperialism arguments, she looks for a way to account for a Canadian form of popular culture. She compares and contrasts how two Canadian television programs—*Street Legal* and *Due South*—reveal the possibility of a Canadian popular culture. She singles out the latter's playfulness with Canadian national identity, where the lead character is a formally dressed Canadian Mountie working with a violent ragtag American cop in Chicago. Although the program is the first Canadian program to succeed in American markets, its use of Canadian humor and nationally specific references undercut the popular image of America as a superior nation. The irony of the program allows the Canadians to create their own popular televisual community whose interpretation proudly differs from the American one.

Catherine Palmer looks at the Tour de France—France's premier bicycle race—from a more traditional academic distance to examine how the event constructs cultural identity, or "Frenchness." Here, home is a complex postmodern construction called "France" designed just for the Tour de France. The event transforms everyday life in the country with its vast commercialism, and it entails a form of consumerism. The Tour de France actually alters landscapes and territories as it proceeds across France giving the landscape "a life of its own." Nevertheless, in this postmodern world the commodities sold are selected based on their ability to evoke "Frenchness" as defined as "sophistication, style, and exuberance." The Tour de France becomes an exercise of national self-reflectivity: "The Tour experiences France and France experiences the Tour" as a chance to come to terms with what is France even if it was constructed just for the race.

Ellen Strain looks at how travel via CD-ROM allows a would-be traveler to play out the lust for the original experience of foreign lands without ever leaving home. Such CD-ROMS perpetuate anti-tourism—convincing oneself that one is not really a glib tourist with a voyeuristic gaze, but rather an individual who experiences a culture from within. These virtual trips play on the user's desire for authenticity that results from a nostalgia for an idealized or past culture that no longer and may never have existed. Strain analyzes how the spatial design of the games attempts to satisfy both the anti-tourist's desire for this authentic experience as well as need for distance to understand a country. Here, the world becomes a material world based on product availability and how the products position the user to identify with Western travelers. The central pleasure of these CD-ROMS is that they make comprehensible "a world that is no longer mappable."

Finally, John Hartley pulls together autobiography, national identity, postmodern play, and popular culture with his playful account of the geography of cultural studies. Caught between two homes—Australia and Britain—he sets out to understand the spatial world and his travel between countries and knowledges. He dubs the process "a vehicular theory" that defies intellectual rigidities and exclusions. This requires him to "twock"—to steal or borrow ideas in a pastiche style avoiding a clearly defined position ideologically or spatially. Ultimately, Hartley makes a case for breaking rules and opening up notions of community, nation, and homeland to follow the richer and ever-changing landscape of culture.

"The Last Truly British People You Will Ever Know": Skinheads, Pakis, and Morrissey

Nabeel Zuberi

Worked upon and reinterpreted, the landscape becomes a historical landscape; but only through continual and active reworking.
—CAROLYN STEEDMAN, *LANDSCAPE FOR A GOOD WOMAN*

I am now
a central part
of your mind's landscape
Whether you care
or do not
—MORRISSEY, "THE MORE YOU IGNORE ME THE CLOSER I GET"

Britain is still convulsed by its postwar, postcolonial identity crisis. Most of Britain's dominions have been liberated from colonial rule since 1945. The end of empire and the need for cheap labor brought many migrants from the former colonies to the "mother country." This settlement has unsettled older conceptions of the white body politic. The nation coughs and splutters into a new Europe. The British Union faces the challenge of devolution from Irish, Scottish, and Welsh nationalisms. British nationalism (largely defined on English terms) is no longer the feisty bulldog of Churchillian features, but a (J)anus-faced pug, wheezing after years of inbreeding. At seemingly regular intervals, it froths at the mouth and barks from the Tory backbenches and inky blots of the tabloid press. In the late 1990s, cricket, mad cows, and the national lottery became issues to test the boundaries of who we are as a people, who belongs and who doesn't in this small island off the coast of continental Europe. These rabid excesses apart, the dog is generally content with its own lamppost to piss on.

One of the taken-for-granted ways the English mark territory is through the notion of Little England, "our patch," a white place with a sedimented, continuous way of life in which the Englishness or Britishness of things is so thoroughly ingrained, ordinary, specific, so nuanced in its details and hierarchies that it's impossible for an outsider to truly master its repertoire and gain membership of this "imagined community." As George Mikes writes in the bestselling satirical classic *How to be an Alien* (1946): "A criminal may improve and become a decent member of society. A foreigner cannot improve. Once a foreigner, always a foreigner. There is no way out for him. He may become British; he can never become English." He goes on to add in a footnote that "[w]hen people say England, they sometimes mean Great Britain, sometimes the United Kingdom, sometimes the British Isles—but never England."[1]

For a nation that prides itself on its sense of irony, one of the most British of ironies might be that many Brits (from a range of political persuasions) have turned repeatedly to their own versions of this Little England of the imagination at the same time as the nation-state has been reduced to a corporate agency that facilitates the movement of transnational finance capital. John Major's "Back to Basics" campaign to promote Britain as the heritage land of warm beer and village green cricket and Tony Blair's nation-branding exercise of "Cool Britannia" still imagine quite narrow and sentimental versions of the national community. In this context, a Scot, Tom Nairn, writes that the English are captivated by the "glamour of backwardness."[2] Other foreigners might be forgiven for believing that England is like an old curiosity shop with one of those closing-down sales that never ends.

"They [the Germans] make good cars. All Britain is good at these days is pop music" says Chris Lowe of the Pet Shop Boys.[3] "Selling England by the sound," popular music and the myriad cultural activities surrounding it form one cultural arena in which "the national" is informally debated. In what Michael Bracewell calls "England's unofficial commentary on itself," musicians interrogate and jostle with ideas of Englishness and Britishness in the constant reevaluation of national identity.[4] They draw upon inherited truths, invented traditions, and common sense. Pop music plays upon nostalgic yearnings. This looking backward cannot simply be dismissed as a desire to escape to the past and freeze history. The *retro* mode in certain strands of British pop music reveals white Englishness to be in a state of flux. This may not be the "passing of whiteness," but a signal of a shift in white ethnicity.

The memory work of Britpop, for example, is part of a reaction to both U.S. cultural hegemony and multi-cultural Britain, a turning inward to familiar narratives, images, musical tropes, and ways of representing England. During the mid-nineties tabloid-fueled rivalry between Oasis and Blur, familiar scenes of white working-class life and lower middle-class suburbia saturated their songs and product packaging, which captured the sounds and shapes of a "timeless" British popular culture. The landscapes on CD covers have been reproduced countless times before as immediate signifiers of Englishness: the greyhound races, the canal lock, the country mansion, the semi-detached suburban house. The characteristically British device of irony allows young Britons to revel in the familiar continuities of "our way of life" while claiming some critical distance from clichéd versions of the past. In an ambiguous fluctuation between intimacy and distance Britpop's camp gestures are part of an ironic attitude to national history that suits a decadent nation, more content to deal with the archives than to grasp the possibilities of an uncertain future. Musically, most Britpop groups revived the tried-and-trusted riffs and motifs of English pop and its high points, from the Beatles and Kinks to Bowie and Cockney Rebel's 1970s glam rock and post-Sex Pistols punk. Britpop was a (re)invention of a specifically British guitar rock/pop tradition, an assertion of an indigenous national version of U.S. rock. Britpop acts have vied for attention in megastore displays alongside a number of rapidly multiplying and hybridizing dancefloor genres and subgenres such as techno, jungle/drum 'n' bass, bhangra, and trip hop. Representing a multi-racial, multi-cultural Britain which includes Caribbean and Asian elements, musicians like Goldie, Massive Attack, Bally Sagoo, Tricky, Talvin Singh, and even Britpop-sounding groups like the Voodoo Queens and Echobelly, have challenged pervasive, banal nationalisms, and helped to redefine the "British" in British music.[5]

Britpop shares something of its fetishization of things English and British with Morrissey, former lead vocalist with Manchester guitar group the Smiths (1983–87). Morrissey is currently a major recording artist in Britain, the United States, and other large markets for Anglo-American pop. In Morrissey's body of work, the nature of Englishness or Britishness is an obsession as deep and murky as the waters of the Manchester-Liverpool canal. His particular fascination with an almost exclusively white English working class can be mapped through record sleeves, songs, videos, and the visuals of his gigantic concert stage backdrops.

Popular music has the power to construct a sense of place. The northern landscapes of Smiths' songs present a proletarian past of back-to-back houses and grimy, rain-sodden streets. Many of the group's plaintive guitar motifs and geographical references in lyrics conjure up a Manchester beautifully sorry for itself and its post-industrial urban wasteland.[6] In her book *And God Created Manchester*, Sarah Champion notes that Johnny Marr's psychedelic Bo Didley guitar riff in the Smiths's "How Soon Is Now" evokes the wet Manchester streets as powerfully as Ry Cooder's blues twang does the desert terrain of Paris, Texas.[7]

As a solo artist, Morrissey's perspective on the white working class shifts south to London's East End, and those landscapes (of the mind) where white working-class boys will always be white working-class boys. In this essay, I'm concerned with Morrissey's representation of the skinhead in songs and the photographic imagery of music packaging, t-shirts, and concert backdrops. In the early 1990s, skins (mainly male, but some female) appeared in his iconography at the same moment as extreme right-wing groups like the British National Party underwent a revival and actively recruited skinheads. As a Pakistani-born British fan of the Smiths and Morrissey, my discomfort with the star's apparent fascination with English fascism leads me to examine the skinhead's role as quintessential working-class English figure in popular culture. The skinhead also has a secure place as a subcultural working-class subject in the discourse of (British) cultural studies. I examine the gendered, racialized, and ethnic assumptions behind some of this writing.

Rather than just lay out yet another history of discourse about the subcultural skinhead, I trace out his representation in relation to his antithesis, the *Paki*—the South Asian in Britain—the object of the right-wing skinhead's wrath, the body at the receiving end of the Doc Marten boot. The stereotypical contours of the Paki emerge at the same time the skinhead is created as a folk devil in the late 1960s. The Paki is a figure in the white youth's shadow. Where is this British Asian, the designated Paki, to be situated in the national landscape?

Morrissey's pop strategies in music and image provocatively and ambiguously riff on discourse about the skinhead and the British Asian. As a longtime fan, I pose these underlying questions of the pop star: Are you really racist or have you just been brave enough to confront certain realities that British people on the right and left want to dismiss as "politically incorrect" or find too troubling to face honestly? Are you a trickster figure forcing British folks to confront painful fractures in the national body? Or are you just another miserable Little Englander who wishes Britain was still white? Are the answers to these questions mutually exclusive?

Here popular music is not the primary object of interpretation, but something that enables interpretation of a cultural situation.[8] This essay essentially explores how my fascination with an English pop star can reveal something of the ways in which Pakistani-British subjects, often derided as Pakis, are positioned in British culture and its "cultural studies."

Paki is the pejorative four-letter word that names the south Asian in Britain, though racist Canadians have also borrowed the term for south Asians in north America. An abbreviation of *Pakistani,* in racist parlance the term is also applied to Bangladeshis and Indians: "They all look the same." Like the skinhead, the British Asian or more commonly known *Asian* is the object of official language. Conservative and Labour governments and a race-relations industry promising institutional multiculturalism may not use the word *Paki* to describe south Asians but they draw upon a reservoir of English "common sense." We have a history of official identities. In the 1960s and early 1970s Britain's Asians were "immigrants," often presumed illegal. "How many you got in your loft then?" jested my primary school mates, conjuring up a clutch of unwashed subcontinentals, potential social security scroungers, reeking of garlic, and breeding like rabbits in the attic. "They stick to their own. They don't want to be like us," summed up the insularity of alien "ethnic minorities" in the heart of English cities. Asians were passive wimps whereas West Indians were hard; Pakis took the beatings quietly from the white racists, whereas Jamaicans fought back. Asians sat besieged in their homes waiting for the shit and burning paper to come through front door letterboxes. Bricks wrapped in Union Jacks crashed through their shop windows. Asians were the Stakhanovites of the corner shop and the late-night takeaway restaurant, quiet exemplars of

Thatcherite free enterprise or tight-fisted acquisitive bastards. When the kids weren't behind the shop counter developing entrepreneurial skills, they would be upstairs doing school homework, passing exams which took them to college or uni, and studying to become doctors, engineers, lawyers, and chartered accountants. Asians were religious fanatics, burning books and bombing bookshops. They wrapped themselves in oppressive family pathologies that promised only failed parents, wounded children, and arranged marriages. Some of these stereotypes have colonial antecedents, some have sprung forth in the context of migration, settlement, and post-imperial British racism. Through these representations, British Asians have been defined as immutably different, "alien cultures" threatening to "swamp us" in one of Margaret Thatcher's infamous soundbites.

Where does the Paki fit into the histories of British popular music culture and cultural studies? Not many places, and only seriously considered since the 1980s with Apache Indian, Bally Sagoo, and the bhangra explosion, hip hop acts like the Kaliphz, Hustlers HC, and Fun^Da^Mental, and guitar groups such as the Voodoo Queens, Cornershop, and Echobelly, and musicians such as Asian Dub Foundation, Talvin Singh, Black Star Liner, and State of Bengal, associated with the Asian Underground. Before that the Asian is largely invisible in pop music, unredeemably uncool in comparison with Afro-Caribbean youth. No wonder then that some of the early 1990s Asian music was branded the New Asian Kool in response to this uncool history. In "multi-racist Britain," Philip Cohen points out that "many White working-class boys discriminate positively in favour of Afro-Caribbean subcultures as exhibiting a macho proletarian style, and against Asian cultures as being 'effeminate' and 'middle-class.' Such boys experience no sense of contradiction in wearing dreadlocks, smoking ganja and going to reggae concerts whilst continuing to assert that 'Pakis stink.'"[9]

I attempt to place the male Paki on the national map by looking at the representation of his nemesis, the skinhead. Without the skinhead, we wouldn't have the Paki in the form he has taken. They appeared as part of national discourse on race at about the same time in the late 1960s. As a Paki(stani) who grew up in Britain during the late 1960s, 1970s, and early 1980s, I've been produced as a British citizen ("naturalized," in official terms, in 1973) in significant measure by the presence of the skinhead.[10] My family migrated to Britain in 1968. I was five years old. This was the year that Enoch Powell, the godfather of New Right cultural racism and a Member of Parliament from the Midlands where we first lived, made his infamous speech predicting civil war and "rivers of blood" if immigration from the former colonies in the Caribbean and the Indian subcontinent were to continue. According to Powell, allowing more black people into the country was also like piling bodies on a funeral pyre. By 1968, the skinhead was emerging from its subcultural precursor the "hard mod." Powell's public statements gave skins the license to indulge in "Paki-bashing." I only remember getting beaten up once for being a Paki, but the threat of violence seemed ever present during all my years in England. I was reminded that I was a Paki by children, teenagers, and adults, who verbally abused me innumerable times at bus stops, in the school playground, outside the school gates, at the football match, in the park, and pub.

"Where is the place that you move into the landscape and can see yourself?" poses Carolyn Steedman in her analysis of the failures of marxism and psychoanalysis to account for the experiences of working-class women and girls.[11] "What binds together images and sounds in personal memory with images and sounds in collective memory?" asks Annette Kuhn.[12] Writing the self in academia is discomfiting. According to some of my peers and advisers, it's a luxury earned only by those with credentials established with more "objective" scholarship. For years I've anguished

over whether "the personal" is valid in serious/academic criticism, pondering if writing my self is an indulgent exercise or justified because it has some typicality that can stand for something greater than the experience of a single individual/subject. Am I trapped in identity-thinking, forever gazing at my middle-class postcolonial diasporic Pakistani-English navel, unable to move on to a more grown-up objective, broader political perspective? After all, as feminist critics have pointed out, sometimes the personal is not political, but just personal.

However, while still ambivalent about the autobiographical in academia, I believe that writing the self can question the claims of grand, overarching theories of culture, can point out their absences and ellisions, and bring to voice neglected subjects. Experience theorized can also, as Elspeth Probyn suggests, lead the critic to the social formation: "As I have found in the sometimes sobering experience of teaching, the absence of a reason to theorize is soon filled by students wanting to know, quite rightly, how theories about culture can help them to understand their own experiences. Put very bluntly, our experience as critics and teachers can articulate and allow for expressions of experience, both our own and others,' 'one's feeling in and through another.'"[13] I have no wish to represent my "experience" as emblematic of British Asian life; I don't know any "typical British Asian." I don't wish to reproduce the false cultural binary of Pakistani diasporic identity against white Englishness nor to proclaim right-on militant Asianness against racist whiteness. On the other hand, I have no desire to act as a cheerleader for British metropolitan hybridity either. Though we're all hodge-podge black white brown, the pain and bitterness, anger and self-doubt of growing up in-between in a "third space" within a deeply racist society are often bypassed in the rush to validate and celebrate the hybrid and hyphenated self. By taking apart white Englishness in this essay, I also acknowledge that aspects of both cultural whiteness and destructive forms of knowledge and discourse that produced "the Paki" have shaped my identity.

It is worth reiterating in these times of cultural absolutism that British Asians consume, use, and abuse white popular culture for their own needs, purposes, and despite themselves. Where are the histories of our reception of "white texts"? Grappling with Morrissey involves an unravelling of my Britishness and Englishness, my sense of belonging and unbelonging—a problem which I haven't been able to escape, despite some distance and time away from dear old Blighty. Writing myself in relation to the discourses of skinhead, the Paki, and British cultural studies *through* Morrissey is one attempt toward a solution.

In the cultural studies classic *Subculture: The Meaning of Style,* Dick Hebdige suggests that we can observe "played out on the loaded surfaces of British working-class youth cultures, a phantom history of race relations since the War." Where to locate the British Asian in this dynamic? In a troubling passage, Hebdige describes the interaction between Pakistanis and reggae-loving skinheads in the late 1960s and early 1970s. The activity of "Paki-bashing" is an outcome of the awkward alliance of Afro-Caribbean and white youth:

> "Paki-bashing" can be read as a displacement manoeuvre whereby the fear and anxiety produced by limited identification with one black group was transformed into aggression and directed against another black community. Less easily assimilated than the West Indians into the host community . . . sharply differentiated not only by racial characteristics but by religious rituals, food taboos and a value system which encouraged deference, frugality and the profit motive, the Pakistanis were singled out for the brutal attentions of skinheads, black and white alike. Every time the boot went in, a contradiction was concealed, glossed over, made to "disappear."[14]

In other words: "We don't have to kick each other's heads in, if we can beat someone else up."

The objects of this violence are represented as a catalogue of anthropological details that fix their difference from the host nation. It's unclear whether Hebdige is reciting these cultural traits as received wisdom to be critiqued or just assuming that they have an empirical truth. As to the violence, while black and white unite, even if temporarily, the Pakistanis "disappear" like the "contradiction" itself. The tentative love affair between black and white youth cultures effaces the agency of the Pakistani, and race relations continue at the expense of the alien, unassimilable Asian. A playground racist joke I remember stretches this vanishing to its limit: "What's transparent, and lies in the gutter? A Paki with the shit kicked out of him?"

Pete Fowler's 1972 article on the emergence of the skinhead explains that Asians basically stick to themselves, and have middle-class values. He is hopeful that the skinhead love of reggae and appropriation of working-class macho Jamaican rude boy style signals a coming together of the races through shared class experiences. Asians are excluded from this racial and class-based compact. Des, a "garage worker and a Skin of three years standing," explains his antipathy to Asian settlers:

> I'll tell you why I hate the bloody Paks. I'll tell you a story. A week or so ago I was walking down the street with a couple of mates. I wanted a light for my fag, so I walk up to this Paki git and ask him, "You got a light, mate?" And what do you think the fucker did? I'll tell you. He walks—no, runs—into this shop and buys me a box of matches! Now I ask you! What the fuck could I do with a bleeder like that but hit him? And another thing. Have you ever been in their restaurants? Have you seen the way they *grovel* round you, the way they're always trying to please you? I hate them, that's all.[15]

The Paki here is an obsequious creature. His reluctance to resort to violence is seen as a weakness. His emasculation is doubly assured when one compares him to Afro-Caribbean youth. White male identification with (and desire for) the black male often involves a worship of certain tropes and images: black cool, machismo, the Stagger Lee/gangsta/outlaw figure, the natural, strong, physical, sensual self with rhythm.

In another example of mid-1970s cultural studies writing on the skinhead, John Clarke explains: "Paki-bashing involved the ritual and aggressive defence of the social and cultural homogeneity of the community against its most obviously scapegoated outsiders—partly because of their particular visibility within the neighbourhood (in terms of shop ownership patterns, etc) by comparison with West Indians, and also because of their different cultural patterns (*especially in terms of their unwillingness to defend themselves and so on*)—again by comparison with West Indian youth" (my emphasis).

Left-wing culture in the 1970s often measured "political resistance" by the individual and collective aptitude and readiness for violence if necessary. Spectacular forms of protest form part of a romantic ideal of praxis that permeates popular cultural forms. The Clash capture this urge for glamorous action, taking to the streets, and "manning" the barricades in their 1977 punk single "White Riot." [16] Singer Joe Strummer wishes that he could have a riot like the black people had in Notting Hill during the previous year's carnival. In leftist pop culture mythology, the "hardness" or toughness of the working-class male (black or white) is lumpen-potential for class action. In popular music culture, particularly the influential British music press circa 1977–78, "street credibility" and working-class credentials were a boon. Being middle class was decidedly unhip, something to keep quiet about. In the post-punk era, the skinhead's seduction by the far Right proves an unfortunate embarrassment for the Left. In skinhead music and culture, the rhetoric of class becomes increasingly articulated through ideas of race and nation. [17] Notions of a macho white mas-

culinity are essential to these far-right fantasies. Since Asians are not hard, have been emasculated, and "stuck in their own ways," they are even less fit for identification as integrated members of the nation. In contrast, for many English academics and journalists, the skin, however politically misguided he may be, is still the genuine article, as British as fish and chips and a pint of bitter.

In 1975 under the influence of Althusserianism at the Birmingham Centre for Contemporary Cultural Studies, Clarke states that skinhead style "represents an attempt to re-create through the 'mob' the traditional working class community as a substitution for the *real* decline of the latter." [18] Rock critic Paul Du Noyer explains that the skins "were aggressively working class, taking traditional styles (big boots, braces, short hair) up to the point of parody. In fact it was the exaggerated uniform of an old proletariat that had vanished along with the blitz." [19] Subcultural analysis in the 1970s took skinheads as ethnographic subjects and texts to be deciphered, recording some of their speech, compiling their fashion fetishes, expanding on their other activities. This research was concerned with how the skinhead embodied a structural change in the English working class. The focus was male skins, rarely female skins. [20] The skinhead's style was a mark of his agency, an act of partial, if misplaced resistance. He was a semiotically charged naif that signified the breakdown of post-war social consensus.

The 1970s saw the rise of the National Front and British Movement, far-right political parties actively recruiting skinheads. The NF's youth paper was sold outside the Leeds United soccer ground. When I was a student in Leeds in the early 1980s, *Bulldog* could be found at gigs by Oi! bands (a kind of skinhead punk) and at certain local pubs. Confrontation with fascist skins was always a possibility during anti-racist events and marches in support of the IRA hunger strikers. In fact, just walking in Leeds streets, not engaged in any political activity, you could get your head kicked in. Before being aware of Dick Hebdige or "cultural studies," I was taught how to identify the socialist skin from the fascist skin by the colour of the laces on Doc Martens: red for fascist, white for socialist. Or was it the other way around?

A bitingly cold February night, 1984 in front of the Georgian facade of Leeds University. My sister and I wait alone for the last bus home to Ilkley after seeing the Smiths in concert, our ears still humming from the loudness of the PA system. Across the street, the neon sign for the Islamabad Restaurant glows red. Suddenly four white skinheads burst into the street through the restaurant's doors, hurtling toward us like toppling skittles. Two Pakistani waiters in white jackets storm out of the doors. They trip one skin, and kick him repeatedly as he lies jerking around on the pavement. His mates gawp at the scene from our side of the street, only a few feet away from us, unsure whether to enter the fray or give their comrade up to the Pakistani kicks.

A number of thoughts raced through my head. The three skins might kick the shit out of us in revenge and frustration. Worse still, they might hover interminably, spit abuse, or just mutter "Paki" at us like a thousand and one times before. I hoped that silence and deference would assuage the fist and the boot. Sometimes it seems eminently reasonable to comply to the passive, emasculated middle-class Asian stereotype when you're middle-class, Asian, outnumbered, and scared shitless. Fortunately the skins retreated up the street. Safely on the 783 bus, fear turned to exhilaration. Our fellow Pakistanis had wrought justice on some of those bastards sons of Enoch. The waiters had really hurt the skins, who doubtless had tried to disturb the peaceful consumption of curries. This was like payback for all the years of schoolyard abuse. Though I was a mute witness to the violence, the incident proved that we Asians were not the passive race the whites made us out to be. The Smiths's "Barbarism Begins at Home,"

which Morrissey had sung only minutes earlier, seemed shockingly appropriate. Morrissey had a way of pinpointing the violence that was normal in northern homes, schools, and streets. My near run-in with the skinheads in Leeds also presaged the solo Morrissey song, "Asian Rut,' in which the narrator passively watches an Asian boy getting beaten up by white youths. Though I, of course, had watched a white skin being assaulted.

Like me, the Smiths were northern. Morrissey, Marr, Rourke, and Joyce came from Manchester. Their music photographed the industrial north in economic decline. Morrissey's lyrics and Johnny Marr's plaintive guitar arrangements lovingly drew a bleak urban landscape of bus stops, bedsit flats, disused railway lines, canals and iron bridges. On the inner sleeve of their album *The Queen Is Dead,* the Smiths stand in front of Salford Lads Club on the corner of Coronation Street, the original setting for Granada TV's long-running soap opera. *Coronation Street* represents the quintessential northern working-class street and neighborhood.[21] In the 1930s, the photographs and ethnographic descriptions of Mass Observation and George Orwell's *The Road to Wigan Pier* revealed the poverty of the mythical working-class street. For Richard Hoggart in *The Uses of Literacy* (1957), this "landscape with figures" and its neighborly working-class culture were threatened by mass American-style consumerism. In the early 1960s, the "kitchen sink" films turned this urban landscape into a poetic mirror for the existential desolation and class resentments of angry young men (but very few angry young women). By the 1980s, this vision of the north had been pastiched and parodied endlessly to the point of cliché: aye, we all knew "it was grim up north." However, this mythology of "northernness" still asserted a defiant regionalism in a period when the north was suffering most from Thatcherite policies.[22]

The Smiths adopted many of these representational tropes. Record sleeves reproduced photographs of Rita Tushingham and Terence Stamp, stars of some of these kitchen-sink films. The group cited snatches of film dialogue in songs, even directly sampled from these films on their recordings. Teenage playwright Shelagh Delaney, writer of *A Taste of Honey,* was a favorite reference in record sleeves and songs. Pat Phoenix, star of *Coronation Street,* was the "cover star" for the Woolfian single "Shakespeare's Sister." The group's few videos included clips of vintage British films and often surveyed this classic working-class landscape.

Morrissey's romance with this iconography reworked popular memory, looking back at a past that had almost disappeared, at a landscape transformed from satanic mills to shopping malls. Working through the mythical tropes of English northern "ordinariness" with wit and invention, the Smiths' images and sounds responded both to Thatcherism's assault on working-class people, and expressed a regional solidarity against the false glitter and yuppie consumerism of a more prosperous south in its temporary economic boom.[23] In the north, middle-class university students and graduates seemed downwardly mobile, spending intermittent and sometimes long periods on the dole in an economic climate where academic qualifications didn't translate into employment. Higher education kept at bay the dole's mind-deadening subsistence lifestyle, the privatized hell of the thriving service and financial sectors, and provided some kind of narrative of a future. Hugo Young notes in his biography of Margaret Thatcher that in 1981 a "Tory backbencher returned from a visit to Hartlepool, in North-east England, with the intelligence that according to the town's director of education it was now statistically more probable that a young person would get to university than get a job."[24] However, with cuts in government spending on education throughout the 1980s, some chose to escape to foreign parts, "refugees from Thatcher-

ism" as Janet Wolff puts it.[25] On the BBC's *Top of the Pops* in 1984, Morrissey caught the narrowing possibilities with close-to-the-bone humor when he sang, "I was looking for a job and now I've found a job / But heaven knows I'm miserable now."[26]

Morrissey seemed to dissolve the distance between public and private space in his songwriting. His lyrics obsessed over adolescent angst, everyday humiliations, and the misery of not belonging. But personal traumas were always placed in a concrete public context, usually the landscape of the northern city. In rock mythology, the street is where the boys are, where the action is, the road to empowerment, or at least the place where the lads hang out and look good. But Smiths songs with their plangent guitar lines articulated the loneliness, danger, and violence of city streets. On *The Queen Is Dead* (1986), Morrissey sings that "you walk without ease on these the very streets where you were raised."[27] "The Death of a Disco Dancer," a song from the Smiths' last studio album *Strangeways, Here We Come,* suggests that "if you think peace is a common goal, it goes to show how little you know."[28] This had a particular resonance for a fan like me, familiar with everyday racist indignities, and the brutalities that had left British Asians insulted, bruised, seriously maimed, or dead.

Rock encyclopedias might describe the Smiths's meteoric career as garnering fifteen Top Thirty singles and seven Top Ten albums, including a Number One in *The Queen Is Dead.* The Smiths achieved national success and international "alternative" appeal on independent label Rough Trade. In the United States their recordings were licensed to Sire, part of the Time-Warner empire. From 1987, Morrissey solo product was sold on the EMI label in Britain (under the Beatles' former label Parlophone for that vintage British look), and Sire in the United States. He has developed his career as an international pop artist fairly typically with regular album releases, video promotion, television appearances, tours, carefully timed press interviews, and so on. As he has gotten older, less scrawny, and more affluent, the imagery on his record sleeves reflects an increasing narcissism. While the sleeve for the Smiths's second single "This Charming Man" (1983) had featured Jean Marais gazing at a mirror-pool in Cocteau's *Orphee,* now Morrissey is the singular photographic subject on single sleeves, seemingly obsessed with the camera's every angle on his face, the dimensions of his quiff, the jewelry adorning the hairs on his chest.[29] "Fame, fame, fatal fame, it can play hideous tricks on the brain," he'd quipped in "Frankly, Mr. Shankly" on *The Queen Is Dead,* and like many a pop star before him, he began now to sing more about the psychological perils of fame, the need for love, and the dynamic between star and audience. In his body of work, now in its mannerist stage, loneliness and unrequited love sit alongside homoerotic paeans to working-class young men. The Smiths had recorded songs about Rusholme Ruffians and Sweet and Tender Hooligans, mixing fear, envy, and adoration, with a sarcastic edge; now characters like the Kray Twins, the Artful Dodger, and the gangsters of Grahame Greene's *Brighton Rock* form part of Morrissey's gallery of lovable rogues.

The solo work has achieved moderate chart success in the UK, while Morrissey's star continues to rise in North America. In Britain, he generated some controversy with a song that appeared to tell Asians that they didn't belong in Britain. "Bengali in Platforms" uses the fashion ineptitude of a settler in the 1970s to say, "Shelve your western plans / Life is hard enough when you belong here."[30] Another song, "Asian Rut" describes a violent encounter between white youths and an Asian. The doubts about Morrissey's Little Englandism were seriously compounded by the 1992 release of the album *Your Arsenal* and an outdoor concert that summer.

On Saturday, August 8, 1992 in Los Angeles,

California, tickets for Morrissey's show at the Hollywood Bowl sold out in twenty-three minutes, breaking a longstanding record held by the Beatles.[31] Meanwhile, in Finsbury Park, north London, Morrissey played support slot for English pop group Madness at its "Madstock" reunion concert. Dressed in blue jeans and an open-necked gold lamé shirt, he sashayed across the stage against a huge projected backdrop of two skinhead girls. During the song "Glamorous Glue," he swirled a Union Jack flag around himself and lyrically lamented, "We look to Los Angeles for the language we use. London is dead! London is dead!"

This performance of Britishness resulted in a volley of homophobic insults, sieg-heils, and small projectiles hurled by neo-Nazi skinhead fans of Madness. Morrissey's use of the loaded signifiers of National Flag and Skinhead also sparked various forms of abuse from antiracist sections of the audience concerned with the rise in racist attacks, and the renewed and vigorous recruitment of skinheads by extreme right-wing organizations. Just outside Finsbury Park that Saturday, National Front and British Movement supporters held aloft Union Jacks in opposition to a Troops Out (of Northern Ireland) march. Upset with the Madstock crowd's response, Morrissey stormed off stage, never to return that night. A press statement issued the next day claimed that he was forced to abandon his performance after being hit in the face by an orange-juice carton and a fifty-pence coin thrown by "National Front skinheads."

This musical moment spilled over with local/national/ transnational ironies: a pop star in London tells his audience that local language and culture are dead at the hands of American cultural imperialism while he spectacularly sells out a concert in Los Angeles; a performer known for this androgyny and Oscar Wilde obsession is abused by the macho, determinedly hetero English skins he seems to celebrate; and the war in Northern Ireland looms large (if offstage) as an English singer of Irish-Catholic descent wraps himself in the Union Jack.

Following the Madstock debacle, the nominally left-liberal British music papers almost uniformly pounced on Morrissey's flirtation with nationalist imagery. When he refused to respond to charges of racism, they exhumed all questionable song references to Asian immigrants, black music, Americanization, National Front youth, and football hooligans. Contentious interview statements about reggae, the Channel Tunnel, and Englishness made during Morrissey's career were cited as evidence for the prosecution. Morrissey seemed to have worryingly racist tendencies. His former fans Anglo-Asian rock group Cornershop burnt a poster of Morrissey outside EMI's offices in London, admittedly to get some press coverage for themselves as pop situationists, but the gesture was also motivated by genuine hurt and disgust at the singer's brush with fascinatin' fascism at a moment of increased racist violence. Morrissey graffiti was found and photographed alongside British National Party scrawlings on a wall in London's East End where British fascists have had some electoral success since the 1930s days of Oswald Mosley and his blackshirts. Bangladeshi British residents face daily attacks to their bodies, homes, and businesses in these neighborhoods. Photographs in the music press showed Morrissey smirking at the camera in a t-shirt with a photograph of an angry skinhead defiantly sticking two fingers up at the camera. Like the skinhead, the pop star shared a desire to provoke; though with a large fan base on both sides of the Atlantic, he didn't need to court controversy purely for publicity's sake. In one photograph, Morrissey wore a shirt emblazoned with the St. George's cross of the English flag, in another he proudly displayed a Britain-shaped badge on his denim jacket. Concert performances were heralded with a recording of William Blake's "Jerusalem," a hymn appropri-

ated as another national anthem. The case for the prosecution seemed, however, to rest predominantly on a couple of provocative tracks from *Your Arsenal*. "We'll Let You Know" and "The National Front Disco" deal with well-known aspects of working-class nationalism: football hooligans and far-right political organizations. The songs do not refer directly to skinheads (of course, not all skinheads are right-wing and vice versa), but in dominant media discourse in Britain the association is clear. For many people, it's a thin line between shaven-headed youth, soccer hooligans, and neo-Nazism.

Your Arsenal, track three: "We'll Let You Know" responds to official "documentary" discourse that marginalizes skinheads as the most abject of the English working class. The words and music accentuate the pathos of their plight. "How sad are we? / And how sad have we been? / We'll let you know / But only if you're really interested," sings Morrissey over a plaintive acoustic guitar. The voice of the singer is the collective voice of the football hooligans. However, the defense for bad behavior is couched in ironic terms: "We're all smiles / And honest, I swear it's the turnstiles / That make us hostile / And the songs we sing / They're not supposed to mean a thing . . . la la la / We will descend on anyone unable to defend / Themselves." Football supporters go through the "turnstiles" to enter the stadium, but this also suggests that the fans are coralled like animals. A long instrumental break follows these words as an electric guitar wails tremulously. A faint sample of the words, "Get off the roof" can be heard during this part of the song. The soundbite is taken from Peter Medak's film *Let Him Have It*, about the execution of hapless working-class teenager Derek Bentley by the machinery of the British state in the early 1950s, after his involvement in the killing of a policeman. The previously subdued music builds up to a crescendo as a sample of football fans chanting on the terraces provides a kind of melancholic chorus. The acoustic guitar is drowned out by more dissonant electric chords. Morrissey then intones: "We may seem cold / Or we may even be the most depressing people you will ever know / But at heart we sadly know / That we are the last truly British people you will ever know." The music comes to a shuddering halt as he repeats, "The last truly British people you will ever, never, want to know." The music shifts momentarily to the kind of military pipe-and-drum band march heard at Protestant, Orange Day parades in Northern Ireland. Here it evokes a hardline, right-wing British nationalism. Then the music fades away into silence almost as soon as it begins, a decaying echo of the past to match the doomed end of "the last truly British you will ever know."

Repeated listening to the song suggests that Morrissey is not celebrating acts of football violence or nationalism. First, the song comments on discourse about the hooligan. Notions of the "British hooligan" have cemented themselves in the public consciousness for several reasons: supporters are held mainly responsible for the 1980s football disasters at Heysel and Hillsborough, even though unsafe facilities and bad policing were at least partially responsible for the deaths in Brussels and Sheffield respectively. British soccer fans have developed a reputation for going abroad, getting drunk, and pissing in the fountains of Europe's city squares before fighting pitched battles with opposing fans and local police. The football hooligan has become a national institution. When England plays another national football team, home or abroad, sociologists, police experts, and various pundits appear in the media to explain this "English disease." Since the soccer disasters of the late 1980s, grounds have become better equipped, clubs are more corporate and tickets more expensive. Soccer fans are more organized. These factors contribute to football once again becoming hip as popular culture. Book-

stores are even full of autobiographical accounts of "my years as a hooligan," amounting to almost a literary/journalistic genre. Stories about football hooligans provide middle-class British readers with a salacious kick, a dose of the ultra-violence similar to the thrill of gangsta rap for a white suburban audience in the United States. These tales allow the audience the vicarious thrill of working-class laddish transgressions from a safe distance.[32]

On his 1995 album *Southpaw Grammar*, "Reader Meets Author" rips apart those who seek to "understand" the working class but have no clue. There may be a hint of self-deprecation in the words. If not, Morrissey has overlooked his own romantic fascination with the working class *yob:* "You don't know a thing about their lives / They live where you wouldn't dare to drive. . . . Books don't save them / Books aren't Stanley knives / And if a fight broke out tonight / You'd be the first away, because you're not that type. . . . So safely with your soft way / Miles from the front line / You hear their sad voices / And you start to imagine things."

Your Arsenal, track four: "The National Front Disco" is as aggressive in its rock guitar sound and forward-looking in its lyrics as "We'll Let You Know" is musically restrained and elegiac in tone. The song describes the enthusiasm of a boy who wants to join the NF despite the anguished protestations of his parents. Morrissey voices the boy's racist slogans like "England for the English" as if they were nursery rhymes. He offers an understanding commentary and empathic commentary on the boy's revenge fantasies: "You look forward to the day you can settle the score." Then he wails the parental worries: "Where is my boy? I've lost my boy. He's going to the National aaaghhh!" The parents are so exasperated, they cannot come to utter the horrible full name of the right-wing party. Morrissey identifies the disillusion that turns the boy toward an organization that promises to give him a sense of belonging. His marginalized, outsider status marks him with a certain pathos. As Armond White puts it, Morrissey "risks the anger of people who want to pretend that the kids are always all right or that fascism has no attraction."[33] Morrissey rationalizes for the boy: "There's a country / You don't live there / But someday you would like to / And you might do / If you show them what you're made of / Then one day you might do." Then Morrissey mimics the voice of "reason" and skepticism as the parents explain, "David, we wonder / If the thunder / Is ever really gonna begin." Shifts in point of view common to Morrissey songs make it difficult to pin down his position on the issue. The power of the recording lies in the way it presents the boy's desire. He longs for independence from his parents and yearns for a utopian elsewhere, back to the future of the white British nation-state. Adolescent freedom is equated with nationalist longing.

"We'll Let You Know" and "The National Front Disco" work through the discursive terrain outlined by Hebdige in his essay "Hiding in the Light." By the late 1980s, there has been a subtle shift in the cultural studies approach to the skin. The style in which the skinhead is represented becomes more important than the way the skin represents himself or herself. Regimes of representation have taken precedence over the skinhead's agency. Discursive power becomes the focus. Hebdige concludes that "youth" is janus-headed: youth-as-fun, youth-as-trouble. He uses photographs of skinheads and punks to explain their position in the documentary photography tradition as either a criminal threat or as victims in the inner-city concrete jungle. The skinhead is the "object of Our fear" or "object of Our compassion."[34] These are the "two skinheads" we encounter most often in the familiar regimes of representation within news media and the academic domains of sociology and cultural studies.[35]

Maybe Morrissey is the Jean Genet of the football terraces. Skinheads are beautiful losers. They embody a dying Britishness. The skinhead is also attractive because he is unsullied by matters of the mind, a common fantasy about the working class. He is not intellectual but physical. In a 1993 press interview with Tony Parsons, Morrissey says: "They don't need to use their imaginations all that much—they act upon impulse—and that's very enviable. Theirs is a naturalness which I think is a great art form, which I can't even aspire to."[36] Morrissey's skinheads are noble savages. Supporting him on this matter, Parsons states that his attraction to "shaven-headed machismo has nothing to do with right-wing tendencies and everything to do with the grudging admiration he feels for lives that can be lived without angst. The attraction is not political but psychological."[37]

Apart from not giving the skinhead much credit for brains, this perspective too neatly separates the political from the psychological. Morrissey's approach is aesthetic and erotic, but has political implications too. Despite a long history of representing the skinhead's homosocial world, its homosexual implications are rarely acknowledged. Morrissey opens up this possibility, and this is why he met with skinhead homophobia at the Madstock concert. His love affair with "hardness," a tough working-class masculinity, is politically ambiguous. Eroticizing and aestheticizing the skin's hypermasculinity may question that masculinity's very construction, but such a gesture of serious camp may also fail to undermine masculine power. The preoccupation with macho working-class lads is part of an important history of transgressive sexual desire that crosses class boundaries. However, the attractions of the hard skinhead are not easily separated from often racist and nationalist politics.[38]

Pat Kane describes the ambiguous politics of this romance in his review of a Morrissey concert at Glasgow Barrowlands in February 1995. After a lacklustre start the band and Morrissey only warm up when they begin the song "The National Front

Disco." Kane notices that some people in the audience sing along weakly with the chorus line of "National Front . . . National Front":

> At that moment, something smelled extremely rotten in the state of adult rock. But as the song appropriately dissolved into white noise frenzy, Morrissey adjusted his jacket, stepped forward and began to croon, rather beautifully, "Moon River," the old tear-jerker covered on the current CD.
>
> I'm gagging at his audacity. Is Morrissey taking this anthem of the white trash, Enoch Powellite, sixties-seventies generation and forcing us to confront how the most virulent hatreds can seethe alongside the most gauzy and romantic fantasies? Are we being presented with both the banality of England's evil, and the evil of England's banality? One dearly hopes so: for what also gives these seven minutes their queasy power is the faint possibility that Morrissey perhaps understands this tumorous England, and its skin-headed carcinogens, far too well. "We're after the same rainbow's end," runs "Moon River"'s key line.[39]

Julian Evans suggests that other songs on *Your Arsenal* which appear to be about love—"It's gonna happen someday" and "Tomorrow"—could just as well articulate a "totalitarian longing" for a white England.[40] Evans defends Morrissey's prying open of this can of worms: "To have any kind of discussion about Englishness, as he has discovered, is practically impossible now—though it may be worth remembering in the future Claude Lévi-Strauss's warning in his autobiography: we should question carefully, even sadly if we wish, "the future of a world whose cultures, all passionately fond of one another, would aspire only to celebrate one another in such confusion that each would lose any attraction it could have for the others and its own reasons for existing."[41]

It's doubtful that we are anywhere near this state of affairs, or that "globalization" has dissolved national cultural distinctions. The ambiguities in Morrissey's "nationalist" position become less ambiguous and more troubling when he makes statements that wouldn't sound amiss on the lips of Enoch Powell or Margaret Thatcher. On the Bengali inhabitants of London's East End, Morrissey remarks: "I suppose there has been a complete invasion." When interviewer Tony Parsons suggests that this has enriched the national culture, he replies: "No, not at all." Then Morrissey suggests, like Evans, that "it's a subject that can't really be discussed. Because if you try to open it out and have the broad discussion it's almost like admitting that there is a case for racism." There's a reluctance on Morrissey's part to admit that cultural nationalism may be a form of racism. He does admit the limits of his own Little Englandism: "I think it's the village atmosphere, the small-mindedness, which is still very much a part of me. I can't shake it off. I can't become internationalised and I don't think of the world as a place that is mine. I don't feel that I can go anywhere I choose to go. But I think I've pounded my Englishness into the ground. It's just me. I don't claim to have a copyright on the English stamp."[42]

But what claim does the British Asian have on the English stamp? In "Bengali in Platforms" from 1988's *Viva Hate* (1998), the Bengali who wears unfashionable platform shoes is trying to make the English love him through a (failed) impersonation of westernness. He's a pathetic creature: "he only wants to impress you . . . and embrace your culture . . . and to be your friend forever." According to Morrissey, the integration of such a sorry sight into the national way of life is impossible. He addresses the Bengali directly: "I break the news to you gently / Shelve your western plans / Bengali, Bengali / It's the touchy march of time that binds you / don't blame me / don't hate me / just because I'm the one to tell you / that life is hard enough when you belong here." I have to admit that Morrissey's description of the sartorial inadequacies of the Bengali reminds me of the recent Asian migrants we saw in post-punk Birmingham and Bradford, who always seemed to dress in unfashionable seventies gear (dodgy color-coordination, bell-bottoms, and platforms) and about whom my brothers, sister, and I would have a supercilious middle-class assimilated laugh. But according to Morrissey, the Bengali must be reminded that he will *never* belong; a sense of belonging is hard enough to achieve for the alienated local, so the outsider has little chance of ever feeling at home in England.

"Asian Rut" from 1991's *Kill Uncle* (1991), about an Asian boy fighting with white thugs to avenge the killing of his friend further suggests Morrissey's attitude to Britain as a multiracial nation. The plight of the Asian is dealt with pathos and dark comic rhyming: "Tough and hard and pale / Oh, they may impale you on railings." The melodrama of the scene is pushed to the max with mawkish, melancholic music that recalls the northern brass band soundtrack from old Hovis Bread television ads set in a vintage heritage north. "Asian Rut" ends with Morrissey observing, "I'm just passing through here / On my way to somewhere civilized / And maybe, I'll even arrive."[43] The tone is one of sadness and inevitability. The Asian will get beaten up because he doesn't belong. That's the way it is. Violence isn't celebrated, simply deemed the only possible consequence of the presence of non-whites in the nation.

Morrissey's staging of the white working class in Little England shares some of the features of George Orwell's representation of the "proles" in *1984*. Patrick Wright suggests that in Orwell's activation of popular memory about the working class in his novel, "the past is imagined as the hopelessly redemptive trace of values which are all but totally buried by a destructive and inferior present. Thus human value comes to be associated with an everyday life which has been shredded and is no longer capable of supporting anything except particularistic argument and quarrel."[44] In a 1990 interview Morrissey opines: "Even people who are quite level-headed and quite capable of happiness feel that this country is absolutely shamboli-

cally doomed."[45] His work suggests, not so much how wonderful the past was (though at least it was *our* white English past), but how awful the present is, and how dreadful the future will be. This apocalyptic approach to the British way of life is a response to Britain's diminishing power and the myriad local and national transformations brought about by globalization. In an era of uncertainty, the myth of a Little England and its white ethnicity reveals a poverty of vision, an inability to imagine a different future for Britain that isn't defined by its whiteness and cultural insularity. As Jesus-Martin Barbero points out, in the search for the quintessentially national—in this case, "the last truly British people you will ever know"—that which is native is defined within stricter limits: "transformed into the touchstone of identity, the indigenous would seem to be the only thing which remains for us of the "authentic," that secret place in which the purity of our cultural roots remains and is preserved. All the rest is contamination and loss of identity."[46]

In this regard, as a studious fan I want to concede to Morrissey the escape clause of irony—that he doesn't really mean it, and he's just provoking Brits to think about the past, juggling the images, sounds, notions and potions of collective memory. This is the attraction of tricksters. Repeated listening to the songs suggests that Morrissey is a ventriloquist, posing different voices against each other. You're never very sure which voice belongs to him. On the other hand, the ambiguities of this kind of queer English tricksterism leave me frustrated too. I sometimes feel that it's about bloody time the British got beyond irony as a device to deal with their limited repertory of the national. As much as an ironic mode has the potential to critique certain versions of history, irony can serve to evade realities and new possibilities as it takes apart the same decaying body of national cultural concerns again and again with its blunt scalpel. I remain stuck in an ambivalent bind: irony can be exasperating, but who wants politically correct music! You can't escape the ironies of being English or British, whether you're Morrissey, a skinhead, or a Paki. Maybe irony is a necessary mechanism through which certain versions the national must be invoked and thus disempowered, before being eventually disavowed. One hopes that camping the national robs it of its power. But irony and camp can also keep the crushing ordinariness of English racism at bay without destroying it. As Hanif Kureishi remarks: "Very few people in England would want to be considered not to have a sense of humor, and the English are very self-conscious about not being considered to be stony-faced about things. So if someone says, 'You fuck off home, you Paki,' you have to laugh about it, and that works all the way through. The levels of irony—you would get lost in them over here." [47]

Notes

I would like to thank the following people for their help with this essay: the editors of this anthology, Mia Carter, Mary Desjardins, Shuchi Kothari, and Neil Nehring.

1 George Mikes, *How to Be an Alien* (London: Andre Deutsch, 1946), reprinted in *How to Be a Brit* (Harmondsworth: Penguin, 1986), 18–20.

2 Tom Nairn, *The Enchanted Looking-Glass: Britain and Its Monarchy* (London: Radius, 1988).

3 Quoted in Chris Heath, *Pet Shop Boys: Literally* (London: Viking 1990), 59.

4 Michael Bracewell, "Selling England by the Sound," in *England Is Mine: Pop Life in Albion from Wilde to Goldie* (London: HarperCollins, 1997), 211–36.

5 See Michael Billig, *Banal Nationalism* (London: Sage, 1995), for a discussion of the everyday, routine ways that belonging to the nation is signaled in the media and society.

6 Mancunians will report that large parts of the city of Manchester have since been gentrified and redeveloped in the 1990s (with the help of European money).

7 Sarah Champion, *And God Created Manchester* (London: Wordsworth, 1990).

8 See the discussion of Greil Marcus's work in John Street, *Rebel Rock: The Politics of Popular Music* (Oxford: Basil Blackwell, 1986), 157.

9 Philip Cohen, "The Perversions of Inheritance: Studies in the Making of Multi-Racist Britain," in *Multi-Racist Britain,* ed. Philip Cohen and Harbajan S. Bains (London: Macmillan, 1988), 83.

10 A memorable photograph by Nick Knight taken in the early 1980s shows a skinhead facing an elderly gray-bearded Pakistani Muslim man and giving him the Nazi salute. They stand just a few feet away from each other, alone on a piece of urban wasteland. The caption notes that the Pakistani returned the salute a few minutes later. See Nick Knight, *Skinhead* (London: Omnibus, 1982).

11 Carolyn Steedman, "Landscape for a Good Woman," in *Truth, Dare, or Promise: Girls Growing up the 1950s,* ed. Liz Heron (London: Virago, 1985), 122.

12 Annette Kuhn, *Family Secrets* (London: Verso, 1995), 107.

13 Elspeth Probyn, *Sexing the Self: Gendered Positions in Cultural Studies* (London: Routledge, 1993), 20.

14 Dick Hebdige, *Subculture: The Meaning of Style* (London: Methuen, 1979), 58.

15 Pete Fowler, "The Emergence of the Skinhead" in *The Faber Book of Pop,* ed. Hanif Kureishi and Jon Savage (London: Faber and Faber, 1995), 378–84.

16 The better version of the song can be found on the debut album *The Clash* (CBS, 1977).

17 See the excellent discussion of cartoonish Oi! punk and the "degeneration of the punk rock dialectic" in more loathsome "fascist" skinhead bands like Skrewdriver in Stewart Home, *Cranked Up Really High: An Inside Account of Punk Rock* (London: Codex, 1995).

18 John Clarke, "The Skinheads and the Magical Recovery of Community," in *Resistance through Rituals: Youth Subcultures in Post-War Britain,* ed. Stuart Hall and Tony Jefferson (London: Routledge, 1993), 99–102.

19 Paul Du Noyer, "The Seventies: Rebellion, Revival, and Survival," in *Cool Cats: 25 Years of Rock 'n' Roll Style,* ed. Tony Stewart (New York: Delilah Press, 1982), 104.

20 See Angela McRobbie, "Settling Accounts with Subcultures: A Feminist Critique," in *On Record: Rock, Pop, and the Written Word,* ed. Simon Frith and Andrew Goodwin (New York: Pantheon, 1990), 66–80.

21 Richard Dyer, Christine Geraghty, Marion Jordan, Terry Lovell, Richard Patterson, and John Stewart, *Coronation Street* (London: BFI, 1981).

22 Listen to the Justified Ancients of Mu Mu's hit "It's Grim Up North" in which a list of northern towns is read ominously over a propulsive electronic beat, sounding to London ears as foreign as a Latin litany in the Vatican.

23 Simon Reynolds, "Miserabilism: Morrissey" in *Blissed Out: The Raptures of Rock* (London: Serpent's Tail, 1990), 15–29.

24 Hugo Young, *One of Us* (London: Macmillan, 1991), 317.

25 Janet Wolff, *Resident Alien: Feminist Cultural Criticism* (London: Polity Press, 1995), 1–22.

26 The Smiths, "Heaven Knows I'm Miserable Now," Rough Trade UK 45, 1984.

27 The Smiths, "Never Had No One Ever," from *The Queen Is Dead*, Rough Trade UK, 1986.

28 The Smiths, *Strangeways, Here We Come*, Rough Trade UK, 1987.

29 See the book of tour photographs taken by Linder Sterling, Morrissey's friend, former lead singer of Ludus, and graphic artist, in *Morrissey Shot* (New York: Hyperion, 1992).

30 Morrissey, *Viva Hate*, EMI UK, 1988.

31 *New Musical Express* (August 22, 1992).

32 One such text, Bill Buford's *Among the Thugs* (London: Martin Secker and Warburg, 1991), works in the tradition of Orwell. The roving male journalist enters the nether world of proletarian life and emerges with a vivid piece of literary journalism for review in the Sunday supplements. Buford's book is gripping, mainly for its laconic detailing of the perils of participant observation. Buford gets beaten up too, often by police. However, like many a study before it, *Among the Thugs* resorts to dubious quasi-sociological concepts of the "mob" and the "crowd" in order to understand working-class behavior. Buford also describes a nervous night out at a pub in East Anglia where a National Front disco is held. Maybe the description of this disco inspired the Morrissey song "The National Front Disco."

33 Armond White, "Anglocentric: Morrissey," *Village Voice* (September 1, 1992): 70.

34 Dick Hebdige, *Hiding in the Light: On Images and Things* (London: Routledge, 1988), 17–36.

35 *Cracker*, Granada Television's detective show starring Robbie Coltrane as a drinking, gambling, but brilliant police psychologist, theatricalized the continuing crisis in white working-class power with a 1994 storyline that brought skinheads, Pakistanis, and football together in an ideologically ambiguous and charged space. "To Be a Somebody" centered on Alby, a white working-class Liverpool fan who works the nightshift at a factory. He is frustrated with life after the death of his father from cancer, the break-up of his marriage, and problems with his fellow workers on the shopfloor. On his way home from work one morning, he stops by a corner- shop to pick up a newspaper and a bottle of milk, which together cost him one pound and four pence. He only has a pound, and the fastidious Pakistani owner will not let him take the goods until he has produced the four pence. They argue and Alby storms out of the shop empty handed. At home he shaves his head, returns to the shop with his late father's British army bayonet, throws the four pence at the Pakistani, calls him a "thieving Paki" repeatedly, then stabs him to death. After the murder, Alby scrawls the number 9615489 in blood on the shop wall. We learn later that this refers to the 96 Liverpool fans killed in the Hillsborough disaster on 15 April 1989. Alby intends to kill exactly 96 people. He targets a tabloid journalist who had written a story blaming Liverpool supporters for the Hillsborough disaster. A university criminologist who comes up with a psychological profile of the Pakistani's murderer is also confronted by Alby. The profile describes the killer as a typical white racist skinhead. Alby tells him that he listens to Mozart and is nothing like this stereotype, then stabs him to death and photocopies his head. He kills a police detective, and turns up at a Manchester United v. Liverpool match in the Manchester end, before finally being apprehended. We learn that Alby and his father witnessed the terrible events at Hillsborough and Alby's father could not bear to go to another football match after this disaster. During interrogation, Alby tells the police psychologist that he became a skinhead because that's what everyone—the police, the politicians, and the media—expects of white working-class football fans. He has transformed himself into this folk devil as a protest against a discourse that marginalizes the white working class. At one point, Alby says that the bizzies (politicians) and the bourgeois lefties listen to the blacks, Pakis, and queers but have no time for the white working class. This *Cracker* story, with all its contrived plotting, does theatricalize a "structure of feeling" among the disenfranchised white working class.

36 Tony Parsons, *Dispatches from the Front Line of Popular Culture* (London: Virgin, 1994), 93–96.

37 Quoted in Jo Slee, *Peepholism: Into the Art of Morrissey* (London: Sidgwick and Jackson, 1994), 159.

38 For a provocative reading of this history of upper-class men and working-class young men's sexual relations, see Alan Hollinghurst's novel *The Swimming-Pool Library* (New York: Vintage, 1988).

39 *Guardian* (February 1995).

40 Julian Evans, "The Object of Love," *Guardian Weekend* (February 26, 1994): 6–11.

41 Ibid., 6.

42 Parsons, *Dispatches from the Front Line*, 95–96.

43 Morrissey, *Kill Uncle*, EMI UK, 1990.

44 Patrick Wright, "The Ghosting of the Inner City," in *On Living in an Old Country: The National Past in Contemporary Britain* (London: Verso, 1985), 243.

45 Nick Kent, "The Deep End," an interview in the *Face* (March 1990).

46 Quoted in David Morley and Kevin Robins, "Spaces of Identity: Communications, Technologies, and the Reconfiguration of Europe," *Screen* (autumn 1989): 34.

47 Quoted in Jonathan Wilson, "A Very English Story," *New Yorker* (March 1995).

FINDING ONE'S WAY HOME: *I DREAM OF JEANNIE* AND DIASPORIC IDENTITY

Maria Koundoura

Beginnings

I came to dream of Jeannie through a very circuitous route. My family, wanting to leave the economic and political situation of junta-ruled Greece, took advantage of the post–World War II immigration accord between Greece and Australia and joined the 650,000 Greeks already in Australia.[1] We arrived November 10, 1970, on the immigrant ship ironically named *Patris*, homeland. Our passage to Australia was paid for by the Australian government out of the surplus generated from capital exports, the prospect of available labor that encouraged capital holders to move to Australia.[2] The Australian government, in order to guarantee the constancy of this labor, brought in immigrants to fill the factories.

With their passage paid for in the immediate present, and their two-year minimum residency clause and the incremental repayment of that passage in the distant future, my parents decided to ignore the reports from the "battlefront"—stories from friends of friends who were already in Australia—of hardship, of an uncouth wilderness, of immense distance and of not so welcoming natives. They threw in their lot with the Department of Immigration and Ethnic Affairs and its portrait of Australia as a land full of opportunity where, if you worked hard, you could comfortably support your family. Although my parents were alarmed by the rumors, their reason prevailed. It was fueled by their belief that things could not be economically worse for them in such a rich land nor could they be politically worse off because Australia did not have Greece's long history of internal and external strife. Thus, my father came to work for General Motors and my mother for Tom Pappas, a canning plant that was part of the Greek American tycoon's global empire.

It did not take long after our arrival for us to realize that both stories were true: we were not so very welcome—"wogs" that we were—and we had an income that we could only dream of in Greece.[3] Thus, as with many immigrants, we immediately benefited from our exile: we drowned our sorrow at leaving home in a frenzy of consumerism that only the buying power of the "lucky country" could offer.[4] Among other things, we acquired our first-ever TV set—a used black-and-white Phillips that I boasted about in my letters back home.

Like other children of immigrants whose parents worked long hours on the production line, the television set was my babysitter. I came to know *The Jetsons, Tom and Jerry, Speed Racer,* and *The Roadrunner Show,* among others. My younger brother and I began this viewing marathon at 3:30 in the afternoon, after walking home from school, and it continued until six when our parents returned home from work. Six, however, heralded not only my joy at my parents arrival, but also the viewing time of my favorite show, *I Dream of Jeannie.* I loved the theme music, the cartoon of Jeannie coming out of her bottle, her dancing, her costume, her playfulness, Major Nelson's astonishment, his exasperation with her, Dr. Bellows's suspicions about Nelson, and Major Healy's support of the pair. But, most of all, I was transfixed with Jeannie's magical powers. I wanted to be Jeannie. To my mother's chagrin, I walked around the house wearing a long scarf as a veil, folding my arms and blinking at anything in sight.

Looking back, rueful nostalgia aside, I realize that, from the perspective of an eight-year-old Greek girl recently migrated to Australia, watching television, especially *I Dream of Jeannie,* was more than a way to fill time until my parents came home from work. It was one of the ways through which I learned English and a means to transport myself (metaphorically at least) out of my new Australian reality and into the timeless, locationless (for me then) place of the imagination, the place where I wasn't teased for looking different or beaten up because I couldn't speak English. That half-hour show, foreign as it was, allowed me to forget my foreignness and, with the blink of an eye, imagine myself in my grandmother's arms being told stories of heroes and gods.

Though my odyssey of academic legitimization has brought me to the United States, I still dream of Jeannie, but now I can use the cultural capital gained in the intervening years to argue that the show facilitated my displacement from home even as it enabled a double displacement back "home." Jeannie, in other words, in her foreignness made my foreignness to others all the more obvious to me. She also showed me the way to belong. If I could, like her, hide my "difference" in the guise of modernity, I too could pass as a thoroughly modern and not "new Australian" (the official label for immigrants like myself).

This desire, which manifested itself as the need to fit in and resulted in conflicting dual (at best), multiple (at worst), cultural identities, has been the dominant factor in the construction of my identity not only as a diasporic but also as an intellectual. I have spent my life, since that first migration, moving between Greece and Australia (and now the United States) every five years and, as a consequence, in my academic training I have focused on theories of displacement as they are discussed in the most recent critical debates: postcolonialism, multiculturalism, cultural studies. Throughout both my personal and academic experience my main focus has been culture's influence in the construction of narratives of the nation.

I am not unusual in my use of my personal experience in my academic work. As Elspeth Probyn points out, there is a "small industry of theorists [who] turn to themselves, their own difference, trying to explicate the world metonymically from their own." Probyn argues that in contemporary cultural criticism this has been "stretched to the limit."[5] Although, to a degree, I agree with Probyn, nevertheless, I believe that there is still much to be learned from the use of the personal in critical accounts of cultural practices. Through an account of my fascination with *Jeannie,* I want to explore in this chapter the question of the relationship of theory to lived experience. Given the multinational rootlessness of my life, my pleasure with popular culture in general, but especially with *I Dream of Jeannie,* has been a surprising constant, one whose stability was guaranteed by the flow of multinational capital that enabled me to watch the show not only in Australia for the first time but also in Greece and now in the United States. Unlike that initial "innocent" consumption, however, now I wonder whether the very same cultural capital that enables me to recount my experience with the show also impedes my pleasure in it. Then, I "identified" with the show; now, I can either engage it with the high cultural mode of theory and argue with Baudrillard against the possibility of not only identity formation but also representation or, I can enter the world of identity politics and have *Jeannie* represent my otherness either as the twice-migrated Greek Australian living in the United States, or as the Greek, or the Australian.[6] Nowhere in any of these theoretical accounts is there a place for that early consumption of popular culture, its pleasures and especially my use of it in the construction of my imaginary homeland.

Finding a Place from Which to Speak

Illustrating their common genealogy in the circuit of Anglo-American cultural studies, most cultural critics in their readings of popular culture are caught on one side of the dilemma Fredric Jameson identifies when he argues that, under multinational capitalism, "if individual experience is authentic, then it cannot be true; and . . . if a scientific or cognitive model of the same content is true, then it escapes individual experience."[7]

Anxious to portray "authentic experience" and avoid the elitism of theory, critics of one type emphasize their and others' enjoyment of popular culture by stressing, in mostly empirical studies, audience reception without reading the complicated ideological structures behind that reception. Meanwhile, despite the risk of being perceived as practicing a paternalistic politics, other critics read cultural imperialism as an ideological property of the text itself, condemn it and the people who consume it as participating in "false consciousness," and attempt to "speak for" the culture as a whole.[8]

These two poles represent the scope of the methodological and theoretical context available to me in this essay. I, with my added trait of the "native informant"—a trait so valuable in ethnographic research—want to step outside current readings on the use of television in my identity formation and find a place for the pleasure I had and have in watching *I Dream of Jeannie.* I am neither the "duped" and uncritical consumer of the cultural imperialism of the United States (also of Anglo-Australia) that these readings would have me be, nor, because of my training, the literate and savvy producer of politico-theoretical critiques of such consumption which, by necessity, because of their theoretical distance, are not "authentic."

I Dream of Jeannie was not only the place where I saw my otherness in the form of the exoticized djin but also the place where I saw that otherness as empowering. It not only inducted me into the dominant culture, it was also the means through which I maintained my otherness by "blinking" a passage home, however fleeting and imaginary. Such a double use and a double pleasure, with all its contradictions, cannot be accounted for in the practices of Anglo-American cultural studies that would have me explore my pleasure in the popular through what Kobena Mercer calls "the all-too-familiar mantra of race, gender, ethnicity, sexuality."[9] In focusing on any one of these, I would have to negate at least one of my multiple identities. My class status, for example, changes according to which country I live in and how my identity is read there: in Greece I am part of the petit bourgeoisie, in Australia, as an immigrant, I am generally seen as working class, while in the United States, because of my academic credentials, I am seen as upper middle class or part of the intellectual elite. A postcolonial or multicultural critique, on the other hand, would read my pleasure in watching *Jeannie* as a product of the imperial dominance of the single integrated market dominated by the United States and have me, as a person of the diaspora, be the victim of this globality. The fact that *Jeannie* functioned as a "school" of English and a lesson in "home" building for me is not taken into account in this equation.

In those early days in Australia, lost in the interstices of the global cultural and economic networks, more acutely felt because of my recent migration, my experience of the present was hampered by the nostalgic return to another more "authentic" present—Greece and its memory of psychological, cultural, and experiential unity. In the abstract space framed by the television set, my window to the world, and its timeless, because foreign, context of 1960s American popular culture, I forgot the foreignness of my present Australian culture and dreamed of the lost past and its recapture in the utopian future. My experience of *I Dream of Jeannie* is a perfect example of Fredric Jameson's argument that "the truth of experience no longer coincides with the place in which it takes place" but is spread-eagled across the world's spaces.[10] For Jameson, in the saturated space of multinational capitalism, place no longer exists except at a "much feebler level," drowned by the other, more powerful abstract spaces of communications networks.

Watching the show was a sign of abstraction for me. Despite my desire to return to Greece, my sense of place was indeed drowned by the more powerful abstract space of the communication network. The Greece that I dreamed of was neither the one I left behind nor the one that developed in my absence; it was, instead, the abstract place of my imagination. Mediated by my vicarious life with *Jeannie,* it was an imaginary place, one in which the reasons for my departure did not exist. Politics and economics, in other words, had no place in that magical kingdom nor did the pain of migration.

Watching the show, however, was also a sign of distraction. Alienated by my Australian reality, I turned to *I Dream of Jeannie* and transformed the abstract space of the communication network into the place of my lived experience. In Jeannie's foreignness I saw mine, in her limited world of the bottle I saw my limited world of the Greek Australian community, and in her constant efforts to hide her otherness I saw my constant battle to fit in. Thus, unlike Jameson's singular and negative reading of the power of communication networks, the show functioned as both a "feeble" and a strong marker of place for me: "feeble" when that place was the Greece of my imagination, strong when that place was the Australia of my then everyday life.

I watched the show in 1970s Australia, a time of political upheaval that led to changes in government and its policies toward immigration, the economy, culture, and the media. For example, 1972 saw the fall of the very popular Whitlam Labour government through an act that reminded Australians of the sovereignty of the queen: her representative, the Governor General, fired Gough Whitlam. His was a government that immigrants felt was sympathetic and helpful to them. In one of its last pieces of legislation, it introduced the multicultural Australia policy to replace the assimilationist policies of the past. For ethnic Australia this meant that, through the establishment of the Department of Immigration and Ethnic Affairs, they could lobby for legislation more sensitive to their needs, they could get funding for their various organizations, and their different cultural and ethnic backgrounds could, on paper at least, be celebrated as contributing to the mosaic of Australian culture.

The early 1970s also saw the end of the post–World War II policy of mass immigration and the introduction of smaller scale and more specialized immigration: family reunions and, most importantly, the encouragement and continuation of capital import driven immigration. Part of this later policy was the encouragement of overseas investment in the Australian film industry, an encouragement that, together with generous government investment in the form of grants and tax breaks, led to the industry's revival.[11]

All of these changes had a huge impact on the up until then quite insular and isolated Australian reality: Australians began to think not only of the identities of their immigrants but also of their own identities. Indicative of its time, the inspiration for the founding of an Australian film industry was the desire to have a cinema that could speak of the national and the local, to have films in which, in the words of an early industry campaigner, "the workaday world is integrated with the world of one's imagination."[12] Thus, from the onset, the industry was heavily protected by the government in the form of subsidies and legislation that mandated the presence of minimum Australian content in foreign co-produced films and television programs, Australian themes in Australian films, and the use of Australian crew members and actors in the films' production. The government also established various agencies to police these mandates: the Australian Broadcasting Tribunal, the Australian Film Commission, and the Australian Council for the Arts.

In 1969 in an Interim Report, the Film Committee of the Australian Council for the Arts, already feeling the pressure of Jameson's abstract spaces and betraying the nationalism that characterizes Australian cultural policy of the time, wrote the following about the role of film and television in the lives of the nation and of government's responsibility to both:

It is in the interests of this nation to encourage its local film and television industry so as to increase the quantity and improve the quality of local material in our cinema and on our television screens. . . . Our audiences are subjected to the ever-increasing sociological influence of imported material, and our writers, actors and film-makers are unable to fulfil their creative potential. . . . This situation hampers Australia's efforts to interpret itself to the rest of the world.

Continuing in this tradition, the Australian Film Commission wrote in 1975:

Australia, as a nation, cannot accept, in this powerful and persuasive medium, the current flood of other nations' production on our screens without it constituting a very serious threat to our national identity.

In 1977 the Australian Broadcasting Tribunal concluded:

An Australian television service which looks unmistakenly Australian has long been regarded as a highly desirable ideal.[13]

Clearly, the discourse underlying these official positions is nationalist. As Elizabeth Jacka has argued, it is nationalist in its protectionism and nationalist in its construction of "Australian-ness."[14] Meanwhile, as I found out at the age of eight, protection from "foreign-ness" did not apply only to the threat posed mostly by American cultural practices and products. (English cultural imports were not seen as foreign at the time since England was, and for a great many Australians still is, considered the "mother country.") "Foreign-ness" was also what all immigrants carried with them, despite the fact that a substantial number of them were second- and third-generation Australians. Thus, there were no Greek-speaking or immigrant theme shows on television and, if there was any portrayal of immigrants, it was generally as uneducated or backward—the colorful comic relief to authentic Australians like those portrayed in shows such as the cop series *Division 4* and the more risqué, because of its adult theme, *Number 96* (both on television in the 1970s). It was only much later (in the 1980s) that the government founded SBS (Special Broadcasting System), whose budget was minuscule compared to the ABC's (Australian Broadcasting Corporation). Available to 75 percent of the population, SBS broadcasts programs from the country of origin of all of Australia's multicultural community and, at the same time, produces original Australian-made shows (news and entertainment) with a multicultural theme.

Against this background, then, I watched *I Dream of Jeannie*. None of the shows on television reflected my Australian reality, and the Australia that they did represent was the one that hurt me: I regularly returned home from school with cuts and bruises, the unwanted trophies from schoolyard scuffles between my name-calling Australian tormentors and myself. Apart from the physical bruising, there was the psychological trauma of muteness: I left Greece a very articulate child and a good student and became in Australia the frustrated and silent non-English-speaking student. Thus, the foreign (initially I did not even register the fact that it was American) and exotic (yet familiar from fairy tales) show about a genie was the one that I could not help but identify with: it spoke to my reality of being both foreign and exotic. It alone reflected my desire to vanish and be somewhere else.

Displaced Fantasies/Fantasies of Displacement

I watched every episode of *I Dream of Jeannie*. Mine was a wholesale acceptance of the show, no discernment there. Individual shows had no lasting effect; it was the constant reminder of the power of her magic that I was after. Her magic was the source of my fascination and my constant fantasies of displacement. My favorite, and the most

baffling episode, however, was one that involved her brunette, and hence, evil, twin. In it, the twin, jealous of Jeannie's fortune in having such a handsome master and living in 1960s Cocoa Beach, manages to dupe Jeannie into switching places and masters with her. The forever gullible Jeannie falls for the trick and finds herself trapped in Baghdad with an old master, archaic in his cruel ways. Initially, Major Nelson cannot tell the difference between the twins, especially since the brunette turned herself into a blonde. After she ends up being too obvious about her advances toward him, however, he realizes that some blondes are more authentic than others: this blonde is not his servile Jeannie but a woman who knows what she wants—him. He refuses her advances, she gets angry and blinks him to Baghdad. A bewildered Major Nelson finds himself in a Baghdad that is timeless: the bazaar with its peddlers and thieves, errant boys, and cruel emissaries of the emir, all in "ancient costume." What a difference from NASA headquarters and 1960s Cocoa Beach! It is here, however, that he manages to find Jeannie, rescue her—and thus himself—and go back home to oust the evil impostor.

When I first saw this episode I certainly didn't see the sexism, orientalism, and imperialism at work in it. I didn't see the problem of having two very powerful, but literally "old fashioned," women fight over the favors of a man who didn't really respect them and who certainly used them, however bumblingly, as a means of shoring up his manhood. I didn't see the strangeness in having Baghdad be timeless, forever ancient, and the United States be the mark of modernity. I also didn't see the problem with having Major Nelson teach both women how to behave, how to learn American ways, how to forget their cultures, and how to stand up for themselves (on his terms, of course). Instead, true to my good Greek upbringing, my anger was directed at the evil twin who fooled poor Jeannie and her master and took something that was not hers. I felt gratified when she was put in her place, sent where she belonged, Baghdad, where masters were masters and djins knew their place.

Apart from this moral, there was another lesson for me in this show, one that didn't play itself out in the field of plot convention and the creation of suspense and resolution in the space of a half hour television show. Jeannie's unwilling return to Baghdad represented the fear that most immigrants have of being sent "back to where they came from." It was a common taunt, one that I heard every day in the schoolyard, and one that left a lasting impression on me: "wogs go home." Could I be forced into going back home? Wasn't going home all I wanted, which is why I imagined that I was Jeannie and could blink my way home to continue the life I had left behind?

My mixed feelings and the contradictory nature of this return were what helped me assimilate into the culture of my new home. I wanted to go back to Greece not as the ousted or failed immigrant but as the triumphant Odysseus coming back from his journey. My dreams of being Jeannie always involved showing off my newfound modernity to the people I left behind, stuck in their "archaic" time. I had all the accoutrements of a growing capitalist economy: television, modern clothes, a new language and multiple stories of places and things that I had seen. My family and friends in Greece, on the other hand, could only show me what I already knew: my place.

Thus I, like Jeannie, was trapped in the bottle of time. Like hers, my place was the world of arabesques: the fake and orientalist interior of her bottle for her, the petrified time of departure from Greece for me. To both of these places she and I staged a continuous return only to turn back dissatisfied with our old selves. After living with Major Nelson, the show implied, she couldn't be happy with her old-fashioned master. After Australia, I couldn't be happy with Greece. And yet that's what I wanted. Like Jeannie's, my "bottle" was always left open: I could come and go as I pleased (after the obligatory two-year stay). I

could be as Australian as the rest; in fact, it was expected that I assimilate. Yet why, like her, did I not choose to live outside my "bottle" in the comfort of my new modern life? I fear that it was because, like her, I always bore the mark of difference in my ways. I wasn't in projected or real ethnic costume like Jeannie, but I might as well have been since I will always be "ethnic" in Australia.

It would seem that the less enlightened and segregated past is behind us now. Yet, as recently as 1987, a report by the Committee to Review Australian Studies at the Tertiary Level, whose purpose was to "enhance citizenship, patriotism and nationalism; secure a productive culture; increase international awareness; bring intellectual enrichment and lead to cultural broadening," placed "understanding and studying the cultures from which all and not only Anglo-Celtic Australians come from" under the goal of "increasing international awareness" and not under "enhancing citizenship."[15] It seems that, for Australia, naturalized Australian citizens like myself will always be foreign. Foreign enough for some of my teachers at the University of Melbourne to marvel at the fact that I, a Greek, was in the English department and not the department of Modern Greek. Foreign enough for "fair dinkum Aussies" to mutter "bloody wogs" whenever we perform a public display of our cultural heritage.

Jeannie's evil twin presented me with another problem: was I, like her, being evil in wanting to assimilate, in wanting to be modern, in throwing off the shackles of a more traditional family and embracing the role of the independent young woman who knows what she wants? Would the past—in the form of her old master in Jeannie's twin's case and Greece and my family in mine—draw me back and leave me nostalgic for my new found ways? Was I not already nostalgic for precisely just that past when I imagined I could blink myself back from my Australian reality? Trapped in this double nostalgia, all I could do was to trick both sides into believing in my "authenticity." Unlike Jeannie's twin, I did not dye my hair blonde, although I did what all blonde Australian kids did: I played cricket, watched football, ate meat pies, wore the same clothes, and developed the typical Australian attitude of nonchalance when being praised for doing well in school—I didn't want to "shine" in difference.[16] Meanwhile, I also had to be the good Greek girl: I went to Saturday Greek school so I wouldn't forget my language, I was properly behaved around adults, and, above all, I tried harder than anyone at school to show those Australians who made fun of immigrants like myself that I wasn't just a "dumb wog." Thus, unlike Jeannie's sister, I wasn't found out, I wasn't sent back home in disgrace, and I certainly could not be labeled "bad." I was the best impostor of them all.

I Dream of Jeannie taught me dissimulation: like her, I could pass as an "ordinary" girl because, like her, I could change my exotic ways with the blink of an eye. It was that very same blink that also made me exotic at home in Greece. In my dreams of return, I regaled my friends and family with the stories of my new home and, like Jeannie, I was always generous with my powers: I shared my knowledge of the new world, I gave them all that they wanted and literally lacked—TVs, new clothes, music, and all the products of the "lucky country." No wonder I took such delight in the show: it confirmed both the reality that I was experiencing and the reality that I wished for, and, along the way, it also taught me some survival tips.

Safe Places: A Theoretically Personal Story

Today I struggle to maintain the specificity of my story and to make sense of the forces that make that story not only peculiar to me but also the story of anyone living in the age of multinational capital. It is difficult. Constantly read as "cosmopolitan," my specialty as a critic working on postcoloniality often used as proof of this cosmopolitanism and my dislocated existence as further proof, there seems to be no place where the "truth" of my story and the "truth" of my theoretical expertise can meet. If Jameson is right and individual experience and cognitive models cancel out each other's truth, then my struggle is essentially quixotic. I will have to choose between my personal experience as a child of eight watching "Jeannie" and my exploration of the methodological and historical context of my viewing of the show. My intention in this essay was neither to add to the work that I have already done as a critic working on postcoloniality nor to write as an innocent-from-theory consumer. Neither my account of my favorite episode of *Jeannie* now nor my then-eight-year-old viewing self are free of critical consciousness. To map out the difference between these two moments in my life as a viewer was also not my intention: what else could that narrative be but a banal stating of the obvious differences in age, location, and training between myself then and now.

I loved watching *Jeannie* then, and I love it now. *Jeannie* was a useful tool for survival in my new home of Australia. Living in the interstices of the dominant culture, I used *Jeannie* as a means of maintaining my identity and my difference. I watch the show now, not in the campy or retro way of most of my friends and—I suspect—most of the viewing public, nor via the ethnographic or semiotic methodological practices of cultural studies. I watch it, instead, with the fondness and familiarity that one has when one finds a favorite old toy. After all, the show created a place for me to make sense of such an abstract, at least to me, space as "Australia."

To the dehistoricizing vacuum of activities like cultural theory, the show helps me to rehistoricize my experience of theoretically abstracted concepts like "identity," "nation," "home." At the same time, as I have argued, those abstracted concepts were understood as such only through my experience of their very real implications: home was not something I questioned until I was forced to think about what "wogs go home" meant, identity was not an issue until I saw that mine was recognized as foreign. *I Dream of Jeannie*, then, far from diminishing my sense of place in the abstract space occupied by communication networks like television, became the tool through which I could occupy that space and turn it into the place of my lived experience.

Postmodern theory would call this practice the effect of the simulacrum that is today's experience of the real. My training in postcolonial theory—and its criticism of postmodernism's culturally insular announcement of the death of the subject and the birth of historical fragments of discourse—halts this prematurely euphoric celebration of the subject's freedom. At the risk of being accused of naïveté at best, modernist belatedness at worst, my turning on/off (being) Jeannie was and is not a historical and fragmented practice. As I have shown in my account of my viewing of the show, it is a practice very much rooted in the "national, the global, and the historical, as well as the contemporary diasporic" that make up "the story of the development of [my] cosmopolitanism"—the cosmopolitanism, that is, of the migrant and not the tourist.[17] As such, it is not the temporary and full-of-pleasure visit to other places and other times of the postmodern subject, but the always never-quite-permanent stay of the "guest worker," the illegal, the immigrant. Jeannie for me represents not the souvenir or the postcard from a temporary visit, but the temporary and hastily built house of the nomad.

In representing the temporary, Jeannie retains its initial function: it still is the means through which I can blink my way home, in the current instance, through this personally theoretical narrative. The show represents my "as if" self, my ability to transport myself to a better place, a place that is both familiar and foreign: the imagined community of the nation which, in my case, can only be represented by the multiple cultures in which I have lived. Since, to paraphrase Raymond Williams, a culture cannot be reduced to its artifacts while it is being lived, only now do I understand the past role of Jeannie in my life: the show

provided me with what Michel Foucault calls a "technology of self." "Technologies of self," writes Foucault, "permit individuals to effect by their own means or with the help of others a certain number of operations on their bodies and souls, thoughts, conduct, and a way of being, so as to transform themselves."[18] I Dream of Jeannie gave me a place from which to speak and an image-repertoire of metaphorical selves with which to speak. In other words, I Dream of Jeannie taught me to theorize, a practice I used and enjoyed then just as much as I do now.

Notes

1 The migration of Greeks to Australia dates back to 1827 but most Greeks in Australia today came after World War II.

2 This policy has a long history in Australia. Known as the Wakefield project, after its author Edward Gibbon Wakefield who dedicated his treatise on the "art of colonisation" to John Hutt the then governor of Western Australia, it was popularized by J. S. Mill in *Principles of Political Economy*. The Wakefield project of colonization was the means through which white settler colonies like Australia, Canada, New Zealand, and South Africa were settled by the British. For a more detailed account of this see my "Multiculturalism or Multinationalism?" in *Multicultural States: Rethinking Difference and Identity*, ed. David Bennett (New York: Routledge, 1998), 69–87.

3 "Wog" was a pejorative term used against "new Australians," immigrants like myself.

4 "The lucky country" is the term that Australians use to refer to their nation. Part an attempt to persuade themselves (immigrants all) of the wisdom of their choice of a new home, part wonder at the vastness and plenitude of this new home, the term was popularized and passed into everyday usage by Donald Horne's book *The Lucky Country* (Baltimore: Penguin, 1964).

5 Elspeth Probyn, "Technologizing the Self," in *Cultural Studies*, ed. Lawrence Grossberg, Cary Nelson, and Paula Treichler (New York: Routledge, 1992), 501–11, 202.

6 Jean Baudrillard, "The Masses: The Implosion of the Social in the Media," in *Selected Writings*, ed. Mark Poster (Stanford: Stanford University Press, 1988), 207–19.

7 Fredric Jameson, "Cognitive Mapping," in *Marxism and the Interpretation of Culture,* ed. Cary Nelson and Lawrence Grossberg (Urbana: University of Illinois Press, 1988), 349.

8 John Fiske, in his seminal book *Television Culture* (London: Methuen, 1987), gives us a classic example of both sides of this equation when he suggests a dual strategy for cultural studies, that of using semiotics to read texts and ethnography to read subjects/fans. Virginia Nightingale has written quite eloquently on the impossibility of this project, especially its ethnographic part. She demonstrates how Fiske's apparently simple formula of "using semiotics to study texts and ethnography to study audiences depends for its coherence on a refusal to acknowledge the theoretical and methodological inadequacies inherent in the enterprise." See "What's 'Ethnographic' about Ethnographic Audience Research?" in *Australian Cultural Studies,* ed. John Frow and Meaghan Morris (Urbana: University of Illinois Press, 1993), 150. Graeme Turner, meanwhile, in an essay that critiques the parochialism of British cultural studies and the colonial genuflecting of some of its Australian practitioners, demonstrates the Eurocentrism of much work. See "'It Works for Me': British Cultural Studies, Australian Cultural Studies, Australian Film," in *Marxism and the Interpretation of Culture,* ed. Nelson and Grossberg, 642.

9 Kobena Mercer, "Welcome to the Jungle: Identity and Diversity in Postmodern Politics," in *Identity, Community, Culture, Difference,* ed. J. Rutherford (London: Lawrence and Wishart, 1990), 43–71.

10 Jameson, "Cognitive Mapping," 349.

11 For an account of the Australian film industry and Australia's cultural policies toward it, see Elizabeth Jacka, "Australian Cinema: An Anachronism in the 1980s?" in *Nation, Culture, Text: Australian Cultural and Media Studies,* ed. Graeme Turner (London: Routledge, 1993), 106–22.

12 Tom Weir, "No Daydreams of Our Own: The Film as National Expression," as quoted in *Nation, Culture, Text,* ed. Turner, 106.

13 All quoted in ibid., 107–8.

14 Jacka, "Australian Cinema," 108–10.

15 *Windows onto Worlds: Studying Australia at Tertiary Level* (Canberra) (June 1987): 12.

16 Eating meat pies and watching football were used then and are used now to invoke images of essential Australianness. The interesting thing about this slogan of essential Australianness is that its origin was an advertising slogan developed by General Motors in the 1970s in Australia to sell their cars. Inserting their message into the connotational strings that made up the (already problematic in its exclusion of immigrant and Aboriginal communities) stock of knowledge that constituted the national cultural identity of Australia, General Motors' aim was to appeal to Australians' sense of patriotism, hiding, in the process, its own multinational corporate identity. The slogan said: "Football, meat pies, kangaroos, and Holden cars. They go together under the southern stars."

17 Gayatri Chakravorty Spivak, "The Question of Cultural Studies," in *Outside in the Teaching Machine* (New York: Routledge, 1993), 255–84.

18 Cited in Probyn, "Technologizing the Self," 504.

As Canadian as Possible . . . : Anglo-Canadian Popular Culture and the American Other

Aniko Bodroghkozy

"The State or the United States!"

Thus proclaimed Canadian nationalist and early broadcast lobbyist Graham Spry to a Parliamentary committee in the early 1930s investigating public broadcasting options for the young nation. Either the federal government must create and oversee a national broadcasting system or, inevitably, private American interests would take over the new medium and further colonize the culturally and economically fragile country north of the all too permeable border at the 49th parallel. In 1936 Spry and his allies got their wish. Parliament created the Canadian Broadcasting Corporation (CBC), a federally funded Crown corporation. Its mandate was to provide radio (and later television) programming to a small population scattered over a vast land mass encompassing five time zones, a forbidding climate, at least six geographically and culturally distinct regions, two separate, official languages, and a citizenry always inclined to prefer the exports of their southern neighbour's culture industries.

Broadcasting was to be the latest technology to assist in nation-building and cultural unification. The regular dissemination and consumption of made-in-Canada media messages would assist in the creation of what historian Benedict Anderson has called an "imagined community." If the heterogeneous occupants of this vast territory from the Pacific to the Prairies to the Arctic to the Atlantic to the industrial centre could all imagine each other engaging with the same media discourses, an imagined notion of "Canadian" would

surely result.[1] This cultural and fictive project of constructing a "Canadian-ness" went hand-in-hand with another technology of national creation. Back in the 1860s when the country severed its colonial ties to Mother England, the Fathers of Confederation had proclaimed that the transcontinental railroad, which they envisioned binding the nation together with bands of steel, would encourage Canadians to trade and communicate with each other east-west rather than north-south with their American cousins. Thus a top-down construction of an economic structure would be complemented by (an equally) top-down mandated communications system that would somehow elicit bottom-up allegiances to an agreed upon sense of shared identity and national purpose. Public broadcasting would also, crucially, serve as a weapon to keep seductive American mass culture on the other side of the border. The constructing of a Canadian-ness could never succeed if the nation's inhabitants were perpetually being enticed to participate in the fictions that helped to solidify the imagined community to the south.

At the close of the twentieth century, it would be hard to argue that the Canadian project of creating a viable imagined community has been an unqualified success. The nation recently teetered on the brink of disintegration when a referendum in the province of Québec on its separation or sovereignty (these terms are semiotically loaded and often undecidable in the local context) resulted in a whisker-thin "victory" for Canadian nationalist forces. The country's ongoing, perpetual low-level crisis of national unity has now been ratcheted up to a much higher level of on-going crisis. Arguably related to this situation, the nation finds itself with not one system of broadcasting encouraging a homogenizing sense of national identity, but with several, including two linguistically separate public and private systems—French and English. The francophone systems have been quite successful in encouraging the francophone Québécois in imagining themselves "un peuple distinct." Francophone television—drama, comedy, public affairs, talk shows—frequently draw on American formulas and rework them for Québécois audiences who watch in huge numbers. While some dubbed-into-French American programmes are popular, nine out of ten of the most watched offerings on francophone Quebec television are home-grown productions.[2] The broadcasting situation in English-speaking Canada (on which this chapter will focus) has been much more problematic. Rather than using the medium successfully to promote a shared national culture while limiting access to that of the United States, one Canadian broadcast critic has argued that "the United States today dominates the television environment of English speaking Canada, which, especially during prime-time, appears to exist as a mini-replica of the American system."[3] Statistics on Anglo-Canadian television viewing seem to bear out Richard Collins's assertion that Canadian programming carries a "cultural discount" among indigenous viewers: English-speaking Canadians actively avoid watching entertainment programming produced by their own countrymen and women.[4] An A. C. Nielsen survey of the top twenty most watched programmes broadcast on the CBC and the private CTV and GLOBAL networks in English Canada for the 1994–95 season appear to support the argument. With one notable exception, the top ten programmes were all American comedies and dramas. The only Canadian offering was the CTV-CBS coproduction *Due South,* which garnered a position as the fifth most watched show with an average Canadian audience of 1,750,000. We will discuss the phenomenon of this show in more detail later. The only other Canadian offerings included the CBC stalwart, *Hockey Night in Canada,* in eleventh place and the CTV national news in twelfth. Rounding out the list at the very bottom of the top twenty were a group of four CBC public affairs and political satire offerings.[5]

It is commonplace in Canada to bemoan the degree to which our popular imagination has been colonized by the United States. Cultural commentators such as Morris Wolfe, TV critic for English Canada's cultural magazine, *Saturday Night,* coined the much used term "jolts-per-minute (jpm)" to disparage American programming (for having too many) and to extol the less-popular Canadian offerings (for having admirably few). Morris proclaims, "Much of the American television (and film) is about the American dream—the world as we wish it could be, a place in which goodness and reason prevail and things work out for the best. Much of Canadian television (and film) on the other hand, is about reality—the grey world as we actually find it."[6] Cultural elites like Wolfe may prefer the "documentary" or quotidian quality they attribute to Canadian stories, but the evidence of Canadian popular tastes indicates that "the grey world" is not the stuff of popular culture.

If, after a century of attempts to carve out a space of cultural sovereignty, the bulk of Canadian citizens still prefer to engage with high "jpm" American dreams rather than sedate northern greyness for their entertainment, is it possible to speak of a "Canadian popular culture?" Or is that term the ultimate oxymoron? Has American cultural imperialism so colonized Canadians' collective imagination that we no longer have (if we ever had) the narrational tools to conceive of a uniquely Canadian community? In a postmodern landscape characterized by heterogeneity, multiple and fluid identities, blurred boundaries, and the globalization of culture, is it useful even to ask such questions about specific national configurations?

For those of us located out in the margins, perhaps it still is. Graeme Turner, an Australian cultural studies critic, has argued that we can re-think the project of national identity in progressive ways to embrace post-colonial attributes of struggle against (imperial) domination, recognition of diversity and difference within the national formation, and a nationalism that celebrates pluralism and hybridity.[7] The national identity and cultural problems that Turner, along with other Australian cultural theorists such as Meaghan Morris, grapple with resonate in familiar ways with questions that obsess many of their postcolonial Commonwealth cousins in the Northern Hemisphere. Questions that animate my discussion in this paper have provided grist for recent explorations of nation and popular culture in Antipodean scholarship and publishing. I would like to consider this work as part of a larger dialogue among Canuck, Aussie, Kiwi, and other postcolonial First World nations negotiating the relationship between their British and American "parent" formations.[8]

The questions I want to explore here concern what happens when Canadian cultural producers mimic the forms and conventions of American popular culture. Such activity has been largely uncontroversial in Québec where francophone television has, for example, produced a Québécois *Wheel of Fortune,* a wildly popular version of *Candid Camera* called *Surprise, Surprise,* and most recently a David Lettermanesque late-night talk show. These kinds of appropriations of "American" forms have been far more contentious in English Canada. Socially and culturally, what are the circulated meanings of these appropriations? Along with that, what happens when Canadians consume made-in-America popular culture? Does such activity indicate that Canadians are the ultimate cultural dupes, avidly gobbling up the imperializer's messages, disempowering, if not obliterating, themselves in the process? Or is something more complicated—more negotiated—going on? Are Canadian cultural producers and consumers engaged in uniquely post-colonial strategies of meaning-making similar to those analysed by Meaghan Morris? In an analysis of the hugely popular Aussie-export film, *Crocodile Dundee,* Morris discusses the positive value of the film's "unoriginality"—borrowing, stealing, plunder

ing, as well as recoding, rewriting, and reworking American forms.[9] Can we see something similar happening in the Canadian context?

This chapter will also map out the often contentious debates about (Americanized) popular culture in Canada. Long standing and almost hegemonic has been the argument that Canadians' voracious appetite for American mass culture has crippled Canada's ability to assert a sense of national identity (typically seen as singular), perhaps even to maintain itself as an independent nation-state. More recent theorizing, influenced by the bottom-up, audience-focused approaches of cultural studies methodologies, are beginning to question that "common sense." From a more reader-oriented standpoint this paper will explore the possibilities that Canadian popular audiences may be engaged in more locally empowering and self-defining activities than the "American-TV-is-bad-for-you-and-will-rot-your-Canadian-brain" arguments can countenance. Using a number of examples of popular "Americanized" television series produced in Canada for indigenous viewers, I will examine ways in which Canadian audiences may use popular texts as sites for working through a sense of what it means to be Canadian in relation to a feared, but always desired, mythic American Other.

Mapping Canadian Media Studies

Engaged theorizing about popular culture—as opposed to condemnations of "mass (read: American, read: debased) culture"—has not elicited much interest from Canadian cultural theorists and critics historically. In *Continental Divide,* a groundbreaking comparative study of U.S. and Canadian values and institutions, Seymour Martin Lipset argues that Canada has traditionally been more elitist, culturally conservative, and suspicious of populist tendencies.[10] While this heritage has promoted a more stable and non-violent social order, it has not nurtured an intellectual class inclined to embrace popular tastes—at least not in English Canada. In his sweeping survey of Canadian broadcasting, Richard Collins notes Anglo-Canadian intellectuals' deep-seated distaste for mass culture and the dearth of serious writing about Canadians' engagement with entertainment media. Morris Wolfe's knee-jerk loathing of American fare and his frankly snobbish championing of "good-for-you" cultural material serve, for Collins, as emblematic of popular culture analysis in English Canada.[11] Of course, this suspicion is not unique to the Canadian intellectual formation. The British academic and intellectual tradition has evidenced similar anxieties that recent inroads by British cultural studies have not succeeded in thoroughly displacing. The tenaciousness of moral panics about the popular among Anglo-Canadian elites suggests the extent to which these elites are still clinging to particular colonial ties that bind.

It is not just a mass/elite, cultural snob attitude among Canadian intellectuals that has discouraged engagements with the potential meanings of "the popular" in Canada. Leftist media analysis has largely been dominated by a "political economy" paradigm heavily influenced by the work of Canadian economic historian Harold Innis. His scholarly legacy to communications and media studies critics focuses on his analysis of metropolis-hinterland relationships and the trap of dependency seen as fundamental to such relations. In this argument, Canada is an economic and cultural dependent of the United States. Seen as periphery to the American centre in cultural production, Canadians are helpless in asserting their own independence. The American economic and cultural colossus reduces the disempowered nation to a position of vassal-state and colony. Unable to produce cultural products in the hinterland, creative artists and producers must relocate to the American centre, assimilate its dominant genres, and, thereby, perpetuate a cycle of dependency.[12] Not only do we import someone else's products, but, according to Dallas Smythe's provocative argument, we end up exporting Canadian audiences as a commodity to the American culture industries.[13] From this perspective, American television programming popular with Canadian viewers is nothing more than a manifestation of monopoly capitalism. Like other Canadian raw materials such as lumber, wheat, or codfish, Canadian television audiences are merely products for export to enrich American business.

While it is currently fashionable to criticize the economic determinism and totalizing nature of these arguments, they cannot be dismissed entirely. It does *matter* that mass communications outlets are being concentrated in fewer and fewer hands as transnational conglomerates, through mergers and acquisitions, oligopolize the media.[14] Many of these conglomerates are not even "American" any more in any unproblematized definition of the word. Media corporations are now global entities. Whose culture and meanings, then, are being exported to this global audience by Time-Warner or Paramount-Viacom? For that matter, whose culture and meanings are being disseminated by the home-grown colossus, Maclean-Rogers, a recent mega-merger of Canada's most powerful cable companies (Rogers Cablesystems) and the country's most powerful publishing empire (Maclean-Hunter)? Despite CEO Ted Rogers's rhetoric about preserving a "Canadian voice" on the much ballyhooed information superhighway, the particularities of region or the voices of minorities have little place to assert themselves in the global strategies of these communication giants.[15] In fact, Rogers can be no more interested in encouraging the creation and distribution of local articulations of identity and cultural meanings than the other mega-corps he is emulating. All need to maximize profits by maximizing audience. As these conglomerates gobble up more and more of the means, not only of mass cultural production, but distribution and exhibition as well, national cultural sovereignty increasingly becomes challenged. Richard Collins points out that Europeans, faced with the new realities of globalized communications, satellite technology, and their lack of respect for national borders, have come to see the situation in Canada vis-à-vis American mass communication as a metaphor for a general threat to national communication sovereignty.[16]

While postmodernist globalization and blurring of national boundaries seems a clear threat to traditional notions of the nation-state, the process need not herald the death-knell of nationalist-oriented imagined communities. Graeme Turner usefully points out that in the wake of global capitalism and phenomena such as the European Economic Union, nationalisms—especially within Europe—have been flourishing (although not necessarily in progressive ways). Arguing against the notion that globalized media industries are irresistible and inevitably successful in eradicating cultural differences, Turner emphasizes that the process is dialectic, uneven, and often results in an increase in nationalist feeling among diverse ethnic and political communities.[17]

Turner's nuancing of the situation might provide a more compelling explanation for Canada's continued existence as a nation-state in the face of over a hundred years of American cultural influence. Nevertheless, in dominant discourse, Canada has been served up as a paradigm case of media imperialism. An industrial powerhouse by global standards, a charter member of the Group of Seven economic powers, regularly ranked by the United Nations as one of the world's most livable societies, and yet, according to much of Canadian communications theory, Canada wallows in dependency and dubious sovereignty, always on the verge of being dismantled as a failed experiment in nation-building. And our taste for American popular culture serves as one of the villainous culprits. Such gloomy pessimism, circulated with variations since the birth of the country, may in it-

self be uniquely Canadian, differentiating us from the nation of optimists to the south. Yet these top-down, monolithic, economically and technologically deterministic arguments fly in the face of Canada's continued viability as a nation-state (a tad shaky at the moment because of the uncertainty in Québec) and as a social formation distinct from the United States.

New Approaches: How the Beaver Bites Back

Some recent work in Canadian media study attempts to nuance and problematize the grimness of previous explorations of Canadians' seeming infatuation with American cultural products. It may be almost inevitable that one of the most hopeful and cheerful studies of Canadian television should come from a non-Canadian. Richard Collins, a British telecommunications scholar (now teaching Down Under) argues that Canada is a viable nation-state—and in fact a harbinger for others—by the very fact that it does not have a common symbolic culture. Arguing that political sovereignty and a strong sense of cultural identity are not necessarily congruent, Collins suggests that "political institutions are more important than television and culture, or even language, in producing and reproducing a solid sentiment of national identity among Canadians."[18] Such an argument is heresy to cultural nationalists for whom localized cultural production is the sine qua non of national identity formation. As an outsider, unafflicted by the supposed "misérabilism" inherent in the Canadian point of view, Collins sees a robust and stable social order characterized by low levels of crime and heightened tolerance for difference mandated by official policies of bilingualism and multiculturalism. Such qualities are the fruits of a lack of strong nationalism. If Canadians choose to relax and entertain themselves with American television programming rather than Canadian alternatives, the activity does nothing to threaten Canada's viability as a sovereign nation. This "How I Learned to Stop Worrying and Love American TV" argument is certainly refreshing in the ways it questions the thesis of a controlling and totalitarian American consciousness rolling over the weaker country, obliterating difference as it does so. However, Collins's optimistic book was written before the Québec sovereignty referendum and before federal Parliamentary elections resulted in the separatist Bloc Québécois finding itself as Her Majesty's Loyal Opposition. It remains to be seen whether Collins's faith in Canada's political institutions and their viability was misplaced or not.

Collins's questioning of the American cultural imperialism argument has been echoed by Canadian media historian Paul Rutherford who asserts that "mass culture in itself does not pose, and never has posed, a direct threat to the Canadian identity, because consumers have 'read' its message through a special lens made in Canada."[19] This viewpoint suggests a cultural studies perspective. Rather than seeing Canadian audiences of American mass entertainment as duped by and subjected to the imperializing strategies of these texts and their producers, audiences negotiate with and struggle against texts in active and self-interested ways. Cultural studies theorists such as John Fiske and Stuart Hall have provided useful correctives to the "mass/elite" and "culture industry" paradigms that have for so long functioned as hegemonic common sense among Canada's Anglo intelligentsia. As Hall has insisted, the vast numbers of people who consume and enjoy the products of the culture industry are not passive "cultural dopes" living in a permanent state of false consciousness.[20] The products of mass culture, while carrying the discourses of dominant ideology, are decoded variously depending on the social subjectivities of readers. As John Fiske has argued, "To be made into popular culture, a commodity must also bear the interests of the people.

Popular culture is not consumption, it is culture—the active process of generating and circulating meanings and pleasures within a social system."[21] If, as Fiske suggests, formations of the people are adept at taking *their* commodities and turning them into *our* culture, then one can argue that American mass culture becomes Canadian at the point of reading. Rutherford points to a survey of Canadian audiences of American mass culture conducted in the mid 1930s that provides some clues about how Canadians were using American popular culture at the dawn of broadcasting. Anglophones appeared to appropriate images of American life pouring over the border to construct their own country as superior. "Americans were seen as excitable, even 'childlike,' 'money-mad,' lawless, 'more corrupt,' and 'less moral,' boastful, and 'less cultured,' although they were given credit for being 'daring and enterprising' or generous. By contrast, Canadians appeared more honourable, law-abiding, and conservative, and their society, 'quieter, slower, in tempo and saner in quality.'"[22] Rather than a means to indoctrinate vassal-like dupes into an American hegemonic worldview, these texts provided readers a way to subvert the preferred meanings and construct locally useful ones.

Tamar Liebes and Elihu Katz employ a similar paradigm to show that different national-ethnic groups will decode mass media texts in culturally local and distinct ways. Focusing on the worldwide success of the American night time television soap opera, *Dallas,* they employ a cross-cultural analysis to examine the show's unique meanings among different cultural communities including Russian, Moroccan, and kibbutzim Israelis in contrast to Japanese and Californians. Questioning the media imperialism thesis, they argue that the openness to negotiation of so many American television shows and their ability to be reworked by disparate cultural groupings explains some of the success of these texts.[23] While American media

texts may be encoded with hegemonic and imperializing messages, decodings may actually subvert
that political project. Liebes and Katz's work provides a useful new avenue for considering how
Canadian viewers decode American media texts.

However, a caveat: since Canadians are not a
culturally homogenous and unified bunch, it is
problematic to speak of a univocal "Canadian" approach to meaning making. As a nation without a
strong sense of identity and with distinct regions
constantly challenging Ottawa's calls for "national
unity," singular definitions of Canadian-ness have
remained elusive, despite the attempts of some
nationalists to promote them. Such attempts suggest an essentialist notion of some ultimate, uniform, and national type—what Turner calls "the
old nationalism." This old nationalism, which has
always been problematic when applied to post-
colonial nation-state formations, can no longer
be supported in the postmodern age—if it ever
could be.[24] Nevertheless, while meanings of "Canadian" may need to be constantly inflected by region, language, and ethnicity, I would argue that
there is one experience all residents of the True
North Strong and Free share (if diversely): an ambivalent relationship to a fictive American Other.
Debates about (American) mass culture in Canada are so heated and obsessive by virtue of the
fact that they require a continual working and reworking of the unresolvable dilemma of how Canadians can construct their imagined community
as ultimately different from an intensively desired,
but just as deeply loathed made-in-Canada construction of "America."

This irresolvable contradiction forms the
foundation of Canadian popular culture. Cultural
studies theorists have argued that popular culture
functions as a terrain for the working through
of social contradictions. It is a site, not where
dominant (in this case, "American") ideology is
triumphantly displayed, but rather, where it is negotiated, played, and struggled with, at times sub-

verted, and, at other times, acceded to. Mass culture texts become popular to the extent that they
help socially situated readers work through fundamental dilemmas. They are the myths of elaborated capitalist societies. So, while it remains important to pay attention to what American, and
increasingly global, culture industries "do" to
Canada—such as prevent the flourishing of an indigenous film industry, for instance—it is also
important to pay attention to what Canadians
"do" with the products of those industries.

What Canadians do with their popular culture
is to work through imaginatively their relations
with their southern neighbours. If, as Seymour
Martin Lipset observes, "Canadians have tended
to define themselves not in terms of their own national history and traditions but by reference to
what they are *not*: Americans," then their hardy
appetite for American cultural products makes a
great deal of sense. As "not-American," Canadians
are the ultimate anti-Americans.[25] A particularly
fruitful way to work through this central binary
opposition at the core of what it means to be Canadian is to engage with popular texts that provide
a productive space for that cultural work. One
could argue that most of the indigenously produced Canadian cultural texts, which tend to be
rooted in the particularities of region, do not provide either the polysemy needed or the "American" signifier necessary to be broadly useful in
pan-Canadian strategies of meaning-making. This
is not to suggest that made-in-Canada mass entertainment texts cannot serve this function. Later
on in this paper, I will examine two Canadian
produced television series that were hugely popular and, in their own distinctive ways, successful precisely because they served as home-grown
vehicles for thinking through a Canadian sense
of difference from the American Other. Unfortunately, perhaps in part because anti-popular
cultural snobs like Morris Wolfe and his ilk still
help determine broadcast policy in Canada, much

made-in-Canada cultural production continues to be regionally limited in appeal at best or elitist, irrelevant, and dogmatic at worst.

How can we productively think through Canadians' use of popular culture in ways that do not perpetuate "mass/elite" theories of victimization and passivity in the face of culture industry onslaught? Very little work has been done in Canada that assumes an active audience perspective. Even less ethnographic work or discursive analysis of popular audience reading strategies have been conducted. Canada's top-down, state-funded public service approach to culture, along with its traditional suspicions of anything smacking of populism may account for the situation. However, a recently published anthology delightfully titled *The Beaver Bites Back? American Popular Culture in Canada* may herald a new era in media studies analysis in the Frozen Northland. Many of the volume's contributors, especially its co-editor, Frank E. Manning, argue that Canadian audiences do not merely survive or endure the aggressiveness of American cultural power, but devise ways to "bite" the imperialistic hand that feeds. Arguing that Canadian popular audiences adopt a tactic of "reversible resistance," Manning writes that their popular culture is "a relational phenomenon that assumes its significance vis-à-vis a particular Canadian conception of the United States. The relationship is both symbiotic and dialectic. Symbiotically, Canadian popular culture needs its American partner as an ambiguous and reversible opposite. Dialectically, Canadian popular culture imposes a particular construction on the United States and then defines and redefines itself in terms of ambivalently held differences."[26]

Canadians' "pragmatic, localized, episodic and fluid" sense of themselves and their culture needs an "absolute, forceful, and mystified 'Other'" for useful comparison.[27] Using case studies of Canadian versions of baseball, football, Olympic sport, televangelism, television lawyer shows, among other examples, the anthology shows the ambivalent ways in which Canadians respond to and appropriate American forms and styles. There is an ironic, self-parodying doubleness to the process. Literary theorist Linda Hutcheon has argued that irony may be a particularly Canadian discursive mode. She points out that irony "allows speakers to address and at the same time slyly confront an 'official' discourse, that is, to work *within* a dominant tradition but also to challenge it— without being utterly co-opted by it."[28] Canadian readings of American culture and reworkings as Canadian popular culture may, then, be subtle and often playful counterhegemonic tactics of asserting difference.

SCTV, a hugely popular satiric look at American television that succeeded with both Canadian and American audiences, is a useful case in point. The Toronto-based Second City troupe was parodying the huckster-like American border stations with their cheap, at times embarrassing, local programming and commercials. To a lesser extent they also lampooned home-grown personalities and familiar Canadian shows. To many Canadian viewers there was little doubt that this was a uniquely Canadian take on their own continuing fascination with even the dregs of American popular culture. Unfortunately, CBC officials were not as sophisticated about such ironized Canadian humour and demanded that the show's producers insert at least two minutes of "Canadian content" when the public broadcaster agreed to begin screening the series.[29] Thus was born the "contentless" two-minute continuing sketch, "The Great White North," whose hosts, Bob and Doug McKenzie, were stereotypical Canuck airheads in toques who could do nothing but drink beer and argue inanities in suitably exaggerated Canadianisms, eh?

The series' popularity in the United States with viewers who were most likely unaware of the Canadian meanings of the show complicates its readings among viewers back home. Having turned *their* television into *our* satire, we exported it back to them, but the beaver's bite would most likely go unnoticed. One might suggest that Canadian viewers, who are typically highly conscious of which of their cultural creations achieve favour with the folks down south, ended up constructing more complicated, doubled responses to *SCTV.* Like female spectators who adopt and fluidly move between "masculine" and "feminine" viewing positions while watching narratives supposedly constructed for a "male gaze," Canadian viewers might also adopt a doubled spectatorship.[30] If, as Bernard Ostry suggests, Canadians are to some extent already American because of the extent to which Canadians have learned American values, then it is relatively easy for Canadians to adopt an American subject position when necessary or desirable.[31] Canadians may thus be uniquely skilled at the disempowered's game of what John Caughie calls "playing at being American."[32] By watching *SCTV* in the wake of its American success, Canadian fans could, by the very fact of their ability to move fluidly between an "American" and a "Canadian" subject position, gain a certain amount of ironic pleasure from the meanings lost on American viewers who could not also adopt a Canadian subjectivity. If the beaver bit back, only Canadian viewers were aware of it—but therein lay some of the pleasure.

Cross-border successes like *SCTV* that allow Canadian audiences to ridicule both the imagined national self and the imagined mythic American Other, all the while preserving a certain amount of ironic protective covering, are unfortunately rare in the annals of Canadian broadcasting. Broadcast regulators with mandates to assure a minimal amount of Canadian content grace Canadian television screens may, along with cultural critics, have constrained views of what "Canadian" can mean. Rather than recognize the extent to which Canadians are "American" and eagerly, if ambivalently, participate in American generic forms, nar-

ratives, myths, and dreams, Cultural Policemen due north attempt to assert a decisive and absolute sense of difference. Therefore, texts that engage with signifiers connoting "American" can only raise suspicions. So, as Mary Jane Miller's analytical history of CBC English-language drama programming, *Turn Up the Contrast,* notes, the "Mother Corp" historically avoided mimicking successful American genre formats such as the cop show or the soap opera, and eschewed cultivation of a home-grown star system. CBC's offerings also shied away from constructing a Canadian heroic mythos.[33]

Nevertheless Canadian viewers appear to crave myths and ritual experiences that encourage a sense of cultural collectivity whether such experiences are created at home or not. Reid Gilbert observes, "Canadians seeking such myths will accept the rituals of their neighbours as entertainment, will overlay the homogeneity of American life on their own silent sense of regional self, and will look to U.S. imports for the collective experience their own more pragmatic culture does not provide."[34] Canadians from one end of the country to the other may share little in common culturally beyond their collective "outsider" engagement with American popular culture. More pessimistic cultural commentators would argue that this makes it more difficult for Canadians to work out the perennial dilemma of "where is here."[35] David Taras gloomily argues that "American dominance is now so great that Canadians have become not only 'strangers in television's land of the imagination' but strangers to themselves."[36] Yet Canadians do know that "here" is not the American "there." By engaging with the Other's popular media, inflected with the particularities of Canadian subjectivities during the process of reading, Canadians recode those texts as their own popular culture. Frank Manning notes that Canadians "reconstitute and recontextualize [American cultural products] in ways representative of what consciously, albeit ambivalently, distinguishes

Canada from its powerful neighbour: state capitalism, social democracy, middle-class morality, regional identities, official multiculturalism, the True North, the parliamentary system, institutionalized compromise, international neutrality, and so on."[37]

Canadians may be adept at using American cultural texts to remind themselves that "here" is quite different in fundamental ways from the American "there," but Taras and other pessimistic critics are right in pointing out the imaginative poverty inherent in the heavy reliance on someone else's national myths and narratives for collective cultural experiences. Nevertheless, Canada does, in fact, have a popular, indigenously produced television. One could argue that broadcast news and public affairs programming are Canada's shared popular culture. As well-known CBC broadcaster and anchorman Knowlton Nash has pointed out, Canadians are inveterate "infomaniacs." As the top-twenty Nielsen rated programmes for 1994–95 showed, five out of the six Canadian-produced programmes were all news/public affairs-oriented. Two of CBC's comedy stalwarts, *The Royal Canadian Air Farce* and *This Hour Has 22 Minutes*, are both satires and spoofs of Canadian politics. To the extent that the country has a star system, it is peopled with journalists, interviewers, and other public affairs/documentary personalities.[38] CTV's *Evening News* with Lloyd Robertson or *The National* on CBC, both coast-to-coast programmes heavily viewed by Anglo-Canadians may be the closest Canadians come to a shared common culture. However, because of the linguistically divided nature of the broadcasting system in Canada, this common culture does not tend to include Québécois viewers. They watch their own made-in-Québec news with their own made-in-Québec news personalities. Thereby, broadcasting reenforces the "two solitudes."

What about fictional programming? Besides *SCTV*, what other home-grown offerings have provided useful grounds for a collective explo-

ration of national self-in-relation to the American Other? Canadian television has produced a number of recent successes, including the broadcast newsroom drama, *ENG*; the long-lived CBC high school kids series, *DeGrassi High*; and *Road to Avonlea*, the CBC-Disney coproduction about life in bucolic nineteenth-century Prince Edward Island. However, I want to focus on two series that succeeded by Nielsen measures and which were, in different ways, thoroughly preoccupied with working through the "American-not American" binary: *Street Legal*, a CBC lawyer drama which ran from 1987 until its retirement from the air in 1994, and *Due South*, produced for Canada's private CTV network in conjunction with the American CBS, which ran on both networks for two years from 1994 to 1996.

Legal Beavers: Struggling over "Americanization"

Street Legal did not begin its long CBC run as a successful show. Debuting the same year as *L.A. Law*, the show suffered blistering comparisons to the American hit in the Canadian press. Where the American show was glamorous and sophisticated, *Street Legal* suffered all the markers of much-maligned Canadian earnestness and sobriety. CBC publicity material for the show's debut depicted its three stars under a caption reading, "Their only crime is they care too much."[39] Initial ratings were poor and, according to the CBC's "enjoyment index," the series scored a low 51 out of 100.[40] The series followed the courtroom and personal drama of a trio of lawyers: left-wing, idealistic Leon Robinovich, hard-headed and ambitious Chuck Tchobanian, and tender, caring Carrie Barr. They set up practice in Toronto's gentrifying but still somewhat seedy Queen Street West neighbourhood where, according to a CBC press release, the series could explore "the streets and neighbourhoods of Toronto from high-life to low-life."[41]

The series stumbled along for two years before

hitting its stride and becoming not only a sudden popular hit, but also a flashpoint for commentary, criticism, and anxiety about the show's "Americanization." In 1988 the sexy, scheming Olivia Novak joined the law firm. As described by the television critic for the *Globe and Mail* (the self-proclaimed "national newspaper" of Canada), she was "all lacquered talons and shellacked hair. She may well prove a positive addition; the show and its characters have so far been altogether too nice, too dully—dare we say it?—Canadian."[42] When the show was plodding, earnest, and boring it was "Canadian" and, thus, worthy of contempt. However, by 1990 the series was hot enough for the CBC to launch a massive ad campaign of posters and billboards provocatively proclaiming "THE HEAT IS ON THE STREET" with images of cast members locked in steamy embraces. Suddenly the *Globe* critic found the show too un-Canadian. He argued that the series "looks like a masters thesis in American prime-time TV. It has been the public network's most successful and shameless homage to Television City, California since the unproclaimed policy of Americanization first took hold at the corporation about four years ago."[43] Yet a few years later this very same critic was eulogizing the series for "reflecting the urban Canadian reality as authentically and entertainingly as possible while trying to emulate the U.S. prime-time form." And rather than representing CBC's alleged policy of Americanization, now the show "was the flagship of the network's renewed and ambitious commitment to Canadianizing prime-time."[44] The critic's incoherence over what "Canadianization" and "Americanization" meant provides some clues about how *Street Legal* functioned as a terrain for discursive struggle in publicly circulated commentary over those semiotically undecidable concepts. Both terms, but in particular the latter, were used almost obsessively in publicly circulated commentary about the series. The reactions the show generated indicate a particular constellation of anxieties about changing definitions of "Canadian" in this period.

One of the anxieties provoked by the series was that it did not provide enough suitable markers of difference. Much of Canadian elite cultural discourse persists in privileging a notion of Canada as "Landscape," "Weather," "Wilderness" in opposition to America's "huddled masses" and cities teaming with urban life. Imagined as a country of forbidding Nature, the Great White North is either empty of human presence or constantly victimizes its puny human settlers. Canada's canonical narratives include the nineteenth-century settler Susanna Moodie's whining memoir, *Roughing It in the Bush*, and Farley Mowatt's wilderness adventures. *Street Legal*, situated in present day Toronto—and insisting on the fact by lovingly showing off the city in skillfully chosen establishing shots—encourages a complex of anxieties about how this place is different from *their* space across the border. Many of these anxieties are provoked by the meanings of "Toronto" in the Canadian context. As Canada's biggest city and financial headquarters, Toronto has come to stand for brashness, hustle, money-madness, careerism, superficiality—in a word: "Americanization." As an industrial-information-service-financial powerhouse, Toronto is a "centre" to the rest of Canada's "hinterland." Thus, it is "America" north of the 49th parallel. Equally crucial to this complex of meanings is the popular knowledge that Toronto has stood in for and masqueraded as any number of American cities in countless films and television programmes shot there by American production crews lured north by the cheap Canadian dollar and Toronto's excellent production facilities. Therefore, in the Canadian imaginary, Toronto, to some extent, is not "Canadian" at all, but chock full of the attributes of the American Other. If Canadians are American already in some ways, then a show like *Street Legal* insisting on all the "American" meanings of the nation's premier city could not help but churn up anxieties about the blurring of the boundaries between the two.

Street Legal also functioned as a flashpoint for debate about Canadian identity because, as the

Globe's critic correctly (if confusingly) noted, the show was the cornerstone of major programming policy changes that were going on at the time in the corporation's English television section. Whether these changes were part of a process of "Canadianizing" or "Americanizing" was, indeed, the question. The late 1980s were a period of crisis for the public broadcaster. The hostile Tory government of Brian Mulroney had saddled the CBC with draconian budget cuts, leading to the wholesale dismantling of much regional programming, the selling off of a number of TV stations, and the laying off of hundreds of creative staffers.[45] In an attempt to generate audiences and advertising revenue to compete with the burgeoning choices Canadian audiences now had in their television offerings from American networks, cable, specialty channels, and home video, the Mother Corp hired hip, young Ivan Fecan in 1988 to head programming for the English Television Network. In press discourse, Fecan's most significant attribute was his status as a former protégé of Brandon Tartikoff at NBC. The (at times) snooty arts and politics magazine, the *Canadian Forum,* surveyed the situation and in a cover story asked rhetorically whether the CBC was now "Just Another American Network?"[46] The more populist *TV Guide* was willing to give Fecan the benefit of the doubt about whether he was planning to sell the public broadcaster down the commercialism river. In a mostly sympathetic profile, the magazine noted: "Critics have panned him for being ratings driven, for following the American model in what he calls the 'Darwinian environment' of commercial television. But Fecan believes that while CBC shouldn't be only ratings driven, it should not be entirely 'intelligentsia driven,' either." He was quoted arguing that the Canadian intelligentsia were more difficult to deal with than "the sharks of L.A." because of the former's sniffing at popular television and their "loser talk" about Canada's ability to produce top-quality entertainment.[47] In the discursive struggle to determine what the CBC now "meant," the lines were being drawn between elite culture-vulture snobbism on the one hand, and "lowest common denominatorism" on the other. At stake in this battle, ultimately, was the definition of "Canadian."

Reworking *Street Legal* was one of Fecan's major goals. Press articles made much of the fact that a former CBS executive (who, conveniently, carried a Canadian passport) had been flown up from Los Angeles to fine-tune the series.[48] Another former CBS staffer, New Yorker Brenda Greenberg, who had worked on *As the World Turns,* took over as executive producer, promising to give the series "more punch and energy."[49] "Los Angeles-based" Canadian-born actors were added to the cast. For those used to considering Canada a cultural hinterland that could only lose top rate talent to the American centre, the reversal in the migration of talent might seem confusing—or another indication of how "free trade" between the two countries would further infect the smaller one with "Americanism." The perceived "spicing up" of the series by American imports left some critics uneasy. Slickness, sex, passion, and intrigue were just not—well, Canadian. *Toronto Life* magazine stated, "Well, of course what makes *Street Legal* seem a touch un-Canadian, no matter how many shots of city hall and the CN Tower it features, is its entertaining luridness."[50] The critic for the *Financial Post* noted the cast's new wardrobe, the "decadent luxury" of the sets with items such as silk sheets, and the fact that "the good guys are nicer, the villains are nastier and the bitches are bitchier." To him this was all a disaster: "The result is what always happens when a Canadian series tries to mimic an American counterpart [*L.A. Law*]: it falls between two stools, and manages to be bad American *and* bad Canadian television at the same time." He went on to contrast the "muck" of *Street Legal* to the far preferable "family-based" CBC offerings such as *Road to Avonlea.* "Does this say something about the warm, cuddly Canadian stereotype? Is it true? Are we all more comfortable with stories about a 12-year-old boy kissing a girl than ones about a

35-year-old man screwing a client?"[51] Presumably in the True North, Canadians did not cavort on silk sheets, fornicate, engage in bitchy behaviour, or pursue lurid affairs—at least not in its fictional narratives. *Road to Avonlea* or *Anne of Green Gables*, situated in the (safe) rural past in isolated Prince Edward Island and concerned with pre-pubescent children untouched by modernity, reinforced a notion of Canada as somehow removed from the realities of urban life and capitalism. American narratives could grapple with the raw and dangerous but enticing challenges and disasters of the modern age. When these "American" concerns were brought into a Canadian setting, confusion reigned. How could "sexiness" and "slickness" be Canadian? Canadian cultural "protectors," having essentialized certain narrative conventions and themes as American, seemed loathe to see them taken up into home-grown productions. Rather than see this hybridization as the inevitable process of creative cultural struggle and dialogue in the postmodern era, they saw only Canadian surrender to the feared Outside Imperializer.

We should also look more closely at the appeal of "traditional" Canadian fare such as the veritable cultural industry around the *Avonlea* and *Green Gables* narratives. Generally overlooked by Canadian nationalists is the extent to which those narratives can be appropriated in colonialist ways by our neighbours to the south. American fans of these stories can end up constructing "Canada" as a mythically innocent, comforting reminder of what "America" used to be. Discussing the appeal to Americans of particular Australian films, Graeme Turner notes, "Australian films speak not so much of Australia itself as of a highly idealised, deeply nostalgic vision of America." Americans seek refuge from their own cynicism and pessimism in Australian period pieces that suggest "old frontier values" now lost, but presumably robust and flourishing out there in the unsophisticated, pre-modern colonies.[52] Both Canada and Australia end up as bucolic, frontier theme parks

for American tourists who (perhaps inevitably) graft American meanings onto what they see and read. Canadian cultural critics who were so nonplussed with material like *Street Legal* may themselves have been more comfortable with colonialist fare that, while seeming to construct a palpable sense of difference from the American Other, also worked to deny Canadian post-colonial postmodernity.

While *Street Legal* generated a great deal of concern over its "American-ness," other commentators insisted on its absolute Canadian-ness. Labeled "The Great Canadian TV Series" by one journalist, the programme served as a site for meditating on perennial questions about national character and identity.[53] Despite the slick, high "jolts-per-minute" look of the series that made it so "American" to some, other critics pointed out how Canadian it looked. In a eulogy marking the show's retirement from the air, the *Toronto Star* noted, "We certainly will cherish our memories of Toronto portrayed, for once, as Toronto—not as some generic Anywhere City, North America. *Street Legal* was bold enough, brash enough, Canadian enough to give us Queen St., old city hall, Toronto Island, Osgoode Hall, Harbourfront and, yes, The Toronto Star. Through the bubbles of soap, it also gave us our country—Bay Street bashing, the hated Tories, stuffy Ottawa bureaucrats, and the ever-whimsical NDP."[54] If part of Canada's national dilemma is that the country is so "hard to see" next to the avalanche of American cultural imagery, then a key pleasure offered by the series was making Toronto so easy to see. By insisting on its locale, the series appeared to have done exactly what Canadian culture is supposed to do: answered the question "where is here?"

Making Toronto *as* Toronto easy to see would, however, have different meanings for Torontonians compared to, let's say, Edmontonians. A staff writer at the *Edmonton Journal* had this to say about the star status of the Queen City: "Toronto's patina of narcissism is buffed to a sparkle usually reserved for polished silver. There's trendy York-ville. There's the Yonge Street strip. Look at all those street musicians. Real streetcars. Hip dudes in red shoes. Wow, am I impressed! Street Legal reminds me of the CBC publicist who once asked me to a trendy rooftop bistro for a cappuccino. Sorry, I said, too busy. Maybe when I come to Edmonton, she offered, adding with the inevitable twist of Toronto condescension: 'Do they have cappuccino in Edmonton?' 'Yes,' I replied. 'We find that it goes very well with bannock and pem-mican.'" [55] In this reading, we see a representation of Toronto from the Canadian "hinterland." The *Toronto Star* and *Toronto Life* may have found "T.O.-specific" pleasures in seeing their city displayed in all its glory. To Canadians outside the self-satisfied metropolis, *Street Legal*'s paean merely marginalized them further. On the other hand, the Edmontonian's reading (involving the Prairie beaver biting back with superb dry, Ca-nuck irony) could not have been possible had he been responding to Toronto's many featured roles as generic Anytown. Canadians residing outside the ever-expanding bounds of the former "Hog-town" are known for engaging in frequent dis-cursive Toronto-bashing sessions. *Street Legal* provided a popular culture space to practice a pleasurable Canadian pastime.[56]

Besides the disparate joys of seeing Toronto as Toronto, there were other pleasures of national self-recognition. As most Canadians know, the Canadian judicial system is different for the American. The Anglo-Canadian system is closer to the British model (albeit without the white wigs), while the Québec judicial system is based on the French Napoleonic Code. This allowed the *Ottawa Citizen* to note: "The legal setting meant there were Canadian flags everywhere. It featured courtroom terms and procedures including the use of legal robes, that instantly set it apart from the U.S. competition, and gave it a special edge with a Canadian audience." [57] Michael Valpy, columnist for the *Globe and Mail*, rhapsodized,

"Its actors . . . have always had that special defining Canadian softness. They look Canadian and walk Canadian. They talk Canadian, use Canadian body language and live in Canadian houses and apartments with Canadian furniture arrange-ments." [58] Whether Canadians have a special body language or manner of displaying household fur-nishing that distinguishes them from their cross-border cousins may be debatable. What both of these reading strategies point to, however, are pleasures in the perception of difference in detail. *Street Legal* was so enjoyably "Canadian" because of its subtle variations in look, tone, and style from comparable American offerings. As Bernard Ostry has pointed out, "It is because our culture is so close to the American one that we feel we must insist on the differences, small though they may seem." [59] It is a foundation of fine details, typically unnoticed by non-Canadians, upon which Cana-dians have built their shaky edifice of national identity.

Other critics saw the show's themes, its charac-ters, and plots as thinly veiled allegories about Canada itself. During the period of the much de-bated (at least north of the border) Canada-U.S. Free Trade negotiations, Barr, Robinovich, Tcho-banian, and Novak decided to merge with a big U.S. law firm and subsequently spent much of the season dealing with their loss of independence. The lawyers were themselves seen as personifica-tions of the conflicting impulses of the imagined national character. In a perceptive cover story in *Broadcast Week*, the television listings magazine of the *Globe and Mail*, John Doyle argued that Leon and Carrie represented the nation's "socially con-scious and nationalistic impulse." Yet, for all their underdog proclivities and "anti-establishment grandstanding, they are virulently conformist Ca-nadians and they're gallingly complacent." Chuck and Olivia, on the other hand, were money-mad and needed "to be as glamorously amoral as the Americans." Olivia's role as an entertainment law-yer "trying to guide American producers around the dumb Canadian regulations that stopped wealth spreading to American producers and Canadian entertainment lawyers" was a particularly useful symbol. For Doyle, Chuck was the most sympathetic character. On the one hand suspicious of Leon and Carrie's goody-goodiness and, on the other hand, leery of Olivia's Hollywood scheming, Chuck was "conscious that he's at the mercy of a force much greater than himself. That's why he's so appealing—his mood mirrors the querulous attitude of most Canadians." [60] The addition of the reptilian slimeball of a Crown prosecutor named Brian Malony also seemed to represent something beyond his own villainy. His name sounded awfully similar to the, by then, much loathed Prime Minister. [61]

The CBC's decision to cancel the series at the height of its popularity with Canadian viewers led to an avalanche of letters and phone calls to the network, newspapers, and radio call-in shows protesting the action. One of the dominant circulated meanings of the decision constructed the CBC as uncaring about its audiences and incapable of dealing with popularity. A fan from Fredericton, New Brunswick, said: "If it had gotten a little stale or something like that, maybe we could have seen it coming. . . . It just seems so popular that it's hard to imagine they would cut it off." [62] Toronto's right-wing, populist tabloid, the *Sun*, saw a Mother Corp conspiracy to set the show up for a fall. By taking away key creative people, the paper opined, the network expected the show would deteriorate, thus providing a reason to cancel it. The paper also reported the corporate brick wall one (and presumably others) of the show's outraged fans encountered when trying to protest directly to the network. The fan kept trying to reach a CBC programme head "but I was put on to audience relations, and that was like talking to a machine. It's like CBC's saying to those million people, 'You don't matter.'" [63] In this reading, popular tastes didn't count. The CBC, a grim, stodgy Canadian cultural arbiter with a suspiciously un-Canadian

creation on its hands, all glitzy, glamorous, and successful, could do nothing but sabotage its "too American" problem child. While CBC programming executives argued that the show had peaked, and could only go downhill, the dominant discourse about the situation painted a Mother Corp thoroughly indifferent to popular tastes and audience desires.

Playing at Being Canadian Due South

While *Street Legal* was a popular Canadian hit and while it was successfully sold to a global television market in such countries as Germany, Austria, Switzerland, Spain, Norway, Greece, and Turkey, the series was not sold to American syndication. [64] The figure of "America" may have loomed large in the show's cultural significance, but viewers in Canada were not sharing the show and thus ways of making sense of it with the feared and desired Others south of the border. Such was not the case with *Due South*. Produced by Canadian-born Paul Haggis who had achieved some renown for his work on *thirtysomething*, the series was the first Canadian-made television programme ever to play on American prime-time. In its first year (1994–95), CBS provided two-thirds of its financing, but production was all done in Canada. After CBS decided not to renew the series for a second year, the show's Canadian production company, Alliance, decided to go it alone and scraped together financing from its Canadian broadcaster, CTV and from Telefilm Canada (a government-sponsored film and media production funding organization). Luckily for all concerned, CBS decided to pick up *Due South* again as a mid-season replacement. Unfortunately, at the end of the 1995–96 season, the American network again decided to remove the series from its schedule for the upcoming season and the series met its apparent demise. [65] As the Nielsen ratings referred to earlier indicate, the show was wildly and unprecedentedly successful among Canadian viewers. It received respectable ratings among American audiences and generated a fiercely loyal and active fandom.[66]

While *Street Legal* implicitly concerned itself with Canada's relation to the American Other, *Due South* wore that concern on the red serge sleeve of its main character, Mountie Benton Fraser. The show's premise, which producer Haggis admitted "sounds like a really stupid idea," involved the unfailingly polite Mountie Fraser, almost always decked out in full traditional uniform, his deaf, lip-reading pet wolf named Diefenbaker, and their partnership with a tough-talking, pistol-packing Chicago cop named Vecchio. They fought crime together and engaged in male bonding on the mean streets of the Windy City.[67] Fraser, the colonial naïf, more at home in the snow-swept landscape of the Northwest Territories than the big city, nevertheless was able to use his wilderness training to prevail over anything Chicago could throw at him.

As an American-Canadian coproduction, *Due South* provided Canadian viewers a unique opportunity to "play at being Canadian," as well as American, within the space of the American Other, all the while engaging in a sly mining of the semiotic markers of difference. Satirizing American stereotypes of Canadians and Canadian stereotypes of Americans, the series was a fine example of the "forked tongue of irony" and "inherent doubleness" that Linda Hutcheon finds in Canadian literary and artistic productions.[68] On the other hand, taking this tactical ironic play into the Americans' sandbox, resulted in some tradeoffs and constraints.

The textual strategies employed in *Due South* would be very familiar to filmgoers who remember the mid-1980s Australian export hit *Crocodile Dundee*. Both narratives involved a backwoods (or backbush) white man, steeped in the wisdom of the indigenous population (Canadian Indians in Fraser's case, Aboriginals in Mike Dundee's) who managed to conquer the wilds of the violent, ul-

tramodern American Megalopolis. Dundee was the quintessential Aussie "national type:" laconic, brawny, and macho, but self-deprecating.[69] Fraser was the quintessential Canuck type: precise and softly spoken, gentle and nonviolent, polite, thoroughly well-mannered, and self-abnegating. These "types" exported to the American market seemed to work because of the ways in which they both acknowledged and fed American stereotypes of seemingly more innocent colonial Others. And since these Others were emphatically white and male, no criticisms of racist infantilization would likely result. While both "types" were innocent and seemingly naive, both were emphatically masculine. Both the Aussie film and the Canadian television series made much of their heroes' sexual desirability to members of the opposite sex.

Meaghan Morris has called *Crocodile Dundee* an "export-drive allegory."[70] With a population, like Canada's, too small to support an elaborate indigenous film and television industry, Australian producers needed to find narrative strategies that would appeal to American audiences, while also allowing for articulations of Aussie senses of identity and difference. *Crocodile Dundee* thus appropriated codes and conventions familiar to American audiences, but reworked them in particularly Aussie ways. Morris argues that the film can be read as a post-colonial comedy of survival as well as a "*takeover* fantasy of breaking into the circuit of media power, to invade the place of control."[71] *Due South* clearly appropriated the same post-colonial strategy for survival. If Canada has traditionally been so "hard to see," what better way to change that than by making a kind of "Canada" so visible in the very place where Canada has been most invisible—American television? Unfortunately this tactic presents a range of dilemmas. The only "Canada" or "Australia" on view is a decidedly patriarchal one. Both national "types" are idealized macho men, even if the Canadian one is oh-so-polite and politically correct. In these myths of survival, it is Canuck and Aussie white men who get to see themselves triumphing in the space of the Other. This form of post-colonial nationalism, if we can call it that, displays none of the pluralism and hybridity that Turner has called for in reconceptualizing new nationalisms.

Another major dilemma in this strategy is evident in the struggles *Due South* had to weather in staying on the air. Canadian fans of the show found themselves dependent on the decisions of their southern neighbours about the show's future. Economically tied to the American market, export-driven products like *Due South* cannot survive no matter how hugely successful they are in the domestic market. It may be hard to sustain fantasies of takeover and control in the space of the Other when the Other has the power to obliterate one at any moment.

Nevertheless, *Due South* as exported Canadian popular culture provided viewers up north with unique pleasures. Canadian press accounts reveal the extent to which a doubled spectatorial position—watching as a "knowing" Canadian as well as an "ignorant" American—could supply a great deal of the show's appeal. Almost all press accounts made mention of the choice of "Diefenbaker" as Fraser's wolf's name, as well as the fact that a supporting player, a female reporter, was called Mackenzie King. Most Canadians would be familiar with those names. Yet, a report on a gathering of a hundred and fifty American and Canadians reporters at a CBS press conference on the upcoming series made clear, some knowledges were reserved for Canadians only. The article highlighted American reporters' inevitable questions about how series star Paul Gross handled working in the snow. Producer Haggis declared that the significance of "Diefenbaker" and "Mackenzie King" were among the show's jokes "that are just for Canadians."[72] Into its second year on the air, popular press reports in Canada continued to delight in the name game. Paul Gross was quoted asserting that he was getting letters from some American viewers asserting "My mother was

Canadian and I know why your dog's called Diefenbaker."[73] The only reason why the use of these two names would be funny to Canadians (or to Americans with a suitable "Canadian connection") was because such references would be unknown to Americans whom Canadian viewers knew would be watching the show in the United States. In a piece of self-deprecating irony, Canadian viewers could take their conditioned sense of insignificance in relation to their self-centered neighbours, showing up the latter's ignorance on their own territory. As with the pleasures of *SCTV*, the beaver was at work taking another chunk out of the American Other, while the Other remained largely oblivious.[74]

The show's premise of a Mountie attired in full dress uniform and riding boots, even when out on every day assignment, also served as a significant site for mediating difference, identity, and questions about the constructedness of iconic Canadian images. Canadians tend to have a complicated relationship to the image of the Mountie. In quotidian, daily life ("the grey world as we actually find it"), the RCMP is a federal police force, corrupt at times, secretive, and slow to respond to social change, certainly not a group of mythic crime fighters. Recent issues that have swirled around the "real" Mounties include controversy over Sikh members of the force wearing turbans with their uniforms and the apparent appearance of some officers at an American gathering of white supremacists called "The Good Ole' Boy Roundup." Race and gender issues have been a site of much debate. Currently in a force of almost 16,000 regular members, women, Aboriginals, and other visible minorities account for only about 2,500 members.[75] However, as Reid Gilbert notes, "citizens of Canada respond to the power of the image even while rejecting it as phony."[76] A law enforcement official as the country's major symbol to the world suggests Canada's self-definition as law abiding and orderly, a place devoted to "peace, order, and good government." On the other hand, the

Mountie is largely a construct for American tourists who expect to see police in red serge when they visit Canada in order, perhaps, to convince themselves that they have indeed been to another country. This tourist Mountie has much to do with another recent controversy around the force. The RCMP recently sold exclusive rights for worldwide marketing of its likeness and image (the scarlet tunic, the Stetson, the tall riding boots) to the American entertainment conglomerate, Disney. Disney now is the sole licenser of any goods carrying the Mountie image. The move set off a moral panic about the selling off of whatever remains of Canadian cultural independence to the Americans. Certainly the Disney interests in Mounties, as well as the Disney stake in *Road to Avonlea* suggest a process of turning the country into one big Disneyland theme park: "Canadaland." An interview with *Due South*'s RCMP technical advisor reveals a telling example of the process of erecting a hyperreal image to satisfy Americans' expectations of the Canadian Other. Arguing that it was not completely unheard of to see officers doing regular patrol in the uniform, the RCMP adviser said, "I know in St. Andrew [New Brunswick], in the summertime, there is always a member who walks the beat in uniform because there are a lot of tourists and it's part of the Canadian image."[77] Part of the Canadian image for *Americans*. From their doubled spectator positions, Canadian audiences of *Due South* might be able to take pride and pleasure in this fictive figure (who, of course, does not wear a turban and is certainly not female or "ethnic"), while on the other hand, dismissing it as a pleasing American construct of an imaginary "Canada." Such postmodernist playing with hyperreal touristy images does have consequences, though. Discussing the mobilization of particular images of a *Crocodile Dundee*-inspired Australia by the tourism industry, Graeme Turner warns, "Tourism advertising is peddling precisely those singular versions of national identity that in other contexts we have spent at least two decades contesting. While we are arguing at home about blurring and broadening our definitions of national identities, our identity overseas may have actually sharpened and narrowed."[78]

Due South, because of its need to appeal to the "tourist trade" of American viewers, put on display numerous singular versions of Canada. However, the series was also playing upon Canadian assumption of how America constructs Canada as Other. As portrayed in the opening credit sequence, "Canada" was a snowy, empty wilderness, a far cry from the sleek, sophisticated urbanism emphasized in the credits of *Street Legal*. Fraser, the lone human figure, walked out of this pristine, vast whiteness with the sound of a Native voice in a traditional chant on the soundtrack. The credit sequence moved to images of a frenetic urban milieu that could only connote "America" as the binary opposite to a precivilized Canada of snow. Fraser as a mythic figure with almost supernatural skills of observation and physical prowess led to a certain amount of discomfort from some commentators. Reporters on a CBC radio arts programme compared Fraser to a Mountie lead character in CBC English television's drama series, *North of 60*. The commentators, noting that both series had been nominated for Gemini awards as best Canadian television programmes, were frankly dismissive of *Due South*'s Mountie and praiseworthy of *North of 60*'s version. The latter Mountie was both female and Native. The series, about a largely Native community in northern Alberta and produced with numerous Native personnel on both sides of the camera, is a good example of the public broadcaster's attempt to depict the regional quality of Canadian life, as well as representing the diversity of Canada's multicultural richness. However, neither Fraser, nor *North of 60*'s Michelle, are "realistic" or representative of the RCMP. Both are cultural constructs, pleasing and useful for different reasons. *Due South*'s Fraser may have been more broadly popular because, unlike Michelle, his representation helped mediate pervasive unresolved dilemmas about Canadian identity and self in relation to the American Other. That is not *North of 60*'s fundamental concern. The series is far more preoccupied with working through Native-white contradictions (including the traditional tensions between Natives and the RCMP) from a generally Native point of view. While the show is successful and engaging on its own terms, the localism of its themes—in many ways what makes it so refreshing, satisfying, and important—tends to prevent it from achieving the textual polysemy necessary to be broadly popular.[79]

Due South's polysemy seems particularly wide-ranging. According to Paul Haggis, the show was popular with gay communities in California (some of whom gathered to watch the show in bars while dressed in Mountie attire) and with the Christian right.[80] The "wholesomeness" and "family values" quality of the show provided a certain amount of protective cover for other meanings that may have been less easily activated by non-Canadian readers. For Canadian viewers, Fraser's partner, Vecchio, could be read as the ultimate Ugly American. Unlike Fraser, Vecchio was rude, loud, quick tempered, brash, and dressed in showy, somewhat sleazy outfits. While American viewers might have read Vecchio as just another cop character, in Canada he would have far more archetypal connotations. While Fraser was every bit as stereotyped, he was the more attractive of the two. To the delight of the Canadian news media, the matinee idol good looks of Paul Gross got him the moniker "Studly Do-Right" in an American magazine.[81] Ironically, when *Street Legal* producers sexualized their characters, the result was supreme discomfort from commentators. When the American press acknowledged the sexualized Mountie, the response up north was delight: "Maybe we *can* be sexy—if the Americans say so!" Fraser's polite and non-violent ways (coded as "Canadian") succeeded where Vecchio's more aggressive shoot-'em-ups did not. As a meditation on difference, Canadian audiences in 1995 would likely come to

the same conclusion their grandparents came to back in the 1930s in the study Paul Rutherford referred to: here again Canadians could use popular media to reassure themselves that, after all, Canadian society really was superior and preferable to the mayhem south of the 49th.

Such readings, however, could only be deeply ironic ones, considering the fact that the series was partially funded by American production dollars and kept on the air mostly by its (precarious) success with American audiences. Describing the work of Wayne Booth on irony, Linda Hutcheon argues that, rather than being elitist (by excluding readers who aren't "in the know" about a text's ostensible meaning), irony actually creates communities.[82] Within the larger context of an American broadcast environment, northern viewers of *Due South* could construct themselves as a Canadian community through their collective knowledge that their reading strategies would be fundamentally different from those of the American majority. The show's "in-jokes" acknowledged and rewarded Canada-specific knowledges and assuaged Canada-specific anxieties about self-in-relation to the Other.

Conclusions

Drawing on the work of Michel de Certeau, John Fiske has argued that "the 'art of being in between' is the art of popular culture."[83] Canadians are perhaps the ultimate in-betweeners: a nation built on compromises, in between two colonial empires, the British and the American, and in between two founding cultures, anglophone and francophone. In its relationship to and use of mass culture, Canadians also practice the art of being in between. Finding ways to adapt to the imposed system of Americanized (now globalized) popular culture, Canadians tactically find ways to make do. While the country's cultural arbiters and policy makers have traditionally been blind to the activity, Canadians have managed to assert an ambivalent but ultimately affirming sense of national self using the materials at hand. Often those materials are provided by the colonialist Other or are fashioned at home using tactically deployed tools appropriated from the Other, but they become fundamentally Canadianized at their moment of use. CBC's *Street Legal* may have been an Americanized Canadian show and CTV's *Due South* may have been a Canadianized American show, but in their very "in-between-ness" they revealed their popular cultural power.[84]

This more optimistic view should not, however, blind us to the economic realities of popular cultural production in the global marketplace. Canadian cultural producers and audiences may "make do" with what it imposed, but this making do tends to accept as given numerous ideological positions that are not particularly emancipatory. In order to be an acceptable export product, *Due South* perpetuated patriarchal notions of the action hero. In order to garner big ratings points, *Street Legal* mimicked glitzy, big city "American" TV dramas thus marginalizing Canadian viewers who were not sophisticated urbanites and who were not well-heeled Yuppies driving BMWs. And while it is important to emphasize that Canadians *do* construct their own made-in-Canada readings of American programming, that argument should not lead us to a position of complacency and "what-me-worry?" about the fact that localized cultural production, ever precarious in this country, is now fundamentally threatened here as well as in every other national and ethnic formation around the world. McLuhan's Global Village may be upon us, but this doesn't mean that the transnational media conglomerates who have helped construct this village have any interest in letting us all tell our stories from our locales.

However, acknowledging the power of imposed systems doesn't mean that we ignore or marginalize how Canadian or other national/ethnic formations negotiate those systems. For too long, Canadian cultural commentators have done precisely that. Debates about imperializing (American) mass culture in Canada are almost as old as

the phenomenon of mass culture itself. However, the tenacious arguments that equate "the popular" with "the American" and lump both together as threatening to Canadian sovereignty need to be questioned. Francophone Québécois appear to have little fear that by adopting "American" genres and conventions in their entertainment forms their distinct culture will be obliterated by the American Other. Unlike anglophone Canadians, the Québécois have a truly popular, indigenously produced cultural industry. Canadians in English Canada may have good reason to avoid much of what passes for home-grown "entertainment" offerings. As an industry insider dryly noted, "Canadian entertainment television has become the cod liver oil of television broadcasting."[85] The top-down mandating of a culture that is "good for" the country makes for terrible entertainment. Canadians did not watch *Street Legal, Due South,* or *SCTV* because any of these programmes would strengthen the national health of the country. They watched because of the useful and immediately relevant ways in which the show mediated, appropriated, subverted, and played with the markers of the American Other. And they were fun.

Notes

This chapter was written in 1996. I would like to thank Lorna Roth, Kim Sawchuk, and Marty Allor, former colleagues at Concordia University in Montreal, for influencing my thinking. I'd especially like to thank students in various sections of my Introduction to Mass Communications course at Concordia for sparking ideas and debating with me about some of the issues in this article. Thanks also to Pierre Belanger at the University of Ottawa. Finally, thanks to my partner Elliot for putting up with this when he'd rather be watching PBS.

1 Benedict Anderson, *Imagined Communities: Reflections on the Origin and Spread of Nationalism* (London: Verso, 1983). Anderson discusses how the spread of newspapers assisted in creating a sense of the nation. The daily ceremony of reading, knowing that thousands or millions of others were engaged in the same

activity assures the individual reader that he or she is part of a larger community rooted in everyday experience and living. Thus, a sense of the nation is created from the bottom up via the social circulation of shared fictions (see 39–40).

2 I would like to thank Pierre Belanger for this observation.

3 Bruce Feldthusen, "Awakening from the National Broadcasting Dream: Rethinking Television Regulation for National Cultural Goals," in *The Beaver Bites Back? American Popular Culture in Canada*, ed. David H. Flaherty and Frank E. Manning (Montreal and Kingston: McGill-Queen's University Press, 1993), 42.

4 A note on how I am using the terms "Anglo" or "English" Canadian. These signifiers can be troublesome in a nation of immigrants, many of whom do not have English as a first language. In the context of this article, I am referring to Canadians who do not perceive themselves as part of the Québécois imagined community. Thus, I am referring to residents of Canada, inside and outside Québec, for whom English is either their mother tongue or their most frequently used acquired tongue. In general, the arguments I pursue here are restricted to the situation in English-speaking Canada. The case of popular television and constructions of community in francophone Québec is a unique and, shall we say, "separate" phenomenon that is outside the parameters of this paper. I am also retaining Anglo-Canadian spelling (e.g., neighbour).

5 See table in appendix A in *Seeing Ourselves: Media Power and Policy in Canada*, 2nd ed., ed. Helen Holmes and David Taras (Toronto: Harcourt Brace, 1996), 334.

6 Morris Wolfe, *Jolts: The TV Wasteland and the Canadian Oasis* (Toronto: James Lorimer and Co., 1985), 78.

7 See Graeme Turner, *Making It National: Nationalism and Australian Popular Culture* (St. Leonards, Australia: Allen and Unwin, 1994), especially 119–39. See also his edited volume: *Nation, Culture, Text: Australian Cultural and Media Studies* (London: Routledge, 1993).

8 This dialogue was put into practice in a major gathering of cultural studies practitioners from Australia, New Zealand, and Canada in 1993 at Griffith University in Brisbane.

9 Meaghan Morris, "Tooth and Claw: Tales of Survival and *Crocodile Dundee*," in *The Pirate's Fiancée: Feminism, Reading, Postmodernism* (London: Verso, 1988), 241–69.

10 Seymour Martin Lipset, *Continental Divide: The Values and Institutions of the United States and Canada* (New York: Routledge, 1990). Lipset's book received a huge amount of attention in Canada when it was published. Had the author and publisher been Canadian rather than American, and had the book not received major write-ups in the American media, it is unlikely Lipset's book would have caused such a stir in the Great White North.

11 Richard Collins, *Culture, Communication, and National Identity: The Case of Canadian Television* (Toronto: University of Toronto Press, 1990), 205–14.

12 Rowland Lorimer and Jean McNulty, *Mass Communication in Canada*, 2d ed. (Toronto: McClelland and Stewart, 1991), 311. An anecdotal example: My husband's Canadian brother-in-law is a successful film director living and working in the Los Angeles area. He and his wife wanted to relocate to Toronto for family and quality of life reasons. He was advised that having a Toronto address would be career suicide. The non-L.A., non-centre address would connote "second-rater." He would be considered a marginal filmmaker who couldn't "make it" in the centre. Among successful Canadian filmmakers, David Cronenberg is among the very few who have been able to cultivate international reputations while remaining in Canada.

13 Dallas Smythe, *Dependency Road: Communication, Capitalism, Consciousness, and Canada* (Norwood, NJ: Ablex, 1981).

14 See, in particular, Ben Bagdikian, *The Media Monopoly* (Boston: Beacon Press, 1990), and Herbert Schiller, *Culture, Inc.: The Corporate Takeover of Public Expression* (New York: Oxford University Press, 1989).

15 Brenda Dalglish, "King of the Road: Ted Rogers' Communication Empire Is Growing. But Is He Building a Highway or a Monopoly?" *Macleans* (Mar. 21, 1994): 36–40.

16 Collins, *Culture, Communication, and National Identity*, ix.

17 Turner, *Making It National*, 121. Turner draws on the ideas of Anthony Giddens in *The Consequences of Modernity* (Stanford, CA: Stanford University Press, 1993).

18 Collins, *Culture, Communication, and National Identity*, 329.

19 Paul Rutherford, "Made in America: The Problem of Mass Culture in Canada," in *The Beaver Bites Back?* ed. Flaherty and Manning, 280.

20 Stuart Hall, "Notes on Deconstructing 'the Popular,'" in *People's History and Socialist Theory*, ed. Raphael Samuel (London: Routledge and Kegan Paul, 1981), 232.

21 John Fiske, *Understanding Popular Culture* (Boston: Unwin Hyman, 1989), 23.

22 Rutherford, "Made in America," 270.

23 Tamar Liebes and Elihu Katz, *The Export of Meaning* (New York: Oxford University Press, 1990), 4.

24 Turner, *Making It National,* 10. Turner discusses "old nations" and "new nations" and the construction of identity in ways that suggest the Canadian and Australian dilemma are remarkably similar: "I regard the dominance of the 'cultural purity' model of national identity as a trap laid for the new nations by the old nations: it proposes the old nations' primacy, endowing them with a naturally coherent identity which throws ours into negative relief as especially constructed and spurious. Of course, *all* nations are 'constructed'—indeed, all forms of collective identity are culturally produced. The older nations, however, have more densely mythologised histories from which explanations or legitimations can more implicitly emerge. The newer nations have to undertake the process of nation formation explicitly, visibly, defensively, and are always being caught in the act—embarrassed in the process of construction. Traditional definitions of nationhood deny the legitimacy of such societies and of such processes" (122–23).

25 Lipset, *Continental Divide,* 53. He draws on the observations of Frank Underhill, *In Search of Canadian Liberalism* (Toronto: Macmillan, 1960), 222.

26 Frank E. Manning, "Reversible Resistance: Canadian Popular Culture and the American Other," in *The Beaver Bites Back?* ed. Flaherty and Manning, 9. Manning died prematurely while this anthology was in press. Tragically, Canadian cultural studies has lost a vibrant and trail-blazing critic.

27 Ibid., 19.

28 Linda Hutcheon, *As Canadian as . . . Possible . . . Under the Circumstances!* (Toronto: ECW Press and York University, 1990), 9.

29 Martin Knelman, "The Inner Networkings of SCTV," *Toronto Life* (October 1983): 36.

30 Laura Mulvey explores, from a psychoanalytical framework, this notion of female double spectatorship in "Afterthoughts on 'Visual Pleasure and Narrative Cinema' Inspired by *Duel in the Sun,*" in *Visual and Other Pleasures* (Bloomington: Indiana University Press, 1989).

31 Bernard Ostry, "American Culture in a Changing World," in *The Beaver Bites Back?* ed. Flaherty and Manning, 36.

32 John Caughie, "Playing at Being American," in *Logics of Television: Essays in Cultural Criticism,* ed. Patricia Mellencamp (Bloomington: Indiana University Press, 1990).

33 Mary Jane Miller, *Turn Up the Contrast: CBC Television Drama since 1952* (Vancouver: University of British Columbia Press and CBC Enterprises, 1987).

34 Reid Gilbert, "Mounties, Muggings, and Moose: Canadian Icons in a Landscape of American Violence," in *The Beaver Bites Back?* ed. Flaherty and Manning, 186.

35 This is a question Margaret Atwood has argued to be at the heart of the Canadian literary imagination. See her analysis of Canada-as-victim, *Survival: A Thematic Guide to Canadian Literature* (Toronto: Anansi, 1972). Her work is heavily indebted to Canadian literary critic Northrop Frye and his book *The Bush Garden* (Toronto: Anansi, 1971).

36 David Taras, "Defending the Cultural Frontier: Canadian Television and Continental Integration, in *Seeing Ourselves: Media Power and Policy in Canada,* ed. Helen Holmes and David Taras (Toronto: Harcourt Brace Jovanovich, 1992), 176.

37 Manning, "Reversible Resistance," 8.

38 Along with Nash, such down home broadcast luminaries include David Suzuki, the late Barbara Frum, Lloyd Robertson, Sandy Rinaldo, Peter Mansbridge, Patricia Wallin, Patrick Watson, Hana Gartner, Moses Znaimer, etc. Except for Suzuki, whose long-running CBC programme *The Nature of Things* is syndicated on many American PBS stations, it is unlikely any of these names are known due south.

39 *TV Guide* [Montreal region] (Sept. 26, 1987): P-23.

40 CBC clipping file for *Street Legal:* "Poor Ratings for Street Legal have Programmers Worried," *Toronto Star* (Feb. 6, 1987?).

41 CBC Television Program Release dated November 28, 1986 in *Street Legal* clipping file.

42 CBC clipping file: John Haslett Cuff, "Promising Legal Series Could Lead the Way for Canadian Drama," *Globe and Mail* (Oct. 8, 1988?).

43 CBC clipping file: John Haslett Cuff, "Taking it to the Sheets, *Globe and Mail* (Oct. 1, 1990?).

44 CBC clipping file: John Haslett Cuff, "We've Grown Accustomed to Their Faces," *Globe and Mail* (no date).

45 The impact of the cuts to the CBC—and to Canada—are eloquently discussed in Wayne Skene, *Fade to Black: A Requiem for the CBC* (Vancouver: Douglas and McIntyre, 1993). Despite raised hopes that the new Liberal government might be more generous with the Mother Corp, the current policies of Prime Minister Jean Chré-

tien and his cabinet have merely continued the Tory cuts. Thousands more CBC employees are due to be laid off in the next few years. The current CBC president, Perrin Beatty, is a former Tory cabinet member and does not appear to be particularly disposed to protest or challenge the inexorable dismantling of public broadcasting in Canada.

46 *Canadian Forum* (March 1993).

47 Linda Aisenberg, "Is This Ivan So Terrible?" *TV Guide* [Montreal region] (September 23, 1989): 20.

48 CBC clipping file: Mike Boone, "Street Legal Season off to Shaky Start—Again," *Montreal Gazette* (Oct. 7, 1988): C11.

49 CBC clipping file: John Haslett Cuff, "Taking the Law into Her Own Hands," *Globe and Mail* (October 13, 1989?).

50 Martin Knelman, "Legal Appeal," *Toronto Life* (Mar. 1993): 30.

51 Richard Ouzounian, "Overhaul of Street Legal a Disaster," *Financial Post* (Nov. 26, 1990): 44.

52 Turner, *Making It National,* 115. In this discussion, Turner draws on Peter Hamilton and Sue Matthews, *American Dreams, Australian Movies* (Sydney: Currency Press, 1986).

53 CBC clipping file: John Doyle, "Case Closed," *Broadcast Week* (Feb. 12, 1994). *Broadcast Week* is the television listings magazine of the *Globe and Mail.*

54 CBC clipping file: "So Long, Olivia," *Toronto Star* [editorial?] (Feb. 19, 1994?). Bay Street is Toronto's version of Wall Street. The New Democratic Party (NDP) is Canada's version of a socialist party. At the provincial level, the NDP ran Ontario with a majority government for much of the time *Street Legal* was on the air.

55 CBC clipping file: Bob Remington, "T.O. Keeps Condescension Intact in Legal Eagle Show," *Edmonton Journal* (January 4, 1987): A20.

56 Having recently accepted a teaching position in Edmonton, I plan to hone my own skills in creatively bashing my former hometown.

57 CBC clipping file: Tony Atherton, "Last Rites for Street Legal Give CBC Show an Almost Perfect Ending," *Ottawa Citizen* (Nov. 5, 1994): E6.

58 CBC clipping file: Michael Valpy, "Chuck and Olivia and Leon and Alana," *Globe and Mail* (Jan. 14, 1994).

59 Ostry, "American Culture in a Changing World," 36.

60 CBC clipping file: John Doyle, "Street Legal," *Broadcast Week,* (Jan. 18, 1992): 7.

61 CBC clipping file: Shirley Knott, "Trials and Tribulations," *Broadcast Week* (Nov. 5, 1994): 7.

62 Wendy McCann, "Out of Steam or Too Costly?" *Montreal Gazette* (Feb. 17, 1994): B5.

63 CBC clipping file: Jim Slotek, "So Was It a Sneaky CBC Conspiracy?" *Toronto Sun* (Jan. 14, 1994). I can sympathize with the fan's complaint about Audience Relations. In researching this article, I contacted the department at the CBC Toronto Broadcast Centre about viewing audience letters related to the show. While the department has folders fat with letters for this, and presumably many other CBC programmes, scholarly researchers have been denied access to this material— documentation of rich importance for historians wanting to pursue reception histories of the "public" broadcaster. The most I was allowed was a perusal of the *Street Legal* clipping file. One can only hope for an eventual reversal of policy.

64 CBC press release dated December 7, 1990, in *Street Legal* clipping file.

65 As this chapter went to press in 1996, Alliance was hopeful about working out a production deal with broadcasters in Britain and other European countries where *Due South* has also been hugely popular. The show could possibly go back into production to be screened in non-American markets for non-American viewers who, like Canadians, may find pleasure in constructing their own meanings about the American Other.

66 The show's online fandom is apparently quite active. It also has a grassroots fanzine, *Even Steven,* soliciting fannish fiction, poetry, and artwork. The show has also inspired "slash" fiction—fan-written stories about the homoerotic interactions of the two leading men, Mountie Fraser and Detective Vecchio. When the series faced cancellation, fans coordinated a mass mailing effort to persuade CBS to reconsider its decision. Thanks to Henry Jenkins for this information.

67 Tony Atherton, "'Stupid Idea' Steals Ratings," *Calgary Herald* (Nov. 2, 1994): D6. The article was reprinted from the *Ottawa Citizen.*

68 Hutcheon's work tends to focus on irony within domains traditionally considered "high culture" rather than popular culture. Nevertheless, I find her arguments extremely useful in discussing the textual operations of popular Canadian television.

69 Turner, *Making It National,* 115.

70 Morris, "Tooth and Claw," 248.

71 Ibid., 250.

72 Wendy McCann, "Canucks Cause Kerfuffle as New Shows Beam South," *Winnipeg Free Press* (July 27, 1994): C8. "Kerfuffle" is a Canadianism meaning a stir or commotion.

73 Jim Bawden, "The South Shall Rise Again," *Starweek* (Mar. 2, 1996): 78.

74 By the way, Diefenbaker and King were two of Canada's most important and long-serving prime ministers in the twentieth century. If called upon to list recent leaders of the United States's most important trading partner, most Americans would be hard pressed to come up with any names beyond Pierre Elliot Trudeau. Large numbers of Americans could not say who the current prime minister is.

75 Tim Harper, "Hiring Policies Changing Face of Mounties," *Toronto Star* (Aug. 8, 1995): A1. As the article emphasizes, the RCMP is in the midst of an affirmative action recruitment drive, strongly favouring female, Native, and visible minority recruits.

76 Gilbert, "Mounties, Muggings, and Moose," 187.

77 Brian McKenna, "Mountie Always Gets His Laughs," *Vancouver Sun* (Jan. 19, 1995): C10.

78 Turner, *Making It National,* 117.

79 For theorizing about the need for popular relevance in order for mass media texts to be taken up by differently situated social formations, see Fiske, *Understanding Popular Culture.*

80 Jane Stevenson, "Cross Border Hit Due South Rushes for More Shows," *Montreal Gazette* (Dec. 3, 1994): D11.

81 Richard Helm, "'Studly Do-Right': Paul, Paul, He's Our Man Catching U.S. Viewers Like No Canadian Can," *Calgary Herald* (Jan. 11, 1995): B6.

82 Hutcheon, *As Canadian,* 19. She refers to Wayne Booth's *A Rhetoric of Irony.*

83 Fiske, *Understanding Popular Culture,* 36.

84 For an autobiographical discussion of my own in-between-ness as a popular culture scholar and a Canadian, please see my contributor's statement in this volume.

85 Sheelah D. Whittaker, "Canadian Programs are the Cod Liver Oil of TV," *Canadian Speeches* (March 1990), 56. Whittaker was president of Canadian Satellite Communications, Inc. and delivered this speech to The Empire Club of Canada.

WHEELS OF FORTUNE: NATION, CULTURE, AND THE TOUR DE FRANCE

Catherine Palmer

Even if there was another Chernobyl disaster twenty kilometres from Paris, the Tour would still go on. The race is unstoppable. You almost don't need the riders anymore.

—JEAN-CLAUDE COLOTTI

In the following pages, I examine the transformation of landscape that is accomplished by the Tour de France; a bicycle race that occurs annually in July, dramatically impacting upon the social and symbolic territory of France. Given that this "mega-event"[1] involves a capital investment of some 150 million francs ($40 million), requires a cast of thousands, and mobilizes cultural and commercial resources on a scale without precedent, unraveling the range and reach of its impact is beyond the scope of any single ethnographer. This chapter thus focuses on one dimension of the Tour, namely the cultural consequences that are effected by it as it moves across France. By paying particular attention to the role that consumer activity plays in the restructuring of symbolic and territorial landscapes, I look at the various ways in which the Tour de France—and France itself— are *socially* constructed. The extreme commercialization of the event presents a range of images of "Frenchness," out of which consumers can construct an enduring cultural identity. As I develop in this chapter, the Tour de France involves a deep transformation of everyday life that is inextricable from the practices of consumer activity.

Before expanding this argument ethnographically, there is some preliminary theoretical territory to negotiate. The emphasis placed on the central role of consumerism in transforming national culture points to a need to shift the focus of anthropology (and other social sciences) so as to take into account the climate of postmodern times. While the relationship between nation and culture has been a longstanding concern for anthropologists, the increasingly media-rich and commodity-replete nature of social life in the late twentieth century offers an unprecedented range of possibilities for exploring this association. The ubiquity of the media, and the sheer quantity of commodities which circulate in contemporary society, provide a new set of provisions for articulating identity. Through their ongoing encounters with goods, commodities, and the media, consumers are continually presented with, and produce for themselves, images of their nation.

While social agency remains central to the construction of national identity, it is now mediated by consumer involvement.[2] This being the case, anthropologists must focus their attention on those sites of experience which are saturated by commercial activity, for it is here that members of nations collectively produce versions of themselves. As Peace recognizes, there is a "need to eschew the cliché ridden, metaphor replete formulae which reify national cultures and national identities to the point of inaccessible abstraction. The analytical focus must shift toward the ethnography of events, processes and encounters."[3] It is precisely the collective and commodity-rich nature of contemporary ceremonies, be they rock concerts, art expositions, or sporting contests, that provides valuable data with which to orient ethnographic inquiries into "national identity." At these events, consumers are provided with a special opportunity to work through what it means to belong to a nation. As I demonstrate in this chapter, the national festival of the Tour de France provides a fine example of the interpretive potential that grand-scale events can hold for reading culture.

My emphasis on the central role that consumerism plays in the transformation of public culture vis-à-vis the Tour de France is a key point of entry to the main theme of this chapter, namely that the Tour de France dramatically alters landscapes and territory as it moves around France. The logical progression from this assertion is to develop the argument that far from being pre-given and inalienable—there simply to be traversed—landscape and territory are *socially* constructed and are the product of sustained involvement and accomplishment by those who live in the nation. As Bender recognizes, "landscapes are created by people—through their experience and engagement with the world around them."[4] The landscape of France is repeatedly worked upon by the producers and consumers of public culture to yield a range of narratives that are brought into being and progressively elaborated by the Tour de France. Its annual return provides a particularly compelling account of the ways in which the spatial landscape of France is constructed by social relations. In moving around the country, the Tour presents an unfolding cartography that ultimately fetishizes France by defining her composition, aesthetic, and ambience. The Tour reorders, reframes, and restructures the cultural territory of France; it gives the landscape a life of its own. Through commercial activity particularly, the Tour capitulates and reinvents a particular social map of France; a specific construction of "Frenchness." As I elaborate in the following pages, the Tour de France provides a key site, albeit one of many, at and toward which new trajectories for nation building can be articulated and directed.

This chapter has two concerns: First, to trace the Tour as it transforms the spatial landscapes it encounters and, second, to elaborate the ways in which this social mapping of France promotes particular imaginings of the nation. In packaging and presenting France through a range of stock images of national identity, the country is invested with style, flair, and sophistication; attributes of "Frenchness" that are reinforced by the annual return of the Tour. Being French is distilled in commercial activity, and the Tour de France provides an ideal site from which to attempt a reading of this construction.

The Calm before the Storm

Before addressing the representations of Frenchness that are articulated by and through the Tour, it is necessary first to provide some sense of the commercial activity that enables and inspires these imaginings of national identity. The Tour brings to France a barrage of media personnel and an avalanche of commercial activity which trigger a manifest transformation of her social and spatial landscapes. To illustrate the capacity of the Tour to redefine territory through consumer intervention, I pay particular attention to the transformation of those stage or host villages that oversee the arrival and departure of each of its daily stages, for it is these *villes-étapes* that most notably bear the brunt of its power. By sustaining a veritable pummeling from the Tour, the stage villages that it visits serve to spatially record the history of the event through the rich tapestry of social relations that unfurl in each town.

My privileging of the *ville-étape* to highlight the effects of the Tour upon France is not to deny its impact upon other towns, nor is it to deny that towns and villages exist independently of the Tour de France, for like all communities, they are involved in a daily process of self-construction. Certainly, the Tour operates as an imperative cultural force when moving throughout the country, however its social, economic, and political ramifications are most obvious for those towns that host its arrivals and departures. It is in response to these social, political, and economic influences that indigenous actors—be they spectators, shop owners, or local dignitaries—articulate their impressions of the Tour in France. Host villages most obviously (although, of course, not exclusively) provide a stage upon which local actors can do some highly interpretive, culturally constitutive work on being both proudly parochial and pub-

licly French. The stage villages that the Tour de France visits provide a succession of sites for the "cultural praxis of national identity."[5]

It is at this juncture that I raise an important methodological issue: the material that I have assembled here is drawn from my fieldwork between June 1993 and August 1994. During this time, I saw two Tours de France. The first I spent as a guest of SBS Australia, traveling virtually the entire race with the television crew. The second I spent immersed in French appreciations of the race; reading about it in papers, watching it on television, and talking about it in bars, cafés, post offices, and laundromats. One week of this second Tour I also spent with the Festina professional cycling team. In between Tours I was most immediately concerned with the actions and interactions of those cyclists living and riding in the *département* of Isère and the neighboring ones of Savoie, Haute-Savoie, and Hautes-Alpes. Most of my fieldwork was conducted in this far eastern corner of France; participating in daily cycling excursions to a range of towns including Villard-de-Lans, Serre Chevalier, Alpe d'Huez, Bourg d'Oisans, Val-Thorens, Moûtiers, and Cluses—those stage villages in Isère and in neighboring *départements* that welcomed the Tour in 1993 and 1994. While the emphasis in this chapter is on the relationship between nation and culture as articulated and commodified by and through the Tour de France, it comes out of my sustained involvement with local cycling lives.[6] As I elaborate in the following pages, national identity is mediated by local experiences, and regularly riding to the aforementioned places enabled me, with my fellow cyclists, to witness their progressive transformation as they prepared for the arrival of this national festival. By undertaking periodic cycling excursions to these stage villages it was possible to trace their systematic reconstruction as they prepared for the arrival of the Tour de France.

While I do not propose to provide a comprehensive description of these towns prior to the arrival of the Tour de France, there are, nonetheless, certain features that make their encounter with the Tour all the more remarkable. While stage villages can be major metropolitan or urban centers such as Bordeaux or Montpellier, those in Isère and the neighboring *départements* are characteristically small, provincial towns, often betwixt and between alpine serenity and the incursions of consumer culture. Alpe d'Huez, Serre Chevalier, and Val-Thorens are custom-built ski resorts, while Bourg d'Oisans and Villard-de-Lans are market towns which service the smaller *communes* dotted throughout the Massif de l'Oisans and the Massif du Vercors; key mountain ranges in the regional topography. Although small in size, these *villes-étapes* remain parochial landmarks that provide key sites for the production, distribution, and, above all, the consumption of cultural products associated with the Tour de France. The *villes-étapes* throughout Isère and elsewhere represent important places at which to manufacture and sustain, through the agency of the Tour de France, a particularly commodified representation of the country it embodies on a national level.

The calm air of alpine serenity that characterizes life in Isère and neighboring *départements* is shattered as the arrival of the Tour de France becomes increasingly imminent. From the month of May onward, both cultural and commercial landscapes are razed and replanted with the seeds of the Tour de France. An enormous swath of consumer activity precedes the Tour, which, once put in place, then leaves the landscape "pure" for the race action itself. The order in which the Tour unfolds is a theme I will pick up on shortly, but suffice it to say here that the coming of the Tour triggers a period of high consumerism in which its imminent arrival is elevated to a position of preeminence in the material concerns of daily life in France. The iconography of the everyday is surrendered to the Tour. Most notably, a veritable flood of advertising saturates the prosaic backdrop of routine life with images of the Tour de France. As Foster notes, "any commodity, under certain conditions, can function as a medium for objectifying the nation,"[7] and the flurry of media activity that surrounds the Tour de France provides many examples of the ways in which commodities can produce new cultural trajectories for a nation.

In the month before the event, television, radio, and newspaper advertising becomes increasingly Tour-oriented. Every conceivable product or business is given a second use value: to promote the Tour de France. For the 1993 Tour, for example, *télécartes* and a special issue of the 100- and 500-franc note feature the faces of past Tour greats, while a set of commemorative dinner plates, made in conjunction with Michelin Maps, is embossed with the route for that year. A survey of advertisements in the French popular press reveals that Coca-Cola becomes "*la boisson officielle du Tour de France,*" Festina watches are now "*les chronométreurs professionnel,*" while France 2/3 Télévision defines itself as "*l'image du Tour*" when featured in newspapers such as *Le Dauphiné-Libéré* or *Le Parisien.* Television advertising is similarly packaged to promote the Tour. In one commercial for the Quick hamburger chain, a young girl is featured riding her bicycle into a Quick restaurant wearing the distinctive red-and-white polka dot jersey of the King of the Mountains. The text which accompanies the widely screened commercial for the then newly released Coupé and la Punto Cabrio models of Fiat cars reads: "Cette année, avec 47,7km/h de moyenne nos croma ont battu un record. Rouleur au ralenti sous un soleil de plomb, pendant des heures, descendre le col d'Izoard à la poursuite d'un coureur échappé à 120 km/h, puis attaquer la montée d'Isola 2000 à fond de seconde. Nous remercions donc les hommes du Tour, et surtout les coureurs, qui nous permettent chaque année d'aller un peu plus loin. PARTENAIRE OFFICIEL DU TOUR DE FRANCE."[8] The semiotics of this text are easy to decode: attempting to follow the riders in the Tour de France has given Fiat a nationwide test track for its cars. Commodity fetishism lies at the heart of the interpretive structure of all advertisements, and this one is no different. Here the Tour is granted with the powers of being and doing. Thanks to the Tour de France, these cars have become better than ever. If it was not for the descent from the Col d'Izoard or the climb to Isola 2000, then Fiat would not be able to showcase the stylish handling of its Coupé and Punto Cabrio. The Tour de France has injected new life into Fiat; it has created opportunities for which advertisers are publicly grateful. Supporting newspaper advertising picks up on this notion of commercial reciprocity: the closing sentence in one advertisement reads: "Le Tour de France aime Fiat, Fiat aime le Tour, la Grande Boucle est bouclée."[9] As Goldman notes: "A dialectic of interpretive contestation and ideological reincorporation unfolds in a commodity culture."[10]

While the increase in media coverage is not, in itself, peculiar to stage villages—indeed, it is nationally omnipresent—the incorporation of consumer products into everyday streetscapes is. The landscape of a host town is peppered with images from the Tour. Billboards, posters, advertising in bus shelters, and promotions in store windows are all dominated by representations of the Tour de France: clothing shops hang cycling uniforms on their mannequins, and the cover sheets from old editions of *L'Equipe* [11] are included in the window displays of *tabacs* and cafés. Even haberdashery and lingerie stores get in on the act, with lengths of material draped over bicycles and scantily clad models posing across their bikes. Corporations such as Coca-Cola and GAN Assurances offer promotions and special deals, while Crédit Lyonnais touts itself as *"la banque du maillot jaune."* Castorama features "yellow jersey specials," and Supermarché Champion, the PMU, Bricomarché, and Bosch all shape their advertising campaigns in terms of the Tour de France. The most mundane of commodities are used to promote the Tour, with groceries in supermarkets being incorporated into this commodity bricolage. Frozen dinners are endorsed by the Chazal racing team, while brands of fruit juice and soft drinks are similarly supported by other teams including WordPerfect and GB-MG Boys.

Given the sheer quantity of images to choose from, it is interesting to note which goods and icons are selected to promote the Tour, and which are ignored. The privileging of certain commodities over others provides an index of national identity in which the selection of certain images reflects salient national archetypes. As Braudel notes, "a nation will consistently recognize in itself certain stock image."[12] Most notably, the theme of sophistication—in both fashion and technology—is repeatedly amplified by the media. Television commercials and newspaper advertisements for France Télécom and France 2/3 Télévision elaborate the hi-tech vision of France,[13] while the esteemed virtues of beauty, finery, elegance, and physical perfection are espoused in advertisements for everything from cars to perfume. In one series of television advertisements for Chanel No. 5, a woman, dressed in the style of haute couture, exudes luxury and elegance. With blood-red lipstick, glittering jewelry, and no doubt smelling like a million bucks, she embodies the stereotype of a chic and sophisticated France.

When promoting the Tour de France, advertisers employ a similar range of iconic images which perpetuate the notion of a sophisticated and sexy France. As in most Western commodity cultures, *la pub* in France trades on the maxim that "sex sells." When advertising everything from sunscreens to telephones, romantic and sexual imagery is customary. Cellular phones from Motorola are the ideal way to say *"je t'aime,"* Cacharel is "the forbidden fragrance," while Tendre Poison is advertised as a "playful and seductive" perfume. In both print and electronic media, thin, languid, and semi-naked bodies abound, with *doubles entendres* plentiful. A television advertisement for Perrier mineral water, for example, features a female hand with long red talons caressing the neck of a bottle. Above the steamy soundtrack, punctuated by heavy breathing, the bottle begins to grow until it blows its top; an unashamed allusion to ejaculation. Such images grace French screens and pages on a daily basis, confirming the centrality of sex to imaginings of a general "French cultural style."[14]

In promoting the Tour de France, the populist press trades on both the sensuality of cycling and the sophisticated nature of French society at one and the same time. A newspaper advertisement, again for Fiat cars, features a woman, clad in evening wear and a pearl necklace, drinking out of a *bidon* and wearing a pair of cycling gloves. The accompanying text reads: "l'élégance, c'est savoir faire les choses les plus folles et les faire jusqu'au bout. Personne ne sait si l'auteur de cette définition était un amateur de cyclisme, toujours est-il qu'elle convient admirablement aux héros du Tour."[15] The juxtaposition of cycling and elegance in this advertisement is striking—a common strategy when packaging and promoting the Tour de France for popular consumption. Similarly, tourist pamphleteering exploits sexual imagery in the selling of the Tour de France. Publicity brochures for the stage finish at Serre Chevalier—*le Toit du Monde* invited one to *"monter au septième ciel,"* to climb to seventh heaven—while one women's magazine featured the young French riders Richard Virenque and Jacky Durand in a pictorial spread entitled *"les mecs à saut,"* literally "guys to jump." In each example the sexual connotation is explicit, reinforcing the carnal and hedonistic nature of life in France.

Transformation of Place and Space

The flood of Tour-oriented media advertising that saturates a stage village gives way to a transformation of place and space as the encounter between the traveling circus and the *ville-étape* draws near.[16] A town awaiting the race is totally restructured as Tour space. Prior to its arrival, the race organization La Société du Tour de France submits a detailed report on what transformations need to be made, right down to how many tables and chairs, flower bouquets, and telephone lines will be required. When the race arrives, bollards, signposts, benches, and rubbish bins are taken out for the time that the Tour spends in a stage town. In Moûtiers in 1994, it was decided that the road surface would be a hazard for the riders, so local officials roughened the surface of the cobblestones in the finishing straight to provide the necessary grip, while in Montluçon in 1993, the town was ordered to take up fifteen traffic islands and roundabouts.

The physical transformation of urban space by the Tour de France is striking as entire towns become engulfed by the race. Common garden areas metamorphose as the Village Départ, car and furniture showrooms become the *salle de presse*, and soccer pitches and rugby grounds are turned into helicopter landing pads. Differently colored arrows strategically placed throughout the town direct the media and other vehicles toward the finish area. Press cars park haphazardly on the footpaths and technical vehicles scream recklessly through the streets. In Cluses, a few shoppers grumble and one elderly woman shakes her fist at the latest driver to jump the curb. He just smiles back, knowing full well that the bicycle race comes first, far ahead of such mundane concerns as being able to pass on the footpath. The entire landscape of a town is transformed by the presence of the Tour. Streets are closed off, traffic is diverted, and barricades are erected, marking the route of the riders through the town. To quote Jean-Marie Leblanc, the Directeur Général du Tour, "We close towns for a living." For one stage finish in 1994, the funnel-shaped church in the ski resort of Alpe d'Huez was converted into the press room. Nôtre Dame des Neighs was probably the only church where, for one day of the year at least, there were ashtrays in the nave and a bar in the vestry, and where, as local opinion has it, an organist was asked to leave because he was disturbing the journalists' concentration. In every possible way, "normal" life is suspended or displaced to accommodate the "abnormality" of the Tour de France.

In each stage village, a range of sites is provided from which to experience the enormous and ever-expanding nature of the Tour de France. In addition to permanent bars and cafés, food and drink stalls are set up selling overpriced Kronenbourg, Coke, and Evian and, in merchandise stalls, t-shirts, windbreakers, pullovers, posters, minibicycles, maps of the route, videos, bottles of commemorative wine, and copies of team jerseys, including *le maillot jaune,* can all be bought and flaunted as evidence of participation in this supremely entrepreneurial event. Around these stalls, a veritable army of workers busy themselves by erecting scaffolding, placing portable toilets, and installing tiers of seating in anticipation of the swell of people that will wash over the stage village. In keeping with the commercial carnival of the Tour, pubs and clubs offer Tour promotions such as cheap drinks and half-priced entry passes. After-dark activities include street parties, fireworks displays, and concerts by prominent French and international artists such as Jean-Michel Jarre, Roch Voisine, and D:REAM. The restructuring of a *ville-étape* to accommodate not only a vast number of Tour workers but also their sound systems, lighting rigs, stage scaffolding, and fireworks detonators demonstrates the transformative capacities of the Tour to impact upon territory by annually introducing a complex web of interlinked social relations to new (and old) regions of France.

While the range of sites from which one can experience the Tour de France is indeed diverse, the arrival of the riders refocuses the gaze that the transformation of place and space disperses. Whether perusing the merchandise stalls, ogling the scantily clad publicity girls, or "talking Tour"

with one's neighbor in the beer tent, all conversations stop and all enthusiasms are redirected toward the race action the moment Daniel Mangeas, "the Voice of the Tour," announces that the riders have entered a town. For all its extravagances, the transformation and commercialization of space by the entourage of the Tour is no more than a necessary preface to the arrival of the riders themselves.

The order with which the package of the Tour unfolds is critical, for having dispensed with commercial activity, the road is then left clear, literally, for the riders to enact a contest that is surely one of unsurpassed sporting authenticity.[17] As the riders descend upon a stage town, the "mega-event" becomes the territory of "mega men." The flood of advertising, the removal of street signs, the takeover of hotels and restaurants, and the sheer extravagance of the publicity caravan, set the stage for the arrival of the riders—the central actors—and their supporting cast of team managers, drivers, *soigneurs,* and publicists.

As the prime performers, the riders get the biggest reaction when they descend upon a stage village. The repeated cry of "*allez! allez!*" echoes throughout the stage town as the riders race toward *l'arrivée.* When they appear in the finishing straight, the thousands of fans pressed into this section of roadway beat their hands against the barricades that keep them from spilling into the road. The din is deafening and crescendic, climaxing in an explosive roar of approval and applause as the jostling sprinters surge across the finish line. Place and space as customarily imagined are reinstalled, barricades and scaffolding are dismantled, and the start and finish areas, the television commentary boxes, the race jury headquarters, the medical center, and the portable toilets are all removed. Even the row of Fiat logos stenciled onto the finishing straight are blasted off with a high-pressure water hose. The riders are now elevated to a position of symbolic preeminence in the unfolding order of the Tour de France. Interviews with the winning riders and the key players in the day's racing become the main focus, with television and radio commentaries being presented from the finishing straight, the commentator often appearing breathless and windblown, as if to simulate the frenetic pace of the race itself. The Tour has a building momentum that culminates with the arrival of the riders themselves.

Mapping France

So far, this chapter has focused on the commercialization of place and space that the Tour de France brings to and imposes upon stage villages. By paying particular attention to the towns that the Tour visits in Isère and neighboring *départements* I have shown the ways in which it recasts spatial landscapes in new cultural and commercial terms. While the ways in which commodities and advertisements are employed and fetishized to denote a *ville-étape* as Tour territory provide a compelling account of the transformative capacities of the Tour de France, they also provide an indispensable means of articulating a particular French cultural style. The absence of traditional rituals of national representation—there are no national colors, no national flags, and no national anthems—mean that those who follow the Tour's progress in France must draw upon other resources to articulate their cultural identity. It is through reading, interpreting, and reappropriating the icons used to promote the Tour de France that this is most consistently done. The remainder of this chapter is thus concerned to examine the Tour de France as a key site for both the commodification and the consumption of national culture. Drawing on the ethnographic terrain covered when examining the transformation of place and space, this chapter now looks at the ways in which the blitz of media activity that accompanies the Tour supplies a range of images and representations of "being French." The customary

assumptions of the French as being stylish, exuberant, and xenophobic are borne out in the annual return of the Tour de France. The Tour is a distinctly French focus of distinctly French interests, and it is when articulated through commercial activity and media coverage that these cultural traits become most pronounced.

The recognized ability of the Tour to produce a social cartography of France is of special note when detailing French appreciations of the Tour de France. As de Certeau notes, "any map is a manipulation of space,"[18] and it is the ways in which the Tour manipulates the map of France that contribute to the making of a distinctive social reality. Through the annual return of its emblematic bike race, France is constructed through a range of complementary cartographies against or through which the elaboration of French national character can be done. The Tour provides a map of France, drawn anew daily, which engages its followers in a variety of ways through which commitment and belonging to the nation can be conferred. The various narrative threads produced in commercial and media activity come together in the one race, the one nation. It is my aim now to identify and elaborate the dimensions of this national map of France which are constructed and negotiated by the Tour de France.

The physical movement of the riders and their entourage across the countryside provides the first grid in this Tour-mediated map of France. The progress of the Tour around France is clearly charted. In its daily coverage, *L'Equipe* features a "progress to date" map, while tourist offices, *tabacs*, and cafés post the expected times that the race will pass through the various towns and villages on its itinerary. When it moves into each new *pays*, the local newspaper prints a listing of the roads that will be closed as the race steams through. While the progress of the riders is charted by media sources, it is also mapped by the strategic placement of personnel along the course. Road closures, for example, are policed vigilantly, with a *gendarme* covering every crossroad to ensure that no unauthorized personnel stray onto the course. France as a territorial construct is now the hostage of the army of workers who ensure the safe passage of the Tour de France. Local roads become national roads, the Tour's intended takeover clearly stated to the public. According to Didier, an Isèrois cyclist and part-time *pompier* who has marshaled several Tours, "when we see the *pilote* we know that the right of way is given to every car carrying a Tour sticker."[19] Such expressions give voice to the power of the Tour to transform the landscapes of France. Roads, streets, and other territorial features are recast as Tour space. The landscape of France becomes an "ethnoscape"; "a landscape of persons"[20] that is totally dependent on social relations for its geographical definition. France as territory does not exist without the agency of individuals. It is not a neutral spatial grid, but a space charged with cultural salience which is made visible by the extravagant excesses of the Tour de France.

Of course, the movement of Tour personnel could not be charted if it were not for the inescapable involvement of the media in packaging, promoting, and presenting the Tour de France. The progress of the riders throughout France constitutes one dimension of the cartography of France that is augmented and amplified by the intense media coverage that the Tour receives. The inescapability of television, radio, and newspaper coverage produces another cartography against or through which the elaboration of French national character can be done; a landscape of people exists alongside a landscape of images which are routinely negotiated and appropriated in ways that reflect national identity. As Blair et al. note, "the media take aspects of sporting competition and reconstitute them into a wider cultural and ideological construction of national stability."[21]

Considering the role of the media is unavoidable in any discussion of a sporting event and the Tour de France is no exception. The Tour could

not exist without the media: it is an event induced by the media and by which the media are seduced. Journalists from just about every major sporting newspaper and magazine in the world fill the Tour village, mobile radio stations carry the race into the homes of people in Bogota, Madrid, Adelaide, and cities worldwide, while television networks from the United States, Japan, England, Australia, and of course, France, transmit their images around the world. While the "global ecumene" within which these images circulate warrants discussion in itself, the concerns of this chapter lie elsewhere.[22] I am more interested in the ways in which the *French* media coverage both constructs and confirms particular messages and motifs of national belonging, for as Hargreaves notes, "a sense of unity, conferred by the feeling of belonging to the nation, cutting across class, ethnic, gender and other loyalties, is perhaps the very linchpin of a hegemonic system, and the media are, arguably, the most important instrument of reproducing national unity today."[23] Despite the internationalism of media personnel and sources, the Tour de France exists as a uniquely French event in that the media coverage provided in France offers, for those who reside there, a range of national (and transnational) character types through which they can constitute a distinctive cultural presence. The vast communications network which carries the Tour around the globe does not diminish the ability of the French media to foster a particularly insular view of national importance, for those who receive these images ultimately control their interpretation in ways that reflect salient national archetypes.

As detailed elsewhere, the media in Isère and neighbouring *départements* are intensely parochial, emphasizing local events over national ones.[24] However, the horizons of media consumers are significantly broadened with the arrival of the Tour de France. On the first Saturday in July listeners tune into Radio Tour, which is transmitted across France, while supporters now read *L'Equipe* in preference to *Le Dauphiné-Libéré;* as Laurent notes, "I feel like I know what is happening wherever the Tour is in France." The standardization of media coverage across the nation functions to mediate the partial and provincial nature of regional media sources. The local becomes national, with followers, irrespective of where they reside, all receiving the same information. And they receive vast quantities of information: television coverage alone attracts between 3.3 million and 4.6 million viewers who tune in daily for the live finishes. Broadcasting begins *en direct* at midday and continues uninterrupted until 9 P.M., alternating between the channels of TF1, France 2, and France 3. Highlights from the stage, interviews with the riders, and excerpts from Vélo-Club are packaged for late-night programs, giving a perpetual, inescapable quality to the Tour. Radio and newspaper coverage are equally comprehensive. Europe 1 Radio Tour is broadcast across France, providing live commentary as the events of the Tour unfold, and the circulation of *L'Equipe* is estimated at over 500,000 copies for each of the twenty-three days of the Tour. Like all "media events," the coverage that the Tour de France receives is monopolistic in that "all channels switch away from their regularly scheduled programming in order to turn to the great event." [25] In doing so, they compel viewers to tune into the Tour. The unanimity of the networks in presenting the same event underlines the worth, even the obligation, of viewing.

The sheer volume of media coverage is acknowledged by the media themselves and incorporated into advertising campaigns to comprise yet another dimension of the Tour-mediated cartography of France. A four-page newspaper advertisement for France 2/3 Télévision charts the comprehensive mapping of France by the media: "Pour suivre 180 mecs qui ne pensent qu'à s'échapeer, il fallait bien 9 motos, 40 voitures, 6 cars-vidéo et 3 helicoptères. Avec 3800km parcou-

rus et 10 millions de téléspectateurs, ça fait 2632 téléspectateurs au km. 120 techniciens, 25 caméramen, 22 journalistes qui parlent alors que 180 coureurs pédalent pour 3800km de route, il faut 80 heures de retransmission en direct et 3 rendez-vous quotidiens. Finalement, à quelques détails près, le Tour de France est une véritable histoire de vélos. France Télévision . . . le plus grand terrain de sports" [26] As detailed in this advertisement, a vast cavalcade of personnel and technology are introduced to the territory of France when charting the Tour's progress around the nation. The distribution of media personnel, and the images that are created by them, comprise what Appadurai defines as a "mediascape"; an environment in which events are experienced as a "complicated and interconnected repertoire of print, celluloid, electronic screens and billboards." [27]

One Race, One Nation

The effect of the unfolding and overlapping cartographies that are designed and traced by both the riders in the Tour de France and the media personnel who chart their every movement is to produce an "imagined community" in which the members of the nation-state of France are bound together by shared cultural imaginings of sameness.[28] Popular sentiment particularly reflects the ability of the Tour de France to unite the nation as one: Jean-Luc, a rider in Isère maintains, "it is a race that we all have in common. It is a communion between us that has lasted since the time of Maurice Garin." [29] Whether watching the race from a vantage point along the route, reading about it in the newspaper or discussing it in a bar or a café, the annual return of the Tour connects people in ways that customary links cannot. "The triumph of the Tour de France" is, as Vigarello notes, "the image of a France unified by the soil, stronger, without a doubt, than the France unified by language or morals." [30]

The idea of the nation as one is the leitmotif par excellence of the Tour de France. The populist media pick up on the power of the Tour to unite multiple personnel across multiple registers of interpretation. An article in *Le Parisien* on July 24, 1994, describes the Tour as producing "*une France réconciliée*," while an advertisement for France 2/3 Télévision in the same newspaper announces: "France 2/3 Supervision. Super! La boucle, encore plus grande sur France Supervision, l'arrivée du Tour comme si vous y étiez."[31] Journalists from *L'Equipe* adopt phrases such as "all of France is speaking of Virenque," "a nation rejoices," or "a nation is plunged into despair" when reporting on the unfolding events of the Tour de France. If, as Anderson suggests, the nation is an imagined community, then the media play important roles in the process by which this community is constructed. The sheer inescapability of the media provides an "arena in which individuals who have never met, can feel part of a wider community."[32] The ubiquity of the media, particularly advertising, provides an important basis for interaction when the Tour comes to France.

The Tour de France provides a fine example of not only an imagined community, but also ways of imagining community. The circulation of commodities and media images are constituent features in this process. When people interact with the goods on sale in the merchandising stalls, discuss the events as reported in *L'Equipe,* or buy the products endorsed by the professionals (among other things) they share a sense of being in common, of a "we-ness" despite their dispersal throughout France. A person in Grenoble can have a sense of familiarity when in Bordeaux or Paris, for he or she is surrounded by the same advertisements, listens to the same radio personalities, and watches the same television programs when moving between these very different sites of experience. As Hannerz notes: "The defining feature of the media is the use of technology to achieve an externalization of meaning in such a way that people can communicate with one another without being in one another's immediate presence; media are machineries of meaning."[33] The media products which are routinely appropriated by consumers do not disappear when the consumer enters a new cultural space; they circulate within a wider system which people move in and out of. The importance of social agency is again stressed, for it is when working with media texts that one's sense of belonging to a community or a nation is both felt and expressed. While cultural membership in France is formalized and institutionalized at the level of the State, it is in the everyday encounters with advertising, goods, and media products where this imagining is most consistently done.

Indeed, the media offer a key mechanism by which to fabricate a sense of cultural unity out of massive regional diversity. As Braudel writes, "France is a "dazzling triumph of the plural, of the heterogeneous, of the never quite the same, of the never quite what you find elsewhere,"[34] and it is precisely this variety that the movement of the Tour around France magnifies. While there are major cycling Tours in most European countries, it is the Tour de France that consistently employs geographical variations for dramatic advantage.

In mapping France, the Tour both exploits the geographical features of individual regions and links each with France at large. National identity is mediated by local experiences to construct the nation as one; a nation that is built out of geographical and cultural diversity. Described by Vigarello as a "valorization, above all, of the landscape," the Tour de France is the perfect showcase for cultural and regional diversity.[35] The tranquility of the Alps stands in opposition to the urban landscape of Paris, the dramatic coastline of Brittany is most pronounced when compared to the lapping shores of the Mediterranean, and the single-story whitewashed villas of Rousillon are distinctive in opposition to the gaudy high-rise complexes that line the Côte d'Azur. The climate and terrain of each region presents its own individual character, which is elevated by virtue of global media coverage to a position of international prominence. As the Tour moves across the countryside, it highlights the contrasting landscapes of France; it constructs a variety of "Frances" for popular consumption.

The cultural and geographical diversity of France is, of course, made most visible by the media. As the Tour unfolds, a range of new archetypal images are highlighted, the cumulative effect producing an enduring pattern of Frenchness. Each day the television program *Autour du Tour* features a segment entitled "*La Découverte de la Ville de sa Région*" which provides an overview of the towns and regions that come under the Tour spotlight. By mentioning its food, produce, and notable historic sites, each region is elevated to a state of temporary preeminence as the Tour moves across France. When the Tour returned to Brittany from its two-day sojourn in England, the television cameras for France 2/3 zoomed in on a field of artichokes growing along the road's edge. The commentator mentioned that artichokes were one of the great crops of Brittany's productive farmland; their export being the catalyst for the foundation of Brittany Ferries, who returned the Tour from Britain. The distinctive qualities of individual *départements* are placed under the national spotlight as the Tour moves through each *pays*.

The analytical point to emphasize is that while the Tour de France is emblematic of national character, its iconic status as a festival of France is frequently enhanced and articulated at the local level. In other words, the Tour de France opens up a range of opportunities at which expressions of regional competitiveness can be played out. The resources through which local identities articulate themselves are various: intricate flower arrangements painstakingly assembled by townsfolk welcome the Tour in Avranches; in Livarot, a gigantic wheel of cheese, prominently displayed alongside

the finish line, draws attention to Normandy's dairy industry. Commemorative bottles of wine are used to mark the passage of the Tour through Villard-de-Lans, and artwork on t-shirts, coffee mugs, cigarette lighters, cufflinks, refrigerator magnets, and postcards, among other things, are used to highlight individual regions. Far from the national simply swamping the local, the annual return of the Tour de France opens up a range of spaces through which locals can articulate their identity vis-à-vis the national.

The tourist industry particularly picks up on these impressions of regional identity, incorporating them into brochures and pamphlets. The various leaflets, newsletters, and magazines that detail the Tour's itinerary contribute to the cultural cartography of France. One brochure available from the tourist office in Limoges offers a menu du jour of local specialties. Through such representations, one discovers that *perdreau* (partridge) and *pineau* (a brandy-fortified wine) are delicacies of the Limousin region, and that Pau, at the foot of the Pyrénées, is the center of the Armagnac industry. Other pamphleteering advises that "while in Perigord, one must sample the regional delicacies of *foie gras* and *foie d'oie*," and "while waiting for the riders, perhaps one could spend the morning searching for the elusive 'black diamonds' [truffles] of the region."[36] When the Tour traveled through Provence in both 1993 and 1994, the local *vignobles* seized upon the opportunity to contribute to this culinary cartography of France. A general brochure announcing road closures, accommodation listings, and the names of local restaurants was put out by the wine makers from the Côtes du Rhône under the heading: "Wines here are like the ambience—light and sunny—but are best enjoyed in their native environment, so raise a glass to the passing *peloton*." Given that wine is, in many ways, emblematic of France, the juxtaposition of the national bike race and the national drink is a particularly appropriate means of uniting one nation through the one race.

As befitting this national festival of France, these iconic imaginings of regional identity culminate when the Tour reaches the nation's capital. In the popular imagination, Paris equals France; it is the center for the production of French cultural style. It is in Paris where the national stereotype of chic sophistication is expressed and embellished, as wealthy Parisians parade their haute couture, haute cuisine, and *savoir vivre*. While the stage villages that the Tour visits—and the regions that it passes through—provide a succession of sites for nation building, it is Paris that provides the supreme site for the cultural praxis of national identity. The movement of the Tour around France peaks in Paris, for it is there where understandings of being French are most obviously distilled and displayed.

The Tour de France has always finished in Paris. For ninety-three years, the nation's capital has received this final, largely ceremonial, stage finish. While the precise location has changed over the years—from the Parc de Princes of its early days, to La Cipale in 1968, and since 1975, the Champs-Elysées—the city of Paris remains a central feature in the iconography of the Tour. The landmarks of Paris become crucial for marking the conclusion of the Tour de France. One rider, Jean-Claude Colotti, remembers that "my suffering melted into the past the moment I entered the Champs-Elysées in Paris," while Paul Sherwin, a former rider and now commentator for the British television station Channel Four, remarked in his commentary for the 1996 race: "The riders have waited for three weeks to see that sight [the Eiffel Tower]. They've been all over France, and finally, when you see that sight, you know that you've made it."

On reaching Paris, the riders head toward the Champs-Elysées where they complete seven laps of the boulevard. The normal chaos of traffic attempting to negotiate the ten-lane confusion around the Arc de Triomphe, the noise of the late-night drag races, and the wealthy extravagances of the boulevard's many *flâneurs* disappear when the riders cross the Place de la Concorde and clatter onto the cobblestones of the Champs-Elysées. For the last Sunday in July the Champs-Elysées becomes Tour territory, the sacred space of the riders. They glide across it, not once, but seven times, their actions given strength through repetition. The Champs-Elysées, such an integral part of Parisian iconography, is imbued with a different set of meanings once the Tour comes to town. As one elderly gentleman remarked to me, "I'm glad it's cyclists and not tanks here today." In following the banks of the river Seine, in turning in the shadow of the Arc de Triomphe, in racing along the Champs-Elysées, the landscape that the Tour negotiates is so familiar that it could only be Paris and thus France where this event is raced. By incorporating such internationally recognizable symbols of France into its repertoire of icons and images, the Tour presents itself in a manner that is self-evidently and unmistakably French.

Media accounts in particular inscribe the significance of Paris for the Tour de France. On July 24, 1994, *Le Parisien* writes of "*une grand finale sur les Champs-Elysées,*" while *L'Equipe* predicts "*la course au podium.*" The emphasis placed on the events that will unfold in Paris means that the three weeks spent mapping France are concertedly directed toward the victory dais on the Champs-Elysées. The regional diversity previously highlighted by the media is now replaced with an emphasis on this very recognizable symbol of France. The national event is the product of local variations and regional differences that combine to assert a national unity. The media construct a sense of national belonging out of local distinctiveness by appealing both to provincial sentiments and to the image of Paris at one and the same time. In reporting the win by Eddy Seigneur on July 25, 1994, *L'Equipe* described it as "le dernier vainqueur d'étape français sur les Champs-Elysées, en 1982, s'appelait Hinault. Hier, le Beauvasien lui a succédé. Un bonheur fou pour ce débutant sur le

Tour." Here, Tour fans can be both proudly parochial and publicly French as they read of the victory claimed by this Beauvasien along the Champs-Elysées.[37] Cultural unity is fabricated out of regional diversity by simultaneously appealing to Seigneur's home *département*, the French hero Bernard Hinault, and the Champs-Elysées, a symbolic juxtaposition that strikes at the heart of French national sentiment. As one rider, Thierry Claveyrolat, maintains, "for a Frenchman, there is no greater stage to win than the Champs-Elysées. It's a 'champagne' stage, better even than Bastille Day."

Paris remains an enduring location not only for the itinerary of the Tour de France but also for representations of being French. Given that Paris is, in many ways, the point of reference for stereotypes of French style, class, flair, romanticism, and excitability, it can perhaps be anticipated that sponsors and advertisers play with these images of France to promote their products. The stereotype of the French as being excitable and enthusiastic is incorporated by the PMU to advertise its latest system of horse race betting. The pamphlets distributed by their float in *la caravane publicitaire* read: "*Un peu de calme, voyons, le Tour est là!*" ("calm down, the Tour is here"). Along the Champs-Elysées, publicity girls for Mercier Champagne dispense free tastings and distribute leaflets proclaiming (in English): "What better way to celebrate the end of a Tour than with a glass or two of champagne? Mercier Champagne: "*C'est le Tour, c'est la France, c'est la vie.*" Being French is distilled in these consumer-driven iconic imaginings of national identity. The ready availability of commercial products provides a resource through which one can imagine, recognize, and articulate belonging within a complex commodity culture such as France.

Like all national stereotypes, the bundle of cultural characteristics that is used to define "Frenchness" unravels in opposition to a range of cultural

Others. What is French is articulated in terms of what or who is not French. Media coverage of the Tour when in Paris picks up on these cultural imaginings of belonging and otherness. A cartoon in *Aujourd'hui* on July 24, 1994, features a triumphant Spanish cyclist emerging from under the Arc de Triomphe. One voice bubble from the crowd contains the phrase, "After the Germans, there are the Spanish on the Champs-Elysées." A second voice retorts, "Yes, but we are yet to be reconciled with the Germans." As Blair et al. note: "Media coverage of sport attempts to construct a sense of social stability by offering an experience with which individuals can relate in such a way so as to encourage them to work out one country from another."[38] The media coverage of the Tour, whether it be in the form of factual reporting in *L'Equipe* or in humorous accounts such as that displayed in *Aujourd'hui*, unites the imagined community of France in a collective heartbeat that evokes a loyalty to the nation through highlighting its position within the wider European community.

To return to the starting point of this chapter, although anthropologists have long been concerned with the relationship between nation and culture, the social climate of postmodern times offers a new set of resources through which to explore this association. As I have argued in this chapter, the quantity of commodities and media images produced and consumed by the Tour de France provide important means through which these imaginings of Frenchness can be done. The commodities presented for national consumption are carefully chosen representations of national identity, for they promise nothing less than the appropriation of qualities deemed essentially "French." The qualities of sophistication, style, and exuberance are all reflected in the Tour de France. The Tour thus becomes a site of extreme self-reflexivity; an event to which people can turn to make sense of themselves. In moving around the country, the Tour experiences France and France experiences the Tour; it provides an annual occasion for a very public period of reflection and contemplation. As Myerhoff and Ruby note: "All societies have created occasions for reflecting upon themselves, regularly engineered crises, collective ceremonies, celebratory rites of passage, public performances and the like—times when the society tells itself who it is (or how it would like to be) or should have been."[39] The Tour de France provides a resource through which what it means to be French can be annually articulated and authenticated.

Notes

1 P. Little, "Ritual, Power, and Ethnography at the Rio Earth Summit," *Critique of Anthropology* 15(3) (1995): 265–88.

2 R. Handler, *Nationalism and the Politics of Culture in Quebec* (Madison: University of Wisconsin Press, 1988), for example, provides a compelling analysis of the social processes that are employed by the Québécois when constructing their national identity.

3 A. Peace, "Grand Prix, Global Culture: Critical Notes on Popular Culture at the Periphery," paper presented at the Popular Culture Association/American Culture Association Conference, Honolulu, Hawaii, January 9–11, 1996.

4 B. Bender, *Landscape: Politics and Perspectives* (Oxford: Berg, 1993), 1.

5 O. Löfgren, "The Nationalization of Culture," *Ethnologia Europaea* 19(1) (1989): 5–24, 105.

6 As a further note on presentation of ethnographic material, when I cite individuals in the text by their first names it is to signal their membership within this regional cycling community. Unless appropriately acknowledged and cited in the text, all quoted exchanges are personal communication.

7 R. Foster, "Making National Cultures in the Global Ecumene," *Annual Review of Anthropology* 20 (1991): 249.

8 Translation: "With an average speed of 47.7 kph, this year we have beaten our record. Racing for hours under the blazing sun, descending the Col d'Izoard in pursuit of a rider who has broken away at 120 KPH, then attack-

ing the climb to Isola 2000, out of the valley in a flash. We thank the organizers of the Tour, and above all, we thank the riders who allow us to, each year, go a little bit further. Official sponsor of the Tour de France."

9 *L'Equipe* (July 24, 1995): 9. Translation: "The Tour de France likes Fiat, Fiat likes the Tour. The Big Lap is complete."

10 R. Goldman, *Reading Ads Socially* (London: Routledge, 1992), 2.

11 *L'Equipe* is France's daily sports newspaper.

12 F. Braudel, *The Identity of France: History and Environment* (New York: Harper and Row, 1986), 23.

13 Since the brothers Auguste and Louis Lumière made their first motion picture in 1895, France has prided herself on her technological vision. In recent years, the developments of the microchip-driven *télécarte,* the nationwide information system Minitel, the nuclear energy programs, the digital flight control systems in the Airbus 320 jetliners, and the SPOT imaging satellite that gave the world its first detailed look at the Chernobyl nuclear disaster in the former Soviet Union have positioned France at the cutting edge of the technology and information service industries.

14 R. Chartier, "Text, Symbol, Frenchness," *Journal of Modern History* 57 (1985): 687.

15 *L'Equipe* (July 24, 1994): 9. Translation: "Elegance is knowing how to do the craziest things to the limit." Nobody knows whether the author of this definition was an amateur cyclist; still, it describes admirably the heroes of the Tour de France.

16 I use the term "space" to denote the territorial areas that the Tour moves into. I use the term "place" to refer to the spaces that have been personalized; invested with symbolic resonance by virtue of the intervention of the Tour de France. In other words, place is space that holds meaning for the social actors who occupy it.

17 While I deal with this elsewhere (C. Palmer, "A Life of Its Own: The Social Construction of the Tour de France," Ph.D. thesis, University of Adelaide, Australia, 1996, chap. 1), it is important to realize here that for those who line the road of the Tour, watch it on television, or read about it in the newspaper, the Tour de France symbolizes a gluttonous feast of sporting combat that both demands and demonstrates complete cycling competence. With its death-defying sprints at more than seventy kilometers an hour, with its solitary

suffering as the riders endure the individual time trial, and with its back-breaking climbs through the Pyrénées and the Alps, the Tour tests every facet of cycling.

18 M. de Certeau, *The Practice of Everyday Life* (Berkeley: University of California Press, 1984), 119.

19 In each *département,* local police and *pompiers* are brought in to boost the corps of troops (La Garde Républicaine) who travel with the race proper. The *pilote* is the first officer from La Garde Républicaine who signals the arrival of *la caravane publicitaire,* which marks the arrival of the Tour itself.

20 A. Appadurai, "Global Ethnoscapes: Notes and Queries for a Transnational Anthropology," in *Recapturing Anthropology: Working in the Present,* ed. R. Fox (Santa Fe, NM: School of American Research Press, 1991), 198.

21 N. Blair et al., *Sport and National Identity in the European Media* (Leisser: Leisser University Press, 1993), 52.

22 The term belongs, of course, to U. Hannerz, "Notes on the Global Ecumene," *Public Culture* 1(2) (1989): 66–75. While the global character of the Tour de France is indeed compelling, I deal with it elsewhere (see Palmer, "A Life of Its Own," chap. 7). Here I am more immediately concerned with the representations of local and national character that are articulated through the Tour de France.

23 J. Hargreaves, *Sport, Power, and Culture: A Social and Historical Analysis of Sport in Britain* (Cambridge: Polity Press, 1986), 154.

24 Palmer, "A Life of Its Own."

25 D. Dayan and E. Katz, *Media Events: The Live Broadcasting of History* (Cambridge, MA: Harvard University Press, 1992), 5.

26 *Le Parisien* (July 25, 1993): 9. Translation: "To follow the 180 guys who think nothing of a breakaway, it takes 9 motorbikes, 40 cars, 6 outside broadcast vans, and 3 helicopters. With 3,800 kilometers to cover and 10 million television viewers, that equals 2632 viewers per kilometer. The 25 cameramen and 22 journalists who interview the 180 riders need 80 hours of live broadcast time and 3 daily up-dates. Finally, the Tour de France is a great history of cycling, and France Television offers the greatest coverage of the sport."

27 A. Appadurai, "Disjuncture and Difference in the Global Cultural Economy," *Public Culture* 2(2) (1990): 299.

28 B. Anderson, *Imagined Communities: On the Origins and Spread of Nationalism* (London: Verso, 1983).

29 Maurice Garin won the first Tour de France in 1903.

30 G. Vigarello, "Le Tour de France, Une Passion Nationale," *Sport-Histoire* 4 (1989): 163.

31 *Le Parisien* (July 26, 1993): 5. Translation: "France 2/3 Supervision . . . the biggest lap is on France Supervision. The arrival of the Tour is like you are there."

32 Blair et al., *Sport and National Identity,* 5.

33 U. Hannerz, *Cultural Complexity: Studies in the Social Organization of Meaning* (New York: Columbia University Press, 1992), 26.

34 Braudel, *The Identity of France,* 38.

35 Vigarello, "Le Tour de France."

36 *Les Evénements du Limousin* (Fall 1994): 1.

37 The Beauvais region lies about 100 kilometers to the north of Paris.

38 Blair et al., *Sports and National Identity,* 43.

39 B. Myerhoff and J. Ruby, *A Crack in the Mirror: Reflexive Perspectives in Anthropology* (Philadelphia: University of Pennsylvania Press, 1982), 3.

Ellen Strain

While 1995 witnessed the introduction of the computer game sensation *Myst*, consumers by 1997 could purchase *Pyst*, a parody of the 1995 game offering a trek through a litter-strewn, tourist-ridden island plagued by overcommercialization. *Pyst* plays upon one of the *Myst* phenomenon's central ironies: despite the game's commercial success and the millions of computer game players who have made their way across the island's alluring landscape and through its mysterious portals, the island remains perpetually deserted. Like a modern archeologist unsealing an ancient tomb, each consumer of *Myst* finds an uninhabited island and a series of undisturbed clues which unlock the secrets of its past. Thus, while various sectors of cyberspace are shared spaces where virtual communities burgeon, cyberspace also offers new frontiers for journeys of a highly private nature. The territories of *Myst* and of other computer games with exploration or colonialist narratives are infinitely renewable as every visitor at her own computer is positioned as a lone trail-blazer amidst an untouched landscape.

Our private journeys through the forever virgin terrains of computer adventure games illustrate the paradoxes of what we might call anti-touristic tourism. We yearn for the kind of travel experience that preceded the neon signs of *Pyst* and the high admission costs of our own world's tourist traps. We seek an escape from the superficiality of the organized tour and hope for a kind of communion with an elusive entity known as authenticity. This authenticity appears to retreat from the industrialized world, residing primarily in the time warps of the globe's primitive cultures. Acknowledging primitives' existence as a construct only, we are then led to seek out authenticity in the past. And as our fascination with computer games' re-creations of Egyptian pyramids and medieval fortresses illustrates, our desire to reaccess that past drives us even further into a world of simulation and artificiality, a post-modern playground in which artifice parades as authenticity.

The quality of authenticity seems particularly inaccessible to the widely disdained figure of the tourist, a figure believed to be a superficial consumer of foreign culture and a despoiler of the world's unique treasures. In fact, if authenticity is a type of purity which exists before or outside of commercialism, then like King Midas, the tourist as a global carrier of commercialism reaches out for authenticity but taints all she touches. Or at least this is the common tale told by the anti-tourist.

Sociologists, semioticians, and literary critics alike have commented on anti-tourism's pervasiveness and its long history.[1] For instance, James Buzard suggests that the word "tourist," as opposed to the less disliked traveler, has had negative connotations as far back as 1792.[2] A few of these thinkers have also suggested the most likely

Pyst's cluttered landscape: tourism run rampant.

group to express anti-touristic sentiments: tourists themselves. As Jonathan Culler explains, the anti-touristic distinction between tourist and traveler has functioned primarily "to convince oneself that one is not a tourist . . . the desire to distinguish between tourists and real travelers [being] a part of tourism—integral to it rather than outside or beyond it."[3] The anti-touristic desire to enjoy the sights and privileges of tourism from a position other than that of the tourist hints at yet another property of tourism: its transmutability or ability to surface in other practices and under other guises. In the same way that some computer games invite players to live out a tourist's fantasy all while pretending to be something far more lofty than a crass tourist just out for a few exotic thrills, various realms of culture offer touristic pleasures while eschewing the label of tourism. For instance, in the contemporary critique of ethnography, even anthropologists have been accused of being tourists hiding under academicians' clothing.[4] And indeed it could be argued that anthropologists and popular culture consumers both employ a series of viewing strategies common to tourists, yet in the context of cultural practices distinct from tourism itself. Thus, to acknowledge the transmutability of tourism is to recognize the surfacing of touristic desires and touristic viewing strategies outside the confines of commercialized travel.

Although the term "the tourist gaze" was first employed by John Urry in his book *The Tourist Gaze: Leisure and Travel in Contemporary Society,* elsewhere I have elaborated on the concept to refer to much more than Urry's more literal reference to the visual perspective of the tourist. By juxtaposing the viewing patterns and epistemological strategies of anthropology, actual travel, and popular culture's representation of the cultural Other, I have arrived at a number of continuities across these diverse practices, continuities that I collectively refer to as the tourist gaze. Like Laura Mulvey's gaze well known to film scholars,

the tourist gaze is a culturally-constructed dynamic of sight and representation tied to a larger power structure and economic framework.[5] Primarily, it is a question of positionality, i.e., the taking up of a psychic and visual perspective in relation to an Other, whether that Other be defined as a foreign person, an exoticized culture, or an unfamiliar landscape. Like Mulvey's gaze, it involves a position of mastery, an underscoring of distance and difference. And perhaps most importantly, with its roots in colonialism and its surfacing in practices as diverse as academia and pop culture, the tourist gaze is both enduring and portable.

While there is not space here to explore in detail the theoretical underpinnings of the tourist gaze as a concept, many of its constituent parts will become evident as the touristic component of computer adventure games is examined. Three intertwined elements of the touristic stance—anti-tourism, the search for authenticity, and nostalgia—have already been mentioned and will be pursued in further depth in relation to particular games. However, the goal of this article is not only to elucidate the strands that connect computer adventure games to other manifestations of the tourist gaze but also to speak to the specificity of CD-ROMS as a medium. In particular, I explore the mediated understandings of space that are integral to the tourist gaze and the multimedia formats of computer games that make this aspect of the tourist gaze particularly pronounced. More specifically, computer games' mediation of space is an attempt to satisfy the tourist's desire to both be immersed in a space and understand it from a distance. As will be shown, a game's various tools for understanding place and orienting oneself within a space are both a reaction to the pressures of immersive travel in general and to the new rules of simulated mobility forged by CD-ROM adventure games. Additionally, I address the overlay of narrative and mobility in these games, an overlay that further defines a relationship of mastery between game player and the represented Other.

However, as a way of beginning it seems appropriate to address a couple of more basic questions: how have computer technologies become devices of mobility (i.e., tools for the armchair traveler) and how can we define the nature of mobility within these games?

Into Orbit with Our Hands on the Controls

Touting a medium's ability to bring you somewhere, to show you some part of the world, fictional or actual, past or present, is an old technique for introducing a new technology. For instance, one early motion picture studio advertised their collection of films with the line, "the world at your fingertips."[6] Similarly, when televisions were marketed to American consumers, advertisers used European tourist attractions as backdrops for displaying their console models.[7] Of course, the computer in its earliest embodiments was not an armchair traveler's companion but a scientist's tool for computing and storing information. Only with recent technological developments has the home computer been transfigured into a device of mobility, delivering the user to cyberspaces and virtual destinations. Actual locations become tangible either through "link-up" capabilities or through interactive representations of these locales. Multi-user interfaces create new virtual spaces defined not by walls but by signals and supporting hardware. And imaginative worlds incarnated through computer graphics suggest a range of fictional paraspaces beyond our more earthly existence, paraspaces that entice and engulf in their illusion.

The employment of metaphors of motion have become commonplace in describing new computer technologies. The term "information superhighway" was quickly incorporated into colloquial language, launching a host of travel analogies ranging from discussion of internet highway patrols to jokes about roadkill and wrong exits. The meaning of a computer's speed, i.e., its ability to quickly complete procedures, has converged with the idea of getting from one place to another in a short time—traveling the Web, navigating cyberspace, barreling down the highway in a high-powered machine. One ad in *PC Magazine* reads, "386MAX runs Windows so fast you'll need a seatbelt. With QEMM, you may need something else." The accompanying photograph features a home computer with an inflated air bag protruding from the screen. Another ad bragging about quick acceleration shows a personal computer with red flame detailing and dual, fire-shooting tail pipes of polished chrome.

However, it is not just about speed. A number of ads highlight alluring destinations and "enterable" spaces. Ads for high-resolution monitors, for instance, routinely show exotic locales from Barbados to Hawaii to Paris displayed on screen, suggesting the foreign environment as the ideal testing ground for an apparatus's enhanced reality effects. Moving toward the idea that the computer can offer a virtually enterable space, a cartoon featured in a software ad reads, "Bob, now totally into his computer, was beyond Windows—way, way beyond." Like other computer ads, the monitor displays a blissful, tropical beach scene, only "Bob" is drawn sitting on this beach wearing a flowered shirt and leaning outside the screen to manipulate the mouse which sits on his desk next to the computer. Ads for CD-ROM applications further the suggestion of immersive cyberspace with repeated appeals to the consumer: "enter," "explore," or, as ads for Microsoft's CD-ROM encyclopedia *Encarta* entreat, "Where do you want to go today?"

Even in games that would not be categorized as travel games, exotica or references to actual cultures of the past or present frequently serve as spice to liven up the game. In *Lemmings Chronicles* (Psygnosis), the player can lead landing parties of Egyptian lemmings or ninja lemmings to three newly discovered islands. Vague references to European and Polynesian locales are encountered in *Freddi Fish and the Case of the Missing Kelp Seeds* (Humongous Entertainment) as the player leads Freddi through an underwater castle, volcano, and theater starring Helga the Singing Mermaid. Other CD-ROMs more explicitly marketed as travel games are entirely situated in a single locale rendered in textured, three-dimensional graphics; ancient Sumeria, the African veldt, the Amazon, the American West of the 1850s, medieval Europe, Antarctica, the Australian outback, and ancient Egypt are just some of the environments depicted on CD-ROMs. Often times such games create cartoon-like universes that simply replicate the popular imagination's envisioning of such locales with little or no claim to authenticity: medieval castles filled with armored knights, Egyptian slaves building pyramids while high priests record their secrets in hieroglyphics, and gun-toting cowboys borrowed as much from the silver screen as from history books.

An equal number of CD-ROM applications do boast of some kind of engagement with the actual world, past or present. Photography is still the most sure-fire way of delivering the distant locale to the computer monitor and satiating the home tourist's desire for authenticity. Games like *Where in the World Is Carmen Sandiego* and *Wrath of the Gods* intertwine animated figures and still photographic backgrounds taken from actual locations. Some games, on the other hand, employ the strategy used by *Africa Trail* (MECC), an educational adventure game whose not quite photo-realistic graphics were nonetheless created from footage taken on actual expeditions to Africa. A number of CD-ROM applications designed to educate as well as entertain combine photography with an appeal to an authoritative body which endows the application with the air of authenticity. For instance, *Carmen Sandiego*'s music and photos come from two renowned experts on the non-Western world: the Smithsonian Institution and *National Geographic* magazine. *Voyage in Egypt* (E.M.M.E.) is advertised as having been developed from the internationally respected SCALA archives. *Antarc-*

tica: The Last Continent (Cambrix Publishing) cites connections to the International Antarctica Research Center just as *Material World* foregrounds its links to the United Nations. *Scientific American* magazine and the Discovery Channel have both used their established authority in popular science to sponsor CD-ROM applications. And Robyn Davidson has used the publicity and adventurer status garnered from her trip across Australia, documented by *National Geographic* photographer Rick Smolan, to compile the CD-ROM *From Alice to Ocean*.

As is apparent in this amalgam of CD-ROM games, a wide range of strategies exists for representing place and space—that is, actual photographed *places* from around the world and *spaces* that may be modeled on actual places but that are rendered in computer graphics and are more amenable to the illusion of three-dimensionality and player movement through space. At this point in time, fairly clear differentiations between the depiction of place and space can be maintained since the technological capability for rendering photographed place as navigable space is very limited. Some golf and flight simulation games have come the closest in replicating actual spaces with graphics that approach photorealism and in simulating the movement of an aircraft or golf ball through that space. For example, Looking Glass Technology's *Flight Unlimited* is one technologically sophisticated example of this merging of place and space with its flight simulation using actual footage from Arizona sites mapped onto 3-D terrain. One titillating development has been Apple's QuickTime VR and Microsoft's Surround Video, which offer fluid movement over 360-degree, wrap-around panoramas and which are already replacing the "full-frame slide shows" of games like *Myst*.[8]

Defining Movement through Space

Most CD-ROM games that depict 3-D spaces provide some means of simulating continuous movement through space using a first-person film-like perspective. The ability to determine the direction and speed of this movement adds an element of interactivity that brings CD-ROM technologies a step closer to the player-controlled navigability of virtual reality. However, one could argue that this illusion of motion through a simulated 3-D space is neither the only nor the predominant type of movement in CD-ROM games. In fact, another type of "movement" stems from CD-ROMs' unique history within the development of home computer technologies. Unlike film, computer technologies are perhaps most notable in their combination of disparate materials, a capability that has consistently grown in sophistication over the past twenty years. From home publishing software, the development of which has brought a greater ease in creating and importing nontextual items, to the World Wide Web with its similar combinatory possibilities, computer applications have incorporated photographic representation, animation, text, voice annotation, music, sound effects, and visual depictions of information in the form of graphs, charts, and maps to a greater extent than commonly employed in any other medium. Thus, interactivity and movement within CD-ROM games—in many ways an extension of previous computer applications—often involves a scurrying between media, between experiential modalities. A CD-ROM may imitate placement within space using optical point of view, provide a means of activating "movement," and then simulate that desired movement through the representation of the same space from slightly altered perspectives. However, with a single command, this immersion may be temporarily abandoned while a map screen is consulted or textually conveyed information is sought. The virtual traveler thus pauses to become reader or alters her interpretation of flat image as three dimensional space in order to engage in another type of spatial interpretation, that required by map-reading. Thus, the CD-ROM traveler may click her mouse, moving in one of four directions, through doors, and into new rooms, but a click of

the mouse could also "move" her into another way of seeing, into a different way of representing the world, or from a seeing mode into a listening mode.

It is worthwhile to ponder why this movement between viewing modalities, or these brief respites from three-dimensionally modeled spaces, are so common in travel games that promise above all else the pleasures of "being there." Perhaps "being there" is not unceasingly pleasurable. New and unfamiliar spaces can be daunting at the same time that they are enthralling. In fact, actual tourism is characterized by a number of behaviors designed to counteract disorientation and culture shock by giving travelers a sense of mastery over the space and the culture. These behaviors, which shape the nature of the tourist gaze, include the use of maps, the translation of space into picture or photograph, the pursuit of elevated/aerial perspectives, and the use of guided tours. In this respect, my fleshing out of the tourist gaze draws in part upon Timothy Mitchell's concept of the traveler's "double demand," that is, the desire to be in the midst of an exotic place while still being able to digest the space as flat, framed image.[9] Again the similarities between the tourist gaze and Mulvey's analysis of the gaze within Hollywood film become evident; a flattening process which reduces signs of difference into consumable spectacle is a mechanism for defusing threat. Confrontation with a way of life radically different from one's own is turned into a pleasurable affair as the spectacle of difference is contained and framed within the postcard or snapshot. The sublime landscape is tamed by the photograph which freezes, miniaturizes, and typically imposes Western aesthetic standards on a chaotic environment. Most importantly, the photograph, the map, and the aerial perspective produce the illusion of separation from a potentially engulfing and disorienting environment. Touristic pleasure is therefore achieved by a precarious balance between these two extremes: surrendering to complete immersion within an environment and the extraction of oneself from that environment in order to see and understand the environment as a flattened whole.[10]

Supplementing Mitchell's concept of the double demand, we could add that the tourist's desire to experience an exotic locale as both flattened spectacle and occupiable three-dimensional space is mirrored by a related set of twin demands which seem similarly at odds with one another: the desire to perceive foreign culture as a play of surfaces without depth or meaning and the urge to view foreign culture as a layered structure requiring decoding and demystifying. The camera is the tool for recording the former whether it be the mealy brilliance of face paint smeared onto the cheek of a Native American dancer or the robust colors of an intricately woven African textile product. Even while digesting culture as an accumulation of tastes, colors, and textures, the tourist views this foreign culture as hieroglyph, awaiting translation. The tourist gaze thus seeks a vision of the foreign site as annotated spectacle. Guidebooks, maps, translators, tour guides, and labels provide the annotation, or one might say, a ready supply of information about the unfamiliar culture which transforms puzzling foreign-ness into distantiated knowledge. A distillation process occurs as the map with its godlike perspective and the guidebook collapse a complex body of history, geography, and daily practice into a picture of the whole painted in broad strokes and marked with simple labels. With these tools at hand, the tourist circumvents the loss of self-placement inherent in culture shock by positioning herself as viewer and knower who stands apart from a masterable culture.

A similar process of defusing the threat of unfamiliarity takes place in CD-ROM games as maps and a ready flow of information provide forms of spatial mastery, control, geographical orientation, and an assurance of the objects' and locations' knowability. A number of CD-ROMs could be used to illustrate this touristic gaze and how its maintenance of spatial mastery and cultural distancing ensures the pleasures of immersion. For instance, games like Broderbund's *Where in the World Is Carmen Sandiego?* maintain touristic mastery by straddling the two aforementioned modes of experience—the belief in image as immersive 3-D space and the distanced understanding of place as a flow of information. Within the game, some level of touristic immersion is guaranteed by the illusion of real space and multisensory simulation. The game's featured photographs are foregrounded as static images or as postcards which tame, appropriate, and capture the world's sights. At the same time, animated sequences suggest that these images constitute real space through which one could pass, or at least through which a cartoon character, Carmen herself or one of her henchpeople, could pass. Folk music appropriate to the locale accompanies the player's voyage and continues for the duration of the visit, contributing to the illusion of immersion and authenticity. The player might visit eight locations around the world in the course of tracking down a single criminal, all while linked to a steady flow of information about the locales and the pursued thieves. A portable video phone, a criminal database with a robotic interface, and a computer readout with constant information about the destinations and the ongoing crime-fighting efforts occupy the majority of the screen and provide this stream of information. These technological tools are aligned with the player and stand in contrast to the less industrialized cultures portrayed by the game as picturesquely exotic.

A similar formula shapes multimedia atlases. Within Electronic Arts' *3-D Atlas,* a technologically aided omnipotent visuality allows users to view the earth as abstracted map, to manipulate the flat geographic image through nine zoom levels, and to access satellite images. The thousands of statistics contained within the software converts countries and locales into facts, numbers, hard data. The 800-plus color photographs or "country postcards" occupy a middle ground between the distanced perspective which renders the world as flat, manipulatable image and the immersed, first-person perspective provided by the software's 3-D flights over world terrains.

The vacillation between the illusion of being there and separation from an image-world is even more apparent in games within which the player is positioned as tourist-photographer. In *From Alice to Ocean: alone Across the Outback* (Claric Clear Choice), for example, the invitation to feel like a fellow traveler on Robyn Davidson's seven-month journey across the Australian outback is clear and redundantly referenced. The written materials included with the CD-ROM offer the words of the publisher, "The enclosed CD-ROM lets you join Robyn in her travels." A letter from photographer Rick Smolan appearing in the same pamphlet reiterates, "With this interactive CD-ROM, imagine yourself joining Robyn. . . . I wish you good luck and Godspeed on your own journey." Spoken journal entries, video clips, still photographs, and a map that allows the home traveler to join in on the trip at any point are designed to flesh out a sense of the place and communicate the excitement of the journey. The photographs serve as entryways into the represented space and as documentation of Smolan's and Davidson's presence in the exotic space. Yet, the artifice of the photograph is simultaneously foregrounded through Smolan's commentary on photographic technique. In an effort to educate the player and prepare the tourist for her next adventure, Smolan doles out advice on how to capture action and how to create silhouettes, dissecting his own images and revealing the tale of their creation. A similar backstory inhabits *Material World* (StarPress Multimedia) as the dominant discourse on the lives of the world's families is accompanied by the narratives of the photographers who captured *Material World*'s images.

Such behind-the-scenes looks exhibit the photographers' expertise and remind CD-ROM users of Smolan's and others' presence on the scene, and

Adventurer Robyn Davidson documents her travels across Australia in the CD-ROM *From Alice to Ocean.*

therefore, of their authority to deliver the world to users. In the absence of any other Western character, the photographer as traveler provides a figure for identification, positioning the game-player as a looker and an image-capturer, rather than as an indigene. To the degree that this incorporation of the photographers' stories into CD-ROM narratives details cross-cultural contact, its inequities, and awkwardness, such discourses can reveal the constructed nature of a CD-ROM's cultural depiction. Yet when the photos themselves become virtual souvenirs that can be downloaded, as in *Material World,* or when the artful compositions and silhouettes romanticize and objectify indigenes who become less important than the successful capture of a Kodak moment, then the image-world takes a dangerous precedence over the political realities of the actual world.

Animated Worlds: The Tomb of Qin

While *Carmen Sandiego, 3-D Atlas, Material World,* and *From Alice to Ocean* all rely on photographic representation to deliver touristic pleasures within a primarily educational format, it is important to note that a similar manifestation of the tourist gaze can be found in less educationally directed games which simulate exotic spaces using computer graphics and 3-D animation rather than photographs. One such game worthy of a more sustained analysis due to its interesting content and unusual blend of fact and fiction is *Qin* (Time Warner Electronic Publishing). *Qin* focuses on a single location using a lush graphic style and a highly atmospheric feel reminiscent of *Myst.* In fact, the game has been accurately described by one reviewer as "Indiana Jones meets *Myst.*" The game's title refers to Qin Shi Huangdi, China's first emperor and occupant of the subterranean tomb available for exploration by the game player. As a player of *Qin,* you are simultaneously pulled into the future and the past as you learn that the year is 2010 and that you have volunteered for the excavation of the tomb of Qin, buried deep in the earth for the past two millennia. As an archeologist, you are the (anti-) tourist par excellence, able to witness what no one else has seen, if you can outwit Qin's booby traps and locking devices.

The game begins with an animated opening sequence, which is quickly becoming a convention of computer adventure games. A small-frame, noninteractive sequence initiates your journey by drawing you into another world. In this case, similar to *Myst,* it is a fall through a crevice that precipitates the adventure, leaving you bruised and shocked fifteen stories beneath the surface locked inside the tomb of the man who united China and began the construction of the Great Wall in the third century B.C. The opening sequence thus sweeps you across the landscape of the excavation site interrupted only by a dizzying drop through this crevice. When the sequence ends you are staring upward at the cracked rock above through which you entered and which is now unreachable.

Due to the efforts of a team of fifteen artists, the graphics are remarkably engaging as you tap the arrow keys to move up, down, left, and right in this mysterious environment. Of equal noteworthiness is the music that, according to the accompanying documentation, is an original soundtrack based on traditional melodies using so-called authentic instruments in an attempt to replicate the spirit of Qin dynasty music. However, the CD-ROM publishers admit that many of the instruments and melodies postdate Qin. The music changes to match the various environments as you move through not just a tomb but a virtual empire constructed underground. Doors and gates to new realms remain impassable until certain puzzles are solved. The resolution of puzzles and the resultant movement through space bring you closer to the game's final goal: to discover the secrets of Qin Shi Huangdi, a powerful man obsessed with the possibility of immortality.

As with many such games, movement through the game space is quite compelling at first, that is, until the novelty wears off, leaving you increasingly aware of its awkwardness and the tedium of transversing the same space to manipulate pieces of the game's puzzles. Disorientation is one net effect of inconsistent movement commands. Clicking the left arrow may sometimes spin you around 90 degrees, while other times it initiates a 180-degree turn. Forward movement may unpredictably propel you a few feet or several yards into the space in front of you. Add to this the general effort required to constantly connect the dots, stitching together different perspectives of a particular scene in order to conceive of it as a three-dimensional space. Since this process is never seamless, *Qin* provides a couple of orientation tools: a compass in the bottom right of the screen and a map which charts your progress. The player's view of the game space is letterboxed with various controls accessible in the black areas above and below the image, areas referred to by the game documentation as the DataVisor. The compass is always in view indicating your current direction with a yellow line and using two blue dots to indicate the directions you would be facing were you to turn left or right. The maps accessed via the DataVisor involves a temporary removal from the space of the tomb but conveniently provides a "you are here" indicator as well as Transport Nodes, i.e.,

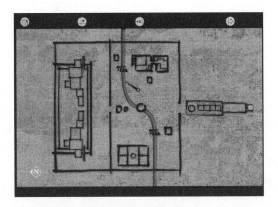

The maps of *Qin* both alleviate travel tedium and mediate the player's experience of game space.

markers on the map which you can click to return to an area you have already explored. In this way, the maps' functions alleviate travel tedium and they mediate the player's experience of the game space. The pull-down maps for each realm also provide an overview of the game's narrative to the extent that narrative progression is charted by spatial movement through the tomb. Thus not only do the maps provide orientation (a glimpse of the whole seen from above) but they help direct your movement toward the tomb's central point and beyond.

Choosing the Archive function in the DataVisor may also change experiental modalities. Through the Archive, the illusion of spatial immersion is abandoned while textual information on ancient Chinese history, culture philosophy, and science is sought. One of the Archive's two functions, the Room Index, provides information on Chinese culture related to objects or puzzles within that particular room. For instance, one environment includes a number of water wheels and the ruins of other machinery. The Archive's Room Index provides information on Qin's efforts to build roads and aqueducts and on irrigation methods during the Qin dynasty. The information proves to be useful in triggering the gate-opening mechanism which then leads the player to the

realm just beyond this system of wheels, bridges, and waterways. The second Archive function, the Encyclopedia, contains a list of categories and related subcategories which link to illustrated text searchable using the Find function. The various categories of information include among others: Myths and Rituals, Science and Technology, the Afterlife and Occult, and Manufacturing and Crafts.

The effect of the annotated environment is intensified by another element of the DataVisor, the Interpreter. Many of the *Qin* environments are dotted with Chinese language inscriptions and labels which can be instantaneously translated with the aid of the Interpreter. When the Interpreter is activated, a gray box drops from the DataVisor and a light gray grid is imposed over your view of the game space. The entire inscription is translated or a Chinese character appearing in the scene is shown along with a pronunciation guide and the character's meaning. When Mandarin is spoken, a translation simultaneously appears as a subtitle at the bottom of the screen.

The past tense of the Qin Dynasty effectively framed within the technologically advanced future tense of 2010 allows for an ideal (anti-) touristic arrangement. The mystery and splen-

Qin's Interpreter adds to the CD-ROM's annotated environment.

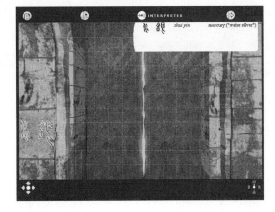

dor of the past (or at least a fantasy version of it seeped in Orientalist imaginings yet couched in an aura of authenticity due to the accompanying historical material) is abundantly accessible to the tourist-turned-explorer enjoying a private journey through Mount Li, China of 210 B.C. The game documentation even tells us that Qin's tomb actually exists and still quietly rests beneath Mount Li due to insufficient excavation funds. Within the world of *Qin,* excavation has begun, and lucky for the tourist, technology has dispensed with the need for a bilingual tour guide. One only needs to strap on a handy-dandy DataVisor and embark on a sojourn through uncharted territory.

This unexplored world is meant to be appreciated for its rich texture and color as artifacts such as sculpted dragons and exquisitely crafted musical instruments can be examined in isolation. When the cursor is passed over an object and changes from its neutral marker to a yellow squiggle, the object can be scrutinized in detail with a click of the mouse. The art object or historical artifact is magnified and isolated against a black screen. The arrow keys may then be used to rotate the item as if you were circling a museum case to see all possible views of a particularly curious or beautiful object. Each perspective on the interior of the tomb is also generated with concerted attention to aesthetics and balance. The gray grid of the Interpreter function dividing a view into a series of perfect squares furthers this sense of a beautiful and ordered environment despite the strangeness of its splendors. Yet at the same time that this empire is presented as exotic spectacle and the culture presented as surface beauty, the game promotes the interpretation of Chinese culture as mystery. However, the game provides a set of guiding principles for deflating its perplexing nature. Animals are invested with mythical meanings and environments are perfectly ordered through the rules of *feng shui.* Culture is boiled down to a set of meanings and rules that can be used to decipher the game's puzzles

and to unlock the protected realms of Qin's underground resting place. The DataVisor thus acts like a decoder ring for your adventure. Of course, for the player who decides not to sort through the Archive's kernels of knowledge for that metaphorical decoder ring, a bit of persistence in rearranging chopsticks and clicking random Chinese symbols will often bring the same results.

Qin is somewhat unusual in that the accumulation of knowledge about an actual culture assists the player in moving through the game space. A number of games such as *Carmen Sandiego* provide cultural information but such material remains incidental to the game. Even on educational CD-ROMs like *Material World* and *From Alice to Ocean,* the casual player can glide through the images while learning very little about the represented cultures. But perhaps what most closely links each of these games is the privileged position assigned to the player who either enters these exotic worlds as detective or archeologist or is given a Western identificatory figure in the form of a photographer, journalist, or adventurer. Undoubtedly, much of the popularity of adventure CD-ROMs has been due to the games' delivery of picture-perfect scenery and their staving off of traveler disorientation. Yet, these very pleasures, secured through cultural distancing devices, foreclose the opportunity for the perspective-altering experience of culture shock in which spatial disorientation takes on larger proportions as the assumed inevitability of one's own culture is shaken. The privileged role of the Western explorer or excavator offers an entry point into a distant land and fulfills the requirements for an anti-touristic adventure; however, such choices pass over more interesting and possibly decentering inductions into a culture. To date, no sophisticated CD-ROM game has been released which allows a player to assume the position of an indigene and meet the challenges of cross-cultural role-playing. Instead games like *Qin* ask the player to learn about another culture in order to better annihilate the enemy and exit the tomb.

Constructing Travel Tales

The relationship between the player and an unfamiliar culture is constructed not only through spatial orientation and a gaze which separates viewer from viewed. Another type of framing is created through narrative. The player participates in the creation of a narrative but must act within a structure of goals created by the game. Narrative theory may offer the best tools for analyzing the implications of such goals and the relationship between player and foreign environment.

Michel de Certeau has described narratives as "spatial trajectories" that regulate changes in space, placing locations within a linear series.[11] Based on this sparse definition of narrative structure, the player, traveling through represented space with its illusion of three dimensionality or through the more inclusive game space, thus maps a trajectory and engages in the spatial weaving of narrative. Jurij Lotman's concepts supplement de Certeau's notion of narrative by defining character types: "Characters can be divided into those who are mobile, who enjoy freedom with regard to plot space . . . and those who are immobile, who represent, in fact, a function of this space."[12] Applying this rule to CD-ROM games, it is possible to differentiate these two categories of characters. The player consistently enters the narrative as a character who possesses the ability to move or navigate through the game space. When the game does not provide a subjective point of view and the illusion of the player's own movement through space, an identificatory figure is often provided. The player as puppet-master may direct the movements of a young man in *Wrath of the Gods,* a female fish in *Freddi Fish,* Phileas Fogg in *Around the World in 80 Days,* or two high school girls in *Hawaii High.* In such cases, the player may not be an actual game character but is aligned with a mobile character. Belonging to Lotman's second category are the game's obstacles or antagonists, "immobile enemy-characters fixed at particular points in the plot space."[13] Although a number of exceptions exist, for the most part the appearance of certain obstacles and enemies are anchored to particular points within the game space. For instance, each time a player visits Spain in the game *Around the World in 80 Days,* a charging bull will have to be dodged, and each visit to France will bring the unfortunate encounter with a rude waiter.

Working from Lotman's character groups as applied to the story of Oedipus, Teresa de Lauretis theorizes, "The work of narrative, then, is a mapping of differences, and specifically, first and foremost, of sexual difference into each text."[14] Within the Oedipal tale, the male, mobile hero is differentiated from the female Sphinx or mother who serves as "an element of plot-space, a topos, a resistance, matrix, and matter."[15] Similar analyses have been applied to the structure of the travel narratives in literature and film. For instance, Eric J. Leed describes the "spermatic journey" as a travel tale which mirrors the narrative of reproduction. The traveler's journey from place to place, encountering stationary women in each locale, leaves a trail of descendants in every port. This journey plot replicates the female immobility/male mobility dichotomy as witnessed in the sperm's spatial trajectory into the female body and through the ovum's outer surface or in the spatial trajectory of the baby-subject's "escape" from the female body-space.[16] Ella Shohat has similarly written about the travel film, noting the preponderance of gendered narratives of military and epistemological conquest over female-obstacle-boundary-space and the sexualized unveilings of the immobile exotic woman.[17] Although each of these analyses focus on narratives plucked from very different realms— history, film, literature, and biology—the conclusions converge at the repaired binarisms of female/male and stasis/mobility.

Gender, thus differentiated via levels of mobility, can be a difficult category for analysis within the CD-ROM narrative in that the primary mobile character is often the player, whose gender is not determined by the game but by who sits down to play. In most cases where a game's subjective perspective creates the illusion of first-person travel, the player's gender is designed to be irrelevant to the game's actions. Nonetheless, gender cues are often still apparent. For example, in *Gadget*, the first-person traveler's suitcase (i.e., the player's suitcase) gets switched for a case full of mysterious gadgets, but not before the player glimpses the contents of the original luggage: men's clothing. In *Myst*, the player's gender is not (mis)represented within the game in the same way as in *Gadget*, but the trail charted by the island's former explorers/time travelers, who are explicitly coded as male, is the text's founding movement which the player retraces. In *From Alice to Ocean*, the player may identify with either the male photographer or the female adventurer. However, while Robyn Davidson, and her movement across the continent, is presumably the focal point of the *From Alice to Ocean*, Rick Smolan's own story of following Davidson through the outback assumes a more dominant position on the CD-ROM. Smolan's video clips give his presence an immediacy absent from Davidson's journal entries, and authorial control is given over to the male photographer as the images take precedence to the written materials.

A comprehensive gender analysis conducted in the same spirit as de Lauretis's study of Oedipal narrative would contribute significantly to an understanding of the story patterns which may characterize CD-ROM games. However, the limits of a conceptual framework grounded in the Oedipal narrative should be noted. Various travel narratives could indeed be considered "Oedipal" to the extent that they involve a search for self, a visit to the birth place of civilization, a return to the site of one's ancestry, or a journey to one's death as a cyclical return to one's origin.[18] However, the Oedipal narrative with its long journey—only to find a place of unrecognized familiarity followed by blindness—hardly accounts for the sight-seeing journey's manifest content—the search for the strange. Or at the very least, the travel tale seeks not solely a gendered strangeness but a strangeness defined by cultural difference. Nonetheless, one can apply narrative theory to travel tales and investigate the unevenly distributed privileges of mobility within such stories.

De Certeau describes the search for the space of the Other as the motivating force of the travel account: "This *a priori* of difference, the postulate of the voyage, results in a rhetoric of distance in travel accounts. It is illustrated by a series of surprises and intervals (monsters, storms, lapses of time, etc.) which at the same time substantiate the alterity of the savage, and empower the text to speak from elsewhere and command belief."[19]

The outbound journey frames the encounter with the Other, and the length of the voyage, its hardships and distance traveled, authenticates the Otherness of the people and objects encountered. Only some CD-ROMS, which choose to include some element of the outbound journey, rely on this rhetoric of distance to assure the strangeness of the Other. In other CD-ROM applications, the Other is experienced as abundantly and instantaneously available. Digital atlases, *Material World*, and *Carmen Sandiego*, to name a few, are characterized by easily accessed exoticism; views of the Other can be triggered with a simple click, and glimpses of various parts of the world can be had by the dozens. The framing of the exoticism in these cases is accomplished through the CD-ROM's introductory material. To provide an example, *Voyage in Egypt* requires the player to enter the game through an animated sequence which serves as a lengthy introduction or passageway which can not be bypassed. The player experiences the illusion of being sucked into the game as a small picture frame features a moving image against a black background. The white outlines of a pharaoh on either side of the frame push themselves to the foreground, increasing the illusion of depth. Due to its dynamic movement within an otherwise static screen, this central image box quickly becomes dominant as it features movement through the complex architecture of an unnamed Egyptian structure. The player is visually pulled through corridors deep into the recesses of the monument until entrance is finally announced by the slow opening of heavy stone doors and the scattering of light into the deep interior which lies beyond. This passage initiates the viewer into the space of the Other where travel down the Nile is instantaneous and a click on any map label immediately elicits exotic images and accompanying text.

Regardless of the nature of the passage into game space, from *Qin's* precarious drop into a dark crevice to *Voyage into Egypt's* feeling of being sucked into a tomb, the mouse-clicking tourist pursues expectations formed by reading the CD-ROM box's promise of strange, secret, distant worlds. The player's own mobility contrasts with the immobility of those objects and individuals encountered in the space of the Other—the world on the other side of the CD-ROM's passageway. Thus, the player's narrative-making maps cultural difference. The Australian aborigine is an anchored image bound to a single locale within *From Alice to Ocean.* The matador of *Around the World in 80 Days* must always remain in the same spot. And Qin himself will not be found randomly wandering through the tomb's various levels.

Carmen Sandiego more accurately represents a world in transit: an Asian "helper" character can be encountered in South America and an Italian in Africa. Within a single game, these characters appear to be stable, but after multiple solved cases, the same characters reappear in different parts of the world. The villains, who are definitely mobile as in any traditional chase story, are of various ethnicities and nationalities. However, the goal is to curtail their mobility, to imprison them with the help of a police officer and a judge, both of whom are white American males regardless of the location of the arrest or trial. While the title character Carmen Sandiego, presumably a Latina or Hispanic woman, seems to be forever on the loose, the immobility of the game's photographically depicted individuals should also be noted. Only the

cartoonish characters (and the player herself) have powers of mobility, while the more material people are photographically captured in all their exoticism and are rendered immobile by the mechanics of the camera and of the game.

One could argue that a character's movement through space does not constitute narrative in and of itself. Even de Certeau identifies three stages of the travel narrative; in his formula, the outbound journey, the encounter with the Other, and the homecoming form the travel tale's necessary components.[20] In the CD-ROM game what determines the point where the journey ends and the homecoming begins? Narratologists have also expounded upon the role of the goal-directed protagonist. What are the goals that propel the player's movement through game space? A number of CD-ROM games do assign goals the player must achieve; their fulfillment marks the conclusion and the traveler's homecoming is enacted by the "exit" option. These goals contain the narrative possibilities and the myriad of possible spatial paths through the game space. Certain paths and actions are rewarded while others may even bring the disincentive of death and aborted narrative.

The variety of game goals is vast: build the Great Pyramid, unravel the ancient mystery that has fallen upon an Indian village, help rescue a law student's time-traveling fiancée, get the inhabitants of Zarg to dig up precious stones faster than your opponent, destroy a doomsday machine, outwit the master computer in a game of psychological warfare, find the stowaway, defeat the Chinese emperor. However, often the means to the goals are relatively similar involving comprehensive spatial exploration and accumulation, two pastimes none too foreign to the tourist. Movement toward the goal can often be spatially plotted, and successful transversal of a space is often awarded through the discovery of some item or clue which can be virtually acquired by the player and which may become necessary at some later point. Or in a game such as *Diggers,* the movement is downwards into the earth, and the accumulation of precious gems allows the purchase of more sophisticated equipment which facilitates even greater movement and accumulation of precious gems. Although the game may not prescribe a certain order or itinerary, the failure to explore a certain space and add a certain object to a player's bag of tricks may prevent further movement and thus prevent the goal from being achieved. In *Gadget,* the train may fail to depart on time unless the player has explored the destination thoroughly and added any new gadgets to her suitcase. The player proceeds in a "gone there, done that" fashion, scanning the environment for trophies and treasures, any item which may be snatched from the premises and later benefit the traveler. The acquired objects punctuate the player-spun narrative in much the same way that souvenirs may launch narratives of the tourist's overseas adventure. As Susan Stewart concludes, the souvenir authenticates experience and documents achievement: "Removed from its context, the exotic souvenir is a sign of survival—not its own survival, but the survival of the possessor outside his or her own context of familiarity." [21] The intangibility of experience is converted into the tangibility of possession. However, within the game, possession is as intangible as experience, thus souvenirs are easily traded to perpetuate the game experience.

A similar materialist gaze even inhabits many CD-ROM applications with more educational leanings. In *Material World,* each family's prized possessions are displayed in front of their place of abode in what could be called the spread-eagle style of exterior decorating. A family's home appears to be turned inside-out, exposing the interior and its inhabitants to the gaze of the passerby. At times, the manner of display is even suggestive of a yard sale, evoking a consumerist gaze. The CD-ROM user can peruse the items and even use a magnifying glass icon for a closer look. Unsurprisingly, many educational "trips" through

past cultures focus on the valued treasures they left behind, allowing the CD-ROM user to view the past in material terms, much like the museum effect experienced through *Qin's* artifact examination function. Interestingly, CD-ROMs such as *Ancient Lands* adds to this museum formula a degree of voyeurism otherwise foreclosed by a past emptied of its inhabitants. *Ancient Lands* reincarnates and repopulates the past beginning with an overview movie featuring a living mummy who plays *Ancient Lands* on his computer. He exclaims, "Finally, I've found a way to discover ancient lands without ever leaving the tomb." The reincarnated mummy is only the first tour guide or informant. The user may choose between several guides including a coy-looking slave girl who promises to provide the native's point of view on the "back regions" of Rome. The tour guide can be abandoned at any point so that the player may pursue an alternate path or may look more closely at a particular aspect of Egyptian, Greek, or Roman life. The interactive, multi-leveled structure of *Ancient Lands* and other CD-ROM applications facilitates this penetrating gaze, as people's personal objects are made available for scrutiny. Icons such as the microscope in *Material World* or the eyeball in *Freak Show* invite the player to click her way to an intimate perspective which may bring a new level of information visually or textually conveyed. Whether rifling through a circus member's diary hidden in his trailer, shuffling through the prized belongings of a Brazilian family, or scrutinizing an Egyptian woman's cosmetics, the world's people, past and present, fictional and actual, are accessed through a voyeuristic perusal of their material possessions.

The Digitalized Past

The assignment of goals or a motivating question such as "Where in the world is Carmen Sandiego?" may direct the player's movement and contain the narrative possibilities provided by interactivity. However, the use of an existent narrative or the placing of the player in the shoes of a historical figure also acts as a force of containment. To the extent that most players are aware of the exploits of Marco Polo, a narrative and a set of goals suggest themselves to the player of the CD-ROM *Marco Polo*. The supranarrative of history provides a model for the player's path down the Silk Route and contextualizes the game's places.

In their analysis of Nintendo games, Mary Fuller and Henry Jenkins comment on the use of colonization narratives and new frontier metaphors in new game technologies. Jenkins speculates that the re-creation of a New World open for exploration represents a desire to return to "a mythic time when there were worlds without limits and resources beyond imagining."[22] Tourism to less industrialized nations and to geographical locations seemingly untouched by the passing of centuries is often motivated by the desire to capture the romance long since drained from our over-industrialized nation, to catch sight of an unspoiled world as past figures must have seen it, to find unpopulated, undeveloped expanses of land where one can imagine that she is the first to set foot. The anti-touristic notion that the tourist despoils land and culture by her presence has gained currency over the past years, giving strength to the eco-tourism movement. Additionally, time travel through tourism appears to be less and less possible as computers, American products, and English-language television become ubiquitous even in the remotest of locations. The goals of tourism thus get shifted into simulated forms of travel where a denial of this loss is enacted, where historical recovery through retroactive environmentalist control over the land and vivification of past events appear feasible.

In past centuries, literature offered one form of simulation which could place the reader in the shoes of previous explorers thereby recapturing the past. By the end of the last century, preservation of the past through documentary film and re-

suscitation of the past through cinematic spectacle became possible. Even today we can watch the 1898 footage captured by anthropologist A. C. Haddon in Australia's Torres Straits and imagine being on the location witnessing some of the first exchanges between Australia's indigenous people and Europeans. Yet, in the spectator's inability to be seen by the participants and in the spectator's inability to swing her gaze around to see all that lies offscreen, she is like a ghost in the camera, unseen and incapacitated. And in return, all that she views has an ephemeral quality, inhabiting the unalterable past through its ghost-like image captured on celluloid.

The CD-ROM game offers an opportunity to enter the past as something more than a specter. The digital re-creation of the past may be a poor visual imitation, but nonetheless, its very pliability, the opportunity to explore, and the illusion of infinite possibilities in terms of space and action compensate for its frequent lack of photorealism. Additionally, the material nature of the CD-ROM does not change; its encoded possibilities and the mapped spaces are forever renewable, as long as the CD-ROM itself does not wear out. The actual tourist may lament that her visit may be the last time she witnesses a certain locale in its current state or that a place is simply not the same as before, now crowded with scenery-blocking hotels and overrun with tourists. Meanwhile, the CD-ROM game, as the home tourist's personal playground, may be saved; we may continually return to its pristine starting point. Digital realities present the illusion of coming into being; nascent possibilities are brought to life by a player's decision-making. The allure of a past without fixity, pouring out like the present tense, is clear; loss is negated as the past can be entered and changed.

The promise of a resuscitated past is realized with varying degrees of satisfaction and at varying levels of technological finesse in actual CD-ROM games. *Wrath of the Gods* almost accomplishes the tricky task of photographically depicting ancient history within an interactive game. The game's temporal placement is clearly in the past with references to kingdoms, ancient Greek costumes, and revitalized myths from centuries past; yet, they all find a place within photographs of Greece from a more modern era. Similarly, *Voyage in Egypt* invites players to "Visit the most important archeological sites and view photographs of the ruins accompanied by 3-D reconstructions which will allow you to enter the buildings as they once were." And *Qin* reconstructs the tomb of Qin Shi Huangdi from accounts of its construction and evidence from other archeological sites. Furthermore, the game suggests that undiscovered sites still exist, that the world's mysteries have not been exhausted, and that journeys into the past are still possible.

In another example, *Carmen Sandiego* illustrates how CD-ROM games and other contemporary armchair voyages may also function as atonement, easing historical anxiety over lost ecosystems, decimated tribes, and the more general disappearance of unknown lands and buried secrets. Within the game, lost items are consistently recovered and returned to their proper owners. This narrative of loss and recovery seemingly reverses the past flow of artifacts, prized possessions, and historical items from indigenous hands into European museums and private collections. Additionally, through the game's crime information network, cellular phone, computer database, and the always accessible robotic warrant-issuer, *Carmen Sandiego* accomplishes something akin to the effect of a recent series of IBM commercials. These commercials, filled with Greek fishermen, Italian nuns, Japanese dancers, and elderly French men all bragging about their computer technologies, suggest a world conveniently linked by compatible computers; yet, the picturesque images of these unique cultures, within which virtually no computers are actually visible, imply that this technological globalization can take place without moving toward worldwide

homogeneity and the obliteration of local culture. Similarly, in *Carmen Sandiego,* the player-crime-fighter can experience all the advantages of a global communication system while the exotic images remain pristine, free from any signs of industrialization and Westernization.

Other CD-ROMs focus on environmental concerns and atone for the loss of delicate ecologies and the species they once supported. The *3-D Atlas* commands not only space but also time, offering time-lapse photography of urbanization, pollution, and deforestation. In a kind of *fort-da* process of loss, mourning, and mastery, these time-lapse sequences can be repeatedly returned to their starting points and re-observed. Mirroring the recent surge in ecotourism, many CD-ROM games embark on exotic expeditions in the name of environmental care-taking. One of the most popular CD-ROM treks through Africa to date has been a game called *Eco East Africa* (Viridis). A player still experiences the touristic: "three-dimensional animals, stunning landscapes, and changing seasons all in unbelievable photorealistic detail." In fact, one of the game's options involves a choice between being a tourist or a game warden. If the player chooses the latter, the beauty of Ethemba, *Eco East Africa*'s fictional game park, may be fleeting unless the player effectively manages the game park's precarious eco-system. However, even if poachers, disease, drought, and park mismanagement ravages the environment, the forests, grasslands, savannas, and highlands can be instantaneously restored using the restart button.

By way of closing, it seems appropriate to ask exactly what the armchair tourist will discover in looking to CD-ROM travel games to fulfill the yearnings that impel touristic exploration. Some software will undoubtedly be purchased for their markers of authenticity, and many will serve some educational function. Yet, in other cases, the game's structure encourages viewing the globe as a "material world," a world defined by the products available for collection and consumption, a world defined by the logic of accumulation. Rather than taking advantage of the role-playing elements of such games in order to position a player as an inhabitant of a distant land, most games still deliver mobility and promote identification with Western travelers. Thus, the virtual tourist, aligned with technologies of both mobility and information-retrieval, stands in counter-distinction to the static inhabitants of touristic destinations, frozen by photographs or viewed as tools, maybe impediments, to the continued collection of booty and to the conquering of terrain. In short, in a world which, according to Fredric Jameson, is no longer mappable, travel CD-ROMs will provide environments which can be comprehensively mapped, explored, understood, and consumed from the privileged position of the tourist.

Notes

1 Dean MacCannell, *The Tourist: A New Theory of the Leisure Class* (1976; New York: Schocken Books, 1989); Jonathan Culler, "Semiotics of Tourism," in *Framing the Sign: Criticism and its Institutions* (Norman: University of Oklahoma Press, 1988); James Buzard, *The Beaten Track: European Tourism, Literature, and the Ways to Culture 1800–1918* (Oxford: Clarendon Press, 1993); Erik Cohen, "Authenticity and Commoditization in Tourism," *Annals of Tourism Research* 15(4) (1988): 371–86.

2 Buzard, *The Beaten Track*, 1.

3 Jonathan Culler, "Semiotics of Tourism," *American Journal of Semiotics* (1981): 156.

4 For a relatively comprehensive list of sources that compare anthropology and tourism, see Deborah Gewertz and Frederick Errington, "Anthropology and Tourism," *Oceania* 60(1) (September 1989): 37–54.

5 Laura Mulvey, "Visual Pleasure and Narrative Cinema," in *Movies and Methods*, vol. 2, ed. Bill Nichols (Berkeley: University of California Press, 1985).

6 Virginia Wright Wexman, "The Critic as Consumer: Film Study in the University, *Vertigo*, and the Film Canon," *Film Quarterly* 39 (spring 1986): 35.

7 Lynn Spigel, "Installing the Television Set: Popular Discourses on Television and Domestic Space, 1948–55," *Camera Obscura* 16 (January 1988): 17.

8 Gregg Keizer, "The Next Generation of Multimedia Software," *Multimedia World* 2(6) (May 1995): 66–72.

9 Timothy Mitchell, *Colonising Egypt* (Cambridge: Cambridge University Press, 1988), 27.

10 For more information about these impulses within the field of anthropology, see Martin Heidegger, "The Age of the World Picture," in *The Question Concerning Technology and Other Essays*, trans. William Lovitt (New York: Harper Colophon, 1977), and Christopher Pinney, "Future Travel," in *Visualizing Theory: Selected Essays from V.A.R. 1990–1994*, ed. Lucien Taylor (New York: Routledge, 1994).

11 Michel de Certeau, *The Practice of Everyday Life*, trans. Steven Rendell (1984; Berkeley: University of California Press, 1988), 115.

12 Jurij M. Lotman, "The Origin of Plot in the Light of Typology," trans. Julian Graffy, *Poetics Today* 1(1–2) (autumn 1979): 167.

13 Ibid.

14 Teresa de Lauretis, *Alice Doesn't: Feminism, Semiotics, Cinema* (Bloomington: Indiana University Press, 1984), 121.

15 Ibid., 119.

16 Eric J. Leed, *The Mind of the Traveler: From Gilgamesh to Global Tourism* (New York: Basic Books, 1991).

17 Ella Shohat, "Gender and Culture of Empire: Toward a Feminist Ethnography of the Cinema," in *Discourse of the Other: Postcoloniality, Positionality, and Subjectivity*, ed. Hamid Naficy and Teshome H. Gabriel, special issue of *Quarterly Review of Film and Video* 13(1 and 3) (1991): 45–84.

18 The anthropologist's voyage could be considered Oedipal in its search for a mirror image of Western civilization's pre-civilization savagery and in its contemplation of some essential human nature.

19 Michel de Certeau, *Heterologies: Discourse on the Other*, trans. Brian Massumi (Minneapolis: University of Minnesota Press, 1986), 69.

20 Ibid.

21 Susan Stewart, *On Longing: Narratives of the Miniature, the Gigantic, the Souvenir, the Collection* (1984; Durham: Duke University Press, 1993), 148.

22 Mary Fuller and Henry Jenkins, "Nintendo7 and New World Travel Writing: A Dialogue," in *CyberSociety: Computer Mediated Communication and Community*, ed. Steven G. Jones (Thousand Oaks, CA: Sage Publications, 1995), 58.

Hotting, Twocking, and Indigenous Shipping: A Vehicular Theory of Knowledge in Cultural Studies

John Hartley

The treaty takes the place of love.
Hardly attempted, the dance degenerates.
The festival becomes war. And already at the water
hole . . .

—JACQUES DERRIDA, *OF GRAMMATOLOGY*

This chapter is about family (race) and travel (writing) in cultural studies; the problem that it wanders (wonders) about is the relationship between origins and destinations, and between writers and readers, in the production of knowledge.

There There

Thor Heyerdahl's account of his 1955–56 research expedition to Easter Island, in search of "centuries-old secrets," is a book called *Aku-Aku,* which opens with a chapter called "Detectives Off to the End of the World."[1] It belongs to the genre of academic adventure, where the account of the travel is as thrilling as the secrets discovered at the "End." The getting of wisdom is the thing, not the wisdom itself. Still today, despite the transformation of international travel and tourism since Heyerdahl's day, academic knowledge is valued for its distance from self. Not only do we compete eagerly for grants to get us out of our home territories to do research, but academics are also the most active conference-goers of all professional groups, at least in Australia. The distribution as well as the production of knowledge is a thoroughly mobile practice, and this extends to the

textual form taken by academic knowledge; traces of travel suffuse the *writing* so pervasively that knowledge and travel seem to be metaphors for each other.

There's something compelling and curious about intellectual travel—as a biographical event, a cultural practice, and as a genre of writing[2]—and in Heyerdahl's case its appeal is enough to warrant a series of regularly reissued popular bestsellers, still in print after more than forty years.[3] But the bodily mobility of research and its writing can also be a *destination* for analysis as well as its *vehicle.* Knowledge is travelogue, bringing to the diectic "here" of reading some exotic "there" of observation, experience, or intellection (writing), whose truthfulness seems to be dependent on distance: the closer Our Hero has been to the End of the World and the more difficult the adventure, then the more convincing is the resultant revelation. Accounts of intellectual travel still conform to a Renaissance model—the authorial pilgrim's progress to colonize a discursive Newfoundland.[4] For the reader, the veracity and scarcity value of the knowledge so produced seems to be guaranteed by the distance traveled and the difficulties encountered in the getting, so that, for instance, Heyerdahl's theories and conclusions seem to be valuable *because* (as a latterday Jason the argonautist) he brings them back (golden fleece-style) from the "End of the World."

Meanwhile, the role of the reader is to mark whatever stationary "here" it is that forms the point of departure—the origin—of intellectual travel. It seems to me that the displacement of knowledge to some exotic elsewhere is a version of the "origin of society" problem discussed by Derrida in *Grammatology,* where the idea of a fixed point of origin always implies a "before," which therefore unfixes the point.[5] In the realm of knowledge, it seems that there's an endless repetition of the problem of indeterminacy by projecting knowledge from the here of the reader to anywhere else (a Galaxy Long Ago and Far Away, or some other Orient), its power to command being suddenly an effect of distance not truth.

Do readers still have to rely on traveler's tales, endless reruns of authorial indeterminacy, or is reading itself the mobility of knowledge? In particular, can the reader, rather than the writer, be *mobilized* as the locus of sense-making? If so, it may at last be time to set a period at the close of these premodern (renaissance/classical) metaphors of exploration.[6] Modernism is no help here, since its idea of progress is Tennyson's *Ulysses;*[7] it has retained distance as a criterion for truth but added eyewitness observation/speculation, transforming the traveler's tall story into the scientific expedition, and taking the skills of the pirate and graverobber into the laboratory and the museum collection. Perhaps it is time to consider a new concept of knowledge, a vehicular theory, centered on reading not writing, on petty theft not the expropriation of whole domains, and interested in the pervasive sense-making practices of popular media, not in preserving the hierarchies of arcane sciences. It's a move from there to here; an antipodean inversion of the polar-relations of knowledge; it's asking, with Stephen Hawking, the impossible question (which is also Derrida's): what's North of the North Pole?

Offense: t.w.o.c.

In what follows, I am interested (as a reader) in the mode of discursive transport used in the getting of wisdom in various writings. But instead of starting (as a writer) with the familiar exploratory travel-space metaphors, which would simply be to set off on a generically predetermined path, I am going to do something which is called, in British police-court terminology (and thence in the slang of those so charged), "*twocking*"—from the initials, as written in charge-sheets, of a common, petty, vehicular offence: t.w.o.c.: "T(aking) W(ith)O(ut) C(onsent)."

Most familiarly, juveniles twoc cars. Here, metaphorically, readers twoc writings. In both cases the offenders are mobile, traveling for the sake of it, in vehicles not belonging to them, without instrumental purpose. Twocking requires a moral code at variance with that of possessive individualism; it's an offense to ownership, intellectual or vehicular, being in the end a kind of pure or total gesture of travel, wherein the vehicle, the streets, moving quickly and being out of accountable time, are enjoyed for themselves, foregrounding the act and skill of driving (reading), not the possession of the car (text) or the promise of a destination (closure). In a twocked vehicle (book), driving (reading) is its own reward, travel (sense-making) is its own end, and time is the duration of the trip itself, not the steady state that travel disrupts. Twocking (of cars or texts) is not a glamorous crime of cultural politics or personal passion, not epic or heroic; it's a routine, low-grade, show-off offense. It is also called *joyriding*—joyreading—and in that spirit I begin; by twocking Thor Heyerdahl's expeditionary metaphors, hot-wiring his vehicular theories, so I can take some ideas for a ride.

The End of the World

Not long ago (as I write, but not necessarily as you read, when "not long ago" may have become "once upon a time"), I too went off to the "End of the World," and like Heyerdahl I went as a "Detective," also searching for "centuries-old secrets." My own forensic investigations were trying to identify secrets not in Easter Island's caves but in the shadow of Plato's, since I was looking for traces of the classical public forum within modern media readerships.[8] Like Heyerdahl, I went not only as researcher, but also as family. He was accompanied by his wife Yvonne and two children, Thor Jr. and Anette, who are all duly indexed in *Aku-Aku;* we too (two parents and two toddlers) mixed study and domesticity by going on a four-month Outside Studies Program from Australia to Britain *en famille.*

Thor Heyerdahl was the adventurer-academic

of his age; no one in the twentieth century managed to combine quite so successfully as he did the eyewitness ideology of science, the thrill of Viking voyages, the exoticism of the South Seas, and the racial fantasies of those for whom civilization has white skin and a red beard. Pursuing a Nordic quest for whiteness to a little island in the Pacific may seem quixotic (it may seem altogether nastier too, though you wouldn't guess this from the chatty *Aku-Aku*) but it is the very uselessness, the harebrained outlandishness of Heyerdahl's quest, that makes it good copy—so the "Kon-Tiki Man" got a year, a crew, a vessel, and a bestseller out of his conspicuously unscientific project, on the strength of his own red-bearded narrative appeal. This is how readers were enticed to read all about it, in a big display ad in the [London] *Daily Sketch* (Thursday April 10 1958):

THE MYSTERY OF EASTER ISLAND
FROM THE MAN WHO WROTE KON-TIKI
Thor Heyerdahl, famous author of *Kon-Tiki,* has written *another* magnificent true adventure story that you can't put down.
It's about a strange, remote island in the Pacific—Easter Island, where giant god-like statues brood over the countryside.
With the powerful help of a devil—Aku-Aku—Heyerdahl solved the mysteries of Easter Island that had puzzled the world for centuries.
He rolled back the years to uncover amazing facts about the colossal, glowering statues.
He brought to light treasures that had lain hidden in caves for generations.
He has discovered the secrets of the lonely inhabitants in a way that only Heyerdahl can do.
This is a thrilling adventure you must not miss!
It starts this Sunday. Reserve your copy now.
STARTING IN THIS WEEK'S SUNDAY DISPATCH.[9]

A generation later, I too was looking for antecedents to contemporary global society, trying to "roll back the years" in order to "uncover amaz-

ing facts" about something that has "puzzled the world for centuries," namely what—and indeed where—is the public? I was looking for evidence of the diffusion of democracy, not of white skins; my investigations concerned prosaic, profane, pervasive, contemporary texts, not epic, sacred, secret, ancient statues; I was digging through the mysteries of popular media, not literally digging up a lonely, windswept island. I was trying to make sense of journalism, not ju-jus, but Heyerdahl's evidence was made of rock, mine of discourses; his treasures in the cave were things, mine were ideas, and even though those ideas help to organize the government of selves and societies throughout the contemporary world, they are not reckoned "real" in the same way as a good old cave-load of buried treasure that can be grasped and photographed and cataloged and produced in evidence. Ironically, the eventual significance of Easter Island's treasure, if any, is precisely textual—textual traces, on stone and wood and landscape, of discourses and of governing ideas about selves and society. The "detective" skill required of the adventurer-academic at the "end of the world" is the same, i.e., to be able to read such evidence for meanings which help to explain how things got to be the way they are; indeed, in the official account of my "findings" I coined the term "forensic analysis" to describe the methodology of cultural studies.[10]

A Race for Time

But rocks is rocks and race is race, as Kipling might have said, while democracy and the public are just words, and so, even though the Australian Research Council application form does specify "a vessel" as an allowable piece of "research equipment," I was unable to call on the services of a ship to take me on my quest from Australia to a small, secretive island at the (Other) End of the World. We could just about afford Aeroflot, but the university travel agent wouldn't let us use it, so we spent a little more and traveled by Malaysian Airlines instead.[11] On board a packed jumbo with puking children, I was unable to check out my theoretical hypotheses by chatting, as Heyerdahl does in the last chapter of *Aku-Aku*, with my own personal familiar spirit, or "aku-aku" in Polynesian. But in the little island I visited—I want to call it Uka-Uka, but UK will have to do—the spirit of racial purity was all too real; not the still small voice of what Heyerdahl calls a "moderate form of ancestor worship" as on Easter Island,[12] but media full of stories about Maastricht,[13] as the European Community changed itself into the European Union and inaugurated the new fantasy of a "common" European "heritage," where much of what was paraded as "European tradition" and "heritage" was merely euphemized white racism.

Unlike Heyerdahl, I was preoccupied with reading the papers and watching the TV news, so I never had the leisure of a conversation with an aku-aku about the gap between scientific knowledge and racial fantasy: "I felt sorry for my own *aku-aku*," writes Heyerdahl:

> It had followed me for a year on a lead, without the freedom to wing its way into the unbounded universe. I thought I could hear its complaining voice. "You're getting stale, and too prosaic," it said. "You're no longer interested in anything but dry facts." . . . "This is a scientific expedition," I said. "I've lived most of my life among scientists and have learnt their first commandment: the task of science is pure research. No speculation, no attempt to prove one thing or another." "Break that commandment," said my *aku-aku*. "Tread on their toes."[14]

You probably remember Thor Heyerdahl, if at all, for his exploits on research vessels; not only Kon-Tiki but also the reed boat Ra. What is less well remembered is that these Boy's Own adventures with indigenous shipping had a *purpose,* namely to demonstrate the possibility that an advanced, white-skinned, red-bearded people could have sailed from Peru to Polynesia (*Kon-Tiki*), and

previously from an outpost of ancient Egypt to South America (*Ra*), ending up on Easter Island (*Aku-Aku*), thereby encircling the globe with a civilization that predates but exceeds the cultural competence of the known or surviving indigenous society.[15] What Heyerdahl was looking for on Easter Island was a "red-haired strain" within the indigenous population that could be traced back to a white-skinned, statue-building, "long-eared" ancestry. His conversation with his imaginary aku-aku culminates in this:

> "We were talking about a possible link between Malays and short-ears," I said. "What would your view be, as an *aku-aku*, if language said yes and race said no?" "If language suggested that Harlem negroes and Utah Indians came from England, I'd back the race expert.[16]

It seems that what's sauce for the *aku-aku* is source for the scientist, so Heyerdahl collects from various unsuspecting Polynesian islands "a bag full of test tubes filled with blood":

> Chiefs, elders, and local authorities had helped [the expedition's doctor] select those who could still be considered pure blooded. We had sent the samples by air in ice-filled thermos bottles from Tahiti to the Commonwealth Serum Laboratories in Melbourne. . . . never before had living blood from natives in these islands reached a laboratory in such good condition that all the hereditary genes could be studied and determined.[17]

The point of this archaeological vampirism was to isolate "all the hereditary factors arguing Polynesian descent from the original population of the American continent and at the same time clearly separating the Polynesians from all Malays, Melanesians, Micronesians, and other Asiatic peoples of the West Pacific."[18] Such an argument, for blood over language, wanting the great precontact civilizations of the Americas and the Pacific to be *white,* is the *purpose* of Heyerdahl's expeditions. The argument is presented as having something to do with science, even when it wishes to tread on scientific toes with its fantasy-speculations; the gist of the book's last chapter is to achieve *in narrative* what cannot be "proven" by normal archaeological and anthropological methods, but to do this, paradoxically, with a combination of traditional ethnographic research and modern high-tech forensic-science (blood-testing) methods.

A Moderate Form of Ancestor Worship

However, narrative is the clear winner over science. What *drives* Heyerdahl's quest in *Aku-Aku* is much more personal than the "prosaic . . . dry facts . . . of pure research"; it's the combination of red hair, family, travel, and race. His acknowledgment of his family's presence on the expedition is more than mere cutesy parental pride. The family serves a crucial narrative purpose, since the book closes with an anecdote about how his daughter Anette's flower wreath, thrown from the departing Research Vessel as the expedition left Polynesia, failed to clear the ship's rail. Heyerdahl relates how he retrieves the garland and tosses it overboard to join the others—a superstitious gesture that earns him the approval (and symbolic integration with the culture) of his *aku-aku.*[19]

Heyerdahl's *aku-aku* was assigned to him by Easter Island's "mayor," the only descendant of the "long-ears," a man who wanted his grandson to be christened "Thor Heyerdahl Kon-Tiki El Salvador de Niños Atan"—a boy whose "skull was covered with stiff, flaming red hair," who was "the last scion of the long-ears' race" and over whom Heyerdahl claims symbolic parenthood—at his christening "I was to be godfather and sat on the first bench on the women's side." There's more, including an account of the death of an unnamed granddaughter of the mayor from the flu that was brought to Easter Island annually by the Chilean navy, and for whom the "strapping grandson" was "compensation."[20] All of this, including the un-

self-consciously patriarchal and quite cheerful sacrifice of a young female child in favor of a masculine "scion," tends to overwhelm Heyerdahl's "science" with his *desire* for *his* red-haired, white, male, Nordic seafaring strain to be fused with that of the indigenous population he studies. The Heyerdahl family sails the seven seas with dad not to keep itself intact but to provide racial purism with a local habitation and a name.

It only remains for you to know that one of the secrets of my past is that I was given *Aku-Aku* (the book) while at an orphanage in 1960, and I still have the same copy. Its tales of an intact family pottering about "trying to prove one thing or another" in the South Seas clearly had some sort of impact on me, since that's what I went on to do for a living. However, although I remember reading and being enthralled by the travel aspect of the book (and its strange ethnographic-tourism color pictures), I don't remember noticing at the time either the Heyerdahl family (irrelevant to the adventure), or the Heyerdahl thesis (ditto). Reading it again, after all these years, the book's narrative desire for the globalization of a patriarchal white family is *all* I can see in it. My own desire on rereading it, namely to recognize the identity of my "erstwhile theoretical self"[21]—a pre-teenage fatherless white male, institutionalized in Wolverhampton but dreaming of Rapa Nui—was thwarted, however, since I am confronted only by a yellowing, loose-leaved, unglued book, inscribed with a dedication that reads:

TO

HIS ROYAL HIGHNESS
CROWN PRINCE OLAV
THE PATRON OF THE
EXPEDITION

Underneath this is my personalization of the book; my possessive individualist aspiration (i.e., to make it my own) was both marked and mocked by a signature that prioritizes my orphanage number over my individual name, for this is what is written in wobbly capitals:

56

HARTLEY

The sight of which leaves me with an impression not of Proustian recall (nostalgia) but of Derridean duplicity (textuality); not the comfort of origin but "hopelessly mediated" writing.[22] Across the divide of time and distance, I do not experience self-presence with the ghost of my "erstwhile theoretical self," I only wonder retrospectively whether the ambitions which tutor my current professional practices are founded on a twocked *misreading:* I read *Aku-Aku* in 1960 for *its* aspirations, made them mine, and in the 1990s discover that adventure, education, travel, discovery, and academic popularization are, after all, merely a species of racist fantasizing about an intact family.[23]

Vehicular Theory

Everyone I've asked, without exception, has heard of Heyerdahl and many have even read one of his books,[24] even those who weren't born when he was drifting through the currents of twentieth-century intellection, but not a single one of them remembers *why* he went on his expeditions. Heyerdahl has crossed the Derridean divide—the distance between self and identity, between subjectivity and text—shorn of his own purposes and endowed with a later generation's racial preferences. He's remembered as being a Good Guy vis-à-vis indigenous peoples, since he demonstrated that they could do a great many technological, navigational, and spectacular traveling tricks of their own, never mind modern science. Heyerdahl's perverse desire to have human migration go from east to west (i.e., not from Africa via Asia to the Americas but from Egypt via Peru to Polynesia), actually helps him—it reads as if the ancient *virachochas* were privy to knowledges that modern

science scarcely suspects. Perhaps it no longer matters that these prehistoric wanderings were, for Heyerdahl, racially motivated, white-skinned, long-eared, Nordic-type journeys. His overseas study trips are remembered *for themselves*—not at all for their intellectual content or scientific rigor, but for their status *as travel.* What has survived is not a collective memory of a wonderful racial theory, but of wonderful *indigenous shipping.*

Here "taking without consent"—twocking—is raised to the level of historical practice, engaged in by a popular readership. Of course Heyerdahl himself is also twocking; traveling in a series of indigenous designs that don't belong to him, he attracts the admiration of the crowd for his devotion to pure travel, without instrumental purpose. Like so many other popular performers, he's embarrassing when he confides his own beliefs, but when he does wheelies in a balsa raft and handbrake turns with a reed boat, we know we're watching pure talent. But this isn't the end of the story, for Heyerdahl's own vehicle—his *text*—is twocked by his readership. The meaning of the performance turns out, as always, to be in the hands of the driver (reader), not the intentions of the manufacturer (author). Heyerdahl's readership has "misunderstood" Heyerdahl's purposes so thoroughly that while he was tracing diachronic, longitudinal connections among humans—i.e. origins in time, blood-flows through generations, authenticity in racial "stock"—his public has simply flipped the theory sideways, and taken him to be a Derridean whose voyages *perform* the synchronic, latitudinal connections between peoples; erasing the *différance* between indigenous and western, primitive and advanced, magic and science. Heyerdahl was talking nineteenth-century grand narrative of origins, but his popular readership has been hearing twentieth-century structuralist relations, positing humanity not temporally but spatially, not as ancestors but as a simultaneous network. This is vehicular the-

628 HOP ON POP

ory, where the motive intentions of the author (pure race), embodied in the purposes of the institution (pure science), upholstered in the colours of rhetoric (pure narrative), become but an empty vehicle which is parked, keys in the ignition (published), ready to be twocked by the popular readership (pure travel). Vehicular theory presupposes in principle that meanings are stolen, but for use only, not possession. Heyerdahl's readership *takes him to mean* what they want, not what he argues, and this seems to be a collective, social "reading," not (indeed, over-riding, over-writing) an individual one.

Meanwhile, we arrived intact in hideous Heathrow, after a day's delay in Kuala Lumpur, where the "mechanical fault" in the plane seemed designed simply to shake extra foreign currency out of 400 stranded tourists; a kind of corporate twocking from helpless captives. But at last, after endless queues and endless walking, we were on the road, thirsty for knowledge. We set off in search of the public, hoping that the "public sphere" was not in fact that grim, grey, airport, busiest international hub in the world, which no one loves but everyone visits sometime.

Half a Dozen Postcards from the M62

"*Welcome*" to Breaston, a dormitory "village" right underneath the M1 Motorway on the Nottinghamshire-Derbyshire border. Here, between the Trent Canal and a large out-of-town Sainsbury's supermarket, where everything is labelled by country of origin except petrol and South African apples (in this period they were called "Cape Produce" instead of "Apartheid Produce"), is the house we stay in. It has lobelias and my sister's sculpture in the garden, Jessye Norman CDs and a well-stocked kitchen inside, also a big beech tree, several oaks, and a privet to shield us from the neighbors, though some sycamores on one boundary fence are inexplicably dying, and my

sister suspects neighborly poison (*her* leaves fall on *his* path). Here we house-sit for her while she takes a family holiday in Spain, while our children get to know Rover the dog and Florence the fish. The house is a big toy, as is the countryside; redolent English destinations are a stone's throw away, including Chatsworth, Hardwick Hall, Haddon Hall (our favorite), the Peak District, Arbor Low stone circle, Peverill Castle, Mam Tor, Blue John Cavern, The Trip to Jerusalem (a pub in Nottingham Castle rock), Elvaston Park, Sherwood Forest and Major Oak (major disappointment), and constant glimpses of this country's industrial underbelly, giant coal pits, some closed, with only their *aku-aku*s to rebuke the Thatcherite traffic whizzing by on the M1.

"*Greetings*" from Tufnell Park, a London suburb whose only claim to fame is HM Women's Prison Holloway, in the news at the time of our stay because of the imminent release of yet another wrongly convicted "IRA terrorist," this time Judith Ward, convicted of the so-called M62 bombing seventeen years earlier, during which time the prison itself had changed from Victorian Gothic castle (one crenellated turret of whose imposing gate-tower was the laundry chimney) to redbrick modernism of the new brutalist school, with prison as an architectural cross between college of education and window-free office block. But here, in the People's Republic of Camden, the yellow-brick houses and aphid-shitting lime trees do somehow cohere or confuse into a tolerant, grimy urbanity. Council blocks (soon to be sold off to private ownership), where radio music and car maintenance are the chief outdoor pursuits, back on to private flats in formerly bourgeois terraces, and in both cases the occupants are mixed— race, age, and family circumstance mottle the community. The Caribbean single mother chats with the self-employed psychotherapist, while the cab-repair firm's blue-serged mechanics hail the Sri Lankan proprietor of the corner shop, and fifteen people of fifteen different ethnic backgrounds (but mutually unremarkable) trudge silently through the garbage and chewing-gum goo and aphid shit from Holloway Road tube station to destinations that are geographically close but culturally unconnected.

"Wish you were here" in Trenowth, Cornwall, where primeval oak forest, farming, and traditional English values are maintained, along with the miller's house we stayed in, several hundred years old and solid granite (i.e., a couple of feet thick), right under an Isambard Kingdom Brunel viaduct of 1837 which still carries the London-Penzance Express, the whole idyllic scene resting solidly on EU subsidy. "Europe" seems an unlikely champion of Englishness, but it is the only line of defense between this garden of Eden and a fall from grace known elsewhere merely as economic unviability. (The reason for the oak forest's survival is the same—it is "unproductive" land too steep to farm.) Visible from the ancient British hill fort that is perched above the farm (a "turfy mountain, where live nibbling sheep"),[25] lies a vast white horizon; mounds of kaolin tailings like monstrous long barrows over the English China Clay Company's declining industrial heartland. A breeze wafts one of my favorite smells, that of the kaolin-impregnated stiff white paper used in the most stylish fashion and photographic magazines like *Australian Style,* across the intervening valley, up the nearer slope of which we can see our friend and her two small sons toiling behind a flock of sheep which she is driving up to be ceremoniously introduced to us (and the children sing, Maddy Prior-style: "And how do you do, and how do you do, and how do you do again!").

"Come on in the water's lovely" at Nailsea, a dormitory suburb of Bristol and our stop-over between Land's End and London; all new housing estate and kempt gardens, with time for a chat and a meal with old friends and mutual admiration of the suddenly numerous children, a quick trip to sightsee Bristol docks (waxed fat on the slave and tobacco trades) and Isambard Kingdom Brunel's *SS Great Britain,* being careful to pass under his spectacular Clifton Suspension Bridge en-route, and then on past grassy perturbations which hardly disturb the natural contours of the landscape; singularities which bespeak the fantasy racial origins of Englishness: Cadbury Castle (probable site of the "real" Arthurian Camelot), Silbury Hill (largest neolithic structure in Europe—a huge white chalk mound containing nothing at all), and on via Kennett Long Barrow, Avebury Circle, Stonehenge, and such places where you stop and are windswept with wonder, but where you certainly can't stay longer than to pick up a feather here, a piece of redolent chalk there, a postcard, and a guidebook, and then we and the children are off again, destination another London suburb with room for four.

"Having a lovely time" in Swiss Cottage, in London's northern inner suburbia, where posh preparatory schools and the Freud Museum rub shoulders with the Finchley Road, a busy and grim metropolitan artery. Just off this six-lane conduit to the electoral heart of Thatcherism (Finchley being Mrs. Thatcher's parliamentary constituency), there's the Central School of Speech and Drama, vibrating slightly with fame-seeking hormones inside as the fire hydrant outside oozes precious summer water for the third straight week, and traffic piles up while some poor student's battered Peugeot is craned on to a truck for a parking infringement, and we pick our way over the dribbling pavement to the children's playground, where a pair of Afro-Caribbean-English sisters dressed like fashion models frolic with their daughters while we do the same with ours, glancing admiringly at the locals' stylish agility, as they defy their confinement in the coralled and dog-dabbed concrete that passes for children's space in this rapidly undeveloping metropolis.

"Kiss me quick" in Lancashire (or, as the Devel-

opment Corporation ad puts it: "Thanks, Central Lancs"), way up north on the M1 to Leeds, then across the Peaks on the exposed and dangerous M62 (whose persistent terrorist is not the IRA but the weather), up the M66 to Padiham, another dormitory suburb/village somewhere between Blackburn and Burnley, facing Pendle Hill, home since the seventeenth century of the Lancashire Witches, to stay with my elder sister, the North-of-North endpoint of our journey, furthest away from Australia and darkening with November chill, as our younger daughter catches something that leaves her crumpled in Blackburn Hospital overnight, starting a race between her bugs and our departure date that did nothing for parental stress levels but left the doughty, no-nonsense, African-English bearers of the Thatcherized NHS completely unflurried as they checked her for meningitis and we just had to wait.

OSPitality

Now, what I want is, Facts. Teach these boys and girls nothing but Facts. Facts alone are wanted in life. . . . You can only form the minds of reasoning animals upon Facts. . . . This is the principle on which I bring up my own children.[26]

Ever since medieval times, travel and knowledge have been seen as so similar that each is understood through metaphors of the other.[27] Travel broadens the mind, and the most trusted knowledge (i.e., science) is still that of the eyewitness who's "been there, done that." Meanwhile, knowledge is figured as a place, area, "domain," "terrain" or "field," which we "explore" or "survey," undertaking "archaeologies" of the "sites" of discourses and institutions, or "pursuing" some truth which is itself "elusive" and "fleeting," always traveling faster than trudging scholarship. In fact the language of travel is nowadays more important than actual footslogging; the itinerant jobbing academic, hawking knowledge from town to town like a medieval colporteur, is nowadays mostly a citizen of the imagination. Although the academic mind—such as the brain of Einstein[28]—is still occasionally valued in popular culture, it has withered in importance in intellectual life as a thing in itself, since its unique capacity to carry around (in something weighting mere kilos) all the "facts wanted in life" has been usurped by extrasomatic technologies. Postmedieval academics usually conduct their travels via the vehicle of metaphor, communicating with the rest of the planet by publication, air-mail, and e-mail.[29] As Charlie Chaplin might have put it, we live in Modem Times; as Charles Dickens nearly did, the one thing needful (in these hard times) is *faxes.*

Occasionally, however, their administrative minders do let academics out into the world, not just in metaphorical vehicles but in their own physical bodies. These they send expensively to far-flung continents in a quaint pre-Derridean hope that if you put the subject of knowledge (the academic brain) and its object (some distant datum) together into the same space then you'll get some sort of metaphysical fusion of the twain, which con-fusion then returns to the home university replete with the one thing needful that it (the university) could not otherwise afford—original knowledge. Storing this priceless good in the brains of jet-lagged academics may seem precisely quixotic (though it may also be cheaper than storing the stuff in the library). Nevertheless, the practice does at last solve the age-old problem of where exactly the origin of knowledge is located. This sacred fountainhead turns out to be a body with an exotic name, as you'd expect, but an all-too-prosaic function: at the university that was destined to send me to the End of The World it is called "OSP," being the body that awards study leave; the O(utside) S(tudies) P(rogram) committee.

Since it makes no attempt to cover the actual costs incurred, OSP requires itinerant academics to spend most of their intellectual ingenuity and research skill on survival; in my case, how to keep two adults and two children alive, fed, sheltered (etc., etc.) on one side of the planet for four months, while on the other side a 17.5 percent mortgage rate and all the other financial tapeworms of family-building demanded their dinner as usual, never mind all this junketing. The question of how to feed the knowledge-seeking self and family is much more compelling on a daily basis than the question the four of us were collectively sent by OSP to investigate. And so we spent most of our time, perforce, in unscholarly places where we could find free beds; that is to say, in suburbia.

The children's insatiable quest for knowledge had to be slaked before OSP could be initiated, much less propitiated. We headed compulsively for parks and playgrounds, and they got on with their research, collecting an amazing array of leaves, pebbles, wet things, and novel microorganisms, all of which adhered tightly to their own physical bodies, fusing together and to their faces, confusing yesterday's peach, today's muddy acorn, and tomorrow's cold, in a childish parody (or was it proof?) of the metaphysics of presence. But none of the resulting insights, collections, empirical samples, or taxonomies could be reported to the OSP committee, even though OSP paid half the children's air fares. It is impossible, for reasons of genre, to tell the truth about a trip, because your "findings" may be scientific, or they may adhere to the sole of your shoe, but you cannot report both in the same piece of writing. So *this* piece of writing, which is indeterminate and wandering (though not purposeless), is not a research report with its stately rhetoric of distortion and suppression (pretending that what you found out on the trip was confined to disciplinary knowledge), but it's not really a holiday postcard either, partly because most of the places we stayed in are those for which there are no postcards. We weren't nomads, explorers, tourists, or field-tripping ethnogra-

phers, and this isn't even a traveler's tale. Let it be generically in-between and not-quite; a "Research Postcard," addressed to no one in particular, not even Derrida;[30] part image, part message, it is a marker of movement, but unsure of its destination.

Dreaming Spires . . . Screaming Tires

Here then, poised precariously on the brink of financial disaster—our own matched by the post-Thatcherite landscape's—somewhere between suburbia and the mythical English village so often quoted in suburban housing, thirstily imbibing information by watching TV and keeping up with the gossip in the style and fashion magazines, at the edge of the known epistemological universe (in a place called "cultural studies"), I started my formal research by doing a little participant observation of popular culture, in these places less renowned for their scholarly resources than is, say, Oxford.

Even so, it was straight to Oxford that my research led, via the inexpensive medium of the nightly TV news. There are bits of Oxford that no scholar enters, of which there are few if any postcards, where no dreaming spires can be seen. A car factory perhaps, or the remains of one, waiting for the last skilled workers to unbolt the presses and machine tools for scrap, a football club of declining fortune, and interminable housing estates for the workers, the ex-workers, their families, and the random drifts of underemployed youth, undercapitalized young couples, underachieving productive assets. Here, rather than in the Oxford of scholarly mythology, occurred the most important event in Britain of that year, the emblem of the British summer, which was both long and hot.

On TV the nation saw for the first time, direct from the council estates of Oxford, the newest pastime of popular culture; it was called "hotting." And with it, a little rioting. Hotting is the practice of driving hotted-up cars flamboyantly in suburban streets at night to impress the onlookers and to tease the police. The TV shows a glint of red paint, the guttural noise of an over-revved engine, knots of suburbanite bystanders on the gray pavements, arms folded against the glare of the camera lights, looking like latecomers to a Guy Fawkes bonfire party. That's all, apart from the usual spattering of journalists, politicians, and police, with the collective gravity and cranial capacity of Winnie the Pooh.[31] Hardly a political crisis, and only a riot because the police media release said it was.

The crisis wasn't easily legible as such because it took place not in the traditional binary context of mainstream adversarial politics, but in (or between) more ambiguous domains: lifestyle (cars), class (lower middle to working), location (suburbia). It was "produced" not as a public event by metropolitan political vanguardists, but literally produced as a media event by media crews with deadlines and the usual hunger for daily visuals, even in summer when the public sphere proper is on holiday. Was there more to hotting (and rioting) than mere silly season journalism? Was the elevation of tacky, unglamorous, politically naive and stylistically inept suburbia to the status of national preoccupation evidence of a political crisis after all? Or is summer rioting just another diary event in British journalism; Notting Hill, Brixton, Toxteth, Moss Side, St. Pauls, . . . Oxford—a summer irritation, like aphid shit underfoot and with the same political significance? Traditional British summer rioting is usually explained away in the popular media not as popular disaffection with the political system but as "race riots." This one, as so often in fact, couldn't be blamed on the ethnic minorities, even if, like so many other forms of popular entertainment, it borrowed from them some stylistic elements.

"Shell Suit Shauns and Lycra Lindas"

As well as hotting, that year in Britain was noteworthy for some other emblematic cultural icons.

These were twocking itself, ramraiding, and Essex girls. Essex girls won pride of place—a cover mention—in *The Face*'s review of the year. Since it liked to think of itself as world's greatest style magazine, *The Face* could hardly bring itself to share Essex girl jokes with its readers, but it gestured to the genre with this:

> Q: What do Gorby and an Essex girl have in common?
>
> A: They both went on holiday and got (that's enough, *Ed*).[32]

"Essex girl" is a taste/class category, denoting lack of both, applied to young working women from outer metropolitan suburbs, who became culturally visible as their spending power began to outstrip the readiness of style-setters to accept their purchasing choices. Notorious for what they do in cars—cars that may well have been twocked—Essex girls get fucked, literally, or (like Gorby on holiday) metaphorically. ("Get fucked," incidentally, is Australian for "go away," so the phrase is another metaphor of *travel* where the "tenor" [make distance] uses a "vehicle" [make love] whose literal meaning is to *join together,* resulting in a figure of difference in sameness, distance in conjunction.) This was not only the year of the Essex girls' joke (which was also generic— outside Britain the same genre circulated as "blonde jokes"), but also their sitcom, *Birds of a Feather* (pronounced "fevvah"), which explored the domestic space between petty bourgeois suburban-respectable Essex girls and crime, petty or otherwise, as the two sisters cope with the vicissitudes of a comfortable lifestyle while their blokes are banged up in the nick for armed robbery.[33]

A twocked car may be taken down to one's own housing estate for a bit of hotting in the light summer evening, or more seriously it may be used for ramraiding. Ramraiding is the latest form of window shopping, where a twocked vehicle—preferably an upper-class Range Rover or an haute-bourgeois Volvo estate (wagon)—is rear-ended into a shop window at high speed, often in full view of the security cameras, using the arse end of the very image of smug fat-bummed class supremacy to facilitate the removal of quick-sale consumer-desirables. All this is duly relayed to the nation on the evening news bulletins, with the aid of videotape from the said security cameras (the latest and cheapest signifier of "gritty reality" on TV),[34] and small riots ensue in the housing estates where "shell-suit Shauns and Lycra Lindas"[35] hang out, waiting for something other than John Major to happen.

Cars and Class

I was about to suffer the fate of Gorby and Essex girls before me. We never went to Oxford—we just saw it being hotted on TV—but we did get around. I got a car from the newspaper classifieds in Nottingham. After looking at two or three dispiriting examples of what neglect and weather can do to cars, and visiting several car yards whose salesmen reminded me of why I'd emigrated, a more promising prospect appeared in the paper. Off we go to another grotty, downmarket housing estate; the kind whose streets have been given a helical twist by some crazed bureaucrat planner, so you're always on a bend, but never going anywhere. The local youths' creative response to this Kafkaesque topography is to use cars to go nowhere too, giving them the flamboyant helical twist of the handbrake turn, and doing noisy, flashy, rally-style declutching, hotting off into the next cul-de-sac. The houses are rendered in gray concrete, and they are being sold off, so this isn't a council estate pure and simple; some houses have been clad in fake stone, others in yellow paint, and one over there is exuberantly ethnicized in the gaudy manner of an Indian restaurant, complete with spy-hole and buzzer in the front door to monitor would-be guests for obvious signs of rac-

ism. The one we're looking for is in a Gramscian state of "moving equilibrium" as two forces fight it out for stylistic hegemony; the neat aspirations of DIY handyman-dad vying with the random derangements of the children, the opposing forces engaged in noisy negotiations as we arrive.

Naturally, we're in my sister's subcompact Metro, not her husband's company BMW, whose presence would add at least £100 if spotted by the vendor. We look at a beige Mark IV Cortina. Fatal attraction. I'm a fan of the Ford Cortina as such, having had (in my youth) no less than five of them, of varying vintage. In those days the Cortina was *the* British volume car—the biggest selling and most stolen car in the U.K., and Cardiff (where I then lived) was the city with the most car thefts. Unsurprisingly I lost two Cortinas that way, twocked, burned, and dumped. My favorite had been a fast, tight, beige Mark IV with tan acrylic roof. It had been, as a passing African Welshman remarked when I parked it one day outside a pawn shop in Butetown (the so-called Tiger Bay of film and Shirley Bassey fame) on my way to buy an Italian coffee maker called the Atomic (£5), a "nice tool."

This one was not. It had suffered the fate of the Essex girl. It was neat enough looking (from across the street); but on closer inspection it had black paint on the tyres, a dreadful portent. It had beige paint on the rubber seals, silver paint on the engine. It had been Gorbied. But it had rear seatbelts, and it was Proustianly beige, and it even had a little booster seat for one of the children, and the young couple who sold it to me were nice enough, not sleazebags, just a little hasty to close the deal and get on with their lives, and they just happened to have a spare wheel in the loungeroom that would fit it. Would it last four months? Shaun and Linda just smiled a lot.

We barely made it to London. The car stopped somewhere in an inner northern suburb, oozing wetly over the anonymous short street, a car with the vehicular equivalent of emphysema, gasping for breath and with no force in its movements. At this point, class takes over. My classy London friend, who drives a classy silver Saab, has a personal mechanic who may be turned to in a crisis; he's in the Filofax. His business card puns gently on his forename. Mark One Motors is tucked in a mews off Eton Avenue; and while you're waiting just walk down England's Lane to Maitland Park Road and there, Number 41, is where Karl Marx lived and where he died.

The Point Is, to Change It

Well, of course they know about class in that part of London. Mark had a car that he himself used to carry parts in; a midnight blue Volvo estate automatic—your average class supremacist's wife's runabout. He'd get it through its "MOT" roadworthiness test and let me have it for £350. No, he didn't want the Cortina in part exchange, and would I kindly move it out of his mews? On top of the £320 I'd already paid for the beige bomb this wasn't really a bargain. But of course I bought it, driving it away with an old piece of popular class analysis ringing in my ears:

Q: What's the difference between a Volvo and a porcupine?
A: Porcupines have the pricks on the outside.

Like any art object a car has a provenance, meticulously recorded by the state in the so-called log book. When I looked at the Volvo's book I was in for a shock. Sure, this is bourgeois north London, and the Volvo is that kind of car, and this one had never been owned further out of London than Golders Green, but still, you don't expect *literature* from a *log book,* and so the name "Walter De La Mare" as previous owner was unsettling. It's as close as I've ever been to a real (literary) author. But while the Volvo was a 1970s car, Walter De La Mare himself had died in 1956, after being awarded

honorary degrees by the universities of Oxford, Cambridge, London, St. Andrews, and Bristol. He'd married in 1899, and he had two sons, one of whom, Richard, went on to become chairman of Faber and Faber, which was Walter De La Mare's publisher. Perhaps Richard had a son or a brother called Walter, or perhaps not (the *Dictionary of National Biography* is silent on the matter), but at any rate there was in fact a Walter De La Mare wandering the streets of North London around Dartmouth Park Hill (where my own publisher also lived), in a midnight blue Volvo 144 estate with a *Blue Guide to England* in the side pocket and a Royal Automobile Club *GB* sign under the dash, for most of the 1970s.[36] Did he play Abba on the 8-track cassette while he pressed a flared trouser leg down on the Volvo's flabby throttle? Did he know about *Grease,* vehicular or disco-cinematic, or was his mind devoted to higher things; the Althusserian Detour through High Theory, perhaps, or the Gramscian Digression through subcultural style? Or was "Walter De La Mare" just a nom de plume for someone who likes to use the names of famous English authors, especially on car log books, as a revenge against literary authenticity—a twocker of other people's names, as well as their cars? Who can tell these days?

Now I have Walter De La Mare's Volvo with Mark One's MOT parked outside Karl Marx's house, and a Cortina, sans everything, parked in an haute-bourgeois street where no Cortina has dared to park before. Soon, with the help of complaining neighbors and the local council's Dead Cortina Officer, the déclassé embarrassment will be humanely put down and recycled into a small, useful metal cube. The Volvo, for its part, will take us all over England—uncomplainingly, reliably, and close to the speed limit. I begin to wonder about porcupines.

If there's a lesson about class in this tale of two cars, perhaps Walter De La Mare can enlighten us. Among other things he wrote children's stories, the pre-Second World War equivalent of kids' TV; well-meaning, interesting, didactic, and ultimately strange visions of a class society into whose mysteries Walter would initiate generations of preteen girls. I do possess one book by him, preserved unread from my own childhood. Here it is; published the year one of my sisters was born, with a short story about three daughters (sometimes I think my biography was written in advance in the books I've unwittingly collected), called "Lucy." [37] Lucy is an imaginary friend, a sort of white modernist *aku-aku*, belonging to one of three girls who live in the mansion built by their jute-manufacturing capitalist grandfather, until the day when their spendthrift father's collapsed speculative investments force them into poverty. The girls' relationship with this history is entirely textual, since they know their forebears only by portraits on the dining room wall, and they know their financial situation (up or down) only via letters from Four Lawyers.

Jean Elspeth and her sisters are no Essex girls, but they are *Birds of a Feather;* beholden to absent men for inexplicable riches and unaccountable losses, while they more or less cope with home and each other. Jean Elspeth, youngest and least worldly sister, discovers her imaginary Lucy at the age of seven, when the family is still rich and time hangs heavily in a house where everyone works hard keeping order but nobody has time for talk. The story is about how a family fails to cope with changes in class, from active (manufacturing) to passive (investment) capitalists, thence to market collapse and the sale of all moveable effects. Lucy is Jean Elspeth's confidante right up until the moment when material ruin transforms their house from a monument to money into an empty, airy shelter for nesting robins and "a marvelous bush of Traveler's Joy" flowering in what had once been the boot cupboard.

A "narrative of enlightenment" this may be,[38] with an improving moral too (you'll find mad-

ness/misery in high society, but happiness in nature/poverty): "How very odd, then, that the moment it [the manor-house] ceased to be a place in which *any* fine personage would be proud to be offered a pillow, [Jean-Elspeth] began to be friends with it." Her personal freedom and identity come to her, and Lucy disappears, at the very moment when material wellbeing departs. "Lucy" is a tale that uses class analysis to criticize capitalism (ever so slyly, so you can miss it if you wish) in favor of a vision of sororal solidarity held in place by an empty house, the symbolic legacy of their patriarch the grandfather, who was born poor and whose surviving granddaughters live long enough to be "taken in" to the home of their kindly erstwhile scullery maid. "Lucy" is a gentle critique of patriarchy too, and it seems that what Walter De La Mare really valued was oddity, which is a kind of integrity that survives physical displacement and mental derangement. Jean Elspeth is outwardly a simpleton suffering hallucinations, and she ends up as a dotty old lady staring at her own reflection in a dank pond. But that, Walter seems to be saying, is OK, even a truth; in the end it's a more moderate and worshipful vision of English ancestry than the conventional respect given to money and manors.

Masculine Understanding

This is literally kids' stuff, written by a man who got honorary doctorates from all the best universities for doing it, and whose eponymous Volvo is even now on the road, a few minutes up the M1 from my sister's house, parked outside the "curious little church of *Ault Hucknall,* with early Norman details, in which is buried Thomas Hobbes (1588–1679), author of Leviathan," according to the entry in Walter De La Mare's own copy of the *Blue Guide to England.* We go inside the picture-postcard church and one of us transcribes the great possessive individualist's black flagstone inscription while the children dart about right over the top of the "repute of his learning":

Condita hic sunt ossa
Thomae Hobbes
Malmesburiensis
Qui per multo annos servivit
Duobus Devoni comitibus
Patri et Filio
Vir Probus et Fama Eruditionis
Domi Forisque bene cognitus
Obiit Anno Domini 1679
Mensis Decembris die 40
Aetatis Sui 91

. . .

Preserved here are the bones
of Thomas Hobbes
of Malmesbury,
who for many years served
two households of [the earls of] Devonshire,
father and son.
The virtue of the man and the repute of his learning
are well-known at home and abroad.
He died in the Year of Our Lord 1679,
on the fourth day of the month of December,
in the 91st year of his age.[39]

Hobbes died in the imperious Hardwick Hall, having tutored the second and third earls of Devonshire—patri et filio—son and grandson of Hardwick's builder, Bess of Hardwick, of whom it has been said:

A woman of masculine understanding and conduct, proud, furious, selfish and unfeeling. She was a builder, a buyer and seller of estates, a moneylender, a farmer and a merchant of lead, coals and timber; when disengaged from these employments, she intrigued alternately with [Queen] Elizabeth and Mary [Queen of Scots], always to the prejudice and terror of her husband.[40]

Bess of Hardwick married four times, laying the foundations of four future dukedoms (Devonshire, Newcastle, Portland and Kingston) with her second marriage to Sir William Cavendish, and securing her own eminence in her fourth marriage in 1567 to George Talbot, sixth earl of Shrewsbury. Of him it has been said:

By the side of his formidable wife he tends to seem a rather colourless character, but it would be a mistake to under-rate him. He used his inherited wealth as a basis on which he became perhaps the biggest tycoon in England. He was a farmer on an enormous scale, an exploiter of coal mines and glassworks, an ironmaster and shipowner with interests in lead and steel. . . . To some extent their marriage can be seen as the merging of two companies. The deal was clinched by a triple marriage; not only did Lord Shrewsbury marry Bess, but his second son married her daughter Mary, and his daughter married her eldest son Henry.[41]

Hobbes thus had firsthand experience of bourgeois possessive individualism as it was being invented within the persons and families of the existing aristocracy; it was this "merging of two companies" (feudal dynasticism with modern capital) into the thing incarnate that gave him lifelong patronage and protection, which itself may be seen as a wise investment by the Cavendishes, since the "repute of his learning" has certainly outlived theirs:

The second earl's main claim to fame is that Thomas Hobbes . . . entered his service when they were both young men just down from Oxford. According to John Aubrey, although ostensibly the earl's tutor, Hobbes mainly "rode a hunting and hawking with him and kept his privy purse. . . . His lord, who was a waster, sent him up and down to borrow money, and to get gentlemen to be bound for him, being ashamed to speak himself."[42]

This wastrel died within two years of inheriting Hardwick, and so his eleven-year-old son, the third earl, inherited house and Hobbes, and continued to patronize him for half a century. As for Hobbes:

At Hardwick he used to sing prick-song very badly in his bed at night and to walk up and down the hill "till he was in a great sweat, and then give the servants some money to rub him."[43]

In fact Thomas Hobbes was a merry old soul, and the contemporary diarist John Aubrey reminds us that this greatest of English political philosophers owed his wits to his ability to puke, a fact that went down well with my travel-sick children:

'Tis not consistent with an harmonicall soule to be a woman-hater, neither had he an Abhorrescense to good wine but he was, even in his youth (generally) temperate, both as to wine and women. . . . When he did drinke, he would drinke to excesse to have the benefit of Vomiting, which he did easily; by which benefit neither his wit was disturbt longer than he was spuing nor his stomach oppressed.[44]

Visiting DWEMS

We visited two other Dead White European Males on our trip. Karl Marx's grave is in Highgate, a pleasant walk from where we were staying in London, to see the man who thought the point of philosophy was to change things, lying peacefully among ragged oaks and behatted matrons who charge you £1 a head to visit the heavy marble and cast iron monument erected in 1956—the year when Walter De La Mare died, Hardwick Hall was taken over by the National Trust, and Thor Heyerdahl returned from Easter Island—and we stand there, world socialism collapsing about our ears, admiring the man with three sisters and three daughters,[45] who in the year of his own death visited his eldest daughter Jenny, "seeking rest in the noise of the children, this 'microscopic world' that is much more interesting than the 'macroscopic.'"[46] When Jenny herself died in January 1883, Marx's biographer says that, "Irredeemably shattered by the death of his "first born, the daughter he loved most," Marx returned to London to die."[47] It is not often remembered that Karl Marx

died of a broken heart for the love of a daughter, nor, perhaps, that his last recorded words on the country where he had lived and worked most of his life, but which had refused him naturalization as a "subject" in 1874 on the grounds that he was a "notorious German agitator" who "had not been loyal to his own King and Country," were: "To the devil with the British."[48]

We also visited my father John William Hartley's grave in Margate Municipal Cemetery. It looked somewhat battered after a recent and very un-British hurricane, with felled trees untactfully exposing the view to the recycling garbage plant next door, although they had restored the headstone to an upright position. In truth the visit to the cemetery was a flying one, to show the grave to my new family and vice versa, en route to that most English of summer pastimes, a day-trip to the seaside, in this case to Ramsgate, where I had lived (post-orphanage) in the mid-1960s. Karl Marx's daughters were, according to their mother, "attached body and soul to London and have become fully English in customs, manners, tastes, needs and habits," and one of their customs was the annual holiday by the sea in Ramsgate:

[In 1857] Jenny [Marx] went to Ramsgate with Lenchen [Helene Demuth, housekeeper and mother of Marx's unacknowledged illegitimate son Frederick Demuth] and the children for several weeks to recuperate and this eventually became an annual occurrence: the Marx family had great faith in the health of sea air, and at one time or another visited practically every resort on the south-east coast. In Ramsgate Jenny had, so Marx informed Engels, "made acquaintance with refined and, *horribile dictu,* intelligent English ladies. After the experience of bad society, or none at all, for years on end, the society of her equals seems to suit her."[49]

And so we sat on the refined and intelligent sand and, as I remember, made some pretty pointed comments on the quality of the sea air (in comparison to Fremantle's). But the children were delighted by water-rounded chalk pebbles and flint nodes, some of which went into the collection, and Ramsgate is a pleasant enough place to drive a Volvo round, looking for the undemolished sacred sites of (my) childhood. However, having subjected Volvo, family and reader alike to this unscholarly diversion along the byways of moderate ancestor-worship, I spare you further patrilinearity, and return to History, and Australia.

Overkill

It turned out we needn't have left. As we got off the plane in Perth, Western Australia was in the grip of an orchestrated media campaign that proved to be an exemplary case study of the very issues I had gone to Europe to research. It had everything: a public domain created by popular media, readerships mobilized as citizens, twocking, hotting, indigenous peoples, patriarchal racists, pure travel, and class relations played out in fictional form. History and death were colliding in the accidental juxtaposition of family saloons. Unfortunately, while this amounted to a vindication of my own reading of the current phase of the textualization of politics, it was not such a confirming experience for those who were being textualized in this way. For some of them, it seemed more like genocide. While the campaign was directed against "juvenile car crime," everyone knew (though no-one in government or media said) that this meant Aboriginal children's car crimes.[50] In fact, although white youths were quite capable of the most serious vehicular offences, up to and including the murder of a young Aboriginal man called Louis Johnson, who was run over by a carload of white youths (male and female) and left to die "because he was black,"[51] it was the lesser but more identifiably indigenous crime of twocking that seemed to inspire a fear in the organs of public enlightenment that the whole fabric of society was under threat. The police policy of high-speed pursuit of stolen cars, was defended to the death

(fifteen people were killed in high-speed chases over a two-year period). The police commissioner maintained that "to do otherwise would be conceding to the actions of a few, which would lead to a breakdown of law and order" (*West Australian* (December 5, 1991).

On Christmas night, while the premier of Western Australia Dr. Carmen Lawrence was on holiday in Italy, a pregnant woman and her one-year-old son were killed in a collision with a stolen car containing three Aboriginal minors, which was being pursued at high speed by the police at the time. That was the pretext for "family men" to turn on indigenous children, literally with a vengeance:

GET TOUGH ON CAR LOUTS: TAYLOR
Acting Premier Ian Taylor has called for juveniles with records of car theft and violence to be given long jail terms. . . . Mr Taylor, a family man with two sons and a daughter, is at odds with the Premier, Dr Lawrence, and the Community Services Minister, Mr Ripper. They both believe long sentences do not deter young criminals. (*Sunday Times*, December 29, 1991)

The Rupert Murdoch-owned *Sunday Times* ran an editorial, a New Year's message to the Western Australian community, which spelt out why the matter was so serious. Aboriginal car theft, it transpires, undermines the entire basis of Western binarism:

The *Sunday Times* is on the side of the police. Their job is to uphold the law and they deserve total community support. Not to chase hopped-up young car thieves would be to invite traffic anarchy, surrendering the roads to young criminals and making hostage a community that already cannot put its trust in traffic lights. (December 29, 1991)

Being able to trust the difference between binary oppositions (red-green) is one of the fundamantal premises of Western thought (as well as being the most commonplace exemplar of meaningful opposition in Saussurian semiotic theory), so a challenge to it in the form of feral Commodore sedans crashing through red lights at over 100 KPH is naturally seen in terms of social dissolution—"anarchy . . . surrender . . . hostage . . . cannot trust." The *Sunday Times* reckons that the "time is long overdue to stop rapping offenders over the knuckles with a feather duster." What's needed is "tougher sentences . . . long periods of secure detention for violent young offenders." The *Sunday Times* has no time for "anyone who has more consideration for offenders than for their victims," or "misguided critics" who "bring allegations of press and television hysteria and charges that the media are somehow to blame for it all" (*Sunday Times*, December 29, 1991).

A week later the boundaries were all tidied up: "WE'LL LOCK THEM UP," promised the *Sunday Times* headline; "'This small group is waging war on society' (Acting Premier)." The paper ran a series of stories on "tragedy dad," the survivor of the most recent crash:

> 10,000 AT VIGIL FOR FATHER
> *Tragedy dad swamped by letters*
> *Sympathetic public gives $20,000*
>
> PERTH has opened its heart to accident victim Peter Blurton.
>
> The young father has been inundated with offers of help, notes of sympathy, gifts and $20,000 in cash.
>
> The Blurtons expressed amazement yesterday after a week in which they were on the receiving end of a huge show of support.
>
> Organizers at 6PR radio station, which has conducted an appeal for the Bayswater man, also spoke out about the public generosity which has seen thousands of dollars collected and pledged to help get Mr Blurton's in-laws to Australia [from England].
>
> The radio station and Royal Perth Hospital have received hundreds of letters and cards.
>
> The State Government Insurance Commission donated two of the return air-tickets, worth about

$5000, and several others were paid for by the Bullcreek Lions Club which raised $7000.

> The Airways Hotel donated a week's free accommodation for the Dawbers [the dead woman's family], and Budget has thrown in two vehicles for their use in Perth.
>
> There have been offers of free funerals and hundreds of dollars sent by different police squads. (*Sunday Times*, January 1, 1992)

This vision of a united community—"Perth" showing its true pecuniary colors with "donations" that just happen to get free press for various publicity-hungry institutions (Radio 6PR, SGIO Insurance, Airways Hotel, Budget car rental, the police)—is imagined by local media that have collectively done a Heyerdahl sidestep. The story is about community, support, an open heart, and "public generosity" for those *within* the pale; but such a vision is only possible if something else, literally unspeakable, is placed *beyond* the pale. Insisting that the campaign was against "hopped-up young car thieves" and "criminals" who are also described as "violent," neatly sidesteps the need to address an Australian racial fantasy that sees English in-laws as "us" and indigenous children as "them." Trust in traffic lights is restored, via the exclusionary tactics of racial binarism.

As for Carmen Lawrence, the state premier who less than two months earlier had said that "the prison system had proved a cataclysmic failure in the case of juvenile crime" (*West Australian*, November 18, 1991); she returned early from her trip to Italy and got off the plane to announce the victory of a small coup d'etat, duly and dispassionately recorded on the front page of the state newspaper: "People Power Won: Premier" (*West Australian*, January 6, 1992).

The government, ramraided by the local media, crumpled: a new draconian law was pushed through a hastily recalled parliament, and some commercial enterprises got free advertorial out of all the publicity. The new law was immediately criticized as contravening Australia's position as a signatory to the UN charter on the rights of the child.

Here Here

Deconstruction is therefore the means by which one operates from the "inside" in order to reach an "outside." Derrida is unable to stand somewhere else and explain how the change is going to come about—for there is nowhere else to stand; we are, of necessity, here.

—Hilary Lawson, *Reflexivity: The Post-Modern Predicamenti*

This piece of writing started with the racial fantasies of a Nordic anthropologist, and it ends with those of Perth media. It illustrates what Mark Gibson has called the "increasing confusion between "here" and "there" in a world where positionality (associating "here," "us" and "now" with a *place*) doesn't confer strength or the power to "lay down the law."[52] Certainly in the case of the Perth campaign against twocking, laying down the law proved to be ineffective and flawed from the start (at the time of writing no-one had been convicted under the new laws), and the attempt to enforce "law and order" proved lethal not only to "they"—offenders but also to random individuals among the approved family model of "we"—citizens too. Conversely, the weakness and dispossession of a few dozen Aboriginal kids and their mates was not seen as weak at all when they turned twocking and joyriding into class war; it was treated as a fundamental threat to society, and it mobilized the full array of Repressive State Apparatuses, cheer-led by the local press, talk-back radio and TV news.

I began to take an interest in "vehicular theory" in Britain, where hotting seemed to be the latest aestheticization of politics for young people in housing estates—it was newsworthy enough, but was it politics? On returning to Perth I found that twocking can be something much more dangerous. It inspired populist revenge in the ugly shape of a mob of shop-keepers trying to convert Aboriginal people from citizens into a fencing problem ("KEEP OUT"). This shows that twocking is more than mere hooliganism; it is a challenge to the petit-bourgeois discourse of "law 'n' order," and thence to the "basic premise of Western thought" which declares that "strength lies always and only in a recognizable position" (Gibson). The fear that things might be otherwise, i.e., that "ours" and "here" are also "theirs" and "there," and that the relationship between the majesty of the law and despised Aboriginal youths is precisely one of circulation, gives rise to a classic over- and undervaluing (i.e., overvaluing the threat of undervalued people). Long ago in 1758, at the point of invention of journalism as the textual system of modernity, Dr. Johnson concluded that the very "duty of the journalist" was to point out such up/down deviations from any social norm; a conceptualization which is still theorized as the general discursive function of the news in society.[53] In this instance "society" turns out to be a petit-bourgeois clean-up which expresses "support" for a bereaved father by totting up the dollar-value and commercial sponsors of his gifts, and which would rather have its children die or spend twenty years in jail than have its "trust in traffic lights" shaken.

The Origin of Society

Accidental juxtapositions are of the essence in vehicular theory; though some are the kind of accidents you try to avoid. In my case, it was a relief that just as the new "car crime" laws were passed, I had booked in my battered old 1968 Chevrolet Impala for a complete body restoration costing a Veblenesque $7000. It came back a month later a shocking shade of pop-culture green, with a Jimmy Pike/Desert Designs Aboriginal pattern called "Billabong Country" for its upholstery (luckily misread by the not-very-tolerant Italian-Australian bodyshop boys as merely "hippy"), and one very pleased possessive-individualist owner. However, partly because it is what it is—a "nice tool"—it has never been locked, and never been twocked. It's just vehicular theory on wheels; circulating in the synchronistic spatial network of latitudinal connections between peoples, alert for intersectional crises and police cars at traffic lights, a Derridean vehicle that has become almost pure signifier; it is so old that the same metal now merely *quotes* the thing that it once *was,* namely the modernist American commitment to freedom and comfort via applied science, consumer mobility and a productive steel industry. It is also, like the indigenous shipping of Thor Heyerdahl, entirely emancipated from its American ancestry, being explicable now only as an Australian car, dedicated to the delights of antipodean *différance,* taking meanings from "there" to "here" without either pole of this deixis being identified as origin or destination. The turns I take in it are not entirely rhetorical, but they are communicative—along with several other "yank-tanks," the restored vehicle was soon featured nationally on the Australian Broadcasting Corporation's nightly TV current affairs show *The 7.30 Report* as an example of the continuing appeal, in the age of postmodern poached-egg cars, of going to the supermarket in something that by comparison feels like driving around in a tennis court.

Interestingly, the Perth media (together with other control agencies like the police, government and various lobby groups) locate the source of the social at the point of intersection between divergent pathways; society is constituted or originated at the moment of control—the traffic light. Without control ("law and order") to enforce stops to travel, society cannot be(come). This theory of the social is a theory of point, moment, origin; but it is refuted in a collision with a countermanding theory of twocking—non-citizens (minors) driving across the path of order in a dispossessed ve-

hicle. The necessity for traffic lights at points of intersection, together with the inevitability of transgression, leaves us not with a theory of society, but, as Derrida has already mentioned, a theory of writing (pure travel) as movement, and society as writing:

> Language, passion, society, are neither of the North nor of the South. They are the movement of supplementarity by which the poles substitute each other *by turn.* . . . Local difference is nothing but the différance between desire and pleasure.[54]

This is the antipodean difference between writing and reading: authorial red lights being run by hopped-up readers in twocked texts. Let's call it joyreading.[55]

Notes

Extracts of an earlier version of this essay have been published as "Twocking and Joyreading," *Textual Practice* 8(3) (1994): 399–413.

1   Thor Heyerdahl, *American Indians in the Pacific* (London: Allen and Unwin, 1958), chap. 1.

2   See my "Been There—Done That: On Academic Tourism," *Communication Research* 14(2) (April 1987): 251–61, which considers genres of academic writing in terms of exploration/travel/tourism, the village raid, and the difference between oedipal and narcissistic/fetishistic modes of transport; and my "Expatriation: Useful Astonishment as Cultural Studies," *Cultural Studies* 6(3) (1992): 449–67, which discusses cultural studies itself as a form of disciplinary "expatriation," and Englishness as a migratory term that must be explained by reference to its destinations not its origins.

3   I thought my interest in Thor Heyerdahl was ideolectic, outmoded, and perverse—a generation out of date at least. But while I was writing this my colleague Steve Mickler handed me a catalog from a local bookshop, which announced the rerelease of three of Heyerdahl's books (*Kon-Tiki, Tigris, Ra*) in a uniform edition. The blurb reckoned that these "very popular titles," covering "thirty years of adventure and discovery," will be "best sellers for a new generation of readers. Certainly they are riveting reading" (*New Editions Bulletin* 13

[April-June 1993]). As for *Aku-Aku*, it was on offer in the same bookshop's $10 bargain bin.

4   The "ur-texts" here would certainly be John Bunyan's *The Pilgrim's Progress*, ed. G. B. Harrison (London: Dent/Dutton, 1678), and his earlier, autobiographical-spiritual journey, *Grace Abounding to the Chief of Sinners*, ed. G. B. Harrison (London: Dent/Dutton, 1666). As for Newfoundland, how about John Donne's "Elegie: To His Mistris Going to Bed"?:

> Licence my roving hands, and let them goe
> Behind, before, above, between, below.
> Oh my America, my new found lande,
> My kingdome, safeliest when with one man man'd,
> My myne of precious stones, my Empiree,
> How blest am I in this discovering thee. (*The Metaphysical Poets*, ed. Helen Gardner [Harmondsworth: Penguin, 1966], 1966)

5   Jacques Derrida, *Of Grammatology*, trans. Gayatri Spivak (Baltimore: Johns Hopkins University Press), 7.

6   See a section on the illustrated book in the seventeenth century, by Claudine Lemaire, in *The Book through Five Thousand Years*, ed. Hendrik D. L. Vervliet (London: Phaidon, 1972), 393–409, where an explicit connection is made between the expansion of knowledge, the expansion of geographical horizons, and the development of literacy and science, up to and during the seventeenth century: "Works on geography, topography, cartography and accounts of voyages grew apace to satisfy a widespread curiosity about newly discovered countries. . . . The accounts of voyages, an ever popular literary genre . . . are very numerous and especially revealing of the attitudes of an age. . . . Voyages of exploration considerably enlarged the known world from the end of the fifteenth century. Gradually, fantastic accounts, their facts often based on Classical authors, became rare, and a more scientific spirit appeared. Writers take an almost sensuous delight in describing sumptuous festivals and ceremonies, and the more sensational tortures inflicted in distant lands" (396–97). The "scientific spirit" and its concomitant "sensuous delight" are illustrated by a Vlad-like scene of impalement, pyramids, a dissected hand and a fetus done as a flower on/in a woman who poses—standing—in a landscape complete with beached ship; the latter from the important Amsterdam firm of Blaeu, who published town plans for Italy and Holland, a book on as-

tronomy, atlases and marine charts (in Dutch, French, German, and Spanish), as well as literary works. Thus was early-modern knowledge imagined literally as a landscape for the roving eye of the traveler.

7   Tennyson is preoccupied with the "untravell'd world" (i.e., death) which gleams through the arch of experience, using it as a point of destination to oppose to the (Derridean) point of origin of society, which, however, is projected into the future via Ulysses' son Telemachus (who is "centred in the sphere / Of common duties"). As for Ulysses himself, despite the fact that Tennyson borrowed him from (Renaissance) Dante, where he burns in the Eighth Ring of Hell for seeking sacrilegious knowledge and immoderate experience, his project is that of modernism:

> . . . I cannot rest from travel . . .
> And this gray spirit yearning in desire
> To follow knowledge like a sinking star,
> Beyond the utmost bound of human thought.
> . . . for my purpose holds
> To sail beyond the sunset, and the baths
> Of all the western stars, until I die. (*Tennyson: Poems and Plays*, ed. T. Herbert Warren [Oxford: Oxford University Press, 1971]: 89–90.)

See also Bruce Chatwin and Paul Theroux, *Patagonia Revisited* (London: Jonathan Cape, 1985), 52–58. It is conventional, and instructive, to compare the death-defying overreaching of the 1842 Ulysses with the death wish of the 1864 *Tithonus*, in which the immortalized Tithonus envies the "happy men that have the power to die, / And grassy barrows of the happier dead" (90–91). Tennysonian modernism seems happy enough with infinity of space (Ulysses), less so with that of time (Tithonus). This is partly a matter of deictics—"here/there" and "this/that" are latitudinal shifters that place and orientate (map) the subject of history, but "above/below" and "ground/sky" produce not distance (knowledge) but death.

8   The results of this research were published as a book; see Hartley, *The Politics of Pictures: The Creation of the Public in the Age of Popular Media* (London: Routledge, 1992), especially chapters 2, 5, and 8.

9   Plug for serialization of *Aku-Aku*, *Daily Sketch* (London) (Apr. 10 1958): 6.

10   See Hartley, *The Politics of Pictures*, especially 29ff.

11   Because we went in July 1991, this meant we missed the

opportunity of traveling via pre-coup Soviet Union on our outward leg, and post-coup Russia on the return leg. In compensation we bought a Gorby doll in London's Camden Market; a £45 Russian doll comprising, in ever-decreasing size, models of Gorbachev, Brezhnev, Khrushchev, Stalin, Lenin, Nicholas II, Catherine the Great, Peter the Great, and Ivan the Terrible. And when we got home to Perth, we took the children to see the Moscow Circus.

12 Thor Heyerdahl, *Aku-Aku: The Secrets of Easter Island* (Harmondsworth: Penguin, 1958), 339.

13 We visited Britain just as the Maastricht Treaty, which transformed the European Community (EC) into the European Union (EU), was signed. Maastricht meant, we were told, full integration within the EU; but by the same token it meant sharpening the distinction between people *inside* the Union and those left *outside* the new "Europe." Events since then, for instance in France and Germany, which include rioting, terrorism against "guest workers" (in Germany), and police harassment of ethnic minorities such as Algerians (in France), have demonstrated that the line between insiders and outsiders is *empirically* (on the street) a matter of skin color, not citizenship.

14 Heyerdahl, *Aku-Aku,* 324. The last chapter is called "My Aku-Aku Says . . . "

15 Heyerdahl, *American Indians;* this book contains an entire section, 217–345, called "Traces of Caucasian-like Elements in Pre-Inca Peru," which concludes:

> When the Norman and Spanish conquerors reached the Canary Islands a few generations before the discovery of America, they found an aboriginal population part of which was of Caucasian race, light-skinned and tall, with blond hair, blue eyes, hooked nose and beard. . . . Any people living on the shores of the Atlantic, with vessels and maritime ambition capable of leaving racial vestiges on the Canary Islands, *may* run the risk of setting similar migrants or castaways ashore in the Gulf of Mexico. One may look east or north—or even for a local evolution— when searching for the origin of the Caucasian-like elements in aboriginal America; it is incautious only to close one's eyes to their existence. (345)

East or north (i.e., toward white Europe) . . . but not *black:* "there is a popular but erroneous belief that black people, if anything, would be all that Central America could receive with the African current in prehistoric

times. Let us not forget there are vestiges of a former people . . . who still have naturally red hair, blue eyes, beard, hooked nose and light skin" (ibid). Even if migration to the Americas came from Africa, for Heyerdahl the whole point was it was still *white.*

16 Heyerdahl, *Aku-Aku,* 331.

17 Ibid.

18 Ibid.

19 Ibid., 333.

20 Ibid., 275–76, 201, 245.

21 This lovely phrase is Tony Bennett's, as recorded by Tom O'Regan, "(Mis)taking Policy: Notes on the Cultural Policy Debates," *Cultural Studies* 6(3) (1992): 419. It refers to textual evidence of "one's own past history," especially where it contradicts one's current enthusiasms.

22 Hilary Lawson, *Reflexivity: The Post-Modern Predicament* (London: Hutchison, 1985), 100.

23 I wonder in retrospect about the tactfulness of being sent (by my mother) a book about an adventurous family traveling the world together while I was away at an orphanage. But my enthusiasm for it obviously started something; I also still possess a follow-up present from my mother's live-in lover, a woman who took pride in being able to procure for me Heyerdahl's magnum opus (1952). This huge tome, a royal octavo hardback costing 75 shillings (1960s prices) and containing 820 pages, had to be ordered from a mysterious acquaintance who knew how to get hold of such outlandish things. Its extravagance was her offering to our household just around the time when I finally left the orphanage to return to a home life and day school in my mid-teens. Having begged for it I forced myself to read the whole thing over the next year or two, but despite wanting Heyerdahl to be right about the globalizing potential of indigenous shipping I *still* didn't notice what he was driving at, racially.

24 One of my colleagues (Toby Miller) was so pleased with my question that he dredged up an anecdote about sporting-telebrity Lisa Curry-Kenny (Olympic swimmer and TV promoter of Uncle Toby's breakfast cereals), who is reputed to have written more books than she's read but who counts *Kon-Tiki* among the few that she remembers. I don't know if this is true, but even if it's an apocryphal story it demonstrates the pervasion of Heyerdahl's popular academic adventurism.

25 William Shakespeare, *The Tempest* (IV.i.62). For a timely and persuasive analysis of this line, showing how

its idyllic pastoralism is simultaneously a record of land enclosure, agrarian capitalization, the invention of wage labor and concomitant unemployment, in all of which Shakespeare the landlord had some personal investment, see the essay by Terence Hawkes, "Playhouse-Workhouse," in *That Shakespeherian Rag* (London: Methuen, 1986), 1–26.

26 Charles Dickens, *Hard Times for These Times* (1854; Harmondsworth: Penguin, 1969), 47.

27 Metaphors of knowledge as travel can also be traces of the histories of colonization. See Ali Behdad, "Traveling to Teach: Postcolonial Critics in the American Academy," in *Race, Identity, and Representation in Education,* ed. C. McCarthy and W. Crichlow (New York: Routledge, 1993). See also James Clifford, "Traveling Cultures," in *Cultural Studies,* ed. Larry Grossberg, Cary Nelson, and Paula Teichler (New York: Routledge, 1992), and Janet Wolff, "On the Road Again: Metaphors of Travel in Cultural Criticism," *Cultural Studies* 7(2) (1993): 224–39.

28 See the chapter of that name in Roland Barthes, *Mythologies* (London: Paladin: 1973), 68–70. Einstein's brain has also starred in an episode of the mid-1990s TV spin-off version of *Weird Science,* where it was conjured into existence to assist in the successful resolution of that most important remaining problem of American screen intellection—how can nerds date teenage ice queens?

29 Communicating requires not only the *writing* of knowledge, but also the *reading* of books, and for some it is the *readership* that distinguishes Western modernism from the rest of the planet. For a straightforward statement of the idea that reading literally maps "progress," note this editorial comment by Herman Liebaers, writing as the chairperson of the UNESCO Support Committee for the International Year of the Book, as director of the Bibliotheque Royale, Brussels, and as president of the International Federation of Library Associations. From this perspective, he writes: "One fifth of the population of the globe produces four fifths of its books. . . . Is then the unassuming book to be the line of demarcation between industrialized countries and developing nations? The divisions of the map suggest it. Progress can be read" (introduction to Vervliet, *The Book through Five Thousand Years,* 14).

30 Jacques Derrida, *The Postcard: From Socrates to Freud and Beyond* (Chicago: University of Chicago Press, 1987).

31 Hotting came to my hometown, Perth, in January 1992, in the middle of the "juvenile car crime" hysteria described below. As usual the *Sunday Times* was first on the scene, even though it couldn't find the right word for it: "Police move on beach 'drags.' Two hundred youths cheered as hooligan drivers did dangerous high-speed stunts in a Scarborough Beach car park early yesterday. Police moved in after oil was poured on the ground. . . . Drivers spun their wheels in burn-outs before racing off—some appearing close to losing control . . . some youths jeered at police officers and accused them of heavy-handed action. But Acting Inspector Eddie Giumelli said, 'It is dangerous. . . . It is not something police can ignore. Otherwise, this week there are 200 here and next week 400'" (*Sunday Times,* January 12, 1992).

32 *The Face* 40 (January 1992): 92. (The phrase "that's enough, *Ed*" is an homage to British satirical magazine *Private Eye.*)

33 *Birds of a Feather* (BBC) was first shown in Australia on ABC-TV in May 1993. It has since gone to seven series.

34 So "generic" is the footage that I saw the tape of the 1991 British ramraiding being used—labeled onscreen as "file vision"—to illustrate a story about the phenomenon in Western Australia (*ABC News,* May 12, 1993). This journalistically unethical invention gave the clear impression that what we saw on screen was "in Perth" as the voice-over said, despite the fact that the shop, the arcade, and the Range Rover all looked oddly familiar. Evidently, in TV semiosis, ten thousand kilometers of distance and two years in time are not enough to separate a good story from available pictures, rendering "there" as "here," and thus "different" as "same."

35 Among the list of "Best We Forget" phenomena of 1991: "1991 in Review," *The Face* 40 (January 1992): 86.

36 *The Blue Guide to England,* first published in 1920, is itself a national institution of Englishness; witness the opening of J. B. Priestley's book *English Journey: being a rambling but truthful account of what one man saw and heard and felt and thought during a journey through England during the autumn of the year 1933* (1934; Harmondsworth: Penguin, 1977):

> I will begin, I said, where a man might well first land, at Southampton. There was a motor coach going to Southampton . . . and I caught it with the minimum of clothes, a portable typewriter, the usual paraphernalia of pipes, notebooks, rubbers, paper fasteners, razor blades, pencils, Muirhead's *Blue Guide to England,* Stamp and Beaver's *Geographic and Economic*

Survey, and, for reading in bed, the tiny thin paper edition of the *Oxford Book of English Prose.* (9)

See also *The Blue Guide to England,* ed. Stuart Rossiter (London: Ernest Benn; Chicago: Rand McNally, 1972).

37 "Lucy," in Walter De La Mare, *The Dutch Cheese and Other Stories* (London: Faber and Faber, 1946), 16–51.

38 Wolff, "On the Road Again," 235.

39 Translated from the Latin with the help of Tina Horton.

40 Edmund Lodge, *Illustrations of British History* (1790), quoted in Mark Girouard, *Hardwick Hall* (London: National Trust, 1989), 4.

41 Girouard, *Hardwick Hall,* 6–7.

42 Ibid., 38–39.

43 Ibid. The internal quotation is from John Aubrey, *Aubrey's Brief Lives,* ed. O. L. Dick (Harmondsworth: Penguin, 1972), 305–20.

44 Ibid., 314–15.

45 David McLellan, *Karl Marx: His Life and Thoughts* (London: Macmillan, 1973). Marx "seems to have been particularly attached" to his elder sister Sophie in his childhood, and later married Sophie's "best friend" (8, 15, 21). I too have three sisters (though I haven't seen my half-sister since childhood) and three daughters, the youngest of whom is called Sophie.

46 Ibid., 449. The internal quotation is a letter from Marx to Jenny Marx.

47 Ibid., 450. The internal quotation is from Marx's youngest daughter Eleanor.

48 Ibid., 426, 447.

49 Ibid., 329. See also 271 for Freddy Demuth.

50 Western Australia Premier Carmen Lawrence reported in November 1991 that Aboriginal children were 33 times more likely to be put in detention than whites (*West Australian,* Nov. 18, 1991). Two days after the new "juvenile crime" laws were passed in February 1992, a small item in the *Sunday Times* revealed the same "latest" figures:

> Aboriginal youths who break the law are 33 times more likely to end up in custody than young non-Aboriginal law breakers. . . . While Aboriginal youths comprise 16 per cent of all offenders who appeared before the Children's Court in 1990/1, they made up 59 per cent of young people whose most recent punishment was detention. . . . The figures also show that Aboriginal offending rates dropped 11 per cent in 1990/1.

All this is printed under a headline which reads: "DCS [Department of Community Services] figures show youth crime is up" (*Sunday Times,* Feb. 9, 1992) despite the report showing that Aboriginal offending rates had *dropped*—the *Sunday Times* can't (be bothered to) distinguish detention rates from crime rates.

51 See Steve Mickler, *Gambling on the First Race: A Comment on Racism and Talk-Back Radio* (Perth: Louis St. John Johnson Memorial Trust/Centre for Research in Culture and Communication, 1992). This report documents the death of Louis Johnson in January 1992 at the height of the media campaign against car crime, and shows how his murder was treated quite differently from Aboriginal car crime (i.e., it wasn't mentioned) by Perth's leading talk-back host and anti-juvenile campaigner on Radio 6PR).

52 Mark Gibson, "A Centre of Flux: Japan in the Austrialian Business Press," *Continuum: The Australian Journal of Media and Culture* 8(2) (1994): 102. Gibson questions "one of the most fundamental premises of Western thought: that strength always and only lies in a recognisable position" (85); for him differences between "here" and "there" cannot be explained by the received geopolitical metaphors of territoriality, strength, groundedness and location, since the strength of "Japanese" (postmodern) economies is not based on them, but on fluidity, flux, indeterminacy, deterritoriality, and even "weakness" (as understood from a territorial perspective). Gibson points out also that such "Japanese" indeterminacy is often feminized in discourse. (It therefore follows that "weaknesses" imputed to "feminine" unpositionality may simply be a case of mistaken lack-of-identity, missing strengths which are not visible from "masculine" metaphors.) This note is a summary of an argument developed more fully in Hartley, "Twocking and Joyreading," *Textual Practice* 8(3) (1994): 399–413.

53 See Hartley, *The Politics of Pictures,* 141ff. and 161–63 for Dr. Johnson on "the duty of a journalist" (1758); see also Richard Ericson, Patricia Baranek, and Janet Chan, *Visualizing Deviance: A Study of News Organization* (Milton Keynes: Open University Press, 1987). They characterize journalists as "playing a key role in constituting visions of order, stability and change, and in influencing the control practices that accord with these visions" (3–4).

54 Derrida, *Of Grammatology,* 268.

55 Talking of joy, I'd like to name names in the OSPitality

(staying alive) department: without Frances O'Brien and Anna Patterson in particular, who lent us their houses, happiness, and hours of company, we wouldn't have made the trip at all; and thanks to Rose Barnecut, Malcolm and Maureen Brady, and Mary Hartley, friends and sisters whose hospitality shone like beacons across the English countryside, lighting our way from South to North. The incomparable Tina Horton (leaves), Karri Hartley (pebbles), Rhiannon Hartley (wet things and novel microorganisms) were the rest of the "we" who made the travel (knowledge) so memorable; and thanks to Sophie Hartley for not being born until it was all over.

HOP ON POP

WHY ARE TEARS EQUATED WITH FEMI-
ninity and weakness? Sentiment condenses the
way gender still operates as the political unconscious within criticism to trigger shame, embarrassment, and disgust. Yet central tenets of intellectual work—objectivity and proof—are two impossible conceits. And psychology often writes off
intense emotion as an abnormality—feminine
hysteria or "treatable" depression. Politics perceives emotion as a sign of a need for control (antiwar activity as "the days of rage"), weakness
(Geraldine Ferraro's tears as "proof" of her inability to be vice president), or obsession ("Muslim
aggression"). But can emotion be rational?

In this section we examine this complex world
of emotion and question the classical embrace of
distance and proof. Feminism with its slogan of
"the political is personal" has called for a reexam-
ination of the realm of the personal and therefore
the emotional in political change. Melodrama
studies has looked at the disgust and shame involved within sentiment. It also asks why the emotion in the great works of political change—*Uncle
Tom's Cabin* and *Battleship Potemkin*—has been
discounted. The historians make the case that
emotion has always been an ingredient in the
power of political persuasion.

Great writing has grown out of great feeling.
Our writers look at emotion within its context to
spin out all its intellectual complexity, political
persuasiveness, and physicality. They offer evidence but it is woven into a web of their different
rhetorical voices full of their own emotion and rationality. Robyn Warhol offers a complexly woven
history of the performances of and publicity surrounding the powerful American jeremiad *Uncle
Tom's Cabin* to reveal how the changing image of
"Uncle Tom" signals the transformations in the
dominant culture's collective memory of slavery.
As the icon of Uncle Tom moved from a written to
a visual construction in its century-and-a-half's
existence, it has lost its social power. It has
gone from an image of the violence done to virile
black masculinity under slavery to a wordless and
powerless figure of a weak black man in the twentieth century. Warhol concludes with a powerful
comparison of the depiction of violence done to
a physically and verbally powerful nineteenth-
century Uncle Tom to a silenced Rodney King depicted in the 1991 videotape of his beating.

Kathleen Green provides an account of the
seductive nature of the stress management industry. It has spawned a highly profitable business of
popular books and activities to alleviate stress.
However, this ability to exercise has become the
provision of the middle classes who have the
leisure time and of women who are the focus of
stress management ideology. Oddly, American
feminism has bought into the language and methods of this questionable self-help industry. Oprah
Winfrey has offered many programs devoted to
women de-stressing under the guise of womanly
solidarity. But more unexpectedly, bell hooks
participates in the stress management industry
through her *Sisters of Yam*—a self-help book for
African American women. Green points out that
hooks fails to consider how poverty does not allow
many women the time and money to carry out her
advice about these emotions.

Eric Freedman isolates the milk carton and the
ubiquitous image of the missing child to create a
horrific meditation on fear and how this child
campaign fabricates fear to garner support for the
surveillance of American behavior. Whether as
mailbox circulars or milk cartons, the photo of the
missing child enters our homes without invitation
to intone a vague sense of institutional failure in
America. These ads threaten the reader/viewer
with the statistical likelihood and frequency of the
kidnapping of children. In the 1980s the media
jumped on the issue with women's magazine stories and reality TV segments on, ads about, and
sightings of disappeared kids. Not surprisingly, this
burgeoning menace led to a new American growth
industry: products to trace one's child through
photographic records. Freedman asks why photography would function to dispel the fear of loss
when parents turn over to others photographs that

they have no control of. The photo or video more often becomes a substitute for action or thought. And in the end fear becomes more virtual than real.

Finally, Charles Weigl evokes the issues in horror film by creating fear. He artfully steps across the traditional division between criticism and fiction by writing a critical study of the horror genre that is more of a Poeian nightmare than a classic argument. He asks "What is horror?" and his answer becomes a short story about the potential horror surrounding his life as a lone writer. Switching back and forth from regular type to italics, he presents a metacommentary on how contemporary critics of horror film might analyze the developments in his story. He concludes that the question should be "What isn't horror?" given the breadth of the meaning of the term. As his story demonstrates so well, fear is omnipresent.

"Ain't I de One Everybody Come to See?!": Popular Memories of Uncle Tom's Cabin

Robyn R. Warhol

Late-twentieth-century readers approaching Harriet Beecher Stowe's *Uncle Tom's Cabin* (1851–52) for the first time are often in for a surprise.[1] "Uncle Tom" survives in American popular memory as an aged, ineffectual, emasculated slave who stoops to conciliate the white master, but the figure of Uncle Tom in Stowe's text—represented as virile, outspoken, principled, and physically powerful—provides a sharp contrast to the legacy his name carries. Over the second half of the nineteenth century, the collective memory transformed "Uncle Tom" from a literary character to an icon, a voiceless visual emblem of the male slave's condition. The consequences of that transformation range from the damage it has caused Harriet Beecher Stowe's literary-political reputation to the blueprint it has provided for the dominant culture's image of African American masculinity. And while "collective memory" must necessarily be various and fragmented in reference to an issue so divided and divisive as race in the United States, the consistency of the popular memory of "Uncle Tom" in the late twentieth century is remarkable. I will argue that this icon grew out of the making of slavery into a spectacle in the Victorian American theater, and that this memory of "Uncle Tom" exemplifies the results of what Michael Rogin calls the "political amnesia" that goes hand in hand with imperialist spectacle.[2] I will follow Rogin's example to think about how spectacle functions as cultural amnesia, or "motivated forgetting" (507), wiping out collective memories of the very phenomena it hides "in

Cover of a 1932 children's book, depicting the twentieth-century idea of Tom as an aged, bent, powerless man. (Private collection.)

plain sight" (503). As America remembers Uncle Tom this way, it forgets not just Stowe's text, but the lived experience of slavery.[3]

Studies of collective or popular memory typically focus on the recollection of historical persons or events, people who "really lived" or things that "really happened." Michael Schudson's 1992 study *Watergate in American Memory,* for example, or Barry Schwartz's 1991 essay "Lincoln's Image in the American Mind" analyze the politics of recalling presidential personae in varying ways, or of interpreting polysemic historical narratives from competing perspectives.[4] Maurice Halbwachs has defined collective memory as "essentially a reconstruction of the past [that] adapts the image of ancient facts to the beliefs and spiritual needs of the present."[5] As Schwartz concludes, collective memory is the joint product of personal and structural influences upon culture. "Images of the past bear the imprint of the present not because of an impersonal affinity between them," he argues, "but because of the actions of people who feel deeply about both, and in some measure successfully impose their convictions upon contemporaries" (317). However, as Schwartz argues, individuals seeking to reshape the collective memory are limited to representing what is plausible, given "the available past" (Schudson's phrase). "Since this available past reflects fundamental qualities of the social structure, believable individual conceptions of the past are not boundless. Two social forces dialectically shape collective memory: different people bearing different images of the past and social structures imposing limitations on those images" (317).

An additional force is operating, however, when the "past" being recalled is itself a discursive construction, or—in the case of "Uncle Tom"—a fictional character. Whereas events and persons operating in the world must always be represented, through narratives or icons, at one remove from "reality," a fictional character has no existence outside of representation. While it is impossible to measure the distance between the "real" Abraham Lincoln and the representation of his character in commemorative statuary, for instance, the origins of "Uncle Tom" are traceable to Stowe's text. Of course, that source, too, is polysemic, and the many versions of "Uncle Tom" that have survived through the past century can be seen as competing readings of *Uncle Tom's Cabin.* But the visual image of Uncle Tom that exists in the popular memory is remarkable, both for its consistency across "high" and "low" American culture, and for its difference from the way the figure is described in the novel.

Equally remarkable is the cultural authority the icon "Uncle Tom" appears to hold. In a study of the collective memory of undergraduate history students in the 1970s and 1980s, Michael Frisch asked his classes to make lists of names they recalled "in response to the prompt, 'American History from its beginning through the end of the Civil War.'"[6] The first ten names students produced were typically those of "presidents, generals, statesmen, etc.," so Frisch asked them to make a second list, excluding people from those categories. Frisch has found (in refutation of those who worry that contemporary college curricula are undermining "cultural literacy") a notable consistency among the names students have recalled since 1975. According to Frisch, "the free association producing the lists is tapping a very particular kind of cultural memory" (1141), the content of which is "the stuff of popular culture rather than school curricula" (1138). Ranked in order of frequency, the names his students produced in 1988 of persons other than politicians and statesmen include authors, explorers, inventors, suffragists, and other figures, including only one fictional character: "Uncle Tom" (1140).

Frisch calls his study "A Modest Exercise in Empirical Iconography," suggesting that the historical figures who live in students' memories take visual form. "Uncle Tom" is not the only icon of a slave that the students recalled; Harriet Tubman occurred with more consistency and frequency on their lists (she ranked sixth, while "Uncle Tom" was fortieth). Tubman, remembered by Frisch's students as the courageous slave who escaped and then returned to help others to freedom, fits well into the "ongoing fixation on creation myths of origin and innovation" that Frisch identifies as a motivating force structuring the collective memory in mainstream America (1143). The icon of Harriet Tubman stands for the origin of the empowerment and emancipation of African Americans. What, then, does the icon of "Uncle Tom" stand for? And what does the pseudo-historical status of the figure mean for the dominant culture's collective memory of slavery?

Toward answering these questions, I will describe the evolution of the visual image of "Uncle Tom" and of Uncle Tom's Cabin since 1852, focusing on tableaux, playbills, and posters for productions of plays bearing that title through the nineteenth century. First, I will demonstrate iconographic variations in popular and literary-critical accounts of Uncle Tom's Cabin in the 1980s, and I will conclude with a consideration of what happens when the icon of "Uncle Tom" gains a speaking voice in a contemporary "New Jack" revision of the play. The icon of "Uncle Tom," implicated as it has been in the spectacularization and amelioration of the history of slavery, stands in a space in the collective memory that I propose to "empty out" (to use Stephen Greenblatt's phrase), in order to sketch a cultural backdrop against which the collective obsession with such spectacles as the notorious videotape of Rodney King's beating can be reframed. The figure of "Uncle Tom" mediates contemporary notions of African American men's historical experience. After tracing the evolution of the "Uncle Tom" icon through the nineteenth century, I propose to refill that space in the cultural memory with contemporary re-writings of "Uncle Tom" that may enable dominant culture to perform more complex and multiple "rereadings" of black masculinity.

Uncle Tom and the "Image Problem"

For an illustration of the mainstream popular memory of Uncle Tom's Cabin, consider the account in American Theatre magazine of "Cabin Fever," as they call the phenomenon of African American adaptors presenting radically revised productions of Uncle Tom's Cabin in the 1990s. Describing Bill T. Jones's The Last Supper at Uncle Tom's Cabin and the San Francisco Mime Troupe's I Ain't Yo' Uncle, the magazine's account of these productions' relations to Stowe's novel and its nineteenth-century dramatizations illustrates the common conflation of the nineteenth-century stage versions of the character of "Uncle Tom" with his counterpart in Stowe's text.[7] Showing no sign of familiarity with the novel, the reporter takes it on faith that "Stowe's already broad characterizations of African-Americans" only "grew more exaggerated in the theatre" (21), and that *Uncle Tom's Cabin* is "a novel of the evil South" whose "gripping plot, many picaresque (if one-dimensional) characters, cornball humor and moral urgency contributed to its popularity" (21). Anyone who has recently read the novel (or the growing body of scholarly commentary upon it) will have difficulty recognizing Stowe's text in this comic-book caricature of it. But the *American Theatre* reporter does not seem to know the novel, nor really even make reference to it. The substance of the article consists of secondhand reports and comments on *Uncle Tom's Cabin,* most of them referring, explicitly or indirectly, to the many dramatized versions of Stowe's material rather than the original text. As a result, the article (unwittingly) offers a glimpse at the popular memory of that icon, "Uncle Tom."

Referring to that popular memory, Stanley E. Williams of the Lorraine Hansberry Theatre—the group that collaborated with the San Francisco Mime Troupe to produce Robert Alexander's *I Ain't Yo' Uncle*—told the magazine that the NAACP and many of his troupe's subscribers "didn't like the idea" of reviving *Uncle Tom's Cabin,* even in a revisionist version. "I think people react to the title—Uncle Tom is a figure no black wants to identify with because he couldn't be a man—he couldn't have principles, or hold his head up high, or even look whites in the eye" (21). Anyone who were to read Stowe's novel outside the context of twentieth-century collective memories of "Uncle Tom" might be startled to see Stowe's hero described in such terms: the first Uncle Tom may not have much, but he has certainly got principles.[8] When, for instance, Chloe and Eliza suggest Tom should escape before Mr. Shelby can sell him to Haley, Tom's principles forbid it: "Mas'r always found me on the spot—he always will. I never

have broke trust, nor used my pass no ways contrary to my word, and I never will. It's better for me alone to go, than to break up the place and sell all" (90). And as for holding up his head, or looking whites in the eye, Stowe's Tom is represented as interacting with each of his white "masters" with dignity and self-possession; even after Legree has kicked and beaten him, Tom "gained his feet, and was confronting his master with a steady, unmoved front" (539). But it would be pointlessly pedantic to argue that Williams is "wrong" when he says, "Uncle Tom . . . couldn't be a man." The entity signified by his "Uncle Tom" exists more vitally in the popular memory than does the figure Stowe created.

Indeed, the "New Jack Revisionist" play, as written by Robert Alexander, begins with a consideration of the "image problem" Uncle Tom suffers from. The character of Uncle Tom "enters through the audience, like a shuffling janitor; with a handkerchief in his hand, he wipes the arms of the theatre chairs," saying, "Excuse me y'all . . . pardon me, ma'am . . . excuse me, suh . . ." When the other African American characters—who are conducting a tribunal against Harriet Beecher Stowe for having misrepresented them in her novel—tell him to leave, Tom turns to the audience to say, "Ain't I de one everybody come to see?! Don't y'all want to see me stoop, shuffle and bend over backwards with a smile for every white person I meet?!" (ms. p. 2). Tom's emphasis in this speech on himself as spectacle, as the object set up to be seen, points to the iconographic status of the part he plays in American culture. In this play, however, Tom refuses to continue in that role. Taunted by the other characters, Tom adjusts his posture and joins them in turning against "Harriet": standing up tall, he turns to the white woman in the Victorian dress and says, "Let's get a few things straight, Ms. Stowe. First of all, I ain't yo' Uncle!" Tom's personal rebellion gets played out in his physical appearance, as he is transformed from the "shuffling janitor" to an energetic man in his prime. He elaborates on the accusation: "Yeah, your book turned some folks against slavery, but it created a big image problem for me" (ms. 2). This prelude to Alexander's revisionist version of the play addresses the concern Williams had raised about what the audience would expect from a character named "Uncle Tom." The figure that "everybody come to see" is bent, aged, ineffectual, conciliatory, ridiculous; in short, he is conceived in perfect opposition to the 1990s model of African American masculinity that the new Tom (intelligent, virile, politically self-conscious, and powerful) turns out to embody in Alexander's play.

The fact that the "New Jack Revisionist" play calls into question the relative age and (implicit) virility of Uncle Tom points to a central disagreement among twentieth-century commentators over who and what "Uncle Tom," the character, is. Some critics present portraits of Tom that are different from the descriptions other critics employ, as well as different from the description of Tom in Stowe's text. Depending on the source of the description, we can picture Uncle Tom as a physically powerful man or an aged, weak one; as self-respecting and dignified or as shuffling and scraping; as sexless or manly or feminine. Stowe describes Tom as

> a large, broad-chested, powerfully-made man, of a full glossy black, [with] a face whose truly African features were characterized by an expression of grave and steady good sense, united with much kindliness and benevolence. There was something about his whole air self-respecting and dignified, yet united with a confiding and humble simplicity. (68)

There is certainly much to object to in this description, from a late-twentieth-century, anti-racist perspective: some of the language Stowe's narrator uses to evoke the visual image of Tom would be equally appropriate in describing a draught animal ("large," "broad-chested," "powerfully made," "full, glossy black"). My point is

not that Stowe's Uncle Tom is not a racist portrait, for he certainly is, in the sense that his personality is presented—according to the principles of physiognomy—as being legible in his physical features, which are stereotyped as "truly African." However, the appearance of Stowe's Uncle Tom hardly resembles the old, shuffling man who appears in the opening scene of *I Ain't Yo' Uncle*. At the end of Stowe's novel, Tom is still relatively young and physically strong: some time passes between Legree's final assault on Tom and Tom's death, "for the laws of a powerful and well-knit frame would not at once release the imprisoned spirit" (588).

Although Stowe's descriptions of the character's appearance are consistent throughout her own text, literary and cultural critics writing about *Uncle Tom's Cabin* disagree in their assumptions about what "Uncle Tom" is like. James Baldwin's version selects and interprets certain details of Stowe's description: "The figure from whom the novel takes its name, Uncle Tom, who is a figure of controversy yet, is jet-black, woolyhaired, illiterate; and he is phenomenally forbearing. . . . Tom, [Stowe's] only black man, has been robbed of his humanity and divested of his sex."[9] Ann Douglas works a further variation on the characteristic Baldwin highlights, Tom's forbearance, placing quotation marks around an adjective Stowe's narrator never attributes to Tom: "Uncle Tom's docility is docility only in the sense that Stowe considers it 'feminine,' but it is 'feminine' only in that it represents adherence to spiritual values—and this adherence, for Stowe, is strength" (25). ("Feminine" is Douglas's importation into the text: when Stowe's Tom must leave his wife and children, the narrator does not call his tears "feminine," but underlines his "brave, manly heart" [163] and "manly disinterestedness" [169].) Alex Haley's vision of Tom is even further removed from the novel's description: "Mrs. Stowe's hero is a white-haired, pious, loyal slave-foreman"[10] The icon Haley invokes resembles what *American The-atre* says "Uncle Tom" means: "the stock figure of the aged, Bible-spouting slave who shuffles and scrapes before white bosses." The magazine goes on to say that "the new, authoritative Tom [in *I Ain't Yo' Uncle*] is a robust, vigorous man in his forties, and a shrewd observer of those around him" (22). The image of the "new, authoritative Tom" is, of course, much closer to "Stowe's hero" than is the popular conception of what that hero was like. That popular conception evolved through theatrical adaptations of Stowe's story, produced around the United States throughout the second half of the nineteenth century. Those plays—rather than the novel—are the source of the early cinematic versions of *Uncle Tom's Cabin,* and of the assumptions about the icon, "Uncle Tom," that led to the phrase's use as one of the ultimate put-downs one African American can level at another.

The general impact the plays had upon the popular memory of *Uncle Tom's Cabin* was to emasculate the figure of Tom and to eviscerate the anti-slavery sentiment of Stowe's novel. Gradually, over the second half of the nineteenth century, the publicity for the plays came to present *Uncle Tom's Cabin* as a story of the pitiful martyrdom of a helpless victim (the aged, shuffling Tom), downplaying or even eliminating the novel's parallel plot, in which George and Eliza Harris escape to Canada, and eventually emigrate to Liberia. During and after the Civil War, plays based on *Uncle Tom's Cabin* offered up slavery as an entertaining spectacle for the public delectation, suggesting a nostalgic attitude toward antebellum plantation life. To the extent that Robert Alexander and the San Francisco Mime Troupe follow James Baldwin's lead in holding Harriet Beecher Stowe personally responsible for the cultural fact of that nostalgia, Stowe—as an author—is getting a bum rap. As feminist commentary on Stowe's novel has recently emphasized, there is a great deal at stake both for gender politics and for race politics, in reconsidering the role Stowe's authorial act played in creating Uncle Tom's "image problem."[11]

The Iconic Text: Playbills

If, as Thomas Gossett has asserted, it is true that fifty people would eventually see "the play" (whichever of the many and varied productions that might signify) of *Uncle Tom's Cabin* for every one who read the novel, then the preponderance of theatrical versions of the story can certainly help account for the variety of impressions Uncle Tom has left upon the popular memory.[12] As no copyright law existed to give Harriet Beecher Stowe the right to control the material of her novel in 1852, adaptors and producers had unlimited access to her characters' names, her title, and her plot, and they had unlimited license to alter those in accordance with their own ideas about what would appeal to American theatrical audiences (not to mention their own ideas about slavery). The result was a plethora of plays called *Uncle Tom's Cabin,* some of them claiming Stowe's approval, some disavowing her; some of them following parts of her novel's plot and characterizations, some varying wildly from the original.

From a literary-critical perspective, one could compare the plots of Stowe's novel and of the various adaptations to look for ways that the content of the plays departed from the stance the novel takes on Uncle Tom and on the institution of slavery in general. But my focus on the popular memory makes me less interested here in what actually took place on the stage of nineteenth-century productions called *Uncle Tom's Cabin* than in the way they were represented to the public through playbills, posters, and newspaper reviews. If more people saw the play in the nineteenth century than read the novel, then surely even more people saw the advertisements and notices than saw the actual productions. Reflecting the emphasis of the play versions they are touting, the playbills highlight certain moments in the story of *Uncle Tom's Cabin* (when, indeed, the productions follow the novel at all) which were played up on stage, though many of the moments hold no marked emphasis in Stowe's text. The scenes which came to form the traditional "tableaux," or frozen visual images ending each scene in the play, loom large in the iconography of *Uncle Tom's Cabin*, and even tend to dominate recent criticism of the novel. Advertising posters, too, served to crystallize tableaux that stood in synecdochal relation to the entire productions they were designed to promote, which, in turn, have come in the collective memory to stand in for the novel. A close look at a chronologically arranged selection of playbills and posters shows that the visual images they foster are largely responsible for the twentieth-century memory of *Uncle Tom's Cabin* as an entertaining, death-obsessed, spectacular trivialization of slavery, and for the reputation of "Uncle Tom" as an aged, shuffling slave who "couldn't be a man."[13]

Playbills for nineteenth-century productions of *Uncle Tom's Cabin* follow a standard set of conventions for this form of print advertisement. The playbill always carries the play's title in enormous, bold type, sometimes including certain words or phrases ("Bress de ladies!" or "I Golly!," for example) or the names of prominent cast members in type nearly matching that of the title. A cast list usually appears in small type, with stars' names in boldface; the list is generally followed by a synopsis of scenes, sometimes denoted by their setting ("Interior of Uncle Tom's Cabin," "Exterior of the Ferry House on the River Ohio"), sometimes by famous lines spoken in the scenes ("Friend, thee is not wanted here," "I specks I'se jes' wicked"), and sometimes by summaries of their action. Playbills for the version written by George Aiken and produced by George C. Howard—the first, most faithful, and phenomenally successful staging of Stowe's material, which premiered in 1852—usually list the tableaux that ended each scene, in large enough type to render these visual images promi-

nent on the bill. After the list of tableaux comes either the advertisement for another play being produced at the same showing (which did not often happen with *Uncle Tom's Cabin,* save for a few notable exceptions I will mention later), or an explanation for *Uncle Tom's Cabin*'s being the only play on the program. Playbills for the National Theatre production in Philadelphia began in 1853 by explaining "In Consequence of the great length of the drama, there will be NO OTHER PERFORMANCE connected with it," but by 1856 the same theater's bills were saying, "In order not to erase the deep impression this Sublime Entertainment leaves upon the memory, NO OTHER PERFORMANCE will be connected with it." An 1857 bill for that theater elaborates, explaining that *Uncle Tom's Cabin* is on the bill alone so "that the audience may keep in their 'Memory Lock'd' the Pleasing Recollections of this Great Modern Drama."

As the evolution of that explanation implies, the playbills provide an interpretive frame for the productions, attempting to fix an idea of the play's meaning in the public memory. The same 1856 playbill from Philadelphia provides an unusually discursive example of this directive mode of description. Citing "S. E. Harris as 'The Poor Slave,' in his original Dramatization of Uncle Tom's Cabin," the bill goes on to call the play an

AFFECTING MORAL DRAMA
which, for brilliancy and success, stands unequalled
in the City.
Overflowing Audiences, in Smiles and Tears,
nightly hail the beautiful scenes in Mrs. Harriet
Beecher Stowe's
"Life Among the Lowly!"
with unbounded LAUGHTER and APPLAUSE.
The Trials of Poor Uncle Tom—the Simplicity of
the Gentle Eva—the Quaint Humor of Topsy—the
Heroism of Eliza and George—the Cruelty of
Legree—the Delightful Songs and Choruses—the
Plantation Sports.

The interpretations this offers for the characters' experience are relatively consistent with the novel's narrator's attitudes toward them (Eliza's and George's "heroism," Eva's "simplicity"), although the reduction of Uncle Tom's position to that of "the Poor Slave," "Poor Uncle Tom" certainly diminishes the connotative stature the novel grants him. Still, a reader of Stowe's novel might be unsurprised by the images presented here, until encountering the "delightful songs and choruses" and "the plantation sports." These promise an injection of the kind of light-hearted entertainment that playbills for *Uncle Tom's Cabin* performances came increasingly to associate with the slave experience, a mode that is completely antithetical to the "grimness" (as Hortense Spillers calls it) of Stowe's presentation of slavery.[14]

In addition to the playbills' directives on how to interpret the story of *Uncle Tom's Cabin,* each playbill's list of tableaux provides a summary of the notable and memorable scenes. These lists, too, function as interpretations of the material by foregrounding selected iconic images. The Philadelphia playbill quoted above lists nine tableaux that were common to the Harris and Howard productions during the 1850s, and that simultaneously constituted and reinforced the popular notion of what *Uncle Tom's Cabin* is about:

1st—Escape of Eliza

2nd—The Trappers Entrapped

3rd—The Freeman's Defence

4th—Death of Little Eva

5th—The Death of St. Clair [*sic*]

6th—Topsy Butting the Yankee [a comic interpolation]

7th—Cassy Helping Uncle Tom

8th—Death of Uncle Tom

9th—Grand Allegorical Representation

[listed on some bills as "Little Eva in Heaven"]

The Aiken-Howard version adds a tableau at the beginning, giving slightly more emphasis to the George-and-Eliza-Harris plot—which ends in their triumphant escape—and less to Uncle Tom's story, which ends with his death at Simon Legree's hands. Nevertheless, as the list suggests, scenes

of death and scenes from the second half of the novel dominate the playbills' version of the story. In the Aiken version, "The Freeman's Defence" (the scene where George Harris and Phineas foil the slave catchers) is a death scene, as Loker is killed in the action. (In Stowe's version, Loker recovers from his wounds.) Four of the ten tableaux in the Aiken and Harris versions represent deaths, whereas death is the central subject of only three of the novel's forty-five chapters. Appropriate to the stage genre of melodrama, this adjustment in the story's emphasis is in large part responsible for the melodramatic associations the title *Uncle Tom's Cabin* carries today.

To perceive shifts in emphasis from the novel's comparatively balanced treatment of the escape motif (in the George and Eliza plot) and the forbearance-unto-death motif (in the Uncle Tom plot), we can look to the amount of space devoted to each motif on the lists of tableaux. Eventually, the martyrdom plot overcame the escape plot in the discourse of the playbills. The proportion of George/Eliza scenes (associated with the escape theme) to Eva/Tom scenes (associated with the death theme) is almost consistent with that which prevails in the novel: twelve of forty-four narrative chapters are devoted to the Harrises, as are three of the nine tableaux. But by making Tom's death and Eva's ascension into heaven the ultimate images, leaving out the Harris's eventual reunion with Cassy and migration to Liberia, the play-bill places heavy emphasis on the martyrdom plot to the detriment of the escape plot; and by presenting "the freeman's defense" as eventuating in a white man's death, the playbill makes George Harris's path a considerably more threatening one from the point of view of the white mainstream audience.

These nine or ten tableaux remained constant on playbills through the 1850s and 1860s, although later productions added scenes highlighting specific performers.[15] When the number of tableaux rose over twenty, as it did in one 1867 production, the added scenes focused on the increasingly popular figures of Topsy and Eva-in-heaven. Scenes from the escape plot featuring the Harrises remained stable at three; hence, scenes from the martyrdom plot, totaling eighteen, strongly dominated the images evoked by the playbills. Significantly, two of the tableaux on this 1867 playbill depict a subject peculiarly absent from the original list of nine: "Sale of the Slaves" and "Life on the Plantation." Before the Civil War, playbills for American productions of *Uncle Tom's Cabin* made next to no reference to slavery, unless—like P. T. Barnum's production of the Conroy version— they purported to show "slavery as it is" and, in so doing (according to a contemporary review of Barnum's show in the Liberator), offered "a version of the great story . . . which omits all the strikes at the slave system and . . . so shaped [the] drama as to make it quite an agreeable thing to be a slave."[16] In this respect the plays followed the tradition of minstrel shows, which—as Eric Lott puts it—"pretend[ed] that slavery was amusing, right, and natural."[17]

The suppression of the topic of slavery from pre-1865 American playbills other than Barnum's becomes evident when they are contrasted with a British example. In 1853 the Theatre Royal Birmingham advertised a version of *Uncle Tom's Cabin* whose plot (judging by the synopsis of scenes) diverged quite a bit from Stowe's novel. The impression created by the bold-face type on the Birmingham playbill would be dramatically different from the standard American advertisements of the same period. Alongside images that would be familiar to American audiences (for instance, "The Ice Blocks—perilous situation and miraculous escape of Eliza," and "Death of Poor Uncle Tom"), references to slavery are predominant: the first headline reads, "The Buyer and Seller of Human Flesh!" Eliza and Harry are called "The Slave Mother and her Infant," a locution that never appears on an American playbill before the Civil War. The third act descriptors include "The Slave Market, New Orleans," "Horrors of an American Slave Sale," and "The Plantation," in ad-

dition to "Death of Poor Uncle Tom" and "Impressive Denouement." This playbill treats George and Eliza more frankly than do the American bills as a married couple, implying that their relationship is taken more seriously in this production than in the American versions. They figure here in "Stolen Interview between George Harris and his beloved Wife" and in "Fearful Situation of George and his Wife." Furthermore, the absence of emphasis on Eva's friendship with Tom reduces the potential for images that glamorize or ameliorate slavery as an institution.[18]

One American show calling itself *Uncle Tom's Cabin* in 1861 emphasizes the subject of slavery in the icons its advertisement invokes, but it takes some stunning departures from Stowe's original material. A playbill for Sanford's Opera House in Philadelphia lists a long program of songs, flute solos, and a play called *Bridget's Trouble!,* then adds in small type, "To conclude with Sanford's Southern Version of," and then, in extremely bold type, "UNCLE TOM'S CABIN!" The cast list contains such familiar names as Uncle Tom, Master George Shelby, George, Topsy, Chloe, and "Lize," among others. But the synopsis of scenes bears no resemblance to those on other *Uncle Tom's Cabin* playbills. For example, the first scene is described thus:

> UNCLE TOM'S CABIN. Aunt Chloe very industrious. A tale about the Abolitionists. Aunt Chloe don't like Cincinnati! "I'd radder be on de Old Plantation." SONG—"Dere's no use talking when a Nigger wants to go." Topsy. Uncle Tom's Return from Camp Meeting and happy time and plenty money. SONG AND DANCE—"Dere's a Nigger in de Tent" . . . Banjo Solo, Topsy.

The last scene ends with George and Lize's getting married ("Dey both Jump de Broom. Such a Happy Time. Congo Dances, Reels, Camp Meeting Chants, Corn-Shucking Reel"). In other words, while the names of the characters are consistent with the novel and other, ostensibly abolitionist versions of the play, the visual images of slavery invoked by this advertisement could hardly be more different from those depicted in Stowe's text. To be sure, the playbill includes, in extremely tiny type, the lyrics to a song admitting the lack of relationship between the novel and this show:

> Oh! White Folks, we'll have you to know,
> Dis am not de version of Mrs. Stowe;
> Wid her de Darks am all unlucky.
> But we am de boys of Old Kentucky.
> Den hand de Banjo down to play,
> We'll make it ring both night and day;
> And we care not what de white folks say,
> Dey can't get us to run away.

The playbill, however, is arranged to make it possible for a person who did not read the small print to believe that *this* is what *Uncle Tom's Cabin* is about. Even a spectator who, having read the novel or seen an anti-slavery version of the play, might "know better" is here being offered a drastically revisionary reading of Stowe's novel. In no way could George and Eliza's escape, or even Tom's death (in the Christian teleology within which Stowe presents it) be constructed as "unlucky": George and Eliza realize their rewards in this life, and Tom is, by Stowe's reasoning, assured of meeting his in the next. The novel figures all three as "fortunate" in the highest Christian sense. But the impact of seeing this play—or indeed, seeing only the advertisement for it—might be the same as that of looking at a *Mad* magazine parody of a familiar film: the original never looks quite the same thereafter.[19]

Slavery eventually made its way into the visual images invoked on playbills for "serious" productions of *Uncle Tom's Cabin* during and after the Civil War, but the further into the period of Reconstruction the playbills go, the more spectacularly entertaining the topic of slavery is presented as being. While the melodramatic forms popular on the stage of the period might suggest the spectacle

would have been based on the more sensational aspects of slavery (the rape, torture, and humiliation that dominate Stowe's novel's representation of the institution, for instance), *Uncle Tom's Cabin* plays came to be more like minstrel shows than melodramas. Slavery was presented as something surpassingly pleasant. One example is a playbill from a production starring "Lotta" (Charlotte Crabtree) as Topsy that traveled to Montreal in 1865 and appeared three years later at Pike's Opera House in Cincinnati.[20] The larger type on its 1865 playbill emphasizes "SONGS, DANCES, and SOLOS on the BANJO" as the show's main attraction, and banjo performances receive equal billing, as it were, with the traditional tableaux associated with the story:

ESCAPE OF ELIZA AND CHILD

UPON THE ICE!

THRILLING TABLEAU

BANJO SOLO AND SONG

ECCENTRICITIES OF TOPSY

THE POINT OF ROCKS

ESCAPE OF GEORGE HARRIS, ELIZA, AND HARRY

DEATH OF EVA

DEATH OF ST. CLAIR [*sic*]

The Slave Mart. Sale of Uncle Tom

THRILLING TABLEAU

REMORSE, Cassy and Legree

DEATH OF LEGREE!

DEATH OF UNCLE TOM!!

APOTHEOSIS OF EVA!!!

Death and apotheosis still dominate the picture (as the exclamation points insist), but the "slave mart" and "sale of Uncle Tom" enter the North American representation of the play hand-in-hand with the banjo.

By 1876, the playbill for *Uncle Tom's Cabin* as produced at the Museum Theater ("formerly Col. Wood's, Corner of Ninth and Arch Streets") unabashedly emphasizes the slavery themes and mixes them with cheerful predictions of their entertainment value. The bill promises "a grand realistic PLANTATION SCENE introducing 100 Genuine SOUTHERN COLORED FOLKS, Men, Women and Children, in a Holiday on the Old Time Cotton Plantation—a Scene never before witnessed in any Theatre. In order to give effect to this Great Moral Drama, a Special Engagement has been effected with the OLD ORIGINAL SOUTHERN JUBILEE SINGERS." The typeface for that last phrase is huge, drawing attention to the explanation that follows it: "All the members of this Troupe were slaves prior to the War, and they sing the Melodies of the South as they were sung upon the Southern Plantation." The value of the former slaves' experience gets presented as inhering in its entertainment potential. Like Uncle Tom in *I Ain't Yo' Uncle,* they were the ones "everybody [should] come to see."

Even the 1870s productions of *Uncle Tom's Cabin* involving the Howards—who might have been supposed to hold some allegiance to the "original" Aiken version they made famous—took this spectacular turn. (According to Harry Birdoff, the first chronicler of what he calls "the world's greatest hit," "It now became almost fatal to stage the play without colored singers" [235]). Mrs. Howard as Topsy shared the stage at Ford's opera House in 1878 with "Little Sawney (aged six years). The best Colored Boy Dancer in the World," "Warren Griffin! The Greatest Living Banjo Player, who was formerly a slave at Milledgeville, Georgia, before the war," and "100 Genuine Southern Colored People (who were slaves before the war)." The bill promises instruments to be played by "Genuine Plantation Darkies," as well as a "plantation scene" and "camp meeting" "redolent of ante-bellum slave life, the characters being represented by veritable colored persons, without the aid of burned cork." The tableaux listed for this production include Eliza's escape, the deaths of Eva and Tom, and the "Allegory of Eva in heaven"—not surprisingly the visual images that seem to have survived most strongly in the popular memory of what *Uncle Tom's Cabin* is about.[21] The other five original tableaux are replaced by the "slave market in New Orleans," the "Great Plantation Scene," and "Warren Griffin." Even if the 1870s plays themselves were only partly as jolly as the advertisements, the tone of the public representation of what *Uncle Tom's Cabin* meant had changed dramatically over a quarter of a century. Notably, the "authenticity" these plays claim makes no reference to Stowe's text, but rather to the historical experience of the persons appearing on the stage. That these blacks— among the first to appear on American stages— were "real" African Americans, now "really" free but formerly "real" slaves is what, the playbill implies, makes them worth looking at. Of course, the minstrel-show emphasis of these advertisements reproduced Sam Sanford's anti-abolitionist claim that slavery "as it actual existed" was actually a singing and dancing jamboree.

Nevertheless, the Howards's later stagings— resembling the shows of their early competitor for *Uncle Tom's Cabin* audiences, P. T. Barnum— were mild compared to the "double mammoth" versions of *Uncle Tom's Cabin* that took to the road in the latter part of the century, sprinkling playbills in their wake that unabashedly make the play out to be a circus. A memorable example is the double-sided leaflet, suitable for distribution rather than posting, for "Abbey's Double Mammoth Uncle Tom's Cabin Co., Brass Band, and Royal Bell Ringers." One side is dominated by a large sketch of the head and shoulders of Harriet Beecher Stowe, accompanied by her signature and the phrase, "presented with the special approval of . . . " The veracity of that claim is questionable, given the details that follow.

After declaring "THE CLERGY UNANIMOUS IN ITS PRAISE," the large type cites "2—FAMOUS FUNNY TOPSYS—2, with songs and dances," "2— COMICAL ECCENTRIC LAWYERS—2, Marks Sr.

and Marks Jr.," and "The Celebrated South Carolina Jubilee Singers." Apparently such companies promoted the idea that audiences would be doubly amused if the production doubled the comic figures on stage: Topsy thus becomes a pair of slaves, Marks a pair of slave catchers (the tradition held that Marks, singly or doubly, had a lot of trouble with a recalcitrant donkey ridden out onto the stage). Reviews of the Aiken-Howard version had praised Caroline Howard's portrayal of Topsy for its complexity, for the "something almost tragic," as one reviewer put it, in Mrs. Howard's depiction of Topsy's "fiendish glee."[22] But any connotations of poignancy the figure of Topsy acquired from earlier reviews focusing upon the character's individual plight, her social and spiritual isolation, and eventual conversion are entirely blotted out in this process of reproducing her as if a slave were to be perceived, in playbills as in political history, as a commodity instead of a person.[23] The icon of singing, dancing, funny Topsy had—by century's end—entirely displaced any notion of Topsy as a fictional person with more than one dimension. Like Topsy, the icon "jes' growed," with no awareness of or reference to its origins.

The playbill for the "double mammoth" production is far more visual in its conception than its predecessors. Rather than relying on verbal descriptions of tableaux, this bill enumerates the wonders to be seen on stage (including "Manuel Trujillo's Negro-hunting Siberian and Cuban bloodhounds," "Eva's Intelligent Pony," "the sagacious Trick Donkey, Oscar," "Edison's Electric

Back of playbill for "Abbey's Double-Mammoth Uncle Tom's Cabin Co., Brass Band, and Royal Bell Ringers." The shadow of a bust of Harriet Beecher Stowe shows through the thin paper from the reverse side, implying the author's (fictitious) endorsement of the images in the show. Harry Ransome Humanities Research Center, the University of Texas at Austin.

Parlor Light," "Exciting Steamboat Race and Collision," "Grand realistic Cotton Field Scene," and the more familiar but considerably melodramatic "Thrilling Floating Ice Scene, introducing the Same Bloodhounds in the realistic, blood-curdling chase." The largest type is still reserved for "GORGEOUS TABLEAU AND TRANSFORMATION: Eva in the Heavenly Realms!" But the audience is advised immediately after that "DO NOT FAIL TO SEE THE STREET PARADE given daily by Jubilee Singers, Eva and her Pony, Marks and his Donkey, and the Savage Bloodhounds." The reverse side includes, in tiny type, a list of "scenery and incidents," but they are overpowered by four sketches at the top of the page, showing a black man holding bloodhounds on leashes, the two Markses and their uncooperative donkey, the two Topsys joking together, and Eva cantering on her clever pony. This is political amnesia in action: when the popular memory is dominated by images of the circus, the spectacle is everything: slavery disappears in the process of its representation.

The Synecdochal Image: Posters

Uncle Tom himself is nowhere to be seen among the sketches on the "double mammoth" playbill. By this time his name had become a synecdoche for the spectacles associating slavery with street parades, performing animals, jubilee singers, and fun. His iconographic image existed, of course, on the stages where these exaggerated versions of his story were being played out. It received even more circulation, however, in posters serving as advertisements for the plays. If the posters are read as visual interpretations of the material of *Uncle Tom's Cabin,* they bring forward a valence of class ideology that is not present in the playbills, and that has contributed to the character, Uncle Tom's "image problem." Visual images of scenes from the play isolate certain features of the material, just as the descriptions of the tableaux on the playbills do, fixing those moments as representative of the whole of *Uncle Tom's Cabin.* Downplaying the violent realities of slavery, typical post-Civil War posters emphasize the domestic and spiritual aspects of the story. One might look at the posters that have survived (a few beautifully preserved examples exist in the Albert Davis collection at the University of Texas, Austin, and are reprinted by kind permission with this essay), and never register the idea that any of the characters being represented are supposed to be "property," owned by others. The posters are about family crisis, death, and Christian faith, and while the character of Uncle Tom figures heroically in most of them, the posters seldom even implicitly associate him or his predicaments with his enslaved condition. These visual images turn the story of one racial group's oppression of another into a middle-class fable about "everyone's" desire for upward mobility. In so doing, they perform spectacle's function of political amnesia, hiding the fact of slavery in plain sight. They remove the icon of Uncle Tom from the arena of racial politics, divesting him of his ethnic specificity, as well as of his historical condition.

A reproduced painting entitled "Uncle Tom Bidding His Children Farewell," undated but probably from the last quarter of the nineteenth century, illustrates very well the disproportionate emphasis on bourgeois domesticity that dominates the posters, effacing the topic of slavery altogether. The setting is the interior of Uncle Tom's cabin, which Stowe's text represents as comfortable, though decorated in a style distinctly different— her narrator implies—from that which would be approved by the middle-class reading audience. Stowe's description of the cabin shows Chloe's middle-class pretensions, including one carpeted corner

treated with distinguished consideration, and made, so far as possible, sacred from the marauding inroads and desecrations of little folks. In fact that corner was the *drawing room* of the establishment. . . .

The wall over the fireplace was adorned with some very brilliant scriptural prints, and a portrait of General Washington, drawn and colored in a manner which would certainly have astonished that hero, if ever he happened to meet with its like. (68)

The heavy irony of the italicized phrase, like the arch description of the hopelessly *déclassé* artwork, points to the crucial difference (from the middle-class audience's perspective) of Chloe's "home": she and Tom are not bourgeois householders but slaves, and that difference between them and their comfortably situated white readers is what will lead, in the diegesis, to the destruction of their conjugal arrangements. This difference is supposed to be funny: as Christina Zwarg has observed, in Stowe's text "the appropriation of white values by the slave community always assumes dark comedic hues" (277). At first glance, then, that difference between Chloe's "drawing room" and the intended reader's presents the "comical" face of slavery, in the form of a burlesque of middle-class interior decorating. But in the larger frame of the novel's plot, that difference is also the scandal, the violence of the institution of slavery which—at the same time that it upholds bourgeois norms in white American society—renders Chloe's aspirations so hopeless.[24]

By contrast, the interior depicted in the poster is indistinguishable from any lower middle-class American dwelling of the period. Lace half-curtains hang in the windows; the mantle-piece is decorated with a pitcher, a china cup, and a miniature grandfather clock. A very healthy dog—wearing a collar!—lies before the roaring fire, looking with a lolling-tongued "smile" at two tiny black boys who lie (somewhat incongruously for the setting) under an orange blanket spread on the floor. One of the boys sleeps while the other props himself up to wave, at Tom or perhaps at Eliza, both of whom are standing with Chloe in the picture's center. Tom is the aged figure the play versions made him out to be: gray-haired and bald-

Poster: "Uncle Tom Bidding His Children Farewell." Harry Ransome Humanities Research Center, the University of Texas at Austin.

ing, but extremely respectably dressed, in necktie, white waistcoat figured with red clover, a frock coat with tails, matching trousers, and good shoes. Chloe, in brightly colored dress, apron, and kerchief and gold hoop earrings, wears a dazed expression: aside from the boys, she is the only figure whose position and attire are not thoroughly middle-class. Eliza, in an un-bustled gray traveling dress, high-necked and long-sleeved, looks—with her distinctly Hispanic features—alertly toward Tom's back, which is turned to her as he looks down at the boys. The scene could be any nineteenth-century American family's parting out of externally imposed exigency: the idea that every figure in the frame, the man as well as the dog, is owned by someone else is absent: invisible. What this poster suggests is that *Uncle Tom's Cabin* is a bourgeois domestic drama, no more and no less.[25]

It achieves the remarkable effect of erasing slavery by making it into a spectacle for the viewer's gaze.

A poster in similar style from the same period depicts Tom and the St. Clare household at Eva's deathbed. Again, nothing in the image suggests Tom's enslaved condition; on the contrary, he stands in the picture's foreground, at the foot of Eva's bed, his bald head—fringed with white hair—bowed respectfully, his body clothed in the most elegant butler's garb imaginable. St. Clare kneels at the dying, blonde-haired Eva's side, as does Marie, her face covered by her handkerchief, at a slight distance. The rest of the room is filled with somber or weeping African Americans, all focusing their gazes upon Eva, and all standing immediately behind the family, suggesting the status of devoted servants.

This poster, however, does more than imply that slaves are in exactly the same position as any working-class Americans. It makes a visual suggestion that slaves are closer than their owners are to angels, a suggestion that does not conflict with Stowe's treatment of "spiritually awakened" slaves, but that takes on valences of racism in the poster that go beyond the prejudices such critics as Hortense Spillers and Richard Yarborough have pointed out in Stowe's text. As Yarborough sees it, "In Stowe's world, to be born black is to be born a pagan, but paradoxically close to a state of grace" (50). The poster makes that supposed relation of blacks to grace manifestly clear, but it stops short of Stowe's novels' optimism about the ultimate fate of Christian blacks.

Here, a flock of a dozen or so winged beings hovers in a beam of light over Eva's bed. The praying or crying black women and men standing behind the bed are each more indistinctly drawn than the last, until the figure at the bottom of the column of light is entirely blurred. This proximity to angels effaces the slaves' individuality: the viewer cannot distinguish even the gender of that last slave. The poster seems to suggest that slaves are sanctified by their position at the same time that it

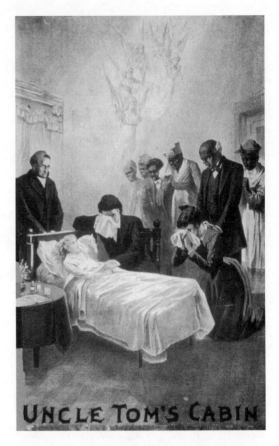

Poster: Eva on her deathbed, surrounded by the St. Clare household and heavenly hosts. Harry Ransome Humanities Research Center, the University of Texas at Austin.

says their individual identity (not to mention their sexuality) is of no importance. And yet the image does not assert an identity between slave and angel—while the slaves are all drawn with distinctly African coloration, every angel is as pale and blond as Eva herself. The implication is that the pious slave might get next to heaven, but the white spectator need not worry about seeing any black faces on the other side of the pearly gates. The suggestion reproduces the gesture that ends Stowe's story, in which the Harrises, now free, leave America (to the whites, as it were) and move on to Liberia,[26] but radically (that is to say, conservatively) transforms that gesture by translating it into the world beyond. At the bottom of this poster, the only text is the phrase "UNCLE TOM'S CABIN," in extended rustic type. The poster conveys, much more subtly, the same message as its contemporaneous playbills: *Uncle Tom's Cabin* is about how much better the blacks had it under slavery, and about how spectacularly picturesque slavery itself used to be. This is the version that prevails in the American popular memory, for the most part uncomplicated by the dialectics Stowe's text sets up between spirituality and politics, resignation and activism, martyrdom and renunciation.[27]

Contradictions abound in the iconography of another striking poster, but the conclusions they point to are significantly far from the novel's. This poster bears three images of black men. On the left is an aged version of Uncle Tom in very formal butler's dress, his white head bowed, his gaze downcast, a bible in his hand. On the right, the same, elderly Tom is shown in colorful, rustic clothing in good repair, holding a soft hat and gazing up, off the right hand edge of the page. Between them is a figure in much larger scale, a bust of a young, naked black man with rippling chest muscles and a facial expression of supremely calm self-confidence. This bust, surrounded by spiky laurel leaves, sits atop a plaque engraved with a motto:

> HONOUR and SHAME
>
> FROM
>
> NO CONDITION
>
> RISE;
>
> ACT WELL YOUR
>
> PART
>
> THERE ALL
>
> THE HONOUR LIES

In large type below the figures is "PETER JACKSON," the name of the black Australian prizefighter who played Tom in "Chas. E. Davies' Spectacular Production" of the play. The motto draws

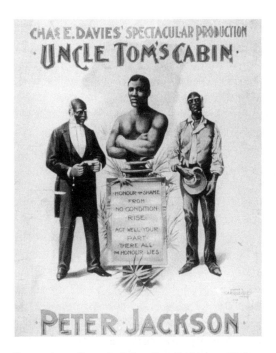

Poster: Australian prizefighter Peter Jackson as Uncle Tom. Harry Ransome Humanities Research Center, the University of Texas at Austin.

an explicit analogy between the slave and the actor: if Tom is honorable in the degree to which he fills the role assigned to him as the chattel property of another man (a notion in line with the "principles" Stowe's text attributes to him), Jackson is honorable insofar as he does justice to Tom's part on stage. On the face of it, the poster is a strong statement for the dignity of black manhood, pre- and post-Civil War. But the poster's capacity to convey this message to the nineteenth-century viewer would depend upon that viewer's ignorance of Jackson's identity and of the particular adaptation of the play that he was starring in. For, according to Birdoff, the curtain would come down after Tom's being sold to Legree, Jackson would step forward to box a few rounds with the actor who played Mr. Shelby, then the play's action would resume (330–31). Peter Jackson earned his laurels as an exhibition pugilist; as Peter Jackson, he embodies youth, aggressive physical power, and virility. As Uncle Tom, he wears a gray wig and receives blows without returning them. The change of costume, along with the boxing match, would confirm Uncle Tom's iconic status as commodified spectacle: the (aged) black man whose primary function in the culture is to be viewed, particularly in the context of a scene of violence.

The icon of Uncle Tom that emerges from the playbills and posters, then, maintains the blackness, the "African features" of Stowe's hero, but divests the figure of youth and virility—those twin twentieth-century signifiers of power—as well as of the signs of his enslavement. The icon also has no voice. These visually oriented texts downplay the historical experience of African Americans who were owned as property by emphasizing the spectacular aspects of slavery and by glossing over both the scandal it represents in Stowe's text and the African Americans' own testimony to that scandal. As Tom's status in American culture shifted from verbal, textual construct to visual icon, his "image problem" became entrenched. Without making an explicit argument about the experience of slavery, the aggregate of iconic representations of "Uncle Tom" taught the dominant culture to read the sign of African-American masculinity in this particular way.

American Scenes of Violence: Uncle Tom and Rodney King

To turn in conclusion to a more recent icon of the African American male that has taken hold in the American collective memory, consider the image invoked by the name "Rodney King." For anyone who even casually followed the American mass media after March 1991, the name signifies an extended and horrific scene reproduced on an amateur's grainy videotape, a spectacle of uniformed police officers heavily wielding batons and boots as they repeatedly beat and kick a prone human

figure. The figure rises (weakly? stubbornly? The viewer cannot be sure.), and the officers beat it down again. During the period immediately after the videotape's release to the press, during the criminal trial of the officers for using excessive force (and the riots that followed the verdict of "not guilty"), and during the second trial of the officers for violating King's civil rights, the most brutal segment of the tape was played again and again on television, frozen in stills in the print media, and imprinted upon the American popular memory.

The videotape frames the scene from a distance; caught as they are in the remote gaze of someone who was not supposed to see or to record the spectacle, the figures bear no visible signs of race, although the violence of the scene suggests something about the participants' gender. The narrative that came with the tape as it entered the collective consciousness, however, made the racial facts (if not the relative culpability) clear: those were white, male police officers beating a black, male suspect. During the first trial, in which the officers were acquitted, only the police gave words to the story; the person who received the beating did not testify. Until the second trial, two years after the incident, Rodney King had no input into the public narrative that formed the official interpretive frame for the videotape; even though he spoke briefly during the Los Angeles riots—to make a plea for "just getting along"—in the matter of his own experience at the hands of the police he might be said to have had no voice. The videotape—and the courtroom strategies of the lawyers involved—made King into a wordless icon, a visual sign of African American men's presumed relation to the dominant culture. As Houston Baker puts it:

> There was virtually no call for the "fugitive" himself to record his story before white audiences. He had merely to be wheeled out for television cameras and turned silently before outraged courts of American

opinion in all of his bandaged, swollen, and bruised victimization. . . . King was always already silent. Moral pundits and paparazzi alike took up his cause. Not only was there a scene of violence, but an overseen one.[28]

Baker calls this visual framing of King's victimization the "sceneing" of violence, to underscore the iconic, silent role the black man plays in it.

The historical context of the "sceneing" of such violence becomes vivid in a scene near the end of *I Ain't Yo' Uncle,* when the drama arrives at one of the iconic legacies of the nineteenth-century playbills: the spectacle of Uncle Tom lying prostrate before the slaveholder Simon Legree, who beats him with a whip. As Legree stands over Tom, with whip raised, the stage is suddenly filled with an enormous backdrop projection, a still reproduction of the scene of King's beating. The iconic connection is striking. For all of the twentieth-century African American man's difference from the nineteenth-century slave, the visual image of his subjugation to white power is eerily the same.

These two icons, Uncle Tom and Rodney King, are closely, harrowingly related. As Frisch's study shows, the collective American memory remembers "Uncle Tom" well. In remembering him, American culture substitutes a spectacular version of a fictional image of a slave for the lived experience of actual slaves. That image mediates slavery through multiple filters: the romantic racialism of Stowe, the spectacularization of the plays, the amelioration of the playbills and posters, and the conclusions of reviewers and critics. All these influences have combined to form the surviving image of "Uncle Tom"—the old, gray, bent, shuffling, emasculated black man who enjoys his servility, and therefore is perceived as deserving it. Although Stowe's Tom is already a racist portrait, the culture's process of making him into an icon is even more insidious: it is an act of violence, through which the figure is drained of his moral and physical power. Making slavery look cozy,

fun, and entertaining, then making this revisionist image of slavery into an icon that America remembers most vividly, is one of the culture's lingering crimes against African Americans. This collective violence is analogous to the beating of Rodney King, just as the continual repetition of the videotape of that beating in the mass media is analogous to the process the image of "Uncle Tom" has undergone. The making of the videotape into a repeated public spectacle constituted an enactment of spectacle as political amnesia. The more we saw the video, the more we were supposed to forget how representative this fetishized incident actually was.

Houston Baker construes King's problem as the imposition of silence that comes with iconic status. The process of redressing that problem—both for Uncle Tom and for Rodney King—would seem to call for a reintroduction of textual voice into their public identities. In *I Ain't Yo' Uncle,* Harriet Beecher Stowe stands accused of "writing stuff she couldn't possibly know about. A slave's experience. The black experience" (ms. p. 2). Her novel's narrator speaks from a specifically white, middle-class, feminine position to an audience of her social peers; the "engaging" narrative stance (as I have called it elsewhere) of *Uncle Tom's Cabin* allows her to seem to speak directly, out of the pages of her text, into American society on the African Americans' behalf.[29] In Robert Alexander's play, the character of Stowe never addresses the audience, but the character of Tom frequently does. His asides and monologues give his voice unmediated access to his spectators. To bestow the character of Tom with a voice is to begin to overturn his iconic status as passive spectacle.

Yet what about that icon who is not a character, but a person, Rodney King? While King did testify in the second trial—where two of the officers were finally found guilty of depriving him of his civil rights—his words have hardly replaced the visual image of his victimization in the collective memory. Baker turns not to King himself but to rap music for a voicing of the contemporary African American man's predicament: "we might actually gain a hearing from rap of what precisely it *sounds* like to be violently *scened* in the United States" (ms. p. 20). And while Baker (himself a powerful speaker) holds out another figure of black manhood as a source of potential inspiration—the pointedly verbal and vocal Frederick Douglass—one might ask with Gayatri Spivak whether indeed the subaltern *can* speak.[30] Anything Rodney King might or could say is always already mediated by "Uncle Tom," anyway. The persistence in American popular memory of visual versions of Uncle Tom, of Rodney King, over verbal renditions of them suggests that American conceptions of race are at the heart of the violent "sceneing" that makes the two figures into wordless icons. Deeply embedded in American culture is the notion that race itself can be seen, that "color" and facial features are visible revelations of an "essential" difference. Until America can see race differently, violence like the Los Angeles riots ought inevitably to be the reaction to the violence of racism itself.

Notes

1 Parenthetical page references to Stowe's novel in this chapter are from the 1981 Penguin edition: Harriet Beecher Stowe, *Uncle Tom's Cabin* (1851–52; Harmondsworth: Penguin, 1981).

2 Michael Rogin, "Make My Day! Spectacle as Amnesia in Imperial Politics," in *Cultures of United States Imperialism,* ed. Amy Kaplan and Donald E. Pease (Durham: Duke University Press, 1993).

3 In an excellent chapter published since this essay was written, Turner confirms my contention that Tom's image has undergone erosion throughout the nineteenth and twentieth centuries and that this erosion has important ramifications for American race politics. Patricia Turner, *Ceramic Uncles and Celluloid Mammies: Black Images and Their Influence on Culture* (New York: Anchor, 1994).

4 Schudson lists "the ambiguity of stories" among nine factors that influence popular recollection of past events, including "institutionalization of memory,"

"the past as scar," and other matters impinging on historiography in *Watergate in American Memory: How We Remember, Forget, and Reconstruct the Past* (New York: Basic Books, 1992), 207–8.

5 Quoted by Schwartz from *La Topographie Légendaire des Évangiles* (Paris: Presses Universitaires de France, 1941), 7. See Barry Schwartz, "Iconography and Collective Memory: Lincoln's Image in the American Mind," *Sociological Quarterly* 32.3 (1991):301–19.

6 Michael Frisch, "American History and the Structures of Collective Memory: A Modest Exercise in Empirical Iconography," *Journal of American History.* 75(4) (19xx): 1130–55.

7 Misha Berson, "Cabin Fever," *American Theatre* 8.2 (1991): 16–23, 71–73, and Robert Alexander, *I Ain't Yo' Uncle: The New Jack Revisionist "Uncle Tom's Cabin,"* typescript of play, November 20, 1991, San Francisco Mime Troupe touring version.

8 Yarborough is one critic who thus credits Stowe's Tom: "Tom's principled refusal to strike out aggressively for his freedom grows out of his unimpeachable personal integrity and his staunch faith in Providence" (54). See Richard Yarborough, "Strategies of Black Characterization in *Uncle Tom's Cabin* and the Early Afro-American Novel" in *New Essays on Uncle Tom's Cabin,* ed. Eric J. Sundquist (Cambridge: Cambridge University Press, 1986), 45–84.

9 Elizabeth Ammons, *Critical Essays on Harriet Beecher Stowe* (Boston: G. K. Hall, 1980), 94.

10 Quoted in Thomas Gossett, *Uncle Tom's Cabin and American Culture* (Dallas: Southern Methodist University Press, 1985), 280.

11 Feminist interpretations of Stowe's text have been among the most illuminating, though they are not always presented as defenses of Stowe's intentions. Ann Douglas's, "Introduction: The Art of Controversy," in Stowe, *Uncle Tom's Cabin,* 7–34, and Jane P. Tompkins's *Sensational Designs: The Cultural Work of American Fiction, 1790–1860* (New York: Oxford University Press, 1985) offer noncanonical (though contradictory) readings of the novel. For insights into the discourses of domesticity in the novel, see Lora Romero, "Bio-Political Resistance in Domestic Ideology and *Uncle Tom's Cabin,*" *American Literary History* 1(4) (1989): 715–34; Gillian Brown, *Domestic Individualism: Imagining Self in Nineteenth-Century America* (Berkeley: University of California Press, 1990); and Myra Jehlen, "The Family Militant: Domesticity versus Slavery in *Uncle Tom's*

Cabin," *Criticism: A Quarterly for Literature and the Arts* 31(4) (1989): 383–400. For alternative gender- (and language-) centered readings, see Helena Michie, "'Dying Between Two Laws': Girl Heroines, Their Gods, and Their Fathers in *Uncle Tom's Cabin* and the *Elsie Dinsmore* Series," in *Refiguring the Father: New Feminist Readings of Patriarchy,* ed. Patricia Yeager and Beth Kowaleski Wallace (Carbondale: University of Southern Illinois Press, 1989), 188–206, and Christina Zwarg, "Fathering and Blackface in *Uncle Tom's Cabin,*" *Novel* 22(3) (1989): 274–87.

12 Gossett, *Uncle Tom's Cabin and American Culture,* 260. Gossett is not alone among commentators of the mid-1980s who generalize about the impact of vastly disparate versions of "the play"; for another example, see Robson. Other discussions of the theatrical tradition of *Uncle Tom's Cabin* include David Grimsted, "Uncle Tom from Page to Stage: Limitations of Nineteenth-Century Drama," *Quarterly Journal of Speech* 56 (1970): 235–44, and Bruce McConachie, "Out of the Kitchen and into the Marketplace: Normalizing *Uncle Tom's Cabin* for the Antebellum Stage," *Journal of American Theatre and Drama* 3 (1991): 5–28.

13 The playbills and posters cited in this article are all in the Albert Davis and Howard-Fox collections in the Harry Ransom Humanities Research Center at the University of Texas at Austin, unless otherwise noted.

14 Hortense Spillers, "Changing the Letter: The Yokes, the Jokes of Discourse, or, Mrs. Stowe, Mr. Reed," in *Slavery and the Literary Imagination,* ed. Deborah E. McDowell and Arnold Rampersad (Baltimore: Johns Hopkins University Press, 1989), 25–61.

15 The bill for the 1867 production starring Caroline (Mrs. George) Howard, who originated the part of Topsy in the first stagings of the Aiken version, lists a whopping twenty-one tableaux, including the original nine, as well as "Wild Topsey} [*sic*], "Tame Topsey," "Singing Topsey," "Dancing Topsey," "Topsey & the Stocking," and "Civilized Topsey," obviously showcases for Caroline Howard's critically lauded interpretation of the role. See Gossett, *Uncle Tom's Cabin and American Culture,* 266.

16 Harry Birdoff, *The World's Greatest Hit: Uncle Tom's Cabin* (New York: S. F. Vanni, 1947), 88.

17 Eric Lott, *Love and Theft: Blackface Minstrelsy and the American Working Class* (New York: Oxford University Press, 1993), 3.

18 To imply that the British production's more serious treatment of slavery is unmixed would be, however, to oversimplify. *Uncle Tom's Cabin* is followed on the playbill by a burlesque version of Othello, the description of which is racist in the extreme. The effect of the juxtaposition of the two plays on the bill would be to undercut the seriousness of the first play.

19 Gossett attributes the song to a minstrel show producer, Sam Sanford, who says that he first did the show in Philadelphia in 1853: "I did a piece called 'Rebuke to Uncle Tom' in which I tried to depict slave life as I knew it, and as it actually existed at the time. I took in $11,000 in nine weeks" (*Uncle Tom's Cabin and American Culture,* 276). That this satirical anti-abolitionist material could be running (still? again?) in Philadelphia as late as 1861, under Stowe's title rather than Sanford's, is surprising.

20 The show did well in Montreal: Winks mentions the extraordinary popularity of *Uncle Tom's Cabin* plays in Canada, observing that their "hold . . . on the public imagination was secure and long-lasting—certainly longer in British North America than in the United States." Considering the positive connotations of "Canada" in all abolitionist versions of *Uncle Tom's Cabin,* the appeal for a popular Canadian audience is understandable. Robin W. Winks, "The Making of a Fugitive Slave Narrative: Josiah Henson and Uncle Tom—A Case Study," in *The Slave's Narrative,* ed. Charles T. Davis, Henry Louis Gates, Jr. (Oxford: Oxford University Press, 1985), 112–46, 121.

21 Consider, for example, the basic material used by Tuptin, one of the King of Siam's wives, in her adaptation of *Uncle Tom's Cabin* in the 1950s American musical, *The King and I:* her dramatization concentrates on images of Eliza's escape, Tom's happiness with Eva and Topsy, and Eva's death and apotheosis.

22 Kesler, title and pub info to come, 187.

23 As Gillian Brown has argued, the commodification of African Americans is a pattern present in Stowe's text, too, where "conjunctions of market value and color underscore the identity of blacks with commodities that Stowe retains even as her ethic of sentimental possession offers a way of transforming commodities into citizens" (*Domestic Individualism,* 59).

24 Jehlen notes this theme in Stowe's text, observing that since "the best of the slaves in *Uncle Tom's Cabin* are models of upward mobility . . . slavery may do its worst in breaking up families, but a close second is its denial of social advancement" ("The Family Militant," 387). Brown points out that for Stowe, skin color limits char-

acters' upward mobility even after their emancipation (*Domestic Individualism,* 55).

25 The poster's implications are, in this respect, in direct opposition to Stowe's version where, as Gillian Brown remarks, "The distinction between work and family is eradicated in the slave, for whom there is no separation between economic and private status" (*Domestic Individualism,* 15).

26 As Yarborough reads it, "Stowe's tragic failure of imagination prevented her from envisioning blacks (free or slave, mulatto or full-blood) as viable members of American society, so she deports the most aggressive, intelligent, 'acceptable' ones to Africa" ("*Strategies of Black Characterization,*" 65).

27 Kenneth T. Rainey argues that American theatrical productions of plays other than Uncle Tom's Cabin served to reinforce racist and nostalgic attitudes toward slavery, contributing to making "the period between 1877 and 1901 . . . the 'nadir' of American attitudes towards Negroes" ("Race and Reunion in Nineteenth-Century Reconciliation Drama," *American Transcendental Quarterly* 2[2] (1988): 156).

28 Houston A. Baker, Jr., "The American Scene of Violence: Reading Frederick Douglass and Rodney King," talk delivered at International Conference for the Study of Narrative Literature, Albany, NY, April 1993.

29 See Robyn R. Warhol, "Women's Narrators Who Cross Gender: *Uncle Tom's Cabin* and *Adam Bede,*" in *Gendered Interventions* (New Brunswick, NJ: Rutgers University Press, 1989), 101–33.

30 Thanks to Stephen DaSilva for making this connection for me (Gayatri Spivak, *Selected Subaltern Studies* [New York: Oxford University Press, 1988]). Thanks also to Roxanne Lin, Helena Michie, Scott Derrick, Colleen Lamos, Beth Kowaleski-Wallace, Joseph Won, Wolfgang Mieder, and this volume's editors for comments that contributed to this essay.

STRESS MANAGEMENT IDEOLOGY AND THE OTHER SPACES OF WOMEN'S POWER

Kathleen Green

In an episode from the 1994–95 season of *The Oprah Winfrey Show,* psychologist Ellen McGrath, Ph.D., on a book tour for her latest medical self-help book, *When Feeling Good Is Bad,* explained how exercise can relieve bouts of mild depression and energize even the slightly frazzled:

> If you're feeling down, Stressed-Depressed, the best one [action strategy] that we have is the ten minute energy walk. This one really works. All you do is get up. You don't have to do aerobics; you just get up. You walk back and forth in a room or around the block, count your steps one-two, one-two or one to ten, and it does two things: it's a meditation effect, it lowers stress and it raises energy. And the research showed that an hour later, it was better than talking to a friend or eating a candy bar.

McGrath's "action strategy" of walking for ten minutes is typical of the expert advice that claims exercise is a stress reducer. Certainly, physical exercise has been an important theme in U.S. culture since industrialization created a sedentary middle class. But the tenacity with which women have clung to exercise in recent decades marks a new phase in the U.S. obsession with fitness. This new exercise imperative is a key element in the construction of the U.S. stress management culture.

According to McGrath, the ten-minute energy walk does more to increase self-esteem, mastery, and control than "talking to a friend or eating a candy bar."[1] In her comparison between talking to a friend and the ten-minute energy walk, McGrath articulates something that is inherent but rarely explicit in women's stress management discourse: that exercise has replaced talk between women. This is a significant point considering that, in women's history, talking to a friend has often been the first step toward consciousness raising, political action, and improvements in the conditions of women's lives. The energy walk is more expedient than conversation; it readies a woman to continue her tasks without questioning them. Thus, McGrath implies that individual solutions are better than collective ones and that being "Stressed-Depressed" is more a personal than a social problem. It is especially ironic that this is the underlying message of the country's leading talk show for women, hosted and produced by one of the most powerful women in the United States. As Wendy Kaminer puts it in her critique of self-help, "Feminism is women talking, but it is not women only talking and not women talking only about themselves."[2]

Oprah responds to McGrath's advice with her own more "down to earth" version of this advice:

Now, I know it's hard to believe. Because there are days too, like, I just don't feel like working out, and you *really, really, really,* don't feel like it. But something happens once you start doing it. The days when I'm the most pissed off about doing it, and I'll start doing it, like today for instance, and you start doing it and something in your body physically changes and you feel better.

Regular *Oprah* viewers will notice immediately a familiar tactic: the guest expert talks and then Oprah vouches for her by presenting her own personal experience in a form that shows she's just as much the expert—if not at medicine, then at life. For Oprah always seems to know more than the experts she brings on the show; her questions seem designed to provoke the expert to say what Oprah already knows. And when the expert does speak first, as in this example, Oprah can follow with her own advice.

As this exchange between Oprah and McGrath shows, women are among the "experts" of stress management culture. Yet, the tension between

professional expertise and women's personal experience—which has been a key feature in U.S. medical history since the professionalization of medicine in the mid-nineteenth century—still arises even when the experts are female. Few of Oprah's audience members (studio and home viewers) are likely to "talk back" to medical experts as Oprah does (in this case, very subtly, but in others quite explicitly). Oprah can "talk back," can claim discursive space, because she is Oprah—because she has money and power, but also, because she is an African American woman who does not push too hard against the limits of hegemonic discourse, who does not challenge white, corporate culture enough to lose ratings.[3]

The theme of McGrath's and Oprah's advice is a familiar one, for it is halfway through the 1994–95 season, and the audience has heard this much slimmer Oprah tell her story of psycho-spiritual recovery and extol the virtues of exercise for several weeks now. Oprah tries to downplay the specifics of her own social position in order to highlight the similarities between her situation and those of other women. Women audience members might experience this as an oppressive move or a feminist one, depending on their own subject position in relation to any given show. Oprah knows that this advice and her own success story are difficult for many of her audience members to take. She begins with the phrase "Now, I know it's hard to believe," in an effort to identify with her audience members' skepticism, itself a recurring motif in her self-portrayal as "everywoman." She admits that even she sometimes still "gets pissed off about" exercising. The lesson to be learned from her example of coming out of depression, exercising, and losing weight, as Oprah has said earlier in the show, is "simply that it can be done."

The Oprah Winfrey Show resonates with the issues of mastery, energy, expertise, and happiness that have come to be key matters in the formation of women's subjectivities in the 1980s and 1990s.

This show both helps create and is the product of ideas about womanhood that permeate U.S. culture, and it is through such texts as *The Oprah Winfrey Show* and the lifestory of Oprah that many women come to define themselves. The cultural construction of "womanhood" emerges from the interaction of a number of themes prevalent in what Mimi White has called the therapeutics of television: narratives of recovery; television's role as therapy service; the contention over expertise among host, guest, and viewers; the class conflict between those on television and those watching it; and the master narrative of self-definition and power as the path to happiness. Though stress management is clearly not the only topic of discussion in the popular psychology of Oprah, its fundamental concepts underlie much of what is circulated on and through the show.

Stress management culture has become one of the most compelling threads in late-twentieth-century United States culture; it is crucial to the economy of money and bodies upon which our consumer culture is based. While many scholars assume stress management to be oppressive, none have explained the specificity of its ideological workings. This paper shows how the concepts of "power" and "burnout" define the parameters of women's health in stress management, and how this mandates individual change almost always to the exclusion of collective political change. Throughout this essay, I am not concerned with whether or not stress management "works" for individual women. (Certainly it does, which is one reason it has taken hold so thoroughly. Sadly, for many women it is the only way they can care for and value themselves; it is a necessary part of women's survival in late-twentieth-century culture.) Rather, my concern in this outline of the history and politics of stress management is to investigate how and why stress management has become such an integral part of our understanding of power and to question the impact this formulation has on feminism today.

One of the reasons stress management culture is so fascinating is its engagement with popular culture and social change. Women's stress management texts—from *The Oprah Winfrey Show* to women's popular print media to bell hooks's *Sisters of the Yam: Black Women and Self-Recovery* (1993)[4]—share a common attempt to negotiate the complicated matrix of feminism and popular culture. In their own ways and with differing degrees of success in different contexts, each of these stress management texts makes an appeal to women's collectivity *through* a particular configuration of "the popular." For instance, as we have seen, Oprah tries to bridge class and racial differences between women by showing their similar plights: low self-esteem, the difficulty of exercising, their common struggles with sexism. Ultimately, these appeals to collectivity cannot be realized from within stress management discourse, which brings with it a history and structure that is antithetical to women's collective resistance. Again, in the example of *The Oprah Winfrey Show,* this desire for collectivity is voiced through what television theorist Mimi White calls "new voices and new subjectivities" of television therapy, voices "that nonetheless remain in fee to consumer culture."[5] By reading these very diverse women's stress management texts in relation to one another—montage style, if you will—I hope to analyze the political ramifications of women's embrace of stress management discourse; I hope to show how and why the cultural net of stress management discourse has managed to capture the imaginations of so many woman who identify, in one way or another, as feminists.

Thus, my specific analysis of women's stress management discourse has wider implications for feminism and cultural studies. In terms of the present volume's concerns with questions of agency and resistance through popular culture, it might be useful to think of stress management itself as a metaphor for the new modes of subjectivity-formation that have come to shape women's lives in the last fifteen years or so. In its depiction of a constant ebb and flow of coping, stress management seems a particularly apt analogy for the often confusing and contradictory movements of power in postmodern culture. Stress management is a seductive model for feminists because it is always contextually bound and is predicated on the details of everyday life, which, as cultural studies feminists have shown, have too long been ignored in many radical movements and theories of social change. Yet, ultimately, stress management discourse hinges on mistaking self-help for mutual aid. As I show below, stress management is inherently individualizing; it configures a woman's relationship to power only through her coping mechanisms, her ability to negotiate and eventually adapt to structures of domination. In stress management culture, for some women to gain power requires the disempowerment of others. This is hardly a feminist model of agency or resistance, and because it is often advocated in the name of feminism, it bears close scrutiny.

"Adaptation Energy" and Dominant Stress Management Discourse

In the late 1930s, Hans Selye, a young medical scientist then conducting experiments at McGill University, discovered that a specific and predictable hormonal reaction occurred when laboratory rats were subjected to extreme temperatures. He called this phenomenon "stress." In 1956, Selye published *The Stress of Life,* the book that laid down the foundation of stress theory and that would garner him the title of the "father of stress." [6] Selye's immense production of scientific books and articles, popular writings, and autobiographies has provided the foundation for the development of stress management. Taking the results of his experiments with rodents as a scientific basis and his own life as a concrete example, Selye formulated the key concept of "adaptation energy" as a way to achieve right living.

Selye's "adaptation energy" concept offered a way to see organisms in terms of continuous processes of change. He described the stress response as a three-part chain reaction that occurs whenever an organism is subjected to stimuli. This three phase process, the "general adaptation syndrome" (GAS), consists of the introduction of a stressor (the alarm stage), the body's adjustment or response to the stressor (the resistance stage), and the body's eventual failure to respond indefinitely to the stressor (the exhaustion stage), which results in exhaustion and, if this state is reached repeatedly over time, in death. [7] The most important bodily force, "adaptation energy" is, according to Selye, the body's ability to respond to good and bad stressors appropriately. "The real strength of life," wrote Selye, "is not the fuel (food) we take, but adaptability, because the living machine can make considerable repairs and adjustments *en route,* as long as it has adaptation energy." [8] There is, of course, no physiological substance known as "adaptation energy." It affects the hormones, but is not one; it is influenced by nutrition, but is not food or calories. A vague but crucial concept in the theory of stress, "adaptation energy" is the force—like faith, motivation, and other such forces were to previous generations—that makes personal experiences good or bad.

Selye subdivided stress into "eustress" (Good Stress) and "distress" (Bad Stress) to show that stress itself was not good or bad, but that one's experience of it would depend upon the subject's reaction to it. Further, he advocated that eliminating stress would lead to death (if only from boredom), and that the best way to manage the amount of tension in one's life would be to seek a happy medium between hypostress (too little) and hyperstress (too much), to find "one's own best stress level." As one of Selye's popularizers, Nancy Gross, described it, each individual has an innate internal and instinctual pace at which he or she should live. [9] To best handle stress, one should not attempt to live beyond one's innate—and genetically pre-disposed—personal pace. Or, as Selye put it:

> Our goal should be to strike a balance between the equally destructive forces of hypo- and hyper-stress, to find as much eustress as possible, and to minimize distress. Clearly, we cannot run away timidly from every unpleasant experience; in order to achieve our purposes, we must often put up with unhappiness, at least for a time. Here faint-heartedness would in the long run prove even more distressing by depriving us of the joy of ultimate success. . . .
>
> It is a biological law that man, like the lower an-imals, must fight and work for some goal that he considers worth while. . . . Only through effort, of-ten aggressive egoistic effort, can we maintain our fitness and assure our homeostatic equilibrium with the surrounding society and the inanimate world.[10]

By introducing these distinctions and the con-cept of "adaptation energy," Selye opened the door to a flood of popular ideas about stress and its management. If the experience of stress de-pended on the subject, who could ostensibly con-trol certain factors, then the subject—and possi-bly those surrounding him or her—could be held accountable for the level of tension in his/her life. The value-laden rhetoric that pervades this pas-sage, as well as much of Selye's writing and of most popular writing on stress, hints at the potential political repercussions of stress management. Many of Selye's conclusions are based on his direct and untheorized application of biochemical pre-cepts to psychological functioning and social in-teraction. Selye's language here—we mustn't be "fainthearted," we must strive with "aggressive egoistic effort" to "maintain fitness and assure our homeostatic equilibrium with the surrounding society and the inanimate world"—is the end re-sult of this slippery slope.[11] Through this maneu-ver, he inscribes into the science of stress what have come to be viewed (by critics and supporters alike) as the classic U.S. values of productivity, self-reliance, and individualism.

The emphasis in Selye's rhetoric on what are usually understood as "masculine" traits is no coincidence. Although since the early 1970s stress has been very much a "woman's problem," earlier uses of the stress concept were obsessed with mas-culinity. Whether described in terms of the ego-psychology of combat aviators in World War II or the cardiac health of Type A and Type B business-men in the 1950s and 1960s, stress was a man's dis-ease for the first few decades of its existence in medical discourse and popular culture.[12] While stress has remained important to the construction of masculinity ever since, the early 1970s ushered in a new era of stress research, one that included women and that began to revise the theoretical models that had previously held sway. New re-searchers and popularizers, many of them women, began to describe the impact stress has on women. They emphasized daily stressors over tragic life events, and they concentrated on the role conflict that emerged for many middle-class married women with children who were entering the paid workforce for the first time. By the early 1980s, stress was commonly used in both medical and popular discourses to describe women's experi-ences. Despite new models of psychological stress and coping that provide for more nuanced analy-ses of the subject's relationship to society, popular stress advice literature for women and men has re-lied almost exclusively on Selye's concept of "adaptation energy."[13]

Stress management discourse, which has been a mainstay of both corporate and mainstream cul-ture since the early 1980s, relies on the slippage be-tween the physiological, the psychological, and the social inherent in Selye's popularization of "adaptation energy." Its central premises are that one can never rid the body of stress and that one must learn to manage it. Stress management in-cludes a number of forms of discourse and occurs in a variety of social spaces, ranging from costly corporate seminars at exotic resorts to inexpensive self-help books, tapes, and videos that can be bor-rowed from libraries or used by social and medical service organizations. As its critics have pointed out, it is especially useful to corporate interests—and oppressive to workers—in the service industries and in lower-level white collar jobs. Corporate stress management programs are often used in place of other forms of employee health care because they are more cost effective.[14] At the same time that health benefits have been cut inside corporate America, the number of work-related stress management programs has increased. According to one source, by 1988 over half of U.S. Fortune 500 companies had health-and-fitness plans intended to reduce stress-related productivity losses.[15] Often explicitly goal-directed, the message of such programs is that one should maintain physical and emotional health in order to be productive in business, and that placing oneself and one's goals above all else is the most effective way to do so. These programs serve the very immediate interests of workers—certainly, it is good to feel healthy and sane—while simultaneously fulfilling corporate goals.

There are literally hundreds of examples of corporate stress management, and most of them share the same approaches. Most of these texts assert the additional difficulty of "modern life" as compared to life in the past, citing the influence of computers, the women's movement, global economies, and the like. The logic of these texts, which is circular, is that employees need to work harder to be successful and that high productivity is success. One of the most profitable stress management companies has been CareerTrack Publications from Boulder, Colorado. CareerTrack runs "personal growth" seminars such as Roger Mellott's "Stress Management for Professionals: How to Feel Better and Perform Better on the Job" (1987) and Jacquelyn Ferguson's "Stress Reduction Workshop for Women" (1992). These employee-participation seminars are then audiotaped and sold in bookstores and distributed through public libraries. Often consisting of four to six one-hour tapes, the seminars feature an ostensibly charismatic host who outlines the major principles of stress management and provides long case histories as examples. There is also an audience participation component; the listener is instructed to turn off the tape at certain points to do the activity along with the studio audience. Stress management discourse is also circulated in print format. For instance, *Vitality* magazine is a monthly magazine geared toward secretaries, data entry personnel, and other female-dominated occupations. It offers general advice about "health, wellness, and happiness" clearly intended to make happy, healthy, and therefore productive employees. The October 1993 "Less Stress Issue" was devoted almost entirely to stress management. In addition to quizzes designed to measure stress, relaxation and exercise hints, and suggestions on how to give yourself an "attitude adjustment," the magazine sells the Vitality company's own stress management products, such as the "Hot and Cold Therapy Pillow." *Vitality* is purchased in bulk by corporations to distribute free of charge to employees; according to their own blurb, as of 1993, 26 percent of Fortune 500 companies provided *Vitality* to their employees.

The crucial question in analyzing this advice is one that scholars often overlook: to what extent do workers need to be so productive? As economist Juliet Schor argues, in the post–World War II U.S. economy, "progress" is marked by excessive production and continual but unnecessary increases in the workday that also result in rising unemployment.[16] "Since 1948, . . ." writes Schor, "the level of productivity of the U.S. worker has more than doubled."[17] When an economy has an increase in worker productivity, two things can happen: each worker's worktime can be decreased, which also means that overall employment could increase (that is, the workforce can move to a part-time workweek at nearly full-time wages), or production can continue at the same pace to sell products and services in new markets. U.S. society has taken the latter option, which benefits corporations rather than workers. The rise of consumer culture (what many have called the "work and spend" cycle) and the decline in labor union efforts to work for a reduction in the workday have made this option possible, according to Schor.[18]

The result of this emphasis on productivity is that the employed are hyperemployed, and stress management seems particularly applicable to their lives. As Schor explains, "Nationwide, people report their leisure time has declined by as much as one third since the early 1970s. Predictably, they are spending less time on the basics, like sleeping and eating."[19] Equally, the number of unemployed or underemployed continually rises, since employers tend to hire fewer employees but work them more. The un- and under-employed face the material stressors of poverty, yet rarely have access to high levels of health services or the social status of stress. Their experiences are rarely intelligible when viewed from the stress management culture in which most Americans are, sometimes unwittingly, positioned.

Given that overwork and unemployment are the two options with which most U.S. employees are presented, it is not surprising that many seek stress management's short-term, individual, and ostensibly feasible approach to the problems of an overextended body and mind. Stress management is appealing to these overworked employees because it makes a big promise: it endeavors to teach coping skills that will make one better able to handle more tasks quickly and easily. It teaches how to increase one's "adaptation energy"; such a skill would seem to improve the quality of every aspect of life. Stress management claims to offer the gift of time and its management, and to provide the semblance of security in what many people (are taught to) believe to be their chaotic, late-twentieth-century lives.

Corporate stress management discourse, though an important cultural force, is not entirely self-sustaining. On the contrary, corporate stress management programs are highly dependent on the circulation of the ideals of stress management in other discursive and social spaces. Certainly, publications, workshops, and seminars endorsed by companies and distributed directly to workers are crucial to the success of corporate productivity programs. But the staying power of corporate culture's stress management programs is largely the result of the widespread circulation of such discourse outside of the workplace. Essentially, stress management discourse itself has become a desirable commodity with a wide open market potential.

Women and the Power-Burnout Continuum

Women, especially, seem drawn to the ideology of stress management. Women consume literally hundreds of popular books, magazine articles, and audiovisuals about stress every year. Fashion magazines regularly feature columns by medical experts, many of them female. *Vogue* and *Mademoiselle*, for example, published articles about stress throughout the 1970s, and by the early 1980s each ran a multi-page article at least three to four times a year and a short, one-page advice column every second or third issue. Magazines aimed at homemakers, such as the *Ladies' Home Journal*, *Good Housekeeping*, and *Woman's Day*, followed suit beginning in the mid-1980s. Such specialty publications as *Working Woman* depend on stress-related discussions for a large percentage of their annual page count, and ethnic group-oriented magazines, such as *Essence*, also regularly publish on stress. While the middle-class offers an important market for the commodities (information and services) of stress management, working class women are also very much part of this economy, through magazines and grocery store "mini-mags" (those little booklets that are available for 59 and 89 cents at checkout counters) and through more obviously prescriptive forms, such as government pamphlets, school textbooks, and the like. As even this quick overview shows, when women look to texts that feature stress, they find an illusion of choice. There is information designed to appeal to whatever social or economic position a female reader occupies, whether she defines herself as a young career woman, a business executive, a single mother, or a partner, among many others. Yet, despite its currency in a wide range of forms, most stress management for women nevertheless functions to support and create the dominant ideology of late-twentieth-century womanhood as ultimately defined by role conflict.

In terms of women's stress management discourse, "adaptation energy" is mapped onto a continuum of women's health that positions power and burnout at opposite ends of the spectrum. Within the logic of this spectrum, women must learn to balance hypo- and hyper-stress, to reduce distress and increase eustress in order to experience life at the power, rather than the burnout, end of the continuum. Power and burnout have become important cultural icons in narratives of women's experience in the 1980s and 1990s.[20]

The word "power" evokes such images as the "powerwalk," the "powerlunch," the 1980s "superwoman," and the 1990s new age "goddess within." Women's magazines of the 1980s and 1990s—particularly the advertisements—are full of photographs of women in motion or women otherwise coded as being capable of physical, sexual, or financial shows of power. Exercise is perhaps the primary way that women believe they can access "power" in U.S. culture. The majority of U.S. women regularly exercise walk, swim, practice aerobics, run, or otherwise work out recreationally.[21] Like Oprah, many women believe that exercise wards off stress, thereby helping them gain "power" and thus stay sane, healthy, and in control of their lives. Medical research, as it is disseminated in women's mass culture, supports these beliefs: "Studies confirm," writes one *Vogue* columnist, "that regular aerobic exercise . . . not only improves one's physiological state by conditioning the heart and lowering blood pressure but also relieves depression and fatigue."[22] Exercise in this context is not leisure but therapy, emotional "work."

Selye's "adaptation energy" is the crucial concept, I would argue, that forms this circuit be-

tween women and power by bypassing feminism. For instance, in a 1986 *Redbook* column on stress, the author makes an analogy between women's experiences and "recharged batteries":

> when we are involved in an activity that excites and challenges us, we may in fact be increasing our energy store. We all know that if we come home exhausted after a hard day's work and just flop onto the couch and watch TV, we keep feeling tired. But if we get up and jog or play tennis or take part in some other sport we enjoy, we start feeling more alert and alive—and we can recharge our psychological batteries in much the same way. So it's not just how much a woman does that's important but also how she feels about what she does.[23]

The author does not explicitly refer to Selye; importantly, she relies mostly on female experts, such as the frequently quoted psychologists Grace Baruch and Rosalind Barnett from the Wellesley Center for Research on Women. The use of women experts is typical of 1980s and 1990s publications on stress, but it does little to change the foundation of the "adaptation energy" model. The last sentence of this passage shows how thoroughly indebted to Selye this author's concept of "recharged batteries" is. The author downplays differences between women's material lives—"it's not just how much a woman does that's important"—and privileges attitude—"how she feels about what she does."[24] By positing television and sport as the two alternatives, the author obliterates the possibility of the energizing effects of collective activity, such as the forms of talking back and talk among women that might lead to political action. The "recharged batteries" model of women's subjectivity springs from stress management notions about the female body's relationship to work. The goal is to become productive again, and the work that makes that possible (tennis, jogging) is presented as play, though it does not function as such in social life.

Educational theorist Alfie Kohn points out in his analysis of competition in U.S. society that "our leisure activities no longer give us a break from the alienating qualities of the work we do; instead, they have come to resemble that work."[25] Exercise as it is understood in this "recharged batteries" model is a prime example of this process of alienation. While such exercise often begins as fun, it seldom remains so because of the way it is positioned in the structure of daily life. For middle-class women, it is part of the routine of body care that has come to be expected and accepted as part of being a woman, not unlike housework. Exercise is part of what makes us "competitive"—as an employee (good-looking and healthy people are rewarded) and as a person (we rate ourselves vis-à-vis others' bodies). Kohn argues that this competitiveness is central to the fabric of capitalism, and he mourns the transformation of play into work that has marked U.S. society.

This process of alienation through exercise is blatant in women's stress management advice. For instance, one article from *Working Woman,* "The Exercise Edge," claims that exercise is not just an added edge, but a mandatory part of a successful lifestyle. Most successful managers, the article explains, work at least sixty-hour weeks, and

> exercise is one way you can develop the energy to meet that kind of schedule. If, like so many busy women, you think you're too tired to exercise, think again. The reason you're tired may well be your lack of exercise. Aerobic exercise is an energy enhancer because it boosts the level of oxygen in the bloodstream.[26]

In addition, the article continues, exercise can boost creativity, give a woman confidence, help her manage her time better, and teach her how to stick to a routine.[27] In a common tactic, the author appeals to science—another power discourse—to explain why "aerobic exercise is an energy enhancer." She explains in some detail the microbiology of exercise—especially the production of the magical beta-endorphins, the anti-stress hormones that have been touted as a miracle substance by medical popularizers—in order to show how exercise can increase one's ability to handle stress. And, as one of the many medical experts she quotes says, "the ability to handle stress is as important, if not more important than, native managerial ability in rising to the top and functioning effectively once there."[28]

Inherently anticollective, such advice clearly privileges individual success (at any cost) over collective gains and long-term social change. There is no critique here of the fact that working sixty-hour weeks in corporate America is counterproductive to social change, nor is there any mention made of changes in labor laws and regulations. While this may not be surprising, arising as it does from a piece of consumer culture, it is significant that the exercise imperative, and the overall construction of "power" in stress management discourse, is made in the name of feminism and is understood by many women to be a feminist strategy. Like the texts that Susan Bordo describes so eloquently in *Unbearable Weight,* such understandings of women's power reinscribe cultural norms of beauty under the guise of resistance to such norms. Bordo analyzes the post-1987 hardbody Madonna and the exercising bodies in the quasifeminist Reebok "I Believe" ad campaign to show how the link between women and power has been stripped of its feminist politics and coopted by commodity culture in recent years.[29] As Bordo is concerned to point out, "postmodern and other celebrations of 'resistant' elements in these images" efface "the social contexts and consequences of images from popular culture."[30]

To be fair, in some contexts the icon of the powerful exercising woman has positive effects. As Susan Willis asserts, the public presence of women as exercisers, the visible evidence of their strong bodies in spandex, is a symbol of a freedom of movement that was not available even a generation previously. According to Willis and many exercising women, exercise has "positive features" such as "the development of independence and the opportunity for bonding between women."[31] But even Willis cautions that exercise in U.S. culture is also bound up with class and consumer culture—exercise and stress management are the prerogative of and the commodities for the overworked middle classes. In that it participates in maintaining hierarchical class divisions between women, the stress management imperative to exercise for power enables sexism to continue unabated. In Willis's example of 1980s workout videos, she concludes:

> The workout focuses women's positive desires for strength, agility, and the physical affirmation of self and transforms these into competition over style and rivalry for a particular body look and performance.[32]

In the context of stress management, this rivalry can be understood as that between individual women, say for a particular job, but more fundamentally, it is an intense but largely invisible class divide.

Part of the success of late capitalism is due to the fact that stress management discourse provides a medium through which women appear to transcend class, and often race, group identification. They leave behind, of course, class and race consciousness and struggle as well. Working-class women's popular culture discusses stress just as frequently as middle-class women's popular culture, though it rarely mentions the particularities of working-class women's lives. While some working-class women might perceive a difference between themselves and middle-class women in terms of access to some of the accoutrements of middle-class stress management, the guiding force behind stress management ideology is that it appears to link all women by their common enemy, stress. Such a conception of women's collectivity is significantly different from that which second-wave feminism attempted to make real. The point is that feminism itself has become easily commodified, particularly by therapeutic discourses such as those of stress management and exercise, which are meant to help women achieve an individualized form of power in dominant culture.[33] The psychologist McGrath's words return: the ten-minute energy walk is better than talking to a friend. Such advice is a stop-gap measure for gaining power as an individual woman, which is always a limited notion of power. The frame of this advice—the television talk show where therapy is consumerism and competition between women masquerades as mutual aid—provides a social context for this inherently anti-feminist message. Through stress management, women rewrite the "personal is political" slogan of earlier feminism to mean that personal change is equivalent to political involvement, and hence they sever the connection between personal and social change.[34]

At the other end of the continuum of health lies "burnout," which is bound to the notion of "relaxation" in the same ways that "power" and exercise are joined. Essentially, by applying the principles of "adaptation energy" that assert that perspective is more crucial than material reality, relaxation becomes, exactly like exercise, another way to achieve self mastery and power. "Active relaxation gives you ways to make your life your own," writes Janette Scandura in her introduction to Working Woman's April 1988 special section on "body management." The oxymoronic quality of "active relaxation" seems lost on most writers and readers of stress management discourse, as is the disciplining force, to use Foucault's rhetoric, of the term "body management." Like exercise, relaxation functions as work within a woman's daily life. It is part of "body management" and one must do it actively—often with a credit card. In women's magazines, articles about "burnout" are usually accompanied by images of women in repose, engaged in therapies to prevent "burnout." A key part of the service economy, "burnout" sells preventive measures. At the spa, in a bath, getting a massage, these figures are representations not of "burnout" itself but of the pleasure that comes from preventing "burnout." The explosion in the U.S. health spa industry and the proliferation of body care products in shopping malls and catalogues are prime examples of this commodification of relaxation. Far beyond the "Calgon take me away" days, women spend millions of dollars on lotions, bath salts, and other products that claim to relax the body and thus reduce stress.

Images of "burnout" are not as revered as those of "power" because they are not as useful in selling products, but they are nevertheless crucial to women's stress management in that they embody the "other" of the coping woman. In certain instances, the representation of "burnout" can be seen as an attempt to smooth over—and sometimes trivialize—the contradictions of women's lives. This is true of the plethora of cartoon and coffee cup images of stressed women that are circulated within the office gift economy. (The constantly frazzled comic strip character "Cathy" is a prime example.) More important, though, "burnout" is also used in the iconography of women who are more seriously destabilizing to dominant culture—such as the white, middle-class "working mother." Though many mothers have been employed for years—and housework and childrearing go unrecognized for the labor that they are—the post-1970s boom in middle-class women's employment had significant repercussions for stress management discourse. The "working mother" embodies the frightening limit of womanhood—that point at which a woman would become incapable of caring for herself and her children.[35]

One long *Redbook* article from 1983, "More Power to You" by Maggie Strong, describes "working-mother burnout" and points to some of the implications of it:

> Combat soldiers, intensive-care nurses and overburdened executives have long suffered from what has only recently come to be called burnout. The new candidate for this state of depletion is the '80s working mother, who lives under constant stress, who continually caters to the needs of others and who finds herself used up even at the start of the day. It's the nature of the double role. Whether at home or on the job, we give and give. We run through our emotional cash flow and find ourselves in deficit spending.[36]

Again, it is easy to see the class—and often, by extension, racial—implications of this historiography of working mothers. For it is mostly middle and upper class women who are new to paid work in the 1980s. The economic metaphor of the working mother's "emotional cash flow," with burnout meaning "deficit spending," is an apt comparison in that it highlights the political stakes involved in such representations of "burnout." As the following passage from the same article makes clear, the problem of "working mother burnout" is that it makes the woman unable to play her role as mother to the nuclear family:

> the burnout victim is confronted by too many demands too often. But she takes the step into the second stage herself. "Instead of taking a break," says Dr. Walker [Duke University psychiatrist and author of *Everybody's Guide to Emotional Well Being*], "burnout victims eliminate exercise and recreational time in a desperate attempt to meet the demands placed on them."[37]

This may work in the short run, the experts quoted in this article agree, but if such coping strategies continue over a period of time, the result is burnout, the last stage of which is illness. And, if a woman is a "burnout victim" she cannot care for her family properly. Furthermore, since a woman "takes the step into the second stage herself," it is largely her own fault, the result of her inability to live by the principle of stress management, that cause this situation. This underlying conservative approach to childcare, where everything is once again "mom's fault," is at odds with the other constant refrain in women's magazines: that partners need to share childcare responsibilities. This subtly masks a blame-the-victim approach to stress. Like the "pull yourself up by your bootstraps" advice given to many young people born into poverty, this call for the working mother's attitude adjustment epitomizes the shape of capitalism and patriarchy after the second wave of feminism.

Neither exercise, which is meant to increase power, nor relaxation, which is meant to ward off burnout, change the material conditions of women's lives that cause stress. Indeed, for many women they may increase potential stressors, as they always take time and often money too, and they certainly work to maintain the systems of sexual and class inequality that create the conditions for stress. That is precisely why the rhetoric of stress management is one of individual, rather than social change. Exercise and relaxation techniques are not intended to change material conditions. They are intended to change a woman's appraisal of such conditions, to help her cope better, to accept material reality. And they do often succeed in this task. The price of a high standard of individual health for some, however, is the perpetuation of the gulf between women of different classes.

Self-Recovery Feminism

While stress management discourse is an extension of patriarchal and capitalist ideology, some forms of it function in the spaces that, according to Teresa de Lauretis, enable feminist agency: "those other spaces both discursive and social that exist, since feminist practices have (re)constructed them, in the margins . . . of hegemonic discourses and in the interstices of institutions, in counterpractices and new forms of community." [38] The success of women's stress management discourse is partly due to its links to these alternative spaces. The cultural icons and rhetoric of stress management are circulated in those spaces where women

speak to other women. The stress management model is flexible enough to appeal to feminists and nonfeminists alike. Thus, it offers the *possibility* for women to speak with other women—and to supplement, if not replace, the ten minute energy walk with feminist models of talk.

One academic feminist who has explicitly tried to situate her work on women's psychology within an "other space" of feminist subjectivity is bell hooks, whose *Sisters of the Yam: Black Women and Self-Recovery* outlines a program for self-actualization that interweaves mainstream self-help—including stress management discourse—with radical politics. The book begins with a theoretical preface that locates the project within the contexts of African American revolutionary struggle, mainstream self-help, and white feminism, which she views as mostly racist. The introduction explains that the book emerged from a support group for African American women at Yale University. Thereafter, each chapter deals with one theme that hooks believes to be important to African American women's mental and spiritual health—for instance, work, addiction, beauty, and eroticism.

By examining how hooks uses stress management ideology and comparing this to the more obviously corporate and mass media uses of such ideology described earlier, we can see the depth and breadth of stress management in our culture and in women's conceptions of power. *Sisters of the Yam* resonates with many of the same issues of power and agency that other stress management texts try to address, but hooks adopts a manner more appropriate for radical politics.

hooks criticizes the white and heterosexist assumptions of popular women's advice literature.[39] She notes that of the plethora of therapeutic books for women published in the 1980s and 1990s, few of them even mention race, much less provide detailed analyses of how the experience of race in U.S. culture is an important factor in mental health. hooks tries to address this silence with *Sisters of the Yam*. She writes that African American women need to heal themselves so that they can participate fully in social change movements:

> Black female self-recovery, like all black self-recovery, is an expression of a liberatory political practice. . . . Before many of us can effectively sustain engagement in organized resistance struggle, in black liberation movement, we need to undergo a process of self-recovery that can heal individual wounds that may prevent us from functioning fully.[40]

Here she positions *Sisters of the Yam* within the space of agency and resistance and asserts the text's power to politically reshape black female identities. Her argument, which draws on long-standing traditions of feminist consciousness-raising, assumes a new meaning within the contexts of hooks's book, her career, and the larger culture of stress management.

While hooks's inclusion of African American women's experiences represents an important intervention, she does not fundamentally question the ideological implications of the self-help genre and its configurations of "power" and "burnout." For instance, in the chapter "Work Makes Life Sweet," hooks links her recognition of her own "burnout" to a self-help book quiz:

> I remember finding a self-help book that listed twelve symptoms of "burn-out," encouraging readers to go down the list and check those that described their experience. At the end, it said, "If you checked three or more of these boxes, chances are you are probably suffering from burn-out." I found I had checked all twelve! That let me know it was time for a change.[41]

hooks does not critique the concept of "burnout" and its deployment in U.S. culture. Rather, here as elsewhere, she takes what she can use from self-help and stress management discourse. She refers to nearly thirty conventional self-help books as useful in her own experience, often quoting from her favorites, Marsha Sinetar's *Do What You Love, The Money Will Follow* and Su-

san Jeffers's *Feel the Fear and Do It Anyway*. These books influenced hooks's own decision to take an academic leave to work solely on writing and her sister's less-lucrative decision to quit a job that was too stressful.[42]

The conflict between hooks's radical politics and her indebtedness to stress management culture is most visible in the chapter "Knowing Peace: An End to Stress." As the chapter's title hints, hooks's approach differs from Selye's conception of stress in that hooks believes stress can end. Here she rejects the productivist logic of contemporary capitalism. Yet, as her reference to "burnout" makes clear, hooks cannot escape other aspects of stress management ideology. The chapter is concerned with two fundamental themes, knowing when to quit and how to stop worrying. Her examples in this chapter—which spring from her own life, from a fellow sister of the Yam who was a lawyer, and from her sister's life—are about the need to quit stressful jobs that endanger mental health. African American women must conquer their worry about loss of status and economic security and replace it with positive thinking.[43]

The first theme, knowing when to quit, does much to resist the dominant ideology of stress management. African American women do not know and appreciate their own value, according to hooks, which is why they do not take care of themselves. Stress comes when African Americans "can no longer assert meaningful, transformative agency in our lives, when we are doing too much, when we experience an ongoing impending sense of doom."[44] This is a fairly conventional understanding of stress, though hooks takes it in a direction opposed to stress management. She does not advocate the exercise or relaxation strategies designed to ready the subject for the productivity mill, but instead calls for what seems (in theory if not in practice) the much more radical move of resistance. She says that African American women need to learn when to quit.

The second major theme of the chapter is that

African American women worry too much; hooks advises them to replace worry with positive thinking. This arises squarely out of dominant stress management assumption that the subject's attitude and perception—not material reality—are the problem. hooks would in no way deny that racism makes the material realities of African Americans more stressful than those of whites. However, she argues that in order to become mentally healthy, African Americans need to change their thoughts:

> The vast majority of black people, particularly those of us from non-privileged class backgrounds, have developed survival strategies based on imagining the worst and planning how to cope. Since the "worst" rarely happens, there is a sense of relief when we find ourselves able to cope with whatever reality brings and we don't have to confront debilitating disappointment.[45]

By replacing this worry with "positive thinking," hooks asserts, African American women might be able to "change the outcome of events."[46] She cites Rev. Martin Luther King Jr. and Shirley Chisholm as leaders who have used positive thinking for social change, but the real impetus for hooks's understanding of the concept is self-help author Susan Jeffers, whom she quotes at length on the subject.[47] Essentially, she returns to the individualistic approach to women's problems that pervades most self-help advice.

For many women, *Sisters of the Yam* works precisely in the ways that hooks would like it to: as a tool for women's resistance to patriarchy and racism. For instance, Vanessa Northington Gamble, an African American medical doctor, begins her review of the book with her own narrative of depression during her residency. The point of relating this account is to offer personal testimony to hooks's description of African American women's experiences and to illustrate hooks's point that African American women have been partly to blame for silencing their own pain. Long after her depres-

sion, Gamble had wanted to write an account of it to show, she writes, "how it had disrupted my life. How I had to struggle, and occasionally still have to struggle, against it. . . . I also wanted my story to offer hope to those who were still suffering."[48] Gamble did not write or publish this account, however, because an African American female colleague "criticized [her] for 'wanting to put [her] business out in the street.'"[49] Gamble's own description of her experiences with depression and her use of *Sisters of the Yam* as a therapeutic tool is very powerful and convincing. It attests to the need for books like *Sisters of the Yam* and illustrates how the text does work to develop alternative, political subjectivities.

Yet such liberatory uses of *Sisters of the Yam* must be contextualized within the wider self-help and stress management culture. hooks has been known for her "sustained allegiance to her own working-class background,"[50] but her advice on coping with stress buttresses the class division that mainstream stress management discourse helps to inscribe in U.S. culture. Throughout *Sisters of the Yam,* hooks weaves in and out of a class-based analysis, at times pointing to the devastating and stressful effects of poverty, yet elsewhere simply asserting that "poverty itself need not be a condition that promotes nihilism and despair."[51] Keith Byerman, editor of the *African American Review,* calls hooks to task for failing to sustain a class analysis. He argues that *Sisters of the Yam*'s advice is rather unsubtly limited to middle-class professionals such as teachers, lawyers, and business women, "that significant but still not typical group of black women entering the American middle class."[52] In response to hooks's "know when to quit" advice, Byerman writes: "The issue of agency is crucial. How are black women . . . to find the personal and economic resources to even begin to do the kinds of things hooks recommends? . . . For those on welfare or in minimum wage positions such recommendations are irrelevant."[53] To the extent that it does use middle-class women as a starting point, *Sisters of the Yam* participates in the denial of class differences upon which U.S. stress management culture is predicated.[54]

Certainly, conventional self-help is not the only tradition of women's writing on which hooks draws. *Sisters of the Yam* shows how the fiction and autobiography of African American women such as Audre Lorde, Alice Walker, and Paule Marshall can be used therapeutically. hooks believes that such writers have filled the "space of longing" that the feminist movement in general has failed to fill.[55] Moreover, hooks points to the long tradition of mutual aid in African American culture and politics. Nevertheless, she feels compelled to supplement that tradition with the mostly white, mainstream self-help books that she had disparaged a few years earlier as "narratives that suggest we are responsible for male domination."[56] hooks makes this odd coupling of African American writers and mainstream self-help writers because she is angry with "popular" (read "white") feminism. She dismisses "popular feminism" on the second page of her book when she takes Susan Faludi to task for erasing race from the bestselling book *Backlash*. But in doing so, hooks seems to reject almost all non-African American feminism as well.[57] She rarely refers to the non-African American feminist writers who have similarly dealt with self-recovery, despite the fact that the work of women like Nancy Mairs, Maxine Hong Kingston, and others might easily be situated in the same radical but sophisticated consciousness-raising vein as *Sisters of the Yam*.[58] Essentially, hooks rejects "popular feminism" in favor of mainstream women's self-help literature without adequately attending to the rhetorical or political positioning of the latter genre, particularly its use of female experts and feminist language, and without recognizing the extent to which feminist consciousness-raising has been present in women's creative and critical writing.

Part of what is at stake in hooks's relationship to both "popular feminism" and mainstream self-help is the issue of female expertise.[59] I would argue that hooks is not alone, as she seems to think she is, in her attempt to write a politically engaged investigation of women's experiences for a wide audience. Rather, she joins a cacophony of divergent voices about female subjectivity and self-recovery with *Sisters of the Yam*. To best understand hooks's work, we must situate her writing within the wider contexts of feminist writing and mainstream advice literature, and examine her own position as an "expert."[60]

One of the most salient characteristics of the new female experts (those women who do not simply "talk back" to the experts, but are themselves part of the knowledge-production industry) is that their narratives defy the personal-professional split. On this point we can compare hooks to Oprah Winfrey, whose personal experience of depression supplemented—even usurped—her guest expert's mere professional knowledge. For both hooks and Winfrey, movement in and out of various communities has created the framework for representing their personal experiences and professional lives. In an earlier essay "On Self-Recovery," hooks charts her own path from southern black woman to professional academic, and that trajectory is still very much at issue in *Sisters of the Yam,* where she explores her ambivalence about the academic community. hooks contrasts the "segregated Southern black world" where "black folks collectively believed in 'higher powers,' knew that forces stronger than the will and intellect of humankind shaped and determined our existence," with the intellectual world, which offers her little "new community, new kin."[61] Oprah, as well, uses this contrast between past and present in her self construction as "everywoman." She often juxtaposes her "down home" self with her famous self: her personal chef Rosie now makes her a low calorie sweet potato pie. After 1994, she also compares her previous stressed-depressed, overweight self with her new mentally heathy, thin self. She has been on both sides of every situation, which grants her the wisdom to offer advice to millions.

For both hooks and Oprah, this self-positioning substantially influences both their relationship to their audiences and the advice they offer. Ideally, such representations allow both hooks and Oprah access to audiences across class lines. Oprah moves with the rich and famous, but is moved by her audience members' stories of everyday life. hooks asserts her unique ability to translate between the university and the rest of the world. In *Sisters of the Yam,* hooks endeavors to address the African American section of the popular audience—a mass rather than a middle-class academic audience—that it is widely believed Oprah has already garnered. hooks wants to politicize this space, make it into an "other space" that would appeal to women across class divisions and create new feminist communities. Yet in her reliance on conventional self-help and stress management, and the resulting problems with class issues and feminist community, hooks reinscribes the dominant ideology while she attempts to undermine it. It is a testament to the pervasiveness of stress management ideology in U.S. culture that even a radical theorist such as hooks would use its concepts of "burnout" and "power." hooks is just as much a participant in stress management culture as she is a cultural critic of its ideology.

Notes

Many thanks to Patrice Petro for extensive comments on this essay and her unwavering support of my research.

1   The candy bar comparison is a stock feature of advice on how to be energetic. For, as women's prescriptive literature maintains, the instant gratification of food, especially chocolate, lasts only a short while and ultimately leads to fat, thought to be one of the biggest stress-inducers. According to a *Vogue* magazine columnist, "So intertwined are eating and relaxing that many women *replace* rest with food, particularly when they're tired. The classic example is the woman who reaches for a candy bar to curb a mid-afternoon slump when a brisk walk—or even a brief nap—would probably be more energizing" (see "Food for Mood," *Vogue* [October 1988]: 411). Clearly, McGrath's "action strategy" for the "Stressed-Depressed" is in line with the advice voiced in other prescriptive literatures.

2   Wendy Kaminer, *I'm Dysfunctional, You're Dysfunctional: The Recovery Movement and Other Self-Help Fashions* (Reading, MA: Addison-Wesley, 1992), 31.

3   By saying this, I do not mean to prescribe what radicalism would look like in every context. In the case of Oprah, her late 1990s move only to do "positive" shows, which was accompanied by a plunge in ratings, might be indicative of a move toward the limits of white, corporate culture.

4   bell hooks, *Sisters of the Yam: Black Women and Self-Recovery* (Boston: South End Press, 1993).

5   Mimi White, *Tele-Advising: Therapeutic Discourse in American Television* (Chapel Hill: University of North Carolina Press, 1992), 186.

6   Hans Selye, *The Stress of Life* (1956; New York: McGraw-Hill, 1976).

7   These phases take place in the adrenal gland, the pituitary gland, and the stomach, and several hormones are involved in the process.

8   Selye, *The Stress of Life,* 437.

9   Ibid., 182.

10 Ibid., 18–19.

11 Indeed, most of Selye's later writings (he wrote, among scores of scientific reports and books, two autobiographies, several popular articles, and his bestseller *Stress without Distress*) are devoted to expounding and circulating his "code of altruistic egoism," a philosophy of life that asserts the individual's social responsibility to meet their own needs.

12 *Men under Stress* (Philadelphia: Blakiston, 1945), published in May 1945 by Army Air Force psychologists Roy R. Grinker and John P. Spiegel, brought the effects of stress on the male ego to the attention of medical specialists and the lay public. In this book, Grinker and Spiegel explain what it takes to be a member of a World War II aviation combat unit; they do so by detailing the case studies of numerous aviator breakdowns due to the grueling physical and emotional stresses of flying missions. The subtext of *Men under Stress* is the horrifying idea that stress poses a serious threat to many U.S. soldiers, whose masculinities are too fragile to take the pressures of combat.

In the postwar years, a way of framing masculinity through stress arose with the formulation of Type A and B personalities. First described for a lay audience by cardiologists Meyer Friedman and Ray Rosenman, Type A and B behavior quickly came to be thought the most deadly stress-related disorder for men (see *Type A Behavior and Your Heart* [New York: Knopf, 1974]). Barbara Ehrenreich argues that the formation of the Type A and B categories was integral to the postwar shift in the construction of gender roles:

> In the 1950s, medical opinion began to shift from genetic to psychosocial explanations of men's biological frailty [manifested in their shorter life spans relative to women's]: There was sometime wrong with the way men lived, and the diagnosis of what was wrong came increasingly to resemble the popular (at least among men) belief that men "died in the harness," destroyed by the burden of responsibility. The disease which most clearly indicted the breadwinning role . . . was coronary heart disease. (*The Hearts of Men* [New York: Doubleday, 1983], 70)

Thus, stress in the postwar years was part of the burden of masculinity.

13 The most important researcher to theorize psychological stress is Richard Lazarus, whose 1966 book *Psychological Stress and the Coping Process* provided the springboard for a number of studies on psychological stress, including women's stress. Lazarus articulated a more well-grounded theory of threat and coping that could, possibly, be used to argue against the prescriptions to social norms that Selye's theory embraces. However influential Lazarus's work has been in many medical circles, the stress management texts under discussion in this essay, unfortunately, tend to rely almost exclusively on Selye's theory, and not those that came later.

14 See Kenneth Pelletier and Robert Lutz, "Healthy People—Healthy Business: A Critical View of Stress Management Programs in the Workplace," in *Stress and Coping: An Anthology* (New York: Columbia University Press, 1991).

15 Janette Scandura, "Mastering the Art of Mellow: A High Achiever's Guide to Stress," *Working Woman* (April 1988): 121.

16 Schor writes, "If present trends continue, by the end of the century Americans will be spending as much time at their jobs as they did back in the nineteen twenties. The rise of worktime was unexpected. For nearly a hundred years, hours had been declining. When this decline abruptly ended in the late 1940s, it marked the beginning of a new era in worktime. But the change was barely noticed. Equally surprising, but also hardly recognized, has been the deviation from Western Europe" (Juliet B. Schor, *The Overworked American: The Unexpected Decline of Leisure* [New York: Basic Books, 1991], 1).

17 Ibid., 2.

18 The shift from a workday-based to a benefits-based approach to union organizing is reflective of both these conditions, I would argue.

19 Schor, *The Overworked American*, 5.

20 This idea is taken from Anson Rabinbach's wonderful book, *The Human Motor: Energy, Fatigue, and the Origins of Modernity* (Berkeley: University of California Press, 1990), which argues that the turn-of-the-century obsession with productivity was figured in the cultural icon of the human motor, the body as part of a machine.

21 Exact data on the number of women who exercise is hard to compile, as some women participate in more than one form of exercise. According to the *Statistical Abstract of the United States 1995*, 59 percent of adult females participate in an exercise program and 29 percent play sports (U.S. Department of Commerce, 115th ed. [Washington, D.C.: Government Printing Office], 257).

22 "The Aerobic Antidote," *Vogue* (October 1988): 413.

23 Caryl Rivers, "Why Are You a Bundle of Nerves," *Redbook* (March 1986): 97.

24 This raises serious questions about class and divisions between women. For, while a game of tennis is a great stress reliever for many, it is not a possibility for all. Identity politics theory has done much to point out the effects of such omissions in popular culture, and it is integral to my analysis. However, what is even more disturbing than this rather obvious and familiar ignorance of class issues are the underlying implications of the "solutions" to stress, even for middle-class women.

25 Alfie Kohn, *No Contest: The Case Against Competition* (Boston: Houghton-Mifflin, 1992), 82.

26 Mary E. King, "The Exercise Edge," *Working Woman* (March 1991): 115.

27 Ibid., 116.

28 Ibid., 115.

29 Susan Bordo, *Unbearable Weight: Feminism, Western Culture, and the Body* (Berkeley: University of California Press, 1993), 272, 297–300.

30 Ibid., 275.

31 Susan Willis, *A Primer for Daily Life* (New York: Routledge, 1991), 65.

32 Ibid.

33 Barbara Ehrenreich makes this point in her discussion of the "marketplace psychology" of such writers as Helen Gurley Brown and Dr. Joyce Brothers who, she argues, "amplified the youthful voice of a new feminism: It's OK to be angry; it's OK to be a woman; it's OK to be *you*," but this commitment to feminism was superficial and short-lived (*For Her Own Good* [New York: Doubleday, 19xx], 298). Ehrenreich explains that the ideology of this new marketplace psychology was "willing to accept the values of the marketplace as *universal* principles" (299). Gone were the sexual stereotypes about women's passive femininity, but gone as well were the values of community, responsibility, and love that had been a function of that femininity. For Ehrenreich, the key issue is political commitment. Feminism was just one more thing to be subsumed by popular psychology. Consumerism conquered the incipient feminism almost before it got a foothold.

34 Researchers have begun to analyze how people use self-help as a genre, though none have extensively studied stress management advice alone. Steven Starker's *Oracle and the Supermarket: The American Preoccupation with Self-Help Books* (New Brunswick, NJ: Transaction Publishers, 1989) provides a solid history of self-help books. In his research, he found that many self-help readers found self-help books useful, and many psychologists suggested that their patients read them. He concludes that self-help books do not usually harm readers' mental health, but he finds no evidence that they help them either. Wendy Kaminer's 1992 critique of self-help, *I'm Dysfunctional, You're Dysfunctional* argues that

> the self-help tradition has always been covertly authoritarian and conformist, relying as it does on a mystique of expertise, encouraging people to look outside themselves for standardized instructions on how to be, teaching us that different people with different problems can easily be saved by the same techniques. It is anathema to independent thought. (6)

A more forgiving critique can be found in Wendy Simonds, *Women and Self-Help: Reading between the Lines* (New Brunswick, NJ: Rutgers University Press, 1992), which was inspired by Janice Radway's *Reading the Romance*. Simonds does not emphasize stress management advice in her survey of women readers, though she does note that books about stress and anxiety, alongside those on love and relationships and weight loss, are the types of self-help books most often read by women (23). Through her ethnographies of women self-help readers, writers, and editors, Simonds concludes that

> Though self-help readers do feel a sense of commonality with other women through their reading, the genre fails them in that it encourages individually oriented and adaptive endeavors to achieve personal change. . . . Like romance reading, self-help reading can be said to enable women to express dissatisfactions with gendered interactions, while it also represses a definitive challenge to the ways in which the social construction of gender works against women. (48)

35 Though the employed mother is still a threat, recently, this icon has been superseded in political and popular rhetoric by an even more threatening image of "burned out" womanhood, the single "welfare mother," who is usually characterized as a "burned-out" African American teenager.

36 Maggie Strong, "More Power to You," *Redbook* (September 1983): 103.

37 Ibid.

38 Teresa de Lauretis, *Technologies of Gender: Essays on Theory, Film, and Fiction* (Bloomington: Indiana University Press, 1987), 26.

39 I use the term "self-help," following hooks's language, to refer to the entire genre of prescriptive literature of which stress management is a major part.

40 hooks, *Sisters of the Yam*, 14–15.

41 Ibid., 49.

42 Ibid., 50.

43 The similarities between hooks's advice and the plot of Terry McMillan's novel, *How Stella Got Her Groove Back* (New York: Viking, 1996), are astonishing, but unfortunately I do not have the space here to enumerate them or to compare the texts and their critical receptions.

44 hooks, *Sisters of the Yam*, 54.

45 Ibid., 62.

46 Ibid., 64.

47 Ibid.

48 Vanessa Northington Gamble, "The Political Is the Personal," *Women's Review of Books* (October 1993): 12.

49 Ibid.

50 Isaac Julien, "bell hooks," *Artforum* (November 1994): 64.

51 hooks, *Sisters of the Yam*, 12.

52   Keith Byerman, "Review of *Sisters of the Yam: Black Women and Self-Recovery* by bell hooks," *College Literature* 22.2 (1995): 134.

53   Ibid.

54   Byerman's critique goes further than simply the question of inclusiveness. Indeed, he is suspicious of hooks's very conceptualization of self-recovery: Self-recovery as a discursive practice assumes a middle-class audience of individuals operating in a competitive, stressful world with few communal resources. It projects a norm of self-control and self-assertion lost through acceptance of the demands of some Other, which could be family, personal relationship, social status, occupation, or addiction. The self must be returned to some "natural" state of primacy in order for healing to occur.

55   bell hooks, *Talking Back: Thinking Feminist, Thinking Black* (Boston: South End Press, 1989), 33, 34.

56   Ibid., 34.

57   In a vituperative review for the *Village Voice Literary Supplement,* Michele Wallace has argued that in recent years hooks has become more interested in self-promotion and fame than in scholarship or critical analysis. She argues that the white media promotes bell hooks as "the only black feminist that matters" and thus erases the long history of black feminism in America (Michele Wallace, "For Whom the Bell Tolls: Why America Can't Deal with Black Feminist Intellectuals," *Village Voice Literary Supplement* [September 19, 1995]: 20).

58   Elsewhere, hooks has referred to such writers. For instance, in her reflections on the roles and responsibilities of criticism for *Artforum,* she quotes Mairs's refusal to distinguish creative from critical writing (bell hooks, "Critical Reflections," *Artforum* [November 1994]: 65).

59   This is not to say, of course, that her expertise goes unchallenged by many on the right, a fact to which she alludes several times when she mentions the experiences of discrimination that prompted her to write *Sisters of the Yam.* Nor is it to say, as Michele Wallace points out, that hooks stands alone in her black feminism. Indeed, Wallace challenges hooks's self-promotion, arguing that hooks's recent work "is clearly trying to drive a wedge into the current white market for books on race and the recent upsurge in the black market for books on spirituality and self-recovery" ("For Whom the Bell Tolls," 20). Questioning whether she is a "Black feminist or poststructuralist Oprah" ("For Whom the Bell Tolls," cover), Wallace raises one of the fundamental issues about how and why conventional stress management discourse and radical politics are, ultimately, incompatible.

60   hooks has been called a "cultural critic/feminist poohbah" (Lisa Jones, "Rebel without a Pause," *Village Voice Literary Supplement* [October 13, 1992]: 3). She has published many books, and several have sold over 50,000 copies, quite a large number for academic books. According to her editor at South End Press, *Sisters of the Yam* had sold over 35,000 copies by March 1995 and is still in print (Calvin Reid, "Books—and More Books—From bell hooks," *Publisher's Weekly* [March 27, 1995]: 25). Again, it is doing well as an academic book, but with such a small circulation and a $14.00 paperback price tag, it does not compete with trade self-help books for women.

61   hooks, *Sisters of the Yam,* 8, 10.

"HAVE YOU SEEN THIS CHILD?" FROM MILK CARTON TO *MISE-EN-ABÎME*

Eric Freedman

The use of video in criminology by commercial enterprise (the "video fingerprint") has created a rather unique form of virtual community of virtual bodies—a community created through the archiving of images of potential kidnap victims. Confronting the popular understanding of the video/audio ontology, my project focuses on the work of Child Shield, U.S.A., a company that trains people to videotape their own children and stores these tapes in the event that their children are ever missing.

Claiming that video provides a more accurate and detailed "portrait" of a subject than still photography, Child Shield contrasts its services to photo IDs, milk cartons, and commercial mailers. The accuracy and detail ascribed to the video image can be correlated with an assumed mastery of the subject, maintained through particular attention to sound and movement, to unique (vocal) inflections and gestures. Yet what are the correlative shifts in perception and memory as we move from a static to a moving image, and from a filmic medium to an electronic one? On a more general level, what notions are embedded in these tapes themselves and in the minds of those who both create and see a need for their creation? In addition, what can be said of the mapping out of a second imaginary, that of the potential crime suspect, and what are the possible points of intersection between these two imagined communities of victims and victimizers?

Using Raymond Williams's categorical distinction between technological determinism and symptomatic uses of technology, I examine here the motive behind this particular use of video and its relation to similar uses of video framed by the need for surveillance, and justified by traditional concerns for public interest and public safety. As a concluding note, through a consideration of Blockbuster Video's foray into this arena, and its further contribution to this particular "imaginary" of video (naturalizing it within the family—partially effectuated by marketing this service as an ancillary to home video rentals), I also look at the domestication of the apparatus, and the particular ideological residues with which it (and our vision) has been saturated.

> All it takes to endow the possible as such with a reality all its own is to speak, and to say "I am afraid" (even if it is a lie). (From Gilles Deleuze and Félix Guattari, *Qu'est-ce que la philosophie?*)

I want to talk about fear. Or maybe I don't really want to talk about fear, but I am afraid that I actually have nothing to talk about. I analyze texts not to understand them but to understand myself; again it is my fear of not knowing myself rather than an active, positivistic pursuit of knowledge (or perhaps one limited to self-knowledge) that drives me onward.

As one subject of analysis, consider the milk carton, its sides not only acknowledging its contents, but self-reflexively acknowledging its own production (a hierarchy of dairy and distributor); not only does it engage in self-analysis (calories, fat, cholesterol, sodium, carbohydrate, protein—each considered in terms of a percentage of a daily value based on a 2,000 calorie diet), but it does so in a mode that acknowledges "you," the consumer (a form of personal address, considering "your" calorie needs, markedly allowing room for an "other" or "others" requiring more or less than 2,000 calories a day). At the top is an expiration date, and although I am not quite certain what relation this date has to the date of production, I can situate this carton of milk temporally; in fact to make the most of my dollar, I have to consider not only my present patterns of consumption, but those of the near future as well. How much milk will I be drinking in the coming week? Will I be eating at home or traveling? And I guess if I had a family—how much milk will my kids consume by week's end? As I ask myself these questions, I turn the milk carton around to consider its other face—in recent years more often than not, a literal face. Though the back—and I hesitate to call it a back, because I am not really certain which is the front of the milk carton (indeed there are presumably two potential fronts—mirror images of the product label)—of the carton that is the subject of my present analysis bears a printed advertisement for a local radio station, popular memory (if I read it correctly) recalls a time when most of these backsides were populated by missing children.

But the missing children still appear in my home. Now they are stuffed into my mail slot, smiling up at me from the floor of my apartment when I get home in the evening, framed by the all too familiar question: "Have you seen me?" (sometimes "Have you seen us?"). Frontside or backside, the "other" side features advertisements for carpet care services, home shopper merchandise (such as the Baby Boombox), the regional Goodyear dealer, and other local merchants; the majority of these mailers (about eighty of my stack of one hundred) do in fact feature carpet cleaning services, perhaps appropriate since I usually find myself picking these things up off the floor (stooped low enough to do a quick visual inspection of my carpet). I personally have never responded to these product ads; and I've never responded to the ads on the other side, have never seen any of these children, have never phoned the 800 number, though presumably someone has—the statistics at the bottom of the mailer state that one out of every 7 children featured have been recovered. Yet it is unclear what role if any these ads have played in their recovery; and the return on these ads from a marketing standpoint—ninety-nine kids found, how many of these mailers distributed nationally—is incredibly low. But how can one put a value on the life of a child? Well at least I know how much I can get my carpet cleaned for.

> The moment a population is identified as a risk, everything within it tends to become—necessarily becomes—just that. Risk has an allusive, insidious potential existence that renders it simultaneously present and absent, doubtful and suspicious. Assumed to be everywhere, it founds a politics of prevention. The term *prevention* does not indicate simply a practice based on the maxim that an ounce of prevention is worth a pound of cure, but also the assumption that if prevention is necessary it is because danger exists—it exists in a virtual state before being actualized in an offense, injury, or accident. This entails the further assumption that the responsible institutions are guilty if they do not detect the presence, or actuality, of a danger even before it is realized. (From François Ewald, "Two Infinities of Risk")

Someone has failed; some institution or institutions are at fault. Children are missing, and Mailbox Values tells me so. But the crisis has been constructed. In his discussion of epidemics—another form of crisis situation—Michel Foucault points out that the determination that a situation is epidemic is typically a political determination, one made by those with access to statistical data and the authority to make and circulate such determinations.[1] Such an authoritative discourse governs the missing children epidemic, allowing the mobilization of bodies, the dispensation of resources, and the justification of tactics of surveillance and regulation.[2] Children are indeed being victimized, but the labeling of the situation as a crisis has depended upon the collection of (scientific) data—tabulated and interpreted by "experts." Though anecdotes do not provide scientific evidence, they are nonetheless critical to keeping the crisis alive; they give the epidemic a face. Visibility is simultaneously problem and solution. The campaign's visibility has focused public concern on the crisis (in a sense bringing the crisis into existence by making it visible—though the campaign is certainly not responsible for the incidents themselves) and allowed the authoritative discourse to take hold (most significantly the mobilization of dollars and resources); and citizens willingly surveil each other, though apparently in the interest of recovering lost (or stolen) children.

With such an interest in mind, we have come to privilege particular technological devices that aid us in surveillance; moreover, we are asked to accept surveillance as the principal raison d'être of certain new technologies (such as the camcorder). Outside of an immediate use for surveillance, we rely on technology to help us define, identify, and evaluate risks (and preventive mechanisms).[3] Yet in both scenarios (of observation/data collection and evaluation/assessment) the technology is not politically or ideologically neutral.

To expose the ideological underpinning of the technology in relation to its use, I focus on risk, for as François Ewald notes the mere recognition of risk depends on the shared values of the group threatened by it.[4] Though certain objective risks do exist, they are given effective existence only when accepted by a population. We may know a risk exists, but are faced with the problem of having to choose whether or not to accept it.[5] In line with the science of probability, we reconsider risk as a "quantifiable presence."

The odds are one in forty-two that your child could be kidnapped. Every forty seconds, another child becomes lost or missing in America (Vanishing Children's Alliance). Each year kidnapped, lost, missing and runaway children number almost two million (National Center for Missing and Exploited Children). If your child is not found in twenty-four hours, s/he is either dead or out of the area (Durham police officer).

The birth of the missing child problem has resulted from an intriguing combination of social forces that include: (1) media attention given to several spectacular cases, (2) intense political pressure from influential lobbyists, and (3) an outpouring of sympathy and concern from individuals around the country for victims and families.[6] These forces came together in the late 1970s and early 1980s, shaping the missing child problem into an epidemic of national proportions; what catalyzed the crisis were several sensational crimes occurring both decades, some of which were clear cases of kidnapping and homicide, and others which involved child homicide under unclear circumstances. These cases, though all different, were somehow melded together in media reports and institutional surveys (and concomitantly in the popular imagination) as missing children cases. The Adam Walsh story is perhaps the most well-known among the first cases of younger missing children. Adam disappeared on July 27, 1981, while he and his mother were in a shopping center in Hollywood, Florida. Despite a massive search led by law enforcement officials, Adam's body was not found until two weeks later, recovered from a ditch about one hundred miles from the site of his disappearance.

The media have been instrumental in not only informing the general public of the factual events associated with specific cases of missing children, but also in shaping the public's reaction to what would otherwise be individual acts. In the early 1980s, stories of missing children began appearing in popular magazines such as *Ladies' Home Journal, Reader's Digest,* and *Redbook.* Although many of these articles had a semblance of newsworthiness, and proactively and productively positioned personal anecdotes alongside preventative tips and evidentiary statistics, most of the hard crime stats and figures presented were of unclear origin and were grossly exaggerated.[7] Nonetheless, the net effect of this fury of coverage in the popular press was to elevate human interest stories to the status of a social problem. An article in the December 1985 *Parents* magazine claims that "no one knows exactly how many children are abducted by strangers each year, but estimates range from

4,000 to 20,000."[8] These statistics were supported by the National Center for Missing and Exploited Children which, in one of its early publications, estimated the number of stranger kidnappings as high as fifty thousand per year.

Television, as well, acted to stimulate the public's interest in the "problem." The most widely viewed made-for-TV movie on missing children was the docudrama *Adam,* based on the Adam Walsh case, which first aired in October 1983. The program closed with photographs of fifty missing children and made an appeal to viewers to call local authorities if they had information on the whereabouts of the featured children.[9] The program was aired on three separate occasions with different children featured each time, and an estimated fourteen children were located as a result of the broadcasts. *Adam* was closely followed by two other television dramas: *Adam, His Song Continues* and *Missing: Have You Seen This Child?* Missing children were found elsewhere on television during the same decade. *Child Search* was a two-minute spot featuring missing children which aired on NBC affiliates. Magazine shows such as *Good Morning America* and *Hour Magazine* also featured segments on missing children. Coverage spilled over into other television genres, including local news broadcasts, true-crime shows (including *America's Most Wanted* and *Unsolved Mysteries*), and talk shows (such as *Donahue*).[10]

Through print and broadcasting, missing children groups received the media's help in launching a national campaign to publicize the names, faces, and descriptive statistics of missing children. The goals of this campaign were both retrieval and prevention. As groups and individuals in the private sector began to develop strategies to further the campaign, their activities stimulated political and governmental entities to take action as well. On May 22, 1985, Senator Howard Metzenbaum introduced S. 1195. This act authorized the use of Senate mail to disseminate pictures of and information about missing children. A 1992 report from the Senate Committee on Rules and Administration found no evidence that a child had been recovered as a direct result of his or her picture appearing on a piece of Senate mail. "Nevertheless, the National Center [for Missing and Exploited Children] believes that the widespread dissemination of such pictures on Senate mail produces approximately 20 to 30 leads per photo used." Moreover, "the use of Senate and other official mail keeps the general public aware of the problem of missing children."[11]

One of the most visible strategies organized by private companies involved putting the photographs of missing children on a variety of products. The Chicago dairyman Walter Woodbury was the first person to propose the now familiar photographs of missing children on milk cartons, and in January 1985 Hawthorn Melody Farm Dairy in Chicago began running the ads.[12] By the end of the month almost four hundred dairies around the country were participating in this program.[13] The milk carton strategy prompted other industries to place photos of missing children on their products—cereal boxes, grocery bags, egg cartons—and to place displays of these photos in a variety of locations, including supermarkets, airports, post offices, bus stops, on municipal buses and subway cars, and on junk mail coupons.[14]

More recent publicity efforts have been developed with the assistance of several of NCMEC's corporate sponsors. Pizza Hut is the official sponsor of the missing children kiosk program; this national program will place kiosks in airports, bus terminals, shopping malls, and train stations to provide viewers with pictures of missing children, as well as safety tips and information on community action programs. Polaroid's KidCare ID provides free identification and safety information to families nationwide, with the partnership of Chrysler, Kmart, Sears, and Toys 'R' Us. Details of these programs are available on NCMEC's Web site, which also includes a searchable database of missing children.

Concern for missing children created a new growth industry of its own, with a complete line of products related to missing children. For example, in 1989 two medical illustrators at the University of Illinois, Chicago—Scott Barrows and Lewis Sadler—developed a computer simulation system to project changes in physical appearance over time. The computer system, which utilizes scanning and digitized facial mapping, can create a copy of an original photograph and generate new photographs of what a child would look like at any time after his or her disappearance. In its earliest configuration the system was sensitive to the differences between males and females (presumably differences in bone structure) yet did not register racial differences (in mapping facial dimensions the two illustrators relied on data drawn from a study of Caucasian children in Iowa).[15]

Like the computer industry, the videotaping industry has also benefited from the missing children campaign, expanding its applications and markets. During the late 1980s, many private studios began offering videotaping services to parents wanting a visual and audio record to help identify their children (in the event of an "incident").

> When a child turns up missing, the ability to positively identify that child becomes critical. Our unique VIDEOTAPE REGISTRATION SERVICE provides the highest level of identification record available. Unlike a still photograph, a properly prepared Identification Videotape gives the authorities and concerned citizens so much more to go on when searching for a missing child. Familiarity with characteristics of voice, manner, motion, and others can greatly improve the likelihood that someone may remember having seen the child. Such a recollection could be the all-important clue that leads to a reunion of child and family. (From an informational packet published by Child Shield, U.S.A.)

Through its national team of independent registered agents, Child Shield, U.S.A. offers parents the protection of its unique Videotape Registration Service; in toto, the program is based on preventive education first, and effective organized recovery second. Parents shoot their own child's

Identification Videotape using the easy to follow instruction guide (completed tapes must be no longer than five minutes). Safe delivery of the completed videotape to Child Shield headquarters is guaranteed using a protective preaddressed Videotape Mailer; tapes are placed in secure storage, each marked with a unique Identification Code Number known only to the parents. Child Shield maintains a separate facility outside of its office to ensure the safe storage of all videotapes. For security purposes, the location of the videotapes is known only to Child Shield officers, its insurance company, and the chief legal counselor for the law firm which represents Child Shield. In the event a child is missing, the parent contacts Child Shield. The agency duplicates the missing child's tape and proceeds to distribute copies, first to local and state law enforcement agencies, then to neighboring states, and finally to the FBI. Videotapes are also provided to several national missing persons organizations and a variety of nationally syndicated and network television news programs. (Efficient videotape duplication facilities enable Child Shield to produce more than one hundred high-quality videotape copies per hour.) Blockbuster Video and local law enforcement agencies offer similar but not equivalent services, providing videography but not storage and distribution.[16]

The services of Child Shield naturalize the state of emergency that is the central concern of the National Center for Missing and Exploited Children. Danger exists. The milk carton ad—more generally, the print ad—is a precedent to the Child Shield ad—the video ad. The danger exists. The documentation attests to it. The records quantify it. The photographic evidence is there, to be taken at face value. We are not allowed to consider the still photograph as a site of analysis; some would say we cannot afford the "luxury" of such hesitation. The danger that Child Shield seeks to curtail does not appear to us as virtual, but visible; there is proof—the proof of the still photo. Moreover, the photo is part of a national campaign; images

from New York, Michigan, Colorado, Illinois, and Texas resurface in my Florida residence; these are decontextualized images, and on a fundamental level, depict children and families I do not know. My community takes on new dimensions. My family grows. Danger is nowhere and everywhere, as it circulates through the printing presses, along postal routes, and through my front door (not unlike the nowhere and everywhere of the broadcast image). I can see the breach in my nation's security; my home is being invaded.

Please remember that you are shooting a moving videotape with sound, not a silent still photograph. The more your child moves and talks, the easier it may be for someone to identify him/her from viewing the tape. It is best to videotape your child while engaged in a game, hobby, or some other favorite activity. This will allow your child to act more naturally and it can make the camera seem less imposing. Get your child talking by asking open-ended questions about familiar topics like school, pets, toys, hobbies, etc. You may even want to ask your child to sing a song. Many people will remember a voice better than they can remember a face. Shoot a ten second CLOSE UP of your child's face from the front, and another from the side (profile). Also, take close up shots of any identifying marks or scars. (From an informational packet published by Child Shield, U.S.A.)

In *The Burden of Representation*, John Tagg considers the ideological contradiction that was negotiated so that photographic practice could be divided between the domain of art, whose privilege is a function of its lack of power, and the scientific/technical domain, whose power is a function of its renunciation of privilege.[17] The Foucauldian framework that I began to sketch out earlier places the body at the center of a certain political economy; it can be mobilized or made immobile. It can be trained, supervised or forced to emit signs. The body is a social body, readily subjected to control, to tactics of regulation and surveillance. The formation of knowledge is inextricably bound up with power relations ("those who know, can"), and since the late eighteenth century the refinement of such power relations has been made possible through new technologies which provided the means to secure new forms of knowledge.

> From the eighteenth and nineteenth centuries onward, an immense police text came increasingly to cover society by means of a complex documentary organization. But this documentation differed markedly from the traditional methods of judicial or administrative writing. What was registered in it were forms of conduct, attitudes, possibilities, suspicions: a permanent account of individuals' behaviour.[18]

More than a picture of a supposed criminal, the standardized image of criminology (proper pose, lighting, placement) is a portrait of the product of the disciplinary method, of those devices that serve to objectify, divide and study the body, enclosing it in a cellular structure of space: the image-frame.[19] In the case of the mailbox ad there are multiple architectures: the square photo, the rectangular mailer, the postal box. Each of these formal devices in turn forces the image (and figure) to yield up its truth, separates and individuates it, sets apart layers of reality as external to it. When accumulated, such images amount to a new representation of society, though that same society is responsible for the assumptions which underpin this particular use of photography, assumptions concerning "the reality of the photograph and the real 'in' the photograph."[20]

The link between Tagg's history of police photography in the eighteenth and nineteenth centuries, and more contemporary practices of a particular type of "portraiture" is found in the codes that shape these exercises. Though not police photos (photos taken by the police), are the codes of the family photo of the child nonetheless the same (to the extent that they embody a disciplinary method)? Are the codes bound up with the act of taking the photo? Or are these photos different (in process) but made to read the same when taken on as police documents (in distribution and exhibition)? Does the family photo look the same as a mug shot, conceived by similar mechanisms, or is it simply reworked to stand in (after the fact of its production) as a mug shot? Is the family photo a form of surveillance and subjugation, to the extent that children are told what is appropriate behavior in front of the camera? Are the enforced codes (parenting) of early childhood (experiencing how to sit in front of the camera at Sears, and at school) later internalized? Do children learn to willingly surveil themselves?

By referring to the "mechanisms" of production (both physical and psychical), I am not suggesting that all home modes (of video and photography) are handed down to the general public, determined by our governing institutions (to include corporate America). We are not simply told how to shoot, and in any case such directives are not simply written into camera manuals (popular television programs bear some of this responsibility). Rather, there is a form of negotiation at work here. In addition, I do not intend to move away from arguments about medium specificity, and have perhaps oversimplified portraiture, eliding for the moment the mode of production (video or photography) and the distinct features of each mode (grounded in the technology and its prescribed uses). I do want to suggest, however, that certain mechanisms of "fear production" can work to more closely align home modes (in any medium) with a dominant discourse; and the disciplinary method (and any negotiation of that method) can be read not only into the relative subjugation of the actor, but the director as well.

Stylistically, the Advo photo and the mug shot share some basic features. Each is typically a head shot (close-up) with a neutral background; the framing excludes details that would give the subject an identifiable context. Unable to be situated in space and time, the subject becomes a free-floating signifier, and can be inserted into an endless assortment of narratives. The criminal (in the photo) is fixed to the crime scene when recognized by a viewer; his/her identity as a criminal is tied to the act of recognition. The "wanted" poster must be reattached to a story line. Likewise, the images on Advo mailers conjure up a host of suppositions. When there are two photos, one of the child and the other of the person last seen with the child, the latter is presumably the guilty victimizer and the former the innocent victim, though the production codes of each photo are almost identical (and the conditions of the disappearance largely unspecified). It is only the age and physiognomy of the former subject (identified as a child) that positions him or her as the victim. The narrative cues found in the photo boxes are bound only to the text below them, which reveals the date and location of the disappearance (letting us know how long the subjects have been missing, and how recently they can be attached to our popular memory) as well as the possible relationship of the two subjects (assessable if by chance they share the same last name). What most clearly separates the Advo photo from the mug shot is the attitude of the sitter; the photo appropriated for the Advo ad is typically an occasional portrait, with the subject posed accordingly; most are smiling for the camera, and those that aren't appear more guilty (if only because of their sour demeanor).

Child Shield has rules of conduct (for taking the video—what the shot should contain and look like). Here, no longer do the police enforce partic-

ular attitudes, rather they are embraced by the family in a form of self-censorship/self-control that is willful. The law is being taken on by commercial enterprises/services that replicate particular codes and bring them to bear on family life—all the more acceptable because this form of governance does not read as government, and all the more beneficial for companies like Blockbuster, being the good parent, caring for families, preserving family values and developing a kinship base (as family photographer) with their clientele.

As a hard-sell, the service that Child Shield provides to local "re-sellers" is an example of the private sector taking over what is referred to as the government's responsibility—a grassroots action towards preventing/solving child abduction cases. The police are ill-equipped to duplicate videotapes, while missing child agencies are reported to have inferior databases. Yet what information is being recorded in these tapes produced by families throughout the country?

As I pour over the images of missing children on my desk, I see that most of these kids were last seen with family members, perhaps abducted by family members. What I have found is a crisis of representation as well as the representation of a crisis. What I don't see are the statistics on runaways, those missing on a voluntary basis. What I don't see are the statistics on the number of kids abducted by relatives.[21] What I don't see are families in crisis, broken homes. However concrete these images, their circulation yields only an abstraction: a pervasive threat to the American family.

Child Shield offers protection from that threat—a threat whose evidence is the still photo. Child Shield distances its product from the still photo, distances its product from the threat; as prevention it cannot signify the threat though it simultaneously acknowledges its existence—a slippage perhaps made evident only when the videotape is called into action, leaves the security of the vault, is broadcast and circulated. But still, somehow, its presence, its action is a distancing mechanism; the liveness of the image is a testament to the liveness of the missing child. After all, wouldn't the still photo suffice if the child were no longer walking, talking, playing games? The videotaped image will literally not hold still, will not allow itself to simply stand in as a positive ID. Still photographs and some circulated home video images have the awkward status as private records becoming public domain, images taken innocently at parties and gatherings which then become the most recent records of children that at a later date are reported missing. The videotapes produced by Child Shield are created specifically for the public domain (though privately stored); issues of family safety are thus relegated to a separate domain, are recorded on different tapes. One can buy peace of mind. "I have done what I should do to ensure the safety of my child. I have detected the danger before it has been realized. I am free from guilt."

It is no coincidence that both the still photograph and the videotape of the missing child circulate along pre-existing paths of commerce (in the grocery store or on TV). We are faced with yet another system of distribution guided by the economy. Missing children photos follow the flow of milk, that bone-building staple of the American diet found on breakfast tables across the country; while missing children tapes circulate along the pre-existing channels of broadcasting, the medium dictating their form and content (for images must adhere to the production standards that define "broadcast quality").

The production of the tape secures the child; it dispels the threat; anxiety is displaced. The primary concern of those parents registered with Child Shield does not seem to be the possible disappearance of their children, but rather the disappearance or exploitative use of the videotape (thus the need for it to be locked away in secrecy). Yet the concern for the safety of the tape, the need for its privacy, its anonymity, is no longer an issue once the child disappears; called into action, the

tape fulfills its destiny; it becomes public property. What we have are two sites of anxiety—the tape and the child—the latter of which seems, at least on the surface, to be a more appropriate point (or object) of investiture. Yet it is only through a particular commodity fetishism that this duality is realized.[22] While we are disdainful of the need to worry about our children—"the world should be a safer place; child molesters should be locked up"—it is only through a financial investment that the healthy fixation becomes possible. We do not want our children exploited and we do not want their images used for the wrong purposes. Yet when our children disappear, so does the possibility for the misuse of their images (or so we would like to believe), for now the tapes must be removed from the vault, circulated, and seen. What becomes apparent is that the image may either be consumed by no one or everyone—the no one of the vault or the everyone of the public sphere (of television). What is not allowable is the consumption of the image by a few, by individuals who are nevertheless read collectively, who constitute a (deviant) community engaged in private activities—they are deviant if only because of the privacy of their actions (first, because a community is thought to be appropriately a public body; and second, in violation of this premise, "we" as the true and healthy community proper want to, indeed have a right to know—"they" are guilty not because of what they do, but because of their need to do so without our knowing, even if we are unaware that our knowing/our knowledge/our science/our truths govern and make their actions unlawful).[23] Within this imagined community (of victimizers), abductors and molesters are often linked together; the call to action is strengthened by this vision, as sexual abuse is one of the most radical forms of violation. *Parents* magazine warns that "while kidnapping is terrifying to contemplate, sexual molestation is far more common, and most molesters are known to the child and parents."[24] Abduction and (sexual) violation are fused in the 1995 made-for-TV movie *The Face on the Milk Carton* (a Family Channel production based on Caroline B. Cooney's book of the same title and its first sequel). As the two affected families assess blame, the kidnapper herself, variously described as a cult member, a prostitute, and "God knows what else" remains blameless and largely unrepresented in the text. The kidnapper's mother confesses that her daughter fled the cult and turned the abducted child over to her, for "there were rumors that the cult members were doing things to the children."[25] Though not the face of the film's title, the kidnapper too is a missing person; however, unlike Janie (the face on the milk carton), she is inevitably unredeemable (as perhaps dictated by the conventions of the genre); she turns up dead from hepatitis.

Brian Massumi notes in his preface to *The Politics of Everyday Fear,* that "fear is a staple of popular culture and politics."[26] American social space has been saturated by mechanisms of fear production, a process perhaps hastened by the role mass media has come to assume in this country. From a Foucauldian perspective, the materiality of the body is the ultimate object of technologies of fear, and from a meta-critical vantage point it is these technologies that naturalize social boundaries and hierarchies. Moreover, the use of these technologies has itself been naturalized. I share the concern voiced by media activists such as Dee Dee Halleck over the manner in which *a* home mode (of video production) has been sanctified by *America's Funniest Home Videos* (though this mode has been *appropriated* not *created* by the program); participants all too willingly turn their tapes over to the networks, allowing their lived moments to be narrativized by someone else, while the flow of this narrative is itself determined by product placement.[27] Yet I am more concerned with home modes that more directly simulate control through surveillance and separation, in which we scrutinize ourselves and our neighbors without thinking about a laugh track, and in

which the lived moment is taped only to provide a form of evidence. In the worst scenario, the tape is a substitute for action or contemplation. It provides evidence but not insight. It is a sign that only someone else can decipher.

Fear and the public sphere are illusive (and intimately bound to one another); and as the statistics on missing children suggest, fear is not simply outside the home, but down the hallway. Felt though not measured, our fears remain more virtual than empirical; and though it is the very (virtual) nature of fear and of the public sphere that drives us toward empiricism, what we may finally discover is that what we fear most is lying beside us.

Notes

1 Michel Foucault, *The Birth of the Clinic: An Archaeology of Medical Perception,* trans. A. M. Sheridan Smith (New York: Vintage Books, 1973), 23.

2 Ibid., 25.

3 François Ewald, "Two Infinities of Risk," in *The Politics of Everyday Fear,* ed. Brian Massumi (Minneapolis: University of Minnesota Press, 1993), 224.

4 Ibid., 225.

5 Ibid., 224–225.

6 Martin L. Forst and Martha-Elin Blomquist, *Missing Children: Rhetoric and Reality* (New York: Lexington Books, 1991), 55.

7 Ibid., 62–63.

8 Gay Norton Edelman, "Kids and Kidnapping," *Parents* 60, no. 12 (Dec. 1985): 81. In the same article Dr. Lawrence Balter (a child psychologist) reminds us that "a little fear is a good thing. Without it we wouldn't have caution." And Dr. Katherine Yost (a clinical therapist) suggests "children are naturally prone to fear because they're little and powerless." Fear is unproblematically naturalized in clinical discourse.

9 Forst and Blomquist, *Missing Children,* 65–66.

10 The same subject—missing children—was fodder for a number of distinct television genres (each with its own conventions), some more grounded in fiction than others; this slippage invites further study.

11 Senate Report No. 102–303, Committee on Rules and Administration, *Printing Pictures of Missing Children on Senate Mail,* 25 June 1992. Appendix D of the report in-

cludes an attachment listing the names of 190 missing children recovered through pictures. The word "pictures" refers to a variety of media, including posters, direct mail postcards, and both local (news) and national television programs. The attachment indicates that each of the program types I have discussed (docudrama, news, magazine, true-crime, and talk) was instrumental in the recovery of at least one missing child.

12 "Milk-Carton Hunt for Lost Children," *U.S. News and World Report* 98, no. 5 (11 Feb. 1985): 12.

13 Ironically, the first beneficiary of the milk carton program was a thirteen-year-old runaway (Doria Yarbrough), not an abducted child. Yarbrough's case was perhaps the inspiration for Caroline B. Cooney's book (for young adult readers), *The Face on the Milk Carton,* which was followed by two sequels: *Whatever Happened to Janie?* and *The Voice on the Radio.*

14 Advo, Inc. has been working with the National Center for Missing and Exploited Children since 1985. Its direct mail fliers are sent to sixty million households on a weekly basis. Each flier contains a fixed-inventory postage mark, the cost of which is offset by the advertisement on the reverse of the NCMEC "ad." Advo's shared mail advertising program, previously distributed under the Mailbox Values brand, was repackaged as Shop Wise in January 2000.

15 Geoffrey Cowley and Karen Springen, "Faces from the Future," *Newsweek* 113, no. 7 (13 Feb. 1989): 62. In reference to this new technology and it beneficiaries, Barrows states, "This opens the files again. They can be considered alive again." More recently, Sony, IBM, and CompuAge have donated age-enhancing technology to NCMEC. The initiative is supported by the Special Projects Unit of the Federal Bureau of Investigation and the Forensic Services Division of the U.S. Secret Service through their technical support of NCMEC's video laboratory. Current age progression techniques rely in part on data from heredity, using the photographs of parents and siblings and merging these gathered facial features with those of the missing child. In this act of convergence, it is possible that victim and victimizer may literally be mapped onto one another (if the case is one of family abduction), in an all too literal act of bodily co-optation.

16 Blockbuster Video's service, sponsored by NCMEC (and, in 1996, Marvel Comics), is registered as Kidprint; the Kidprint Identification Video, unlike the Child Shield video, is offered at no cost to parents (though the fees charged by Child Shield seem to be justified by the more-extended offerings of the contract—access to duplication and distribution).

17 John Tagg, *The Burden of Representation: Essays on Photographies and Histories* (Minneapolis: University of Minnesota Press, 1988), 67.

18 Ibid., 74.

19 Ibid., 76.

20 Ibid., 76.

21 In the 1984 Missing Children's Act, Congress mandated that the Office of Juvenile Justice and Delinquency Prevention conduct national incidence studies to determine various statistics, including the number of juvenile "victims of abduction by strangers" and the number of "parental kidnappings." While the act provided a statutory definition of "missing children," the expression became a catchall in the public mind. NCMEC now differentiates between: (1) attempted abductions of children by nonfamily members, (2) abductions by nonfamily members reported to police, (3) abductions by nonfamily members where the children were gone for long periods of time or were murdered, (4) children abducted by family members, (5) children who ran away, (6) children who were thrown away, and (7) children who were lost, injured, or otherwise missing. In May 1990 the U.S. Department of Justice released the following numbers (for the year 1988): (1) 450,700 children who ran away, (2) 354,000 children abducted by family members, (3) 114,600 attempted nonfamily abductions, (4) 4,600 nonfamily abductions, (5) 300 nonfamily abductions resulting in long period absence or murder. What these statistics make clear is that the number of children abducted by family members far exceeds the number abducted by nonfamily members (three times as many children were abducted by family members than by nonfamily members), while the number of runaways exceeds both family and nonfamily abductions. Indeed, there seems to be a significant (though only vaguely identified) threat looming inside the family circle.

22 This commodity fetishism is all too readily assessable given the abundance of corporate sponsors that support NCMEC's programs, all of whom would agree that their own products are a more desirable point of investiture (a luxury we could all enjoy if only the world were a better place).

23 The inappropriate consumption of the child's image is a risk that NCMEC is willing to take in posting photos on

the Internet. In any case, these photos all conform to a certain production code (a prescribed form and content—what is to be contained within the box of the photo and what must be excluded) that perhaps limits the possibility of an incorrect reading.

24 Edelman, "Kids and Kidnapping," 83. In the same sidebar, Edelman also gives the assailant a voice: "Abductors and molesters often play on a child's natural desire to help, by asking for directions or making up stories such as, 'I lost my dog and I need your help to find him.' . . . Another kidnapper's lure is to say, 'Your mommy is hurt and needs you.'"

25 The mother assumed the child was her natural granddaughter; she was not aware that her daughter had actually kidnapped a child and claimed her as her own.

26 Brian Massumi, "Preface," in *The Politics of Everyday Fear,* ed. Massumi, vii.

27 See, for instance: Dee Dee Halleck, "Towards a Popular Electronic Sphere, or Options for Authentic Media Expression beyond *America's Funniest Home Videos,*" in *A Tool, A Weapon, A Witness: The New Video News Crews,* ed. Mindy Faber (Chicago: Randolph Street Gallery, 1990).

Introducing Horror

Charles E. Weigl

So that, thus it is that natural men are held in the hand of God, over the pit of hell . . . neither is God in the least bound by any promise to hold them up one moment . . . there are no means within reach that can be any security to them. In short, they have no refuge, nothing to take hold of; all that preserves them every moment is the mere arbitrary will and uncovenanted, unobliged forbearance of an incensed God.

—JONATHAN EDWARDS

Nor is it an accident that the horror story ends so often with an O. Henry twist that leads straight down a mine shaft. When we turn to the creepy movie or the crawly book, we are not wearing our "Everything works out for the best" hats. We're waiting to be told what we so often suspect—that everything is turning to shit.

—STEPHEN KING

What is horror? According to the Oxford English Dictionary, *it is "a painful emotion compounded of loathing and fear; a shuddering with terror and repugnance." It is a hybrid feeling, a fusion of fear and revulsion. And this fusion takes place on the surface of the body: "'Tis taken for a shivering and trembling of the Skin over the whole Body." Hence the word's origins in the Latin,* horrere, *to bristle.*

In The Philosophy of Horror, *Noel Carroll quite reasonably defines the horror genre as that which evokes an emotional response of fear and revulsion. However, he immediately goes on to distinguish that response from the emotions we feel when confronted by real horrors in the world around us. For Carroll, "natural horror" is an emotional response to actual monstrosities, such as war, murder, or ecological destruction. "Art-horror," on the other hand, is a response evoked by visual or textual representations— a product, in short, of fictions.*[1]

A SUDDEN, WEIGHTLESS descent. He jerks upright, nearly knocking his laptop from its perch on his knees. His gasp is echoed throughout the plane as a hundred men and women hastily measure the 30,000 feet between themselves and the ground. Cocktails spill over glass rims, puddling in fold-out trays. Somewhere behind him, a woman's scream is abruptly cut off as if she, or someone else, had slapped a hand over her mouth.

Then, just as suddenly, it is over. The 747 rediscovers whatever keeps 747s aloft and his internal organs slosh indelicately into their original positions. The plane levels off with groans and shudders that conjure images of buckling metal and loosening bolts. He pushes his glasses to the tip of his nose and peers over their wire frames. Outside the tiny window to his left, a pale, gray wing lay on the darkness, immobile and apparently intact. Two red lights blink indifferently at its outermost tip.

The smell of whiskey and a voice almost in his ear: "Looking for gremlins?"

Startled for a second time, he turns to face a wiry young man in a loose-fitting black t-shirt leaning over from the next seat. Unkempt blonde hair hangs around a sallow face that still holds its smirking question. He responds, flustered, "Uh, no, I hadn't considered that."

His companion raises a tiny bottle of Jack Daniels to his chapped lips and empties it without seeming to swallow. Above the word "MEGA-DEATH" in gothic letters, a skull grins from his bicep. "You seen that *Twilight Zone*, right? The one with whassisname . . . the guy from *Star Trek*, Captain Kirk?"

"William Shatner," he answers automatically.

"Yeah, him. The show where he's on this plane and he keeps looking out the window and seeing this ugly gremlin fucking with the engine, but everyone thinks he's crazy . . ."

"'Nightmare at 20,000 Feet.'"

"Huh?"

"That's the title of the episode: 'Nightmare at 20,000 Feet.'"

"I didn't know those things *had* titles. But, whatever it was called, it scared the hell outta me when I was a kid." A grin splits the gaunt face, making it seem, in the wan light of the overhead lamp, like a poor imitation of the tattoo. "I still think about it every time I get on a plane."

The plane shudders again, rises slightly, then dips. With a soft electronic *ping*, the FASTEN SEAT-BELT sign lights up. Other cabin lights flicker and he resists the urge to look out his window. Instead, he focuses on the back of the seat in front of him, the pleated pocket that holds *America in Flight*, the airline magazine, as well as an air-sickness bag and a laminated *Passenger Safety Card*. The card pokes from the top of the pocket, revealing two frames of its colorful apocalypse. In one, an expressionless mother reaches to place an oxygen mask over her child's face. The little boy is smiling. In the other, mother and child assume the crash position: arms folded, heads to knees. Serene supplicants to the dark god of Descent.

The plane lurches. His companion laughs and slaps the armrests as if he were on an amusement park ride. He leans his forehead against the scratched plexiglass window, gazing into the immeasurable, moonless night. The plane tilts sharply to the left, but the darkness doesn't move. Somewhere behind him a serving cart topples and he thinks, *I'm going home.*

Nine years old I was scrubbing floors and I ain't dead yet.

Who else was gonna do it? My mother was in that wheelchair for thirty-five years with her arthritis. The pain got so bad sometimes, she'd just sit there and cry all day long. The doctor finally took pity on her, gave her a shot with gold in it. Tiny flakes of gold. The only thing that ever stopped the pain she said. She said you couldn't imagine how good it felt—that gold inside you going straight to the pain.

We couldn't afford to keep something like that up, though, not with all those mouths to

feed. Things were bad enough already and my mother knew it. Never asked for another shot, but she remembered the one she got. A world of good she said. She kept saying it right up to the day she died.

HE STANDS IN THE kitchen doorway watching his grandmother push a mop back and forth across the spotless, worn linoleum. Groggy with lack of sleep after his aptly named "red-eye" flight, a mug of black coffee in his hand, he listens to the flow of words, knowing it will continue whether he stands there or not.

He moves into the small living room, dim with the shades still drawn, and sits in an old recliner. He leans forward, elbows on the patched armrests, unwilling to sink into the threadbare hollows and grooves left by his grandfather. The shape of a dead man. Death and madness. Home.

And pain. And gold. The abundance of one, the endless search for the other. Longitude and latitude on the map of this family. His family.

He closes his eyes and listens to the sound of ticking clocks. There are three of them in this room, all set to different times. He trusts only the one set by his own watch; the watch he carries in his pocket, brought here from Outside. The watch that measures the distance between him and his own past. The watch that proves he knows what time it is.

Carroll's distinction between natural horror and art-horror (which is essentially a distinction between truth and fiction) is the first of many lines he draws in the course of his study. These lines are consistent with the nature of his project: a functionalist philosophy of mind in the tradition of Western analytic philosophy.

In terms of the emotion itself, Carroll makes a clear division between horror's physical and cognitive dimensions, arguing that shudders and screams are secondary reactions caused by the evaluations readers/viewers make about monstrous fictional beings. He also erects categorical boundaries within the

process of the reading or viewing experience itself. The most resolute of these is between fictional characters and real audiences, each of whom react to objects of fear and revulsion with different "ontological statuses": characters confront (fictional) realities while audiences confront (real) fictions. Related to this is Carroll's ongoing attempt to, as he says, "vaporize" the paradox between thought and belief, the paradox of "how anyone can be frightened by what they know does not exist."[2]

And here the reader might hesitate. Carroll's study—in effect a meticulous exercise in the identification and resolution of a series of logical paradoxes within and around a popular genre of film and fiction—is well-suited to the needs of a philosophy lecture. But what relation or relevance does it have to the genre it seeks to explain? Certainly, to any horror fan, it would seem like something had been lost or, more likely, lopped off in the translation.

In the encounter between text and critic, Carroll assumes that he is the only one producing theory. He assumes that the object of his inquiry does not contain an implicit or, quite often, explicit theorization of both the world and its place in that world. Such assumptions are hard to sustain when considering a genre like horror. Not only is horror utterly self-referential, but it also asks many of the same questions Carroll himself asks. Horror repeatedly explores the relationship between thought and belief, truth and fiction. It investigates (rather than simply assumes) the configuration of "that which we know does not exist." And, in so doing, it produces a body of knowledge that destabilizes the very methodology that Carroll employs.

HE WAKES BEFORE dawn to an argument. In the kitchen, his grandmother remonstrates with two small children who refuse to eat their breakfast:

"What's the matter with you? You better eat whatever I put in front of you. And drink your coffee. I can't be making coffee just to pour it out. You're gonna get me in trouble. They keep asking me why I go through coffee so fast."

He rises slowly, pulls on a pair of pants and trudges toward the kitchen. The children again. They are bad children. They hide beneath the furniture, smoke cigarettes in the closets. They are finicky eaters. Sometimes, late at night, they lock her out of the bathroom, giggling behind the closed door, refusing to let her in until she begs and pleads.

In the kitchen, his grandmother stands with her back to him, hands on the hips of her polyester slacks, frail shoulders hunched in exasperation. Stepping to one side, he looks at the table: two bowls of Corn Flakes, two cups of coffee, two empty chairs.

This ritual never fails to unnerve him. He faces it every day wondering if this is the morning he will wake to find those chairs inhabited by pale children with sinister smiles and dirty fingernails.

It is not. He tries to control his voice when he speaks, not wanting to startle her, to wrench her too abruptly from one world to another. "Morning, Grandma," he says, then adds, a bit more forcefully, as he heads down the hall to the bathroom, "There's no one here but you and me."

They're calling it senility, but I still say it's a bad dream. Like someone took a key and opened the top of my head.

Honey,

Well, I'm here. In more ways than one. Frozen into this tiny apartment by two terrible snow storms in the last four days. More predicted, of course. The sky is low, solid and gray; the same flat inexorability from dawn to dusk.

My grandmother's condition is pretty much as I feared. Maybe a little worse. What else could I expect? It's been a year since I've spent this much time with her, a year since my grandfather's funeral, since she woke to find herself sharing her bed with a stiffening corpse. A year since she began her descent into hallucination and paranoia.

I thought that my aunt and uncle had made a mistake when they moved her into the apartment

above them, dragging her from familiar surroundings. But they were right: she can't function on her own. They deserve more than a month's vacation.

Before I go to bed, I lock the doors from the inside to keep her from walking "Hannah" or "Lulu" home. I hide the key and sleep fitfully on the sofabed, one ear open for rattling doorknobs, the howl of a nightmare, or the clanging pots of a 3:00 A.M. dinner party. Otherwise, my job is merely to give her a pill every evening, to make sure she eats three meals a day, and to try convincing her that the things she sees are not real. Failing that, I protect her from the intruders who creep from closets or slink down the attic stairs. None of which is beyond my capability, however upsetting, and I think I can manage to survive this month with my sanity intact.

Predictably, my writing—or, as my grandmother insists, my "homework"—has slowed to a trickle. I barely produce a paragraph per day and what I do come up with is written in a language that seems less and less substantial amidst these ghosts and ticking clocks. I'm hoping that this is temporary, just a matter of getting adjusted, but I'm not sure how well "Cultural Studies" can hold up against the flood of memories and emotions unleashed by coming home.

Is this home? No, home is with you and I count the days till I get there.

Yours,

HE ESCAPES HIS responsibilities by going to the empty apartment downstairs. Every morning, he spends a few hours in front of his computer trying to gather his increasingly disordered thoughts. But even this relative privacy offers little reprieve. Downstairs has its own memories, wraiths that flicker in the corners of the room as his grandmother's incessant, now muted, monologue drips from the ceiling. There is one memory in particular, one so oppressive as to crowd out any pleasant reminiscence he might have. The rooms that surround him, stark and surreal in the morning light, are the same rooms he inhabited as a child in the hours immediately following his father's death.

Twenty years ago he sat in this same chair, numb and terrified, staring into a mug of hot cocoa and listening to the unfamiliar sound of weeping adults. The room off the kitchen, currently an office, had been his cousin Timmy's bedroom, and he can almost see the small boy now, kneeling before a plastic racetrack, his back to the door and the tableau of a horror he is too young to understand, watching the electric cars speed around and around . . .

He shakes his head in an attempt to clear it. Memories and personal pain: these have no place on his LCD screen. The hum of the computer mixes with the muffled drone of his grandmother's voice, and he tries to concentrate on the task at hand: the introduction to a series of essays on horror film and fiction. He lights a cigarette and hunches over the keyboard, shoulders braced as if for a blow. He writes.

But what is the theory of horror and how does one evaluate it? To answer that question we must assume that horror speaks and does not simply lie mute upon our well-lit dissection table. Second, we must be willing to enter horror rather than merely study it, to abandon the standard protocol of detached and masterful criticism. As even Carroll admits, horror operates by blurring cultural categories. How could we hope to understand the genre by keeping those same categories intact? How can we judiciously interpret a genre for which, in tale after tale, the person (usually a professor or scientist) who insists that "there's nothing to be afraid of" or "there must be a reasonable explanation for all this" is the one most likely to have his head ripped off in the next scene?

HIS GRANDMOTHER SHOUTS downstairs to let him know that lunch will be ready in half an hour. She calls him by his father's name.

He looks at the screen, frowning as if words have appeared on it in a foreign language. *Horror speaks? Enter horror?* He watches as meaning seeps from his words. Blood down a shower drain. Above him his grandmother flushes the toilet and shuffles from the bathroom, muttering angrily. He can't hear what she is saying. He can't remember where his words were supposed to lead. He stubs out his cigarette and rests his fingers lightly on the delete key. He pauses and then switches files. He writes:

Massive Coronary Thrombosis. They were for me three words of dark magic, conjuring images of my father's heart exploding like a bomb in his chest as he sat behind the wheel of his 1969 Rambler. A windshield splattered with blood. A traffic light that shifts from red to green as his car rolls toward the curb, ponderous and unmanned, stopping a few feet from the gates of the cemetery where he would soon be buried.

My uncle and I waited at that same traffic light two hours later, rain beating against the roof of his Camaro. We were driving from the church youth group meeting I had been attending to his home, where friends and relatives had gathered to share the shock. I remember looking at the scene of the event, amazed at how innocent it seemed. Yet there was something suspect about its very innocence. The whole intersection, and the world that spread out from it like a stain, seemed contrived. A major piece had been ripped from reality, but everything shimmered, straining to look exactly as it had before.

What finally gave it away was the people on the street. There were far too many of them out on such a stormy October night. The rain came down in torrents and, still, they lined the sidewalks as if for a parade, as if they had a reason for being there. They moved restlessly to and fro, collars up, heads down, as if they had no idea what had happened.

But they knew. I realized this as I watched them through the passenger-side window, my face averted from my silently crying uncle. I studied them through rivulets of rain, their faces warping and dividing. I noticed how deliberate their indifference seemed. They were too nonchalant. They were bending closer and closer to the ground, wrapping their coats and their knowledge more tightly around themselves.

Of course they knew. And my discovery of their cloaked-but-bulging truth was causing them to mutate before my eyes, to become feral and dwarfish. The streets were filled with these misshapen creatures, deformed by the effort of their artifice, limping busily and secretly gleeful alongside our car. I began to notice an occasional furtive glance, a face rough and unfinished in the glow of a streetlight. Then, as we waited for that traffic light to change, one young-old thing, its face melting inside the hood of its ratty sweatshirt, looked directly at me and smiled.

I don't remember the rest of the trip, only our arrival, the way the house seemed threatening and alien as we approached, carved from the darkness surrounding it by a sharp, angry blade. I remember the women silhouetted in the doorway murmuring among themselves in a language I had never heard before, the way I was crushed in one desperate embrace after another, the way "comfort" ceased to have any meaning now that the world had revealed its terrible face. Red-eyed, drunk adults reeled around me, some wailing demons, others numb and dead, all looking more like monsters than the family and friends I thought I had known. And, through the smoke and babble, the stinging fog of alcohol and anguish, I watched reality transform around me, like a body with its skin removed, like the nightmares everyone said would never hurt me.

I don't know who he is, but he comes in here everyday. At three-thirty on the nose, right in the middle of General Hospital. He sits in your grandfather's chair. He won't say anything, just sits there smiling with his arms folded. I tell him to go away. I tell him I gave them his name down at the precinct, but he keeps on smiling. He knows I don't know his name. There's nothing I can do about it.

THE RITUAL OF LUNCH: two bowls of Campbell's Chicken Soup, a platter of cold cuts, a loaf of Wonder Bread, a quart of Darilee milk. They sit at one corner of the aluminum and formica table, heads nearly touching as they lean over their

bowls. The other end is taken up by the black-and-white television his grandmother turns on at noon every day, just as they sit down to eat. CBS Midday News with lunch, Eyewitness News with dinner and, filling the spaces in between, News Radio 88: the brutal soundtrack of life in his grandmother's apartment.

"I've been here at three-thirty every day," he says, speaking loudly enough to be heard over a commercial for *Promise*, the dish-washing liquid that cuts right through grease. "Why don't I ever see this guy?"

She tells him that the stranger knows how to sit in a way that makes him hard to see.

"You gotta look."

He raises his eyebrows. "Alright, I'll be sure to do that today." The commercial ends and the news begins.

MORE BLOODSHED TODAY IN FORMER YUGOSLAVIA AS THE BOSNIAN/SERB CEASE-FIRE AGREEMENT IS VIOLATED FOR THE THIRD TIME IN AS MANY DAYS. A hand-held camera pans shakily across a recently bombed marketplace. Bodies strewn among the shattered stalls. A leg twitches and the camera pauses, then zooms like a descending hawk. AS THE DEATH TOLL MOUNTS . . . Cut to a woman, covered in blood, screaming, lifted into an ambulance. The sound of heavy artillery in the hills.

ALSO TODAY, A TRAGEDY CLOSER TO HOME: AN ELEVEN-YEAR-OLD BOY ON HIS WAY TO SCHOOL WAS BEATEN, RAPED, AND SEXUALLY MUTILATED IN A PLAYGROUND IN BROOKLYN. RON DIAZ HAS THE STORY. Medium shot of Ron Diaz, breath steaming from the hood of his heavy parka, strategically positioned in front of the playground's swingset. LITTLE JIMMY WILLIAMS DID NOT SHOW UP FOR ST. SEBASTIAN JUNIOR HIGH'S SCIENCE FAIR TODAY, WHERE HE PLANNED TO EXHIBIT HIS MODEL OF THE SOLAR SYSTEM. AT TEN O'CLOCK THIS MORNING, A PARKS DEPARTMENT EMPLOYEE FOUND JIMMY'S RAVAGED BODY IN A DUMPSTER NEAR THE ENTRANCE TO THIS PLAYGROUND IN BEN-

SONHURST. Cut to a haggard middle-aged man standing next to a green Parks Department van. "I KEPT FINDING THESE STYROFOAM BALLS ON THE GROUND. THEY WERE PAINTED LIKE LITTLE PLANETS. I WENT TO THROW THEM OUT AND . . .THAT'S WHEN I FOUND . . . THE BODY."

He turns to watch his grandmother, her head shaking as the horror unfolds on their lunch table. It is amazing, he thinks, that she can still be shocked. She has performed this call and response of atrocity and anxiety for as long as he can remember.

"What's this world coming to? Can't even walk down the street without getting shot or stabbed. They'll even come right into your house."

It seems that as she gets older, rather than becoming inured, she is affected more and more personally by the news. Things that once remained at a relatively safe distance are now jiggling the doorknob and prying up the windows. The man who visits at three-thirty. The two women in green dresses who stare up at her window from the street. The bad children.

He stands up and carries his dirty dishes to the sink, lights the flame under the tea kettle. As the water heats, he moves across the room to stand in front of the window. Outside, more snow falls on an already suffocating world. The third major snowfall of the month. Weather that keeps them both indoors: she because she cannot negotiate the drifts and icy patches, he because he is afraid to leave her alone.

"If this keeps up much longer, we're gonna be buried."

He doesn't answer, not completely sure whether she's talking about the carnage on the television or the snow outside. A lace curtain twitches in a window across the street, and he catches a glimpse of a white-haired head before it recedes into darkness. A lone figure struggles through the frozen wasteland, head bent against the wind, a plastic shopping bag in each hand. Snow drifts have made it impossible to distinguish the street from the sidewalk. As he watches, the figure slips, loses its balance and goes down onto one knee. It remains in that position long enough for snow to begin piling on its shoulders.

He wonders if his grandmother's is the more reasonable response. Her inability to distance herself from mass-mediated images of violence and cruelty is also her inability to let the events they describe pass unacknowledged, unmourned. It's almost funny. *He* is the one who was raised on TV, a member of the allegedly postmodern generation that has lost the ability to distinguish between symbol and reality. You'd expect him to be far more upset by the news, to read it as *real*. Yet the opposite seems to be true. He apparently finds it more difficult to see the human beings behind the images. To feel the pain of the bleeding woman. To understand the vacuum left behind when a boy is viciously subtracted from this world. Which is the greater madness: to be wounded by the news or to ignore it? To see what everyone claims isn't there, or to fail to see what so obviously is?

Outside, the sky darkens as if the storm clouds, which were already blocking the sun, have suddenly grown more dense. He removes his glasses and rubs his eyes as the wind rises to a scream and television children sing a happy song about the breakfast cereal that is both good and good for them. The cereal is called Life.

"You gonna go out there and shovel the walk again? The paperboy'll be coming soon. Don't want him to slip on the ice and sue us. They're all just waiting for the chance, y'know. Them and the lawyers."

On cue, the paperboy appears down the block, a black speck against endless white. He turns off the tea kettle and hurries down the hall for his coat.

Because we remember pain and the menace of death more vividly than pleasure, and because our feelings toward the beneficent aspects of the unknown have from the first been captured and formalized by conventional religious rituals, it has fallen to the lot of the darker and more maleficent side of cosmic mystery to figure chiefly in our popular supernatural folklore.[3]

Despite its stylistic idiosyncracies, H. P. Lovecraft's 1927 Supernatural Horror in Literature *still offers a useful view of the horror genre. One of its more awkward attributes—namely, the pompous tone that is so indicative of Lovecraft's extravagant elitism—is especially telling. Lovecraft was a man of contradictions. A pulp writer who scorned most of the pulp magazines he wrote for, he would tear the offensively lurid covers off volumes that contained his own luridly excessive prose. Yet he also believed that such magazines provided one of the last refuges from which thinkers "of the requisite sensitiveness" could refuse "calls for a didactic literature to 'uplift' the reader toward a suitable degree of smirking optimism."*[4] *As he writes: "Relatively few are free enough from the spell of the daily routine to respond to rappings from outside."*[5]

Horror literature, which is for Carroll (the critic) a realm of that-which-we-know-does-not-exist, is for Lovecraft (the practitioner) a place where spells are lifted and senses are heightened. But those spells are not lifted to "uplift" and vision is improved only so that we might gaze into a previously unadmitted, seething darkness. The best of the genre, as he puts it, excites in the reader "a profound sense of dread, and of contact with unknown spheres and powers; a subtle attitude of awed listening, as if for the beating of black wings or the scratching of outside shapes and entities on the known universe's utmost rim."[6]

What Lovecraft gives us is a theory of knowledge. It is not, admittedly, a very precise epistemology, but, since precision is not what Lovecraft is after, it should not be the main criterion by which we judge his work. And, in any case, the contours are clear enough. There are shapes and spheres, powers and entities all around us. They reside outside, at the edges of the known, but if we listen we can hear them, if we look we can see. But the act of hearing and

looking, of knowing, requires "a malign and particular suspension or defeat of those fixed laws of Nature which are our only safeguard against the assaults of chaos and the daemons of unplumbed space."[7]

AT NIGHT, AFTER his grandmother has gone to bed, he slips back downstairs to watch horror movies on his aunt and uncle's VCR. He sits cross-legged on the floor—ashtray, cold Budweiser, notebook, and remote control, all within easy reach. It is a comfortable habit, one that stretches back to a time before beer and VCRs, a childhood fascination sanctioned in recent years, cloaked in the respectable robes of academic research.

Truth be told, it has always been more of an obsession than a fascination. When he was a boy, from the moment he was able to read the television listings in the newspaper, he spent almost every Saturday afternoon glued to the set for that afternoon's line-up of old horror films. For four, sometimes six, hours he would sit there, unmoved by his mother's pleas that he "go out and get some air," watching *The Creature from the Black Lagoon*, or *Donovan's Brain*, or any number of gory Hammer vampire movies. His graduate work in American popular culture has tempered his obsession somewhat. It has forced him to slow down, to replay certain scenes, to break down shot sequences, to hit the Pause button in order to take notes.

Although the institutional legitimization of his tastes has forced him to watch with two sets of eyes—those of the fan and those of the theorist— the boundary between the two has been steadily eroding since he came to stay with his grandmother. More and more during the past two weeks, the cultural theorist has bowed to the fan, analysis has bled into obsession. He has been watching two or three films every night, allowing himself to become fully absorbed by each narrative, to sit quietly and nearly oblivious, not once reaching for the remote control. Only afterwards does he guiltily pick up his notebook.

Tonight is no different. He has watched *Invaders from Mars* twice: John Cameron Menzies's 1953 version and Tobe Hooper's 1986 remake. Both films ran in their entirety, with one short intermission between them to grab another beer from the refrigerator. Now that they are finished, he picks up the remote control and turns the VCR off. Film credits are replaced by the maniacal blare of a late-night infomercial. A loud, athletic-looking woman with very little hair stomps aggressively across the screen, gesturing wildly with a calculated passion so insincere that it is strangely moving. Her arm muscles ripple as she points toward him, exhorting him to invest in the ultimate health plan. His self-esteem is low, his body is a nest of filth and disease, but she, this sweat-glistening dominatrix of vitality, will cast out those demons, filling him with the same sterile light that dances in her frenzied eyes. She cares about him and, if *he* cares about himself, she will send him a specially priced video called *Stop the Madness!*

He lowers the sound and opens his notebook.

The invasion is a dream, the dream is real. Reality and illusion, love and deception, security and monstrosity, all change places.

A little boy wakes in the middle of the night to see a UFO land just over a dune on the beach behind his house. His kind and gently disbelieving father agrees to go investigate. Dad is gone most of the night and, when he returns after dawn, he is changed: disheveled, five o'clock shadow, one shoe missing, dead unblinking eyes. And he is mean. Within seconds of his arrival, he is angrily demanding coffee from his wife and slapping his son.

Two cops are next, then the little girl down the street, then Mom: all sucked beneath the sand to an unknown fate that leaves them with open wounds on the backs of their necks and rotten dispositions. The boy runs all over town seeking help, only to find more Martian slaves and a series of disbelieving adults. Eventually, a kindly nurse believes him and, with the help of her astronomer boyfriend, convinces a colonel at the airforce base. The troops are gathered.

The original film is interesting not for how it plays on Cold War paranoia (which it certainly does), but for the way it reveals how that paranoia is structured around and relies upon another set of fears. The film is, in fact, two films. The first is a horror film. In it, a boy realizes that the world is not what he thought it was. Nothing is what it seems; or, rather, what everything seems is only a thin layer of deceit stretched over a horrible truth. The fact that the terror this involves is congruent with Cold War propaganda does not mean that the two are the same.

The second film within Invaders from Mars *is a war movie concerned almost entirely with fire-power and troop movements. Structurally very different from the first, this section is composed largely of carelessly montaged stock footage of rolling tanks and marching soldiers. The same clips are sometimes used two or three times, highlighting the fact that the Cold War theme need only be gestured toward, that it is an ideological superstructure built on a foundation of fears much closer to home.*

The horror movie occupies the first third of the film; the war movie the second. In a textbook example of the way personal fears are channeled into more abstract political objectives, the final third of the film weaves the two themes together, however awkwardly. The tone of horror is revived when the boy and the nurse are sucked beneath the sand to face the horrible truth that lives beneath their town—a disembodied head in a glass jar giving telepathic commands to humanoid servants in velour jumpsuits—and this, in turn, is intercut with more stock footage and a few desultory scenes of military strategizing. The film ends, after the green horde has been blown to smithereens, with the boy waking up, realizing it was all a dream, and then looking out his window to see another UFO landing behind the dunes.

We are left to believe that our worst nightmares are true. But what are our worst nightmares? Not Martians or even the Commies they supposedly represent. The most frightening scenes in this film are also the most prosaic: an angry father, a little girl in a pretty dress who gives flowers to her mother just before burning their house down, cops who seem to lack any human emotion. The fears that this film plays on are not fears of invaders from outer space (despite the title), but of the invaders who are already here: the fear of the things Dad is capable of, the fear that there's something sinister about your next-door neighbor, the fear that the police are not there simply to protect and serve. The fear, in short, that the ground you stand upon is a thin crust over a vast network of underground tunnels occupied by forces that want to destroy you, that can suck you and everyone you know down whenever they want.

HE PAUSES, SCRIBBLES "Long American tradition—cf. Jonathan Edwards" in the margin, then awkwardly crawls, stiff from sitting for so long, to a pile of books near the couch. He chooses one and returns to his notebook.

If critics of the horror genre are slow to understand this, the genre itself is not. In Robert McCammon's Boy's Life, *two young boys, Cory and Ben, attend a Saturday matinee of* Invaders from Mars. *After the terrifying movie, Ben invites Cory to spend the night at his house. Once there, Cory witnesses a strange family scene: Ben's father decides to go out with one of his friends, but Ben begs him to stay at home. The father ignores his son's tearful pleas. Cory assumes that his friend, still caught up in the movie they watched earlier, is afraid that his father will be captured by Martians. He reassures Ben that it "was just a movie . . . It's all made up. You don't have to be scared. See?"*

When the boys are later awakened by the father's return, Cory realizes that he misread his friend's anguish. The father is stumbling drunk, violent and abusive. After Dad eventually passes out in a chair, Cory decides:

> *There are some things much worse than monster movies. There are horrors that burst the bounds of screen and page, and come home all twisted up and grinning behind the face of somebody you love. At that*

moment I knew Ben would have gladly looked into that giant glass bowl at the tentacled Martian head rather than into his father's drunk-red eyes . . .

> *Never again would we mention to each other the movie where Martians plotted to conquer the earth, town by town, father by mother by child. We had both seen the face of the invader.*[8]

IT IS IMPORTANT TO BREATHE as if he were asleep. Mouth closed, lips pressed together lightly. Draw the air in, slowly, through the nose. Hold it. Let it out again—not too fast! A barely audible hiss. Again.

He is not sure why this is important until, as if his efforts have somehow engaged the grinding gears of a terrible machine, he hears the harsh sound of keys being dropped on the front porch, followed by a low growl of anger.

Daddy's home.

His breath quickens before he can control it, struggles in his grip like a scared animal. Heart pounding. The panic of panic. He thinks, *play possum play possum,* and burrows more deeply beneath his blanket, willing his muscles to unclench, his lungs to expand.

Downstairs, the front door is thrown open to slam against the wall. The entire house trembles. More muttering precedes the second slam, the fumbled lock. Muddy workboots thunder down the narrow hallway to the back of the house, stopping in the kitchen. His mother's tired murmur of greeting, the growled response. A chair scrapes.

Then a silence that is not silence; a silence he knows is filled with whispers. The hiss and spit of his daily transgressions. Anger sealed all day in the tomb of her resentment and frustration, marked with the epitaph: "When Your Father Gets Home . . ." Released now in a miasma of decay. The rasp of leathery wings, a dark cloud swirling beneath the bulb in the kitchen ceiling, shadows on his father's face.

One Mississippi. Two Mississippi. He counts his breaths, knows that the gap between his lashes ruins the facade of innocent slumber, but he cannot tear his gaze from the door. He knows it is futile anyway. It makes no difference whether he is awake or asleep; the storm will break. The storm *always* breaks.

The rumble of a mountain uprooting itself. The toys on his shelf rattle against one another as the stairs outside groan. Breathe.

The room opens. High noon glare against the slit of his eye. Dark beast silhouetted in the doorway, shoulders nearly touching either side. He decides some things are better left unseen. Darkness. Eyes clamped shut and ears open to the slightest sound. Don't screw up your face like that. Don't brace for the blow you know will fall. Relax in your terror.

The blanket is torn away and the massive hands descend, close into fists, one at the seat of his pants, the other at his collar. He is lifted, arms and legs flailing, all pretense gone, breath sucked now in desperate liquid clumps. He wails as he chants *imsorryimsorryimsorry* to a god—white t-shirt, anchor tattoo, belt buckle, stale smoke—that couldn't care less.

"Son . . . of . . . a . . . bitch," and with that last snarled syllable he is flung across the room, feeling a mixture of relief and despair. The brief escape of weightless flight, but arms outstretched, warding off the inevitable impact.

And lands in another bed. Face down, tangled in blankets and still flailing. He spins around and sits up abruptly, gasping in his grandmother's living room, just in time to see a small white shape dart across the doorway in the hall.

No. That last part didn't happen. The nightmare is over. He is awake, sweat cooling on his skin to make him shiver. There was no white shape and it was not the size of a child.

He leans toward the coffee table next to the bed and fumbles for his cigarettes. He lights one with shaking hands, and then freezes as he hears a quiet giggle from the kitchen. He listens. Everything is silent again except for the ticking clocks. Then, a sound: the soft scrape of a chair against linoleum.

"Grandma?" he whispers.

Another giggle.

He pulls the blanket up to his chest and cranes his neck, trying to see into the kitchen. He is about to speak again, when a small figure in white steps into the doorway, causing his heart to leap. It is his grandmother.

"Jesus," he gasps, "you scared the hell outta me."

"You were having a bad dream."

"Yeah, I was. It's over now."

One final giggle as she moves back to her bedroom.

"*I'm* the one who's supposed to have the bad dreams."

ANOTHER DAWN ARGUMENT. An exhaustion coffee cannot erase. More snow.

His watch has stopped.

After breakfast, he looks out the window as his grandmother paces her bedroom, talking to her reflection in the large mirror atop her dresser. Through swirling white, he sees two motionless women in long green dresses staring up at him.

"Shrubs," he mutters, turning away. "They're just shrubs."

Honey,

Jesus Christ, I miss you. You who might help me keep some perspective in all of this, who might give me something to hold onto as everything shifts and dissolves. Don't worry: it's not as bad as it sounds. I haven't lost it—sanity, control, whatever. But I have, perhaps, forgotten the qualities that defined "it" in the first place.

This ice-encrusted prison of duty and compassion is a chrysalis. Everything inside it mutates to become something else. Things move in the shadows. Around me, in me, something takes shape. But what? Dread? Understanding? Madness? By now, these things are impossible to distinguish and it may be that impossibility that defines me. The impossibility of separating sense from terror, terror from theory, theory from pain. Sound crazy? I can't judge. Maybe I can explain.

Once upon a time, before I met you, I worked as a counselor in a home for schizophrenic women. It was a horrible place: green cinder-block walls; ratty second-hand furniture; vacant-eyed, over-medicated residents wandering the halls like ghosts. It's purpose was profit, not therapy. The only "counseling" I was expected to do during my graveyard shift was to tell women to go back to bed or, if they got out of hand, threaten a return to the overcrowded hell of the state hospital. Young and idealistic, I did neither. Unlike my co-workers, I didn't lock myself in my office. Unlike my co-workers, I listened.

Over the course of six months, I sat in the florescent-lit haze of the smoking room, filling ashtrays and heard one 4:00 A.M. set of so-called delusions after another. The women told me of worlds filled with huge mechanical devices that hunted, trapped and tortured them. They saw their doctors as enemy spies, agents of larger, darker forces bent on their annihilation. They were Christ, dying over and over for the sins of others. Or the Virgin Mary, "blessed" among women, impregnated by an immaculate and inhuman Purpose that could lay its seed without ever deigning to touch.

And they were absolutely right. These women were describing their lives in an accurate, even literal manner. Some of their stories could be sifted from the manila folders of their "case histories"—abusive parents, rape, dead-end jobs, brutal marriages—but never were they rendered with the canny precision the women themselves employed. I was shocked by the realization, so obvious in hindsight, that the mental health industry operated through a systematic denial of what these women knew. In fact, what they knew had been designated as their problem: madness resided not in pervasive violence and alienation, but in the convulsive strategies that the violated and alienated used to make sense of their pain.

Doesn't it seem strange that I've taken so long to recall these experiences? I mean, they were my only previous exposure to a "madness" comparable to my grandmother's. This makes me suspicious. Perhaps I'm afraid to grant my grandmother the same empathy, the same respect I once granted a few dozen strangers. That sort of generosity is more dangerous with the people you love. There's a helluva lot more at stake.

But respect precludes the idea of delusion, right? Or at least redefines it so as to efface whatever comfort it might offer the ostensibly sane. Yet, if my grandmother is not delusional and her vision of the world contradicts my own, where does that leave me? Where do I stand? Right here, I suppose, at her side. Her pain is real. Her paranoia is justified. The dead walk. The living maim and abuse. The air is filled with voices, webs of force and significance. Listen. Feel. The universe is held together by lies and malice. The exercise of power. The theft of hope. It's not so hard to admit, really: I have known it all along. My first tottering steps were taken with her down those dark, echoing halls.

Can you see how this relates to my academic work, or is that connection just a symptom of my own delusional decomposition? It seems quite obvious to me: respect is also something that most academic critics of popular culture seem to lack. The spectrum of their discourtesy runs from the lifeless titillation of "slumming" to the blind violence of denial and denunciation. Even the least offensive theoretical work stands above mass-produced culture, supposedly reading texts and films more subtly, more profoundly than the people who read and watch for "pleasure." The language of criticism, like the language of mental health, presumes to expose rather than share, to define rather than listen—none of which, in any case, is even conceivable to me without believing the stories you hear, without respect, without a certain border-blurring madness.

My grandmother has taught me this. She's forcing me to live the difficulties of translation; the graceless, at times injurious, ignorance with which one stands between two languages, a traitor to every interpretive and communicative effort, subtracting sense, mutilating meaning in the effort to understand and make understood.

I'm in the same position when I write about horror. What I want to say, what I continually dance around, lost in the schizophrenic translation be-

tween fan and theorist, confidant and cop, is that horror is not metaphorical. Only in the most obvious and theoretically manageable sense does it operate as allegory. Its central power resides in . . . and here vocabulary begins to fail me . . . an intensification, rather than metaphorization, of experience; a simultaneous distillation and amplification of the structures and relations of daily existence.

Do you remember watching Brian Yuzna's Society with me? It's the one in which the upper class of the film's fictional community literally devours members of the working class. Through special effects, doctors, ceos, judges, crew-necked sons, and debutante daughters mutate, liquefy and merge into a single, gelatinous organism of perversity and hunger. The film's hero, a working-class boy adopted as an infant and fattened into adolescence, realizes the true nature of the "contribution" he is expected to make to society as he is dragged toward this many-mouthed embodiment of social power. The scene is not fantastic. It is absolutely realistic, utterly accurate. Certainly as accurate, and no more metaphorical, than a Marxist tale of expropriated surplus value. It is cinema verite with a vengeance.

The sense of horror is predicated on a willful conflation of symbol and reality, a calculated refusal to abstract, a blurring of the categories we critics hold so dear. Word becomes flesh, identity is embodied and vague suspicions take deadly shape at the "utmost rim" of the known. Relations, the previously "empty" spaces between human beings, become as palpable as tumors. Violence is literal, visible: it opens wounds, tears off limbs, crushes, swallows and digests.

How can I retrieve such sense? How can I stand between two languages—the popular and the academic, the scream and the lecture—in order to make one hear the other? How do I carry anything back from that maelstrom of viscera, not as varnished booty in some intellectual flotilla, but as a monstrous gift that stains the page, bloody and still throbbing?

"GET IN THE CAR, you bitch!"

He has left the house for the first time in over three weeks to enter a nightmare. The wind drives snow into his face as he stands on the frozen sidewalk between a McDonald's and a 7–11. His mustache is stiff with frozen snot, and he cannot feel his feet. One hand holds the plastic bag filled with videotapes he has just rented, the other holds his coat collar tight against his neck.

"I'm warning you: the longer it takes for you to get in this fucking car, the worse it's gonna be!"

He should not be here. He should be at home with his grandmother and her ghosts. But he has watched all the videos he brought from home and cannot bear the thought of a single night without his ritual. He was afraid to lock her in while he made the mile and a half trek to Blockbuster Video—visions of flames and smoke, arthritic hands clawing at the door—but made her promise to sit quietly in front of the television until he returned.

And now another dilemma. A woman stands about five yards in front of him on the sidewalk, crying, shivering in her short skirt and open-toed shoes. In the street, atop a pile of filthy ice left behind by a snowplow, a man bellows down at her: he is a mammoth silhouette of rage, backlit by the glare of traffic, coat whipped by snow-laden gusts of wind. The entire scene seems staged, a counterfeit world that is nonetheless frightening, as if he somehow exists both within and beyond the frame of a film. He thinks of the "Night on Bald Mountain" sequence from Fantasia, the demon rising slowly to spread its wings, and takes one step forward.

The demon sees his movement and turns. The red glow of brake lights, and the soundtrack turn ominous.

"What the fuck you starin' at?"

He doesn't answer, but shifts his gaze to the woman, mascara smeared and then frozen against her cheeks, lower lip swollen, her eyes somehow pleading and resigned at the same time. He looks back up at the demon, who suddenly laughs and begins descending the mountain.

"You got somethin' to say, little man? Huh? You want some of what she's gonna get?"

He doesn't. All he wants is to be back home with his grandmother, safe behind locked doors. He also wants to articulate this but can't seem to open his mouth. The demon reaches the sidewalk and starts lumbering toward him, swaggering as much as the icy ground allows. The face is visible now. It is the face of anyone, of everyone, utterly nondescript. The quintessential character actor.

He puts his bag down, rubs his frozen hands together, and hears his father's voice: *On the outside. Your thumb goes on the outside when you make a fist. You wanna punch like a girl?* He struggles against the wind that pushes like callused hands on his back.

He doesn't want to punch at all. Lips mashed between knuckle and tooth. The crunch of cartilage, the snap of bone. Broken celery stalks in a sound editor's lab. He doesn't want to replay scenes of those paternally sadistic boxing lessons in a damp basement. The lessons of manhood beneath a swinging light bulb. His father slapping his face repeatedly, telling him to keep his guard up, getting more and more angry, each blow a little harder than the last.

"I . . ." He manages to find his voice as the demon stops in front of him. *It don't matter if they're bigger than you. Kick 'em in the balls.* The creature is fury and shadow, leaning closer. The music is discordant now, sliding imperceptibly from Disney to Dario Argento. *And when you got 'em down, keep 'em down. Go for the kidneys. Kick 'em in the head.* "I don't fight."

Sudden silence. Reality holds its breath and, as the demon considers this strange sentence, a police car pulls into the McDonald's parking lot. They both look at it: one with relief, the other with annoyance. The woman's expression does not change.

"You're gettin' off lucky, little man. Real lucky." The demon turns and strolls nonchalantly toward the woman, opening his coat wide to engulf her. To keep her warm.

Stop crying, boy. You're lucky I don't really hit you.

HE STOPS ON THE front walk, just short of the rectangle of light thrown from the gaping door onto the glistening snow. There are no aunts waiting on the threshold, no murmurs of grief, but the feeling is the same as it was twenty years ago. Tragedy. Upheaval.

He drops his bag and runs up the stairs, calling for his grandmother. The house absorbs his cries but doesn't respond. He searches every room, the attic, the closets, the places where the children hide. She is gone.

He stumbles back downstairs, losing his footing once and twisting his ankle. He limps outside, searching the snow for footprints, but sees only his own. The street is empty in both directions, the streetlights obscure orbs diminishing in the white haze. He moves back toward the house, muttering "Jesus" over and over in a child's voice.

He pauses at the front steps, wondering what to do, when he hears a name called from behind the house.

"Kurt!" His grandfather's name. His grandmother's voice.

He hurries down the driveway. In the small backyard, he finds her standing next to his uncle's toolshed, a pale ghost on white, her nightgown billowing. Her feet are bare.

"Grandma," he calls, freezing snow filling his shoes as he struggles toward her. "What the hell are you doing?"

She whirls toward him, eyes aflame, then gestures toward the shadows behind the shed. "It's your father. He won't come inside." She turns back and screams into the darkness: "Kurt! Who do you think you are, spending all night in your goddamn bars. What kind of family do you expect to raise? Leaving us alone every night. I don't want to be alone!"

The shadows shift and rustle. He does not, will not, look. He wants only to sink into the snow, to curl up at his grandmother's tiny feet and sleep forever. Instead, he puts an arm around her trembling shoulders and guides her gently toward the house. "C'mon, Grandma. It's cold. We'll get him later."

Once inside, he settles her on the recliner and finds a blanket to wrap around her. He kneels on the carpet and rubs her frigid feet between his hands. She kicks out at him.

"Stop that. Just get me a pair of socks and go bring your father in. He's drunk again."

"He's not my father. He's . . ." He pauses, confused, struggling to remember the actual structure of their lives, then looks up at her. "Grandma, your husband is dead. Your son is dead. I'm your grandson. I . . . I'm sorry." There is nothing else to say.

Her eyes still burn. She opens her mouth to tell him never to say such things. But the spark goes out and is replaced by bewilderment. Her back, momentarily straight with indignation, bends with age. She looks around at the familiar furniture in an unfamiliar room.

"You're right. I know you're right. But . . . they were here."

He resumes rubbing her feet, concentrating on the task so as not to see her tears. "I know they were, Grandma. I know they were."

In 1937, as Europe teetered on the brink of another World War, director Abel Gance finished his film, J'Accuse. The story concerns a veteran-turned-scientist who creates a device he believes will prevent future wars. When the government confiscates his invention and puts it to military use, the man takes his revenge by summoning dead soldiers back from the grave. To portray the hideous resuscitated soldiers, Gance turned not to make-up artists, but to the Union des Gueules Cassees, The Union of Bashed Faces: a group of disfigured war veterans who traditionally led French Armistice parades.[9]

Make-up artist Tom Savini was disappointed at being unable to work on George Romero's Night of the Living Dead. *He had been conscripted as an army photographer in Vietnam. Ten years later, after producing the grisly effects for Romero's sequel,* Savini told an interviewer, "*Much of my work for* Dawn of the Dead *was like a series of portraits of what I had seen for real in Vietnam.*"[10]

WHEN HE FIRST arrived, his uncle had been waiting for him, anxious to leave, suitcase in hand and dark circles beneath his eyes. In the midst of their simultaneous hellos and goodbyes, his uncle informed him, "The bar downstairs is stocked. You'll need it." He laughed at the time, pretending it was a joke, as fragments of an angry one-sided conversation drifted from his grandmother's apartment. It would be the first of many denials.

And here he is, dressed in his long coat and wool hat, sitting on a stool at the bar in a half-finished basement, sipping his half-finished scotch. The house crouches above him. Two floors of creaking and rustling—none of it, as far as he can tell, coming from his grandmother's bedroom.

The basement is a crumbling sculpture of deferred dreams. The sporadically tiled dropped ceiling leaves barely enough room to stand. The cement walls of the house's foundation are lined with evenly spaced two-by-four studs that have waited fruitless years for fiberglass insulation, sheetrock and cheap paneling. The bar itself is intact—polished oak and brass, bought years ago at a flea market—but the festive decor around it has decayed. A coconut hangs from a wooden support beam, its surface, carved to resemble a human face, barely visible beneath a layer of dust. A travel poster of a sunny beach in Jamaica is stained and wrinkled by damp-rot. The bulbs have burned out in half the plastic lanterns that line the mirror behind the bar. The other half produce a somber, muddy glow.

Outside the wind howls, shouting down any vestige of cheer the basement might have held. The storm is the worst of the season and the weatherman has warned, with ill-concealed glee, of frozen pipes and downed power-lines. He tops off his drink and leans over to read a print-out of something he wrote, it feels, years ago.

Contemporary critics of horror film often link the genre's formulaic cycles to specific social and political events. It is common, as I have noted, to see the horror/sci-fi "invasion" films of the 1950s as illustrations of McCarthy-era fears of the advancing Red horde. In a similar reading of the "stalk-and-slash" films of the late 1970s and early 1980s, Vera Dika sees them as expressing a "national mood . . . of outrage and impotence." These films, she says, appeared in the wake of the Vietnam War and in the midst of the Iranian hostage crisis, finding a certain resonance in the media images of an impotent Jimmy Carter and an outraged, get-tough Ronald Reagan. Dika concludes that once the madman's terror(ism) in these films is terminated by a resourceful and previously powerless heroine, "the cheers at the end of the film are for an enfeebled but still strong America."[11]

Such analyses are useful insofar as they maintain that the horror genre is inextricably tied to the events in our lives and that it should not be written off as simply tasteless, sensationalist, or otherwise dismissible. At the same time, accounts like Dika's leave one with a sense of only having skimmed the surface or even, at times, of having been the victim of a sophisticated sleight-of-hand. After all, what part did "communism" play in the lives of most people watching Invasion of the Body Snatchers at drive-ins in 1956? What did "terrorism" mean to the teenagers who saw Halloween twenty-two years later? Is it accurate to describe political terminology as "events in people's lives?"

Perhaps, but only as events constructed, mediated and undergone in much the same way that one "undergoes" a horror film. For most Americans, communism and terrorism are (or, in the case of communism, were) horror stories of only a slightly different sort: tales of terror in the service of national security interests and Nielsen ratings. Even the phrase "national mood of outrage" sounds as if it were lifted from a newscaster's teleprompter: the same device that scrolls its own species of relentless horror, a nightly narrative of catastrophe and violence that— despite the sympathetic, head-shaking dismay of reporters—unfolds with the gruesome eagerness of an early Wes Craven film. To accept the buzz-words of the media as sources of American anxiety is to reduce most horror criticism to tautology.

AND WHAT OF HIS OWN WRITING? He looks up from the page, stares at the shrouded coconut face. Is his own work any less tautological? It certainly feels redundant, driving the same point home over and over. He thinks of the characters in Stephen King's Salem's Lot. Confronted by an entire town of vampires, they wonder if they can face the task of destroying the creatures, of tracking them down one by one, driving stake after stake into heart after heart, drenched in black blood, maddened with rage and revulsion.

And never finished.

He pushes the print-out away and rubs his face with shaking hands. Who wrote those words? Who imagined that he could corral this madness, that he could get anything to stand still long enough to even point to, let alone define?

He can't keep things straight. Is that the shuffle of feet in the room above him, or the echo of a movie he has watched? He feels drenched. Contaminated. His words squirm on a page of flesh. Categories mutate and merge; world, film, and criticism exchange places continually, but so subtly that he is never sure where he stands. The storm outside. The storm in his head. The storm of a genre that Wes Craven once described as "rage against the horror of life itself."[12] Fighting horror with horror. Massive storm fronts collide and he stands there like an idiot, trying to gather pages as the wind rips them from his grasp.

He retrieves the print-out, turns it over and writes on the back.

I watched Night of the Living Dead tonight. Or tried to. The images started getting to me. They hit, as it were, too close to home. Home as fortress, as deathtrap. As pathetic and illusory asylum in a world gone mad.

Outside, a holocaust waits, hungry in the darkness. It wants in. It wants you. Lock the doors. Nail *boards across the windows. Keep it out. Psychoanalytic theorists claim that these are gestures of repression, that "outside" is, in reality, "inside." They argue that victims, through the arcane displacements of projection, are victims of themselves, barricading their psyches to imprison their own inadmissible desires, further protecting their shameful secrets by casting them outward in distorted form.*

It is sometimes a tough call. But doesn't that very difficulty suggest a more humane, not to mention parsimonious, hypothesis: one that gives the victims the benefit of the doubt? Did the daughters of Viennese society unconsciously long for their own molestation or had they actually felt that hateful paw beneath their skirts?

THE WIND IS A CHORUS of tortured women. It circles the house with screams, seeking entry. Inside, the house is filled with whispers and stealthy movement. A cold draft caresses his neck with fingers of ice, and he turns up his collar. His face floats in the filthy mirror like a featureless ghost, making the shadows behind him seem more substantial, congealed into shapes he can almost name. When he turns, nothing is there. Nothing but his uncle's sad, incomplete project.

One of his childhood homes had a similar basement—the second one, the one in the suburbs. The one his father had worked two, sometimes three, jobs to afford, moving them from Staten Island's decaying, crime-infested north shore to the converted farms and landfill of its south. The basement was to be the house's crown, the embodiment of an imagined salvation. It would have a seafaring motif: fishing nets and plastic lobsters, liquor bottles shaped like pirates, a fish tank with its bubbling chest of treasure. It would convey the sense of *going somewhere.*

And his father would die before it was complete, betrayed by an overworked body. He would die like a character in a cheaply inked story from *Weird Tales*, survived by sawdust and stacked lumber, scattered tools that smirked in their lair beneath the house. Be careful what you wish for. Hope can close like a remorseless talon around your heart.

The living and the dead. Disfigurement. Desolate resurrection. We all live in foxholes. Haunted by events that are still unfolding.

Night of the Living Dead poses a question quite familiar to the horror genre: What is to be done? How do we survive our seemingly endless ordeal? It is a question I cannot avoid. Turning off the VCR does no good; I have seen the film so often that it is always playing somewhere inside me. I watch as Barbara sinks into catatonia, reviving only in time to scream as pale hands drag her into the darkness. I know that Harry wants to barricade himself and his family in the basement, to bar the door and huddle in a corner until the nightmare passes. I listen as Ben, the group's sole Afro-American, argues for remaining upstairs where there is more room to maneuver, where they can see the enemy, fight it and, perhaps, prevail long enough to elude it.

Night of the Living Dead is a film about the strategic decisions we make every day; choices between fight or flight, fortification or guerilla warfare, catatonia or rage. However, the fact that its horrors are embodied in the form of zombies does not mean, as Douglas Kellner says of the supernatural elements in Poltergeist, *that the film "displaces" or "obfuscates" American anxieties, directing "the audience toward occult horror rather than the actual horrors of contemporary American life."*[13] Night of the Living Dead *does not provide a detailed political or economic investigation of American society. At the same time, however, a methodical Marxist analysis is unlikely to capture the actual horrors of contemporary American life. Even Marx, searching for a language appropriate to his subject, periodically relied on phrases like "werewolf hunger" to describe the capitalist's driving greed.*[14]

The emotions that Night of the Living Dead *both speaks to and elicits—fear, dread, revulsion, despair, rage—are not very amenable to rational* analysis. In a strict, and, therefore, limited sense, Romero's lumbering, cannibalistic corpses are "fantastic" constructions. However, their presence in the film ensures a precise and phenomenologically accurate rendering of the inexorable brutality of the world we live in: there is something horrible out there; it is about to break down the door; and what it feels like to be watching that door buckle and crack cannot be understood, can barely be gestured toward, in a language that makes arrogantly clear distinctions between truth and false consciousness, between reality and what Adorno calls "the metaphysics of dopes."[15]

HE GRIPS HIS PEN more tightly as he, in turn, is gripped by an emotion he can't name. Or, perhaps, it is several emotions fused into a single monstrous amalgam, a tentacled thing, unresolved and writhing. Traces of anger twist through him. Adorno's arrogant disdain merges with the haughty faces of the rich men and women for whom his father did yardwork and then spreads out to cover the face of reality like a bloody caul. Despair embraces him, a succubus, a desiccated mouth that whispers his grandmother's name, mocks the futility of his words, and offers another drink.

And fear. The barometric sense of forces gathering, gelatinous, pressing in from all sides. The world, the basement, its shadows, seem to lean toward him, breathing, alive with venomous intention. Something will happen. The ground will open. Pale arms will reach for him.

What is horror? That is a dangerously misleading question. We should ask instead, what isn't?

A young woman buckles her two sons into their car-seats, moves the gearshift to neutral and watches as the car rolls into a lake. She later tells the authorities that her wealthy boyfriend did not like children, that he wanted her but not her little boys. How many horrors does this single event hold, how many nightmares within nightmares? The uncomprehending terror of children betrayed by the person they trusted most, screams silenced as lungs fill with water. A woman maddened by a life of intolerable options, believing she must choose between happiness predicated on murder and loneliness as reward for motherhood. A boyfriend who has been, by whatever means, sufficiently drained of compassion to issue such inhuman ultimatums. Who is the monster? Who is the victim? Who isn't?

"You know the word autopsy," horror author/ director Clive Barker once asked. "It means the act of seeing with one's own eyes. The work of a horror writer is actually in a sense a kind of extended autopsy. The act of seeing with your own eyes and saying I can look at that."[16]

And the work of a horror writer is not all that difficult. It takes only a slight shift in perspective for the quotidian to turn monstrous. A minor tilt of the head, and woven into the tapestry of normality is a panorama so hideous it makes Bosch look like the Sunday comics. Alongside the obvious atrocities are images of infinite subtlety, scenes of apparent innocence that are made up of a thousand tiny tragedies.

Men and women—the lucky ones—spend half their waking hours at jobs they hate, jobs that drain and degrade them. They produce far more wealth than they receive in wages in order to satisfy an insatiable race of vampires. This is called making a living.

Demon fathers bequeath legacies of violence to their sons, hardening them into zombies, teaching them how to dish out and receive pain without betraying a single emotion. This is called becoming a man.

Wives wear long sleeves to hide the bruises. They make up tales of falling down stairs and walking into walls. They move like ghosts as they take responsibility for their suffering. This is love.

"You gotta look."

But looking, we are told, is a bad idea. Medusa's mass of writhing snakes will turn you to stone. In polite society—the domain of committees and task forces—the repeated refrain is that images of horror *are the problem, that "violence in the media" habituates its viewers to actual violence.*

What a strange and insidious inversion: genteel murmurs of moral dismay uttered from atop a mountain of skulls. If anything can habituate a human being to violence—a dubious proposition in the first place—it is violence itself. Like rats quivering in their Skinner boxes, shocked into learned helplessness, our bodies are etched and scarred by violence from the moment we are born into a culture of domination. Physical abuse, psychological torture, degradation, humiliation, crushing boredom and despair: these are the means by which the world reproduces itself, the building-blocks of identity and culture. The horror genre knows this and, even worse, refuses to look away, rejects the fraudulent solace of carefully constructed ignorance. Which is one reason it is reviled: it insists on conducting Barker's autopsy, on plunging its hands into wounds no one is supposed to have, on, as Bataille might say, "hollowing out chambers in a decomposed soil repugnant to the delicate nose of the utopians."[17]

THE HOUSE TREMBLES in the storm's grip. Behind the bar, the lights flicker. The power remains on, but the shadows around him do not recede accordingly. "Too much booze," he confides to whatever approaches.

His muscles tense as he reaches for the bottle of Dewar's, anticipating the grip of a heavy hand on his shoulder. Snow hurls itself against the ground-level windows with an accusing hiss. The door at the top of the stairs opens almost, but not quite, silently. It's just the wind. It's just the house settling. It's just *them* coming for him. He does not look up.

Does this even need to be written down? What could be more obvious? The horror genre exists because horror exists.

Is it possible to practice cultural criticism and not become filled with rage and pity, with terror and despair? Is it possible to look into the corners of this room, this culture, and not see small shapes with

sharp claws and hungry eyes? Judging from the books that line my shelves at home, it is.

My grandmother's lonely madness. My father's anger and frustration like a bomb in his chest. A slaughterhouse masquerading as a civilization. Crimes more vicious and bloody than even the most extreme splatter film. Who wrote this screenplay? Who can deny their role, the axe whistling its downward arc, the bodies piling up around them? Who can sit in this theater and calmly take notes?

THE BASEMENT STAIRS creak beneath an unknown weight. He lays down his pen but doesn't turn, refusing to believe his ears, refusing to face what he believes. His glass is empty and the shadows are full; they move over his hands, over the half-filled page, living things that obliterate his words. The lights dim as the wind rises to an intolerable scream, and the house feels as if it is about to be ripped out like a rotten tooth.

Then, another scream joins in: his grandmother's hoarse voice echoing suddenly through the heating ducts. It is not a howl of dreams but the sound of conscious, wide-eyed terror.

He stands quickly and the room tilts. His glass slides from the bar and falls in slow-motion, glancing off his shoe to roll purposefully toward the stairs. He follows it with failing eyes and takes an unsteady step forward. The lights flicker once and the glass stops before a pair of muddy work boots; twice and his grandmother resumes her screaming; three times and his gaze moves upward against his will.

The lights go out and shadows descend.

I don't need no monster movies. I got plenty of monsters already.

Notes

This chapter was written before September 11, 2001.

1 Noel Carroll, *The Philosophy of Horror, or Paradoxes of the Heart* (New York: Routledge, 1990), 89.

2 Ibid., 8.

3 H. P. Lovecraft, *Supernatural Horror in Literature* (New York: Dover, 1973), 14.

4 Ibid., 12.

5 Ibid.

6 Ibid., 16.

7 Ibid., 15.

8 Robert R. McCammon, *Boys Life* (New York: Pocket, 1991), 50.

9 David J. Skal, *The Monster Show: A Cultural History of Horror* (New York: Penguin, 1993), 66, 206.

10 Bob Martin, "Tom Savini: A Man of Many Parts," *Fangoria* (19xx): 50.

11 Vera Dika, "The Stalker Film, 1978–81," in *American Horrors: Essays on the Modern American Horror Film,* ed. Gregory A. Waller (Chicago: University of Illinois Press, 1987), 97, 99.

12 Christopher Sharrett, "'Fairy Tales for the Apocalypse': Wes Craven on Horror Film," *Literature/Film Quarterly* 13 (1985): 141.

13 Douglas Kellner, "Fear and Trembling in the Age of Reagan: Notes on *Poltergeist,*" *Socialist Review* 13(3) (May/June 1983): 129.

14 Karl Marx, *Grundrisse: Foundations of the Critique of Political Economy* (Middlesex, Eng.: Penguin, 1973), 706.

15 Theodor Adorno, *Minima Moralia* (London: New Left Books, 1974), 241 (cited in Kellner, "Fear and Trembling," 129).

16 Michael Beeler, "Clive Barker: Horror Visionary." *Cinefantastique* 26(3) (April 1995).

17 Georges Bataille, *Visions of Excess: Selected Writings 1927–39* (Minneapolis: University of Minnesota Press, 1985).

ABOUT THE CONTRIBUTORS

JOHN BLOOM

My work on baseball card collecting begins from an interest in the ways that sports provide images, icons, spectacles, and cultural references through which people understand their daily lives. Of course, I would like to say that my interest in sports stems from my superior athletic talents; that after being offered generous scholarships in football, baseball, basketball, and track, after turning down a promising career as a major league pitcher, and after winning a bronze medal in the two-man luge in Innsbruck, I decided that I was tired of being treated like a piece of meat, and that I wanted to search for greater meaning in life. In actuality, my greatest athletic achievement was a chin-up I managed to sweat out in eighth grade during those terrible President's Physical Fitness tests. However, I have long had an active fantasy life in which I have been all of the things mentioned above and more. Perhaps it is the wide disparity between my skills on one hand, and my desires and passions for sports on the other, that has led me to examine their social meanings.

John Bloom is the author of *A House of Cards: Baseball Card Collecting and Popular Culture* and *To Show What an Indian Can Do: Sports at Native American Boarding Schools,* both published by the University of Minnesota Press.

GERRY BLOUSTIEN

Where does my love of film and my passion for its magic and mimetic transformative power come from? Perhaps it emerges from my early childhood in England when Saturday afternoon at the cinema was a regular step into the fantasy and drama of other worlds. The quiet and dutiful daughter of migrant parents, I lived the usual schizophrenic existence of such a life; inside the home was noise, color, and drama. Outside the home was the studied attempt to emulate British refinement and Otherness. Excitingly, the cinema seemed to blend these two separate worlds for me. Every weekend I vicariously explored the complexities of these *other*

ways of seeing and being until I felt that only a thin veneer of respectability divided *my* experiences from those of the Stars; I would wait and watch tremulously and expectantly (though inevitably with mounting disappointment!) for the moment when *my* determinedly refined family would suddenly throw aside their public facades and, like my fabulous icons on the screen, suddenly launch into spontaneous song and dance in the street. I don't think I have ever lost that expectation that under the normal and the explicable lies the imaginary and the uncanny—if we could but *see* it! My ethnographic research, grounded in the disciplines of anthropology and cultural studies, continues to explore the ways in which the mimetic power of film, music, and play facilitates that experience of wonder and magic in so many everyday lives and cultures.

Gerry Bloustien is a senior lecturer and program director of Communication, Culture, and New Media Studies at the University of South Australia. Her writing on youth, film, and popular culture, published in the United Kingdom, the United States, and Europe, focuses on youth cultures, fandom, and aspects of representation and gender, particularly those that intersect with music and new technologies. Her essay is drawn from her larger ethnographic study of teenage girls, *Girl Making: A Cross-Cultural Ethnography on the Processes of Growing Up Female* (Berghahn Books, 2003).

ANIKO BODROGHKOZY

My life has been a series of border crossings. Literally. I've hopped back and forth between the United States and Canada since I was seven years old. Pittsburgh for three years during my childhood. New York City during my early and mid-twenties. Wisconsin in my early thirties. Every border crossing, either south or north, involved a culture and identity shock. "Who am I now?" "Where is here now?" Each return to Canada following a period of living in the States forced me to reconsider what my "Canadian-ness" meant on home territory. Whenever I found myself back in Canada, either on a visit or for an extended stay, I voraciously consumed Canadian television shows—public affairs and news shows to try to catch up on all the Canadian politics and current affairs I'd missed, but also entertainment programming. Watching Canadian television allowed me to "play at being Canadian" and served as one useful site to work at determining what that might mean for me.

My contribution to this volume also arises from my desire to think through how the cultural studies-media studies approaches I learned during my Ph.D. studies at the University of Wisconsin–Madison could be put to use in analyzing Canadian media and Canadian popular culture. While I was teaching Canadian students, I felt the need to suggest how the critical insights provided by cultural studies and the engaged study of popular culture can yield fruitful new ways of thinking about Canadian popular media. In 2001, I crossed the border again. I am negotiating my "Canadian-ness" yet again in Virginia.

Aniko Bodroghkozy, formerly an assistant professor at the University of Alberta, is now at the University of Virginia. She is the author of *Groove Tube: Sixties Television and Youth Rebellion* (Duke University Press, 2001).

DIANNE BROOKS

This piece is both deeply personal and professional, representing turning points for me in a couple of different ways. I teach in a legal studies department and until this time have tried to make all of my writing about media have some, if sometimes vaguely, legal relevance. So here, for the first time, I am writing something that has no real legal analysis—a dangerous yet exciting attempt to step beyond some of my own boundaries. I also see this piece as a turning point because it serves as both a tribute and a step away from my own operatic relationship to my mom. Mom looms large in this work and, through Leontyne Price, I can give her my tribute as a great black lady herself. At the same time, I'm done—now I can get on with the more subtle tributes to parents that work themselves out in one's own independent thought and existence. Finally, this piece helps me to acknowledge that I am a black lady, without apology, and really proud of the great ones who came before me like the glorious Leontyne Price.

PETER A. CHVANY

My work on Klingons extends a twenty-seven-year meditation on my own ethnic identity. Introduced to

the show by my parents at six (what were they thinking?), growing up with an unpronounceable surname in an ethnically fractured family ("Russian" on my father's side, "Anglo" on my mother's), I often felt like an outsider caught between worlds. Only later did I realize how ordinary such feelings are among science fiction fans; I began to ponder the frequent cliqueishness of "outsiders" and the in-differences of the "different." Meanwhile, Klingons shifted from a Soviet to a black typology just as I began to understand that "white ethnic" identity, however troublesome and ironic, had never affected me as race had affected friends not privileged to be white; this moment coincided with my commitment to antiracist cultural criticism. *Star Trek* is cheap, as therapy goes, and therefore exhilarating and disappointing by turns, like all processes of growth. My aim has been to take the show's therapeutic potential out of the realm of the strictly personal and into the social.

ELANA CRANE

Until graduate school, I was not particularly interested in consumer culture, nor was I much of a shopper. But at the end of my first year as a grad student the Body Shop opened at the Grand Avenue Mall in Milwaukee. I spent what seemed at the time to be an unbelievable amount of money on soap, and I think it was then that I started thinking about what it means to be a consumer. Shopping became for me both a form of recreation and a subject of scholarly inquiry. In contrast to historical and theoretical work that views shopping as being about distraction, I believe that shopping has a great deal more to do with contemplation. As I wrote my dissertation, shopping offered a way to reduce anxiety, not through its mindlessness, but through the scrutinizing and decision making it involved.

Elana Crane is Visiting Assistant Professor of English at Miami University, where she teaches courses in writing and American Literature.

ALEXANDER DOTY

Where did it all begin? At that muscle-bound matinee of *Hercules* when I was six? Playing Marilyn Monroe to my sister's Robert Mitchum after a *Saturday Night at the Movies* television showing of *The River of No Re-*

turn? Dragging my high school best friend to a midnight double bill of *The Golddiggers of 1933* and *Freaks?* Or perhaps it was when I caught myself using a line from *Stage Door* to put down someone at a college party. Whatever the turning point was, I'm still here, still queer, and still ready to confront the mainstream and "read" it—in both senses of the word, honey!

Alexander Doty is Professor of Film, Television, Popular Culture, and Gay/Lesbian/Queer Studies in Lehigh University's English Department. He has written *Making Things Perfectly Queer* and *Flaming Classics: Queering the Film Canon* and coedited *Out in Culture: Gay, Lesbian and Queer Essays on Popular Culture.*

ROBERT DREW

Like most lost souls I was a literature major in college. I plunged into the great books, but couldn't shake the feeling that these were no longer the voices that compelled most people, and that there were equally compelling voices closer to home. Our erudite, late-night gabfests always turned on the same sources: movies, TV shows, pop songs. Communication seemed a natural field for graduate study, and amid all the hand wringing about "media effects" and conniving about "persuasion," I had the luck to take a class in aesthetic communication with Larry Gross. Larry taught that art, like love, was only realized in the sharing, and that there was artfulness to be found in places scholars rarely visited. He also taught me, and many other students, to follow the threads of our questions wherever they led us. In 1991, scouting for a dissertation topic, I wandered into a karaoke bar for the first time, observed briefly, and volunteered almost immediately. Thus began a six-year joyride of which this essay is one result.

Robert Drew is Assistant Professor of Communication at Saginaw Valley State University. His book *Karaoke Nights: An Ethnographic Rhapsody* was published by AltaMira Press in 2001.

STEPHEN DUNCOMBE

Stephen Duncombe writes about bohemian "losers" with both love and self-identification. Having played guitar in several obscure—and thus truly authentic—punk bands in the early 1980s, he graduated to working as a political activist for equally noble and hopeless causes. Somewhere along the way he fell into academia, lured by the promise of a life of endless pontificating and perpetual slack. His work on the politics of alternative culture is an attempt to weave together the disparate parts of his life into a seamless whole.

Stephen Duncombe teaches the history and politics of media and culture at the Gallatin School of New York University. He is the author of *Notes from Underground: Zines and the Politics of Alternative Culture* (Verso, 1997) and the editor of *Cultural Resistance Reader* (Verso, 2002). He is also a lifelong political activist, most recently working with the Lower East Side Collective and Reclaim the Streets/New York City.

NICHOLAS M. EVANS

Having played guitar in punk bands before and during college, I never thought I'd be interested in jazz. Depending on its vintage, that music had seemed either old-fashioned or overly complex and abstract. For reasons still mysterious to me, I became an avid jazz listener in my postgraduate days as a Southwesterner in Boston. I began attending as many performances and collecting as many recordings as I could afford, and I started haunting libraries and bookstores in search of jazz criticism. Now I can say I "love" jazz in all its forms, but I don't fully understand what that means—in terms of, say, racial/cultural politics or consumer culture. My essay in this volume attempts to explore these issues by returning to one of the earliest historical moments when formations of whiteness entwined with jazz as pop culture.

Nicholas M. Evans has served as Visiting Assistant Professor of English at the University of Texas at San Antonio. His essays have appeared in the *Minnesota Review, Library Chronicle of the University of Texas,* and *ATQ,* and his book *Writing Jazz* explores the cultural and literary significance of early jazz. He is now a technical writer and editor.

ERIC FREEDMAN

I can trace my engagement with photography back to my role as family photographer during summer vacations. I willingly embraced the task, toting my trusty Polaroid One Step to national parks and monuments across the United States, posing members of my clan in front of token landmarks. Though my photos have long since turned deep shades of blue, I am still enthralled with these relics of my youth and their shifting evidentiary status—at once a record of numerous regions, a marker of my family's travels, a testament to our conquest of the great frontier, a cultural trace of a decade, a document of each member of my family during a particular past moment, and, on close inspection, a map of our interpersonal dynamics. Perhaps my fascination with images formed over those summers in the seventies as I longingly watched the chemicals of overheated instant film develop into an exquisite corpus.

Eric Freedman is Assistant Professor in the Department of Communication at Florida Atlantic University. An independent video artist and former public access producer, he is currently at work on a manuscript on the aesthetics and politics of public access cable television, excerpts of which are included in *The Television Studies Book* and the journal *Television and New Media*. His experimental video work has shown at such venues as the Long Beach Museum of Art, the American Film Institute, and Ars Electronica in Linz, Austria.

TONY GRAJEDA

Tony Grajeda holds a B.A. and M.A. in American studies from SUNY–Buffalo and a Ph.D. in modern studies from the University of Wisconsin–Milwaukee. In a previous life he played bass with Buffalo's legendary anarcho-punk band the Painkillers, and also worked at Ani DiFranco's Righteous Babe Records. He now labors as Assistant Professor of Cultural Studies in the English Department at the University of Central Florida. His book manuscript, "Machines of the Audible: A Cultural History of Sound, Technology, and a Listening Subject," is informed by British cultural studies and the Frankfurt School theory of cultural critique.

KATHLEEN GREEN

Kathleen Green is an English instructor at Pasadena City College. She is currently at work on a book about women, stress, and mass culture in the United States. She learned to be skeptical about the relationship between feminism and mainstream self-help discourse in her years as a rape crisis counselor, women's self-defense instructor, and counselor at a women's health center.

JOHN HARTLEY

Since this chapter was completed, John Hartley has relocated to Australia to take up a position as Dean of the Creative Industries Faculty, Queensland University of Technology, Brisbane. At the time of writing he was Head of the School of Journalism, Media, and Cultural Studies, and Director of the Tom Hopkinson Centre for Media Research, at Cardiff University, Wales. Previously he was Foundation Professor of Media Studies at Edith Cowan University in Western Australia, and held posts at Murdoch University and at the Polytechnic of Wales. He is author of *Communication, Cultural and Media Studies: The Key Concepts* (Routledge, 2002), *Uses of Television* (Routledge, 1999), *Popular Reality: Journalism, Modernity, Popular Culture* (Arnold, 1996), *The Politics of Pictures: The Creation of the Public in the Age of Popular Media* (Routledge, 1992), *Teleology: Studies in Television* (Routledge, 1992), and *Understanding News* (Routledge, 1982); coauthor of *The Indigenous Public Sphere: The Reporting and Reception of Aboriginal Issues in the Australian Media* (Oxford University Press, 2000), and *Reading Television* (Routledge, 1978); and coeditor of *American Cultural Studies: A Reader* (Oxford University Press, 2000). He is founding editor of the *International Journal of Cultural Studies* (Sage, London).

Having emigrated to Australia, eventually to become an Australian citizen, I began to build a family life with an Australian partner and two (eventually three) Australian children. In the middle of all this I was intrigued to return to Britain on study leave. But in fact the realities of traveling with a family, into a land that had become strange to my Australianized eyes, turned the trip into an "ethnographic" experience, where the exploration of the "peculiarities of the English" became just as important to me as was the formal process of gathering research materials for a book, *The Politics of Pictures*. Everyday experience began to infiltrate the work I was doing, to the extent that the customary boundaries between my personal life and more public questions dissolved. What constitutes citizenship, nation, knowledge, even "society" itself, and where to look for these things in the era of popular media, were questions that were addressed not in scholarly libraries but in the suburban, private, familial, personal setting of our immediate affairs as we drove around the country and as we listened to speech-radio (i.e., the BBC), watched TV, or admired the plenitude of magazines that between them seemed to constitute a grand, if virtual, public arena for the democratization of culture and semiosis. I wanted to catch and record the intense dialogue between public and private life, formal and informal knowledge, as we conducted it in our vehicular travels, because these lived conversations with popular media and everyday culture in ordinary places were decisive in forming my "authorial speaking position" (my "current theoretical self," as Tony Bennett might say). In this paper I "read" cars, class, race, and family by the simple process of driving around in or with them. From there it is but a short step to a general theory of reading (as constitutive of "society") based on the metaphor of petty theft (of cars and indigenous shipping).

Several years later I returned to Wales from Australia, along with the family and my pop-green Chevy, to take up a new job in Cardiff. It was not a case of "going native," nor even of returning to the ancestors, since it was just the next job for the itinerant jobbing academic (a "movement of supplementarity," as Derrida might say), and since then I have emigrated for the third time—back to Australia, this time to live on the east coast in Brisbane, without the Chevy, alas, which was last seen living in Somerset. International popular culture and international academic job markets follow some of the same trade routes, but as Tom Paine did say, in *Rights of Man* (1791), international commerce is a "pacific system, operating to cordialize mankind, by rendering nations, as well as individuals, useful to each other." In the name of useful cordialization, then, I'm continuing the international turn-taking in intellectual ideas about popular culture by writing a personal travelogue about a theoretical quest.

HEATHER HENDERSHOT

I grew up in the heart of the Bible Belt. My first direct encounter with fundamentalism occurred when a clinic doctor denied me birth control pills. She informed me that my body, like a vacuum cleaner, came with an in-struction manual. God authored my manual, and, according to Him, sex outside of marriage would void my warrantee for eternal life.

Visiting Birmingham more than a decade later, I find myself struggling to decipher the relationship between my research on Christian culture and the sick feeling I get when I drive past the clinic. I only begin to grasp at the connection between this personal memory and my intellectual work when I run into an old Quaker friend. It was Quakers who taught me that religion and social justice could be intertwined, and it was my internalized Quaker "manual" that had enabled me to articulate that the clinic doctor was not just a "wacko": she was "denying me reproductive choice." Adulthood and scholarly research have expanded my understanding of reproductive politics, while a Quaker-inspired understanding of ethics and human dignity reminds me why the academic work matters.

Heather Hendershot is Assistant Professor of Media Studies at Queens College/CUNY. Her teaching and research focus on media censorship and Christian fundamentalist culture. She is the author of *Saturday Morning Censors: Television Regulation before the V-Chip* (Duke University Press, 1998) and *Shaking the World for Jesus: Media and Conservative Evangelical Culture* (University of Chicago Press, forthcoming).

HENRY JENKINS

When I was a child, I used to grill my mother and father mercilessly for information about "what the world was like when you were children." I watched old movies, listened to their old 78s and old radio shows, studied old photographs, and flipped through the crumbling pages of old *Life* magazines and personal artifacts we found in the attic of my grandmother's house. Yet, somehow, I never found a satisfactory answer that linked their personal experiences to the larger collective history of the Depression and the Second World War. This work on the good doctors, Seuss and Spock, reflects a similar inquiry into the realm of my own childhood, again an investigation of my parent's generation but also an investigation of the way their culture impinged upon my own life. You might read it as my attempt to answer for my son the questions my parents never answered to my satisfaction. For me, the writing of history, no less than other modes of studying popular culture, stems from a need to better understand the place of media within my own family.

Henry Jenkins is Director of the Comparative Media Studies Program at MIT. His most recent books have centered around the cultural studies of childhood. He is the editor of *The Children's Culture Reader* (New York University Press, 1998) and coeditor of *From Barbie to Mortal Combat: Gender and Games* (MIT Press, 1998). He is currently working on two books on postwar children's culture, one an intellectual biography of Dr. Seuss, the other a study of the influence of permissive child-rearing doctrines on popular culture.

EITHNE JOHNSON

My interest in pornography stems from the ways in which civic and domestic discourses intersected in my family's home in Boston in the 1960s and 1970s. My liberal parents subscribed to *Evergreen* magazine and the recently available pornographic "classics" distributed by Grove Press. Along with "sexy" pictures, *Evergreen* featured articles about the New Left and against the Vietnam War, topics that were a staple of family discussions. While urging us to read widely, my parents were conflicted over whether or not we should have access to everything they did. Though my parents were not opposed to X-rated movies, they joined in the liberal effort to create the Combat Zone. Thus my parents' participation in a civic discourse to legitimize "adult entertainment" through containment reflected their own domestic discourse to regulate the circulation of "adult" materials within our home. Perhaps both discourses speak to a desire to carve out child-free zones for adults. Though my parents remained liberal on pornography, they shielded us from the "wasteland" of television by barring it from the home. Now, to their amusement, I've studied not only pornography but television, both of which are more readily available in the home.

Eithne Johnson and Eric Schaefer have also published an essay on the "snuff" film controversy in the *Journal of Film and Video*.

LOUIS KAPLAN

I've always been interested in the subversive power of Jewish humor—subverting even Jewish identity itself—as well as its deployment as a popular way to transmute suffering into laughter. I guess that's what fascinates me about Ringelblum's diaries and Holocaust humor in general.

Louis Kaplan is Assistant Professor of the History and Theory of Photography and New Media in the Department of Fine Art at the University of Toronto. He is the author of *Laszlo Moholy-Nagy: Biographical Writings* (Duke University Press, 1995) and has published and lectured widely in such fields as modern visual culture, film and media studies, Jewish studies, and popular culture. From 1993 to 1995, he was a Franz Rosenzweig Postdoctoral Fellow at the Hebrew University of Jerusalem, where he worked on the discourse of the Jewish joke in twentieth-century Germany. His current research is concerned with imaging and imagining community in twentieth-century American photography.

MARIA KOUNDOURA

Truly bicultural, I have moved between Greece and Australia all of my life, spending five years in each country at regular intervals until I moved to the United States ten years ago. As a result, I started my B.A. in Greece, finished it and my M.A. degree at the University of Melbourne in Australia, and received my Ph.D. from Stanford University in 1993. I'm a specialist in late-nineteenth- and early-twentieth-century British literature as well as in the most recent cultural debates found in postcolonial theory, multiculturalism, and cultural studies. In 1987 I organized the inaugural *Antipodes* cultural festival funded by the Ministry of Culture of Greece and the Victorian Ministry for the Arts.

Maria Koundoura is Associate Professor of Cultural Criticism and Literature at Emerson College in Boston. Her most recent articles examine the discourses of orientalism and philhellenism (in *The Eighteenth Century: Theory and Interpretation*) and the postcolonial critique of the discourse on modernity (in *Journal X*).

SHARON MAZER

"Who would have imagined that I'd end up claiming 'men with muscles' as my area of expertise?" Sharon Mazer is Head of the Department of Theatre and Film Studies at the University of Canterbury in Christchurch, New Zealand. She is the author of *Professional Wrestling: Sport and Spectacle* (University Press of Mississippi, 1998). When a passage of her book was read to Stone Cold Steve Austin, a WWF wrestler, in a 1998 interview for *Rolling Stone,* he said: "Why do people with such levels of intelligence . . . come up with such absurd theories?"

ANNA MCCARTHY

I wish I could trace my interest in burlesque back to the exhibitionist days of my childhood, when my sister and I spent hours devising performances we called "ballets." These involved sliding solemnly across a hardwood section of the living room floor in underpants and stockinged feet while gesturing gracefully to the beat of such hi-fi classics as "Raindrops Keep Falling on My Head," but unfortunately, this essay connects with those days only in the sense that both reveal my investment in music's power to channel fantasies and transform environments. It's strange, perhaps, that the twists and turns of the research path led me to express this investment through a study of something I'll never have the chance to experience directly. Still, I've derived much pleasure, both solitary and collective, from acts of listening to and playing music over the years; this essay is only a first attempt to think seriously about the sensual nature of listening, and it's made me excited about doing more work like this in the future.

Anna McCarthy teaches in the Department of Cinema Studies at New York University. She is the author of *Ambient Television: Visual Culture and Public Space* (Duke University Press, 2001).

TARA MCPHERSON

Given that I grew up sharing my name with Scarlett's plantation, it probably should have come as no surprise that I ended up writing a dissertation on southern race, place, and femininity. But it did surprise me, for I had left the South for a northern graduate school intent on leaving the "backward" region of my birth behind. Of course, such migrations are never as simple nor as complete as they might seem (or as we might hope), and within a year or two of graduate study I found myself (like many southern expatriates before me) drawn to southern topics, writing term papers on the sitcom *De-*

signing Women and the documentary *Sherman's March.* What I discovered in the process was a way to begin to work through many of the realities of southern life— including its sexism and racism—that I found troubling. I also found that my own writing style was shaped by the South and its patterns of storytelling, a style that did not easily conform to the theoretical models I was studying in seminars. Gradually, I've learned to live with certain pasts without completely jettisoning them and also to know that it's okay to write theory without sounding like Deleuze.

Tara McPherson is Associate Professor of Critical Studies in USC's School of Cinema-TV. Her writing has appeared in *Camera Obscura, Velvet Light Trap, Discourse,* and *Screen,* and in several anthologies. She recently completed *Reconstructing Dixie* for Duke University Press and is currently editing two anthologies examining the role of new technologies in the construction of everyday life.

ANGELA NDALIANIS

Angela Ndalianis is Head of the Cinema Studies Program at the University of Melbourne, Australia. She has published widely on such topics as contemporary-effects cinema, computer games, and theme park attractions. She coedited *Stars in Our Eyes: The Star Phenomenon in the Contemporary Era* (Praeger, 2002). In *Neo-Baroque Aesthetics and Contemporary Entertainment Media* (MIT Press, 2003), she explores the parallels between contemporary entertainment forms and the baroque. Her enthusiasm for these topics stems from her unabashed love of engagement with the wild and wonderful world of entertainment.

EDWARD O'NEILL

Edward O'Neill was raised by wolves. Wanting a better life for him among the goyim, the wolves (who were Jewish) put him in a basket and put the basket in the river. But the wolves' plan went awry; the child drifted downstream toward Manhattan, where a bunch of drag queens discovered him in the bulrushes near the now-defunct Greenwich Village Pier. They took the child in as one of their own, weaned him of the wolves' Kabbalistic dialectical materialism, and fed him Camel Lights and ontology. Eventually, the queens sent him to a

Swiss boardingschool, but he boarded the wrong plane and wound up studying poststructuralism in Paris. His UCLA dissertation, *Of Fags and Femmes Fatales,* engages with theory, fiction, autobiography, and criticism as both textual modes and theoretical objects. All the same, Mr. O'Neill insists his identity is untrammeled by fantasy.

Edward O'Neill is currently Mellon Postdoctoral Fellow at Bryn Mawr. He has been a Visiting Guest Lecturer at both UCLA and the USC School of Cinema-TV. Mr. O'Neill has published on queer theory, identity politics, and "reality" television in *Strategies, CineAction,* and *Spectator.* His next project is entitled *Phantasmatic Communities:* it confronts the paradoxical unrepresentability of mediated communities by tracing the textual figures used to construct images of community at those sites at which existing and emerging media engage one another.

CATHERINE PALMER

As the sort of cyclist who rides through the pouring rain and in searing heat, I have long been interested in the politics, presentation, and sheer fanaticism of sporting cultures and events. My more recent incarnation as a social anthropologist allows me to indulge this passion on a sustained and critical basis. More than just a self-indulgence on my part, the Tour de France provides an ideal and timely point of entry to a range of issues facing anthropologists and other social scientists, including perceptions of belonging and identity and the relationship between nation, culture, and social reflexivity. Although issues of nation and culture have been long-standing concerns for anthropologists and others, the ubiquity of the media and the sheer quantity of commodities that circulate at the Tour de France provide an entirely new set of provisions for reading, interpreting, and reflecting upon public life.

Catherine Palmer teaches anthropology and cultural studies at the University of Adelaide. Her research interests include consumption and identity, particularly as played out in contemporary sporting culture(s). She is currently at work on a manuscript that looks at the increasing involvement of global identities and influences in the staging of the Tour de France, particularly the responses of local and regional communities to an event that is now dominated by powerful,

non-French, transnational corporations. When not looking at cyclists, her work examines perceptions of risk and danger, again within the context of contemporary sporting experiences, and work so far has focused on skaters, mountain climbers, and other extreme athletes.

ROBERTA E. PEARSON

I have been fascinated by history since I was a child and consumed vast quantities of historical novels, films, and television programs. My great regret is that a viable method of time travel probably won't be discovered in my lifetime, although I keep hoping! In the meantime I am consoled by immersing myself in historical archives and walking around the streets of lower Manhattan, trying to imagine what it would have been like in 1908.

Roberta E. Pearson is Reader in Media and Cultural Studies at Cardiff University. She is the author, co-author, and coeditor of numerous books, articles, and edited collections. Among her favorite publications are *The Many Lives of Batman* (Routledge, 1992), *Reframing Culture: The Case of the Vitagraph Quality Films* (Princeton University Press, 1993), *Worlds Apart: Essays on Cult Television* (University of Minnesota Press, 2003), and *Small Screen, Big Universe: Star Trek as Television* (University of California Press, forthcoming).

ELAYNE RAPPING

I can't remember a time when popular culture wasn't central to my life—a source of pleasure, meaning, dreams, and desires. Nor did I ever—despite the deleterious influence of a "good" education—seriously doubt, in my heart of hearts, the legitimacy of my cultural preferences. However, I did learn to keep them to myself as I moved through college, graduate school, and a position teaching literature, for I was carefully and traditionally trained to do it.

But when the sixties hit, and Left and feminist politics became my primary activities—obsessions, really—I turned my critical attentions back to pop culture. For, along with all the other things that suddenly made sense to me as a result of "being politicized" and "having my consciousness raised" about things like history, class, race, and gender, my early instincts about the importance and value of movies, TV, pop music, and the powerful if contradictory emotions they evoked, suddenly also made sense and seemed worth thinking and writing about.

During those heady years, although I kept my day job, most of my energies went into politics. And it was the Left and feminist press to which I sent my reviews, articles, and manuscripts, all of which focused on the politics of popular culture from the point of view of an engaged, radically activist agenda. Those days, of course, are gone (although hopefully not forever). But my hardbitten activist, political perspective—"pessimism of the intellect, optimism of the will" as Gramsci so eloquently put it—has stubbornly remained with me, no matter the shifts in intellectual fashion. This is why the opportunity to contribute to this volume, which so insistently links the pleasures and politics of pop culture and in so personal a way, seemed so inviting to me. Writing my very personal piece on the role of soap opera in my own life felt to me like a "coming out," a way of summing up the various discordant strands of experience, emotion, and thought by which my own identity has been forged and developed. It's been fun.

Elayne Rapping is Professor of Media Studies and Women's Studies at SUNY–Buffalo.

ERIC SCHAEFER

In 1978 I made a trip to Boston to visit two friends attending college in the city. I was still bumming around, having graduated from high school, feeling that college had nothing to offer me. I remember standing on the corner of Boylston and Tremont streets—now the location of the college where I teach—staring down Boylston into the heart of the Combat Zone. At the time I considered the Zone, and my own curiosity about it, unworthy of a second thought. Just like college. So as I wrote this paper with my partner, Eithne Johnson, it was not without some sense of irony, an irony that now seems to guide my life: Didn't want to go to college; became a college professor. Wanted to study the "masterpieces" of cinema; ended up specializing in trashy movies. Vowed to always work alone; enjoy collaborating with Eithne. Just goes to show, you never really know. . . .

Eric Schaefer is Associate Professor of Visual and Media Arts at Emerson College in Boston. He is the author of *Bold! Daring! Shocking! True! A History of Exploitation Films, 1919–1959* (Duke University Press, 1999) and is currently working on "Massacre of Pleasure: A History of Sexploitation Films, 1960–1979."

JANE SHATTUC

The telephone rang in the middle of writing my article on expertise for this anthology. It was the head of the legal department at Warner Bros. asking me to be the expert on talk shows in the upcoming civil suit against the *Jenny Jones Show* and its parent company Time/Warner. The responsibilities of cultural studies expertise (however much I had previously deflected it) crashed down on me. A media conglomerate was asking me to legitimize its television practices because of the concept of the "active audience" I had developed in my book *The Talking Cure: TV Talk Shows and Women*. Jon Schmitz, the straight man who had killed the gay man, was in Warners' eyes an active or "knowing" participant and therefore was not "ambushed" by the program. Could I participate in this trial? Was my interest in Warners' offer a result of the lucrative rewards of expertise? Or had the academic Left (myself included) changed in a post-1989 world to become more pragmatic and less programmatic? My academic work and participation in this volume reflect this growing ambivalence about my once-strict adherence to Marxist theory. I still question the limits of popular reception and inequity of economic power in America, but now I also focus on political contradictions. How could the shooting of a gay man by an angry heterosexual friend after a talk show appearance not be about corporate power and responsibility? But then, could it be one of those contradictory moments where a more complex, less morally smug understanding is called for? I have not decided.

GREG M. SMITH

I'd like to be able to argue that I was a visionary in the 1980s, that I got my bachelor's degree in computer science and my higher degrees in media studies because I anticipated the coming convergence of computers, film, and television. If I had been that much of a soothsayer, I'd be rich now. As with many people who never quite knew what they wanted to do when they grew up,

I lurched from one career to another, from software designer to media academic. Now as I try to unite the two halves of my professional life, my career wanderings look more like a career path. Or at least that's what I'm telling people.

Greg M. Smith is Assistant Professor of Communication and graduate director of the Moving Image Studies Program at Georgia State University. He is editor of *On a Silver Platter: CD-ROMs and the Promises of a New Technology* (New York University Press, 1999) and coeditor of *Passionate Views: Film, Cognition, and Emotion* (Johns Hopkins University Press, 1999). His book *Film Structure and the Emotion System* is forthcoming from Cambridge University Press, and he is currently working on a book about Ally McBeal.

ELLEN STRAIN

Raised and schooled alternately in Silicon Valley and Los Angeles, Ellen Strain appropriately works in the intersection between the stock-in-trade of these two regions: computer-based media and film. Her book *Public Place, Private Journeys: Ethnographic Spectacle and the Tourist Gaze* and her NEH-funded CD-ROM on D. W. Griffith's *The Birth of a Nation* represents two facets of her blending of film and new media while engaged in the study of cross-cultural immersion. The latter project, undertaken with coauthor and southern studies scholar Gregory VanHoosier-Carey, was the result of the "cross-cultural" experience of moving from familiar California to that part of the nation commonly known as the South. Despite this attempt to understand southern culture from the perspective of a film historian, in addition to six years in Atlanta, she remains unassimilated and to date has not been spotted in a floral sundress with parasol in hand at a Buckhead tearoom. More likely, she can be found commuting between Atlanta and New York, where she does consulting on educational software for Pearson Education. Sometimes she has also been known to show up on the Georgia Tech campus, where she is an assistant professor of film and interactive design.

THE THRIFTERS

We went to graduate school in Pittsburgh, Pennsylvania, the epicenter of American twentieth-century industrial production, after capital had pretty much left there to go to Asia and back to New York (or so we were told). The previously robust economy of steel, coal, and glass left behind an astonishing amount of debris, much of which clothed, furnished, and educated us about the current historical moment. Even more important, it left behind a remarkable society of women and men whose lives tell us about how capital is lived in the everyday. We would like to thank the citizens of western Pennsylvania for all their kindnesses and good humor as they helped us to see the world anew, one rack of old sweaters at a time.

Matthew Tinkcom teaches in the English Department and the graduate program in Communication, Culture, and Technology at Georgetown University.

Joy Van Fuqua teaches television and cultural studies in the Department of Communication at Tulane, and is working on a book on the culture and economy of HIV/AIDS.

Amy Villarejo teaches film in the Department of Theatre, Film, and Dance and also in the Women's Studies and Lesbian, Gay, Bisexual Studies programs at Cornell University.

WILLIAM URICCHIO

I spend quite a bit of time moving between Cambridge in the United States and Utrecht in the Netherlands, two homes that compel a confrontation with media's rich and complex history. Utrecht's thirteenth- and fourteenth-century church bells, for example, serve as a reminder of digital culture's long history. Add to this the Dutch predilection for punch-card-driven street organs, or the many antique shops with perforated metal polyphone disks, and the notion that there is much to be learned from "old" media when they were new seems inescapable. By contrast, MIT is a place where many of tomorrow's media systems are taking form and where the discourses that inform and shape them abound. Positioned between this artifact-intensive history and a discursive present, it is no surprise that much of my research concerns the transformation of media technology into cultural practice. I've long been interested in why certain technological capacities are developed or suppressed, and how these have been understood and deployed by various social groups and to what ends. At the heart of my interest is the ongoing reorganization of knowledge and publics—a reorganization that, as demonstrated by my essay in the current collection, has sometimes surprising political consequences.

William Uricchio is Professor of Comparative Media Studies at MIT and Professor of Media and Representation at Utrecht University.

ROBYN R. WARHOL

Growing up in Taos, New Mexico, and Las Vegas, Nevada, I used to read a lot of nineteenth-century British and American novels and feel as far away from the centers of culture they represented as if I had been living on the moon. Although the "high culture" education I got at Pomona College and Stanford University from the mid-1970s through the early 1980s was very traditional, nineteen years into my career as an English professor I am still much more at home in a shopping mall than an art museum. Give me the choice between watching the latest installment of *Masterpiece Theater* and today's episode of *As the World Turns,* and I'll take that second option every time. Unless, that is, PBS is presenting a series based on a good Victorian soap opera, like a Trollope novel. My feminism means that I see the lines between "high" and "popular" culture as increasingly blurred, arbitrary, and contingent.

My interest in *Uncle Tom's Cabin* grew out of my puzzlement, when I read the novel for the first time in graduate school, over how profoundly it moved me. If it was such a bad book how could it make me cry like that? Either there was something wrong with my working definition of a "good novel" or there was something wrong with me. The question became the topic of my first book, *Gendered Interventions;* since then I have concentrated on identifying and "rehabilitating" feminine (or what I am now calling "effeminate") cultural forms and feelings.

Robyn R. Warhol is Professor of English and Chair of the Department of English at the University of Vermont.

CHARLES E. WEIGL

My earliest memory: *Leave It to Beaver* on a wall-mounted television in the children's ward of St. Vincent's Hospital. The first dream I remembered upon waking: a nightmare involving the Three Stooges and a bloody pitchfork. Dreams are "like going inside your own ear," I told my mother that morning. So is the study of popular culture.

Charles E. Weigl is one of those "independent scholars." A senior staff writer for dELiA*s, he is the author of *how2 write love poems that don't suck* and other instructional books for teen girls. Before that he was a bartender in Honolulu. He can be reached at *cweigl@telocity.com.*

ALAN WEXELBLAT

Alan Wexelblat has been a *Babylon 5* fan since the pilot aired. He's also been a Net geek since he got his first Usenet access in 1983, braving wave after wave of newcomers over the succeeding years. Currently he reads a lot, posts little, and moderates a newsgroup dedicated to reviews of SF works. He bought a Worldcon membership in part so he could vote for Bab5's first Hugo award.

In his secret identity as a researcher, he completed his Ph.D. at the MIT Media Lab, working for Pattie Maes in the Software Agents group. He works in the area of interaction design, trying to build systems that can adapt to how communities of people actually do tasks in the real world.

PAMELA ROBERTSON WOJCIK

Having spent most of my youth watching Gidget movies and Hollywood musicals virtually nonstop on Saturdays and Sundays—and knowing there were probably more productive ways to spend my time—I still sometimes can't believe that I make my living talking and writing about movies. When our students assume that a film class is going to be a fluff course, we all have reasoned arguments about the cultural importance of film studies and the rigorous training required to analyze films. And, of course, those arguments are true. Still, in my heart of hearts, I have to admit that watching *Gold Diggers of 1933* to prepare a class or write an essay isn't a bad way to earn a living. However, I do not think the point of academic work on popular culture is, or should be, simply to indulge ourselves in unreflective celebrations of our own pleasure. It may seem old fashioned, but I still believe that our job is, at some level, to destroy pleasure. While we may wish, for the sake of candor, to admit our own pleasure in popular culture, we should nonetheless aim to denaturalize it and consider its ramifications and effects. I still love Gidget, but, really, who cares?

Pamela Robertson Wojcik is Associate Professor in the Department of Film, Television, and Theatre at the University of Notre Dame. She is the author of *Guilty Pleasures: Feminist Camp from Mae West to Madonna* (Duke University Press, 1996) and coeditor of *Soundtrack Available: Essays on Film and Popular Music* (Duke University Press, 2001).

NABEEL ZUBERI

Pop music helped to orient me in Britain as the child of Pakistanis. It made sense of the place and was a channel for my disaffection, anger, and desire. References to Nietzsche, Derrida, and Barthes in pretentious record reviews in the music press of the early 1980s led me to a more academic interest in media and popular culture. An obsession with the exotic American Other as a way

of (not) being British led to an American studies degree in Nottingham, which then provided a means to escape Thatcherite Britain for Michigan and then Texas. In Austin, I finally became English while writing the Englishness out of myself through pop fandom.

Nabeel Zuberi is Senior Lecturer in Film, Television, and Media Studies at the University of Auckland, Aotearoa/New Zealand. He is the author of *Sounds English: Transnational Popular Music* (University of Illinois Press, 2000), and his essay on British (South) Asian documentary, music, and video is included in *Soundtrack Available: Essays on Film and Popular Music*, edited by Pamela Robertson Wojcik and Arthur Knight (Duke University Press, 2001). He has also published reviews and articles on popular music, film, and cultural studies in the student press, arts weeklies, and academic journals, and from 1995–96 he hosted "Roots and Routes" on KVRX 91.7 FM in Austin. He is currently researching contemporary South Asian diaspora media and the impact of digital technologies on music cultures.

NAME INDEX

Library of Congress Cataloging-in-Publication Data
Hop on pop : the politics and pleasures of popular
culture / edited by Henry Jenkins, Tara McPherson,
and Jane Shattuc.
p. cm.
Includes bibliographical references and index.
ISBN 0-8223-2727-9 (cloth : alk. paper)
ISBN 0-8223-2737-6 (pbk. : alk. paper)
1. United States—Civilization—1970—Study and
teaching.   2. Popular culture—Study and teaching—
United States.   3. United States—Civilization—1970–
4. Popular culture—United States.   5. United States—
Social life and customs—1971–   I. Jenkins, Henry.
II. McPherson, Tara.   III. Shattuc, Jane.
E169.12 .H666 2002
306´.0973—dc21   2001008590